W9-CNM-448

Left tail

α

Critical *t* score
(negative)

Student *t* distribution
Right tail

α

Critical *t* score
(positive)

Two tails

α/2   α/2

Critical *t* score   Critical *t* score
(negative)   (positive)

TABLE A-3	*t* Distribution

			α			
Degrees of freedom	.005 (one tail) .01 (two tails)	.01 (one tail) .02 (two tails)	.025 (one tail) .05 (two tails)	.05 (one tail) .10 (two tails)	.10 (one tail) .20 (two tails)	.25 (one tail) .50 (two tails)
1	63.657	31.821	12.706	6.314	3.078	1.000
2	9.925	6.965	4.303	2.920	1.886	.816
3	5.841	4.541	3.182	2.353	1.638	.765
4	4.604	3.747	2.776	2.132	1.533	.741
5	4.032	3.365	2.571	2.015	1.476	.727
6	3.707	3.143	2.447	1.943	1.440	.718
7	3.500	2.998	2.365	1.895	1.415	.711
8	3.355	2.896	2.306	1.860	1.397	.706
9	3.250	2.821	2.262	1.833	1.383	.703
10	3.169	2.764	2.228	1.812	1.372	.700
11	3.106	2.718	2.201	1.796	1.363	.697
12	3.054	2.681	2.179	1.782	1.356	.696
13	3.012	2.650	2.160	1.771	1.350	.694
14	2.977	2.625	2.145	1.761	1.345	.692
15	2.947	2.602	2.132	1.753	1.341	.691
16	2.921	2.584	2.120	1.746	1.337	.690
17	2.898	2.567	2.110	1.740	1.333	.689
18	2.878	2.552	2.101	1.734	1.330	.688
19	2.861	2.540	2.093	1.729	1.328	.688
20	2.845	2.528	2.086	1.725	1.325	.687
21	2.831	2.518	2.080	1.721	1.323	.686
22	2.819	2.508	2.074	1.717	1.321	.686
23	2.807	2.500	2.069	1.714	1.320	.685
24	2.797	2.492	2.064	1.711	1.318	.685
25	2.787	2.485	2.060	1.708	1.316	.684
26	2.779	2.479	2.056	1.706	1.315	.684
27	2.771	2.473	2.052	1.703	1.314	.684
28	2.763	2.467	2.048	1.701	1.313	.683
29	2.756	2.462	2.045	1.699	1.311	.683
Large (*z*)	2.575	2.327	1.960	1.645	1.282	.675

elementary statistics

second canadian edition

Mario F. Triola
Dutchess Community College

William M. Goodman
Durham College

Richard Law
Humber College

Addison
Wesley
Longman

Toronto

National Library of Canada Cataloguing in Publication Data

Triola, Mario F.
    Elementary statistics

2nd Canadian ed.
Includes bibliographical references and index.
ISBN 0-201-75209-3

1. Statistics II. Goodman, William Martin, 1950– II. Law, Richard, 1949– III. Title.

QA276.12.T74 2001   519.5   C2001-900826-0

Copyright ©, 2002, 1999 Pearson Education Canada Inc., Toronto, Ontario

Original edition published by Addison Wesley Longman, Inc., a division of
Pearson Education, Needham Heights, MA. Copyright ©2000 by Addison Wesley
Longman, Inc. This edition is authorized for sale in Canada only.

All Rights Reserved. This publication is protected by copyright, and permission should
be obtained from the publisher prior to any prohibited reproduction, storage in a
retrieval system, or transmission in any form or by any means, electronic, mechanical,
photocopying, recording, or likewise. For information regarding permission, write to
the Permissions Department.

ISBN 0-201-75209-3

Vice President, Editorial Director: Michael Young
Acquisitions Editor: Dave Ward
Marketing Manager: Peter Luke
Developmental Editor: Veronica Tomaiuolo
Production Editor: Julia Hubble
Copy Editor: Tally Morgan
Production Coordinator: Patricia Ciardullo
Page Layout: Phyllis Seto, Debbie Kumpf
Photo Research: Susan Wallace-Cox
Art Director: Julia Hall
Interior Design: Zena Denchik
Cover Design: Jennifer Federico
Cover Image: Robert Karpa/Masterfile

5   06 05

Printed and bound in the U.S.A.

Photo Credits: page 3, PhotoDisc; page 31, Comstock; page 109, Corel; page 167, Corel;
page 209, Dave Sandford/Hockey Hall of Fame; page 271, Mehau Kulyk and Victor de
Schwanberg/Science Photo Library/Photo Researchers; page 329, Corel; page 397, G.
Moore/First Light; page 463, Stone; page 523, Corel; page 561, PhotoDisc; page 599,
Mark Antman/Image Works; page 629, Corel; page 699, Corel

Contents

9 Correlation and Regression 462

10 Multinomial Experiments and Contingency Tables 522

11 Analysis of Variance 560

12 Statistical Process Control 598

13 Nonparametric Statistics 628

14 Time Series 698

15 Project and Epilogue 742

Appendices 748

Preface

About This Book

The authors and publishers of this book share a common goal: to provide the best possible introductory statistics book for both students and professors. *Elementary Statistics*, Second Canadian Edition, incorporates the latest technological and teaching advances, an abundance of pedagogical features, and real, meaningful, and interesting applications, such as those related to these questions:

- Are commercial vehicles more likely to be involved in accidents than non-commercial vehicles?
- Do hockey players weigh more than they used to?
- Is the mean body temperature really 37°C (98.6°F), as is commonly believed?
- Does "El Nino" really affect the weather (as reported by the media)?
- Are people spending more time on the Internet?
- How can we forecast next year's Canadian retail sales?

Audience and Prerequisites

Elementary Statistics, Second Canadian Edition, is written for students majoring in any field except mathematics. A strong mathematics background is not necessary, but students should have completed a high school or college elementary algebra course. Although underlying theory is included, this book does not stress the mathematical rigour more suitable for mathematics majors. Because the many examples and exercises cover a wide variety of different and interesting statistical applications, *Elementary Statistics* is appropriate for students pursuing majors in a wide range of disciplines, ranging from business and economics to the social sciences, physical and biological sciences, and humanities.

This new edition was prepared especially for the Canadian market and includes an extensive use of Canadian data. Where possible, the text presents data using metric measurement; however, because some industries use imperial measurements, this is also conveyed in selected data.

Professors are given great flexibility to choose how much detail to include in the course: Subsections on the "rationale" for statistical procedures, and on specifics of related computer software, can easily be included or omitted in the course content.

Content and Organization Changes in the Second Canadian Edition

- Each chapter has been tightened and reorganized to better reflect key topics throughout.
- Sections 2-3 and 8-2 are just two examples of increased emphasis on *describing*, *exploring*, and *comparing* data throughout the book.
- Section 5-7 (Determining Normality) is a new section that describes methods for determining whether a set of sample data appears to come from a population having a normal distribution.
- Chapter 7: Hypothesis Testing has been revised, particularly the sections on the fundamentals of hypothesis testing and testing claims.
- Throughout the book there is also increased emphasis on *interpreting* results. Instead of simply obtaining an answer, the consequences of the answer are more often considered. For example, when discussing probability in Chapter 3, we don't simply find probability values, we interpret them by differentiating between events that are usual and those that are unusual. With hypothesis testing, we don't simply end with a conclusion of rejecting or failing to reject a null hypothesis; we proceed to state (or ask for) a practical conclusion that addresses the real issue. Students are encouraged to *think* about the implications of results instead of cranking out cookbook results.
- Details on using specific computer technology (Excel and STATDISK) have been consolidated, in separate subsections at the end of main chapter sections. These computer details are now easier to reference—or bypass—as desired by your instructor.
- Similarly, discussions of mathematical rationales for particular techniques have been clearly marked near the ends of the sections, allowing for a more simplified presentation of the statistical methods in the main text.
- This edition features over 140 examples and exercises that are entirely new, as well as three new chapter problems that reflect a variety of disciplines. Many other questions have been expanded to include requests for interpretation.

New Features

- Internet Projects included at the end of each chapter involve the student with applications using data found on the Internet. The projects can be found at **www.pearsoned.ca/triola**.
- ActiveStats icons throughout the text encourage students to go to the ActivStats CD when encountering difficult concepts.

AS

- The CD-ROM, packaged free with the text, contains:
  - STATDISK statistical software
  - Data Desk/XL statistical software (an Excel "add in")
  - Data Sets (Appendix B) in Excel and text file formats.

Hallmark Features

Beyond an interesting and accessible (and sometimes humorous) writing style, great care has been taken to ensure that each chapter of *Elementary Statistics* will help students understand the concepts presented. The following features are designed to help meet that objective:

Chapter opener: A list of chapter sections with a brief description of their contents previews the chapter for the student; a chapter-opening problem, using real data, then motivates the chapter material; and a chapter overview provides a statement of the chapter's objectives.

Solved examples: Each section contains one or more solved examples (based on real data) that demonstrate the concept or method under discussion.

Exercises: This edition contains even more new exercises based on Canadian data. There is also an increased focus on applications in business and the physical and biological sciences. Exercises are arranged in order of increasing difficulty by dividing them into two groups: (a) Basic Skills and Concepts and (b) Beyond the Basics. The Beyond the Basics exercises address more difficult concepts or require a somewhat stronger mathematical background.

Sidebars: Sidebars introduce the uses and abuses of statistics in real, practical applications. Topics include the use of statistics in political polls, quality control, sports, and medicine.

Flowcharts: Flowcharts appear throughout the text to simplify and clarify complex concepts and procedures.

End-of-chapter features

- Vocabulary list of important terms.
- Chapter Review, which summarizes the key concepts and topics of the chapter
- Review Exercises for practice on the chapter concepts and procedures
- Culmulative Review Exercises to reinforce earlier material
- Technology Projects for use with Excel and STATDISK softwares
- From Data to Decision, a final review problem requiring critical thinking and a writing component
- Cooperative Group Activities to encourage active learning in groups
- Internet Project, which applies important chapter concepts

Appendices

- Appendix A provides the statistical tables required for the procedures covered in the text.

- Appendix B lists 22 data sets, 12 of which are Canadian and 5 are new to this edition. These are used extensively throughout the entire book, in Chapter Problems, examples, and exercises. These data sets are provided in printed form in Appendix B and in electronic form on the CD packaged with the text.

- Appendix C lists some Web sites that provide information on statistics or data sets.

- Appendix D is a bibliography of recommended texts and reference books.

- Appendix E contains answers to all the odd-numbered section exercises, as well as answers to Review Exercises and Culmulative Review Exercises.

Quick-reference tables

Tables A–2 and A–3 (the normal and t distributions) are reproduced on the front inside cover for quick reference. A symbol table is included for quick reference on the back inside cover pages.

Canadian Data Sets

Data Set 2:   Body Temperatures of Healthy Adults in Varied Postures

Data Set 4:   Temperature and Precipitation for Canadian Cities

Data Set 5:   Sitting Days and Durations of Sessions of Parliament

Data Set 6:   *The Financial Post* Top 100 Companies

Data Set 7:   Temperature and Precipitation Departures from Seasonal Means

Data Set 10: Annual Rate of Return of 40 Mutual Funds

Data Set 12: Lotto 6/49 Results

Data Set 14: Labour Force 15 Years and Over by Occupation by Province

Data Set 17: Sample Dates of Last Spring Frost at Two Groups of Alberta Locations

Data Set 18: Body Temperatures of Adults Accepted for Voluntary Surgical Procedures

Data Set 20: Person-Days Lost in Labour Stoppages in the Transportation Industry

Data Set 22: Canadian Exports and Imports by World Area

Technology

Elementary Statistics, Second Canadian Edition, can be used without reference to any specific technology. For those who choose to supplement the course with technology, sections called Using Technology provide written descriptions and screen grabs to help students access the statistical capabilities of Excel (including the DDXL add-in) and STATDISK.

STATDISK is an easy-to-use statistical software package developed specifically for use with *Elementary Statistics*. The Canadian STATDISK package, available free to adopters with the Instructor's Guide and Solutions Manual, includes Version 7.0 of the software and files for the data sets in Appendix B. STATDISK may be loaded on school computers or copied onto disks for student use.

For students using other statistical software, the data CD included with the book has plain text files for the data sets in Appendix B. Graphing calculators may also be used for many of the exercises.

Supplements

A number of supplements are now available for this edition. Instructors should contact their local Pearson Education Canada sales representative to order these.

Instructor's Guide and Solutions Manual: contains solutions to all in-text exercises; quizzes (with answers); and other instructor's material. ISBN 0-201-75212-7

Electronic Transparencies in PowerPoint: provides lecture material that follows the text's sequence and theory. ISBN 0-201-75211-5

Test Bank (print and electronic versions): instructors can view and edit test bank questions and transfer them to tests. ISBN 0-201-75214-X (print); ISBN 0-201-75213-1 (electronic).

Companion Website: **New** to this edition, the Web site can be found at **www/pearsoned.ca/triola**. It provides resources for instructors and students, including multiple choice, true and false, and short essay questions, as well as internet projects. ISBN 0-201-75883-0

The ActivStats CD-ROM presents material commonly found in introductory statistics courses, using video, sound, animation, narration, text, web links, and the Data Desk statistics package. Contact your sales representative for further information about ActivStats and other supplements, such as G. Zabowski's *Using Excel for Statistics and Data Analysis*.

Acknowledgments

The publishers and authors would like to thank Canadian users and reviewers of previous editions of *Elementary Statistics* for their feedback on developing this edition. Many colleagues and associates have contributed to the first and second editions of this text. Among many we wish to thank: Rick Hird and Tony Rahilly of Durham College, Murray Walsh, Ken MacKenzie, Jeff Bakal, Irving Bansfield, John Dukhia, Gerard Leung, Brian Lim, Henry McLean, John Wilson, and Ginny Campbell,

Special thanks to Mario F. Triola, who provided an excellent base for the Canadian editions, and to editors and contributors, including Dave Ward, Veronica Tomaiuolo, Trish Ciardullo, and Julia Hubble.

For all their help in the search for Canadian examples, we are grateful to Carol Mittlestead and Doug Willford and the reference librarians at Durham and Humber colleges. Thanks also to many paid and unpaid Webmasters across Canada, who have posted such a wealth of useful and intriguing information.

We also gratefully acknowledge the contributions of Michael B. Ducharme and Allan Keefe of the Defence and Civil Institute of Environmental Medicine; the *Financial Post*; David Chamberlain and Andrew McRae of the Research Institute; Rudy Chernecki and Lakeview Health, Oshawa; and Jake Thomas of Statistics Canada.

Dedications

To Kathryn, my wife, and to my children, Rachel and Aleksey. Even through the chaos, you have added a rich balance to my life.

W.M.G.

I thank my intelligent and resourceful wife, Beth. She kept me focused and inspired when the need arose, and was a helpful source of original ideas.

R.L.

The Pearson Education Canada

companion Website...

Your Internet companion to the most exciting, state-of-the-art educational tools on the Web!

The Pearson Education Canada Companion Website is easy to navigate and is organized to correspond to the chapters in this textbook. The Companion Website comprises these distinct, functional features:

Customized Online Resources

Interactivities

Communication

Table of Contents

Explore these areas in this Companion Website. Students and distance learners will discover resources for indepth study, research, and communication, empowering them in their quest for greater knowledge and maximizing their potential for success in the course.

A NEW WAY TO DELIVER EDUCATIONAL CONTENT

Course Management

Our Companion Websites provide instructors and students with the ability to access, exchange, and interact with material specially created for our individual textbooks.

- **Syllabus Manager** provides instructors with the option of creating online classes and constructing an online syllabus linked to specific modules in the Companion Website.

- **Grader** allows the student to take a test that is automatically marked by the program. The results of the test can be e-mailed to the instructor and then added to the student's record.

- **Help** includes an evaluation of the user's system and a tune-up area that makes updating browsers and plug-ins easier. This new feature will facilitate the use of our Companion Websites.

Instructor Resources

This section features modules with additional teaching material organized by chapter for instructors. Downloadable PowerPoint Presentations, Electronic Transparencies, and an Instructor's Manual are just some of the materials that may be available in this section. Where appropriate, this section will be password protected. To get a password, simply contact your Pearson Education Canada representative or call Faculty Sales and Services at 1-800-850-5813.

General Resources

This section contains information that is related to the entire book and that will be of interest to all users of the site. A Table of Contents and a Glossary are just two examples of the kind of information you may find in this section.

The General Resources section may also feature *Communication facilities* that provide a key element for distributed learning environments:

- **Message Board** – This module takes advantage of browser technology to provide the users of each Companion Website with a national newsgroup to post and reply to relevant course topics.

- **Chat Room** – This module enables instructors to lead group activities in real time. Using our chat client, instructors can display website content while students participate in the discussion.

Visit **www.pearsoned.ca/triola**
for great student resources

**Pearson
Education
Canada**

Want some practice before an exam?

The Student Resources section contains the modules that form the core of the student learning experience in the Companion Website. The modules presented in this section may include the following:

- Learning Objectives
- Multiple-Choice Questions
- True/False Questions
- Essay Questions

- Internet Exercises
- Destinations
- Net Search

The question modules provide students with the ability to send answers to our grader and receive instant feedback on their progress through our Results Reporter. Coaching comments and references to the textbook may be available to ensure that students take advantage of all available resources to enhance their learning experience.

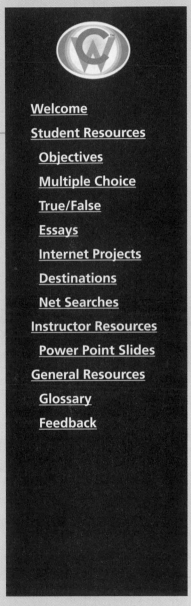

Welcome

Student Resources

Objectives

Multiple Choice

True/False

Essays

Internet Projects

Destinations

Net Searches

Instructor Resources

Power Point Slides

General Resources

Glossary

Feedback

PEARSON EDUCATION CANADA

26 Prince Andrew Place
Toronto, Ontario M3C 2T8

To order:
Call: 1-800-567-3800
Fax: 1-800-263-7733

For samples:
Call: 1-800-850-5813
Fax: (416) 299-2539
E-mail:
phabinfo_pubcanada@pearsoned.com

Companion Websites are currently available for:

- Griffin: *Business*
- Solomon: *Consumer Behaviour*
- Miller: *Economics Today*

Note: Companion Website content will vary slightly from site to site depending on discipline requirements.

The Companion Website for this text can be found at:

www.pearsoned.ca/triola

Introduction to Statistics

1-1 Overview

The term *statistics* is defined along with the terms *population*, *sample*, *parameter*, and *statistic*.

1-2 The Nature of Data

Quantitative data and qualitative data are defined along with discrete data and continuous data. The four levels of measurement (nominal, ordinal, interval, ratio) are also defined.

1-3 Uses and Abuses of Statistics

Examples of beneficial uses of statistics are presented, along with some of the common ways in which statistics are used to deceive. Deceptive uses include small samples, precise numbers, distorted percentages, loaded questions, misleading graphs, and bad samples.

1-4 Design of Experiments

Observational studies and experiments are described, along with good statistical methodology. The importance of good sampling is emphasized. Different sampling methods are defined and described, including random sampling, stratified sampling, systematic sampling, cluster sampling, and convenience sampling.

CHAPTER PROBLEM:

As a student, are you in the most dangerous profession?

On his fourth day of work, a young worker is fatally burned by a highly flammable chemical. While guiding a truck into a loading bay, another worker is crushed to death when the truck driver loses sight of him. A forklift driver is crushed when his forklift topples over. Sadly, these are among the hundreds of Canadian workers (about three a day, according to North American Occupational Safety and Health (NAOSH) statistics) who are killed as a result of occupational injuries.

Some professions are inherently more dangerous than others. Fatal injuries are sometimes suffered by police officers in car crashes or firefighters in collapsed buildings. Taxicab drivers are sometimes killed by passengers determined to steal fares. Some miners' lives have been shortened by dangerous levels of coal dust.

For obvious reasons, governments and health workers around the world take a serious interest in collecting and analyzing statistics relating to these hazards. The Swiss physician H.C. Lombard, for example, once compiled longevity data for different professions. He used death certificates that included name, age at death, and profession. He then proceeded to compute the average (mean) length of life for the different professions, and he found that students were lowest with the mean of only 20.7years! (See "A Selection of Selection Anomolies" by Wainer, Palmer, and Bradlow in *Chance*, Volume 11, No. 2.) Similar results would be obtained if the same data were collected today in Canada. Could being a student really be more dangerous than working in a chemical plant, upholding the law, working in a mine, or driving a taxicab? Not likely, as you will see in the *Uses and Abuses of Statistics* section of this chapter.

1-1 Overview

We begin our study of *statistics* by noting that the word has two basic meanings. In the first sense, the term is used in reference to actual and specific numbers derived from data, such as the results of a Canadian Automobile Association survey, according to which 58% of the respondents paid cash for their used vehicles.

A second meaning refers to statistics as a method of analysis.

DEFINITION

Statistics is a collection of methods for planning experiments, obtaining data, and then organizing, summarizing, presenting, analysing, interpreting, and drawing conclusions based on the data.

AS Statistics involves much more than simply drawing graphs and calculating averages. In this book, we will learn how to develop generalized and meaningful conclusions that go beyond the original data. In statistics, we commonly use the terms *population* and *sample*. These terms are at the very core of statistics and we define them now.

DEFINITIONS

A **population** is the complete collection of all elements (scores, people, measurements, and so on) to be studied.

A **census** is the collection of data from *every* element in a population.

A **sample** is a subcollection of elements drawn from a population.

For example, a typical Nielsen television survey uses a *sample* of 1700 households, and the results are used to form conclusions about the *population* of all 10,820,050 households in Canada. Every five years, Statistics Canada tries to obtain a complete census, with information on every Canadian; but in practice, it is impossible to reach everyone.

Closely related to the concepts of population and sample are the concepts of *parameter* and *statistic*. The following definitions are easy to remember if we recognize the alliteration in "population parameter" and "sample statistic."

DEFINITIONS

A **parameter** is a numerical measurement describing some characteristic of a *population*.

A **statistic** is a numerical measurement describing some characteristic of a *sample*.

The State of Statistics

The word statistics is derived from the Latin word *status* (meaning "state"). Early uses of statistics involved compilations of data and graphs describing various aspects of a state or country. In 1662, John Graunt published statistical information about births and deaths. Graunt's work was followed by studies of mortality and disease rates, population sizes, incomes, and unemployment rates. Households, governments, and businesses rely heavily on statistical data for guidance. For example, unemployment rates, inflation rates, consumer indexes, and birth and death rates are carefully compiled on a regular basis, and the resulting data are used by business leaders to make decisions affecting future hiring, production levels, and expansion into new markets.

EXAMPLES

1. **Parameter:** According to the 1881 Canada Census, 12.4% of the population of Yale District, British Columbia, belonged to the Buddhist religion. Assuming that the list of 8951 residents for that region did not overlook anyone, then the 12.4% is a *parameter*, not a statistic.

2. **Statistic:** In a survey of 1031 tournament-level golfers, 44% had the career-threatening condition known as the "yips" (*The Globe and Mail*, January 8, 2001). The figure 44% is a *statistic* because it is based on a sample, not the entire population of all professional golfers.

An important consideration when evaluating sample statistics is whether the data were collected in an appropriate way, such as through a process of *random* selection. If sample data are not collected appropriately, then no amount of statistical torturing can salvage the data.

We are convinced that if you apply yourself diligently, and with an open mind, to the materials in this book, you will discover that statistics is an interesting and rich subject—with many real and meaningful applications within your grasp.

1–2 The Nature of Data

Data are observations (such as measurements, genders, and survey responses) that have been collected. Some data sets consist of numbers (such as heights), and others are nonnumerical (such as gender). The terms *quantitative data* and *qualitative data* are often used to distinguish between these two types.

DEFINITIONS

Quantitative data consist of numbers representing counts or measurements.

Qualitative (or **categorical** or **attribute**) **data** can be separated into different categories that are distinguished by some nonnumeric characteristic.

Data Set 4 in Appendix B includes amounts of precipitation in different Canadian cities. Those amounts are quantitative data, but the names of the cities are qualitative data.

AS We can further describe quantitative data by distinguishing between the discrete and continuous types.

What can we conclude from this survey?

The Toronto Star has a readers' service called StarPhone. Readers with touch-tone phones can call a selected extension number to vote on various topics. On one occasion, after the Canadian dollar had dropped in value to less than 67 cents US, readers were asked to vote on whether the dollar should be propped up by government intervention or left alone to find its true value in the currency marketplace. Of the 287 people who responded 157, or 54.7%, favoured intervention. Based on the results of this poll, what can we conclude about the way Canadians feel about the value of their currency?

DEFINITIONS

Discrete data result from either a finite number of possible values or a countable number of possible values. (That is, the number of possible values is 0, or 1, or 2, and so on.)

Continuous (numerical) data result from infinitely many possible values that can be associated with points on a continuous scale in such a way that there are no gaps or interruptions.

When data represent counts, they are discrete; when they represent measurements, they are continuous. The numbers of eggs that hens lay are *discrete* data because they represent counts; the amounts of milk that cows produce are *continuous* data because they are measurements that can assume any value over a continuous span. (For convenience, continuous quantitative data are often scaled into seemingly discrete units, such as "to the nearest litre," or "in 1000s of dollars.")

Another common way to classify data is to use four levels of measurement: nominal, ordinal, interval, ratio. In applying statistics to real problems, the level of measurement of the data is an important factor in determining which procedure it is appropriate to use.

DEFINITION

The **nominal level of measurement** is characterized by data that consist of names, labels, or categories only. The data cannot be arranged in an ordering scheme (such as low to high).

● **EXAMPLES**   The following are examples of sample data at the nominal level of measurement:

1. Survey responses of yes, no, and undecided
2. The "kingdoms" into which life forms can be classified

Because nominal data lack any ordering or numerical significance, they cannot be used for calculations. Numbers are sometimes assigned to categories (especially when data are computerized), but these numbers lack any real computational significance. However, you *can* count how often different nominal categories occur.

DEFINITION

The **ordinal level of measurement** involves data that may be arranged in some order, but differences between data values either cannot be determined or are meaningless.

EXAMPLES
The following are examples of data at the ordinal level of measurement:

1. An editor rates some manuscripts as "excellent," some as "good," and some as "bad." (We can't find a specific quantitative difference between "good" and "bad.")
2. An Olympic screening committee ranks Gail 3rd, Diana 7th, and Kim 10th. (We can find a difference between ranks of 3 and 7, but the difference of 4 doesn't mean anything.)

Ordinal level data provide information about relative comparisons, but not about the degrees of differences. They are restricted in the types of calculations they can be used for.

DEFINITION

The **interval level of measurement** is like the ordinal level, with the additional property that we can determine meaningful amounts of differences between data. However, there is no inherent (natural) zero starting point (where *none* of the quantity is present).

EXAMPLES   The following are examples of data at the interval level of measurement.

1. Body temperatures of 37.0°C and 36.39°C. Such values are ordered, and we can determine their difference (often called the *distance* between the two values). However, there is no natural starting point. The value of 0°C might seem like a starting point, but it is arbitrary and does not represent "no heat." It is wrong to say that 50°C is twice as hot as 25°C. (Temperature readings on the Kelvin scale are at the ratio level of measurement; that scale has an absolute zero.)

2. The years 1000, 2002, 1867, and 1944. (Time did not begin in the year 0, so the year 0 is arbitrary instead of being a natural zero starting point.)

Measuring Disobedience

How are data collected about something that doesn't seem to be measurable, such as people's level of disobedience? Psychologist Stanley Milgram devised the following experiment: A researcher instructed a volunteer subject to operate a control board that gave increasingly painful "electrical shocks" to a third person. Actually, no real shocks were given, and the third person was an actor. The volunteer began with 15 volts and was instructed to increase the shocks by increments of 15 volts. The disobedience level was the point at which the subject refused to increase the voltage. Surprisingly, two-thirds of the subjects obeyed orders even though the actor screamed and faked a heart attack.

> ### DEFINITION
>
> The **ratio level of measurement** is the interval level modified to include the inherent zero starting point (where zero indicates that *none* of the quantity is present). For values at this level, differences and ratios are both meaningful.

EXAMPLES   The following are examples of data at the ratio level of measurement:

1. Weights of plastic discarded by households (0 kg does represent no plastic discarded, and 10 kg does weigh twice as much as 5 kg).
2. Distances (in kilometres) travelled by cars in a test of fuel consumption. (A distance of 0 km is possible, and it would be meaningful to calculate that one car drove three times as far as another.)

This level is called the ratio level because the starting point makes ratios meaningful. Because a 200-kg weight is *twice* as heavy as a 100-kg weight, but 50°C is *not* twice as hot as 25°C, weights are at the ratio level while Celsius temperatures are at the interval level. For a concise comparison and review, study Table 1-1 to see the differences among the four levels of measurement.

1–2 Exercises A: Basic Skills and Concepts

In Exercises 1–4, identify each number as discrete *or* continuous.

1. Each regular strength Dristan tablet has 325 mg of acetaminophen.
2. An Air Canada altimeter reports a height of 10,000 m.
3. A poll of 1015 people shows that 40 of them now subscribe to an on-line computer service.
4. Radar indicated that Paul Tracy reached a top speed in the straight-away of 275 km/h.

In Exercises 5–8, determine whether the given value is a statistic or a parameter.

5. A sample of students is selected, and the average (mean) age is 20.7 years.
6. 93% of those questioned in a consumer survey recognized the Campbell's Soup brand name.
7. According to the latest census, 4.83% of families in Calgary have an annual income less than $10,000.
8. The average (mean) of the atomic numbers for the elements that are listed on a student's chemistry data tables is 51.79.

In Exercises 9–18, determine which of the four levels of measurement (nominal, ordinal, interval, ratio) is most appropriate.

9. Ratings of superior, above average, average, below average, or poor for blind dates
10. Phenylephrin contents (in milligrams) of Dristan tablets
11. Social insurance numbers (SIN)

TABLE 1-1	Levels of Measurement of Data	
Level	Summary	Example
Nominal	Categories only. Data cannot be arranged in an ordering scheme.	Student cars: Corvettes Ferraris Porsches } Categories or names only.
Ordinal	Categories are ordered, but differences cannot be determined or they are meaningless.	Student cars: compact mid-size full-size } An order is determined by "compact, mid-size, full-size."
Interval	Differences between values can be found, but there is no inherent starting point. Ratios are meaningless.	Campus temperatures: 15°C 20°C 30°C } 90°C is not twice as hot as 45°C.
Ratio	Like interval, but with an inherent starting point. Ratios are meaningful.	Weights of university football players: 150 lb 195 lb 300 lb } 300 lb is twice 150 lb.

12. Temperatures (in degrees Celsius) of a sample of angry taxpayers who are being audited
13. Years in which the Winnipeg Blue Bombers won the Grey Cup
14. Final course grades (A, B, C, D, F) for statistics students
15. Telephone area codes
16. Annual incomes of nurses
17. Cars described as subcompact, compact, intermediate, or full-size
18. Colours in a handful of M&M candies

1-2 Exercises B: Beyond the Basics

19. A pollster in Saskatchewan surveys 200 people and asks them their preference of political party. He codes the responses as 0 (for Canadian Alliance), 1 (for Liberal), 2 (for New Democratic Party), and 3 (for Progressive Conservative). He then calculates the average (mean of the numbers) and gets 1.78. How can that value be interpreted?
20. In the "The Born Loser" cartoon strip, Brutus expresses joy over an increase in temperature from 1° to 2°. When asked what is so good about 2°, he answers, "It's twice as warm as this morning." Why is Brutus wrong once again?

Are Older Drivers Safer Drivers?

Alberta Transportation compiled statistics on car accidents involving casualties and found that drivers aged 18–19 had a rate of 27.3 per thousand, while drivers over 65 had a rate of only 10.3 per thousand. Does this mean that older drivers are safer drivers?

University of Alberta psychology professor Allen Dobbs studied whether the decline in mental competence experienced by some seniors affects their ability to drive safely. In an article in *Alberta Report*, Dobbs is quoted as saying that the statistics create a misleading picture, because "seniors drive less, avoid rush-hour traffic, winter snowstorms, and longer trips." When the numbers are adjusted to take into account the number of kilometres driven, the younger and older drivers actually have about the same rate of accidents involving casualties; for seniors, the rate continues to rise as they get older. Dobbs's recommendation is that more stringent testing of older drivers be implemented, especially since a demographic shift is resulting in more seniors on the road.

1-3 Uses and Abuses of Statistics

Uses of Statistics

The applications of statistics have grown so that practically every field of study now benefits in some way from the use of statistical methods. Manufacturers now provide better products at lower costs through the use of statistical quality control techniques. Diseases are controlled through analyses designed to anticipate epidemics. Endangered species of fish and other wildlife are protected through regulations and laws that react to statistical estimates of changing population sizes. By pointing to lower fatality rates, legislators can better justify laws such as those governing air pollution, auto inspections, seat belt and air bag use, and drunk driving. We will cite only these few examples, because a complete compilation of the uses of statistics would easily fill the remainder of this book (a prospect not totally unpleasant to some readers).

AS As you proceed with this course, you will encounter many different applications of statistics.

Abuses of Statistics

Abuses of statistics have occurred for some time. For example, about a century ago, statesman Benjamin Disraeli famously said, "There are three kinds of lies: lies, damned lies, and statistics." It has also been said that "figures don't lie; liars figure," and that "if you torture the data long enough, they'll admit to anything." Historian Andrew Lang said that some people use statistics "as a drunken man uses lampposts—for support rather than illumination." These statements refer to abuses of statistics in which data are presented in ways that may be misleading. Some abusers of statistics are simply ignorant or careless, whereas others have personal objectives and are willing to suppress unfavourable data while emphasizing supportive data. We will now present a few examples of the many ways in which data can be distorted.

Bad Samples   A major source of deceptive statistics is inappropriate methods of collecting data. One very common sampling method allows the sample subjects to decide for themselves whether to be included.

DEFINITION

A **self-selected survey** is one in which the respondents themselves decide whether to be included.

In such surveys, people with strong opinions are more likely to participate, so the responses obtained do not necessarily represent the whole population. Phone-in polls are good examples of **self-selected samples** because the callers themselves decide whether to be included in the survey.

A self-selected sample is only one way in which the method of collecting data can be seriously flawed. As another example, consider our Chapter Problem, which described how Swiss physician H.C. Lombard once compiled longevity data for different professions and found that students ranked lowest, with a mean of only 20.7 years. The problem is that the sample is not appropriate, because most people are students when they are relatively young; they are no longer students when they become a little older and are employed in some other profession. Also, all of the students in the Lombard study *died*, so the 20.7-year longevity figure merely suggests that if students die, they are likely to be young. A similar error would be made if you computed the average age of teenagers who died. That figure could not possibly be more than 19 years, but this does not really mean that being a teenager is more dangerous than being a test pilot, a profession in which members rarely join at ages younger than 19 years.

AS **Small Samples**   In Chapter 6 we will see that small samples are not necessarily bad, but small sample results are sometimes used as a form of statistical "lying." The toothpaste preferences of only 10 dentists should not be used as a basis for a generalized claim such as "Covariant toothpaste is recommended by 7 out of 10 dentists." Even if a sample is large, it must be unbiased and representative of the population from which it comes. Sometimes a sample might seem relatively large (as in a survey of "2000 randomly selected adult Canadians"), but if conclusions are made about subgroups, such as the Catholic male Conservatives in the survey, such conclusions might be based on very small samples.

Precise Numbers   Sometimes the numbers themselves can be deceptive. A very precise figure, such as an annual salary of $37,735.29, might be used to sound precise, so that people assume incorrectly that it is also *accurate*. In this case, the number is an estimate, so it would be better to state that the number is about $37,700.

Guesstimates   Another source of statistical deception involves estimates that are really guesses and can therefore be in error by substantial amounts. We should consider the source of the estimate and how it was developed. At a recent demonstration in Ottawa, organizers estimated the crowd size to be 50,000, but the media used aerial photographs and grids to come up with a more accurate estimate that was much smaller.

Distorted Percentages   Misleading or unclear percentages are sometimes used. An airline ran full-page ads boasting better service. In referring to lost baggage, these ads claimed that this was "an area where we've already improved 100% in the last six months." An editorial criticizing this statistic interpreted the 100% improvement figure to mean that no baggage is now being lost—an accomplishment not yet achieved.

Partial Pictures   "Ninety percent of all our cars sold in this country in the last 10 years are still on the road." Millions of consumers heard that impressive commercial message. What the manufacturer failed to mention was that 90% of the cars had been sold within the last three years. The claim was technically correct, but it was very misleading by not presenting the complete story.

The Literary Digest Poll

In the 1936 presidential race, *Literary Digest* magazine ran a poll and predicted an Alf Landon victory, but Franklin D. Roosevelt won by a landslide. Maurice Bryson notes, "Ten million sample ballots were mailed to prospective voters, but only 2.3 million were returned. As everyone ought to know, such samples are practically always biased." He also states, "Voluntary response to mailed questionnaires is perhaps the most common method of social science data collection encountered by statisticians, and perhaps also the worst." (See Bryson's "The *Literary Digest* Poll: Making of a Statistical Myth," *The American Statistician*, Vol. 30, No. 4.)

Deliberate Distortions   In the book *Tainted Truth,* Cynthia Crossen cites an example of the magazine *Corporate Travel* that published results showing that among car rental companies, Avis was the winner in a survey of people who rent cars. When Hertz requested detailed information about the survey, the actual survey responses disappeared and the magazine's survey coordinator resigned. Hertz sued Avis (for false advertising based on the survey) and the magazine; a settlement was reached.

Loaded Questions   Survey questions can be worded to elicit a desired response. For example, the *Toronto Star*'s StarPhone poll asked, "Should the provincial government change the law to make it easier to get squeegee kids off our streets?" The results were 69% in favour of changes to the law. The so-called squeegee kids had just been at the centre of some very negative press. The wording of the question appealed to those *Star* readers who had very strong negative feelings toward these individuals. It might have been more appropriate to word the question, "Should the government change the law to discourage street vendors from approaching motor vehicles?" Sometimes questions are unintentionally loaded by such factors as the order of the items being considered. For example, one German poll asked these two questions:

- Would you say that traffic contributes more or less to air pollution than industry?

- Would you say that industry contributes more or less to air pollution than traffic?

When traffic was presented first, 45% blamed traffic and 27% blamed industry; when industry was presented first, those percentages changed dramatically to 24% and 57%, respectively.

Misleading Graphs   Many visual devices—such as bar graphs and pie charts—can be used to exaggerate or de-emphasize the true nature of data. (Such devices will be discussed in Chapter 2.) The two graphs in Figure 1-1 depict the *same data* from Statistics Canada, but part (b) is designed to exaggerate the

Figure 1-1   Earnings of Full-Time Professional Workers

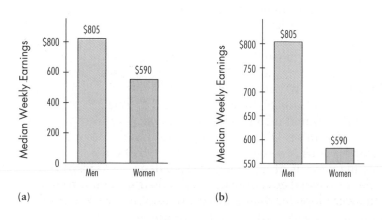

difference between the earnings of men and women. By not starting the vertical axis at zero, the graph in part (b) tends to produce a misleading subjective impression. Figure 1-1 carries an important lesson: We should analyse the *numerical* information given in the graph, so that we won't be misled by its general shape.

Pictographs   Drawings of objects, called *pictographs*, may also be misleading. Some objects commonly used to depict data include moneybags, stacks of coins, army tanks (for military expenditures), cows (for dairy production), barrels (for oil production), and houses (for home construction). When drawing such objects, artists can create false impressions that distort differences. If you double each side of a square, the area doesn't merely double; it increases by a factor of four. If you double each side of a cube, the volume doesn't merely double; it increases by a factor of eight. If taxes double over a decade, an artist may depict tax amounts with one moneybag for the first year and a second moneybag that is twice as deep, twice as tall, and twice as wide. Instead of appearing to double, taxes will appear to increase by a factor of eight, so the truth will be distorted by the drawing.

Entire books have been devoted to such abuses of statistics, including Darrell Huff's classic *How to Lie with Statistics,* Robert Reichard's *The Figure Finaglers,* and Cynthia Crossen's *Tainted Truth*. Understanding these practices will be extremely helpful in evaluating the statistical data found in everyday situations.

1-3 Exercises A: Basic Skills and Concepts

1. You've been hired to research recognition of the Roots brand name, and you must conduct a telephone survey of 1500 consumers in Canada. What is wrong with using telephone directories as the population from which the sample is drawn?
2. A slight majority—57 percent—of the 415 respondents to the *Toronto Star*'s web site survey wanted the Bank of Canada to step in to halt the dollar's slide. What is wrong with this survey?
3. A report sponsored by British Columbia fruit farmers concluded that cholesterol levels can be lowered by eating fruit products. Why might the conclusion be suspect?
4. An employee has an annual salary of $40,000 but is told that she will be given a 10% cut in pay because of declining company profits. She is also told that next year, she will be given a 10% raise. This doesn't seem too bad because the 10% cut seems to be offset by the 10% raise.
   a.   What is the annual income after the 10% cut?
   b.   Use the annual income from part (a) to find the annual income after the 10% raise. Did the 10% cut followed by the 10% raise get the employee back to an annual salary of $40,000?
5. Sixty-nine percent of those who responded to a StarPhone question said that the provincial government should change the law to make it easier to get squeegee kids off the streets. How valid is the 69% result?

6. McLaren NightVision, a manufacturer of "night-vision" lenses for drivers, claims in an ad that darkness is the cause of most highway mayhem. Their advertisement stated that "according to Ministry of Transportation statistics, over 25% of highway fatalities occur between midnight and 6 A.M." What is misleading about this statement?

7. In a study on campus crimes committed by students high on alcohol or drugs, a mail survey of 1875 students was conducted. A report on the survey noted, "Eight percent of the students responding anonymously say they've committed a campus crime. And 62% of that group say they did so under the influence of alcohol or drugs." Assuming that the number of students responding anonymously is 1875, how many actually committed a campus crime while under the influence of alcohol or drugs?

8. A study conducted by the Insurance Institute for Highway Safety found that the Chevrolet Corvette had the highest fatality rate—5.2 deaths for every 10,000. The car with the lowest fatality rate was the Volvo, with only 0.6 death per 10,000. Does this mean that the Corvette is not as safe as the Volvo?

9. An East Coast newspaper claims that pregnant mothers can increase their chances of having healthy babies by eating lobster. That claim is based on a study showing that babies born to lobster-eating mothers have fewer health problems than babies born to mothers who don't eat lobsters. What is wrong with this claim?

10. A survey includes this item: "Enter your height in inches." It is expected that actual heights of respondents can be obtained and analysed. Identify the two major problems with this item.

11. "According to a nationwide survey of 250 hiring professionals, scuffed shoes was the most common reason for a male job seeker's failure to make a good first impression." Newspapers carried this statement based on a poll commissioned by Kiwi Brands, producers of shoe polish. Comment on why the results of the survey might be questionable.

12. The increases in expenditures made by the Newfoundland government for pollution abatement are shown in the graph below (based on data from Statistics Canada). What is wrong with the figure?

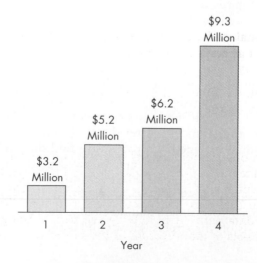

Year

1–3 Exercises B: Beyond the Basics

13. A study noted that the mean life span for 35 male symphony conductors was 73.4 years, in contrast to the mean of 69.5 years for males in the general population. The longer life span was attributed to such factors as fulfillment and motivation. There is a fundamental flaw in concluding that male symphony conductors live longer. What is it?

14. A researcher at the Sloan-Kettering Cancer Research Center was once criticized for falsifying data. Among his data were figures obtained from 6 groups of mice, with 20 individual mice in each group. These values were given for the percentage of successes in each group: 53%, 58%, 63%, 46%, 48%, 67%. What's wrong?

15. Try to identify each of the four major flaws in the following. A daily newspaper ran a survey by asking readers to call in their response to this question: "Do you support the development of atomic weapons that could kill millions of innocent people?" It was reported that 20 readers responded and 87% said "no," while 13% said "yes."

16. A chart caption in an advertisement described a dental rinse as one that "reduces plaque on teeth by over 300%."
    a. If you remove 100% of some quantity, how much is left?
    b. What does it mean to reduce plaque by over 300%?

1–4 Design of Experiments

Sometimes we have an interesting and important data set, but we do not have a particular objective in mind, so we want to *explore* the data to see what insights we might acquire. (The basic tools for exploring and describing data sets are presented in Chapter 2.) More often, though, we do have a specific objective, and we want to collect the data and do the analysis that will help us to meet that objective. We typically get our data from two common sources: *observational studies* (such as polls) and *experiments* (such as using irradiation to improve the shelf life of food products).

DEFINITIONS

In an **observational study,** we observe and measure specific characteristics, but we don't attempt to manipulate or modify the subjects being studied.

In an **experiment,** we apply some *treatment* and then proceed to observe its effects on the subjects.

For example, an observational study might involve a survey of citizens to determine what percentage of the population favours the registration of handguns. An experiment might involve a drug treatment given to a group of patients in order to determine its effectiveness as a cure. With the handgun survey, we collect data without modifying the people being polled, but the drug treatment consists of modification of the subjects.

Political Polls Grow

The publication of political polls during the period leading up to an election has been a controversial issue; some people believe that such polls have too much influence on voters' decisions. The use of polls, however, has grown over the last two decades. In the lead-up to the 1980 federal election, only 4 polls were published; that number grew to 24 in the period before the 1988 election. Polling is complicated by answering machines and people who refuse to cooperate, but good polls include repeated attempts to get responses from those who are not at home and those who refuse to answer. Ignoring those who don't answer or respond could result in a sample that is not representative of the population.

When designing an experiment, there are a few basic steps that should be followed:

1. *Identify your objective.* Identify the exact question to be answered, and clearly identify the relevant population. (For example, "Is the Salk vaccine effective in reducing the incidence of polio in the population of children?")

2. *Collect sample data.* The way in which sample data are collected is absolutely critical to the success of the experiment. The sample data must be representative of the population in question, the sample must be large enough so that the effects of the treatment can be known, and the question should be addressed without interference from extraneous factors.

3. *Use a random procedure that avoids bias.* (In the Salk vaccine experiment, for example, children were assigned to the two groups through a process of random selection.)

4. *Analyse the data and form conclusions.*

Controlling the Effects of Variables

When conducting an experiment, it is all too easy to receive interference from variable factors that are not relevant to the issue being studied. These effects can be controlled through good experimental design. Careful experiments often involve one group that is given a particular treatment (called a *treatment group*) and a second *control group* that is not given the treatment. For example, a 1954 polio experiment involved a treatment group of children who were injected with the Salk vaccine and a control group of children who were injected with a placebo that contained no medicine or drug. In experiments of this type, a **placebo effect** occurs when an untreated subject incorrectly believes that he or she is receiving a treatment and reports an improvement in symptoms. The placebo effect can be countered by using **blinding**, a technique in which the subject doesn't know whether he or she is receiving a treatment or a placebo. The polio experiment was *double-blind* in that the children being injected didn't know whether they were given the Salk vaccine or a placebo, and the doctors who gave the injections and evaluated the results didn't know either.

AS   When designing an experiment to test the effectiveness of one or more treatments, you should be careful to assign the *experimental units* (or subjects) to the different groups in such a way that those groups are very similar. (Such similar groups of experimental units are called **blocks.**) One effective approach is to use a **completely randomized experimental design**, which requires that the experimental units be divided into different groups through a process of *random* selection. For example, such a design might involve random assignment of people to a group treated with aspirin and a control group that is not treated. Another approach is to use a **rigorously controlled design**, with experimental units carefully chosen so that the different groups (or blocks) are carefully arranged to be similar. With a rigorously controlled design, you might try to design treatment and control groups to include people similar in age, weight, blood pressure, and so on. The polio experiment was a completely randomized experimental design because the subjects in both the treatment group and the control group were selected randomly. It incorporated replication by including very large (200,000) numbers of subjects in each group to reduce the effects of chance sample variation.

When conducting experiments, results are sometimes ruined because of *confounding*.

> **DEFINITION**
>
> **Confounding** occurs when the effects from two or more variables cannot be distinguished from each other.

For example, if you're conducting an experiment to test the effectiveness of a new fire retardant on a brush fire but it begins to rain, then confounding occurs because it's impossible to distinguish between the effect from the retardant and the effect from the rain.

One of the worst mistakes is to collect data in a way that is inappropriate. We cannot overstress this very important point:

Data carelessly collected may be so completely useless that no amount of statistical torturing can salvage them.

As well as being chosen appropriately, your sample must be sufficiently large to avoid misleading results, which can arise from the erratic behaviour of very small samples. Repetition of an experiment to increase sample size is called **replication**.

Randomization

We have just stressed the importance of selecting samples by appropriate techniques. In five of the more common methods, described below, *randomization* plays a crucial role in how the samples are chosen.

> **DEFINITIONS**
>
> In a **random sample,** members of the population are selected in such a way that each individual has an *equal chance* of being selected.
>
> A **simple random sample** of n subjects is selected in such a way that every possible sample of size n has the same chance of being chosen.

Random samples have been selected by a variety of methods, including using computers to generate random numbers and using tables of random numbers. With random sampling, we expect all groups of the population to be (approximately) proportionately represented in the sample. Careless or haphazard sampling can easily result in a biased sample with characteristics very unlike the population from which the sample came. Random sampling, in contrast, is carefully designed to avoid any bias. For example, using telephone directories automatically eliminates anyone with an unlisted number, and ignoring that segment of the population could easily yield misleading results. Pollsters commonly circumvent this problem by using computers to generate phone numbers so that all numbers are possible. They must also be careful to include those who are initially unavailable or initially refuse to comment. One polling company has found that the refusal rate for telephone interviews is generally at least 20%. If you ignore those people who initially refuse, you run a real risk of having a biased sample.

DEFINITION

With **stratified sampling,** we subdivide the population into at least two different subpopulations (or strata) that share the same characteristics (such as gender), then we draw a sample from each stratum.

In surveying views on pay equity, we might use gender as a basis for creating two strata. After obtaining a list of men and a list of women, we use some suitable method (such as random sampling) to select a certain number of people from each list. When the various strata have sample sizes that reflect the general population, we say that we have *proportionate* sampling. If it should happen that some strata are not represented in the proper proportion, then the results can be adjusted or weighted accordingly.

Given a fixed sample size, if you randomly select subjects from different strata, you are likely to get more consistent (and less variable) results than by simply selecting a random sample from the general population. For that reason, stratified sampling is often used to reduce the variation in the results.

DEFINITION

In **systematic sampling,** we select some starting point and then select every kth (such as every 50th) element in the population.

For example, if Noranda wanted to conduct a survey of its 33,000 employees, it could begin with a complete roster, then select every 100th employee to obtain a sample of size 330. This method is simple and is often used.

DEFINITION

In **cluster sampling,** we first divide the population area into sections (or clusters), then randomly select a few of those sections, and then choose *all* the members from those selected sections.

One important way that cluster sampling differs from stratified sampling is that cluster sampling uses *all* members from selected clusters, whereas stratified sampling uses a *sample* of members from each strata. An example of cluster sampling can be found in a pre-election poll, whereby we randomly select 30 election ridings and then survey all the people from each of those chosen ridings. This would be much faster and much less expensive than selecting one person from each of the many ridings in the population area. The results can be adjusted or weighted to correct for any disproportionate representations of groups. Cluster sampling is used extensively by government and private research organizations.

DEFINITION

With **convenience sampling,** we simply use results that are readily available.

In some cases results from convenience sampling may be quite good, but in other cases they may be seriously biased. In investigating the proportion of left-handed people, it would be convenient for a student to survey his or her classmates, because they are readily available. Even though such a sample is not random, the results should be quite good. In contrast, it might be convenient for CBC Radio to ask people to call the a toll-free number to register their opinions, but this would be a self-selected survey and the results would likely be biased.

Figure 1-2 illustrates the five common methods of sampling just described. The descriptions are intended to be brief and general. Thoroughly understanding these different methods so that you can successfully use them requires much more extensive study than is practical in a single introductory course. To keep this section in perspective, we should note that this text will make frequent reference to "randomly selected" data, and you should understand that such data are carefully selected so that all members of the population have the same chance of being chosen. Although we will not make frequent reference to the other methods of sampling, you should understand that they exist and that the method of sampling requires careful planning and execution. Note that if you are obtaining measurements of a characteristic (such as height) from people, you will get more accurate results if you do the measuring yourself instead of asking the subjects for the value. Asking tends to yield a disproportionate number of rounded results, as well as many results that reflect *desired* values instead of *actual* values.

No matter how well you plan and execute the sample collection process, there is likely to be some error in the results. For example, randomly select 1000 adults, ask them if they graduated from high school, and record the sample percentage of "yes" responses. If you randomly select another sample of 1000 adults, it is likely that you will obtain a *different* sample percentage. This unavoidable error is called **sampling error** and you should take it into account when interpreting sample results.

Meta-Analysis

The term *meta-analysis* refers to a technique of doing a study that essentially combines results of other studies. It has the advantage that separate smaller samples can be combined into one big sample, making the collective results more meaningful. It also has the advantage of using work that has already been done. Meta-analysis has the disadvantage of being only as good as the studies that are used. If the previous studies are flawed, the "garbage in, garbage out" phenomenon can occur. The use of meta-analysis is currently popular in medical research and psychological research; articles using meta-analysis have appeared in such journals as the *Canadian Journal of Cardiology* and the *Canadian Journal of Behavioural Science.*

Figure 1-2   Common Sampling Methods

Random Sampling

Each member of the population has an equal chance of being selected. Computers are often used to generate random telephone numbers.

Stratified Sampling

Classify the population into at least two strata, then draw a sample from each.

Systematic Sampling

Select every *k*th member.

Cluster Sampling

Divide the population area into sections, randomly select a few of those sections, and then choose all members in them.

Convenience Sampling

Use results that are readily available.

Hey! Do you believe in the death penalty?

DEFINITIONS

A **sampling error** is the difference between a sample result and the true population result; such an error results from chance sample fluctuations.

A **nonsampling error** occurs when the sample data are incorrectly collected, recorded, or analysed (such as by selecting a nonrandom and biased sample, using a defective measuring instrument, or copying the sample data incorrectly).

If we carefully collect a sample so that it is representative of the population, we can use the methods in this book to analyse the sampling error, but we must exercise extreme care so that nonsampling error is minimized.

1–4 Exercises A: Basic Skills and Concepts

In Exercises 1–4, determine whether the given description corresponds to an observational study or an experiment.

1. Temperatures and amounts of precipitation and snowfall are recorded in different locations across the country (as in Data Set 4 in Appendix B).
2. People who smoke are asked to halve the number of cigarettes consumed each day so that any effect on pulse rate can be measured.
3. In a physical education class, the effect of exercise on blood pressure is studied by requiring that half of the students walk a mile each day while the other students run a mile each day.
4. The relationship between weights of bears and their lengths is studied by measuring bears that have been anesthetized.

In Exercises 5–16, identify which of these types of sampling is used: random, stratified, systematic, cluster, or convenience.

5. When she wrote *Women and Love: A Cultural Revolution*, author Shere Hite based her conclusions on 4500 responses from 100,000 questionnaires distributed to women.
6. A psychologist at the University of Saskatchewan surveys all students from each of 20 randomly selected classes.
7. A sociologist at Grant MacEwen Community College selects 12 men and 12 women from each of 4 English classes.
8. Sony selects every 200th compact disc from the assembly line and conducts a thorough test of quality.
9. A tobacco lobbyist writes the name of each Member of Parliament on a separate card, shuffles the cards, and then draws 10 names.
10. The marketing manager for Sympatico tests a new sales strategy by randomly selecting 250 consumers with less than $50,000 in gross income and 250 consumers with gross income of at least $50,000.
11. Planned Parenthood polls 500 men and 500 women about their views concerning the use of contraceptives.

Hawthorne and Experimenter Effects

The well-known *placebo effect* occurs when an untreated subject incorrectly believes that he or she is receiving a real treatment and reports an alleviation of symptoms. The *Hawthorne effect* occurs when treated subjects somehow respond differently, simply because they are part of an experiment. (This phenomenon is called the "Hawthorne effect" because it was first observed in a study of factory workers at Western Electric's Hawthorne plant.) An *experimenter effect* (sometimes called a Rosenthall effect) occurs when the researcher or experimenter unintentionally influences subjects through such factors as facial expression, tone of voice, or attitude.

12. A market researcher for Air Canada interviews all passengers on each of 10 randomly selected flights.
13. A medical researcher from Acadia University interviews all leukemia patients in each of 20 randomly selected hospitals.
14. A reporter for the *Financial Post* interviews every 25th chief executive officer identified in that magazine's listing of the 500 companies with the highest stock market values.
15. A reporter for *Report on Business* obtains a numbered listing of the 1000 companies with the highest stock market values, uses a computer to generate 20 random numbers between 1 and 1000, and then interviews the chief executive officers of companies corresponding to these numbers.
16. In conducting research for the Ottawa evening news, a reporter for CBC interviews 15 people as they leave Revenue Canada audits.
17. Describe a procedure for obtaining a simple random sample of 200 students from the population of full-time students at your college.
18. Describe a procedure for obtaining a simple random sample of 100 eligible voters from your local riding.

1-4 Exercises B: Beyond the Basics

19. Two categories of survey questions are *open* and *closed*. An open question allows a free response, while a closed question allows only a fixed response. Here are examples:

    Open question: What do you think can be done to reduce crime?
    Closed question: Which of the following approaches would be most effective in reducing crime?
    - Hire more police officers.
    - Get parents to discipline children more.
    - Correct social and economic conditions in slums.
    - Improve rehabilitation efforts in jails.
    - Give convicted criminals tougher sentences.
    - Reform courts.
    a. What are the advantages and disadvantages of open questions?
    b. What are the advantages and disadvantages of closed questions?
    c. Which type is easier to analyse with formal statistical procedures, and why is that type easier?
20. Among the 10 provinces, one province is randomly selected. Then, a province-wide voter registration list is obtained and one name is randomly selected. Does this procedure result in a randomly selected voter?
21. We noted that systematic sampling could result in a random sample, but not a simple random sample.
    a. Does stratified sampling result in a random sample? A simple random sample? Explain.
    b. Does cluster sampling result in a random sample? A simple random sample? Explain.

Using Technology

We will make frequent reference to two particular software packages: Excel and STATDISK. STATDISK has two advantages: (1) it is easy-to-use software designed specifically as a supplement to this textbook, and (2) it's *free* to colleges that adopt this textbook. Excel is a higher-level statistical software package, but it is also relatively easy to use. Separate workbook/manuals for Excel and STATDISK are available as supplements to this book.

With Excel and STATDISK, programs are selected from a main menu bar at the top of the screen, as shown:

Excel: **File Edit View Insert Format Tools Data Window Help**

STATDISK: **File Edit Analysis Data Help**

To enter a *new* data set:

Excel: Select **File** from the main menu bar, then select the option of **New**, or click the **New File** icon on the toolbar.

STATDISK: Select **Data** from the main menu bar, then select the option of **Sample Editor.**

To *save* and name a data set:

Excel: Select **File** from the main menu bar, then select the option of **Save As**, or click the **Disk** icon on the toolbar, which brings up a **Save As** dialog box.

STATDISK: Select **File** from the main menu bar, then select the option of **Save As.**

To retrieve (or *open*) a previously stored data set:

Excel: Select **File** from the main menu bar, then select the option of **Open**, or click the **Open File** icon on the toolbar.

STATDISK: Select **File** from the main menu bar, then select the option of **Open.** In procedures where STATDISK is expecting input, you can also import data that have been stored in a column of an Excel spreadsheet. Open the relevant Excel file, and highlight the column containing the data; click on **Edit** then on **Copy.** Then open STATDISK, and place the cell pointer at the top of the column that requires the data; click on **Edit** then on **Paste.**

To *print* results:

Excel: Select **File** from the main menu bar, then select the option of **Print**, or select the **Printer** icon on the toolbar.

STATDISK: Select **File** from the main menu bar, then select the option of **Print.**

Leave Computers On

Some people turn off their computer whenever they finish an immediate task, whereas others leave it on until they know they won't be using it again until the next day. The computer's circuit board and chips do suffer from repeated on/off electrical power cycles. However, the monitor can be damaged when the same image is left on a screen for very long periods of time. The mean time between failures (MTBF) for hard disk drives was once around 5000 hours, but it's now up to about 30,000 hours. Considering the bad effects of on/off cycles on circuit boards and chips and the large MTBF for hard drives, it does make sense to leave computers on until the end of the day, provided the monitor's screen can be protected by making it blank or by using a screen-saver program. Many people use this strategy, which evolved in part from a statistical analysis of past events.

To *quit* the program:

Excel: Select **File** from the main menu bar, then select the option of **Exit.**

STATDISK: Select **File** from the main menu bar, then select the option of **Quit.**

Excel and STATDISK are each capable of performing almost all of the important operations discussed in this book.

The use of these programs is discussed further in *Using Excel for Statistics and Data Analysis* and the STATDISK *Student Laboratory Manual and Workbook* (7th edition).

Some statistics professors prefer to use other software packages, such as SPSS, SAS, BMDP, Execustat, Systat, Mystat, or Statgraphics. Whichever software package is chosen, students will generally benefit by improving the computer skills that have become so important in today's world.

• •

Vocabulary List

statistics
population
census
sample
parameter
statistic
data
quantitative data
qualitative data
categorical data
attribute data
discrete data
continuous data
numerical data
nominal level of measurement
ordinal level of measurement
interval level of measurement
ratio level of measurement
self-selected survey

observational study
experiment
placebo effect
binding
block
completely randomized experimental
    design
rigorously controlled design
replication
confounding
random sample
simple random sample
stratified sampling
systematic sampling
cluster sampling
convenience sampling
sampling error
nonsampling error

Review

This chapter began with a general description of the nature of statistics, then discussed different aspects of the nature of data. Uses and abuses of statistics were illustrated with examples. We then discussed the design of experiments, emphasizing the importance of good sampling methods. On completing this chapter, you should be able to do the following:

- Distinguish between a population and a sample
- Distinguish between a parameter and a statistic
- Identify the level of measurement (nominal, ordinal, interval, ratio) of a set of data
- Recognize the importance of good sampling methods, as well as the serious deficiency of poor sampling methods
- Understand the importance of good experimental design, including the control of variable effects, sample size, and randomization

Review Exercises

1. The Consumer Product Testing Laboratory selects a dozen batteries (labelled 9 volts) from each company that makes them. Each battery is tested for its actual voltage level.
   a. Are the values obtained discrete or continuous?
   b. Identify the level of measurement (nominal, ordinal, interval, ratio) for the voltages.
   c. Which type of sampling (random, stratified, systematic, cluster, convenience) is being used?
   d. Is this an observational study or an experiment?
   e. What is an important effect of consumers using batteries that are labelled 9 volts when, in reality, the voltage level is very different?

2. Researchers at the Consumer Product Testing Laboratory test samples of electronic surge protectors to find the voltage levels at which computers can be damaged. For each of the following, determine which of the four levels of measurement (nominal, ordinal, interval, ratio) is most appropriate.
   a. The measured voltage levels that cause damage
   b. Rankings (first, second, third, and so on) in order of quality for a sample of surge protectors
   c. Ratings of surge protectors as "recommended, acceptable, not acceptable"
   d. The room temperatures of the rooms in which the surge protectors are tested
   e. The countries in which the surge protectors were manufactured

3. *Report on Business* magazine conducts a survey by mailing a questionnaire to 5000 people known to invest in securities. On the basis of the results, the magazine editors conclude that most investors in Canada are pessimistic about the economy. What is wrong with that conclusion?

4. You plan to conduct an experiment to test the effectiveness of Statistiszene, a new drug that allegedly improves performance in learning statistics. You will use a sample of subjects who are treated with the drug and another sample of subjects who are given a placebo.
   a. What is blinding, and how might it be used in this experiment?
   b. Why is it important to use blinding in this experiment?
   c. What is a completely randomized block design?
   d. What is a rigorously controlled block design?
   e. What is replication, and why is it important?

5. Identify the type of sampling (random, stratified, systematic, cluster, convenience) used in each of the following.
   a. A sample of products is obtained by selecting every 100th item on the assembly line.
   b. Random numbers generated by a computer are used to select serial numbers of cars to be chosen for sample testing.
   c. An auto parts supplier obtains a sample of all items from each of 12 different randomly selected retail stores.
   d. A car maker conducts a marketing study involving test drives performed by a sample of 10 men and 10 women in each of 4 different age brackets.
   e. A car maker conducts a marketing study by interviewing potential customers who request test drives at a local dealership.

6. Census takers have found that in obtaining people's ages, they get more people of age 50 than of age 49 or 51. Can you explain how this might occur?

7. You plan to conduct a survey on your campus. What is wrong with selecting every 50th student leaving the cafeteria?

8. The *Ottawa Citzen* reports that a pro-choice rally was attended by 8725 people. Comment.

• •

Cumulative Review Exercises

This book's cumulative review exercises are designed to incorporate some material from preceding chapters, a feature that will be implemented in the following chapters. The exercises in this section use concepts learned before beginning the study of this book.

1. The following survey question raised concerns when responses suggested that about 22% of respondents thought that the Holocaust might not have occurred:

   "Does it seem possible or does it seem impossible to you that the Nazi extermination of the Jews never happened?"

   A subsequent poll showed that respondents were probably confused by the double negative in the wording of the question. Here is the wording used in a subsequent Roper poll:

   "Does it seem possible to you that the Nazi extermination of the Jews never happened, or do you feel certain that it happened?"

Is this second version substantially less confusing? Can you write the question in a way that is clearer than both of these versions?

2. Refer to the figure that follows. It is similar to one that Edwin Tufte, author of *The Visual Display of Quantitative Data*, refers to in observing: "This may well be the worst graphic ever to find its way into print." He notes that the graph reports "almost by happenstance, only five pieces of data (since the division within each year adds to 100 percent)." First examine this graph and identify the information it attempts to relate. Then design a new graph that relates the same information.

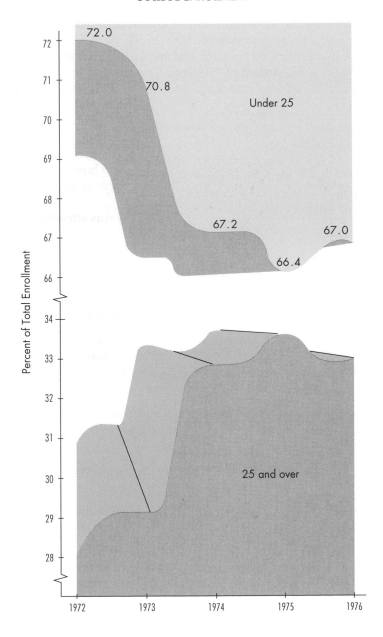

AGE STRUCTURE OF
COLLEGE ENROLLMENT

Technology Project

The objective of this project is to introduce the technology resources that can assist in collecting simple random samples. Suppose that the 108 temperatures in Data Set 18 in Appendix B were, instead of a sample, the complete data listing from a population. Use your statistics software to select a simple random sample of size 6 from this population.

Excel: In an empty cell, type in the Excel formula =randbetween (**1108**). This results in an integer in that range. Copy/paste this formula down a column. (*Hint:* paste to a larger number of cells than the intended size *n* of the sample.)

STATDISK: Click on **Data**, then on **Uniform Generator**. In the dialog box, input a **Sample Size (n)** which is larger than the actual *n* intended for your sample, and input a **Minimum** of 1 and a **Maximum** of 108, and 0 (zero) for **Number of Decimals**. Click on **Generate**.

In either of the two preceding methods, you have generated a list of random integers in the range 1 to 108. Each *distinct number* in the output represents one selected member of the sample; simply pick out the patient whose patient number corresponds. If a patient number has already been used, skip to the next number in the output, until all members of the sample have been chosen.

Adapt the method just shown to select a sample of size 5 from the "population" of Bonus numbers listed in Data Set 12 in Appendix B.

⋯⋯⋯⋯⋯ FROM DATA TO DECISION ⋯⋯⋯⋯⋯

Misrepresented Data

Collect an example from a current newspaper or magazine in which data have been presented in a deceptive manner. Identify the source (including the publication date) from which the example was taken. Explain the way in which the presentation is deceptive, and suggest how the data might be presented more fairly.

⋯⋯⋯⋯ COOPERATIVE GROUP ACTIVITIES ⋯⋯⋯⋯

1. *Out-of-class activity:* Divide into groups of 5, then collect 50 data values by using random sampling as described in Section 1-4. Then repeat the collection of 50 data values for each of the other four methods of sampling: stratified, systematic, cluster, convenience. In each case, calculate the "mean." (The mean is defined in Chapter 2 as the average obtained when the scores are added, and the total is then divided by the number of scores.) First describe in detail the procedure used for each method of sampling, then list the scores, then compare the five means. Does it appear that the different methods of sampling produce the same results? The sample data should be selected from a population such as the ages of books in your college library or the ages of cars in the student parking lot.

2. *In-class activity:* Divide into groups of three or four and use the data given below to construct a graph that exaggerates the increases in the high points of the TSE 300 Composite Index. Also construct a graph that de-emphasizes those increases, and construct a third graph that represents the data fairly.

Time Period	TSE 300 High
1980–84	2598.3
1985–89	4112.9
1990–94	4609.9
1995–98	7835.8

3. *In-class activity:* Divide into groups of three or four. Assume that you must conduct a survey of full-time students at your college. Design and describe in detail a procedure for obtaining a *random* sample of 100 students.

INTERNET PROJECT

In this section of each chapter, you will usually be directed to

http://www.pearsoned.com/triola

where a great variety of chapter-related activities, simulations, and examples (and links to other, related sites) await you. These activities will help you to explore and understand the rich nature of statistics and its importance in our world. So visit this Web site often and enjoy the activities!

Describing, Exploring, and Comparing Data

2-1 Overview

This chapter presents important tables, graphs, and measurements that can be used to describe a data set, explore a data set, or compare two or more data sets. Later chapters will use many of the important concepts introduced in this chapter.

2-2 Summarizing Data with Frequency Tables

The construction of frequency tables, relative frequency tables, and cumulative frequency tables is described. These tables are useful for condensing a large set of data to a smaller and more manageable summary.

2-3 Pictures of Data

Methods for constructing histograms, relative frequency histograms, stem-and-leaf plots, pie charts, Pareto charts, and scatter plots are presented. These graphs are extremely helpful in visually displaying characteristics of data that cannot be seen otherwise.

2-4 Measures of Centre

Measures of centre are attempts to find values that are representative of data sets. The following measures of centre are defined: mean, median, mode, midrange, and weighted mean. The concept of skewness is also considered.

2-5 Measures of Variation

Measures of variation are numbers that reflect the amount of scattering among the values in a data set. The following measures of variation are defined: range, standard deviation, mean deviation, and variance. Such measures are extremely important in statistical analyses.

2-6 Measures of Position

The standard score (or z score) is defined and used to illustrate how unusual values can be identified. Also defined are percentiles, quartiles, and deciles that are used to compare values within the same data set.

2-7 Exploratory Data Analysis (EDA)

Techniques for exploring data with 5-number summaries and boxplots are described. Boxplots are especially useful for comparing different data sets.

CHAPTER PROBLEM:

Can 12-oz aluminum cans be made thinner to save money?

Data Set 15 in Appendix B includes these two samples:

1. 12-oz aluminum cans that are 0.0109 in. thick (reproduced as Table 2-1)

2. 12-oz aluminum cans that are 0.0111 in. thick

We will explore the values in Table 2-1, which lists the axial loads (in pounds) of the sample of aluminum cans that are 0.0109 in. thick. This data set was supplied by a student who used a previous edition of this book. She is an employee of the company that manufactures the cans considered here, and she uses methods she learned in her introductory statistics course. The authors are grateful for her contributions.

The axial load of a can is the maximum weight supported by its sides, and it is measured by using a plate to apply increasing pressure to the top of the can until it collapses. It is important to have an axial load high enough so that the can isn't crushed when the top lid is pressed into place. In this particular manufacturing process, the top lids are pressed into place with pressures that vary between 158 lb and 165 lb.

Thinner cans have the obvious advantage of using less material so that costs are lower, but thinner cans are probably not as strong as the thicker ones. The company manufacturing these cans is currently using a 0.0111-in. thickness, but is testing to determine if the thinner cans could be used. Using the methods of this chapter, we will explore the data set (reproduced in Table 2-1) for these thinner cans (0.0109 in. thick). Ultimately, we will determine whether these thinner cans could be used.

Table 2-1   Axial Loads of 0.0109-in. Cans

270	273	258	204	254	228	282
278	201	264	265	223	274	230
250	275	281	271	263	277	275
278	260	262	273	274	286	236
290	286	278	283	262	277	295
274	272	265	275	263	251	289
242	284	241	276	200	278	283
269	282	267	282	272	277	261
257	278	295	270	268	286	262
272	268	283	256	206	277	252
265	263	281	268	280	289	283
263	273	209	259	287	269	277
234	282	276	272	257	267	204
270	285	273	269	284	276	286
273	289	263	270	279	206	270
270	268	218	251	252	284	278
277	208	271	208	280	269	270
294	292	289	290	215	284	283
279	275	223	220	281	268	272
268	279	217	259	291	291	281
230	276	225	282	276	289	288
268	242	283	277	285	293	248
278	285	292	282	287	277	266
268	273	270	256	297	280	256
262	268	262	293	290	274	292

2-1 Overview

We sometimes collect data in order to address a specific issue. For example, a safety study of the elevators in the CN Tower would require data concerning the average weight of the people who ride the elevators. In other cases, we collect or obtain data without having a specific objective, but because we wish to explore the data to see what might be revealed. A geologist may wonder about the time intervals between eruptions of the Old Faithful geyser—are they equally distributed over the range of times or do some time intervals occur more often than others? In both circumstances, we need a variety of tools that will help us *understand* the data set. This chapter presents those tools.

When analysing a data set, we should first determine whether we have a *sample* or a complete *population*. That determination will affect both the methods we use and the conclusions we form. We use methods of **descriptive statistics** to summarize or describe the important characteristics of an available set of data, and we use methods of **inferential statistics** when we specifically use sample data to make inferences (or generalizations) about a population. When your professor calculates the final exam average for your statistics class, that result is an example of a descriptive statistic. However, if we state that the result is an estimate of the final exam average for all statistics classes, we are making an inference that goes beyond the known data.

Descriptive statistics and inferential statistics are the two general divisions of the subject of statistics. This chapter deals with the basic concepts of descriptive statistics.

Important Characteristics of Data

When describing, exploring, and comparing data sets, the following characteristics of data are usually most important.

1. *Centre:* A representative or average value that indicates where the middle of the data set is located
2. *Variation:* A measure of the amount that the values vary among themselves
3. *Distribution:* The nature or shape of the distribution of the data (such as bell-shaped, uniform, or skewed)
4. *Outliers:* Sample values that lie very far away from the vast majority of the other sample values
5. *Time:* Changing characteristics of the data over time

In this chapter we begin showing how the tools of statistics can be applied to these characteristics of data to provide instructive insights. The chapter includes detailed steps for important procedures, although it is recognized that, today, a computer or calculator can automate many of these. We recommend that in each case you perform a few of the calculations manually, to enhance your understanding of the underlying techniques. (But using Excel to help with repetitive multiplying and so on is a handy compromise—if your computer is nearby.)

Summarizing Data with Frequency Tables

When investigating large data sets, it is generally helpful to organize and summarize the data by constructing a frequency table.

DEFINITION

A **frequency table** lists classes (or categories) of values, along with frequencies (or counts) of the number of values that fall into each class.

Table 2-2 is a frequency table with 10 classes. The **frequency** for a particular class is the number of original values that fall into that class. For example, the first class in Table 2-2 has a frequency of 9, indicating that there are 9 values between 200 and 209 inclusive.

We will first present some standard terms used in discussing frequency tables, and then we will describe a procedure for constructing them.

DEFINITIONS

Lower class limits are the smallest numbers that can actually belong to the different classes. (Table 2-2 has lower class limits of 200, 210, . . . , 290.)

Upper class limits are the largest numbers that can actually belong to the different classes. (Table 2-2 has upper class limits of 209, 219, . . . , 299.) For continuous data, these upper class limits actually represent the largest values in the classes—*when rounded to the indicated number of decimal places*. For example, the class 200–209 may, in fact, include a can with an axial load of 209.49, which has been rounded to 209; but a can with an axial load of 209.50 will have been rounded to 210 and included in the next class.

Class boundaries are the numbers used to separate classes, but without the gaps created by class limits. They are obtained as follows: Find the size of the gap between the upper class limit of one class and the lower class limit of the next class. Add half of that amount to each upper class limit to find the upper class boundaries; subtract half of that amount from each lower class limit to find the lower class boundaries. (Table 2-2 has class boundaries of 199.5, 209.5, 219.5, . . . , 299.5.)

Class midpoints are the midpoints of the classes. (Table 2-2 has class midpoints of 204.5, 214.5, . . . , 294.5.) Each class midpoint can be found by adding the lower class limit to the corresponding upper class limit and dividing the sum by 2.

Class width is the difference between two consecutive lower class limits or two consecutive lower class boundaries. (Table 2-2 uses a class width of 10.)

TABLE 2-2

Frequency Table of Axial Loads of Aluminum Cans

Axial Load	Frequency
200–209	9
210–219	3
220–229	5
230–239	4
240–249	4
250–259	14
260–269	32
270–279	52
280–289	38
290–299	14

The definitions of class midpoints and class boundaries are tricky. Be careful to avoid the easy mistake of making the class width the difference between the lower class limit and the corresponding upper class limit. See Table 2-2 and note that the class width is 10, not 9. You can simplify the process of finding class boundaries by understanding that they basically fill the gaps between classes by splitting the difference between the end of one class and the beginning of the next class. Carefully examine the definition of class boundaries, and spend some time until you understand it.

Constructing Frequency Tables

The main reason for constructing a frequency table is to use it for constructing a graph that effectively shows the distribution of the data (for example, see *histograms*, introduced in the following section.) It is important to observe the following *guidelines* when constructing a frequency table—whether manually or by using technology.

1. *Be sure that the classes are mutually exclusive.* That is, each of the original values must belong to exactly one class.
2. *Include all classes,* even if the frequency is zero.
3. *Try to use the same width for all classes,* although sometimes open-ended intervals such as "65 years or older" are impossible to avoid.
4. *Select convenient numbers for class limits.* Round up to use fewer decimal places or use numbers relevant to the situation.
5. *Use between 5 and 20 classes.*
6. *The sum of the class frequencies must equal the number of original data values.*

If you are constructing a frequency table manually, follow the procedure given below. (While some instructors include these detailed steps, others may skip them, perhaps preferring a computer-based approach.)

Step 1: *Decide on the number of classes your frequency table will contain.* As a guideline, the number of classes should be between 5 and 20. The actual number of classes may be affected by the convenience of using round numbers or other subjective factors.

Step 2: *Determine the class width by dividing the range by the number of classes.* (The range is the difference between the highest and the lowest scores.) Round the result *up* to a convenient number and to guarantee that all of the data will be included in the frequency table.

$$\text{class width} = \text{round } up \text{ of } \frac{\text{range}}{\text{number of classes}}$$

Step 3: *Select as the lower limit of the first class either the lowest score or a convenient value slightly less than the lowest score.* This value serves as the starting point.

Step 4: *Add the class width to the starting point to get the second lower class limit.* Add the class width to the second lower class limit to get the third, and so on. If you need to add one more class in order to include all the data, that is generally not a problem.

Step 5: *List the lower class limits in a vertical column, and enter the upper class limits, which can be easily identified at this stage.*

Step 6: *Represent each data value by a tally in the appropriate class, then use those tally marks to find the total frequency for each class.*

Determination of the number of classes is not yet part of federal law, so it is generally okay to use a different number of classes, which will result in a different frequency table, providing it has convenient and understandable values. (Exercise 25 in this section is about a possible exception.)

EXAMPLE   Construct a frequency table for the 175 axial loads of aluminum cans given in Table 2-1.

SOLUTION   We will list the steps that lead to the development of the frequency table shown in Table 2-2.

Step 1: We begin by selecting 10 as the number of desired classes. (Within the guideline of 5–20 classes, choose a small number of classes with smaller data sets and a larger number of classes with larger data sets.)

Step 2: With a minimum of 200 and a maximum of 297, the range is $297 - 200 = 97$, so

$$\text{class width} = \text{round up of } \frac{97}{10}$$
$$= \text{round up of } 9.7 \approx 10$$

Step 3: The lowest value is 200. Because it is a convenient value, it becomes the starting point and we use it for the lower limit of the first class.

Step 4: Add the class width of 10 to the lower limit of 200 to get the next lower limit of 210. Continuing, we get the other lower class limits of 220, 230, and so on.

Step 5: These lower class limits suggest these upper class limits

200   209
210   219
etc.

(the raw data are all rounded to the nearest whole unit).

Step 6: Count up the data values in each class, and enter the frequencies as shown in the right column of Table 2-2.

Table 2-2 provides useful information by making the list of axial loads more intelligible, but we cannot reconstruct the original 175 axial loads from the frequency table. We have traded the exactness of the original data for a better understanding of the data.

TABLE 2-3	
Relative Frequency Table of Axial Loads of Aluminum Cans	
Axial Load	Relative Frequency
200–209	0.051
210–219	0.017
220–229	0.029
230–239	0.023
240–249	0.023
250–259	0.080
260–269	0.183
270–279	0.297
280–289	0.217
290–299	0.080

Relative Frequency Table

An important variation of the basic frequency table uses **relative frequencies,** which are easily found by dividing each class frequency by the total of all the frequencies. The **relative frequency table** includes the same class limits as a frequency table, but relative frequencies are used instead of actual frequencies. The relative frequencies are often expressed as percentages.

$$\text{relative frequency} = \frac{\text{class frequency}}{\text{sum of all frequencies}}$$

Table 2-3 shows the relative frequencies for the 175 axial loads summarized in Table 2-2. The first class has a relative frequency of 9/175 = 0.051, or 5.1%. The second class has a relative frequency of 3/175 = 0.017, or 1.7%, and so on. If constructed correctly, the sum of the relative frequencies should total 1 (or 100%), with small discrepancies allowed for rounding errors.

Relative frequency tables make it easier for us to understand the distribution of the data and to compare different sets of data.

Cumulative Frequency Table

Another variation of the standard frequency table is used when cumulative totals are desired. The **cumulative frequency** for a class is the sum of the frequencies for that class and all previous classes. Table 2-4 is an example of a **cumulative frequency table,** with cumulative frequencies used instead of the individual class frequencies. For example, (in the first row) there are 9 values less than 210, and (in the second row) there are 9 + 3 = 12 values less than 220, and so on. If constructed correctly, the last cumulative frequency should be equal to the total number of values in the data set.

Using Technology

J	K
Bin	Frequency
209	9
219	3
229	5
239	4
249	4
259	14
269	32
279	52
289	38
299	14
More	0

Excel Display

Excel: Although Excel cannot generate a frequency distribution table from scratch, it can automate the job of tallying the frequencies within each class. Follow the guidelines of this section to decide on the best set of class limits. Input the *upper class limits* into an Excel column (for example, J5:J14). Input the raw data into a column or block of cells (for example, B4:H28). On Excel's menu bar, click **Tools,** then select **Data Analysis,** then **Histogram.** For *Input Range,* type in the address range for the raw data; for *Bin Range,* type in the address range for the column of upper class limits. For *Output Range,* type in the desired cell address for the *upper left corner* of the output. The output that corresponds to the chapter problem is shown here.

Exercises A: Basic Skills and Concepts

In Exercises 1–4, identify the class width, class midpoints, and class boundaries for the given frequency table.

1.

Absences	Frequency
0–5	39
6–11	41
12–17	38
18–23	40
24–29	42

2.

Absences	Frequency
0–9	22
10–19	40
20–29	71
30–39	44
40–49	23

3.

Weight (kg)	Frequency
0.00–1.99	20
2.00–3.99	32
4.00–5.99	49
6.00–7.99	31
8.00–9.99	18

4.

Weight (kg)	Frequency
0.0–4.9	60
5.0–9.9	58
10.0–14.9	61
15.0–19.9	62
20.0–24.9	59

TABLE 2-4

Cumulative Frequency Table of Axial Loads

Axial Load	Cumulative Frequency
Less than 210	9
Less than 220	12
Less than 230	17
Less than 240	21
Less than 250	25
Less than 260	39
Less than 270	71
Less than 280	123
Less than 290	161
Less than 300	175

In Exercises 5–8, construct the relative frequency table that corresponds to the frequency table in the exercise indicated.

5. Exercise 1   **6.** Exercise 2   **7.** Exercise 3   **8.** Exercise 4

In Exercises 9–12, construct the cumulative frequency table that corresponds to the frequency table in the exercise indicated.

9. Exercise 1   **10.** Exercise 2   **11.** Exercise 3   **12.** Exercise 4

13. Compare the *distribution* of the data in Exercise 1 to the *distribution* of the data in Exercise 2. What is the basic difference?

14. Compare the *distribution* of the data in Exercise 3 to the *distribution* of the data in Exercise 4. What is the basic difference?

In Exercises 15–16, use the given information to find upper and lower limits of the first class. (The data are in Appendix B, but there is no need to refer to the appendix for these exercises.)

15. A data set consists of weights of metal collected from households for one week. Those weights range from 0.26 lb to 4.95 lb. You wish to construct a frequency table with 10 classes.

16. A sample of M&M candies has weights that vary between 0.838 g and 1.033 g. You wish to construct a frequency table with 12 classes.

In Exercises 17–20, construct the frequency table and answer the associated questions.

17. Refer to the labour force data in Data Set 14 in Appendix B, using the column for male Newfoundlanders. Construct a frequency table of the sizes of occupational groups—interpreting the "size" of an occupational group as the number of male Newfoundlanders having a given SOC code. Use 12 classes, beginning with a lower class limit of 0. Describe two different notable features of the result.

18. Refer to the TEMPAGE column in Data Set 18 in Appendix B, and construct a frequency table of the ages of patients admitted for voluntary surgery. Start at age 13 and use a class width of 17.5. Does the result violate any of the guidelines for constructing frequency tables?

19. Refer to Data Set 20 in Appendix B, and construct a frequency table with 10 classes of the annual unemployment rates for Canada. The table you construct will have no reference to time or year. Compare the table with the original data, and evaluate whether the unemployment numbers appear random with respect to time, or whether time is associated in some way with the results of the frequency distribution.

20. Refer to Data Set 21 in Appendix B. A set of high-price diamonds is sold at auction. Construct a frequency table for the variable colour of the diamonds. If the colour of diamonds which fetch over $50,000 is never greater than 3, are these diamonds likely to be bought at prices over $50,000?

21. Below are two frequency tables for 32 cities, showing annual precipitation and annual snowfall. First construct the corresponding relative frequency tables, and then use those results to compare the two samples.

Precipitation (mm)	Frequency	Snowfall (cm)	Frequency
266 up to 492	8	32 up to 68	2
492 up to 718	4	68 up to 104	1
718 up to 944	7	104 up to 140	5
944 up to 1170	6	140 up to 176	3
1170 up to 1396	2	176 up to 212	4
1396 up to 1622	4	212 up to 248	4
1622 up to 1848	0	248 up to 284	2
1848 up to 2074	0	284 up to 320	4
2074 up to 2300	0	320 up to 356	5
2300 up to 2526	1	356 up to 392	2

2-2 Exercises B: Beyond the Basics

22. Listed below are two sets of scores that are supposed to be heights (in inches) of randomly selected adult males. One of the sets consists of heights actually obtained from randomly selected adult males, but the other set consists of numbers that were fabricated. Construct a frequency table for each set of heights. By examining the two frequency tables, identify the set of data that you believe to be false, and state your reason.

a. 70 73 70 72 71 73 71 67 68 72 67 72 71 73
72 70 72 68 71 71 71 73 69 73 71 66 77 67

b. 70 73 70 72 71 66 74 76 68 75 67 68 71 77
66 69 72 67 77 75 66 76 76 77 73 74 69 67

23. Refer to Data Set 15 in Appendix B. The axial loads are the weights that were applied before the cans collapsed. Construct two separate frequency tables for the cans that are 0.0111 in. thick. In the first table, do not include the value of 504 lb. Start the first class at 200 lb and use a class width of 20 lb. The load of 504 lb is called an outlier because it is far away from all the other values. Construct a second frequency table which does include that value. Compare the results, and interpret the effect of the outlier on the results.

24. In constructing a frequency table, Sturges' guideline suggests that the ideal number of classes can be approximated by $1 + (\log n) / (\log 2)$, where n is the number of values. Use this guideline to suggest a tentative number of classes (rounded off) for constructing a frequency table from a data set with this many values.

    a. 50   **b.** 100   **c.** 150
    d. 500   **e.** 1000   **f.** 50,000

25. Is it possible that the number of classes in a frequency table can have a dramatic effect on the apparent distribution of the data? If so, construct a data set for which a change from five classes to six results in a dramatic change in the apparent distribution of the frequencies.

2–3   Pictures of Data

In Section 2-2 we showed how frequency tables can be used to describe, explore, or compare distributions of data sets. In this section we continue the study of distributions by introducing graphs that show the distributions of data in pictorial form. As you read through this section, keep in mind that the objective is not simply to construct a graph, but rather to learn something about a data set—that is, to understand the nature of the distribution.

Histograms

A common and important graphic device for presenting frequency of information is the histogram.

DEFINITION

A **histogram** is a bar graph in which the horizontal scale represents classes and the vertical scale represents frequencies. The heights of the bars correspond to the frequency values, and the bars are drawn adjacent to each other (usually without gaps—at least for manually drawn versions).

We generally construct a histogram after we have first completed a frequency table representing a data set. Each bar of a histogram is marked with its lower class boundary at the left and its upper class boundary at the right. Improved readability, however, is often achieved by using class midpoints instead of class boundaries. The histogram in Figure 2-1 corresponds directly to the frequency table (Table 2-2) in the previous section.

Before constructing a histogram from a completed frequency table, we must give some consideration to the scales used on the vertical and horizontal axes. The maximum frequency (or the next highest convenient number) should suggest a value for the top of the vertical scale; 0 should be at the bottom. In Figure 2-1 we designed the vertical scale to run from 0 to 60. The horizontal scale should be designed to accommodate all the classes of the frequency table. Ideally, we should try to follow the rule of thumb that the vertical height of the histogram should be about three-fourths of the total width. Both axes should be clearly labelled.

AS Relative Frequency Histogram

A **relative frequency histogram** has the same shape and horizontal scale as a histogram, but the vertical scale is marked with *relative frequencies* instead of actual frequencies, as in Figure 2-2.

Frequency tables and graphs such as histograms enable us to see how our data are distributed, and the distribution of data is an extremely important characteristic. Figure 2-3 is roughly bell-shaped in the sense that it resembles the shape shown in the margin. Many procedures in statistics require that a distribution have a bell-shaped distribution similar to the one shown in Figure 2-3, and one way to check that requirement is to construct a histogram.

Compare the ideal bell shape with Figure 2-1, the axial loads of aluminum cans. The fact that the left tail of the distribution extends far to the left, showing that a number of cans had apparently low values for their axial loads, might be an indicator of a quality problem.

Bell Shape

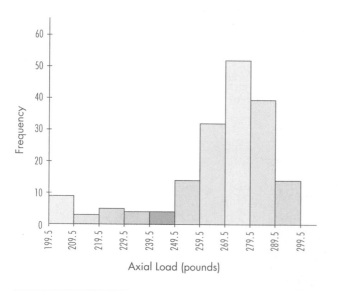

Figure 2-1 Histogram of Axial Loads of Aluminum Cans

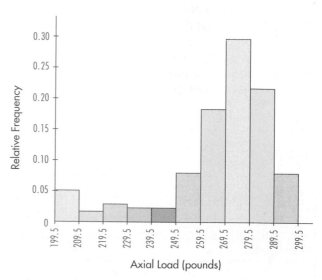

Figure 2-2 Relative Frequency Histogram of Axial Loads of Aluminum Cans

Figure 2-3 Histogram of Weights of Quarters

Frequency Polygon

A **frequency polygon** uses line segments connected to points located directly above the class midpoint values for a frequency distribution. Figure 2-4 shows the frequency polygon corresponding to Table 2-2. The heights of the points correspond to the class frequencies, and the line segments are extended to the left and right so that the graph meets the x axis at one class width below the lowest class midpoint, and at one class width above the largest class midpoint.

Ogive

An **ogive** (pronounced "oh-jive") is a line graph that depicts cumulative frequencies, just as the cumulative frequency table (see Table 2-4 in the preceding section) lists cumulative frequencies. Figure 2-5 is an ogive corresponding to Table 2-4. Note that the ogive uses class boundaries along the horizontal scale and that the graph begins with the lower boundary of the first class and ends with the upper boundary of the last class. Ogives are useful for determining the number of values *less than* some particular class boundary. For example, Figure 2-5 shows that about 160 of the values are less than 289.5.

Figure 2-4 Frequency Polygon for Axial Loads of Aluminum Cans

Figure 2-5 Ogive of Axial
Loads of Aluminum Cans

Stem-and-Leaf Plots

In a **stem-and-leaf plot** we sort data according to a pattern that reveals the underlying distribution. The pattern involves separating a number (such as 257) into two parts, usually the first one or two digits (25) and the other digits (7). The stem consists of the leftmost digits (in this case, 25), and the leaves consist of the rightmost digits (in this case, 7). The method is illustrated in the following example.

EXAMPLE   Use the axial loads of aluminum cans listed in Table 2-1 to construct a stem-and-leaf plot.

SOLUTION   If we use the two leftmost digits for the stem, the stems consist of 20, 21, . . . , 29. We then draw a vertical line and list the leaves as shown below. The first value in Table 2-1 is 270, and we include that value by entering a 0 in the stem row for 27. We continue to enter all 175 values, and then we arrange the leaves (the digits positioned to the right) so that the numbers are arranged in increasing order. The first row represents the numbers 200, 201, 204, 204, 206, and so on.

Stem	Leaves
20	014466889
21	578
22	03358
23	0046
24	1228
25	01122466677899
26	0122222333334555677888888889999
27	0000000011222223333334444555566666777777778888888999
28	0001111222222333333444455566667789999
29	00011222334557

By turning the page on its side, we can see a distribution of these data. Here's the great advantage of the stem-and-leaf plot: We can see the distribution of the data and yet retain all the information in the original list; if necessary, we could reconstruct the original list of values.

You might notice that the rows of digits in a stem-and-leaf plot are similar in nature to the bars in a histogram. One of the guidelines for constructing histograms is that the number of classes should be between 5 and 20, and that same guideline applies to stem-and-leaf plots for the same reasons. Stem-and-leaf plots can be *expanded* to include more rows and can also be *condensed* to include fewer rows. The stem-and-leaf plot of the preceding example can be expanded by subdividing rows into those with the digits 0 through 4 and those with digits 5 through 9. This expanded stem-and-leaf plot is shown here.

When it becomes necessary to *reduce* the number of rows, we can *condense* a stem-and-leaf plot by combining adjacent rows, as in the following illustration. Note that we separate digits in the leaves associated with the numbers in each stem by an asterisk. Every row in the condensed plot must include exactly one asterisk so that the shape of the plot is not distorted.

Stem	Leaves
20	0144
20	66889
21	
21	578
22	033
22	58
23	004
23	6
24	122
24	8
25	011224
25	66677899
26	0122222333334
26	5556778888888889999
27	000000001122222333334444
27	5555666667777777778888888999
28	0001111222222333334444
28	555666677899999
29	00011222334
29	557

    78-79   07*4 ← This row represents 780, 787, 794.
    80-81   *55   ← This row represents 815, 815.
    82-83   9*   ← This row represents 829.
    84-85   *   ← This row has no data.
    86-87   79*0 ← This row represents 867, 869, 870.

AS Another advantage of stem-and-leaf plots is that their construction provides a fast and easy procedure for *sorting* data (arranging data in order). Data must be sorted for a variety of statistical procedures, such as finding the median (discussed in Section 2-4) and finding percentiles or quartiles (discussed in Section 2-6).

Pareto Charts

Consider this statement: Among 186,291 deaths in Canada in 1995, 79,107 were attributable to heart disease, 58,817 to cancer, 18,886 to respiratory diseases, 15,537 to stroke, 7723 to accidents, 3968 to suicide, 1764 to AIDS, and 489 to murder (based on data from Statistics Canada). The information contained in this statement concerning the relationships among the data would be much more effectively conveyed in a Pareto chart. A **Pareto chart** is a bar graph for qualitative data, with the bars arranged in order according to frequencies. As in histograms, vertical scales in Pareto charts can represent frequencies or relative frequencies. The tallest bar is at the left, and the smaller bars are at the right, as in Figure 2-6. By arranging the bars in the order of frequency, the Pareto chart focuses attention on the more important categories. From Figure 2-6 we can see that heart disease is a problem that is much more prevalent than the other categories.

Florence Nightingale

Florence Nightingale (1820–1910) is known to many as the founder of the nursing profession, but she also saved thousands of lives by using statistics. When she encountered an unsanitary and undersupplied hospital, she improved those conditions and then used statistics to convince others of the need for more widespread medical reform. She developed original graphs to illustrate that, during the Crimean War, more soldiers died as a result of unsanitary conditions than were killed in combat. Florence Nightingale pioneered the use of social statistics as well as graphics techniques.

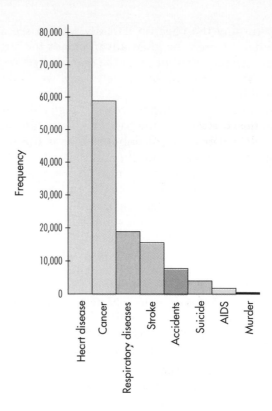

Figure 2-6   Pareto Chart of Deaths by Type

Pie Charts

Like Pareto charts, pie charts are used to depict qualitative data in a way that makes them more understandable. Figure 2-7 shows an example of a **pie chart,** which graphically depicts qualitative data as slices of a pie. Construction of such a pie chart involves slicing up the pie into the proper proportions. If the category of heart disease represents 42.5% of the total, then the wedge representing heart disease should be 42.5% of the total. (The central angle should be $0.425 \times 360° = 153°$.)

The Pareto chart of Figure 2-6 and the pie chart of Figure 2-7 depict the same data in different ways, but a comparison will probably show that the Pareto chart does a better job of showing the relative sizes of the different components.

Scatter Diagrams

A **scatter diagram** is a plot of paired (x, y) data with a horizontal x-axis and a vertical y-axis. The data are paired in a way that matches each value from one data set with a corresponding value from a second data set. To manually construct a scatter diagram, construct a horizontal axis for the values of the

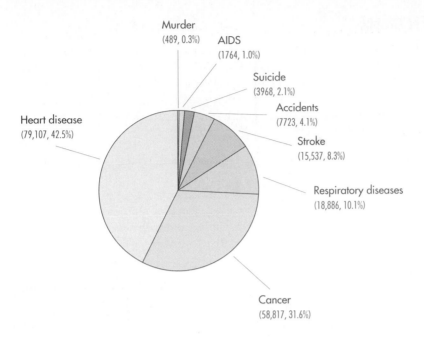

Figure 2-7 Pie Chart of Deaths by Type

first variable, construct a vertical axis for the values of the second variable, then plot the points. The pattern of the plotted points is often helpful in determining whether there is some relationship between the two variables. (This issue is discussed at length when the topic of correlation is considered in Section 9-2.)

Using the data on Canadian exports and imports to and from Europe in Data Set 22 in Appendix B, we used Excel to generate the scatter diagram shown in Figure 2-8. On the basis of that graph, there does appear to be a relationship between the dollar values of imports and imports, as shown by the pattern of the points.

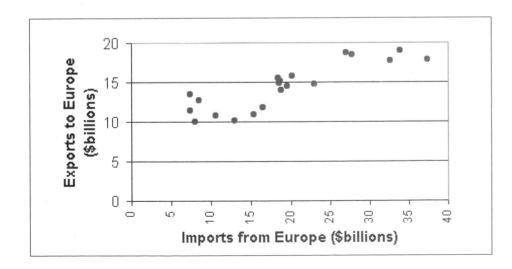

Figure 2-8 Scatter Diagram Comparing Canadian Imports and Exports

Invisible Ink

The *National Observer* once hired a firm to conduct a confidential mail survey. Editor Henry Gemmill wrote in a cover letter that "each individual reply will be kept confidential, of course, but when your reply is combined with others from all over this land, we'll have a composite picture of our subscribers." One clever subscriber used an ultra-violet light to detect a code written on the survey in invisible ink. That code could be used to identify the respondent. Gemmill was not aware that this procedure was used, and he publicly apologized. Confidentiality was observed as promised, but anonymity was not directly promised, and it was not maintained.

Other Graphs

Numerous pictorial displays other than the ones just described can be used to represent data dramatically and effectively. Section 2-7 will present boxplots, which are very useful for seeing the distribution of data. Pictographs depict data by using pictures of objects, such as soldiers, tanks, airplanes, stacks of coins, or moneybags. Various graphs in Chapter 12 and Chapter 14 depict patterns of data over time.

Conclusion

In this section we have focused on the nature or shape of the distribution of data and methods of graphically depicting data. When we create meaningful pictures of data, we are really doing the following:

Describing data: In a histogram, for example, we consider the shape of the distribution, whether there are extreme values, and any other notable characteristics. We note the overall shape of the distribution. Are the values evenly distributed? Is the distribution skewed (lopsided) to the right or left? Does the distribution peak in the middle? We observe any outliers (values located far away from most of the other values) that might hide the true nature of the distribution.

Exploring data: We look for any features of the graph that reveal useful and/or interesting characteristics of the data set. In Figure 2-9, for example, we see a common distribution pattern among graphs of *severities*—such as the severities of loss or damage caused by different storms or accidents. Based on Data Set 20 in Appendix B, it appears that for both the air and rail transportation industries, most stoppages result in relatively few person-days lost; but there is an extended tail of work stoppages that involve many more people.

Comparing data: Figure 2-9 allows us to compare the person-days-lost distributions for work stoppages in the air and rail transportation industries. It appears that the air transportation industry has been more prone to work stoppages that involve 62,500 or more person-days lost.

 ## Using Technology

Excel: Excel can generate many of the graphs discussed in this section. In fact, Figure 2-4 (frequency polygon), Figure 2-5 (ogive), Figure 2-8 (scatter diagram), and Figure 2-9 (histogram comparisons) were all created with Excel. (Pie charts can also be generated in Excel.) For any of these graph types, begin by entering the relevant data in separate Excel columns. (For a histogram, for example, enter the class [or category] labels in one column, and the corresponding data values in another.) Click on Excel's "Chart Wizard" icon, and proceed by using the dialog box which appears.

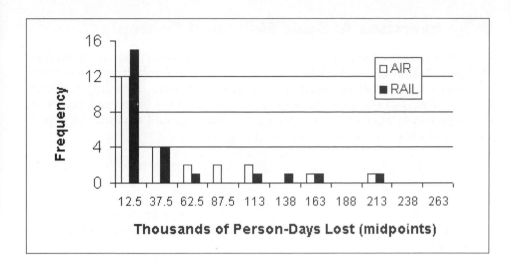

Figure 2-9   Person-Days Lost Through Work Stoppages (Air vs. Rail Transportation Industries)

STATDISK: An advantage of STATDISK is that you can generate histograms directly from the raw data—without needing to first construct a frequency table. Click to select **Data**, then **Histogram**. The data can be input on the right side of the dialog box, either directly or by cutting and pasting from another data source, such as a spreadsheet column. Then click the **Evaluate** button. As displayed in the figure, you have the choice of specifying the class width and class start (i.e., the lowest lower class limit), or you can click on **Auto Fit** and let STATDISK decide on these values for you. You can also click **Data**, then **Scatter Diagram**, to generate a scatter diagram from the raw data for two paired variables.

STATDISK Display

2-3 Exercises A: Basic Skills and Concepts

1. Visitors to Yellowstone National Park consider an eruption of the Old Faithful geyser to be a major attraction that should not be missed. The given frequency table summarizes a sample of times (in minutes) between eruptions. Construct a histogram corresponding to the given frequency table. If you're scheduling a bus tour of Yellowstone, what is the minimum time you should allocate to Old Faithful if you want to be reasonably sure that your tourists will see an eruption?

Time	Frequency
40–49	8
50–59	44
60–69	23
70–79	6
80–89	107
90–99	11
100–109	1

2. Samples of student cars and faculty/staff cars were obtained at the author's college, and their ages (in years) are summarized in the accompanying frequency table. Construct a relative frequency histogram for student cars and another relative frequency histogram for faculty cars. Based on the results, what are the noticeable differences between the two samples?

Age	Students	Faculty/Staff
0–2	23	30
3–5	33	47
6–8	63	36
9–11	68	30
12–14	19	8
15–17	10	0
18–20	1	0
21–23	0	1

3. The given group data were collected on the amount of income tax payable for the clients of an accounting firm. Construct a histogram corresponding to this frequency table.

Income Tax Payable	Number of Clients
$0 to less than $1000	15
$1000 to less than $2000	21
$2000 to less than $3000	35
$3000 to less than $4000	12

4. Canadian Automated Electronics (CAE) did a study of time to complete tasks entailing simulation control for 25 employees. Construct a relative frequency histogram that corresponds to the given frequency table. The data are a summary of the study. What does the histogram suggest about the time taken to complete a task?

Minutes	Frequency
100 up to 200	1
200 up to 300	8
300 up to 400	5
400 up to 500	1
500 up to 600	0
600 up to 700	1
700 up to 800	4
800 up to 900	5

In Exercises 5 and 6, list the original numbers in the data set represented by the given stem-and-leaf plots.

5.

Stem	Leaves
57	017
58	13349
59	456678
60	23

6.

Stem	Leaves
10	21 45 91
11	11 32 77 83
12	04 22 49
13	69

In Exercises 7 and 8, construct the stem-and-leaf plots for the given data sets found in Appendix B.

7. The lengths (in inches) of the bears in Data Set 3. (*Hint:* First round the lengths to the nearest inch.)

8. Weights (in pounds) of plastic discarded by 62 households as listed in Data Set 1. Start by rounding the listed weights to the nearest tenth of a pound (or one decimal place). (Use an expanded stem-and-leaf plot with about 11 rows.)

9. A study was conducted to determine how people get jobs. The table below lists data from 400 randomly selected subjects. Construct a Pareto chart that corresponds to the given data. If someone would like to get a job, what seems to be the most effective approach?

Job Sources of Survey Respondents	Frequency
Help-wanted ads	56
Executive search firms	44
Networking	280
Mass mailing	20

10. Refer to the data given in Exercise 9, and construct a pie chart. Compare the pie chart to the Pareto chart, and determine which graph is more effective in showing the relative importance of job sources.

11. A local power commission sent a survey to homeowners to determine household power efficiency. Following is a list of major electrical appliances and their total kilowatt-hour (kWh) usage for one year. Construct a pie chart representing the given data.

Appliance	Total Use (kWh)
Refrigerator	1525
Freezer	1206
All other	1190
Lights	1109
Heating fan/pump	1082
Laundry	750
Air conditioning	725
Cooking	547
Television	189
Stereo	186
Dishwasher	176
Microwave oven	94

12. Refer to the data given in Exercise 11 and construct a Pareto chart. Compare the Pareto chart to the pie chart, and determine which graph is more effective in showing the relative power consumption of the appliances.

13. Refer to the labour force data in Data Set 14 in Appendix B, using the two columns for Male and Female Newfoundlanders. Compare the sizes of the occupational groups for each of the two genders by constructing two frequency polygons on the same axis. (Interpret the "size" of an occupational group as the number of individuals having a given SOC code.) (Compare Exercise 17 in Section 2-2.) Does the distribution of job-group sizes appear to differ substantially for male and female members of the Newfoundland labour force? Can we tell from the results if it is the same job groups for both genders that have the higher frequencies?

14. Construct an ogive based on the sizes of occupational groups for Male Newfoundlanders in the labour force. (See Exercise 13.) As above, interpret the "size" of an occupational group as the number of individuals having a given SOC code. Use the ogive to estimate the median size of the occupational groups (that is, the size below which half of the sizes of occupational groups fall).

In Exercises 15–16, use the given paired data from Appendix B to construct a scatter diagram.

15. In Data Set 4, use average annual temperature for the horizontal scale and use precipitation for the vertical scale. Based on the result, does there appear to be a relationship between average annual temperature and precipitation?

16. In Data Set 3, use the distances around bear necks for the horizontal scale and use the bear weights for the vertical scale. Based on the result, what is the relationship between a bear's neck size and its weight?

In Exercises 17–20, refer to the data sets in Appendix B.

   a. Construct a histogram.
   b. Describe the general shape of the distribution, such as bell-shaped, uniform, or skewed (lopsided).

17. Data Set 3 in Appendix B: weights of bears (use 11 classes with a class width of 50 and begin with a lower class boundary of -0.5).

18. Data Set 11 in Appendix B: weights of 100 M&Ms (use 12 classes with a class width of 0.017 and begin with a lower class boundary of 0.8375.)

19. Data Set 1 in Appendix B: weights of paper discarded by 62 households in one week (use 10 classes).

20. Data Set 12 in Appendix B: the 300 numbers selected in the Lotto 6/49 (not the bonus numbers).

2-3 Exercises B: Beyond the Basics

21. Frequency tables are given for the first 100 digits in the decimal representation of π and the first 100 digits in the decimal representation of 22/7.

π			22/7	
x	f		x	f
0	8		0	0
1	8		1	17
2	12		2	17
3	11		3	1
4	10		4	17
5	8		5	16
6	9		6	0
7	8		7	16
8	12		8	16
9	14		9	0

a. Construct histograms representing the frequency tables, and note any differences.

b. The numbers π and 22/7 are both real numbers, but how are they fundamentally different?

22. In an insurance study of motor vehicle accidents, fatal crashes are categorized according to time of day, with the results given in the accompanying table.

a. Complete the circular bar chart and construct a histogram.

b. Which is more effective in depicting the data? Why?

c. Because the time period 4:00 A.M. to 6:00 A.M. has the lowest number of fatal crashes, is that time period the safest time to drive? Why or why not?

Time of Day	Number of Fatal Crashes
A.M. 12–2	194
2–4	149
4–6	100
6–8	131
8–10	119
10–12	160
P.M. 12–2	152
2–4	221
4–6	230
6–8	211
8–10	223
10–12	178

23. Using a collection of sample data, we construct a frequency table with 10 classes and then construct the corresponding histogram. How is the histogram affected if the number of classes is doubled but the same vertical scale is used?

24. In "Ages of Oscar-Winning Best Actors and Actresses" (*Mathematics Teacher* magazine) by Richard Brown and Gretchen Davis, stem-and-leaf plots are used to compare the ages of actors and actresses at the time they won Oscars. Here are the results for 34 recent winners from each category:

Actors: 32 37 36 32 51 53 33 61 35 45 55 39
            76 37 42 40 32 60 38 56 48 48 40
            43 62 43 42 44 41 56 39 46 31 47

Actresses: 50 44 35 80 26 28 41 21 61 38 49 33
            74 30 33 41 31 35 41 42 37 26 34
            34 35 26 61 60 34 24 30 37 31 27

a. Construct a back-to-back stem-and-leaf plot for the above data. The first two scores from each group have been entered below.

Actors' Ages	Stem	Actresses' Ages
	2	
72	3	
	4	4
	5	0
	6	
	7	
	8	

b. Using the results from part (a), compare the two different sets of data, and explain any differences.

2-4 Measures of Centre

The main objective of this section is to present the important measures of centre, and to show how to compute them.

DEFINITION

A **measure of centre** is a value at the centre or middle of a data set.

Whereas Sections 2-2 and 2-3 considered frequency tables and graphs that reveal the nature or shape of the *distribution* of a data set, this section focuses on finding values that are typical or at the *centre* of a data set. There are different criteria for determining the centre, and so there are different definitions of measures of centre, including the mean, median, mode, and midrange. We begin with the mean.

Mean

The (arithmetic) mean is generally the most important of all numerical descriptive measurements, and it is what most people call an average. In Figure 2-10 we illustrate that the mean is at the centre of the data set in the sense that it is a balance point for the data.

DEFINITION

The **arithmetic mean** of a set of values is the number obtained by adding the values and dividing the total by the number of values. This particular measure of central tendency will be used frequently throughout the remainder of this text, and it will be referred to simply as the **mean**.

This definition can be expressed as Formula 2-1, where the Greek letter Σ (uppercase Greek sigma) indicates *summation* of values, so that Σx represents the sum of all data values. Also, the symbol n denotes the **sample size**, which is the number of values in the data set.

Formula 2-1
$$\text{mean} = \frac{\Sigma x}{n}$$

The mean is denoted by $\bar{x}$ (pronounced "x-bar") if the available values are a sample from a larger population; if all values of the population are available, then we can denote the computed mean by μ (lowercase Greek mu).

Class Size Paradox

There are at least two ways to obtain the mean class size, and they can have very different results. At one college, if we take the numbers of students in 737 classes, we get a mean of 40 students. But if we were to compile a list of the class sizes for each student and use this list, we would get a mean class size of 147. This large discrepancy is due to the fact that there are many students in large classes, while there are few students in small classes. Without changing the number of classes or faculty, we could reduce the mean class size experienced by students by making all classes about the same size. This would also improve attendance, which is better in smaller classes.

2–4   Measures of Centre   53

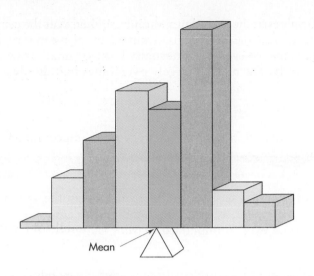

Figure 2-10 Mean as a Balance Point

Figure 2-10 Mean as a Balance Point
If a fulcrum is placed at the position of the mean, it will balance the histogram.

Mean

Notation	
Σ	denotes the *addition* (called the *summation*) of a set of values.
x	is the *variable* usually used to represent the individual data values.
n	represents the *number of values in a sample*.
N	represents the *number of values in a population*.
$\bar{x} = \dfrac{\Sigma x}{n}$	is the *mean of a set of sample values*.
$\mu = \dfrac{\Sigma x}{N}$	denotes the *mean of all values in a population*.

EXAMPLE   A potato chip packaging plant selects 10 bags for a quality control check. The weights in grams are listed below. Find the mean for this sample.

454.1 455.0 454.2 454.9 454.7 454.4 455.1 454.6 454.4 455.2

SOLUTION
The mean is computed by using Formula 2-1. First add the values:

$$\Sigma x = 454.1 + 455.0 + 454.2 + 454.9 + 454.7 + 454.4$$
$$+ 455.1 + 454.6 + 454.4 + 455.2 = 4546.6$$

Now divide the total by the number of values present. Because there are 10 values, we have $n = 10$ and get

$$\bar{x} = \frac{4546.6}{10} = 454.66$$

The mean value is therefore 454.66 g.

Six Degrees of Separation

Social psychologists, historians, political scientists, and communications specialists are among those interested in the "Small World Problem": Given any two people in the world, how many intermediate links are required in order to connect the two original people? Social psychologist Stanley Milgram conducted an experiment using the U.S. mail system. Subjects were instructed to try to contact other target people by mailing an information folder to an acquaintance who they thought would be closer to the target. Among 160 such chains that were initiated, only 44 were completed. The number of intermediate acquaintances varied from 2 to 10, with a median of 5. A mathematical model was used to show that if those missing chains were completed, the median would be slightly greater than 5. (See "The Small World Problem," by Stanley Milgram, *Psychology Today*, May 1967.)

For the 10 values in the preceding example, 454.66 is at the centre, according to the definition of the mean. One disadvantage of the mean is that it is sensitive to every data value, so even one unusually large or small value can affect the mean dramatically. The median largely overcomes that disadvantage.

Median

DEFINITION

The **median** of a data set is the middle value when the values are arranged in order of increasing (or decreasing) magnitude. The median is often denoted by $\tilde{x}$ (pronounced "x-tilde").

To find the median, first sort the values (arrange them in order), then use one of these two procedures:

1. If the number of values is odd, the median is the number that is located in the exact middle of the list.
2. If the number of values is even, the median is found by computing the mean of the two middle numbers.

EXAMPLE   Find the median of the weights of the first five bags of potato chips in the previous example.

$$454.1 \quad 455.0 \quad 454.2 \quad 454.9 \quad 454.7$$

SOLUTION   Begin by rearranging the scores so that they are in order from lowest to highest:

$$454.1 \quad 454.2 \quad 454.7 \quad 454.9 \quad 455.0$$

Because the number of values is an odd number (5), we find the number that is at the exact middle. The number 454.7 is in the middle, so the median for this data set is 454.7 g.

EXAMPLE   The following values are the incomes (in dollars) that performers received for one rock concert. The mean is $8900. Find the median.

$$500 \quad 600 \quad 800 \quad 50,000 \quad 1000 \quad 500$$

SOLUTION   Begin by rearranging the values so that they are in order:

$$500 \quad 500 \quad 600 \quad 800 \quad 1000 \quad 50,000$$

Because the number of values is an even number (6), we find the two values that are at the middle and then find their mean. The two values at the middle are 600 and 800, so the median is found by adding these two values and dividing by 2. The median is $700.

For this data set, the mean of $8900 was strongly affected by the extreme value of $50,000, but that extreme value did not affect the median of $700.

Mode

> **DEFINITION**
>
> The **mode** of a data set is the value that occurs most frequently. When two values occur with the same greatest frequency, each one is a mode and the data set is **bimodal**. When more than two values occur with the same greatest frequency, each is a mode and the data set is said to be **multimodal**. When no value is repeated, we say that there is no mode. The mode is often denoted by M.

EXAMPLE   Find the modes of the following data sets.

a. 5 5 5 3 1 5 1 4 3 5
b. 1 2 2 2 3 4 5 6 6 6 7 9
c. 1 2 3 6 7 8 9 10

SOLUTION

a. The number 5 is the mode because it is the value that occurs most often.
b. The numbers 2 and 6 are both modes because they occur with the same greatest frequency. The data set is bimodal.
c. There is no mode because no value is repeated.

Among the different measures of central tendency we are considering, the mode is the only one that can be used with data at the nominal level of measurement, as illustrated in the next example.

EXAMPLE   A study of reaction times involved 30 left-handed subjects, 50 right-handed subjects, and 20 ambidextrous subjects. Although we cannot numerically average these characteristics, we can report that the mode is right-handed, because that is the characteristic with the greatest frequency.

Midrange

DEFINITION

The **midrange** is the value midway between the highest and lowest values in the data set. It is found by adding the highest value to the lowest value and then dividing the sum by 2, as in the following formula:

$$\text{midrange} = \frac{\text{highest value} + \text{lowest value}}{2}$$

EXAMPLE   Find the midrange of the weights of the 10 bags of potato chips in the sample.

454.1   455.0   454.2   454.9   454.7   454.4   455.1   454.6   454.4   455.2

SOLUTION   The midrange is found as follows:

$$\frac{\text{highest value} + \text{lowest value}}{2} = \frac{455.2 + 454.1}{2} = 454.65 \text{ g}$$

The midrange isn't used much (it is too sensitive to a single extreme value), but we include it mainly to emphasize the point that there are several different ways to define the centre of a set of data. (For two other methods, see Exercises 20–22.) Figure 2-11 illustrates the differences among the mean, median, mode, and midrange. (Assume the boxed numbers are six original data values.)

Figure 2-11   Measures of Centre

MODE = 2
Value that occurs most often

MEDIAN = 20
Middle Value with 3 above and 3 below

MEAN = 45
Balance point

MIDRANGE = 106
Midway between highest and lowest

2

2

2   20   34   45   210

Unfortunately, the term *average* is sometimes used for any measure of centre and is sometimes used for the mean. Because of this ambiguity, we should avoid using the term *average* when referring to a particular measure of centre. Instead, we should use the specific term, such as mean, median, mode, or midrange. Also, be cautious when you encounter a value reported by someone as an average; unless we are told specifically, the value could have been computed by any one of several different approaches.

● **EXAMPLE**   Refer to Table 2-1, where we list 175 axial loads of aluminum cans. Find the (a) mean, (b) median, (c) mode, and (d) midrange.

SOLUTION

a. Mean: The sum of the 175 values is 46,745, so

$$\bar{x} = \frac{46{,}745}{175} = 267.1 \text{ lb}$$

b. Median: After arranging the values in increasing order, we find that the 88th value of 273 is in the exact middle, so the median is 273.0 lb. We express the result with an extra decimal place by using the round-off rule that follows this example.

c. Mode: The most frequent axial load is 268 lb, which occurs 9 times. It is therefore the mode.

d. Midrange: We use the following formula to find the midrange:

$$\text{midrange} = \frac{\text{highest value} + \text{lowest value}}{2} = \frac{297 + 200}{2} = 248.5 \text{ lb}$$

We now summarize these results:

mean: 267.1 lb

median: 273.0 lb

mode: 268 lb

midrange: 248.5 lb

Previously, we constructed a frequency table and histogram for the data in Table 2-1 and we saw the distribution of the data. We now have important information about the centre of the data.

Round-Off Rule
A simple rule for rounding answers is this: **Carry one more decimal place than is present in the original set of data.**

The Earned Run Average

A weighted mean is used in baseball's earned run average (ERA), which is a measure of a pitcher's effectiveness. It is computed as follows: Multiply the number of earned runs scored against the pitcher by 9, then divide by the total number of innings pitched. (Earned runs do not include runs scored by players who got on base because of errors.) The ERA represents the total number of runs a pitcher would yield in nine innings. It has the advantage of being weighted to correspond to a full game, so different pitchers can be compared. However, it is criticized because it does not take into account the very different circumstances faced by starting pitchers and relief pitchers.

When implementing this rule, we round only the final answer and not intermediate values. For example, the mean of 2, 3, 5 is 3.33333333 . . . , and it can be rounded as 3.3. Because the original data were whole numbers, we rounded the answer to the nearest tenth. As another example, the mean of 2.1, 3.4, 5.7 is rounded to 3.73 with two decimal places (one more decimal place than was used for the original values).

Mean from a Frequency Table

When data are summarized in a frequency table, we can approximate the mean by replacing class limits with class midpoints and assuming that each class midpoint is repeated a number of times equal to the class frequency. In Table 2-2, for example, the first class of 200–209 contains 9 values that fall somewhere between those class limits, but we don't know the specific values of those 9 values. We make calculations possible by assuming that all 9 values are the class midpoint of 204.5. With 9 values of 204.5, we have a total of $9 \times 204.5 = 1840.5$ to contribute toward the grand total of all values combined. The number of values is equal to the sum of the frequencies, so Formula 2-2 can be used to find the mean from a frequency table. Formula 2-2 is not really a new concept; it is simply a variation of Formula 2-1.

First multiply each frequency and class midpoint, then add the products

Formula 2-2 $$\bar{x} = \frac{\Sigma(f \cdot x)}{\Sigma f}$$ ← *Mean from frequency table*

Sum of the frequencies

The aluminum can axial load data from Frequency Table 2-2 have been entered in Table 2-5, where we apply Formula 2-2. When we used the original collection of values to calculate the mean directly, we obtained a mean of 267.1, so the value of the estimated mean obtained from the frequency table is just a little off.

Weighted Mean

In some situations the values vary in their degree of importance, so we may want to compute a **weighted mean**, which is a mean computed with the different values assigned different weights. In such cases, we can calculate the weighted mean by assigning different weights to different values, as shown in Formula 2-3:

TABLE 2-5	Finding Σf and $\Sigma(f \cdot x)$		
Axial Load (lb)	Frequency f	Class Midpoint x	$f \cdot x$
200–209	9	204.5	1,840.5
210–219	3	214.5	643.5
220–229	5	224.5	1,122.5
230–239	4	234.5	938.0
240–249	4	244.5	978.0
250–259	14	254.5	3,563.0
260–269	32	264.5	8,464.0
270–279	52	274.5	14,274.0
280–289	38	284.5	10,811.0
290–299	14	294.5	4,123.0
Total	$\Sigma f = 175$		$\Sigma(f \cdot x) = 46,757.5$

$$\bar{x} = \frac{\Sigma(f \cdot x)}{\Sigma f} = \frac{46,757.5}{175} = 267.2$$

Formula 2-3 weighted mean: $\bar{x} = \dfrac{\Sigma(w \cdot x)}{\Sigma w}$

For example, suppose we need a mean of 5 test scores (85, 90, 75, 80, 95), but the first 4 tests count for 15% each, while the last score counts for 40%. We can simply assign a weight of 15 to each of the first 4 tests, and a weight of 40 to the last test, then proceed to calculate the mean by using Formula 2-3 as follows:

$$\bar{x} = \frac{\Sigma(w \cdot x)}{\Sigma w}$$

$$= \frac{(15 \times 85) + (15 \times 90) + (15 \times 75) + (15 \times 80) + (40 \times 95)}{15 + 15 + 15 + 15 + 40}$$

$$= \frac{8750}{100} = 87.5$$

As another example, college grade-point averages can be computed by assigning each letter grade the appropriate number of points (A = 4, B = 3, etc.), then assigning to each number a weight equal to the number of credit hours. Again, Formula 2-3 can be used to compute the grade-point average.

The Best Measure of Centre

So far, we have considered the mean, median, mode, and midrange as measures of centre. Which one of these is best? Unfortunately, there is no single best answer to that question because there are no objective criteria for determining the most representative measure for all data sets. The different measures of centre have different advantages and disadvantages, some of which are summarized in Table 2-6. An important advantage of the mean is that it takes every value into account, but an important disadvantage is that it is sometimes dramatically affected by a few extreme values. This disadvantage can be overcome by using a trimmed mean, as described in Exercise 25.

Skewness

A comparison of the mean, median, and mode can reveal information about the characteristic of skewness, defined below and illustrated in Figure 2-12.

> **DEFINITION**
>
> A distribution of data is **skewed** if it is not symmetric and extends more to one side than the other. (A distribution of data is **symmetric** if the left half of its histogram is roughly a mirror image of its right half.)

TABLE 2-6   Comparison of Mean, Median, Mode, and Midrange

Average	Definition	How Common?	Existence	Takes Every Score into Account?	Affected by Extreme Scores?	Advantages and Disadvantages
Mean	$\bar{x} = \dfrac{\Sigma x}{n}$	most familiar "average"	always exists	yes	yes	uses all the data; works well with many statistical methods; sensitive to extreme values
Median	middle value	commonly used	always exists	no	no	often a good choice if there are some extreme scores
Mode	most frequent value	sometimes used	might not exist; may be more than one mode	no	no	appropriate for data at the nominal level
Midrange	$\dfrac{\text{high} + \text{low}}{2}$	rarely used	always exists	no	yes	very sensitive to extreme values

General comments:
- For a data collection that is approximately symmetric with one mode, the mean, median, mode, and midrange tend to be about the same.
- For a data collection that is obviously asymmetric, it would be good to report both the mean and median.
- The mean is relatively *reliable*. That is, when samples are drawn from the same population, the sample means tend to be more consistent than the other averages (consistent in the sense that the means of samples drawn from the same population don't vary as much as the other averages).

Figure 2-12   Skewness

(a) Skewed to the Left (Negatively Skewed): The mean and median are to the *left* of the mode.

(b) Symmetric (Zero Skewness): The mean, median, and mode are the same.

(c) Skewed to the Right (Positively Skewed): The mean and median are to the *right* of the mode.

Data skewed to the *left* are said to be **negatively skewed**; the mean and median are to the left of the mode. Although not always predictable, negatively skewed data generally have the mean to the left of the median. (See Figure 2-12(a).) Data skewed to the *right* are said to be **positively skewed**; the mean and median are to the right of the mode. Again, although not always predictable, positively skewed data generally have the mean to the right of the median. (See Figure 2-12(c).)

If we examine the histogram in Figure 2-1 for the axial loads of aluminum cans, we see a graph that appears to be skewed to the left. In practice, many distributions of data are symmetric and without skewness. Distributions skewed to the right are more common than those skewed to the left because it's often easier to get exceptionally large values than values that are exceptionally small. With annual incomes, for example, it's impossible to get values below the lower limit of zero, but there are a few people who earn millions of dollars in a year. Annual incomes therefore tend to be skewed to the right, as in Figure 2-12(c).

Using Technology

Many computer programs allow you to enter a data set and use one operation to get several different sample statistics, referred to as descriptive statistics. (See Section 2-6 for sample Excel and STATDISK displays.)

Excel: First enter the relevant data in a spreadsheet range (such as A1:A20). Select **Tools**, then **Data Analysis**, then select **Descriptive Statistics** and click **OK**. In the dialog box, enter the data input range, click on **Summary Statistics**, then click **OK**. (If Data Analysis does not appear in the Tools menu, it must be installed using Add-Ins.) Excel also offers a set of useful statistical functions that can be used individually as needed. Suppose the raw data are in range A1:A20; to find the mean, median, mode, count (n), or largest or smallest value, respectively, type the corresponding function into an empty cell: **=average**(A1:A20), **=median**(A1:A20), **=mode**(A1:A20), **=count**(A1:A20), **=max**(A1:A20), or **min**(A1:A20). (*Caution:* **=mode**() returns only one mode, even if there is actually more than one.)

STATDISK: Click to select **Data**, then **Descriptive Statistics**. The data can be input on the right side of the dialog box, either directly, or by cutting and pasting from another data source, such as a spreadsheet column. Then click the **Evaluate** button to get the mean, median, midrange, and other descriptive statistics.

2-4 Exercises A: Basic Skills and Concepts

In Exercises 1–4, find the (a) mean, (b) median, (c) mode, and (d) midrange for the given sample data.

1. A sample of 20 chocolate chip cookies was taken from a box. The cookies were examined for the number of chocolate chips in each cookie. The numbers recorded were

   18   15   17   17   16   18   16   15   16   14
   16   17   18   15   14   16   15   18   17   16

2. A survey of families in a particular neighbourhood showed the number of children in each household:

   0   3   4   7   2   2   3   0   1   5   2   4   1   2   3
   3   2   1   6   1   3   2   9   2   3   2   1   0   6   2

3. Prices of a set of windshield wiper blades vary from store to store. Listed are the prices of blades for a particular make and model of car (in dollars):

   7.45   5.51   4.96   5.62   6.26   5.10   8.29   6.82   5.34   7.00   5.19

4. Based on data from Statistics Canada, the average annual snowfall (in centimetres) for 15 Canadian cities is

   359   271   208   290   271   293   387   320
   227   131   170   122   195   138   60

In Exercises 5–8, find the mean, median, mode, and midrange for each of the two samples, then compare the two sets of results.

5. Weights (in kg) of samples of the contents in cans of regular Coke and diet Coke:

   Regular   0.3724   0.3705   0.371   0.3732   0.3719   0.3749
   Diet   0.3533   0.3526   0.3589   0.3576   0.3565   0.3573

   Does there appear to be a significant difference between the two data sets? How might such a difference be explained?

6. Weights (in kg) of samples of the contents in cans of regular Coke and regular Pepsi:

   Coke: 0.3724   0.3705   0.371   0.3732   0.3719   0.3749
   Pepsi: 0.3754   0.3707   0.3732   0.3714   0.3735   0.3774

   Does there appear to be a significant difference in the weights of the two different brands?

7. Maximum breadth of samples of male Egyptian skulls from 4000 B.C. and 150 A.D. (in mm, based on data from *Ancient Races of the Thebaid* by Thomson and Randall-Maciver):

   4000 B.C.:   131 119 138 125 129 126 131 132 126 128 128 131
   150 A.D.:   136 130 126 126 139 141 137 138 133 131 134 129

   Changes in head sizes over time suggest interbreeding with people from the other regions. Do the head sizes appear to have changed from 4000 B.C. to 150 A.D.?

8. The annual values of Canadian exports to Europe and to the areas designated Far East/Oceania (in $millions) were collected in independent random samples:

Far E./ Oceania	19407	16889	16688	15887	13262	8288
Europe	17834	15794	14686	14490	13928	9946

   Does there appear to be a significant difference between the export amounts to these two regions? Do they differ by another measure, besides a measure of centre?

In Exercises 9–12, refer to the data set in Appendix B, and find the (a) mean, (b) median, (c) mode, and (d) midrange.

9. Data Set 2 in Appendix B: 22 body temperatures for supine position
10. Data Set 4 in Appendix B: the average annual temperature of all cities listed
11. Data Set 3 in Appendix B: the weights of the bears
12. Data Set 11 in Appendix B: the weights of the red M&M plain candies

In Exercises 13–16, find the mean of the data summarized in the given frequency table.

13. Visitors to Yellowstone National Park consider an eruption of the Old Faithful geyser to be a major attraction that should not be missed. The given frequency table summarizes a sample of times (in minutes) between eruptions.

Time	Frequency
40–49	8
50–59	44
60–69	23
70–79	6
80–89	107
90–99	11
100–109	1

14. Samples of student cars and faculty/staff cars were obtained at the author's college, and their ages (in years) are summarized in the accompanying frequency table (page 64). Find the mean age of student cars and find the mean age of faculty/staff cars. Based on the results, are there any noticeable differences between the two samples? If so, what are they?

Age	Students	Faculty/Staff
0–2	23	30
3–5	33	47
6–8	63	36
9–11	68	30
12–14	19	8
15–17	10	0
18–20	1	0
21–23	0	1

15. The given frequency table shows the distribution in megatonnes (Mt) of carbon dioxide emissions from fossil fuel in Canada over the 30-year period from 1965 to 1994. If the level this year is 492 Mt, how does that compare to the average of the 30-year period?

Carbon Dioxide Emissions (Mt)	Frequency
250 to less than 300	3
300 to less than 350	4
350 to less than 400	12
400 to less than 450	9
450 to less than 500	2

16. Canadian Automated Electronics (CAE) did a study of time to complete tasks entailing simulation control for 25 employees. The data shown are a summary of the study. What do you conclude from the result?

Minutes	Frequency
100–200	1
200–300	8
300–400	5
400–500	1
500–600	0
600–700	1
700–800	4
800–900	5

17. A student receives quiz grades of 60, 84, and 90. The final exam grade is 88. Find the weighted mean if the quizzes each count for 20% and the final exam counts for 40% of the final grade.

18. A student's transcript shows an A in a 4-credit course, an A in a 3-credit course, a C in a 3-credit course, and a D in a 2-credit course. Grade points are assigned as follows: A = 4, B = 3, C = 2, D = 1, F = 0. If grade points are weighted according to the number of credit hours, find the weighted mean (grade-point average).

Exercises B: Beyond the Basics

19. a. Find the mean, median, mode, and midrange for the following labour force populations (based on data from Statistics Canada):

Halifax: 186,600   Quebec City: 356,800   Oshawa: 148,100
Winnipeg: 381,300   Saskatoon: 121,600   Victoria: 164,600

b. If a constant value k is added to each population, how are the results from part (a) affected?

c. If each population given in part (a) is multiplied by a constant k, how are the results from part (a) affected?

d. Data are sometimes transformed by replacing each score x with $\log x$. For the given x values, determine whether the mean of the $\log x$ values is equal to $\log \bar{x}$.

20. The **harmonic mean** is often used as a measure of central tendency for data sets consisting of rates of change, such as speeds. It is found by dividing the number of scores n by the sum of the **reciprocals** of all scores, expressed as

$$\frac{n}{\sum \frac{1}{x}}$$

(No score can be zero.) For example, the harmonic mean of 2, 4, 10 is

$$\frac{n}{\sum \frac{1}{x}} = \frac{3}{\frac{1}{2} + \frac{1}{4} + \frac{1}{10}} = \frac{3}{0.85} = 3.5$$

a. Four students drive from Toronto to Saint John (1440 km) at a speed of 60 km/h and return at a speed of 100 km/h. What is their average speed for the round trip? (The harmonic mean is used in averaging speeds.)

b. Jacques Villeneuve posted the average speeds (in kilometres per hour) shown below for his last 10 laps of practice, and in doing so qualified for the Canadian Grand Prix at Montreal. What was Villeneuve's average speed for these 10 laps?

192.8 191.6 197.5 198.2 199.1 197.6 196.5 197.5 193.5 190.0

21. The **geometric mean** is often used in business and economics for finding average rates of change, average rates of growth, or average ratios. Given n scores (all of which are positive), the geometric mean is the nth root of their product. For example, the geometric mean of 2, 4, 10 is found by first multiplying the scores to get 80, then taking the cube root (because there are 3 scores) of the product to get 4.3. The **average growth factor** for money compounded at annual interest rates of 10%, 8%, 9%, 12%, and 7% can be found by computing the geometric mean of 1.10, 1.08, 1.09, 1.12, and 1.07. Find that average growth factor.

22. The **quadratic mean** (or **root mean square**, or **R.M.S.**) is usually used in physical applications. In power distribution systems, for example, voltages and currents are usually referred to in terms of their R.M.S. values.

The quadratic mean of a set of scores is obtained by squaring each score, adding the results, dividing by the number of scores n, and then taking the square root of that result. For example, the quadratic mean of 2, 4, 10 is

$$\sqrt{\frac{\Sigma x^2}{n}} = \sqrt{\frac{4 + 16 + 100}{3}} = \sqrt{\frac{120}{3}} = \sqrt{40} = 6.3$$

Find the R.M.S. of these power supplies (in volts): 151, 162, 0, 81, −68.

23. Frequency tables often have open-ended classes, such as the accompanying table (based on data for Ontario from Statistics Canada), which summarizes annual household incomes for a sample of 5197 families of 3–4 persons. Formula 2-2 cannot be directly applied because we can't determine a class mark for the class "more than 80,000." Calculate the mean by assuming this class is really (a) 80,000 up to 100,000, (b) 80,000 up to 110,000, and (c) 80,000 up to 120,000. What can you conclude?

Annual Household Income ($)	Frequency
0 up to 20,000	404
20,000 up to 40,000	1081
40,000 up to 60,000	982
60,000 up to 80,000	1310
More than 80,000	1420

24. When data are summarized in a frequency table, the median can be found by first identifying the *median class* (the class that contains the median). We then assume that the scores in that class are evenly distributed and we can interpolate. This process can be described by

$$(\text{lower limit of median class}) + (\text{class width})\left(\frac{\left(\dfrac{n + 1}{2}\right) - (m + 1)}{\text{frequency of median class}}\right)$$

where n is the sum of all class frequencies and m is the sum of the class frequencies that *precede* the median class. Use this procedure and the frequency data in Table 2-2 to find the median axial load.

25. Because the mean is very sensitive to extreme scores, it is accused of not being a *resistant* measure of central tendency. The *trimmed mean* is more resistant. To find the 10% trimmed mean for a data set, first arrange the data in order, then delete the bottom 10% of the scores and the top 10% of the scores, and calculate the mean of the remaining scores. For the weights of the bears in Data Set 3 from Appendix B, find (a) the mean, (b) the 10% trimmed mean, and (c) the 20% trimmed mean. How do the results compare?

26. Using an almanac, a researcher finds the average teacher's salary for each province and territory (including Nunavut, created in 1999). He adds those 13 values, then divides by 13 to obtain their mean. Is the result equal to the national average teacher's salary? Why or why not?

Measures of Variation

This section deals with the characteristic of variation, which is one of the most important topics in the entire book. The following key concepts should be mastered: (1) Variation refers to the amount that values vary among themselves, and it can be measured with specific numbers; (2) values that are relatively close together have low measures of variation, whereas values that are spread farther apart have measures of variation that are larger; (3) the standard deviation is a particularly important measure of variation, which can be computed; (4) the values of standard deviations must be *interpreted* correctly.

Many banks once required that customers wait in separate lines at each teller's window, but most have now changed to one single main waiting line. Why did they make that change? The mean waiting time does not necessarily change, because the waiting-line configuration doesn't affect the efficiency of the tellers. They changed to the single line because customers prefer waiting times that are more *consistent* with less variation. Thus thousands of banks made a change that resulted in lower variation (and happier customers), even though the mean was not affected. The listed values are waiting times (in minutes) of customers:

| Humber Valley Credit Union (Single line) | 6.5 | 6.6 | 6.7 | 6.8 | 7.1 | 7.3 | 7.4 | 7.7 | 7.7 | 7.7 |
| Durham Credit Union (Multiple lines) | 4.2 | 5.4 | 5.8 | 6.2 | 6.7 | 7.7 | 7.7 | 8.5 | 9.3 | 10.0 |

In Figure 2-13 we compare frequency polygons for both data sets, and we include the measures of centre. A comparison of the measures of centre does

Figure 2-13 Frequency Polygons of Waiting Times

Humber Valley Credit Union (single line)	Durham Credit Union (multiple lines)
Mean = 7.15	Mean = 7.15
Median = 7.20	Median = 7.20
Mode = 7.7	Mode = 7.7
Midrange = 7.10	Midrange = 7.10

Good Advice for Journalists

"Most schools of journalism give statistics short shrift and some let students graduate without any numbers training at all. How can such reporters write sensibly about trade and welfare and crime, or air fares, health care and nutrition? The media's sloppy use of numbers about the incidence of accidents or disease frightens people and leaves them vulnerable to journalistic hype, political demagoguery, and commercial fraud." (Max Frankel, *New York Times*)

not reveal any differences between the two data sets, but their compared frequency polygons provide clear and strong visual evidence that the Humber Valley Credit Union has waiting times with substantially less variation than the times for the Durham Credit Union.

Let us now proceed to develop some specific ways of actually *measuring* variation. We begin with the range.

Range

The **range** of a set of data is the difference between the highest value and the lowest value. To compute it, simply subtract the lowest value from the highest value. For the Humber Valley customers, the range is $7.7 - 6.5 = 1.2$ min. Durham has waiting times with a range of 5.8 min, and this larger value suggests greater variation.

The range is very easy to compute, but because it depends on only the highest and the lowest values, it is not as useful as the other measures of variation that use every value. (See Exercise 25 for an example in which the range is misleading.)

Standard Deviation of a Sample

The standard deviation is the measure of variation that is generally the most important and useful. We define the standard deviation in the following box, but to understand this concept fully you will need to read the remainder of this section very carefully.

DEFINITION

The **standard deviation** of a set of sample values is a measure of variation of values about the mean. It is calculated by using Formula 2-4 or Formula 2-5.

Formula 2-4

$$s = \sqrt{\frac{\Sigma (x - \bar{x})^2}{n - 1}}$$ sample standard deviation

Formula 2-5

$$s = \sqrt{\frac{n\Sigma(x^2) - (\Sigma x)^2}{n(n - 1)}}$$ shortcut formula for standard deviation

Formulas 2-4 and 2-5 are equivalent in the sense that they will always yield the same result. Formula 2-4 has the advantage of reinforcing the concept that the standard deviation is a type of average deviation. Formula 2-5 is a "shortcut" (i.e., easier to calculate) if you must calculate standard deviations on your own. Formula 2-5 also has the advantages of eliminating rounding errors when the exact value of the mean is not used, and (for calculators and statistical software) it requires only three memory locations to calculate (for Σn, Σx, and Σx^2), instead of one location per data value. So which formula should you use? We advise the following: Use Formula 2-4 for a few examples, then learn how to find standard deviations on your calculator or by using statistical software; you might want to consult your calculator manual now to find the procedure that yields the value of the standard deviation.

Why define a measure of variation in the way described by Formula 2-4? In measuring variation in a set of sample data, it's reasonable to begin with the individual amounts by which values deviate from the mean. For a particular value x, the amount of **deviation** is $x - \overline{x}$, which is the difference between the value and the mean. However, the sum of all such deviations is always zero, which really doesn't do anything for us. To get a statistic that measures variation (instead of always being zero), we could take absolute values, as in $\Sigma|x - \overline{x}|$. If we find the mean of that sum, we get the **mean absolute deviation** described by the following expression:

$$\text{Mean absolute deviation} = \frac{\Sigma\,|\,x - \overline{x}\,|}{n}$$

Instead of using absolute values, we can obtain an alternative, and more commonly used, measure of variation by making all deviations $(x - \overline{x})$ nonnegative by squaring them. Finally, we take the square root to compensate for that squaring. As a result, the standard deviation has the same units of measurement as the original scores. For example, if customer waiting times are in minutes, the standard deviation of those times will also be in minutes. On the basis of the format of Formula 2-4, we can describe the procedure for calculating the standard deviation as follows.

Procedure for Finding the Standard Deviation with Formula 2-4

Step 1:   Find the mean of the values $(\overline{x})$.

Step 2:   Subtract the mean from each individual value $(x - \overline{x})$.

Step 3:   Square each of the differences obtained from Step 2. [This produces numbers of the form $(x - \overline{x})^2$.]

Step 4:   Add all of the squares obtained from Step 3 to get $\Sigma(x - \overline{x})^2$.

Step 5:   Divide the total from Step 4 by the number $(n - 1)$; that is, 1 less than the total number of values present.

Step 6:   Find the square root of the result of Step 5.

More Stocks, Less Risk

In their book *Investments*, authors Zvi Bodie, Alex Kane, and Alan Marcus state that "the average standard deviation for returns of portfolios composed of only one stock was 0.554. The average portfolio risk fell rapidly as the number of stocks included in the portfolio increased." They note that with 32 stocks, the standard deviation is 0.325, indicating much less variation and risk. The authors make the point that with only a few stocks, a portfolio has a high degree of "firm-specific" risk, meaning that the risk is attributable to the few stocks involved. With more than 30 stocks, there is very little firm-specific risk; instead, almost all of the risk is "market risk," attributable to the stock market as a whole. They note that these principles are "just an application of the well-known law of averages."

● **EXAMPLE** Find the standard deviation of the Humber Valley Credit Union customer waiting times. Those times (in minutes) are reproduced below:

6.5 6.6 6.7 6.8 7.1 7.3 7.4 7.7 7.7 7.7

SOLUTION We will follow the six steps just given. (See Table 2-7, where the steps are executed.)

Step 1: Obtain the mean of 7.15 by adding the values and then dividing by the number of values:

$$\bar{x} = \frac{\Sigma x}{n} = \frac{71.5}{10} = 7.15 \text{ min}$$

Step 2: Subtract the mean of 7.15 from each value to get these values of $(x - \bar{x})$: $-0.65, -0.55, \ldots, 0.55$.

Step 3: Square each value obtained in Step 2 to get these values of $(x - \bar{x})^2$: $0.4225, 0.3025, \ldots, 0.3025$.

Step 4: Sum all of the preceding values to get the value of

$$\Sigma(x - \bar{x})^2 = 2.0450$$

TABLE 2-7	Calculating Standard Deviation for Humber Valley Credit Union Customers	
x	$x - \bar{x}$	$(x - \bar{x})^2$
6.5	-0.65	0.4225
6.6	-0.55	0.3025
6.7	-0.45	0.2025
6.8	-0.35	0.1225
7.1	-0.05	0.0025
7.3	0.15	0.0225
7.4	0.25	0.0625
7.7	0.55	0.3025
7.7	0.55	0.3025
7.7	0.55	0.3025
Totals: 71.5		2.0450

$$\bar{x} = \frac{71.5}{10} = 7.15 \text{ min} \qquad s = \sqrt{\frac{2.0450}{10 - 1}} = \sqrt{0.2272} = 0.48 \text{ min}$$

Step 5:   There are $n = 10$ values, so divide by 1 less than 10:

$$2.0450 \div 9 = 0.2272$$

Step 6:   Find the square root of 0.2272. The standard deviation is

$$\sqrt{0.2272} = 0.48 \text{ min}$$

Ideally, we would now interpret the meaning of the resulting standard deviation of 0.48 min, but such interpretations will be discussed a little later in this section.

EXAMPLE   This time use Formula 2-5 to find the standard deviation of the Humber Valley Credit Union customer waiting times (in minutes) (assuming the same data as before).

SOLUTION   Formula 2-5 requires that we find the values of n, Σx, and Σx^2. Because there are 10 scores, we have $n = 10$. The sum of the 10 scores is 71.5, so $\Sigma x = 71.5$. The third required component is calculated as follows:

$$\begin{aligned}
\Sigma x^2 &= 6.5^2 + 6.6^2 + 6.7^2 + \cdots + 7.7^2 \\
&= 42.25 + 43.56 + 44.89 + \cdots + 59.29 \\
&= 513.27
\end{aligned}$$

Formula 2-5 can now be used to find the value of the standard deviation.

$$s = \sqrt{\frac{n(\Sigma x^2) - (\Sigma x)^2}{n(n-1)}} = \sqrt{\frac{10(513.27) - (71.5)^2}{10(10-1)}}$$

$$= \sqrt{\frac{20.45}{90}} = 0.4766783 = 0.48 \text{ min (rounded)}$$

A great self-test is to stop here and calculate the standard deviation of the waiting times for the Durham Credit Union. Follow the same procedures used in the preceding two examples and verify that the standard deviation is 1.82 min. Although the interpretations of those standard deviations will be discussed later, we can now compare them and note that the standard deviation of the times for Humber Valley (0.48 min) is much lower than the standard deviation for Durham (1.82 min). This supports our subjective conclusion that the waiting times at the Humber Valley Credit Union have much less variation than those at the Durham Credit Union.

Standard Deviation of a Population

In our definition of standard deviation, we referred to the standard deviation of *sample* data. A slightly different formula is used to calculate the standard deviation σ (lowercase Greek sigma) of a *population*: Instead of dividing by $n - 1$, divide by the population size N, as in the following expression.

$$\sigma = \sqrt{\frac{\Sigma(x - \mu)^2}{N}} \quad \text{population standard deviation}$$

For example, if the 10 scores in Table 2-7 constitute a *population,* the standard deviation is as follows:

$$\sigma = \sqrt{\frac{\Sigma(x - \mu)^2}{N}} = \sqrt{\frac{2.0450}{10}} = 0.45 \text{ min}$$

Because we generally deal with sample data, we will usually use Formula 2-4, in which we divide by $n - 1$. Many calculators do both the sample standard deviation and the population standard deviation; but for some creative but strange reason, calculators use a variety of different notations. Be sure to identify the notation used by your calculator.

Variance of a Sample and Population

If we omit Step 6 (taking the square root) in the procedure for calculating the standard deviation, we get the **variance,** defined in Formula 2-6:

Formula 2-6 $$s^2 = \frac{\Sigma(x - \bar{x})^2}{n - 1} \quad \text{sample variance}$$

Similarly, we can express the population variance as

$$\sigma^2 = \frac{\Sigma(x - \mu)^2}{N} \quad \text{population variance}$$

DEFINITION

The **variance** of a set of values is a measure of variation equal to the square of the standard deviation.

Sample variance: Square of the sample standard deviation s.

Population variance: Square of the population standard deviation σ.

The variance is an important statistic used in some important statistical calculations, such as analysis of variance (discussed in Chapter 11). The sample variance s^2 is an **unbiased estimator** of the population variance σ^2, which means that values of s^2 tend to target the value of σ^2 without systematically tending to overestimate or underestimate σ^2. As useful as variance is, we should concentrate first on the concept of standard deviation as we try to get some sense of this statistic. A major difficulty with the variance is that it is not in the same units as the original data. For example, a data set might have a standard deviation of $3.00 and a variance of 9.00 square dollars. Because a square dollar is an abstract concept that we can't relate to directly, we find variance difficult to understand.

Here is the notation and round-off rule we are using.

Notation

s denotes the standard deviation of a set of *sample* data
σ denotes the standard deviation of a set of *population* data
s^2 denotes the variance of a set of *sample* data
σ^2 denotes the variance of a set of *population* data
Note: Articles in professional journals and reports often use SD for standard deviation and Var for variance.

Round-Off Rule

As in Section 2-4, we use this rule for rounding final results:

Carry one more decimal place than was present in the original data.

We should round only the final answer and not intermediate values. (If it's absolutely necessary to round intermediate results, we should carry at least twice as many decimal places as will be used in the final answer.)

Finding Standard Deviation from a Frequency Table

We sometimes need to compute the standard deviation of a data set that is summarized in the form of a frequency table, such as Table 2-2 in Section 2-2. If the original list of sample values is available, use those values with Formula 2-4 or 2-5 (or with the help of your calculator or statistical software) so that the result will be more exact. If the original data are not available, we can use the following formula (where the x's are not the individual data values—

Where Are the 0.400 Hitters?

The last baseball player to hit above 0.400 was Ted Williams, who hit 0.406 in 1941. There were averages above 0.400 in 1876, 1879, 1887, 1894, 1895, 1896, 1897, 1899, 1901, 1911, 1920, 1922, 1924, 1925, and 1930, but none since 1941. Are there no longer great hitters? Stephen Jay Gould notes that the mean batting average has been steady at 0.260 for about 100 years, but the standard deviation has been decreasing from 0.049 in the 1870s to 0.031, where it is now. He argues that today's stars are as good as those from the past, but consistently better pitchers now keep averages below 0.400. Dr. Gould discusses this in Program 4 of the series *Against All Odds: Inside Statistics.*

which are not available to us—but the class midpoints in the frequency table that *is* available).

$$s = \sqrt{\frac{\Sigma f \cdot (x - \bar{x})^2}{n - 1}}$$

We will express this formula in an equivalent expression that usually simplifies the actual calculations.

Formula 2-7 $s = \sqrt{\dfrac{n[\Sigma\,(f \cdot x^2)] - [\Sigma\,(f \cdot x)]^2}{n(n - 1)}}$ standard deviation for frequency table

where x = class midpoint
             f = class frequency
             n = sample size (or Σf = sum of the frequencies)

EXAMPLE   Estimate the standard deviation of the 175 axial loads of aluminum cans by using Formula 2-7 with the frequency table (Table 2-2).

SOLUTION   Application of Formula 2-7 requires that we find the values of n, $\Sigma(f \cdot x^2)$, and $\Sigma(f \cdot x)^2$. After finding those values from Table 2-8, we apply Formula 2-7 as follows:

$$s = \sqrt{\frac{n[\Sigma\,(f \cdot x^2)] - [\Sigma\,(f \cdot x)]^2}{n(n - 1)}} = \sqrt{\frac{175(12{,}579{,}173.75) - (46{,}757.5)^2}{175(175 - 1)}}$$

$$= \sqrt{\frac{15{,}091{,}600}{30{,}450}} = \sqrt{495.6190476} = 22.3 \text{ lb}$$

The 175 axial loads have a standard deviation estimated to be 22.3 lb. (The exact value calculated from the original set of data is 22.1 lb, so the result obtained here is quite good.)

Interpreting and Understanding Standard Deviation

We will now attempt to make some intuitive sense of the standard deviation. First, we should clearly understand that the standard deviation measures the variation among values. Values close together will yield a small standard deviation, whereas values spread farther apart will yield a larger standard deviation. Refer again to Figure 2-13, which illustrates samples with clearly different amounts of variation.

Because variation is such an important concept and because the standard deviation is such an important tool in measuring variation, we will consider three different ways of developing an interpretation of standard deviations. The first is the **range rule of thumb,** a very rough estimate. (We could improve the accuracy of this rule by taking into account such factors as the size of the sample and the nature of the distribution, but we prefer to sacrifice accuracy

TABLE 2-8	Calculating Standard Deviation from a Frequency Table			
Axial Load	Frequency f	Class Midpoint x	$f \cdot x$	$f \cdot x^2$
200–209	9	204.5	1,840.5	376,382.25
210–219	3	214.5	643.5	138,030.75
220–229	5	224.5	1,122.5	252,001.25
230–239	4	234.5	938.0	219,961.00
240–249	4	244.5	978.0	239,121.00
250–259	14	254.5	3,563.0	906,783.50
260–269	32	264.5	8,464.0	2,238,728.00
270–279	52	274.5	14,274.0	3,918,213.00
280–289	38	284.5	10,811.0	3,075,729.50
290–299	14	294.5	4,123.0	1,214,223.50
Total	$\Sigma f = 175$		$\Sigma(f \cdot x) = 46{,}757.5$	$\Sigma(f \cdot x^2) = 12{,}579{,}173.75$

Range Rule of Thumb

For estimation: For typical data sets, the range of a set of data is approximately 4 standard deviations ($4s$) wide, so the standard deviation can be approximated as follows:

$$\text{standard deviation} \approx \frac{\text{range}}{4} \quad \text{range rule of thumb}$$

where range = (highest* value) – (lowest* value)
*but if the actual highest or lowest value appears clearly to be an outlier, then use the next highest or lowest value—because we are looking here for the range that holds most of the data.

For interpretation: If the standard deviation s is known, we can use it to find rough estimates of the minimum and maximum "usual" sample values as follows:

$$\text{minimum "usual" value} \approx (\text{mean}) - 2 \times (\text{standard deviation})$$
$$\text{maximum "usual" value} \approx (\text{mean}) + 2 \times (\text{standard deviation})$$

for the sake of simplicity. We want a simple rule that will help us interpret values of standard deviations; later methods will produce more accurate results.)

When calculating a standard deviation using Formula 2-4 or 2–5, you can use the range rule of thumb as a check on your result, but realize that although the approximation will get you in the general vicinity of the answer, it can be off by a fairly large amount.

Mail Consistency

Canada Post's stated standard delivery times are two days for local mail, three days within a province, and four days between provinces. In a letter to the editor of the *Globe and Mail*, a Victoria woman complained that in her recent experience, delivery times were much longer: seven days for a letter from Mississauga (between provinces), eight days from Calgary (between provinces), and twelve days from Vancouver (within a province).

In dealing with organizations such as Canada Post, people want some assurance of a consistent level of service, so that they can plan when to send out birthday cards, bill payments, and other time-sensitive material. The level of consistency can be measured by the standard deviation of the delivery times. A lower standard deviation reflects more consistency. The standard deviation is often a critically important tool used to monitor and control the quality of goods and services.

EXAMPLE   Use the range rule of thumb to find a rough estimate of the standard deviation of the sample of 175 axial loads of aluminum cans listed in Table 2-1.

SOLUTION   In using the range rule of thumb to estimate the standard deviation of sample data, we find the range and divide by 4. By scanning the list of scores, we find that the lowest is 200 and the highest is 297, so the range is $297 - 200 = 97$. The standard deviation s is estimated as follows:

$$s \approx \frac{\text{range}}{4} = \frac{97}{4} = 24.3 \text{ lb}$$

Interpretation This result is in the ballpark of the correct value of 22.1 lb that is obtained by calculating the exact value of the standard deviation with Formula 2-4 or 2-5.

The preceding example illustrated how we can use known information about the range to estimate the standard deviation. The following example is particularly important as an illustration of one way to *interpret* the value of a standard deviation.

EXAMPLE   The average weekly earnings for manufacturing industries in Canada in 1997 was $736.69 and the standard deviation was $110.25. Using the range rule of thumb, estimate the highest and lowest "usual" weekly earnings of these industries.

SOLUTION   The lowest and highest "usual" earnings are estimated from the range rule of thumb as follows:

$$\text{minimum} \approx (\text{mean}) - 2 \times (\text{standard deviation})$$
$$= \$736.69 - 2(\$110.25)$$
$$= \$516.19$$
$$\text{maximum} \approx (\text{mean}) + 2 \times (\text{standard deviation})$$
$$= \$736.69 + 2(\$110.25)$$
$$= \$957.19$$

Interpretation We expect that most workers in these industries will earn between $516.19 and $957.19 in weekly wages, although there may be a few workers with unusually low or high wages. We now have a much better understanding of how the wages vary.

Another rule that is helpful in interpreting a standard deviation is the **empirical rule,** *which applies only to a data set having a distribution that is approximately bell-shaped,* as in Figure 2-14.

> ### Empirical (or 68–95–99.7) Rule for Data with a Bell-Shaped Distribution
>
> - About 68% of all scores fall within 1 standard deviation of the mean.
>
> - About 95% of all scores fall within 2 standard deviations of the mean.
>
> - About 99.7% of all scores fall within 3 standard deviations of the mean.

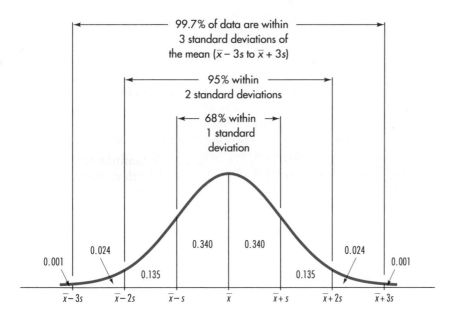

Figure 2-14   The Empirical Rule

AS

EXAMPLE   Adult IQ scores have a bell-shaped distribution with a mean of 100 and a standard deviation of 15. Use the empirical rule to find the percentage of adults with IQ scores between 55 and 145.

SOLUTION   The key to solving this problem is to recognize that 55 and 145 are each exactly 3 standard deviations away from the mean of 100. (Because the standard deviation is $s = 15$, it follows that $3s = 45$, so 3 standard deviations below the mean is $100 - 45 = 55$, and 3 standard deviations above the mean is $100 + 45 = 145$.) The empirical rule states that 99.7% of all scores are within 3 standard deviations of the mean, so it follows that 99.7% of adults should have IQ scores between 55 and 145. Because values outside of that range are so rare, someone with an IQ above 145 or below 55 is considered exceptional.

A third concept helpful in understanding or interpreting a standard deviation is **Chebyshev's theorem.** The empirical rule applies only to data sets with a bell-shaped distribution. Chebyshev's theorem applies to *any* data set, but its results are very approximate.

Chebyshev's Theorem

The proportion (or fraction) of *any* set of data lying within K standard deviations of the mean is always *at least* $1 - 1/K^2$, where K is any positive number greater than 1. For $K = 2$ and $K = 3$, we get the following two specific results:

- At least 3/4 (or 75%) of all scores will fall within the interval from 2 standard deviations below the mean to 2 standard deviations above the mean ($\overline{x} - 2s$ to $\overline{x} + 2s$).
- At least 8/9 (or 89%) of all scores will fall within 3 standard deviations of the mean ($\overline{x} - 3s$ to $\overline{x} + 3s$).

Using IQ scores with a mean of 100 and a standard deviation of 15, Chebyshev's theorem tells us that at least 75% of IQ scores will fall between 70 and 130, and at least 89% of IQ scores will fall between 55 and 145.

After studying this section, you should understand that the standard deviation is a measure of variation among values. Given sample data, you should be able to compute and interpret the standard deviation. You should recognize that for typical data sets, it is unusual for a score to differ from the mean by more than 2 or 3 standard deviations.

Using Technology

Computer programs which can output descriptive statistics generally include some measures of variation. (See Section 2-6 for sample Excel and STATDISK displays.)

Excel: First enter the relevant data in a spreadsheet range (such as A1:A20). Select **Tools**, then **Data Analysis**, then select **Descriptive Statistics** and click **OK**. In the dialog box, enter the data input range, click on **Summary Statistics**, then click **OK**. (Excel also offers some related statistical functions that can be used individually as needed. Suppose the raw data are in range A1:A20. To find the sample standard deviation, population standard deviation, sample variance, or population variance, respectively, type the corresponding function into an empty cell: **=stdev**(A1:A20), **=stdevp**(A1:A20), **=var**(A1:A20), **=varp**(A1:A20).)

STATDISK: Click to select **Data**, then **Descriptive Statistics**. Type or copy/paste the data onto the right side of the dialog box, then click the **Evaluate** button.

2-5 Exercises A: Basic Skills and Concepts

In Exercises 1–4, find the range, variance, and standard deviation for the given data. (The same data were used in Section 2-4 where we found measures of central tendency. Here we find measures of variation.)

1. A sample of 20 chocolate chip cookies was taken from a box. The cookies were examined for the number of chocolate chips in each cookie. The numbers recorded were

   18 15 17 17 16 18 16 15 16 14
   16 17 18 15 14 16 15 18 17 16

2. A survey of families in a particular neighbourhood showed the number of children in each household:

   0 3 4 7 2 2 3 0 1 5 2 4 1 2 3
   3 2 1 6 1 3 2 9 2 3 2 1 0 6 2

3. Prices of a set of windshield wiper blades vary from store to store. Listed are the prices of blades for a particular make and model of car (in dollars):

   7.45 5.51 4.96 5.62 6.26 5.10 8.29 6.82 5.34 7.00 5.19

4. Based on data from Statistics Canada, the average annual snowfall (in centimetres) for 15 Canadian cities is

   359 271 208 290 271 293 387 320
   227 131 170 122 195 138 60

In Exercises 5–8, find the range, variance, and standard deviation for each of the two samples, then compare the two sets of results.

5. Weights (in kg) of samples of the contents in cans of regular Coke and diet Coke:

   Regular 0.3724 0.3705 0.371 0.3732 0.3719 0.3749
   Diet   0.3533 0.3526 0.3589 0.3576 0.3565 0.3573

6. Weights (in kg) of samples of the contents in cans of regular Coke and regular Pepsi:

   Coke: 0.3724 0.3705 0.371 0.3732 0.3719 0.3749
   Pepsi: 0.3754 0.3707 0.3732 0.3714 0.3735 0.3774

7. Maximum breadth of samples of male Egyptian skulls from 4000 B.C. and 150 A.D. (in mm, based on data from *Ancient Races of the Thebaid* by Thomson and Randall-Maciver):

   4000 B.C.: 131 119 138 125 129 126 131 132 126 128 128 131
   150 A.D.:   136 130 126 126 139 141 137 138 133 131 134 129

8. The annual values of Canadian exports to Europe and to the areas designated Far East/Oceania (in $millions) were collected in independent random samples:

   Far E./ Oceania 19407 16889 16688 15887 13262 8288
   Europe   17834 15794 14686 14490 13928 9946

In Exercises 9–12, refer to the data set in Appendix B and find the standard deviation.

9. Data Set 2 in Appendix B: 22 body temperatures for supine position
10. Data Set 4 in Appendix B: the average annual temperature of all cities listed
11. Data Set 3 in Appendix B: the weights of the bears
12. Data Set 11 in Appendix B: the weights of the red M&M plain candies

In Exercises 13–16, find the standard deviation of the data summarized in the given frequency table.

13. Visitors to Yellowstone National Park consider an eruption of the Old Faithful geyser to be a major attraction that should not be missed. The given frequency table summarizes a sample of times (in minutes) between eruptions.

Time	Frequency
40–49	8
50–59	44
60–69	23
70–79	6
80–89	107
90–99	11
100–109	1

14. Samples of student cars and faculty/staff cars were obtained at the author's college, and their ages (in years) are summarized in the accompanying frequency table. Find the standard deviation in age of student cars and of faculty/staff cars. Based on the results, are there any noticeable differences between the two samples? If so, what are they?

Age	Students	Faculty/Staff
0–2	23	30
3–5	33	47
6–8	63	36
9–11	68	30
12–14	19	8
15–17	10	0
18–20	1	0
21–23	0	1

15. The given frequency table shows the distribution in megatonnes (Mt) of carbon dioxide emissions from fossil fuel in Canada over the 30-year period from 1965 to 1994.

Carbon Dioxide Emissions (Mt)	Frequency
250 to less than 300	3
300 to less than 350	4
350 to less than 400	12
400 to less than 450	9
450 to less than 500	2

16. The frequency table opposite indicates the weekly earnings of 46 students.

Weekly Wages ($)	Number of Students
80 to less than 90	6
90 to less than 100	10
100 to less than 110	14
110 to less than 120	6
120 to less than 130	10

17. If you must purchase a replacement battery for your car, would you prefer one that comes from a population with $\sigma = 1$ month, for time to failure, or one that comes from a population with $\sigma = 1$ year? (Assume that both populations have the same mean and price.) Explain your choice.

18. As a manager, you must purchase lightbulbs to be used in a hospital. Should you choose Ultralight bulbs that have lives with $\mu = 3000$ h and $\sigma = 200$ h, or should you choose Electrolyte bulbs with $\mu = 3000$ h and $\sigma = 250$ h? Explain.

19. If a data set consists of the prices of textbooks expressed in dollars, what are the units used for standard deviation? What are the units used for variance?

20. A data set consists of 20 values that are fairly close together. Another value is included, but this new value is an outlier (very far away from the other values). How is the standard deviation affected by the outlier? No effect? A small effect? A large effect?

21. A typing-competency test yields scores with $\bar{x} = 80.0$ and $s = 10.0$, and a histogram shows that the distribution of the scores is roughly bell-shaped. Use the empirical rule to answer the following:
    a. What percentage of the scores should fall between 70 and 90?
    b. What percentage of the scores should fall within 20 points of the mean?
    c. About 99.7% of the scores should fall between what two values? (The mean of 80.0 should be midway between those two values.)

22. Heights of adult women have a mean of 63.6 in. and a standard deviation of 2.5 in. What does Chebyshev's theorem say about the percentage of women with heights between 58.6 in. and 68.6 in.? Between 56.1 in. and 71.1 in.?

2-5 Exercises B: Beyond the Basics

23. a. Find the range and standard deviation s for the following labour force populations (based on data from Statistics Canada):

Halifax: 186,600	Quebec City: 356,800	Oshawa: 148,100
Winnipeg: 381,300	Saskatoon: 121,600	Victoria: 164,600

   b. If a constant value k is added to each population, how are the results from part (a) affected?
   c. If each population given in part (a) is multiplied by a constant k, how are the results from part (a) affected?
   d. Data are sometimes transformed by replacing each score x with $\log x$. For the given x values, determine whether the standard deviation of the $\log x$ values is equal to $\log s$.
   e. The following exercise summarizes parts (a)–(d): For the body temperature data listed in Data Set 18 of Appendix B (first 10 scores), $\bar{x} = 36.36°C$ and $s = 0.35°C$. Find the values of $\bar{x}$ and s for the data after each temperature has been converted to the Fahrenheit scale. [*Hint:* $F = (C \times 9) \div 5 + 32$.]

24. If we consider the values $1, 2, 3, \ldots, n$ to be a population, the standard deviation can be calculated by the formula

$$\sigma = \sqrt{\frac{n^2 - 1}{12}}$$

This formula is equivalent to Formula 2-4 modified for division by n instead of $n - 1$, where the data set consists of the values 1, 2, 3, . . . , n.

a. Find the standard deviation of the population 1, 2, 3, . . . , 100.

b. Find an expression for calculating the sample standard deviation s for the *sample* values 1, 2, 3, . . . , n.

c. Computers and calculators commonly use a random-number generator that produces values between 0.00000000 and 0.99999999. In the long run, all values occur with the same relative frequency. Find the mean and standard deviation for the *population* of those values.

25. Two different sections of a statistics class take the same surprise quiz and the scores are recorded below. Find the range and standard deviation for each section. What do the range values lead you to conclude about the variation in the two sections? Why is the range misleading in this case? What do the standard deviation values lead you to conclude about the variation in the two sections?

Section 1:	1	20	20	20	20	20	20	20	20	20	20
Section 2:	2	3	4	5	6	14	15	16	17	18	19

26. a. The **coefficient of variation,** expressed as a percent, is used to describe the standard deviation relative to the mean. It allows us to compare variability of data sets with different measurement units (such as centimetres versus kilograms), and it is calculated as follows:

$$\frac{s}{\bar{x}} \cdot 100 \quad \text{or} \quad \frac{\sigma}{\mu} \cdot 100$$

Find the coefficient of variation (C.V.) for the following two samples:

Sample A (Service in years of 10 employees):

$$10 \quad 35 \quad 40 \quad 12 \quad 15 \quad 11 \quad 17 \quad 16 \quad 15 \quad 25$$

Sample B (Number of new cars sold at a dealership over 7 days):

$$8 \quad 5 \quad 12 \quad 3 \quad 0 \quad 6 \quad 3$$

b. Genichi Taguchi developed a method of improving quality and reducing manufacturing costs through a combination of engineering and statistics. A key tool in the Taguchi method is the **signal-to-noise ratio.** The simplest way to calculate this ratio is to divide the mean by the standard deviation. Find the signal-to-noise ratio for the sample data given in part (a).

27. In Section 2-4 we introduced the general concept of skewness. Skewness can be measured by **Pearson's index of skewness:**

$$I = \frac{3(\bar{x} - \text{median})}{s}$$

If $I \geq 1.00$ or $I \leq -1.00$, the data can be considered to be *significantly skewed.* Find Pearson's index of skewness for the axial loads of the aluminum cans listed in Table 2-1, and then determine whether there is significant skewness.

28. a. A sample consists of 6 scores that fall between 1 and 9 inclusive. What is the largest possible standard deviation?

b. For any data set of n scores with standard deviation s, every score must be within $s\sqrt{n-1}$ of the mean. A statistics teacher reports that the test scores in her class of 17 students had a mean of 75.0 and a standard deviation of 5.0. Kelly, the class's self-proclaimed best student, claims that she received a grade of 97. Could Kelly be telling the truth?

2-6 Measures of Position

In this section we introduce z scores, which enable us to standardize values so that they can be compared more easily. We also introduce quartiles, percentiles, and deciles, which help us better understand data by showing their positions relative to the whole data set.

z Scores

Most of us are reasonably familiar with IQ scores, and we recognize that an IQ of 102 is fairly common, whereas an IQ of 170 is rare. The IQ of 102 is fairly common because it is very close to the mean of 100, but the IQ of 170 is rare because it is so far above 100. This might suggest that we can differentiate between typical scores and rare scores on the basis of the difference between the score and the mean $(x - \overline{x})$. However, the size of such differences is relative to the scale being used. With IQ scores, a 2-point difference is insignificant, but for college grade-point averages, the 2-point difference between 2.00 and 4.00 is very significant, especially to parents. It would be much better if we could use a standard that doesn't require an understanding of the scale being used. With the standard score, we get such a result.

DEFINITION

The **standard score,** or **z score,** is the number of standard deviations that a given value x is above or below the mean. It is found by using

$$\text{Sample} \qquad \text{Population}$$

$$z = \frac{x - \overline{x}}{s} \quad \text{or} \quad z = \frac{x - \mu}{\sigma}$$

(Round z to two decimal places.)

EXAMPLE   Heights of all adult males have a mean of $\mu = 69.0$ in., a standard deviation of $\sigma = 2.8$ in., and a distribution that is bell-shaped. Basketball player Michael Jordan earned a giant reputation for his skills, but at a height of 78 in., is he exceptionally tall when compared to the general population of adult males? Find the z score for his 78-in. height.

SOLUTION   Because we are dealing with population parameters, the z score is calculated as follows:

$$z = \frac{x - \mu}{\sigma} = \frac{78 - 69.0}{2.8} = 3.21$$

Interpretation Michael Jordan's height of 78 in. is 3.21 standard deviations above the mean, that is, he is unusually tall.

The role of z scores in statistics is extremely important because they can be used to differentiate between ordinary values and unusual values. Values with standard scores between 22.00 and 2.00 are ordinary, and values with z scores less than 22.00 or greater than 2.00 are unusual. (See Figure 2-15.) Michael Jordan's height converts to a z score of 3.21, so we consider it unusual because it is greater than 2.00. In comparison to the general population, Michael Jordan is exceptionally tall.

Figure 2-15   Interpreting
z Scores
Unusual values are those
with z scores less than
$z = -2.00$ or greater than
$z = 2.00$.

Our criterion for unusual z scores follows from the empirical rule and Chebyshev's theorem. Recall that for data with a bell-shaped distribution, about 95% of the values are within 2 standard deviations of the mean. Also, Chebyshev's theorem states that for any data set, at least 75% of the values are within 2 standard deviations of the mean.

We noted earlier that z scores are also useful for comparing values from dissimilar populations. The following example illustrates this use of z scores.

EXAMPLE   A statistics professor gives two different tests to two sections of her course. Which score is relatively better: an 82 on the Section 1 test, or a 46 on the Section 2 test?

Section 1: $\bar{x} = 75$ and $s = 14$
Section 2: $\bar{x} = 40$ and $s = 8$

SOLUTION   We can't directly compare the scores of 82 and 46 because they come from different scales. Instead, we convert them both to z scores. For the score of 82 on the Section 1 test, we get a z score of 0.50, because

$$z = \frac{x - \bar{x}}{s} = \frac{82 - 75}{14} = 0.50$$

For the score of 46 on the Section 2 test, we get a *z* score of 0.75, because

$$z = \frac{x - \bar{x}}{s} = \frac{46 - 40}{8} = 0.75$$

AS **Interpretation** A score of 82 on the Section 1 test is 0.50 standard deviation above the mean, whereas a score of 46 on the Section 2 test is 0.75 standard deviation above the mean. This implies that the 46 on the Section 2 test is the better relative score, when considered in the context of the other test results.

The preceding example illustrated that z scores provide useful measurements for making comparisons between different sets of data. Likewise, quartiles, deciles, and percentiles are measures of position useful for comparing scores within one set of data or between different sets of data.

Quartiles, Deciles, and Percentiles

Just as the median divides the data into two equal parts, the three **quartiles**, denoted by Q_1, Q_2, and Q_3, divide the *sorted* values into four equal parts. (Values are sorted when they are arranged in order.) Roughly speaking, Q_1 separates the bottom 25% of the sorted values from the top 75%, Q_2 is the median, and Q_3 separates the top 25% from the bottom 75%. To be more precise, at least 25% of the data will be less than or equal to Q_1, and at least 75% will be greater than or equal to Q_1. At least 75% of the data will be less than or equal to Q_3, while at least 25% will be equal to or greater than Q_3.

Quartiles are useful for exploring and describing the distribution of a data set. We describe a procedure for finding quartiles after we discuss percentiles. No procedure for calculating quartiles is universally approved (not even ours), so be aware that different techniques and computer programs can yield different results (and may not agree with our answers at the back of the book). For example, if you use the data set of 1, 3, 6, 10, 15, 21, 28, and 36, Excel would calculate Q_1 at 5.25, but STATDISK would return an answer of 4.5.

Just as there are three quartiles separating a data set into four parts, there are nine **deciles**, denoted by D_1, D_2, D_3, . . . , D_9, which partition the data into 10 groups with about 10% of the data in each group. There are also 99 **percentiles**, which partition the data into 100 groups with about 1% of the scores in each group. (Quartiles, deciles, and percentiles are examples of **quantiles**—or **fractiles**—which partition data into parts that are approximately equal.)

The process of finding the percentile that corresponds to a particular value *x* is fairly simple, as indicated in the following expression:

percentile of value $x = \dfrac{\text{number of values less than } x}{\text{total number of values}} \cdot 100$

Buying Cars

For buying a new or used car, an excellent reference is the reliability data compiled and reported by *Consumer Reports* magazine. Frequency-of-repair data are based on 10 million pieces of data collected from thousands of readers. Statisticians analyse the data for patterns that lead to lists of both reliable cars and cars that should be avoided. Consumers Union President Rhoda Karpatkin writes, "Because numbers describe so much of our work, it should be no surprise that statisticians are key to that process."

EXAMPLE   Table 2-9 lists the 175 axial loads of aluminum cans, sorted from lowest to highest. Find the percentile corresponding to 241.

SOLUTION
From Table 2-9 we see that there are 21 values less than 241, so

$$\text{percentile of } 241 = \frac{21}{175} \cdot 100 = 12$$

The axial load of 241 is the 12th percentile.

TABLE 2-9		*Ranked* Axial Loads of Aluminum Cans												
200	201	204	204	206	206	208	208	209	215	217	218	220	223	223
225	228	230	230	234	236	241	242	242	248	250	251	251	252	252
254	256	256	256	257	257	258	259	259	260	261	262	262	262	262
262	263	263	263	263	263	264	265	265	265	266	267	267	268	268
268	268	268	268	268	268	268	269	269	269	269	270	270	270	270
270	270	270	270	271	271	272	272	272	272	272	273	273	273	273
273	273	274	274	274	274	275	275	275	275	276	276	276	276	276
277	277	277	277	277	277	277	277	278	278	278	278	278	278	278
279	279	279	280	280	280	281	281	281	281	282	282	282	282	282
282	283	283	283	283	283	283	284	284	284	284	285	285	285	286
286	286	286	287	287	288	289	289	289	289	289	290	290	290	291
291	292	292	292	293	293	294	295	295	297					

The preceding example illustrated the procedure for finding the percentile corresponding to a given value. There are several different methods for the reverse procedure of finding the value corresponding to a particular percentile, but the one we will use is summarized in Figure 2-16, which uses the following notation.

Notation
n number of values in the data set
k percentile being used (Example: For the 25th percentile, $k = 25$.)
L locator that gives the *position* of a value (Example: For the 25th value in a sorted list, $L = 25$.)
P_k kth percentile (Example: P_{25} is the 25th percentile.)

EXAMPLE   Refer to the 175 axial loads of aluminum cans in Table 2-9, and find the value corresponding to the 25th percentile. That is, find the value of P_{25}.

SOLUTION   We refer to Figure 2-16 and observe that the data are already sorted from lowest to highest. We now compute the locator L as follows:

$$L = \left(\frac{k}{100}\right)n = \left(\frac{25}{100}\right) \cdot 175 = 43.75$$

We answer no when asked in Figure 2-16 if 43.75 is a whole number, so we are directed to round L up (not off) to 44. The 25th percentile, denoted by P_{25}, is the 44th score, counting from the lowest. Beginning with the lowest score of 200, we count through the list to find the 44th score of 262, so $P_{25} = 262$.

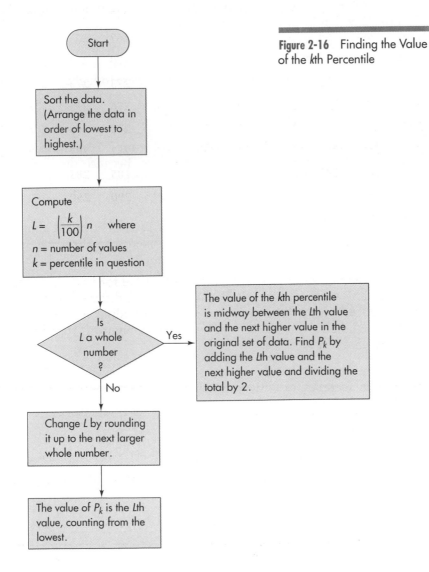

Figure 2-16   Finding the Value of the *k*th Percentile

Cost of Laughing Index

There really is a Cost of Laughing Index (CLI), which tracks costs of such items as rubber chickens, Groucho Marx glasses, admission to comedy clubs, and 13 other leading humour indicators. This is the same basic approach used in developing the Consumer Price Index (CPI), which is based on a weighted average of goods and services purchased by typical consumers. While standard scores and percentiles allow us to compare different values, they ignore any element of time. Index numbers, such as the CLI and CPI, allow us to compare the value of some variable to its value at some base time period. The value of an index number is the current value, divided by the base value, multiplied by 100.

Suppose we want to find the percentile corresponding to a score of 262. Verify that there are 41 scores below 262; be sure to count each individual score, including duplicates. Finding the percentile for 262 therefore yields $(41/175) \cdot 100 = 23$ (rounded). There is a small discrepancy: In the preceding example we found the 25th percentile to be 262, but when we reverse the process we find that 262 is the 23rd percentile. As the amount of data increases, such discrepancies become smaller. We could eliminate the discrepancy by using a more complicated procedure that includes interpolations instead of rounding.

Because of the sample size in the preceding example, the locator L first became 43.75, which was rounded to 44 because L was not originally a whole number. In the next example we illustrate a case in which L does begin as a whole number. This condition will cause us to branch to the right in Figure 2-16.

EXAMPLE   Refer to the axial load data for aluminum cans, as listed in Table 2-9. Find P_{40}, which denotes the 40th percentile.

SOLUTION   Following the procedure outlined in Figure 2-16 and noting that the data are already sorted from lowest to highest, we compute

$$L = \left(\frac{k}{100}\right)n = \left(\frac{40}{100}\right) \cdot 175 = 70 \quad \text{(exactly)}$$

We note that 70 is a whole number, and Figure 2-16 indicates that P_{40} is midway between the 70th and 71st values. Because the 70th and 71st values are both 269, we conclude that the 40th percentile is 269.

Once you have mastered these calculations with percentiles, similar calculations for quartiles and deciles can be performed with the same procedures by noting the relationships given in the margin.

Using these relationships, we can see that finding Q_1 is equivalent to finding P_{25}. In an earlier example we found that $P_{25} = 262$, so it follows that the first quartile can be described by $Q_1 = 262$. If we need to find the third quartile, Q_3, we can restate the problem as that of finding P_{75}, and we can then proceed to use Figure 2-16.

In addition to the measures of central tendency and the measures of variation already introduced, other statistics are sometimes defined using quartiles, deciles, or percentiles, as in the following:

Quartiles	Deciles
$Q_1 = P_{25}$	$D_1 = P_{10}$
$Q_2 = P_{50}$	$D_2 = P_{20}$
$Q_3 = P_{75}$	$\vdots$
	$D_9 = P_{90}$

$$\text{interquartile range } = Q_3 - Q_1$$

$$\text{semi-interquartile range} = \frac{Q_3 - Q_1}{2}$$

$$\text{midquartile } = \frac{Q_1 + Q_3}{2}$$

$$\text{10–90 percentile range } = P_{90} - P_{10}$$

Using Technology

Procedures to generate *descriptive statistics* in Excel or STATDISK have been described in Sections 2-4 and 2-5, in the Using Technology sections. STATDISK's display also includes some measures of position. (In Excel, quartile values can be generated by the function **=quartile**(*range,quartile*), where *range* is the Excel range containing the raw data, and *quartile* indicates the quartile number (for example 1, for Q_1).) The Excel and STATDISK outputs, based on the 175 axial loads listed in Table 2-1, are shown here.

STATDISK **Display**   Descriptive Statistics

Excel **Display**   Descriptive Statistics

Mean	267.1143
Standard Error	1.67153
Median	273
Mode	268
Standard Deviation	22.11227
Sample Variance	488.9524
Kurtosis	1.679651
Skewness	-1.4777
Range	97
Minimum	200
Maximum	297
Sum	46745
Count	175
Confidence Level(95.0%)	3.299083
Minimum	200
Maximum	297
Sum	46745
Count	175
Confidence Level(95.0%)	3.299083

2-6 Exercises A: Basic Skills and Concepts

In Exercises 1–4, express all z scores with two decimal places.

1. The Goodstone Tire Company claims that the useful life of its tires is an average of 68,000 km with a standard deviation of 10,000 km. Find the z scores corresponding to the following:
   a. A tire that lasts 50,000 km
   b. A tire that lasts 78,000 km
   c. A tire that lasts 70,000 km

2. Student cars at the author's college have ages with a mean of 7.90 years and a standard deviation of 3.67 years. Find the z scores for cars with the given ages:
   a. A 12-year-old Corvette
   b. A 2-year-old Ferrari
   c. A brand-new Porsche

3. A large airline found that, on average, each passenger's luggage weighed 50.6 kg with a standard deviation of 8.8 kg. Find the z score for a passenger whose luggage weighed 75 kg.

4. The mean score on a statistics test was 70 and the standard deviation was 5.5. Find the z score for students scoring 80 or better on the test.

In Exercises 5–8, express all z scores with two decimal places. Consider a score to be unusual if its z score is less than −2.00 or greater than 2.00.

5. The Beanstalk Club is limited to women and men who are very tall. The minimum height requirement for women is 70 in. Women's heights have a mean of 63.6 in. and a standard deviation of 2.5 in. Find the z score corresponding to a woman with a height of 70 in. and determine whether that height is unusual.

6. According to Statistics Canada, the monthly earnings of workers in the mining industry was $3840, with a standard deviation of $240. A mine worker claims to earn $4325 each month. Find the z score corresponding to this worker's wage. Is the amount unusual?

7. One of the few working vending machines is located and is found to accept quarters with weights that are not unusual. Weights of quarters have a mean of 5.67 g and a standard deviation of 0.070 g. Find the z score for a quarter weighing 5.50 g. Will it be accepted by this vending machine?

8. For men aged between 18 and 24 years, serum cholesterol levels (in mg/100 mL) have a mean of 178.1 and a standard deviation of 40.7. Find the z score corresponding to a male, aged 18–24 years, who has a serum cholesterol level of 275.2 mg/100 mL. Is this level unusually high?

9. Which of the following two scores has the better relative position?
   a. A score of 60 on a test for which $\bar{x} = 50$ and $s = 5$
   b. A score of 250 on a test for which $\bar{x} = 200$ and $s = 20$

10. Two similar groups of students took equivalent language facility tests. Which of the following results indicates the higher relative level of language facility?
    a. A score of 65 on a test for which $\bar{x} = 70$ and $s = 10$
    b. A score of 455 on a test for which $\bar{x} = 500$ and $s = 80$

11. Three prospective employees take equivalent tests of critical thinking. Which of the following scores corresponds to the highest relative position?
    a. A score of 37 on a test for which $\bar{x} = 28$ and $s = 6$
    b. A score of 398 on a test for which $\bar{x} = 312$ and $s = 56$
    c. A score of 4.10 on a test for which $\bar{x} = 2.75$ and $s = 0.92$

12. Three students take equivalent tests of a sense of humour and, after the laughter dies down, their scores are calculated. Which is the highest relative score?
    a. A score of 2.7 on a test for which $\bar{x} = 3.2$ and $s = 1.1$
    b. A score of 27 on a test for which $\bar{x} = 35$ and $s = 12$
    c. A score of 850 on a test for which $\bar{x} = 921$ and $s = 87$

In Exercises 13–16, use the 175 ranked axial loads of aluminum cans listed in Table 2-9. Find the percentile corresponding to the given value.

13. 254   14. 265   15. 277   16. 288

In Exercises 17–24, use the 175 ranked axial loads of aluminum cans listed in Table 2-9. Find the indicated percentile, quartile, or decile.

17. P_{70} 18. P_{20} 19. D_6 20. D_3
21. Q_3 22. Q_1 23. D_1 24. P_1

In Exercises 25–28, use the annual values for person-days lost in the truck-based transportation industry due to work stoppages (listed in Data Set 20 in Appendix B). Find the percentile corresponding to the given number of person-days lost.

25. 1000   26. 54000   27. 12000   28. 40000

In Exercises 29–36, use the annual values for person-days lost in the truck-based transportation industry due to work stoppages (listed in Data Set 20 in Appendix B). Find the indicated percentile, quartile, or decile.

29. P_{85} 30. P_{35} 31. Q_1 32. Q_3
33. D_9 34. D_3 35. P_{50} 36. P_{95}

2-6 Exercises B: Beyond the Basics

37. Use the ranked axial loads of aluminum cans listed in Table 2-9.
    a. Find the interquartile range.
    b. Find the midquartile.
    c. Find the 10–90 percentile range.
    d. Does $P_{50} = Q_2$? If so, does P_{50} *always* equal Q_2?
    e. Does $Q_2 = (Q_1 + Q_3)/2$? If so, does Q_2 *always* equal $(Q_1 + Q_3)/2$?

38. When finding percentiles using Figure 2-16, if the locator L is not a whole number, we round it up to the next larger whole number. An alternative

to this procedure is to interpolate so that a locator of 23.75 leads to a value that is 0.75 (or 3/4) of the way between the 23rd and 24th scores. Use this method of interpolation to find P_{35}, Q_1, and D_3 for the weights of bears listed in Data Set 3 of Appendix B.

39. Distribution of z Scores:
    a. A data set has a distribution that is uniform. If all of the values are converted to z scores, what is the shape of the distribution of the z scores?
    b. A data set (whose units are cm) has a distribution that is bell-shaped. If all the values are converted to z scores, what is the shape of the distribution of z scores?
    c. In general, how is the shape of a distribution affected if all values are converted to z scores?
    d. If all the values in the data set mentioned in (b) are converted from cm into inches, what is the effect on the distribution of z scores?

40. Using the scores 2, 5, 8, 9, and 16, first find $\bar{x}$ and s, then replace each score by its corresponding z score. (Don't round the z scores; carry as many decimal places as your calculator can handle.) Now find the mean and standard deviation of the five z scores. Will these new values of the mean and standard deviation result from every set of z scores?

2-7 Exploratory Data Analysis (EDA)

The theme of this chapter is describing, exploring, and comparing data; the focus of this section is exploration. We will first define exploratory data analysis, then introduce some new tools—outliers, 5-number summaries, and box-plots. We can then add these to the techniques presented earlier in this chapter.

DEFINITION

Exploratory data analysis is the process of using statistical tools (such as graphs, measures of centre, and measures of variation) to investigate data sets in order to understand their important characteristics.

Recall that in Section 2-1 we introduced these three important characteristics of data: (1) *centre*, a representative or average value; (2) *variation*, a measure of the amount of spread among the sample values; and (3) *distribution*, the nature or shape of the distribution of the data. When exploring a data set, we usually want to calculate the mean and the standard deviation and to generate a histogram, but we should not stop there. Are there any other notable features—especially features that could have a strong effect on results and conclusions? One such feature is the presence of outliers.

Outliers

An **outlier** is a value that is located very far away from almost all the other values. Relative to the other data, an outlier is an *extreme* value. The following example illustrates the possible effects if an outlier is included in a data set.

EXAMPLE   When using computer software it is easy to make typing errors. Referring to the axial loads listed in Table 2-1, suppose that the first entry of 270 was incorrectly entered as 2700. How does that affect your data set?

SOLUTION   After the first entry of 270 is mistakenly replaced with the value of 2700, the data in Table 2-1 will result in a mean of 281.0 (instead of the correct value of 267.1), and a standard deviation of 185.2 (instead of the correct value of 22.1). The accompanying STATDISK display shows the histogram for the mistakenly modified data set. Compare this histogram with the correct version, shown in Figure 2-2 of Section 2-3, and you can clearly see the difference.

Our example demonstrates these important principles:

1. An outlier can have a dramatic effect on the mean.

2. An outlier can have a dramatic effect on the standard deviation.

3. An outlier can have a dramatic effect on the scale of the histogram so that the true nature of the distribution is totally obscured.

An easy way to find outliers is to examine a *sorted* list of the data. In particular, look at the minimum and maximum sample values and determine whether they are very far away from the other typical values. In the preceding example, the outlier of 2700 is an error. When such an error is identified, we should either correct it or delete it. Remember, however, that some data sets include outliers that are correct values, not errors. (It is often useful to "troubleshoot" exactly where and how the specific extreme value was collected—in order to judge if an error was made.) When exploring data, we might study the effects of outliers by constructing graphs and calculating statistics with and without the outliers. (See Exercise 12 for a way to depict outliers on boxplots.)

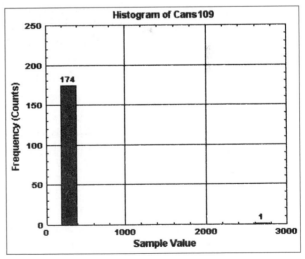

STATDISK Display   Incorrect Data

Boxplots

Boxplots are graphs that are useful for revealing central tendency, the spread of the data, the distribution of the data, and the presence of outliers (extreme values). The construction of a boxplot requires that we obtain the minimum value, the first quartile Q_1, the median (or second quartile Q_2), the third quartile Q_3, and the maximum value (together these are called the **5-number summary**.) Because medians are used to reveal central tendency and quartiles are used to reveal the spread of data, boxplots have the advantage of not being as sensitive to extreme values as other devices based on the mean and standard deviation. Boxplots don't show as much detailed information as histograms or stem-and-leaf plots, so they might not be the best choice when dealing with a single data set. However, boxplots are often more useful when comparing two or more data sets. When using two or more boxplots for comparing different data sets, it is important to use the same scale so that the comparisons can be made.

AS

DEFINITIONS

For a set of data, the **5-number summary** consists of the the minimum value, the first quartile Q_1, the median, the third quartile Q_3, and the maximum value.

A **boxplot** (or **box-and-whisker diagram**) is a graph of data that consists of a line extending from the lowest score to the highest, and a box with lines drawn at the first quartile Q_1, the median, and the third quartile Q_3.

EXAMPLE   Refer to Data Set 9 of Appendix B and use the pulse rates of smokers.

a. Find the values constituting the 5-number summary.
b. Construct a boxplot for the pulse rates of smokers.

SOLUTION

a. The 5-number summary consists of the minimum, Q_1, median, Q_3, and maximum. To find those values, we should first arrange the pulse rates of smokers in order from low to high. Here is the *sorted* list of the 22 pulse rates of smokers from Data Set 9:

52	52	60	60	60	60	63	63	66	67	68
69	71	72	73	75	78	80	82	83	88	90

    From this sorted list, it is easy to identify the minimum of 52 and the maximum of 90. Using the flowchart of Figure 2-16, we find that the first quartile Q_1 (or P_{25}) is 60, which is located by calculating $L = (25/100)22 = 5.5$ and rounding up the result to 6. Q_1 is the 6th value in the sorted list, namely 60. The median is 68.5, which is the number midway between the 11th and 12th values. We also find that $Q_3 = 78$ by using Figure 2-16 for the 75th percentile. The 5-number summary is therefore 52, 60, 68.5, 78, and 90.

b. In Figure 2-17 we graph the boxplot for the data. We use the minimum (52) and the maximum (90) to determine a scale of values, then we plot the values from the 5-number summary as shown.

Figure 2-17   Boxplot of Pulse Rates (Beats per Minute) of Smokers

In Figure 2-18 we show some generic boxplots along with common distribution shapes.

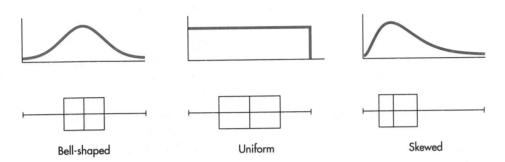

Bell-shaped   Uniform   Skewed

Figure 2-18   Boxplots Corresponding to Bell-Shaped, Uniform, and Skewed Distributions

Exploring

Including the options from this section, we now have the following arsenal of tools for data exploration:

- *Measures of centre:* mean, median, and mode
- *Measures of variation:* standard deviation and range
- *Measures of spread and relative location:* minimum and maximum values, and quartiles
- *Unusual values:* outliers
- *Distribution:* histograms, stem-and-leaf plots, and boxplots

Now that you have all these tools in hand, begin to *think creatively!* Rather than simply cranking out statistics and graphs, try to identify those that are particularly interesting or important. As a first step, investigate outliers and consider their effects by finding measures and graphs with and without the outliers.

EXAMPLE   If you have spent time in the four Atlantic provinces, it is easy to conclude that they have (on average) more annual rainfall than do other provinces. Later in this book we will describe statistical methods that can be used to formally address such a claim, but for now, let us explore the related data in Data Set 4 in Appendix B, to see what can be learned. (Even if we know the more formal statistical tests, it is useful to explore the data first.) We will use the Average Precipitation column, and assume that the selected cities are representative of areas within Atlantic or non-Atlantic Canada.

SOLUTION   In the following table and STATDISK display we apply our arsenal of data exploration tools, listed above this example. Note that the table (based on Excel) and the display disagree about the first and third quartiles for the two groups of provinces; but since we are just exploring the data, this is not a great concern.

Excel Display   Data Exploration

	Atlantic Provinces	Other Provinces
Mean	1313.250	772.583
Standard Deviation	171.873	453.035
Minimum	1097.000	266.000
Q_1	1154.000	463.750
Median	1341.000	737.000
Q_3	1455.750	908.250
Maximum	1514.000	2523.000

STATDISK Display   Boxplots

Interpretation   Examining and comparing the statistics and graphs, we make the following important observations.

- *Outliers:* The maximum value of 2523 for precipitation in non-Atlantic Canada stands out as a possible outlier. A further check by sorting the data for non-Atlantic Canada shows that this maximum value is more than double the next largest value (of 1174). Because the data source (Environment Canada) is generally reliable, it is probable that this outlier is not a mistaken value, but indicates that at least one city (Prince Rupert, B.C.) may have an atypical value, compared to the average precipitations in other non-Atlantic cities.

- *Means:* Comparison of means (1313 for Atlantic Canada, and 773 for other provinces) may support the claim of higher precipitation in Atlantic Canada, but this may be misleading, given the large standard deviation (453) for non-Atlantic provinces. However, if the mean and standard deviation for non-Atlantic cities are recalculated, omitting the apparent outlier (2523), they become 696 and 263, respectively— further strengthening the claim of difference from Atlantic Canada.

- *Variation:* Data from the non-Atlantic provinces have a larger standard deviation (453 *with* the outlier, 263 *without*) than data from the Atlantic provinces (172). This is logical, since the former are drawn from a greater diversity of geographical and meteorological contexts.

- *Distributions and 5-number summaries:* In comparison with the non-Atlantic provinces, data from the Atlantic provinces appear to have a more symmetrical distribution, with less variation; and the measures of location and position clearly suggest (except for the outlier) greater precipitation values for cities from the Atlantic region.

We have now gained considerable insight into the comparative values for "average precipitation" from cities in two parts of Canada (Atlantic provinces, the other provinces). Based on our exploration we can conclude that, in general, the Atlantic cities experience the greater levels of precipitation, but in the broad expanse of "the other provinces" there are some notable exceptions to the rule.

Using Technology

We have already seen how Excel and STATDISK can generate measures of location, variation, and position. These are their procedures for generating boxplots.

Excel: To generate boxplots with Excel, use the Data Desk XL add-in that is a supplement to this book. In a block of cells (such as M1:N24) enter the data for each desired box plot (if there is more than one column, Excel will generate one box plot per column). Data columns should start on the same row, but do *not* need to contain the same number of values. Click on **DDXL** and select **Charts** and **Plots**. Under **Function Type**, select the option **Boxplot**. In the dialog box, click on the pencil icon and enter the range of data (the range should be large enough to include all the data values in the input block; it does not matter if some cells are empty). Click on **OK**. The result is actually a modified box plot, as described in Exercise 12.

STATDISK   Choose the main menu item of **Data**, then select **Boxplot**. On the right of the screen, input data manually or copy/paste from another source, then click the **Evaluate** button.

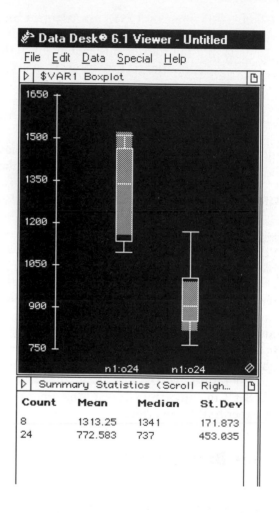

2-7 Exercises A: Basic Skills and Concepts

Include values of the 5-number summary in all boxplots.

1. Refer to Data Set 4 in Appendix B and construct a boxplot for the average annual temperatures of the cities listed.
2. Refer to Data Set 4 in Appendix B and construct a boxplot for the annual precipitation of the cities listed.
3. In "Ages of Oscar-Winning Best Actors and Actresses" (*Mathematics Teacher* magazine) by Richard Brown and Gretchen Davis, boxplots are used to compare the ages of actors and actresses at the time they won

Oscars. The results for 34 recent winners from each category are listed below. Use boxplots to compare the two data sets.

Actors:	32	37	36	32	51	53	33	61	35	45	55	39
	76	37	42	40	32	60	38	56	48	48	40	
	43	62	43	42	44	41	56	39	46	31	47	
Actresses:	50	44	35	80	26	28	41	21	61	38	49	33
	74	30	33	41	31	35	41	42	37	26	34	
	34	35	26	61	60	34	24	30	37	31	27	

4. Refer to Data Set 9 in Appendix B for these two data sets: pulse rates of those who smoke and pulse rates of those who don't smoke. Construct a boxplot for each data set. Based on the results, do pulse rates of the two groups appear to be different? If so, how? Is this the result you would expect? (Exclude the 8 and 15, which must be errors.)

5. Refer to Data Set 9 in Appendix B for these two data sets: pulse rates of males and pulse rates of females. Construct a boxplot for each data set. Based on the results, do pulse rates of the two groups appear to be different? If so, how? (Exclude the 8 and 15, which must be errors.)

6. Refer to Data Set 10 in Appendix B. Use boxplots to compare the one-year return of U.S. equity funds to that of the funds other than U.S. equity.

7. Refer to Data Set 11 in Appendix B. Use boxplots to compare the weights of red M&M candies to the weights of yellow M&M candies.

8. Refer to Data Set 13 in Appendix B. Construct a boxplot for the weights of quarters. Compare the shape of the resulting boxplot to the generic shapes shown in Figure 2-18. Based on the boxplot, what do you conclude about the nature of the distribution?

9. Refer to Data Set 12 in Appendix B. Construct a boxplot for the 50 digits from the Lotto 6/49 bonus draw. Compare the shape of the resulting boxplot to the generic shapes shown in Figure 2-18. Based on the boxplot, do the Lotto 6/49 results appear to be occurring as expected?

10. Refer to Data Set 1 in Appendix B. Use boxplots to compare the weights of discarded paper to the weights of discarded plastic.

2–7 Exercises B: Beyond the Basics

11. Compare the two boxplots from Exercises 1 and 2. How would you describe the shape of the distribution in the two sets of data? Are they uniform, skewed, or bell-shaped?

12. The boxplots discussed in this section are often called *skeletal (or regular)* boxplots. **Modified boxplots** are constructed as follows:
   a. Calculate the difference between the quartiles Q_3 and Q_1 and denote it as *IQR (interquartile range)*, so that $IQR = Q_3 - Q_1$.
   b. Draw the box with the median and quartiles as usual, but when extending the lines that branch out from the box, go only as far as the scores that are within 1.5 *IQR* of the box.
   c. *Mild outliers* are scores above Q_3 by an amount of 1.5 *IQR* to 3 *IQR*, or below Q_1 by an amount of 1.5 *IQR* to 3 *IQR*. Plot mild outliers as solid dots.

d. *Extreme outliers* are scores that exceed Q_3 by more than $3\ IQR$ or are below Q_1 by an amount more than $3\ IQR$. Plot extreme outliers as small hollow circles.

The accompanying figure is an example of the boxplot described here. Use this procedure to construct the boxplot for the given scores, and identify any mild outliers or extreme outliers.

3   15   17   18   21   21   22   25   27   30   38   49   68

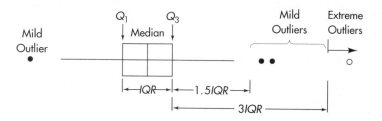

- -

Vocabulary List

descriptive statistics
inferential statistics
frequency table
frequency
lower class limits
upper class limits
class boundaries
class midpoints
class width
relative frequency
relative frequency table
cumulative frequency
cumulative frequency
   table
histogram
relative frequency
   histogram
reltive frequency
   polygon
ogive
stem-and-leaf plot
Pareto chart
pie chart
scatter diagram

measure of centre
arithmetic mean
mean
sample size
median
mode
bimodal
multimodal
midrange
weighted mean
skewed
symmetric
negatively skewed
positively skewed
harmonic mean
geometric mean
quadratic mean
root mean square
range
standard deviation
deviation
mean absolute deviation
variance
unbiased estimator

range rule of thumb
empirical rule
68–95–99.7 rule
Chebyshev's theorem
coefficient of variation
signal-to-noise ratio
Pearson's index of
   skewness
standard score
z score
quartiles
deciles
percentiles
quantiles
fractiles
exploratory data
   analysis (EDA)
outlier
5-number summary
boxplot (or box-and-
   whisker diagram)
modified boxplots

Review

Chapter 2 considered methods and techniques of describing, exploring, and comparing data. We noted these important characteristics of data:

1. *Centre:* A representative or average value
2. *Variation:* A measure of the amount that the values vary
3. *Distribution:* The nature or shape of the distribution of the data (such as bell-shaped, uniform, or skewed)
4. *Outliers:* Sample values that lie very far away from the vast majority of the other sample values
5. *Time:* Changing characteristics of the data over time

After completing this chapter, you should be able to do the following:

- Summarize the data by constructing a frequency table or relative frequency table (Section 2-2)
- Visually display the nature of the distribution by constructing a histogram, stem-and-leaf plot, pie chart, or Pareto chart (Section 2-3)
- Calculate measures of centre by finding the mean, median, mode, and midrange (Section 2-4)
- Calculate measures of variation by finding the standard deviation, variance, and range (Section 2-5)
- Compare individual scores by using z scores, quartiles, deciles, or percentiles (Section 2-6)
- Investigate and explore the spread of data, the centre of the data, and the range of values by constructing a boxplot (Section 2-7)

In addition to obtaining the above tables, graphs, and measures, we should *understand* and *interpret* those results. For example, we should clearly understand that the standard deviation is a measure of how much the data vary, and we should be able to use the standard deviation to distinguish between scores that are usual and those that are unusual.

Review Exercises

1. A family living in Ontario collected the data from their natural gas bills to monitor their consumption of gas and to try to save money. The following values are the cubic feet of gas used each month for five years. Using the lowest volume as the lower limit of the first class, construct a frequency table with 10 classes.

Month	Year 1	2	3	4	5
Jan.	303	263	260	104	219
Feb.	192	212	254	170	176
Mar.	126	125	156	142	102
Apr.	57	83	83	38	70
May	34	42	31	40	27
June	24	18	15	19	20
July	18	15	17	19	18
Aug.	17	14	17	19	18
Sept.	58	75	60	48	62
Oct.	116	118	91	102	104
Nov.	181	203	200	205	223
Dec.	254	292	206	200	223

2. Construct a relative frequency table (with 10 classes) for the data in Exercise 1.
3. Construct a histogram that corresponds to the frequency table from Exercise 1.
4. For the data in Exercise 1, find (a) Q_1, (b) P_{45}, and (c) the percentile corresponding to the volume of 125 cu. ft.
5. Use the range rule of thumb to estimate the standard deviation of the data in Exercise 1.
6. Use the frequency table from Exercise 1 to find the mean and standard deviation for the volumes.
7. Use the data from Exercise 1 for the first two years to construct a stem-and-leaf plot with 7 rows.
8. Use the data from Exercise 1 to construct a boxplot.
9. Given below are times (in seconds) between an order being placed and the food being received at a McDonald's drive-through window. Find the (a) mean, (b) median, (c) mode, (d) midrange, (e) range, (f) standard deviation, and (g) variance.

    135   90   85   121   83   69   87   159   177   135   227

10. Given below are numbers taken from the hydro bills of the family mentioned in Exercise 1. The numbers represent the usage of hydro (in kilowatt-hours) every two months for six years.

    22   21   20   22   27   25   19   18   18   18   23   21
    26   24   16   15   23   24   35   32   18   28   31   45
    24   23   20   23   23   25   19   19   18   19   23   24

    Find the (a) mean, (b) median, (c) mode, (d) midrange, (e) range, (f) standard deviation, (g) variance, (h) Q_1, (i) P_{30}, and (j) D_7.

11. Scores on a test of depth perception have a mean of 200 and a standard deviation of 40.
    a. Is a score of 260 unusually high? Explain.
    b. What is the z score corresponding to 185?
    c. Assuming that the scores have a bell-shaped distribution, what does the empirical rule say about the percentage of scores between 120 and 280?
    d. What is the mean after 20 points have been added to every score?
    e. What is the standard deviation after 20 points have been added to every score?

12. The accompanying table lists times (in years) required to earn an honours bachelor's degree for a sample of undergraduate students. Use the table to find the mean and standard deviation. Based on the results, is it unusual for an undergraduate to require 8 years to earn a bachelor's degree? Explain.

Time (years)	Number
4	147
5	81
6	27
7	15
7.5–11.5	30

13. Using the frequency table given in Exercise 12, construct the corresponding relative frequency histogram.

14. An industrial psychologist gave a subject two different tests designed to measure employee satisfaction. Which score is better: a score of 57 on the first test, which has a mean of 72 and a standard deviation of 20, or a score of 450 on the second test, which has a mean of 500 and a standard deviation of 80? Explain.

15. Refer to the two boxplots below. The first boxplot represents a sample of skulls of male Egyptians from about 4000 B.C., whereas the second boxplot represents a sample of male Egyptian skulls from about 150 A.D. (in mm, based on data from *Ancient Races of the Thebaid* by Thomson and Randall-Maciver). A shift in head sizes would suggest some societal changes, such as interbreeding with other cultures. By comparing the two boxplots, is there a shift in the maximum skull breadth? Explain.

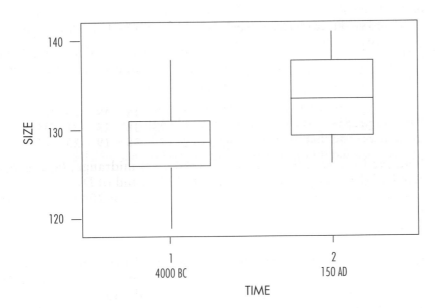

16. Statistics Canada did a study of environmental impacts on health in five provinces. Listed below are five age-standardized mortality rates selected by cause (per 100,000 population). Construct a Pareto chart summarizing the given data.

Lung cancer: 296   Heart disease: 959

Respiratory disease: 297   Chronic liver disease: 45

All accidents: 303

Cumulative Review Exercises

1. The amounts of time (in hours) spent on paperwork in one day were obtained from a sample of office managers with the results given below:

3.7	2.9	3.4	0.0	1.5	1.8	2.3	2.4	1.0	2.0
4.4	2.0	4.5	0.0	1.7	4.4	3.3	2.4	2.1	2.1

   a. Find the mean, median, mode, and midrange.
   b. Find the standard deviation, variance, and range.
   c. Are the given scores from a population that is discrete or continuous?
   d. What is the level of measurement of these scores? (nominal, ordinal, interval, ratio)

2. a. A set of data is at the nominal level of measurement and you want to obtain a representative data value. Which of the following is most appropriate: mean, median, mode, or midrange? Why?
   b. A sample is obtained by telephoning the first 250 people listed in the local telephone directory. What type of sampling is being used? (random, stratified, systematic, cluster, convenience)
   c. An exit poll is conducted by surveying everyone who leaves the polling booth at 30 randomly selected election ridings. What type of sampling is being used? (random, stratified, systematic, cluster, convenience)

3. Auto dealer A sold 5 Volkswagen Beetles for $28,000 each; auto dealer B sold 9 Beetles for $31,000 each; and dealer C sold 3 Beetles for $27,000 each. Can the dealers state that the mean selling price of VW Beetles is $28,666.67? If not, how should they calculate the mean price of this vehicle?

Technology Project

It is commonly believed that the mean body temperature of healthy adults is 37.0°C. Refer to Data Set 18 in Appendix B and consider the body temperatures there. Open the data file that you created for the Chapter 1 Computer Project in Excel or STATDISK. Proceed to obtain a histogram, measures of central tendency, measures of variation, Q_1, Q_3, the minimum, and the maximum values. Use the results to describe important characteristics of the data set. Based on this sample, what do you conclude about the common belief that the mean body temperature is 37.0°C? Is this the result you would have expected?

•••••••• FROM DATA TO DECISION ••••••••

Garbage In, Insight Out

Refer to Data Set 1 in Appendix B. That data set consists of weights of different categories of garbage discarded by a sample of 62 households. With such data sets, there are often several different issues that can be addressed. In Chapter 9 we will consider the issue of whether there is some relationship between household size and amount of waste discarded so that we might be able to predict the size of the population of a region by analysing the disposed-of garbage. For now, we will work with descriptive statistics based on the data.

a. Construct a Pareto chart and a pie chart depicting the relative amounts of the total weights of metal, paper, plastic, glass, food, yard waste, textile waste, and other waste. (Instead of frequencies, use the total weights.) Based on the results, which categories appear to be the largest components of the total amount of waste? Is there any single category that stands out as being the largest component?

b. A pie chart depicted metal, paper, plastic, glass, food, yard waste, and other waste with the percents of 14%, 38%, 18%, 2%, 4%, 11%, and 13%, respectively. Do these percentages appear to be consistent with Data Set 1 in Appendix B?

c. For each category, find the mean and standard deviation, and construct a histogram of the 62 weights. Enter the results in the table below.

d. The amounts of garbage discarded are listed by weight. Many regions have household waste collected by commercial trucks that compress it, and charges at the destination are based on weight. Under these conditions, is the volume of the garbage relevant to the problem of community waste disposal? What other factors are relevant?

e. Based on the preceding results, if you had to institute conservation or recycling efforts because your region's waste facility was almost at full capacity, what would you do?

	Metal	Paper	Plastic	Glass	Food	Yard	Textile	Other
Mean								
Standard deviation								
Shape of distribution								

········ COOPERATIVE GROUP ACTIVITIES ········

1. *Out-of-class activity:* Are estimates influenced by anchoring numbers? In the article "Weighing Anchors" in *Omni* magazine, author John Rubin observed that when people estimate a value, their estimate is often "anchored" to (or influenced by) a preceding number, even if that preceding number is totally unrelated to the quantity being estimated. To demonstrate this, he asked people to give a quick estimate of the value of $8 \times 7 \times 6 \times 5 \times 4 \times 3 \times 2 \times 1$. The average answer given was 2250, but when the order of the numbers was reversed, the average became 512. Rubin explained that when we begin calculations with larger numbers (as in $8 \times 7 \times 6$), our estimates tend to be larger. He noted that both 2250 and 512 are far below the correct product, 40,320. The article suggests that irrelevant numbers can play a role in influencing real estate appraisals, estimates of car values, and estimates of the likelihood of nuclear war.

Conduct an experiment to test this theory. Select some subjects and ask them to quickly estimate the value of

$$8 \times 7 \times 6 \times 5 \times 4 \times 3 \times 2 \times 1$$

Then select other subjects and ask them to quickly estimate the value of

$$1 \times 2 \times 3 \times 4 \times 5 \times 6 \times 7 \times 8$$

Record the estimates along with the particular order used. Carefully design the experiment so that conditions are uniform and the two sample groups are selected in a way that minimizes any bias. Don't describe the theory to subjects until after they have provided their estimates. Compare the two sets of sample results by using the methods of this chapter. Provide a typewritten report that includes the data collected, the detailed methods used, the method of analysis, any relevant graphs and/or statistics, and a statement of conclusions. Include a critique of reasons why the results might not be correct and describe ways in which the experiment could be improved.

A variation of the preceding experiment is to survey people about their knowledge of the population of Kenya. First ask half of the subjects whether they think the population is above 5 million or below 5 million, then ask them to estimate the population with an actual number. Ask the other half of the subjects whether they think the population is above 80 million or below 80 million, then ask them to estimate the population. (Kenya's population is 29 million.) Compare the two sets of results and identify the "anchoring" effect of the initial number that the survey subjects are given.

••••••• COOPERATIVE GROUP ACTIVITIES •••••••

2. *In-class activity:* In each group of three or four students, find the total value of the coins possessed by each individual member. Find the group mean and standard deviation, then exchange those statistics with the other groups. Using the group means as a separate data set, find the mean, standard deviation, and shape of the distribution. How do these results compare to the mean and standard deviation originally found in the group?

3. *In-class activity:* Given below are the ages of motorcyclists at the time they were fatally injured in traffic accidents. If your objective is to dramatize the dangers of motorcycles for young people, which would be most effective: histogram, Pareto chart, pie chart, mean, median, . . . ? Construct the graph and find the statistic that best meets that objective. Is it okay to deliberately distort data if the objective is one such as saving lives of motorcyclists?

```
17  38  27  14  18  34  16  42  28  24  40  20  23  31
37  21  30  25  17  28  33  25  23  19  51  18  29
```

INTERNET PROJECT   Data on the Internet

The Internet is a host to a wealth of information. Much of that information comes in the form of raw data, which can be studied and summarized using the statistics introduced in this chapter. The Internet Project for this chapter, located at

   http://www.pearsoned.ca/triola

will point you to data sets in such areas as sports, finance and the weather. (When you reach the site, click on Internet Project, then on Chapter 2.) Once you have assembled a data set you can use the methods in this chapter to summarize and classify the data.

3

Probability

3-1 Overview

Chapter objectives are identified. The importance of probability is discussed, along with its role in basic statistical methods.

3-2 Fundamentals

The relative frequency and classical definitions of probability are both presented and illustrated. Methods are given for finding probabilities of simple events. The law of large numbers is described, and the complement of an event is defined and illustrated. Odds are also considered.

3-3 Addition Rule

The addition rule is described as a method for finding the probability that either one event *or* another event (or both events) occurs when an experiment is conducted. Mutually exclusive events are defined. In applying the addition rule, we avoid or correct for double counting of events that are not mutually exclusive. The rule of complementary events is also introduced.

3-4 Multiplication Rule and Conditional Probabilities

The multiplication rule is described as a method for finding the probability that one event occurs in one experiment *and* some other event occurs in another experiment. Independent events are defined. The probability of getting at least one outcome of some event is described. Conditional probability is defined and illustrated.

3-5 Probabilities Through Simulations

Probabilities can often be estimated from simulations that emulate experiments. Methods for creating simulations are described and illustrated.

3-6 Counting

The following important counting techniques are described: the fundamental counting rule, factorial rule, permutations rule (when all items are different), permutations rule (when some items are identical to others), and combinations rule. Such counting devices are used to find the total number of outcomes.

CHAPTER PROBLEM:

Do you have a better chance of being hit by lightning or winning the lottery?

Many of us take action based on the likelihood of events occurring. Some of us fly in airplanes recognizing that while there is a chance of a crash, the likelihood of this happening is really quite small. Some of us sprint to our cars during a thunderstorm knowing that we could be struck by lightning, but, again, the likelihood of that event is actually quite small. Many of us buy lottery tickets knowing that we could win, although the likelihood of that event is very small, but do we really understand just how small? Is the chance of winning the lottery actually smaller than the chance of being struck by lightning? In this chapter we discuss *probability* as we determine specific ways of measuring the chance of various events. Among other things, we will find probabilities for being struck by lightning and for winning a lottery. We will then know which event is more likely.

3-1 Overview

In Chapter 2 we described the method of *inferential statistics,* which uses sample evidence to make inferences or conclusions about a whole population. Inferential decisions are based on **probabilities**—or likelihoods—of events. Suppose, for example, that a check of your college's employee records reveals that of the last 100 people hired, all are men. The probability that 100 consecutive men would be selected with a hiring policy that is unbiased is so low that most reasonable people would conclude that men were favoured. This example illustrates the following important principle, which will be a foundation of our reasoning in several of the chapters to come:

Rare Event Rule for Inferential Statistics
If, under a given assumption (such as a fair hiring practice), the probability of a particular observed event (such as 100 hired men) is exceptionally small, we conclude that the assumption is probably not correct.

The primary objective of this chapter is to develop a sound understanding of probability values, which we will build upon in subsequent chapters. A secondary objective is to develop the basic skills necessary to solve simple probability problems.

3-2 Fundamentals

In considering probability problems, we deal with procedures that produce outcomes (these are sometimes called experiments).

DEFINITIONS

An **event** is any collection of results or outcomes of a procedure.

A **simple event** is an outcome or an event that cannot be broken down into simpler components.

The **sample space** for a procedure consists of all possible *simple* events. That is, the sample space consists of all outcomes that cannot be broken down any further.

EXAMPLES

Procedure	Event	Sample Space
Roll one die	A 3 is rolled (simple event)	{1, 2, 3, 4, 5, 6}
Roll two dice	Dice add to 7 (not a simple event)	{1-1, 1-2,..., 6-6}

When rolling one die, rolling a 3 is a *simple event* because it cannot be broken down any further, and the *sample space* consists of these simple events: 1, 2, 3, 4, 5, 6. When rolling a pair of dice, the result of 7 is not itself a simple event because it can be broken down into simple events, such as 3-4 and 6-1. In rolling a pair of dice, the sample space consists of 36 simple events: 1-1, 1-2, . . . , 6-6.

There are different ways to define the probability of an event, and we will present three approaches. We begin by listing some basic notation.

Notation for Probabilities

P denotes a probability. A, B, and C denote specific events. $P(A)$ denotes the probability of event A occurring.

Rule 1: Relative Frequency Approximation of Probability

Conduct (or observe) a procedure a large number of times, and count the number of times that event A actually occurs. Then $P(A)$ is *estimated* as follows:

$$P(A) = \frac{\text{number of times } A \text{ occurred}}{\text{number of times trial was repeated}}$$

Rule 2: Classical Approach to Probability

Assume that a given experiment has n different simple events, each of which has an *equal chance* of occurring. If event A can occur in s of these n ways, then

$$P(A) = \frac{\text{number of ways } A \text{ can occur}}{\text{number of different simple events}} = \frac{s}{n}$$

Rule 3: Subjective Probabilities

$P(A)$, the probability of event A, is found by simply guessing or estimating its value based on knowledge of the relevant circumstances

---

It is very important to note that *the classical approach* (Rule 2) *requires equally likely outcomes*. If the outcomes are not equally likely, we must use the relative frequency estimate or rely on our knowledge of the circumstances to make an *educated* guess. Figure 3-1 illustrates this important distinction.

How Probable?

How do we interpret such terms as *probable, improbable,* or *extremely improbable?* The FAA interprets these terms as follows. *Probable:* A probability on the order of 0.00001 or greater for each hour of flight. Such events are expected to occur several times during the operational life of each airplane. *Improbable:* A probability on the order of 0.00001 or less. Such events are not expected to occur during the total operational life of a single airplane of a particular type, but may occur during the total operational life of all airplanes of a particular type. *Extremely improbable:* A probability on the order of 0.000000001 or less. Such events are so unlikely that they need not be considered ever to occur.

Figure 3-1 Comparison of Relative Frequency and Classical Approaches

(a)   **(b)**   **(c)**

Figure 3-1 Comparison of Relative Frequency and Classical Approaches

(a) Relative Frequency Approach (Rule 1): When trying to determine P(the tack lands point up), we must repeat the experiment of tossing the tack many times and then find the ratio of the number of times the tack lands with the point up to the number of tosses. That ratio is our estimate of the probability.

(b) Classical Approach (Rule 2): When trying to determine $P(2)$ with a balanced and fair die, each of the six faces has an equal chance of occurring.

$$P(2) = \frac{\text{number of ways 2 can occur}}{\text{total number of simple events}}$$

$$= \frac{1}{6}$$

(c) Subjective Probability (Rule 3): When trying to estimate the probability of rain tomorrow, meteorologists use their expert knowledge of weather conditions.

When finding probabilities with the relative frequency approach (Rule 1), we obtain an *approximation* instead of an exact value. As the total number of observations increases, the corresponding approximations tend to get closer to the actual probability. This property is stated as a theorem commonly referred to as the **law of large numbers**.

Law of Large Numbers

AS As a procedure is repeated again and again, the relative frequency probability (from Rule 1) of an event tends to approach the actual probability.

The law of large numbers tells us that the relative frequency approximations from Rule 1 tend to get better with more observations. This law reflects a simple notion supported by common sense: A probability estimate based on only a few trials can be off by substantial amounts, but with a very large number of trials, the estimate tends to be much more accurate. For example, if you conduct an opinion poll of only a dozen people, your results could easily be in error by large amounts, but if you poll thousands of *randomly selected* people your sample results will be much closer to the true population values.

Figure 3-2 illustrates the law of large numbers by showing computer-simulated results. Note that as the number of births increases, the proportion of girls approaches the 0.5 value.

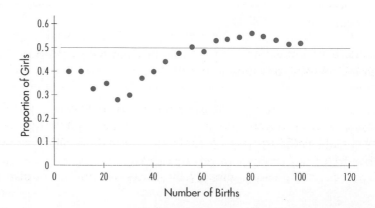

Figure 3-2 Illustration of the Law of Large Numbers

After examining Rules 1 and 2, it might seem that we should always use Rule 2 when a procedure has equally likely outcomes. It frequently happens, though, that many procedures are so complicated that the classical approach (Rule 2) is impractical to use. Instead, we can more easily get estimates of the desired probabilities by using the relative frequency approach (Rule 1). In such cases simulations are often helpful. (A **simulation** of a procedure is a process that behaves in the same ways as the procedure itself, thus producing similar results.) For example, it's much easier to use Rule 1 for estimating the probability of winning at solitaire—that is, to play the game many times (or to run a computer simulation)—than to perform the extremely complex calculations required with Rule 2.

The examples that follow are intended to illustrate the use of the three rules. In some of these examples we use the term *random*. Recall these definitions from Section 1-4: In a **random sample of one element** from a population, all elements available for selection have the same chance of being chosen; a sample of *n* items is a **random sample** (or a simple random sample) if it is selected in such a way that every possible sample of *n* items from the population has the same chance of being chosen. The general concept of randomness is extremely important in statistics. When making inferences based on samples, we must have a sampling process that is representative, impartial, and unbiased. If a sample is not carefully selected, it may be totally worthless.

EXAMPLE   Find the probability that a person will achieve a hole-in-one when playing a round of golf.

SOLUTION   It is extremely unlikely that a person will get a hole-in-one when playing a round of golf. We can, though, use a relative frequency approximation, as described in Rule 1, to find the approximate probability of this event. Recently, a Canadian golf course did a hole-in-one survey. They found 8 holes-in-one scored in 64,000 rounds of golf played at the course. The probability of a hole-in-one during a round of golf at that course is estimated to be

$$\frac{8}{64,000} = 0.000125$$

EXAMPLE   A typical multiple-choice question on a test has 5 possible answers. If you make a random guess on one such question, what is the probability that your response is wrong?

SOLUTION   There are 5 possible outcomes or answers, and there are 4 ways to answer incorrectly. Random guessing implies that the outcomes in the sample space are equally likely, so we apply the classical approach (Rule 2) to get

$$P(\text{wrong answer}) = \frac{4}{5} = 0.8$$

Shakespeare's Vocabulary

According to Bradley Efron and Ronald Thisted, Shakespeare's writings included 31,534 different words. They used probability theory to conclude that Shakespeare probably knew at least another 35,000 words that he didn't use in his writings. The problem of estimating the size of a population is an important problem often encountered in ecology studies, but the result given here is another interesting application. (See "Estimating the Number of Unseen Species: How Many Words Did Shakespeare Know?" in *Biometrika*, Vol. 63, No. 3.)

In basic probability problems of the type we are now considering, it is very important to examine the available information carefully and to identify the total number of possible outcomes correctly. In some cases the total number of possible outcomes is directly available, but in other cases we must process the available information to determine that total. The preceding example included the information that the total number of outcomes is 5, but the following examples require us to calculate the total number of possible outcomes.

EXAMPLE   A survey of songs played by three Vancouver music stations shows the following breakdown of the type of music played:

Rock	Country	Blues
64	43	21

If one of the songs played is randomly selected, find the probability that it is a blues song.

SOLUTION   The total number of songs surveyed is found by computing $64 + 43 + 21 = 128$. With random selection, the 128 songs are equally likely and Rule 2 is applied as follows:

$$P(\text{blues}) = \frac{\text{number of blues songs}}{\text{total number of songs}} = \frac{21}{128} = 0.164$$

There is a 0.164 probability that a song selected at random will be a blues song.

<u>1st</u> <u>2nd</u> <u>3rd</u>

boy-boy-boy

boy-boy-girl

exactly 2 boys

boy-girl-boy

boy-girl-girl

girl-boy-boy

girl-boy-girl

girl-girl-boy

girl-girl-girl

EXAMPLE   Find the probability that a couple with 3 children will have exactly 2 boys. Assume that boys and girls are equally likely and that the gender of any child is not influenced by the gender of any other child.

SOLUTION   We first list the sample space that identifies the 8 outcomes. Those outcomes are equally likely, so we use Rule 2. Of those 8 different possible outcomes, 3 correspond to exactly 2 boys, so

$$P(2 \text{ boys in 3 births}) = \frac{3}{8} = 0.375$$

There is a 0.375 probability that if a couple has 3 children, exactly 2 will be boys.

EXAMPLE   In choosing among several computer suppliers, a purchasing agent wants to know the probability of a personal computer breaking down during the first two years. What is that probability?

SOLUTION   There are only two outcomes: A personal computer either breaks down during the first two years or it does not. Because those two outcomes are not equally likely, the relative frequency approximation must be used. This requires that we somehow observe a large number of personal computers. A *PC World* survey of 4000 personal computer owners showed that 992 of them broke down during the first two years. (The computers broke down, not the owners.) On the basis of that result, we *estimate* that the probability is 992/4000, or 0.248.

EXAMPLE If we select an odd-numbered year at random—for example, 1999—what is the probability it is a leap year?

SOLUTION All leap years (for example, 1996) are divisible by 4, and so a leap year must be even. It is impossible for an odd-numbered year to be a leap year. When an event is impossible, we say the probability is 0. When an event is certain (for example, it will rain at least one day of the year in St. John's, Newfoundland), we say the probability is 1.

Because any event imaginable is impossible, certain, or somewhere in between, it is reasonable to conclude that the mathematical probability of any event is 0, 1, or a number between 0 and 1 (see Figure 3-3).

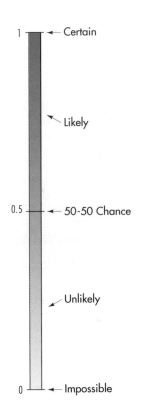

Probability Values

- **The probability of an impossible event is 0.**
- **The probability of an event that is certain to occur is 1.**
- $0 \leq P(A) \leq 1$ **for any event** A.

In Figure 3-3, the scale of 0 through 1 is shown on the left, whereas the more familiar and common expressions of likelihood are shown on the right.

Complementary Events

Sometimes we need to find the probability that an event A does *not* occur.

DEFINITION

The **complement** of event A, denoted by $\overline{A}$, consists of all outcomes in which event A does *not* occur.

Figure 3-3 Possible Values for Probabilities

EXAMPLE A survey of some mutual funds is conducted. A sample group of 20 Canadian equity funds and 30 international equity funds is assembled. If one fund is selected at random from the sample group, find the probability that a Canadian equity fund is *not* selected.

SOLUTION First, observe that the total sample space consists of 50 equity funds. Second, because 20 of the 50 funds are Canadian, it follows that 30 of the 50 funds are international, so

$$P(\text{not selecting a Canadian fund}) = P(\overline{\text{Canadian}})$$
$$= P(\text{international})$$
$$= \frac{30}{50} = 0.6$$

Although it is difficult to develop a universal rule for rounding off probabilities, the following guide will apply to most problems in this text.

Rounding Off Probabilities

When expressing the value of a probability, either give the *exact* fraction or decimal or round off final decimal results to three significant digits. (*Suggestion:* When a probability is not a simple fraction, such as 2/3 or 5/9, express it as a decimal, so it can be better understood.)

All the digits in a number are significant except for the zeros that are included for proper placement of the decimal point.

EXAMPLES

- The probability of 0.0000128506 has six significant digits (128506), and it can be rounded to three significant digits as 0.0000129.
- The probability of 1/3 can be left as a fraction or rounded in decimal form to 0.333, but not 0.3.
- The probability of heads in a coin toss can be expressed as 1/2 or 0.5; because 0.5 is exact, there's no need to express it as 0.500.
- The fraction 7659/32785 is exact, but its value isn't obvious, so express it as the decimal 0.234.

An important concept of this section is the mathematical expression of probability as a number between 0 and 1. This type of expression is fundamental and common in statistical procedures, and we will use it throughout the remainder of this text. A typical computer output, for example, may include a "P-value" expression such as "significance less than 0.001." We will discuss the meaning of P-values later, but they are essentially probabilities of the type discussed in this section. For now, you should recognize that a probability of 0.001 (equivalent to 1/1000) corresponds to an event so rare that it occurs an average of only once in a thousand trials.

Odds

Expressions of likelihood are often given as *odds*, such as 50:1 (or "50 to 1"). A serious disadvantage of odds is that they make many calculations extremely

---

Coincidences?

Edgar Allan Poe's story "The Narrative of Arthur Gordon Pym," published in 1838, tells the story of three shipwreck survivors who kill and eat a cabin boy named Richard Parker; in 1884, three real-life sailors survived a shipwreck by killing and eating a cabin boy named Richard Parker. Canadian authors Adele Wiseman and Marian Engel, unknown to each other, both named characters Odessa Yarker after seeing a sign on the highway for the towns Odessa and Yarker (Sylvia Fraser, *Chatelaine*, October 1996). Fourteen years *before* the sinking of the *Titanic*, a novel described the sinking of the Titan, a ship that hit an iceberg. Martin Gardners, in *The Wreck of the Titanic Foretold?*, states, "In most cases of startling coincidences, it is impossible to make even a rough estimate of their probability."

difficult. As a result, statisticians, mathematicians, and scientists prefer to use probabilities. The advantage of odds is that they make it easier to deal with money transfers associated with gambling, so they tend to be used in casinos, in lotteries, and at racetracks. There are three definitions that apply.

DEFINITION

The actual **odds against** event A occurring are the ratio $P(\overline{A})/P(A)$, usually expressed in the form of $a:b$ (or "a to b"), where a and b are integers having no common factors.

The actual **odds in favour** of event A are the reciprocal of the odds against that event. If the odds against A are $a:b$, then the odds in favour are $b:a$.

The **payoff odds** against event A represent the ratio of net profit (if you win) to the amount bet.

payoff odds against event A = (net profit):(amount bet)

EXAMPLE   Find the actual odds against rolling a 5 when a single die is rolled once.

SOLUTION $P(\text{roll a } 5) = 1/6$ because there is only one way to roll a 5, but 6 simple events in the sample space. With $P(\text{roll a } 5) = 1/6$, we calculate:

$$\text{Actual odds against rolling a } 5 = \frac{P(\overline{\text{roll a } 5})}{P(\text{roll a } 5)} = \frac{5/6}{1/6} = \frac{5}{1}$$

We express this as 5:1, or "5 to 1." Because the actual odds against rolling a 5 are 5:1, the actual odds in favour are 1:5.

See Exercise 31 for conversions from odds into probabilities.

EXAMPLE   If you bet $4 on the number 13 in roulette, your probability of winning is 1/38, and the payoff odds are given by the casino as 35:1.

a. Find the actual odds against the outcome of 13.

b. How much net profit would you make if you win by betting on 13?

c. If the casino were operating just for the fun of it, and the payoff odds were changed to match the actual odds against 13, how much would you win if the outcome were 13?

SOLUTION

a. With $P(13) = 1/38$ and $P(\text{not } 13) = 37/38$, we get

Subjective Probabilities at the Racetrack

Researchers studied the ability of racetrack bettors to develop realistic subjective probabilities. (See "Racetrack Betting: Do Bettors Understand the Odds?", by Brown, D'Amato, and Gertner, *Chance* magazine, Vol. 7, No. 3.) After analysing results for 4400 races, they concluded that although bettors slightly overestimate the winning probabilities of "longshots" and slightly underestimate the winning probabilities of "favourites," their general performance is quite good. The subjective probabilities were calculated from the payoffs, which are based on the amounts bet, and the actual probabilities were calculated from the actual race results.

You Bet

In a typical lottery, the "house" has a 65% to 70% advantage, since only 35% to 40% of the money bet is returned as prizes. The house advantage at racetracks is usually around 15%. In casinos, the house advantage is 5.26% for roulette, 5.9% for blackjack, 1.4% for craps, and 3% to 22% for slot machines. Some professional gamblers can systematically win at blackjack by using complicated card-counting techniques. They know when a deck has disproportionately more high cards, and this is when they place large bets. Many casinos react by ejecting card counters or by shuffling the decks more frequently.

$$\text{Actual odds against } 13 = \frac{P(\text{not } 13)}{P(13)} = \frac{37/38}{1/38} = \frac{37}{1} \text{ or } 37{:}1$$

b. Because the payoff odds against 13 are 35:1, we have

$$35{:}1 = (\text{net profit}){:}(\text{amount bet})$$

so that there is a $35 profit for each $1 bet. For a $5 bet, the net profit is $35 × 5 = $175. The bettor would collect $175 plus the original $5 bet.

c. If the casino were not operating for profit, the payoff odds would be equal to the actual odds against the outcome. If the payoff odds were changed from 35:1 to 37:1, you would obtain a net profit of $37 for each $1 bet, which is a profit of $37 × 5 = $185 for a $5 bet. (The difference between the answers for parts (b) and (c) indicates the profit normally received by the casino.)

3–2 Exercises A: Basic Skills and Concepts

1. Which of the following values *cannot* be probabilities?

$$0, 0.0001, -0.2, 3/2, 2/3, \sqrt{2}$$

2. a. What is $P(A)$ if event A is that February has 30 days this year?
    b. What is $P(A)$ if event A is that November has 30 days this year?
    c. A sample space consists of 500 separate events that are equally likely. What is the probability of each?
    d. On a mid-term exam, each question has 5 possible answers. If you make a random guess on the first question, what is the probability that you are correct?

3. Find the probability that when a coin is tossed, the result is heads.

4. We noted in this section that for the experiment of rolling a pair of dice, there are 36 simple events that form the sample space: 1-1, 1-2, . . . , 6-6. Find the probability of rolling a pair of dice and getting a total of 4.

5. Refer to Data Set 11 in Appendix B. Based on those sample results, estimate the probability that when a plain M&M candy is randomly selected, it will be red.

6. Refer to Data Set 8 in Appendix B. Based on those sample results, estimate the probability that a randomly selected statistics student has at least one credit card.

7. According to a survey sent out by Deloitte & Touche to British Columbia's top CEOs, 20 out of the 80 respondents possess an MBA. What is the estimated probability of a British Columbian top CEO having an MBA? Does it appear that an MBA is a requirement for the position?

8. The Kelly-Lynne Advertising Company is considering a computer campaign that targets teenagers. In a survey of 1066 teens, 181 had a computer on-line service in their household. If a teen is randomly selected, estimate the probability that he or she will have access to an on-line service in his or her household. Would you advise this company to use a computer advertising campaign?

9. In a survey of college students, 1162 stated that they cheated on an exam and 2468 stated that they did not (based on data from the Josephson Institute of Ethics). If one of these college students is randomly selected, find the probability that he or she cheated on an exam.

*In each of Exercises 10–22, you will be asked to calculate the probability of a specific event occurring. Based on your solutions, identify also which of these events would be **unusual** if they occurred—considering an event to be "unusual" if its probability is less than or equal to 0.05.*

10. A survey was done across 5 provinces to determine the mortality rate of lung cancer among male patients. Of 1000 patients who were tracked during this survey, 295 eventually succumbed to the disease (based on data from Statistics Canada). If a male lung cancer patient is selected at random, what is the probability that he will die of the disease?

11. In a study of blood donors, 225 were classified as group O and 275 had a classification other than group O. What is the approximate probability that a person will have group O blood?

12. A recent census by Statistics Canada showed there are 54,946 police officers in Canada. Of this number, 188 serve in Prince Edward Island. If a police officer is randomly selected from across Canada, what is the probability she or he is serving in Prince Edward Island?

13. a. If a person is randomly selected, find the probability that his or her birthday is October 18, which is National Statistics Day in Japan. Ignore leap years.

    b. If a person is randomly selected, find the probability that his or her birthday is in November. Ignore leap years.

14. In a study of brand recognition, 831 consumers knew of Campbell's Soup, and 18 did not (based on data from Total Research Corporation). Use these results to estimate the probability that a randomly selected consumer will recognize Campbell's Soup. How do you think this probability value compares to typical values for other brand names?

15. In a Bruskin/Goldring Research poll, respondents were asked how a fruitcake should be used. One hundred thirty-two respondents indicated that it should be used for a doorstop, and 880 other respondents cited other uses, including birdfeed, landfill, and a gift. If one of these respondents is randomly selected, what is the probability of getting someone who would use a fruitcake for a doorstop?

16. In a survey of Canadian workers who worked more than 50 hours per week, it was found that 334 workers surveyed were under 35 years of age and 401 workers were 35 to 55 years old. If one worker from this survey is selected at random, what is the probability that she or he is 35 years or older? Based on this result, are workers slowing down as they get older?

17. Among 400 randomly selected drivers in the 20–24 age bracket, 136 were in a car accident during the last year (based on data from the National Safety Council). If a driver in that age bracket is randomly selected, what is the approximate probability that he or she will be in a car accident during the next year? Is the resulting value high enough to be of concern to those in the 20–24 age bracket?

18. In a recent survey of Canadians who had just purchased new vehicles, 1521 bought pick-up trucks, 1849 bought sport utility vehicles (SUVs), and 1671 bought passenger vehicles. Use these results to estimate the probability that a new vehicle purchaser will buy an SUV. What would this result indicate to auto manufacturers about the SUV market?

19. When the allergy drug Seldane was clinically tested, 70 people experienced drowsiness and 711 did not (based on data from Merrell Dow Pharmaceuticals, Inc.). Use this sample to estimate the probability of a Seldane user becoming drowsy. Based on the result, is drowsiness a factor that should be considered by Seldane users?

20. A Statistics Canada study of deaths by cancer by age group showed 579 deaths in the 0–29 age group, 10,456 deaths in the 30–59 age group, and 42,928 deaths in the 60-and-over age group. Find the probability that a randomly selected cancer mortality will be a person in the first age group.

21. A study of credit-card fraud was conducted by MasterCard International, and the accompanying table is based on the results. If one case of credit-card fraud is randomly selected from the cases summarized in the table, find the probability that the fraud resulted from a counterfeit card.

Method of Fraud	Number
Stolen card	243
Counterfeit card	85
Mail/phone order	52
Other	46

22. A Gallup survey about tooth brushing resulted in the sample data in the given table. If one of the respondents is randomly selected, find the probability of getting someone who brushes three times per day, as dentists recommend.

Tooth-Brushings per Day	Number
1	228
2	672
3	240

23. A couple plans to have 2 children.
   a. List the different outcomes according to the gender of each child. Assume that these outcomes are equally likely.
   b. Find the probability of getting 2 girls.
   c. Find the probability of getting exactly 1 child of each gender.

24. A couple plans to have 4 children.
   a. List the 16 different possible outcomes according to the gender of each child. Assume that these outcomes are equally likely.
   b. Find the probability of getting all girls.
   c. Find the probability of getting at least 1 child of each gender.
   d. Find the probability of getting exactly 2 children of each gender.

25. On a quiz consisting of 3 true/false questions, an unprepared student must guess at each one. The guesses will be random.
   a. List the different possible solutions.
   b. What is the probability of answering all 3 questions correctly?
   c. What is the probability of guessing incorrectly for all questions?
   d. What is the probability of passing the quiz by guessing correctly for at least 2 questions?

26. Both parents have the brown/blue pair of eye-colour genes, and each parent contributes one gene (for one of those colours) to a child. Assume that if the child has at least one brown gene, that colour will dominate and the eyes will be brown. (Actually, the determination of eye colour is somewhat more complex.)
   a. List the different possible eye-colour gene combinations that the child could have. Assume that these outcomes are equally likely.

b. What is the probability that a child of these parents will have the blue/blue pair of genes?

c. What is the probability that the child will have brown eyes?

27. Find the actual odds against correctly guessing the answer to a multiple-choice question with 5 possible answers.

28. Find the actual odds against randomly selecting someone who is left-handed, given that 10% of us are left-handed.

29. a. The probability of a 7 in roulette is 1/38. Find the actual odds against 7.

b. If you bet $2 on the number 7 in roulette and you win, the casino gives you $72, which includes the $2 bet. First identify the net profit, then find the payoff odds.

c. How do you explain the discrepancy between the odds in parts (a) and (b)?

30. a. In the casino game craps, you can bet that the next roll of the two dice will result in a total of 2. The probability of rolling 2 is 1/36. Find the odds against rolling 2.

b. If you bet $5 that the next roll of the dice will be 2, you will collect $155 (including your $5 bet) if you win. First identify the net profit, then find the payoff odds.

c. How do you explain the discrepancy between the odds in parts (a) and (b)?

3–2 Exercises B: Beyond the Basics

31. If the actual odds against event A are $a:b$, then $P(A) = b/(a + b)$. Find the probability of Horse Cents winning his next race, given that the actual odds against his winning are 10:3.

32. A double-blind experiment is designed to test the effectiveness of the drug Statistiszene as a treatment for number blindness. When treated with Statistiszene, subjects seem to show improvement. Researchers calculate that there is a 0.04 probability that the treatment group would show improvement even if the drug has no effect. What should you conclude about the effectiveness of Statistiszene?

33. The stem-and-leaf plot summarizes the time (in hours) that managers spend on paperwork in one day (based on data from Adia Personnel Services). Use this sample to estimate the probability that a randomly selected manager spends more than 2.0 hours per day on paperwork.

```
0. | 00
1. | 0578
2. | 00113449
3. | 347
4. | 445
```

34. After collecting IQ scores from hundreds of subjects, a boxplot is constructed with this 5-number summary: 82, 91, 100, 109, 118. If one of the subjects is randomly selected, find the probability that his or her IQ score is greater than 109.

35. In part (a) of Exercise 13, leap years were ignored in finding the probability that a randomly selected person will have a birthday on October 18.

a. Recalculate this probability, assuming that a leap year occurs every 4 years. (Express your answer as an exact fraction.)

b. Leap years occur in years evenly divisible by 4, except they are skipped in 3 of every 4 centesimal years (years ending in 00). The years 1700, 1800, and 1900 were not leap years, but 2000 was a leap year. Find the exact probability for this case, and express it as a fraction.

36. a. If 2 flies land on an orange, find the probability that they are on points that are within the same hemisphere.

b. Two points along a straight stick are randomly selected. The stick is then broken at those 2 points. Find the probability that the 3 resulting pieces can be arranged to form a triangle. (This is a difficult problem.)

3-3 Addition Rule

The main objective of this section is to introduce the *addition rule* as a device for finding $P(A \text{ or } B)$, the probability that either event A occurs or event B occurs (or they both occur) as the single outcome of a procedure. The key word to remember is *or*. (Throughout this text we use the *inclusive or*, which means either one or the other or both. Except for Exercise 27, we will not consider the *exclusive or*, which means either one or the other but not both.)

In the previous section we presented the fundamentals of probability, and considered events that could be categorized as *simple*. In this and the following section we consider *compound events*.

Probabilities That Challenge Intuition

In certain cases, our subjective estimates of probability values are dramatically different from the actual probabilities. Here is a classic example: If you take a deep breath, there is a better than 99% chance that you will inhale a molecule that was exhaled in dying Caesar's last breath. In that same morbid and unintuitive spirit, if Socrates' fatal cup of hemlock was mostly water, then the next glass of water you drink will likely contain one of those same molecules. Here's another less morbid example that can be verified: In classes of 25 students, there is a better than 50% chance that at least 2 students will share the same birthday.

DEFINITION

A **compound event** is any event combining two or more simple events.

Notation for Addition Rule

$P(A \text{ or } B) = P(\text{event } A \text{ occurs or event } B \text{ occurs or they both occur})$

Let us begin with a simple example. Survey subjects are often chosen by using computers to randomly select the last digits of telephone numbers, which can be one of the numbers 0, 1, 2, 3, 4, 5, 6, 7, 8, 9. For the next selection, what is the probability that the selected number will be 0 or 1? Using Rule 2 from Section 3-2, we see that the event of getting 0 or 1 can occur in 2 different ways, and the total number of possible outcomes is 10, so

$$P(0 \text{ or } 1) = \frac{2}{10} = 0.2$$

This example suggests a general rule whereby we add the number of outcomes corresponding to each of the events in question.

When finding the probability that event A occurs or event B occurs, find the total of the number of ways A can occur and the total number of ways B can occur, but *find those totals in such a way that no outcome is counted more than once.*

One approach is to combine the number of ways event A can occur with the number of ways event B can occur and, if there is any overlap, compensate by subtracting the number of outcomes that are counted twice, as in the following rule.

Formal Addition Rule

$$P(A \text{ or } B) = P(A) + P(B) - P(A \text{ and } B)$$

where $P(A \text{ and } B)$ denotes the probability that A and B both occur at the same time as an outcome in one procedure.

AS   Although the formal addition rule is presented as a formula, it is generally better to understand the spirit of the rule and apply it intuitively, as follows.

Intuitive Addition Rule

To find $P(A \text{ or } B)$, find the sum of the number of ways event A can occur and the number of ways event B can occur, *adding in such a way that every outcome is counted only once*. $P(A \text{ or } B)$ is equal to that sum, divided by the total number of outcomes.

Figure 3-4 shows a Venn diagram that provides a visual illustration of the formal addition rule. In this figure we can see that the probability of A or B equals the probability of A (left circle) plus the probability of B (right circle) minus the probability of A and B (football-shaped middle region). This figure shows that the addition of the areas of the two circles will cause double counting of the football-shaped middle region. This is the basic concept that underlies the addition rule. Because of the relationship between the addition rule and the Venn diagram shown in Figure 3-4, the notation $P(A \cup B)$ is often used in place of $P(A \text{ or } B)$. Similarly, the notation $P(A \cap B)$ is often used in place of $P(A \text{ and } B)$, so the formal addition rule can be expressed as

$$P(A \cup B) = P(A) + P(B) - P(A \cap B)$$

The addition rule is simplified whenever A and B cannot occur simultaneously, so $P(A \text{ and } B)$ becomes zero. Figure 3-5 illustrates that with no overlapping of A and B, we have $P(A \text{ or } B) = P(A) + P(B)$. The following definition formalizes the lack of overlapping shown in Figure 3-5.

DEFINITION

Events A and B are **mutually exclusive** if they cannot occur simultaneously.

The flowchart of Figure 3-6 shows how mutually exclusive events affect the addition rule.

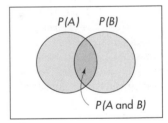

Figure 3-4   Venn Diagram Showing Overlapping Events

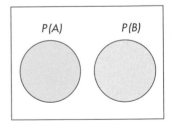

Figure 3-5   Venn Diagram Showing Nonoverlapping Events

Figure 3-6 Applying the Addition Rule

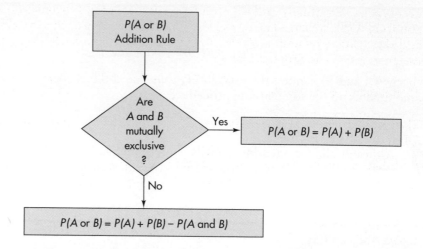

TABLE 3-1	Test of Seldane (based on data from Merrell Dow Pharmaceuticals)			
	Seldane	Placebo	Control Group	**Total**
Headache	49	49	24	**122**
No headache	732	616	602	**1950**
Total	**781**	**665**	**626**	**2072**

EXAMPLE   If one of the 2072 subjects represented in Table 3-1 is randomly selected, find the probability of getting someone who was given a placebo or was in the control group.

SOLUTION   The probability we seek can be denoted by P(placebo or control). Table 3-1 shows that the subjects who used the placebo and those in the control group are mutually exclusive. That is, there is no overlap between those two groups. Consequently, the total number of people who used a placebo or were in the control group is $665 + 626 = 1291$, and the probability we seek is

$$P(\text{placebo or control}) = \frac{665}{2072} + \frac{626}{2072} = \frac{1291}{2072} = 0.623$$

EXAMPLE   If one of the 2072 subjects represented in Table 3-1 is randomly selected, find the probability of getting someone who used Seldane or did not experience a headache.

SOLUTION   The probability we seek can be denoted by P(Seldane or no headache). Table 3-1 shows that there is overlap between the group of Seldane users and the group of subjects who had no headache. That is, the events are not mutually exclusive, and we must be careful to avoid double counting when we calculate our sums. The intuitive approach is to simply add the Seldane column and the "no headache" row in such a way that the entry of 732 is counted only once:

$$P(\text{Seldane or no headache}) = \frac{49 + 732 + 616 + 602}{2072} = \frac{1999}{2072} = 0.965$$

The same result could be obtained by applying the formal addition rule as follows.

$$P(\text{Seldane or no headache}) = P(\text{Seldane}) + P(\text{no headache})$$
$$- P(\text{Seldane and no headache})$$
$$= \frac{781}{2072} + \frac{1950}{2072} - \frac{732}{2072} = \frac{1999}{2072} = 0.965$$

Guess on Tests?

Students preparing for multiple-choice test questions are often told not to guess, but that's not necessarily good advice. Standardized tests with multiple-choice questions typically *compensate* for guessing, but they don't *penalize* it. For questions with five answer choices, one-fourth of a point is usually subtracted for each incorrect response. Principles of probability show that in the long run, pure random guessing will neither raise nor lower the exam score. Definitely guess if you can eliminate at least one choice or if you have a sense for the right answer, but avoid tricky questions with attractive wrong answers. Also, don't waste too much time on such questions.

We can summarize the key points of this section as follows:

1. To find $P(A \text{ or } B)$, begin by associating *or* with addition.
2. Consider whether events A and B are mutually exclusive; in other words, can they happen at the same time? If they are not mutually exclusive (that is, if they can happen at the same time), be sure to avoid (or at least compensate for) double counting when adding the relevant probabilities. If you understand the importance of not double counting when you find $P(A \text{ or } B)$, you don't necessarily have to calculate $P(A) + P(B) - P(A \text{ and } B)$.

Errors made when applying the addition rule often involve double counting. That is, events that are not mutually exclusive are treated as if they were. One indication of such an error is a total probability that exceeds 1; however, errors involving the addition rule do not always cause the total probability to exceed 1.

Complementary Events

In Section 3-2 we defined the complement of event A and denoted it by $\overline{A}$. By definition complementary events must be mutually exclusive because it is impossible for an event both to occur and *not* to occur at the same time. Also, A either does or does not occur. That is, either A or $\overline{A}$ must occur. These observations enable us to apply the addition rule for mutually exclusive events as follows:

$$P(A \text{ or } \overline{A}) = P(A) + P(\overline{A}) = 1$$

We justify $P(A \text{ or } \overline{A}) = P(A) + P(\overline{A})$ by noting that A and $\overline{A}$ are mutually exclusive; we justify the total of 1 by our absolute certainty that A either does or does not occur. This result of the addition rule leads to the following three equivalent forms.

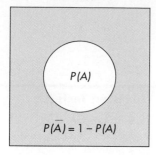

Total Area = 1

$P(\overline{A}) = 1 - P(A)$

Figure 3-7   Venn Diagram for the Complement of Event A

Rule of Complementary Events

$$P(A) + P(\overline{A}) = 1$$
$$P(\overline{A}) = 1 - P(A)$$
$$P(A) = 1 - P(\overline{A})$$

The first form comes directly from our original result. The second (see Figure 3-7) and third variations involve very simple equation manipulations.

EXAMPLE   If $P(\text{rain}) = 0.4$, find $P(\text{no rain})$.

SOLUTION   Using the rule of complementary events, we get

$$P(\text{no rain}) = 1 - P(\text{rain}) = 1 - 0.4 = 0.6$$

A major advantage of the *rule of complementary events* is that its use can greatly simplify certain problems. We will illustrate this advantage in the following section.

3-3 Exercises A: Basic Skills and Concepts

For each part of Exercises 1 and 2, are the two events mutually exclusive (that is, not overlapping) for a single procedure?

1. **a.** Selecting a geometric shape
      Selecting an octahedron
   b. Selecting a survey subject who is a member of the Liberal party
      Selecting a survey subject opposed to all welfare plans
   c. Spinning a roulette wheel and getting an outcome of 7
      Spinning a roulette wheel and getting an even number
2. **a.** Buying a new Corvette that is free of defects
      Buying a car with inoperative headlights
   b. Selecting a math course
      Selecting a course that is interesting
   c. Selecting a person with blond hair (natural or otherwise)
      Selecting a person who is bald
3. **a.** If $P(A) = 2/5$, find $P(\overline{A})$.
   b. According to a recent Interac survey, 28% of consumers use their debit cards in supermarkets. Find the probability that they use debit cards only in other stores or not at all.
4. **a.** Find $P(\overline{A})$, given that $P(A) = 0.228$.
   b. Statistics Canada reports that 30% of Canadians own stocks. If you randomly select someone from Canada, what is the probability that he or she does not own stocks?

5. When playing blackjack with a single deck of cards at Casino Regina, you are dealt the first card from the top of a shuffled deck. What is the probability that you get (a) a club or an ace? (b) an ace or a 2?

6. If someone is randomly selected, find the probability that his or her birthday is not October 18, which is National Statistics Day in Japan. Ignore leap years.

7. Refer to Table 3-1 in this section. If one of the 2072 subjects is randomly selected, find the probability of getting someone who used Seldane or a placebo.

8. Refer to Table 3-1 in this section. If one of the 2072 subjects is randomly selected, find the probability of getting someone who used a placebo or experienced a headache.

9. Pollsters are concerned about declining levels of cooperation among persons contacted in surveys. A pollster contacts 84 people in the 18–21 age bracket and finds that 73 of them respond and 11 refuse to respond. When 275 people in the 22–29 age bracket are contacted, 255 respond and 20 refuse to respond (based on data from "I Hear You Knocking but You Can't Come In," by Fitzgerald and Fuller, *Sociological Methods and Research*, Vol. 11, No. 1). Assume that 1 of the 359 people is randomly selected. Find the probability of getting someone in the 18–21 age bracket or someone who refused to respond.

10. Refer to the data set in Exercise 9, and find the probability of getting someone who is in the 18–21 age bracket or someone who responded.

11. Problems of sexual harassment have received much attention in recent years. In one survey, 420 workers (240 of whom are men) considered a friendly pat on the shoulder to be a form of harassment, whereas 580 workers (380 of whom are men) did not consider that to be a form of harassment (based on data from Bruskin/Goldring Research). If one of the surveyed workers is randomly selected, find the probability of getting someone who does not consider a pat on the shoulder to be a form of harassment.

12. Refer to the data set in Exercise 11, and find the probability of randomly selecting a man or someone who does not consider a pat on the shoulder to be a form of harassment.

13. A survey of 100 businesspeople showed that 25 owned copiers, 50 owned printers, and 13 owned both types of equipment. If a businessperson is selected at random from this sample, find the probability of getting someone who owns a copier or a printer.

14. Refer to the data set in Exercise 13, and find the probability of getting a businessperson who does not own a copier or a printer.

In Exercises 15 and 16, use the data in the accompanying table, which summarizes a sample of 200 times (in minutes) between eruptions of the Old Faithful Geyser in Yellowstone National Park.

Time	Frequency
40–49	8
50–59	44
60–69	23
70–79	6
80–89	107
90–99	11
100–109	1

15. Visitors to Yellowstone naturally want to see Old Faithful erupt, so the interval between eruptions becomes a concern for those with time constraints. If we randomly select one of the times represented in the table, what is the probability that it is at least one hour?

16. If we randomly select one of the times represented in the table, what is the probability that it is at least 70 min or between 60 and 79 min?

In Exercises 17–24, refer to the accompanying figure, which describes the typical blood groups and Rh types of 100 Canadians (based on data from Canadian Blood Services). In each case, assume that 1 of the 100 subjects is randomly selected, and find the indicated probability.

17. $P(\text{not group O})$
18. $P(\text{not type Rh}^+)$
19. $P(\text{group B or type Rh}^-)$
20. $P(\text{group O or group A})$
21. $P(\text{type Rh}^-)$
22. $P(\text{group A or type Rh}^+)$
23. $P(\text{group AB or type Rh}^-)$
24. $P(\text{group A or B or type Rh}^+)$

3-3 Exercises B: Beyond the Basics

25. **a.** If $P(A \text{ or } B) = 1/3$, $P(B) = 1/4$, and $P(A \text{ and } B) = 1/5$, find $P(A)$.
    b. If $P(A) = 0.4$ and $P(B) = 0.5$, what is known about $P(A \text{ or } B)$ if A and B are mutually exclusive events?
    c. If $P(A) = 0.4$ and $P(B) = 0.5$, what is known about $P(A \text{ or } B)$ if A and B are not mutually exclusive events?
26. If events A and B are mutually exclusive and events B and C are mutually exclusive, must events A and C be mutually exclusive? Give an example supporting your answer.
27. How is the addition rule changed if the *exclusive or* is used instead of the *inclusive or*? Recall that the *exclusive or* means either one or the other, but not both.
28. Given that $P(A \text{ or } B) = P(A) + P(B) - P(A \text{ and } B)$, develop a formal rule for $P(A \text{ or } B \text{ or } C)$. (*Hint:* Draw a Venn diagram.)

3-4 Multiplication Rule and Conditional Probabilities

The Basics

In Section 3-3 we presented the addition rule for finding $P(A \text{ or } B)$, the probability that a trial in a procedure or experiment has an outcome of A or B or both. The main objective in this section is to develop a rule for finding $P(A \text{ and } B)$, the probability that event A occurs in a first trial and event B occurs in a second trial.

Notation
$P(A \text{ and } B) = P(\text{event } A \text{ occurs in a first trial and event } B \text{ occurs in a second trial})$

In Section 3-3 we associated *or* with addition; in this section we will associate *and* with multiplication. We will see that $P(A$ and $B)$ involves multiplication of probabilities and that we must sometimes adjust the probability of event B to reflect the outcome of event A.

Probability theory is used extensively in the analysis and design of standardized tests, such as the LSAT (for law) and MCAT (for medicine). For ease of grading, such tests typically use true/false or multiple-choice questions. Let's assume that the first question on a test is a true/false type, while the second question is multiple choice with 5 possible answers (a, b, c, d, e). We will use the following two questions. Try them!

1. True or false: Smoking is one of the leading causes of cancer.

2. The Pearson correlation coefficient is named after

    a. Karl Marx
    b. Carl Friedrich Gauss
    c. Karl Pearson
    d. Carly Simon
    e. Mario Triola

Let us find the probability that if someone guesses the answers to both questions, the first answer will be correct *and* the second answer will be correct. One way to find that probability is to list the sample space as follows:

T,a   T,b   T,c   T,d   T,e
F,a   F,b   F,c   F,d   F,e

If the answers are random guesses, then the 10 possible outcomes are equally likely. The correct answers are T and c, so

$$P(\text{both correct}) = P(\text{T and c}) = \frac{1}{10} = 0.1$$

Considering the individual answers of T and c, respectively, we see that with random guesses we have $P(\text{T}) = 1/2$ and $P(\text{c}) = 1/5$. Since $1/10 = 1/2 \times 1/5$, we see that $P(\text{T and c}) = P(\text{T}) \cdot P(\text{c})$. This suggests that, in general, $P(A$ and $B) = P(A) \cdot P(B)$, but let's consider another example before making that generalization.

For now, we note that tree diagrams are sometimes helpful in determining the number of possible outcomes in a sample space. A **tree diagram** is a picture of the possible outcomes of an experiment, shown as line segments emanating from one starting point. These diagrams are helpful in counting the number of possible outcomes if the number of possibilities is not too large. The tree diagram shown in Figure 3-8 summarizes the outcomes of the true/false and multiple-choice questions. From Figure 3-8 we see that if both answers are random guesses, all 10 branches are equally likely and the probability of getting the correct pair (T, c) is 1/10. For each response to the first question, there are 5 responses to the second. The total number of outcomes is 5 taken 2 times, or 10. The tree diagram in Figure 3-8 illustrates the reason for the use of multiplication.

Composite Sampling

The U.S. Army once tested for syphilis by giving each inductee an individual blood test that was analysed separately. One researcher suggested mixing pairs of blood samples. After the mixed pairs were tested, syphilitic inductees could be identified by retesting the few blood samples that were in the pairs that tested positive. The total number of analyses was reduced by pairing blood specimens, so why not put them in groups of three or four or more? Probability theory was used to find the most efficient group size, and a general theory was developed for detecting the defects in any population. This technique is known as *composite sampling*.

Figure 3-8 Tree Diagram of
Test Answers

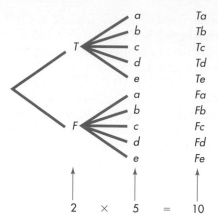

$$2 \quad \times \quad 5 \quad = \quad 10$$

Our first example of the true/false and multiple-choice questions suggested that $P(A \text{ and } B) = P(A) \cdot P(B)$, but the next example will introduce another important element.

● **EXAMPLE**   When drawing two cards from a shuffled deck, find the probability that the first card is an ace and the second card is a king. That is, find $P(\text{ace and king})$. (Assume that the first card is not replaced before the second card is drawn.)

SOLUTION   We can use Rule 2 from Section 3-2 to find the probability of getting an ace on the first selection. Noting that there are 4 aces among the 52 different cards, we get $P(\text{ace}) = 4/52$. For the second selection, we assume that an ace was obtained on the first draw, so we now have 4 kings among only 51 cards and we get $P(\text{king}) = 4/51$. The probability of getting an ace on the first draw *and* a king on the second is

$$P(\text{ace and king}) = \frac{4}{52} \cdot \frac{4}{51} = 0.00603$$

We could confirm this result by listing the sample space or providing a tree diagram. The sample space, however, has 2652 different possibilities, and the tree diagram has 2652 branches. Clearly, working out this example would be a bit overwhelming, but the results would show that there are 16 cases among the 2652 possibilities that consist of an ace followed by a king.

This example illustrates the important principle that *the probability for event B should take into account the fact that event A has already occurred.* This principle is often expressed using the following notation.

Notation for Conditional Probability
$P(B\|A)$ represents the probability of B occurring after it is assumed that the event A has already occurred. (We can read $B\|A$ as "B given A.")

AS   In the preceding example of finding the probability of an ace on the first card and a king on the second card drawn without replacement of the first, we have

$$P(\text{ace on first card}) = \frac{4}{52}$$

$$P(\text{king}|\text{ace}) = \frac{4}{51}$$

where $P(\text{king} | \text{ace})$ denotes the probability of drawing a king on the second card, given that the first card drawn was an ace.

DEFINITIONS

Two events A and B are **independent** if the occurrence of one does not affect the probability of the occurrence of the other. (Several events are similarly independent if the occurrence of any does not affect the probabilities of the occurrence of the others.) If A and B are not independent, they are said to be **dependent**.

For example, flipping a coin and then tossing a die are *independent* events because the outcome of the coin has no effect on the probabilities of the outcomes of the die. On the other hand, the event of having your car start and the event of driving to class on time are *dependent,* because the outcome of trying to start your car does affect the probability of your getting to class on time (unless you're a dorm resident).

Using the preceding notation and definitions, along with the principles illustrated in the preceding examples, we summarize the key concept of this section in Figure 3-9 and the *formal multiplication rule.*

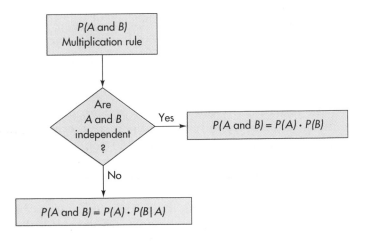

Figure 3-9   Applying the Formal Multiplication Rule

Formal Multiplication Rule

$P(A \text{ and } B) = P(A) \cdot P(B)$ if A and B are *independent*.

$P(A \text{ and } B) = P(A) \cdot P(B|A)$ if A and B are *dependent*.

AS

Intuitive Multiplication Rule

When finding the probability that event A occurs in one trial and B occurs in the next trial, multiply the probability of event A by the probability of event B, but be sure that the probability of event B takes into account the previous occurrence of event A.

Redundancy

Reliability of systems can be greatly improved with redundancy of critical components. Airplanes have two independent electrical systems, and aircraft used for instrument flight typically have two separate radios. The following is from a *Popular Science* article: "One plane built largely of carbon fibre was the Lear Fan 2100 which had to carry two radar transponders. That's because if a single transponder failed, the plane was nearly invisible to radar." Such redundancy is an application of the multiplication rule in probability theory. If one component has a 0.001 probability of failure, the probability of two independent components both failing is only 0.000001.

The multiplication rule is extremely important because it has so many meaningful applications. One area of application involves product testing, as in the following example.

EXAMPLE   A batch of 50 fuel filters is produced by the Windsor Auto Supply Company, and 6 of them are defective. (Optimists would say that 44 are good.) Two of the filters are selected and tested. Find the probability that the first is good and the second is good if the filters are selected (a) with replacement, and (b) without replacement.

SOLUTION

a. If the filters are selected with replacement, the two selections are independent because the second event is not affected by the first outcome. We therefore get

$$P(\text{first good and second good}) = \frac{44}{50} \cdot \frac{44}{50} = 0.774$$

b. If the filters are selected without replacement, the two selections are dependent because the second event is affected by the first outcome. We therefore get

$$P(\text{first good and second good}) = \frac{44}{50} \cdot \frac{43}{49} = 0.772$$

Note that in this case, we adjust the second probability to take into account the selection of a good filter on the first selection. After selecting a good filter the first time, there would be 43 good filters among the 49 that remain. Also note that without replacement, there is a slightly lower chance of getting 2 good filters. If we want to develop a procedure for using samples to test batches of products, we should sample without replacement for two reasons: First, there is a lower chance of getting only good items when some defects are present; second, it doesn't make sense to sample with replacement because it becomes possible to test the same item more than once, and that is a waste.

So far we have discussed two events, but the multiplication rule can be easily extended to several events. In general, the probability of any sequence of independent events is simply the product of their corresponding probabilities. For example, the probability of tossing a coin three times and getting all heads is $0.5 \cdot 0.5 \cdot 0.5 = 0.125$. We can also extend the multiplication rule so that it applies to several dependent events; simply adjust the probabilities as you go along. For example, the probability of getting three aces when three cards are selected without replacement is given by

$$\frac{4}{52} \cdot \frac{3}{51} \cdot \frac{2}{50} = 0.000181$$

In this last example involving three aces, we assumed that the events were dependent because the selections were made without replacement. However, it is a common practice to treat events as independent when *small samples* are drawn from *large populations*. (In such cases, it is rare to select the same item twice.) **A common guideline is to assume independence whenever the sample size is no more than 5% of the size of the population.** When pollsters survey 1200 adults from a population of millions, they typically assume independence, even though they sample without replacement.

The Probability of "At Least One"

The multiplication rule and the rule of complements can be used together to greatly simplify certain types of problems, such as those in which we want to find the probability that among several trials, *at least 1* will result in some specified outcome. In such cases, these two issues of language should be clearly understood:

- "At least 1" is equivalent to "1 or more."
- The complement of getting at least 1 item of a particular type is that you get no items of that type.

A survey of households in Canada found that 22.4% of all households with annual incomes over \$50,000 subscribed to *The Globe and Mail* (based on data from a NADbank study). Assume that 5 households with incomes over \$50,000 are randomly selected. We need to find the probability that at least 1 of the 5 will subscribe to *The Globe and Mail*. See the following interpretations:

At least 1 household will subscribe = 1 or more subscribers
The complement of "at least 1 subscriber" = no subscribers

The direct solution to this problem is complex, but a simple, indirect approach is given in the solution to the following example.

> **EXAMPLE**   Find the probability that at least 1 of 5 Canadian households with incomes over \$50,000 subscribe to the *Globe and Mail*. Assume that newspaper subscriptions are independent and that 77.6% of these households do not subscribe to the newspaper.

Monkey Typists

A classical claim is that a monkey randomly hitting a keyboard would eventually produce the complete works of Shakespeare, assuming that it continues to type century after century. The multiplication rule for probability has been used to find such estimates. One result of 1,000,000,000,000,000, 000,000,000,000,000,000, 000 years is considered by some to be too short. In the same spirit, Sir Arthur Eddington wrote this poem: "There once was a brainy baboon, who always breathed down a bassoon. For he said,'It appears that in billions of years, I shall certainly hit on a tune.'"

SOLUTION

Step 1: Use a symbol to represent the probability desired. In this case, let G = be at least 1 *Globe and Mail* subscriber among 5 households.

Step 2: Identify the complement of the event denoted in Step 1:

$\overline{G}$ = *not* getting at least 1 *Globe and Mail* subscriber in 5 households

= getting 5 nonsubscribers in 5 households

Step 3: Find the probability of the complement from Step 2:

$$P(\overline{G}) = P(5 \text{ nonsubscribers in 5 households})$$
$$= 0.776 \cdot 0.776 \cdot 0.776 \cdot 0.776 \cdot 0.776$$
$$= 0.776^5 = 0.281$$

Step 4: Find the probability of the event desired by subtracting the probability of the complement from 1:

$$P(G) = 1 - P(\overline{G}) = 1 - 0.281 = 0.719$$

Interpretation For any five, randomly selected households among Canadian households with an income over $50,000, there is a 0.719 probability that at least one household subscribes to *The Globe and Mail*.

The principle used in the example can be summarized as follows:

To find the probability of *at least one* of something, calculate the probability of *none*, then subtract that result from 1.

Conditional Probability

Our assessment of probability for an event can be affected by our knowledge of circumstances. For example, if you randomly select someone from the general population, the probability of getting a male is 0.5, but if you know that the selected person frequently changes TV channels with a remote control, the probability is 0.999 (OK, that might be a slight exaggeration). A conditional probability of an event applies when the probability is affected by other, known circumstances. We have already used notation for conditional probability in the formal multiplication rule:

$$P(A \text{ and } B) = P(A) \cdot P(B|A)$$

Now, we solve this equation for $P(B|A)$, by dividing both sides of the equation by $P(A)$.

DEFINITION

The **conditional probability** of B given A is the probability of event B occurring, given that event A has already occurred. It can be found by dividing the probability of events *A* and *B* both occurring by the probability of event *A*.

$$P(B|A) = \frac{P(A \text{ and } B)}{P(A)}$$

This formula is a formal expression of conditional probability, but we can often use the following intuitive approach.

Intuitive Approach to Conditional Probability
The conditional probability of *B* given *A* can be found by assuming that event *A* has occurred and, operating under that assumption, calculating the probability that event *B* will occur.

EXAMPLE   Refer to Table 3-2, and base probability calculations on the frequencies shown in the table.

TABLE 3-2	Relationship of Criminal to Victim			
	Homicide	Robbery	Assault	**Totals**
Stranger	12	379	727	**1118**
Acquaintance or relative	39	106	642	**787**
Relationship unknown	18	20	57	**95**
Totals	**69**	**505**	**1426**	**2000**

a. If one person is randomly selected, what is the likelihood that he or she was victimized by a stranger, given that a robbery victim is selected?

b. Given that an assault victim is selected, what is the likelihood that the criminal is a stranger?

SOLUTION

a. We want *P*(stranger|robbery). If we assume that the person selected was a robbery victim, we are dealing with the 505 people in the second column of values. Among those 505 people, 379 were victimized by strangers, so

$$P(\text{stranger}|\text{robbery}) = \frac{379}{505} = 0.750$$

The same result can be obtained using this formal approach:

Convicted by Probability

A witness described a robber as a Caucasian woman with blond hair in a ponytail who escaped in a yellow car driven by an African-American male with a mustache and beard. Janet and Malcolm Collins fit this description, and they were convicted based on testimony that there is only about 1 chance in 12 million that any couple would have these characteristics. It was estimated that the probability of a yellow car is 1/10, and the other probabilities were estimated to be 1/4, 1/10, 1/3, 1/10, and 1/1000. The convictions were later overturned when it was noted that no evidence was presented to support the estimated probabilities or the independence of the events. However, because the couple was not randomly selected, a serious error was made in not considering the probability of *other* couples being in the same region with the same characteristics.

Bayes' Theorem

Thomas Bayes (1702–1761) said that probabilities should be revised when we learn more about an event. Here's one form of Bayes' theorem:

$$P(A|B) =$$

$$\frac{P(A) \cdot P(B|A)}{P(A) \cdot P(B|A) + P(\overline{A}) \cdot P(B|\overline{A})}$$

Suppose 60% of a company's computer chips are made in one factory (denoted by A) and 40% are made in its other factory (denoted by $\overline{A}$). For a randomly selected chip, the probability it came from factory A is 0.60. Suppose we learn that the chip is defective and the defect rates for the two factories are 35% (for A) and 25% (for $\overline{A}$). We can use the above formula to find that there is a 0.677 probability the defective chip came from factory A.

$$P(\text{stranger}|\text{robbery}) = \frac{P(\text{robbery and stranger})}{P(\text{robbery})}$$

$$= \frac{379/2000}{505/2000} = 0.750$$

b. Here we want $P(\text{stranger}|\text{assault})$. If we assume that the person selected was an assault victim, we are dealing with the 1426 people in the third column. Among those 1426 people, 727 were victimized by strangers, so

$$P(\text{stranger}|\text{assault}) = \frac{727}{1426} = 0.510$$

Again, the same result can be obtained using a formal approach:

$$P(\text{stranger}|\text{assault}) = \frac{P(\text{assault and stranger})}{P(\text{assault})}$$

$$= \frac{727/2000}{1426/2000} = 0.510$$

Interpretation By comparing the results from parts (a) and (b), we see that the probability of being victimized by a stranger is very different for robberies than for assaults, so there is a dependency between the type of crime and the relationship of the criminal to the victim.

Observe that Table 3-2, called a *contingency table*, provides a useful summary for frequency data, which can in turn be used for calculating probabilities. A contingency table is essentially a 2-way frequency distribution table, showing the frequencies for different classes or categories of two different variables—individually (in the Totals) and in their different combinations (in the inner cells). Often, data are presented piecemeal, in various statements, which can form the *basis* for constructing a contingency table of your own.

EXAMPLE A study on the maximum lifespans of animals shows that, of 15 species selected, 3 live no more than 5 years. Nine of the selected species weigh over 10 kg when full grown. Moreover, 3 species in the study live over 5 years and have weights no more than 10 kg. (Based on Data Set 19 in Appendix B.) If a species is selected from those included in this study, what is the probability that it has a maximum lifespan of over 5 years, given that it weighs over 10 kg?

SOLUTION There are lots of numbers here, but no frequencies are given for animals living over 5 years and having a weight over 10 kg. Yet there are enough data to begin construction of a contingency table; the rest can be filled in later. Table 3-3, in the *non-shaded* cells, summarizes what we have been told. Data for the size of the sample (15) can be placed in the "grand total" on the lower right. Frequency data that apply to just one of the variables, with no reference to other variable, are placed in the Totals at the right or bottom. Table 3-3 shows the lifespan variable at the top, with its category frequencies at the bottom, such as a frequency of 3 for species of lifespan up to 5 years. The weight variable is on the left of the table, with its category frequencies on the right, such as the frequency of 9 for species of weight over 10 kg. There is also one case where we know the frequency for a combination of variable values: 3 species with lifespan over 5 years and weight up to 10 kg. 3 is placed in the appropriate cell.

Next, we complete the table in the manner of a puzzle (the correct answers are shaded in the table). All row frequencies have to add up to their row totals on the right, and all column frequencies have to add up to their column totals on the bottom. The sum of row totals should equal the sum of column totals, which in turn should equal the grand total. At last, we are ready to answer the probability question for this exercise: Of the 9 species whose weight is over 10 kg, 9 species have maximum lifespans over 5 years, so

$$P(\text{over 5 yr. } | \text{ over 10 kg}) = \frac{9}{9} = 1.00$$

Interpretation It appears from this sample that all species whose adult weight is over 10 kg. have a maximum lifespan which is over 5 years.

TABLE 3-3	Lifespans of Animals (Years Maximum)		
	Up to 5 yr.	Over 5 yr.	Total
Weight up to 10 kg	3	3	6
Weight over 10 kg	0	9	9
Total	3	12	15

Testing for Independence

In the version of the multiplication rule for dependent events, if $P(B|A) = P(B)$, then the occurrence of event A has no effect on the probability of event B. This is often used as a test for independence. If, however, if $P(B|A) \neq P(B)$, then A and B are dependent events. Another test for independence involves checking for the equality of $P(A \text{ and } B)$ and $P(A) \cdot P(B)$. If they are equal, events A and B are independent. If $P(A \text{ and } B) \neq P(A) \cdot P(B)$, then A and B are dependent events. These results are summarized as follows.

Two events A and B are independent if	Two events A and B are dependent if
$P(B|A) = P(B)$ or $P(A \text{ and } B) = P(A) \cdot P(B)$	$P(B|A) \neq P(B)$ or $P(A \text{ and } B) \neq P(A) \cdot P(B)$

3-4 Exercises A: Basic Skills and Concepts

In Exercises 1 and 2, for each given pair of events, classify the two events as independent or dependent. Some of the other exercises are based on concepts from earlier sections of this chapter.

1. a. Attending classes in a statistics course
      Passing a statistics course
   b. Getting a flat tire on the way to class
      Sleeping too late for class
   c. Events A and B, where $P(A) = 0.40$, $P(B) = 0.60$, and $P(A \text{ and } B) = 0.20$

2. a. Finding your microwave oven inoperable
      Finding your battery-operated smoke detector inoperable
   b. Finding your kitchen light inoperable
      Finding your refrigerator inoperable
   c. Events A and B, where $P(A) = 0.90$, $P(B) = 0.80$, and $P(A \text{ and } B) = 0.72$

3. Using funding from Ontario's "Superbuild" Program, a contractor bought a box of decorative screws. Five of the screws are slotted, four are designed for a Phillips-head screwdriver, and three are designed for a square-tipped screwdriver. If two of the screws are randomly selected from the box, find the probability that they are both slotted.
   a. Assume that the first screw is replaced before the second is selected.
   b. Assume that the first screw is not replaced before the second is selected.

4. Find the probability of answering the first 2 questions on a test correctly if random guesses are made and
   a. The first 2 questions are both true/false types.
   b. The first 2 questions are both multiple choice, each with 5 possible answers.

5. Find the probability of getting 4 consecutive aces when 4 cards are drawn without replacement from a shuffled deck.

6. Remote sensors are used to control each of two separate and independent valves, denoted by p and q, which must both open to provide water for emergency cooling of a nuclear reactor. Each valve has a 0.95 probability of opening when triggered. For the given configuration, find the probability that when both sensors are triggered, water will get through the system so that cooling can occur.

$$\boxed{\text{Water}} \quad \rightarrow \quad p \quad \text{---} \quad q \quad \rightarrow \quad \boxed{\text{Reactor}}$$

7. A student experiences difficulties with malfunctioning alarm clocks. Instead of using 1 alarm clock, he decides to use 3. What is the probability that at least 1 alarm clock works correctly if each individual alarm clock has a 98% chance of working correctly?

8. We have noted that when rolling a pair of dice, there are 36 different possible outcomes: 1-1, 1-2, . . . , 6-6.
   a. What is the probability of rolling a 7?
   b. If you have just entered a friendly neighbourhood game of craps and the person who brought the dice rolls 8 consecutive 7s, what do you conclude? Why?

9. A classic excuse for a missed test is offered by 4 students who claim that their car had a flat tire. On the makeup test, the instructor asks the students to identify the particular tire that went flat. If they didn't really have

a flat tire and randomly select one that supposedly went flat, what is the probability that all 4 select the same tire?

10. Three firms using the same auditor independently and randomly select a month in which to conduct their annual audits. What is the probability that all 3 months are different?

11. A quality control manager uses test equipment to detect defective computer modems. A sample of 3 different modems is to be randomly selected from a group consisting of 12 that are defective and 18 that have no defects. What is the probability that (a) all 3 selected modems are defective, and (b) at least 1 selected modem is defective?

12. When driving to class, a student must pass 2 traffic lights that operate independently. For each light, there is a 0.4 probability that it is green. If he must reach both lights when they are green in order to make class on time, what is the probability that he will be on time?

13. In a market survey of Zellers, a researcher is told that 76% of customers are repeat customers. If 10 customers are selected at random, what is the probability that all 10 are repeat customers? Would this be a very common occurrence?

14. Ignoring leap years, find the probability that 3 randomly selected people were all born on September 24.

15. A Statistics Canada study of environmental impacts on human health in 5 provinces indicates that a male has a 0.133 chance of dying in any type of accident. Find the probability that 5 randomly selected males will all eventually die in an accident.

16. With one method of *acceptance sampling,* a sample of items is randomly selected without replacement and the entire batch is rejected if there is at least one defect. The Niko Electronics Company has just manufactured 5000 CDs, and 3% are defective. If 10 of the CDs are selected and tested, what is the probability that the entire batch will be rejected?

17. A manager can identify employee theft by checking samples of employee shipments. Among 36 employees, 2 are stealing. If the manager checks on 4 different randomly selected employees, find the probability that neither of the thieves will be identified.

18. Seven financial experts participated in a stock market selection game. Their first choice had to be selected from 8 different resource stocks. All 7 experts picked the same resource stock. If the picks were purely at random, what is the probability of this event occurring?

19. As an insurance claims investigator, you are suspicious of 4 brothers who each reported a stolen car in a different region of Montreal. If Montreal has an annual car-theft rate of 4.5%, find the probability that among 4 randomly selected cars, all are stolen in a given year. What does the result suggest?

20. An approved jury list contains 20 women and 20 men. Find the probability of randomly selecting 12 of these people and getting an all-male jury. Under these circumstances, if the defendant is convicted by an all-male jury, is there strong evidence to suggest that the jury was not randomly selected?

21. A blood-testing procedure is made more efficient by combining samples of blood specimens. If samples from 5 people are combined, the mixture will test positive except if all 5 individual samples are negative. Find the

probability of a positive result for 5 samples combined into 1 mixture, assuming the probability of an individual blood sample testing positive is 0.015.

22. An employee claims that a new process for manufacturing VCRs is better because the rate of defects is below 5%, the rate of defects in the past. When 20 VCRs are manufactured with the new process, there are no defects. Assuming that the new method has the same 5% defect rate as in the past, find the probability of getting no defects among the 20 VCRs. Based on the result, is there strong evidence to conclude that the new process is better?

In Exercises 23 and 24, use the data in Table 3-2.

23. a. Find the probability that when 1 of the 2000 subjects is randomly selected, the person chosen was victimized by an acquaintance or relative, given that he or she was robbed.

    b. Find the probability that when 1 of the 2000 subjects is randomly selected, the person chosen was robbed by an acquaintance or relative.

    c. Find the probability that when 1 of the 2000 subjects is randomly selected, the person chosen was robbed or was victimized by an acquaintance or relative.

    d. If two different subjects are randomly selected, find the probability that they were both robbed.

24. a. If one of the crime victims represented in the table is randomly selected, find the probability of getting someone who was victimized by a stranger or who was a homicide victim.

    b. If one of the crime victims represented in the table is randomly selected, find the probability of getting someone who was a homicide victim, given that the criminal was a stranger.

    c. If one of the crime victims represented in the table is randomly selected, find the probability of getting someone who was victimized by a stranger, given that he or she was a homicide victim.

    d. If two different subjects are randomly selected, find the probability that they were both victimized by criminals who were strangers.

In Exercises 25–30, use the following information: Suppose that researchers developed a test to detect a particular disease in the general population. However, the test was not perfect. To determine the accuracy of the test, a study was done on 2000 subjects, 1000 of whom were known to have the disease, and 1000 of whom were known to be free of the disease. Some results are shown in the accompanying table.

Group	Positive	Negative	Total
Subjects with the disease	900		1000
Disease-free subjects			1000
Total		1050	

1141

The researchers indicated that the incidence of the disease in the general population is 0.5%.

25. Based on the study results, what is the probability that if a disease-free person is randomly selected, they will test positive?
26. Based on the study results, what is the probability that if a person with the disease is randomly selected, they will test negative?
27. Based on the study results, what is the probability that if a person without the disease is randomly selected, they will test negative?
28. If a test subject is selected at random, what is the probability that he or she tests negative or is a subject known to be disease-free?
29. If a test subject is selected at random, what is the probability that he or she tests positive or is a subject known to be disease-free?
30. If a test subject is selected at random, what is the probability that he or she tests negative given the subject is known to have the disease?

3–4 Exercises B: Beyond the Basics

31. Find the probability that of 25 randomly selected people,
    a. No 2 share the same birthday.
    b. At least 2 share the same birthday.
32. a. Develop a formula for the probability of not getting either A or B on a single trial. That is, find an expression for $P(\overline{A \text{ or } B})$.
    b. Develop a formula for the probability of not getting A or not getting B on a single trial. That is, find an expression for $P(\overline{A} \text{ or } \overline{B})$.
    c. Compare the results from parts (a) and (b). Are they the same or are they different?
33. Two cards are to be randomly selected without replacement from a shuffled deck. Find the probability of getting a 10 on the first card and a club on the second card.

3–5 Probabilities Through Simulations

Finding probabilities of events is sometimes very difficult. Sometimes the results, even though correct, just don't seem to be what we might expect. Instead of relying solely on the abstract principles of probability theory, we can often benefit from using a simulation.

DEFINITION

A **simulation** of a procedure is a process that behaves the same way as the procedure, so that similar results are produced.

EXAMPLE In testing techniques of gender selection, medical researchers need to know probabilities related to the genders of offspring. Assuming that males and females are equally likely, describe an experiment that simulates genders from births.

SOLUTION   One simulation is simply to flip a coin, with heads representing *male* and tails representing *female*. Another approach is to use a computer program, such as Excel or STATDISK, to generate 0s and 1s, with 0 representing *male* and 1 representing *female*. Those numbers must be randomly generated in such a way that the 0s and 1s are equally likely. Shown below is a typical computer-generated result. On the basis of this result, we could use the relative frequency approximation of probability to estimate P(male) as 6/10, because there are 6 males among the 10 births.

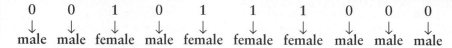

0	0	1	0	1	1	1	0	0	0
↓	↓	↓	↓	↓	↓	↓	↓	↓	↓
male	male	female	male	female	female	female	male	male	male

EXAMPLE   One classic exercise in probability is the *birthday problem,* in which we find the probability that in a class of 25 students, at least 2 students have the same birthday. Ignoring leap years, describe a simulation of the experiment that yields the birthdays of 25 students in a class.

SOLUTION   Begin by representing birthdays by integers from 1 through 365 as follows:

$$1 = \text{January 1}$$
$$2 = \text{January 2}$$
$$\vdots$$
$$365 = \text{December 31}$$

Using this representation, we need only generate integers between 1 and 365, instead of actual months and days. Using any source of equally likely integers (such as the uniform random generators in Excel or STATDISK), we can generate a list of 25 random integers between 1 and 365. That list can be sorted so that it becomes easy to determine whether any of the "birthdays" are the same. If we repeat this process many times, we can simulate many different classes, and we can then estimate the probability that in a class of 25 students, at least 2 students share the same birthday.

EXAMPLE   The Delmarva Communications Company manufactures cellular phones and has been experiencing a 6% rate of defects. The quality control manager knows that the phones are produced in batches of 250 and that, on average, there are 15 defects per batch. She wants to know how much the number of defects will typically vary. Describe a simulation of 250 cell phones that are manufactured with a 6% rate of defects.

SOLUTION   Use Excel or STATDISK to generate 250 integers, where each integer is between 1 and 100. Let the integers 1, 2, 3, 4, 5, 6 represent defective cell phones, while 7, 8, 9, . . . , 100 represent good cell phones. If the 250 integers are sorted, it becomes easy to find the number of "defects," which are the numbers between 1 and 6 inclusive, found at the beginning of the sorted list.

It is extremely important to construct a simulation so that it behaves just like the real procedure. In the next example we demonstrate the right way and a wrong way to construct a simulation.

EXAMPLE   Describe a procedure that simulates the rolling of a pair of dice.

SOLUTION   In the actual procedure of rolling a pair of dice, each of the two dice yields a number between 1 and 6 (inclusive), and those two numbers are then added. Any simulation should do the same thing.

The right way: Randomly generate one number between 1 and 6, randomly generate a second number between 1 and 6, and then add the results.

A wrong way: Randomly generate a number between 2 and 12. This procedure is similar to rolling dice in the sense that it gives the same range of possible results, but in this case, these outcomes between 2 and 12 are equally likely. With real dice, the values between 2 and 12 are **not** equally likely. If this simulation were repeated many times, it would produce misleading results.

Some probability problems can only be solved by estimating the probability from actual observations or by constructing a simulation. Today's widespread availability of powerful calculators and computers has greatly facilitated the use of simulation methods, but as shown in the preceding example, one must be very careful to simulate accurately all the key features of the original procedure.

Using Technology

For all the example simulations in this section, it has been necessary to generate a random sequence of integers, within a certain range (from 0 to 1, for the genders of children, or from 1 to 365 for the birthday problem, and so on). Such sequences can be generated easily by computer

Excel: Click on a cell where the first random integer is to be generated. Then click on the icon *fx*. Select **Math & Trig**, then select **RANDBETWEEN**. In the dialog box, enter the "bottom" integer and the "top" integer (for example, 1 and 365, respectively, in the birthday problem), then click **OK**. The resulting formula (which displays as one of the desired

STATDISK
File Edit Analysis Data Help

Doc17.sdd   _ □ X
Uniform Random Sample Generator

| Rand Unif 569963 |
Sample Size, n: 25 | | |
Minimum: 1   1 | 169 |
Maximum: 365   2 | 246 |
Num Decimals: 0   3 | 28 |
Random Seed: 4 | 221 |
   (if known)   5 | 224 |
                       6 | 232 |
                       7 | 253 |
                       8 | 282 |
                       9 | 299 |
                      10 | 134 |
                      11 | 364 |
                      12 | 42 |
                      13 | 184 |
      Generate   14 | 301 |
                      15 | 57 |
      Help   16 | 187 |
                      17 | 116 |
                      18 | 249 |
                      19 | 269 |
                      20 | 220 |

   Clear | Copy | Paste

integers) can be copy/pasted to as many cells as desired. (*Note:* For more complex simulations, try the sequence **Tools, Data Analysis, Random Number Generation, OK**. In the dialog box you can choose to generate a specified number of values for one or more variables, and random numbers following a variety of distributions, such as the uniform (which we used for the birthday problem) or the normal, and so on.)

STATDISK: Select **Data** from the main menu bar, then select **Uniform Generator** and proceed to enter a sample size, a minimum value, and a maximum value (25, 1, and 365, respectively, for the birthday problem). Enter 0 for the number of decimal places, then click Generate. The resulting values can be copy/pasted to Excel, for example, for sorting and manipulation.

3-5 Exercises A: Basic Skills and Concepts

1. Simulate a procedure of recording the number of girls in families of 3 children by using the Lotto 6/49 results in Data Set 12 in Appendix B. Let the first 3 numbers in each row represent the 3 children in one family, and let an even number be a male and let an odd number represent a female. Based on the 50 simulated families, what is the estimated probability of getting a family with 3 girls when a family with 3 children is randomly selected? How does the simulated result compare with the actual probability, which is 0.125? Is there any aspect of the simulation that could explain the discrepancy?

2. If raw data are collected that show a large number of significant digits, then sometimes (not always) the digits on the right side of the numbers appear to be virtually random. Refer to Data Set 6 in Appendix B, in the column labeled REVENUES, and select the digits in the 10's place and in the 1's place of each number. (For example, in the top number of 34,249,489, use "8" and "9" respectively.) *Skip over, and* DO NOT USE, *any Revenue values for which both the last digits are 0's.* Let each Revenue value that you use represent a family that has two children; let a selected digit from 0–4 represent a female, and a selected digit from 5–9 represent a male. Based on selecting data in this fashion for 50 simulated families, what is the estimated probability of getting a family with 2 girls when a family with 2 children is randomly selected? How does the simulated result compare with the actual probability of 0.25? Explain why it was necessary to not include in the simulation any Revenue values for which both the last digits are 0's. Is there any aspect of the simulation that could still cause a discrepancy?

3. The Jehonkis Company manufactures cellular phones in batches of 6 and has been experiencing a 14.3% overall rate of defects. Refer to the Lotto 6/49 results in Data Set 12 in Appendix B. Let the numbers 1–7 represent a defective cell phone and let the numbers 8–49 represent good cell phones. Let each row of the results represent a simulated batch of cell phones and use 50 simulated batches to estimate the probability of at least 1 defect in each batch. How does the estimated probability compare to the

theoretical result of 0.603? Is there any aspect of the simulation that could cause a discrepancy? If yes, how could you modify the simulation to eliminate the problem?

For Exercises 4–6, use the table of random numbers shown here in the margin.

4. Ten percent of us are left-handed. In a study of dexterity, people are randomly selected in groups of five. Use the random digits in the margin to develop a simulation for finding the probability of getting at least one left-handed person in a group of five people. (*Hint*: Because 10% of us are left-handed, let the digit 0 represent someone who is left-handed, and the other digits represent non-left-handed people.)
5. Use the random digits in the margin to develop a simulation for one roll of a die. Describe the simulation, then use it to estimate the probability of rolling a "1." Compare your result with the classical probability of 1/6 = 0.167 for this situation.
6. A student guesses the answers to each of the 6 true/false questions on a test. Use the random digits in the margin to estimate the probability of getting exactly 2 answers correct among the 6.

3-5 Exercises B: Beyond the Basics

7. Develop a simulation for finding the probability that when 50 people are randomly selected, at least three of them have the same birthday. Describe the simulation and estimate the probability. (*Hint*: Compare the second example in this section.)
8. A classic probability problem involves a king who wants to increase the proportion of women in his kingdom by decreeing that after a mother gives birth to a son, she is prohibited from having any more children. The king reasons that some families will have just one boy, whereas other families will have a few girls and one boy, so the proportion of girls will be increased. Is his reasoning correct? Estimate the proportion of girls if the king's scheme is followed.

3-6 Counting

What are the chances of winning the grand prize in a major lottery like Lotto 6/49? In this lottery, you choose 6 numbers from 49 possible numbers (1 to 49). If you get the same 6-number combination that is randomly drawn, you could potentially win millions of dollars. We could use Rule 2 from Section 3-2 (the classical approach) to find the probability of winning this lottery. That rule, which requires equally likely outcomes, states that the probability of an event *A* can be found using $P(A) = s/n$, where *s* is the number of ways *A* can occur and *n* is the total number of outcomes. With Lotto 6/49, there is only one way to win the grand prize: Choose the same 6-number combination that is drawn in the lottery. Knowing that there is only one way to win, we now need to determine the total number of outcomes; that is, how many 6-number combinations are possible? Writing out all the possible combinations would be an almost impossible task (and boring as well). We could try constructing a tree diagram, but that would require a sheet of paper that would cover

35484
27473
43113
35852
29235
46790
53852
05763
21938
83217
03008
70644
17473
24410
53726
67162
28089
85106
55438
84646

Prince Edward Island and probably Newfoundland too! We need a more practical way of finding the total number of possibilities. This section introduces efficient methods of finding such numbers. We will return to this lottery problem after we first present some basic principles. We begin with the **fundamental counting rule**.

Fundamental Counting Rule

For a sequence of two events in which the first event can occur *m* ways and the second event can occur *n* ways, the events together can occur a total of *m · n* ways.

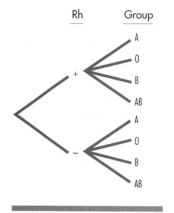

Figure 3-10 Tree Diagram of Blood Types/Rh Factors

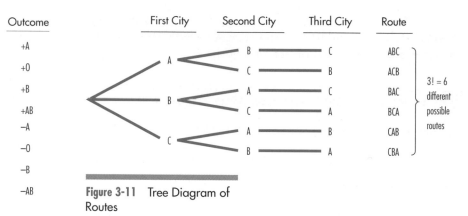

Figure 3-11 Tree Diagram of Routes

For example, if a medical researcher must randomly select 1 of the 2 Rh types (positive, negative) and 1 of the 4 blood groups (A, O, B, AB), the total number of possibilities is $2 \cdot 4 = 8$. We can see the reason for multiplication in Figure 3-10 where we use a tree diagram to depict the different possibilities. The fundamental counting rule easily extends to situations involving more than two events, as illustrated in the following example.

EXAMPLE In designing a computer, if a *byte* is defined to be a sequence of 8 bits and each bit must be a 0 or 1, how many different bytes are possible? (A byte is often used to represent an individual character, such as a letter, digit, or punctuation symbol. For example, one coding system represents the letter *A* as 01000001.)

SOLUTION Because each bit can occur in two ways (0 or 1) and we have a sequence of 8 bits, the total number of different possibilities is given by

$$2 \cdot 2 \cdot 2 \cdot 2 \cdot 2 \cdot 2 \cdot 2 \cdot 2 = 256$$

There are 256 different possible bytes.

EXAMPLE   When designing surveys, pollsters sometimes try to minimize a *lead-in* effect by rearranging the order in which the questions are presented. (A lead-in effect occurs when some questions influence the responses to the questions that follow.) If the Canadian Institute of Public Opinion (CIPO) plans to conduct a consumer survey by asking subjects 5 questions, how many different versions of the survey are required if all possible arrangements are included?

SOLUTION   In arranging any individual survey, there are 5 possible choices for the first question, 4 remaining choices for the second question, 3 choices for the third question, 2 choices for the fourth question, and only 1 choice for the fifth question. The total number of possible arrangements is therefore

$$5 \cdot 4 \cdot 3 \cdot 2 \cdot 1 = 120$$

That is, CIPO would need 120 versions of the survey in order to include every possible arrangement.

In the preceding example, we found that 5 survey questions can be arranged $5 \cdot 4 \cdot 3 \cdot 2 \cdot 1 = 120$ different ways. This particular solution can be generalized by using the following notation for the symbol ! and the following *factorial rule*.

Notation

The **factorial symbol !** denotes the product of decreasing positive whole numbers. For example, $4! = 4 \cdot 3 \cdot 2 \cdot 1 = 24$. By special definition, $0! = 1$. (Many calculators have a factorial key.)

Factorial Rule

A collection of n different items can be arranged in order $n!$ different ways. (This **factorial rule** reflects the fact that the first item may be selected n different ways, the second item may be selected $n - 1$ ways, and so on.)

EXAMPLE   Routing problems often involve application of the factorial rule. Bell Canada wants to route telephone calls through the shortest networks. Federal Express wants to find the shortest routes for its deliveries. Suppose a computer salesperson must visit 3 separate cities denoted by A, B, C. How many routes are possible?

SOLUTION   Using the factorial rule, we see that the 3 different cities (A, B, C) can be arranged in $3! = 6$ different ways. In Figure 3-11 we can

The Random Secretary

One classic problem of probability goes like this: A secretary addresses 50 different letters and envelopes to 50 different people, but the letters are randomly mixed before being put into envelopes. What is the probability that at least one letter gets into the correct envelope? Although the probability might seem like it should be small, it's actually 0.632. Even with a million letters and a million envelopes, the probability is 0.632. The formal solution is beyond the scope of this text—but you can test it using the simulation techniques discussed in Section 3–5. Try it!

see that there are 3 choices for the first city and 2 choices for the second city. This leaves only 1 choice for the third city. The number of possible arrangements for the 3 cities is $3 \cdot 2 \cdot 1 = 6$.

EXAMPLE   In your first assignment as a researcher for Environics, you must conduct a survey in each of the 10 provincial capitals. As you plan your travels, you want to determine the number of different possible routes. How many routes are possible?

SOLUTION   By applying the factorial rule, we know that 10 items can be arranged in order 10! different ways. That is, the 10 provincial capitals can be arranged 10! ways, so the number of different routes is 10! or 3,628,800.

Safety in Numbers

Some hotels have abandoned the traditional room key in favour of an electronic key with a number code. A central computer changes the access code to a room as soon as a guest checks out. A typical electronic key has 32 different positions that are either punched or left untouched. This configuration allows for 2^{32}, or 4,294,967,296, different possible codes, so it is impractical to develop a complete set of keys or try to make an illegal entry by trial and error.

The preceding example is a variation of a classical problem called the *travelling salesman problem*. It is especially interesting because the large number of possibilities (especially if you add a few more stops to the itinerary) means that we can't use a computer to calculate the distance of each route.

Using the factorial counting rule, we determine the number of different possible ways we can arrange a number of items in some type of ordered sequence. The factorial rule tells us how many arrangements are possible when all of n different items are used. Sometimes, however, we want to select only some of the n items.

If we must conduct surveys in provincial capitals, as in the preceding example, but we have time to visit only 4 of the capitals, the number of different possible routes is $10 \cdot 9 \cdot 8 \cdot 7 = 5040$. Another way to obtain this same result is to evaluate

$$\frac{10!}{6!} = 10 \cdot 9 \cdot 8 \cdot 7 = 5040$$

In this calculation, note that the factors in the numerator divide out with the factors in the denominator, except for the factors of 10, 9, 8, and 7 that remain. We can generalize this result by noting that if we have n different items available and we want to select r of them, the number of different arrangements possible is $n!/(n - r)!$, as in 10!/6!. This generalization is commonly called the *permutations rule*.

Some calculators are designed to automatically calculate values of $_nP_r$. If your calculator lacks such a feature, it is still easy to calculate $n!/(n - r)!$ by using the factorial key identified as !.

It is very important to recognize that the permutations rule requires the following conditions:

- We must have a total of n *different* items available. (This rule does not apply if some of the items are identical to others.)

Permutations Rule (When items are all different)

The number of **permutations** (or sequences) of r items selected from n available items (not allowing repetition) is

$$_nP_r = \frac{n!}{(n-r)!}$$

- We must select r of the n items (without repetition).
- We must consider rearrangements of the same items to be different sequences.

When we use the terms *permutations*, *arrangements*, or *sequences*, we imply that *order is taken into account* in the sense that different orderings of the same items are counted separately. The letters *ABC* can be arranged six different ways: *ABC, ACB, BAC, BCA, CAB, CBA.* (Later, we will refer to *combinations*, which do not count such arrangements separately.) In the following example, we are asked to find the total number of different sequences that are possible. That suggests use of the permutations rule.

EXAMPLE   A college student planning her fall timetable must select 6 courses from 30 courses offered. The courses must be selected in order of preference. How many different timetables are possible?

SOLUTION   She needs to select $r = 6$ courses from $n = 30$ courses available. Order is relevant because they must be selected in order of preference. Because order counts, we want the number of permutations, which is found as shown:

$$_nP_r = \frac{n!}{(n-r)!} = \frac{30!}{(30-6)!} = 427{,}518{,}000$$

Because there are 427,518,000 possible timetables, there are too many to consider individually.

The permutations rule can be thought of as an extension of the fundamental counting rule. We can also solve the preceding example by using the fundamental counting rule as follows: With 30 courses available and with a stipulation that 6 are to be selected, we know that there are 30 choices for the first course, 29 choices for the second course, and so on. The total number of possible arrangements is therefore

$$30 \cdot 29 \cdot 28 \cdot 27 \cdot 26 \cdot 25 = 427{,}518{,}000$$

but $30 \cdot 29 \cdot 28 \cdot 27 \cdot 26 \cdot 25$ is actually $30! \div 24!$ [or $30! \div (30-6)!$].

We sometimes need to find the number of permutations, but some of the items are identical to others. The following variation of the permutations rule applies to such cases.

Permutations Rule (When some items are identical to others)

If there are n items with n_1 alike, n_2 alike, . . . , n_k alike, the number of permutations of all n items is

$$\frac{n!}{n_1!\, n_2! \cdots n_k!}$$

● **EXAMPLE**   The classic examples of the permutations rule are those that show that the letters of the word *Mississippi* can be arranged 34,650 different ways and that the letters of the word *statistics* can be arranged 50,400 ways. We will instead consider the letters *DDDDRRRRR*, which are included in a discussion of the runs test for randomness (Section 13-7). Those letters represent a sequence of diet (*D*) and regular (*R*) colas. How many ways can we arrange the letters *DDDDRRRRR*?

SOLUTION   In the sequence *DDDDRRRRR*, we have $n = 9$ items, with $n_1 = 4$ alike and $n_2 = 5$ others that are alike. The number of permutations is computed as follows:

$$\frac{n!}{n_1!\, n_2!} = \frac{9!}{4!\, 5!} = \frac{362,880}{2880} = 126$$

In Section 13-7 we use the fact that there are 126 different possible sequences of *DDDDRRRRR*, and we can now see how that result is obtained.

The preceding example involved n items, each belonging to one of two categories. When there are only two categories, we can stipulate that x of the items are alike and the other $n - x$ items are alike, so the permutations formula simplifies to

$$\frac{n!}{(n - x)!\, x!}$$

This particular result will be used for binomial experiments, which are introduced in Section 4-3.

When we intend to select r items from n different items but *do not take order into account,* we are really concerned with possible combinations rather than permutations. That is, **when different orderings of the same items are to be counted separately, we have a permutation problem, but when different orderings are not to be counted separately, we have a combination problem** and may apply the following rule.

Combinations Rule

The number of **combinations** of r items selected from n different items is

$$_nC_r = \frac{n!}{(n-r)!\,r!}$$

How Many Shuffles?

After conducting extensive research, mathematician Persi Diaconis found that it takes seven shuffles of a deck of cards to get a complete mixture. The mixture is complete in the sense that all possible arrangements are equally likely. More than seven shuffles will not have a significant effect, and fewer than seven are not enough. Casino dealers rarely shuffle as often as seven times, so the decks are not completely mixed. Some expert card players have been able to take advantage of the incomplete mixtures that result from fewer than seven shuffles.

Some calculators are designed to automatically evaluate $_nC_r$.

It is very important to recognize that in applying the combinations rule, the following conditions apply:

- We must have a total of n different items available.
- We must select r of the n items (without repetition).
- We must consider rearrangements of the same items to be the same grouping.

Because choosing between the permutations rule and the combinations rule can be confusing, we provide the following example, which is intended to emphasize the difference between them.

EXAMPLE   The Board of Trustees at the author's college has 9 members. Each year, they elect a 3-person committee to oversee buildings and grounds. Each year, they also elect a chairperson, vice chairperson, and secretary.

a. When the board elects the buildings and grounds committee, how many different 3-person committees are possible?
b. When the board elects the 3 officers (chairperson, vice chairperson, and secretary), how many different slates of candidates are possible?

SOLUTION   Note that order is irrelevant when electing the buildings and grounds committee. When electing officers, however, different orders are counted separately.

a. Here we want the number of combinations of $r = 3$ people selected from the $n = 9$ available people. We get

$$_9C_3 = \frac{n!}{(n-r)!\,r!} = \frac{9!}{(9-3)!\,3!} = \frac{362{,}880}{4320} = 84$$

b. Here we want the number of sequences (or permutations) of $r = 3$ people selected from the $n = 9$ available people. We get

$$_9P_3 = \frac{n!}{(n-r)!} = \frac{9!}{(9-3)!} = \frac{362{,}880}{720} = 504$$

There are 84 different possible committees of 3 board members, but there are 504 different possible slates of candidates.

Voltaire Beats Lottery

In 1729, the philosopher Voltaire became rich by devising a scheme to beat the Paris lottery. The government ran a lottery to repay municipal bonds that had lost some value. The city added large amounts of money with the net effect that the prize values totalled more than the cost of all tickets. Voltaire formed a group that bought all the tickets in the monthly lottery and won for more than a year. A bettor in the New York State Lottery tried to win a share of an exceptionally large prize that grew from a lack of previous winners. He wanted to write a $6,135,756 cheque that would cover all combinations, but the state declined and said that the nature of the lottery would have been changed.

The counting techniques presented in this section are sometimes used in probability problems. The following examples illustrate such applications.

EXAMPLE   In Lotto 6/49, a player wins first prize by selecting the correct 6-number combination when 6 different numbers from 1 through 49 are drawn. If a player selects one particular 6-number combination, find the probability of winning. (The player need not select the 6 numbers in the same order that they are drawn, so order is irrelevant).

SOLUTION   Because 6 different numbers are selected from 49 different possibilities, the total number of combinations is

$$_{49}C_6 = \frac{49!}{(49-6)!6!} = 13,938,816$$

With only one combination selected, the player's probability of winning is only 1/13,983,816.

In the preceding example, we found that the probability of winning Lotto 6/49 is only 1/13,983,816 or 0.0000000715. In Canada, lightning strikes an average of 60 to 70 people and kills an average of 7 people per year. The probability of being struck and killed by lightning is 1/4,285,714 = 0.000000233. A comparison of these two probabilities shows that in a single year, there is a much better chance of being struck and killed by lightning than of winning Lotto 6/49 in a single try. Of course, you could increase your chances of winning the lottery by buying many tickets, a strategy generally deemed to be unwise.

EXAMPLE   A UPS dispatcher sends a delivery truck to 8 different locations. If the order in which the deliveries are made is randomly determined, find the probability that the resulting route is the shortest possible route.

SOLUTION   With 8 locations there are 8!, or 40,320, different possible routes. Among those 40,320 different possibilities, only two routes will be shortest (actually, the same route in two different directions). Therefore, there is a probability of only 2/40,320, or 1/20,160, or 0.0000496 that the selected route will be the shortest one possible.

This section presented five different counting approaches. When deciding which particular one to apply, you should consider a list of questions that address key issues. The following summary may be helpful.

- Is there a sequence of events in which the first can occur m ways, the second can occur n ways, and so on? If so, use the fundamental counting rule and multiply m, n, and so on.

- Are there *n different* items and are *all* of them to be used in different arrangements? If so, use the factorial rule and find *n*!.

- Are there *n different* items and are only *some* of them to be used in different arrangements? If so, evaluate $_nP_r = \dfrac{n!}{(n-r)!}$

- Are there *n* items with some of them *identical* to each other, and is there a need to find the total number of different arrangements of all of those *n* items? If so, use the following expression in which n_1 of the items are alike, n_2 are alike, and so on.

$$\frac{n!}{n_1!\, n_2! \,\cdots\, n_k!}$$

- Are there *n* different items, with *some* of them to be selected, and is there a need to find the total number of combinations (that is, is the order irrelevant)? If so, evaluate $_nC_r = \dfrac{n!}{(n-r)!r!}$

3-6 Exercises A: Basic Skills and Concepts

In Exercises 1–16, evaluate the given expressions.

1. 6!
2. 11!
3. 100!/97!
4. 85!/82!
5. (10 − 4)!
6. (90 − 87)!
7. $_6C_4$
8. $_6P_4$
9. $_{12}P_9$
10. $_{10}C_9$
11. $_{40}C_6$
12. $_{40}P_6$
13. $_nC_0$
14. $_nP_0$
15. $_nP_n$
16. $_nC_n$

17. The author uses a home security system that has a code consisting of 4 digits (0, 1, . . . , 9) that must be entered in the correct sequence. The digits can be repeated in the code.
    a. How many different possibilities are there?
    b. If it takes a burglar 5 seconds to try a code, how long would it take to try every possibility?

18. There are 12 members on the board of directors for Cliffside General Hospital.
    a. If they must elect a chairperson, first vice chairperson, second vice chairperson, and secretary, how many different slates of candidates are possible?
    b. If they must form an ethics subcommittee of 4 members, how many different subcommittees are possible?

19. Each social insurance number (SIN) is a sequence of 9 digits. What is the probability of randomly generating 9 digits and getting your SIN number?

20. A typical "combination" lock is opened with the correct sequence of 3 numbers between 0 and 49 inclusive. How many different sequences are possible? (A number can be used more than once.) Are these sequences combinations or are they actually permutations?

21. In doing a runs test for randomness (Section 13-7), it is found that genders of survey subjects listed in consecutive order are as follows: MMMMMMMMMMMFFFFFFFFF. How many different ways can those letters be arranged?

The Number Crunch

Every so often telephone companies split regions with one area code into regions with two or more area codes because the increased number of area fax and Internet lines has nearly exhausted the possible numbers that can be listed under a single code. A seven-digit telephone number cannot begin with a 0 or 1, but if we allow all other possibilities, we get 8 · 10 · 10 · 10 · 10 · 10 = 8,000,000 different possible numbers! Even so, after surviving for many years with the single area code of 514, the Montreal area was partitioned into the two area codes of 514 and 450. Other regions have also been assigned split area codes.

22. A Federal Express delivery route must include stops at 5 cities.
    a. How many different routes are possible?
    b. If the route is randomly selected, what is the probability that the cities will be arranged in alphabetical order?

23. How many ways can the word *history* be rearranged?

24. a. If a couple plans to have 8 children (it happens), how many different gender sequences are possible?
    b. If a couple has 4 boys and 4 girls, how many different gender sequences are possible?
    c. Based on the results from parts (a) and (b), what is the probability that when a couple has 8 children, the result will consist of 4 boys and 4 girls?

25. Suppose you bought a ticket in a lottery that requires you to select 6 distinct numbers between 1 and 40 inclusive.
    a. How many different selections are possible?
    b. What is the probability of winning with one ticket?
    c. What are the odds against winning such a lottery with one ticket?

26. Refer to the same lottery described in Exercise 25. What is the probability of winning if the rules are changed so that you must select the correct 6 numbers in the same order in which they are drawn?

27. In Denys Parsons' *Directory of Tunes and Musical Themes*, melodies for more than 14,000 songs are listed according to the following scheme: The first note of every song is represented by an asterisk (*), and successive notes are represented by R (for repeat the previous note), U (for a note that goes up), or D (for a note that goes down). Beethoven's Fifth Symphony begins as *RRD. Classical melodies are represented through the first 16 notes. With this scheme, how many different classical melodies are possible?

28. A Canada Post courier must pick up weather summaries from 11 different locations around the city of Winnipeg. He would like to work out the shortest route. How many routes are possible?

29. M.S. and Associates would like to design a mutual fund portfolio from 50 eligible Canadian equity funds. The portfolio must be made up of 4 funds.
    a. How many different portfolios are possible?
    b. If the funds are selected at random (which we hope they are not), what is the probability of getting the 4 best performing Canadian equity funds?

30. You become suspicious when a genetics researcher randomly selects groups of 20 newborn babies and seems to consistently get 10 girls and 10 boys. The researcher explains that it is common to get 10 boys and 10 girls in such cases.
    a. If 20 newborn babies are randomly selected, how many different gender sequences are possible?
    b. How many different ways can 10 boys and 10 girls be arranged in sequence?
    c. What is the probability of getting 10 boys and 10 girls when 20 babies are born?
    d. Based on the preceding results, do you agree with the researcher's explanation that it is common to get 10 boys and 10 girls when 20 babies are randomly selected?

31. The Halifax Music Company has purchased the rights to 15 different songs and it plans to release a new CD with 8 of them. Recognizing that the order of the songs is important, how many different CDs are possible?

32. A supervisor must visit 8 different distribution locations around the country. She can visit them in any order, but wishes to find the most convenient sequence. How many sequences are possible?

33. **a.** How many different postal codes are possible if each code is two sequences, the first sequence being letter-number-letter (for example, E1A) and the second sequence being number-letter-number (for example, 3E9)?
    b. If a computer randomly generates postal codes, what is the probability that it will produce your postal code?

34. Because of recent retirements, 8 management positions became open at the Red River Finance Company. The jobs were all at different levels of management. A total of 22 employees applied for these management positions. How many different ways could the company fill the 8 vacancies?

35. In an age-discrimination case against Darmin, Inc., evidence showed that among the last 40 applicants for employment, only the 8 youngest were hired. Find the probability of randomly selecting 8 of 40 people and getting the 8 youngest. Based on the result, does it appear that age discrimination is occurring?

36. The following excerpt is from *The Man Who Cast Two Shadows,* by Carol O'Connell: "The child had only the numbers written on her palm in ink . . . , all but the last four numbers disappeared in a wet smudge of blood . . . . She would put the coins into the public telephones and dial three untried numbers and then the four she knew. If a woman answered, she would say, 'It's Kathy. I'm lost.'" If it costs Kathy 25¢ for each call and she tries every possibility except those beginning with 0 or 1, what is her total cost?

37. After testing 12 homes for the presence of radon, an inspector is concerned that her test equipment is defective because the measured radon level at each home was higher than the reading at the preceding home. That is, the 12 readings were arranged in order from low to high. If the homes were randomly selected, what is the probability of getting this particular arrangement? Based on the result, is her concern about the test equipment justified?

38. A freight train is to carry 12 coal cars, 5 cars full of lumber, and 4 tankers all carrying kerosene. How many different arrangements are possible?

39. How many 6-digit licence plates are possible? How many plates are possible if no digits can be repeated? How many plates are possible if 1 letter replaces one of the 6 digits (no repeated digits)?

40. The House of Commons would like to set up a committee to investigate foreign investment in Canada. The committee must have 4 members from the government and 4 members from all the opposition parties. If 8 government members and 10 opposition members apply to serve on the committee, how many different ways can it be formed?

3–6 Exercises B: Beyond the Basics

41. A common computer programming rule is that names of variables must be between 1 and 8 characters long. The first character can be any of the 26 letters, while successive characters can be any of the 26 letters or any of the 10 digits. For example, allowable variable names are A, BBB, and M3477K. How many different variable names are possible?

42. a. Five managers gather for a meeting. If each manager shakes hands with each other manager exactly once, what is the total number of handshakes?

   b. If n managers shake hands with each other exactly once, what is the total number of handshakes?

   c. How many different ways can 5 managers be seated at a round table? (Assume that if everyone moves to the right, the seating arrangement is the same.)

   d. How many different ways can n managers be seated at a round table?

43. Many calculators or computers cannot directly calculate 70! or higher. When n is large, $n!$ can be approximated by $n! = 10^K$ where $K = (n + 0.5) \log n + 0.39908993 - 0.43429448n$.

   a. Evaluate 50! using the factorial key on a calculator and also by using the approximation given here.

   b. Canada Post wanted to find the shortest route for delivering to 300 locations in Winnipeg. There are 300! different possible routes. If 300! is evaluated, how many digits are used in the result?

44. Can computers "think"? According to the *Turing test,* a computer can be considered to think if, when a person communicates with it, the person believes he or she is communicating with another person instead of a computer. In an experiment at Boston's Computer Museum, each of 10 judges communicated with 4 computers and 4 people and was asked to distinguish between them.

   a. Assume that the first judge cannot distinguish between the 4 computers and the 4 people. If this judge makes random guesses, what is the probability of correctly identifying the 4 computers and the 4 people?

   b. Assume that all 10 judges cannot distinguish between computers and people, so they make random guesses. Based on the result from part (a), what is the probability that all 10 judges make all correct guesses? (That event would lead us to conclude that computers cannot "think" when, according to the Turing criterion, they can.)

• •

Vocabulary List

probability
rare event rule
event
simple event
sample space
relative frequency approximation of
   probability
classical approach to probability
subjective probabilities
law of large numbers
simulation
random sample
complement
actual odds against
actual odds in favour

payoff odds
addition rule
compound event
mutually exclusive
rule of complementary events
tree diagram
independent events
dependent events
multiplication rule
conditional probability
fundamental counting rule
factorial symbol
permutations rule
permutation
combinations rule
combination

• •

Review

This chapter introduced the basic concepts of probability theory. In Section 3-2 we presented the basic definitions and notation, including the representation of events by letters such as A. We defined probabilities of simple events as

$$P(A) = \frac{\text{number of times } A \text{ occurred}}{\text{number of times experiment was repeated}} \quad \text{(relative frequency)}$$

$$P(A) = \frac{\text{number of ways } A \text{ can occur}}{\text{number of different simple events}} = \frac{s}{n} \quad \text{(for equally likely outcomes)}$$

We noted that the probability of any impossible event is 0, the probability of any certain event is 1, and for any event A, $0 \le P(A) \le 1$. Also, $\overline{A}$ denotes the complement of event A. That is, $\overline{A}$ indicates that event A does not occur.

After Section 3-2 we proceeded to consider compound events, which involve more than one event. In general, associate *or* with addition and associate *and* with multiplication. Always keep in mind the following key considerations.

- When conducting one trial, do we want the probability of event *A or B*? If so, use the addition rule, but be careful to avoid counting any outcomes more than once.

- When finding the probability that event *A* occurs on one trial *and* event *B* occurs on a second trial, use the multiplication rule. Multiply the probability of event *A* by the probability of event *B*. *Caution:* When calculating the probability of event *B*, be sure to take into account the fact that event *A* has already occurred.

In some probability problems, the biggest obstacle is finding the total number of possible outcomes. The last section of this chapter was devoted to the following counting techniques, which are briefly summarized at the end of Section 3-6:

- Fundamental counting rule
- Factorial rule
- Permutations rule (when items are all different)
- Permutations rule (when some items are identical to others)
- Combinations rule

Most of the material in the following chapters deals with statistical inferences based on probabilities. As an example of the basic approach used, consider a test of someone's claim that a quarter used in a coin toss is fair. If we flip the quarter 10 times and get 10 consecutive heads, we can make one of two inferences from these sample results:

1. The coin is actually fair, and the string of 10 consecutive heads is a fluke.
2. The coin is not fair.

The statistician's decision as to which inference is correct is based on the probability of getting 10 consecutive heads, which, in this case, is so small (1/1024) that the inference of unfairness is the better choice. Here we can see the important role played by probability in the standard methods of statistical inference.

• •

Review Exercises

In Exercises 1–8, use the data from Table 3-4, which summarize results of a study to determine if there is a relationship between place of residence and ownership of a foreign car. A random sample of 200 car owners from large cities, 150 from suburbs, and 150 from rural areas was selected.

1. If one of the 500 car owners is randomly selected, find the probability of getting a foreign car owner.
2. If one of the 500 car owners is randomly selected, find the probability of getting a foreign car owner or someone who lives in a large city.
3. If two different car owners are randomly selected, find the probability that both people live in a rural area.

TABLE 3-4	Car Ownership		
	Large City	Suburbs	Rural
Foreign	90	60	25
Domestic	110	90	125

4. If one of the 500 car owners is randomly selected, find the probability of getting a domestic car owner who lives in the suburbs.

5. If one owner is randomly selected, find the probability of getting someone who lives in the suburbs or in a rural area.

6. If three different owners are randomly selected, find the probability that they all own domestic cars.

7. If one owner is randomly selected, find the probability of getting a domestic car owner, given that she or he is from a large city.

8. If one car owner is randomly selected, find the probability of getting someone who lives in a large city, given that her or his car is foreign. Are owning a foreign car and living in large cities independent events? Why or why not?

9. In setting up a manufacturing process for a new computer memory storage device, the initial configuration has a 16% yield: 16% of the devices are acceptable and 84% are defective. If 12 of the devices are made, what is the probability of getting at least 1 that is good? If it is very important to have at least 1 good unit for testing purposes, is the resulting probability adequate?

10. On the basis of past experience, a commuting student knows that when he speeds on any given day, there is a 2% chance of being ticketed. What is the probability of not getting a speeding ticket if he speeds every one of the 150 days in one year of college? If this student cannot afford the increased insurance costs resulting from a speeding ticket, what does the resulting probability suggest about a course of action?

11. The board of directors for the Southern Alberta Insurance Company has 8 members.
    a. If a committee of 3 is formed by random selection, what is the probability that it consists of the 3 wealthiest members?
    b. If the board must elect a chairperson, vice chairperson, and secretary, how many different slates of candidates are possible?

12. You choose 5 Canadian equity mutual funds for your portfolio. The probability that each fund will rise in value next year is 87.5%. What is the probability that all 5 funds will rise in value next year?

13. When betting on *even* in roulette, there are 38 equally likely outcomes, but only 2, 4, 6, . . . , 36 are winning outcomes.
    a. Find the probability of winning when betting on even.
    b. Find the odds against winning with a bet on even.
    c. Casinos pay winning bets according to odds described as 1:1. What is your net profit if you bet $5 on even and you win?

14. A question on a history test requires that 5 events be arranged in the proper chronological order. If a random arrangement is selected, what is the probability that it will be correct?

15. A pollster claims that 12 voters were randomly selected from a population of 200,000 voters (30% of whom are Progressive Conservatives), and all 12 were Progressive Conservatives. The pollster claims that this could easily happen by chance. Find the probability of getting 12 Progressive Conservatives when 12 voters are randomly selected from this population. Based on the result, does it seem that the pollster's claim is correct?

16. In a statistics class of 8 women and 8 men, 2 groups of 8 students are formed by random selection. What is the probability that all of the women are in the first group and all of the men are in the second group? (*Hint:* Find the number of ways of arranging WWWWWWWWMMMMMMMM.)

Cumulative Review Exercises

1. Refer to the accompanying frequency table, which describes the age distribution of Canadians who died of cancer (based on data from the Statistics Canada).

Age	Number
0–4	56
5–14	116
15–24	190
25–44	2,292
45–64	14,605
65–74	16,472
75 and over	20,233

   a. Assuming that the class of "75 and over" has a class midpoint of 80, calculate the mean age of the Canadians who died of cancer.

   b. Using the same assumption given in part (a), calculate the standard deviation of the ages summarized in the table.

   c. If one of the 53,964 ages is randomly selected, find the probability that it is below 15 or above 64.

   d. If one of the 53,964 ages is randomly selected, find the probability that it is below 15 or between 5 and 44.

   e. If two different ages are randomly selected from those summarized in the table, find the probability that they are both between 0 and 4 years.

2. The accompanying boxplot depicts heights (in inches) of a large collection of randomly selected adult women.

   a. If one of these women is randomly selected, find the probability that her height is between 56.1 in. and 62.2 in.

   b. If one of these women is randomly selected, find the probability that her height is below 62.2 in. or above 63.6 in.

   c. If two women are randomly selected, find the probability that they both have heights between 62.2 in. and 63.6 in.

3. A zookeeper is interested in the lengths of pregnancies of mammals. The gestation periods (in days) of 12 randomly selected mammal species are listed below.

260   42   16   350   280   230   337   113   68   44   13   62

   a. Find the mean gestation period for the sample.

   b. Find the median gestation period for the sample.

   c. Find the standard deviation of the given sample gestation periods.

   d. What is the range of the sample gestation periods?

   e. If one gestation period is randomly selected from this sample, find the probability that it is at least 50 days.

   f. If two gestation periods are randomly selected from this sample, find the probability that they are both at least 50 days.

Technology Project

We can often use computers to find probabilities by simulating an experiment or procedure. Recall that a simulation of a procedure is a process that behaves in the same ways as the procedure itself, thus producing similar results. Exercise 31 in Section 3-4 required computation of the probability of getting at least 2 people who share the same birthday when randomly selecting 25 people. Instead of doing theoretical calculations, we will use Excel or STATDISK to simulate the procedure. Instead of generating actual birthdays, we will generate numbers between 1 and 365, which represent the different possible birthdays. (We will ignore leap years.) For example, a generated number of 5 represents January 5, and 364 represents December 30. We can work with the generated numbers; it isn't necessary to identify the actual day and month. After generating 25 such numbers, we can sort them so that it becomes very easy to see if at least 2 of them are the same "birthday."

Use Excel or STATDISK to generate 25 "birthdays," then sort them and observe whether at least 2 are the same. Record the result. Repeat this experiment until you are reasonably confident that your estimated probability is approximately correct.

To use Excel, first enter the numbers 1 to 365 in Column A and the probability for each of the 365 cells (1/365) in Column B. Select **Data Analysis** under the **Tools** menu. Next, select **Random Number Generation**. In the dialog box, enter 1 for **Number of Variables** and 25 for **Number of Random Numbers**. Choose **Discrete** in the **Distribution** pull-down box. In the box for **Value and Probability Input Range**, enter A1:B365. Select **New Worksheet Ply** for **Output Option** and click **OK**. Twenty-five random numbers between 1 and 365 will appear in Column A of a new worksheet. Sort the numbers ascending and view the sorted results.

To use STATDISK, first select **Data** from the main menu bar, then choose **Uniform Generator** and use **Format** to set the number of decimal places to 0 (because we want to generate only whole numbers). Proceed to generate a sample size of 25, with a maximum of 365 and a minimum of 1. Use the **Sample Editor's Format** feature to rank and display the 25 simulated birthdays so you can easily see whether at least 2 are the same.

•••••••• FROM DATA TO DECISION ••••••••

Drug Testing of Job Applicants

Most U.S. companies now test at least some employees and job applicants for drug use. Some Canadian companies have tried to implement similar policies, particularly in industries where security and workplace safety are major issues. Allyn Clark, a 21-year-old college graduate, applied for a job with a transportation company, took a drug test, and was not offered a job. He suspected that he might have failed the drug test, even though he does not use drugs. In checking with the company's personnel department, he found that the drug test has 99% sensitivity, so only 1% of drug users test negative. Also, the test has 98% specificity, meaning that only 2% of nonusers are incorrectly identified as drug users. Allyn felt relieved by these figures because he believed that they reflected a very reliable test that usually provides good results—but should he be relieved? Can the company feel certain that drug users are not being hired? The accompanying table shows data for Allyn and 1999 other job applicants. Based on those results, find the probability of a "false positive"; that is, find the probability of randomly selecting one of the subjects who tested positive and getting someone who does not use drugs. Also find the probability of a "false negative"; that is, find the probability of randomly selecting someone who tested negative and getting someone who does use drugs. Are the probabilities of these wrong results low enough so that job applicants and the company need not be concerned?

	Drug Users	Nonusers
Positive test result	297	34
Negative test result	3	1666

········ COOPERATIVE GROUP ACTIVITIES ········

1. *In-class activity:* Divide into groups of three or four and estimate P(2 girls in 3 births) by using a *simulation* with coins. Describe the exact procedure used and the results obtained.

2. *In-class activity:* Divide into groups of three or four and use actual thumbtacks to estimate the probability that when dropped, a thumbtack will land with the point up. How many trials are necessary to get a result that seems to be reasonably accurate?

3. *In-class activity:* Divide into groups of three or four. In each group, agree on the value of a subjective probability for the event that a woman will be elected as prime minister of Canada in the next federal election. Are the various group values approximately the same, or are they very different? Would agreement among the groups mean that the results are accurate?

4. *In-class activity:* Each student should be given a different page torn from an old telephone directory. Proceed to randomly select 25 simulated "birthdays" by using the last three digits of telephone numbers, ignoring those above 365. After recording the 25 birthdays, check to determine whether any two of them are the same. The class results can be combined to form an estimate of the probability that when 25 people are randomly selected, at least two of them will have the same birthday.

5. *Out-of-class activity: The Capture–Recapture Method.* Marine biologists often use the capture–recapture method as a way to estimate the size of a population, such as the number of fish in a lake. This method involves capturing a sample from the population, tagging each member in the sample, then returning them to the population. A second sample is later captured and the tagged members are counted along with the total size of this second sample. As an example, suppose a random sample of 50 fish is captured and tagged. Also suppose that a second random sample (obtained later) consists of 100 fish with 20 of them tagged, suggesting that when a fish is captured, the probability of it being tagged is estimated to be 0.20. That is, 20% of the fish in the population have been tagged. Because the original sample of 50 fish were tagged, we estimate that the population size is 250 fish (50 ÷ 20/100 = 250).

It's not easy to actually capture and recapture real fish, but we can simulate an experiment using some uniform collection of items such as coloured beads, M&Ms, or Fruit Loop cereal pieces. "Captured" items in the first sample can be "tagged" with a magic marker (or they can be replaced with similar items of a different color). Illustrate the capture–recapture method by designing and conducting such an experiment. Starting with a large package of M&Ms, for example, collect a sample of 50, then use a magic marker to "tag" each one. Replace the tagged items, mix the whole population, then select a second sample and proceed to estimate the population size. Compare the result to the actual population size obtained by counting all of the items.

········ COOPERATIVE GROUP ACTIVITIES ········

6. *In-class activity:* Divide into groups of two. The "Monty Hall" problem has, according to *Chance* magazine, been used to study decision making in business schools. The problem is based on a television game show that was hosted by Monty Hall. Begin by selecting one of the team members to serve as the host. The other team member is the contestant, and there are three doors numbered 1, 2, and 3. The host should *randomly* select one of the doors, and the selection must not be revealed to the contestant. Pretend that the host has put a prize of a new red Corvette behind the door that was randomly selected, but the other two doors have nothing behind them. The contestant should now select one of the three doors. After the contestant reveals which door has been chosen, the host should select an "empty" door and inform the contestant that this particular door has nothing behind it. The host should now offer the contestant a choice of sticking with the original door or switching to the other door that has not been revealed. After the contestant announces his or her decision to stick or switch, the host should announce that the contestant has (or has not) won the Corvette. Record the result along with the contestant's decision to stick or switch. Repeat the game 20 times with the contestant sticking 10 times and switching ten times. Then reverse roles and play the game another 20 times. Find the proportion of times the game was won by sticking and find the proportion of times the game was won by switching. Based on the results, which strategy is better: sticking or switching?

7. *In-class activity:* Divide into groups of two for the purpose of doing an experiment designed to show one approach to dealing with sensitive survey questions, such as those related to drug use, stealing, cheating, or sexual activity. For the purposes of this activity, we will use this innocuous question: "Were you born between January 1 and March 31?" We expect that about 1/4 of all responses should be "yes," but let's assume that the question is very sensitive and subjects are usually reluctant to answer honestly. One team member (the "interviewer") should ask the other (the "survey subject") to flip a coin and write "no" on a piece of paper if the survey subject was *not* born between January 1 and March 31 *and* the coin turns up heads; if the subject was born between those dates or if the coin turns up tails, the response of "yes" should be written. Switch roles so that two responses are obtained from each team. Supposedly, respondents tend to be more honest because the coin flip protects their privacy. Combine all results and analyse them to determine the proportion of people born between January 1 and March 31. The accuracy of the results can be checked against the actual birth dates. The experiment can be repeated with a question that is more sensitive, but such a question is not given here because the author already receives enough mail.

INTERNET PROJECT   What's the Probability of Landing on Boardwalk?

Finding probabilities when rolling dice is easy. With one die, there are six possible outcomes, so each outcome, such as rolling a 2, has a probability 1/6. For a card game the calculations are more involved, but they are still manageable. But what about a more complicated game, such as the board game "Monopoly"? What is the probability of landing on a particular space on the board? The probability depends on the space your piece currently occupies, the roll of the dice, the drawing of cards, as well as other factors. Now consider more true-to-life examples, such as the probability of having an auto accident. The number of factors involved there is too large to even consider, yet such probabilities are nonetheless quoted, for example, by insurance companies.

The Internet Project for this chapter considers methods for computing probabilities in complicated situations. Go to the site

http://www.pearsoned.ca/triola

Click on Internet Project, then on Chapter 3, and then you will be guided in researching probabilities for a board game. Then you will compute such a probability yourself. Finally, you will compute a health-related probability using empirical data.

4

Probability Distributions

4-1 Overview

The objectives of this chapter are identified.
Random variables and probability distributions
are described in general, then some special
probability distributions are examined.

4-2 Random Variables

Discrete and continuous random variables and
probability distributions are described in this
section. Methods for finding the mean, variance,
and standard deviation for a given probability
distribution are also described. The expected
value of a probability distribution is defined.

4-3 Binomial Probability Distributions

Binomial probability distributions are defined.
Probabilities in binomial probability distributions
are calculated using the binomial probability
formula, a table of binomial probabilities, and
statistical software.

4-4 Mean, Variance, and Standard Deviation for the Binomial Distribution

The mean, variance, and standard deviation for a
binomial distribution are calculated.
Interpretation of those values is also discussed.

4-5 The Poisson Distribution

The Poisson distribution is described as another
special and important example of a discrete
probability distribution. A key characteristic of
the Poisson distribution is that it applies to
occurrences of some event over a specified
interval of time, distance, area, or some similar
unit.

CHAPTER PROBLEM:

Is the number of accidents caused by commercial vehicles just a coincidence?

Much publicity has been given lately to the increasing volumes of traffic on our highways and, in particular, the volume of commercial vehicles, which include trucks, buses, and other vehicles. Along with this increase in volume comes an increase in accidents. Large vehicles pose a large risk to those who travel the roads and highways in smaller, lighter passenger vehicles. In 1997 there were 3,720,000 registered commercial vehicles in Canada, representing about 20% of all vehicles on the road (based on data from Transport Canada, *Canadian Motor Vehicle Traffic Collision Statistics, 1997*).

Commercial vehicles have grown in size as well as numbers. We now see trucks pulling two large trailers behind them. With just-in-time inventory control, there is more emphasis on speed and longer operating hours of these commercial vehicles. Are they safe for our roads? How much of a threat are they to drivers and passengers in smaller vehicles?

Recently, accidents involving trucks have claimed more than a few headlines. The public's anxiety level rises whenever there is a cluster of accidents. Suppose, on a specific stretch of highway during a short period of time, 4 of 7 vehicles involved in accidents were commercial vehicles. Given that commercial vehicles represent 20% of all vehicles on the road, can we conclude from these 7 accident reports that commercial vehicles are not as safe or are not being

operated as safely as other vehicles? That determination depends on the *probability* that the given events occur by chance. We will consider these two questions:

1. Given that 20% of all vehicles on the road are commercial vehicles, and assuming that the vehicles are as safe as other vehicles and that accidents are independent events that occur at random, what is the probability that 4 of 7 vehicles involved in a cluster of accidents will be commercial vehicles?

2. In deciding whether commercial vehicles are unsafe or the victims of coincidence, is the probability in the preceding question the *relevant* probability? Instead of asking for the probability that exactly 4 of the 7 involved vehicles are commercial, is there another question that better addresses the real issue of whether commercial vehicles are unsafe?

The first question can easily be answered using methods presented in this chapter. The second question is more difficult and requires serious thought, but it is extremely important to correctly identify the event that is key to the issue. We will address both questions later in the chapter.

4-1 Overview

In Chapter 2 we saw that we could explore and describe a set of data by using graphs (such as a histogram or boxplot), measures of central tendency (such as the mean), and measures of variation (such as the standard deviation). In Chapter 3 we discussed the basic principles of probability theory. In this chapter we combine those concepts as we develop probability distributions that describe what will *probably* happen instead of what actually did happen. In Chapter 2 we constructed frequency tables and histograms using *observed* real scores, but in this chapter we will construct probability distributions by presenting possible outcomes along with the relative frequencies we *expect*, given an understanding of the relevant circumstances.

Suppose that a casino manager suspects cheating at a dice table. He or she can compare the relative frequency distribution of the actual sample outcomes to a theoretical model that describes the frequency distribution likely to occur with a fair die. A fair die should have a relative frequency histogram similar to the one shown in Figure 4-1(a), so if the relative frequency histogram looks like Figure 4-1(b) that may arouse suspicion.

In Figure 4-1(a) we see relative frequencies based not on actual outcomes, but on our knowledge of the probabilities for the outcomes of a fair die. In essence, we can describe the frequency table and histogram for a die rolled an infinite number of times. With this knowledge of the population of outcomes, we are able to determine important characteristics, such as the mean and standard deviation. The remainder of this book and the very core of inferential statistics are based on some knowledge of probability distributions. We begin by examining the concept of a random variable, then we consider important distributions that have many real applications.

4-2 Random Variables

In this section we discuss random variables, probability distributions, and procedures for finding the mean and standard deviation for a probability distribution. We will see that a random variable has a numeric value for each out-

Figure 4-1 Histograms of Dice Outcomes for (a) a Fair Die and (b) a Loaded Die

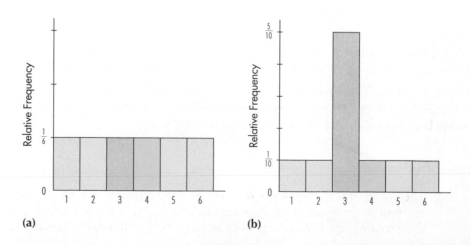

come of a procedure, and a probability distribution associates a probability value with each outcome of a procedure.

DEFINITION

A **random variable** is a variable (typically represented by x) that has a single numerical value (determined by chance) for each outcome of a procedure.

Examples of random variables are the following:

x = The number of women among 10 newly hired employees

x = The number of students absent from statistics class today

x = The height (in cm) of a randomly selected adult male

The word *random* is used to remind us that we don't usually know what the value of x is until we observe or perform a procedure.

> **EXAMPLE**   We randomly select 7 vehicles involved in accidents on public roadways and count how many of these are commercial vehicles. If we let the random variable represent the number of commercial vehicles among 7, this procedure has possible outcomes of 0, 1, 2, 3, 4, 5, 6, 7. (Remember, 0 represents no vehicles are commercial vehicles, 1 represents 1 vehicle is a commercial vehicle, and so on.) The variable is random in the sense that we do not know the value until after the 7 vehicles have been selected.

In Section 1-2 we made a distinction between discrete and continuous data. Random variables may also be discrete or continuous, and the following two definitions are consistent with those given in Section 1-2. This chapter deals with discrete random variables, but the following chapters will deal with continuous random variables.

DEFINITIONS

A **discrete random variable** has either a finite number of values or a countable number of values, that is, they result from a counting process.

A **continuous random variable** has infinitely many values, and those values can be associated with measurements on a continuous scale in such a way that there are no gaps or interruptions.

> **EXAMPLE**
>
> **a.** The count of the number of patrons viewing a movie is a whole number and is therefore a discrete random variable. The counting device shown in Figure 4-2(a) is capable of indicating only whole numbers. It

Sensitive Surveys

Survey respondents are sometimes reluctant to honestly answer questions on a sensitive topic, such as employee theft or sex. Stanley Warner (York University, Ontario) devised a scheme that leads to more accurate results in such cases. As an example, ask employees if they stole within the past year and also ask them to flip a coin. The employees are instructed to answer no if they didn't steal and the coin turns up heads. Otherwise, they should answer yes. The employees are more likely to be honest because the coin flip helps protect their privacy. Probability theory can then be used to analyze responses so that more accurate results can be obtained.

(a) Discrete Random Variable: Count of the number of movie patrons.

(b) Continuous Random Variable: The measured voltage of a smoke detector battery.

Figure 4-2 Discrete and Continuous Random Variables

can therefore be used to obtain values for a discrete random variable.

b. The measure of voltage for a smoke detector battery can be any value between 0 volts and 9 volts and is therefore a continuous random variable. The voltmeter depicted in Figure 4-2(b) is capable of indicating values on a continuous scale, so it can be used to obtain values for a continuous random variable.

After we identify possible values of a random variable, we can often identify a probability for each of those values. When we know all values of a random variable along with their corresponding probabilities, we have a probability distribution, defined as follows.

DEFINITION

A **probability distribution** gives the probability for each value of the random variable.

EXAMPLE   Suppose that 20% of all registered motor vehicles are commercial vehicles, and that all vehicles have the same chance of being involved in an accident. If we let the random variable x represent the number of commercial vehicles among 7 randomly selected vehicles involved in accidents, then the probability distribution can be described by Table 4-1. (In Section 4-3 we will see how the probabilities in Table 4-1 are found.) In the table, we see that the probability that 0 of 7 vehicles in accidents is a commercial vehicle is 0.210, the probability that 1 of 7 is commercial is 0.367, and so on. The values denoted by 0+ represent positive probabilities that are so small that they become 0.000 when rounded to three decimal places. We avoid using 0.000 because it incorrectly suggests an impossible event with a probability of 0.

TABLE 4-1	Probability Distribution for Number of Commercial Vehicles Among Seven Vehicles Involved in Accidents

x	$P(x)$
0	0.210
1	0.367
2	0.275
3	0.115
4	0.029
5	0.004
6	0+
7	0+

Graphs

There are various ways to graph a probability distribution, but we present only the **probability histogram.** Figure 4-3 is a probability histogram that resembles the relative frequency histogram from Chapter 2, but the vertical scale delineates *probabilities* instead of relative frequencies based on actual sample results.

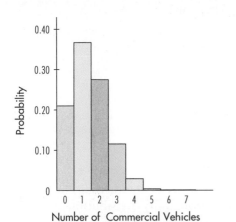

Figure 4-3   Probability Histogram for Number of Commercial Vehicles Among Seven Vehicles Involved in Accidents

Number of Commercial Vehicles Among Seven Vehicles Involved in Accidents

In Figure 4-3, note that along the horizontal axis, the values of 0, 1, 2, . . . , 7 are located at the centres of the rectangles. This implies that the rectangles are each 1 unit wide, so the areas of the rectangles are 0.210, 0.367, and so on. When the total area of such a probability histogram is 1, the *probabilities* are equal to the corresponding rectangular *areas*. We will see in Chapter 5 and future chapters that this correspondence between area and probability is very useful in statistics.

For discrete data every probability distribution must satisfy the following two requirements.

Requirements for a Probability Distribution (for discrete data)
1. $\Sigma P(x) = 1$ where x assumes all possible, distinct values
2. $0 \leq P(x) \leq 1$ for every value of x

The first requirement states that the sum of the individual probabilities must equal 1 and is based on the addition rule for mutually exclusive events. The values of the random variable x represent all possible events in the entire sample space, so we are certain (with probability 1) that one of the events will occur. We use simple addition of the values of $P(x)$ because the different values of x correspond to events that are mutually exclusive. In Table 4-1 we can see that the individual probabilities do result in a sum of 1. Also, the probability rule (see Section 3-2) stating that $0 \leq P(A) \leq 1$ for any event A implies that $P(x)$ must be

Prophets for Profits

Many books and computer programs claim to be helpful in predicting winning lottery numbers. Some use the theory that particular numbers are "due" (and should be selected) because they haven't been coming up often; others use the theory that some numbers are "cold" (and should be avoided) because they haven't been coming up often; and still others use astrology, numerology, or dreams. Because selections of winning lottery number combinations are independent events, such theories are worthless. A valid approach is to choose numbers that are "rare" in the sense that they are not selected by other people, so that if you win, you will not need to share your jackpot with many others. For this reason, the combination of 1, 2, 3, 4, 5, and 6 is a bad choice because many people use it, whereas 12, 17, 18, 33, 40, 46 is a much better choice, at least until it was published in this book.

between 0 and 1 for any value of x. Again, refer to Table 4-1 and note that each individual value of $P(x)$ does fall between 0 and 1. Because Table 4-1 does satisfy both of these requirements, it is an example of a probability distribution. A probability distribution may be described by a table, such as Table 4-1, or a graph, such as Figure 4-3, or a formula, as in the following two examples.

EXAMPLE   Can the formula $P(x) = x/5$ (where x can take on the values of 1, 2, 3) determine a probability distribution?

SOLUTION   If a probability distribution is determined, it must conform to the preceding two requirements. But

$$\Sigma P(x) = P(1) + P(2) + P(3)$$
$$= \frac{1}{5} + \frac{2}{5} + \frac{3}{5}$$
$$= \frac{6}{5} \quad \text{(showing that } \Sigma P(x) \neq 1\text{)}$$

Because the first requirement is not satisfied, we conclude that $P(x)$ given in this example cannot be determining a probability distribution.

EXAMPLE   Can the formula $P(x) = x/3$ (where x can be 1 or 2) determine a probability distribution?

SOLUTION   For the given function, we find that $P(1) = 1/3$ and $P(2) = 2/3$ so that

1. $\Sigma P(x) = \dfrac{1}{3} + \dfrac{2}{3} = \dfrac{3}{3} = 1$

2. Each of the $P(x)$ values is between 0 and 1 inclusive.

Because the two requirements are both satisfied, the $P(x)$ function given in this example is a possible probability distribution.

Mean, Variance, and Standard Deviation

In Chapter 2 we saw that three of the extremely important characteristics of data are:

1. *Centre:* Representative value, such as a mean
2. *Variation:* Measure of scattering or variation, such as a standard deviation
3. *Distribution:* Nature or shape of the distribution, such as bell-shaped

The probability histogram can give us insight into the nature or shape of the distribution. Also, we can often find the mean, variance, and standard deviation of data, which provide insight into the other characteristics. The mean, variance, and standard deviation for a probability distribution can be found by applying Formulas 4-1, 4-2, 4-3, and 4-4.

Formula 4-1 $\mu = \Sigma[x \cdot P(x)]$ Mean for a probability distribution

Formula 4-2 $\sigma^2 = \Sigma[(x - \mu)^2 \cdot P(x)]$ Variance for a probability distribution

Formula 4-3 $\sigma^2 = [\Sigma x^2 \cdot P(x)] - \mu^2$ Variance for a probability distribution

Formula 4-4 $\sigma = \sqrt{[\Sigma x^2 \cdot P(x)] - \mu^2}$ Standard deviation for a probability distribution

Caution: The expression $\Sigma x^2 \cdot P(x)$ is the same as $\Sigma[x^2 \cdot P(x)]$. Evaluate $\Sigma x^2 \cdot P(x)$ by first squaring each value of x, then multiplying each square by the corresponding $P(x)$, then adding.

When using Formulas 4-1 through 4-4, use this rule for rounding results:

Round-Off Rule for μ, σ^2, and σ

Round results by carrying one more decimal place than the number of decimal places used for the random variable x. If the values of x are integers, round μ, σ^2, and σ to one decimal place.

It is sometimes necessary to use a different rounding rule because of special circumstances, such as results that require more decimal places to be meaningful.

When we calculate the mean of a probability distribution, we get the average (mean) value that we would expect to get if the trials could be repeated indefinitely. We *don't* get the value we expect to occur most often. In fact, we often get a mean value that cannot occur in any one actual trial (such as 1.5 girls in 3 births). The standard deviation gives us a measure of how much the probability distribution is spread out around the mean. A large standard deviation reflects considerable spread, whereas a smaller standard deviation reflects lower variability with values relatively closer to the mean. The range rule of thumb (see Section 2-5) may also be helpful in interpreting the value of a standard deviation. According to the range rule of thumb, most values should lie within two standard deviations of the mean; it is unusual for a score to differ from the mean by more than two standard deviations.

● **EXAMPLE**   Table 4-1 represents the probability distribution for the number of commercial vehicles among 7 randomly selected vehicles involved in accidents (assuming that 20% of all registered vehicles are commercial vehicles and that accidents are independent and random events). Using the probability distribution described in Table 4-1, assume that we repeat the procedure of randomly selecting 7 accident vehicles and each time we find the number that are commercial vehicles. Find the mean number of commercial vehicles (among 7), the variance, and the standard deviation. Would it be unusual if 4 of 7 accident vehicles were commercial vehicles?

SOLUTION   In Table 4-2, the two columns at the left describe the probability distribution given earlier in Table 4-1. We create the three columns at the right for the purposes of the calculations required.

Using Formulas 4-1 and 4-3 and the table results, we get

$$\mu = \Sigma[x \cdot P(x)] = 1.398 = 1.4 \text{ commercial vehicles (rounded)}$$
$$\sigma^2 = [\Sigma x^2 \cdot P(x)] - \mu^2$$
$$= 3.066 - 1.398^2 = 1.111596 = 1.1 \text{ commercial vehicles}^2$$
$$\text{(rounded)}$$

TABLE 4-2		Calculating μ, σ^2, and σ for a Probability Distribution		
x	$P(x)$	$x \cdot P(x)$	x^2	$x^2 \cdot P(x)$
0	0.210	0.000	0	0.000
1	0.367	0.367	1	0.367
2	0.275	0.550	4	1.100
3	0.115	0.345	9	1.035
4	0.029	0.116	16	0.464
5	0.004	0.020	25	0.100
6	0+	0.000	36	0.000
7	0+	0.000	49	0.000
Total	1.000	1.398		3.066
	↑	↑		↑
	$\Sigma P(x)$	$\Sigma x \cdot P(x)$		$\Sigma x^2 \cdot P(x)$

The standard deviation is the square root of the variance, so

$$\sigma = \sqrt{1.111596} = 1.054323 = 1.1 \text{ commercial vehicles (rounded)}$$

Interpretation We now know that among 7 accident vehicles, the mean number of commercial vehicles is 1.4, the variance is 1.1 "commercial vehicles squared" and the standard deviation is 1.1 commercial vehicles. Using the range rule of thumb from Section 2-5, we can conclude that most of the time, there should be between 0 and 3.6 commercial vehicles when 7 accident vehicles are randomly selected. (Recall that with the range rule of thumb, we can find rough estimates of minimum and maximum scores by starting with the mean of 1.4 and adding and subtracting 2.2, which is twice the standard deviation.) If, in fact, there were 4 commercial vehicles among 7 accident vehicles, this would appear to be an unusual result.

Rationale for Formulas 4-1 to 4-4

Why do Formulas 4-1 through 4-4 work? A probability distribution is actually a model of a theoretically perfect population frequency distribution. The probability distribution is like a relative frequency distribution based on data that behave perfectly, without the usual imperfections of samples. Because the probability distribution allows us to predict the population of outcomes, we are able to determine the values of the mean, variance, and standard deviation. Formula 4-1 accomplishes the same task as the formula for the mean of a frequency table. (Recall that f represents class frequency and N represents population size.) Rewriting the formula for the mean of a frequency table so that it applies to a population and then changing its form, we get

$$\mu = \frac{\Sigma(f \cdot x)}{N} = \Sigma \frac{f \cdot x}{N} = \Sigma x \cdot \frac{f}{N} = \Sigma x \cdot P(x)$$

In the fraction f/N, the value of f is the frequency with which the value x occurs and N is the population size, so f/N is the probability for the value of x.

Similar reasoning enables us to take the variance formula from Chapter 2 and apply it to a random variable for a probability distribution; the result is Formula 4-2. Formula 4-3 is a shortcut version that will always produce the same result as Formula 4-2. Although Formula 4-3 is usually easier to work with, Formula 4-2 is easier to understand directly. On the basis of Formula 4-2, we can express the standard deviation as

$$\sigma = \sqrt{\Sigma(x - \mu)^2 \cdot P(x)}$$

or as the equivalent form given in Formula 4-4.

Expected Value

The mean of a discrete random variable is the theoretical mean outcome for infinitely many trials. We can think of that mean as the *expected value* in the sense that it is the average value that we would expect to get if the trials could continue indefinitely. The uses of expected value (also called *expectation* or *mathematical expectation*) are extensive and varied, and they play a very important role in an area of application called *decision theory*.

DEFINITION

The **expected value** of a discrete random variable is denoted by E, and it represents the average value of the outcomes. It is found by finding the value of $\Sigma[x \cdot P(x)]$:

$$E = \Sigma[x \cdot P(x)]$$

From Formula 4-1 we see that $E = \mu$. That is, the mean of a discrete random variable is the same as its expected value. Repeat the experiment of flipping a coin five times and the *mean* number of heads is 2.5; when flipping a coin five times, the *expected value* of the number of heads is also 2.5.

Cell Phones Cause Brain Cancer?

In *Discover* magazine, mathematician John Allen Paulos cites the case of a man who sued, claiming that his wife's brain cancer was caused by using a cell phone. That lawsuit attracted considerable media attention and caused a drop in stock prices of cell phone manufacturers.

Paulos concluded that with an annual brain cancer rate of about 0.007%, and with 10 million cell phone users, we expect about 700 brain tumours each year among those who use cell phones. Paulos's conclusion: "Since only a handful have come to public attention, we should conclude that cellular phones might even effectively ward off brain tumours. Absurd, to be sure, but no more so than the reasoning behind the original hysteria." Paulos refers to this as an example of "the psychological obstacles to rational understanding of statistics."

EXAMPLE   Lotteries have become extremely popular with the general public. They might not be so popular with statistics teachers. A ticket in a typical lottery like Lotto 6/49 is usually $1. The probability of winning Lotto 6/49 is 1 in 13,983,816. The payoffs (jackpots) are usually in excess of $1 million. Suppose that you buy one ticket for $1 and the jackpot is $1 million. What is your expected value of gain or loss?

SOLUTION   For this situation there are two simple outcomes: You win or you lose. Your ticket contains one of the 13,983,816 number combinations that could possibly be drawn; your probability of winning is 1/13,983,816 (0.0000000715) and your probability of losing is 13,983,815/13,983,816. Table 4-3 summarizes the situation.

TABLE 4-3	The Numbers Game		
Event	x	$P(x)$	$x \cdot P(x)$
Win	$999,999	0.0000000715	$0.0715
Lose	− $1	0.9999999285	−$0.9999
Total			−$0.93 (or −93¢)

From Table 4-3 we can see that when we buy one ticket for $1, our expected value is

$$E = \Sigma x \cdot P(x) = -93¢$$

Interpretation   This means that in the long run, for each $1 ticket, we can expect to lose an average of 93¢. This is not a very attractive investment scheme. Even if the jackpot were $10 million, the expected value would be −28¢.

In this section we learned that a random variable has a numerical value associated with each outcome of some chance experiment, and a probability distribution has a probability associated with each value of a random variable. We examined methods for finding the mean, variance, and standard deviation for a probability distribution. We saw that the expected value of a random variable is really the same as the mean. We also learned that lotteries are lousy investments.

4-2 Exercises A: Basic Skills and Concepts

In Exercises 1–4, identify the given random variable as being discrete or continuous.

1. The weight of a randomly selected textbook
2. The cost of a randomly selected textbook

3. The number of eggs a hen lays

4. The amount of milk obtained from a cow

In Exercises 5–12, determine whether a probability distribution is given. In those cases where a probability distribution is not described, identify the requirement that is not satisfied. In those cases where a probability distribution is described, find its mean, variance, and standard deviation.

5. When a household is randomly selected, the probability distribution for the number x of automobiles owned is as described in the accompanying table.

x	$P(x)$
0	0.011
1	0.394
2	0.380
3	0.215

6. If your college hires the next 4 employees without regard to gender, and the pool of applicants is large with an equal number of men and women, then the probability distribution for the number x of women hired is described in the accompanying table.

x	$P(x)$
0	0.0625
1	0.2500
2	0.3750
3	0.2500
4	0.0625

7. Statistics Canada found that English is the mother tongue of 62.6% of the residents in the Greater Toronto Area (GTA). A small survey of 8 residents in one area of the GTA will be taken, so the accompanying table describes the probability distribution for the number of residents (among the 8 randomly selected residents) whose mother tongue is English.

x	$P(x)$
0	0.000
1	0.002
2	0.012
3	0.053
4	0.147
5	0.261

8. In assessing credit risks, a bank investigates the number of credit cards people have. With x representing the number of credit cards adults have, the accompanying table describes the probability distribution for a population of applicants (based on data from Maritz Marketing Research, Inc.).

x	$P(x)$
0	0.26
1	0.16
2	0.12
3	0.09
4	0.07
5	0.09
6	0.07
7	0.14

9. The Willford Printing Company conducted a survey to monitor daily absenteeism at the plant. The accompanying table describes the probability distribution for one department at the plant, where x represents the number of employees absent in the department.

x	$P(x)$
0	0.15
1	0.50
2	0.25
3	0.10

10. Big Grack's used car dealership reports that the probabilities of selling 0, 1, 2, 3, 4, and 5 cars in one week are 0.256, 0.239, 0.259, 0.71, and 0.061, respectively.

11. A manufacturing process is continually monitored for defective parts. Every hour 5 samples are taken from the process. Listed here are the number of defective parts in a sample of 5 and the probability associated with each.

Defective	Probability
0	0.5905
1	0.3280
2	0.0729
3	0.0081
4	0.0005
5	0.0000

12. A study of gender bias in television news involves the selection of guests and reporters on CBC's *The National*. The people appearing on air during a certain period are randomly selected in groups of 4 and the numbers of women are recorded. The probabilities of getting 0, 1, 2, 3, and 4 women are 0.4979, 0.3793, 0.1084, 0.0138, and 0.0006, respectively (based on data from NewsWatch Canada).

13. When you give a casino $5 for a bet on the number 7 in roulette, you have a 1/38 probability of winning $175 and a 37/38 probability of losing $5. What is your expected value? In the long run, how much do you lose for each dollar bet?

14. Based on past results found in the *Information Please Almanac*, there is a 0.120 probability that a baseball World Series contest will last four games, a 0.253 probability that it will last five games, a 0.217 probability that it will last six games, and a 0.410 probability that it will last seven games. Find the mean and standard deviation for the numbers of games that World Series contests last. Is it unusual for a team to "sweep" by winning in four games?

15. If the probability of being killed by lightning is 0.000002 for a one-year period, what is the expected value of a one-year insurance policy that would pay $1 million if you are killed by lightning?

16. *Reader's Digest* recently ran a sweepstakes in which prizes were listed along with the chances of winning: $5,000,000 (1 chance in 201,000,000), $150,000 (1 chance in 201,000,000), $100,000 (1 chance in 201,000,000), $25,000 (1 chance in 100,500,000), $10,000 (1 chance in 50,250,000), $5000 (1 chance in 25,125,000), $200 (1 chance in 8,040,000), $125 (1 chance in 1,005,000), and a watch valued at $89 (1 chance in 3774).
    a. Find the expected value of the amount won for one entry.
    b. Find the expected value if the cost of entering this sweepstakes is the cost of a postage stamp.

17. The random variable x represents the number of girls in a family of 3 children. (*Hint:* Assuming that boys and girls are equally likely, we get $P(2) = 3/8$ by examining this sample space: bbb, bbg, bgb, bgg, gbb, gbg, ggb, ggg.) Find the mean, variance, and standard deviation for the random variable x. Also, use the range rule of thumb (from Section 2-5) to approximate the minimum and maximum usual values of x.

18. The random variable x represents the number of boys in a family of 4 children. (See Exercise 17.) Find the mean, variance, and standard deviation for the random variable x. Also, use the range rule of thumb (from Section 2-5) to approximate the usual minimum and maximum values of x.

19. The Don Mills Electronics Company makes switching devices for traffic signals. One batch of 10 switches includes 2 that are defective. If 2 switches are randomly selected from that batch without replacement, let the random variable x represent the number that are defective. Find the mean, variance, and standard deviation for the random variable x.

20. A statistics class includes 3 left-handed students and 24 right-handed students. Two different students are randomly selected for a data collection project and the random variable x represents the number of left-handed students selected. Find the mean, variance, and standard deviation for the random variable x. (*Hint:* Use the multiplication rule of probability to first find $P(0)$ and $P(2)$.)

4–2 Exercises B: Beyond the Basics

21. In each case, determine whether the given function is a probability distribution.
    a. $P(x) = 1/2^x$ where $x = 1, 2, 3, \ldots$
    b. $P(x) = 1/2x$ where $x = 1, 2, 3, \ldots$
    c. $P(x) = 3/[4(3 - x)!x!]$ where $x = 0, 1, 2, 3$
    d. $P(x) = 0.4(0.6)^{x-1}$ where $x = 1, 2, 3, \ldots$

22. The mean and standard deviation for a random variable x are 5.0 and 2.0, respectively. Find the mean and standard deviation if
    a.   each value of x is increased by 3.
    b.   each value of x is multiplied times 3.
    c.   each value of x is multiplied times 3 and then 4 is added.

23. Digits $(0, 1, 2, \ldots, 9)$ are randomly selected for telephone numbers in surveys. The random variable x is the selected digit.
    a.   Find the mean and standard deviation of x.
    b.   Find the z score for each of the possible values of x, then find the mean and standard deviation of the population of z scores.
    c.   Will the same mean and standard deviation as you found in part (b) result from every probability distribution?

24. Assume that the discrete random variable x can assume the values 1, 2, $\ldots, n$, and that those values are equally likely.
    a.   Show that $\mu = (n + 1)/2$.
    b.   Show that $\sigma^2 = (n^2 - 1)/12$.
        (*Hint:* $1 + 2 + 3 + \cdots + n = n(n + 1)/2$ and
        $1^2 + 2^2 + 3^2 + \cdots + n^2 = n(n + 1)(2n + 1)/6$)
    c.   An experiment consists of randomly selecting a whole number between 1 and 50, and the random variable x is the value of the number selected. Find the mean and standard deviation for x.

25. Let the random variable x represent the number of girls in a family of four children. Construct a table describing the probability distribution, then find the mean and standard deviation. (*Hint:* Begin by listing the different possible outcomes.)

4-3 Binomial Probability Distributions

In Section 4-2 we learned that a random variable has a numerical value associated with each outcome of some chance procedure, and a probability distribution has a probability associated with each value of a random variable. In this section we will focus on one specific type of probability distribution: the *binomial distribution*. Binomial probability distributions are important because they allow us to deal with circumstances in which the outcomes belong to either of *two* relevant categories. In manufacturing, parts either fail or they do not. In medicine, a patient either survives a year or does not. In advertising, a consumer either recognizes a product or does not.

DEFINITION

A **binomial probability distribution** results from a procedure that meets all the following requirements:

1. The procedure has a *fixed number of trials (such as 7 coin tosses, or 20 responses to a survey question).*
2. The trials must be *independent*. (The outcome of any individual trial doesn't affect the probabilities in the other trials.)
3. The outcome of each trial must be classifiable into one of *two possible categories*.
4. The probabilities must remain *constant* for each trial.

If a procedure satisfies these four requirements, the distribution of the random variable x is called a *binomial probability distribution* (or *binomial distribution*). The following notation is commonly used.

Notation for Binomial Distributions

S and F (success and failure) denote the two possible categories of all outcomes; p and q will denote the probabilities of S and F, respectively, so

$$P(S) = p \qquad (p = \text{probability of a success})$$

$$P(F) = 1 - p = q \qquad (q = \text{probability of a failure})$$

n denotes the fixed number of trials.

x denotes a specific number of successes in n trials, so x can be any whole number between 0 and n, inclusive.

p denotes the probability of success in *one* of the n trials.

q denotes the probability of failure in *one* of the n trials.

$P(x)$ denotes the probability of getting exactly x successes among the n trials.

The word *success* as used here is arbitrary and does not necessarily describe a desired result. Either of the two possible categories may be called the success S as long as the corresponding probability is identified as p. (The value of q can always be found by subtracting p from 1; if $p = 0.95$, then $q = 1 - 0.95 = 0.05$.) Once a category has been designated as the success S, be sure that p is the probability of a success and x is the number of successes. That is, **be sure that the values of p and x refer to the same category designated as a success.**

One very common application of statistics involves sampling without replacement, as in testing manufactured items or conducting surveys. Strictly speaking, sampling without replacement involves dependent events, which violates the second requirement in the preceding definition. However, the following rule of thumb is based on the fact that if the sample is very small relative to the population size, the difference in results will be negligible if we treat the trials as independent when they are actually dependent.

When sampling without replacement, the events can be considered to be independent if the sample size is no more than 5% of the population size. (That is, $n \leq 0.05N$.)

EXAMPLE   Five percent of the population of Toronto speaks Italian. Find the probability of getting, in a random sample of 15 Toronto residents, exactly 3 residents who speak Italian.

a. Is this a binomial experiment?

b. If this is a binomial experiment, identify the values of n, x, p, and q.

SOLUTION

a. This experiment does satisfy the requirements for a binomial experiment, as shown below:

1. The number of trials (15) is fixed.
2. The trials are independent because one resident speaking Italian doesn't affect the probability of any other randomly selected resident speaking Italian.
3. Each trial has two categories of outcomes: the resident either speaks Italian or does not.
4. The probability of selecting an Italian-speaking resident (0.05) remains constant from trial to trial.

b. Having concluded that the experiment is binomial, we now proceed to identify the values of n, x, p, and q:

1. With 15 residents, we have $n = 15$.
2. We want 3 residents who speak Italian (successes), so $x = 3$.
3. The probability of a resident who speaks Italian (success) is 0.05, so $p = 0.05$.
4. The probability of failure (a resident who does not speak Italian) is 0.95, so $q = 0.95$.

Afraid to Fly?

Many of us tend to overestimate the probability of death from events that make headlines, such as jet crashes, murders, or terrorist attacks. Polls and fatality statistics show that although travel is becoming safer, people are now becoming more fearful of flying than they were in the past. In travelling across North America, your chances of dying are about 1 out of 11 million for a commercial jet, 1 out of 900,000 for a train, and 1 out of 14,000 for a car.

Again, it is very important to be sure that both x and p refer to the same concept of "success." In this example, we use x to count the desired number of residents who speak Italian, and p is the probability of getting a resident who speaks Italian, so x and p do use the same concept of success.

In this section we present three methods for finding probabilities in a binomial experiment. The first method involves calculations using the *binomial probability formula* and is the basis for the other two methods. The second method involves the use of Table A-1, and the third method involves the use of statistical software. (If your instructor is requiring technology-based solutions (Method 3), we recommend that you also work through some examples using Method 1 and Method 2, to ensure you understand the basis for the calculations.)

Method 1: Use the Binomial Probability Formula   In a binomial distribution, probabilities can be calculated by using the **binomial probability formula**:

Formula 4-5 $$P(x) = \frac{n!}{(n-x)!x!} \cdot p^x \cdot q^{n-x} \quad \text{for } x = 0, 1, 2, \ldots, n$$

where n = number of trials

x = number of successes among n trials

p = probability of success in any one trial

q = probability of failure in any one trial ($q = 1 - p$)

The factorial symbol !, introduced in Section 3-6, denotes the product of decreasing factors. Two examples of factorials are $3! = 3 \cdot 2 \cdot 1 = 6$ and $0! = 1$ (by definition). Many calculators have a factorial key, as well as a key labelled $_nC_r$ that can simplify the computations. For calculators with the $_nC_r$ key, use this version of the binomial probability formula (where n, x, p, and q are the same as in Formula 4-5):

$$P(x) = {_nC_x} \cdot p^x \cdot q^{n-x}$$

EXAMPLE   Five percent of the population of Toronto speaks Italian. Use the binomial probability formula to find the probability of getting, in a random sample of 15 Toronto residents, 3 residents who speak Italian. That is, find $P(3)$, given that $n = 15$, $x = 3$, $p = 0.05$, and $q = 0.95$.

SOLUTION   Using the given values of n, x, p, and q in the binomial probability formula (Formula 4-5), we get

$$P(3) = \frac{15!}{(15-3)!3!} \cdot 0.05^3 \cdot 0.95^{15-3}$$

$$= \frac{15!}{12!3!} \cdot 0.000125 \cdot 0.5403601$$

$$= (455)(0.000125)(0.5403601) = 0.031$$

The probability that exactly 3 of 15 residents will speak Italian is .031.

Calculation hint: When computing a probability with the binomial probability formula, it's helpful to get a single number for $n!/(n-x)!x!$, a single number for p^x, and a single number for q^{n-x}, then simply multiply the three factors together. Don't round too much when you find those three factors; round only at the end.

Method 2: Use Table A-1 in Appendix A

In some cases, we can easily find binomial probabilities by simply referring to Table A-1 in Appendix A. First locate n and the corresponding value of x that is desired. At this stage, one row of numbers should be isolated. Now align that row with the proper probability of p by using the column across the top. The isolated number represents the desired probability. A very small probability, such as 0.000000345, is indicated by 0+.

Shown in the margin is part of Table A-1. When $n = 15$ and $p = 0.05$ in a binomial experiment, the probabilities of $0, 1, 2, \ldots, 15$ successes are 0.463, 0.366, 0.135, \ldots, 0+, respectively.

EXAMPLE   In the preceding example, we used the binomial probability formula to find the probability of 3 successes, given that $n = 15, x = 3$, $p = 0.05$, and $q = 0.95$. Use the portion of Table A-1 shown in the margin to find

a. The probability of exactly 3 successes
b. The probability of *at least* 3 successes

SOLUTION

a. The display from Table A-1 shows that when $n = 15$ and $p = 0.05$, $P(3) = 0.031$, which is the same value computed with the binomial probability formula in the preceding example.

b. $P(\text{at least } 3) = P(3 \text{ or } 4 \text{ or } 5 \text{ or } \ldots \text{ or } 15)$
$= P(3) + P(4) + P(5) + \cdots + P(15)$
$= 0.031 + 0.005 + 0.001 + \cdots + 0$
$= 0.037$

In part (b) of the preceding solution, if we wanted to find $P(\text{at least } 3)$ by using the binomial probability formula, we would need to apply that formula 13 times to compute 13 different probabilities, which would then be added. (A shortcut would be to calculate $P(0)$, $P(1)$, and $P(2)$ and subtract their sum from 1, but even this shortcut would take much longer than using Table A-1.) Given this choice between the formula and the table, it makes sense to use the table. Note, however, that Table A-1 includes only limited values of n as well as limited values of p, so the table doesn't always work. We must then find the probabilities by using the binomial probability formula or software.

From Table A-1:

n	x	p .05
15	0	463
	1	366
	2	135
	3	031
	4	005
	5	001
	6	0+
	7	0+
	8	0+
	9	0+
	10	0+
	11	0+
	12	0+
	13	0+
	14	0+
	15	0+

Binomial probability distribution for $n = 15$ and $p = 0.05$

x	$P(x)$
0	0.463
1	0.366
2	0.135
3	0.031
4	0.005
5	0.001
6	0+
7	0+
8	0+
9	0+
10	0+
11	0+
12	0+
13	0+
14	0+
15	0+

Method 3: Use Computer Software Many computer statistics packages and some calculators include an option for generating binomial probabilities. For the details of using Excel or STATDISK, see the Using Technology segment at the end of this section. Your instructor may prefer that you look instead at specific instructions for using Minitab, SPSS, or other such tools.

In general, the following is a good strategy for choosing the best method for finding binomial probabilities:

1. Use computer software or a calculator, if available.
2. If a computer cannot be used, use Table A-1 if possible.
3. If a computer cannot be used and the probabilities can't be found using Table A-1, use the binomial probability formula.

In Section 4-2 we presented Table 4-1 as an example of a probability distribution. The following example illustrates that the probabilities are binomial.

> **EXAMPLE** At the beginning of this chapter we noted that commercial vehicles accounted for 20% of all vehicles registered for the road in Canada and considered a situation in which such vehicles constituted 4 of 7 accident vehicles on a certain stretch of road. We assume that vehicle accidents are independent and random events, and also that commercial vehicles are as safe as any other type of vehicle. Find the probability that when there are 7 motor vehicles in accidents, 4 of them are commercial vehicles.
>
> **SOLUTION** This is a binomial experiment because of the following:
>
> 1. We have a fixed number of trials (7).
> 2. The trials are assumed to be independent.
> 3. There are two categories: Each vehicle either is a commercial vehicle or is not.
> 4. The probability of a selected vehicle being a commercial vehicle (considered a "success" in this example) is 0.20 (because 20% of all vehicles registered are commercial), and it remains a constant for each trial. (We are assuming that accidents are independent and random.)
>
> We begin by identifying the values of n, p, q, and x. We have
>
> | | |
> |---|---|
> | $n = 7$ | Number of trials (accident vehicles) |
> | $p = 0.20$ | Probability of success (an accident vehicle is a commercial vehicle) |
> | $q = 0.80$ | Probability of failure (an accident vehicle is not a commercial vehicle) |
> | $x = 4$ | Number of commercial vehicles among 7 |
>
> Referring to Table A-1 with $n = 7$, $p = 0.20$, and $x = 4$, we find that $P(4) = 0.029$. That is, there is a 0.029 probability that among 7 accident vehicles, exactly 4 are commercial vehicles.

Asking the Right Question

The low probability (0.029) that we found in the preceding example might seem to suggest that it is unlikely that commercial vehicles are operating as safely as other vehicles (because they are overrepresented among the accident vehicles). But are we really addressing the correct issue? Is there another question that better addresses the real issue of whether commercial vehicles are unsafe? Here are some possibilities:

1. What is the probability that *at least* 4 out of 7 accident vehicles are commercial vehicles?
2. What is the probability that any single vehicle type (with 20% of total vehicle registrations) will constitute *exactly* 4 out of 7 accident vehicles?
3. What is the probability that *any* single vehicle type (with 20% of total vehicle registrations) will constitute at least 4 out of 7 accident vehicles?

We eliminate the first question because the real issue concerns the likelihood of *any* vehicle type constituting 4 of 7 accident vehicles. To clarify this point, consider your local lottery in which *your* individual chance of winning is extremely small, but the probability of *somebody* winning is fairly high. When someone does win, we don't conclude that this individual had a better chance than anyone else. Similarly, an accident involving a commercial vehicle doesn't necessarily mean that this type of vehicle isn't as safe as others; like winning the lottery, the accident might be the result of random events that affect all vehicles the same way. We therefore need to find the probability of *any* type of vehicle showing up as 4 out of 7 randomly selected accident vehicles, assuming that each type of vehicle represents 20% of total vehicle registrations.

Next, we should eliminate the second question in our list because it refers to *exactly* 4 accident vehicles out of 7. Our real concern is not the likelihood of getting any specific number of accidents. Instead, the issue rests on the likelihood of getting an outcome *at least as extreme* as the one observed. This is a difficult concept, so let's try to clarify it with another example.

Suppose you were flipping a coin to determine whether it favours heads, and suppose 1000 tosses resulted in 501 heads. Intuition should suggest that this is not evidence that the coin favours heads, because it is quite easy to get 501 heads in 1000 tosses. Yet, the probability of getting exactly 501 heads in 1000 tosses is actually quite small: 0.0252. This low probability reflects the fact that with 1000 tosses, *any specific* number of heads will have a very low probability. However, the result of 501 heads among 1000 tosses is not *unusual* because the probability of getting *at least* 501 heads is high: 0.488.

Similarly, we should be asking for the probability of *at least* 4 accidents, not the probability of exactly 4. That is, we need to find the probability that any single vehicle type (with 20% of total vehicle registrations) will constitute at least 4 of 7 vehicles involved in accidents. If that probability is very low (such as 0.05 or less), it is reasonable to conclude that commercial vehicles are not being operated safely, but if it is high (such as greater than 0.05), it is reasonable to conclude that accidents involving commercial vehicles are a coincidence. First

How Likely Is an Asteroid Strike?

NASA astronomer David Morrison says that there are about 2000 asteroids with orbits that cross Earth's orbit, yet we have found only 100 of them. It's therefore possible for an undetected asteroid to crash into our planet and cause a global catastrophe that could destroy most life. Morrison says that there is a 1/10,000 probability that within a person's lifetime, there will be an asteroid impact large enough to wipe out all agricultural crops for at least a year, with mass starvation following. Some astronomers recommend a 20-year program aimed at observing asteroids with the goal of early detection of those that are dangerous. Early detection could possibly allow us to alter an asteroid's course so that it isn't a fatal threat.

we find the probability of commercial vehicles constituting at least 4 out of 7 accident vehicles. We refer to Table A-1 (with $n = 7$, $p = 0.20$, $x = 4, 5, 6, 7$):

$$
\begin{aligned}
P(\text{commercial vehicles constituting} \\
\text{at least 4 of 7 accident vehicles}) \quad &= P(4) + P(5) + P(6) + P(7) \\
&= 0.029 + 0.004 + 0^+ + 0^+ \\
&= 0.033
\end{aligned}
$$

But suppose there are five different types of vehicles (denoted by A, B, C, D, E), each with 20% of the total motor vehicle registrations. The probability of *any one* of them constituting 4 of 7 vehicles involved in an accident is found by using the addition rule for mutually exclusive events. (The events are mutually exclusive, because only one type of vehicle could constitute 4 of 7 vehicles selected.)

$$
\begin{aligned}
P(\text{A or B or C or D or E}) &= P(\text{A}) + P(\text{B}) + P(\text{C}) + P(\text{D}) + P(\text{E}) \\
&= 0.033 + 0.033 + 0.033 + 0.033 + 0.033 \\
&= 0.165
\end{aligned}
$$

This probability suggests that is hardly rare (it happens over 16% of the time) to have some vehicle type or other constitute 4 of 7 randomly selected accident vehicles, assuming each of the vehicle-type alternatives represents 20% of vehicle registrations. We would not have expected *in advance* that those 4 of 7 would be commercial vehicles (just as I do not really expect to win the next lottery, even though *someone* might win), but it could easily be a coincidence that, yes, some vehicle type constituted 4 of the selected 7 accident vehicles—and it just happened, this time, to be commercial vehicles. (Part of our problem is working with such a small sample.) This analysis is not simple, but it illustrates an important principle: **We should take great care to ask the questions that correctly identify the real issue.**

Rationale for the Binomial Probability Formula

The binomial probability formula is the basis for all three methods presented in this section. Instead of blindly accepting and using that formula, let us see why it works.

In the preceding example we wanted the probability of getting 4 successes among the 7 trials, given a 0.20 probability of success in any one trial. It's correct to reason that for 4 successes among 7 trials, there must be 3 failures. A common error is to find the probability of 4 successes and 3 failures as follows:

4 successes   3 failures

$$(0.20 \cdot 0.20 \cdot 0.20 \cdot 0.20) \cdot (0.80 \cdot 0.80 \cdot 0.80) = 0.000819$$

This calculation is *wrong* because it assumes that the *first* 4 outcomes are successes and the *last* 3 are failures. However, the 4 successes and 3 failures can occur in many different sequences, not only the one given above. In fact, there are 35 different sequences of 4 successes and 3 failures, each with a probability of 0.000819, so the correct probability is $35 \cdot 0.000819 = 0.029$, as we have found. In general, the number of ways in which it is possible to arrange x successes and $n - x$ failures is shown in Formula 4-6:

Formula 4-6 $\quad \dfrac{n!}{(n - x)!x!} \quad$ Number of outcomes with exactly x successes among n trials

The expression given in Formula 4-6 is from Section 3-6. (Coverage of Section 3-6 is not required for this chapter.) Combining this counting device (Formula 4-6) with the direct application of the multiplication rule for independent events results in the binomial probability formula:

The number of outcomes with   The probability of x successes among
exactly x successes among n trials n trials for any 1 particular order

$$P(x) = \frac{n!}{(n - x)!x!} \cdot p^x \cdot q^{n - x}$$

To keep this section in perspective, remember that the binomial probability formula is only one of many probability formulas that can be used for different situations. It is often used in applications such as quality control, voter analysis, medical research, military intelligence, and advertising. Although the main focus of this section is the binomial distribution, other distributions can be found in Exercises 33–35 and Section 4-5.

Using Technology

Excel: In Excel it is possible—but usually not necessary—to reproduce a full binomial probability distribution table for all values of x, for a given n and p. Simply click on *fx* on the toolbar, and select the function category **Statistical** and then the function name **BINOMDIST**. In the dialog box, enter the number of successes x, as well as the values of n (number of trials), and p (the probability of success each trial), plus 0 for the binomial distribution (instead of 1 for the cumulative binomial distribution). The probability value for *exactly x* successes will be displayed. If, instead, you enter a 1 for the cumulative binomial distribution, the value returned is the probability of *up to or including x* successes. (*Hint*: For the probability of "at least x successes," interpret as: 1 − [the probability of "*up to or including* (x − 1) successes"].)

STATDISK: Select **Analysis** from the main menu, then select the **Binomial Probabilities** option. Enter the requested values for n and p, and the entire probability distribution will be displayed. Other columns represent cumulative probabilities obtained by adding the values $P(x)$ as you go down, or up, the column.

Excel Display   Binomial
Probabilities

Statdisk Display   Binomial
Probabilities

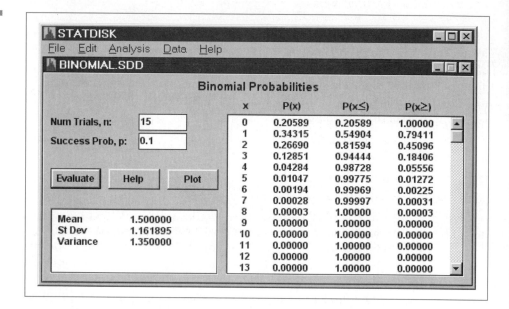

4-3 Exercises A: Basic Skills and Concepts

In Exercises 1–8, determine whether the given experiments are binomial. For those that are not binomial, identify at least one requirement that is not satisfied.

1. Rolling a die 50 times
2. Tossing an unbiased coin 200 times
3. Tossing a biased coin 200 times
4. Surveying 1000 Canadian consumers by asking each one if the brand name Tilley Endurables is recognized
5. Spinning a roulette wheel 500 times

6. Surveying 1067 people by asking each one if he or she voted in the last election
7. Sampling (without replacement) a randomly selected group of 12 different tires from a population of 30 tires that includes 5 that are defective
8. Surveying 2000 television viewers to determine whether they can recall a particular product name after watching a commercial

In Exercises 9–12, assume that in a procedure that yields a binomial distribution, a trial is repeated n times. Find the probability of x successes given the probability p of success on a given trial. (Use the given values of n, x, and p and Table A-1.)

9. $n = 3, x = 2, p = 0.9$
11. $n = 8, x = 7, p = 0.99$
10. $n = 2, x = 0, p = 0.6$
12. $n = 6, x = 1, p = 0.05$

In Exercises 13–16, assume that in a procedure that yields a binomial distribution, a trial is repeated n times. Find the probability of x successes given the probability p of success on a single trial. Use the given values of n, x, and p and the binomial probability formula or statistical software.

13. $n = 3, x = 2, p = 1/4$
15. $n = 10, x = 4, p = 0.35$
14. $n = 6, x = 2, p = 1/3$
16. $n = 8, x = 6, p = 0.85$

In Exercises 17–20, refer to the table in the margin for n = 8 and p = 0.381. When a car buyer is selected at random, there is a 0.381 probability that he or she bought a used car (based on data from a CAA members' survey). In each case, assume that 8 buyers are randomly selected and find the indicated probability.

x	$P(X = x)$
0	0.021554
1	0.106133
2	0.228640
3	0.281460
4	0.216551
5	0.106631
6	0.032816
7	0.005771
8	0.000444

17. Find the probability that 6 car buyers bought a used car.
18. Find the probability that at least 5 car buyers bought used cars.
19. Find the probability that fewer than 7 car buyers bought used cars.
20. Find the probability that more than 4 car buyers bought used cars.

In Exercises 21–32, find the probability requested.

21. Assume that male and female births are equally likely and that the birth of any child does not affect the probability of the gender of any other children. Find the probability of
    a. Exactly 4 girls in 10 births.
    b. At least 4 girls in 10 births.
    c. Exactly 8 girls in 20 births.
22. According to a market-share study, 13% of televisions in use are tuned to *Hockey Night in Canada* on Saturday night. Assume that an advertiser wants to verify that 13% market share value by conducting its own survey, and a pilot survey begins with 20 households having TV sets in use at the time of a *Hockey Night in Canada* broadcast.
    a. Find the probability that none of the households are tuned to *Hockey Night in Canada*.
    b. Find the probability that at least one of the households is tuned to *Hockey Night in Canada*.

    c. Find the probability that at most one household is tuned to *Hockey Night in Canada*.

    d. Suppose at most one household is tuned to *Hockey Night in Canada*. Does it appear that the claimed 13% share value is mistaken? Why or why not?

23. Mars, Inc., claims that 20% of its plain M&M candies are red. Find the probability that when 15 plain M&M candies are randomly selected, exactly 20% (or 3 candies) are red.

24. In a market study for Zellers, a researcher found that 76% of customers are repeat customers. If 12 customers are selected at random, find the probability that at least 11 of them are repeat customers. Suppose at least 11 of the 12 are repeat customers; does it appear that the 76% value found in the study is too low? Why or why not?

25. A statistics quiz consists of 10 multiple-choice questions, each with 5 possible answers. For someone who makes random guesses for all of the answers, find the probability of passing if the minimum passing grade is 60%. Is the probability high enough to make it worth the risk of passing by random guesses instead of by studying?

26. A regional airline has a policy of booking as many as 15 persons on an airplane that can seat only 14. (Past studies have revealed that only 85% of the booked passengers actually arrive for the flight.) Find the probability that if the airline books 15 persons, not enough seats will be available.

27. In a survey, the Canadian Automobile Association (CAA) found that 6.1% of its members bought their cars at a used-car lot. If 15 CAA members are selected at random, what is the probability that 4 of them bought their cars at a used-car lot?

28. Deloitte & Touche surveyed British Columbia's top CEOs. According to the survey, 82% of the respondents have a computer on their desk. Suppose that a conference is being arranged in Montreal for 9 of these CEOs. Unfortunately there are only 7 computers available for their workstations. Find the probability that more computers will be needed for the CEOs. Is that probability high enough so that plans should be initiated to provide more computers?

29. A quality control manager at the Don Mills Electronics Company knows that his company has been making surge protectors with a 10% rate of defective units. He has instituted several measures designed to lower that defect rate. In a test of 20 randomly selected surge protectors, only one is found to be defective. If the 10% defect rate hasn't changed, find the probability that among 20 units, 1 or none is defective. Based on the result, does it appear that the newly instituted measures are effective?

30. The Telektronic Company purchases large shipments of fluorescent bulbs and uses this *acceptance sampling* plan: Randomly select and test 24 bulbs, then accept the whole batch if there is only 1 or none that doesn't work. If a particular shipment of thousands of bulbs actually has a 4% rate of defects, what is the probability that this whole shipment will be accepted?

31. A survey of college statistics students shows that 30% of the students who show up for their 8:00 A.M. classes are late. One statistics professor reports that among 15 of her students selected at random, only 3 were late for her 8:00 A.M. class. Find the probability that this number will be that low. That is, find the probability of getting 3 or fewer students late for class when 15 are selected at random. Based on the result, is the professor's result likely to occur by chance?

32. Nine percent of men and 0.25% of women cannot distinguish between the colours red and green. This is the type of colour blindness that causes problems with traffic signals. If six men are randomly selected for a study of traffic signal perceptions, find the probability that exactly two of them cannot distinguish between red and green.

4–3 Exercises B: Beyond the Basics

33. If a procedure meets all the conditions of a binomial distribution except that the number of trials is not fixed, then the **geometric distribution** can be used. The probability of getting the first success on the xth trial is given by $P(x) = p(1 - p)^{x-1}$ where p is the probability of success on any one trial. Assume that the probability of a defective computer component is 0.2. Find the probability that the first defect is found in the seventh component tested.

34. If we sample from a small finite population without replacement, the binomial distribution should not be used because the events are not independent. If sampling is done without replacement and the outcomes belong to one of two types, we can use the **hypergeometric distribution**. If a population has A objects of one type, while the remaining B objects are of the other type, and if n objects are sampled without replacement, then the probability of getting x objects of type A and $n - x$ objects of type B is

$$P(x) = \frac{A!}{(A - x)!x!} \cdot \frac{B!}{(B - n + x)!(n - x)!} \div \frac{(A + B)!}{(A + B - n)!n!}$$

In Lotto 6/49, a bettor selects 6 numbers from 1 to 49 (without repetition), and a winning 6-number combination is later randomly selected. Find the probability of getting
a. All 6 winning numbers.
b. Exactly 5 of the winning numbers.
c. Exactly 3 of the winning numbers.
d. No winning numbers.

35. The binomial distribution applies only to cases involving 2 types of outcomes, whereas the **multinomial distribution** involves more than 2 categories. Suppose we have 3 types of mutually exclusive outcomes denoted by A, B, and C. Let $P(A) = p_1$, $P(B) = p_2$, and $P(C) = p_3$. In n independent trials, the probability of x_1 outcomes of type A, x_2 outcomes of type B, and x_3 outcomes of type C is given by

$$\frac{n!}{(x_1!)(x_2!)(x_3!)} \cdot p_1^{x_1} \cdot p_2^{x_2} \cdot p_3^{x_3}$$

A genetics experiment involves 6 mutually exclusive genotypes identified as A, B, C, D, E, and F, and they are all equally likely. If 20 offspring are tested, find the probability of getting exactly 5 As, 4 Bs, 3 Cs, 2 Ds, 3 Es, and 3 Fs by expanding the above expression so that it applies to 6 types of outcomes instead of only 3.

4-4 Mean, Variance, and Standard Deviation for the Binomial Distribution

In Chapter 2 we explored actual collections of real data and identified these three important characteristics: (1) the measure of centre, (2) the measure of variation, and (3) the nature of the distribution. A key point of this chapter is that probability distributions describe what will *probably* happen instead of what actually did happen. In Section 4-2, we learned methods for analysing probability distributions by finding the mean, the standard deviation, and a probability histogram. Because a binomial distribution is a special type of probability distribution, we could use Formulas 4-1, 4-3, and 4-4 (from Section 4-2) for finding the mean, variance, and standard deviation. Fortunately, those formulas can be greatly simplified for binomial distributions, as shown below.

For Any Probability Distribution:

Formula 4-1 $\mu = \Sigma[x \cdot P(x)]$

Formula 4-3 $\sigma^2 = [\Sigma x^2 \cdot P(x)] - \mu^2$

Formula 4-4 $\sigma = \sqrt{[\Sigma x^2 \cdot P(x)] - \mu^2}$

For Binomial Distributions:

Formula 4-7 $\mu = n \cdot p$

Formula 4-8 $\sigma^2 = n \cdot p \cdot q$

Formula 4-9 $\sigma = \sqrt{n \cdot p \cdot q}$

Formula 4-7 for the mean makes sense intuitively. If we were to analyse 100 births, we would expect to get about 50 girls, and $n \cdot p$ becomes $100 \cdot 1/2$, or 50. In general, if we consider p to be the proportion of successes, then the product $n \cdot p$ will give us the actual number of expected successes in n trials. The variance and standard deviation are not so easily justified, and we prefer to omit the complicated algebraic manipulations that lead to Formulas 4-8 and 4-9. Instead, the following example illustrates that for a binomial experiment, Formulas 4-7, 4-8, and 4-9 will produce the same results as Formulas 4-1, 4-3, and 4-4.

EXAMPLE   In Section 4-3 we confirmed that the Chapter Problem is really based on the binomial distribution, and Table 4-1 represents a binomial probability distribution for the numbers of commercial vehicles among 7 accident vehicles, randomly selected (assuming that commercial vehicles represent 20% of all registered vehicles on public roads, and that vehicles are "selected" randomly and independently for involvement in accidents). In Section 4-2, we used Formulas 4-1, 4-3, and 4-4 (see Table 4-2) to find these values for the mean, variance, and standard deviation: $\mu = 1.4$ commercial vehicles, $\sigma^2 = 1.1$ "commercial vehicles squared," and $\sigma = 1.1$ commercial vehicles. But given the values we found in

Section 4-3 for this distribution ($n = 7$, $p = .20$, and $q = .80$), we can now use Formulas 4-7, 4-8, and 4-9 to find the mean, variance, and standard deviation. Verify that the results are the same as those obtained by using Formulas 4-1, 4-3, and 4-4.

SOLUTION   Using the values of $n = 7$, $p = 0.20$, and $q = 0.80$, Formulas 4-7, 4-8, and 4-9 provide these results:

$$\mu = n \cdot p = (7)(0.20) = 1.4$$
$$\sigma^2 = n \cdot p \cdot q = (7)(0.20)(0.80) = 1.1 \quad \text{(rounded)}$$
$$\sigma = \sqrt{n \cdot p \cdot q}$$
$$= \sqrt{(7)(0.20)(0.80)} = \sqrt{1.12} = 1.1 \quad \text{(rounded)}$$

These results show that when we have a binomial experiment, Formulas 4-7, 4-8, and 4-9 will produce the same results as Formulas 4-1, 4-3, and 4-4. (There may be small discrepancies in the unrounded values, due to rounding errors in Table 4-2.)

EXAMPLE   Some couples prefer to have baby girls because the mothers are carriers of an X-linked recessive disorder that will be inherited by 50% of their sons but none of their daughters. The Ericsson method of gender selection supposedly has a 75% success rate. Suppose 100 couples use the Ericsson method, with the result that among 100 babies, there are 75 girls.

a. Assuming that the Ericsson method has no effect and assuming that boys and girls are equally likely, find the mean and standard deviation for the number of girls in groups of 100 babies. (The assumption that girls and boys are equally likely is not precisely correct, but it will give us very good results.)

b. Interpret the values from part (a) to determine whether the result of 75 girls among 100 babies supports a claim that the Ericsson method is effective.

SOLUTION

a. Let x represent the random variable for the number of girls in 100 births. Assuming that the Ericsson method has no effect and that girls and boys are equally likely, we have $n = 100$, $p = 0.5$, and $q = 0.5$. We can find the mean and standard deviation by using Formulas 4-7 and 4-9 as follows:

$$\mu = n \cdot p = (100)(0.5) = 50$$
$$\sigma = \sqrt{n \cdot p \cdot q} = \sqrt{(100)(0.5)(0.5)} = 5$$

For groups of 100 couples who each have a baby, the mean number of girls is 50 and the standard deviation is 5.

b. We must now interpret the results to determine whether 75 girls among 100 babies is a result that could easily occur by chance, or

---

Disease Clusters

Periodically, much media attention is given to a cluster of disease cases in a given community. Research of such clusters can be revealing. A study of a cluster of cancer cases near African asbestos mines led to the discovery that asbestos fibres can be carcinogenic.

When doing such an analysis, we should avoid the mistake of artificially creating a cluster by locating its outer boundary so that it just barely includes cases of disease or death. That would be like gerrymandering, even though it might be unintentional.

whether that result is so unlikely that the Ericsson method of gender selection seems to be effective. We will use the range rule of thumb and the empirical rule, both from Section 2-5.

According to the range rule of thumb, rough estimates of the minimum and maximum scores are as follows:

minimum "usual" value ≈ (mean) − 2 × (standard deviation)
= 50 − 2(5) = 40

maximum "usual" value ≈ (mean) + 2 × (standard deviation)
= 50 + 2(5) = 60

Interpretation The range rule of thumb indicates that typical scores are probably between 40 and 60, so 75 girls seems to be a result that is not very likely to occur by chance and may possibly indicate that the Ericsson method is effective.

It is helpful to develop the technical skill to calculate means and standard deviations, but it is especially important to develop an ability to interpret the significance of values of means and standard deviations, as shown in part (b) of the preceding example.

4-4 Exercises A: Basic Skills and Concepts

In Exercises 1–4, find the mean μ, variance σ^2, and standard deviation σ for the given values of n and p. Assume the binomial conditions are satisfied in each case.

1. $n = 64, p = 0.5$
2. $n = 150, p = 0.4$
3. $n = 1068, p = 1/4$
4. $n = 2001, p = 0.221$

In Exercises 5–8, find the indicated values.

5. Several students are unprepared for a true/false test with 25 questions, and all of their answers are guesses. Find the mean, variance, and standard deviation for the number of correct answers that would be expected for such students. Would it be unusual for one of these students to get a good mark by guessing at least 20 correct answers? Why or why not?

6. On a multiple-choice test with 50 questions, each question has possible answers of a, b, c, and d, one of which is correct. For students who guess at all answers, find the mean, variance, and standard deviation for the number of correct answers that would be expected. Would it be unusual for one of these students to get a good mark by guessing at least 40 correct answers? Why or why not?

7. The probability of a 7 in roulette is 1/38. In an experiment, the wheel is spun 500 times. If this experiment is repeated many times, find the mean and standard deviation for the number of 7s. Would it be unusual not to win once in 500 trials? Why or why not?

8. The probability of winning Lotto 6/49 is 1/13,983,816. If someone plays 5200 times over 50 years, find the mean and standard deviation for the number of wins. (Express your answer with three significant digits.)

In Exercises 9–16, consider as unusual any result that differs from the mean by more than two standard deviations. That is, unusual values are either less than $\mu - 2\sigma$ or greater than $\mu + 2\sigma$.

9. When surveyed for brand recognition, 95% of consumers recognize Coke (based on data from Total Research Corporation). A new survey of 1200 randomly selected consumers is to be conducted. For such a group of 1200,
   a. Find the mean and standard deviation for the number who recognize the Coke brand name.
   b. Is it unusual to get 1170 consumers who recognize the Coke brand name?

10. A report to Health Canada indicated that the rate of lung cancer development among males is 9.1%. In one region, an intensive education program is used in an attempt to lower that rate. After running the program, a long-term follow-up study of 200 males is conducted.
    a. Assuming the program has no effect, find the mean and standard deviation for the number of lung cancer cases in groups of 200 males.
    b. Among the 200 males in the long-term follow-up study, 7% (or 14 people) test positive for lung cancer. If the program has had no effect, is that rate unusually low? Does this result suggest that the program is effective?

11. *Maclean's* conducted a marketing solutions poll of mutual funds and fund owners. One question asked fund owners what action they took after the October 1997 market drop. Seventeen percent of respondents said they bought more funds.
    a. Find the mean and standard deviation of the number of respondents who bought more funds, if groups of 900 fund owners were polled.
    b. In one of these polls of 900 fund owners, 140 respondents bought more mutual funds. Is this unusual?

12. According to the same *Maclean's* poll as in Exercise 11, fund owners were asked what they believe will happen to the stock market over the next year. In answer to the question, 46% stated that they believe the market will rise. Assume that this poll was conducted among 900 fund owners.
    a. For such groups of 900 fund owners, find the mean and standard deviation of the number of optimistic fund holders.
    b. In a group of 900 fund owners, 450 show optimism about the future of the stock market. Is this result unusual?

13. According to the CBC, 2.539 million Canadians watched the 1997 Grey Cup game. This figure represents a market share of 29%: that is, 29% of televisions were tuned to the game. Assume that this game is being broadcast and 4000 televisions are randomly selected.
    a. For such groups of 4000, find the mean and standard deviation for the number of televisions tuned to that game.
    b. Is it unusual to find that 1372 of the 4000 televisions are tuned to the game? What is the likely cause of a rate that is considerably higher than 29%?

14. A Calgary observatory records daily the mean counting rates for cosmic rays for that day. If a daily mean rate below 3200 is considered low, then "low" values occur about 3.6% of the time (in no particular sequence). Suppose a sample of 90 mean daily counting rates is randomly selected.

a. Find the mean and standard deviation for the number of "low" daily mean rates in such groups of 90 randomly selected rates.

b. Suppose that in a 90-day period, 9 "low" values for mean daily counting rates were observed. Is this result unusual?

15. Statistics Canada reports that 27.3% of all deaths are attributable to heart disease.

a. Find the mean and standard deviation for the number of such deaths that will occur in a typical region with 5000 deaths.

b. In one region, 5000 death certificates are examined, and it is found that 1500 deaths were attributable to heart disease. Is there cause for concern? Why or why not?

16. One test of extrasensory perception involves the determination of a shape. Fifty blindfolded subjects are asked to identify the one shape selected from the possibilities of a square, circle, triangle, star, heart, and profile of former prime minister Brian Mulroney.

a. Assuming that all 50 subjects make random guesses, find the mean and standard deviation for the number of correct responses in such groups of 50.

b. If 12 of 50 responses are correct, is this result within the scope of results likely to occur by chance? What would you conclude if 12 of 50 responses are correct?

(4-4) Exercises B: Beyond the Basics

17. The Port Arthur Computer Supply Company knows that 16% of its computers will require warranty repairs within one month of shipment. In a typical month, 279 computers are shipped.

a. If x is the random variable representing the number of computers requiring warranty repairs among the 279 sold in one month, find its mean and standard deviation.

b. For a typical month in which 279 computers are sold, what would be an unusually low figure for the number of computers requiring warranty repair within one month? What would be an unusually high figure? (These values are helpful in determining the number of service technicians that are required.)

18. a. If a company makes a product with an 80% yield (meaning that 80% are good), what is the minimum number of items that must be produced to be at least 99% sure that the company produces at least 5 good items?

b. If the company produces batches of items, each with the minimum number determined in part (a), find the mean and standard deviation for the number of good items in such batches.

The Poisson Distribution

If you've ever waited in a line at an amusement park, it's likely that your behaviour was analysed with the Poisson distribution, which is a probability distribution often used as a mathematical model describing arrivals of people in a line. Other applications include the study of vehicle crashes, shoppers arriving at a checkout counter, cars arriving at a gas station, and computer users logging onto the Internet. The Poisson distribution is defined as follows.

Who was Poisson?

Born in 1781, Siméon-Denis Poisson became one of the most respected mathematicians and physicists of his day. Electrostatics and magnetism were his main interests; however, he also dabbled in statistics. Legend has it that he first used the Poisson distribution, or the Poisson law of large numbers, to describe the number of Prussian soldiers who suffered fatal injuries resulting from horse kicks.

> ### DEFINITION
>
> The **Poisson distribution** is a discrete probability distribution that applies to occurrences of some event *over a specified interval*. The random variable x is the number of occurrences of the event in an interval. The interval can be time, distance, area, volume, or some similar unit. The probability of the event occurring x times over an interval is given by Formula 4-10.

Formula 4-10 $$P(x) = \frac{\mu^x \cdot e^{-\mu}}{x!} \quad \text{where } e \approx 2.71828$$

The Poisson distribution has the following requirements:

- The random variable x is the number of occurrences of an event *over some interval*.
- The occurrences must be *random*.
- The occurrences must be *independent* of each other.
- The occurrences must be *uniformly distributed* over the interval being used.

The Poisson distribution has these parameters:

- The mean is μ.
- The standard deviation is $\sigma = \sqrt{\mu}$.

The Poisson distribution differs from the binomial distribution in these important ways:

1. The binomial distribution is affected by the sample size n and the probability p, whereas the Poisson distribution is affected only by the mean μ.

2. In a binomial distribution, the possible values of the random variable x are $0, 1, \ldots, n$, but a Poisson distribution has possible x values of $0, 1, 2, \ldots$ with no upper limit.

Speed Kills

Drivers often lobby provincial governments for increased speed limits, especially on major highways. They claim that they can drive safely at faster speeds (as demonstrated by the fact that they already *do* drive faster!). However, Canadian governments should look at the experience in some American states, where the maximum speed limit was raised from 55 mi/h to 65 mi/h on some interstate highways. A statistical analysis showed that in Iowa, a 20% increase in fatal crashes is attributable to the increased speed limit. (See "Evaluating the Impact of the 65 mph Maximum Speed Limit on Iowa Rural Interstates," by Ledolter and Chan, *The American Statistician*, Vol. 50, No. 1.) This study used the Poisson distribution to find margins of error for estimated changes in fatalities for rural interstates, urban interstates, rural primary roads, and rural secondary roads. The increase in fatalities on rural interstates was found to be statistically significant, but the modest changes on roads with no speed limit changes were not significant.

EXAMPLE   When hits by V-1 buzz bombs in World War II were analysed, South London was subdivided into 576 regions, each with an area of 0.25 km^2. A total of 535 bombs hit the combined area of 576 regions. If a region is randomly selected, find the probability that it was hit exactly twice.

SOLUTION   The Poisson distribution applies because we are dealing with the occurrences of bomb hits over an interval of one region. The mean number of hits per region is $\mu = 535/576 = 0.929$. Because we want the probability of two hits in a region, we let $x = 2$ and use Formula 4-10 as follows:

$$P(x) = \frac{\mu^x \cdot e^{-\mu}}{x!} = \frac{0.929^2 \cdot 2.71828^{-0.929}}{2!} = \frac{0.863 \cdot 0.395}{2} = 0.170$$

The probability of a particular region being hit exactly twice is $P(2) = 0.170$.

In the preceding example, we can also calculate the probabilities for 0, 1, 3, 4, and 5 hits. (We stop at $x = 5$ because no region was hit more than five times and the probabilities for $x > 5$ are 0.000 when rounded to three decimal places.) Those probabilities are listed in Table 4-4. Using the calculated probabilities, we are able to find the expected number of regions with no hits, 1 hit, and so on. For example, the 576 regions each have a probability of 0.395 of not being hit, so we expect that the number of regions with no hits is $576 \cdot 0.395 = 227.5$. (Note that in computing the expected value, we use the number of *regions,* not the number of hits.) This expected value is listed with the others in the third column of Table 4-4. The fourth column describes the results that actually occurred. There were 229 regions that had no hits, 211 regions that were hit once, and so on. We can compare the frequencies *predicted* with the Poisson distribution (third column) to the *actual* frequencies (fourth column) to conclude that there is very good agreement. In this case, the Poisson distribution does a good job of predicting the results that actually occurred. Section 10-2 describes a statistical procedure for determining whether such expected frequencies constitute a good "fit" to the actual frequencies.

Table 4-4	V-1 Buzz Bomb Hits for 576 Regions in South London		
Number of Bomb Hits	Probability	Expected Number of Regions	Actual Number of Regions
0	0.395	227.5	229
1	0.367	211.4	211
2	0.170	97.9	93
3	0.053	30.5	35
4	0.012	6.9	7
5	0.002	1.2	1

The Poisson distribution is sometimes used to approximate the binomial distribution when n is large and p is small. One rule of thumb is to use such an approximation when $n \geq 100$ and $np \leq 10$. When using the Poisson distribution as an approximation to the binomial distribution, the required value of the mean μ can be found from Formula 4-7: $\mu = n \cdot p$. (See Exercises 13 and 14.)

This chapter presented a variety of different *discrete* probability distributions, including binomial (Sections 4-3 and 4-4), Poisson (this section), geometric (Exercise 33 in Section 4-3), hypergeometric (Exercise 34 in Section 4-3), and multinomial (Exercise 35 in Section 4-3). In the following chapter we shift our attention to the extremely important *normal* probability distribution, which is *continuous* instead of discrete.

Using Technology

Excel: Click on *fx* on the toolbar, then select the function category **Statistical** and then **Poisson**, then **OK**. In the dialog box, enter the value of interest for x (number of occurrences), as well as the value of μ, and enter 0 for the "Cumulative" option. The probability value for *exactly x* occurrences will be displayed. (Entering 1 for "Cumulative" will return the probability for values of *x up to and including x occurrences*.)

STATDISK: Select **Analysis** from the main menu, then select the **Poisson Probabilities** option. Enter the requested value for μ, and the entire probability distribution will be displayed. Other columns represent cumulative probabilities obtained by adding the values $P(x)$ as you go down, or up, the column.

4-5 Exercises A: Basic Skills and Concepts

In Exercises 1–4, assume that the Poisson distribution has the indicated mean and use Formula 4-10 to find the probability of the value given for the random variable x.

1. $\mu = 2, x = 3$
2. $\mu = 4, x = 1$
3. $\mu = 0.845, x = 2$
4. $\mu = 0.250, x = 2$

In Exercises 5–12, use the Poisson distribution to find the indicated probabilities.

5. A new tornado-resistant communications tower is being planned for the area around Regina. The area averages 3.25 tornadoes per year. Find the probability that in a one-year period, the number of tornadoes is
   a. 0   b. 1   c. 4
6. According to data from a Calgary observatory, the mean daily counting rate for cosmic rays falls below 3000 about one day per month. Find the probability that in a randomly selected month, the number of days with a mean counting rate below 3000 is
   a. 0   b. 1   c. 2

7. The Townsend Manufacturing Company experiences a weekly average of 0.2 accidents requiring medical attention. Find the probability that in a randomly selected week, the number of accidents requiring medical attention is
   a. 0   **b.** 1   **c.** 2

8. A statistics professor finds that when she schedules an office hour for student help, an average of 2 students arrives. Find the probability that in a randomly selected office hour, the number of student arrivals is
   a. 0   **b.** 2   **c.** 5

9. Careful analysis of magnetic computer data tape shows that for each 150 m of tape, the average number of defects is 2.0. Find the probability of more than one defect in a randomly selected length of 150 m of tape.

10. For a recent year, there were 46 aircraft hijackings worldwide (based on data from the FAA). Using one day as the specified interval required for a Poisson distribution, we find the mean number of hijackings per day to be estimated as $\mu = 46/365 = 0.126$. If the United Nations is organizing a single international hijacking response team, there is a need to know about the chances of multiple hijackings in one day. Use $\mu = 0.126$ and find the probability that the number of hijackings (x) in one day is 0 or 1. Is a single response team sufficient?

11. A classic example of the Poisson distribution involves the number of deaths caused by horse kicks of men in the Prussian Army between 1875 and 1894. Data for 14 corps were combined for the 20-year period, and the 280 corps-years included a total of 196 deaths. After finding the mean number of deaths per corps-year, find the probability that a randomly selected corps-year has the following numbers of deaths:
    a. 0   **b.** 1   **c.** 2   **d.** 3   **e.** 4
    The actual results consisted of these frequencies: 0 deaths (in 144 corps-years); 1 death (in 91 corps-years); 2 deaths (in 32 corps-years); 3 deaths (in 11 corps-years); 4 deaths (in 2 corps-years). Compare the actual results to those expected from the Poisson probabilities. Does the Poisson distribution serve as a good device for predicting the actual results?

12. In 1996, there were 572 homicide deaths in Canada (based on data from Statistics Canada). For a randomly selected day, find the probability that the number of homicide deaths is
    a. 0   **b.** 1   **c.** 2   **d.** 3   **e.** 4

4-5 Exercises B: Beyond the Basics

13. Assume that a binomial experiment has 15 trials, each with a 0.01 probability of success. Find the probability of getting exactly one success among the 15 trials by using (a) Table A-1 and (b) the Poisson distribution as an approximation to the binomial distribution. Note that the rule of thumb requiring that $n \geq 100$ and $np \leq 10$ suggests that the Poisson distribution might not be a good approximation to the binomial distribution.

14. The following is a binomial experiment, but the large number of trials involved creates major problems with many calculators. Overcome that obstacle by approximating the binomial distribution by the Poisson distribution.

    If you bet on the number 7 for one spin of a roulette wheel, there is a 1/38 probability of winning. Assume that bets are placed on the number 7 in each of 500 different spins.
    a. Find the mean number of wins in such experiments.
    b. Find the probability that 7 occurs exactly 13 times.
    c. Compare the result to the probability of 0.111, which is found from the binomial probability formula.

· ·

Vocabulary List

random variable
discrete random variable
continuous random variable
probability distribution
probability histogram
expected value
binomial probability distribution

binomial probability formula
geometric distribution
hypergeometric distribution
multinomial distribution
Poisson distribution

· ·

Review

The central concerns of this chapter were the random variable and the probability distribution. This chapter dealt exclusively with discrete probability distributions. (Chapter 5 will deal with continuous probability distributions.) The following key points were discussed:

- In an experiment yielding numerical results, the *random variable* has numerical values corresponding to different chance outcomes of an experiment.

- A *probability distribution* consists of all values of a random variable, along with their corresponding probabilities. Any probability distribution must satisfy two requirements: $\Sigma P(x) = 1$ and, for each value of x, $0 \le P(x) \le 1$.

- The important characteristics of a *probability distribution* can be investigated by computing its mean (Formula 4-1) and standard deviation (Formula 4-4) and by constructing a probability histogram.

- In a *binomial distribution*, probabilities can be found from Table A-1, they can be calculated with Formula 4-5 or a calculator, or they can be found with software, such as Excel or STATDISK.

- In a *binomial distribution*, the mean and standard deviation can be easily found by calculating the values of $\mu = n \cdot p$ and $\sigma = \sqrt{n \cdot p \cdot q}$.

- A *Poisson probability distribution* applies to occurrences of some event over a specified interval, and its probabilities can be computed with Formula 4-10.

- In the solutions to several problems and exercises, this chapter stressed the importance of interpreting results as being unusual outcomes or simply being a typical outcome that one might expect. One approach is to apply the range rule of thumb, where

$$\text{Maximum usual value} = \mu + 2\sigma$$
$$\text{Minimum usual value} = \mu - 2\sigma$$

By this standard, an "unusual" outcome falls outside these bounds. We can also determine whether outcomes in a binomial distribution are unusual by using probability values.

x successes among n trials is unusually high if $P(\text{at least } x)$ is very small.

x successes among n trials is unusually low if $P(\text{at most } x)$ is very small.

- -

Review Exercise

x	$P(x)$
0	0.0004
1	0.0094
2	0.0870
3	0.3562
4	0.5470

1. a. What is a random variable?
   b. What is a probability distribution?
   c. An insurance association's study of home smoke detector use involves homes randomly selected in groups of 4. The accompanying table lists values and probabilities for x, the number of homes (in groups of 4) that have smoke detectors installed (based on data from the National Fire Protection Association). Does this table describe a probability distribution? Why or why not?
   d. Assuming that the accompanying table does describe a probability distribution, find its mean.
   e. Assuming that the accompanying table does describe a probability distribution, find its standard deviation.

2. Fifteen percent of sport/compact cars are dark green (based on data from DuPont Automotive). Assume that 50 sport/compact cars are randomly selected.
   a. What is the expected number of dark green cars in such a group of 50?
   b. In such groups of 50, what is the mean number of dark green cars?
   c. In such groups of 50, what is the standard deviation for the number of dark green cars?
   d. Is it unusual to get 15 dark green cars in such a group? Why or why not?
   e. Find the probability that there are exactly 9 dark green cars in such a group of 50.

3. In a survey, the Canadian Automobile Association (CAA) found that 58% of its members paid cash for their vehicles. Ten CAA members are selected at random.
   a. Find the probability that exactly half of the 10 members paid cash for their vehicles.
   b. Find the probability that at least half of the 10 members paid cash for their vehicles.
   c. If many different groups of 10 CAA members are selected at random, find the mean and standard deviation for the number (among 10) who paid cash for their vehicles.

4. Inability to get along with others is the reason cited in 17% of worker firings (based on data from Robert Half International, Inc.). Concerned about her company's working conditions, the personnel manager at the Drummondville Fabric Company plans to investigate the 5 employee firings that occurred over the past year. Assuming that the 17% rate applies, find the probability that among those 5 employees, the number fired because of an inability to get along with others is
    a. 0   b. 4   c. 5   d. at least 3
    (Once the actual reasons for the firings have been identified, such probabilities will be helpful in comparing Drummondville Fabric Company to other companies.)

5. Refer to the data given in Exercise 4. Let the random variable x represent the number of fired employees (among 5) who were let go because of an inability to get along with others.
    a. Find the mean value of x.
    b. Find the standard deviation of the random variable x.
    c. Is it unusual to have 4 employees (among 5) fired because of an inability to get along with others? Why or why not?

6. The Western Canada Trucking Company operates a large fleet of trucks. Last year, there were 84 breakdowns.
    a. Find the mean number of breakdowns per day.
    b. Find the probability that for a randomly selected day, 2 trucks break down.

· ·

Cumulative Review Exercises

1. The Sports Associates Vending Company supplies refreshments at a baseball stadium and must plan for the possibility of a World Series contest. In the accompanying frequency table (based on past results), x represents the number of baseball games required to complete a World Series contest.

x	f
4	13
5	22
6	20
7	34

a. Construct the corresponding relative frequency table.
b. Does the result from part (a) describe a probability distribution? Why or why not?
c. Based on the past results, what is the probability that the next World Series contest will last at least 5 games?
d. If two different series included in the table are randomly selected, find the probability that they both lasted 7 games.
e. Find the mean number of games for the World Series contests included in the table.
f. Find the standard deviation for the number of games for the World Series contests included in the table.
g. What is the expected number of games for a World Series contest? If a vendor supplies hot dogs to both stadiums involved, and if each stadium averages 30,000 hot dogs sold per game, what is the expected number of hot dogs that will be required?

2. A casino cheat is caught trying to use a pair of loaded dice. At his court trial, physical evidence reveals that some of the black dots were drilled, filled with lead, then repainted to appear normal. In addition to the physical evidence, the dice are rolled in court with these results:

$$12 \quad 8 \quad 9 \quad 12 \quad 12 \quad 9 \quad 8 \quad 7 \quad 12 \quad 10$$
$$12 \quad 3 \quad 2 \quad 12 \quad 10 \quad 9 \quad 12 \quad 11 \quad 11 \quad 12$$

A probability expert testifies that when fair dice are rolled, the mean should be 7.0 and the standard deviation should be 2.4.

a. Find the mean and standard deviation of the sample values obtained in court.

b. Based on the outcomes obtained in court, what is the probability of rolling a 12? How does this result compare to the probability of 1/36 (or 0.0278) for fair dice?

c. If the probability of rolling a 12 with fair dice is 1/36, find the probability of getting at least one 12 when fair dice are rolled 20 times.

d. If you are the defence attorney, how would you refute the results obtained in court?

Technology Project

An Air Borealis flight from Toronto to Vancouver has seats for 340 passengers. An average of 5% of people with reservations don't show up, so Air Borealis over-books by accepting 350 reservations for the 340 seats. We can analyse this system by treating it as a binomial experiment with $n = 350$ and $p = 0.95$ (the probability that someone with a reservation does show up).

Find the probability that for a particular flight, there are more passengers than seats. That is, find the probability of at least 341 people showing up with reservations. Because of the value of n, Table A-1 cannot be used and the binomial probability formula would be extremely time consuming and painfully tedious to use. Statistical software would be the best tool.

(For instructions on using Excel or STATDISK for this task, see the Using Technology segment at the end of Section 4-3.)

•••••••• FROM DATA TO DECISION ••••••••

Is a Transatlantic Flight Safe with Two Engines?

Statistics is at its best when it is used to benefit humanity in some way. Companies use statistics to become more efficient, increase shareholders' profits, and lower prices. Regulatory agencies use statistics to ensure the safety of workers and clients. This exercise involves a situation in which cost effectiveness and passenger safety are both critical factors. With new aircraft designs and improved engine reliability, airline companies wanted to fly transatlantic routes with twin-engine jets, but the regulations required at least three engines for transatlantic flights. Lowering this requirement was, of course, of great interest to manufacturers of twin-engine jets (such as the Boeing 767). Also, the two-engine jets use about half the fuel of jets with three or four engines. Obviously, the key issue in approving the lowered requirement is the probability of a twin-engine jet making a safe transatlantic crossing. This probability should be compared to that of three- and four-engine jets. Such a study should involve a thorough understanding of the related probabilities.

A realistic estimate for the probability of an engine failing on a transatlantic flight is 1/14,000. Use this probability and the binomial probability formula to find the probabilities of 0, 1, 2, and 3 engine failures for a three-engine jet and the probabilities of 0, 1, and 2 engine failures for a two-engine jet. Because of the numbers involved, carry all results to as many decimal places as your calculator will allow. Summarize your results by entering the probabilities in the two given tables.

Three Engines			*Two Engines*	
x	$P(x)$		x	$P(x)$
0	?		0	?
1	?		1	?
2	?		2	?
3	?			

Use the results from the tables and assume that a flight will be completed if at least one engine works. Find the probability of a safe flight with a three-engine jet, and find the probability of a safe flight with a two-engine jet. Write a report that outlines the key issues, and include a recommendation. Support your recommendation with specific results.

········ COOPERATIVE GROUP ACTIVITIES ········

1. *In-class activity:* Divide into groups of three or four. Let the random variable x be the value of a coin randomly selected from those in possession of a statistics student. On the basis of the coins belonging to the group members, construct a table (similar to Table 4-1) listing the possible values of x along with their probabilities, then find the mean and standard deviation. What is a practical use of the results?

2. *Out-of-class activity:* Divide into groups of three or four. Conduct a survey that includes the following three questions. (Because the first question may be sensitive to some people, use a procedure that provides for anonymity.)

   • How much do you weigh?

   • Enter three random digits (0, 1, 2, 3, 4, 5, 6, 7, 8, 9). A digit may be chosen more than once.

   • Enter the last three digits of your social insurance number.

First, compile a list consisting of the *last digit* of each weight. If the weights are accurate and precise, we would expect those *last* digits to have a uniform distribution, so each digit has a probability of 1/10. Assuming that each digit has a probability of 1/10, construct a table describing the probability distribution for the last digits. Next, construct a relative frequency table from the list of recorded *last digits*. Compare the probability distribution to the relative frequency table. (This procedure is often used as a test to determine whether the subjects were actually weighed, or whether they simply reported their weights.) Use a similar procedure to analyse the random digits that were selected. Do those digits seem to be random? Finally, use a similar procedure to analyse the digits in the social insurance numbers. Do they seem to be random?

INTERNET PROJECT   Probability Distributions and Simulation

Probability distributions are used to predict the outcomes of the events they model. For example, if we toss a fair coin, the distribution for the outcome is a probability of 1/2 for heads and 1/2 for tails. If we toss the coin ten consecutive times, we expect 5 heads and 5 tails. We might not get this exact result, but in the long run, over hundreds or thousands of tosses, we expect the split between heads and tails to be very close to "50–50". Go to the site

http://www.pearsoned.ca/triola

and click on Internet Project, and then on Chapter 4, where you will find two explorations. In the first exploration you are asked to develop a probability distribution for a simple experiment, and use that distribution to predict the outcome of repeated trial runs of the experiment. In the second exploration, we will analyse a more complicated situation: the paths of rolling marbles as they move in pinball-like fashion through a set of obstacles. In each case, a dynamic visual simulation will allow you to compare the predicted results with a set of experimental outcomes.

5 Normal Probability Distributions

5-1 Overview

Whereas Chapter 4 focused on discrete probability distributions, this chapter focuses on the normal distribution, which is continuous. The normal distribution is the most important single distribution in statistics, and it is used often throughout the remainder of this book.

5-2 The Standard Normal Distribution

The standard normal distribution is defined as a normal probability distribution having a mean given by $\mu = 0$ and a standard deviation given by $\sigma = 1$. This section presents the basic methods for determining probabilities by using that distribution, as well as for determining standard scores corresponding to given probabilities.

5-3 Normal Distributions: Finding Probabilities

The z score (or standard score) is used to work with normal distributions in which the mean is not 0, the standard deviation is not 1, or both.

5-4 Normal Distributions: Finding Values

Work with nonstandard normal distributions is continued through methods for finding values that correspond to given probabilities.

5-5 The Central Limit Theorem

As the sample size increases, the sampling distribution of sample means is shown to approach a normal distribution with mean μ and standard deviation $\sigma/\sqrt{n}$, where n is the sample size and μ and σ represent the mean and standard deviation of the population, respectively. The ideas of this section form a foundation for the important concepts introduced in Chapters 6 and 7.

5-6 Normal Distribution as Approximation to Binomial Distribution

Use of the normal distribution to estimate probabilities in a binomial experiment is described and illustrated.

5-7 Determining Normality

Because many statistical methods require that the sample data be collected from a population that has a normal distribution, this section presents techniques for determining whether the available data are normally distributed.

CHAPTER PROBLEM:

How big are they?

There has been much interest in the last few years, among sports writers and hockey enthusiasts, concerning the ever-increasing size of National Hockey League players. A lot of this interest has been generated by the growing number of injuries, particularly head injuries, that players suffer. In an effort to reduce the number of injuries and amount of lost playing time, the NHL and critics of the game have suggested many changes. One suggestion is to enlarge the rink to give players more room to skate and freewheel. However, enlarging the rink would present an economic setback for team owners, since seats near the ice would have to be removed, causing lost ticket revenue. Of course, there are other less costly ways to protect players, such as rule changes and equipment improvement.

How large are the players in today's NHL? Official rosters of the teams of the 1997–98 season reveal that the average height for the league is 72.9 in. and the average weight is 196.0 lb. The Philadelphia Flyers sit at the top of the height and weight list, with an average height of 74.6 in. and an average weight of 208.3 lb. The Flyers are, on average, 8 lb per player heavier than the second team on the list, the Los Angles Kings. On the basis of average height per player, the Toronto Maple Leafs are the third smallest team in the NHL. The Leafs' average height is 72.4 in. and their average weight is 198.8 lb.

It is interesting to look back and see what an NHL team looked like in another era. If we check the roster of the 1944–45 Maple Leafs (a Stanley Cup winning team), the average player's height was 70.2 in. and the average weight was 173.2 lb. The difference over half a century is obvious. Today's Leaf team is 2 in. taller and 25 lb heavier on average.

Anthropometric data, such as height and weight, are important in many aspects of sports, business, and research. The areas in which such data are used extensively include health care, safety research for crash-testing, furniture design, and architecture. This chapter will introduce methods of analysing data such as heights and weights, and methods for calculating percentages such as the percentage of people within one standard deviation of the average height or weight of a population.

Overview

In Chapter 4 we introduced the concept of the *random variable* as a variable having a single numerical value (determined by chance) for each outcome of an experiment. We noted that a *probability distribution* gives the probability for each value of the random variable. Chapter 4 included only *discrete* random variables, such as those in binomial distributions that have a finite number of possible values. The number of quarters produced by the Royal Canadian Mint each day is an example of a discrete distribution. There are also many different *continuous* probability distributions, such as the weights of the quarters produced at the mint. Distributions can be either discrete or continuous, and they can be described by their *shape,* such as a bell shape. This chapter focuses on normal distributions, which are extremely important because they occur so often in real applications. Heights of adult women, weights of adult men, and third-grade reading test scores are some examples of normally distributed populations.

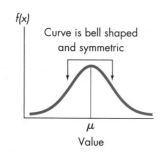

Figure 5-1
The Normal Distribution

DEFINITION

A continuous random variable has a **normal distribution** if that distribution has a graph that is symmetric and bell shaped, as in Figure 5-1, and the distribution fits the equation given as Formula 5-1.

Formula 5-1

$$f(x) = \frac{e^{-\frac{1}{2}\left(\frac{x - \mu}{\sigma}\right)^2}}{\sigma\sqrt{2\pi}}$$

Do not be discouraged by the complexity of Formula 5-1, because it is not really necessary for us actually to use it. What it shows is that any particular normal distribution is determined by two parameters: the mean μ and standard deviation σ. Once specific values are selected for μ and σ, we can graph Formula 5-1 as we would graph any equation relating x and y; the result is a probability distribution with a bell shape. We will see that this normal distribution has many real applications, and we will use it often throughout the remaining chapters.

The Standard Normal Distribution

The Uniform Distribution

Although this chapter focuses on the concept of a normal probability distribution, we begin by looking at a *uniform distribution*, which makes it easier to illustrate some very important properties, which we will then use with normal distributions.

> ### DEFINITION
>
> A continuous random variable has a **uniform distribution** if its values spread evenly over the full range of possibilities. The graph of a uniform distribution results in a rectangular shape.

EXAMPLE   The temperatures in vat #7 of a manufacturing process are controlled so that they range between 0°C and 5°C. The quality control supervisor monitors the temperatures in the vat at randomly selected times, so we will represent the temperature at a selected time as x, which can be any value from 0°C and 5°C. If every possible temperature in that range is equally likely, then x is a continuous random variable with a uniform distribution. (See Figure 5-2.)

In Section 4-2 we identified two requirements for a discrete probability distribution: (1) $\Sigma P(x) = 1$, and (2) $0 \leq P(x) \leq 1$ for all values of x. Also in Section 4-2, we stated that the graph of a discrete probability distribution is called a *probability histogram*. The graph of a continuous probability distribution, such as Figure 5-2, is called a *density curve*, and it must satisfy two properties similar to the requirements for discrete probability distributions, as listed in the definition.

> ### DEFINITION
>
> A **density curve** or **probability density function** is a graph of a continuous probability distribution. It must satisfy the following properties:
>
> 1. The total area under the curve must be 1.
> 2. Every point on the curve must have a vertical height that is 0 or greater.

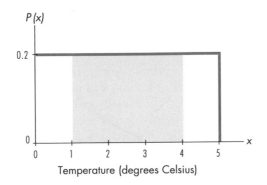

Figure 5-2   Uniform Distribution of Temperatures

New Data Collection Technology

Measuring or coding products and manually entering results is one way of collecting data, but technology is now providing us with alternatives that are not so susceptible to human error. Supermarkets use barcode readers to set prices and analyse inventory and buying habits. Manufacturers are increasingly using "direct data entry" devices such as electronic measuring gauges connected directly to a computer that records results. A third possibility is voice data entry, such as the Voice Data Logger. It consists of a headset connected to a small box that attaches to the speaker's belt. The box transmits the data to a computer.

By setting the height of the rectangle in Figure 5-2 to be 0.2, we force the enclosed area to be $5 \times 0.2 = 1$, as required. This property (area = 1) makes it very easy to solve probability problems, so the following statement is important:

Because the total area under the density curve is equal to 1, there is a correspondence between area and probability.

EXAMPLE   The quality control supervisor must read the temperature in vat #7 at a randomly selected time. Assuming that every temperature in the range from 0°C to 5°C is equally likely, what is the probability that the randomly selected temperature is greater than 0.5 °C?

SOLUTION   In Figure 5-3 the temperatures greater than 0.5°C are represented by the shaded rectangle that has an area of $4.5 \times .2 = 0.9$. Because there is a correspondence here between area and probability, we can conclude that there is a 0.9 probability that a randomly selected temperature will be greater than 0.5°C.

Figure 5-3   Temperatures Greater than 0.5°C

Temperature (degrees Celsius)

The Standard Normal Distribution

While the density curve of a uniform distribution results in a rectangle, the density curve of a normal distribution has the more complicated bell shape shown in Figure 5-1, so it's more difficult to find areas; but the basic principle is the same: There is a correspondence between area and probability.

Just as there are many different uniform distributions, there are also many different normal distributions, with each one depending on two parameters: the population mean μ and the population standard deviation σ. Figure 5-4 shows density curves for heights of female and male college students. Because males have a larger mean height, the density curve for males is farther to the right. Because males have a slightly larger standard deviation, the density curve for males is slightly wider. Figure 5-4 shows two different possible normal distributions. There are infinite possibilities, but one is of special interest.

AS

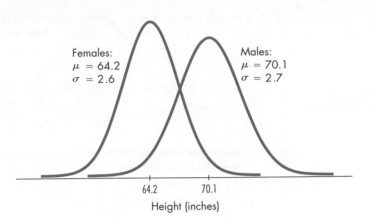

Figure 5-4 Heights of Male and Female College Students

DEFINITION

The **standard normal distribution** is a normal probability distribution that has a mean of 0 and a standard deviation of 1. (See Figure 5-5.)

Suppose that somehow we were forced to perform calculations using Formula 5-1. We would quickly see that the most workable values for μ and σ are $\mu = 0$ and $\sigma = 1$. By letting $\mu = 0$ and $\sigma = 1$, mathematicians have calculated areas under the curve. As shown in Figure 5-5, the area under the curve bounded by the mean of 0 and the score of 1 is 0.3413. Remember, the total area under the curve is always 1; this allows us to make the correspondence between area and probability, as we did in the preceding example with the uniform distribution.

Finding Probabilities When Given *z* Scores

Figure 5-5 shows that the area bounded by the curve, the horizontal axis, and the scores of 0 and 1 is an area of 0.3413. Although the figure shows only one area, we can find areas (or probabilities) for many different regions. Such areas can be found by using Table A-2 in Appendix A or by using statistical software. If you are using Table A-2, it is essential to understand the following points.

1. Table A-2 is designed only for the *standard* normal distribution, which has a mean of 0 and a standard deviation of 1.

2. Each value in the body of the table is an area under the curve bounded on the left by a vertical line above the mean of 0 and bounded on the right by a vertical line above a specific positive score denoted by *z*, as illustrated in Figure 5-6.

3. When working with a graph, avoid confusing *z* scores and areas.

   z score: *distance* along the horizontal scale of the standard normal distribution; refer to the leftmost column and top row of Table A-2

   Area: *region* under the curve; refer to the values in the body of Table A-2

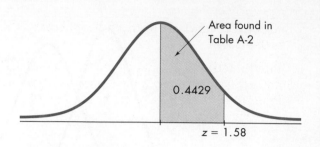

Figure 5-5 Standard Normal Distribution, with Mean $\mu = 0$ and Standard Deviation $\sigma = 1$

Figure 5-6 The Standard Normal Distribution

The area of the shaded region bounded by the mean of 0 and the positive number z can be found in Table A-2.

4. The part of the z score denoting hundredths is found across the top row of Table A-2.

The following example requires that we find the probability associated with a score between 0 and 1.58. Begin with the z score of 1.58 by locating 1.5 in the left column; now find the value in the adjoining row of probabilities that is directly below 0.08, as shown in this excerpt from Table A-2.

z	...	.08
.		.
.		.
.		.
1.5	...	.4429

The area (or probability) value of 0.4429 indicates that there is a probability of 0.4429 of randomly selecting a score between 0 and 1.58. (The following sections will consider cases in which the mean is not 0 or the standard deviation is not 1.)

EXAMPLE   The Precision Scientific Instrument Company manufactures thermometers that are supposed to give readings of 0°C at the freezing point of water. Tests on a large sample of these instruments reveal that at the freezing point of water, some thermometers give readings below 0° (denoted by negative numbers) and some give readings above 0° (denoted by positive numbers). Assume that the mean reading is 0°C and the standard deviation of the readings is 1.00°C. Also assume that the frequency distribution of errors closely resembles the normal distribution. If one thermometer is randomly selected, find the probability that, at the freezing point of water, the reading is between 0° and +1.58°.

SOLUTION   The probability distribution of the readings is a standard normal distribution because the readings are normally distributed with $\mu = 0$ and $\sigma = 1$. We need to find the area between 0 and z (the shaded region) in Figure 5-6 with $z = 1.58$. From Table A-2 we find that this area is 0.4429.

Interpretation The probability of randomly selecting a thermometer with an error between 0° and +1.58° is therefore 0.4429. Another way to interpret this result is to conclude that 44.29% of the thermometers will have errors between 0° and +1.58°.

AS

EXAMPLE Using the thermometers from the preceding example, find the probability of randomly selecting one thermometer that reads (at the freezing point of water) between −2.43° and 0°.

SOLUTION We are looking for the region shaded in Figure 5-7(a), but Table A-2 is designed to apply only to regions to the right of the mean (0) as in Figure 5-7(b). By comparing the shaded area in Figure 5-7(a) to the shaded area in Figure 5-7(b), we can see that those two areas are identical because the density curve is symmetric. Referring to Table A-2, we can easily determine that the shaded area of Figure 5-7(b) is 0.4925, so the shaded area of Figure 5-7(a) must also be 0.4925.

Interpretation The probability of randomly selecting a thermometer with an error between −2.43° and 0° is 0.4925. In other words, 49.25% of the thermometers have errors between −2.43° and 0°.

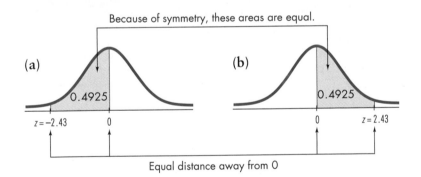

Because of symmetry, these areas are equal.

(a)   0.4925 $z = -2.43$ 0

(b)   0.4925   0 $z = 2.43$

Equal distance away from 0

Figure 5-7 Using Symmetry to Find the Area to the Left of the Mean

The preceding solution illustrates an important principle:

Although a z score can be negative, the area under the curve (or the corresponding probability) can never be negative.

Now recall the empirical rule (presented in Section 2-5) which states that for bell-shaped distributions,

- About 68% of all scores fall within 1 standard deviation of the mean.
- About 95% of all scores fall within 2 standard deviations of the mean.
- About 99.7% of all scores fall within 3 standard deviations of the mean.

If we refer to Figure 5-5 with $z = 1$, Table A-2 shows us that the shaded area is 0.3413. It follows that the proportion of scores between $z = -1$ and $z = 1$ will be $0.3413 + 0.3413 = 0.6826$. That is, about 68% of all scores fall within 1 standard deviation of the mean. A similar calculation with $z = 2$ yields the values of $0.4772 + 0.4772 = 0.9544$ (or about 95%) as the proportion of scores between $z = -2$ and $z = 2$. Similarly, the proportion of scores between $z = -3$ and $z = 3$ is given by $0.4987 + 0.4987 = 0.9974$ (or about 99.7%). These exact values correspond very closely to those given in the empirical rule. In fact, the values of the empirical rule were found directly from the probabilities in Table A-2 and have been slightly rounded for convenience. The empirical rule is sometimes called the *68–95–99 rule*; using exact values from Table A-2, it would be called the *68.26–95.44–99.74 rule,* but then it wouldn't sound as snappy.

Because we are dealing with a density curve for a probability distribution, the total area under the curve must be 1. Now refer to Figure 5-8 and see that a vertical line directly above the mean of 0 divides the area under the curve into two equal parts, each containing an area of 0.5. The following example uses this observation.

EXAMPLE   Once again, make a random selection from the same sample of thermometers. Find the probability that the chosen thermometer reads (at the freezing point of water) greater than $+1.27°$.

SOLUTION   We are again dealing with normally distributed values having a mean of 0° and a standard deviation of 1°. The probability of selecting a thermometer that reads greater than $+1.27°$ corresponds to the shaded area of Figure 5-8. Table A-2 cannot be used to find that area directly, but we can use the table to find that $z = 1.27$ corresponds to the area of 0.3980, as shown in the figure. We now reason that because the area to the right of zero is one-half of the total area, it has an area of 0.5 and the shaded area is $0.5 - 0.3980$, or 0.1020.

Interpretation We conclude that there is a probability of 0.1020 of randomly selecting one of the thermometers with a reading greater than $+1.27°$. Another way to interpret this result is to state that if many thermometers are selected and tested, then 0.1020 (or 10.20%) of them will read greater than $+1.27°$.

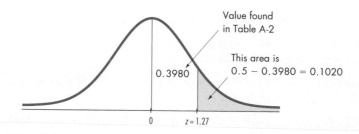

Figure 5-8 Finding the Area to the Right of $z = 1.27$

We are able to determine the area of the shaded region in Figure 5-8 by an indirect application of Table A-2. The following example illustrates yet another indirect use.

EXAMPLE   Assuming that one thermometer in our sample is randomly selected, find the probability that it reads (at the freezing point of water) between 1.20° and 2.30°.

SOLUTION   The probability of selecting a thermometer that reads between +1.20° and +2.30° corresponds to the shaded area of Figure 5-9. However, Table A-2 is designed to provide only for regions bounded on the left by the vertical line above 0. We can use the table to find that $z = 1.20$ corresponds to an area of 0.3849 and that $z = 2.30$ corresponds

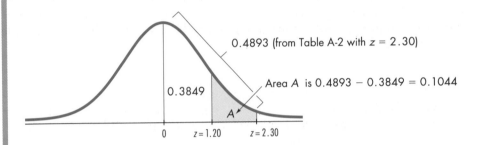

0.4893 (from Table A-2 with $z = 2.30$)

0.3849

Area A is $0.4893 - 0.3849 = 0.1044$

A

0        $z = 1.20$ $z = 2.30$

Figure 5-9   Finding the Area Between $z = 1.20$ and $z = 2.30$

to an area of 0.4893, as shown in the figure. If we denote the area of the shaded region by A, we can see from Figure 5-9 that

$$0.3849 + A = 0.4893$$

so

$$A = 0.4893 - 0.3849 = 0.1044$$

Interpretation   If one thermometer is randomly selected, the probability that it reads (at the freezing point of water) between 1.20° and 2.30° is therefore 0.1044.

The preceding example concluded with the statement that the probability of a reading between 1.20° and 2.30° is 0.1044. Such probabilities can also be expressed with the following notation.

Notation	
$P(a < z < b)$	denotes the probability that the z score is between a and b.
$P(z > a)$	denotes the probability that the z score is greater than a.
$P(z < a)$	denotes the probability that the z score is less than a.
$P(z = a)$	This probability is always equal to 0.

Using this notation, we can express the result of the last example as $P(1.20 < z < 2.30) = 0.1044$, which states in symbols that the probability of a z score falling between 1.20 and 2.30 is 0.1044. With a continuous probability distribution such as the normal distribution, the probability of getting any single *exact* value is 0. That is, $P(z = a) = 0$.

For example, there is a 0 probability of randomly selecting someone and getting a height of exactly 68.16243357 in. In the normal distribution, any single point on the horizontal scale is represented not by a region under the curve, but by a vertical line above the point. For $P(z = 1.33)$, we have a vertical line above $z = 1.33$, but that vertical line by itself contains no area, so $P(z = 1.33) = 0$. With any continuous random variable, the probability of any one exact value is 0, and it follows that $P(a \le z \le b) = P(a < z < b)$. It also follows that the probability of getting a z score of *at most b* is equal to the probability of getting a z score of *less than b*. It is important to interpret correctly key phrases such as *at most, at least, more than, no more than,* and so on. The illustrations in Figure 5-10 provide an aid to interpreting several of the most common phrases, assuming you will be working with Table A-2.

Figure 5-10 Interpreting Areas Correctly

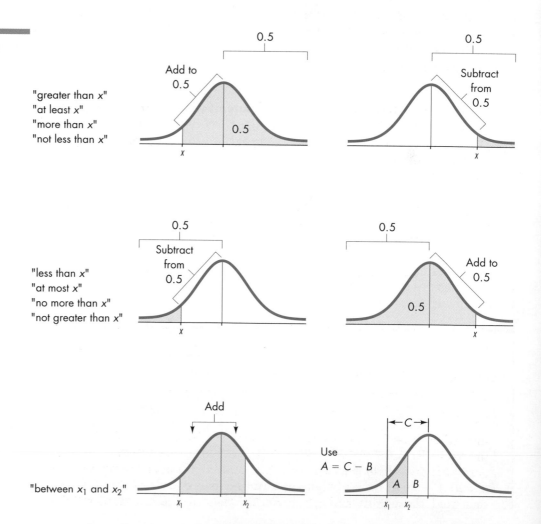

Finding z Scores When Given Probabilities

So far, the examples of this section involving the standard normal distribution have all followed the same format: Given some value, we found areas under the curve, which represent probabilities. In many other cases, we already know the probability, but we need to find the corresponding z score. In such cases, it is very important to avoid confusion between z scores and areas. Remember, the numbers Table A-2 shows in the extreme left column and across the top are z scores, which are *distances* along the horizontal scale, whereas the numbers in the body of Table A-2 are *areas* (or probabilities). Also, z scores to the left of the centreline are always negative (as in Figure 5-7a). If we already know a probability and want to determine the corresponding z score using Table A-2, we find it as follows:

1. Draw a bell-shaped curve, draw the centreline, and identify the region under the curve that corresponds to the given probability. If that region is not bounded by the centreline, work with a portion of the curve that *is* bounded, on one side, by the centreline, and, on the other, by a boundary of the area corresponding to the probability.

2. Using the probability representing the area bounded by the centreline, locate the closest probability in the *body* of Table A-2 and identify the corresponding z score.

3. If the z score is positioned to the left of the centreline, make it negative.

> **EXAMPLE**   Use the same thermometers with temperature readings that are normally distributed with a mean of 0°C and a standard deviation of 1°C. Find the temperature corresponding to P_{95}, the 95th percentile. That is, find the temperature separating the bottom 95% from the top 5%. (See Figure 5-11.)
>
> **SOLUTION**   Figure 5-11 shows the z score that is the 95th percentile, separating the top 5% from the bottom 95%. We must refer to Table A-2 to find that z score, and we must use a region bounded by the centre-

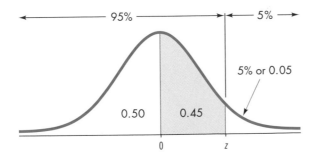

Figure 5-11   Finding the 95th Percentile

line (where $\mu = 0$) on one side, such as the shaded region of 0.45 in Figure 5-11. (Remember, Table A-2 is designed to directly provide only those areas that are bounded on the left by the centreline and on the right by the z score.) We first search for the area of 0.45 *in the body of the table* and then find the corresponding z score. In Table A-2 the area of 0.45 is between the table values of 0.4495 and 0.4505, but there's an asterisk with a special note indicating that 0.4500 corresponds to a z score of 1.645. We can now conclude that the z score in Figure 5-11 is 1.645, so the 95th percentile is the temperature reading of 1.645°C.

Interpretation When tested at freezing, 95% of the readings will be less than or equal to 1.645°C, and 5% of them will be greater than or equal to 1.645°C.

z score	Area
1.645	0.4500
2.575	0.4950

Note that in the preceding solution, Table A-2 led to a z score of 1.645, which is midway between 1.64 and 1.65. When using Table A-2, we can usually avoid interpolation by simply selecting the closest value. There are two special cases involving values that are important because they are used so often in a wide variety of applications (see the accompanying table). Except in these two special cases, we can select the closest value in the table. (If a desired value is midway between two table values, select the larger value.) Also, for z scores above 3.09, we can use 0.4999 as an approximation of the corresponding area.

EXAMPLE   Using the same thermometers, find P_{10}, the 10th percentile. That is, find the temperature reading separating the bottom 10% of all temperatures from the top 90%.

SOLUTION   Refer to Figure 5-12, where the 10th percentile is shown as the z score separating the bottom 10% from the top 90%. Table A-2 is designed for areas bounded by the centreline, so we refer to the shaded area of 0.40 (corresponding to 50% − 10%). *In the body of the table,* we select the closest value of 0.3997 and find that it corresponds to $z = 1.28$. However, because the z score is below the mean of 0, it must be negative. The 10th percentile is therefore −1.28°C.

Interpretation When tested at freezing, 10% of the thermometer readings will be equal to or less than −1.28°C, and 90% of the readings will be equal to or greater than −1.28°C.

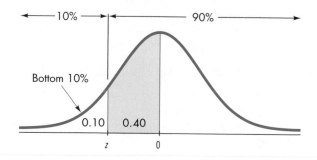

Figure 5-12   Finding the 10th Percentile

The examples in this section were contrived so that the mean of 0 and the standard deviation of 1 coincided exactly with the parameters of the standard normal distribution described in Table A-2. In reality, it is unusual to find such convenient parameters because typical normal distributions involve means different from 0 and standard deviations different from 1. The next section introduces methods for working with such nonstandard normal distributions.

Using Technology

Excel: *To find the probability when given a z score*:

Click on the *fx* icon, and select **Statistical, NORMSDIST**. In the dialog box, enter the z score for a boundary of the region whose probability you are seeking. Excel returns the cumulative area from the left of the curve up to a vertical line above the specified z score. Assuming you input some number as the z score, three cases may apply:

1. For $P(z < a)$, the probability is the value returned by Excel.
2. For $P(z > a)$, the probability is 1 – (the value returned by Excel).
3. For $P(a < z < b)$ (assuming you have used Excel twice, using two separate z scores), the desired probability is $P(z < b) - P(z < a)$.

To find the z score when given a probability:

Click on the *fx* icon, and select **Statistical, NORMSINV**. In the dialog box, enter the probability corresponding to the area to the left of the z score.

STATDISK: *To find the probability when given a z score*:

Select **Analysis, Probability Distributions, Normal Distribution**. Slide the mouse to the right or left, over the approximate value of the z score. STATDISK provides several outputs, including the probability which Table A-2 would return for that z score, as well as the cumulative probabilities to the left, and to the right, of the given z score.

To find the z score when given a probability:

Proceed as described above, but set the mouse position at the point where the desired probability is displayed. Read the corresponding z score from the upper right of the display.

Excel Display

Excel Display

STATDISK Display

5-2 Exercises A: Basic Skills and Concepts

In Exercises 1–4, refer to the continuous uniform distribution depicted in Figure 5-2, assume that one temperature reading is randomly selected, and find the probability of each reading in degrees.

1. Greater than 2
3. Between 2 and 4

2. Less than 3
4. Between 0.8 and 4.7

In Exercises 5–24, assume that the readings on the thermometers are normally distributed with a mean of 0° and a standard deviation of 1.00°. A thermometer is randomly selected and tested. In each case, draw a sketch, and find the probability of each reading in degrees.

5. Between 0 and 3.00
7. Between 0 and −2.33
9. Greater than 2.58
11. Less than −2.09
13. Between 1.34 and 2.67
15. Between −2.22 and −1.11
17. Less than 0.08
19. Greater than −2.29
21. Between −1.99 and 2.01
23. Between −1.00 and 4.00

6. Between 0 and 1.96
8. Between 0 and −1.28
10. Less than −1.47
12. Greater than 0.25
14. Between −1.72 and −0.31
16. Between 0.89 and 1.78
18. Less than 3.01
20. Greater than −1.05
22. Between −0.07 and 2.19
24. Between −5.00 and 2.00

In Exercises 25–28, assume that the readings on the thermometers are normally distributed with a mean of 0° and a standard deviation of 1.00°. Find the indicated probability, where z is the reading in degrees.

25. $P(z > 2.33)$
27. $P(-3.00 < z < 2.00)$

26. $P(2.00 < z < 2.50)$
28. $P(z < -1.44)$

In Exercises 29–36, assume that the readings on the thermometers are normally distributed with a mean of 0° and a standard deviation of 1.00°. A thermometer is randomly selected and tested. In each case, draw a sketch, and find the temperature reading corresponding to the given information.

29. Find P_{90}, the 90th percentile. This is the temperature reading separating the bottom 90% from the top 10%.
30. Find P_{30}, the 30th percentile.
31. Find Q_1, the temperature reading that is the first quartile.
32. Find D_1, the temperature reading that is the first decile.
33. If 4% of the thermometers are rejected because they have readings that are too high, but all other thermometers are acceptable, find the reading that separates the rejected thermometers from the others.
34. If 8% of the thermometers are rejected because they have readings that are too low, but all other thermometers are acceptable, find the reading that separates the rejected thermometers from the others.
35. A quality control analyst wants to examine thermometers that give readings in the bottom 2%. What reading separates the bottom 2% from the others?

36. If 2.5% of the thermometers are rejected because they have readings that are too high and another 2.5% are rejected because they have readings that are too low, find the two readings that are cutoff values separating the rejected thermometers from the others.

5-2 Exercises B: Beyond the Basics

37. Assume that z scores are normally distributed with a mean of 0 and a standard deviation of 1.
    a. If $P(0 < z < a) = 0.3212$, find a.
    b. If $P(-b < z < b) = 0.3182$, find b.
    c. If $P(z > c) = 0.2358$, find c.
    d. If $P(z > d) = 0.7517$, find d.
    e. If $P(z < e) = 0.4090$, find e.
38. For a standard normal distribution, find the percentage of data that are
    a. within 1 standard deviation of the mean
    b. within 1.96 standard deviations of the mean
    c. between $\mu - 3\sigma$ and $\mu + 3\sigma$
    d. between 1 standard deviation below the mean and 2 standard deviations above the mean
    e. Suppose it turns out that the distribution is not exactly normal, but is positively skewed. How does this affect your answers to parts (a), (b), and (d) of this exercise?
39. In a continuous uniform distribution,

$$\mu = \frac{\text{minimum} + \text{maximum}}{2} \text{ and } \sigma = \frac{\text{range}}{\sqrt{12}}$$

Find the mean and standard deviation for the uniform distribution represented in Figure 5-2.

40. Assume that the random variable x has a continuous probability distribution that is *uniform* with $\mu = 0$ and $\sigma = 1$. For this random variable, the minimum is $-\sqrt{3}$ and the maximum is $\sqrt{3}$.
    a. Find $P(x > 1)$.
    b. Find $P(x > 1)$ if you incorrectly assume that the distribution is normal instead of uniform.
    c. Compare the correct result from part (a) to the incorrect result from part (b). Does using the wrong distribution have much of an effect on the result?

5-3 Normal Distributions: Finding Probabilities

Although Section 5-2 introduced important methods for dealing with normal distributions, the examples and exercises included in that section are generally unrealistic because most normally distributed populations have a nonzero mean, a standard deviation different from 1, or both. In this section we include many real and important nonstandard normal distributions. The basic principle we will be explaining in this section is the following:

If we convert values to standard scores using Formula 5-2, then procedures for working with all normal distributions are the same as for the standard normal distribution.

Formula 5-2
$$z = \frac{x - \mu}{\sigma}$$

If you use certain calculators or software programs to find probabilities under the normal curve, the conversion to z scores may not be necessary, because the probabilities can be found directly. Regardless of the method used, however, you need to clearly understand the basic principle of this section, because it is an important foundation for concepts introduced in the following chapters.

See Figure 5-13, where we illustrate the important principle that the area bounded by a score and the population mean is the same as the area bounded by the corresponding z score and the mean of 0. Once we convert a nonstandard score to a z score, we can use Table A-2 the same way it was used in Section 5-2. You can use the following procedure for finding probabilities for values of a random variable with a normal probability distribution:

1. Draw a normal curve, label the mean and the specific x values, then *shade* the region representing the desired probability.
2. For each relevant score x that is a boundary for the shaded region, use Formula 5-2 to find the equivalent z score.
3. Refer to Table A-2 to find the area of the shaded region. This area is the desired probability.

The following example uses these three steps, and it illustrates the relationship between a typical nonstandard normal distribution and the standard normal distribution.

EXAMPLE   The mean value of Canadian imports each year from the Middle East and Africa is $2502 million, according to Statistics Canada data for 1980 to 1999. The standard deviation is $905 million. Assuming there is no trend in the data, and that the annual figures are normally distributed, what is the probability that in a randomly selected year from that period, the value of imports from the Middle East and Africa is between $2502 million and $4312 million?

SOLUTION

Step 1: See Figure 5-14, where we enter the mean of 2502 and the x value of 4312, and we shade the area representing the probability we want.

Step 2: To use Table A-2, we must use Formula 5-2 to convert the nonstandard distribution of import values to the standard normal distribution. The import value of 4312 is converted to a z score as follows:

$$z = \frac{x - \mu}{\sigma} = \frac{4312 - 2502}{905} = \frac{1810}{905} = 2.00$$

This result shows that the import value of $4312 million differs from the mean of $2502 million by 2.00 standard deviations.

(a)   (b)

Figure 5-13 Converting from a Nonstandard Normal Distribution to the Standard Normal Distribution

Figure 5-14 Probability of Imports Between $2502 million and $4312 million.

Step 3: Referring to Table A-2, we find that $z = 2.00$ corresponds to an area of 0.4772.

Interpretation There is a probability of 0.4772 of randomly selecting a year with an import value between $2502 million and $4312 million. This can be expressed in symbols as

$$P(2502 < x < 4312) = P(0 < z < 2.00) = 0.4772$$

Another way to interpret this result is to conclude that 47.72% of years have import values from the Middle East and Africa between $2502 million and $4312 million.

EXAMPLE   Assume that the heights of male college students are normally distributed with a mean of 70.1 in. and a standard deviation of 2.7 in.

a. Find the percentage of male students who fall between the Toronto Maple Leafs' average height of 72.4 in. and the Philadelphia Flyers' average height of 74.6 in.

b. Among 500 randomly selected male college students, how many would fall between the Toronto Maple Leafs' average height and the Philadelphia Flyers' average height ?

SOLUTION

a. The shaded region B in Figure 5-15 represents the proportion of male students who fall between the Maple Leafs' average height and the Flyers' average height. We can't find that shaded region directly because Table A-2 isn't designed for such cases, but we can find it indirectly by using the same basic procedures presented in Section 5-2. Find the shaded area B by subtracting region A from the total area of regions A and B combined. That is,

$$B = (A \text{ and } B \text{ combined}) - A$$

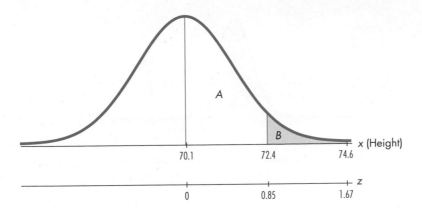

For the area of regions A and B combined:

$$z = \frac{x - \mu}{\sigma} = \frac{74.6 - 70.1}{2.7} = 1.67$$

Using Table A-2, we find that $z = 1.67$ corresponds to an area of 0.4525.

For the area of region A

$$z = \frac{x - \mu}{\sigma} = \frac{72.4 - 70.1}{2.7} = 0.85$$

Again using Table A-2, we find that $z = 0.85$ corresponds to an area of 0.3023. Region *A* has an area of 0.3023.

For the area of region B the shaded area is the difference between 0.4525 and 0.3023:

$$\text{Area } B = (\text{areas of } A \text{ and } B, \text{ combined}) - (\text{area } A)$$
$$= 0.4525 - 0.3023 = 0.1502$$

Interpretation This number indicates that only 15.02% of male college students have heights between the Maple Leafs' average height and the Flyers' average height.

b. Among 500 randomly selected male college students, we expect that 15.02% of them would have heights between the Maple Leafs' average height and the Flyers' average height:

$$500 \cdot 0.1502 = 75.1 \text{ male students}$$

EXAMPLE   Find the percentage of years in which Canadian imports from the Middle East and Africa are between $339 million and $8004 million. Again, assume that the annual import values exhibit no trend, and are normally distributed with a mean of $2502 million and a standard deviation of $905 million.

SOLUTION   Figure 5-16 shows the normal distribution of import values, with the shaded region representing values between $339 million and

Queues

Queuing theory is a branch of mathematics that uses probability and statistics. The study of queues, or waiting lines, is important to businesses such as super-markets, banks, fast-food restaurants, airlines, and amusement parks. A super-market in the Netherlands stakes its reputation and revenues on the reliability of queuing theory: A system electronically monitors the number of customers who enter, and cashiers are brought on duty or sent off based on the customer arrival rate. Customers who cannot find a checkout line with fewer than three people don't have to pay for their purchases. (See Nico M. van Dijk in *Chance*, Vol. 10, No. 1.) Bell Laboratories uses queuing theory to opti-mize telephone network usage, and factories use it to design efficient produc-tion lines.

Figure 5-16 Import Values Between $339 Million and $8004 Million.

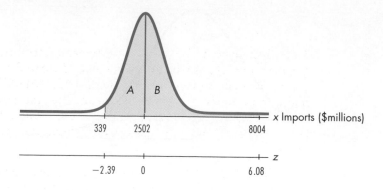

$8004 million. The method for finding the area of the shaded region involves breaking it up into parts A and B as shown. We can use Formula 5-2 and Table A-2 to find the areas of those regions separately; then we can add the results.

For area A only:

$$z = \frac{x - \mu}{\sigma} = \frac{339 - 2502}{905} = -2.39$$

We can use Table A-2 to find that $z = -2.39$ corresponds to 0.4916, so the area A is 0.4916.

For area B only:

$$z = \frac{8004 - 2502}{905} = 6.08$$

Table A-2 does not include z scores above 3.09, but it does include a note that for values of z above 3.09, we should use 0.4999 for the area. (If necessary, more accurate results can be obtained by using special tables or software.) Area B is 0.4999.

For areas of regions A *and* B *combined*: 0.4916 + 0.4999 = 0.9915

Interpretation The proportion of years in which the value of Canadian imports from the Middle East and Africa is between $339 million and $8004 million is 0.9915. That is to say, imports fall within this range 99.15% of all years.

In this section we have extended the concepts of Section 5-2 to include more realistic nonstandard normal probability distributions. However, all of the examples we have considered so far are of the same general type: We are given specific limit values and we must find an area (or probability, or percentage). In many practical and real cases, the probability (or percentage) is known and we must find the relevant value(s). Problems of this type are discussed in the next section.

Using Technology

Excel: To find the probability in a nonstandard distribution when given an x value, use the following procedure in Excel: Click on the *fx* icon, and select **Statistical, NORMDIST**. In the dialog box, enter the value, the mean, the standard deviation, and "true". Excel returns the cumulative area from the left of the curve up to a vertical line above the specified x value.

STATDISK: Like Table A-2, STATDISK requires that you use Formula 5-2 to convert nonstandard values to standard values; then use the STATDISK procedures described in Using Technology for Section 5-2.

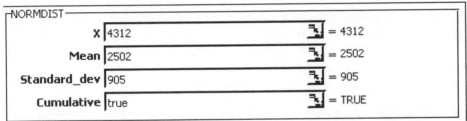

Excel Display

---NORMDIST---

X	4312	= 4312
Mean	2502	= 2502
Standard_dev	905	= 905
Cumulative	true	= TRUE

= 0.977249938

Returns the normal cumulative distribution for the specified mean and standard deviation.

Cumulative is a logical value: for the cumulative distribution function, use TRUE; for the probability mass function, use FALSE.

Formula result = 0.977249938   [OK]   [Cancel]

5-3 Exercises A: Basic Skills and Concepts

In Exercises 1–6, assume that the heights of female students are normally distributed with a mean given by $\mu = 64.2$ in. and a standard deviation given by $\sigma = 2.6$ in. (based on data from a survey of college students). Also assume that a female student is randomly selected. Draw a graph, and find the indicated probability.

1. $P(64.2 \text{ in.} < x < 65.0 \text{ in.})$ 2. $P(x < 70.0 \text{ in.})$
3. $P(x > 58.1 \text{ in.})$ 4. $P(59.1 \text{ in.} < x < 66.6 \text{ in.})$
5. A fashion agency is looking for females between 65.5 in. and 68.0 in. tall to work as models. Find the probability that a randomly selected female student meets the height requirements to be a model.
6. The Beanstalk Club, a social organization for tall people, has a requirement that women must be at least 70 in. (or 5 ft 10 in.) tall. Suppose you are trying to decide whether to open a branch of the Beanstalk Club at your college with 500 female students.
   a. Find the percentage of female students who are eligible for membership because they meet the minimum height requirement of 70 in.

   b. Among the 500 female students in your college, how many would be eligible for Beanstalk Club membership?

   c. Will you open a branch of the Beanstalk Club?

7. Replacement times for TV sets are normally distributed with a mean of 8.2 years and a standard deviation of 1.1 years (based on data from "Getting Things Fixed," *Consumer Reports*). Find the probability that a randomly selected TV set will have a replacement time of less than 7.0 years.

8. Replacement times for CD players are normally distributed with a mean of 7.1 years and a standard deviation of 1.4 years (based on data from "Getting Things Fixed," *Consumer Reports*). Find the probability that a randomly selected CD player will have a replacement time of less than 8.0 years.

9. Assume that the heights of soldiers in the Canadian Armed Forces are normally distributed with a mean height of 70.3 in. and a standard deviation of 3.4 in. Find the probability of one soldier who is selected at random having a height of 77.0 in. or greater

10. Based on the sample results in Data Set 18 of Appendix B, assume that human body temperatures are normally distributed with a mean of 36.4°C and a standard deviation of 0.62°C. If we define a fever to be a body temperature above 37.8°C, what percentage of normal and healthy persons would be considered to have a fever? Does this percentage suggest that a cutoff of 37.8°C is appropriate?

11. One classic use of the normal distribution is inspired by a letter to *Dear Abby* in which a wife claimed to have given birth 308 days after a brief visit from her husband, who was serving in the Navy. The lengths of pregnancies are normally distributed with a mean of 268 days and a standard deviation of 15 days. Given this information, find the probability of a pregnancy lasting 308 days or longer. What does the result suggest?

12. Lengths of pregnancies are normally distributed with a mean of 268 days and a standard deviation of 15 days. If we stipulate that a baby is *premature* if born at least three weeks early, what percentage of babies are born prematurely? Why would this information be useful to hospital administrators?

13. Based on daily summaries from a Calgary observatory (for January to November, 2000), the mean daily counting rates for cosmic rays are approximately normally distributed, with a mean equal to 3465.5 and a standard deviation of 127.7. If one day is randomly selected, what is the probability that the day's observed mean counting rate is at least 3248?

14. According to the International Mass Retail Association, girls aged 13 to 17 spend an average of $31.20 on shopping trips in a month. Assume that the amounts are normally distributed with a standard deviation of $8.27.

If a girl in that age category is randomly selected, what is the probability that she spends between $35.00 and $40.00 in one month? Does the assumption of a normal distribution seem plausible for this population?

15. IQ scores are normally distributed with a mean of 100 and a standard deviation of 15. Mensa is an organization for people with high IQs, and eligibility requires an IQ above 131.5.
   a. If someone is randomly selected, find the probability that he or she meets the Mensa requirement.
   b. In a typical region of 75,000 people, how many are eligible for Mensa?

16. An IBM subcontractor was hired to make ceramic substrates that are used to distribute power and signals to and from computer silicon chips. Specifications require resistance between 1.500 ohms and 2.500 ohms, but the population has normally distributed resistances with a mean of 1.978 ohms and a standard deviation of 0.172 ohms. What percentage of the ceramic substrates will not meet the manufacturer's specifications? Does this manufacturing process appear to be working well?

17. The average household expenditure in Canada on postsecondary books is $53.00, with a standard deviation of $18.61 (based on a study by Statistics Canada on family expenditures). If a household is selected at random, find the probability that its expenditure on postsecondary books is between $60 and $70. Do you expect that the household expenditure on postsecondary books is normally distributed?

18. Measurements of human skulls from different epochs are analysed to determine whether they change over time. The maximum breadth is measured for skulls from Egyptian males who lived around 3300 B.C. Results show that those breadths are normally distributed with a mean of 132.6 mm and a standard deviation of 5.4 mm (based on data from *Ancient Races of the Thebaid* by Thomson and Randall-Maciver). An archeologist discovers a male Egyptian skull and a field measurement reveals a maximum breadth of 119 mm. Find the probability of getting a value of 119 or less if a skull is randomly selected from the period around 3300 B.C. Is the newly found skull likely to come from that era?

19. According to a national health survey, the serum cholesterol levels of men aged 18 to 24 are normally distributed with a mean and standard deviation (in mg/100mL) of 178.1 and 40.7, respectively. One criterion for identifying risk of coronary disease is a cholesterol level above 300. If a man aged 18–24 is randomly selected, find the probability that his serum cholesterol level is above 300. Does this probability warrant serious concern?

20. Some vending machines are designed so that their owners can adjust the weights of the quarters that are accepted. If many counterfeit coins are found, adjustments are made to reject more coins, with the effect that

most of the counterfeit coins are rejected along with many legal coins. Assume that quarters have weights that are normally distributed with a mean of 5.67 g and a standard deviation of 0.070 g. If a vending machine is adjusted to reject quarters weighing less than 5.50 g or more than 5.80 g, what is the percentage of legal quarters that are rejected?

5-3 Exercises B: Beyond the Basics

In Exercises 21–23, refer to the indicated data set in Appendix B.

   a. Construct a histogram to determine whether the data set has a normal distribution.
   b. Find the sample mean $\bar{x}$ and sample standard deviation s.
   c. Use the sample mean as an estimate of the population mean μ, use the sample standard deviation as an estimate of the population standard deviation σ, and use the methods of this section to find the indicated probability.

21. Use the combined list of 100 weights of M&M plain candies listed in Data Set 11, and estimate the probability of randomly selecting one M&M candy and getting one with a weight greater than 1.000 g.
22. Use the total weights of discarded garbage in Data Set 1, and estimate the probability of randomly selecting a household that discards more than 20.0 lb of garbage in a week.
23. Use the chest measurements of bears in Data Set 3, and estimate the probability of randomly selecting a bear with a chest measuring less than 30 in.
24. When you constructed a histogram for total weights of discarded garbage, for Question 22, was the distribution *exactly* normal? If not, do you believe your probability estimate in Question 22 was likely too low or too high? Explain.

5-4 Normal Distributions: Finding Values

In this section we consider problems such as this: If companies' revenues per employee are normally distributed with $\mu = \$310,000$ and $\sigma = \$147,000$, find the revenue per employee separating the bottom 10% from the others. This problem starts from a given probability (0.10). We need to find the appropriate value x. This section reverses the procedure of Section 5-3, where we used a given value to find a probability.

In considering problems of finding values when given probabilities, there are three important cautions to keep in mind.

1. *Don't confuse z scores and areas.* Remember, z scores are *distances* along the horizontal scale, but areas represent *regions* under the normal curve. Table A-2 lists z scores in the left column and across the top row, but areas are found in the body of the table.

2. *Choose the correct (right/left) side of the graph.* A score separating the top 10% from the others will be located on the right side of the graph, but a score separating the bottom 10% will be located on the left side of the graph.

3. *A z score must be negative whenever it is located to the left of the centre-line of 0.*

As in Section 5-3, graphs are extremely helpful and they are strongly recommended. Even if you will be using statistical software to find values when given probabilities, you should understand the graphs and procedures which are presented below.

Procedure for Finding Values Using Table A-2 and Formula 5-2

1. Sketch a normal distribution curve; enter the given probability or percentage in the appropriate region of the graph, and identify the x value(s) being sought.
2. Use Table A-2 to find the z score corresponding to the region bounded by x and the centreline of 0. Observe the following cautions:

    - Refer to the *body* of Table A-2 to find the closest area, then identify the corresponding z score.
    - Make the z score *negative* if it is located to the left of the centreline.

3. Using Formula 5-2, enter the values for μ, σ, and the z score found in Step 2, then solve for x. On the basis of the format of Formula 5-2, we can solve for x as follows:

$$x = \mu + (z \cdot \sigma) \quad \text{(Another form of Formula 5-2)}$$

4. Refer to the sketch of the curve to verify that the solution makes sense in the context of the graph and in the context of the problem.

The following example, which was introduced at the beginning of this section, uses the procedure just outlined. Pay extra attention to Step 2, especially where we make the z score negative because it is to the left of the mean.

EXAMPLE   In its annual lists of the "Top 100 Companies" of Canada, the *Financial Post* uses the companies' revenues as the basis for ranking. There are other company variables which seem, in fact, quite randomly distributed. For example, in 1997, fully $\frac{2}{3}$ of the Top 100 companies appeared to have values for the variable "Revenues per employee" that fell into a normal distribution, with a mean and standard deviation (in $1000s) of 310 per employee and 147 per employee, respectively. (The other $\frac{1}{3}$ of companies truly did distinguish themselves, with values ranging from 3 up to 115 times the mean value for the lower group.) For those lower performing companies, find the value of P_{10}—the revenue per employee separating the bottom 10% from the top 90%.

SOLUTION

Step 1:   We begin with the graph shown in Figure 5-17. We have entered the mean of 310, shaded the area representing the bottom 10%, and identified the desired value as x. The area between 310 and x must be 40% of the total area (because the left half of the area

AS

Figure 5-17 Finding P_{10} for Revenues Per Employee

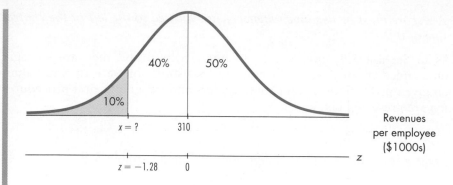

must combine to be 50% of the total). Because the total area is 1, the area constituting 40% of the total must be 0.4.

Step 2: We refer to Table A-2, but we look for an area of 0.4000 in the body of the table. (Remember, Table A-2 is designed to list areas only for those regions bounded on the left by the mean and on the right by some value.) The area closest to 0.4000 is 0.3997, and it corresponds to a z score of 1.28. Because the score is to the left of the mean, we make it negative and use $z = -1.28$.

Step 3: With $z = -1.28$, $\mu = 310$, and $\sigma = 147$, we solve for x either by using Formula 5-2 directly or by using the following version of Formula 5-2:

$$x = \mu + (z \cdot \sigma) = 310 + (-1.28 \cdot 147) = 121.8$$

Step 4: If we let $x = 121.8$ in Figure 5-17, we see that this solution is reasonable because the 10th percentile should be less than the mean of 310.

Interpretation The revenue per employee of $121,800 separates the lowest 10% from the highest 90%.

EXAMPLE   Assume that body temperatures of healthy adults are normally distributed with a mean of 36.39°C and a standard deviation of 0.62°C (based on Data Set 18 in Appendix B). If a medical researcher wants to study people in the bottom 2.5% and people in the top 2.5%, find the temperatures separating those limits.

SOLUTION

Step 1: We begin with the graph shown in Figure 5-18. We have shaded the areas representing the bottom 2.5% and top 2.5% (or 0.025). The areas of 0.475 are found by using the fact that the centreline above the mean divides the total area of 1 into two parts, each with area 0.5. We get $0.5 - 0.025 = 0.475$.

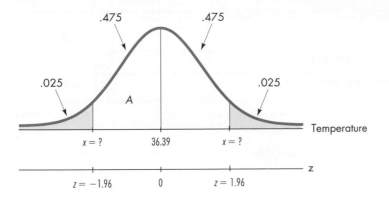

Figure 5-18 Body
Temperatures

Step 2: We refer to Table A-2, but we look for an area of 0.475 in the body of the table. (Remember, Table A-2 is designed to list areas only for those regions bounded on the left by the mean and on the right by some value.) The area of 0.4750 corresponds to $z = 1.96$. For the x value located on the right in Figure 5-18, we use $z = 1.96$; for the x value located on the left we use $z = -1.96$.

Step 3: With $z = 1.96$, $\mu = 36.39$, and $\sigma = 0.62$, we solve for x using a variation of Formula 5-2:

$$x = \mu + (z \cdot \sigma) = 36.39 + (1.96 \cdot 0.62) = 37.61$$

With $z = -1.96$, $\mu = 36.39$, and $\sigma = 0.62$, we solve for x using a variation of Formula 5-2:

$$x = \mu + (z \cdot \sigma) = 36.39 + (-1.96 \cdot 0.62) = 35.17$$

Step 4: If we let $x = 35.17$ and 37.61 in Figure 5-18, we see that our solutions are reasonable.

Interpretation If the researcher's assumptions about the distribution of body temperatures are correct, then he or she should select people with body temperatures below 35.17°C and or above 37.61 °C.

Survey Medium Can Affect Results

In a survey of Catholics, the subjects were asked if contraceptives should be made available to unmarried women. In personal interviews, 44% of the respondents said yes. But among a similar group contacted by mail or telephone, 75% of the respondents answered yes to the same question.

Using Technology

Excel: To find a value given a probability: Click on the *fx* icon, and select **Statistical, NORMINV**. In the dialog box, enter the cumulative probability to the left of the given value, the mean, and the standard deviation. Excel returns the corresponding x value.

STATDISK: Follow the procedures described in Using Technology for Section 5-2. Like Table A-2, STATDISK provides a z score, which you must convert by use of a formula into the corresponding x value.

Excel Display

```
┌─NORMINV────────────────────────────────────────────────────┐
│     Probability │0.025│                    ▛▜ = 0.025        │
│                                                              │
│          Mean │36.39│                      ▛▜ = 36.39        │
│                                                              │
│   Standard_dev │0.62│                      ▛▜ = 0.62         │
│                                                              │
│                                              = 35.17482413   │
│ Returns the inverse of the normal cumulative distribution for the specified mean and standard │
│ deviation.                                                   │
│       Probability is a probability corresponding to the normal distribution, a number │
│                   between 0 and 1 inclusive.                 │
│                                                              │
│    ⟦?⟧        Formula result =35.17482413       ┌────────┐  ┌────────┐ │
│                                                 │   OK   │  │ Cancel │ │
│                                                 └────────┘  └────────┘ │
└──────────────────────────────────────────────────────────────┘
```

⬤5-4 Exercises A: Basic Skills and Concepts

In Exercises 1–4, assume that female college students have heights that are normally distributed with a mean of 64.2 in. and a standard deviation of 2.6 in. Find the height for the given percentile.

1. P_{85} **2.** P_{66} **3.** P_{15} **4.** P_{35}

5. Replacement times for TV sets are normally distributed with a mean of 8.2 years and a standard deviation of 1.1 years (based on data from "Getting Things Fixed," *Consumer Reports*).

    a. Find the replacement time that separates the top 20% from the bottom 80%.

    b. Find the probability that a randomly selected TV will have a replacement time of less than 5.0 years.

    c. If you want to provide a warranty so that only 1% of the TV sets will be replaced before the warranty expires, what length of time would you recommend for the warranty?

6. Replacement times for CD players are normally distributed with a mean of 7.1 years and a standard deviation of 1.4 years (based on data from "Getting Things Fixed," *Consumer Reports*). Find P_{55}, which is the replacement time separating the top 45% from the bottom 55%.

7. Weights of paper discarded by households each week are normally distributed with a mean of 4.3 kg and a standard deviation of 1.9 kg. Find P_{33}, which is the weight that separates the bottom 33% from the top 67%.

8. Based on the sample results in Data Set 18 of Appendix B, assume that human body temperatures are normally distributed with a mean of 36.4°C and a standard deviation of 0.62°C . What two temperature levels separate the bottom 2% and the top 2%? Could these values serve as reasonable limits that could be used to identify people who are likely to be ill?

9. The lengths of pregnancies are normally distributed with a mean of 268 days and a standard deviation of 15 days. If we stipulate that a baby is *premature* if the length of pregnancy is in the lowest 4%, find the length that separates premature babies from those who are not premature.

10. According to the Opinion Research Corporation, men spend an average of 11.4 min in the shower. Assume that the times are normally distributed with a standard deviation of 1.8 min. Find the values of the quartiles Q_1 and Q_3.

11. IQ scores are normally distributed with a mean of 100 and a standard deviation of 15. If we define a genius to be someone in the top 1% of IQ scores, find the score separating geniuses from the rest of us. Are there any jobs where this score could reasonably be used as one criterion for employment?

12. A subcontractor manufactures ceramic substrates for IBM. These devices have resistances that are normally distributed with a mean of 1.978 ohms and a standard deviation of 0.172 ohms. If the required specifications are to be modified so that 3% of the devices are rejected because their resistances are too low and another 3% are rejected because their resistances are too high, find the cutoff values for the acceptable devices.

13. Scores obtained from the Law School Admission Test (LSAT) are normally distributed with a mean score of 550 and a standard deviation of 110.
    a. If a test score is selected at random, find the probability that it is less than 750.
    b. If the top 16% of the test scores are usually good enough for admission to law school, find the cutoff score for gaining admission.

14. Measurements of human skulls from different epochs are analysed to determine whether they change over time. The maximum breadth is measured for skulls from Egyptian males who lived around 3300 B.C. Results show that those breadths are normally distributed with a mean of 132.6 mm and a standard deviation of 5.4 mm (based on data from *Ancient Races of the Thebaid* by Thomson and Randall-Maciver).
    a. Find the probability of getting a value greater than 140 mm if a skull is randomly selected from the period of around 3300 B.C.
    b. Find the value that is D_2, the second decile.

15. Based on daily summaries from a Calgary observatory (for January to November, 2000), the mean daily counting rates for cosmic rays are approximately normally distributed, with a mean equal to 3465.5 and a standard deviation of 127.7. Find the sixth decile D_6, which is the mean daily counting rate that separates the lowest 60% from the highest 40%.

16. Quarters have weights that are normally distributed with a mean of 5.67 g and a standard deviation of 0.070 g.
    a. If a vending machine is adjusted to reject quarters weighing less than 5.53 g or more than 5.81 g, what is the percentage of legal quarters that are rejected?
    b. Find the weights of accepted legal quarters if the machine is readjusted so that the lightest 1.5% are rejected and the heaviest 1.5% are rejected.
    c. If your quarter is rejected from a machine that is set to reject the upper 1.5% and the lower 1.5% of coins, by weight, is it a waste of time to re-insert your coin?

5-4 Exercises B: Beyond the Basics

17. The construction of a histogram for a data set reveals that the distribution is approximately normal and the boxplot is constructed with these quartiles: $Q_1 = 62$, $Q_2 = 70$, $Q_3 = 78$. Estimate the standard deviation.

18. An instructor informs her physics class that a test is very difficult, but the grades will be curved. Scores for the test are normally distributed with a mean of 25 and a standard deviation of 5.

   a. If she curves by adding 50 to each grade, what is the new mean? What is the new standard deviation?

   b. Is it fair to curve by adding 50 to each grade? Why or why not?

   c. If the grades are curved according to the following scheme (instead of adding 50), find the numerical limits for each letter grade.
     A: Top 10%
     B: Scores above the bottom 70% and below the top 10%
     C: Scores above the bottom 30% and below the top 30%
     D: Scores above the bottom 10% and below the top 70%
     F: Bottom 10%

   d. Which method of curving the grades is fairer: Adding 50 to each grade or using the scheme given in part (c)? Explain.

19. According to data from the College Entrance Examination Board, the mean math SAT score is 475, and 17.0% of the scores are above 600. Find the standard deviation, and then use that result to find the 99th percentile. (Assume that the scores are normally distributed.)

20. The College Entrance Examination Board writes that "for the SAT Achievement Tests, your score would fall in a range about 30 points above or below your actual ability about two-thirds of the time. This range is called the standard error of measurement (SEM)." Use that statement to estimate the standard deviation for scores of an individual on an SAT Achievement Test. (Assume that the scores are normally distributed.)

5-5 The Central Limit Theorem

This section presents the central limit theorem, which is one of the most important and useful concepts in statistics. It forms a foundation for estimating population parameters and hypothesis testing—topics discussed at length in the following chapters.

We will not present rigorous proofs in this section, but will instead focus on the concepts and how to apply them. You will need to keep in mind the types of data sets we are considering. Instead of sets of *individual* values—the values of a *random variable* (see Section 4-2)—we will work with data sets in which each value is the *mean* of some other sample. Just as a *probability distribution* describes the probability for each value of a random variable *x*, the *sampling distribution of the mean* describes the probability for each value of the sample mean, when drawing samples of a given size from a population.

Figure 5-19 Distribution of
200 Digits from Social
Insurance Numbers (Last 4
Digits) of 50 Students

Figure 5-20 Distribution of
50 Sample Means for 50
Students

DEFINITION

The **sampling distribution** of the mean is the probability distribution of
sample means, with all samples having the sample size n.

One property of the sampling distribution of sample means is key to this
section:

AS   **As the sample size increases, the sampling distribution of sample
means approaches a normal distribution.**

In other words, if we collect many samples of the same size from the same
population, compute their means, and then draw a histogram of those means,
that histogram will tend to have the bell shape of a normal distribution. This
is true regardless of the shape of the distribution of the original population.
Compare Figure 5-19, which shows a probability distribution for a specific
variable, and Figure 5-20, which shows the sampling distribution for sample
means for the same variable. Figure 5-21 is a general illustration of the same
principle, applied to three different shapes of underlying population distribution. Observations exactly like these led to the formulation of the central limit
theorem, which we will now discuss.

The **central limit theorem** involves two different distributions: the distribution of the original population and the distribution of the sample means. As
in previous chapters, we use the symbols μ and σ to denote the mean and standard deviation of the original population. We now introduce new notation for
the mean and standard deviation of the distribution of sample means.

Figure 5-21 Normal, Uniform, and Skewed Distributions

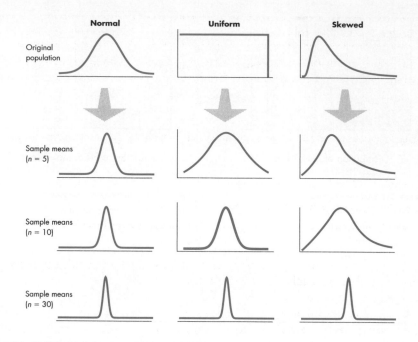

Central Limit Theorem

Given:

1. The random variable x has a distribution (which may or may not be normal) with mean μ and standard deviation σ.

2. Samples of size n are randomly selected from this population. (The samples are selected so that all possible samples of size n have the same chance of being selected.)

Conclusions:

1. The distribution of sample means $\bar{x}$ will, as the sample size increases, approach a *normal* distribution.

2. The mean of this distribution of sample means will be the population mean μ.

3. The standard deviation of this distribution of sample means will be $\sigma/\sqrt{n}$.

Practical Rules Commonly Used:

1. For samples of size n larger than 30, the distribution of the sample means can be approximated reasonably well by a normal distribution. The approximation gets better as the sample size n becomes larger.

2. If the original population is itself normally distributed, then the sample means will be normally distributed for *any* sample size n (not just the sample sizes n larger than 30).

Notation for the Central Limit Theorem

If all possible random samples of size n are selected from a population with mean μ and standard deviation σ, the mean of the sample means is denoted by $\mu_{\bar{x}}$, so

$$\mu_{\bar{x}} = \mu$$

Also, the standard deviation of the sample means is denoted by $\sigma_{\bar{x}}$, so

$$\sigma_{\bar{x}} = \frac{\sigma}{\sqrt{n}}$$

$\sigma_{\bar{x}}$ is often called the **standard error of the mean.**

TABLE 5-1

SIN digits				$\bar{x}$
1	8	6	4	4.75
5	3	3	6	4.25
9	8	8	8	8.25
5	1	2	5	3.25
9	3	3	5	5.00
4	2	6	2	3.50
7	7	1	6	5.25
9	1	5	4	4.75
5	3	3	9	5.00
7	8	4	1	5.00
0	5	6	1	3.00
9	8	2	2	5.25
6	1	5	7	4.75
8	1	3	0	3.00
5	9	6	9	7.25
6	2	3	4	3.75
7	4	0	7	4.50
5	7	5	6	5.75
4	1	5	7	4.25
1	2	0	6	2.25
4	0	2	8	3.50
3	1	2	5	2.75
0	3	4	0	1.75
1	5	1	0	1.75
9	7	4	0	5.00
7	3	1	1	3.00
9	1	1	3	3.50
8	6	5	9	7.00
5	6	4	1	4.00
9	3	9	5	6.50
6	0	7	3	4.00
8	2	9	6	6.25
0	2	8	6	4.00
2	0	9	7	4.50
5	8	9	0	5.50
6	5	4	9	6.00
4	8	7	6	6.25
7	1	2	0	2.50
2	9	5	0	4.00
8	3	2	2	3.75
2	7	1	6	4.00
6	7	7	1	5.25
2	3	3	9	4.25
2	4	7	5	4.50
5	4	3	7	4.75
0	4	3	8	3.75
2	5	8	6	5.25
7	1	3	4	3.75
8	3	7	0	4.50
5	6	6	7	6.00

EXAMPLE   Table 5-1 illustrates the last four digits of the social insurance numbers of each of 50 students.

The last four digits of social insurance numbers are random. If we combine the four digits from each student into one big collection of 200 numbers, we get a mean of $\bar{x} = 4.5$, a standard deviation of $s = 2.8$, and an approximately uniform distribution with the graph shown in Figure 5-19. Now see what happens when we find the 50 sample means, as shown in Table 5-1. Even though the original collection of data has an approximately *uniform* (that is, not normal) distribution, the sample means have a distribution that is approximately *normal*. This can be a confusing concept, so you should stop right here and study this paragraph until its major point becomes clear: The original set of 200 individual numbers has a uniform distribution (because the digits 0–9 occur with approximately equal frequencies), but the 50 sample means have a normal distribution. It's a truly fascinating and intriguing phenomenon in statistics that by sampling from any distribution, we can create a distribution that is normal or at least approximately normal.

Applying the Central Limit Theorem

Many important and practical problems can be solved with the central limit theorem. When working on such problems, remember the following rules.

- If you are working with a random sample of size $n > 30$, or if the original population is normally distributed, treat the distribution of sample means as a normal distribution.

- Treat the mean μ of the original population as the mean of the distribution of sample means.

- Treat the calculated value $\sigma/\sqrt{n}$ (based on the original population) as the standard deviation of the distribution of sample means

In the following example, part (a) involves an individual value, so we use the methods presented in Section 5-3; those methods apply to the normal distribution of the random variable x. Part (b), however, involves the mean for a *group* of 36 Canadian Football League (CFL) players, so we must use the central limit theorem in working with the random variable $\bar{x}$. Observe the significant difference betwen the procedures used in part (a) and part (b).

EXAMPLE   In human engineering and product design, it is often important to consider the weights of people so that airplanes or elevators aren't overloaded, chairs don't break, and other such dangerous or embarrassing mishaps do not occur. Given that the population of players in offensive back positions (including quarterback) in the CFL have weights that are approximately normally distributed, with a mean of 197.5 lb and a standard deviation of 14.2 lb (based on sampling from data on the CFL Web site), find the probability that

a. if one player is randomly selected, his weight is greater than 200 lb.
b. if 36 different players are randomly selected, their mean weight is greater than 200 lb.

SOLUTION

a. *Approach: Use the methods presented in Section 5-3* (because we are dealing with an *individual* value from a normally distributed population). We seek the area of the shaded region in Figure 5-22(a).

$$z = \frac{x - \mu}{\sigma} = \frac{200 - 197.5}{14.2} = 0.18$$

We now refer to Table A-2 to find that region A is 0.0714. The shaded region is therefore $0.5 - 0.0714 = 0.4286$. The probability of the player weighing more than 200 lb is 0.4286.

b. *Approach: Use the central limit theorem* (because we are dealing with the *mean for a group* of 36 values, not an individual value). Because we are now dealing with a distribution of sample means, we must use the parameters $\mu_{\bar{x}}$ and $\sigma_{\bar{x}}$, which are evaluated as follows:

$$\mu_{\bar{x}} = \mu = 197.5$$

$$\sigma_{\bar{x}} = \frac{\sigma}{\sqrt{n}} = \frac{14.2}{\sqrt{36}} = 2.37$$

We want to determine the shaded area shown in Figure 5-22(b), and the relevant z score is calculated as follows:

$$z = \frac{\bar{x} - \mu_{\bar{x}}}{\sigma_x} = \frac{200 - 197.5}{\frac{14.2}{\sqrt{36}}} = \frac{2.5}{2.37} = 1.05$$

Figure 5-22   Distribution of (a) Individual Offensive Backs' Weights and (b) Means of Samples of 36 Offensive Backs' Weights

Referring to Table A-2, we find that $z = 1.05$ corresponds to an area of 0.3531, so the shaded region is $0.5 - 0.3531 = 0.1469$. The probability that the 36 players have a mean weight greater than 200 lb is 0.1469.

Interpretation   There is a 0.4286 probability that an offensive back in the CFL will weigh more than 200 lb, but there is only a 0.1469 probability that 36 offensive backs (collectively) will have a mean weight of more than 200 lb. It is much easier for an individual to deviate from the mean than it is for a group of 36. A single extreme weight among the 36 weights will lose its impact when it is averaged in with the other 35 weights.

Also, remember that the calculated probabilities are usually approximate, although they are displayed here to four decimal places. For example, the solutions based on using Table A-2 will differ slightly, due to rounding, from solutions based on statistical software. Moreover, these calculations assume (especially when working with single x values) that the population is normal—which may not be *exactly* true for your data.

The next example illustrates another application of the central limit theorem, but carefully examine the conclusion that is reached. This example shows the type of thinking that is the basis for the important procedure of hypothesis testing (discussed in Chapter 7), and illustrates the rare event rule for inferential statistics that was presented in Section 3-1.

EXAMPLE   Assume that the population of human body temperatures has a mean of 37.0°C, as is commonly believed. Also assume that the population standard deviation is 0.62°C. If a sample of size $n = 108$ is randomly selected, find the probability of getting a mean of 36.4°C or lower. (The value of 36.4°C was actually obtained; see the 108 temperatures in Data Set 18 of Appendix B.)

A Professional Speaks About Sampling Error

Daniel Yankelovich, in an essay for *Time*, commented on the sampling error often reported along with poll results. He stated that sampling error refers only to the inaccuracy created by using random sample data to make an inference about a population; the sampling error does not address issues of poorly stated, biased, or emotional questions. He said, "Most important of all, warning labels about sampling error say nothing about whether or not the public is conflict-ridden or has given a subject much thought. This is the most serious source of opinion poll misinterpretation."

The Fuzzy Central Limit Theorem

In *The Cartoon Guide to Statistics* by Gonick and Smith, the authors describe the *fuzzy central limit theorem* as follows: "Data that are influenced by many small and unrelated random effects are approximately normally distributed. This explains why the normal is everywhere: stock market fluctuations, student weights, yearly temperature averages, [test] scores: All are the result of many different effects." People's heights, for example, are the results of hereditary factors, environmental factors, nutrition, health care, geographic region, and other influences that, when combined, produce normally distributed values.

SOLUTION   We weren't given the distribution of the population, but because the sample size $n = 108$ exceeds 30, we use the central limit theorem and conclude that the distribution of sample means is a normal distribution with these parameters:

$$\mu_{\bar{x}} = \mu = 37.0$$

$$\sigma_{\bar{x}} = \frac{\sigma}{\sqrt{n}} = \frac{0.62}{\sqrt{108}} = 0.059659$$

Figure 5-23 shows the shaded area (see the left tail of the graph) corresponding to the probability we seek. Having already found the parameters that apply to the distribution shown in Figure 5-23, we can now find the shaded area by using the same procedures developed in the preceding section. We first find the z score:

$$z = \frac{\bar{x} - \mu_{\bar{x}}}{\sigma_{\bar{x}}} = \frac{36.4 - 37.0}{0.059659} = -10.06$$

Referring to Table A-2, we find that $z = -10.06$ (or its positive equivalent) is off the chart, but for absolute values of z above 3.09, we use an area of 0.4999. We therefore conclude that region A in Figure 5-23 is 0.4999 and the shaded region is $0.5 - 0.4999 = 0.0001$.

Interpretation   The result shows that if the mean of our body temperatures is really 37°C, then there is an extremely small probability of getting a sample mean of 36.4°C or lower when 108 subjects are randomly selected. Either the population mean really is 37.0°C and the sample represents a chance event that is extremely rare, or the population mean is actually lower than 37.0°C so the sample is typical. Because the probability is so low, it seems more reasonable to conclude that the population mean is lower than 37.0°C. This is the type of reasoning used in hypothesis testing, to be introduced in Chapter 7. For now, we should focus on the use of the central limit theorem for finding the probability of 0.0001, but we should also observe that this theorem will be used later in developing some very important concepts in statistics.

Figure 5-23   Distribution of Sample Mean Body Temperatures ($n = 108$)

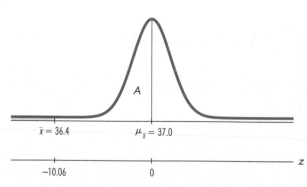

Correcting for a Finite Population

In applying the central limit theorem, our use of $\sigma_{\bar{x}} = \sigma/\sqrt{n}$ assumes that the population has infinitely many members. When we sample with replacement (that is, put back each selected item before making the next selection), the population is effectively infinite. Yet many realistic applications involve sampling without replacement, so successive samples depend on previous outcomes. In manufacturing, quality control inspectors typically sample items from a finite production run without replacing them. For such a finite population, we may need to adjust $\sigma_{\bar{x}}$. Here is a common rule of thumb:

When sampling without replacement and the sample size n is greater than 5% of the finite population size N (that is, $n > 0.05N$), adjust the standard deviation of sample means $\sigma_{\bar{x}}$ by multiplying it by the *finite population correction factor:*

$$\sqrt{\frac{N - n}{N - 1}}$$

Except for Exercises 15, 20, 21 and 23, the examples and exercises in this section assume that the finite population correction factor does not apply, because the population is infinite or the sample size does not exceed 5% of the population size.

It's very important to note that the central limit theorem applies when we are dealing with the distribution of sample means and either the sample size is greater than 30 or the original population has a normal distribution. Once we have established that the central limit theorem applies, we can determine values for $\mu_{\bar{x}} = \mu$ and $\sigma_{\bar{x}} = \sigma/\sqrt{n}$ and then proceed to use the methods presented in the preceding section.

The central limit theorem is so important because it allows us to use the basic normal distribution methods in a wide variety of different circumstances. In Chapter 6, for example, we will apply the theorem when we use sample data to estimate means of populations. In Chapter 7 we will apply it when we use sample data to test claims made about population means. Such applications of estimating population parameters and testing claims are extremely important uses of statistics, and the central limit theorem makes them possible.

5-5 Exercises A: Basic Skills and Concepts

In Exercises 1–4, assume that female students' heights are normally distributed with a mean given by $\mu = 64.2$ in. and a standard deviation given by $\sigma = 2.6$ in.

1. **a.** If one female student is randomly selected, find the probability that her height is between 64.2 in. and 65.2 in.
   b. If 36 female students are randomly selected, find the probability that they have a mean height between 64.2 in. and 65.2 in.

2. **a.** If one female student is randomly selected, find the probability that her height is above 63.0 in.

   b. If 100 female students are randomly selected, find the probability that they have a mean height greater than 63.0 in.

3. **a.** If one female student is randomly selected, find the probability that her height is above 65.0 in.

   b. If 50 female students are randomly selected, find the probability that they have a mean height greater than 65.0 in.

4. **a.** If 4 female students are randomly selected, find the probability that their mean height is between 63.0 in. and 65.0 in.

   b. Why can the central limit theorem be used in part (a), even though the sample size does not exceed 30?

5. Replacement times for TV sets are normally distributed with a mean of 8.2 years and a standard deviation of 1.1 years (based on data from "Getting Things Fixed," *Consumer Reports*). Find the probability that 40 randomly selected TV sets will have a mean replacement time less than 8.0 years.

6. Replacement times for CD players are normally distributed with a mean of 7.1 years and a standard deviation of 1.4 years (based on data from "Getting Things Fixed," *Consumer Reports*). Find the probability that 45 randomly selected CD players will have a mean replacement time of 6.8 years or less. If 45 CD players were, in fact, selected randomly from the past sales of E-Electronics Edmonton, and had a mean replacement time of 6.8 years, would it appear that this store has been given CD players with lower than average quality?

7. The total weights of garbage that households discard weekly is approximately normally distributed, with a mean of 12.5 kg and a standard deviation of 5.7 kg (based on Data Set 1 in Appendix B).

   a. If 120 households are randomly selected, find the probability that the mean weight of their discarded garbage is over 13.5 kg.

   b. If the town's waste transfer station allocates capacity for 1690 kg of temporary garbage storage per 120 households per week, and the typical garbage route is based on 120 households, what percentage of garbage routes will exceed the allocated capacity for their garbage? Is this an acceptable level or should the town council take corrective action?

8. According to the International Mass Retail Association, girls aged 13 to 17 spend an average of $31.20 on shopping trips in a month. Assume that the amounts have a standard deviation of $8.27. If 85 girls in that age category are randomly selected, what is the probability that their mean monthly shopping expense is between $30.00 and $33.00?

9. For females aged 18–24, systolic blood pressures (in mm Hg) are normally distributed with a mean of 114.8 and a standard deviation of 13.1.

   a. If a woman between the ages of 18 and 24 is randomly selected, find the probability that her systolic blood pressure is above 120.

   b. If 12 women in that age bracket are randomly selected, find the probability that their mean systolic blood pressure is greater than 120.

   c. Given that part (b) involves a sample size that is not larger than 30, why can the central limit theorem be used?

10. The *depth* of a diamond signifies 100 times the ratio of its height to its diameter. For many high-priced diamonds, depth appears to be normally distributed, with a mean of 60.83 and a standard deviation of 1.97 (based on Data Set 21 in Appendix B). If 40 high-priced diamonds are randomly selected, find the probability that their mean depth is less than 61.2.

11. The ages of U.S. commercial aircraft have a mean of 13.0 years and a standard deviation of 7.9 years (based on data from Aviation Data Services). If the Federal Aviation Administration randomly selects 35 commercial aircraft for special stress tests, find the probability that the mean age of this sample group is greater than 15.0 years.

12. Information provided by Bell Canada in Winnipeg showed that the average monthly bill for basic service was normally distributed with a mean of $15.30 and a standard deviation of $1.25. If 55 phone bills are randomly selected, find the probability that their mean exceeds $15.

13. The typical computer random-number generator yields numbers in a uniform distribution between 0 and 1 with a mean of 0.500 and a standard deviation of 0.289. If 45 random numbers are generated, find the probability that their mean is below 0.565.

14. A study was made of seat-belt use among children who were involved in car crashes that caused them to be hospitalized. It was found that children not wearing any restraints had hospital stays with a mean of 7.37 days and a standard deviation of 0.79 day (based on data from "Morbidity Among Pediatric Motor Vehicle Crash Victims: The Effectiveness of Seat Belts," by Osberg and Di Scala, *American Journal of Public Health,* Vol. 82, No. 3). If 40 such children are randomly selected, find the probability that their mean hospital stay is greater than 7.00 days.

15. As part of his review for a chemistry test, a student randomly selects (without replacement) 40 out of the 102 elements listed on the standard tables, and tries to guess their atomic numbers. Given that the mean of all 102 atomic numbers is 51.794, and the population standard deviation is 29.804, what is the probability that the mean of the 40 atomic numbers selected by the student will be at least 58.3? (*Hint*: See the discussion of the finite population correction factor.)

16. SAT verbal scores are normally distributed with a mean of 430 and a standard deviation of 120 (based on data from the College Board ATP). Randomly selected SAT verbal scores are obtained from the population of students who took a test preparatory course from a training school. Assume that this training course has no effect on test scores.
    a. If one of the students is randomly selected, find the probability that he or she obtained a score greater than 440.
    b. If 100 students of an SAT preparation course achieve a sample mean of 440, does it seem reasonable to conclude that the course is effective because the students perform better on the SAT?

17. The lengths of pregnancies are normally distributed with a mean of 268 days and a standard deviation of 15 days.
    a. If one pregnant female is randomly selected, find the probability that her length of pregnancy is less than 260 days.
    b. If 25 randomly selected females are put on a special diet just before they become pregnant, find the probability that their lengths of

pregnancy have a mean that is less than 260 days (assuming that the diet has no effect).

   c. If the 25 females do have a mean of less than 260 days, should the medical supervisors be concerned?

18. A survey by Statistics Canada shows the average household expenditure on post-secondary textbooks is $53.00, with a standard deviation of $18.61. A similar poll randomly selects 150 households to find average expenditure on post-secondary textbooks.

   a. Find the probability that the mean is greater than $57.00.

   b. If a sample of 150 households does yield a mean of $57.00 or greater, is there reason to believe that this sample came from a population with a mean that is higher than $53.00?

19. M&M plain candies have a mean weight of 0.9147 g and a standard deviation of 0.0369 g (based on Data Set 11 in Appendix B). The M&M candies used in Data Set 11 came from a package containing 1498 candies, and the package label stated that the net weight is 48.0 oz, or 1361 g. (If every package has 1498 candies, the mean weight must exceed $1361/1498 = 0.9085$ g for the net contents to weigh at least 1361 g.)

   a. If an M&M plain candy is randomly selected, find the probability that it weighs more than 0.9085 g.

   b. If 1498 M&M plain candies are randomly selected, find the probability that their mean weight is at least 0.9085 g.

   c. Given these results, does it seem that Mars is providing M&M consumers with the amount claimed on the label?

20. Weights of players in offensive back positions (including quarterback) in the Canadian Football League are approximately normally distributed, with a mean of 197.5 lb and a standard deviation of 14.2 lb (based on data from the CFL Web site). An elevator at the hotel that is hosting an awards dinner for all CFL offensive backs (there are 90 such players) posts a limit of 32 occupants, but it will be overloaded if the 32 occupants have a combined weight of 6450 lb or over. If a random selection of 32 of the offensive backs happen to get on the elevator at one time, find the probability that their combined weight will exceed 6450 lb, causing the elevator to be overloaded. Based on the value obtained, is there reason for concern?

5-5 Exercises B: Beyond the Basics

21. A *population* consists of these scores: 2, 3, 6, 8, 11, 18.

   a. Find μ and σ.

   b. List all samples of size $n = 2$ that are obtained without replacement.

   c. Find the population of all values of $\bar{x}$ by finding the mean of each sample from part (b).

   d. Find the mean $\mu_{\bar{x}}$ and standard deviation $\sigma_{\bar{x}}$ for the population of sample means found in part (c).

   e. Verify that

$$\mu_{\bar{x}} = \mu \quad \text{and} \quad \sigma_{\bar{x}} = \frac{\sigma}{\sqrt{n}}\sqrt{\frac{N-n}{N-1}}$$

22. An education researcher develops an index of academic interest and obtains scores for a randomly selected sample of 350 college students. The results are summarized in the accompanying boxplot. If 15 of the students are randomly selected, find the probability that their mean score is greater than 55.

23. The finite population correction factor can be ignored when sampling with replacement or when $n \leq 0.05N$. When collecting a sample (without replacement) that is 5% of the population N, what do the values of the finite population correction factor have in common for values of $N \geq 600$? (That is, try calculating the factor for a few values of $N > 600$ and with $n = 0.05N$. What do the results have in common?)

5-6 Normal Distribution as Approximation to Binomial Distribution

In Section 4-3 we introduced the *binomial probability distribution,* which applies to a discrete random variable (rather than to a continuous random variable, as does the normal distribution). We noted that a binomial distribution has these four requirements:

1. The experiment must have a *fixed number of trials.*

2. The trials must be *independent.*

3. Each trial must have all outcomes classified into *two categories.*

4. The probabilities must remain *constant* for each trial.

A typical binomial probability problem involves finding $P(x)$, the probability of x successes among n trials. In Section 4-3 you learned (we hope) how to solve binomial problems by using computer software or Table A-1 or the binomial probability formula. In many cases, however, those methods are not practical. Consider the binomial problem of finding the probability of getting at least 64 men among 100 randomly selected people. Table A-1 doesn't apply because it stops at $n = 15$, and the formula isn't practical because we would have to apply it 37 times (once for each integer from 64 through 100). Such calculations are of the type mathematicians often refer to as "tedious," meaning that they will seriously challenge your sanity. Instead, we will introduce a new method whereby we approximate the binomial distribution by a normal distribution so that the calculations will be greatly simplified. The following box summarizes the key point of this section.

Reliability and Validity

The reliability of data refers to the consistency with which results occur, whereas the validity of data refers to how well the data measure what they are supposed to measure. The reliability of an IQ test can be judged by comparing scores for the test given on one date to scores for the same test given at another time. To test the validity of an IQ test, we might compare the test scores to another indicator of intelligence, such as academic performance. Many critics charge that IQ tests are reliable, but not valid; they provide consistent results, but don't really measure intelligence.

She Won the Lottery Twice!

Evelyn Marie Adams won the New Jersey Lottery twice in four months. This happy event was reported as an incredible coincidence with a likelihood of only 1 chance in 17 trillion. But mathematicians Persi Diaconis and Frederick Mosteller note that there is 1 chance in 17 trillion that a particular person with one ticket in each of two New Jersey lotteries will win both times. However, there is about 1 chance in 30 that someone in the United States will win a lottery twice in a four-month period. Diaconis and Mosteller analysed coincidences and concluded that "with a large enough sample, any outrageous thing is apt to happen."

Normal Distribution as Approximation to Binomial Distribution

If $np \geq 5$ and $nq \geq 5$, then the binomial random variable is approximately normally distributed with the mean and standard deviation given as

$$\mu = np$$
$$\sigma = \sqrt{npq}$$

Review Figure 4-4 (which applies to a binomial distribution with $n = 100$, $p = 0.5$, and $q = 0.5$) and note that this particular binomial distribution does have a probability histogram with roughly the same shape as that of a normal distribution. The formal justification that allows us to use the normal distribution as an approximation to the binomial distribution results from more advanced mathematics, but Figure 4-4 is a visual argument supporting that approximation.

The normal approximation approach involves the following procedure, which is depicted in the flowchart shown in Figure 5-24.

Normal Approximation Procedure

1. Verify that the binomial probability distribution applies.
2. If available, use software such as Excel or STATDISK. (Examples of Excel or STATDISK displays are found in Section 4-3.)
3. If software is not available, try to solve the problem by using Table A-1.
4. If Table A-1 cannot be used, consider the binomial probability formula. If the problem can be *easily* solved with the binomial probability formula, use it. Otherwise, continue with Step 5.
5. Establish that the normal distribution is a suitable approximation to the binomial distribution by verifying that $np \geq 5$ and $nq \geq 5$.
6. Find the values of the parameters μ and σ by calculating $\mu = np$ and $\sigma = \sqrt{npq}$.
7. Identify the discrete value x, which represents the number of successes in the binomial experiment. Modify the *discrete* value x by replacing it with the *interval* from $x - 0.5$ to $x + 0.5$. (See the discussion under the subheading "Continuity Corrections" found later in this section.) Draw a normal curve and enter the values of μ, σ, and either $x - 0.5$ or $x + 0.5$, as appropriate.
8. Modify x by replacing it with $x - 0.5$ or $x + 0.5$, as appropriate, then find the z score: $z = (x - \mu)/\sigma$.
9. Using the z score found in Step 8, refer to Table A-2 to find the area between μ and either $x - 0.5$ or $x + 0.5$, as appropriate. Identify the area corresponding to the desired probability.

We will now illustrate this normal approximation procedure with an example.

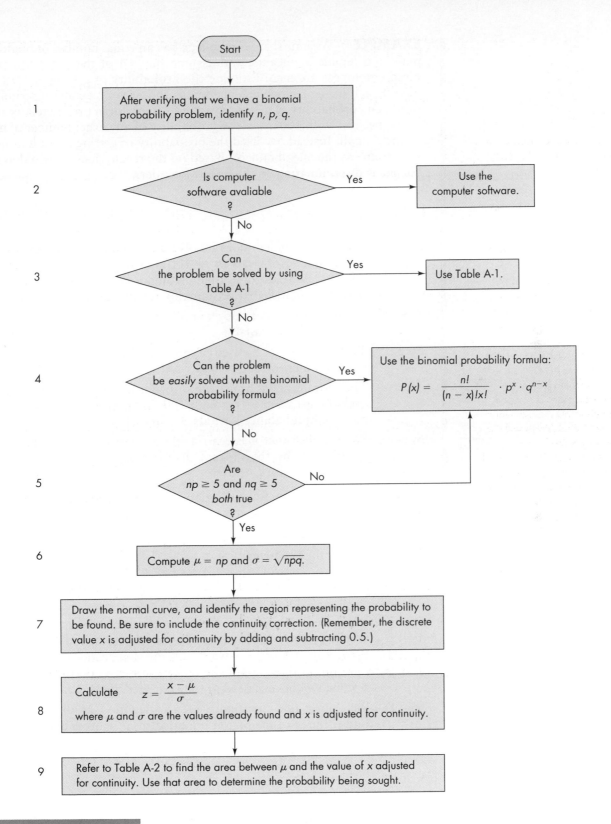

Figure 5-24   Solving Binomial Probability Problems Using a Normal Approximation

EXAMPLE   Assume that your college has an equal number of qualified male and female applicants, and assume that 64 of the last 100 newly hired employees are men. Estimate the probability of getting *at least* 64 men if each hiring is done independently and with no gender discrimination. (The probability of getting *exactly* 64 men doesn't really tell us anything, because with 100 trials, the probability of any exact number of men is fairly small. Instead, we need the probability of getting a result *at least* as extreme as the one obtained.) Based on the result, does it seem that the college is discriminating on the basis of gender?

SOLUTION

Step 1:   The given problem does involve a binomial distribution with a fixed number of trials ($n = 100$), which are presumably independent, two categories (man, woman) of outcome for each trial, and probabilities that presumably remain constant.

Step 2:   For the purposes of this example, we will assume that computer software is not available.

Step 3:   Table A-1 cannot be used because the value of $n = 100$ exceeds the maximum value of $n = 15$ found in the table.

Step 4:   The formula could be used, but then it would have to be used for each integer from 64 through 100. We prefer to avoid using the binomial probability formula 37 times.

Step 5:   We establish that it is reasonable to approximate the binomial distribution by the normal distribution because $np \geq 5$ and $nq \geq 5$, as verified below:

$$np = 100 \cdot 0.5 = 50 \qquad \text{(Therefore } np \geq 5.\text{)}$$
$$nq = 100 \cdot 0.5 = 50 \qquad \text{(Therefore } nq \geq 5.\text{)}$$

Step 6:   We now proceed to find the values for μ and σ that are needed. We get the following:

$$\mu = np = 100 \cdot 0.5 = 50$$
$$\sigma = \sqrt{npq} = \sqrt{100 \cdot 0.5 \cdot 0.5} = 5$$

Step 7:   In Figure 5-25 we show the discrete value of 64 as being represented by the vertical strip bounded by 63.5 and 64.5. Figure 5-26 shows the area we want: It is the shaded area in the extreme right tail of the graph. (The reasons for this "correction" of the x value will be discussed in the next section.)

Step 8:   We cannot find the shaded area in Figure 5-26 directly, so we find the area of the region bounded by $\mu = 50$ and the score of 63.5. This area corresponds to the following z score:

$$z = \frac{x - \mu}{\sigma} = \frac{63.5 - 50}{5} = 2.70$$

Step 9:   Using Table A-2, we find that $z = 2.70$ corresponds to an area of 0.4965, so the shaded area we seek is $0.5 - 0.4965 = 0.0035$.

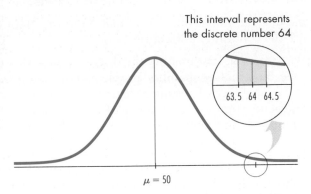

Figure 5-25 Illustration of Continuity Correction

This interval represents the discrete number 64

63.5 64 64.5

$\mu = 50$

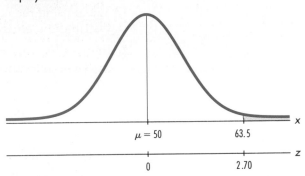

Figure 5-26 Finding the Probability of "At Least" 64 Men Among 100 New Employees

$\mu = 50$ 63.5   x

0   2.70   z

Assuming that men and women have equal chances of being hired, the probability of getting at least 64 men in 100 new employees is approximately 0.0035. (Using the software packages of Excel or STATDISK, we get the answer of 0.0033, so the approximation is quite good here.)

Interpretation Because the probability of getting at least 64 men is so small (0.0035), we conclude that either a very rare event has occurred or the assumption that men and women have the same chance is incorrect. It appears that the college discriminates on the basis of gender. The reasoning here will be considered in more detail in Chapter 7 when we discuss formal methods of testing hypotheses. For now, we should focus on the method of finding the probability by using the normal approximation technique.

Continuity Corrections

Step 7 in the procedure just given (where we add or subtract 0.5 from the discrete value x) is difficult for many people to understand. It is based on the concept of continuity corrections.

DEFINITION

When we use the normal distribution (which is continuous) as an approximation to the binomial distribution (which is discrete), a **continuity correction** is made to a discrete whole number x in the binomial distribution by representing the single value x by the *interval* from $x - 0.5$ to $x + 0.5$ (that is, add and subtract 0.5).

The following practical suggestions should help you use continuity corrections properly.

Procedure for Continuity Corrections

1. When using the normal distribution as an approximation to the binomial distribution, *always* use the continuity correction.

2. In using the continuity correction, first identify the discrete whole number x that is relevant to the binomial probability problem. For example, if you're trying to find the probability of getting at least 64 men in 100 randomly selected people, the discrete whole number of concern is $x = 64$. First focus on the x value itself, and temporarily ignore whether you want at least x, more than x, fewer than x, or whatever.

3. Draw a normal distribution centred about μ, then draw a *vertical strip area* centred over x. Mark the left side of the strip with the number $x - 0.5$, and mark the right side with $x + 0.5$. For $x = 64$, draw a strip from 63.5 to 64.5. *Consider the entire area of the strip to represent the probability of the discrete number x itself.*

4. Now determine whether the value of x itself should be included in the probability you want. (For example, "at least x" does include x itself, but "more than x" does not include x itself.) Next, determine whether you want the probability of at least x, at most x, more than x, fewer than x, or exactly x. Shade the area to the right or left of the strip, as appropriate; also shade the interior of the strip itself *if and only if x itself is to be included.* This total shaded region corresponds to the probability being sought.

To see how this procedure results in continuity corrections, see the common cases illustrated in Figure 5-27.

At least 64

63.5

More than 64

64.5

At most 64

64.5

Fewer than 64

63.5

Exactly 64

63.5 64.5

Figure 5-27 Identifying the Correct Area

EXAMPLE   It is common for chemistry data tables to include the atomic masses of the elements. For 15.7% of the elements, however, the atomic masses cannot be known exactly, unless something is known of a specimen's origin. Suppose a chemistry professor is giving to each of his 150 students an individualized test, such that each student receives the name of one of the elements, which they must discuss. A computer randomly selects an element name for each student independently. What is the probability that exactly 30 students will receive the name of an element for which the atomic mass cannot be known exactly without knowledge of origin?

SOLUTION   This solution follows the steps outlined in Figure 5-24.

Step 1: The conditions described satisfy the criteria for the binomial distribution with $n = 150$, $p = .157$, $q = .843$, and $x = 30$. (The value of q is found from $q = 1 - p = 1 - .157 = .843$.)

Step 2: For the purposes of this example, we assume that computer software is not available.

Step 3: Table A-1 cannot be used because $n = 150$ exceeds the largest table value of $n = 15$.

Step 4: The binomial probability formula applies, but

$$P(30) = \frac{150!}{(150 - 30)!\, 30!} \cdot 0.157^{30} \cdot 0.843^{150 - 30}$$

is difficult to compute because many calculators cannot evaluate 70! or higher.

Step 5: In this problem,

$$np = 150 \cdot 0.157 = 23.55 \qquad \text{(Therefore } np \geq 5.\text{)}$$

$$nq = 150 \cdot 0.843 = 126.45 \qquad \text{(Therefore } nq \geq 5.\text{)}$$

Because np and nq are both at least 5, we conclude that the normal approximation to the binomial distribution is satisfactory.

Step 6: We obtain the values of μ and σ as follows:

$$\mu = np = 150 \cdot 0.157 = 23.55$$

$$\sigma = \sqrt{npq} = \sqrt{(150)(0.157)(0.843)} = 4.4556313$$

Step 7: We draw the normal curve shown in Figure 5-28. The shaded region of the figure represents the probability we want. Use of the continuity correction results in the representation of 30 by the region extending from 29.5 to 30.5.

Step 8: The format of Table A-2 requires that we first find the probability corresponding to the region bounded on the left by the vertical line through the mean of 23.55 and on the right by the vertical line through 30.5. Therefore, one of the calculations required in this step is as follows:

$$z = \frac{30.5 - 23.55}{4.4556313} = 1.56$$

Picking Lottery Numbers

In a typical lottery, you select six different numbers. After a random drawing, any entries with the correct combination share in the prize. Since the winning numbers are randomly selected, any choice of six numbers will have the same chance as any other choice, but some combinations are better than others. The combination of 1, 2, 3, 4, 5, 6 is a poor choice because many people tend to select it. In a Florida lottery with a $105 million prize, 52,000 tickets had 1, 2, 3, 4, 5, 6; if that combination had won, the prize would have been only $1000. It's wise to pick combinations not selected by many others. Avoid combinations that form a pattern on the entry card.

Figure 5-28

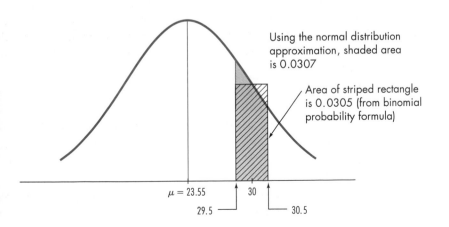

Using the normal distribution approximation, shaded area is 0.0307

Area of striped rectangle is 0.0305 (from binomial probability formula)

$\mu = 23.55$ 30

29.5   30.5

We also need the probability corresponding to the region bounded by 23.55 and 29.5, so we calculate

$$z = \frac{29.5 - 23.55}{4.4556313} = 1.34$$

Step 9:   We use Table A-2 to find that $z = 1.56$ corresponds to a probability of 0.4406 and $z = 1.34$ corresponds to a probability of 0.4099. Consequently, the shaded region of Figure 5-28 depicts a probability of $0.4406 - 0.4099 = 0.0307$. The probability of exactly 30 students (out of 150) getting names of chemical elements whose atomic mass cannot be exactly known without knowledge of origin is 0.0307.

If we solve the preceding example using Excel or STATDISK, we get a result of 0.0305, but the normal approximation method resulted in a value of 0.0307. The discrepancy of 0.0002 occurs because the use of the normal distribution results in an *approximate* value that is the area of the shaded region in Figure 5-28, whereas the correct area is a rectangle centered above 30. (Figure 5-28 illustrates this discrepancy.)

5-6 Exercises A: Basic Skills and Concepts

In Exercises 1–8, use the continuity correction and describe the region of the normal curve that corresponds to the indicated probability. For example, the probability of "more than 47 successes" corresponds to this area of the normal curve: the area to the right of 47.5.

1. Probability of more than 35 defective parts
2. Probability of at least 175 girls
3. Probability of fewer than 42 correct answers to multiple-choice questions
4. Probability of exactly 65 correct answers to true/false questions
5. Probability of no more than 72 cars with defective brakes
6. Probability that the number of baby girls is between 35 and 45 inclusive
7. Probability that the number of Conservative voters is between 125 and 150 inclusive
8. Probability that the number of patients with group A blood is exactly 34

In Exercises 9–12, do the following:

   a. *Find the indicated binomial probability using Table A-1 in Appendix A.*
   b. *If $np \geq 5$ and $nq \geq 5$, also estimate the indicated probability by using the normal distribution as an approximation to the binomial distribution; if $np < 5$ or $nq < 5$, then state that the normal approximation is not suitable.*

9. With $n = 14$ and $p = 0.50$, find $P(8)$.

10. With $n = 10$ and $p = 0.40$, find $P(7)$.

11. With $n = 15$ and $p = 0.80$, find $P(\text{at least } 8)$.

12. With $n = 14$ and $p = 0.60$, find $P(\text{fewer than } 9)$.

13. Estimate the probability of getting at least 55 girls in 100 births.

14. Estimate the probability of getting exactly 32 boys in 64 births.

15. Estimate the probability of passing a true/false test of 50 questions if 60% (or 30 correct responses) represents a passing grade and all responses are random guesses.

16. A multiple-choice test consists of 50 questions with possible answers of a, b, c, d, and e. Estimate the probability of getting at most 30% correct if all answers are random guesses.

17. Based on past records, there is a 3.62% chance that any particular CFL player is a punter or kicker. For 140 randomly selected players, estimate the probability that exactly 3 are punters or kickers.

18. The Angus Reid Group surveyed Ontario residents on what they think will be the most valuable type of education to have in the work force ten years from now. Thirty-five percent of the respondents chose a college diploma in technical occupations. Estimate the probability that if 1000 Ontario residents are selected at random, 350 of them would choose or recommend a college diploma in technical occupations.

19. According to a consumer affairs representative from Mars (the candy company, not the planet), 10% of all M&M plain candies are blue. Data Set 11 in Appendix B shows that among 100 M&Ms chosen, 5 are blue. Estimate the probability of randomly selecting 100 M&Ms and getting 5 or fewer that are blue. Assume that the company's 10% blue rate is correct. Based on the result, is it very unusual to get 5 or fewer blue M&Ms when 100 are randomly selected?

20. John Dukhia plans to place 200 bets of $1 each on the number 7 at roulette. On any one spin there is a probability of 1/38 that 7 will be the winning number. For John to end up with a profit, the number 7 must occur at least 6 times among the 200 trials. Estimate the probability that John finishes with a profit.

21. The Angus Reid Group surveyed Ontario residents on what they think will be the most valuable type of education to have in the work force ten years from now. Eighteen percent of the respondents chose a university degree in science. Estimate the probability that if 400 Ontario residents are selected at random, 70 or fewer would choose or recommend a university degree in science

22. Air Borealis has been experiencing a 7% rate of no-shows on advance reservations. In a test project that requires passengers to confirm reservations, it is found that among 250 randomly selected advance reservations, there are 4 no-shows. Assuming that the confirmation requirement has no effect so the 7% rate applies, estimate the probability of 4 or fewer no-shows among 250 randomly selected reservations. Based on that result, does it appear that the confirmation requirement is effective?

23. In a survey, the Canadian Automobile Association (CAA) found that 38% of respondents had bought used vehicles. A car dealership surveys 150 people at random and finds that 45 of them have bought used vehicles.

Estimate the probability of 45 or more respondents being used-vehicle purchasers. Based on that value, does the CAA survey result seem too high?

24. A successful venture capital firm reports that it finances only 10% of the proposals that it receives. A check of 100 randomly selected proposals shows that 8 of them were financed by the firm. Estimate the probability that among 100 proposals, 8 or fewer were financed by the firm. Based on the result, does it seem that the venture capital firm's claim is correct?

25. A manufacturer of automobile headlights claims that 10% of a batch of these headlights are defective. A quality control inspector tests a random selection of 300 headlights in the batch. The number of defective headlights in this random sample is 35, which is more than expected. Estimate the probability of getting at least 35 defective lights in a random sample of 300. Based on the result, does it appear that the manufacturer's claim of 10% defectiveness is accurate? Was there a problem with the sample?

26. Some couples have genetic characteristics configured so that one-quarter of all offspring have blue eyes. A study is conducted of 40 couples believed to have those characteristics, with the result that 8 of their 40 offspring have blue eyes. Estimate the probability that among 40 offspring, 8 or fewer have blue eyes. Based on that probability, does it seem that the one-quarter rate is correct?

27. Sunnybrook Hospital is conducting a blood drive because its supply of group O blood is low, and it needs 177 donors of group O blood. If 400 volunteers donate blood, estimate the probability that the number with group O blood is at least 177. Forty-six percent of us have group O blood, according to data provided by Canadian Blood Services.

28. Some companies monitor quality by using a method of acceptance sampling whereby an entire batch of items is rejected if, in a random sample, the number of defects is at least some predetermined number. The Macker Machine Company buys machine bolts in batches of 5000 and rejects a batch if, when 50 of them are sampled, at least 2 defects are found. Estimate the probability of rejecting a batch if the supplier is manufacturing the bolts with a defect rate of 10%. Is this monitoring plan likely to identify the unacceptable rate of defects? Explain.

5-6 Exercises B: Beyond the Basics

29. Replacement times for TV sets are normally distributed with a mean of 8.2 years and a standard deviation of 1.1 years (based on data from "Getting Things Fixed," *Consumer Reports*). Estimate the probability that for 250 randomly selected TV sets, at least 15 of them have replacement times greater than 10.0 years.

30. Assume that a baseball player hits .350, so his probability of a hit is 0.350. (Ignore the complications caused by walks.) Also assume that his hitting attempts are independent of each other.
    a. Find the probability of at least 1 hit in 4 tries in 1 game.

    b. Assuming that this batter gets up to bat 4 times each game, estimate the probability of getting a total of at least 56 hits in 56 games.

    c. Assuming that this batter gets up to bat 4 times each game, find the probability of at least 1 hit in each of 56 consecutive games (Joe DiMaggio's 1941 record).

    d. What minimum batting average would be required for the probability in part (c) to be greater than 0.1?

31. Find the difference between the answers obtained with and without use of the continuity correction in each of the following. What do you conclude from the results?

    a. Estimate the probability of getting at least 11 girls in 20 births.

    b. Estimate the probability of getting at least 22 girls in 40 births.

    c. Estimate the probability of getting at least 220 girls in 400 births.

32. Air Borealis works only with advance reservations and experiences a 7% rate of no-shows. How many reservations could be accepted for an airliner with a capacity of 250 if there is at least a 0.95 probability that all reservation holders who show will be accommodated?

5-7   Determining Normality

Many important statistical methods require that the sample data were collected from a population that has a *normal* distribution. It is therefore very important to be able to determine whether we are working with data that are normally distributed. In this section we describe one of many different procedures that could be used for determining whether the population distribution is normal. That procedure follows the definition of a *normal probability plot*.

> **DEFINITION**
>
> A **normal probability plot** compares the original values in a set of sample data with the expected values, for a sample of the given size and assuming the sample were drawn from a normally distributed population.

Procedure for Determining Whether Data Have a Normal Distribution

1. *Histogram*: Construct a histogram. Reject normality if the histogram departs dramatically from a bell shape.

2. *Outliers*: Identify outliers. Reject normality if there is more than one outlier present. (Just one outlier could be an error or the result of chance variation; but be careful, because even a single outlier can have a dramatic effect on results.)

3. *Normal probability plot*: If the histogram is basically symmetric and there is at most one outlier, construct a normal probability plot, using the following steps.

a. First sort the data by arranging the values in order from lowest to highest, and use the sorted data to form the left column of a table (see Figure 5-29).

b. With a sample of size n, each value in the left column represents a proportion of $1/n$ of the sample. The procedure to fill the right column is based on finding the z-score which corresponds to the centre of each successive area under the assumed normal curve. There are two steps:

a) First calculate, for each successive portion of the curve, the area under the normal curve that it represents—that is, the area extending from the extreme left to a line over the z score at the centre of that portion of the curve. For example, the first z score represents an area of $0.5/n$, the next z score represents an area of $1.5/n$, then $2.5/n$, $3.5/n$, and so on.

b) Use Table A-2 (or statistical software) to find the z scores that correspond to each of these areas under the curve. That is, for each portion, find z such that $P(x < z)$ is the value you calculated in step (a).

c. Plot the points (x, y) where the x's are the expected middle z scores for the first, second, third, etc. portions of the normal curve, and the y's are the corresponding values in the original sample. (See Figure 5-30.)

(*Note*: Some details for constructing normal probability plots can vary among different textbooks or software packages—for example, whether to assign the original or the expected values to the x axis, or whether to work with z scores (as we do here) or with t scores (which is recommended if you are working with small samples.)

To interpret the results of this procedure, compare the plot you have created with the ideal of a straight line. If the distribution of the sample is normal, we expect the points to exhibit only a small amount of random variation from a straight-line relationship.

Figure 5-29 Table for Constructing a Probability Plot

(sorted) Imports to Canada from the Middle East and Africa	Middle z-score for the the expected, corresponding portion of the normal curve
1387	−1.960
1490	−1.440
1590	−1.150
1598	−0.935
1691	−0.755
1774	−0.598
1815	−0.454
1937	−0.319
1992	−0.189
2039	−0.063
2283	0.063
2554	0.189
2571	0.319
2840	0.454
3372	0.598
3446	0.755
3503	0.935
3989	1.150
4057	1.440
4103	1.960

Figure 5-30   Normal Probability Plot

EXAMPLE   The *F*-test for comparing variances (Chapter 8) has a strong requirement that each population being compared have a normal distribution. Suppose the data in the rightmost column of Data Set 22 in Appendix B, for imports to Canada from the Middle East and Africa over 20 years, represent one of the samples to be compared. Although the data were collected as a time series (one total is given per year), would it be reasonable to assume that the results are normally distributed?

SOLUTION

Step 1:   We begin by constructing the histogram of the original values, with the result shown in the accompanying Excel (DDXL) display. An examination of the histogram shows that the data appear to be somewhat skewed to the right.

Step 2:   There do not appear to be any outliers.

Step 3:   We construct the normal probability plot, as shown in Figure 5-30.

Interpretation   Both the histogram and the normal probability plot suggest that these data are, at best, loosely approximated by a normal curve. For example, in the normal probability plot, every actual value in the middle part of the data set is below the expected value for that position. Therefore, it would not be valid to apply a technique such as the *F*-test for comparing sample variances, since the test requires a good fit to normality.

For an additional example, see Review Exercise 11. In addition to the procedures discussed in this section, there are other, more advanced procedures, such as the chi-square goodness-of-fit test, the Kolmogorov-Smirnov test, and the Lilliefors test.

DDXL Histogram

d7:d26

DDXL Output

Using Technology

Excel: Thc Data Desk XL add-in (Figure 5-31) can be used to gen-erate a *normal probability plot*. First enter the sample val-ues into an Excel column. (There is no need to sort the data.) Click on **DDXL** on the main menu bar. Select **Charts and Plots,** then select the function type of **Normal Probability Plot.** Click on the pencil icon for "Quantitative Variable," then enter the range of values, such as A3:A22. Click **OK.**

Figure 5-3   Normal Probability Plot Produced by Excel (DDXL add-in)

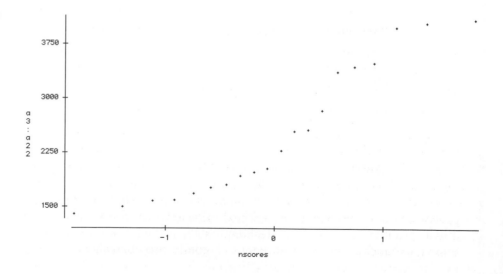

. . . .

Vocabulary List

normal distribution
uniform distribution
density curve
probability density function
standard normal distribution
z score

sampling distribution of sample
   means
central limit theorem
standard error of the mean
finite population correction factor
continuity correction
normal probability plot

. . . .

Review

Chapter 4 introduced the concept of the probability distribution, but included only *discrete* types. This chapter introduced *continuous* probability distributions and focused on the most important category: normal distributions. Normal distributions will be used extensively in the following chapters.

The normal distribution, which appears bell shaped when graphed, can be described algebraically by an equation, but the complexity of that equation usually forces us to use a table of values (Table A-2) or statistical software instead. Table A-2 gives areas corresponding to specific regions under the standard normal distribution curve, which has a mean of 0 and a standard deviation of 1. Those areas correspond to probability values.

In this chapter we worked with standard procedures for applying Table A-2 to a variety of different situations, including those that involve normal distributions that are nonstandard (with a mean other than 0 or a standard deviation other than 1). Those procedures usually involve use of the standard score: $z = (x - \mu)/\sigma$.

In Section 5-5 we presented the following important points associated with the central limit theorem:

1. The distribution of sample means will, as the sample size n increases, approach a normal distribution.

2. The mean of the sample means is the population mean μ.

3. The standard deviation of the sample means will be $\sigma/\sqrt{n}$.

In Section 5-6 we noted that we can sometimes approximate a binomial probability distribution by a normal distribution. If both $np \geq 5$ and $nq \geq 5$, the binomial random variable x is approximately normally distributed with the mean and standard deviation given as $\mu = np$ and $\sigma = \sqrt{npq}$. Because the binomial probability distribution deals with discrete data and the normal distribution deals with continuous data, we apply the continuity correction, which should be used in normal approximations to binomial distributions.

Finally, in Section 5-7 we presented a procedure for determining whether sample data appear to come from a population that has a normal distribution. Many of the statistical methods presented in this book have a loose requirement of a normally distributed population. In such cases, examination of a histogram and outliers might be all that is needed. In other cases, there is a very strict requirement that the distribution be normal, and normal probability plots might be necessary to ensure the requirement is met.

Review Exercises

In Exercises 1–4, assume that college statistics students have normally distributed heights with a mean of 68.0 in. and a standard deviation of 4.36 in. (based on Data Set 8 in Appendix B).

1. You plan to sell sweat suits in the college bookstore. To minimize start-up costs, you will not stock sweat suits for the tallest 5% and the shortest 5% of male students. Find the minimum and maximum heights of the students for whom sweat suits will be stocked.

2. The Beanstalk Club is a social organization for tall people. Students are eligible for membership if they are at least 74 in. tall. What percentage of students are eligible for membership in the Beanstalk Club?

3. The tallest player on the varsity basketball team is 80 in. tall. The shortest player is 69 in. tall. What percentage of students is in this range?

4. If 45 students are randomly selected, what is the probability that their mean height is between 67.0 in. and 71.0 in.?

5. In a survey, the Canadian Automobile Association (CAA) found that 58% of its members paid cash for their vehicles. Estimate the probability that when 500 CAA members are randomly selected, the number who paid cash is between 250 and 290 inclusive.

6. The Gleason Supermarket uses a scale to weigh produce, and errors are normally distributed with a mean of 0 oz and a standard deviation of 1 oz. (The errors can be positive or negative.) One item is randomly selected and weighed. Find the probability that the error is
   a. between 0 and 1.25 oz
   b. greater than 0.50 oz
   c. greater than −1.08 oz
   d. between −0.50 oz and 1.50 oz
   e. between −1.00 oz and −0.25 oz

7. Scores on the biology portion of the Medical College Admissions Test are normally distributed with a mean of 8.0 and a standard deviation of 2.6. Among 600 individuals taking this test, how many are expected to score between 6.0 and 7.0?

8. On the Graduate Record Exam in economics, scores are normally distributed with a mean of 615 and a standard deviation of 107. If a college admissions office requires scores above the 70th percentile, find the cutoff point.

9. According to the *National Hockey League Official Guide and Record Book 1998–1999*, the top goalie in the season let only 6.8% of the shots fired at him into the net for a goal. In a season in which 1739 shots are fired at the goalie, estimate the probability that more than 120 shots will result in a goal.

10. The Chemco Company manufactures car tires that last distances that are normally distributed with a mean of 57,300 km and a standard deviation of 6875 km.
    a. If a tire is randomly selected, what is the probability that it lasts more than 48,000 km?
    b. If 40 tires are randomly selected, what is the probability that they last distances that have a mean greater than 56,300 km?
    c. If the manufacturer wants to guarantee the tires so that only 3% will be replaced because of failure before the guaranteed number of kilometres, for how many kilometres should the tires be guaranteed?

11. Exercises 1 to 4 were based on the assumption that the height data in Data Set 8 are normally distributed. Use the methods presented in this chapter to confirm the assumption of normality. (Be sure to identify and remove the outlier in the data set—you can't miss it.)

Cumulative Review Exercises

1. According to data from Statistics Canada, Chinese is the mother tongue of 8.1% of Toronto residents.
   a. If 3 Toronto residents are randomly selected, find the probability that they all have Chinese as their mother tongue.
   b. If 3 Toronto residents are randomly selected, find the probability that at least one of them has Chinese as his or her mother tongue.
   c. Why can't we solve the problem in part (b) by using the normal approximation to the binomial distribution?
   d. If groups of 100 Toronto residents are randomly selected, what is the mean number of residents whose mother tongue is Chinese in such groups?
   e. If groups of 100 Toronto residents are randomly selected, what is the standard deviation for the number of residents whose mother tongue is Chinese?
   f. Would it be unusual to get 10 people whose mother tongue is Chinese in a randomly selected group of 100 Toronto residents? Why or why not?

2. The sample scores given below are times (in milliseconds) it took the author's disk drive to make one revolution. The times were recorded by a diagnostic software program.

   199.7 200.0 200.1 200.1 200.1 200.3 200.3 200.3 200.3 200.3
   200.3 200.3 200.4 200.4 200.4 200.4 200.4 200.4 200.4 200.4
   200.5 200.5 200.5 200.5 200.5 200.5 200.5 200.5 200.5 200.6
   200.6 200.6 200.6 200.6 200.6 200.7 200.8 201.1 201.2 201.2

   a. Find the mean $\bar{x}$ of the times in this sample.
   b. Find the median of the times in this sample.
   c. Find the mode of the times in this sample.
   d. Find the standard deviation s of this sample.
   e. Convert the time of 200.5 ms to a z score.
   f. Find the actual percentage of these sample scores that are greater than 201.0 ms.
   g. Assuming a normal distribution, find the percentage of *population* scores greater than 201.0 ms. Use the sample values of $\bar{x}$ and s as estimates of μ and σ.
   h. The specifications require times between 197.0 ms and 202.0 ms. Based on these sample results, does the disk drive seem to be rotating at acceptable speeds?

Technology Project

In this chapter we looked at finding the percentage of male college students with heights between the average height of the Toronto Maple Leafs (the third-shortest team in the NHL), at 72.4 in., and the average height of the Philadelphia Flyers (the tallest team), at 74.6 in. We found that only 15.02% of college males were that tall. The solution, given in Section 5-3, involves theoretical calculations based on the assumptions that the heights of male college students are normally distributed with a mean of 70.1 in. and a standard deviation of 2.7 in. (based on data from a survey of Humber College students). This project describes a different method of solution that is based on a simulation technique: We will use a computer to randomly generate 100 heights of male students (from a normally distributed population with $\mu = 70.1$ and $\sigma = 2.7$), then we will find the percentage of those simulated heights that fall between 72.4 in. and 74.6 in. The Excel and STATDISK procedures are described below.

Excel: Choose **Data Analysis** from the **Tools** menu. Select **Random Number Generation**. In the dialog box, specify 1 for Number of Variables and 100 for **Number of Random Numbers**. Select **Normal** from the pull-down **Distribution** menu, and enter 70.1 for **Mean** and 2.7 for **Standard Deviation**. Choose an output option, and click OK. When the 100 numbers have been generated, sort them by choosing **Sort** from the **Data** menu. Once the numbers are sorted, it is not difficult to count the number of heights between 72.4 in. and 74.6 in. Divide that number by 100 to find the percentage of these simulated heights. Compare the value to the theoretical value of 15.02% that was found in Section 5-3.

STATDISK: Select **Data** from the main menu bar, then choose the option of **Normal Generator**. Proceed to generate 100 values with a mean of 70.1 and a standard deviation of 2.7. (Use the **Format** option to specify 1 decimal place.) Next, rank the data by using the options of **Sample Editor**, then **Format**. With this ranked list, it becomes quite easy to count the number of heights between 72.4 and 74.6. Divide that number by 100 to find the percentage of these simulated heights in that range.

•••••••• FROM DATA TO DECISION ••••••••

How Can We Outsmart Users of Counterfeit Coins in Vending Machines?

Operators of vending machines are continually devising strategies to combat the use of counterfeit coins and bills.

Let's develop a strategy for minimizing losses from slugs that are counterfeit quarters. In Data Set 13 of Appendix B, we have a random sample of weights (in grams) of legitimate quarters. Based on that sample, let's assume that for the population of all such quarters, the distribution is normal, the mean weight is 5.622 g, and the standard deviation is 0.068 g. Let's also assume that a supply of counterfeit quarters has been collected from vending machines in downtown Calgary. Analysis of those counterfeit quarters shows that they have weights that are normally distributed with a mean of 5.450 g and a standard deviation of 0.112 g. A vending machine is designed so that coins are accepted or rejected according to weight. The limits for acceptable coins can be changed, but the machine currently accepts any coin with a weight between 5.500 g and 5.744 g. Find the percentages of legitimate coins and counterfeit coins accepted by the machine.

Here's a dilemma: If we restrict the weight limits on the coins too much, we reduce the proportion of legitimate coins that are accepted and business is lost. If we don't restrict the weight limits on coins enough, too many counterfeit coins are accepted and losses are incurred. What are the percentages of legitimate and counterfeit coins accepted if the lower weight limit is changed to 5.550 g? Experiment with different weight settings and identify limits that seem reasonable in that the machine does not accept too many counterfeit coins but still does accept a reasonable proportion of legitimate coins. It might be helpful to construct a reasonably accurate normal distribution graph for legitimate coins and another one for counterfeit coins; use the same horizontal scale and position one graph above the other so that numbers on the horizontal scale are aligned. With these graphs, you want to find limits that include the most legitimate coins and the fewest counterfeit coins. (There isn't necessarily a unique answer here; to some extent, the choices depend on subjective judgments.) Write a brief report that includes the settings you recommend, along with specific reasons for your choices.

−.204
−.202
−.199
−.196
−.194
−.191
−.188
−.185
−.183
−.180
−.177
−.174
−.171
−.168
−.165
−.161
−.158
−.155
−.151
−.148
−.144
−.140
−.137
−.133
−.129
−.125
−.121
−.116
−.112
−.107
−.102
−.097
−.091
−.085
−.079
−.072
−.065
−.056
−.046
−.032

REACTION TIMER

•••••••• COOPERATIVE GROUP ACTIVITIES ••••••••

1. *Out-of-class activity:* Use the reaction timer by following the instructions given below. Collect reaction times for a sample of at least 40 different subjects taken from a homogeneous group, such as right-handed college students. For each subject, measure the reaction time for each hand. Construct a histogram for the right-hand times and another histogram for the left-hand results. Based on the histogram shapes, do the two sets of times each appear to be normally distributed? Calculate the values of the mean and standard deviation for each of the two data sets and compare the two sets of results. Using the right-hand sample mean $\bar{x}$ as an estimate of the population mean μ, and using the right-hand sample standard deviation s as an estimate of the population standard deviation σ, find the quartiles Q_1, Q_2, and Q_3. Repeat that procedure to find Q_1, Q_2, and Q_3 for the left hand. If the right-hand reaction times are to be used to screen job applicants, what time is the cutoff separating the fastest 5% from the slowest 95%?

Instructions for Using the Reaction Timer
   a. Cut the reaction timer along the dashed line.
   b. Ask the subject to hold his or her thumb and forefinger horizontally; those fingers should be spread apart by a distance that is the same as the width of the reaction timer.
   c. Hold the reaction timer so that the bottom edge is just above the subject's thumb and forefinger.
   d. Ask the subject to catch the reaction timer as quickly as possible, then release it after a few seconds.
   e. Record the reaction time (in seconds) corresponding to the point at which the subject catches it.

2. *In-class activity:* Use the chalkboard to construct two stem-and-leaf plots with stem values of 0, 1, 2, . . . , 9. For the stem-and-leaf plot at the left, each student should enter the last four digits of his or her social insurance number. For the stem-and-leaf plot at the right, each student should calculate the mean $\bar{x}$ of those same four digits, round the result to the nearest whole number, and enter it on the stem-and-leaf plot. Groups of three or four should now be formed to analyse the results and state how they illustrate the central limit theorem.

········ COOPERATIVE GROUP ACTIVITIES ········

3. *In-class activity:* Divide into groups of three or four students. For each group member, find the total value of coins that member has in his or her possession. Next, find the group mean. Share the individual values and the mean value with all of the other groups. What is the distribution of the individual values? What is the distribution of the group means? Do the results illustrate the central limit theorem? How?

4. *In-class activity:* Divide into groups of three or four students. Using a coin to simulate births, each group member should simulate 25 births and record the number of simulated girls. Combine all results in the group and record n = total number of births and x = number of girls. Given batches of n births, compute the mean and standard deviation for the number of girls. Is the simulated result usual or unusual? Why?

INTERNET PROJECT   Exploring the Central Limit Theorem

The Central Limit Theorem is one of the most important results in statistics. It also may be one of the most surprising. Basically, the theorem says that the normal distribution is everywhere. No matter what probability distribution underlies an experiment, there is a corresponding distribution of means that will be approximately normal in shape. The best way to both understand and appreciate the Central Limit Theorem, however, is to see it in action. The Internet Project for this chapter can be found at:

http://www.pearsoned.ca/triola

Click on Internet Project, then on Chapter 5. You will be asked to view, interpret and discuss a demonstration of the Central Limit Theorem as part of a dice rolling experiment. In addition, you will be guided in a search through the Internet for other such demonstrations.

6

Estimates and Sample Sizes

6-1 Overview

Chapter objectives are identified. This and the following chapters present topics of *inferential statistics*, characterized by methods of using sample data to form conclusions about population parameters. This chapter focuses on methods of estimating values of population means, proportions, or variances. Methods for determining the sample sizes necessary to estimate those parameters are also presented.

6-2 Estimating a Population Mean: Large Samples

The value of a population mean is approximated with a single value (called a point estimate) and a confidence interval. This section deals with large samples ($n > 30$) only.

6-3 Estimating a Population Mean: Small Samples

This section uses statistics from small samples ($n \leq 30$) to estimate the values of population means. Point estimates and confidence intervals are discussed, and the Student t distribution is introduced.

6-4 Estimating a Population Proportion

The value of a population proportion is estimated with a point estimate and confidence interval. Procedures are described for determining how large a sample must be to estimate a population proportion. This section presents the method commonly used by pollsters to determine how many people must be surveyed in various opinion polls.

6-5 Estimating a Population Variance

The value of a population variance is approximated with a point estimate and confidence interval, and a method for determining the sample size is presented. The chi-square distribution is introduced.

CHAPTER PROBLEM:

Is the mean body temperature really 37.0°C?

Table 6-1 lists 108 body temperatures (from Data Set 18 in Appendix B) obtained courtesy of David Chamberlain and Andrew McRae, Research Institute, Lakeridge Health Oshawa. Using the methods described in Chapter 2, we can obtain the following important characteristics of the sample data set:

- As revealed by a histogram, the distribution of the data is approximately bell shaped.
- The mean is $\bar{x} = 36.39°C$.
- The standard deviation is $s = 0.62°C$.
- The sample size is $n = 108$.

Most people believe that the mean body temperature is 37.0°C, but the data in Table 6-1 seem to suggest that it is actually 36.39°C. We know that samples tend to vary, so perhaps it is true that the mean body temperature is 37.0°C and the sample mean, $\bar{x} = 36.39°C$, is the result of a chance sample fluctuation. On the other hand, perhaps the sample mean of 36.39°C is correct and the commonly believed value of 37.0°C is wrong. On the basis of an analysis of the sample data in Table 6-1, we will see whether the mean body temperature is or is not 37.0°C.

Table 6-1   Body Temperatures (in degrees Celsius) of Adults Accepted for Voluntary Surgery, Measured Before the Surgery

36.4	36.3	36.7	36.3	36.8	36.6	36.6	36.1	36.2	35.6	37.4	36.3
36.2	35.4	36.4	36.3	36.7	36.1	36.0	36.1	36.4	36.4	35.8	36.7
37.3	36.4	37.1	37.1	36.4	36.6	36.6	36.5	36.7	36.5	36.6	36.8
35.5	37.0	36.9	35.2	37.1	36.7	37.4	37.1	37.0	36.4	35.9	36.9
36.3	37.1	36.4	36.8	36.5	37.6	36.1	36.4	36.0	36.7	36.3	36.2
36.4	36.7	35.4	36.1	35.0	39.9	36.6	35.9	36.0	36.0	35.4	36.2
36.0	36.8	37.3	36.3	37.1	35.8	36.0	35.8	36.2	36.9	36.3	36.6
36.0	35.5	36.0	36.1	36.4	35.0	36.5	36.6	35.1	36.4	36.0	36.7
36.3	36.8	36.5	36.5	35.8	36.4	35.9	36.1	36.1	36.2	36.3	36.3

Note that while not all of these temperatures may represent "normal, healthy" temperatures, they are the temperatures of people who were deemed sufficiently nonfevered to undergo voluntary surgery. Temperatures of patients who were operated on but may have had fever are omitted.

6-1 Overview

In Chapter 2 we noted that we use *descriptive statistics* to summarize or describe important characteristics of known population data, but with *inferential statistics* we use sample data to make inferences (or generalizations) about a population. The two major applications of inferential statistics involve the use of sample data to (1) estimate the value of a population parameter and (2) test some claim (or hypothesis) about a population. This chapter presents methods for estimating values of the following population parameters: population means, proportions, and variances. We also present methods for determining the sample sizes necessary to estimate those parameters. The basic methods for testing claims about a population will be introduced in Chapter 7.

As we proceed with methods for using sample data to form inferences about populations, we should recall an extremely important point first made in Chapter 1:

> **Data collected carelessly can be absolutely worthless, even if the sample is quite large.**

The methods used here and in the following chapters require sound sampling procedures.

6-2 Estimating a Population Mean: Large Samples

Consider the 108 body temperatures given in Table 6-1 at the beginning of this chapter. On the basis of those sample values, we want to estimate the mean of *all* body temperatures. We could use a statistic such as the sample median, midrange, or mode as an estimate of this population mean μ, but the sample mean $\overline{x}$ usually provides the best estimate of a population mean. The choice of $\overline{x}$ is based on careful study and analysis of the distributions of the different statistics that could be used as estimators.

DEFINITIONS

An **estimator** is a sample statistic (such as the sample mean $\overline{x}$) used to approximate a population parameter. An **estimate** is a specific value or range of values used to approximate some population parameter.

For example, on the basis of the data in Table 6-1, we might use the *estimator* $\overline{x}$ to conclude that the *estimate* of the mean body temperature of all healthy adults is 36.39°C.

There are two important reasons why a sample mean is a better estimator of a population mean μ than other estimators such as the median or the mode:

1. For many populations, the distribution of sample means $\overline{x}$ tends to be more consistent (with *less variation*) than the distributions of other sample

statistics. (That is, if you use sample means to estimate the population mean μ, those sample means will have a smaller standard deviation than would other sample statistics, such as the median or the mode.)

2. For all populations, we say that the sample mean $\bar{x}$ is an **unbiased estimator** of the population mean μ, meaning that the distribution of sample means tends to centre about the value of the population mean μ. (That is, sample means do not systematically tend to overestimate the value of μ, nor do they systematically tend to underestimate μ. Instead, they tend to target the value of μ itself.)

For these reasons, we will use the sample mean $\bar{x}$ as the best estimate of the population mean μ. Because the sample mean $\bar{x}$ is a single value that corresponds to a point on the number scale, we call it a *point estimate*.

DEFINITION

A **point estimate** is a single value (or point) used to approximate a population parameter.

The sample mean $\bar{x}$ is the best point estimate of the population mean μ.

EXAMPLE Use the sample body temperatures given in Table 6-1 to find the best point estimate of the population mean μ of all body temperatures.

SOLUTION The sample mean $\bar{x}$ is the best point estimate of the population mean μ, and for the sample data in Table 6-1 we have $\bar{x} = 36.39°C$. Based on those particular sample values, the best point estimate of the population mean μ of all body temperatures is therefore 36.39°C.

TV Sample Sizes

A *Newsweek* article described the use of people meters as a way of determining how many people are watching different television programs. The article stated, "Statisticians have long argued that the household samples used by the rating services are simply too small to accurately determine what America is watching. In that light, it may be illuminating to note that 4000 homes reached by the people meters constitute exactly 0.0045% of the wired nation." This implied claim that the sample size of 4000 homes is too small is not valid. Methods of this chapter can be used to show that a random sample size of 4000 can provide results that are quite good, even though the sample might be only 0.0045% of the population.

Why Do We Need Confidence Intervals?

In the preceding example we saw that 36.39°C was our best point estimate of the population mean μ, but we had no indication of just how good our best estimate was. If we knew only the first four temperatures of 36.4°C, 36.3°C, 36.7°C, and 36.3°C, the best point estimate of μ would be their mean ($\bar{x}$ = 36.43°C), but we wouldn't expect this point estimate to be very good because it is based on such a small sample. Statisticians have therefore developed another type of estimate that does reveal how good the point estimate is. This estimate, called a confidence interval or interval estimate, consists of a range (or an interval) of values instead of just a single value.

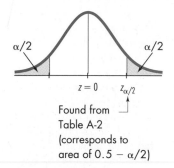

Found from
Table A-2
(corresponds to
area of 0.5 − α/2)

Figure 6-1 The Standard Normal Distribution: The Critical Value $z_{\alpha/2}$

DEFINITION

A **confidence interval** (or **interval estimate**) is a range (or an interval) of values that is *likely* to contain the true value of the population parameter.

A *confidence interval* is associated with a degree of confidence, which is a measure of how certain we are that our interval contains the population parameter. The definition of degree of confidence uses α (lowercase Greek alpha) to describe a probability that corresponds to an area. Refer to Figure 6-1, where the probability α is divided equally between two shaded extreme regions (often called tails) in the standard normal distribution. (We'll describe the role of $z_{\alpha/2}$ later; for now, simply note that α is divided equally between the two tails.)

DEFINITION

The **degree of confidence** is the probability $1 - \alpha$ (often expressed as the equivalent percentage value) that the confidence interval contains the true value of the population parameter. (The degree of confidence is also called the **level of confidence** or the **confidence coefficient**.)

Common choices for the *degree of confidence* are 90% (with $\alpha = 0.10$), 95% (with $\alpha = 0.05$), and 99% (with $\alpha = 0.01$). The choice of 95% is most common because it provides a good balance between precision (as reflected in the width of the confidence interval) and reliability (as expressed by the degree of confidence).

Here's an example of a confidence interval based on the sample data of 108 body temperatures given in Table 6-1:

> **The 0.95 (or 95%) degree of confidence interval estimate of the population mean μ is 36.27°C $< \mu <$ 36.51°C.**

Interpreting a Confidence Interval

We must be careful to interpret confidence intervals correctly. What is the correct interpretation of the confidence estimate 36.27°C $< \mu <$ 36.51°C? We interpret this confidence interval as follows: If we were to select many different samples of size $n = 108$ from the population of all healthy people and construct a similar 95% confidence interval estimate for each sample, in the long run 95% of those intervals would actually contain the value of the population mean μ. We should know that μ is a fixed value, not a random variable, and it is therefore *wrong* to say that there is a 95% chance that μ will fall within the interval. Any particular confidence interval either contains μ or does not, and because μ is fixed, there is no probability that μ falls within an interval. In short, the 95% level refers to the *process* being used to estimate the mean (we have confidence that, 95% of the time, using this process will correctly identify an interval that *contains* the mean); the 95% does *not* refer to the population mean itself.

Critical Values

We know from the central limit theorem that sample means $\bar{x}$ tend to be normally distributed, as in Figure 6-1. Sample means have a relatively small chance of falling in one of the extreme tails of Figure 6-1. Denoting the area of each shaded tail by $\alpha/2$, we see that there is a total probability of α that a sample mean will fall in either of the two tails. By the rule of complements (from Chapter 3), it follows that there is a probability of $1 - \alpha$ that a sample mean will fall within the unshaded region of Figure 6-1. The z score separating the right-tail region is commonly denoted by $z_{\alpha/2}$ and is referred to as a *critical value* because it is on the borderline separating sample means that are likely to occur from those that are unlikely to occur.

Notation for Critical Value

$z_{\alpha/2}$ is the positive z value that is at the vertical boundary separating an area of $\alpha/2$ in the right tail of the standard normal distribution. (The value of $-z_{\alpha/2}$ is at the vertical boundary for the area of $\alpha/2$ in the left tail.)

DEFINITION

A **critical value** is the number on the borderline separating sample statistics that are likely to occur from those that are unlikely to occur. The number $z_{\alpha/2}$ is a critical value that is a z score with the property that it separates an area of $\alpha/2$ in the right tail of the standard normal distribution. (There is an area of $1 - \alpha$ between the vertical borderlines at $-z_{\alpha/2}$ and $z_{\alpha/2}$.)

● **EXAMPLE** Find the critical value $z_{\alpha/2}$ corresponding to a 95% degree of confidence.

SOLUTION A 95% degree of confidence corresponds to $\alpha = 0.05$. See Figure 6-2, where we show that the area in each of the shaded tails is $\alpha/2 = 0.025$. We find $z_{\alpha/2} = 1.96$ by noting that the region to its left (and bounded by the mean of $z = 0$) must be $0.5 - 0.025$, or 0.475. Now refer to Table A-2 and find that the area of 0.4750 (found in the *body* of the table) corresponds exactly to a z value of 1.96. For a 95% degree of confidence, the critical value is therefore $z_{\alpha/2} = 1.96$.

The preceding example showed that a 95% degree of confidence results in a critical value of $z_{\alpha/2} = 1.96$. This is the most common critical value, and it is listed with two other common values in the table that follows:

Estimating Wildlife Population Sizes

British Columbia's Land Use Coordination Office, working with the Ministry of Forests and the Ministry of Environment, Land, and Parks, developed a management plan to protect the spotted owl, which is considered an endangered species. Biologists and statisticians concluded that survival rates and population sizes were decreasing for the female owls, known to play an important role in species survival. Biologists and statisticians have also studied other wildlife, such as penguins in New Zealand. In the article "Sampling Wildlife Populations" (*Chance*, Vol. 9, No. 2), authors Bryan Manly and Lyman McDonald comment that in such studies, "biologists gain through the use of modelling skills that are the hallmark of good statistics. Statisticians gain by being introduced to the reality of problems by biologists who know what the crucial issues are."

Figure 6-2 Finding $z_{\alpha/2}$ for 95% Degree of Confidence

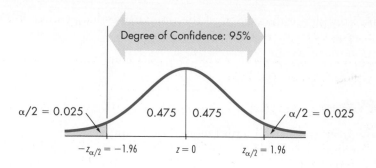

Degree of Confidence	α	Critical Value $z_{\alpha/2}$
90%	0.10	1.645
95%	0.05	1.96
99%	0.01	2.575

Margin of Error

When we collect a set of sample data, such as the set of 108 body temperatures listed in Table 6-1, we can calculate the sample mean $\bar{x}$, and that sample mean is typically different from the population mean μ. The difference between the sample mean and the population mean can be thought of as an error. This is important because we do not know the true value of μ; and although we assume there is some error, we can't know its exact size. In Section 5-5 we saw that $\sigma/\sqrt{n}$ is the standard deviation of sample means. Using $\sigma/\sqrt{n}$ and the $z_{\alpha/2}$ notation, we now define the margin of error E as follows:

DEFINITION

When data from a random sample are used to estimate a population mean μ, the **margin of error**, denoted by E, is the maximum likely (with probability $1 - \alpha$) difference between the observed sample mean $\bar{x}$ and the true value of the population mean μ. The margin of error E is also called the **maximum error of the estimate** and can be found by multiplying the critical value and the standard deviation of sample means, as shown in Formula 6-1.

Formula 6-1
$$E = z_{\alpha/2} \cdot \frac{\sigma}{\sqrt{n}}$$

Given the way that the margin of error E is defined, there is a probability of $1 - \alpha$ that a sample mean will be in error (different from the population mean μ) by no more than E, and there is a probability of α that the sample mean will be in error by more than E. The calculation of the margin of error E as given in Formula 6-1 requires that you know the population standard deviation σ, but in reality it's rare to know σ when the population mean μ is not known. The following method of calculation is common practice.

Calculating E When σ Is Unknown

If $n > 30$, we can replace σ in Formula 6-1 by the sample standard deviation s.

If $n \leq 30$, the population must have a normal distribution and we must know σ to use Formula 6-1. [An alternative method for calculating the margin of error E for small ($n \leq 30$) samples will be discussed more fully in the next section.]

On the basis of the definition of the margin of error E, we can now identify the confidence interval for the population mean μ.

Confidence Interval (or Interval Estimate) for the Population Mean μ (Based on Large Samples: $n > 30$)

$$\bar{x} - E < \mu < \bar{x} + E \quad \text{where} \quad E = z_{\alpha/2} \cdot \frac{\sigma}{\sqrt{n}}$$

Other equivalent forms for the confidence interval are $\mu = \bar{x} \pm E$ and $(\bar{x} - E, \bar{x} + E)$.

The values $\bar{x} - E$ and $\bar{x} + E$ are called **confidence interval limits.**

Procedure for Constructing a Confidence Interval for μ (Based on a Large Sample: $n > 30$)

1. Find the critical value $z_{\alpha/2}$ that corresponds to the desired degree of confidence. (For example, if the degree of confidence is 95%, the critical value is $z_{\alpha/2} = 1.96$.)
2. Evaluate the margin of error $E = z_{\alpha/2} \cdot \sigma/\sqrt{n}$. If the population standard deviation σ is unknown, use the value of the sample standard deviation s provided that $n > 30$.
3. Using the value of the calculated margin of error E and the value of the sample mean $\bar{x}$, find the values of $\bar{x} - E$ and $\bar{x} + E$. Substitute those values in the general format of the confidence interval:

$$\bar{x} - E < \mu < \bar{x} + E$$

or

$$\mu = \bar{x} \pm E$$

or

$$(\bar{x} - E, \quad \bar{x} + E)$$

4. Round the resulting values by using the following round-off rule.

The following example clearly illustrates the relatively simple procedure for actually constructing a confidence interval. The original data from Table 6-1 use one decimal place and the summary statistics use two decimal places, so the confidence interval limits will be rounded to two decimal places.

Reporting Poll Results

The following is an excerpt from an Angus Reid press release on a poll taken prior to the Quebec election in 1998. The poll found that the Parti Québécois had 46% support, with the Liberals at 41% and the Action Démocratique at 11%. This example demonstrates the use of the confidence interval in reporting poll results:

"The results presented here are taken from a telephone survey of 1000 Quebec residents, conducted between November 18 and November 23, 1998. These data are representative of the distribution of the Quebec population along all key demographic variables including mother tongue. As well, the distribution of the interviews across the province is representative of the geographic distribution of the population. A sample of this size is said to be representative of the Quebec voting population ±3.1%, 19 times out of 20." (Note that "19 times out of 20" represents 95% confidence.)

Round-Off Rule for Confidence Intervals Used to Estimate μ

1. When using the *original set of data* to construct a confidence interval, round the confidence interval limits to one more decimal place than is used for the original set of data.

2. When the original set of data is unknown and only the *summary statistics* (n, $\bar{x}$, s) are used, round the confidence interval limits to the same number of decimal places used for the sample mean.

EXAMPLE   For the body temperatures in Table 6-1, we have $n = 108$, $\bar{x} = 36.39$, and $s = 0.62$. For a 0.95 degree of confidence, find both of the following:

a. The margin of error E

b. The confidence interval for μ

SOLUTION

a. The 0.95 degree of confidence implies that $\alpha = 0.05$, so $z_{\alpha/2} = 1.96$, as shown in the preceding example. The margin of error E is calculated by using Formula 6-1 as follows. (Note that σ is unknown, but we can use $s = 0.62$ for the value of σ because $n > 30$.)

$$E = z_{\alpha/2} \cdot \frac{\sigma}{\sqrt{n}} = 1.96 \cdot \frac{0.62}{\sqrt{108}} = 0.12$$

b. With $\bar{x} = 36.39$ and $E = 0.12$, we construct the confidence interval as follows:

$$\bar{x} - E < \mu < \bar{x} + E$$
$$36.39 - 0.12 < \mu < 36.39 + 0.12$$
$$36.27 < \mu < 36.51$$

[This result could also be expressed as $\mu = 36.39 \pm 0.12$ or as (36.27, 36.51).]

Interpretation Based on the sample of 108 body temperatures listed in Table 6-1, the confidence interval for the population mean μ is $36.27°C < \mu < 36.51°C$, and this interval has a 0.95 degree of confidence. This means that if we were to select many different samples of size 108 and construct the confidence intervals as we did here, 95% of them would actually contain the value of the population mean μ.

Note that the confidence interval limits of $36.27°C$ and $36.51°C$ do not contain $37.0°C$, the value generally believed to be the mean body temperature. Based on the sample data in Table 6-1, it seems very unlikely that $37.0°C$ is the correct value of μ.

For interpreting the confidence interval that we derived in the preceding example, Figure 6-3 may be helpful. Suppose that the true mean for body temperatures is really 36.32°C, instead of the 36.39°C that we estimated from our sample. The topmost of the bold line segments in the figure shows the confidence intervals we calculated from our sample. Notice that the interval contains the true mean. The confidence intervals that could have been derived from *other* samples taken from the population are also illustrated. Observe that *most* of the derived confidence intervals contain the population mean—though in a minority of the cases (we expect in about 5% of them) the confidence intervals do not contain the mean.

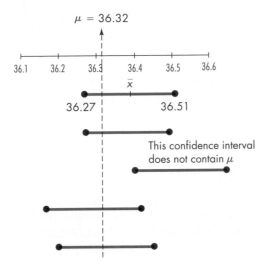

Figure 6-3 Confidence Intervals from Different Samples

The graph shows several confidence intervals, one of which does not contain the population mean μ. For 95% confidence intervals, we expect that among 100 such intervals, 5 will not contain $\mu = 36.32$ while the other 95 will contain it.

Basis for the Procedure of Finding the Confidence Interval

The basic idea underlying the construction of confidence intervals relates to the central limit theorem, which indicates that with large ($n > 30$) samples, the distribution of sample means is approximately normal with mean μ and standard deviation $\sigma/\sqrt{n}$. The confidence interval format is really a variation of the equation

$$z = \frac{\overline{x} - \mu}{\dfrac{\sigma}{\sqrt{n}}}$$

If we solve this equation for μ, we get $\mu = \overline{x} - z\dfrac{\sigma}{\sqrt{n}}$. Using the positive and negative values for z results in the confidence interval limits we are using.

Let's consider the specific case of a 95% degree of confidence, so $\alpha = 0.05$ and $z_{\alpha/2} = 1.96$. For this case there is a probability of 0.05 that a sample mean will be more than 1.96 standard deviations (or $z_{\alpha/2}\sigma/\sqrt{n}$, which we denote by E) away from the population mean μ. Conversely, there is a 0.95 probability that a sample mean will be within 1.96 standard deviations (or $z_{\alpha/2}\sigma/\sqrt{n}$) of μ. (See Figure 6-4.) If the sample mean $\overline{x}$ is within $z_{\alpha/2}\sigma/\sqrt{n}$ of the population

Figure 6-4   Distribution of
Sample Means

There is a $1 - \alpha$ probability that
a sample mean will be in error
by less than E or $z_{\alpha/2}\sigma/\sqrt{n}$

There is a probability of α that a
sample mean will be in error
by more than E (in one of the
shaded tails)

AS

mean μ, then μ must be between $\bar{x} - z_{\alpha/2}\sigma/\sqrt{n}$ and $\bar{x} + z_{\alpha/2}\sigma/\sqrt{n}$; this is expressed in the general format of our confidence interval (with $z_{\alpha/2}\sigma/\sqrt{n}$ denoted as E): $\bar{x} - E < \mu < \bar{x} + E$.

Determining Sample Size

So far in this section we have discussed ways to find point estimates and interval estimates of a population mean μ. We based our procedures on known sample data. But suppose that we haven't yet collected the sample. How do we know how many members of the population should be selected? For example, suppose we want to estimate the mean first-year income of college graduates. How many such incomes must our sample include? Determining the size of a sample is a very important issue, because samples that are needlessly large waste time and money, and samples that are too small may lead to poor results. In many cases we can find the minimum sample size needed to estimate some parameter, such as the population mean μ.

If we begin with the expression for the margin of error E (Formula 6-1) and solve for the sample size n, we get the following.

Sample Size for Estimating Mean μ

Formula 6-2
$$n = \left[\frac{z_{\alpha/2}\sigma}{E}\right]^2$$

where

$z_{\alpha/2}$ = critical z score based on the desired degree of confidence
E = desired margin of error
σ = population standard deviation

Formula 6-2 is quite remarkable because it implies that the sample size does not depend on the size (N) of the population: the sample size depends on the desired degree of confidence, the desired margin of error, and the value of the standard deviation σ.

The sample size must be a whole number, but the calculations for sample size n often result in a value that is not a whole number. When this happens, we observe the following round-off rule. (It is based on the principle that when rounding is necessary, the required sample size should be rounded *up* so that it is at least adequately large as opposed to slightly too small.)

Round-Off Rule for Sample Size n

When finding the sample size n, if the use of Formula 6-2 does not result in a whole number, always *increase* the value of n to the next *larger* whole number.

EXAMPLE   An economist wants to estimate the mean income for the first year of work for a college graduate who has had the profound wisdom to take a statistics course. How many such incomes must be found if we want to be 95% confident that the sample mean is within $500 of the true population mean? Assume that a previous study has revealed that for such incomes, $\sigma = \$6250$.

SOLUTION   We want to find the sample size n given that $\alpha = 0.05$ (from 95% confidence). We want the sample mean to be within $500 of the population mean, so $E = 500$. Assuming that $\sigma = 6250$, we use Formula 6-2 to get

$$n = \left[\frac{z_{\alpha/2}\sigma}{E} \right]^2 = \left[\frac{1.96 \cdot 6250}{500} \right]^2 = 600.25 = 601 \quad \text{(rounded up)}$$

We should therefore obtain a sample of at least 601 randomly selected first-year incomes of college graduates who have taken a statistics course. With such a sample, we will be 95% confident that the sample mean $\bar{x}$ will be within $500 of the true population mean μ.

If we are willing to settle for less accurate results by using a larger margin of error such as $1000, the sample size drops to 150.0625, which is rounded up to 151. Doubling the margin of error causes the required sample size to decrease to one-fourth its original value. Conversely, halving the margin of error quadruples the sample size. What this implies is that if you want more accurate results, the sample size must be substantially increased. Because large samples generally require more time and money, there is often a need for a trade-off between the sample size and the margin of error E.

Captured Tank Serial Numbers Reveal Population Size

During World War II, Allied intelligence specialists wanted to determine the number of tanks Germany was producing. Traditional spy techniques provided unreliable results, but statisticians obtained accurate estimates by analysing serial numbers on captured tanks. As one example, records show that Germany actually produced 271 tanks in June 1941. The estimate based on serial numbers was 244, but traditional intelligence methods resulted in the extreme estimate of 1550. (See "An Empirical Approach to Economic Intelligence in World War II," by Ruggles and Brodie, *Journal of the American Statistical Association,* Vol. 42.)

What If σ Is Unknown?   Formula 6-2 requires that we substitute some value for the population standard deviation σ, but if it is unknown (as it usually is), we may be able to use a preliminary value obtained from procedures such as these:

1. Using the range rule of thumb (see Section 2-5) to estimate the standard deviation as follows: $\sigma \approx$ typical range/4.

2. Conducting a pilot study by starting the sample process. Based on the first collection of at least 31 randomly selected sample values, calculate the sample standard deviation σ and use it in place of σ. That value can be refined as more sample data are obtained.

3. Estimate the value of σ by using the results of some other study that was done earlier.

If in doubt when calculating the sample size n, any errors should always be conservative in the sense that they make n too large instead of too small.

In the two examples that follow, the first uses the range rule of thumb to estimate σ and the second uses a pilot study consisting of sample data found in Appendix B.

● **EXAMPLE**   You plan to estimate the mean incubation period (in days) for sea birds. How many incubation periods of sea birds must you sample if you want to be 95% confident that the sample mean is within 3 days of the true population mean μ?

SOLUTION   We seek the sample size n given that $\alpha = 0.05$ (from 95% confidence, so $\alpha = 1 - 0.95$), so $z_{a/2} = 1.96$. We want to be within 3 days, so $E = 3$. We do not know the standard deviation σ of incubation periods for all sea birds, but we can estimate σ by using the range rule of thumb: If past experience suggests that these incubation periods typically range from 23 to 78 days (disregarding outliers), the range becomes 55 days so that

$$\sigma \approx \frac{\text{(typical range)}}{4} = \frac{(78 - 23)}{4} = 13.75$$

With $z_{\alpha/2} = 1.96$, $E = 3$, and $\sigma \approx 13.75$, we use Formula 6-2 as follows:

$$n = \left[\frac{z_{\alpha/2}\sigma}{E}\right]^2 = \left[\frac{1.96 \cdot 13.75}{3}\right]^2 = 80.70 = 81 \quad \text{(rounded up)}$$

We must randomly select 81 incubation periods of seabirds and then find the value of the sample mean $\bar{x}$. We will be 95% confident that the resulting sample mean is within 3 days of the true mean incubation period.

EXAMPLE   If we want to estimate the mean weight of plastic discarded by households in one week, how many households must we randomly select if we want to be 99% confident that the sample mean is within 0.250 lb of the true population mean?

SOLUTION   We seek the sample size n given that $\alpha = 0.01$ (from 99% confidence), so $z_{\alpha/2} = 2.575$. We want to be within 0.250 lb of the true mean, so $E = 0.250$. The value of the population standard deviation σ is unknown, but we can refer to Data Set 1 in Appendix B, which includes the weights of plastic discarded for 62 households. Using that sample as a pilot study, we can calculate the value of the standard deviation to get $s = 1.065$ lb; because this sample is large ($n > 30$), we can use the value of $s = 1.065$ as an estimate of the population standard deviation σ, as shown below:

$$n = \left[\frac{z_{\alpha/2}\sigma}{E}\right]^2 = \left[\frac{2.575 \cdot 1.065}{0.250}\right]^2 = 120.3 = 121 \quad \text{(rounded up)}$$

On the basis of the population standard deviation estimated from Data Set 1 in Appendix B, we must sample at least 121 randomly selected households to be 99% confident that the sample mean is within 0.250 lb of the true population mean.

This section dealt with the construction of point estimates and confidence interval estimates of population means and presented a method for determining sample sizes needed to estimate population means to the desired degree of accuracy. All of the examples and exercises in this section involve large ($n > 30$) samples. The following section describes procedures to be used when the samples are small ($n \le 30$).

Using Technology

Excel: *Confidence Intervals:* Excel's built-in tools can calculate the margin of error E. You must then subtract this result from $\bar{x}$ and add it to $\bar{x}$ so that you can identify the lower and upper limits of the confidence interval. First, use techniques from Chapter 2 to identify the sample size n and the sample standard deviation s. Then click on the *fx* icon, select the function category of **Statistical**, and then select the item **Confidence**. In the dialog box, enter the value of α (called the significance level), the standard deviation, and the sample size. The margin of error E will be displayed.

Estimating Sugar in Oranges

In Florida, members of the citrus industry make extensive use of statistical methods. One particular application involves the way in which growers are paid for oranges used to make orange juice. An arriving truckload of oranges is first weighed at the receiving plant, then a sample of about a dozen oranges is randomly selected. The sample is weighed and then squeezed, and the amount of sugar in the juice is measured. Based on the sample results, an estimate is made of the total amount of sugar in the entire truckload. Payment for the load of oranges is based on the estimate of the amount of sugar because sweeter oranges are more valuable than those less sweet, even though the amounts of juice may be the same.

Alternatively, you can use the Data Desk XL add-in that is a supplement to this book. Click on **DDXL** and select **Confidence Intervals**. Under the Function Type options, select **1 Var z Interval**. Click on the pencil icon and enter the Excel range containing the data. Click on **OK**. In the dialog box, set the level of confidence, enter the standard deviation, and click on **Compute Interval**. The confidence interval will be displayed, as shown below.

STATDISK: *Confidence Intervals:* First, use techniques from Chapter 2 to identify the sample size n, the sample mean $\bar{x}$, and the sample standard deviation σ. Select **Analysis** from the main menu bar, select **Confidence Intervals**, then select **Population Mean**. Proceed to enter the items in the dialog box, then click the **Evaluate** button.

Sample Size: Select **Analysis** from the main menu bar at the top, then select **Sample Size Determination**, followed by **Estimate Mean**. You must now enter the confidence level (such as 0.99, for the second example, above), the error E, and the actual or estimated population standard deviation σ. There is also an option that allows you to enter the population size N, if you are sampling without replacement from a finite population (see Exercise 29).

Excel Display

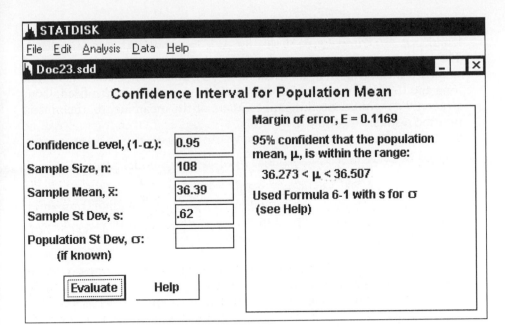

STATDISK Display

(6-2) Exercises A: Basic Skills and Concepts

In Exercises 1–4, find the critical value $z_{\alpha/2}$ that corresponds to the given degree of confidence.

1. 99%   **2.** 94%   **3.** 98%   **4.** 92%

In Exercises 5–8, use the given degree of confidence and sample data to find (a) the margin of error and (b) the confidence interval for the population mean μ.

5. Heights of female students: 95% confidence; $n = 50$, $\bar{x} = 64.2$ in., $s = 2.6$ in.
6. Grade-point averages: 99% confidence; $n = 75$, $\bar{x} = 2.76$, $s = 0.88$
7. Test scores: 90% confidence; $n = 150$, $\bar{x} = 77.6$, $s = 14.2$
8. Cost of basic phone service: 92% confidence; $n = 64$, $\bar{x} = \$15.30$, $s = \$1.25$
9. A sample of 35 skulls is obtained for Egyptian males who lived around 1850 B.C. The maximum breadth of each skull is measured with the result that $\bar{x} = 134.5$ mm and $s = 3.48$ mm (based on data from *Ancient Races of the Thebaid* by Thomson and Randall-Maciver). Using these sample results, construct a 95% confidence interval for the population mean μ. Write a statement that interprets the confidence interval.
10. A sample consists of 75 TV sets purchased several years ago. The replacement times of those TV sets have a mean of 8.2 years and a standard deviation of 1.1 years (based on data from "Getting Things Fixed," *Consumer Reports*). Construct a 90% confidence interval for the mean replacement time of all TV sets from that era. Does the result apply to TV sets currently being sold?

11. A Lyman Electronic Digital Caliper was used to accurately measure the lengths of 40 Triton Quik-Shok 380 ACP 90 grain cartridges (bullets). The results (in millimetres) are listed below. The cartridges are supposed to have a mean length of 0.950 mm and they must be between 0.945 mm long and 0.955 mm, otherwise they could be dangerous when fired. Construct a 90% confidence interval estimate of the mean length, then interpret the results.

0.951	0.954	0.954	0.953	0.953	0.953	0.952	0.955	0.951	0.949
0.950	0.950	0.954	0.950	0.948	0.948	0.945	0.947	0.950	0.954
0.951	0.951	0.952	0.943	0.952	0.952	0.949	0.946	0.949	0.949
0.953	0.953	0.953	0.950	0.949	0.950	0.950	0.949	0.950	0.951

12. An economist is studying the annual revenues of top Canadian companies. The results of a random sample of such revenues (in billions of dollars) is listed below (based on Data Set 6 in Appendix B). Construct a 95% confidence interval estimate of the mean annual revenue for "Top 100" companies. Based on these results, would you expect to find a company on the list with an annual revenue of $350 million?

1.718	6.017	1.681	2.520	1.800	3.678	4.583	2.052	3.795	6.813
3.150	3.149	1.778	2.458	8.509	3.277	2.653	7.312	2.411	4.000
17.161	1.843	2.043	3.076	3.432	3.058	2.683	3.643	3.307	4.148
2.424	1.717	9.512	7.013	33.191

13. The standard IQ test is designed so that the mean is 100 and the standard deviation is 15 for the population of normal adults. Find the sample size necessary to estimate the mean IQ score of statistics students. We want to be 98% confident that our sample mean is within 1.5 IQ points of the true mean. The mean for this population is clearly greater than 100. The standard deviation for this population is probably less than 15 because it is a group with less variation than a group randomly selected from the general population; therefore, if we use $\sigma = 15$, we are being conservative by using a value that will make the sample size at least as large as necessary. Assume then that $\sigma = 15$ and determine the required sample size.

14. The McLean Vending Machine Company must adjust its machines to accept only coins with specified weights. We will obtain a sample of quarters and weigh them to determine the mean. How many quarters must we randomly select and weigh if we want to be 99% confident that the sample mean is within 0.025 g of the true population mean for all quarters? If we use the sample of quarters in Data Set 13 of Appendix B, we can estimate that the population standard deviation is 0.068 g.

15. If we refer to the weights (in grams) of quarters listed in Data Set 13 in Appendix B, we will find 50 weights with a mean of 5.622 g and a standard deviation of 0.068 g. Based on this random sample of quarters in circulation, construct a 98% confidence interval estimate of the population mean of all quarters in circulation. Is the claim that quarters are minted to yield a mean weight of 5.670 g consistent with the confidence interval? If not, what is a possible explanation for the discrepancy?

16. Data Set 18 in Appendix B gives the body temperatures in degrees Celsius of adults accepted for voluntary surgery. For that sample, the mean is 36.39°C and the standard deviation is 0.62°C. Construct a 99% confidence interval for the mean body temperature of the general population and interpret the results.

17. A psychologist has developed a new test of spatial perception, and she wants to estimate the mean score achieved by male pilots. How many people must she test if she wants the sample mean to be in error by no more than 2.0 points, with 95% confidence? An earlier study suggests that $\sigma = 21.2$.

18. To plan for the proper handling of household garbage, the city of Fredericton must estimate the mean weight of garbage discarded by households in one week. Find the sample size necessary to estimate that mean if you want to be 96% confident that the sample mean is within 2 lb of the true population mean. For the population standard deviation σ, use the value of 12.46 lb, which is the standard deviation of the sample of 62 households included in Data Set 1.

19. A large sample of data ($n = 335$) from a Calgary observatory produced a mean daily counting rate for cosmic rays of 3465.46, and a standard deviation of 127.72. Use these sample data to find the 90% confidence interval for the mean of the daily counting rates. Suppose a scientist claims that the mean of the daily counting rates is actually 3525. Would that claim be consistent with the confidence interval?

20. A random sample of 250 Ontario households using natural gas heating shows that the mean monthly consumption of natural gas is 107.73 cu. ft., with a standard deviation of 13.94 cu. ft. Use these statistics to construct a 94% confidence interval for the mean monthly consumption for the population of all Ontario households.

21. Nielsen Media Research wants to estimate the mean amount of time (in hours) that full-time college students spend watching television each weekday. Find the sample size necessary to estimate that mean with a 0.25 h (or 15 min) margin of error. Assume that a 96% degree of confidence is desired. Also assume that a pilot study showed that the standard deviation is estimated to be 1.87 hours.

22. In deciding whether to attend university, many students are influenced by the increased earnings potential that a university degree is likely to create. A recent census study by Statistics Canada shows that the mean annual income of high-school graduates is $22,846, whereas the mean annual income of university graduates is $42,054. Find the sample size necessary to estimate next year's mean annual income of university graduates. Assume that you want 94% confidence that the sample mean will be within $1000 of the true mean, and assume that the population standard deviation is estimated to be $32,896.

23. You have just been hired by the Stampeder Marketing Company to conduct a survey to estimate the mean amount of money spent by movie patrons (per movie) in Alberta. First use the range rule of thumb to make a rough estimate of the standard deviation of the amounts spent. It is reasonable to assume that typical amounts range from $3 to about $15. Then use that estimated standard deviation to determine the sample size corresponding to 98% confidence and a 25¢ margin of error.

24. Estimate the minimum and maximum ages for typical textbooks currently used in college courses, then use the range rule of thumb to estimate the standard deviation. Next, find the size of the sample required to estimate the mean age (in years) of textbooks currently used in college courses. Assume a 96% degree of confidence that the sample mean will be in error by no more than 0.25 year.

25. Refer to Data Set 1 in Appendix B for the 62 weights (in pounds) of *paper* discarded by households. Using that sample, construct a 92% confidence interval estimate of the mean weight of paper discarded by all households.

26. Refer to Data Set 1 in Appendix B and construct a 92% confidence interval for the mean weight in pounds of discarded plastic goods per household for one week. Compare these results with your solution to Exercise 25, and interpret. Which is more of an ecological problem: discarded paper or discarded plastic?

27. Refer to Data Set 11 in Appendix B and construct a 97% confidence interval for the mean weight of brown M&M plain candies. Can the methods of this section be used to construct a 97% confidence interval for the mean weight of blue M&M plain candies? Why or why not?

28. Refer to Data Set 8 in Appendix B and construct a 98% confidence interval for the mean value of coins in possession of statistics students. Is there reason to believe that this value is different from the mean value of coins in possession of people randomly selected from the general population of adult Canadians?

6–2 Exercises B: Beyond the Basics

29. In Formula 6-1 we assume that the population is infinite, that we are sampling with replacement, or that the population is very large. If we have a relatively small population such that $n > 0.05N$, and sample without replacement, we should modify E to include a *finite population correction* factor as follows:

$$E = z_{\alpha/2} \frac{\sigma}{\sqrt{n}} \sqrt{\frac{N - n}{N - 1}}$$

where N is the population size.

a. Find the 95% confidence interval for the mean of 100 IQ scores if a sample of 31 of those scores produces a mean and standard deviation of 132 and 10, respectively.

b. If you are determining a sample size, and realize that the population size N is relatively small, then the sample-size calculation should be revised to:

$$n = \frac{N\sigma^2 (z_{\alpha/2})^2}{(N - 1)E^2 + \sigma^2(z_{\alpha/2})^2}$$

For a challenge, try solving the expression given at the beginning of this question for n to produce the formula given here. Repeat Exercise 13, assuming that the statistics students are randomly selected without replacement from a population of $N = 200$ statistics students.

30. Test the effect of an outlier as follows: Use the sample data in Table 6-1 to find a 95% confidence interval estimate of the population mean, but change the first entry from 36.4 to 364. Nobody can really have that high a body temperature, but such an error can easily occur when a decimal point is inadvertently omitted when the sample values are entered.
 a. Find the 95% confidence interval.
 b. By comparing the result from part (a) to the confidence interval found in this section, describe the effect of an outlier on a confidence interval. Are the confidence interval limits sensitive to outliers?
 c. Based on part (b), how should you handle outliers when they are found in sample data sets that will be used for construction of confidence intervals?

31. In many of the preceding examples, confidence intervals are used toward the ultimate goal of estimating the value of a population parameter. Confidence intervals can also be used as a data-exploration tool, for describing and comparing data sets. Consider the following descriptive statistics, taken from two samples:

Men: $n = 100$ $x = 1.747$ m $s = 0.0744$m
Women: $n = 100$ $x = 1.610$ m $s = 0.0620$m

Construct 95% confidence intervals for the estimates of the population mean of each group. Do the intervals overlap? Based on your answer to the preceding question, would you conclude that the populations of men's and of women's heights are likely to be the same or different? Explain.

32. A 95% confidence interval for the lives (in minutes) of Kodak AA batteries is $430 < \mu < 470$. (See Program 1 of *Against All Odds: Inside Statistics*.) Assume that this result is based on a sample of size 100.
 a. Construct the 99% confidence interval.
 b. What is the value of the sample mean?
 c. What is the value of the sample standard deviation?
 d. If the confidence interval $432 < \mu < 468$ is obtained from the same sample data, what is the degree of confidence?

6-3 Estimating a Population Mean: Small Samples

In Section 6-2 we began our study of inferential statistics by considering point estimates and confidence intervals as methods for estimating the value of a population mean μ. All of the examples and exercises in Section 6-2 involved samples that were large, with sample sizes n greater than 30. Factors such as cost and time often severely limit the size of a sample, so the normal distribution may not be a suitable approximation of the distribution of means from small samples. In this section we investigate methods for estimating a population mean μ when the sample size n is small, where *small* is considered to be 30 or fewer.

Assumptions for This Section

1. $n \leq 30$
2. The sample has been collected by a valid random-sampling technique
3. The sample is from a normally distributed population. (This is a loose requirement, which can be met if the population has only one mode and is basically symmetric.)

If the first assumption is not satisfied, we have a large sample, and we can use the methods described in Section 6-2. If the second assumption is not satisfied, we cannot use the methods described in this book, but it might be possible to use more advanced methods. If the third assumption is not satisfied because the population has a distribution that is very nonnormal, we cannot use the methods of this section, but we might be able to use nonparametric methods (see Chapter 13) or bootstrap resampling methods (see the Computer Project at the end of this chapter).

As explained in Section 6-2, *the sample mean $\bar{x}$ is generally the best point estimate of the population mean μ*, because the distribution of sample means $\bar{x}$ tends to be more consistent (with less variation) than distributions of other sample measures of centre, and the sample mean $\bar{x}$ is an *unbiased estimator* of the population mean μ, that is, its distribution tends to centre around the value of the population mean.

As we also saw in Section 6-2, however, the point estimate does not reveal how good that estimate is, and that led us to develop confidence interval estimates for μ. In fact, confidence intervals can be constructed for small samples by using the normal distribution with the same margin of error from the preceding section, **provided that** the original population has a normal distribution and the population standard deviation σ is known (a condition not very common in real applications).

If we have a small ($n \leq 30$) sample but do not know σ, we can sometimes use the Student t distribution, developed by William Gosset (1876–1937), for constructing a confidence interval. Gosset was a Guinness Brewery employee who needed a distribution that could be used with small samples. The Irish brewery where he worked did not allow the publication of research results, so Gosset published under the pseudonym *Student*. As a result of his early experiments and studies of small samples, we can now use the Student t distribution.

AS

Student t Distribution

If the distribution of a population is essentially normal (approximately bell shaped), then the distribution of

$$t = \frac{\bar{x} - \mu}{\frac{s}{\sqrt{n}}}$$

is essentially a **Student t distribution** for all samples of size n. The Student t distribution, often referred to as the t **distribution,** is used to find critical values denoted by $t_{\alpha/2}$.

Table A-3 lists values of the t distribution along with areas denoted by α. Values of $t_{\alpha/2}$ are obtained from Table A-3 by locating the proper value for *degrees of freedom* in the left column and then proceeding across the corresponding row until reaching the number directly below the applicable value of α for two tails.

DEFINITION

The number of **degrees of freedom** for a data set corresponds to the number of sample values that can vary after certain restrictions have been imposed on all data values.

For example, if 10 students have quiz scores with a mean of 80, we can freely assign values to the first 9 scores, but the 10th score is then determined. The sum of the 10 scores must be 800, so the 10th score must equal 800 minus the sum of the first 9 scores. Because those first 9 scores can be freely selected to be any values, we say that there are 9 degrees of freedom available. For the applications of this section, the number of degrees of freedom is simply the sample size minus 1:

$$\text{degrees of freedom} = n - 1$$

EXAMPLE   A sample of size $n = 15$ is a simple random sample selected from a normally distributed population. Find the critical value $t_{\alpha/2}$ corresponding to a 95% degree of confidence.

SOLUTION   Because $n = 15$, the number of degrees of freedom is given by $n - 1 = 14$. Using Table A-3, we locate the 14th row by referring to the column at the extreme left. As in Section 6-2, a 95% degree of confidence corresponds to $\alpha = 1 - 0.95 = 0.05$, so we find the column with the heading "0.05 (two tails)." The value in the 14th row and the "0.05 (two tails)" column is 2.145, so $t_{\alpha/2} = 2.145$.

It might seem a bit strange that with a normally distributed population, we sometimes use the t distribution to find critical values, but when σ is unknown, the use of s from a small sample incorporates another source of error. To maintain the desired degree of confidence, we compensate for the additional variability by widening the confidence interval through a process that replaces the critical value $z_{\alpha/2}$ (found from the standard normal distribution values in Table A-2) with the larger critical value of $t_{\alpha/2}$ (found from the t-distribution values in Table A-3).

Important Properties of the Student t Distribution

1. The Student t distribution is different for different sample sizes. (See Figure 6-5 for the cases $n = 3$ and $n = 12$.)

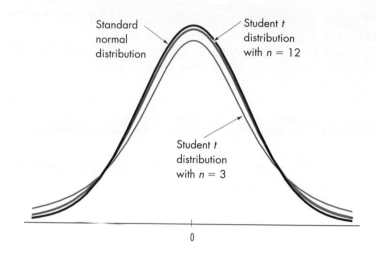

Figure 6-5 Student t Distributions for $n = 3$ and $n = 12$

The Student t distribution has the same general shape and symmetry as the standard normal distribution, but it reflects the greater variability that is expected with small samples.

2. The Student t distribution has the same general symmetric bell shape as the standard normal distribution, but it reflects the greater variability (with wider distributions) that is expected with small samples.

3. The Student t distribution has a mean of $t = 0$ (just as the standard normal distribution has a mean of $z = 0$).

4. The standard deviation of the Student t distribution varies with the sample size, but it is greater than 1 (unlike the standard normal distribution, which has $\sigma = 1$).

5. As the sample size n gets larger, the Student t distribution gets closer to the standard normal distribution. For values of $n > 30$, the differences are so small that we can use the critical z values instead of developing a much larger table of critical t values. (The values in the bottom row of Table A-3 are equal to the corresponding critical z values from the standard normal distribution.)

 Following is a summary of the conditions indicating use of a t distribution instead of the standard normal distribution. (These same conditions will also apply in Chapter 7.)

Conditions for Using the Student t Distribution

1. The sample is small ($n \leq 30$); and

2. σ is unknown; and

3. The parent population has a distribution that is essentially normal. (Because the distribution of the parent population is often unknown, we often estimate it by constructing a histogram of sample data.)

We can now determine values for the margin of error E in estimating μ when a t distribution applies. This margin of error can be used for constructing confidence intervals.

> **Margin of Error for the Estimate of μ**
> [Based on a Small Random Sample ($n \leq 30$) and Unknown σ from an Approximately Normally Distributed Population]
>
> Formula 6-3 $E = t_{\alpha/2} \dfrac{s}{\sqrt{n}}$ where $t_{\alpha/2}$ has $n - 1$ degrees of freedom

> **Confidence Interval for the Estimate of μ**
> [Based on a Small Random Sample ($n \leq 30$) and Unknown σ from an Approximately Normally Distributed Population]
>
> $$\bar{x} - E < \mu < \bar{x} + E$$
>
> where $E = t_{\alpha/2} \dfrac{s}{\sqrt{n}}$

● **EXAMPLE**   With *destructive testing,* sample items are destroyed in the process of testing them. Crash testing of cars is one very expensive example of destructive testing. If you were responsible for such crash tests, there is no way you would want to tell your supervisor that you must crash and destroy more than 30 cars so that you could use the normal distribution. Let's assume that you have crash tested 12 Dodge Viper sports cars under a variety of conditions that simulate typical collisions. Analysis of the 12 damaged cars results in repair costs having a distribution that appears to be bell shaped, with a mean of $\bar{x} = \$26{,}227$ and a standard deviation of $s = \$15{,}873$ (based on data from the Highway Loss Data Institute). Find the following:

a. The best point estimate of μ, the mean repair cost for all Dodge Vipers involved in collisions

b. The 95% interval estimate of μ, the mean repair cost for all Dodge Vipers involved in collisions

SOLUTION

a. The best point estimate of the population mean μ is the value of the sample mean $\bar{x}$. In this case, the best point estimate of μ is therefore $\$26{,}227$.

b. We will proceed to construct a 95% confidence interval by using the t distribution because the following three conditions are met: (1) The sample is small ($n \leq 30$), (2) the population standard deviation σ is unknown, and (3) the population appears to have a normal distribution because the sample data have a bell-shaped distribution.

   We begin by finding the value of the margin of error as shown below. Note that the critical value of $t_{\alpha/2} = 2.201$ is found from Table A-3 in the column labelled ".05 two tails" (from 95% confidence) and the row corresponding to 11 degrees of freedom (from $n - 1 = 11$).

$$E = t_{\alpha/2} \frac{s}{\sqrt{n}} = 2.201 \frac{15,873}{\sqrt{12}} = 10,085.29$$

We can now construct the 95% interval estimate of μ by using $E = 10,085.29$ and $\bar{x} = 26,227$. Because the summary statistics are rounded to the nearest dollar, the confidence interval limits will also be rounded to the nearest dollar.

$$\bar{x} - E < \mu < \bar{x} + E$$
$$26,227 - 10,085.29 < \mu < 26,227 + 10,085.29$$
$$\$16,142 < \mu < \$36,312$$

[This result could also be expressed in the format of $\mu = \$26,227 \pm \$10,085$ or as ($16,142, $36,312).]

Interpretation On the basis of the given sample results, we are 95% confident that the limits of $16,142 and $36,312 actually do contain the value of the population mean μ. These repair costs appear to be quite high. Such information is important to companies that insure Dodge Vipers against collisions.

Choosing the Appropriate Distribution

It is sometimes difficult to decide whether to use Formula 6-1 (and the standard normal distribution) or Formula 6-3 (and the Student t distribution). Figure 6-6 summarizes the traditional approach to making this decision when constructing confidence intervals for estimating μ, the population mean. In Figure 6-6, note that if we have a small ($n \le 30$) sample drawn from a very nonnormal distribution, we can't use the methods described in this chapter. One alternative is to use nonparametric methods (see Chapter 13), and another alternative is to use the computer-oriented bootstrap method, which makes no assumptions about the original population. This method is described in the Computer Project at the end of this chapter.

   Another Approach Rather than using *sample size* as the major criterion for choosing between the normal (z) and Student t distributions, some statisticians and software use *knowledge of the population standard deviation σ* as the major criterion—namely, if the sample is from a normally distributed population, then use the *Student t distribution* (regardless of sample size) *unless σ* is known (which is rarely the case). But using the Student t distribution with a large sample size results in a large number of degrees of freedom, so the value of $t_{\alpha/2}$ is, for all practical purposes, the same as the value of $z_{\alpha/2}$. When depending on tables, the normal distribution allows more precision in calculating P-values than does the t table—but if you are using computers, this limitation no longer applies.

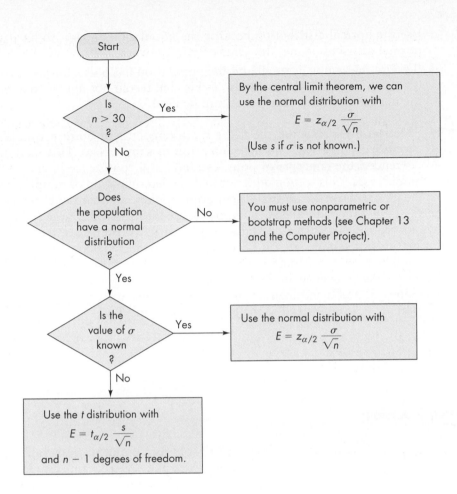

Figure 6-6   Choosing Between Normal (z) and t Distributions to Calculate the Margin of Error E for Estimating μ (Traditional Approach)

EXAMPLE   Assuming that you plan to construct a confidence interval for the population mean μ, use the given data to determine whether the margin of error E should be calculated using the normal distribution, the t distribution, or neither (so that the methods of this chapter cannot be used).

a. $n = 50, \bar{x} = 77.6, s = 14.2$, and the shape of the distribution is skewed.

b. $n = 25, \bar{x} = 77.6, s = 14.2$, and the distribution is bell shaped.

c. $n = 25, \bar{x} = 77.6, \sigma = 14.2$, and the distribution is bell shaped.

d. $n = 25, \bar{x} = 77.6, \sigma = 14.2$, and the distribution is extremely skewed.

SOLUTION   Refer to Figure 6-6 and use the flowchart to determine the following.

a. Because the sample is large ($n > 30$), use the normal distribution. When calculating the margin of error E, use Formula 6-1, where the sample standard deviation s is used for σ.

b. Use the t distribution because (1) the sample is small, (2) the population appears to have a normal distribution, and (3) σ is unknown.

Small Sample

The Children's Defense Fund was organized to promote the welfare of children. The group reported that in one area, 37.5% of the 16- and 17-year-old children were out of school. This statistic received much press coverage, but it was based on a sample of only 16 children. Another statistic was based on a sample size of only 3 students. (See "Firsthand Report: How Flawed Statistics Can Make an Ugly Picture Look Even Worse," *American School Board Journal*, Vol. 162.)

c. Use the normal distribution because the population appears to have a normal distribution and the value of σ is known.

d. Because the sample is small and the population has a distribution that is very nonnormal, the methods of this chapter do not apply. Neither the normal nor the t distribution can be used.

 Section 6-2 presented the three main concepts of point estimate, confidence interval, and determination of sample size. This section extended the concepts of point estimate and confidence interval to small sample cases. This section does not include determination of sample size because with known σ the normal distribution applies, and with unknown σ we need a large sample to justify estimation of σ with s, but the large sample allows us to use the normal distribution again. We therefore base our determinations of sample size on Formula 6-2 only and include no circumstances in which the t distribution is used.

The following section again considers the concepts of point estimate, confidence interval, and determination of sample size, but we will focus on the population proportion instead of the population mean.

Using Technology

Excel: *Caution:* Excel's built-in tools for confidence intervals are based on finding critical values of $z_{\alpha/2}$. To obtain confidence intervals that require critical values of $t_{\alpha/2}$, use the Data Desk add-in that is a supplement to this book. Click on **DDXL**, select **Confidence Intervals**, and select **1 Var t Interval** under the options listed under Function Type. Click on the pencil icon and enter the Excel range containing the data, such as A1:A12. Click on **OK**. In the dialog box, select the level of confidence, then click on **Compute Interval**, and the confidence interval will be displayed.

STATDISK: Select **Analysis** from the main menu, then select **Confidence Intervals**, followed by **Population Mean**, and enter the items in the dialog box. After you click on **Evaluate**, the confidence interval will be displayed.

6-3 Exercises A: Basic Skills and Concepts

In Exercises 1–4, find the critical value $t_{\alpha/2}$ that corresponds to the given degree of confidence and sample size n.

1. 99%; $n = 10$ 2. 95%; $n = 16$
3. 98%; $n = 21$ 4. 90%; $n = 8$

In Exercises 5–8, use the given degree of confidence and sample data to find (a) the margin of error and (b) the confidence interval for the population mean μ. In each case, assume that the population has a normal distribution.

5. Heights of female students: 95% confidence; $n = 10$, $\bar{x} = 64.2$ in., $s = 2.6$ in.
6. Grade-point averages: 99% confidence; $n = 15$, $\bar{x} = 2.76$, $s = 0.88$
7. Test scores: 90% confidence; $n = 16$, $\bar{x} = 77.6$, $s = 14.2$
8. Cost of basic phone service: 98% confidence; $n = 19$, $\bar{x} = \$15.30$, $s = \$1.25$

In Exercises 9–20, be sure to determine correctly whether the confidence intervals are calculated with the normal distribution or the t distribution. (In some cases, you may have a choice.)

9. In crash tests of 15 Honda Odyssey minivans, collision repair costs are found to have a distribution that is roughly bell shaped, with a mean of $1786 and a standard deviation of $937. Construct the 99% confidence interval for the mean repair cost in all such vehicle collisions.
10. Data Set 18 in Appendix B includes 108 body temperatures. Suppose that we have only the first 10 temperatures given below. For these scores, $\bar{x} = 36.36$ and $s = 0.35$. Construct the 95% confidence interval for the mean of all body temperatures. (A prior study has shown that body temperatures are normally distributed.)

    36.4   36.3   36.7   36.3   36.8   36.6   36.6   36.1   36.2   35.6

11. In a time-use study, 20 randomly selected managers were found to spend a mean of 2.40 h each day on paperwork. The standard deviation of the 20 scores is 1.30 h (based on data from Adia Personnel Services). Also, the sample data appear to have a bell-shaped distribution. Construct the 95% confidence interval for the mean time spent on paperwork by all managers. If the organization requires its managers to have a mean of 5.60 hours available each day (out of 8 hours) for non-desk work, should they be satisfied with the results of the time study? Why or why not?
12. In a study relating the amounts of time required for room-service delivery at a newly opened Radisson Hotel, 20 deliveries had a mean time of 24.2 min and a standard deviation of 8.7 min. The sample data appear to have a bell-shaped distribution. Construct the 90% confidence interval for the mean time of all deliveries.
13. In a study relating physical attractiveness and mental disorders, 231 subjects were rated for attractiveness. The resulting sample mean and standard deviation for that variable were 3.94 and 0.75, respectively. (See "Physical Attractiveness and Self-Perception of Mental Disorder," by Burns and Farina, *Journal of Abnormal Psychology*, Vol. 96, No. 2.) Use these sample data to construct the 95% confidence interval for the population mean.
14. A survey was conducted to estimate the annual income of CEOs of large corporations. Twenty companies were surveyed and the mean income for this group was $220,000 with a standard deviation of $21,000, and the distribution of this group appeared normal. Construct the 99% confidence interval for the mean annual income of all CEOs of large corporations.

15. A manufacturer of AAA batteries wants to estimate the mean life expectancy of the batteries. A sample of 25 such batteries shows that the distribution of life expectancies is roughly normal with a mean of 44.25 h and a standard deviation of 2.25 h. Construct a 98% confidence interval for the mean life expectancy of all the AAA batteries made by this manufacturer.

16. Off-season football players often participate in community events and charity fundraisers. Suppose a firm is bidding to provide T-shirts for players who are representing the CFL in such events. The firm has randomly sampled CFL quarterbacks and running backs, with these results (based on data from the CFL web site):

Quarterbacks: n = 10 $\bar{x}$ = 192.7 lb.   s = 11.7 lb
Running backs: n = 9 $\bar{x}$ = 199.7 lb.   s = 11.8 lb

Construct a 95% confidence interval for the mean weight of both populations. Assuming that weight is a rough indicator of required T-shirt size, should the firm consider making separate sizes for quarterbacks and running backs? Explain.

17. In a study of the use of hypnosis to relieve pain, sensory ratings were measured for 16 subjects, with the results given below (based on data from "An Analysis of Factors That Contribute to the Efficacy of Hypnotic Analgesia," by Price and Barber, *Journal of Abnormal Psychology*, Vol. 96, No. 1). Use these sample data to construct the 95% confidence interval for the mean sensory rating for the population from which the sample was drawn.

8.8   6.6   8.4   6.5   8.4   7.0   9.0   10.3
8.7   11.3   8.1   5.2   6.3   8.7   6.2   7.9

18. Refer to Data Set 11 in Appendix B and use only the sample of *red* M&M plain candies to construct a 95% confidence interval for the mean weight of all M&Ms.

19. Refer to Data Set 11 in Appendix B and use the entire sample of 100 plain M&M candies to construct a 95% confidence interval for the mean weight of all M&Ms. How does the result compare to the confidence interval for Exercise 18?

20. Refer to Data Set 10 in Appendix B.
   a. Construct a 95% confidence interval for the mean annual return over three years of U.S. equity funds.
   b. Construct a 95% confidence interval for the mean annual return over three years of Canadian equity funds and European funds.
   c. Compare and interpret the results of parts (a) and (b).

6-3 Exercises B: Beyond the Basics

21. Assume that a small ($n \leq 30$) sample is randomly selected from a normally distributed population for which σ is unknown. Construction of a confidence interval should use the t distribution, but how are the confidence interval limits affected if the normal distribution is incorrectly used instead?

22. A confidence interval is constructed for a small sample of temperatures (in degrees Celsius) randomly selected from a normally distributed population for which σ is unknown (such as the data set given in Exercise 10).

   a. How is the margin of error E affected if each temperature is converted to the Fahrenheit scale? $[F = \frac{9}{5}C + 32]$

   b. If the confidence interval limits are denoted by a and b, find expressions for the confidence interval limits after the original temperatures have been converted to the Fahrenheit scale.

   c. Based on the results from part (b), can confidence interval limits for the Celsius temperatures be found by simply converting the confidence interval limits from the Celsius scale to the Fahrenheit scale?

23. A simple random sample of Boeing 747 aircraft is selected, and the times (in hours) required to test for structural stress fractures are as follows: 8.1, 9.9, 9.5, 6.9, 9.8. Based on these results, a confidence interval is found to be $\mu = 8.84 \pm 1.24$. Find the degree of confidence.

Estimating a Population Proportion

In this section we apply the same three concepts discussed in Sections 6-2 and 6-3: (1) point estimate, (2) confidence interval, and (3) determining the required sample size. Whereas Sections 6-2 and 6-3 applied these concepts to estimates of a population mean μ, this section applies them to the population proportion p. For example, Nielsen Media Research might need to estimate the proportion of households that tune in to the Grey Cup, a question of great interest to potential television sponsors.

Although this section focuses on the population proportion p, we can also consider a probability or a percentage. Proportions and probabilities are both expressed in decimal or fraction form. When working with percents, convert them to proportions by dropping the percent sign and dividing by 100. For example, the 82.8% rate of Canadians who read newspapers regularly can be expressed in decimal form as 0.828. The symbol p may therefore represent a proportion, a probability, or the decimal equivalent of a percent. We now introduce the new notation of $\hat{p}$ (called "p hat") for the sample proportion.

In previous chapters we stipulated that $q = 1 - p$, so it is natural to note here that $\hat{q} = 1 - \hat{p}$. For example, if you survey 1068 Canadians and find that 673 of them have answering machines, the sample proportion is $\hat{p} = x/n = 673/1068 = 0.630$, and $\hat{q} = 0.370$ (calculated from $1 - 0.630$). In

Push Polling

"Push polling" is the practice of political campaigning under the guise of a poll. Its name is derived from its objective of pushing voters away from opposition candidates or views by asking loaded questions designed to discredit them. Here's an example of one such question that was used by the Ontario Ministry of Education when it was trying to sell its restructuring plan to the public: "Would your opinion about change be affected if you were told that major changes in education have not been made in over 20 years?" Many people see push polls as unethical, but some professional pollsters do not condemn the practice as long as the questions do not include outright lies.

Notation for Proportions
$p = population$ proportion
$\hat{p} = \dfrac{x}{n} = sample$ proportion of x successes in a sample of size n
$\hat{q} = 1 - \hat{p} = sample$ proportion of failures in a sample of size n

some cases, the value of $\hat{p}$ may be known because the sample proportion or percentage is given directly. If it is reported that 1068 Canadian television viewers are surveyed and 25% of them are college graduates, then $\hat{p} = 0.25$ and $\hat{q} = 0.75$.

If we want to estimate a population proportion with a single value, the best estimate is the *point estimate $\hat{p}$.*

Point Estimate

The sample proportion $\hat{p}$ is the best point estimate of the population proportion p.

We use $\hat{p}$ as the point estimate of p (just as $\overline{x}$ is used as the point estimate of μ) because it is unbiased and is the most consistent of the estimators that could be used. It is unbiased in the sense that the distribution of sample proportions tends to centre about the value of p; that is, sample proportions $\hat{p}$ do not systematically tend to underestimate p, nor do they systematically tend to overestimate p. The sample proportion $\hat{p}$ is the most consistent estimator in the sense that the standard deviation of sample proportions tends to be smaller than the standard deviation of any other unbiased estimators.

As we saw when estimating the mean, the point estimate has a major disadvantage: Although it provides the best single-value estimate, in this case for the population proportion p, it gives no indication of just how good the estimate is. The advantage of a confidence interval estimate is that it does contain an indication of how accurate the point estimate is. We first present the *margin of error* (first defined in Section 6-2), which is used for finding a confidence interval, and then we present the format of the confidence interval itself.

Margin of Error of the Estimate of p

Formula 6-4
$$E = z_{\alpha/2} \sqrt{\frac{\hat{p}\hat{q}}{n}}$$

Confidence Interval (or Interval Estimate) for the Population Proportion p

$$\hat{p} - E < p < \hat{p} + E \qquad \text{where } E = z_{\alpha/2} \sqrt{\frac{\hat{p}\hat{q}}{n}}$$

The confidence interval is sometimes expressed in the following formats:

$$p = \hat{p} \pm E$$

or $$(\hat{p} - E, \hat{p} + E)$$

In Chapter 3 we rounded probabilities expressed in decimal form to three significant digits. We use that same rounding rule here.

Round-Off Rule for Confidence Interval Estimates of p
Round the confidence interval limits to three significant digits.

Assumptions for This Section

1. The sample has been collected by a valid random-sampling technique.
2. The four conditions for the binomial distribution are satisfied (see Section 4-3). These are: (1) There is a fixed number of trials; (2) the trials are independent; (3) there are two categories of outcomes; and (4) the probabilities of success remain constant for each trial.
3. The conditions for using the normal distribution to approximate the distribution of sample proportions are satisfied: $np \geq 5$ and $nq \leq 5$. (Because the population values for p and q are unknown, we use the sample proportion to estimate these values. Also, there are procedures for dealing with situations in which the normal distribution is not a suitable approximation. See Exercise 34.)

EXAMPLE   To estimate the percent of all households in Canada with any children, 19,760 households were selected at random. It was found that 7483 of these households had children (based on data from a NADbank study). Using these sample results, find

a. The point estimate of the population proportion of all households in Canada with any children.
b. The 95% interval estimate of the population proportion of all households in Canada with any children.

SOLUTION

a. The point estimate of p is

$$\hat{p} = \frac{x}{n} = \frac{7483}{19{,}760} = 0.379$$

b. Construction of the confidence interval requires that we first evaluate the margin of error E. The value of E can be found from Formula 6-4. We use $\hat{p} = 0.379$ (found above), $\hat{q} = 0.621$ (from $\hat{q} = 1 - \hat{p}$), and $z_{\alpha/2} = 1.96$ (from Table A-2, where 95% converts to $\alpha = 0.05$, which is divided equally between the two tails so that $z = 1.96$ corresponds to an area of 0.4750).

$$E = z_{\alpha/2} \sqrt{\frac{\hat{p}\hat{q}}{n}} = 1.96 \sqrt{\frac{(0.379)(0.621)}{19{,}760}} = 0.0068$$

We can now find the confidence interval by using $\hat{p} = 0.379$ and $E = 0.0068$.

$$\hat{p} - E < p < \hat{p} + E$$

$$0.379 - 0.0068 < p < 0.379 + 0.0068$$

$$0.372 < p < 0.386$$

If we wanted the 95% confidence interval for the true population *percentage,* we could express this result as $37.2\% < p < 38.6\%$. This result is often reported in the following format: "Among Canadian households, the percentage that have children is estimated to be 37.9%, with a margin of error of plus or minus 0.68 percentage points." This is a verbal expression of this format for the confidence interval: $p = 37.9\% \pm 0.68\%$. (The level of confidence should also be reported, but it rarely is in the media. The media typically use a 95% degree of confidence but omit any reference to it.) The confidence interval is also expressed in this format: (0.372, 0.386).

Remember that the population value for p is fixed, and we are not assigning it a probability. In the preceding solution, the "95%" level expresses our confidence that 95% of the time, if we were to randomly select a sample with $n = 19{,}760$, and construct a confidence interval for p using the procedures shown, the true value of p would in fact be included in the calculated interval.

Basis for the Procedure of Finding the Margin of Error

If the assumptions given for this section are satisfied, then our calculations can be based on a normal approximation for a binomial distribution. Therefore, we can use results from Section 5-6 to conclude that μ and σ are given by $\mu = np$ and $\sigma = \sqrt{npq}$. Both of these parameters pertain to n trials, but we convert them to a per trial basis by dividing by n as follows:

$$\text{Mean of sample proportions} = \frac{np}{n} = p$$

$$\text{Standard deviation of sample proportions} = \frac{\sqrt{npq}}{n} = \sqrt{\frac{npq}{n^2}} = \sqrt{\frac{pq}{n}}$$

The first result may seem trivial because we have already stipulated that the true population proportion is p. The second result is nontrivial and is useful in describing the margin of error E, but we replace the product pq by $\hat{p}\hat{q}$ because we don't yet know the value of p (it is the value we are trying to estimate). Formula 6-4 for the margin of error reflects the fact that $\hat{p}$ has a probability of $1 - \alpha$ of being within $z_{\alpha/2}\sqrt{pq/n}$ of p. The confidence interval for p, as given previously, reflects the fact that there is a probability of $1 - \alpha$ that $\hat{p}$ differs from p by less than the margin of error

$$E = z_{\alpha/2}\sqrt{\frac{\hat{p}\hat{q}}{n}}$$

Determining Sample Size

Having discussed point estimates and confidence intervals for p, we will now describe a procedure for determining how large a sample should be when we want to find the approximate value of a population proportion. In the previous section we began with the expression for the margin of error E, then solved for n. Using a similar procedure, we begin with

$$E = z_{\alpha/2}\sqrt{\frac{\hat{p}\hat{q}}{n}}$$

and solve for n to get the sample size, as given in Formula 6-5. Formula 6-5 requires $\hat{p}$ as an estimate of the population proportion p, but if no such estimate is known, we replace $\hat{p}$ by 0.5 and replace $\hat{q}$ by 0.5, with the result given in Formula 6-6.

Sample Size

In 1997, the Angus Reid Group conducted a survey entitled *Canada and the World: An International Perspective on Canada and Canadians.* People from 20 countries, including Canada, were asked about their views of Canada in a number of areas. One component involved identifying prominent Canadians. Of the 1000 people in Canada who were surveyed, 9 out of 10 recognized the name of singer Céline Dion. Given that Canada's population is over 30,000,000, the sample of 1000 represents only 0.0033% of the population. While such a small sample may seem insignificant, the methods of this chapter can be used to show that a random sample size of 1000 can provide results that are quite good, even though that sample may be only 0.0033% of the population.

Sample Size for Estimating Proportion p		
When an estimate $\hat{p}$ is known:	Formula 6-5	$n = \dfrac{[z_{\alpha/2}]^2 \hat{p}\hat{q}}{E^2}$
When no estimate $\hat{p}$ is known:	Formula 6-6	$n = \dfrac{[z_{\alpha/2}]^2 \cdot 0.25}{E^2}$

Round-Off Rule for Determining Sample Size
If the computed sample size is not a whole number, round it up to the next *higher* whole number.

$\hat{p}$	$\hat{q}$	$\hat{p} \cdot \hat{q}$
0.1	0.9	0.09
0.2	0.8	0.16
0.3	0.7	0.21
0.4	0.6	0.24
0.5	0.5	0.25
0.6	0.4	0.24
0.7	0.3	0.21
0.8	0.2	0.16
0.9	0.1	0.09

Use Formula 6-5 when reasonable estimates of $\hat{p}$ can be made by using previous samples, a pilot study, or someone's expert knowledge. When no such guess can be made, we can assign the value of 0.5 to each of $\hat{p}$ and $\hat{q}$, so the resulting sample size will be at least as large as it should be. The underlying reason for the assignment of 0.5 is this: The product $\hat{p} \cdot \hat{q}$ has 0.25 as its largest possible value, which occurs when $\hat{p} = 0.5$ and $\hat{q} = 0.5$. (See the accompanying table, which lists some values of $\hat{p}$ and $\hat{q}$.) Note that Formulas 6-5 and 6-6 do not include the population size N, so the size of the population is irrelevant. (*Exception:* When sampling is without replacement from a relatively small finite population. See Exercise 29.)

● **EXAMPLE** Insurance companies are becoming concerned that increased use of cellular telephones is resulting in more car crashes, and they are considering implementing higher rates for drivers who use such phones. We want to estimate, with a margin of error of three percentage points, the percentage of drivers who talk on phones while they are driving. Assuming that we want 95% confidence in our results, how many drivers must we survey?

a. Assume that we have an estimate of $\hat{p}$ based on a prior study that showed that 18% of drivers talk on a phone (based on data from *Prevention* magazine).

b. Assume that we have no prior information suggesting a possible value of $\hat{p}$.

SOLUTION

a. The prior study suggests that $\hat{p} = 0.18$, so $\hat{q} = 0.82$ (found from $\hat{q} = 1 - 0.18$). With a 95% level of confidence, we have $\alpha = 0.05$, so $z_{\alpha/2} = 1.96$. Also, the margin of error is $E = 0.03$ (the decimal equivalent of "three percentage points"). Because we have an estimated value of $\hat{p}$, we use Formula 6-5 as follows:

$$n = \frac{[z_{\alpha/2}]^2 \hat{p}\hat{q}}{E^2} = \frac{[1.96]^2 (0.18)(0.82)}{0.03^2}$$

$$= 630.0224 = 631 \qquad \text{(rounded up)}$$

We must survey at least 631 randomly selected car drivers.

b. As in part (a), we again use $z_{\alpha/2} = 1.96$ and $E = 0.03$, but with no prior knowledge of $\hat{p}$ (or $\hat{q}$), we use Formula 6-6 as follows:

$$n = \frac{[z_{\alpha/2}]^2 \cdot 0.25}{E^2} = \frac{[1.96]^2 \cdot (0.25)}{0.03^2}$$

$$= 1067.1111 = 1068 \qquad \text{(rounded up)}$$

Interpretation To be 95% confident that our sample percentage is within three percentage points of the true percentage for all car drivers, we should randomly select and survey 1068 drivers. By comparing this result to the sample size of 631 found in part (a), we can see that if we have no knowledge of a prior study, a larger sample is required to achieve the same results as when the value of $\hat{p}$ can be estimated.

Part (b) of the preceding example involved application of Formula 6-6, the same formula frequently used by Nielsen, Gallup, and other professional pollsters. Many people incorrectly believe that we should sample some percentage of the population, but Formula 6-6 shows that the population size is irrelevant. (In reality, the population size is sometimes used, but only in cases in which we sample without replacement from a relatively small population. See Exercise 29.) Most of the polls featured in newspapers, magazines, and broadcast media involve polls with sample sizes in the range of 1000 to 2000. Even though such polls may involve a very small percentage of the total population, they can provide results that are quite good. When Nielsen surveys 1068 TV households from a population of 10 million, only 0.01% of the households are surveyed; still, we can be 95% confident that the sample percentage will be within three percentage points of the population percentage.

Polls have become very important and prevalent in Canada. They affect the television shows we watch, the leaders we elect, the legislation that governs us, and the products we consume. An understanding of the concepts of this section removes much of the mystery and misunderstanding surrounding polls.

Using Technology

Excel: *Confidence Intervals:* Use the Data Desk XL add-in that is a supplement to this book. First enter the number of successes and the total number of trials in two spreadsheet cells (such as A1 and A2). Click on **DDXL** and select **Confidence Intervals**. Under the Function Type options, select **Summ 1 Var Prop Interval** (which is an abbreviation for "confidence interval for a proportion using summary data for one variable"). Click on the pencil icon for "Num successes" and enter the cell address where you input that data. Similarly, click on the pencil icon for "Num trials" and enter the corresponding Excel address. Click on **OK**. In the dialog box, set the level of confidence, then click on **Compute Interval**. The confidence interval will be displayed, as shown below.

STATDISK: *Confidence Intervals:* Select **Analysis** from the main menu bar, select **Confidence Intervals**, then select **Population Proportion**. Enter the required items in the dialog box, then click the **Evaluate** button.

Sample Size: Select **Analysis** from the main menu bar at the top, then select **Sample Size Determination**, followed by **Estimate Proportion**. Proceed to enter the required items in the dialog box.

Excel Display

(6-4) Exercises A: Basic Skills and Concepts

In Exercises 1–4, assume that a sample is used to estimate a population proportion p. Find the margin of error that corresponds to the given values of n and x and the degree of confidence.

1. $n = 800$, $x = 200$, 95%
2. $n = 1400$, $x = 420$, 99%
3. $n = 4275$, $x = 2576$, 98%
4. $n = 887$, $x = 209$, 90%

In Exercises 5–8, use the given sample data and degree of confidence to construct the interval estimate of the population proportion p.

5. $n = 800$, $x = 600$, 95% confidence
6. $n = 2000$, $x = 300$, 99% confidence
7. $n = 2475$, $x = 992$, 90% confidence
8. $n = 5200$, $x = 1024$, 98% confidence

In Exercises 9–12, use the given data to find the minimum sample size required to estimate a population proportion or percentage.

9. Margin of error: 0.02; confidence level: 95%; $\hat{p}$ and $\hat{q}$ unknown
10. Margin of error: 0.01; confidence level: 90%; $\hat{p}$ and $\hat{q}$ unknown
11. Margin of error: four percentage points; confidence level: 99%; $\hat{p}$ is estimated to be 0.20 from a prior study
12. Margin of error: two percentage points; confidence level: 97%; p is estimated to be 0.85 from a prior study
13. Wawanesa Mutual Insurance Company wants to estimate the percentage of drivers who change tapes or CDs while driving. A random sample of 850 drivers results in 544 who change tapes or CDs while driving (based on data from *Prevention* magazine).
    a. Find the point estimate of the *percentage* of all drivers who change tapes or CDs while driving.
    b. Find a 90% interval estimate of the *percentage* of all drivers who change tapes or CDs while driving.

14. When 160 CEOs in British Columbia are randomly selected and surveyed, it is found that 41 of them possess an MBA.
  a. Find the point estimate of the true proportion of all CEOs in British Columbia who possess an MBA.
  b. Find a 95% confidence interval for the true proportion of all CEOs in British Columbia who possess an MBA.
15. The drug Ziac is used to treat hypertension. In a clinical test, 3.2% of 221 Ziac users experienced dizziness (based on data from Lederle Laboratories).
  a. Construct a 99% confidence interval estimate of the percentage of all Ziac users who experience dizziness.
  b. In the same clinical test, people in the placebo group didn't take Ziac, but 1.8% of them reported dizziness. Based on the results in parts (a) and (b), what can we conclude about dizziness as an adverse reaction to Ziac?
16. In a follow-up article on Y2K problems, a reporter wants to conduct a survey of small businesses, in order to estimate the true proportion of small businesses that took some action regarding the Y2K problem—that is, the then-widespread concern that when the date 2000 arrived, it would confuse software that used two-digit dates (such as 99). The reporter wants 95% confidence that her results have a margin of error of 0.03. How many small businesses must be surveyed?
  a. Assume the reporter will estimate $\hat{p}$ based on a 1998 Industry Canada study (taken from the Web site "strategis.ic.gc.ca"), according to which 66% of small businesses were taking action.
  b. Assume, instead, that we do *not* have prior information on which to estimate the value of $\hat{p}$.
17. A random survey of 85 CEOs in British Columbia showed 70 respondents have a computer on their desk. Based on those results, construct a 98% confidence interval for the percentage of all CEOs in British Columbia who have a computer on their desk.
18. Internationally, 53.3% of the candidates who wrote the Certified General Accounting (CGA) exams in December 1995 passed. In Manitoba, out of 781 candidates who wrote those exams, 439 passed (based on data from the Certified General Accountants Association of Manitoba). Assuming that these 1995 results are representative of years in general, construct a 99% interval estimate of the percentage of all Manitoban candidates of the CGA exams who passed. Is there sufficient evidence to indicate that the pass rate in Manitoba is greater than the international pass rate?
19. The Greybar Tax Company believes that its clients are selected for audits at a rate substantially higher than the rate for the general population. Suppose that Revenue Canada audits 4.3% of those who earn more than $100,000, but a check of 400 randomly selected Greybar returns with earnings above $100,000 shows that 56 of them were audited. Using a 99% level of confidence, construct a confidence interval for the percentage of Greybar returns with earnings above $100,000 that are audited. Based on the result, does it appear that the high-income Greybar clients are audited at a rate that is substantially higher than the rate for the general population?

20. The Locust Tree Restaurant keeps records of reservations and no-shows. When 150 Saturday reservations are randomly selected, it is found that 70 of them were no-shows (based on data from American Express). Using a 90% degree of confidence, find a confidence interval for the proportion of Saturday no-shows.

21. How many TV households must Nielsen survey to estimate the percentage that are tuned to *The Late Show with David Letterman*? Assume that you want 97% confidence that your sample percentage has a margin of error of two percentage points. Also assume that nothing is known about the percentage of households tuned in to any television shows after 11 P.M.

22. The Western Canada Communications Company is considering a bid to provide long-distance phone service. You are asked to conduct a poll to estimate the percentage of consumers who are satisfied with their current long-distance phone service. You want to be 90% confident that your sample percentage is within 2.5 percentage points of the true population value, and a Roper poll suggests that this percentage should be about 85%. How large must your sample be?

23. A hotel chain gives an aptitude test to job applicants and considers a multiple-choice test question to be easy if at least 80% of the responses are correct. A random sample of 6503 responses to one particular question includes 84% correct responses. Construct the 99% confidence interval for the true percentage of correct responses. Is it likely that this question is really easy?

24. A random sample of 400 people is taken from a large city in Atlantic Canada. They are asked about their views on the amalgamation of the four provinces in Atlantic Canada. Of the respondents, 190 are in favour of this amalgamation. Construct the 98% confidence interval for the true percentage of Atlantic Canada residents who are in favour of amalgamation. Based on the result, does there appear to be much chance that this amalgamation will ever occur?

25. In a study of store checkout scanners, 1234 items were checked and 20 of them were found to be overcharges (based on data from "UPC Scanner Pricing Systems: Are They Accurate?" by Goodstein, *Journal of Marketing*, Vol. 58).
    a. Using the sample data, construct a 95% confidence interval for the proportion of all such scanned items that are overcharges.
    b. Use the sample data as a pilot study and find the sample size necessary to estimate the proportion of scanned items that are overcharges. Assume that you want 99% confidence that the estimate is in error by no more than 0.005.

26. A health study involves 1000 randomly selected deaths, with 273 of them caused by heart disease (based on data from Statistics Canada).
    a. Using the sample data, construct a 99% confidence interval for the proportion of all deaths caused by heart disease.
    b. Use the sample data as a pilot study and find the sample size necessary to estimate the proportion of all deaths caused by heart disease. Assume that you want 98% confidence that the estimate is in error by no more than 0.01.

27. A climatologist claims that half of Canada's largest towns and cities receive more than 200 cm of snowfall each year. Refer to Data Set 4 in Appendix B and construct the 95% confidence interval for the percentage of cities with snowfall over 200 cm. Is the resulting confidence interval consistent with the climatologist's claim?

28. Refer to Data Set 11 in Appendix B and find the sample proportion of M&Ms that are red. Use that result to construct a 95% confidence interval estimate of the population percentage of M&Ms that are red. Is the result consistent with the 20% rate that is reported by the candy maker Mars?

6-4 Exercises B: Beyond the Basics

29. This section presented Formulas 6-5 and 6-6, which are used for determining sample size. In both cases we assumed that the population is infinite or very large, or that we are sampling with replacement. When we have a relatively small population with size N and sample without replacement, we modify E to include the *finite population correction factor* shown here, and we can solve for n to obtain the result shown to the right. Use this result to repeat Exercise 21, assuming that we limit our population to a town of 5000 people.

$$E = z_{\alpha/2} \sqrt{\frac{\hat{p}\hat{q}}{n}} \sqrt{\frac{N - n}{N - 1}} \qquad n = \frac{N\hat{p}\hat{q}[z_{\alpha/2}]^2}{\hat{p}\hat{q}\,[z_{\alpha/2}]^2 + (N - 1)E^2}$$

30. Consider the following statement: "The results from this poll differ, 19 times out of 20, by no more than 1 percentage point in either direction from the results that would be obtained by surveying all voters in Canada." Find the sample size suggested by this statement.

31. A newspaper article indicates that an estimate of the unemployment rate involves a survey of 47,000 people. If the reported unemployment rate must have an error no larger than 0.2 percentage point and the rate is known to be about 8%, find the corresponding confidence level.

32. Heights of female students are normally distributed with a mean of 64.2 in. and a standard deviation of 2.6 in. How many female students must be surveyed if we want to estimate the percentage who are taller than 5 ft? Assume that we want 98% confidence that the error is no more than 2.5 percentage points.

33. A *one-sided confidence interval* for p can be written as $p < \hat{p} + E$ or $p > \hat{p} - E$, where the margin of error E is modified by replacing $z_{\alpha/2}$ with z_α. If Air Borealis wants to report an on-time performance of at least x percent with 95% confidence, construct the appropriate one-sided confidence interval and then find the percent in question. Assume that a random sample of 750 flights results in 630 that are on time.

34. Special tables are available for finding confidence intervals for proportions involving small numbers of cases where the normal distribution approximation cannot be used. For example, given three successes among eight trials, the 95% confidence interval found in *Standard Probability and Statistics Tables and Formulae* (CRC Press) is $0.085 < p < 0.755$. Find the confidence interval that would result if you were to use the normal distribution incorrectly as an approximation to the binomial distribution. Are the results reasonably close?

(6-5) Estimating a Population Variance

In this section we consider the same three concepts discussed earlier in this chapter: (1) point estimate, (2) confidence interval, and (3) determining the required sample size. Whereas Sections 6-2, 6-3, and 6-4 applied these concepts to estimates of means and proportions, this section applies them to the population variance σ^2 or standard deviation σ. Many real situations, such as quality control in a manufacturing process, require that we estimate values of population variances or standard deviations. In addition to making products with measurements yielding a desired mean, the manufacturer must make products of *consistent* quality that do not run the gamut from extremely good to extremely poor. As this consistency can often be measured by the variance or standard deviation, these become vital statistics in maintaining the quality of products.

Assumptions for This Section

1. The sample has been collected by a valid random-sampling technique.
2. The population must have normally distributed values (even if the sample is large).

The assumption of a normally distributed population was made in earlier sections, but that requirement is more critical here. We describe this sensitivity to a normal distribution by saying that inferences about the population variance σ^2 (or population standard deviation σ) are *not robust*, meaning that the inferences can be very misleading, and lead to gross errors, if the population does not truly have a normal distribution. Consequently, the normal-distribution requirement is much more strict than in previous sections, and we should check the distribution of data first, by constructing histograms and normal probability plots, as described in Section 5-7.

When we considered estimates of means and proportions in Sections 6-2, 6-3, and 6-4, we used the normal and Student t distributions. When developing estimates of variances or standard deviations, we use another distribution, referred to as the *chi-square distribution*. We will examine important features of that distribution before proceeding with the development of confidence intervals.

Chi-Square Distribution

In a normally distributed population with variance σ^2, we randomly select independent samples of size n and compute the sample variance s^2 (see Formula 2-5) for each sample. The sample statistic $\chi^2 = (n-1)s^2/\sigma^2$ has a distribution called the **chi-square distribution.**

Chi-Square Distribution
Formula 6-7 $\qquad\qquad \chi^2 = \dfrac{(n-1)s^2}{\sigma^2}$
where $\qquad n$ = sample size
$\qquad\qquad s^2$ = sample variance
$\qquad\qquad \sigma^2$ = population variance

We denote chi-square by χ^2, pronounced "kigh square." (The specific mathematical equations used to define this distribution are not given here because they are beyond the scope of this text.) To find critical values of the chi-square distribution, refer to Table A-4. The chi-square distribution is determined by the number of degrees of freedom, and in this chapter we use $n-1$ degrees of freedom:

degrees of freedom $= n - 1$

In later chapters we will encounter situations in which the degrees of freedom are not $n-1$, so we should not assume that degrees of freedom are always $n-1$.

Properties of the Distribution of the Chi-Square Statistic

1. The chi-square distribution is not symmetric, unlike the normal and Student t distributions (see Figure 6-7). (As the number of degrees of freedom increases, the distribution becomes more symmetric, as Figure 6-8 illustrates.)

2. The values of chi-square can be zero or positive, but they cannot be negative (see Figure 6-7).

3. The chi-square distribution is different for each number of degrees of freedom (see Figure 6-8), which is determined in this section by df $= n - 1$. As the number of degrees of freedom increases, the chi-square distribution approaches a normal distribution.

Because the chi-square distribution is skewed instead of symmetric, the confidence interval does not fit the familiar format of [**point estimate**] $\pm E$, and we must do separate calculations for the upper and lower confidence interval limits. There is a different procedure for finding critical values, illustrated in the following example. Note the following essential feature of Table A-4:

Figure 6-7 Chi-Square
Distribution

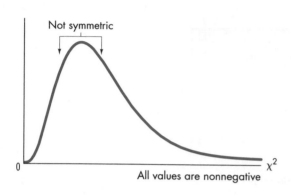

Figure 6-8 Chi-Square
Distribution for 10 and 20
degrees of freedom (df)

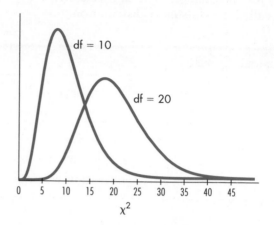

In Table A-4, each critical value of χ^2 corresponds to an area given in the top row of the table, and that area represents the *total region located to the right* of the critical value.

● **EXAMPLE**   Find the critical values of χ^2 that determine critical regions containing an area of 0.025 in each tail. Assume that the relevant sample size is 10 so that the number of degrees of freedom is $10 - 1$, or 9.

SOLUTION   See Figure 6-9 and refer to Table A-4. The critical value to the right ($\chi^2 = 19.023$) is obtained in a straightforward manner by locating 9 in the degrees-of-freedom column at the left and 0.025 across the top. The critical value of $\chi^2 = 2.700$ to the left once again corresponds to 9 in the degrees-of-freedom column, but we must locate 0.975 (found by subtracting 0.025 from 1) across the top because the values in the top row are always *areas to the right* of the critical value. Refer to Figure 6-9 and see that the total area to the right of $\chi^2 = 2.700$ is 0.975.

Interpretation   Figure 6-9 shows that, for a sample of 10 scores taken from a normally distributed population, the chi-square statistic $(n - 1)s^2/\sigma^2$ has a 0.95 probability of falling between the chi-square critical values of 2.700 and 19.023.

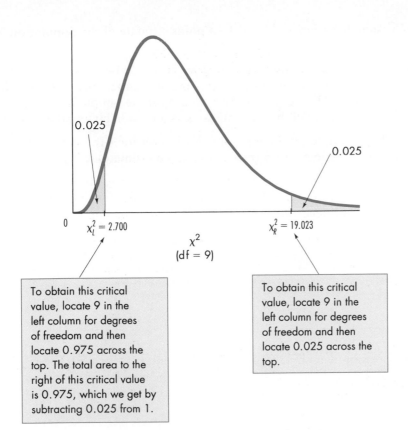

Figure 6-9   Critical Values of the Chi-Square Distribution

0.025

0.025

0 $\chi_L^2 = 2.700$ $\chi_R^2 = 19.023$

χ^2
(df = 9)

To obtain this critical value, locate 9 in the left column for degrees of freedom and then locate 0.975 across the top. The total area to the right of this critical value is 0.975, which we get by subtracting 0.025 from 1.

To obtain this critical value, locate 9 in the left column for degrees of freedom and then locate 0.025 across the top.

When obtaining critical values of chi-square from Table A-4, note that the numbers of degrees of freedom are consecutive integers from 1 to 30, followed by 40, 50, 60, 70, 80, 90, and 100. When a number of degrees of freedom (such as 52) is not found on the table, you can usually use the closest critical value. For example, if the number of degrees of freedom is 52, refer to Table A-4 and use 50 degrees of freedom. (If the number of degrees of freedom is exactly midway between table values, such as 55, simply find the mean of the two χ^2 values.) For numbers of degrees of freedom greater than 100, use the equation given in Exercise 22, a more detailed table, or a statistical software package.

Estimators of σ^2

Because sample variances s^2 (found by using Formula 2-5) tend to centre on the value of the population variance σ^2, we say that s^2 is an *unbiased estimator* of σ^2. That is, sample variances s^2 do not systematically tend to overestimate the value of σ^2, nor do they systematically tend to underestimate σ^2. Instead, they tend to target the value of σ^2 itself. Also, the values of s^2 tend to produce smaller errors by being closer to σ^2 than do other measures of variation. For these reasons, the value of s^2 is generally the best single value (or point estimate) of the various possible statistics we could use to estimate σ^2.

The sample variance s^2 is the best point estimate of the population variance σ^2.

Because s^2 is the best point estimate of σ^2, it would be natural to expect s to be the best point estimate of σ, but this is not the case, because s is a biased estimator of σ (see Exercise 35 in Section 2-5). If the sample size is large, however, the bias is so small that we can use s as a reasonably good estimate of σ.

For large samples, the sample standard deviation s is a reasonably good point estimate of σ (but it is a biased estimate).

Although s^2 is the best point estimate of σ^2, there is no indication of how good it actually is. To compensate for that deficiency, we develop an interval estimate (or confidence interval) that is more informative.

Confidence Interval (or Interval Estimate) for the Population Variance σ^2

$$\frac{(n-1)s^2}{\chi_R^2} < \sigma^2 < \frac{(n-1)s^2}{\chi_L^2}$$

This expression is used to find a confidence interval for variance σ^2, but the confidence interval (or interval estimate) for the standard deviation σ is found by taking the square root of each component, as shown below:

$$\sqrt{\frac{(n-1)s^2}{\chi_R^2}} < \sigma < \sqrt{\frac{(n-1)s^2}{\chi_L^2}}$$

The notations χ_R^2 and χ_L^2 in the preceding expressions are described as follows. (Note that some other texts use $\chi_{\alpha/2}^2$ in place of χ_R^2, and they use $\chi_{1-\alpha/2}^2$ in place of χ_L^2.)

Notation

With a total area of α divided equally between the two tails of a chi-square distribution, χ_L^2 denotes the left-tailed critical value and χ_R^2 denotes the right-tailed critical value. (See Figure 6-10.)

Figure 6-10 Chi-Square Distribution with Critical Values χ_L^2 and χ_R^2
The critical values χ_L^2 and χ_R^2 separate the extreme areas corresponding to sample variances that are unlikely (with probability α).

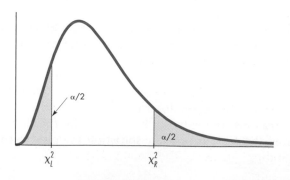

Confidence interval limits for σ^2 and σ should be rounded by using the following round-off rule, which is really the same basic rule given in Section 6-2.

Round-Off Rule for Confidence Interval Estimates of σ or σ^2

1. When using the original set of data to construct a confidence interval, round the confidence interval limits to one more decimal place than is used for the original set of data.

2. When the original set of data is unknown and only the summary statistics (n, s) are used, round the confidence interval limits to the same number of decimal places used for the sample standard deviation or variance.

EXAMPLE   The Qu'appelle Valley Bakery makes doughnuts that are packaged in boxes with labels stating that there are 12 doughnuts weighing a total of 42 oz. If the variation among the doughnuts is too large, some boxes will be underweight (cheating consumers) and others will be overweight (lowering profit). A consumer would not be happy with a doughnut so small that it can be seen only with an electron microscope, nor would a consumer be happy with a doughnut so large that it resembles a tractor tire. The quality control supervisor has found that he can stay out of trouble if the doughnuts have a mean of 3.50 oz and a standard deviation of 0.06 oz or less. Twelve doughnuts are randomly selected from the production line and weighed, with the results given here (in ounces). Construct a 95% confidence interval for σ^2 and a 95% confidence interval for σ, then determine whether the quality control supervisor is in trouble.

3.43   3.37   3.58   3.50   3.68   3.61   3.42   3.52   3.66   3.50   3.36   3.42

SOLUTION   Based on the sample data, the mean of $\bar{x} = 3.504$ seems quite good because it's very close to the desired 3.50 oz. The given scores have a standard deviation of $s = 0.109$, which might seem to be greater than the desired value of 0.06 or less. Let's proceed to find the confidence interval for σ^2.

With a sample of 12 scores, we have 11 degrees of freedom. With a 95% degree of confidence, we divide $\alpha = 0.05$ equally between the two tails of the χ^2 distribution and we refer to the values of 0.975 and 0.025 across the top row. The critical values of χ^2 are $\chi^2_L = 3.816$ and $\chi^2_R = 21.920$. Using these critical values, the sample standard deviation of $s = 0.109$, and the sample size of 12, we construct the 95% confidence interval by evaluating the following:

$$\frac{(12 - 1)(0.109)^2}{21.920} < \sigma^2 < \frac{(12 - 1)(0.109)^2}{3.816}$$

This becomes $0.006 < \sigma^2 < 0.034$. Taking the square root of each part (before rounding) yields $0.077 < \sigma < 0.185$.

Airlines Sample

Airline companies once used an expensive accounting system to split up income from tickets that involved two or more companies. They now use a sampling method in which a small percentage of these "split" tickets are randomly selected and used as a basis for dividing up all such revenues. The error created by this approach can cause some companies to receive slightly less than their fair share, but these losses are more than offset by the clerical savings accrued by dropping the 100% accounting method. This new system saves companies millions of dollars each year.

Interpretation Based on the 95% confidence interval for σ, it appears that the standard deviation is greater than the desired value of 0.06 or less, so the quality control supervisor is in trouble and must take corrective action to make the doughnut weights more consistent.

The confidence interval $0.077 < \sigma < 0.185$ can also be expressed as $(0.077, 0.185)$, but the format of $\sigma = s \pm E$ *cannot* be used because the confidence interval does not have s at its centre.

Basis for the Procedure of Finding the Confidence Interval for σ^2

We now explain why the confidence intervals for σ^2 and σ have the forms just given. If we obtain samples of size n from a population with variance σ^2, the distribution of the $(n-1)s^2/\sigma^2$ values will be as shown in Figure 6-10. For a random sample, there is a probability of $1 - \alpha$ that the statistic $(n-1)s^2/\sigma^2$ will fall between the critical values of χ_L^2 and χ_R^2. In other words (and symbols), there is a $1 - \alpha$ probability that both of the following are true:

$$\frac{(n-1)s^2}{\sigma^2} < \chi_R^2 \qquad \text{and} \qquad \frac{(n-1)s^2}{\sigma^2} > \chi_L^2$$

If we multiply both of the preceding inequalities by σ^2 and divide each inequality by the appropriate critical value of χ^2, we see that the two inequalities can be expressed in the equivalent forms

$$\frac{(n-1)s^2}{\chi_R^2} < \sigma^2 \qquad \text{and} \qquad \frac{(n-1)s^2}{\chi_L^2} > \sigma^2$$

These last two inequalities can be combined into one inequality:

$$\frac{(n-1)s^2}{\chi_R^2} < \sigma^2 < \frac{(n-1)s^2}{\chi_L^2}$$

There is a probability of $1 - \alpha$ that these confidence interval limits contain the population variance σ^2.

Determining Sample Size

The procedures for finding the sample size necessary to estimate σ^2 are much more complex than the procedures given earlier for means and proportions. Instead of using very complicated procedures, we will use Table 6-2.

EXAMPLE   With 95% confidence, you wish to estimate σ to within 10%. How large should your sample be? Assume that the population is normally distributed.

SOLUTION   From Table 6-2, we can see that 95% confidence and an error of 10% for σ correspond to a sample of size 191. You should randomly select 191 values from the population.

TABLE 6-2	Sample Size for σ^2	Sample Size for σ	
To be 95% confident that s^2 is within	of the value of σ^2, the sample size n should be at least	To be 95% confident that s is within	of the value of σ, the sample size n should be at least
1%	77,207	1%	19,204
5%	3,148	5%	767
10%	805	10%	191
20%	210	20%	47
30%	97	30%	20
40%	56	40%	11
50%	37	50%	7
To be 99% confident that s^2 is within	of the value of σ^2, the sample size n should be at least	To be 99% confident that s is within	of the value of σ, the sample size n should be at least
1%	133,448	1%	33,218
5%	5,457	5%	1,335
10%	1,401	10%	335
20%	368	20%	84
30%	171	30%	37
40%	100	40%	21
50%	67	50%	13

Using Technology

First, ensure that the distribution is sufficiently normal, using the procedures described in Section 5-7.

Excel: *Confidence Intervals:* Although Excel has no built-in tool for finding the confidence intervals for σ^2 and σ, a template such as the one illustrated can be created for this purpose. Place the raw data in column A, and type in the desired σ value in cell C11. All other values will be calculated by the template.

STATDISK: *Confidence Intervals:* Select **Analysis** from the main menu bar, select **Confidence Intervals**, then select **Population St Dev**. Enter the required items in the dialog box, then click the **Evaluate** button.

Excel Display Confidence
Intervals About σ or σ^2

	E16	▼	=	
	A	B	C	
1	Weight			
2	3.43	Mean	3.504167	
3	3.37	Std.Dev.	0.109084	
4	3.58	Pop.Var.		
5	3.50	Lower Limit	0.005971	
6	3.68	Upper Limit	0.034303	
7	3.61	Pop.Std.Dev.		
8	3.42	Lower Limit	0.077274	
9	3.52	Upper Limit	0.185211	
10	3.66			
11	3.50	alpha	0.050000	
12	3.36	Chi-square Left	3.815742	
13	3.42	Chi-square Right	21.920023	
14		d.f.	11.000000	

Cell	Formula	Explanation
C2	=AVERAGE(A2:A13)	Mean
C3	=STDEV(A2:A13)	Standard deviation
C5	=((C14*C3^2)/C13)	Lower limit of confidence interval for variance
C6	=((C14*C3^2)/C12)	Upper limit of confidence interval for variance
C8	=SQRT(C5)	Lower limit of confidence interval for standard deviation
C9	=SQRT(C6)	Upper limit of confidence interval for standard deviation
C11	{input alpha here}	
C12	=CHIINV(1-C11/2,C14)	Critical chi-square on left tail
C13	=CHIINV(C11/2,C14)	Critical chi-square on right tail
C14	=COUNT(A2:A13)-1	Degrees of Freedom

Use appropriate cell addresses for data

Sample Size: Select **Analysis** from the main menu bar at the top, then select **Sample Size Determination**, followed by **Estimate St Dev.** Proceed to enter the required items in the dialog box.

6-5 Exercises A: Basic Skills and Concepts

In Exercises 1–4, find the critical values χ_L^2 and χ_R^2 that correspond to the given degree of confidence and sample size.

1. 95%; $n = 26$
2. 99%; $n = 17$
3. 90%; $n = 60$
4. 95%; $n = 50$

In Exercises 5–8, use the given degree of confidence and sample data to find a confidence interval for the population standard deviation σ. In each case, assume that the population has a normal distribution.

5. Heights of female students: 95% confidence; $n = 10$, $\bar{x} = 64.2$ in., $s = 2.6$ in.

6. Grade-point averages: 99% confidence; $n = 15$, $\bar{x} = 2.76$, $s = 0.88$

7. Test scores: 90% confidence; $n = 16$, $\bar{x} = 77.6$, $s = 14.2$

8. Cost of basic phone service: 95% confidence; $n = 19$, $\bar{x} = \$15.30$, $s = \$1.25$

In Exercises 9–12, assume that each sample is obtained by randomly selecting values from a normally distributed population.

9. Find the minimum sample size needed to be 95% confident that the sample standard deviation s is within 5% of σ.

10. Find the minimum sample size needed to be 99% confident that the sample standard deviation s is within 20% of σ.

11. Find the minimum sample size needed to be 99% confident that the sample variance is within 30% of the population variance.

12. Find the minimum sample size needed to be 95% confident that the sample variance is within 40% of the population variance.

In Exercises 13–20, assume that each sample is obtained by randomly selecting values from a population with a normal distribution.

13. A container of car antifreeze is supposed to hold 3785 mL of the liquid. Realizing that fluctuations are inevitable, the quality control manager wants to be quite sure that the standard deviation is less than 30 mL. Otherwise, some containers would overflow while others would not have enough of the coolant. She randomly selects a sample, with the results given here. Use these sample results to construct the 99% confidence interval for the true value of σ. Does this confidence interval suggest that the fluctuations are at an acceptable level?

3761	3861	3769	3772	3675	3861	$n = 18$
3888	3819	3788	3800	3720	3748	$\bar{x} = 3787.0$
3753	3821	3811	3740	3740	3839	$s = 55.4$

14. Refer to Data Set 21 in Appendix B.
    a. Use the range rule of thumb (see Section 2-5) to estimate σ, the standard deviation of values for the "depth" of high-price diamonds.
    b. Use the listed weights to construct a 98% confidence interval for σ.
    c. Does the confidence interval contain your estimated value for σ?

15. A sample of 35 skulls is obtained for Egyptian males who lived around 1850 B.C. The maximum breadth of each skull is measured with the result that $\bar{x} = 134.5$ mm and $s = 3.5$ mm (based on data from *Ancient Races of the Thebaid* by Thomson and Randall-Maciver). Using these sample results, construct a 95% confidence interval for the population standard deviation σ.

16. A sample consists of 75 TV sets purchased several years ago. The replacement times of those TV sets have a mean of 8.2 years and a standard deviation of 1.1 years (based on data from "Getting Things Fixed," *Consumer Reports*). Construct a 90% confidence interval for the standard deviation of replacement times for all TV sets from that era. Does the result apply to TV sets currently being sold?

17. a. The listed values are waiting times (in minutes) of customers at the Humber Valley Credit Union, where customers enter a single waiting line that feeds three windows. Construct a 95% confidence interval for the population standard deviation σ.

    6.5   6.6   6.7   6.8   7.1   7.3   7.4   7.7   7.7   7.7

    b. The listed values are waiting times (in minutes) of customers at the Durham Credit Union, where customers may enter any one of three different lines that have formed at three different teller windows. Construct a 95% confidence interval for σ.

    4.2   5.4   5.8   6.2   6.7   7.7   7.7   8.5   9.3   10.0

    c. Interpret the results found in (a) and (b). Do the confidence intervals suggest a difference in the variation among waiting times? Which arrangement seems better: the single-line system or the multiple-line system?

18. Off-season football players often participate in community events and charity fundraisers. Suppose a firm is bidding to provide T-shirts for players who are representing the CFL in such events. The firm has randomly sampled CFL quarterbacks and slotbacks, with these results based on data from the CFL Web site:

Quarterbacks: $n = 10$ $\bar{x} = 192.7$ lb. $s = 11.7$ lb
Slotbacks: $n = 11$ $\bar{x} = 195.0$ lb. $s = 14.3$ lb

  a. Construct a 95% confidence interval estimate for the standard deviation σ for the quarterbacks.

  b. Construct a 95% confidence interval estimate for the standard deviation σ for the slotbacks.

  c. Assume that weight is a rough indicator of required T-shirt size, and that the firm sells a T-shirt with just enough stretchiness to fit the variation in sizes of quarterbacks. Would it be reasonable to assume that this same style of T-shirts could also fit all of the slotbacks? Explain why or why not.

19. Refer to Data Set 4 in Appendix B.

  a. Use the range rule of thumb (see Section 2-5) to estimate σ, the standard deviation of the annual snowfall (in centimetres) of the first 31 cities (all except Victoria).

  b. Construct a 99% confidence interval for σ.

  c. Does the confidence interval contain your estimated value of σ?

20. Refer to Data Set 11 in Appendix B.

  a. Use the range rule of thumb (see Section 2-5) to estimate σ, the standard deviation of the weights of brown M&M plain candies.

  b. Construct a 98% confidence interval for σ.

  c. Does the confidence interval contain your estimated value of σ?

6-5 Exercises B: Beyond the Basics

21. A journal article includes a graph showing that sample data are normally distributed.

  a. The degree of confidence is inadvertently omitted when this confidence interval is given: $2.8 < \sigma < 6.0$. Find the degree of confidence for these given sample statistics: $n = 20$, $\bar{x} = 45.2$, and $s = 3.8$.

  b. This 95% confidence interval is given: $19.1 < \sigma < 45.8$. Find the value of the standard deviation s, which was omitted from the article.

22. In constructing confidence intervals for σ or σ^2, we use Table A-4 to find the critical values χ_L^2 and χ_R^2, but that table applies only to cases in which $n \leq 101$, so the number of degrees of freedom is 100 or fewer. For larger numbers of degrees of freedom, we can approximate χ_L^2 and χ_R^2 by using

$$\chi^2 = \frac{1}{2}\left[\pm z_{\alpha/2} + \sqrt{2k-1}\right]^2$$

where k is the number of degrees of freedom. Construct the 95% confidence interval for σ by using the following sample data: The measured heights of 772 men between the ages of 18 and 24 have a standard deviation of 2.8 in.

Vocabulary List

estimator

estimate

unbiased estimator

point estimate

confidence interval

interval estimate

degree of confidence

level of confidence

confidence coefficient

critical value

margin of error (E)

maximum error of the estimate

confidence interval limits

Student t distribution

t distribution

degrees of freedom

chi-square distribution

Review

This chapter and the following chapter introduce the fundamental and important concepts of inferential statistics. This chapter focused on *estimates* of parameters as we considered population means, proportions, and variances to develop procedures for each of the following:

- Identifying a point estimate
- Constructing a confidence interval
- Determining the required sample size

We discussed point estimate (or single-valued estimate) and formed these conclusions:

- The best point estimate of μ is $\overline{x}$.
- The best point estimate of p is p.
- The best point estimate of σ^2 is s^2.

As single values, the point estimates don't convey any real sense of how reliable they are, so we introduced confidence intervals (or interval estimates) as more informative estimates. We also considered ways of determining the sample sizes necessary to estimate parameters to within given tolerance factors. This chapter also introduced the Student t and chi-square distributions. We must be careful to use the correct distribution for each set of circumstances.

It is important to know that all of the confidence interval and sample size procedures in this chapter require that we have a population with a distribution that is approximately normal. If the distribution is very nonnormal, we must use other methods, such as the bootstrap method described in the Computer Project at the end of this chapter.

Review Exercises

1. A human resources specialist has compiled annual numbers of person-days of work lost, due to work stoppages, in the water-based transportation industry. These are the results (based on data from Human Resources Canada, Workplace Information Directorate):

$$n = 40 \qquad \bar{x} = 38015.7 \qquad \text{median} = 18240.0 \qquad s = 49288.8$$

   a. Construct a 96% confidence interval estimate for the population mean of annual numbers of person-days lost.
   b. Why can we not use the methods of Section 6-5 to construct confidence interval estimates of the population standard deviation?

2. You have just been hired by General Motors to tour Canada giving randomly selected drivers test rides in a new Corvette (yeah, right). After giving the test drive, you must ask the rider whether he or she would consider buying a Corvette. How many riders must you survey to be 97% confident that the sample percentage is off by no more than two percentage points?

3. An auto parts supplier wants information about how long car owners plan to keep their cars. A random sample of 25 car owners results in $\bar{x} = 7.01$ years and $s = 3.74$ years, respectively (based on data from a Roper poll). Assuming that the sample is drawn from a normally distributed population, find a 95% confidence interval for the population mean.

4. Using the same sample data from Exercise 3, find a 95% confidence interval for the population standard deviation.

5. The Angus Reid Group randomly selected 1000 Ontario residents ages 18 and older by phone. Fifty-four percent of those surveyed believe the private sector should be responsible for ensuring there are jobs for Ontario residents. Construct the 95% confidence interval for the true proportion of Ontario residents who have this opinion. Also, what margin of error (in percentage points) should be reported along with the sample percentage of 54%?

6. In a Gallup poll of 1004 adults, 93% indicated that restaurants and bars should refuse service to patrons who have had too much to drink. If you plan to conduct a new poll to confirm that the percentage continues to be correct, how many randomly selected adults must you survey if you want 98% confidence that the margin of error is four percentage points?

7. In designing a new machine to be used on an assembly line at a General Motors plant, an engineer obtains measurements of arm lengths of a random sample of male machine operators. The following values (in centimetres) are obtained. Construct the 95% confidence interval for the mean arm length of all such employees.

| 76.8 | 75.6 | 69.3 | 75.7 | 75.5 | 71.2 | 72.5 | 71.9 |
| 70.9 | 69.4 | 71.7 | 72.5 | 72.2 | 68.5 | 75.9 | 73.0 |

8. Verbal PSAT scores of a random sample of 40 college-bound high-school juniors have a mean of 40.7, a standard deviation of 10.2, and a distribution that is normal (based on data from Educational Testing Service). Find a 99% confidence interval estimate of the population mean.

9. A company that produces electronic ignition systems for an engine developer wants to select a suitable sample size for monitoring the mean defect-free life

of the ignition systems. The company wants to be 95% confident that the true mean life of these systems will be estimated within ± 300 hours. A test study of these ignition systems provided the data that $s = 1600$ hours. How large must the sample size be to be 95% confident of the true mean?

10. In a Roper survey of 1998 randomly selected adults, 24% included loud commercials among the annoying aspects of television. Construct the 99% confidence interval for the percentage of all adults who are annoyed by loud commercials

• •

Cumulative Review Exercises

1. The college statistics club is reviewing its order for sweat suits for the new fall semester. Its review involves the random sample of heights for 24 students, listed here (in inches):

73.4	66.9	68.2	70.6	67.1	70.4	71.0	65.9
72.5	70.5	71.5	69.5	70.4	68.6	69.7	70.9
72.1	73.3	72.6	67.4	69.4	71.9	69.3	71.6

Find each of the following:

a. mean   b. median   c. mode   d. midrange

e. range   f. variance   g. standard deviation

h. Q_1 i. Q_2 j. Q_3

k. What is the level of measurement of these data? (nominal, ordinal, interval, ratio)

l. Construct a boxplot for the data.

m. Construct a histogram and identify its general shape.

n. Construct a 99% confidence interval for the population mean.

o. Construct a 99% confidence interval for the standard deviation σ.

p. Find the sample size necessary to estimate the mean height so that there is 99% confidence that the sample mean is in error by no more than 0.2 in. Use the sample standard deviation s from part (g) as an estimate of the population standard deviation σ.

q. Based on a prior study (see Data Set 8 in Appendix B), the heights of statistics students are approximately normally distributed with a mean of 68.00 in. and a standard deviation of 4.36 in. Do the heights of the new sample of 24 students (as listed above) agree with the population parameters for statistics students? Explain.

2. A genetics expert has determined that for certain couples, there is a 0.25 probability that any child will have an X-linked recessive disorder.

a. Find the probability that among 200 such children, at least 65 have the X-linked recessive disorder.

b. A subsequent study of 200 actual births reveals that 65 of the children have the X-linked recessive disorder. Based on these sample results, construct a 95% confidence interval for the proportion of all such children having the disorder.

c. Based on parts (a) and (b), does it appear that the expert's determination of a 0.25 probability is correct? Explain.

Technology Project

The *bootstrap method* can be used to construct confidence intervals for situations in which traditional methods cannot (or should not) be used. For example, the following sample of 10 scores was randomly selected from a very nonnormal distribution, so the methods previously discussed cannot be used:

$$2.9 \quad 564.2 \quad 1.4 \quad 4.7 \quad 67.6 \quad 4.8 \quad 51.3 \quad 3.6 \quad 18.0 \quad 3.6$$

The methods of this chapter require that the population have a distribution that is at least approximately normal. The bootstrap method, which makes no assumptions about the original population, typically requires a computer to build a bootstrap population by replicating (duplicating) a sample many times. We can draw from the sample with replacement, thereby creating an approximation of the original population. In this way, we pull the sample up "by its own bootstraps" to simulate the original population. Using the sample data given above, construct a 95% confidence interval estimate of the population mean μ by using the bootstrap method as described in the following Excel steps.

a. Create 500 new samples, each of size 10, by repeatedly selecting 10 scores with replacement from the 10 sample scores given above. To prepare for this, set up a data block with the raw data in the left column and, in the right column, the assumed probability of occurrence for each value if a random sample were taken. [Since there are 10 scores, we assume a 1/10 (0.10) probability that any one score would be selected.]

b. To begin sampling, select **Data Analysis** from **Tools** on Excel's main menu. From the list of tools, select **Random Number Generation**. For the **Number of Variables,** you want to enter the desired number of bootstrapped samples (500), but Excel will give an error message for such a large number. Instead, enter 250 and run the generator twice. Enter 10 (your intended number of scores per sample) as the **Number of Random Numbers.** For **Distribution,** select **Discrete.** For **Value and Probability Input Range,** enter the Excel range for the input data block that was created in part (a). It is usual to enter 0 for the random seed. (If you enter a different seed number, then you can reproduce the same simulated sample by choosing the same seed number later.) Now select an **Output Option,** as a specified **Output Range** on the same spreadsheet, or on a **New Worksheet Ply,** for which a sheet name can be input. Click on **OK** to obtain the results.

 A sample of a partial output is shown. Each column represents one of the 250 10-score samples that would be generated. Run the procedure a second time to generate the remaining 250 samples.

4.8	4.8	3.6	51.3	4.7	...
2.9	564.2	2.9	2.9	3.6	...
564.2	18.0	1.4	1.4	67.6	...
18.0	4.7	67.6	2.9	67.6	...
18.0	3.6	51.3	3.6	2.9	...
4.7	4.8	18.0	4.8	67.6	...
1.4	4.8	67.6	4.7	4.7	...
4.7	2.9	1.4	4.8	51.3	...
51.3	3.6	564.2	67.6	4.8	...
3.6	1.4	3.6	4.7	67.6	...

c. Find the means of the 500 bootstrap samples generated in part (b). For example, if the first sample is entered in Cells A1:A10, the formula =AVERAGE(A1:A10) could be put in Cell A11 to obtain the mean of the first sample; this formula could be copied along Row 11 to obtain the means for all the samples of the output.

    Because the sample generator had to be run twice in part (b), repeat this process for the second set of samples that were generated.

d. Use the "Copy\Paste Special\Values" sequence in Excel to bring all the sample means together in a single block, as shown below. The top row represents the means calculated for the first output of samples, and the bottom row represents the means calculated for the second output of samples.

67.3	61.28	78.16	14.87	34.24
65.9	179.2	125.1	72.31	68.31

e. Find the percentiles $P_{2.5}$ and $P_{97.5}$ for the means that result from the preceding step. To calculate $P_{2.5}$, use the formula =PERCENTILE (____,0.025), replacing the blank with the range for the block of means created in part (d). To calculate $P_{97.5}$, use the formula =PERCENTILE(____,0.975), replacing the blank with the range for the block of means created in part (d).

    Now use the bootstrap method to find a 95% confidence interval for the population standard deviation σ. Use the same steps listed above, but use the formula =STDEV instead of =AVERAGE in part (c), and use these new values for parts (d) and (e). Compare your result to the interval $318.4 < \sigma < 1079.6$, which was obtained by incorrectly using the methods described in Section 6-5. (Their use is incorrect because the population distribution is very nonnormal.) This incorrect confidence interval for σ does not contain the true value of σ, which is 232.1. Does the bootstrap procedure yield a confidence interval for σ that contains 232.1, verifying that the bootstrap method is effective?

    An alternative to using Excel is to use special software designed specifically for bootstrap resampling methods, such as Resampling Stats (available from Resampling Stats, Inc., 612 N. Jackson St., Arlington, VA 22201).

•••••••• FROM DATA TO DECISION ••••••••

He's Angry, But Is He Right?

The following excerpt is taken from a letter written by a corporation president and sent to the Associated Press:

> When you or anyone else attempts to tell me and my associates that 1223 persons account for our opinions and tastes here in America, I get mad as hell! How dare you! When you or anyone else tells me that 1223 people represent America, it is astounding and unfair and should be outlawed.

The writer then goes on to claim that because the sample size of 1223 people represents 120 million people, his letter represents 98,000 people (120 million divided by 1223) who share the same views.

a. Given that the sample size is 1223 and the degree of confidence is 95%, find the margin of error for the proportion. Assume that there is no prior knowledge about the value of that proportion.

b. The writer of the letter is taking the position that a sample size of 1223 taken from a population of 120 million people is too small to be meaningful. Do you agree or disagree? Write a response that either supports or refutes the writer's position that the sample is too small.

c. The writer also makes the claim that because the poll of 1223 people was projected to reflect the opinions of 120 million, any 1 person actually represents 98,000 other people. As the writer is 1 person, he claims to represent 98,000 other people. Is this claim correct? Explain why or why not.

INTERNET PROJECT   Confidence Intervals

The confidence intervals in this chapter illustrate an important point in the science of statistical estimation: Estimations based on sample data are made with certain degrees of confidence. In the Internet project, you will use confidence intervals to make a statement about the temperature in selected geographical areas. Go to the site

http://www.pearsoned.ca/triola

and click on Internet Project, and then on Chapter 6. Here you will find instructions on how to use the Internet to find temperature data collected by the weather stations in a wide variety of cities. Once you have collected a set of available weather data, you will construct confidence intervals for temperatures during different time periods and attempt to draw some conclusions about temperature change in the selected area.

········ COOPERATIVE GROUP ACTIVITIES ········

1. *Out-of-class activity:* Estimate the mean error (in seconds) on wristwatches. First, using a wristwatch that is reasonably accurate, set the time to be exact. Use a radio station or telephone time report that states that "at the tone, the time is. . . ." If you cannot set the time to the nearest second, record the error for the watch you are using. Now compare the time on your watch to the time on others. Record the errors with positive signs for watches that are ahead of the actual time and negative signs for those watches that are behind the actual time. Find point estimates and confidence intervals for the mean error and standard deviation of errors. Does the confidence interval for the mean error contain zero? Based on the results, what do you conclude about the accuracy of people's watches? Are the deviations from the correct time random fluctuations, or are there other factors to consider?

2. *In-class activity:* Divide into groups with approximately 10 students in each group. Get the reaction timer from the first Cooperative Group Activity given in Chapter 5 and measure the reaction time of each group member. (Right-handed students should use their right hand, and left-handed students should use their left hand.) Use the methods of this chapter to estimate the mean reaction time for all college students. Construct a 90% confidence

interval estimate of that mean. Compare the results to those found in other groups.

3. *In-class activity:* Divide into groups of three or four. Assume that you need to conduct a survey of full-time students at your college with the objective of identifying the percentage of students who are eligible for a student loan. Identify a margin of error that is reasonable, select an appropriate degree of confidence, then find the minimum sample size. Describe a sampling plan that is likely to yield good results.

4. *In-class activity:* Divide into groups with approximately 10 students in each group. First, each group member should write an estimate of the mean amount of cash being carried by students in the group. Next, each group member should report the actual amount of cash being held. (The amounts should be written anonymously on separate sheets of paper that are mixed, so that nobody's privacy is compromised.) Use the reported values to find $\bar{x}$ and s, then construct a 95% confidence interval estimate of the mean μ. Describe the precise population that is being estimated. Which group member came closest to the value of $\bar{x}$? Compare the results with other groups. Are the results consistent, or are there large variations among the group results?

Hypothesis Testing

7-1 Overview

Chapter objectives are defined. This chapter introduces the basic concepts and procedures used for testing claims made about population parameters. The hypothesis-testing procedures of this chapter and the estimation procedures of Chapter 6 are two of the fundamental and major topics of inferential statistics.

7-2 Fundamentals of Hypothesis Testing

An informal example of a hypothesis test is presented and its important components are described. The types of errors that can be made are also discussed.

7-3 Testing a Claim About a Mean: Large Samples

The traditional approach to hypothesis testing is presented, along with the *P*-value approach and a third approach based on confidence intervals. This section is limited to cases involving large ($n > 30$) samples only.

7-4 Testing a Claim About a Mean: Small Samples

This section presents the procedure for testing a claim made about the mean of a population, given that the data set is small (with 30 or fewer values) and that the value of the population standard deviation is not known. The *t* distribution will be used in such cases.

7-5 Testing a Claim About a Proportion

The method is described for testing a claim made about a population proportion or percentage. The normal distribution is used for the examples and exercises in this section.

7-6 Testing a Claim About a Standard Deviation or Variance

The method is described for testing a claim made about the standard deviation or variance of a population. The chi-square distribution is used for such tests, and its role is described.

CHAPTER PROBLEM:

The mean body temperature is 37°C, right?

When asked, almost everyone will identify the mean body temperature for healthy adults as 37.0°C (or 98.6°F). But "healthy adults" may not always refer to the same population. Table 7-1 lists 108 measured body temperatures found in Data Set 18 of Appendix B (for patients admitted for voluntary surgery at Lakeridge Health Oshawa). These patients had health issues that brought them to surgery; yet their voluntary surgeries would not have proceeded if they were not judged to be essentially healthy overall. These 108 temperatures have a mean of 36.39°C, and a standard deviation of 0.62°C. In Chapter 6 we used the same set of temperatures to estimate μ, the mean body temperature, and to find the 99% confidence interval: $36.24°C < \mu < 36.54°C$ (see Exercise 16 in Section 6–2).

Here's the problem: The confidence interval limits of 36.24°C and 36.54°C do not contain 37.0°C, the value generally believed to be the mean body temperature. Some researchers believe the concept of 37.0°C as a "normal body temperature" is meaningless. Based on the data from Lakeridge Health Oshawa, should we reject the claim that the mean body temperature for those healthy enough for elective surgery is 37.0°C? There is a standard procedure for testing such claims, and this chapter will describe that procedure.

Table 7-1   Body Temperatures (in Degrees Celsius) of Adults Accepted for Voluntary Surgery, Measured Before the Surgery

36.4	36.3	36.7	36.3	36.8	36.6	36.6	36.1	36.2	35.6	37.4	36.3
36.2	35.4	36.4	36.3	36.7	36.1	36.0	36.1	36.4	36.4	35.8	36.7
37.3	36.4	37.1	37.1	36.4	36.6	36.6	36.5	36.7	36.5	36.6	36.8
35.5	37.0	36.9	35.2	37.1	36.7	37.4	37.1	37.0	36.4	35.9	36.9
36.3	37.1	36.4	36.8	36.5	37.6	36.1	36.4	36.0	36.7	36.3	36.2
36.4	36.7	35.4	36.1	35.0	39.9	36.6	35.9	36.0	36.0	35.4	36.2
36.0	36.8	37.3	36.3	37.1	35.8	36.0	35.8	36.2	36.9	36.3	36.6
36.0	35.5	36.0	36.1	36.4	35.0	36.5	36.6	35.1	36.4	36.0	36.7
36.3	36.8	36.5	36.5	35.8	36.4	35.9	36.1	36.1	36.2	36.3	36.3

Note that while not all of these temperatures may represent "normal, healthy" temperatures, they are the temperatures of people who were deemed sufficiently nonfevered to undergo voluntary surgery. Temperatures of patients who were operated on but may have had fever are omitted.

7-1 Overview

In Chapter 6 we introduced a major topic of inferential statistics: estimating values of population parameters based on sample statistics. This chapter introduces another major topic of inferential statistics: testing claims (or *hypotheses*) made about population parameters.

DEFINITION

In statistics, a **hypothesis** is a claim or statement about a property of a population.

The following statements are examples of hypotheses that will be tested by the procedures we develop in this chapter:

- The mean body temperature for patients admitted to elective surgery is not equal to 37.0°C (a claim about population *mean*).

- Drivers who use cell phones have a car crash rate that is greater than the 13% rate for those who do not use cell phones (a claim about a population *proportion*).

- When new equipment is used to manufacture aircraft altimeters, the variation in the errors is reduced so that the readings are more consistent (a claim about a population *variance*).

Before beginning to study this chapter, you should keep in mind the rare event rule for inferential statistics, first introduced in Section 3-1:

> **If, under a given assumption, the probability of a particular observed event is exceptionally small, we conclude that the assumption is probably not correct.**

Following this rule, we analyse a sample in an attempt to distinguish between results that can easily occur and results that are *highly unlikely*. We can explain the occurrence of highly unlikely results by saying either that a rare event has indeed occurred or that things are not as they are assumed to be. Let us apply that reasoning in the following example (data taken from Environment Canada Web site http://www.ec.gc.ca/press/smog2_b_e.htm):

EXAMPLE   Ground-level ozone is a colourless, unhealthy gas that typically forms in urban areas, from a heated mixture of nitrogen oxide and other air pollutants. In the heavily urbanized corridor from Windsor to Quebec City, it is estimated that 50% of the ozone "smog" is generated locally, and 50% has its origins in the United States. Suppose that Ontario and Quebec take serious steps towards reducing noxious emissions, and that after several years of this program, the proportion of smog generated locally is measured. (Assume that emission rates from United States remain unchanged.)

Using common sense and no formal statistical methods, what should we conclude about the relative effectiveness of Ontario and Quebec's anti-pollution measures if the proportion of locally generated smog is:

a. 48%?
b. 2%?

SOLUTION

a. If the two provinces had not lowered their emissions, we would expect about 50% of the smog still to be generated locally. The result of 48% is close to 50%, so we should not conclude that the anti-pollution measures were effective. If the provinces had taken no special measures, it could easily occur by chance that 48% of the observed smog was locally generated.

b. The result that only 2% of the smog is locally generated is extremely unlikely to happen by chance. We could explain the proportion of 2% in one of two ways: Either an *extremely* rare event has occurred by chance, or the provinces' anti-pollution measures were effective in reducing emissions. Given the extremely low probability that 2% of the smog was locally generated, due simply to chance, the more likely explanation is that the program was effective.

Interpretation   We can only conclude that the provinces effectively reduced the percentage of locally generated ozone if they obtain a *significantly* reduced percentage of locally generated ozone compared to what we would expect under normal circumstances. Although the outcomes 48% locally generated and 2% locally generated are both "below average," and less than the expected 50%, the result of 48% is not significant, whereas 2% locally generated ozone does constitute a significant reduction.

This brief example illustrates the basic approach used in testing hypotheses. The formal method involves a variety of standard terms and conditions incorporated into an organized procedure. We recommend that you begin the study of this chapter by first reading Sections 7-2 and 7-3 casually to obtain a general idea of their concepts and then rereading Section 7-2 more carefully to become familiar with the terminology.

7-2   Fundamentals of Hypothesis Testing

In this section we begin with an informal example, then we identify the formal components of the standard method of **hypothesis testing**: null hypothesis,

---

Large Sample Size Isn't Good Enough

Biased sample data should not be used for inferences, no matter how large the sample is. For example, in *Women and Love: A Cultural Revolution in Progress*, Shere Hite bases her conclusions on 4500 replies that she received after mailing 100,000 questionnaires to various women's groups. A *random* sample of 4500 subjects would usually provide good results, but Hite's sample is biased. It is criticized for overrepresenting women who join groups and women who feel strongly about the issues addressed. Because Hite's sample is biased, her inferences are not valid, even though the sample size of 4500 might seem to be sufficiently large.

alternative hypothesis, test statistic, critical region, significance level, critical value, type I error, and type II error. After studying this chapter, you should be able to:

- Given a claim, identify the *null hypothesis* and the *alternative hypothesis*, and express them both in symbolic form.
- Given a *significance level*, identify the *critical value(s)*.
- Given a claim and sample data, calculate the value of the *test statistic*.
- State the conclusion of a hypothesis test in simple, nontechnical terms.
- Identify the *type I* and *type II* errors that could be made when testing a given claim.

You should study the following example until you thoroughly understand it. Once you do, you will have captured a major concept of statistics.

● **EXAMPLE**   In the Chapter Problem, we found that a population of essentially healthy adults does not appear to have a mean body temperature equal to the commonly assumed value of 37.0°C (98.6°F). A random sample was taken from the recorded body temperatures of individuals judged healthy enough to undergo elective surgery at Lakeridge Health Oshawa. The sample has these characteristics: $n = 108$, $\bar{x} = 36.39°$, $s = 0.62$, and the shape of the distribution is approximately normal. Here is the key question: *Do the sample data (with $\bar{x} = 36.39$) constitute sufficient evidence to warrant rejection of the hypothesis that $\mu = 37.0$ for this population?*

We conclude that there is sufficient evidence to warrant rejection of the belief that $\mu = 37.0$ for at least this one population of people who *are* essentially healthy. For if the mean were really 37.0, the probability of getting the sample mean of 36.39 is less than 0.0001, which is too small. (Later, we will show how that probability value of less than 0.0001 is determined.)

If we were to assume that $\mu = 37.0$ and use the central limit theorem (Section 5-5), we know that sample means tend to be normally distributed with these parameters:

$$\mu_{\bar{x}} = \mu = 37.0 \quad \text{(by assumption)}$$

$$\sigma_{\bar{x}} = \frac{\sigma}{\sqrt{n}} \approx \frac{s}{\sqrt{n}} = \frac{0.62}{\sqrt{108}} = 0.06$$

We construct Figure 7-1 by assuming that $\mu = 37.0$ and by using the parameters just shown. Figure 7-1 also shows that if μ is really 37.0, then 99% of all sample means should fall between 36.85 and 37.15. (The values of 36.85 and 37.15 were found by using the methods of Section 5-5. Specifically, 99% of sample means should fall within approximately 2.575 standard deviations of μ. With $\sigma_{\bar{x}} = 0.06$, 99% of sample means should fall within $2.575 \times 0.06 \approx 0.15$ of 37.0. Falling within 0.15 of 37.0 is equivalent to falling between 36.85 and 37.15.)

Here are the key points:

- The common belief is that $\mu = 37.0$.
- The sample resulted in $\bar{x} = 36.39$.

- Considering the distribution of sample means, the sample size, and the magnitude of the discrepancy between 37.0 and 36.39, we find that a sample mean of 36.39 is unlikely (with less than a 1% chance) to occur if μ is really 37.0.
- There are two reasonable explanations for the sample mean of 36.39: Either a very rare event has occurred, or μ is not really 37.0. Because the probability of getting a sample mean of 36.39 (when $\mu = 37.0$) is so low, we go with the more reasonable explanation: The value of μ is not 37.0 for at least one population of healthy people.

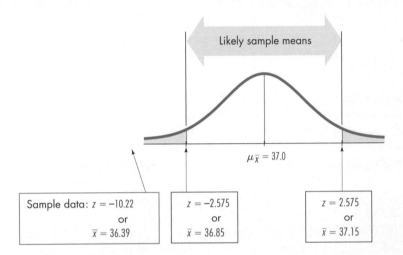

Figure 7-1   Central Limit Theorem
The expected distribution of sample means assuming that $\mu = 37.0$

The preceding example illustrates well the basic line of reasoning that we will use throughout this chapter. Read it several times until you understand it. Try not to dwell on the details of the calculations. Instead, focus on the key idea that although there is an assumption that $\mu = 37.0$, the sample mean is $\bar{x} = 36.39$. By using the central limit theorem, we determine that if the mean is really 37.0, then the probability of getting a sample with a mean of 36.39 is very small, which suggests that, for the sampled population, the belief that $\mu = 37.0$ should be rejected. Section 7-3 will describe the specific procedure used in hypothesis testing, but we will first describe the components of a formal **hypothesis test** or **test of significance**.

Components of a Formal Hypothesis Test

Null and Alternative Hypotheses

- The **null hypothesis** (denoted by H_0) is a statement about the value of a population parameter (such as the mean), and it must contain the condition of equality and must be written with the symbol $=$, $\leq$, or $\geq$. (When actually conducting the test, we operate under the assumption that the parameter *equals* some specific value.) For the mean, the null hypothesis will be stated in one of these three possible forms:

H_0: $\mu =$ some value H_0: $\mu \leq$ some value H_0: $\mu \geq$ some value

For example, the null hypothesis corresponding to the common belief that the mean body temperature is 37.0°C is expressed as H_0: $\mu = 37.0$. We test the null hypothesis directly in the sense that we assume it is true and reach a conclusion either to reject H_0 or fail to reject H_0.

- The **alternative hypothesis** (denoted by H_1) is the statement that must be true if the null hypothesis is false. For the mean, the alternative hypothesis will be stated in only one of three possible forms:

$$H_1: \mu \neq \text{some value} \qquad H_1: \mu > \text{some value} \qquad H_1: \mu < \text{some value}$$

Note that H_1 is the opposite of H_0. For example, if H_0 is given as $\mu = 37.0$, then it follows that the alternative hypothesis is given by H_1: $\mu \neq 37.0$.

Note About Using $\leq$ or $\geq$ in H_0: Even though we sometimes express H_0 with the symbol $\leq$ or $\geq$ as in H_0: $\mu \leq 37.0$ or H_0: $\mu \geq 37.0$, we conduct the test by assuming that $\mu = 37.0$ is true. We must have a single fixed value for μ so that we can work with a single distribution having a specific mean. (Some textbooks and some software packages use notation in which H_0 *always* contains only the equals symbol. Where this and many other textbooks might use $\mu \leq 37.0$ and $\mu > 37.0$ for H_0 and H_1, respectively, some others might use $\mu = 37.0$ and $\mu > 37.0$ instead.)

Note About Forming Your Own Claims (Hypotheses): If you are conducting a study and you want to use a hypothesis test to *support* your claim, you must state it in such a way that it becomes the alternative hypothesis. In other words, your claim must be expressed in one of these formats:

$$\mu \neq \text{some value} \qquad \mu > \text{some value} \qquad \mu < \text{some value}$$

For example, suppose you wish to attract new businesses to Calgary by arguing that the city's average income per capita has surpassed Toronto's level of $28,767 (Conference Board of Canada, October 1998). If you want to provide evidence for this claim, you must state the claim as $\mu > \$28,767$.

(When trying to support the goal of research, the alternative hypothesis is sometimes referred to as the *research hypothesis*. Also in this context, the null hypothesis of $\mu \leq 28,767$ is assumed true for the purpose of conducting the hypothesis test, but it is hoped that the conclusion will be rejection of the null hypothesis so that the claim of $\mu > \$28,767$ is supported.)

Note About Testing the Validity of Someone Else's Claim: Sometimes we test the validity of someone else's claim, such as the claim of the Coca Cola Bottling Company that "the mean amount of Coke in cans is at least 355 mL," which becomes the null hypothesis of H_0: $\mu \geq 355$. In this context of testing the validity of someone else's claim, their original claim sometimes becomes the null hypothesis (because it contains equality), and it sometimes becomes the alternative hypothesis (because it does not contain equality).

Test Statistic

- The **test statistic** is a value that we compute from the sample data and that we use as a step in deciding whether to reject the null hypothesis. The test statistic converts the sample statistic (such as the sample mean $\bar{x}$) to a score (such as the z score) with the assumption that the null hypothesis is true. The test statistic can therefore be used to gauge whether the discrepancy between the sample and the claim is significant. In this section and the following section, we use only large samples in testing claims made about population means. In such cases, we can use the central limit theorem (Section 5-5) with the test statistic based on the discrepancy between the sample mean $\bar{x}$ and the claimed population mean μ, calculated by using Formula 7-1, which is another form of $z = (\bar{x} - \mu_{\bar{x}})/\sigma_{\bar{x}}$.

Formula 7-1 $$z = \frac{\bar{x} - \mu_{\bar{x}}}{\frac{\sigma}{\sqrt{n}}}$$ Test statistic

EXAMPLE   Use the sample data from the Chapter Problem ($n = 108$, $\bar{x} = 36.39$, and $s = .62$), and find the value of the test statistic for the claim that the population mean is given by $\mu = 37$.

SOLUTION   With $n = 108$, $\bar{x} = 36.39$, and $s = .62$, and with the assumption that $\mu = 37$, the test statistic is calculated by using Formula 7-1 as shown below (with s used as an estimate of σ).

$$z = \frac{\bar{x} - \mu_{\bar{x}}}{\frac{\sigma}{\sqrt{n}}} = \frac{36.39 - 37.0}{\frac{0.62}{\sqrt{108}}} = -10.22$$

Critical Region, Significance Level, and Critical Value

- The **critical region** is the set of all values of the test statistic that cause us to reject the null hypothesis. For the preceding example, the critical region is represented by the shaded part of Figure 7-1 and consists of values of the test statistic less than $z = -2.575$ or greater than $z = 2.575$.
- The **significance level** (denoted by α) indicates how rare an event it would be if the test statistic falls in the critical region when the null hypothesis is actually true. If the test statistic falls in the critical region, we will reject the null hypothesis, so α is the probability of making the mistake of rejecting the null hypothesis when it is true. This is the same α introduced in Section 6-2, where we defined the degree of confidence for a confidence interval to be the probability $1 - \alpha$. Common choices for α are 0.05, 0.01, and 0.10. In Figure 7-1 the shaded regions in the tails combine to be $\alpha = 0.01$. The significance level is described as $\alpha = 0.01$.

- A **critical value** is any value that separates the critical region (where we reject the null hypothesis) from the values of the test statistic that do not lead to rejection of the null hypothesis. The critical values depend on the nature of the null hypothesis, the relevant sampling distribution, and the significance level α. For the preceding example, the critical values of $z = -2.575$ and $z = 2.575$ separate the shaded critical regions, as shown in Figure 7-1.

Two-Tailed, Left-Tailed, Right-Tailed

The *tails* in a distribution are the extreme regions bounded by critical values. Some hypothesis tests are two-tailed, some are right-tailed, and some are left-tailed.

- **Two-tailed test:** The critical region is in the extreme regions (tails) under both sides of the curve.
- **Right-tailed test:** The critical region is in the extreme region (tail) under the right side of the curve.
- **Left-tailed test:** The critical region is in the extreme region (tail) under the left side of the curve.

Sign used in H_1: >
Right-tailed test

Sign used in H_1: <
Left-tailed test

Sign used in H_1: ≠
Two-tailed test

In two-tailed tests, the level of significance α is divided equally between the two tails that constitute the critical region. For example, in a two-tailed test with a significance level of $\alpha = 0.05$, there is an area of 0.025 in each of the two tails. In right- or left-tailed tests, the area of the critical region is α.

By examining the null hypothesis H_0, we should be able to deduce whether a test is right-tailed, left-tailed, or two-tailed. The tail will correspond to the critical region containing the values that would conflict significantly with the null hypothesis. A useful check is summarized in the margin figures, which show that the inequality sign in H_1 points in the direction of the critical region. The symbol $\neq$ is often expressed in programming languages as $< >$, and this reminds us that an alternative hypothesis such as $\mu \neq 37.0$ corresponds to a two-tailed test.

> **EXAMPLE**   *Finding critical values:* Many passengers on cruise ships wear skin patches that supply dramamine to the body for the purpose of preventing motion sickness. A claim about the mean dosage amount is tested with a significance level of $\alpha = 0.05$. The conditions are such that the standard normal distribution can be used (because the central limit theorem applies). Find the critical value(s) of z if the test is (a) two-tailed, (b) left-tailed, and (c) right-tailed.
>
> **SOLUTION**
>
> **a.** In a two-tailed test, the significance level of $\alpha = 0.05$ is divided equally between the two tails, so there is an area of 0.025 in each tail. We can find the critical values in Table A-2 as the values corresponding to areas of 0.4750 (found by subtracting 0.025 from 0.5) to the right and left of the mean. We get critical values of $z = -1.96$ and $z = 1.96$, as shown in Figure 7-2(a).

b. In a left-tailed test, the significance level of $\alpha = 0.05$ is the area of the critical region at the left, so the critical value corresponds to an area of 0.4500 (found from $0.5 - 0.05$) to the left of the mean. Using Table A-2, we get a critical value of $z = -1.645$, as shown in Figure 7-2(b).

c. In a right-tailed test, the significance level of $\alpha = 0.05$ is the area of the critical region to the right, so the critical value corresponds to an area of 0.4500 (found from $0.5 - 0.05$) to the right of the mean. Using Table A-2, we get a critical value of $z = 1.645$, as shown in Figure 7-2(c).

Figure 7-2 Finding Critical Values

Conclusions in Hypothesis Testing

We have already noted that the original claim sometimes becomes the null hypothesis and at other times becomes the alternative hypothesis. However, our procedure requires that we always test the null hypothesis. In Section 7-3 we will see that our initial conclusion will always be one of the following:

1. Reject the null hypothesis.
2. Fail to reject the null hypothesis.

Wording of the Final Conclusion

The conclusion of failing to reject the null hypothesis or rejecting it is fine for those of us with the wisdom to take a statistics course, but we should use simple, nontechnical terms in stating what the conclusion really means. Figure 7-3 shows how to formulate the correct wording of the final conclusion. Note that only one case leads to wording indicating that the sample data actually *support* the conclusion. If you want to support some claim, state it in such a way that it becomes the alternative hypothesis and then hope that the null hypothesis gets rejected. For example, to support the claim that the mean body temperature is different from $37.0°C$, make the claim that $\mu \neq 37.0$. This claim will be an alternative hypothesis that will be supported if you reject the null hypothesis of $H_0: \mu = 37.0$. If, on the other hand, you claim that $\mu = 37.0$, you will either reject or fail to reject the claim; in either case, you will not *support* the original claim.

Accept/Fail to Reject

Some texts say "accept the null hypothesis" instead of "fail to reject the null hypothesis." Whether we use the term *accept* or *fail to reject,* we should recognize that *we are not proving the null hypothesis;* we are merely saying that the sample evidence is not strong enough to warrant rejection of the null hypothesis. It's like a jury saying that there is not enough evidence to convict a suspect. The term *accept* is somewhat misleading because it seems to imply incorrectly that the null hypothesis has been proved. The phrase *fail to reject* says more correctly that the available evidence isn't strong enough to warrant rejection of the null hypothesis. In this text we will use the conclusion *fail to reject the null hypothesis,* instead of *accept the null hypothesis.*

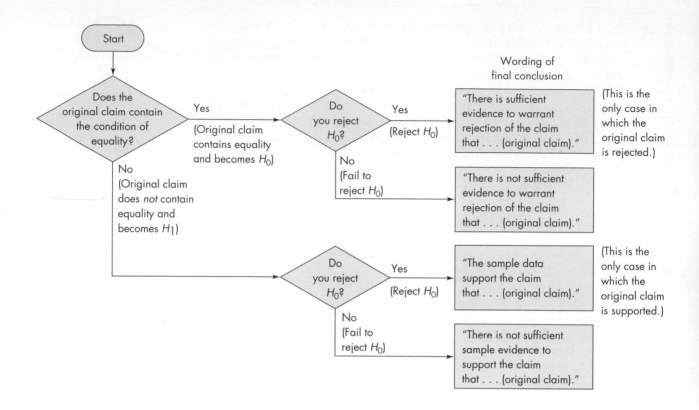

Figure 7-3 Wording of
Conclusions in Hypothesis
Tests

Type 1 and Type 2 Errors

When testing a null hypothesis, we arrive at a conclusion of rejecting it or failing to reject it. Such conclusions are sometimes correct and sometimes not (even if we do everything correctly). Table 7-2 summarizes the different possibilities and shows that we make a correct decision when we either reject a null hypothesis that is false or fail to reject a null hypothesis that is true. However, we make an error when we reject a true null hypothesis or fail to reject a false null hypothesis. The type I and type II errors are described as follows.

- **Type I error:** *The mistake of rejecting the null hypothesis when it is true.* For the chapter problem, a type I error would be the mistake of rejecting the null hypothesis that the mean body temperature is 37.0 when that mean really is 37.0. The type I error is not a miscalculation or procedural misstep; it is an actual error that can occur when a rare event happens by chance. The *probability* of rejecting the null hypothesis when it is true is called the **significance level** and is denoted by the symbol α (alpha).

- **Type II error:** *The mistake of failing to reject the null hypothesis when it is false.* For the Chapter Problem, a type II error would be the mistake of failing to reject the null hypothesis ($\mu = 37.0$) when it is actually false (that is, the mean is not really 37.0). The symbol β (beta) is used to represent the probability of a type II error.

TABLE 7-2	Type I and Type II Errors		
		True State of Nature	
		The null hypothesis is true.	The null hypothesis is false.
Decision	We decide to reject the null hypothesis.	**Type I error** (rejecting a true null hypothesis) α	Correct decision
	We fail to reject the null hypothesis.	Correct decision	**Type II error** (failing to reject a false null hypothesis) β

Notation

α (alpha) = probability of a type I error (the probability of rejecting the null hypothesis when it is true)

β (beta) = probability of a type II error (failing to reject a false null hypothesis)

AS

EXAMPLE   *Identifying components of a hypothesis test:* A concerned citizen is preparing a complaint to the Council of Better Business Bureaus. He has discreetly collected samples from the gasoline pumps of Elite Auto Centre and claims that consumers are being cheated because of this condition: When the meters indicate 1 L, the mean amount of gas actually supplied is less than 1 L.

a. Express in symbolic form the claim that the Elite Auto Centre is cheating consumers.

b. Identify the null hypothesis H_0.

c. Identify the alternative hypothesis H_1.

d. Identify this test as being two-tailed, left-tailed, or right-tailed.

e. Identify the type I error for this test.

f. Identify the type II error for this test.

g. Assume that the conclusion is to reject the null hypothesis. Interpret the conclusion in nontechnical terms; be sure to address the original claim.

h. Assume that the conclusion is failure to reject the null hypothesis. Interpret the conclusion in nontechnical terms; be sure to address the original claim.

SOLUTION

a. The claim that consumers are being cheated is equivalent to claiming that the mean is less than 1 L, which is expressed in symbolic form as $\mu < 1$ L.

b. The original claim of $\mu < 1$ L does not contain equality, as required by the null hypothesis. The original claim is therefore the alternative hypothesis; the null hypothesis is H_0: $\mu \geq 1$.

c. See part (b). The alternative hypothesis is H_1: $\mu < 1$.

d. This test is left-tailed because the null hypothesis is rejected if the sample mean is significantly less than (or to the left of) 1. (As a double check, note that the alternative hypothesis $\mu < 1$ contains the sign $<$, which points to the left.)

e. The type I error (rejection of a true null hypothesis) is to reject the null hypothesis $\mu \geq 1$ when the population mean is really equal to or greater than 1. (This is a serious error, because the business will be charged with cheating consumers when no such cheating is actually happening.)

f. The type II error (failure to reject a false null hypothesis) is to fail to reject the null hypothesis $\mu \geq 1$ when the population mean is really less than 1. (That is, we conclude that there isn't sufficient evidence to charge cheating when cheating is actually taking place.)

g. See Figure 7-3 for interpreting the case where the original claim does not contain equality, but H_0 is rejected. Conclude that there is sufficient evidence to support the claim that the mean is less than 1.

h. See Figure 7-3 for interpreting the case where the original claim does not contain equality, and we fail to reject H_0. Conclude that there is not sufficient evidence to support the claim that the mean is less than 1.

Statistics: Jobs and Employers

Here is a small sample of advertised jobs in the field of statistics: forecaster, database analyst, marketing scientist, credit-risk manager, cancer researcher and evaluator, insurance-risk analyst, educational testing researcher, biostatistician, statistician for pharmaceutical products, cryptologist, statistical programmer.

Controlling Type I and Type II Errors One step in our procedure for testing hypotheses involves the selection of the significance level α, which is the probability of a type I error. However, we do not select β [P(type II error)]. It would be great if we could always have $\alpha = 0$ and $\beta = 0$, but in reality that is not possible so we must attempt to manage the α and β error probabilities. Mathematically, it can be shown that α, β, and the sample size n are all related, so when you choose or determine any two of them, the third is automatically determined. The usual practice in research and industry is to select the values of α and n, so the value of β is determined. Depending on the seriousness of a type I error, try to use the largest α that you can tolerate. For type I errors with more serious consequences, select smaller values of α. Then choose a sample size n as large as is reasonable, based on considerations of time, cost, and other such relevant factors. (Sample size determinations were discussed in Section 6-2.) The following practical considerations may be relevant:

1. For any fixed α, an increase in the sample size n will cause a decrease in β. That is, a larger sample will lessen the chance that you make the error of not rejecting the null hypothesis when it's actually false.

2. For any fixed sample size n, a decrease in α will cause an increase in β. Conversely, an increase in α will cause a decrease in β.

3. To decrease both α and β, increase the sample size.

To make sense of these abstract ideas, let's consider M&Ms (produced by Mars, Inc.) and Bufferin brand aspirin tablets (produced by Bristol-Myers Products). The mean weight of the M&M candies should be at least 0.9085 g (in order to conform to the weight printed on the package label). The Bufferin tablets are supposed to contain a mean weight of 325 mg of aspirin. Because M&Ms are candies used for enjoyment whereas Bufferin tablets are drugs used for treatment of health problems, we are dealing with two very different levels of seriousness. If the M&Ms don't have a population mean weight of 0.9085 g, the consequences are not very serious, but if the Bufferin tablets don't have a mean of 325 mg of aspirin, the consequences could be very serious. If the M&Ms have a mean that is too large, Mars will lose some money but consumers will not complain. In contrast, if the Bufferin tablets have too much aspirin, Bristol-Myers could be faced with consumer lawsuits and actions by Health Canada under the Food and Drugs Act. Consequently, in testing the claim that $\mu = 0.9085$ g for M&Ms, we might choose $\alpha = 0.05$ and a sample size of $n = 100$; in testing the claim that $\mu = 325$ mg for Bufferin tablets, we might choose $\alpha = 0.01$ and a sample size of $n = 500$. The smaller significance level α and larger sample size n are chosen because of the more serious consequences associated with testing a commercial drug.

Power of a Test: We have presented notation indicating that β is the probability of failing to reject a false null hypothesis (type II error). It follows that $1 - \beta$ is the probability of rejecting a false null hypothesis. Statisticians refer to this probability as the *power* of a test, and they often use it to gauge the test's effectiveness in recognizing that a null hypothesis is false.

DEFINITION

The **power** of a hypothesis test is the probability $(1 - \beta)$ of rejecting a false null hypothesis, which is computed by using a particular significance level α and a particular value of the mean that is an alternative to the value assumed true in the null hypothesis.

Suppose we are using a 0.05 significance level to test the null hypothesis that the mean height of men is 1.83 m. Given sample data and given the alternative height of 1.75 m, we can compute the power of a test to reject $\mu = 1.83$ m. If our sample consists of only a few observations, the power will be low, but if it consists of hundreds of observations (or if other adjustments are made to the test), the power can be much higher. Just as 0.05 is a common choice for a significance level, a power of at least 0.80 is a common requirement for determining that a test is effective. Because the calculations of power are really tough, only Exercise 27 deals with power.

In Section 7-3 we will show how the components presented in this section are used in formal procedures for testing hypotheses.

7-2 Exercises A: Basic Skills and Concepts

In Exercises 1–4, what do you conclude? (Do not use formal procedures and exact calculations. Use only the rare event rule described in Section 7-1, and make subjective estimates to determine whether events are likely.)

1. Claim: A coin is fair. Then the coin turns up heads 27 times in 30 tosses.

2. Claim: A die is fair. Then the die turns up a 1 nine times in 60 rolls.

3. Claim: Women who eat blue M&M candies have a better chance of having a baby boy. Then 50 such women give birth to 27 boys and 23 girls.

4. Claim: A roulette wheel is fair. Then the number 7 occurs seven times in seven trials. (A fair roulette wheel has 38 equally likely slots, one of which is a 7.)

In Exercises 5–12, assume that a hypothesis test of the given claim will be conducted. Use μ for a claim about a mean, p for a claim about a proportion, and σ for a claim about variation.

   a. Express the claim in everyday language.
   b. Identify the null hypothesis H_0.
   c. Identify the alternative hypothesis H_1.
   d. Identify the test as being two-tailed, left-tailed, or right-tailed.
   e. Identify the type I error for the test.
   f. Identify the type II error for the test.
   g. Assuming that the conclusion is to reject the null hypothesis, state the conclusion in nontechnical terms; be sure to address the original claim. (See Figure 7-3.)
   h. Assuming that the conclusion is failure to reject the null hypothesis, state the conclusion in nontechnical terms; be sure to address the original claim. (See Figure 7-3.)

5. Health Canada claims that a pharmaceutical company makes cold caplets that contain amounts of acetaminophen with a mean different from the 650 mg amount indicated on the label.

6. The college registrar claims that the times students require to earn a college diploma have a mean less than 5 years.

7. The Canadian Alliance Party M.P. claims that she is currently favoured by more than 1/2 of all voters in her riding.

8. The Home Electronics Supply Company claims that its home circuit breakers trip at levels that have less variation than circuit breakers made by its major competitor, which has variation described by $\sigma = 0.4$ amp.

9. Statistics Canada claims that over 2% of all adults are enrolled in school full time.

10. In explaining the need to attract new business, Antigonish and Guysborough counties claim that, for women, the mean income in that region is $14,000.

11. The Canadian Automobile Association warns that motorists are being seduced by ads to buy higher octane gas than is useful. Test the claim that fewer than 10% of cars on the road have a design that benefits from higher octane gasoline.

12. The buyer for a hospital supply company recommends not buying the new digital thermometers because they vary more than the old thermometers with a standard deviation of 0.33°C.

In Exercises 13–20, find the critical z values for the given conditions. In each case assume that the normal distribution applies, so Table A-2 can be used. Also, draw a graph showing the critical value and critical region.

13. Right-tailed test; $\alpha = 0.05$
14. Left-tailed test; $\alpha = 0.05$
15. Left-tailed test; $\alpha = 0.01$
16. Two-tailed test; $\alpha = 0.01$
17. Two-tailed test; $\alpha = 0.10$
18. Right-tailed test; $\alpha = 0.025$
19. Left-tailed test; $\alpha = 0.025$
20. Two-tailed test; $\alpha = 0.02$

In Exercises 21–24, use Formula 7-1 to find the value of the test statistic z.

21. From a study of consumer buying: The claim is $\mu = 0.21$, and the sample statistics include $n = 32$, $\bar{x} = 0.83$, and $s = 0.24$.

22. From an article on the ages of humans: The claim is $\mu = 73.4$, and the sample statistics include $n = 35$, $\bar{x} = 69.5$, and $s = 8.7$.

23. From research on seatbelt use: The claim is $\mu < 1.39$, and the sample statistics include $n = 123$, $\bar{x} = 0.83$, and $s = 0.16$.

24. From a study of the amounts of Moosehead Beer in cans: The claim is $\mu = 355$, and the sample statistics include $n = 36$, $\bar{x} = 360.6$, and $s = 3.3$.

7-2 Exercises B: Beyond the Basics

25. When testing a claim that a mean is at least 100, the null hypothesis becomes $\mu \geq 100$. When actually conducting the hypothesis test, why is it necessary to assume $\mu = 100$ instead of $\mu \geq 100$?

26. Someone suggests that in testing hypotheses, you can eliminate a type I error by making $\alpha = 0$. In a two-tailed test, what critical values correspond to $\alpha = 0$? If $\alpha = 0$, will the null hypothesis ever be rejected?

27. Assume that you are using a significance level of $\alpha = 0.05$ to test the claim that $\mu < 2$ and that your sample consists of 50 randomly selected values.
    a. Find β, the probability of making a type II error, given that the population actually has a normal distribution with $\mu = 1.5$ and $\sigma = 1$. (*Hint*: With H_0: $\mu \geq 2$, begin by finding the values of the sample means that do not lead to rejection of H_0, then find the probability of getting a sample mean with one of those values.)
    b. Find $1 - \beta$, which is the *power* of the test. If β is the probability of *failing* to reject a false null hypothesis, describe the probability of $1 - \beta$.

7-3 Testing a Claim About a Mean: Large Samples

In this section we combine the components used in the preceding section to create a formal procedure for testing claims made about population means.

We will present three methods of testing hypotheses that appear different but are equivalent in the sense that they always lead to similar conclusions. The first procedure is the traditional method; the second is the *P*-value method; and the third is the confidence interval method, which is based on concepts introduced in Chapter 6.

We begin by identifying the two assumptions that apply to the methods we have already presented in this section.

Assumptions for Testing a Claim About the Mean of a Single Population, from a Large Sample

1. The sample is large ($n > 30$), so the central limit theorem applies and we can use the normal distribution.

2. When applying the central limit theorem, we can use the sample standard deviation *s* as an estimate of the population standard deviation σ whenever σ is unknown and the sample size is large ($n > 30$).

We also assume that the data have been collected by valid random-sampling techniques. Then, our first step is to *explore* the data set, using methods introduced in Chapter 2 to investigate centre, variation, and distribution, and to identify any outliers.

The Traditional Method of Testing Hypotheses

Figure 7-4 summarizes the steps used in the **traditional** (or **classical**) **method** of testing hypotheses. This procedure uses the components described in Section 7-2 as part of a system to identify a sample result that is *significantly* different from the claimed value. The relevant sample statistic (such as $\bar{x}$) is converted to a test statistic, which we compare to a critical value. The following expression can be used for the examples and exercises in this section.

Test Statistic for Claims About μ When $n > 30$
$$z = \frac{\bar{x} - \mu_{\bar{x}}}{\dfrac{\sigma}{\sqrt{n}}}$$

Note that Step 7 in Figure 7-4 uses this decision criterion:

Reject the null hypothesis if the test statistic is in the critical region.

Fail to reject the null hypothesis if the test statistic is not in the critical region.

Section 7-2 presented an informal example of a hypothesis test; the following example formalizes that test.

EXAMPLE   Using the sample data given at the beginning of the chapter ($n = 108$, $x = 36.39°$, $s = 0.62$) and a 0.01 significance level, test the claim that the mean body temperature of adults healthy enough to undergo elective surgery is equal to 37.0°C.

SOLUTION   Refer to Figure 7-4 and follow these steps:

Step 1:   The claim that the mean is equal to 37.0 is expressed in symbolic form as $\mu = 37.0$.

Step 2:   The alternative (in symbolic form) to the original claim is $\mu \neq 37.0$.

Step 3:   The statement $\mu = 37.0$ contains the condition of equality, and so it becomes the null hypothesis. We have

$$H_0\!: \mu = 37.0 \text{ (original claim)} \qquad H_1\!: \mu \neq 37.0$$

Step 4:   As specified in the statement of the problem, the significance level is $\alpha = 0.01$.

Step 5:   Because the claim is made about the population mean μ, the sample statistic most relevant to this test is $x = 36.39$. Because $n > 30$, the central limit theorem indicates that the distribution of sample means can be approximated by a *normal* distribution.

Step 6:   In calculating the test statistic, we can use $s = 0.62$ as a reasonable estimate of σ (because $n > 30$), so the test statistic of $z = -10.22$ is found by converting the sample mean of $x = 36.39$ to $z = -10.22$ through the following computation:

$$z = \frac{x - \mu_{\bar{x}}}{\dfrac{\sigma}{\sqrt{n}}} = \frac{36.39 - 37.0}{\dfrac{0.62}{\sqrt{108}}} = -10.22$$

The critical z values are found by first noting that the test is two-tailed because a sample mean significantly less than or greater than 37.0 is strong evidence against the null hypothesis that $\mu = 37.0$. Because the test is two-tailed, we divide $\alpha = 0.01$ equally between the two tails to get 0.005 in each tail. We then refer to Table A-2 or use statistics software to find the critical values of $z = 2.575$ and $z = -2.575$. The test statistic, critical region, and critical values are shown in Figure 7-5.

Step 7:   The sample mean of $x = 36.39$ is converted to a test statistic of $z = -10.22$, which falls within the critical region, so we reject the null hypothesis.

Interpretation   (By the method of Figure 7-4, this is **Step 8.**)To restate the Step 7 conclusion in nontechnical terms, we might refer to Figure 7-2 in the preceding section. We are rejecting the null hypothesis, which is the original claim. We conclude that there is sufficient evidence to warrant rejection of the claim that the mean body temperature of adults healthy enough to undergo elective surgery is 37.0°C.

Figure 7-4 Traditional Method of Hypothesis Testing

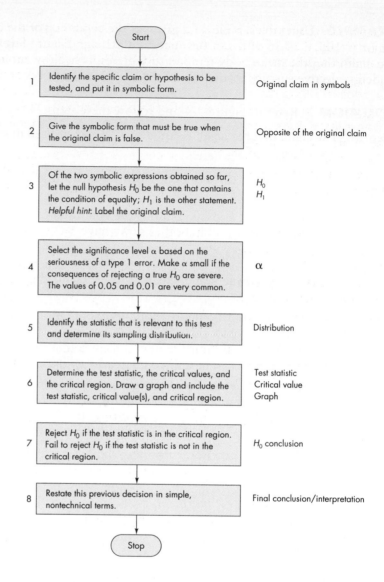

Start

1 Identify the specific claim or hypothesis to be tested, and put it in symbolic form.   Original claim in symbols

2 Give the symbolic form that must be true when the original claim is false.   Opposite of the original claim

3 Of the two symbolic expressions obtained so far, let the null hypothesis H_0 be the one that contains the condition of equality; H_1 is the other statement. *Helpful hint*: Label the original claim. H_0 H_1

4 Select the significance level α based on the seriousness of a type 1 error. Make α small if the consequences of rejecting a true H_0 are severe. The values of 0.05 and 0.01 are very common. α

5 Identify the statistic that is relevant to this test and determine its sampling distribution.   Distribution

6 Determine the test statistic, the critical values, and the critical region. Draw a graph and include the test statistic, critical value(s), and critical region.   Test statistic Critical value Graph

7 Reject H_0 if the test statistic is in the critical region. Fail to reject H_0 if the test statistic is not in the critical region. H_0 conclusion

8 Restate this previous decision in simple, nontechnical terms.   Final conclusion/interpretation

Stop

Figure 7-5 Distribution of Means of Body Temperatures Assuming $\mu = 37.0$

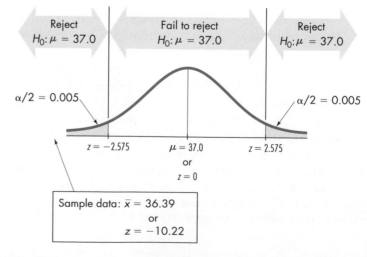

Reject $H_0: \mu = 37.0$ Fail to reject $H_0: \mu = 37.0$ Reject $H_0: \mu = 37.0$

$\alpha/2 = 0.005$ $\alpha/2 = 0.005$

$z = -2.575$ $\mu = 37.0$ $z = 2.575$
or
$z = 0$

Sample data: $\bar{x} = 36.39$
or
$z = -10.22$

In the preceding example, the sample mean of 36.39 was converted to a test statistic of $z = -10.22$. That is, the sample mean is 10.22 standard deviations away from the claimed mean of $\mu = 37.0$. In Chapter 2 we saw that a z score above 5, let alone a z score above 10, is quite large and corresponds to an unusual result if in fact the mean of the null hypothesis applies. This evidence is strong enough to make us believe that the mean is actually different from 37.0. The critical values and critical region clearly identify the range of unusual values that cause us to reject the claimed value of μ.

The preceding example illustrated a two-tailed hypothesis test; the following example illustrates a one-tailed test. The following example also illustrates the difference between *statistical significance* and *practical significance*.

EXAMPLE   According to the Canadian Emitting Devices Act (Regulations C.R.C., C.1370), there is a limit to how much ionizing radiation a television may emit. Under described test conditions, the emission limit corresponds to a maximum X-ray exposure rate of 0.50 milliroentgens per hour (mR/h). A supervisor at a TV superstore claims that their product lines perform better than this standard. To test the claim, 35 televisions are randomly selected from their warehouse. It is found that the average radiation emission from the 35 televisions corresponds to an exposure rate of 0.47 mR/h, with a standard deviation of 0.10 mR/h. Use a 0.05 level of significance to test the supervisor's claim.

SOLUTION   We know that the measured emissions will vary from television to television, based on positions of control knobs, exact supply voltage, and so on. So we need to determine whether the apparent difference in the mean exposure rate of 0.47 mR/h from the expected standard of 0.50 mR/h represents a significant improvement. That is, the claim is supported if the mean exposure in the test is significantly less than the standard limit. Refer to Figure 7-4 and follow these steps:

Step 1:   A significant decrease in exposure from the standard can be expressed as $\mu < 0.50$.

Step 2:   The opposite (in symbolic form) of the original claim is $\mu \geq 0.50$.

Step 3:   The statement $\mu \geq 0.50$ contains the condition of equality, so it becomes the null hypothesis and we have

$$H_0: \mu \geq 0.50 \qquad H_1: \mu < 0.50 \text{ (original claim)}$$

Step 4:   With a 0.05 significance level, we have $\alpha = 0.05$.

Step 5:   The sample mean $\bar{x} = 0.47$ mR/h should be used to test a claim made about the population mean μ. Because $n > 30$, the central limit theorem indicates that the distribution of sample means can be approximated by a normal distribution.

Step 6:   In calculating the test statistic, we can use $s = 0.10$ as a reasonable estimate of σ (because $n > 30$), so the test statistic of $z = -1.77$ is computed as follows:

$$z = \frac{\bar{x} - \mu_{\bar{x}}}{\frac{\sigma}{\sqrt{n}}} = \frac{0.47 - 0.50}{\frac{0.10}{\sqrt{35}}} = -1.77$$

The critical value of $z = -1.645$ is found in Table A-2 as the z score corresponding to an area of 0.4500. (The test is left-tailed because the null hypothesis of $\mu \geq 0.50$ is rejected if the sample mean $\bar{x}$ is *less than* 0.50 by a significant amount.) The test statistic, critical region, and critical value are shown in Figure 7-6.

Step 7:   From Figure 7-6 we see that the sample mean of 0.47 mR/h does fall within the critical region, so we reject the null hypothesis H_0.

Interpretation There is sufficient evidence to support the claim that the mean exposure rate is less than the regulated limit. That is, the supervisor does appear to be truthful. But even though the result is *statistically significant*, it may not have *practical significance* because the difference (0.03) from the standard exposure rate is so small.

Figure 7-6   Distribution of Means of Exposure Rates

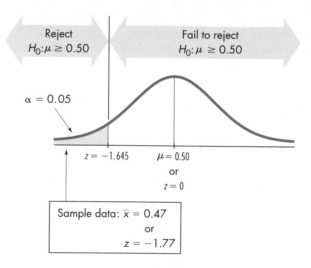

In presenting the results of a hypothesis test, it is not always necessary to show all of the steps included in Figure 7-4. However, the results should include the null hypothesis, the alternative hypothesis, the calculation of the test statistic, a graph such as Figure 7-6, the initial conclusion (reject H_0 or fail to reject H_0), and the final conclusion stated in nontechnical terms. The graph should show the test statistic, critical value(s), critical region, and significance level.

The P-Value Method of Testing Hypotheses

Many professional articles and software packages use another approach to hypothesis testing that is based on the calculation of a *probability*, or *P*-value. Given a null hypothesis and sample data, the *P*-value reflects the likelihood of getting the sample results obtained assuming that the null hypothesis is actually true. A very small *P*-value (such as 0.05 or lower) suggests that the sample results are very unlikely under the assumption of the null hypothesis, so that such a small *P*-value is evidence against the null hypothesis.

DEFINITION

A ***P*-value** (or **probability value**) is the probability of getting a value of the sample test statistic that is *at least as extreme* as the one found from the sample data, assuming that the null hypothesis is true.

Whereas the traditional approach results in a "reject/fail to reject" conclusion, *P*-values measure how confident we are in rejecting a null hypothesis. For example, a *P*-value of 0.0002 would lead us to reject the null hypothesis, but it would also suggest that the sample results are extremely unusual if the claimed value of μ is in fact correct. In contrast, given a *P*-value of 0.40, we fail to reject the null hypothesis because the sample results can *easily* occur if the claimed value of μ is correct.

The *P*-value approach uses most of the same basic procedures as the traditional approach, but Steps 6 and 7 are different:

Step 6:   Find the *P*-value.

Step 7:   Report the *P*-value. Some statisticians prefer simply to report the *P*-value and leave the conclusion to the reader. Others prefer to use the following decision criterion:

- *Reject the null hypothesis* if the *P*-value is less than or equal to the significance level α.

- *Fail to reject the null hypothesis* if the *P*-value is greater than the significance level α.

In Step 7, if the conclusion is based on the *P*-value alone, the following guide may be helpful.

AS

P-Value	Interpretation
Less than 0.01	*Unusual* sample results; highly statistically significant Very strong evidence against the null hypothesis
0.01 to 0.05	Statistically significant Adequate evidence against the null hypothesis
Greater than 0.05	Sample results are *not unusual*; insufficient evidence against the null hypothesis

Many statisticians consider it good practice always to select a significance level *before* doing a hypothesis test. This is a particularly good procedure when using *P*-values because we may be tempted to adjust the significance level based on the results. For example, with a 0.05 level of significance and a

Beware of *P*-Value Misuse

John P. Campbell, editor of the *Journal of Applied Psychology,* wrote the following on the subject of *P*-values: "Books have been written to dissuade people from the notion that smaller *P*-values mean more important results or that statistical significance has anything to do with substantive significance. It is almost impossible to drag authors away from their *P*-values, and the more zeros after the decimal point, the harder people cling to them." Although it might be necessary to provide a statistical analysis of the results of a study, we should place strong emphasis on the significance of the results themselves.

P-value of 0.06, we should fail to reject the null hypothesis, but it is sometimes tempting to say that a probability of 0.06 is small enough to warrant rejection of the null hypothesis. Other statisticians believe that prior selection of a significance level reduces the usefulness of *P*-values. They contend that no significance level should be specified and that the conclusion should be left to the reader. We will use the decision criterion that involves a comparison of a significance level and the *P*-value.

Figure 7-7 outlines the procedure for finding the *P*-value. The figure shows the following:

Right-tailed test:	The *P*-value is the area to the right of the test statistic.
Left-tailed test:	The *P*-value is the area to the left of the test statistic.
Two-tailed test:	The *P*-value is *twice* the area of the extreme region bounded by the test statistic.

Figure 7-7   Finding *P*-Values

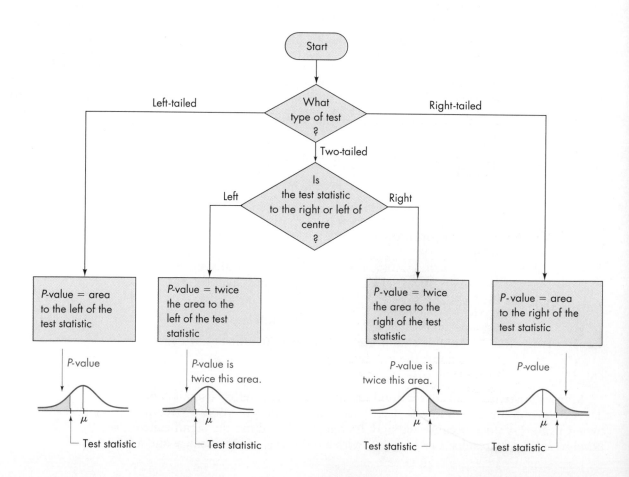

Figure 7-8 summarizes the *P*-value method for testing hypotheses. A comparison of the traditional method (summarized in Figure 7-4) and the *P*-value method (Figure 7-8) shows that they are essentially the same, but they differ in the decision criterion. The traditional method compares the test statistic to the critical values, whereas the *P*-value method compares the *P*-value to the significance level. However, the traditional and *P*-value methods are equivalent in the sense that they will always result in the same conclusion.

Figure 7-8   *P*-Value Method of Testing Hypotheses

Start

1   Identify the specific claim or hypothesis to be tested, and put it in symbolic form.

2   Give the symbolic form that must be true when the original claim is false.

3   Of the two symbolic expressions obtained so far, let the null hypothesis H_0 be the one that contains the condition of equality; H_1 is the other statement.

4   Select the significance level α based on the seriousness of a type 1 error. Make α small if the consequences of rejecting a true H_0 are severe. The values of 0.05 and 0.01 are very common.

5   Identify the statistic that is relevant to this test and determine its sampling distribution.

6   Determine the test statistic and find the *P*-value (see Figure 7-7). Draw a graph and show the test statistic and *P*-value.

7   Reject H_0 if the *P*-value is less than or equal to the significance level α. Fail to reject H_0 if the *P*-value is greater than α.

8   Restate this previous decision in simple, nontechnical terms.

Stop

EXAMPLE   Use the *P*-value method to test the claim that the mean body temperature of adults healthy enough to undergo elective surgery is equal to 37.0°C. As before, use a 0.01 significance level and the sample data summarized in the chapter-opening problem ($n = 108$, $\bar{x} = 36.39°$, $s = 0.62$, and an approximately bell-shaped distribution).

SOLUTION   Except for Steps 6 and 7, this solution is the same as the one developed earlier in this section using the traditional method. Steps 1, 2, and 3 led to the following hypotheses:

$$H_0: \mu = 37.0 \text{ (original claim)} \qquad H_1: \mu \neq 37.0$$

In Steps 4 and 5 we noted that the significance level is $\alpha = 0.01$ and that the central limit theorem indicates use of the normal distribution. We now proceed to Steps 6 and 7.

Step 6:   The test statistic of $z = -10.22$ was already found in a preceding example. We can now find the *P*-value by referring to Figure 7-7. Because the test is two-tailed, the *P*-value is twice the area to the left of the test statistic $z = -10.22$. Using Table A-2, we find the area to the left of $z = -10.22$ is $1 - 0.4999 = 0.0001$. (Actually, the area to the left would be considerably less than 0.0001, but $z = \pm 3.10$ is the limit of the table. A computer or a more precise table than Table A-2 would show a smaller value for the area to the left of $z = -10.22$.) Using 2×0.0001 gives the table-based estimate for the *P*-value: 0.0002. (See Figure 7-9.)

Step 7:   Because the *P*-value of 0.0002 is less than the significance level of $\alpha = 0.01$, we reject the null hypothesis.

Interpretation   As with the traditional method, we conclude that there is sufficient evidence to warrant rejection of the claim that the mean body temperature for adults healthy enough to undergo elective surgery is 37.0°C.

Figure 7-9   *P*-Value Method of Testing H_0: $\mu = 37.0$
Because the test is two-tailed, the *P*-value is *twice* the shaded area.

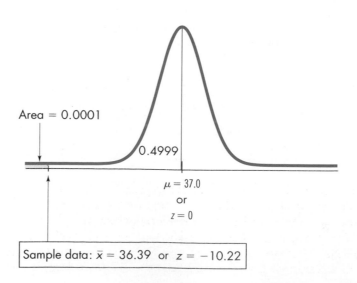

Area = 0.0001

0.4999

$\mu = 37.0$
or
$z = 0$

Sample data: $\bar{x} = 36.39$ or $z = -10.22$

The following example applies the *P*-value approach to the example about television radiation levels discussed in an earlier example in this section.

EXAMPLE   Use the *P*-value approach and a 0.05 significance level to test the claim that the televisions sold at the TV superstore emit radiation at a rate that is under the regulated limit. Recall that the sample data consist of 35 televisions whose mean emissions are 0.47 mR/h with a standard deviation of 0.10 mR/h. The legal limit set by Health Canada's regulation C.1370 is 0.50 mR/h.

SOLUTION   Again, refer to the steps used earlier to solve this problem by the traditional method. Steps 1, 2, and 3 resulted in the following hypotheses:

$$H_0: \mu \geq 0.50 \qquad H_1: \mu < 0.50 \text{ (original claim)}$$

Steps 4 and 5 led to a significance level of $\alpha = 0.05$ and the decision that the normal distribution is relevant to this test of a claim about a sample mean. We now proceed to Steps 6 and 7.

Step 6:   The test statistic of -1.77 was computed in the earlier solution to this same problem. To find the *P*-value, we refer to Figure 7-7, which indicates that for this left-tailed test, the *P*-value is the area to the left of the test statistic. Referring to Table A-2, and looking up the absolute value of z, we find that the area to the left of $z = -1.77$ is $0.5 - 0.4616$, or 0.0384. The *P*-value is therefore 0.0384.

Step 7:   Because the *P*-value of 0.0384 is less than the significance level of $\alpha = 0.05$, we reject the null hypothesis that $\mu \geq 0.50$.

Interpretation   As in the previous solution of this same problem, we conclude that there is sufficient evidence to support the claim that the emission levels of the televisions are lower than the legislated limit. The *P*-value of 0.0384 shows us that it is unlikely that we would get a sample mean of 0.47 if the mean were really 0.50.

The next procedure for testing hypotheses is based on confidence intervals and therefore requires the concepts discussed in Section 6-2.

Testing Claims with Confidence Intervals

Confidence intervals can be used to identify results that are highly unlikely, so we can determine whether there is a *significant* difference between sample results and a claimed value of a parameter. For example, let us consider again the hypothesis-testing problem described at the beginning of the chapter. We want to test the claim that the mean body temperature of adults healthy enough to undergo elective surgery is equal to 37.0°C. Sample data consist of

$n = 108$ temperatures with mean $\bar{x} = 36.39$ and standard deviation $s = 0.62$. Chapter 6 described methods of constructing confidence intervals. In one exercise, we used the body temperature sample data to construct the following 99% confidence interval:

$$36.24 < \mu < 36.54$$

We are 99% confident that the limits of 36.24 and 36.54 contain the population mean μ. (This means that if we were to repeat the experiment of collecting a sample of 108 body temperatures, 99% of the samples would result in confidence interval limits that actually do contain the value of the population mean μ.) This confidence interval suggests that it is very unlikely that the population mean is equal to 37.0. That is, on the basis of the confidence interval given here, we reject the common belief that the mean body temperature of healthy adults is 37.0°C. We can generalize this procedure as follows: First use the sample data to construct a confidence interval, and then apply the following decision criterion:

> **A confidence interval estimate of a population parameter contains the likely values of that parameter. We should therefore reject a claim that the population parameter has a value that is not included in the confidence interval.**

Using this criterion, we note that the confidence interval given here does not contain the claimed value of 37.0, and we therefore reject the claim that the population mean equals 37.0. (*Note:* We can make a direct correspondence between a confidence interval and a hypothesis test only when the test is two-tailed. A one-tailed hypothesis test with significance level α corresponds to a confidence interval with degree of confidence $1 - 2\alpha$. For example, a right-tailed hypothesis test with a 0.05 significance level corresponds to a 90% confidence interval.)

In the remainder of the text, we will apply methods of hypothesis testing to other circumstances, such as those involving claims about proportions or standard deviations or involving more than one population. It is easy to become entangled in a complex web of steps without ever understanding the underlying rationale of hypothesis testing. The key to that understanding lies in the rare event rule for inferential statistics: **If, under a given assumption, the probability of getting the observed sample is exceptionally small, we conclude that the assumption is probably not correct.** When testing a claim, we make an assumption (null hypothesis) that contains equality. We then compare the assumption and the sample results and form one of the following conclusions:

- If the sample results can easily occur when the assumption is true, we attribute any small discrepancy between the assumption and the sample results to chance.

- If the sample results cannot easily occur when the assumption is true, we explain the discrepancy between the assumption and the sample results by concluding that the assumption is not true.

Using Technology

Excel:

Excel does not include a built-in tool for the one- or two-tailed tests described in this section. Instead, use the Data Desk XL add-in that is a supplement to this book. First enter the sample data into an Excel column. (In the text's data set of body temperatures, the data are found in the range B4:B111.) Select **DDXL** on the main menu bar, then select **Hypothesis Tests**. Under the function type options, select **1 Var z Test**. Click on the pencil icon and enter the range of data values, such as B4:B111. Click on **OK**. Follow the four steps listed in the dialog box. After clicking on **Compute** in Step 4, you will get the *P*-value, test statistic, and conclusion.

STATDISK:

If working with a list of the original sample values, first find the sample size, sample mean, and sample standard deviation by using the STATDISK procedure described in Section 2-4. After finding the values of n, $\bar{x}$, and s, proceed to select the main menu bar item **Analysis**, then select **Hypothesis Testing**, followed by **Mean-One Sample**. Enter the data in the dialog box. See the accompanying STATDISK display showing the results from the body temperature example of this section.

Data Desk® 6.1 Viewer - Untitled

File   Edit   Data   Special   Help

$VAR1 z Test

Summary Statistics	
Count	108
Mean	36.39
Pop StDev:	0.62

Test Summary

Ho:	$\mu = 37$
Ha:	2-tailed: $\mu \neq 37$
z Statistic:	-10.228
p-value:	< .001

Test Results

Conclusion

Reject Ho at alpha = 0.01

New Test

Excel Display   Testing a Claim About a Mean (Large Sample)

STATDISK Display Testing a Claim About a Mean (Large Sample)

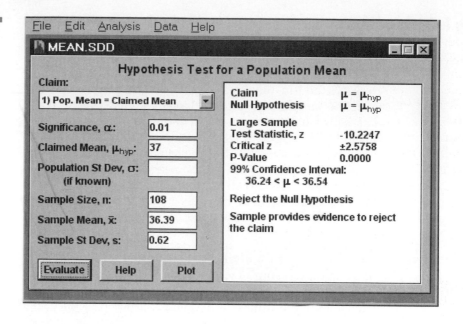

7-3 Exercises A: Basic Skills and Concepts

In Exercises 1–24, test the given claim using the traditional method of hypothesis testing. Clearly identify the following components of the hypothesis test: (a) test statistic, (b) critical value(s), (c) P-value, (d) final conclusion. Check that the P-value method would lead to the same solution as the traditional method. Assume that all samples have been randomly selected.

1. Test the claim that the population mean $\mu = 75$, given a sample of $n = 100$ for which $\bar{x} = 78$ and $s = 15$. Test at the $\alpha = 0.05$ significance level.

2. Test the claim that $\mu > 750$, given a sample of $n = 36$ for which $\bar{x} = 800$ and $s = 100$. Use a significance level of $\alpha = 0.01$.

3. Test the claim that $\mu < 2.50$, given a sample of $n = 64$ for which $\bar{x} = 2.45$ and $s = 0.80$. Use a significance level of $\alpha = 0.02$.

4. Test the claim that a population mean is different from 32.0, given a sample of $n = 75$ for which $\bar{x} = 31.8$ and $s = 0.85$. Use a significance level of $\alpha = 0.01$.

5. In April 1994, during a spring of unusually good hitting in professional baseball, a columnist for the *Toronto Star* hinted at a "conspiracy" by managers in which they "juiced" the baseballs to increase excitement in the game. Suppose that tests of the old balls showed that when dropped 24 ft onto a concrete surface, they bounced an average of 92.14 in. In a test of a sample of 40 new balls, the bounce heights had a mean of 92.67 in. and a standard deviation of 1.79 in. Use a 0.05 significance level to test the claim that the new balls have bounce heights different from 92.14 in. Are these balls "juiced"?

6. The Mackenzie Valley Bottling Company distributes root beer in bottles labelled 32 oz. An inspector randomly selects 50 of these bottles, measures

their contents, and obtains a sample mean of 31.8 oz and a sample standard deviation of 0.75 oz. Using a 0.01 significance level, test the inspector's claim that the company is cheating consumers. Should charges be filed?

7. In a study of consumer habits, researchers designed a questionnaire to identify compulsive buyers. For a sample of consumers who identified themselves as compulsive buyers, questionnaire scores have a mean of 0.83 and a standard deviation of 0.24 (based on data from "A Clinical Screener for Compulsive Buying," by Faber and Guinn, *Journal of Consumer Research,* Vol. 19). Assume that the subjects were randomly selected and that the sample size was 32. At the 0.01 level of significance, test the claim that the self-identified compulsive-buyer population has a mean greater than 0.21, the mean for the general population. Does the questionnaire seem to be effective in identifying compulsive buyers?

8. Planners in Ontario's Durham region compiled data for the value of building permits. The mean for all building permits (in thousands of dollars) was 97. But for a random sample of 38 permits in the smaller Durham region communities of Scugog, Brock, Clarington, and Uxbridge, the mean value was 113.6, with a standard deviation of 70.67 (based on data in the *Durham Business News,* June 1998). Using the 0.05 level of significance, test the hypothesis that these smaller communities have a mean value for building permits that is different from the regional mean of 97.

9. Your investment goal is to choose only from mutual fund groups with at least 10% foreign equity. To determine whether the Canadian equity funds group meets your criterion, you randomly sample 33 of the funds in that category. The mean foreign equity percentage in your sample is 8.386, with a standard deviation of 7.126 (based on data from *Mutual Funds Update,* Bank of Montreal, March 31, 1998). Do the Canadian equity funds fail to meet your criterion? What could be the consequence if your conclusion is a type I or type II sampling error?

10. An ambitious young worker claims that older employees have a better chance of being CEOs than younger employees. To confirm this, he sampled the ages of CEOs for 31 companies. The mean age in the sample was found to be 41.77, with a standard deviation of 10.24 (based on data from *Profit,* May 29, 1996). If the mean age for all workers in the population is 37, and if the significance level 0.01 is used, test the hypothesis that the CEOs have a higher mean age than workers in general. Explain how your answer to this question relates to the young worker's original claim—that older employees have a *better chance* of being CEO.

11. The yearly rates of traffic accidents and violations were studied for a group of 137 young adult males who volunteered for treatment for substance abuse. For the five years before receiving treatment, their mean accident rate was 0.123 with a standard deviation of 0.167 (based on data from "Does Treatment for Substance Abuse Improve Driving Safety? A Preliminary Evaluation," by Mann et al., Addiction Research Foundation). At the 0.01 significance level, test the claim that the sample was drawn from the general driving population with a mean accident rate of 0.075. Do the results suggest that the Ministry of Transportation should take an interest in substance-abuse programs?

12. In a study of distances travelled by buses before the first major engine failure, a sampling of 191 buses resulted in a mean of 154,700 km and a

standard deviation of 60,000 km (based on data in *Technometrics,* Vol. 22, No. 4). At the 0.05 level of significance, test the manufacturer's claim that mean distance travelled before a major engine failure is more than 144,000 km.

13. A poll of 100 randomly selected car owners revealed that the mean length of time that they plan to keep their cars is 7.01 years and the standard deviation is 3.74 years (based on data from a Roper poll). The president of the Kamloops Car Park is trying to plan a sales campaign targeted at car owners who are ready to buy a different car. Test the claim of the sales manager, who authoritatively states that the mean length of time all car owners plan to keep their cars is less than 7.5 years. Use a 0.05 significance level.

14. When 200 convicted embezzlers were randomly selected, the mean length of prison sentence was found to be 22.1 months and the standard deviation was found to be 8.6 months. Kim Patterson is running for political office on a platform of tougher treatment of convicted criminals. Test her claim that prison terms for convicted embezzlers have a mean of less than 2 years. Use a 0.05 significance level.

15. A nighttime cold medicine bears a label indicating the presence of 600 mg of acetaminophen in each fluid ounce of the drug. Suppose that Health Canada randomly selected 65 one-ounce samples and found that the mean acetaminophen content was 589 mg, and the standard deviation was 21 mg. Using $\alpha = 0.01$, test the claim of the pharmaceutical company that the population mean is equal to 600 mg. Would you buy this cold medicine?

16. An insurance company is reviewing the driving habits of women aged 16–24 to determine whether they should pay higher premiums than women in a higher age bracket. In a study of 750 randomly selected women drivers aged 16–24, the mean driving distance for one year is 9750 km and the standard deviation is 4750 km. Use a 0.01 significance level to test the claim that the population mean for women in the 16–24 age bracket is less than 11,490 km, which is the known mean for women in the higher age bracket. If women in the 16–24 age bracket drive less, should they be charged lower insurance premiums?

✓ 17. A fish-processing company is concerned about the shelf life of its new cat food. A quality manager claims that the mean product shelf life of cans from the Dartmouth facility is less than the advertised mean (of 12 months) for its product's shelf life. Test that claim using the 0.005 level of significance. A sample of 40 items produced in Dartmouth had a mean shelf life of 11 months, and a standard deviation of 1.52 months.

18. The true value of one type of degree or diploma cannot be quantitatively measured, but we can measure its relative impact on starting salary. Graduates from Quebec universities with a B.A. or a B.Sc. degree have a mean annual starting salary of $28,300. Sixty-five Quebec graduates with a civil engineering degree are randomly selected. Their starting salaries have a mean of $36,300 (based on "Annual Salary Survey," Peat Marwick Stevenson & Kellogg). If the standard deviation is $1670, use a 0.01 level of significance to test the claim that Quebec graduates with a civil engineering degree have a mean starting salary that is greater than the mean for graduates with a B.A. or B.Sc. degree from Quebec. Is the sample size large enough to reach a conclusion?

19. The mean time between failures (in hours) for a Telektronic Company radio used in light aircraft is 420 h. After 35 new radios were modified in an attempt to improve reliability, tests showed that the mean time between failures for this sample is 385 h and the standard deviation is 24 h. Use a 0.05 significance level to test the claim that the modifications improved reliability. (Note that improved reliability should result in a *longer* mean time between failures.)

20. An investment advisor is trying to persuade an investor to switch from her current fund holdings, claiming that the advisor's portfolio recommendations have had a greater one-year return rate than the investor's current funds. Last year, the investor's annual return rate was 35%. Use a 0.01 level of significance to test the claim that the investments that the advisor recommends have a greater one-year return rate than 35%. Base your calculations on the sample of 40 return rates in the one-year return column of Data Set 10 in Appendix B. Is there sufficient evidence to support the advisor's claim? A real investor is not likely to invest in *all* 40 funds in Data Set 10. What additional statistic would help to portray the *risk* of switching to just a portion of the advisor's portfolio?

21. Refer to Data Set 1 in Appendix B for the *total* weights of garbage discarded by households in one week. For that data set, the mean is 27.44 lb and the standard deviation is 12.46 lb. At the 0.01 level of significance, test the claim that the mean weight of all garbage discarded by households each week is less than 35 lb, the amount that can be handled by the town. Based on the result, is there any cause for concern that there might be too much garbage to handle?

22. If we refer to the weights (in grams) of quarters listed in Data Set 13 in Appendix B, we find 50 weights with a mean of 5.622 g and a standard deviation of 0.068 g. Use a 0.01 significance level to test the claim that the mean weight of quarters in circulation is 5.670 g. If the claim is rejected, what is a possible explanation for the discrepancy?

23. Analysis of the last digits in data sometimes reveals whether the data have been accurately measured and reported. If the last digits are uniformly distributed from 0 to 9, then their mean should be 4.5. The last digits in the published numbers of sitting days for federal Parliaments are used to test the claim they come from a population with a mean of 4.5. (The raw data are in Data Set 5 in Appendix B.) If Excel is used to analyse the results, a table similar to the one shown here could be generated. Using a 0.05 significance level, interpret these results.

Mean (Sample)	4.8286
Mean (Null Hyp.)	4.5000
StDev	2.7277
N	35
Std Error	0.4611
Test Statistic z	0.7135
Critical z	1.9600
P-value	0.4755

24. A package of M&M plain candies is labelled as containing 1361 g, and there are 1498 candies, so the mean weight of the individual candies should be 1361/1498, or 0.9085 g. In a test to determine whether consumers are being cheated, a sample of 33 brown M&Ms is randomly selected. (See Data Set 11 in Appendix B). If Excel is used to analyse the results, a table similar to the one shown here could be generated. Using a 0.05 significance level, for a one-tailed test, interpret these results.

Mean (Sample)	0.91282
Mean (Null Hyp.)	0.90850
StDev	0.03952
N	33
Std Error	0.00688
Test Statistic z	0.62790
Critical z	-1.6450
P-value	0.7350

7-3 Exercises B: Beyond the Basics

25. A journal article reported that a null hypothesis of $\mu = 100$ was rejected because the *P*-value was less than 0.01. The sample size was given as 62, and the sample mean was given as 103.6. Find the largest possible standard deviation.

✓ 26. In Exercise 17, find the *largest* sample mean below 12 months that will support the claim that the mean is less than 12 months. (Use the same sample size and sample standard deviation.)

27. For a given hypothesis test, the probability α of a type I error is fixed, whereas the probability β of a type II error depends on the particular value of μ that is used as an alternative to the null hypothesis. For hypothesis tests of the type found in this section, we can find β as follows:

Step 1: Find the value(s) of $\overline{x}$ that correspond to the critical value(s). In

$$ z = \frac{\overline{x} - \mu_x}{\sigma_x} $$

substitute the critical value(s) for z, enter the values for $\mu_{\overline{x}}$ and $\sigma_{\overline{x}}$, and solve for $\overline{x}$.

Step 2: Given a particular value of μ that is an alternative to the null hypothesis H_0, draw the normal curve with this new value of μ at the centre. Also plot the value(s) of $\overline{x}$ found in Step 1.

Step 3: Refer to the graph in Step 2 and find the area under the new curve (for the new value of μ) which is in the rejection region with respect to the H_0 curve that is being tested. (This involves converting the critical $\overline{x}$ values into z values with respect to the new value of μ.) This is the probability of rejecting the null hypothesis, given that the new value of μ is correct.

Step 4: The value of β is 1 minus the area from Step 3. This is the probability of failing to reject the null hypothesis, given that the new value of μ is correct.

The preceding steps allow you to find the probability of failing to reject H_0 when it is false. You are determining the area under the curve that excludes the critical region in which you reject H_0; this area corresponds to a failure to reject a false H_0, because we use a particular value of μ that goes against H_0. Refer to the body-temperature example discussed in this section and find the value of β corresponding to the following:

    a. $\mu = 37.2$ b. $\mu = 36.6$

28. The *power* of a test is $1 - \beta$, the probability of rejecting a false null hypothesis. Refer to the example in this section that addressed the claim about television radiation emissions. If the test of that claim has a power of 0.8, find the mean μ (see Exercise 27).

7-4 Testing a Claim About a Mean: Small Samples

One great advantage of learning the methods of hypothesis testing that we have described in Sections 7-2 and 7-3 is that those same methods can be easily modified for use in many other circumstances. The previous sections' examples and exercises all use large samples in tests of claims about means, but in this section we will deal with small sample cases—that is, cases where the number of sample values is 30 or fewer. The following assumptions apply to the methods described in this section.

Assumptions

1. The data have been collected by valid random sampling.
2. The sample is small ($n \leq 30$).
3. The value of the population standard deviation σ is unknown. (We seldom know the population standard deviation when we do not know the population mean.)
4. The sample values come from a population with a distribution that is approximately normal.

If these four assumptions are satisfied and we plan to test a hypothesis, then we use the Student t (not the normal) distribution with the test statistic and critical values described as follows.

Test Statistic for Claims About μ When $n \leq 30$ and σ Is Unknown

If a population is essentially normal, then the distribution of

$$t = \frac{\bar{x} - \mu_{\bar{x}}}{\frac{s}{\sqrt{n}}}$$

is essentially a *Student t distribution* for all samples of size n. (The Student t distribution is often referred to as the t *distribution*.)

Critical Values

1. Critical values are found in Table A-3.
2. Degrees of freedom $= n - 1$.
3. After finding the number of degrees of freedom, refer to Table A-3 and locate that number in the column at the left. With a particular row of t values now identified, select the critical t value that corresponds to the appropriate column heading. If a critical t value is located at the left tail, be sure to make it negative.

Polls and Psychologists

Poll results can be dramatically affected by the wording of questions. A phrase such as "over the last few years" is interpreted differently by different people. Over the last few years (actually, since 1980), survey researchers and psychologists have been working together to improve surveys by decreasing bias and increasing accuracy. In one case, psychologists studied the finding that 10% to 15% of those surveyed say they voted in the last election when they did not. They experimented with theories of faulty memory, a desire to be viewed as responsible, and a tendency of those who usually vote to say that they voted in the most recent election, even if they did not. Only the last theory was actually found to be part of the problem.

Important Properties of the Student t Distribution

1. The Student t distribution is different for different sample sizes (see Figure 6-5 in Section 6-3).

2. The Student t distribution has the same general bell shape as the standard normal distribution; its wider shape reflects the greater variability that is expected with small samples.

3. The Student t distribution has a mean of $t = 0$ (just as the standard normal distribution has a mean of $z = 0$).

4. The standard deviation of the Student t distribution varies with the sample size and is greater than 1 (unlike the standard normal distribution, which has $\sigma = 1$).

5. As the sample size n gets larger, the Student t distribution gets closer to the standard normal distribution. For values of $n > 30$, the differences are so small that we can use the critical z values instead of developing a much larger table of critical t values. (The values in the bottom row of Table A-3 are equal to the corresponding critical z values from the standard normal distribution.)

Choosing the Appropriate Distribution

When testing claims about population means, sometimes the normal distribution applies, sometimes the Student t distribution applies, and sometimes neither applies, so we must use nonparametric methods, which do not require a particular distribution. (Nonparametric methods are discussed in Chapter 13.)

Figure 7-10 summarizes the decisions to be made in choosing between the normal and Student t distributions. Studying the figure leads to the following observations.

1. According to the central limit theorem, if we obtain large ($n > 30$) samples (from any population with any distribution), the distribution of the sample means can be approximated by the normal distribution.

2. When we obtain samples (of any size) from a population with a normal distribution, the distribution of the sample means will be approximately normal with mean μ and standard deviation $\sigma/\sqrt{n}$. In a hypothesis test, the value of μ corresponds to the null hypothesis, and the value of the population standard deviation σ must be known. If σ is unknown and the samples are large, we can use the sample standard deviation s as a substitute for σ because large random samples tend to be representative of the populations from which they come.

3. The conditions for using the Student t distribution are as follows:

   a. The sample is small ($n \leq 30$); and

   b. σ is unknown; and

   c. The parent population has a distribution that is essentially normal.

4. If our random samples are small, σ is unknown, and the population distribution is grossly nonnormal, we cannot use the methods of this chapter.

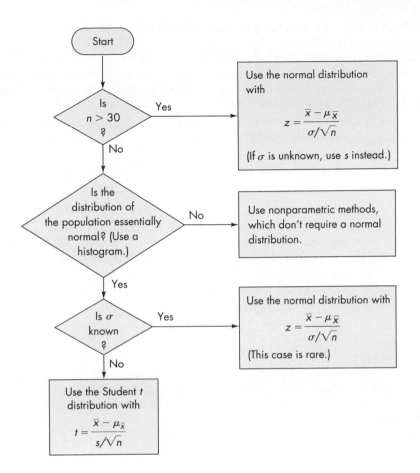

Figure 7-10 Choosing Between the Normal and Student *t* Distributions When Testing a Claim About the Population Mean μ

Instead, we can use nonparametric methods, some of which are discussed in Chapter 13.

The following example involves a small sample drawn from a normally distributed population for which the standard deviation σ is not known. These conditions require that we use the Student *t* distribution.

EXAMPLE   The seven values listed here are axial loads (in pounds) for the first sample of seven 12-oz aluminum cans (see Data Set 15 in Appendix B). An axial load of a can is the maximum weight supported by its sides, and it must be greater than 165 lb, because that is the maximum pressure applied when the top lid is pressed into place. At the 0.01 level of significance, test the claim of the engineering supervisor that this sample comes from a population with a mean that is greater than 165 lb.

270   273   258   204   254   228   282

SOLUTION   Using the given sample data, we apply procedures of Chapter 2 to find that $n = 7$, $\bar{x} = 252.7$, and $s = 27.6$. The mean of 252.7 does seem to be well above the required value of 165, but with only seven scores, do we really have enough evidence to support the supervisor's claim? Let's find out by conducting a formal hypothesis test with the same steps outlined in Figure 7-4.

Steps 1, 2, and 3 result in the following null and alternative hypotheses:

$$H_0: \mu \le 165$$
$$H_1: \mu > 165 \quad \text{(supervisor's claim)}$$

Step 4: The significance level is $\alpha = 0.01$.

Step 5: In this test of a claim about the population mean, the most relevant statistic is the sample mean. Referring to Figure 7-10, we see that the sample is small (because $n = 7$ and does not exceed 30), it's reasonable to conclude that the population distribution is normal (because we're dealing with physical measurements of a product made under standard conditions), and σ is unknown. Figure 7-10 shows that we should use the Student t distribution (not the normal distribution).

Step 6: The test statistic is

$$t = \frac{\bar{x} - \mu_{\bar{x}}}{\frac{s}{\sqrt{n}}} = \frac{252.7 - 165}{\frac{27.6}{\sqrt{7}}} = 8.407$$

The critical value of $t = 3.143$ is found by referring to Table A-3. First locate $n - 1 = 6$ degrees of freedom in the column at the left. Because this test is right-tailed with $\alpha = 0.01$, refer to the column with the heading of 0.01 (one tail). The critical value of $t = 3.143$ corresponds to 6 degrees of freedom and $\alpha = 0.01$ in one tail. The test statistic and critical value are shown in Figure 7-11.

Step 7: Because the test statistic of $t = 8.407$ falls in the critical region, we reject H_0.

Figure 7-11   *t*-Test of Claim That $\mu > 165$

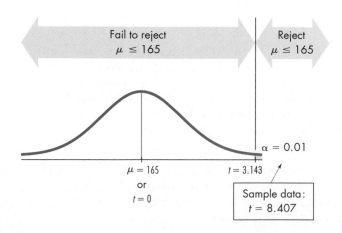

Interpretation (Refer to Figure 7-2 for help in wording the final conclusion.) There is sufficient evidence to support the supervisor's claim that the sample comes from a population with a mean greater than the required 165 lb.

The critical value in the preceding example was $t = 3.143$, but if the sample had been large ($n > 30$), the critical value would have been $z = 2.33$. The larger Student t critical value shows that with a small sample, the sample evidence must be *more extreme* before we consider the difference to be significant.

P-Values

The preceding example followed the traditional approach to hypothesis testing, but Excel, STATDISK, and much of the literature display P-values. Because the t distribution table (Table A-3) includes only selected values of the significance level α, we cannot usually find the specific P-value from Table A-3. Instead, we can use that table to identify limits that contain the P-value. In the last example we found the test statistic to be $t = 8.407$, and we know that the test is one-tailed with 6 degrees of freedom. By examining the row of Table A-3 corresponding to 6 degrees of freedom, we see that the test statistic of 8.407 exceeds the largest critical value in that row. Although we cannot pinpoint an exact P-value from Table A-3, we can conclude that it must be less than 0.005. That is, we conclude that P-value < 0.005. With a significance level of 0.01 and a P-value less than 0.005, we reject the null hypothesis (because the P-value is less than the significance level), as we did with the traditional method in the preceding example.

Better Results with Smaller Class Size

An experiment at a university found that students did significantly better in classes limited to 35 students than in large classes with 150 to 200 students. For a calculus course, failure rates were 19% for the small classes compared to 50% for the large classes. The percentages of A's were 24% for the small classes and 3% for the large classes. These results suggest that students benefit from smaller classes, which allow for more direct interaction between students and teachers.

EXAMPLE Use Table A-3 to find the P-value corresponding to these results: The Student t distribution is used in a two-tailed test with a sample of $n = 10$ scores, and the test statistic is found to be $t = 2.567$.

SOLUTION Refer to the row of Table A-3 with 9 degrees of freedom and note that the test statistic of 2.567 falls between the critical values of 2.821 and 2.262. Because the test is two-tailed, we consider the values of α at the top that are identified with "two tails." The critical values of 2.821 and 2.262 correspond to 0.02 (two tails) and 0.05 (two tails), so we express the P-value as follows.

$$0.02 < P\text{-value} < 0.05$$

With a true null hypothesis, the chance of getting a sample mean (from 10 sample values) that converts to a test statistic of $t = 2.567$ is somewhere between 0.02 and 0.05.

So far, we have discussed tests of hypotheses made about population means only. In the next section we will test hypotheses made about population proportions or percentages, and the last section will consider claims made about standard deviations or variances.

Using Technology

When conducting hypothesis tests using the Student t distribution, the procedures for using Excel and STATDISK are essentially the same as described in Section 7-3, except as noted here.

Excel: When choosing the function type option, select **1 Var t Test** instead of **1 Var z Test.**

STATDISK: (STATDISK proceeds exactly as in Section 7-3. After you have input the data, STATDISK itself will determine (based on the sample size n) whether to use a z test or a t test.)

Note that for the example of the seven axial loads, STATDISK estimates the P-value = 0.0001; Excel concludes the P-value < 0.001.

Excel Display   Testing a Claim
About a Mean
(Small Sample)

7-4 Exercises A: Basic Skills and Concepts

In Exercises 1 and 2, find the critical t values for the given hypotheses, sample sizes, and significance levels.

1. a. $H_0: \mu = 37.0$ b. $H_0: \mu \geq 100$ c. $H_1: \mu > 32$
        $n = 7$ $n = 12$ $n = 9$
        $\alpha = 0.05$ $\alpha = 0.05$ $\alpha = 0.01$

2. a. $H_0: \mu \leq 1.07$ b. $H_1: \mu < 75.2$ c. $H_1: \mu \neq 64$
        $n = 5$ $n = 14$ $n = 10$
        $\alpha = 0.01$ $\alpha = 0.05$ $\alpha = 0.10$

In Exercises 3 and 4, assume that the sample is randomly selected from a population with a normal distribution. Test the given claim by using the traditional method of testing hypotheses, then re-test using the P-value method.

3. Use a significance level of $\alpha = 0.05$ to test the claim that $\mu \neq 64.8$. The sample data consist of 12 scores for which $\bar{x} = 59.8$ and $s = 8.7$.

4. Use a significance level of $\alpha = 0.01$ to test the claim that $\mu < 927$. The sample data consist of 10 scores for which $\bar{x} = 874$ and $s = 57.3$.

5. A student used just one trade publication to price desktops that have at least 20 GB hard drive and a 700 MHZ processor speed. To justify relying on the one source, he took a sample of prices for such systems, as quoted in dealers' ads in the publication. Assume the industry mean price for such a system is $1750. Use a 0.01 significance level to test the claim that the mean quoted price in the sample is no different from the industry average of $1750. Interpret the results from this table.

Mean (sample)	2062.4
Mean (null hypothesis)	1750
Standard deviation	663.58
n	10
Test statistic t	1.489
Critical t	3.250
P-value	0.171

6. Refer to the display in Exercise 5. If the claim is changed from "is no different from the industry average" to "is greater than the industry average," how are the values in the right column of the table affected?

For hypothesis tests in Exercises 7–24, use the traditional approach summarized in Figure 7-4. Draw a graph showing the test statistic and critical values. In each case, assume that the population has a distribution that is approximately normal and that the sample is randomly selected. Note: Some of the exercises meet the requirements for using the normal distribution (as described in the preceding section) instead of the Student t distribution (as described in this section). Actually, you can also use the t tables for large samples as long as σ is not known (just use the bottom row of the tables); but unless you are using software, the t tables are generally less precise for finding P-values.

7. The top 10 punt returners in CIAU football have a mean for total-yards-returned in the season of 377 yards (based on data from the CIAU Football Web page). To support his arguments for a pay raise, a scout claims that punt returners he has recruited have performed *better* than the mean for top athletes in that position. If 5 of the punt returners he has recruited have a mean total-yards-returned for a year of 398.8, with a standard deviation of 77.84, test the recruiter's claim, using a 0.05 level of significance.

8. The expense of moving the storage yard for the Consolidated Package Delivery Service (CPDS) is justified only if it can be shown that the daily mean travel distance will be less than 342 km. In trial runs of 12 delivery trucks, the mean and standard deviation are found to be 318 km and

67 km, respectively. At the 0.01 level of significance, test the claim that the mean is less than 342 km. Should the storage yard be moved?

9. Data Set 2 in Appendix B is derived from research into the effects of cold and other factors on human body temperature. Use just the data in the leftmost column, representing the temperatures of 11 subjects after they sat perfectly still for a period of time. Test the claim that the mean body temperature of all healthy adults who have been sitting still is equal to 37.0°C, using a 0.05 level of significance.

10. Refer to Data Set 2 in Appendix B. In two separate analyses, use the data in the two columns labelled "Supine." Both columns represent the temperatures of 11 subjects after they lay face up for a period of time. (In the first experiment, the subjects sat first, before lying down; in the second experiment, they stood before lying down.) For *each* of these two situations, test the hypothesis that the mean body temperature of all healthy adults who have been lying face up (after sitting or standing) is equal to 37.0°C. Use a 0.05 level of significance. (In the lying-after-sitting case, $\bar{x} = 37.02$ and $s = 0.215$; for the lying-after-standing case, $\bar{x} = 36.97$ and $s = 0.249$.) Compare your results with your answer to Exercise 9. What might this suggest about the usual assumptions about a "normal" body temperature, which does not take posture into account?

11. For each of 12 organizations, the cost of operation per client was found. The 12 scores have a mean of $2133 and a standard deviation of $345 (based on data from "Organizational Communication and Performance," by Snyder and Morris, *Journal of Applied Psychology*, Vol. 69, No. 3). At the 0.01 significance level, test the claim of a stockholder who complains that the mean for all such organizations exceeds $1800 per client.

12. The skid properties of a snow tire have been tested, and a mean skid distance of 47 m has been established for standardized conditions. A new, more expensive tire is developed, but tests on a sample of 17 new tires yield a mean skid distance of 45 m with a standard deviation of 3.7 m. Because of the cost involved, the new tires will be purchased only if it can be shown at the $\alpha = 0.005$ significance level that they skid less than the current tires. Based on the sample, will the new tires be purchased?

13. A major bank is concerned about the amount of debt being accrued by customers using its credit cards. The Board of Directors voted to institute an expensive monitoring system if the mean for all of the bank's customers is greater than $2000. The bank randomly selected 50 credit-card holders and determined the amounts they charged. For this sample group, the mean is $2177 and the standard deviation is $1257. Use a 0.025 level of significance to test the claim that the mean amount charged is greater than $2000. Based on the result, will the monitoring system be implemented?

14. When a poultry farmer uses her regular feed, the chickens attain normally distributed weights with a mean of 1.77 kg. In an experiment with an enriched feed mixture, nine chickens are born that attain the weights (in kg) given below.

    1.74   1.77   1.90   1.80   1.88   1.87   1.79   1.81   1.89

    a. Use a 0.01 significance level to test the claim that the mean weight is higher with the enriched feed.

b. If the farmer can charge an extra 2 cents for each additional gram that her chickens weigh, and if it will cost an extra $1.17 per chicken to feed them the enriched feed, is it a good decision to switch to the enriched feed?

15. In a study of factors affecting hypnotism, visual analogue scale (VAS) sensory ratings were obtained for 16 subjects. For these sample ratings, the mean is 8.33 while the standard deviation is 1.96 (based on data from "An Analysis of Factors That Contribute to the Efficacy of Hypnotic Analgesia," by Price and Barber, *Journal of Abnormal Psychology*, Vol. 96, No. 1). At the 0.01 level of significance, test the claim that this sample comes from a population with a mean rating of less than 10.00.

16. A critic of Canada Post claims that its financial returns are typically $200 million less than forecast. In five of the years of the 1990s, the mean difference (in millions of dollars) between Canada Post's forecast and actual financial positions was 218.8, with a standard deviation of 118.76 (based on Canada Post data reported by Maclean Hunter, 1996). Use a significance level of 0.05 to test the claim that the mean difference between forecasted returns and actual returns was 200.

17. Because of a merger, a Vancouver executive will commute regularly to San Francisco for important meetings. To plan for travel time, she has compiled, as shown, a sample of flight times, in hours, for flights from Vancouver to San Francisco (based on data from Gary Murphy, chief flight dispatcher, Air Canada). The most convenient flight takes off 2.4 hours before she must reach San Francisco. Test the claim that the mean flight time from Vancouver to San Francisco is less than 2.4 hours. Because of the importance of not being mistaken, use a 0.01 level of significance.

2.30	2.20	1.97	2.22	2.12	$\bar{x} = 2.1564$
1.95	2.03	2.30	2.15	2.33	$s = 0.1312$
2.15					

18. A Calgary observatory records daily the mean counting rates for cosmic rays for that specific day (data as found at ftp.ngdc.noaa.gov./STP/ SOLAR_DATA/_COSMIC_RAYS/CALGARY.0). These recorded values are approximately normally distributed. If, for a randomly selected sample of the observatory's records, $\bar{x}$ equals 3455, and $s = 126.7$, test the claim that the mean for daily counting rates is actually equal to 3465.5. Assume that n = 30 and $\alpha = 0.05$.

19. Using the weights of only the *blue* M&Ms listed in Data Set 11 of Appendix B, test the claim that the mean is at least 0.9085 g, the mean value necessary for the 1498 M&Ms to produce a total of 1361 g as the package indicates. Use a 0.05 significance level. For the blue M&Ms, $\bar{x} = 0.9014$ g and $s = 0.0573$ g. Based on the result, can we conclude that the package contents do not agree with the claimed weight printed on the label?

20. Using the weights of only the *brown* M&Ms listed in Data Set 11 of Appendix B, test the claim that the mean is greater than 0.9085 g, the mean value necessary for the 1498 M&Ms to produce a total of 1361 g as the package indicates. Use a 0.05 significance level. For the brown M&Ms, $\bar{x} = 0.9128$ g and $s = 0.0395$ g. Based on the result, can we conclude that the packages contain more than the claimed weight printed on the label?

21. Listed here are the total electric energy consumption amounts (in kWh) for the home of a statistics professor during seven different years:

11,943   11,463   10,789   9907   9012   9942   11,153

The utility company claims that the mean annual consumption amount is 11,000 kWh and offers a budget payment plan based on that amount. At the 0.05 significance level, test the utility company's claim that the mean is equal to 11,000 kWh.

22. Given here are the birth weights (in kilograms) of male babies born to mothers on a special vitamin supplement. At the 0.05 level of significance, test the claim that the mean birth weight for all male babies of mothers given vitamins is equal to 3.39 kg, which is the mean for the population of all males. Based on the result, does the vitamin supplement appear to have an effect on birth weight?

3.73   4.37   3.73   4.33   3.39   3.68   4.68   3.52
3.02   4.09   2.47   4.13   4.47   3.22   3.43   2.54

23. Rita Gibbons is a stand-up comedian who videotapes her performances and records the total of the times she must wait for audience laughter to subside. Given here are the times (in seconds) for 15 different shows in which she used a new routine. Test the claim that the mean time is greater than 63.2 s, the mean time for her old routine. Based on the results, does her new routine seem to be better than the old one? Use the 0.05 level of significance.

86 45 44 78 52 79 86 66 61 57 98 44 61 99 87

24. An umbrella salesperson has moved her base from Winnipeg to Atlantic Canada. Believing that the mean annual precipitation for communities in Atlantic Canada is over twice the annual amount in Winnipeg (526 mm), she expects to do a great business. Refer to the top eight entries for annual precipitation in Data Set 4 in Appendix B. Assuming these data are from a random selection of sites in Atlantic Canada, test the claim that the mean annual precipitation for communities in Atlantic provinces is greater than 1052 mm. Use the 0.05 level of significance.

Suppose the entries from Atlantic Canada in Data Set 4 were *not* selected randomly from all possible sites, but were selected based on population plus convenience of data collection. What would be the implications—theoretical and practical—for using the results of the *t* test?

7-4 Exercises B: Beyond the Basics

25. Refer to the table of summary statistics included with Exercise 5. If the claim were changed from "is not different from the industry average" to "is more than the industry average," how would the values in the right column be affected?

26. Because of certain conditions, a hypothesis test requires the Student t distribution, as described in this section. Assume that the standard normal distribution was incorrectly used instead. Does using the standard normal distribution make you more or less likely to reject the null hypothesis, or does it not make a difference? Explain.

27. When finding critical values, we sometimes need significance levels other than those available in Table A-3. Some computer programs approximate critical t values by

$$t = \sqrt{\mathrm{df} \cdot (e^{A^2/\mathrm{df}} - 1)}$$

where
$$\mathrm{df} = n - 1$$
$$e = 2.718$$
$$A = z\left(\frac{8\,\mathrm{df} + 3}{8\,\mathrm{df} + 1}\right)$$

and z is the critical z score. Use this approximation to find the critical t score corresponding to $n = 10$ and a significance level of 0.05 in a right-tailed case. Compare the results to the critical t value found in Table A-3.

28. Refer to the data in Exercise 23 and assume that you're testing the claim that $\mu > 63.2$ s. Find β (the probability of a type II error), given that the actual value of the population mean is $\mu = 72.1$ s. (Use the procedures described in Exercise 27 in Section 7-3.)

Lie Detectors

Why not require all criminal suspects to take lie detector tests and dispense with trials by jury? While lie detectors are 75–97% accurate in indicating guilt when a person *is* guilty, they also have a high rate of "false positives." A "false positive" is an indication of guilt when the subject is actually innocent. Even with accuracy as high as 97%, the percentage of false positive results can be 50%, so half of the innocent subjects incorrectly appear to be guilty.

7-5 Testing a Claim About a Proportion

In the preceding sections of this chapter we introduced the basic methods of hypothesis testing, but they were used to address claims made about population *means* only. In this section we see how to apply those same basic methods to claims about population *proportions*. Using the methods of this section, we can test a claim about a proportion, percentage, or probability, as illustrated in these examples:

- Based on a sample survey, fewer than 1/4 of all college graduates smoke.
- The percentage of nonmilitary physicians leaving the country who are from Saskatchewan is equal to 5.4%.
- If a driver is fatally injured in a car crash, there is a 0.35 probability that the driver was legally impaired.

Assumptions Used When Testing a Claim About a Population Proportion, Probability, or Percentage

1. As always, we assume that the data have been collected by valid random-sampling techniques.
2. The conditions for a *binomial experiment* are satisfied. That is, we have a fixed number of independent trials having constant probabilities, and each trial has two outcome categories, which we classify as "success" and "failure."

3. The conditions $np \geq 5$ and $nq \geq 5$ are both satisfied, so **the distribution of sample proportions can be derived from the normal approximation of the binomial, with $\mu = np$ and $\sigma = \sqrt{npq}$** (as described in Section 5-6).

If these assumptions are not all satisfied, we may be able to use other methods. In this section, however, we consider only those cases in which the assumptions are satisfied, so the sampling distribution of sample proportions can be approximated by the normal distribution. We will use the following notation and test statistic.

Notation

n = number of trials

$\hat{p} = \dfrac{x}{n}$ (*sample* proportion)

p = *population* proportion (used in the null hypothesis)

$q = 1 - p$

Test Statistic for Testing a Claim About a Proportion

$$z = \frac{\hat{p} - p}{\sqrt{\dfrac{pq}{n}}}$$

The Traditional Method

For using the traditional method of testing hypotheses, follow the steps outlined in Figure 7-4, choosing the test statistic z, to be calculated as shown in this section. Find critical z values from Table A-2 (standard normal distribution) by using the procedures described in Section 7-2, or find critical z values with the aid of statistical software. (Note that our method for calculating z is equivalent to finding $z = (x - \mu)/\sigma$ as in Section 2-5, but we have substituted the binomial equivalents for μ and σ, and divided numerator and denominator by n.)

For example, in a two-tailed test with significance level $\alpha = 0.05$, divide α equally between the two tails, then refer to Table A-2 for the z score corresponding to an area of $0.5 - 0.025 = 0.475$; the result is $z = 1.96$, so the critical values are $z = -1.96$ and $z = 1.96$.

When conducting a test of a claim about a population proportion p, be careful to identify correctly the sample proportion $\hat{p}$. The sample proportion $\hat{p}$ is sometimes given directly, as in the statement that "10% of the observed sports cars are red," which is expressed as $\hat{p} = 0.10$. In other cases, we may need to calculate the sample proportion by using $\hat{p} = x/n$. For example, from the statement that "96 surveyed households have cable TV and 54 do not," we can first find the sample size n to be $96 + 54 = 150$, then we can calculate the value of the sample proportion of households with cable TV as follows:

$$\hat{p} = \frac{x}{n} = \frac{96}{150} = 0.64$$

Caution: The value of 0.64 is exact, but when a calculator or computer display of $\hat{p}$ results in many decimal places, use all of those decimal places when evaluating the z test statistic. Large errors can result from rounding $\hat{p}$ too much.

● **EXAMPLE**   In a study of air-bag effectiveness, it was found that in 821 crashes of midsize cars equipped with air bags, 46 of the crashes resulted in hospitalization of the drivers (based on data from the Highway Loss Data Institute). Use a 0.01 significance level to test the claim that the air-bag hospitalization rate is lower than the 7.8% rate for crashes of midsize cars equipped with automatic safety belts.

SOLUTION   We will use the traditional method of testing hypotheses as outlined in Figure 7-4. Instead of working with percentages, this solution will use the sample proportion of $\hat{p} = 46/821 = 0.0560292$ and the claimed population proportion of $p = 0.078$.

Step 1:   The original claim is that the air-bag hospitalization rate is lower than 7.8%. We express this in symbolic form as $p < 0.078$.

Step 2:   The opposite of the original claim is $p \geq 0.078$.

Step 3:   Because $p \geq 0.078$ contains equality, we have

$H_0: p \geq 0.078$ (null hypothesis)
$H_1: p < 0.078$ (alternative hypothesis and original claim)

Step 4:   The significance level is $\alpha = 0.01$.

Step 5:   The statistic relevant to this test is $\hat{p} = 46/821 = 0.0560292$. The sampling distribution of sample proportions is approximated by the normal distribution. (The requirements that $np \geq 5$ and $nq \geq 5$ are both satisfied with $n = 821$, $p = 0.078$, and $q = 0.922$.)

Step 6:   The test statistic of $z = -2.35$ is found as follows:

$$z = \frac{\hat{p} - p}{\sqrt{\dfrac{pq}{n}}} = \frac{0.0560292 - 0.078}{\sqrt{\dfrac{(0.078)(0.922)}{821}}} = -2.35$$

The critical value of $z = -2.33$ is found from Table A-2. With $\alpha = 0.01$ in the left tail, look for an area of 0.4900 in the body of Table A-2; the closest value is 0.4901 and it corresponds to $z = 2.33$, but it must be negative because it is to the left of the mean. The test statistic and critical value are shown in Figure 7-12.

The Conqueror

The Conqueror is a 1954 movie filmed near St. George, Utah, a year after an atomic bomb was exploded nearby. Among the 220 people who worked on the movie, John Wayne and 97 others eventually died of cancer. Methods of statistics can be used to show that the 45% cancer death rate is significantly higher than the rate that would have been expected under normal circumstances. However, methods of statistics cannot be used to show that the *cause* of the cancer deaths was the explosion of the atomic bomb.

Figure 7-12 Hypothesis Test of Claim That $p < 0.078$

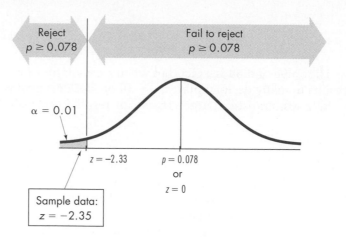

Step 7: Because the test statistic does fall within the critical region, reject the null hypothesis.

Interpretation There is sufficient evidence to support the claim that for crashes of midsize cars, the air-bag hospitalization rate is lower than the 7.8% rate for automatic safety belts.

EXAMPLE In a consumer taste test, 100 regular Pepsi drinkers are given blind samples of Coke and Pepsi; 48 of these subjects preferred Coke. At the 0.05 level of significance, test the claim that Coke is preferred by 50% of Pepsi drinkers who participate in such blind taste tests.

SOLUTION We summarize the key components of the hypothesis test:

$H_0: p = 0.5$ (from the claim that "Coke is preferred by 50%")
$H_1: p \neq 0.5$

Test statistic:

$$z = \frac{\hat{p} - p}{\sqrt{\dfrac{pq}{n}}} = \frac{0.48 - 0.5}{\sqrt{\dfrac{(0.5)(0.5)}{100}}} = -0.40$$

The test statistic, critical values, and critical region are shown in Figure 7-13. Because the test statistic is not in the critical region, we fail to reject the null hypothesis. There is not sufficient evidence to reject the claim that 50% of Pepsi drinkers prefer Coke. (Critics of such taste tests claim that the subjects often cannot observe differences and guess when making their choices.)

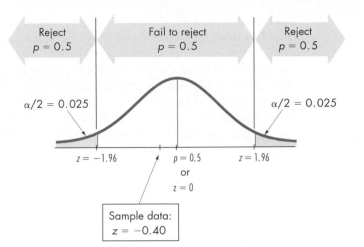

Figure 7-13 Hypothesis Test of $p = 0.5$

The *P*-Value Method

To find the *P*-value corresponding to a z test statistic, use the following procedure, which was shown in Figure 7-8 and described in Section 7-3:

Right-tailed test: *P*-value = area to right of test statistic z

Left-tailed test: *P*-value = area to left of test statistic z

Two-tailed test: *P*-value = *twice* the area of the extreme region
                                   bounded by the test statistic z

As in Section 7-3, we use this decision criterion:

Reject the null hypothesis if the *P*-value is less than or equal to the significance level α.

Applying this method to the last example, which was two-tailed, the *P*-value is twice the area to the left of the test statistic $z = -0.40$. Table A-2 indicates that the area between $z = 0$ and $z = -0.40$ is 0.1554, so the area to the left of the test statistic ($z = -0.40$) is $0.5 - 0.1554 = 0.3446$. The *P*-value is $2 \times 0.3446 = 0.6892$. Because the *P*-value of 0.6892 is not less than or equal to the significance level of 0.05, we fail to reject the null hypothesis and again conclude that there is not sufficient evidence to reject the claim that 50% of Pepsi drinkers prefer Coke. Again, the *P*-value method is simply another way of arriving at the same conclusion reached using the traditional approach.

Using Technology

Excel: First enter the number of successes and the total number of trials into separate spreadsheet cells (for example A1 and B1, respectively). Use the Data Disk XL add-in by clicking on **DDXL** on the main menu bar, and then select **Hypothesis**

Tests. Under the function type options, select **Summ 1 Var Prop Test** (for testing a claimed proportion for one variable, using summary data). Click on the pencil icon for "Num successes" and enter the appropriate cell address (e.g., A1). Click on the pencil icon for "Num trials" and enter the cell address for this data (e.g., B1). Click **OK**. Follow the four steps listed in the dialog box. After clicking on **Compute** in Step 4, you will get the *P*-value, test statistic, and conclusion.

STATDISK: Select **Analysis, Hypothesis Testing, Proportion—One Sample**, then proceed to enter the data in the dialog box.

Excel Display   Testing a Claim About a Proportion

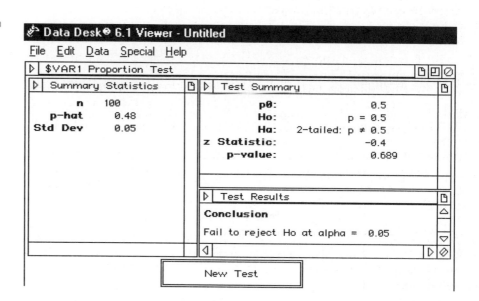

7-5 Exercises A: Basic Skills and Concepts

In Exercises 1–20, test the given claim, and draw the appropriate graph. Use the traditional method or the P-value method of testing hypotheses (or your instructor may specify which method to use with assigned exercises). Assume that all samples have been randomly selected.

1. In a study of store checkout scanners, 1234 items were checked and 20 of them were found to be overcharges (based on data from "UPC Scanner Pricing Systems: Are They Accurate?" by Goodstein, *Journal of Marketing,* Vol. 58). Use a 0.05 level of significance to test the claim that with scanners, 1% of sales are overcharges. (Before scanners were used, the overcharge rate was estimated to be about 1%.) Based on these results, do scanners appear to actually increase occurences of overcharges?

2. Environmental concerns often conflict with modern technology, as is the case with birds that pose a hazard to aircraft during takeoff. An environmental group states that incidents of bird strikes are too rare to justify

killing the birds. A pilots' group claims that among aborted takeoffs leading to an aircraft's going off the end of the runway, 10% are due to bird strikes. Use a 0.05 level of significance to test that claim. Sample data consist of 74 aborted takeoffs in which the aircraft overran the runway. Among those 74 cases, 5 were due to bird strikes (based on data from the Airline Pilots Association and Boeing).

3. The quality control manager at the Telektronic Company considers production of telephone-answering machines to be "out of control" when the overall rate of defects exceeds 4%. Testing of a random sample of 150 machines revealed that 9 are defective, so the sample percentage of defects is 6%. The production manager claims that this is only a chance difference, so production is not really out of control and no corrective action is necessary. Use a 0.05 significance level to test the production manager's claim. Does it appear that corrective action is necessary?

4. In a recent year, 64% of all formal complaints to government institutions were resolved. The other complaints were unresolved, discontinued, or not substantiated. A spokesperson for Revenue Canada claims that they had a more positive record. In a sample of 58 complaints received, 42 were resolved (based on Information Commissioner of Canada, Annual Report, 1995–1996). Do the data suggest that more than 64% of complaints to Revenue Canada were resolved? Use the 0.01 level of significance.

5. Ralph Carter is a high-school history teacher who says that if students are not aware of the Holocaust, then the curriculum should be revised to correct that deficiency. A Roper survey of 506 high-school students showed that 268 of them did not know that the term "Holocaust" refers to the Nazi killing of about 6 million Jews during World War II. Using the sample data and a 0.05 significance level, test the claim that most (more than 50%) students don't know what "Holocaust" refers to. Based on these results, should Ralph Carter seek revisions to the curriculum?

6. Refer to Data Set 8 in Appendix B and consider only those statistics students who are 21 or older. Find the sample percentage of smokers in that age group, then test the claim that statistics students aged 21 or over smoke at a rate that is less than 32%, which is the smoking rate for the general population of persons aged 21 and over. Is there a reason that statistics students 21 and over would smoke at a rate lower than the rate for the general population in that age group?

7. In past years, the percentage of civilian medical doctors leaving the country who are from Saskatchewan has been equal to 5.4%. In a more recent sample of 120 civilian doctors leaving the country, 10 were from Saskatchewan (based on data from the Southam Medical Database). At the 0.05 level of significance, test the claim that the percentage of non-military doctors leaving the country who are from Saskatchewan is now greater than 5.4%.

8. A mutual funds specialist claims that two-year return rates are greater than one-year return rates for 35% of funds on the market. Test that claim using a 0.05 significance level. For sample data, refer to Data Set 10 of Appendix B. (*Hint*: You must first identify and count the records that are "successes.")

9. Based on seven years of data collected by Transport Canada, 45.8% of all bird strikes on moving aircraft involve gulls. Suppose that the next year, planes are asked to emit gull-repelling sound effects, and that of 364 bird-strike incidents, 150 involve gulls. Test the claim that the sound effects have been effective in reducing the proportion of air-strike incidents that involve gulls. Use the 0.05 level of significance.

10. "Bystanders perform CPR correctly less than half the time," according to a newspaper article that noted that among 662 cases in which bystanders gave CPR, 46% performed the CPR correctly. Use a 0.025 significance level to test the article's claim.

11. Auto insurance companies are beginning to consider raising rates for those who use cell phones while driving. A consumer group claims that the problem really isn't too serious because only 10% of drivers use cell phones. The insurance industry conducts a study and finds that among 500 randomly selected drivers, 90 use cell phones (based on data from *Prevention* magazine). At the 0.02 level of significance, test the consumer group's claim.

12. Many researchers consider that a 75% response rate to a survey is quite good. In spring 1998, Statistics Canada surveyed thousands of representatives of businesses, governments, and institutions regarding their capital spending plans. At the same time, they wished to study the response rates. Of 500 who were contacted for the spending survey, 395 returned a response (based on data in *The Globe and Mail*, July 23, 1998). At the 0.05 level of significance, test the claim that this survey had a response rate greater than 75%.

13. In clinical studies of the allergy drug Seldane, 70 of the 781 subjects experienced drowsiness (based on data from Merrell Dow Pharmaceuticals, Inc.). A competitor claims that 8% of Seldane users experience drowsiness. Use a 0.10 significance level to test that claim.

14. Late in the campaign for the June 1997 federal election, the Angus Reid Group conducted an opinion poll of public preferences. The poll found the Liberals had the support of 42% of the 3208 voters surveyed. In the election, the Liberals won 38.4% of the popular vote (based on reports by Reuters Limited). Test whether the public support in the poll was greater than on election day. Use the 0.05 level of significance. Did Liberal support drop in the last weeks before the election?

15. Dr. Kelly Roberts is dean of a medical school and must plan courses for incoming students. The college president is encouraging her to increase the emphasis on pediatrics, but Dr. Roberts argues that fewer than 10% of medical students prefer pediatrics. She refers to sample data indicating that 64 of 1068 randomly selected medical students chose pediatrics. Is there sufficient sample evidence to support her argument (at the 0.01 significance level)?

16. Several dentist offices were concerned with their 8% rate of no-shows for appointments. The Canadian Dental Association recommended that to reduce these no-shows, the receptionist should call each patient a day before his or her scheduled appointment, as a reminder and confirmation. A study was then made of 125 randomly selected appointments that were made under the new system. If 5 no-shows were recorded, test the claim that the no-show rate is lower with the new system. Does the new system appear to be effective in reducing no-shows? Use the 0.05 level of significance.

17. In one study of 71 smokers who tried to quit smoking with nicotine patch therapy, 32 were not smoking one year after the treatment. Use a 0.10 level of significance to test the claim that among smokers who try to quit with nicotine patch therapy, the majority are smoking a year after the treatment. Do these results suggest that the nicotine patch therapy is not effective?

18. In a study of the risks to children of automobile accidents, 400 records were randomly selected for the ages of children who died as occupants in motor vehicles. Of these, 285 were teenagers from 15 to 19 years old (based on data from Health Canada). At the 0.03 level of significance, test the claim that more than 2/3 of the children who died in automobile accidents were teenagers from 15 to 19 years old.

19. A research poll of 1012 adults showed that among those who used fruit-cakes, 28% ate them and 72% used them for other purposes, such as doorstops, birdfeed, and landfill. This surprised fruitcake producers, who believe that a fruitcake is an appealing food. The president of the Tombits Food Company claims that the poll results are a fluke and, in reality, half of all adults eat their fruitcakes. Use a 0.01 level of significance to test that claim. Based on the result, does it appear that fruitcake producers should consider changes to make their product more appealing as a food or better suited for its uses as a doorstop, birdfeed, and so on?

20. A *Prevention* magazine article reported on a poll of 1257 adults. The article noted that among those polled, 27% smoke, and 82% of those who smoke have tried to stop at least once. How many of the surveyed people are smokers who have tried to stop at least once? At the 0.05 significance level, test the claim that less than 25% of adults are smokers who have tried to stop at least once.

7–5 Exercises B: Beyond the Basics

21. In a study of the prevalence of cold/flu symptoms in December 2000, 44 residents of Ottawa are tested in December, and 5 of them have the symptoms (based on data from *The Globe and Mail*, December 20, 2000). We want to use a 0.01 significance level to test the claim that the percentage of Ottawans suffering from cold/flu symptoms in December is greater than the national rate of 11.1%.

    a. Why can't we use the methods of this section?

    b. Assuming that the percentage of Ottawans suffering from cold/flu symptoms in December is equal to the national rate of 11.1%, find the probability that among 44 Ottawans randomly selected in December, 5 will be suffering from the symptoms.

    c. Based on the result from your part (b), what do you conclude?

22. Chemco, a supplier of chemical waste containers, finds that 3% of a sample of 500 units are defective. Being fundamentally dishonest, the Chemco production manager wants to make a claim that the rate of defective units is no more than some specified percentage, and he doesn't want that claim

rejected at the 0.05 level of significance if the sample data are used. What is the *lowest* defective rate he can claim under these conditions?

23. A researcher claimed that when 20 small businesses were opened, the success rate was equal to 47%. Describe a basis for rejecting that claim?

24. Refer to Exercise 9. If the true value of p is 0.45, find β, the probability of a type II error (see Exercise 27 from Section 7-3). (*Hint:* In Step 3 use the values of $p = 0.45$ and $pq/n = (0.45)(0.55)/364$.)

7-6 Testing a Claim About a Standard Deviation or Variance

Quality control engineers want to ensure that a product is, on the average, acceptable, but they also want to produce items of *consistent* quality so that there will be few defective products. Consistency is improved by reducing variation. For example, the consistency of dental X-ray tube operation is governed by the Radiation Emitting Devices Regulations (C.R.C., C.1370), administered by Health Canada. Besides requiring that operating X-ray tube voltage must be at least 50 kV (peak value), the regulations specify a maximum allowable deviation: The standard deviation can be no more than 5% of the mean voltage. Even if the mean voltage is perfectly acceptable, an excessively large standard deviation could result in individual voltages that are outside the safe operating range.

While the preceding sections of this chapter introduced methods of testing claims made about population means and proportions, this section uses the same basic procedures to test claims made about a population standard deviation σ or variance σ^2. The following assumptions must be met for such tests.

Assumptions

1. The data have been collected by valid random-sampling techniques.
2. The population has values that are normally distributed.

Other methods of testing hypotheses have also required a normally distributed population, but tests of claims about standard deviations or variances are not as *robust,* meaning that the inferences can be very misleading if the population does not have a normal distribution. Therefore, the condition of a normally distributed population is a much stricter requirement in this section. Given the assumption of a normal distribution, we can use the following notation for the chi-square test statistic.

Test Statistic for Testing Hypotheses About σ or σ^2
$$\chi^2 = \frac{(n-1)s^2}{\sigma^2}$$

where n = sample size
    s^2 = sample variance
    σ^2 = population variance (given in the null hypothesis)

Critical Values

1. Critical values are found in Table A-4.
2. Degrees of freedom = $n - 1$.

Do not be confused by the use of both the normal and the chi-square distributions. After verifying that the sample data themselves come from a normally distributed population, we should then shift gears and think "chi-square." The chi-square distribution was introduced in Section 6-5, where we noted the following important properties.

Properties of the Chi-Square Distribution

1. All values of χ^2 are nonnegative, and the distribution is not symmetric (see Figure 7-14).
2. There is a different distribution for each number of degrees of freedom (see Figure 7-15).
3. The critical values are found in Table A-4 using

degrees of freedom = $n - 1$

Critical values are found in Table A-4 by first locating the row corresponding to the appropriate number of degrees of freedom (where df = $n - 1$). Next, the significance level α is used to determine the correct column as described in the following list:

Right-tailed test:	Locate the area at the top of Table A-4 that is equal to the significance level α.
Left-tailed test:	Calculate $1 - \alpha$, then locate the area at the top of Table A-4 that is equal to $1 - \alpha$.
Two-tailed test:	Calculate $1 - \alpha/2$ and $\alpha/2$, then locate the area at the top of Table A-4 that equals $1 - \alpha/2$ (for the left critical value) and locate the area at the top equal to $\alpha/2$ (for the right critical value). (See Figure 6-9 and the example on pages 312 and 313.)

Ethics in Experiments

Sample data can often be obtained by simply observing or surveying members selected from the population. Many other situations require that we somehow manipulate circumstances to obtain sample data. In both cases ethical questions may arise. Researchers in Tuskegee, Alabama, withheld the effective penicillin treatment from syphilis victims so that the disease could be studied. This experiment continued 27 years!

Figure 7-14 Properties of the Chi-Square Distribution

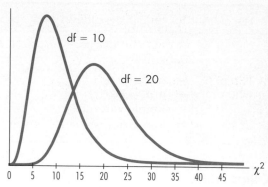

Figure 7-15 Chi-Square Distributions for 10 and 20 Degrees of Freedom
There is a different distribution for each number of degrees of freedom.

EXAMPLE   The Stewart Aviation Products Company has been success-fully manufacturing aircraft altimeters with errors normally distributed with a mean of 0 ft (achieved by calibration) and a standard deviation of 43.7 ft. After the installation of new production equipment, 30 altimeters were randomly selected from the new line. This sample group had errors with a standard deviation of $s = 54.7$ ft. Use a 0.05 significance level to test the claim that the new altimeters have a standard deviation different from the old value of 43.7 ft.

SOLUTION   We will use the traditional method of testing hypotheses as outlined in Figure 7-4.

Step 1:   The claim is expressed in symbolic form as $\sigma \neq 43.7$ ft.

Step 2:   If the original claim is false, then $\sigma = 43.7$ ft.

Step 3:   The null hypothesis must contain equality, so we have

$$H_0: \sigma = 43.7 \qquad H_1: \sigma \neq 43.7 \text{ (original claim)}$$

Step 4:   The significance level is $\alpha = 0.05$.

Step 5:   Because the claim is made about σ, we use the chi-square distribution.

Step 6:   The test statistic is

$$\chi^2 = \frac{(n-1)s^2}{\sigma^2} = \frac{(30-1)(54.7)^2}{43.7^2} = 45.437$$

The critical values are 16.047 and 45.722. They are found in Table A-4, in the 29th row (degrees of freedom = $n - 1 = 29$) in the columns corresponding to 0.975 and 0.025. See the test statistic and critical values shown in Figure 7-16.

Step 7:   Because the test statistic is not in the critical region, we fail to reject the null hypothesis.

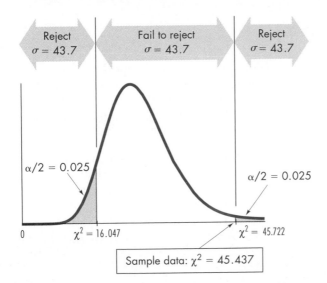

Figure 7-16   Hypothesis Test of Claim That $\sigma \neq 43.7$

Interpretation   There is not sufficient evidence to support the claim that the standard deviation is different from 43.7 ft. (For help in wording the final conclusion, refer to Figure 7-2.) However, it would be wise to continue monitoring and testing the new product line.

The *P*-Value Method

Instead of the traditional approach to hypothesis testing, we can also use the P-value approach summarized in Figures 7-7 and 7-8. If we use Table A-4, we usually cannot find *exact* P-values because the chi-square distribution table includes only selected values of α. Instead, we use the table to identify limits that contain the P-value. The test statistic from the last example is $\chi^2 = 45.437$, and we know that the test is two-tailed with 29 degrees of freedom. Refer to the 29th row of Table A-4 and see that the test statistic of 45.437 is between the table critical values of 42.557 and 45.722, indicating that the area to the right of the test statistic is between the corresponding areas of 0.05 and 0.025. However, Figure 7-7 shows that in a two-tailed test with a test statistic to the right of the centre, the P-value is *twice* the area to the right of the test statistic. The P-value is therefore between 0.10 and 0.05, which can be expressed as

Ethics in Reporting

Statistics quoted out of context can be misleading. Public opinions gathered in surveys may easily be distorted by people who are trying to present an issue in a particular light. Ethical reporting of survey results will present details about the information-gathering process, including the following:

1. Identification of the survey sponsor
2. Date the survey was conducted
3. Size of the sample
4. Nature of the population sampled
5. Type of survey used
6. Exact wording of survey questions

$$0.05 < P\text{-value} < 0.10$$

Because the P-value is not less than or equal to the significance level of $\alpha = 0.05$, we again fail to reject the null hypothesis. Again, the traditional method and P-value method are equivalent in the sense that they always lead to the same conclusion. Note that if statistical software is used, the exact P-value (in this example, 0.0533) is usually displayed directly.

Using Technology

STATDISK: Select **Analysis**, then **Hypothesis Testing**, then **StDev—One Sample**. Proceed to provide the required entries in the dialog box, then click on **Evaluate**. STATDISK will display the test statistic, critical value, P-value, conclusion, and confidence intervals.

Excel: Since there is no Excel Data Analysis or DDXL tool for testing claims about a standard deviation, create a formula-based template, such as the one illustrated below. The template is shown here as being placed in Cells B19 to C27. You must modify the underlying formulas shown in the table based on where the data and the template appear on

Excel Display   Testing a Claim About a Standard Deviation

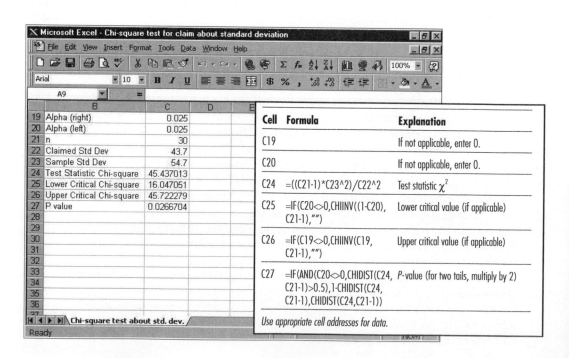

your own spreadsheet. Enter the right-tailed and left-tailed portions of α. If you are conducting a two-tailed test, then input the value of $\alpha/2$ in both cells. Enter the sample size n, the claimed standard deviation, and the sample standard deviation where indicated. When the underlying formulas are entered into the cells labelled here as C24 to C27, then the test statistic χ^2, lower critical χ^2, upper critical χ^2, and P-value will all be displayed. (For a one-tailed test, the lower or upper critical χ^2 will be omitted, as appropriate.) For a two-tailed test, multiply the displayed P-value by 2.

7–6 Exercises A: Basic Skills and Concepts

In Exercises 1 and 2, use Table A-4 to find the critical values of χ^2 based on the given information.

1. a. H_0: $\sigma = 15$ b. H_1: $\sigma > 0.62$ c. H_1: $\sigma < 14.4$
        $n = 10$ $n = 27$ $n = 21$
        $\alpha = 0.01$ $\alpha = 0.01$ $\alpha = 0.05$
2. a. H_1: $\sigma < 1.22$ b. H_1: $\sigma > 92.5$ c. H_0: $\sigma = 0.237$
        $n = 23$ $n = 12$ $n = 16$
        $\alpha = 0.025$ $\alpha = 0.10$ $\alpha = 0.05$

In Exercises 3–14, use the traditional method to test the given hypotheses. Follow the steps outlined in Figure 7-4, and draw the appropriate graph. In all cases, assume that the population is normally distributed and that the sample has been randomly selected.

3. The Stewart Aviation Products Company uses a new production method to manufacture aircraft altimeters. A random sample of 81 altimeters resulted in errors with a standard deviation of $s = 52.3$ ft. At the 0.05 level of significance, test the claim that the new production line has errors with a standard deviation different from 43.7 ft, which was the standard deviation for the old production method. If it appears that the standard deviation has changed, does the new production method appear to be better or worse than the old method?

4. The incubation periods for different, common bird families of the type Hole Nesters have a standard deviation of 6.8 days. The incubation periods for a sample of 5 different, common bird families of the type Open Nesters have a standard deviation of 2.0. Use a 0.05 significance level to test the claim that Open Nesters have less variation of incubation period than Hole Nesters. Can you suggest a biological explanation for your result?

5. With individual lines at its various windows, the Humber Valley Credit Union found that the standard deviation for normally distributed waiting times on Friday afternoons was 6.2 min. The credit union experimented with a single main waiting line and found that for a random sample of 25 customers, the waiting times have a standard deviation of 3.8 min. On the

basis of previous studies, we can assume that the waiting times are normally distributed. Use a 0.05 significance level to test the claim that a single line causes lower variation among the waiting times. Why would customers prefer waiting times with less variation? Does the use of a single line result in a shorter wait?

6. Do men's heights vary more than women's? The nurse at a women's college has collected data from physical exams. The standard deviation of women's heights is found to be 2.5 in. The college has now become coed and the first 20 male students have heights with a standard deviation of 2.8 in. Use a 0.025 significance level to test the claim that men's heights vary more than women's. If that claim is not supported, does this mean that men's heights do not vary more than women's?

7. Xtron Electrics manufactures dental X-ray tubes. Health Canada has warned that they are not fulfilling regulations for Radiation Emitting Devices. For a sample of 20 X-ray tubes in operation, their mean peak-value voltage ($\bar{x} = 52$ kV) is acceptable, but it is claimed that the standard deviation is greater than the 2.6 kV allowed (based on Federal Regulation C.R.C., C.1370). The standard deviation for the sample was 2.8 kV. At the 0.05 level of significance, test the claim that Xtron's product is failing to meet the requirement of a maximum standard deviation of 2.6 kV.

8. The St. Lawrence Investment Company finds that if the standard deviation for the weekly downtimes of their computer is 2 h or less, then the computer is predictable and planning is facilitated. Twelve weekly downtimes for the computer were randomly selected, and the sample standard deviation was computed to be 2.85 h. The manager of computer operations claims that computer access times are unpredictable because the standard deviation exceeds 2 h. Test her claim, using a 0.025 significance level. Does the variation appear to be too high?

9. The Medassist Pharmaceutical Company uses a machine to pour cold medicine into bottles in such a way that the standard deviation of the weights is 0.15 oz. A new machine was tested on 71 bottles, and the standard deviation for this sample is 0.12 oz. The Dayton Machine Company, which manufactures the new machine, claims that it fills bottles with a lower variation. At the 0.05 significance level, test the claim made by the Dayton Machine Company. If Dayton's machine is being used on a trial basis, should its purchase be considered?

10. For randomly selected adults, IQ scores are normally distributed with a mean of 100 and a standard deviation of 15. A sample of 24 randomly selected college professors resulted in IQ scores having a standard deviation of 10. A psychologist is quite sure that college professors have IQ scores that have a mean greater than 100. He doesn't understand the concept of standard deviation very well and claims the standard deviation for IQ scores of college professors is equal to 15, the same standard deviation as in the general population. Use a 0.05 level of significance to test that claim. Based on the result, what do you conclude about the standard deviation of IQ scores for college professors?

11. Systolic blood pressure results from contraction of the heart. In comparing systolic blood pressure levels of men and women, Dr. Jane Taylor obtained readings for a random sample of 50 women. The sample mean

and standard deviation were found to be 130.7 and 23.4, respectively. If systolic blood pressure levels for men are known to have a mean and standard deviation of 133.4 and 19.7, respectively, test the claim that women have more variation. Use a 0.05 level of significance. (All readings are in millimetres of mercury.)

12. A study examined the effects of a stay in the Arctic on a person's tolerance for cold. After a stay in the Arctic, three subjects were exposed to cold in experimental conditions and the effects noted. The subjects' mean skin temperatures had a standard deviation of 2.11°C after their exposure to cold (based on data in *International Journal of Biometeorology*, 1996). Supposing the expected standard deviation for mean skin temperature is 1.06°C, test whether the stay in the Arctic has had an effect on the variance of the subjects' mean skin temperature. Test the claim at the 0.05 level of significance.

13. Based on data from a health survey, men aged 25–34 have heights with a standard deviation of 2.9 in. Test the claim that men aged 45–54 have heights with a different standard deviation. The heights of 25 randomly selected men in the 45–54 age bracket are listed below.

```
66.80  71.22  65.80  66.24  69.62  70.49  70.00  71.46  65.72
68.10  72.14  71.58  66.85  69.88  68.69  72.77  67.34  68.40
68.96  68.70  72.69  68.67  67.79  63.97  67.19
```

14. An investor claims that the variability between the two-year return rates of different mutual funds is greater than when she began investing. Refer to the two-year return column in Data Set 10 in Appendix B. If the two-year return rates for different funds had a standard deviation of 10.11 when she began investing, test the claim that the current standard deviation for two-year return rates ($s = 12.845$) is greater. Use the 0.01 level of significance.

7–6   Exercises B: Beyond the Basics

15. Use Table A-4 to find the range of possible *P*-values in the given exercises.

    a. Exercise 3   b. Exercise 5   c. Exercise 9

16. For large numbers of degrees of freedom, we can approximate critical values of χ^2 as follows:

$$\chi^2 = \frac{1}{2} (z + \sqrt{2k - 1})^2$$

Here k is the number of degrees of freedom and z is the critical value, found in Table A-2. For example, if we want to approximate the two critical values of χ^2 in a two-tailed hypothesis test with $\alpha = 0.05$ and a sample size of 150, we let $k = 149$ with $z = -1.96$, followed by $k = 149$ and $z = 1.96$.

    a. Use this approximation to estimate the critical values of χ^2 in a two-tailed hypothesis test with $n = 101$ and $\alpha = 0.05$. Compare the results to those found in Table A-4.

b. Use this approximation to estimate the critical values of χ^2 in a two-tailed hypothesis test with $n = 150$ and $\alpha = 0.05$.

17. Repeat Exercise 16 using this approximation (with k and z as described in Exercise 16):

$$\chi^2 = k\left(1 - \frac{2}{9k} + z\sqrt{\frac{2}{9k}}\right)^3$$

18. Refer to Exercise 5. Assuming that σ is actually 4.0, find β (the probability of a type II error). See Exercise 27 from Section 7-3 and modify the procedure so that it applies to a hypothesis test involving σ instead of μ.

19. When using the hypothesis testing procedure of this section, will the result be dramatically affected by the presence of an outlier? Describe how you arrived at your response.

20. The last digits of sample data are sometimes used in an attempt to determine whether the data have been measured or simply reported by the subject. Reported data often have last digits with disproportionately more 0s and 5s. Measured data tend to have last digits with a mean of 4.5 , a standard deviation of about 3, and the digits should occur with roughly the same frequency.

   a. How is the standard deviation of the data affected if there are disproportionately more 0s and 5s?

   b. Why can we not use the methods of this section to test that the last digits of the sample data have a standard deviation equal to 3?

• •

Vocabulary List

hypothesis

formal hypothesis test

test of significance

null hypothesis

alternative hypothesis

test statistic

critical region

significance level

critical value

two-tailed test

right-tailed test

left-tailed test

type I error

type II error

alpha (α)

beta (β)

power

traditional method

classical method

P-value

• •

Review

Chapters 6 and 7 introduced two important concepts in using sample data to form inferences about population data: estimating values of population parameters (Chapter 6), and testing claims made about population parameters (Chapter 7). The parameters considered in Chapters 6 and 7 are means, proportions, standard deviations, and variances.

Section 7-2 presented the fundamental concepts of a hypothesis test: null hypothesis, alternative hypothesis, type I error, type II error, test statistic, critical region, critical value, and significance level. We also discussed two-tailed tests, left-tailed tests, right-tailed tests, and the statement of conclusions. Section 7-3 used those components in identifying three different methods for testing hypotheses:

1. The traditional method (summarized in Figure 7-4)

2. The P-value method (summarized in Figure 7-8)

3. Confidence intervals (discussed in Chapter 6)

Sections 7-3 through 7-6 discussed specific methods for dealing with the different parameters. Because it is so important to be correct in selecting the distribution and test statistic, we provide Figure 7-17, which summarizes the key decisions to be made.

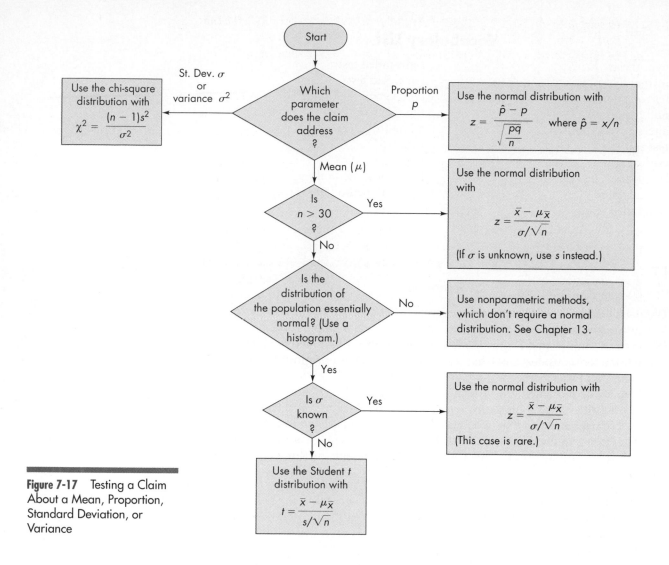

Figure 7-17 Testing a Claim About a Mean, Proportion, Standard Deviation, or Variance

Review Exercises

In Exercises 1 and 2, find the appropriate critical values. In all cases, assume that the population standard deviation σ is unknown.

1. **a.** $H_1: \mu < 27.3$
    $n = 10$
    $\alpha = 0.05$

    b. $H_1: p \neq 0.5$
    $n = 150$
    $\alpha = 0.01$

    c. $H_1: \sigma \neq 15$
    $n = 20$
    $\alpha = 0.05$

2. **a.** $H_0: \mu = 19.9$
    $n = 40$
    $\alpha = 0.10$

    b. $H_0: \sigma \leq 0.93$
    $n = 10$
    $\alpha = 0.025$

    c. $H_0: p \geq 0.25$
    $n = 540$
    $\alpha = 0.01$

In Exercises 3 and 4, respond to each of the following:
  a. Give the null hypothesis in symbolic form.
  b. Is this test left-tailed, right-tailed, or two-tailed?

    c.   In simple terms devoid of symbolism and technical language, describe the type I error.

    d.   In simple terms devoid of symbolism and technical language, describe the type II error.

    e.   Identify the probability of making a type I error.

3. The claim that statistics consultants have a mean income of $90,000 is to be tested at the 0.05 significance level.

4. The claim that lengths of CBC commercials have a standard deviation less than 15 s is to be tested at the 0.01 significance level.

5. According to the National Population Health Survey for 1996–97, 28% of those with dental insurance did not have their teeth checked during the survey period (based on data from *The Globe and Mail*). Assume that there were 2014 people in the survey group with dental insurance. Test the claim that more than one quarter (25%) of people with dental insurance do not have their teeth checked annually. Use the 0.01 significance level.

6. A Telektronics dental X-ray machine bears a label stating that the machine gives radiation dosages with a mean of less than 5.00 milliroentgens (mR). Sample data consist of 36 randomly selected observations with a mean of 4.13 mR and a standard deviation of 1.91 mR. Using a 0.01 level of significance, test the claim stated on the label.

7. Using the same sample data from Exercise 6, use a 0.01 significance level to test the claim that the radiation dosages have a standard deviation less than 2.50 mR. What is a practical consequence of a standard deviation that is too high in this case?

8. In the 1991 Census of Agriculture, 26.7% of all farms had gross farm receipts over $100,000. In a more recent sample of 75 farms, 23 had that level of gross income. Using the 0.01 level of significance, test the claim that the proportion of farms with gross farm receipts over $100,000 is greater than it was 1991.

9. The Cape Breton Bottling Company distributes cola in cans labelled 355 mL. Measurement Canada randomly selected 24 cans, measured their contents, and obtained a sample mean of 348.69 mL and a sample standard deviation of 11.21 mL. Use a 0.01 significance level to test the claim that the company is cheating consumers.

10. The Medassist Pharmaceutical Company makes a pill intended for children susceptible to seizures. The pill is supposed to contain 20.0 mg of phenobarbital. A random sample of 20 pills yielded the amounts (in milligrams) listed here. Are these pills acceptable at the $\alpha = 0.01$ significance level?

27.5	26.0	22.9	23.4	23.0
23.9	32.6	20.9	22.9	24.3
24.8	16.1	24.3	17.3	18.9
20.7	33.0	15.6	24.3	23.3

11. Has the number of times the House sits in each session of federal Parliament grown more variable? The overall standard deviation of days the House sits per Parliament is 188.3. But in a sample of 9 Parliaments since World War II, the standard deviation of days the House sits per Parliament is 224.8 (based on data from *Duration of Sessions of Parliament*, Library of Parliament). Test, at the 0.05 level of significance, the claim that the standard deviation for the number of sittings per Parliament is no longer equal to 188.3.

Cumulative Review Exercises

1. For healthy women aged 18–24, systolic blood pressure readings (in millimetres of mercury) are normally distributed with a mean of 114.8 and a standard deviation of 13.1.

   a. If a healthy woman is randomly selected from the general population of all women aged 18–24, find the probability of getting one with systolic blood pressure greater than 124.23.

   b. If 16 women are randomly selected, find the probability that the mean of their systolic blood pressure readings is greater than 124.23.

2. A medical researcher obtains the systolic blood pressure readings (in millimetres of mercury) in the accompanying list for women aged 18–24 who have a new strain of viral infection. (As in Exercise 1, healthy women in that age group have readings that are normally distributed with a mean of 114.8 and a standard deviation of 13.1.)

   | 134.9 | 78.7 | 108.9 | 133.0 | 123.7 | 96.1 | 126.9 | 89.8 |
   | 132.0 | 134.7 | 132.1 | 121.7 | 112.3 | 150.2 | 158.3 | 154.4 |

   a. Find the sample mean $\bar{x}$ and standard deviation s.

   b. Use a 0.05 significance level to test the claim that the sample comes from a population with a mean equal to 114.8.

   c. Use the sample data to construct a 95% confidence interval for the population mean μ. Do the confidence interval limits contain the value of 114.8, which is the mean for healthy women aged 18–24?

   d. Use a 0.05 significance level to test the claim that the sample comes from a population with a standard deviation equal to 13.1, which is the standard deviation for healthy women aged 18–24.

   e. Based on the preceding results, does it seem that the new strain of viral infection affects systolic blood pressure?

3. A student majoring in psychology designs an experiment to test for extrasensory perception (ESP). In this experiment, a card is randomly selected from a shuffled deck, and the blindfolded subject must guess the suit (clubs, diamonds, hearts, spades) of the card selected. The experiment is repeated 25 times, with the card replaced and the deck reshuffled each time.

   a. For subjects who make random guesses with no ESP, find the expected mean number of correct responses.

   b. For subjects who make random guesses with no ESP, find the expected standard deviation for the numbers of correct responses.

   c. For subjects who make random guesses with no ESP, find the probability of getting more than 12 correct responses.

   d. If a subject gets more than 12 correct responses, test the claim that he or she made random guesses. Use a 0.05 level of significance.

   e. You want to conduct a survey to estimate the percentage of adult Canadians who believe that some people have ESP. How many people must you survey if you want 90% confidence that your sample percentage is in error by no more than four percentage points?

4. An important requirement in Sections 7-4 and 7-6 is that the sample data must come from a population that is normally distributed.

   a. Refer to the body temperatures of females listed in Data Set 18 of Appendix B and construct a stem-and-leaf plot.

b. Based on the result, does the distribution appear to be normal?
c. What other method could be used to determine whether the distribution is normal?

· ·

Technology Project

Refer to the body temperatures (in °C) summarized in the given stem-and-leaf plot. (The sample is a subset of the body temperatures listed in Table 7-1.) Use Excel or STATDISK and a 0.05 significance level for the following tests.

a. Test the claim that the sample comes from a population with a mean of 37.0°C.
b. Add 5 to each of the original temperatures listed in the stem-and-leaf plot, then test the claim that the sample comes from a population with a mean of 42.0. Compare the results to those found in part (a). In general, what changes when the same constant is added to every score?
c. After multiplying each of the original temperatures by 10, test the claim that the sample comes from a population with a mean of 370. Compare the results to those found in part (a). In general, what changes when every score is multiplied by the same constant?
d. Celsius temperatures can be converted to Fahrenheit temperatures by using $F = (9/5)C + 32$. That is, multiply each Celsius temperature by 9/5, then add 32. Because the conversion from the Celsius scale to the Fahrenheit scale involves adding the same constant (32) and multiplying by the same constant (9/5), can you predict what will happen when the original temperatures are converted and the claim of $\mu = 98.6°F$ is tested? (Note that 37.0°C = 98.6°F.) Verify or disprove your prediction by converting the original temperatures to the Fahrenheit scale and testing the claim that $\mu = 98.6°F$.
e. When testing the claim that the mean weight of men is now greater than the known mean from men who lived 100 years ago, does it make any difference if the weights are measured in pounds or kilograms?

```
35. | 02
35. | 688
36. | 011223
36. | 67
37. | 1
```

••••••••• FROM DATA TO DECISION •••••••••

Are Slices of the Venture Capital Pie Getting Smaller?

An increasingly popular way for risk capital companies to raise money is to attract venture capital investment. However, as the number of companies in Canada receiving these moneys has increased, has the mean amount of such funding available to a given recipient decreased? In the first quarter of 1997, the mean amount received was $2150. (All amounts are in thousands of dollars.) Given the sample data below for the first quarter of 1998 (based on data from "The Venture Capital Survey"

in the *Financial Post*, June 27–29, 1998), use a 0.05 significance level to test the claim that the amounts received by venture capital companies in the first quarter of 1998 were less than the mean amount received in the first quarter of 1997. Based on these results, should agents who arrange venture capital investments expect smaller commissions per transaction? Should companies who depend on this type of funding plan on receiving smaller amounts than they might have in previous years?

250	7000	4500	6000	1000	500	250	600	1500	2000	375	5000
3500	750	3000	250	175	500	250	500	2800	150	215	75
1000	150	420	1000	1000	2000	6000	2500	250	50	650	200

•••••••• COOPERATIVE GROUP ACTIVITIES ••••••••

1. *Out-of-class activity:* A group activity suggested for Chapter 6 involved estimating the mean error (in seconds) on people's wristwatches. Use the same data collected in that activity to test the claim that the mean error of all wristwatches is equal to 0. Recall that some errors are positive (because the watch reads earlier than the actual time) and some are negative (because the watch reads later than the actual time). Describe the details of the test and include a graph showing the test statistic and critical values. Do we collectively run on time, or are we early or late? Also test the claim that the standard deviation of errors is less than one minute. What are the practical implications of a standard deviation that is excessively large?

2. *In-class activity:* In a group of three or four people, conduct an ESP experiment by selecting one of the group members as the subject.

Draw a circle on one small piece of paper and draw a square on another sheet of the same size. Repeat this experiment 20 times: Randomly select the circle or the square and place it in the subject's hand behind his or her back so that it cannot be seen, then ask the subject to identify the shape (without looking at it); record whether the response is correct. Test the claim that the subject has ESP because the proportion of correct responses is greater than 0.5.

3. *In-class activity:* Divide into groups of 10 to 20 people. Each group member should record the number of heartbeats in one minute. After calculating $\bar{x}$ and s, each group should test the claim that the mean is greater than 59, which is the author's result. (When people exercise, they tend to have lower pulse rates, and the author runs five miles a few times each week. What a guy.)

INTERNET PROJECT

Hypothesis Testing

This chapter discussed the important method of inferential statistics known as hypothesis testing. This Internet Project will have you conduct tests using a variety of data sets. For each data set, you will be asked to

- Collect data available on the Internet.
- Formulate a hypothesis based on a given question.
- Conduct the test at a specified level of significance.
- Summarize your conclusions.

The Internet Project for this chapter can be found at this site:

http://www.pearsoned.ca/triola

Click on Internet Project, then on Chapter 7. There you will find instructions outlining tasks that use data from business and economics, education and sports, as well as a classic example from the physical sciences.

Inferences from Two Samples

8-1 Overview

Chapters 6 and 7 presented the two major activities of inferential statistics: estimating a population parameter and testing a hypothesis about a population. Whereas those chapters considered cases involving only a single population, this chapter deals with two populations. Methods for hypothesis testing and the construction of confidence intervals are described for cases involving two populations.

8-2 Inferences About Two Means: Dependent Samples (Matched Pairs)

Two dependent samples (consisting of paired data) are used to test hypotheses about the means of two populations. Methods are presented for constructing confidence intervals as estimates of the difference between two population means.

8-3 Inferences About Two Means: Independent and Large Samples

Independent and large ($n > 30$) samples are used to test hypotheses about the means of two populations. Methods are presented for the construction of confidence intervals used to estimate the difference between two population means.

8-4 Comparing Two Variances

A method is presented for testing hypotheses made about two population variances or standard deviations.

8-5 Inferences About Two Means: Independent and Small Samples

This section deals with cases in which two samples are independent and small ($n \leq 30$). Procedures for testing hypotheses about the difference between two population means are discussed. Also discussed are methods for constructing confidence intervals used to estimate the difference between two population means.

8-6 Inferences About Two Proportions

This section deals with methods of inferential statistics applied to two population proportions. Methods are presented for testing claims about the difference between two population proportions. Confidence intervals are constructed for estimating the difference between two population proportions.

CHAPTER PROBLEM:

Does El Niño really affect the weather, or is it just a lot of hype with little or no significance?

In Table 8-1 we list temperature and precipitation departures from springtime norms for the strongest El Niño years on record and compare these with data from other randomly selected springs. Temperature departures are in degrees Celsius and precipitation departures are expressed as percents. In Figure 8-1 we use boxplots to compare different stages of El Niño years to other years. The boxplots suggest that there may be some distinct differences, particularly for temperatures in the middle of an El Niño (that is, the second spring). But the number of samples is small (only 7 El Niño samples), so we might question whether these apparent differences are significant. In this section, we will consider the data from Table 8-1 as we test the equality of population means.

Table 8-1   Temperature and Precipitation Departures from Seasonal Means for Spring in the Strongest El Niño Years

Spring of El Niño Onset		Second Spring of El Niño		Spring of Other Years	
Departure in Temperature (in degrees Celsius)	Departure in Precipitation (as a percent)	Departure in Temperature (in degrees Celsius)	Departure in Precipitation (as a percent)	Departure in Temperature (in degrees Celsius)	Departure in Precipitation (as a percent)
0.5	−15.9	1.5	−11.1	0.6	−2.3
0.2	−6.8	0.0	−4.5	−0.4	−4.0
−1.2	2.9	0.9	2.0	0.0	28.8
−1.0	4.5	−0.5	10.6	0.0	−5.7
0.6	11.6	1.0	2.2	−0.3	−2.8
1.3	6.4	0.1	3.9	0.8	8.1
−0.4	1.6	3.1	−4.7	1.6	3.0
				1.1	−4.7
				−1.2	−21.3
				−0.3	10.9
				0.0	−7.1
				1.4	9.0
				−0.6	−15.1
				1.1	11.4
				1.0	−0.7
				1.9	26.0
				0.3	−4.5
				−1.8	6.7
				−1.6	−7.0
				2.0	7.1

Based on data from Environment Canada

Figure 8-1   Comparisons of El Niño and Non–El Niño Springs

Research in Twins

Identical twins occur when a single fertilized egg splits in two, so that both twins share the same genetic makeup. There is now an explosion in research focused on those twins. Speaking for the Centre for Study of Multiple Birth, Louis Keith notes that now "we have far more ability to analyze the data on twins using computers with new, built-in statistical packages." A common goal of such studies is to explore the classic issue of "nature versus nurture." For example, Thomas Bouchard, who runs the Minnesota Study of Twins Reared Apart, has found that IQ is 50%-60% inherited, while the remainder is the result of external forces.

Identical twins are matched pairs that provide better results by allowing us to reduce the genetic variation that is inevitable with unrelated pairs of people.

8-1 Overview

Chapter 6 introduced an important activity of inferential statistics: Samples were used to construct confidence intervals, which are used to estimate values of population parameters. Chapter 7 introduced a second important activity of inferential statistics: Samples were used to test hypotheses about population parameters. In both of those chapters all examples and exercises involved the use of *one* sample to form an inference about *one* population. In reality, however, there are many important and meaningful situations in which it becomes necessary to compare *two* sets of sample data. The following are examples typical of those found in this chapter, which presents methods for using data from two samples so that inferences can be made about the populations from which they came:

- Determine whether there is a difference between the mean amounts of nicotine from filtered cigarettes and nonfiltered cigarettes.
- Determine whether women employees exposed to ethyl glycol ethers have a rate of miscarriage that is different from the rate for women not exposed to those chemicals.

8-2 Inferences About Two Means: Dependent Samples (Matched Pairs)

In this section we consider methods for testing hypotheses and constructing confidence intervals for two samples that are dependent, which means that they are paired or matched. We begin by formally defining *independent* and *dependent*.

DEFINITION

Two samples are **independent** if the sample values selected from one population are not related to or somehow paired with the sample values selected from the other population. If the values in one sample are related to the values in the other sample, the samples are **dependent**. Such samples are often referred to as **matched pairs** or **paired samples**.

EXAMPLE   **Dependent samples:** Subjects' weights are measured before and after undergoing a regimen of training, with the results in the following table. The sample of pretraining weights and the sample of post-training weights are *dependent samples,* because each pair is matched according to the person involved. "Before/after" data are usually matched and are usually dependent.

Subject	A	B	C	D	E	F
Pretraining weights (kg)	99	62	74	59	70	73
Posttraining weights (kg)	94	62	66	58	70	76

Based on data from the *Journal of Applied Psychology,* Vol. 62, No. 1.

Independent samples: Weights are taken from two separate groups of subjects. These two samples are *independent* because the sample of females is not related to the sample of males. The data in this table are not matched.

Weights of females (lb)	115	107	110	128	130	
Weights of males (lb)	128	150	160	140	163	155	175

Assumptions

For the hypothesis tests and confidence intervals described in this section, we make the following assumptions:

1. The sample data consist of matched pairs.
2. The sample has been selected by a valid random-sampling technique.
3. If the number of pairs of sample data is small ($n \leq 30$), then the population of differences between the paired values must be approximately *normally distributed*. (If the population of differences departs radically from a normal distribution, we should not use the methods given in this section. We may be able to use nonparametric methods, discussed in Chapter 13.)

Prior to attempting formal inferences with the data, it is advisable to *explore* the data sets, as discussed in Chapter 2. For example, is a data pair an *outlier* that should be removed from further calculations? Have all values been rounded consistently? What are the means and distributions of the two samples?

Hypothesis Tests

In dealing with two dependent samples, we base our calculations on the differences (d) between the pairs of data, as illustrated in the table in the margin. (Comparing the two sample means $\bar{x}$ and $\bar{y}$ would waste important

x	10	8	5	20
y	7	2	9	20
d	3	6	-4	0

Notation for Two Dependent Samples
μ_d = mean value of the differences d for the *population* of paired data
$\bar{d}$ = mean value of the differences d for the paired *sample* data (equal to the mean of the $x - y$ values)
s_d = standard deviation of the differences d for the paired *sample* data
n = number of *pairs* of data in the sample

Crest and Dependent Samples

In the late 1950s, Procter & Gamble introduced Crest toothpaste as the first such product with fluoride. To test the effectiveness of Crest in reducing cavities, researchers conducted experiments with several sets of twins. One of the twins in each set was given Crest with fluoride, while the other twin continued to use ordinary toothpaste without fluoride. It was believed that each pair of twins would have similar eating, brushing, and genetic characteristics. Results showed that the twins who used Crest had significantly fewer cavities than those who did not. This use of twins as dependent samples allowed the researchers to control many of the different variables affecting cavities.

information about the paired data.) The notation on page 439 is based on those differences.

We now describe the test statistic to be used in hypothesis tests of claims made about the means of two populations, given that the two samples are dependent. If we have random paired sample (i.e., dependent) data from populations in which the paired differences have a normal distribution, we use the sample differences and proceed with a single test. We use the following test statistic with a Student t distribution.

Test Statistic for Two Dependent Samples (Matched Pairs)

$$t = \frac{\bar{d} - \mu_d}{\dfrac{s_d}{\sqrt{n}}}$$

where degrees of freedom $= n - 1$

If the number of pairs of data is large ($n > 30$), the number of degrees of freedom will be at least 30, so critical values will in effect be z scores (Table A-2) instead of t scores (Table A-3).

EXAMPLE Using a reaction timer similar to the one described in the Cooperative Group Activities of Chapter 5, subjects are tested for reaction times with their left and right hands. (Only right-handed subjects were used.) The results (in thousandths of a second) are given in the accompanying table, and the distribution of the paired differences is approximately normal. Use a 0.05 significance level to test the claim that there is a difference between the mean of the right- and left-hand reaction times. If an engineer is designing a fighter-jet cockpit and must locate the ejection-seat activator to be accessible to either the right or the left hand, does it make a difference which hand she chooses?

Subject	A	B	C	D	E	F	G	H	I	J	K	L	M	N
Right	191	97	116	165	116	129	171	155	112	102	188	158	121	133
Left	224	171	191	207	196	165	177	165	140	188	155	219	177	174
Difference	−33	−74	−75	−42	−80	−36	−6	−10	−28	−86	33	−61	−56	−41

SOLUTION Using the traditional method of hypothesis testing, we will test the claim that there is a difference between the right- and left-hand reaction times. Because we are dealing with paired data, begin by finding the differences $d = $ right $-$ left. Then follow the steps summarized in Figure 7-4.

Step 1:   If there is a difference, we expect the mean of the d values to be different from 0. This is expressed in symbolic form as $\mu_d \neq 0$.

Step 2:   If the original claim is not true, we have $\mu_d = 0$.

Step 3:   The null hypothesis must contain equality, so we have

$$H_0: \mu_d = 0 \qquad H_1: \mu_d \neq 0 \text{ (original claim)}$$

Step 4:   The significance level is $\alpha = 0.05$.

Step 5:   Because we are testing a claim about the means of paired dependent data, we use the Student t distribution.

Step 6:   Before finding the value of the test statistic, we must first find the values of $\overline{d}$ and s_d. The difference d for each subject is shown in the preceding table.

We now use Formulas 2-1 and 2-6 as follows:

$$\overline{d} = \frac{\Sigma d}{n} = \frac{-595}{14} = -42.5$$

$$s_d = \sqrt{\frac{n(\Sigma d^2) - (\Sigma d)^2}{n(n-1)}} = \sqrt{\frac{14(39,593) - (-595)^2}{14(14-1)}} = 33.2$$

With these statistics and the assumption that $\mu_d = 0$, we can now find the value of the test statistic:

$$t = \frac{\overline{d} - \mu_d}{\frac{s_d}{\sqrt{n}}} = \frac{-42.5 - 0}{\frac{33.2}{\sqrt{14}}} = -4.790$$

The critical values of $t = -2.160$ and $t = 2.160$ are found from Table A-3; use the column for 0.05 (two tails), and use the row with degrees of freedom of $n - 1 = 13$. Figure 8-2 shows the test statistic, critical values, and critical region.

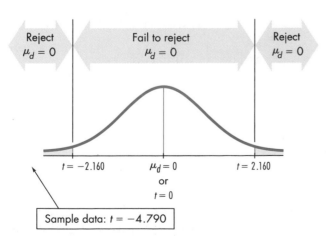

Figure 8-2   Distribution of Differences Between Right- and Left-Hand Reaction Times

Step 7:   Because the test statistic does fall in the critical region, we reject the null hypothesis of $\mu_d = 0$.

Interpretation There is sufficient evidence to support the claim of a difference between the right- and left-hand reaction times. Because there does appear to be such a difference, an engineer designing a fighter-jet cockpit should locate the ejection-seat activator so that it is readily accessible to the faster hand, which appears to be the right hand with seemingly lower reaction times. (We could require special training for left-handed pilots if a similar test of left-handed pilots shows that their dominant hand is faster.)

The preceding example is a two-tailed test, but left-tailed tests and right-tailed tests follow the same basic procedure. For example, if we want to test the claim that the right-hand reaction times are lower than the left-hand times, we have a claim that $\mu_d < 0$ (because the values of "right–left" would tend to be negative).

The preceding two-tailed example used the traditional method, but the P-value approach could be used by modifying Steps 6 and 7. In Step 6, use the test statistic of $t = -4.790$ and refer to the 13th row of Table A-3 to find that 4.790 is beyond the largest table value of 3.012. The P-value in the two-tailed test is therefore less than 2(0.005) or 0.01; that is, P-value < 0.01. In Step 7, we again reject the null hypothesis because the P-value is less than the significance level of $\alpha = 0.05$.

Confidence Intervals

We can develop a confidence interval estimate of the population mean difference μ_d by using the sample mean $\overline{d}$, the standard deviation of sample means $\overline{d}$ (which is $s_d/\sqrt{n}$), and the critical value $t_{\alpha/2}$.

Confidence Intervals

The confidence interval estimate of the mean difference μ_d is as follows:

$$\overline{d} - E < \mu_d < \overline{d} + E$$

where $E = t_{\alpha/2} \dfrac{s_d}{\sqrt{n}}$ and degrees of freedom = $n - 1$

EXAMPLE   Use the sample data from the preceding example to construct a 95% confidence interval estimate of μ_d.

SOLUTION   Using the values of $\overline{d} = -42.5$, $s_d = 33.2$, $n = 14$, and $t_{\alpha/2} = 2.160$, we first find the value of the margin of error E:

$$E = t_{\alpha/2} \frac{s_d}{\sqrt{n}} = 2.160 \frac{33.2}{\sqrt{14}} = 19.2$$

The confidence interval can now be found:

$$\bar{d} - E < \mu_d < \bar{d} + E$$
$$-42.5 - 19.2 < \mu_d < -42.5 + 19.2$$
$$-61.7 < \mu_d < -23.3$$

The result is sometimes expressed as $\mu_d = -42.5 \pm 19.2$ or as $(-61.7, -23.3)$.

Interpretation In the long run, 95% of such samples will lead to confidence interval limits that actually do contain the true population mean of the differences. Note that the confidence interval limits do not contain 0, indicating that the true value of μ_d is significantly different from 0. That is, the mean value of the "right − left" differences is different from 0. On the basis of the confidence interval, we conclude that there is sufficient evidence to support the claim that there is a difference between the right- and left-hand reaction times. This conclusion agrees with the conclusion in the preceding example.

Using Technology

Excel: From the **Tools** menu, select **Data Analysis.** Choose **t-Test: Paired Two Sample for Means**. Enter these details in the dialog box that appears: For **Variable 1 Range,** specify the worksheet range that contains the first variable's data; for **Variable 2 Range,** specify the worksheet range that contains the second variable's data (the data in these two ranges should be arranged in corresponding order). Also enter the appropriate choice for **Alpha.** Then select an **Output Option,** and click on **OK** to obtain the results. Note that both the one-tailed and the two-tailed solutions are provided. (Only positive t values are output, but they may be interpreted as negative where appropriate.)

Although Excel cannot calculate confidence intervals directly for paired samples, the Data Desk XL add-in can be

Excel Display   Two Dependent Samples

	A	B	C
1	t-Test: Paired Two Sample for Means		
2			
3		Variable 1	Variable 2
4	Mean	139.57143	182.07143
5	Variance	984.41758	567.45604
6	Observations	14	14
7	Pearson Correlation	0.3020121	
8	Hypothesized Mean Difference	0	
9	df	13	
10	t Stat	-4.793725	
11	P(T<=t) one-tail	0.0001754	
12	t Critical one-tail	1.7709317	
13	P(T<=t) two-tail	0.0003508	
14	t Critical two-tail	2.1603682	

used. Click on **DDXL**. Select **Confidence Intervals** and **Paired *t* Interval**. In the dialog box, click on the pencil icon for the first quantitative column and enter the range for the first sample's data. Then click on the pencil icon for the second quantitative column and enter the range for the second sample's data. Click on **OK**. Follow the steps in the next dialog box that appears.

STATDISK: Select **Analysis**, then **Hypothesis Testing**, then **Mean-Two Dependent Samples**. The result will be the display shown here. (STATDISK automatically provides confidence interval limits for two-tailed hypothesis tests.)

We used Table A-3 to conclude that the *P*-value is less than 0.01, but from the Excel and STATDISK displays we can see that the *P*-value is actually 0.0004.

STATDISK **Display**   Two Dependent Samples

8-2 **Exercises A: Basic Skills and Concepts**

In Exercises 1 and 2, assume that you want to test the claim that the paired sample data come from a population for which the mean difference is $\mu_d = 0$. Assuming a 0.05 level of significance, find (a) $\bar{d}$ (b) s_d, (c) the t test statistic, and (d) the critical values.

1.

x	8	8	6	9	7
y	3	2	6	4	9

2.

x	20	25	27	27	23	29	30	26
y	20	24	25	29	20	29	32	29

3. Using the sample paired data in Exercise 1, construct a 95% confidence interval for the population mean of all differences $x - y$.

4. Using the sample paired data in Exercise 2, construct a 99% confidence interval for the population mean of all differences $x - y$.

5. Do strong El Niño phenomena change the weather as much as people claim?

   a. Using the data in the following table (aggregate temperature departures from spring norms in degrees Celsius), test the claim that the progression of a strong El Niño, from the spring of onset to the next spring, affects Canadian temperature departures from seasonal norms. Use a 0.05 level of significance.

   b. Construct a 95% confidence interval for the mean difference of the "onset" minus "second spring" departures from norms. Write a statement that interprets the resulting confidence interval.

El Niño Cycle	A	B	C	D	E	F	G
Spring of El Niño Onset	0.5	0.2	–1.2	–1	0.6	1.3	–0.4
Second Spring of El Niño	1.5	0.0	0.9	–0.5	1.0	0.1	3.1

Based on data from Environment Canada.

6. Captopril is a drug designed to lower systolic blood pressure. When subjects were tested with this drug, their systolic blood pressure readings (in millimetres of mercury) were measured before and after the drug was taken, with the results given in the accompanying table.

   a. Use the sample data to construct a 99% confidence interval for the mean difference between the before and after readings.

   b. Is there sufficent evidence to support the claim that Captopril is effective in lowering systolic blood pressure?

Subject	A	B	C	D	E	F	G	H	I	J	K	L
Before	200	174	198	170	179	182	193	209	185	155	169	210
After	191	170	177	167	159	151	176	183	159	145	146	177

Based on data from "Essential Hypertension: Effect of an Oral Inhibitor of Angiotensin-Converting Enzyme" by MacGregor et al., *British Medical Journal*, Vol. 2.

7. Does past growth in a company translate to continued growth in the future? In 1988, *Profit* magazine identified the 50 fastest-growing companies in Canada. In 1998, it revisited these companies. Of the companies for which relevant data were available, 10 have been randomly selected. Compare their sales in 1987 and 1997 (in $1,000,000s).

   a. At the 0.05 significance level, test the claim that fast-growing companies do grow in sales after 10 years. Does the fact that some companies in the 1987 survey went out of business or would not report their sales for 1997 affect the validity of the sample? (Consider the issues raised in Section 1-3.)

   b. Construct a 95% confidence interval for the mean of the difference between 1987 sales and 1997 sales.

Company	A	B	C	D	E	F	G	H	I	J
1987 Sales	1.0	1.0	3.1	2.7	4.2	7.8	7.6	2.0	7.0	6.0
1997 Sales	5.0	2.5	1.7	4.5	19.0	17.0	17.0	1.2	64.0	8.0

Based on data from *Profit*, Vol. 17, No. 3.

8. According to a report in *The Globe and Mail*, the Canadian oil and gas industry "ramped up" investment spending in the period from 2000 to 2001 ("Energy Sector Ramps Up Spending," *The Globe and Mail*, January 29, 2001, p. B14). The accompanying table shows the spending levels (in millions of dollars) in each of those years for nine top oil and gas companies.

    a. Using a 0.01 level of significance, is there sufficient evidence to support the claim that spending is greater in 2001 than in 2000?

    b. Construct a 98% confidence interval for the mean of the differences. Do the confidence interval limits contain 0, indicating that there is not a significant difference between the two years' spending levels?

Company	A	B	C	D	E	F	G	H	I
2000 spending	1685	1153	1190	1415	1125	1203	954	957	1998
2001 spending	1940	1800	1710	1500	1500	1410	1320	1200	935

9. A study was conducted to examine differences in starting salaries for university graduates in Ontario and Quebec. Because starting salaries are in different ranges based on type of degree, the Ontario and Quebec results are paired with respect to degree earned in the following table.

    a. At the 0.05 significance level, test the claim that starting salaries in Ontario and Quebec are equal. What do you conclude about the effect of province on the starting salary for graduates?

    b. Construct a 95% confidence interval for the mean of the differences between Ontario and Quebec starting salaries for various types of degrees earned.

Degree	Ontario	Quebec
B.A. or B.Sc.	$28,900	$28,300
B. Comm.	$29,500	$28,500
M.A. or M.Sc.	$34,600	$31,900
M.B.A.	$36,600	$34,100
Chem. Eng.	$32,900	$34,400
Civil Eng.	$33,700	$36,300
Elec. Eng.	$34,000	$32,300
Mech. Eng.	$33,700	$34,300
Structural Eng.	$33,500	$35,100

Based on "Annual Salary Survey," Peat Marwick Stevenson & Kellogg.

10. In May 1997, Calgary-based Bre-X Minerals collapsed when its gold assets were revealed to be dramatically less than had been claimed. Did this collapse affect the prices of other mining stocks?
   a. Using the price data below, construct a 98% confidence interval for the mean difference of their pre-crash prices minus their prices three months later.

Stock	A	B	C	D	E
Before the crash	1.4	1.2	1.15	0.280	2.73
After the crash	0.7	0.5	0.41	0.225	2.06

   b. At the 0.01 level of significance, does the evidence support a claim that the prices of mining stocks dropped during the period?

11. People who use Internet browsers to find helpful Web sites often get hundreds or thousands of references in reply, many of them irrelevant. Does it solve the problem simply to add more words to the search string (that is, to the text being searched for)? An experiment was conducted using 8 randomly selected two-word strings as inputs into the Yahoo Canada Web browser. Then, a randomly selected third word was added to each two-word string, resulting in a three-word search string. The number of results that Yahoo Canada returned was noted in each case (in thousands).
   a. Using a 0.05 significance level, test whether adding the third word had any effect on the number of search results returned.
   b. Construct a 95% confidence interval for the mean of the "two-word search string" minus "three-word search string" differences.

Trial	Two-Word Search String	Three-Word Search String
A	3.6	3.6
B	1071.6	794.0
C	387.8	695.9
D	88.5	72.5
E	71.6	66.3
F	1.4	1.9
G	236.1	166.1
H	208.4	315.5

12. If a t- test were run on Excel at the 0.01 confidence level, using the data in Exercise 10, the following output would be produced.

	A	B	C
1	t-Test: Paired Two Sample for Means		
2			
3		Variable 1	Variable 2
4	Mean	1.352	0.779
5	Variance	0.77857	0.54203
6	Observations	5	5
7	Pearson Correlation	0.951423	
8	Hypothesized Mean Difference	0	
9	df	4	
10	t Stat	4.4084749	
11	P(T<=t) one-tail	0.0058072	
12	t Critical one-tail	3.7469363	
13	P(T<=t) two-tail	0.0116144	
14	t Critical two-tail	4.6040805	

Could a person who ran this test validly reject a null hypothesis that there is no difference in means? Is this the same answer as is reached in Exercise 10(b)? If not, explain how these answers could be different.

13. Refer to Data Set 2 in Appendix B. Use the paired data consisting of the body temperatures of "initially standing" subjects in the standing posture (column STAND1) and after lying down (column SUPINE2).
   a. Construct a 95% confidence interval for the mean difference of the STAND1 temperatures minus the SUPINE2 temperatures.
   b. Using a 0.05 significance level, test the claim that for those temperatures the mean difference is 0. Based on the result, do the body temperatures in the two postures appear to be about the same?

14. A company offers a daily list of stock picks to paid subscribers. Its "Track Record for TSE" Web page shows the prices of stocks it has recommended (1) on the day the "buy" recommendation was made, and (2) on a subsequent day within the next week or two. The accompanying table is a sample from this data, for November to December 2000. (Based on data from the Web site www.active-trading-global.com.)
   a. At the 0.05 significance level, do the data support the company's claim that, for stocks bought and sold at the prices cited, their prices show an increase during the period?
   b. Suppose the company recommends good stock buys, but leaves it up to the client to decide *when actually to sell* the stocks. Is the displayed data sufficient to support a claim that the actual clients of this company made money? Explain.

Stock Pick No.	1	2	3	4	5	6	7	8	9	10	11	12
Entry price	4.87	22.85	14.05	13.80	22.70	10.00	25.45	18.90	20.90	4.50	31.30	14.00
Exit price	5.35	23.65	14.25	14.80	25.25	9.65	26.70	20.50	25.25	9.15	41.25	14.40

8-2 Exercises B: Beyond the Basics

15. Re-examine the data presented in Exercise 7. Is there any data value that may possibly be an outlier? How would the results be affected if that value were excluded from the analysis? In general, can an outlier have a dramatic effect on the hypothesis test and confidence interval?

16. Exercise 13 used temperatures given in degrees Celsius. Suppose we express all of the temperatures in their equivalent Fahrenheit value. Is the hypothesis test affected by such a change in units? Is the confidence interval affected by such a change in units? How?

17. The 95% confidence interval for a collection of paired sample data is $0.0 < \mu_d < 1.2$. Based on this confidence interval, the traditional method of hypothesis testing leads to the conclusion that the claim of $\mu_d > 0$ is supported. What is the smallest possible value of the significance level of the hypothesis test?

8-3 Inferences About Two Means: Independent and Large Samples

Section 8-2 described methods of using inferential statistics for dependent (paired) data. In this section our two samples are *independent*, that is, the sample selected from one population is not related to the sample selected from the other population. This section is also restricted to large ($n > 30$) samples. For the hypothesis tests and confidence intervals described in this section, we make the following assumptions.

Assumptions

1. The two samples are *independent*.
2. The two sample sizes are large. That is, $n_1 > 30$ and $n_2 > 30$.
3. Both samples have been selected by valid random-sampling techniques.

Exploring the Data Sets

Before we jump into a formal hypothesis test or construction of a confidence interval, it is often enlightening to *explore* the two samples, using the techniques described in Chapter 2. For example, Figure 8-3 shows the value of box-plots for comparing the axial loads of a sample of cans 0.0109 in. thick and another sample of cans 0.0111 in. thick. (An axial load of a can is the maximum weight supported by its sides, (based on Data Set 15 in Appendix B.)

The axial load of 504 lb (for the cans that are 0.0111 in. thick) stands out as a possible outlier, and indeed it is very far away from all of the other values. If that outlier is deleted, the long right tail (or "whisker") on the bottom boxplot is shortened to the value identified as 317. A comparison of the two boxplots shows that the spread of the data is about the same, but the values for the 0.0111 in. cans appear to be farther to the right, suggesting that those cans have larger axial loads and are stronger. We can now use a hypothesis test to determine whether that apparent difference is significant.

Figure 8-3 Boxplots of Axial Loads (in Pounds) of Cans 0.0109 in. Thick and 0.0111 in. Thick

Hypothesis Tests

In testing a claim about the difference $\mu_1 - \mu_2$, we use the following test statistic.

Test Statistic for Two Means: Independent and Large Samples
$$z = \frac{(\bar{x}_1 - \bar{x}_2) - (\mu_1 - \mu_2)}{\sqrt{\dfrac{\sigma_1^2}{n_1} + \dfrac{\sigma_2^2}{n_2}}}$$

Except for the form of this test statistic, the method of hypothesis testing is essentially the same as that described in Chapter 7. (Later in this section, we will discuss the rationale for the form of the given test statistic.) As in Chapter 7, if the values of σ_1 and σ_2 are not known, we can use s_1 and s_2 in their places, provided that both samples are large. If σ_1 and σ_2 are known, we use those values in calculating the test statistic, but realistic cases will usually require the use of s_1 and s_2.

Axial Loads (lb) of 0.0109 in. Cans

$n_1 = 175$
$\bar{x}_1 = 267.1$
$s_1 = 22.1$

Axial Loads (lb) of 0.0111 in. Cans

$n_2 = 175$
$\bar{x}_2 = 281.8$
$s_2 = 27.8$

● **EXAMPLE**   Use a 0.01 significance level to test the claim that cans 0.0109 in. thick have a lower mean axial load than cans that are 0.0111 in. thick. The original data are listed in Data Set 15 of Appendix B, and the summary statistics are listed in the margin.

SOLUTION

Step 1:   The claim can be expressed symbolically as $\mu_1 < \mu_2$.

Step 2:   If the original claim is false, then $\mu_1 \geq \mu_2$.

Step 3:   The null hypothesis must contain equality, so we have

$$H_0: \mu_1 \geq \mu_2 \qquad H_1: \mu_1 < \mu_2 \text{ (original claim)}$$

We now proceed with the assumption that $\mu_1 = \mu_2$, or $\mu_1 - \mu_2 = 0$.

Step 4: The significance level is $\alpha = 0.01$.

Step 5: Because we have two independent and large samples and we are testing a claim about the two population means, we use a normal distribution with the test statistic given earlier in this section.

Step 6: The values of σ_1 and σ_2 are unknown, but the samples are both large, so we can use the sample standard deviations as estimates of the population standard deviations, and the test statistic is calculated as follows:

$$z = \frac{(\bar{x}_1 - \bar{x}_2) - (\mu_1 - \mu_2)}{\sqrt{\dfrac{\sigma_1^2}{n_1} + \dfrac{\sigma_2^2}{n_2}}} = \frac{(267.1 - 281.8) - 0}{\sqrt{\dfrac{22.1^2}{175} + \dfrac{27.8^2}{175}}} = -5.48$$

Because we are using a normal distribution, the critical value of $z = -2.33$ is found from Table A-2. (With $\alpha = 0.01$ in the left tail, find the z score corresponding to an area of $0.5 - 0.01$, or 0.4900.) The test statistic, critical value, and critical region are shown in Figure 8-4.

Step 7: Because the test statistic does fall within the critical region, reject the null hypothesis $\mu_1 \geq \mu_2$.

Interpretation There is sufficient evidence to support the claim that the 0.0109 in. cans have a mean axial load that is lower than the mean for the 0.0111 in. cans. We might have expected the thinner cans to be weaker, but we now know that the difference is statistically significant. The *practical* significance of that difference is another issue not addressed by this hypothesis test, and to assess practical significance would require additional information—for example, about the *actual* loads typically applied to such cans, and whether these are at all close to the cans' *maximum* loads.

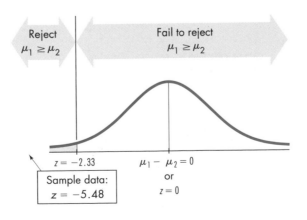

Figure 8-4 Distribution of Differences Between Means of Axial Loads for 0.0109 in. Cans and 0.0111 in. Cans

Drug Screening: False Positives

Some Canadian companies have implemented employee drug-testing programs. For a job applicant undergoing drug screening, a *false positive* is an indication of drug use when he or she does not use drugs. A *false negative* is an indication of no drug use when he or she is a user. The *test sensitivity* is the probability of a positive indication for a drug user; the *test specificity* is the probability of a negative indication for a nonuser. Suppose that 3% of job applicants use drugs, and a test has a sensitivity of 0.99 and a specificity of 0.98. The high probabilities make the test seem reliable, but 40% of the positive indications will be false positives.

P-Values

Determination of *P*-values is easy here because the test statistics are *z* scores from the standard normal distribution. Simply follow the method outlined in Figures 7-7 and 7-8. For the preceding left-tailed hypothesis test, the *P*-value is the area to the left of the test statistic $z = -5.48$. Referring to Table A-2, we find that the area to the left of $z = -5.48$ is 0.0001. (Because the *z* score is beyond 3.09, we use an area of 0.4999 as indicated in the footnote to Table A-2.) Because the *P*-value of 0.0001 is less than the significance level of $\alpha = 0.01$, we again reject the null hypothesis and conclude that the 0.0109 in. cans have a mean that is lower than the mean for the 0.0111 in. cans.

Confidence Intervals

We can construct confidence interval estimates of the difference between two population means, which we denote as $\mu_1 - \mu_2$.

Confidence Intervals

The confidence interval estimate of the difference $\mu_1 - \mu_2$ is as follows:

$$(\bar{x}_1 - \bar{x}_2) - E < (\mu_1 - \mu_2) < (\bar{x}_1 - \bar{x}_2) + E$$

where

$$E = z_{\alpha/2}\sqrt{\frac{\sigma_1^2}{n_1} + \frac{\sigma_2^2}{n_2}}$$

As with hypothesis testing, if $\sigma_1 - \sigma_2$ are not known, use $s_1 - s_2$ in their places, provided that both samples are large.

EXAMPLE   Using the sample data given in the preceding example, construct a 99% confidence interval estimate of the difference between the means of the axial loads of the 0.0109 in. cans and the 0.0111 in. cans.

SOLUTION   We first find the value of the margin of error *E*:

$$E = z_{\alpha/2}\sqrt{\frac{\sigma_1^2}{n_1} + \frac{\sigma_2^2}{n_2}} = 2.575\sqrt{\frac{22.1^2}{175} + \frac{27.8^2}{175}} = 6.9$$

We now find the desired confidence interval as follows:

$$(\bar{x}_1 - \bar{x}_2) - E < (\mu_1 - \mu_2) < (\bar{x}_1 - \bar{x}_2) + E$$
$$(267.1 - 281.8) - 6.9 < (\mu_1 - \mu_2) < (267.1 - 281.8) + 6.9$$
$$-21.6 < (\mu_1 - \mu_2) < -7.8$$

Interpretation We are 99% confident that the limits of -21.6 and -7.8 actually do contain the difference between the two population means. This result could be more clearly presented by stating that μ_2 exceeds μ_1 by an amount that is between 7.8 lb and 21.6 lb. Because those limits do not contain 0, it is very unlikely that the two population means are equal.

Rationale: Why Do the Test Statistic and Confidence Interval Have the Particular Forms Presented?

Both forms are based on a normal distribution of $\bar{x}_1 - \bar{x}_2$ values with mean $\mu_1 - \mu_2$ and standard deviation $\sqrt{\sigma_1^2/n_1 + \sigma_2^2/n_2}$. This follows from the central limit theorem introduced in Section 5-5. The central limit theorem tells us that sample means $\bar{x}$ are normally distributed with mean μ and standard deviation $\sigma/\sqrt{n}$. Also, when samples have a size of 31 or larger, the normal distribution serves as a reasonable approximation to the distribution of sample means. By similar reasoning, the values of $\bar{x}_1 - \bar{x}_2$ also tend to approach a normal distribution with mean $\mu_1 - \mu_2$. When both samples are large, the following property of variances leads us to conclude that the values of $\bar{x}_1 - \bar{x}_2$ will have a standard deviation of

$$\sqrt{\frac{\sigma_1^2}{n_1} + \frac{\sigma_2^2}{n_2}}$$

The variance of the *differences* between two independent random variables equals the variance of the first random variable *plus* the variance of the second random variable.

That is, the variance of sample values $\bar{x}_1 - \bar{x}_2$ will tend to equal

$$\sigma_{\bar{x}_1}^2 + \sigma_{\bar{x}_2}^2$$

provided that $\bar{x}_1$ and $\bar{x}_2$ are independent. (See Exercise 21.) For large random samples, the standard deviation of sample means is $\sigma/\sqrt{n}$, so the variance of sample means is σ^2/n. If we combine the additive property of variances with the central limit theorem's expression for variance of sample means, we get the following:

$$\sigma_{\bar{x}_1 - \bar{x}_2}^2 = \sigma_{\bar{x}_1}^2 + \sigma_{\bar{x}_2}^2 = \frac{\sigma_1^2}{n_1} + \frac{\sigma_2^2}{n_2}$$

Taking the square root, we see that the standard deviation of the differences $\bar{x}_1 - \bar{x}_2$ can be expressed as

$$\sqrt{\frac{\sigma_1^2}{n_1} + \frac{\sigma_2^2}{n_2}}$$

The Placebo Effect

It has been a common belief that when patients are given a placebo (a treatment with no medicinal value), about one-third of them show some improvement. However, a more recent study of 6000 patients showed that for those with mild medical problems, the placebos seemed to result in improvement in about two-thirds of the cases. The placebo effect seems to be strongest when patients are very anxious and they like their physicians. Because it could cloud studies of new treatments, the placebo effect is minimized by using a *double-blind* experiment in which neither the patient nor the physician knows whether the treatment is a placebo or a real medicine.

Because z is a standard score that corresponds in general to

$$z = \frac{(\text{sample statistic}) - (\text{population mean})}{(\text{standard deviation of sample statistics})}$$

we get

$$z = \frac{(\bar{x}_1 - \bar{x}_2) - (\mu_1 - \mu_2)}{\sqrt{\dfrac{\sigma_1^2}{n_1} + \dfrac{\sigma_2^2}{n_2}}}$$

by noting that the sample values of $\bar{x}_1 - \bar{x}_2$ will have a mean of $\mu_1 - \mu_2$ and the standard deviation previously given.

Using Technology

Excel: From the **Tools** menu, select **Data Analysis**. Choose **z-Test: Two Sample for Means**. Enter these details in the dialog box that appears: For Variable 1 Range, specify the worksheet range that contains the first variable's data; for Variable 2 Range, specify the worksheet range that contains the second variable's data. Also enter the appropriate choice for Alpha (in this example, 0.01). Enter the Variances for the two variables (which you must calculate separately, for example by using the **= VAR**() function) Now select an **Output Option**, and click on **OK** to obtain the results.

Excel Display   Hypothesis Test

	A	B	C
1	z-Test: Two Sample for Means		
2			
3		Variable 1	Variable 2
4	Mean	267.11429	281.80571
5	Known Variance	488.9524	771.4333
6	Observations	175	175
7	Hypothesized Mean Difference	0	
8	z	-5.474334	
9	P(Z<=z) one-tail	2.201E-08	
10	z Critical one-tail	2.3263419	
11	P(Z<=z) two-tail	4.402E-08	
12	z Critical two-tail	2.5758345	

Note that both the one-tailed and the two-tailed solutions are provided, although you should determine in advance which version will apply. As in a printed *z* table, only positive critical *z* values are output, but they may be interpreted as negative where appropriate.

Although Excel cannot calculate a confidence interval directly for the data, the Data Desk XL add-in can be used. Click on **DDXL**. Select **Confidence Intervals** and **2 Var t Interval**. In the dialog box, click on the pencil icon for the first quantitative column and enter the range for the first sample's data. Then click on the pencil icon for the second quantitative column and enter the range for the second sample's data. Click on **OK**. Follow the steps in the next dialog box that appears. (In Step 1, select **2 Sample**.)

STATDISK: Select **Analysis**, then **Hypothesis Testing**, then **Mean-Two Independent Samples**. Confidence interval limits are included with hypothesis test results.

Capture–Recapture

Ecologists need to determine population sizes of endangered species. One method is to capture a sample of some species, mark all members of this sample, and then free them. Later, another sample is captured, and the ratio of marked subjects, coupled with the size of the first sample, can be used to estimate the population size. This capture–recapture method was used with other methods to estimate the blue whale population, and the result was alarming: The population was as small as 1000. That led the International Whaling Commission to ban the killing of blue whales to prevent their extinction.

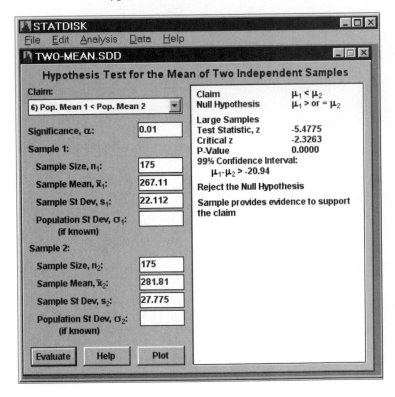

STATDISK **Display**   Hypothesis Test and Confidence Interval

8-3 Exercises A: Basic Skills and Concepts

In Exercises 1 and 2, use a 0.05 significance level to test the claim that the two samples come from populations with the same mean. In each case, the two samples are independent and have been randomly selected.

1.

Control Group	Experimental Group
$n_1 = 50$	$n_2 = 100$
$\bar{x}_1 = 75$	$\bar{x}_2 = 73$
$s_1 = 15$	$s_2 = 14$

2.

Math Majors	English Majors
$n_1 = 60$	$n_2 = 75$
$\bar{x}_1 = 8.75$	$\bar{x}_2 = 9.66$
$s_1 = 2.05$	$s_2 = 2.88$

3. Using the sample data given in Exercise 1, construct a 95% confidence interval estimate of the difference between the two population means. Do the confidence interval limits contain 0? What do you conclude about the difference between the control group and experimental group?

4. Using the sample data given in Exercise 2, construct a 95% confidence interval estimate of the difference between the two population means. Do the confidence interval limits contain 0? What do you conclude about the difference between the math majors and the english majors?

Canadian Equity Funds

$n_1 = 33$

$\bar{x}_1 = 8.386$

$s_1 = 7.126$

Canadian Balanced Equity Funds

$n_2 = 33$

$\bar{x}_2 = 9.233$

$s_2 = 7.454$

5. For comparison purposes, mutual funds are often grouped into various categories. Do Canadian equity funds and Canadian balanced equity funds differ with respect to percentage of foreign holdings within the funds?
   a. Using the data shown, and a 0.01 level of significance, test the claim that there is no difference in foreign content between these fund groups.
   b. Construct a 99% confidence interval for $\mu_1 - \mu_2$, where μ_1 is the mean foreign content (in percent) in Canadian equity funds. (Based on data from *Mutual Funds Update*, published by the Bank of Montreal, March 31, 1998.)

New Brunswick	Nova Scotia
$n_1 = 31$	$n_2 = 38$
$\bar{x}_1 = 37.054$	$\bar{x}_2 = 60.973$
$s_1 = 49.046$	$s_2 = 76.602$

6. Provincial governments across Canada have been re-examining their delivery of services, such as health care. A researcher compared the number of beds in long-term care centres in New Brunswick and in Nova Scotia. Her sample results are summarized in the margin, based on data in *Guide to Canadian Healthcare Facilities 1998-1999*, Vol. 6 (Canadian Healthcare Association, Ottawa). Testing at the 0.05 significance level, is there sufficient evidence to support a claim that the mean number of beds per centre is greater in Nova Scotia than in New Brunswick? Do the results support a claim that there are more long-term care beds per person in Nova Scotia than in New Brunswick? Why or why not?

7. The Medassist Pharmaceutical Company wants to test Dozenol, a new cold medicine intended for night use. Tests for such products often include a "treatment group" of people who use the drug and a "control group" of people who don't use the drug. Fifty people with colds are given Dozenol, and 100 others are not. The systolic blood pressure is measured for each subject, and the sample statistics are as given in the margin. The head of research at Medassist claims that Dozenol does not affect blood pressure—that is, the treatment population mean μ_1 and the control population mean μ_2 are equal.

a. Test that claim using a significance level of 0.01. Based on the result, would you recommend advertising that Dozenol does not affect blood pressure?

b. Construct a 99% confidence interval for $\mu_1 - \mu_2$, where μ_1 and μ_2 represent the mean for the treatment group and the control group, respectively.

Treatment Group	Control Group
$n_1 = 50$	$n_2 = 100$
$\bar{x}_1 = 203.4$	$\bar{x}_2 = 189.4$
$s_1 = 39.4$	$s_2 = 39.0$

8. A group of college students randomly selected 217 student cars and found that they had ages with a mean of 7.89 years and a standard deviation of 3.67 years. They also randomly selected 152 faculty cars and found that they had ages with a mean of 5.99 years and a standard deviation of 3.65 years.

a. Use a 0.05 significance level to test the claim that student cars are older than faculty cars.

b. Construct a 95% confidence interval for the mean $\mu_1 - \mu_2$, where μ_1 is the mean age of student cars.

9. In April 1996, *The Globe and Mail* listed the salaries of the hundreds of University of Toronto staff who earn at least $100,000 annually. On studying this article, several disgruntled staff (whose last names begin with S, V, and Q) concluded that top staff whose names begin with S to Z earn less than their counterparts.

Names A to R	Names S to Z
$n_1 = 40$	$n_2 = 40$
$\bar{x}_1 = 118.980$	$\bar{x}_2 = 117.580$
$s_1 = 27.050$	$s_2 = 15.796$

a. Based on the sample data shown, construct appropriate null and alternate hypotheses, and test the employees' claim, at the 0.05 significance level. Mean salaries are in $1000s.

b. Construct a 95% confidence interval for $\mu_1 - \mu_2$, where μ_1 is the mean salary of the reported staff with last names starting with the letters A to R. Do the confidence interval limits contain 0? Does this indicate that there is or is not a significant difference between the two means?

10. A fish-processing company is concerned about the shelf life of its new cat food. A sample examined in Halifax ($n = 35$) had an acceptable mean shelf life of 13 months, with a standard deviation of 1.44 months. But a second sample, examined in Dartmouth ($n = 40$), had a mean shelf life of only 11 months, with a standard deviation of 1.52 months. The manager in Dartmouth claims that there is no significant difference between these two means.

a. Test her claim at the 0.05 level of significance. Based on the result, should the operation in Dartmouth be subjected to a special review?

b. Construct a 95% confidence interval for the difference between the population means $(\mu_1 - \mu_2)$, where μ_1 is the mean shelf life of cat food in Halifax and μ_2 is the mean shelf life of cat food in Dartmouth. Do the confidence interval limits contain 0? Does this suggest that there is not a significant difference between the two population means?

11. Data Set 9 in Appendix B contains measured levels of serum cotinine (in ng/mL) for two samples of nonsmokers—nonsmokers with no environmental tobacco smoke exposure at home or at work, and nonsmokers who *are* exposed to environmental tobacco smoke at home or at work.

a. Testing at the 0.02 level of significance, do the data support a claim that nonsmokers with exposure to environmental tobacco smoke have higher levels of serum cotinine than nonsmokers without such exposure?

b. Construct a 96% confidence interval for $\mu_1 - \mu_2$, where μ_1 is the mean for exposed nonsmokers and μ_2 is the mean for nonexposed nonsmokers. Do the confidence interval limits contain 0? Assuming that raised levels of serum cotinine are undesirable, do the results suggest that exposure to environmental tobacco smoke poses a possible health hazard?

12. Data Set 11 in Appendix B contains weights of 100 randomly selected M&M plain candies. Those weights have a mean of 0.9147 g and a standard deviation of 0.0369 g. A previous edition of this book used a different sample of 100 M&M plain candies, with a mean and standard deviation of 0.9160 g and 0.0433 g, respectively. Is the discrepancy between the two sample means significant?

13. Two samples are used to compare building permit values for larger communities versus smaller ones in the regional municipality of Durham, in Ontario. For both samples n is 38. Expressed in thousands of dollars, the mean value per building permit for the larger communities is 102.008, with a standard deviation of 25.546. The mean value per permit for smaller communities is 113.637, with a standard deviation of 70.670. At the 0.05 significance level, test the claim that the population of smaller communities has a higher mean value for the building permits issued (based on data in the *Durham Business News*, June 1998).

14. As an aid to farmers, the Alberta government records freezing dates for over a hundred locations around the province. Based on average last-frost dates for spring, a researcher has proposed dividing the province into early last-frost locations and late last-frost locations. Refer to Data Set 17 of Appendix B. Use the day-of-the-year columns to test, at the 0.01 significance level, the claim that the late last-frost locations have a different mean date for last spring frost than the early last-frost locations.
   a. Conduct the hypothesis test using the traditional method.
   b. Conduct the hypothesis test using the *P*-value method.
   c. Conduct the hypothesis test by constructing a 99% confidence interval for the difference $\mu_1 - \mu_2$.
   d. Compare the results from parts (a), (b), and (c).

15. Refer to the pulse rates in Data Set 8 from Appendix B. First identify and delete the two outliers that are unrealistic pulse rates for living and reasonably healthy statistics students.
   a. Use a 0.05 level of significance and the traditional method of testing hypotheses to test the claim that male and female statistics students have the same mean pulse rate.
   b. Use the *P*-value method to test the claim given in part (a).
   c. Construct a 95% confidence interval for the difference $\mu_1 - \mu_2$, where μ_1 and μ_2 are the mean pulse rates for male and female statistics students, respectively.
   d. Compare the results from parts (a), (b), and (c).

16. When testing for a difference between the means of a treatment group and a group given a placebo, the accompanying Excel display is obtained. Using a 0.05 significance level, is there sufficient evidence to support the claim that the treatment group (Variable 1) comes from a population with a mean that is less than the mean for the placebo population? Explain.

	A	B	C
1	z-Test: Two Sample for Means		
2			
3		Variable 1	Variable 2
4	Mean	152.0739	154.9669
5	Known variance	438.4388	239.1461
6	Observations	50	50
7	Hypothesized mean difference	0	
8	z	-0.7858	
9	P(Z<=z) one-tail	0.215991	
10	z Critical one-tail	1.644853	
11	P(Z<=z) two-tail	0.431982	
12	z Critical two-tail	1.959961	

Excel Display

17. When testing for a difference between the means of a treatment group and a group given a placebo, the accompanying Excel display is obtained. Using a 0.02 significance level, is there sufficient evidence to support the claim that the treatment group (Variable 1) comes from a population with a mean that is different from the mean for the placebo population? Explain.

	A	B	C
1	z-Test: Two Sample for Means		
2			
3		Variable 1	Variable 2
4	Mean	75.34798	73.81763
5	Known variance	1.55383	11.65292
6	Observations	50	50
7	Hypothesized mean difference	0	
8	z	2.199422	
9	P(Z<=z) one-tail	0.013924	
10	z Critical one-tail	1.644853	
11	P(Z<=z) two-tail	0.027848	
12	z Critical two-tail	1.959961	

Excel Display

8-3 Exercises B: Beyond the Basics

18. Refer to Exercise 5. If the actual difference between the population means is 1.5, find β, the probability of a type II error. (See Exercise 27 in Section 7-3.) *Hint:* In Step 1, replace $\bar{x}$ by $(\bar{x}_1 - \bar{x}_2)$, replace $\mu_{\bar{x}}$ by 0, and replace $\sigma_{\bar{x}}$ by

$$\sqrt{\frac{\sigma_1^2}{n_1} + \frac{\sigma_2^2}{n_2}}$$

19. The examples in this section used the axial loads of a sample of cans 0.0109 in. thick and a second sample of cans 0.0111 in. thick. (The original data are listed in Data Set 15 of Appendix B.) We noted that the second sample includes an outlier of 504 lb. How are the boxplots of Figure 8-3, the hypothesis test, and the confidence interval affected if we decide that the outlier is actually an error that should be deleted?

20. The examples in this section used the axial loads of cans, where the loads were given in pounds. How are the boxplots, hypothesis test, and confidence interval affected if the loads are all converted to kilograms?

21. a. Find the variance for this *population* of x scores: 5, 10, 15. (See Section 2-5 for the variance σ^2 of a population.)

    b. Find the variance for this *population* of y scores: 1, 2, 3.

    c. List the *population* of all possible differences $x - y$, and find the variance of this population.

    d. Use the results from parts (a), (b), and (c) to verify that $\sigma^2_{x-y} = \sigma^2_x + \sigma^2_y$. (This principle is used to derive the test statistic and confidence interval for this section.)

    e. How is the *range* of the differences $x - y$ related to the range of the x values and the range of the y values?

8-4   Comparing Two Variances

Because the characteristic of variation among data is extremely important, this section presents a method for using two samples to compare the variances of the populations from which the samples are drawn. The method we use requires the following assumptions.

Assumptions

1. The two populations are *independent* of each other. (Recall from Section 8-2 that two samples are independent if the sample selected from one population is not related to the sample selected from the other population.)

2. The two populations are each *normally distributed*. (This assumption is important, because the test statistic is extremely sensitive to departures from normality.)

Exploring the Data Sets

As in previous sections of this chapter, it is important to explore the data sets before undertaking formal hypothesis tests or constructing confidence intervals. In this section, because the requirement of a normal distribution is quite strict, procedures such as the construction of *normal probability plots* to test for normality (see Section 5-7) become especially important, as does the identification and removal of outliers.

Hypothesis Tests

The computations of this section will be greatly simplified if we stipulate that s_1^2 represents the *larger* of the two sample variances. It doesn't really make any difference which sample is designated as sample 1, so we use the following notation.

Notation for Hypothesis Tests with Two Variances (or Standard Deviations)

$s_1^2 = $ *larger* of the two sample variances

$n_1 = $ size of the sample with the *larger* variance

$\sigma_1^2 = $ variance of the population from which the sample with the *larger* variance was drawn

The symbols s_2^2, n_2, and σ_2^2 are used for the other sample and population.

For two normally distributed populations with equal variances (that is, $\sigma_1^2 = \sigma_2^2$), the sampling distribution of the following test statistic is the **F distribution** shown in Figure 8-5 with critical values listed in Table A-5. If you continue to repeat an experiment of randomly selecting samples from two normally distributed populations with equal variances, the distribution of the ratio s_1^2/s_2^2 of the sample variances is the F distribution. In Figure 8-5, note these properties of the F distribution:

- The F distribution is not symmetric.
- Values of the F distribution cannot be negative.
- The exact shape of the F distribution depends on two different degrees of freedom.

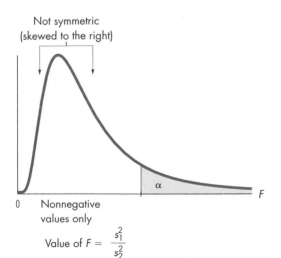

Not symmetric
(skewed to the right)

0   Nonnegative
values only

Value of $F = \dfrac{s_1^2}{s_2^2}$

Figure 8-5   F Distribution
There is a different F distribution for each different pair of degrees of freedom for numerator and denominator.

Commercials

Television networks have their own clearance departments for screening commercials and verifying claims. The Council of Better Business Bureaus also investigates advertising claims. In the past, Firestone had to drop a claim that its tires resulted in 25% faster stops, and Warner Lambert had to spend $10 million informing customers that Listerine doesn't prevent or cure colds. Many deceptive ads are voluntarily dropped, and many others escape scrutiny simply because the regulatory mechanisms can't keep up with the flood of commercials.

Test Statistic for Hypothesis Tests with Two Variances

$$F = \frac{s_1^2}{s_2^2}$$

If the two populations really do have equal variances, then $F = s_1^2/s_2^2$ tends to be close to 1 because s_1^2 and s_2^2 tend to be close in value. But if the two populations have radically different variances, s_1^2 and s_2^2 tend to be very different numbers. Denoting the larger of the sample variances by s_1^2, we see that the ratio s_1^2/s_2^2 will be a large number whenever s_1^2 and s_2^2 are far apart in value. Consequently, a value of F near 1 will be evidence in favour of the conclusion that $\sigma_1^2 = \sigma_2^2$, but a large value of F will be evidence against the conclusion of equality of the population variances.

This test statistic applies to a claim made about two variances, but we can also use it for claims about two population standard deviations. Any claim about two population standard deviations can be restated in terms of the corresponding variances.

Critical Values

Using Table A-5, we obtain critical F values that are determined by the following three values:

1. **The significance level α.** (Table A-5 has six pages of critical values for $\alpha = 0.01$, 0.025, and 0.05.)
2. **Numerator degrees of freedom $= n_1 - 1$**
3. **Denominator degrees of freedom $= n_2 - 1$**

To find a critical value, first refer to the part of Table A-5 corresponding to α (for a one-tailed test) or $\alpha/2$ (for a two-tailed test), then intersect the column representing the degrees of freedom for s_1^2 with the row representing the degrees of freedom for s_2^2. Because we are stipulating that the larger sample variance is s_1^2, all one-tailed tests will be right-tailed and all two-tailed tests will require that we find only the critical value located to the right. Good news: We have no need to find a critical value separating a left-tailed critical region. (If you would like to try anyway, see Exercise 15.)

We often have numbers of degrees of freedom that are not included in Table A-5. We could use linear interpolation to approximate the missing values, but in most cases that's not necessary because the F test statistic is either less than the lowest possible critical value or greater than the largest possible critical value. For example, Table A-5 shows that given $\alpha = 0.025$ in the right tail, 20 degrees of freedom for the numerator, and 34 degrees of freedom for the denominator, the critical F value is between 2.0677 and 2.1952. Any F test statistic below 2.0677 will result in failure to reject the null hypothesis, any F test statistic above 2.1952 will result in rejection of the null hypothesis, and interpolation is necessary only if the F test statistic falls between 2.0677 and 2.1952. (See Exercise 13 in this section.) The use of a statistical software package such as Excel or STAT-DISK eliminates this problem by providing critical values or P-values.

EXAMPLE In the preceding section we used a sample of 175 aluminum cans that are 0.0109 in. thick and a second sample of 175 aluminum cans that are 0.0111 in. thick. Data Set 15 lists the axial loads of the cans in those samples, and the summary statistics are listed in the margin. Use a 0.05 significance level to test the claim that the samples come from populations with the same variance.

Axial Loads (lb) of 0.0109 in. Cans	Axial Loads (lb) of 0.0111 in. Cans
$n = 175$	$n = 175$
$\bar{x} = 267.1$	$\bar{x} = 281.8$
$s = 22.1$	$s = 27.8$

SOLUTION Because we stipulate in this section that the larger variance is denoted by s_1^2, we reverse the subscript notation used in the preceding section, and we let $s_1^2 = 27.8^2$, $n_1 = 175$, $s_2^2 = 22.1^2$, and $n_2 = 175$. We now proceed to use the traditional method of testing hypotheses as outlined in Figure 7-4:

Step 1: The claim of equal population variances is expressed symbolically as $\sigma_1^2 = \sigma_2^2$.

Step 2: If the original claim is false, then $\sigma_1^2 \neq \sigma_2^2$.

Step 3: Because the null hypothesis must contain equality, we have

$$H_0: \sigma_1^2 = \sigma_2^2 \text{ (original claim)} \qquad H_1: \sigma_1^2 \neq \sigma_2^2$$

Step 4: The significance level is $\alpha = 0.05$.

Step 5: Because this test involves two population variances, we use the F distribution.

Step 6: The test statistic is

$$F = \frac{s_1^2}{s_2^2} = \frac{27.8^2}{22.1^2} = 1.5824$$

For the critical values, first note that this is a two-tailed test with 0.025 in each tail. As long as we are stipulating that the larger variance is placed in the numerator of the F test statistic, we need to find only the right-tailed critical value. From Table A-5 we get a critical value of $F = 1.4327$, which corresponds to 0.025 in the right tail, with 174 degrees of freedom for the numerator and 174 degrees of freedom for the denominator. (Actually, the table does not include 174 degrees of freedom, so we chose the closest value of 120 degrees of freedom. If the difference in sample variances is significant based on sample sizes of 121, that difference would certainly be significant with sample sizes of 175.)

Step 7: Figure 8-6 shows that the test statistic $F = 1.5824$ falls within the critical region, so we reject the null hypothesis.

Interpretation There is sufficient evidence to warrant rejection of the claim that the two variances are equal. However, we should recognize that the F test is extremely sensitive to distributions that are not normally distributed—and the distributions of axial loads are by no means perfectly normal. Therefore, the apparent result of this test (that the variances are not equal) cannot be accepted as definitive.

Lower Variation, Higher Quality

Ford and Mazda were producing similar transmissions that were supposed to be made with the same specifications. But the American-made transmissions required more warranty repairs than the Japanese-made transmissions. When investigators inspected samples of the Japanese transmission gearboxes, they first thought that their measuring instruments were defective because they weren't detecting any variability among the Mazda transmission gearboxes. They realized that although the American transmissions were within the specifications, the Mazda transmissions were not only within the specifications, but consistently close to the desired value. By reducing variability among transmission gearboxes, Mazda reduced the costs of inspection, scrap, rework, and warranty repair.

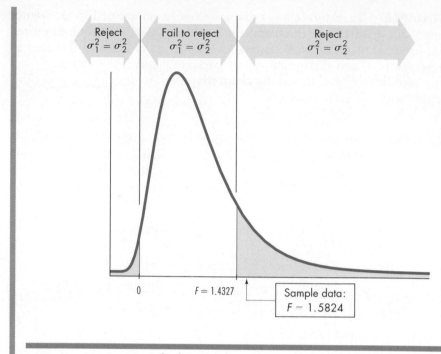

Figure 8-6   Distribution of s_1^2/s_2^2 for Axial Loads of 0.0111 in. Cans and 0.0109 in. Cans

In the preceding example we used a two-tailed test for the claim of equal variances. A right-tailed test of the claim that the 0.0111 in. cans have a larger variance would yield the same test statistic of $F = 1.5824$, but a different critical value of $F = 1.3519$ (found from Table A-5 with $\alpha = 0.05$). We would have sufficient evidence to support the claim of a larger variance.

We have described the traditional method of testing hypotheses made about two population variances. Exercise 14 deals with the P-value approach, and Exercise 16 deals with the construction of confidence intervals.

Using Technology

Excel: From the **Tools** menu, select **Data Analysis**. Choose **F-Test Two-Sample for Variances**. Enter these details in the dialog box that appears: For Variable 1 Range, specify the worksheet range that contains the data for the variable with the larger variance; for Variable 2 Range, specify the worksheet range that contains the other variable's data. Also enter the appropriate choice for the right-tail Alpha (in this example, 0.025). For a two-tailed hypothesis test, enter $\alpha/2$ at this point. Then select an **Output Option**, and click on **OK** to obtain the results. The Data Analysis tool returns the critical F value for the right tail.

Excel formulas can be also used for constructing confidence intervals for the *F* ratio, based on the calculations described in Exercise 16 of this section.

The following figure is Excel's solution to the solved example for this section. There are minor differences from the text version because (1) in the text-based solution, 174 degrees of freedom had to be approximated by 120 degrees of freedom in the tables, and (2) the text has rounded off the *s* terms in the intermediate calculations. Excel, on the other hand, can work from the full data set. Below the example output from the Data Analysis tool are sample formulas for finding the left-tail critical *F* and the confidence interval.

STATDISK: Select Analysis from the main menu, then select **Hypothesis Testing**, then **St. Dev.-Two Samples**.

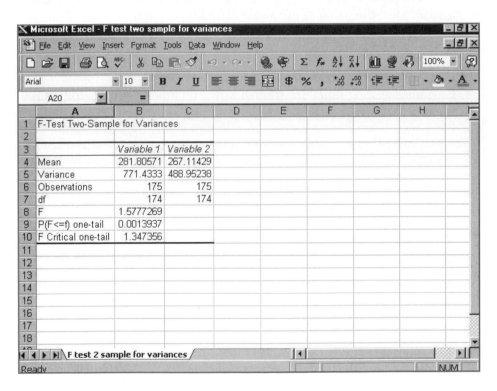

Excel Display   Comparing Two Variances

Cell	Formula	Result	Explanation
B12	=FINV(1-0.025,B7,C7)	0.742193862	Critical *F*, left tail, for two-tail test
B13	=B5/C5*(1/B10)	1.170979939	Lower bound of confidence interval
B14	=B5/C5*(1/B12)	2.125761115	Upper bound of confidence interval

Use appropriate cell addresses for data. Formula in B12 assumes α = 0.05.

8-4 Exercises A: Basic Skills and Concepts

In Exercises 1 and 2, test the given claim. Use a significance level of $\alpha = 0.05$, and assume that all populations are normally distributed. Use the traditional method of testing hypotheses outlined in Figure 7-4, and draw the appropriate graphs.

1. Claim: Populations A and B have different variances ($\sigma_1^2 \neq \sigma_2^2$).
   Sample A: $n = 25, \bar{x} = 175, s^2 = 900$
   Sample B: $n = 31, \bar{x} = 200, s^2 = 2000$

2. Claim: Population A has a larger variance than population B.
   Sample A: $n = 50, \bar{x} = 77.4, s = 18.1$
   Sample B: $n = 15, \bar{x} = 75.7, s = 7.0$

Nonstress	Stress
$n_1 = 40$	$n_2 = 40$
$\bar{x}_1 = 53.3$	$\bar{x}_2 = 45.3$
$s_1 = 11.6$	$s_2 = 13.2$

3. An experiment was conducted to investigate the effect of stress on the recall ability of police eyewitnesses. The experiment involved a nonstressful interrogation of a cooperative suspect and a stressful interrogation of an uncooperative and belligerent suspect. The numbers of details recalled a week after the incident are summarized in the margin (based on data from "Eyewitness Memory of Police Trainees for Realistic Role Plays," by Yuille et al., *Journal of Applied Psychology*, Vol. 79, No. 6). Use a 0.10 level of significance to test the claim that the samples come from populations with different standard deviations.

4. Customer waiting times are studied at the Humber Valley Credit Union. When 25 randomly selected customers enter any one of several waiting lines, their times have a mean of 6.896 min and a standard deviation of 3.619 min. When 20 randomly selected customers enter a single main waiting line that feeds the individual teller stations, their waiting times have a mean of 7.460 min and a standard deviation of 1.841 min. Use a 0.01 significance level to test the claim that waiting times for the single line have a lower standard deviation.

5. A study was done of 137 young adult males who had been treated for substance abuse. The study compared their yearly rates of traffic accidents before treatment and after treatment. For the pre-treatment group, the mean accident rate was 0.123, with a standard deviation of 0.167. For the post-treatment group, the mean accident rate was 0.068, with a standard deviation of 0.223 (based on data from "Does Treatment for Substance Abuse Improve Driving Safety? A Preliminary Evaluation," by Mann et al., Addiction Research Foundation). At the 0.05 significance level, test the claim that the standard deviation for the post-treatment group is greater than that for the pre-treatment group.

6. Canadian equity funds and Canadian balanced equity funds can be compared for their percentages of foreign holdings. At the 0.05 significance level, test the claim that both types of funds have the same variance.

Canadian Equity Funds	Canadian Balanced Equity Funds
$n_1 = 33$	$n_2 = 33$
$\bar{x}_1 = 8.386$	$\bar{x}_2 = 9.233$
$s_1 = 7.126$	$s_2 = 7.454$

Based on data from *Mutual Funds Update*, published by the Bank of Montreal, March 31, 1998.

7. A fish-processing company is concerned about the shelf life of its new cat food. A sample examined in Halifax ($n = 35$) had an acceptable mean shelf life of 13 months, with a standard deviation of 1.44 months. But a second sample, examined in Dartmouth ($n = 40$), had a mean shelf life of only 11 months, with a standard deviation of 1.52 months. At the 0.05 level of significance, test the claim that shelf lives at both plants have the same standard deviation.

8. An investor is comparing the variability of estimates by stock analysts, when they analyze the earnings potentials of U.S. and Canadian firms. For a sample of estimates (by different analysts) of the earning potentials of Canadian firms, the standard deviation is 0.0204, whereas the standard deviation for a sample of earnings estimates for U.S. firms is 0.0076 (based on data from "The Seasonal Impact of Institutional Investors (The January Effect)", Vol. 11, *Canadian Investment Review*, 09-01-1998, pp. 28-31). Suppose that n (the number of analysts making the projections) is 12 for each sample. At the 0.02 significance level, test the claim that the variability in analysts' earnings forecasts is different for firms in the two countries. If you base your investment decisions on earnings forecasts, would it be wiser to listen to a forecaster of Canadian or of U.S. firms? Explain.

9. Because of wind patterns, Air Canada flights between Vancouver and San Francisco can take different times in each direction. Sample times for flights between these cities, from March 8 to March 18, 1997, are shown. Test the claim that both sets of times come from populations with the same variance. Use a 0.05 level of significance.

Vancouver to San Francisco	San Francisco to Vancouver
2.30 2.20 1.97 2.22 2.12	1.80 1.68 2.03 1.83
1.95 2.03 2.30 2.15 2.33	1.77 1.98 1.85
2.15	

Based on data from Gary Murphy, chief flight dispatcher, Air Canada.

10. Provincial governments across Canada have had to reexamine their delivery of services, such as health care, to avoid expensive duplication, and yet provide fair access to their citizens. The following table is based on one random sample of hospitals in New Brunswick and another in Nova Scotia, and shows the total number of beds in each hospital (*Guide to Canadian Healthcare Facilities*, 1998–99, Vol. 6, Canadian Healthcare Association, Ottawa). At the 0.05 significance level, test the claim that the two given samples come from populations with the same variance. If the variances are different, could this have implications for the equity of services around each province? Explain why it would be useful to know the population served by each hospital in order fully to answer the preceding question.

New Brunswick		Nova Scotia	
23	47	15	13
153	47	27	136
397	15	8	26
12	500	85	311
15	56	12	132
398			

11. Sample data were collected to compare the ages of CEOs of top growth companies in western Canada and Quebec. Because of small sample sizes, techniques introduced later in this chapter would be needed to compare group means. One such method assumes equal variances for the two groups. At the 0.05 significance level, test the claim that these two sample groups come from populations with the same variance.

Western Canada	38 54 35 40 41 34 59 37 35 48 35 59
Quebec	50 31 38 49 34 36 35 33 39 38

Based on data from *Profit,* May 29, 1996.

12. Refer to Data Set 11 in Appendix B and use a 0.10 level of significance to test the claim that red and yellow M&M plain candies have weights with different standard deviations. If you were responsible for controlling production so that red and yellow M&Ms have weights with the same amount of variation, would you take corrective action?

8–4 Exercises B: Beyond the Basics

13. A hypothesis test of the claim $\sigma_1^2 = \sigma_2^2$ is being conducted with a 0.05 level of significance. What do you conclude in each of the following cases?
    a. Test statistic is $F = 2.0933$; $n_1 = 50$; $n_2 = 35$
    b. Test statistic is $F = 1.8025$; $n_1 = 50$; $n_2 = 35$
    c. Test statistic is $F = 2.3935$; $n_1 = 40$; $n_2 = 20$
14. To test a claim about two population variances by using the P-value approach, first find the F test statistic, then refer to Table A-5 to determine how it compares to the critical values listed for $\alpha = 0.01$, $\alpha = 0.025$, and $\alpha = 0.05$. For example, if the F test statistic (for a one-tailed test) is greater than the table value for $\alpha = 0.05$ but *not* greater than the value for $\alpha = 0.025$, then $0.025 < p < 0.05$. That is, p is between 0.025 and 0.05. Also recall that for two-tailed tests, the significance level in the actual problem is halved for purposes of using the F distribution tables. Therefore, in these cases, if the test statistic exceeds the critical value for F on a table, the p indicated is *2 times* the α shown at the top of that table. For example, an F just above the critical F on the $\alpha = 0.025$ table represents (for a two-tailed test) $p < 0.05$. Referring to Exercises 4 and 13(a), what can be concluded about the P-values?

15. For hypothesis tests in this section that were two-tailed, we found only the upper critical value. (Recall that for two-tailed tests, the significance level that you look up in the F distribution tables is in fact $\alpha/2$.) Let's denote that value by F_R, where the subscript suggests the critical value for the right tail. The lower critical value F_L (for the left tail) can be found as follows: First interchange the degrees of freedom, and then take the reciprocal of the resulting F value found in Table A-5. (F_R is often denoted by $F_{\alpha/2}$, and F_L is often denoted by $F_{1-\alpha/2}$.) Find the critical values F_L and F_R for two-tailed hypothesis tests based on the following values.

   a. $n_1 = 10$, $n_2 = 10$, $\alpha = 0.05$ b. $n_1 = 10$, $n_2 = 7$, $\alpha = 0.05$
   c. $n_1 = 7$, $n_2 = 10$, $\alpha = 0.05$ d. $n_1 = 25$, $n_2 = 10$, $\alpha = 0.02$
   e. $n_1 = 10$, $n_2 = 25$, $\alpha = 0.02$

16. In addition to testing claims involving σ_1^2 and σ_2^2, we can also construct interval estimates of the ratio σ_1^2/σ_2^2 using the following expression:

$$\left(\frac{s_1^2}{s_2^2} \cdot \frac{1}{F_R}\right) < \frac{\sigma_1^2}{\sigma_2^2} < \left(\frac{s_1^2}{s_2^2} \cdot \frac{1}{F_L}\right)$$

   Here F_L and F_R are as described in Exercise 15. Construct the 95% confidence interval estimates for the ratios between group variances for the data in (a) Exercise 9 and (b) Exercise 11.

17. Sample data consist of temperatures recorded for two different groups of items that were produced by two different production techniques. A quality control specialist plans to analyse the results. She begins by testing for equality of the two population standard deviations.
   a. If she adds the same constant to every temperature from both groups, how is the value of the test statistic F affected?
   b. If she multiplies every score from both groups by the same constant, how is the value of the test statistic F affected?
   c. If she converts all temperatures from the Celsius scale to the Fahrenheit scale, how is the value of the test statistic F affected?

8–5 Inferences About Two Means: Independent and Small Samples

In this section we present methods of inferential statistics for situations involving the means of two independent populations, when (unlike Section 8-3) at least one of the two samples is small (with $n \leq 30$). We describe methods for testing hypotheses and constructing confidence intervals for situations in which the following assumptions apply.

Assumptions

1. The two samples are *independent*.
2. The two samples are *randomly selected from normally distributed* populations.
3. At least one of the two samples is small ($n \leq 30$).

When these conditions are satisfied, we use one of three different procedures corresponding to the following cases:

Case 1: The values of both population variances are known. (In reality, this case rarely occurs.)

Case 2: The two populations appear to have equal variances. (That is, $\sigma_1^2 = \sigma_2^2$.)

Case 3: The two populations appear to have unequal variances. (That is, $\sigma_1^2 \neq \sigma_2^2$.)

Case 1: Both Population Variances Are Known

In reality, Case 1 doesn't occur very often. Usually, the population variances are computed from the known population data, and if we could find σ_1^2 and σ_2^2, we should be able to find the values of μ_1 and μ_2, so there would be no need to test claims or construct confidence intervals. If some strange set of circumstances allows us to know the values of σ_1^2 and σ_2^2 but not μ_1 and μ_2, then we can use the same methods as described in Section 8-3 for large samples. Because this case of known population variances is so unlikely to occur, we will not pursue it here.

Choosing Between Cases 2 and 3: How Do We Decide That Two Populations Have Equal or Unequal Variances?

If the three assumptions listed at the beginning of this section are satisfied, inferences about the two population means are made with the procedures we will describe in Cases 2 and 3. Case 2 applies when the two populations have equal variances, and Case 3 applies when the two populations have *different* variances. But how do we determine whether the two population variances are equal?

In Section 8-4 we described a procedure for testing the claim that two populations have equal variances, and this approach, which we will now call the *preliminary F test approach*, is preferred by some statisticians. Not all statisticians agree: Some argue that if we apply the F test with a certain significance level and then do a t test at the same level, the overall result will not be at the same level of significance. The F statistic also is much more sensitive to departures from normal distributions than is the t statistic—so there are samples for which the t test is appropriate, but the F test is not appropriate for the preliminary analysis. (For one argument against the preliminary F test, see "Homogeneity of Variance in the Two-Sample Means Test," by Moser and Stevens, *The American Statistician*, Vol. 46, No. 1.) Different textbooks address this difficulty in different ways. In this text, we provide some *tools* that different strategies can utilize, and your instructor may recommend a specific approach. Here are two options:

1. *Preliminary F test approach*:

   Use the *F* test described in Section 8-4 to test the null hypothesis that $\sigma_1^2 = \sigma_2^2$. Use the conclusion of that test as follows:

   - *Fail to reject* $\sigma_1^2 = \sigma_2^2$: Treat the populations as if they have equal variances (Case 2).
   - *Reject* $\sigma_1^2 = \sigma_2^2$: Treat the populations as if they have unequal variances (Case 3).

2. *Assume unequal variances*: Assume that the two populations have *unequal* variances $\sigma_1^2 \neq \sigma_2^2$ and use the methods of Case 3. (Remember, this assumption applies only to cases in which we have two independent samples, at least one of which is small, and the population variances are not known.)

You might also consider making inferences using *both* methods (for equal variances and for unequal variances). If the two sets of results agree, your conclusion is probably OK.

Case 2: The Two Populations Appear to Have Equal Variances

If we are working on the assumption of equal variances, we calculate a **pooled estimate of σ^2** that is common to both populations; that pooled estimate is denoted by s_p^2 and is a weighted average of s_1^2 and s_2^2, as shown in the box. (Excel is one of many systems using the "pooled" option of this case.) Hypotheses about μ_1 and μ_2 can be tested and confidence interval estimates of $\mu_1 - \mu_2$ can be constructed by using the following methods.

EXAMPLE   Refer to the data listed in Table 8-1 in the Chapter Problem. Use a 0.05 significance level to test the claim that, for the initial and for the subsequent spring seasons of strong El Niño events, the mean departures in temperatures from seasonal norms were equal. (Temperature departures are in degrees Celsius.)

Test Statistic (Small Independent Samples and Equal Variances)

$$t = \frac{(\bar{x}_1 - \bar{x}_2) - (\mu_1 - \mu_2)}{\sqrt{\dfrac{s_p^2}{n_1} + \dfrac{s_p^2}{n_2}}}$$

where $s_p^2 = \dfrac{(n_1 - 1)s_1^2 + (n_2 - 1)s_2^2}{(n_1 - 1) + (n_2 - 1)}$

and the degree of freedom is given by df $= n_1 + n_2 - 2$

> **Confidence Interval (Small Independent Samples and Equal Variances)**
>
> $$(\bar{x}_1 - \bar{x}_2) - E < (\mu_1 - \mu_2) < (\bar{x}_1 - \bar{x}_2) + E$$
>
> where
> $$E = t_{\alpha/2}\sqrt{\frac{s_p^2}{n_1} + \frac{s_p^2}{n_2}}$$
>
> and s_p^2 is as given in the test statistic

Temperature Departures (°C)

Second Spring	Spring of Onset
$n_1 = 7$	$n_2 = 7$
$\bar{x}_1 = 0.88$	$\bar{x}_2 = 0$
$s_1 = 1.20$	$s_2 = 0.91$

SOLUTION   In Figure 8-1 we used boxplots to compare weather deviations at different stages of El Niño events. The boxplots representing temperature deviations seem to suggest an increase in temperature deviations from the norm in the second spring of an El Niño compared to the initial spring, but let's use a formal hypothesis of the claim that the two mean amounts are equal. We will use the sample statistics listed in the margin.

The samples are independent (because they are separate and are not matched), the sample sizes are small, and we don't know the values of σ_1 and σ_2, so we are dealing with either Case 2 or Case 3. If we use a preliminary F test (described in Section 8-4) to choose between Case 2 and Case 3, we test $H_0: \sigma_1^2 = \sigma_2^2$ with the test statistic

$$F = \frac{s_1^2}{s_2^2} = \frac{1.20^2}{0.91^2} = 1.7389$$

With $\alpha = 0.05$ in a two-tailed F test and with 6 degrees of freedom for both the numerator and denominator, we use Table A-5 to find the critical F value of 5.8198. Because the computed test statistic of $F = 1.7389$ does *not* fall within the critical region, we fail to reject the null hypothesis of equal variances and proceed by using the approach outlined in Case 2.

In using the Case 2 approach, we test the claim that $\mu_1 = \mu_2$ with the following null and alternative hypotheses:

$$H_0: \mu_1 = \mu_2 \ (\text{or } \mu_1 - \mu_2 = 0) \qquad H_1: \mu_1 \neq \mu_2$$

The test statistic for this case of equal variances requires the value of the pooled variance s_p^2, so we find that value first:

$$s_p^2 = \frac{(n_1 - 1)s_1^2 + (n_2 - 1)s_2^2}{(n_1 - 1) + (n_2 - 1)} = \frac{(7 - 1) \cdot 1.20^2 + (7 - 1) \cdot 0.91^2}{(7 - 1) + (7 - 1)}$$

$$= 1.134$$

We can now find the value of the test statistic:

$$t = \frac{(\bar{x}_1 - \bar{x}_2) - (\mu_1 - \mu_2)}{\sqrt{\frac{s_p^2}{n_1} + \frac{s_p^2}{n_2}}} = \frac{(0.88 - 0) - 0}{\sqrt{\frac{1.134}{7} + \frac{1.134}{7}}} = 1.546$$

The critical values of $t = -2.179$ and $t = 2.179$ are found from Table A-3 by referring to the column for $\alpha = 0.05$ (two tails) and to the row for df $= 12$ (the value of $7 + 7 - 2$). Figure 8-7 shows the test statistic, critical values, and critical region. We see that the test statistic does not fall within the critical region, so we fail to reject the null hypothesis that $\mu_1 = \mu_2$.

Interpretation Despite localized effects and subjective reports about El Niño, there is not sufficient evidence to warrant rejection of the claim that the mean temperature deviations in Canada are the same during the first and second springs of El Niños. The tentative conclusion we formed by intuitively analysing Figure 8-1 was, in this case, not upheld by a formal hypothesis test. If instead of using the preliminary F test approach, we used the approach of automatically assuming *unequal* variances (Case 3), we would again fail to reject the null hypothesis of equal population means.

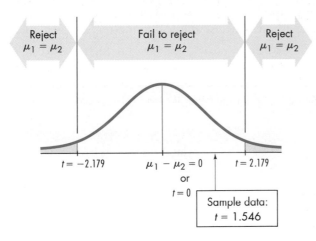

Figure 8-7 Distribution of Differences Between Means of Temperature Deviations

EXAMPLE   Using the data in the preceding example, construct a 95% confidence interval estimate of $\mu_1 - \mu_2$.

SOLUTION   It is easy to find that $\bar{x}_1 - \bar{x}_2 = 0.88 - 0 = 0.88$. Next, we find the value of the margin of error E:

$$E = t_{\alpha/2}\sqrt{\frac{s_p^2}{n_1} + \frac{s_p^2}{n_2}} = 2.179\sqrt{\frac{1.134}{7} + \frac{1.134}{7}} = 1.240$$

With $\bar{x}_1 - \bar{x}_2 = 0.88$ and with $E = 1.240$, we proceed to construct the confidence interval as follows:

$$(\bar{x}_1 - \bar{x}_2) - E < (\mu_1 - \mu_2) < (\bar{x}_1 - \bar{x}_2) + E$$
$$0.88 - 1.240 < (\mu_1 - \mu_2) < 0.88 + 1.240$$
$$-0.36 < (\mu_1 - \mu_2) < 2.12$$

This confidence interval contains zero, which means that the apparent difference in means for temperature deviations, for the first and second springs of El Niños, could be the result of chance. We fail to reject the hypothesis that the difference in means is zero.

Case 3: The Two Populations Appear to Have Unequal Variances

If we are working on the assumption of unequal variances, there is no exact method for testing equality of means and constructing confidence intervals. An *approximate* method is to use the following test statistic and confidence interval.

Test Statistic (Small Independent Samples and Unequal Variances)

$$t = \frac{(\bar{x}_1 - \bar{x}_2) - (\mu_1 - \mu_2)}{\sqrt{\dfrac{s_1^2}{n_1} + \dfrac{s_2^2}{n_2}}}$$

where df = smaller of $n_1 - 1$ and $n_2 - 1$

Confidence Interval (Small Independent Samples and Unequal Variances)

$$(\bar{x}_1 - \bar{x}_2) - E < (\mu_1 - \mu_2) < (\bar{x}_1 - \bar{x}_2) + E$$

where
$$E = t_{\alpha/2}\sqrt{\dfrac{s_1^2}{n_1} + \dfrac{s_2^2}{n_2}}$$

and df = smaller of $n_1 - 1$ and $n_2 - 1$

This test statistic and confidence interval give the number of degrees of freedom as the smaller of $n_1 - 1$ and $n_2 - 1$, but this is a more conservative and simplified alternative to computing the number of degrees of freedom by using Formula 8-1.

Formula 8-1
$$df = \frac{(A + B)^2}{\dfrac{A^2}{n_1 - 1} + \dfrac{B^2}{n_2 - 1}}$$

where

$$A = \frac{s_1^2}{n_1} \quad \text{and} \quad B = \frac{s_2^2}{n_2}$$

AS More exact results are obtained by using Formula 8-1, but they continue to be only approximate. (*Note:* Excel and STATDISK use Formula 8-1 instead of the "smaller of $n_1 - 1$ and $n_2 - 1$," so their results will be a little more precise than those included in this text.)

EXAMPLE Refer to the companies in Data Set 6 in Appendix B, which are taken from the *Financial Post* list of top 500 companies for 1997. Conglomerates (marked "f") are clearly major employers, some having as many as 50,000 and 83,000 employees. Wholesale distributors (marked "dd") do not appear on the list until row 60, and appear to have fewer employees. Use a 0.05 significance level to test the claim that for *all* 500 companies on this list, the mean number of employees in conglomerates is greater than the mean number of employees in wholesale distributors.

SOLUTION A visual scan of Data Set 6 in Appendix B suggests that conglomerates are bigger employers than wholesale distributors, but let's justify that observation with a formal hypothesis test based on the sample statistics listed in the margin. Note that these samples were drawn randomly from the *complete* list of top 500 companies, not just those in Data Set 6.

The two samples are independent (because they are separate and are not matched), the sample sizes are small, and we don't know the values of σ_1 and σ_2, so we are dealing with either Case 2 or Case 3. If we use a preliminary F test to choose between Case 2 and Case 3, and we test $H_0: \sigma_1^2 = \sigma_2^2$ with the test statistic

Employees (00s)	
Conglo-merates	Wholesale Distributors
$n_1 = 10$	$n_2 = 11$
$\bar{x}_1 = 105.77$	$\bar{x}_2 = 17.77$
$s_1 = 143.643$	$s_2 = 29.003$

$$F = \frac{s_1^2}{s_2^2} = \frac{143.643^2}{29.003^2} = 24.5292$$

With $\alpha = 0.05$ in a two-tailed F test and with 9 and 10 degrees of freedom for the numerator and denominator, respectively, we use Table A-5 to find the critical F value of 3.7790. Because the computed test statistic of $F = 24.5292$ does fall within the critical region, we reject the null hypothesis of equal variances and proceed by using the approach outlined in Case 3.

In using the Case 3 approach, we test the claim that $\mu_1 > \mu_2$ with the following null and alternative hypotheses:

$$H_0: \mu_1 \leq \mu_2 \,(\text{or } \mu_1 - \mu_2 \leq 0) \qquad H_1: \mu_1 > \mu_2 \,(\text{original claim})$$

The test statistic for this case of unequal variances is

$$t = \frac{(\bar{x}_1 - \bar{x}_2) - (\mu_1 - \mu_2)}{\sqrt{\frac{s_1^2}{n_1} + \frac{s_2^2}{n_2}}} = \frac{(105.77 - 17.77) - 0}{\sqrt{\frac{143.643^2}{10} + \frac{29.003^2}{11}}} = 1.902$$

The critical value of $t = 1.833$ is found from Table A-3 by referring to the column for $\alpha = 0.05$ (one tail) and to the row for df $= 9$ (the smaller of $10 - 1$ and $11 - 1$). Because this right-tailed test has a test statistic of $t = 1.902$ and a critical value of $t = 1.833$, the test statistic does fall within the critical region, so we reject the null hypothesis that $\mu_1 \leq \mu_2$.

Interpretation There is sufficient evidence to support the claim that the mean number of employees for top conglomerates in Canada is greater than the mean number of employees for top wholesale distribution companies. (If we use the same data with the methods of Case 2 for equal variances, we again reject the null hypothesis, and reach the same conclusion, that $\mu_1 > \mu_2$.)

EXAMPLE Using the data in the preceding example, construct a 95% confidence interval estimate of $\mu_1 - \mu_2$.

SOLUTION With $\bar{x}_1 - \bar{x}_2 = 105.77 - 17.77 = 88.0$, we proceed to find the value of the margin of error E:

$$E = t_{\alpha/2}\sqrt{\frac{s_1^2}{n_1} + \frac{s_2^2}{n_2}} = 2.262\sqrt{\frac{143.643^2}{10} + \frac{29.003^2}{11}} = 104.636$$

With $\bar{x}_1 - \bar{x}_2 = 88.0$ and with $E = 104.636$, we now construct the confidence interval as follows:

$$(\bar{x}_1 - \bar{x}_2) - E < (\mu_1 - \mu_2) < (\bar{x}_1 - \bar{x}_2) + E$$
$$88.0 - 104.636 < (\mu_1 - \mu_2) < 88.0 + 104.636$$
$$-16.6 < (\mu_1 - \mu_2) < 192.6$$

Interpretation Based on this result, we are 95% confident that the mean number of employees in conglomerates (in hundreds) exceeds the mean number of employees in wholesale distributors (in hundreds) by an amount that is between 192.6 and *minus* 16.6. That is, there *may* actually be a higher mean for the wholesale distributors. Note the apparent discrepancy of this result with the previous example, which concluded, based on a one-tailed test, in favour of conglomerates having the greater mean number of employees. The one-tailed test achieved, just barely, the required 0.05 level of significance. A confidence-interval approach corresponds more closely with a two-tailed test: The p region under each tail is only $\alpha/2$ (0.025). It is important to decide *before* calculating results which approach will be considered to represent sufficient evidence for a difference in means, if the test is passed.

This section, Section 8-2, and Section 8-3 all deal with inferences about the means of two populations. Determining the correct procedure can be difficult because we must consider issues such as the independence of the samples, the sizes of the samples, and whether the two populations appear to have equal variances. Figure 8-8 is designed to simplify the decisions that lead to the correct procedure.

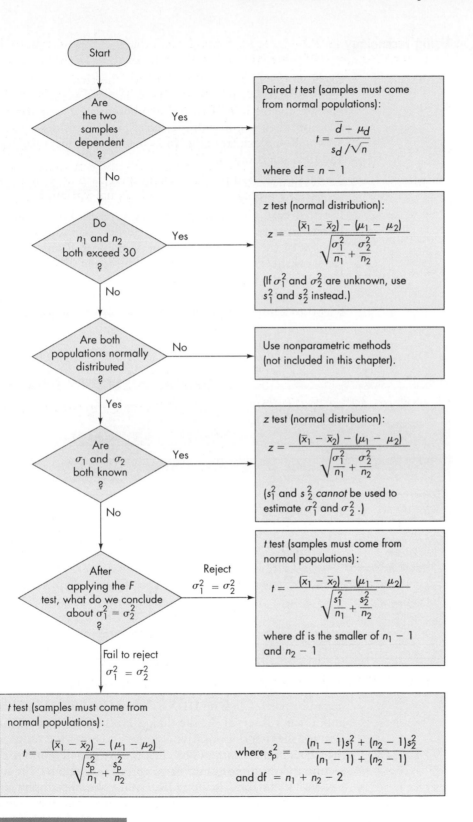

Start

Are the two samples dependent?

— Yes →

Paired t test (samples must come from normal populations):

$$t = \frac{\overline{d} - \mu_d}{s_d / \sqrt{n}}$$

where df $= n - 1$

↓ No

Do n_1 and n_2 both exceed 30?

— Yes →

z test (normal distribution):

$$z = \frac{(\overline{x}_1 - \overline{x}_2) - (\mu_1 - \mu_2)}{\sqrt{\dfrac{\sigma_1^2}{n_1} + \dfrac{\sigma_2^2}{n_2}}}$$

(If σ_1^2 and σ_2^2 are unknown, use s_1^2 and s_2^2 instead.)

↓ No

Are both populations normally distributed?

— No →

Use nonparametric methods (not included in this chapter).

↓ Yes

Are σ_1 and σ_2 both known?

— Yes →

z test (normal distribution):

$$z = \frac{(\overline{x}_1 - \overline{x}_2) - (\mu_1 - \mu_2)}{\sqrt{\dfrac{\sigma_1^2}{n_1} + \dfrac{\sigma_2^2}{n_2}}}$$

(s_1^2 and s_2^2 *cannot* be used to estimate σ_1^2 and σ_2^2.)

↓ No

After applying the F test, what do we conclude about $\sigma_1^2 = \sigma_2^2$?

— Reject $\sigma_1^2 = \sigma_2^2$ →

t test (samples must come from normal populations):

$$t = \frac{(\overline{x}_1 - \overline{x}_2) - (\mu_1 - \mu_2)}{\sqrt{\dfrac{s_1^2}{n_1} + \dfrac{s_2^2}{n_2}}}$$

where df is the smaller of $n_1 - 1$ and $n_2 - 1$

↓ Fail to reject $\sigma_1^2 = \sigma_2^2$

t test (samples must come from normal populations):

$$t = \frac{(\overline{x}_1 - \overline{x}_2) - (\mu_1 - \mu_2)}{\sqrt{\dfrac{s_p^2}{n_1} + \dfrac{s_p^2}{n_2}}}$$

where $s_p^2 = \dfrac{(n_1 - 1)s_1^2 + (n_2 - 1)s_2^2}{(n_1 - 1) + (n_2 - 1)}$

and df $= n_1 + n_2 - 2$

Figure 8-8 Testing Hypotheses Made About the Means of Two Populations

Using Technology

Excel:

Excel works from the raw data for the two samples, and requires that you first determine whether Case 2 or Case 3 applies. If you intend to use a *preliminary F test* for that decision, then begin with the Excel procedures described in Section 8-4. Next, from the **Tools** menu, select **Data Analysis**, and then select one of:

t-test: Two-Sample Assuming Equal Variances
t-test: Two-Sample Assuming Unequal Variances

In either case, the same dialog box appears. For **Variable 1 Range**, specify the worksheet range that contains the data for one of the two variables; for **Variable 2 Range**, specify the worksheet range that contains the other variable's data. Unlike for the Excel *F* test, the appropriate choice for **Alpha** is the *full* intended α, not just the right-tailed portion. Next, select an **Output Option**, and click on **OK** to obtain the results. The illustration shows the results for Case 2 and Case 3 types of output.

Excel Display Testing Two Samples, with Equal or Unequal Variances

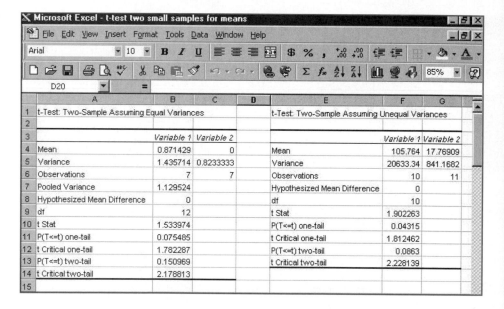

	Variable 1	Variable 2			Variable 1	Variable 2
t-Test: Two-Sample Assuming Equal Variances				**t-Test: Two-Sample Assuming Unequal Variances**		
Mean	0.871429	0		Mean	105.764	17.76909
Variance	1.435714	0.8233333		Variance	20633.34	841.1682
Observations	7	7		Observations	10	11
Pooled Variance	1.129524			Hypothesized Mean Difference	0	
Hypothesized Mean Difference	0			df	10	
df	12			t Stat	1.902263	
t Stat	1.533974			P(T<=t) one-tail	0.04315	
P(T<=t) one-tail	0.075485			t Critical one-tail	1.812462	
t Critical one-tail	1.782287			P(T<=t) two-tail	0.0863	
P(T<=t) two-tail	0.150969			t Critical two-tail	2.228139	
t Critical two-tail	2.178813					

To generate confidence intervals, the Data Desk XL add-in can be used. Click on **DDXL**. Select **Confidence Intervals** and **2 Var t Interval**. In the dialog box, click on the pencil icon for the first quantitative column and enter the range for the first sample's data. Then click on the pencil icon for the second quantitative column and enter the range for the second sample's data. Click on **OK**. Follow the steps in the next dialog box that appears. (In Step 1, select **2 Sample** if assuming unequal population variances, or **Pooled** if assuming equal variances.)

STATDISK: Unlike Excel, STATDISK works from summary data. Begin by selecting the menu items **Analysis, Hypothesis Testing,** and **Mean-Two Independent Samples.** STATDISK, itself, determines whether to assume Case 2 or Case 3, based on automatically performing a preliminary F test. The output from STATDISK includes both the test results and a confidence interval.

8-5 Exercises A: Basic Skills and Concepts

In Exercises 1 and 2, test the given claim. Use a significance level of $\alpha = 0.05$, and assume that all populations are normally distributed. Use the traditional method of testing hypotheses outlined in Figure 7-4.

1. Claim: Populations A and B have the same mean ($\mu_1 = \mu_2$).
   Sample A: $n_1 = 10$, $\bar{x}_1 = 75$, $s_1 = 15$
   Sample B: $n_2 = 20$, $\bar{x}_2 = 80$, $s_2 = 12$
2. Claim: Populations A and B have the same mean ($\mu_1 = \mu_2$).
   Sample A: $n_1 = 15$, $\bar{x}_1 = 150$, $s_1 = 40$
   Sample B: $n_2 = 5$, $\bar{x}_2 = 140$, $s_2 = 10$
3. Using the sample data in Exercise 1, construct a 95% confidence interval estimate of the difference between the means of the two populations.
4. Using the sample data in Exercise 2, construct a 95% confidence interval estimate of the difference between the means of the two populations.
5. The equality of Air Canada flight times (in hours) between Vancouver and San Francisco is tested using Excel. A preliminary F test shows that there is no significant difference between the two sample variances, so, as shown in the accompaning figure ($\alpha = 0.05$) the t-test assuming equal variances was used.
   a. Based on the displayed results (see next page), construct a 95% confidence interval for the difference $\mu_1 - \mu_2$, where μ_1 denotes the mean flight time from Vancouver to San Francisco. Do the confidence intervals contain 0? What can you conclude about equality of the mean flight times in both directions?
   b. Use elements from the Excel display on the next page to answer these questions: At the 0.05 significance level, test the claim that flights from Vancouver to San Francisco take a longer time than flights in the other direction. What is the test statistic? What is the critical value? What is the P-value?

Vancouver to San Francisco	San Francisco to Vancouver
2.30 2.20 1.97 2.22 2.12	1.80 1.68 2.03 1.83
1.95 2.03 2.30 2.15 2.33	1.77 1.98 1.85
2.15	

Based on data from Gary Murphy, chief flight dispatcher, Air Canada.

	A	B	C
1	t-Test: Two-Sample Assuming Equal Variances		
2			
3		Variable 1	Variable 2
4	Mean	2.1560606	1.85
5	Variance	0.0173485	0.0148148
6	Observations	11	7
7	Pooled Variance	0.0163984	
8	Hypothesized Mean Difference	0	
9	df	16	
10	t Stat	4.943293	
11	P(T<=t) one-tail	7.338E-05	
12	t Critical one-tail	1.7458842	
13	P(T<=t) two-tail	0.0001468	
14	t Critical two-tail	2.1199048	

6. Employees who work with electronic components at Canadian Automated Electronics are required to undergo special training. Training includes completing tasks under simulated conditions and recording completion times. A supervisor claims he has found some star performers among a new group of trainees.

   a. Based on the data shown, test the claim at the 0.01 significance level that the star-performers group has a mean completion time less than the other group (based on data from Canadian Automated Electronics). The assumption of equal variances for the groups has been rejected ($p < 0.01$).

   b. Construct a 99% confidence interval estimate of the difference between the mean task completion time for the two groups.

   Star performers: $n = 15$, $\bar{x} = 286$, $s = 71.93$
   Other trainees: $n = 10$, $\bar{x} = 873.7$, $s = 259.26$

7. In a sample of the driving records of 137 young adult males who underwent treatment for substance abuse in a Toronto clinic, the mean accident rate after treatment was 0.068, with a standard deviation of 0.223 (based on data from "Does Treatment of Substance Abuse Improve Driving Safety? A Preliminary Evaluation," by Mann et al., Addiction Research Foundation). Suppose a competing clinic claims that those who complete its substance-abuse program have better driving records. In a random sample of 20 of its past clients, the mean accident rate after treatment was 0.061, with a standard deviation of 0.210.

   a. At the 0.05 level of significance, test the claim that the past clients of both clinics have the same mean accident rate. Based on this result, is the competing clinic entitled to make the assertion that it does?

   b. Construct a 95% confidence interval for the difference between the mean accident rates for the client groups from the two clinics.

8. Assume that Data Set 21 in Appendix B represents sample prices and characteristics of high quality diamonds sold at auction. A vendor claims that near-colourless diamonds sell at a higher price than yellower ones. Based

on the data summarized in the margin (from Data Set 21, with colours 5–9 interpreted as "More Yellow"), use a 0.05 level of significance to test the vendor's claim. Assume unequal variances for the two groups. Should a buyer for the auction house avoid buying the yellower diamonds? Is more information needed to answer that question? Explain.

9. Assume that Data Set 21 in Appendix B represents sample prices and characteristics of high quality diamonds sold at auction. A vendor claims that nearly flawless diamonds sell at a higher price than noticeably flawed ones. Based on the data summarized in the margin (from Data Set 21, with clarity 4–5 interpreted as "More Flawed"), use a 0.05 level of significance to test the vendor's claim. Assume equal variances for the two groups. Should a buyer for the auction house avoid buying the noticeably flawed diamonds? Is more information needed to answer that question? Explain.

10. A simple random sample of 21 peanut M&M candies is selected, and each candy is weighed. The mean is 2.4658 g and the standard deviation is 0.3127 g. The 100 M&M plain candies listed in Data Set 11 in Appendix B have a mean of 0.9147 g and a standard deviation of 0.0369 g. Is there sufficient evidence to support the claim that there is a difference between the mean weight of peanut M&Ms and the mean weight of plain M&Ms?

11. Data Set 11 in Appendix B includes a sample of 21 red M&Ms with weights having a mean of 0.9097 g and a standard deviation of 0.0275 g. The data set also includes a sample of 8 orange M&Ms with weights having a mean of 0.9251 g and a standard deviation of 0.0472 g. Use a 0.05 level of significance to test for equality of the two population means. If you were responsible for controlling production so that red and orange M&Ms have weights with the same mean, would you take corrective action?

12. Refer to Data Set 11 in Appendix B and test the claim that yellow M&Ms and green M&Ms have the same mean weight. If you were part of a quality control team with responsibility for ensuring that yellow M&Ms and green M&Ms have the same mean weight, would you take corrective action?

13. Refer to Data Set 4 in Appendix B. If the Ontario–Manitoba border is taken as the boundary between East and West, test the claim that in comparing provincial averages, there is no difference in mean annual precipitation between western and eastern provinces. Use the 0.05 level of significance.

14. Provincial governments have been re-examining their delivery of services, such as health care. The accompanying table is based on one random sample of hospitals in New Brunswick and another in Nova Scotia, and shows the total number of beds in each hospital (*Guide to Canadian Healthcare Facilities*, 1998–99, Vol. 6, Canadian Healthcare Association, Ottawa). At the 0.05 significance level, test the claim that the two given samples come from populations with the same mean (assume unequal variances). If the means are different, what are the possible implications for the equity

Less Yellow

$n_1 = 13$

$\bar{x}_1 = \$30{,}638.31$

$s_1 = \$28{,}346.06$

More Yellow

$n_2 = 17$

$\bar{x}_2 = \$14{,}541.00$

$s_2 = \$11{,}297.64$

Less Flawed

$n_1 = 13$

$\bar{x}_1 = \$27{,}083.23$

$s_1 = \$25{,}644.35$

More Flawed

$n_2 = 17$

$\bar{x}_2 = \$17{,}259.59$

$s_2 = \$17{,}660.96$

of services between these two provinces? If the means are different, do we have sufficient information to conclude that the numbers of hospital beds per person are different in the two provinces? Explain.

New Brunswick		Nova Scotia	
23	47	15	13
153	47	27	136
397	15	8	26
12	500	85	311
15	56	12	132
398			

15. Sample data were collected to compare the ages of CEOs of top growth companies in western Canada and Quebec, shown in the table below. Exercise 11 in Section 8-4 looked at the variances for these two groups. Assuming the populations have equal variances, test at the 0.05 significance level the claim that these two samples come from populations with the same mean.

Western Canada	38 54 35 40 41 34 59 37 35 48 35 59
Quebec	50 31 38 49 34 36 35 33 39 38

Based on data from *Profit*, May 29, 1996.

16. An experiment was conducted to test the effects of alcohol. The errors were recorded in a test of visual and motor skills for a treatment group of people who drank ethanol and another group given a placebo. The results are shown in the accompanying table. Use a 0.05 significance level to test the claim that the two groups come from populations with the same mean. Do these results support the common belief that drinking is hazardous for drivers, pilots, ship captains, and so on?

Treatment Group	Placebo Group
$n_1 = 22$	$n_2 = 22$
$\bar{x}_1 = 4.20$	$\bar{x}_2 = 1.71$
$s_1 = 2.20$	$s_2 = 0.72$

Based on data from "Effects of Alcohol Intoxication on Risk Taking, Strategy, and Error Rate in Visuomotor Performance," by Streufert et al., *Journal of Applied Psychology*, Vol. 77, No. 4.

8-5 Exercises B: Beyond the Basics

17. An experiment was conducted to test the effects of alcohol. The breath alcohol levels were measured for a treatment group of people who drank ethanol and another group given a placebo. The results are given in the accompanying table. Use a 0.05 significance level to test the claim that the two groups come from populations with the same mean.

Treatment Group	Placebo Group
$n_1 = 22$	$n_2 = 22$
$\bar{x}_1 = 0.049$	$\bar{x}_2 = 0.000$
$s_1 = 0.015$	$s_2 = 0.000$

Based on data from "Effects of Alcohol Intoxication on Risk Taking, Strategy, and Error Rate in Visuomotor Performance," by Streufert et al., *Journal of Applied Psychology*, Vol. 77, No. 4.

18. Assume that two samples have the same standard deviation and that both are independent, small, and randomly selected from normally distributed populations. Also assume that we want to test the claim that the samples come from populations with the same mean.
    a. Is it necessary to conduct a preliminary F test?
    b. If both samples have standard deviation s, what is the value of s_p^2 expressed in terms of s?

19. Refer to the two examples of this section that used the number of employees in key industry groups. (See the Case 3 subsection.) How are the hypothesis test and confidence interval affected if the number of degrees of freedom is calculated with Formula 8-1, instead of using the smaller of $n_1 - 1$ and $n_2 - 1$?

20. Suppose that the sample data for the ages of CEOs displayed for Exercise 15 had omitted one data point because it was viewed as an outlier. This extra data value was an 11th CEO from Quebec, who is 80. How are the hypothesis test and confidence interval affected if this apparently extreme value is re-included?

8-6 Inferences About Two Proportions

Although this section appears last in the chapter, it is arguably the most important because this is where we describe methods for using two sample proportions to make inferences (hypothesis testing and confidence interval construction) about two population proportions.

When testing a hypothesis made about two population proportions—such as the proportions of cured patients in a population given some treatment and a second population given a placebo—or when constructing a confidence interval for the difference between two population proportions, we make the following assumptions and use the following notation.

Assumptions

1. We have two *independent* sets of randomly selected sample data.

2. For both samples, the conditions $np \geq 5$ and $nq \geq 5$ are satisfied. That is, there are at least 5 successes and 5 failures in each of the two samples. (In many cases, we will test the claim that two populations have equal proportions so that $p_1 - p_2 = 0$. Because we assume that $p_1 - p_2 = 0$, it is not necessary to specify the particular value that p_1 and p_2 have in common. In such cases, the conditions $np \geq 5$ and $nq \geq 5$ can be checked by replacing p by the estimated pooled proportion $\bar{p}$, which will be described later.)

Notation for Two Proportions

For population 1 we let

$p_1 = $ *population* proportion

$n_1 = $ size of the sample

$x_1 = $ number of successes in the sample

$\hat{p}_1 = \dfrac{x_1}{n_1}$ (the *sample* proportion)

$\hat{q}_1 = 1 - \hat{p}_1$

The corresponding meanings are attached to $p_2, n_2, x_2, \hat{p}_2,$ and $\hat{q}_2,$ which come from population 2.

How do we find the values of x_1 and x_2? Sometimes we are told directly the numbers of successes x_1 and x_2. In other cases, we may have to calculate the values of x_1 and x_2, which can be found by noting that $\hat{p}_1 = x_1/n_1$ implies that

$$x_1 = n_1 \cdot \hat{p}_1$$

For example, if we know that sample 1 consists of 500 treated patients and 30% of them were cured, the actual number of cured patients is $x_1 = 500 \cdot 0.30 = 150$. In this case, $n_1 = 500$, $\hat{p}_1 = 0.30$, and $x_1 = 150$.

Hypothesis Tests

In Section 7-5 we discussed tests of hypotheses made about a single population proportion. We will now consider tests of hypotheses made about two population proportions, but *we will be testing only claims that $p_1 = p_2$* and we will use the following pooled (or combined) estimate of the value that p_1 and p_2 have in common. (For claims that the difference between p_1 and p_2 is equal to a nonzero constant, see Exercise 17 of this section.)

Pooled Estimate of p_1 and p_2

The **pooled estimate of p_1 and p_2** is denoted by $\bar{p}$ and is given by

$$\bar{p} = \frac{x_1 + x_2}{n_1 + n_2}$$

We denote the complement of $\bar{p}$ by $\bar{q}$, so $\bar{q} = 1 - \bar{p}$.

Test Statistic for Two Proportions

The following test statistic applies to null and alternative hypotheses that fit one of these three formats:

$$H_0: p_1 = p_2 \qquad H_0: p_1 \geq p_2 \qquad H_0: p_1 \leq p_2$$
$$H_1: p_1 \neq p_2 \qquad H_1: p_1 < p_2 \qquad H_1: p_1 > p_2$$

$$z = \frac{(\hat{p}_1 - \hat{p}_2) - (p_1 - p_2)}{\sqrt{\dfrac{\bar{p}\,\bar{q}}{n_1} + \dfrac{\bar{p}\,\bar{q}}{n_2}}}$$

where $p_1 - p_2 = 0$ (assumed in the null hypothesis), and

$$\hat{p}_1 = \frac{x_1}{n_1} \quad \text{and} \quad \hat{p}_2 = \frac{x_2}{n_2}$$

$$\bar{p} = \frac{x_1 + x_2}{n_1 + n_2}$$

$$\bar{q} = 1 - \bar{p}$$

The following example will help clarify the roles of x_1, n_1, $\hat{p}_1$, $\bar{p}$, and so on. In particular, you should recognize that under the assumption of equal proportions, the best estimate of the common proportion is obtained by pooling both samples into one big sample, so that $\bar{p}$ becomes a more obvious estimate of the common population proportion.

EXAMPLE   Johns Hopkins researchers conducted a study of pregnant IBM employees. Among 30 employees who worked with glycol ethers, 10 (or 33.3%) had miscarriages, but among 750 who were not exposed to glycol ethers, 120 (or 16.0%) had miscarriages. At the 0.01 significance level, test the claim that the miscarriage rate is greater for women exposed to glycol ethers.

SOLUTION   For notation purposes, we stipulate that sample 1 is the group that worked with glycol ethers and sample 2 is the group not exposed, so the sample statistics can be summarized as shown here:

	Exposed to Glycol Ethers	Not Exposed to Glycol Ethers
	$n_1 = 30$	$n_2 = 750$
	$x_1 = 10$	$x_2 = 120$
	$\hat{p}_1 = \dfrac{10}{30} = 0.333$	$\hat{p}_2 = \dfrac{120}{750} = 0.160$

We will now use the traditional method of hypothesis testing, as summarized in Figure 7-4.

Step 1: The claim of a greater miscarriage rate for women exposed to glycol ethers can be represented by $p_1 > p_2$.

Step 2: If $p_1 > p_2$ is false, then $p_1 \leq p_2$.

Step 3: Because our claim of $p_1 > p_2$ does not contain equality, it becomes the alternative hypothesis, and we have

$$H_0: p_1 \leq p_2 \qquad H_1: p_1 > p_2 \text{ (original claim)}$$

Step 4: The significance level is $\alpha = 0.01$.

Step 5: We will use the normal distribution (with the test statistic previously given) as an approximation to the binomial distribution. We have two independent samples, and the conditions $np \geq 5$ and $nq \geq 5$ are satisfied for each of the two samples. To check this, we note that in conducting this test, we assume that $p_1 = p_2$, where their common value is the pooled estimate $\bar{p}$, calculated as

$$\bar{p} = \frac{x_1 + x_2}{n_1 + n_2} = \frac{10 + 120}{30 + 750} = 0.1667$$

With $\bar{p} = 0.1667$, it follows that $\bar{q} = 1 - 0.1667 = 0.8333$. We verify that $np \geq 5$ and $nq \geq 5$ for both samples as follows:

Sample 1	Sample 2
$n_1 p = (30)(0.1667) = 5 \geq 5$	$n_2 p = (750)(0.1667) = 125 \geq 5$
$n_1 q = (30)(0.8333) = 25 \geq 5$	$n_2 q = (750)(0.8333) = 625 \geq 5$

Step 6: We can now find the value of the test statistic:

$$z = \frac{(\hat{p}_1 - \hat{p}_2) - (p_1 - p_2)}{\sqrt{\dfrac{\bar{p}\,\bar{q}}{n_1} + \dfrac{\bar{p}\,\bar{q}}{n_2}}}$$

$$= \frac{(0.333 - 0.160) - 0}{\sqrt{\dfrac{(0.1667)(0.8333)}{30} + \dfrac{(0.1667)(0.8333)}{750}}} = 2.49$$

The critical value of $z = 2.33$ is found by observing that we have a right-tailed test with $\alpha = 0.01$. The value of $z = 2.33$ is found from Table A-2 as the z score corresponding to an area of $0.5 - 0.01 = 0.4900$.

Step 7:   In Figure 8-10 we see that the test statistic falls within the critical region, so we reject the null hypothesis of $p_1 \leq p_2$.

Interpretation We conclude that there is sufficient evidence to support the claim that the miscarriage rate is greater for women exposed to ethyl glycol. Johns Hopkins researchers concluded that women employees exposed to glycol ethers "have a significantly increased risk of miscarriage." On the basis of these results, IBM warned its employees of the danger, notified the Environmental Protection Agency, and greatly reduced its use of glycol ethers.

(These results could also be reached with the P-value approach. In Step 6, instead of finding the critical value of z, we would find the P-value by using the procedure summarized in Figures 7-7 and 7-8. With a test statistic of $z = 2.49$ and a right-tailed test, we get

$$P\text{-value} = (\text{area to the right of } z = 2.49) = 0.0064$$

Again, we reject the null hypothesis because the P-value of 0.0064 is less than the significance level of $\alpha = 0.01$.)

Figure 8-10   Distribution of Differences Between Proportions for Group Exposed to Glycol Ethers and Group Not Exposed

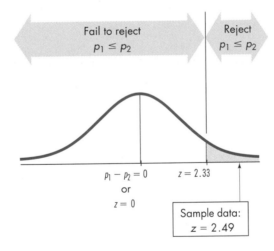

Confidence Intervals

In the preceding example we found that there appears to be a larger miscarriage rate for women exposed to glycol ethers, so we now proceed to estimate the amount of the difference. Is the difference large enough to justify extensive and expensive changes in manufacturing procedures?

With the same assumptions given at the beginning of this section, a confidence interval for the difference between population proportions $p_1 - p_2$ can be constructed by evaluating the following:

Polio Experiment

In 1954 an experiment was conducted to test the effectiveness of the Salk vaccine as protection against the devastating effects of polio. Approximately 200,000 children were injected with an ineffective salt solution, and 200,000 other children were injected with the vaccine. The experiment was "double blind" because the children being injected didn't know whether they were given the real vaccine or the placebo, and the doctors giving the injections and evaluating the results didn't know either. Only 33 of the 200,000 vaccinated children later developed paralytic polio, whereas 115 of the 200,000 injected with the salt solution later developed paralytic polio. Statistical analysis of these and other results led to the conclusion that the Salk vaccine was indeed effective against paralytic polio.

Confidence Interval Estimate of $p_1 - p_2$

The confidence interval estimate of the difference $p_1 - p_2$ is:

$$(\hat{p}_1 - \hat{p}_2) - E < (p_1 - p_2) < (\hat{p}_1 - \hat{p}_2) + E$$

where
$$E = z_{\alpha/2} \sqrt{\frac{\hat{p}_1 \hat{q}_1}{n_1} + \frac{\hat{p}_2 \hat{q}_2}{n_2}}$$

● **EXAMPLE**   Use the sample data given in the preceding example to construct a 99% confidence interval for the difference between the two population proportions.

SOLUTION   With a 99% degree of confidence, $z_{\alpha/2} = 2.575$ (from Table A-2). We first calculate the value of the margin of error E as shown below:

$$E = z_{\alpha/2} \sqrt{\frac{\hat{p}_1 \hat{q}_1}{n_1} + \frac{\hat{p}_2 \hat{q}_2}{n_2}} = 2.575 \sqrt{\frac{(0.333)(0.667)}{30} + \frac{(0.160)(0.840)}{750}}$$

$$= 0.2242$$

With $\hat{p}_1 = 0.333$, $\hat{p}_2 = 0.160$, and $E = 0.2242$, the confidence interval is evaluated as follows:

$$(\hat{p}_1 - \hat{p}_2) - E < (p_1 - p_2) < (\hat{p}_1 - \hat{p}_2) + E$$
$$(0.333 - 0.160) - 0.2242 < (p_1 - p_2) < (0.333 - 0.160) + 0.2242$$
$$-0.0512 < (p_1 - p_2) < 0.3972$$

Interpretation   The confidence interval limits contain 0, suggesting that there is not a significant difference between the two proportions. Similar to what occurred in a solved example in Section 8-5 (for employment numbers by industry), the confidence-interval results appear to contradict the conclusions from the related hypothesis-testing procedure. In this instance, the discrepancy is attributable to two factors: (1) The hypothesis test was right-tailed with a 0.01 significance level, so it corresponds to a 98% confidence interval (but the above confidence interval has a 99% degree of confidence); (2) the variance used for the hypothesis test (based on an assumption of equal proportions) is different from the variance used for the confidence interval (where the proportions are not assumed to be equal).

As always, we should be careful when interpreting confidence intervals. Because p_1 and p_2 have fixed values and are not variables, it is wrong to state that there is a 99% chance that the value of $p_1 - p_2$ falls between

−0.0512 and 0.3972. It is correct to state that if we repeat the same sampling process and construct 99% confidence intervals, in the long run 99% of the intervals will actually contain the value of $p_1 − p_2$.

Rationale for the Procedures Used in This Section

The test statistic given for hypothesis tests is justified by the following:

1. With $n_1 p_1 \geq 5$ and $n_1 q_1 \geq 5$, the distribution of $\hat{p}_1$ can be approximated by a normal distribution with mean p_1, standard deviation $\sqrt{p_1 q_1 / n_1}$, and variance $p_1 q_1 / n_1$. These conclusions are based on Sections 5-6 and 6-4 and they also apply to the second sample.

2. Because $\hat{p}_1$ and $\hat{p}_2$ are each approximated by a normal distribution, $\hat{p}_1 − \hat{p}_2$ will also be approximated by a normal distribution with mean $p_1 − p_2$ and variance

$$\sigma^2_{(\hat{p}_1 − \hat{p}_2)} = \sigma^2_{\hat{p}_1} + \sigma^2_{\hat{p}_2} = \frac{p_1 q_1}{n_1} + \frac{p_2 q_2}{n_2}$$

(In Section 8-2 we established that the variance of the differences between two independent random variables is the sum of their individual variances.)

3. Because the values of p_1, p_2, q_1, and q_2 are typically unknown and from the null hypothesis we assume that $p_1 = p_2$, we can pool (or combine) the sample data. The pooled estimate of the common value of p_1 and p_2 is $\bar{p} = (x_1 + x_2)/(n_1 + n_2)$. If we replace p_1 and p_2 by $\bar{p}$ and replace q_1 and q_2 by $\bar{q} = 1 − \bar{p}$, the variance from Step 2 leads to the following standard deviation:

$$\sigma_{(\hat{p}_1 − \hat{p}_2)} = \sqrt{\frac{\bar{p}\,\bar{q}}{n_1} + \frac{\bar{p}\,\bar{q}}{n_2}}$$

4. We now know that the distribution of $p_1 − p_2$ is approximately normal, with mean $p_1 − p_2$ and standard deviation as given, so that the z test statistic has the form given earlier.

The form of the confidence interval requires an expression for the variance different from the one given in Step 3. In Step 3 we are assuming that $p_1 = p_2$, but if we don't make that assumption (as in the construction of a confidence interval), we estimate the variance of $\hat{p}_1 − \hat{p}_2$ as

$$\sigma^2_{(\hat{p}_1 − \hat{p}_2)} = \sigma^2_{\hat{p}_1} + \sigma^2_{\hat{p}_2} = \frac{\hat{p}_1 \hat{q}_1}{n_1} + \frac{\hat{p}_2 \hat{q}_2}{n_2}$$

and the standard deviation becomes

$$\sqrt{\frac{\hat{p}_1 \hat{q}_1}{n_1} + \frac{\hat{p}_2 \hat{q}_2}{n_2}}$$

The Lead Margin of Error

Authors Stephen Ansolabehere and Thomas Belin wrote in their article "Poll Faulting" (*Chance* magazine) that "our greatest criticism of the reporting of poll results is with the margin of error of a single proportion (usually ±3%) when media attention is clearly drawn to the *lead* of one candidate." They point out that the lead is really the *difference* between two proportions $(p_1 − p_2)$ and go on to explain how they developed the following rule of thumb: The lead is approximately $\sqrt{3}$ times larger than the margin of error for any one proportion. For a typical pre-election poll, a reported ±3% margin of error translates to about ±5% for the lead of one candidate over the other. They write that the margin of error for the lead should be reported.

In the test statistic

$$z = \frac{(\hat{p}_1 - \hat{p}_2) - (p_1 - p_2)}{\sqrt{\dfrac{\hat{p}_1 \hat{q}_1}{n_1} + \dfrac{\hat{p}_2 \hat{q}_2}{n_2}}}$$

let z be positive and negative (for two tails) and solve for $p_1 - p_2$. The results are the limits of the confidence interval given earlier.

Using Technology

Excel: In Excel, you must use the Data Disk XL add-in, which is a supplement to this book. In four spreadsheet cells, input these numbers, respectively: the number of successes in Sample 1, the number of trials for Sample 1, the number of successes in Sample 2, and the number of trials for Sample 2. Click on **DDXL**. For the hypothesis test, select **Hypothesis Tests** and **Summ 2 Var Prop Test**; or for the confidence interval, select **Confidence Intervals** and **Summ 2 Var Prop Interval**. In the dialog box, click on the each of the four pencil icons in turn, and enter the corresponding cell addresses (for example, in the first input box, enter the cell address containing the number of successes in Sample 1). Click **OK**. Proceed to complete the new dialog box.

STATDISK: Select **Analysis**, then **Hypothesis Testing**, then **Proportion-Two Samples**. Enter the required items in the dialog box. Confidence interval limits are included with the hypothesis test results.

8-6 Exercises A: Basic Skills and Concepts

In Exercises 1 and 2, assume that you plan to use a significance level of $\alpha = 0.05$ to test the claim that $p_1 = p_2$. Use the given sample sizes and numbers of successes to find (a) the pooled estimate $\bar{p}$, (b) the z test statistic, (c) the critical z values, and (d) the P-value.

1. Sample 1	Sample 2		2. Sample 1	Sample 2
$n_1 = 50$	$n_2 = 100$		$n_1 = 500$	$n_2 = 200$
$x_1 = 25$	$x_2 = 55$		$x_1 = 300$	$x_2 = 150$

In Exercises 3 and 4, find the number of successes x suggested by the given statement.

3. From Health Canada: Of 2429 industrial radiographers whose exposures to radiation were monitored for a year, 2.0% of them had radiation doses above 20 mSv.

4. Based on a list of major bridges (BlackDog Media, 2000, www.swish-web.com): Of a random selection of 10 major continuous truss bridges, 10% are in Canada.

5. The Composting Council of Canada requires that type AA compost must comprise less than 1% foreign matter. A ministry inspector uses random sampling to test two commercial composting facilities against the standards. Of 50 samples collected at Facility A, 15 had less than half of the allowable level of foreign matter. Facility B attained this quality in 7 of 55 samples. Test the claim that Facility A has a greater proportion of product containing less than half of the allowable level of foreign matter than Facility B. Use the 0.05 significance level. If the claim is true, does it follow that Facility A consistently produces better quality compost?

6. According to the *Annual Report of the Correctional Investigator* (1995–1996), this agency was able to resolve or provide assistance for 88 of the 280 complaints received about the prison grievance procedure. On the other hand, they were able to resolve or provide assistance for 55 of 232 complaints received about private family visits. At the 0.05 level of significance, and assuming that data for the years covered in the report are representative of future years, test the claim that the Correctional Investigator has more success in resolving or assisting complaints about the grievance procedure than complaints about private visits. Is it reasonable to treat the reported data as a sample of a larger population of future years or years in general?

7. Based on a random survey of 1000 adult Canadians conducted in January 2001, a headline in *The Globe and Mail* (February 5, 2001) concluded that "fewer Canadians support free trade." In the survey, 64% of the respondents supported the North American free trade agreement, but in a 1999 survey 70% supported the agreement. Testing at the 0.01 level of significance, is there sufficient evidence to support the claim in the headline? (Assume that the number of Canadians surveyed in 1999 was 1000.) We are not told in the article how many Canadians were surveyed in 1999. Could it make a difference to our conclusion if our assumption of $n = 1000$ is incorrect? Explain.

8. In initial tests of the Salk vaccine, 33 of 200,000 vaccinated children later developed polio. Of 200,000 children vaccinated with a placebo, 115 later developed polio. At the 0.01 level of significance, test the claim that the Salk vaccine is effective in lowering the polio rate. Does it appear that the vaccine is effective?

9. A random sample was taken from the *Financial Post* list of top 500 companies for 1998. Of 26 food- and beverage-related industries in the sample, 12 had at least 10% foreign ownership. Of 29 wholesale distribution firms in the sample, 15 had at least 10% foreign ownership.

   a. Use a 0.01 significance level to test the claim that both industry groups sampled had the same proportion of companies with a foreign ownership level of at least 10%.

   b. Construct the 99% confidence interval for the difference between proportions of companies that are significantly (at least 10%) foreign-owned, in top food- and beverage-related companies versus top wholesale distribution firms.

10. During the campaign for the June 1997 federal election, many opinion polls were conducted. Early in the campaign, a poll found that 47.6% of voters supported the Liberals. Then in May 1997 an Angus Reid poll found that of 3208 voters surveyed, 42% supported the Liberals (based on a report conducted for the CTV television network and the Southam newspaper chain). Some analysts suggested that this difference was within the margin of error for the polls.

  a. Assuming that 3100 voters participated in the earlier poll, test the claim that there was no change in support for the Liberals between the two polls. Based on the result, did the Liberals need to change campaign strategies?

  b. Construct a 95% confidence interval for the difference between the proportions of voters who supported the Liberals in the earlier poll and those who supported the Liberals in the May poll.

11. Karl Pearson, who developed many important concepts in statistics, collected crime data in 1909. Of those convicted of arson, 50 were drinkers and 43 abstained. Of those convicted of fraud, 63 were drinkers and 144 abstained. Use a 0.01 significance level to test the claim that the proportion of drinkers among convicted arsonists is greater than the proportion of drinkers convicted of fraud. Does it seem reasonable that drinking might have an effect on the type of crime? Why?

12. An initial public offering (IPO) of a company's stock is considered "underpriced" if there is a large percentage difference between its issuing price and its closing price after one day of trading. A Canadian study based on a sample of 399 IPOs, over 25 years, showed that approximately 8% of those stocks were underpriced when they were issued (The Mixed Results of Canadian IPOs, *Canadian Investment Review*, vol. 10, 12-01-1997, pp. 22–26). Suppose that a study of 430 U.S. IPOs had shown that 66 of those issues were underpriced.

  a. Use the 0.05 level of significance to test the claim that fewer Canadian IPOs have been underpriced than U.S. IPOs.

  b. "Day traders" like underpriced IPOs, because if bought early and sold late on their day of issuance, the trades make a profit. Do the results from (a) support a claim that day traders who knew which IPOs were underpriced could have made more money by investing in U.S. IPOs? What additional information, if any, is needed to answer the question?

  c. Construct a 95% confidence interval for the difference in proportions of underpriced IPOs for Canadian and U.S. stocks.

13. Professional pollsters are becoming concerned about the growing rate of refusals among potential survey subjects. In analysing the problem, there is a need to know if the refusal rate is universal or if there is a difference between the rates for central-city residents and those not living in central cities. Specifically, it was found that when 294 central-city residents were surveyed, 28.9% refused to respond. A survey of 1015 residents not in a central city resulted in a 17.1% refusal rate (based on data from "I Hear You Knocking But You Can't Come In," by Fitzgerald and Fuller, *Sociological Methods and Research*, Vol. 11, No. 1). At the 0.01 significance level, test the claim that the central-city refusal rate is the same as the refusal rate in other areas.

14. A mining company conducted a safety analysis for workers at a Saskatchewan site. Of 450 sample records in January, 16 revealed undesirable safety conditions. Of 660 sample records in February/March, 10 showed undesirable conditions. Is there sufficient sample evidence to support the site manager's claim, at the 0.02 level of significance, that safety conditions improved between the two sample periods?

15. When games were sampled from throughout a season, it was found that the home team won 127 of 198 professional *basketball* games, and the home team won 57 of 99 professional *football* games (based on data from "Predicting Professional Sports Game Outcomes from Intermediate Game Scores," by Cooper et al., *Chance,* Vol. 5, No. 3–4). Construct a 95% confidence interval for the difference between the proportions of home wins. Do the confidence interval limits contain 0? Based on the results, is there a significant difference between the proportions of home wins? What do you conclude about the home field advantage?

8–6 Exercises B: Beyond the Basics

16. Ziac is a Lederle Laboratories drug developed to treat hypertension. Lederle Laboratories reported that when 221 people were treated with Ziac, 3.2% of them experienced dizziness. It was also reported that among the 144 people in the placebo group, 1.8% experienced dizziness.
    a. Can you use the methods of this section to test the claim that there is a significant difference between the two rates of dizziness? Why or why not?
    b. Can the given information be correct? Why or why not?

17. To test the null hypothesis that the difference between two population proportions is equal to a nonzero constant c, use the test statistic

$$z = \frac{(\hat{p}_1 - \hat{p}_2) - c}{\sqrt{\dfrac{\hat{p}_1(1 - \hat{p}_1)}{n_1} + \dfrac{\hat{p}_2(1 - \hat{p}_2)}{n_2}}}$$

As long as n_1 and n_2 are both large, the sampling distribution of the test statistic z will be approximately the standard normal distribution. Refer to the sample data included with the example presented in this section, and use a 0.05 significance level to test the claim of a medical expert that when women are exposed to glycol ethers, their percentage of miscarriages is 10 percentage points more than the percentage for women not exposed to glycol ethers.

18. Sample data are randomly drawn from three independent populations, each of size 100. The sample proportions are $\hat{p}_1 = 40/100$, $\hat{p}_2 = 30/100$, and $\hat{p}_3 = 20/100$.
    a. At the 0.05 significance level, test H_0: $p_1 = p_2$.
    b. At the 0.05 significance level, test H_0: $p_2 = p_3$.
    c. At the 0.05 significance level, test H_0: $p_1 = p_3$.
    d. In general, if hypothesis tests lead to the conclusions that $p_1 = p_2$ and $p_2 = p_3$ are reasonable, does it follow that $p_1 = p_3$ is also reasonable? Why or why not?

19. The *sample size* needed to estimate the difference between two population proportions to within a margin of error E with a confidence level of $1 - \alpha$ can be found as follows. In the expression

$$E = z_{\alpha/2} \sqrt{\frac{p_1 q_1}{n_1} + \frac{p_2 q_2}{n_2}}$$

replace n_1 and n_2 by n (assuming that both samples have the same size) and replace each of p_1, q_1, p_2, and q_2 by 0.5 (because their values are not known). Then solve for n.

Use this approach to find the size of each sample if you want to estimate the difference between the proportions of men and women who own cars. Assume that you want 95% confidence that your error is no more than 0.03.

Vocabulary List

independent samples
dependent samples
matched pairs
paired samples
F distribution

significance level
numerator degrees of freedom
denominator degrees of freedom
pooled estimate of σ^2
pooled estimate of p_1 and p_2

Review

Chapters 6 and 7 introduced two major concepts of inferential statistics: the estimation of population parameters and the methods of testing hypotheses made about population parameters. Whereas those chapters considered only cases involving a single population, this chapter considered two samples drawn from two populations.

- Section 8-2 considered inferences made about the means of (dependent) population data consisting of matched pairs.

- Section 8-3 considered inferences made about two independent populations, but the involved samples were both large ($n > 30$).

- Section 8-4 presented methods for testing claims about two population standard deviations or variances.

- Section 8-5 described procedures for making inferences about two independent populations, with at least one of the samples being small ($n \leq 30$). Sections 8-2, 8-3, and 8-5 dealt with a variety of different cases for making inferences about two population means; those cases were summarized in Figure 8-8 (for hypothesis tests) and Figure 8-9 (for confidence intervals).

- Section 8-6 discussed the procedures for making inferences about two population proportions.

Review Exercises

1. In a study of people who stop to help drivers with disabled cars, researchers hypothesized that more people would stop to help someone if they first saw another driver with a disabled car getting help. In one experiment, 2000 drivers first saw a woman being helped with a flat tire and then saw a second woman who was alone, farther down the road, with a flat tire; 2.90% of those 2000 drivers stopped to help the second woman. Among 2000 other drivers who did not see the first woman being helped, only 1.75% stopped to help (based on data from "Help on the Highway," by McCarthy, *Psychology Today*). At the 0.05 significance level, test the claim that the percentage of people who stop after first seeing a driver with a disabled car being helped is greater than the percentage of people who stop without first seeing someone else being helped.

2. Twelve Dozenol tablets are tested for solubility before and after being stored for one year. The indexes of solubility are given in the table below.

Before	472	487	506	512	489	503	511	501	495	504	494	462
After	562	512	523	528	554	513	516	510	524	510	524	508

   a. At the 0.05 significance level, test the claim that the Dozenol tablets are more soluble after the storage period.
   b. Construct a 95% confidence interval estimate of the mean difference of after − before.

3. In clinical tests of adverse reactions to the drug Viagra, 7% of the 734 subjects in the treatment group experienced dyspepsia (indigestion), but 2% of the 725 subjects in the placebo group experienced dyspepsia (based on data from Pfizer Pharmaceuticals).
   a. Is there sufficient evidence to support the claim that dyspepsia occurs at a higher rate among Viagra users than those who do not use Viagra?
   b. Construct a 95% confidence interval estimate of the difference between the dyspepsia rate for Viagra users and the dyspepsia rate for those who use a placebo. Do the confidence interval limits contain 0, and what does this suggest about the two dyspepsia rates?

4. Having just been charged more to fly from Toronto to Saint John than from Toronto to Britain, an annoyed passenger claims there is no difference in price between domestic and international flights. Using ads in the *Toronto Star*, his travelling companion compiles a random sample of prices for domestic flights from Toronto and flights from Toronto to Europe. Based on his results, shown below, test the disgruntled passenger's claim that there is no difference in price between these two types of flight. Use the 0.02 level of significance. Assume unequal standard deviations for the two samples.

Domestic	International
$n_1 = 12$	$n_2 = 16$
$\bar{x}_1 = 354.8$	$\bar{x}_2 = 522.6$
$s_1 = 76.8$	$s_2 = 179.3$

5. To conduct the means test in Exercise 4, it was assumed that the two samples had unequal variances. Test whether the evidence supports that assumption, at the 0.02 level of significance.

6. A test question is considered good if it discriminates between prepared and unprepared students. The first question on a test was answered correctly by 62 of 80 prepared students and by 23 of 50 unprepared students. At the 0.05 level of significance, test the claim that this question was answered correctly by a greater proportion of prepared students.

7. In a study of techniques used to measure lung volumes, physiological data were collected for 10 subjects. The values given in the accompanying table are in litres, representing the measured forced vital capacities of the 10 subjects in a sitting position and in a supine (lying) position. At the 0.05 significance level, test the claim that the position has no effect, so the mean difference is zero.

Subject	A	B	C	D	E	F	G	H	I	J
Sitting	4.66	5.70	5.37	3.34	3.77	7.43	4.15	6.21	5.90	5.77
Supine	4.63	6.34	5.72	3.23	3.60	6.96	3.66	5.81	5.61	5.33

Based on data from "Validation of Esophageal Balloon Technique at Different Lung Volumes and Postures," by Baydur et al., *Journal of Applied Physiology*, Vol. 62, No. 1.

8. A major airline is experimenting with its training program for flight attendants. With the traditional six-week program, a random sample of 60 flight attendants achieves competency test scores with a mean of 83.5 and a standard deviation of 16.3. With a new ten-day program, a random sample of 35 flight attendants achieve competency test scores with a mean of 79.8 and a standard deviation of 19.2. At the 0.01 significance level, test the claim that the ten-day program results in scores with a lower mean.

9. Researchers are testing commercial air-filtering systems made by the Winston Industrial Supply Company and the Barrington Filter Company. Random samples are tested for each company, and the filtering efficiency is scored on a standard scale, with the results shown in the margin. (Higher scores correspond to better filtering.) At the 0.05 level of significance, test the claim that both systems have the same mean.

Winston	Barrington
$n = 18$	$n = 24$
$\bar{x} = 85.7$	$\bar{x} = 80.6$
$s = 2.8$	$s = 9.7$

10. Data Set 18 in Appendix B shows body temperatures (in degrees Celsius) of adults accepted for voluntary surgical procedures in an urban hospital. Sample data for men are summarized by these statistics: $n = 12, \bar{x} = 36.275$, $s = 0.561$. Sample data for women are summarized by these statistics: $n = 12$, $\bar{x} = 36.533, s = 0.365$.
   a. At the 0.05 significance level, test the claim that both men and women who have been accepted for voluntary surgical procedures have the same mean temperature. Use a preliminary F test to determine whether the two populations have equal variances.
   b. Construct a 95% confidence interval for the difference between the two population means.

Cumulative Review Exercises

1. The data in the table on the next page were obtained through a survey of randomly selected subjects.
   a. If one of the survey subjects is randomly selected, find the probability of getting someone ticketed for speeding.
   b. If one of the survey subjects is randomly selected, find the probability of getting a male or someone ticketed for speeding.
   c. Find the probability of getting someone ticketed for speeding, given that the selected person is a man.
   d. Find the probability of getting someone ticketed for speeding, given that the selected person is a woman.
   e. Use a 0.05 level of significance to test the claim that the percentage of women ticketed for speeding is less than the percentage for men. Can we conclude that men generally speed more than women?

	Ticketed for Speeding Within the Last Year?	
	Yes	No
Men	26	224
Women	27	473

Based on data from R.H. Bruskin Associates.

2. The Newton Scientific Instrument Company manufactures scales with its day shift and night shift. Random samples are routinely tested with errors recorded as positive amounts for readings that are too high or negative for readings that are too low.

   a. A random sample of 40 scales made by the day shift is tested and the errors are found to have a mean of 1.2 g and a standard deviation of 3.9 g. Use a 0.05 significance level to test the claim that the sample comes from a population with a mean error equal to 0.

   b. A random sample of 33 scales made by the night shift is tested and the errors are found to have a mean of −1.4 g and a standard deviation of 4.3 g. Use a 0.05 significance level to test the claim that the sample comes from a population with a mean error equal to 0.

   c. Use a 0.05 significance level to test the claim that both shifts manufacture scales with the same mean error.

   d. Construct a 95% confidence interval for the mean error of the day shift.

   e. Construct a 95% confidence interval for the mean error of the night shift.

   f. Construct a 95% confidence interval for the difference between the means of errors for the day shift and night shift.

   g. If you want to estimate the mean error for the day shift, how many scales must you check if you want to be 95% confident that your mean is off by no more than 0.5 g? (*Hint:* Use the sample standard deviation in part (a) as an estimate of the population standard deviation σ.)

Technology Project

Refer to Data Set 1 in Appendix B and use Excel or STATDISK to retrieve the weights of discarded metal and plastic, which are already stored on a disk. Use Excel or STATDISK for each of the following.

a. Test the claim that the weights of discarded metal and the weights of discarded plastic have the same mean. Record the test statistic and *P*-value, and state your conclusion. Also construct a 95% confidence interval for the difference $\mu_m - \mu_p$, where μ_m is the mean weight of discarded metal and μ_p is the mean weight of discarded plastic.

b. The weights used in part (a) are given in pounds. They can be converted to kilograms by multiplying each value by 0.4536. Convert all of those weights from pounds to kilograms and then repeat part (a). Compare the results to those originally found in part (a). In general, are the results affected if a different scale is used?

c. The first weight of discarded metal is 1.09 lb. Change that value to 109 lb by deleting the decimal point. The value of 109 lb is clearly an outlier, but it is only one wrong entry among the 62 metal weights. After making that change, repeat part (a). How are the results affected by this outlier?

•••••••• FROM DATA TO DECISION ••••••••

Does Aspirin Help Prevent Heart Attacks?

In a recent study of 22,000 male physicians, half were given regular doses of aspirin while the other half were given placebos. The study ran for six years at a cost of $4.4 million. Among those who took the aspirin, 104 suffered heart attacks. Among those who took the placebos, 189 suffered heart attacks. (The figures are based on data from *Time* and the *New England Journal of Medicine,* Vol. 318, No. 4.) Do these results show a statistically significant decrease in heart attacks among the sample group who took aspirin? The issue is clearly important because it can affect many lives.

Use the methods of this chapter to determine whether the use of aspirin seems to help prevent heart attacks. Write a report that summarizes your findings. Include any relevant factors you can think of that might affect the validity of the study. For example, is it noteworthy that the study involved only male physicians? Is it noteworthy that aspirin sometimes causes stomach problems?

········ COOPERATIVE GROUP ACTIVITIES ········

1. *Out-of-class activity:* Are estimates influenced by anchoring numbers? Refer to the related Chapter 2 Cooperative Group Activity. In Chapter 2 we noted that, according to author John Rubin, when people must estimate a value, their estimate is often "anchored" to (or influenced by) a preceding number. In that Chapter 2 activity, subjects were asked to quickly estimate the value of $8 \times 7 \times 6 \times 5 \times 4 \times 3 \times 2 \times 1$, while others are asked to quickly estimate the value of $1 \times 2 \times 3 \times 4 \times 5 \times 6 \times 7 \times 8$.

   In Chapter 2, we compared the two sets of results by using statistics (such as the mean) and graphs (such as boxplots). The methods of Chapter 8 now allow us to compare the results with a formal hypothesis test. Collect sample data and test the claim that when we begin with larger numbers ($8 \times 7 \times 6$), our estimates tend to be larger.

2. *In-class activity:* In Exercise 15 from Section 8-3, we used pulse rates in Data Set 8 to test the claim that male and female statistics students have the same mean pulse rate. Divide into groups according to gender, with about 10 or 12 students in each group. Each group member should record his or her pulse rate by counting the number of heartbeats in one minute, and the group statistics (n, $\bar{x}$, s) should be calculated. The groups should exchange their results and test the same claim given in Exercise 15 from Section 8-3. Is there a difference? Why?

3. *In-class activity:* Divide into groups of about 10 or 12 students and use the same reaction timer included with the Chapter 5 Cooperative Group Activities. Each group member should be tested for right-hand reaction time and left-hand reaction time. Using the group results, test the claim that there is no difference between the right-hand and left-hand reaction times. Compare the conclusion to the conclusion reached by other groups. Is there a difference?

INTERNET PROJECT   Hypothesis Testing

Whereas Chapter 7 presented methods for testing hypotheses about a single population, the methods of this chapter extend those methods to two populations. Similarly, the Internet Project for this chapter differs from that of Chapter 7 through the use of two data sets in each of the hypothesis tests. The project can be found at

http://pearsoned.ca/triola

After choosing "Internet Projects" and then "Chapter 8" from the menus, you will find several hypothesis-testing problems that examine population demographics, salary fairness, and a traditional superstition. In each case you will formulate the problem as a hypothesis test using the notation of the chapter, seek out appropriate data, conduct the test, and then interpret the results with a summarizing conclusion.

Correlation and Regression

9-1 Overview

This chapter describes methods for dealing with relationships between two variables. The important concepts of correlation and regression are discussed.

9-2 Correlation

The relationship between two variables is investigated with a graph (called a scatter diagram) and a measure (called the linear correlation coefficient).

9-3 Regression

Linear relationships between two variables are described using the equation and graph of a straight line, called the regression line. A method for determining predicted values of a variable is also presented. The general concept of mathematical modelling is introduced.

9-4 Variation and Prediction Intervals

A method is presented for analysing the differences between the predicted values of a variable and the actual observed values. Prediction intervals, which are confidence interval estimates of predicted values, are constructed.

9-5 Multiple Regression

Methods are presented for finding a linear equation that relates three or more variables. The multiple coefficient of determination is presented as a measure of how well the sample points fit that linear equation. Because of the calculations involved, this section emphasizes the use of computer software and the interpretation of computer displays.

CHAPTER PROBLEM:

Do earthquakes at all latitudes have the same magnitude?

To most Canadians, earthquakes are probably viewed as rare occurrences, which usually strike somewhere else, such as in California. If a tremor is noticeable nearby (as has happened a few times in the Toronto area), it is treated as a newsworthy event. In fact, "seismic activity" or earthquakes are quite common. In just one month in 2001, Natural Resources Canada recorded 215 separate earthquakes that affected Canada, from Vancouver Island, B.C. to Wager Bay, Nunavut, to the Labrador Sea.

Not all earthquakes have the same strength either at their centre or in how they spread their energies. The commonly known Richter Scale (officially the Magnitude Local, or ML, scale) is one system for measuring earthquake magnitudes; but other systems may be preferred in certain circumstances.

The 215 earthquakes referred to above were spread across the whole of Canada. But was their magnitude the same in all locations? In particular, were the magnitudes greater at higher latitudes?

The data in Table 9-1 represent 13 randomly selected cases of seismic activity (earthquakes) from among those recorded between January 9 and February 8, 2001. (Only events whose magnitudes are recorded in the ML scale were selected.) For reasons of clarity, we use this abbreviated data set, but better results could be obtained if we used a more complete set of sample values. Based on these data, does there appear to be a relationship between the recorded magnitude and the recorded latitude of seismic activity? If so, what is that relationship? If we learn that an earthquake has occurred at a latitude of 64°N, how can we use that information to predict the magnitude of the event? These questions will be addressed in this chapter.

Table 9-1   Latitudes and Magnitudes of Seismic Activity

x Latitude (°N)	60.0	77.5	50.7	65.6	48.2	63.5	49.2	60.3	52.6	52.8	64.3	49.3	48.3
y Magnitude (ML)	4.1	4.0	2.6	2.8	0.9	2.2	3.0	4.1	1.2	1.1	5.5	2.7	0.9

Based on data from the Natural Resources Canada Web site

9-1 Overview

The main focus of this chapter is to form inferences based on sample data that come in *pairs*. Given such paired data, we want to determine whether there is a relationship between the two variables and, if so, identify what the relationship is. For example, using the data in Table 9-1, we want to determine whether there is a relationship between the latitude of recorded seismic activity and its magnitude. If such a relationship exists, we want to identify it with an equation so that we can predict the magnitude of seismic activity if we are informed of the latitude where it occurred.

We begin in Section 9-2 by considering the concept of correlation, which is used to determine whether there is a statistically significant relationship between two variables. We investigate correlation using the scatter diagram (a graph) and the linear correlation coefficient (a measure of the strength of linear association between two variables). Section 9-3 investigates regression analysis, where we construct an explanation that mathematically describes the relationship between two variables. We show how to use that equation to predict values of a variable.

In Section 9-4 we analyse the differences between predicted values and actual observed values of a variable. Sections 9-2 through 9-4 deal with relationships between two variables, but Section 9-5 uses concepts of multiple regression to describe the relationship among three or more variables. Throughout this text we deal only with linear (or straight-line) relationships between two or more variables.

9-2 Correlation

In this section we address the issue of determining whether there appears to be a relationship between two variables. In statistics, we refer to such a relationship as a *correlation*.

DEFINITION

A **correlation** exists between two variables when one of them is related to the other in some way.

Table 9-1, for example, consists of paired data (sometimes called **bivariate data**). We will determine whether there is a correlation between the variable x (length) and the variable y (weight).

As we work with sample data and develop methods of forming inferences about populations, we make the following assumptions.

Assumptions

1. The sample of paired (x, y) data is a *random* sample.
2. The pairs of (x, y) data have a **bivariate normal distribution.** (Normal distributions are discussed in Chapter 5, but this assumption basically

requires that for any fixed value of x, the corresponding values of y have a distribution that is bell shaped, and for any fixed value of y, the values of x have a distribution that is bell shaped.)

The second assumption is usually difficult to check, but a partial check can be made by determining whether the values of both x and y have distributions that are basically bell shaped.

Exploring the Data

Before working with the more formal computational methods of this section, we should first explore the data set to see what we can learn. We can often see a relationship between two variables by constructing a graph called a *scatterplot*, or *scatter diagram*.

DEFINITION

A **scatterplot** (or **scatter diagram**) is a graph in which the paired (x, y) sample data are plotted with a horizontal x-axis and a vertical y-axis. Each individual (x, y) is plotted as a single point.

As an example, see the Excel display of the 13 pairs of data listed in Table 9-1. When we examine such a scatterplot, we should study the overall pattern of the plotted points. If there is a pattern, we should note its direction: That is, as one variable increases, does the other seem to increase or decrease? We should observe whether there are any outliers which, in this context, means points that lie very far away from all the other points. The Excel-generated display does seem to reveal a pattern showing that larger recorded magnitudes

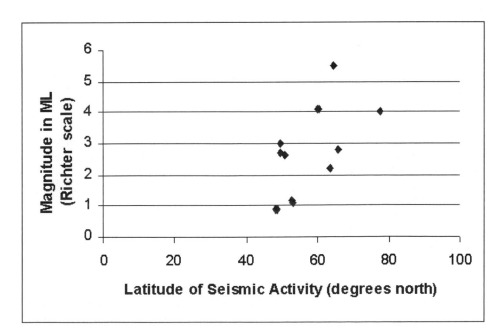

Excel Display Scatter Diagram Showing Correlation

Figure 9-1   Scatter Diagrams

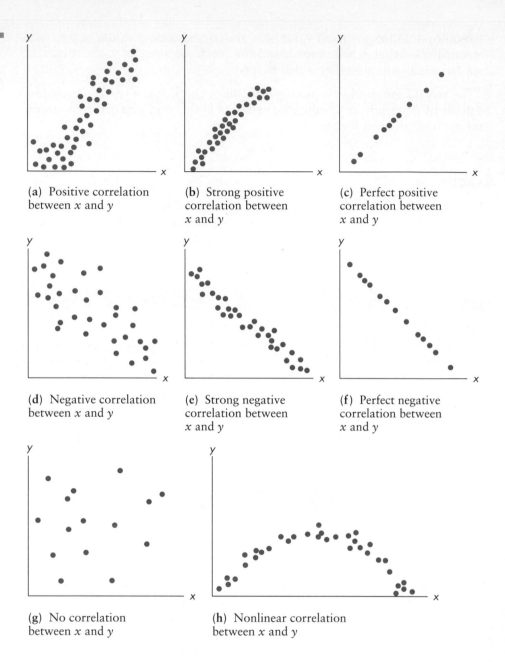

(a) Positive correlation between x and y

(b) Strong positive correlation between x and y

(c) Perfect positive correlation between x and y

(d) Negative correlation between x and y

(e) Strong negative correlation between x and y

(f) Perfect negative correlation between x and y

(g) No correlation between x and y

(h) Nonlinear correlation between x and y

for seismic activity tend to go along with higher recorded latitudes for the activity. There do not appear to be any outliers.

Other examples of scatter diagrams are shown in Figure 9-1. The graphs in Figure 9-1(a), (b), and (c) depict a pattern of increasing values of y that correspond to increasing values of x. As you proceed from (a) to (c), the dot pattern becomes closer to a straight line, suggesting that the relationship between x and y becomes stronger. The scatter diagrams in (d), (e), and (f) depict patterns in which the *y* values decrease as the *x* values increase. Again, as you proceed from (d) to (f), the relationship becomes stronger. In contrast to the first six graphs, the scatter diagram of (g) shows no pattern and suggests that there is no correlation (or relationship) between *x* and *y*. Finally, the scatter diagram of (h) shows a pattern, but it is not a straight-line pattern.

Linear Correlation Coefficient

Because conclusions drawn from scatter diagrams are largely subjective, we need more precise and objective methods. We will use the linear correlation coefficient, which is useful for detecting straight-line patterns.

DEFINITION

The **linear correlation coefficient** *r* measures the strength of the linear relationship between the paired *x* and *y* values in a *sample*. Its value is computed by using Formula 9-1, which follows. [The linear correlation coefficient is sometimes referred to as the **Pearson product moment correlation coefficient** in honour of Karl Pearson (1857–1936), who originally developed it.]

Formula 9-1

$$r = \frac{n\Sigma xy - (\Sigma x)(\Sigma y)}{\sqrt{n(\Sigma x^2) - (\Sigma x)^2}\ \sqrt{n(\Sigma y^2) - (\Sigma y)^2}}$$

Because *r* is calculated using sample data, it is a sample statistic used to measure the strength of the linear correlation between *x* and *y*. If we had every pair of population values for *x* and *y*, the result of Formula 9-1 would be a population parameter, represented by ρ (pronounced "rho").

We will describe how to compute and interpret the linear correlation coefficient *r* given a list of paired data, but we will first identify the notation relevant to Formula 9-1. Later in this section we will present the underlying theory that led to the development of Formula 9-1.

Rounding the Linear Correlation Coefficient *r*

Round the linear correlation coefficient *r* to three decimal places (so that its value can be directly compared to critical values in Table A-6). In the social sciences *r* is often rounded off to two decimal points. When calculating *r* and other statistics in this chapter, rounding in the middle of a calculation often creates substantial errors, so try using your calculator's memory to store intermediate results and round off only at the end. Many inexpensive calculators have Formula 9-1 built in so that you can automatically evaluate *r* after entering the sample data.

Cell Phones and Crashes

Because some countries have banned the use of cell phones in cars while other countries are considering such a ban, researchers studied the issue of whether the use of cell phones while driving increases the chance of a crash. A sample of 699 drivers was obtained. Members of the sample group used cell phones and were involved in crashes. Subjects completed questionnaires and their telephone records were checked. Telephone usage was compared to the time interval immediately preceding a crash to a comparable time period the day before. Conclusion: Use of a cell phone was associated with a crash risk that was about four times as high as the risk when a cell phone was not used. (See "Association between Cellular-Telephone Calls and Motor Vehicle Collisions," by Redelmeier and Tibshirani, New England Journal of Medicine, Vol. 336, No. 7.

Notation for the Linear Correlation Coefficient

n	represents the number of pairs of data present.
Σ	denotes the addition of the items indicated.
Σx	denotes the sum of all x values.
Σx^2	indicates that each x value should be squared and then those squares added.
$(\Sigma x)^2$	indicates that the x values should be added and the total then squared. It is extremely important to avoid confusing Σx^2 and $(\Sigma x)^2$.
Σxy	indicates that each x value should be first multiplied by its corresponding y value. After obtaining all such products, find their sum. (Note: each product of corresponding x and y values is called a **cross product**.)
r	represents the linear correlation coefficient for a *sample*.
ρ	represents the linear correlation coefficient for a *population*.

EXAMPLE   Using the data in Table 9-1, find the value of the linear correlation coefficient r. (A later example will use this value to determine whether there is a relationship between the recorded latitudes and magnitudes of seismic activity.)

SOLUTION   For the sample paired data in Table 9-1, $n = 13$ because there are 13 pairs of data. The other components required in Formula 9-1 are found from the calculations in Table 9-2. Note how this vertical format makes the calculations easier.

Using the calculated values and Formula 9-1, we can now evaluate r as follows:

$$r = \frac{n\Sigma xy - (\Sigma x)(\Sigma y)}{\sqrt{n(\Sigma x^2) - (\Sigma x)^2}\sqrt{n(\Sigma y^2) - (\Sigma y)^2}}$$

$$= \frac{13(2100.84) - (742.3)(35.1)}{\sqrt{13(43344.79) - (742.3)^2}\sqrt{13(119.87) - (35.1)^2}}$$

$$= \frac{1256.19}{\sqrt{12472.98}\sqrt{326.3}} = 0.623$$

These calculations get quite messy with large data sets, so it's fortunate that the linear correlation coefficient can be found automatically with many different calculators and computer programs. For example, see "Using Technology" at the end of this section.

TABLE 9-2	Finding Statistics Used to Calculate r			
Latitude (°N)	Magnitude (ML)			
x	y	$x \cdot y$	x^2	y^2
60.0	4.1	246.00	3600.00	16.81
77.5	4.0	310.00	6006.25	16.00
50.7	2.6	131.82	2570.49	6.76
65.6	2.8	183.68	4303.36	7.84
48.2	0.9	43.38	2323.24	0.81
63.5	2.2	139.70	4032.25	4.84
49.2	3.0	147.60	2420.64	9.00
60.3	4.1	247.23	3636.09	16.81
52.6	1.2	63.12	2766.76	1.44
52.8	1.1	58.08	2787.84	1.21
64.3	5.5	353.65	4134.49	30.25
49.3	2.7	133.11	2430.49	7.29
48.3	0.9	43.47	2332.89	0.81
Total 742.3	35.1	2100.84	43344.79	119.87
↑	↑	↑	↑	↑
Σx	Σy	Σxy	Σx^2	Σy^2

Interpreting the Linear Correlation Coefficient

We need to interpret a calculated value of r, such as the value of 0.623 found in the preceding example. Given the way that Formula 9-1 was developed, the value of r must always fall between -1 and $+1$ inclusive. If r is close to 0, we conclude that there is no significant linear correlation between x and y, but if r is close to -1 or $+1$, we conclude that there is a significant linear correlation between x and y. Interpretations of "close to" 0 or 1 or -1 are vague, so we use the following very specific decision criterion:

> If the absolute value of the computed value of r exceeds the value in Table A-6, conclude that there is a significant linear correlation. Otherwise, there is not sufficient evidence to support the conclusion of a significant linear correlation.

AS When there really is no actual linear correlation between x and y, Table A-6 lists values that are "critical" in this sense: They separate *usual* values of r from those that are *unusual*. For example, Table A-6 shows us that with $n = 13$ pairs of sample data, the critical values are 0.553 (for $\alpha = 0.05$) and 0.684 (for $\alpha = 0.01$). Critical values and the role of α are carefully described in Chapters 6 and 7. Here's how we interpret those numbers: With 13 pairs of data and no actual linear correlation between x and y, there is a 5% chance that the absolute value of the computed linear correlation coefficient r will exceed 0.553. With $n = 13$ and no actual linear correlation, there is a 1% chance that $|r|$ will exceed 0.684.

Power Lines Correlate with Cancer

Interesting, surprising, and useful results sometimes occur when correlations are found between variables. Several scientific studies suggest that there is a correlation between exposure to electromagnetic fields and the occurrence of cancer. Epidemiologists from Sweden's Karolinska Institute researched 500,000 Swedes who lived within 300 metres of a high-tension power line during a 25-year period. They found that the children had a higher incidence of leukemia. Their findings led Sweden's government to consider regulations that would reduce housing in close proximity to high-tension power lines. In an article on this study, *Time* magazine reported: "Although the research does not prove cause and effect, it shows an unmistakable correlation between the degree of exposure and the risk of childhood leukemia."

EXAMPLE   Given the sample data in Table 9-1 for which $r = 0.623$, refer to Table A-6 to determine whether there is a significant linear correlation between the recorded latitudes and magnitudes of seismic activity. In Table A-6, use the critical value for $\alpha = 0.05$. (With $\alpha = 0.05$, we will conclude that there is a significant linear correlation only if the sample is unlikely in the sense that such a value of r occurs less than 5% of the time.)

SOLUTION   Referring to Table A-6, we locate the row for which $n = 13$ (because there are 13 pairs of data). That row contains the critical values of 0.553 (for $\alpha = 0.05$) and 0.684 (for $\alpha = 0.01$). Using the critical value for $\alpha = 0.05$, we see that there is less than a 5% chance that with no linear correlation, the absolute value of the computed r will exceed 0.553. Because $r = 0.623$, its absolute value does exceed 0.553, so we conclude that there is a significant linear correlation between recorded latitudes and magnitudes of seismic activity.

We have already noted that the format of Formula 9-1 requires that the calculated value of r always falls between -1 and $+1$ inclusive. We list that property along with other important properties.

Properties of the Linear Correlation Coefficient r

1. The value of r is always between -1 and 1. That is,
$$-1 \leq r \leq 1$$

2. *The value of r does not change if all values of either variable are converted to a different scale.* For example, if the latitudes in Table 9-1 are given in minutes instead of degrees, the value of r will not change.

3. *The value of r is not affected by the choice of x or y.* Interchange all x and y values and the value of r will not change.

4. *r measures the strength of a linear relationship.* It is not designed to measure the strength of a relationship that is not linear.

Common Errors Involving Correlation

We now identify three of the most common errors made in interpreting results involving correlation.

1. *A common source of error involves concluding that correlation implies causality.* One study showed a correlation between the salaries of statistics professors and per capita beer consumption, but those two variables are affected by the state of the economy, a third variable lurking in the background. (A **lurking variable** is formally defined as one that affects the variables being studied, but is not included in the study.)

AS

2. *Another source of error arises with data based on rates or averages.* Averages suppress the variation among the individuals or items, and this may lead to an inflated correlation coefficient. One study produced a 0.4 linear correlation coefficient for paired data relating income and education among individuals, but the linear correlation coefficient became 0.7 when regional averages were used.

3. *A third source of error involves the property of linearity.* The conclusion that there is no significant linear correlation does not mean that x and y are not related in any way. The data depicted in Figure 9-2 result in a value of $r = 0$, which is an indication of no *linear* correlation between the two variables. However, we can easily see from Figure 9-2 that there is a pattern reflecting a very strong *nonlinear* relationship. (Figure 9-2 is a scatter diagram that depicts the relationship between distance above ground and time elapsed for an object thrown upward.)

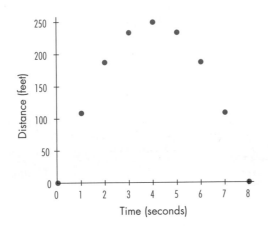

Figure 9-2 Scatter Diagram of Distance Above Ground and Time for Object Thrown Upward

Formal Hypothesis Test (requires coverage of Chapter 7)

We present two methods (summarized in Figure 9-3) for using a formal hypothesis test to determine whether there is a significant linear correlation between two variables. Some instructors prefer Method 1 because it reinforces concepts introduced in earlier chapters. Others prefer Method 2 because it involves easier calculations.

Figure 9-3 shows that the null and alternative hypotheses will be expressed as follows:

H_0: $\rho = 0$ (no significant linear correlation)

H_1: $\rho \neq 0$ (significant linear correlation)

For the test statistic, we use one of the following methods.

Method 1: Test Statistic Is t   This method follows the format presented in earlier chapters. It uses the Student t distribution with a test statistic having the form $t = (r - \mu_r)/s_r$, where μ_r and s_r denote the claimed value of the mean and the sample standard deviation of r values. Because we assume that $\rho = 0$, it follows that $\mu_r = 0$. Also, it can be shown that s_r, the standard deviation of linear correlation coefficients, can be expressed as $\sqrt{(1 - r^2)/(n - 2)}$. We can therefore use the following test statistic.

Test Statistic t for Linear Correlation

$$t = \frac{r}{\sqrt{\dfrac{1 - r^2}{n - 2}}}$$

Critical values: Use Table A-3 with degrees of freedom $= n - 2$.

Figure 9-3   Testing for a Linear Correlation

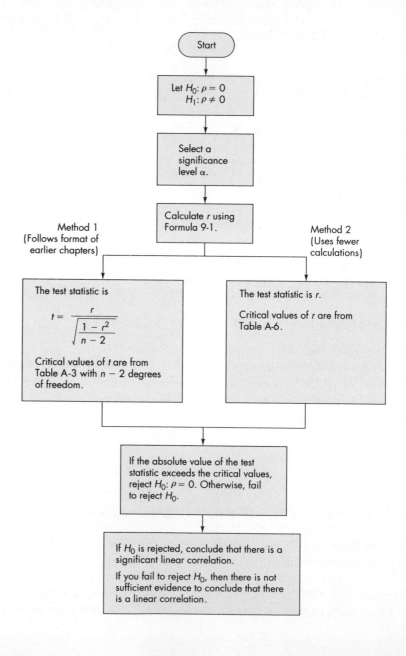

Method 2: Test Statistic Is r   This method requires fewer calculations. Instead of calculating the test statistic just given, we use the computed value of r as the test statistic. Critical values are found in Table A-6.

Test Statistic r for Linear Correlation
Test statistic: r **Critical values:** Refer to Table A-6.

Figure 9-3 shows that the decision criterion is to reject the null hypothesis of $\rho = 0$ if the absolute value of the test statistic exceeds the critical values; rejection of $\rho = 0$ means that there is sufficient evidence to support a claim of a linear correlation between the two variables. If the absolute value of the test statistic does not exceed the critical values, then we fail to reject $\rho = 0$; that is, there is not sufficient evidence to conclude that there is a linear correlation between the two variables.

EXAMPLE   Using the sample data in Table 9-1, test the claim that there is a linear correlation between the recorded latitudes and magnitudes of seismic activity. For the test statistic, use both (a) Method 1 and (b) Method 2.

SOLUTION   Refer to Figure 9-3. To claim that there is a significant linear correlation is to claim that the population linear correlation ρ is different from 0. We therefore have the following hypotheses:

$$H_0: \rho = 0 \quad \text{(no significant linear correlation)}$$
$$H_1: \rho \neq 0 \quad \text{(significant linear correlation)}$$

No significance level α was specified, so use $\alpha = 0.05$.

In a preceding example we already found that $r = 0.623$. With that value, we now find the test statistic and critical value, using each of the two methods just described.

a. *Method 1:* The test statistic is

$$t = \frac{r}{\sqrt{\dfrac{1 - r^2}{n - 2}}} = \frac{0.623}{\sqrt{\dfrac{1 - 0.623^2}{13 - 2}}} = 2.642$$

The critical values of $t = -2.201$ and $t = 2.201$ are found in Table A-3, where 2.201 corresponds to 0.05 divided between two tails (with 0.025 in each tail) and the number of degrees of freedom is $n - 2 = 11$. See Figure 9-4 for the graph that includes the test statistic and critical values.

b. *Method 2:* The test statistic is $r = 0.623$. The critical values of $r = -0.553$ and $r = 0.553$ are found in Table A-6 with $n = 13$ and

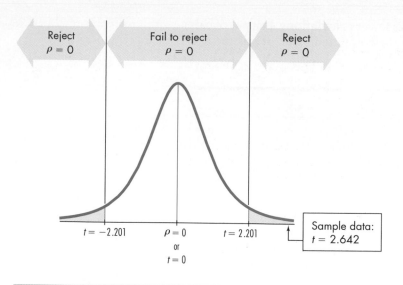

Figure 9-4   Testing H_0: $\rho = 0$ with Method 1

Figure 9-5   Testing H_0: $\rho = 0$ with Method 2

$\alpha = 0.05$. See Figure 9-5 for a graph that includes this test statistic and critical values.

Using either of the two methods, we find that the absolute value of the test statistic does exceed the critical value (Method 1: $2.642 > 2.201$; Method 2: $0.623 > 0.553$); that is, the test statistic does fall within the critical region. We therefore reject H_0: $\rho = 0$.

Interpretation   There is sufficient evidence to support the claim of a linear correlation between the recorded latitudes and magnitudes of seismic activity. Seismic activity detected and recorded at higher latitudes tends to have a higher magnitude than activity at lower latitudes.

One-tailed tests: The preceding example and Figures 9-4 and 9-5 illustrate a two-tailed hypothesis test. The examples and exercises in this section will generally involve only two-tailed tests, but one-tailed tests can occur with a claim of a positive linear correlation or a claim of a negative linear correlation. In such cases, the hypotheses will be as shown here.

Claim of Negative Correlation (Left-tailed test)	Claim of Positive Correlation (Right-tailed test)
H_0: $\rho \geq 0$	H_0: $\rho \leq 0$
H_1: $\rho < 0$	H_1: $\rho > 0$

For these one-tailed tests, Method 1 can be handled as in earlier chapters. For Method 2, either calculate the critical value as described in Exercise 25 or modify Table A-6 by replacing the column headings of $\alpha = 0.05$ and $\alpha = 0.01$ by the one-sided critical values of $\alpha = 0.025$ and $\alpha = 0.005$, respectively.

Palm Reading

Some people believe that the length of their palm's lifeline can be used to predict longevity. M.E. Wilson and L.E. Mather refuted that belief with a study of cadavers. Ages at death were recorded, along with the lengths of palm lifelines. The authors concluded that there is no significant correlation between age at death and length of lifeline. Palmistry lost, hands down.

Explanation for formula for calculating r:

We have presented Formula 9-1 for calculating r and have illustrated its use; we will now give a justification for it. Formula 9-1 simplifies the calculations used in this equivalent formula:

$$r = \frac{\Sigma(x - \bar{x})(y - \bar{y})}{(n - 1)s_x s_y}$$

We will temporarily use this latter version of Formula 9-1 because its form relates more directly to the underlying theory. We will consider the following paired data, which are depicted in the scatter diagram shown in Figure 9-6:

x	1	1	2	4	7
y	4	5	8	15	23

Figure 9-6 includes the point $(\bar{x}, \bar{y}) = (3, 11)$, which is called the centroid of the sample points.

DEFINITION

Given a collection of paired (x, y) data, the point $(\bar{x}, \bar{y})$ is called the centroid.

The statistic r, sometimes called the Pearson product moment, was first developed by Karl Pearson. It is based on the product of the moments $(x - \bar{x})$ and $(y - \bar{y})$; that is, Pearson based his measure of scattering on the statistic $\Sigma(x - \bar{x})(y - \bar{y})$. In any scatter diagram, vertical and horizontal lines

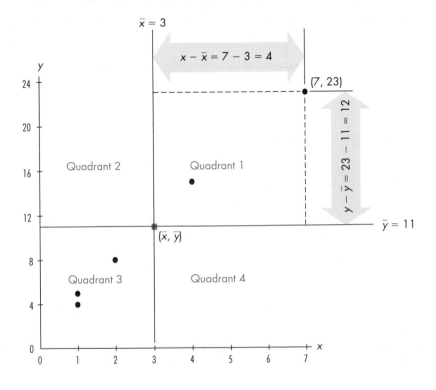

Figure 9-6   Scatter Diagram Partitioned into Quadrants

Student Ratings of Teachers

Many colleges equate high student ratings with good teaching—an equation often fostered by the fact that student evaluations are easy to administer and measure.

However, one study that compared student evaluations of teachers with the amount of material learned found a strong *negative* correlation between the two factors. Teachers rated highly by students seemed to induce less learning.

In a related study, an audience gave a high rating to a lecturer who conveyed very little information but was interesting and entertaining.

through the centroid $(\bar{x}, \bar{y})$ divide the diagram into four quadrants, as in Figure 9-6. If the points of the scatter diagram tend to approximate an uphill line (as in the figure), individual values of the product $(x - \bar{x})(y - \bar{y})$ tend to be positive because most of the points are found in the first and third quadrants, where the products of $(x - \bar{x})$ and $(y - \bar{y})$ are positive. If the points of the scatter diagram approximate a downhill line, most of the points are in the second and fourth quadrants, where $(x - \bar{x})$ and $(y - \bar{y})$ are opposite in sign, so $\Sigma(x - \bar{x})(y - \bar{y})$ is negative. Points that follow no linear pattern tend to be scattered among the four quadrants, so the value of $\Sigma(x - \bar{x})(y - \bar{y})$ tends to be close to 0.

The sum $\Sigma(x - \bar{x})(y - \bar{y})$ depends on the magnitude of the numbers used. For example, if you change x from inches to feet, that sum will change. To make r independent of the particular scale used, we include the sample standard deviations as follows:

$$r = \frac{\Sigma(x - \bar{x})(y - \bar{y})}{(n - 1)s_x s_y}$$

This expression can be algebraically manipulated into the equivalent form of Formula 9-1.

Preceding chapters discussed methods of inferential statistics by addressing methods of hypothesis testing, as well as methods for constructing confidence interval estimates. A similar procedure may be used to find confidence intervals for ρ. However, because the construction of such confidence intervals involves somewhat complicated transformations, that process is presented in Exercise 26 (Beyond the Basics).

We can use the linear correlation coefficient to determine whether there is a linear relationship between two variables. Using the data in Table 9-1, we have concluded that there is a linear correlation between the recorded latitudes and magnitudes of earthquakes. Having concluded that a relationship exists, we would like to determine what that relationship is so that we can calculate the magnitude of an earthquake when we know only its latitude. This next stage of analysis is addressed in the following section.

Using Technology

Excel: Excel has a function that calculates the value of the linear correlation coefficient. First enter the paired sample data in two adjacent columns (such as A1:A13 for x and B1:B13 for y). Click on the **fx** function key located on the main menu bar. Select the function category **Statistical** and the function name **CORREL**, then click **OK**. In the dialog box, enter the cell range of values for x, and the cell range of values for y.

To obtain a scatterplot, click on the Chart Wizard icon, and then select the chart type identified as **XY(Scatter)**. In the dialog box, enter the input range of the data, such as A1:B13. Click **Next** and proceed to use the dialog boxes to modify the graph as desired.

STATDISK: Select **Analysis** from the main menu bar, then use the option **Correlation and Regression.** Enter the paired data, or use Copy/Paste to copy in the data (from Excel, for example). Click on the **Evaluate** button. The display will include the value of the linear correlation coefficient along with the critical value of r, the conclusion of a hypothesis test, and other results to be discussed in later sections. Graphs, including a scatterplot, can also be obtained by clicking on the Plot 1 and Plot 2 buttons.

9-2 Exercises A: Basic Skills and Concepts

In Exercises 1 and 2, assume that a sample of n pairs of data results in the given value of r. Is there is a significant linear correlation between x and y? Explain.   What proportion of the variation in y can be explained by the variation in x?

1. a. $n = 32, r = 0.992$
   b. $n = 50, r = -0.333$
   c. $n = 17, r = 0.456$

2. a. $n = 22, r = -0.087$
   b. $n = 40, r = 0.299$
   c. $n = 25, r = -0.401$

In Exercises 3 and 4, (a) use a scatterplot to determine whether there is a significant linear correlation between x and y, and (b) find the values of n, Σx, Σx^2, $(\Sigma x)^2$, Σxy, and the linear correlation coefficient r.

3.
x	2	3	5	5	10
y	6	9	14	16	30

4.
x	2	3	5	5	10
y	6	0	15	5	2

In Exercises 5–18,
a. *Construct the scatterplot.*
b. *Find the value of the linear correlation coefficient r.*
c. *Determine whether there is a significant linear correlation between the two variables. (Use $\alpha = 0.05$.)*
d. *Save your work because some of the same data will be used in the next section.*

5. When bears were anesthetized, researchers measured the distances (in inches) around their chests and they weighed the bears (in pounds). The results are given below for 8 male bears. Based on the results, does a bear's weight seem to be related to its chest size? Do the results change if the chest measurements are converted to feet, with each of those values divided by 12?

x Chest (in.)	26	45	54	49	41	49	44	19
y Weight (lb)	90	344	416	348	262	360	332	34

Based on data from Gary Alt and Minitab.

6. The accompanying table lists the number of Christmas trees (in thousands) exported from New Brunswick in one year and the dollar value

(also in thousands) of those exports. Based on the results, can New Brunswick depend on receiving a greater dollar value for tree exports when it exports more trees? Do the results change if the tree numbers are entered as 358,000, 341,000, 364,000, and 367,000?

x Trees	358	341	364	367
y Dollars	3978	3729	4073	4564

Based on data from Statistics Canada.

7. The accompanying table lists weights (in kilograms) of plastic discarded by a sample of households, along with the sizes of the households (adapted from Data Set 1). Is there a significant linear correlation? This issue is important because the presence of a correlation implies that Statistics Canada could predict population size by analysing discarded garbage.

Plastic	0.12	0.64	0.99	1.28	0.99	0.82	0.39	1.38
Household size	2	3	3	6	4	2	1	5

8. The paired data below consist of weights (in kilograms) of discarded paper and sizes of the households.

Paper	1.09	3.43	4.33	4.00	3.96	3.16	3.10	5.18
Household size	2	3	3	6	4	2	1	5

9. A study was conducted to compare the incubation periods and fledgling periods (in days) of different bird species. Sample data are given below for randomly selected species.
   a. Do the incubation and fledgling periods appear to be related?
   b. Each of the numbers shown in the table is itself a mean—for the incubation or fledgling periods *of an entire species*. Suppose the data gave the incubation and fledgling periods of randomly selected *individual* birds. Would you expect r to be larger or smaller than you obtained in part (a)? Explain.

Incubation	23	13	53	23	30	17	78	49	15	12	18
Fledgling	35	11	360	30	53	28	280	49	17	22	28

10. An investor is considering whether to add a mining stock to his portfolio as a long-term investment. In his research he compares, for the years 1995–2000, the year's closing price for a Toronto-based mining firm and the year's closing value for the TSE 300 index, an indicator of general price trends for stocks traded on the Toronto Stock Exchange (based on data from *Management Information Circular*, January 26, 2001, TWIN Mining Corporation, Toronto).
    a. Does the stock price appear to be related to the TSE 300 index?
    b. These data were collected during a long period of general increase in TSE 300 values. If the TSE 300 begins to drop, is it reasonable to rely on the results found in part (a)? Why or why not?

Mining stock	0.450	0.600	0.210	0.160	0.335	0.400
TSE 300	9397.97	12061.95	13868.54	13648.84	17977.46	19309.36

11. To investigate the relationship between a person's education level and his or her salary, these variables were compared for people in selected occupations. Salaries are shown in thousands of dollars. Based on these results, does salary appear to depend on years of education?

12. A stock-market investor is seeking clues to pick the most profitable companies. The accompanying table lists, for each of 11 companies, its profit margin (as a percent) versus its ratio of current assets to current liabilities. Are higher profit margins associated with higher ratios of current assets to current liabilities? Would it be advisable for the investor to rely heavily on this indicator?

Profit margin	3.9	2.9	9.4	6.1	–0.6	3.6	2.7	1.0	2.2	8.3	3.9
Assets/liabilities	1.3	1.3	1.1	1.5	1.7	1.5	1.6	1.5	1.0	1.1	0.9

Based on data from Statistics Canada.

Years of education	salary
16	61.10
10	26.53
11	29.57
11	28.38
13	37.62
13	27.22
12	36.70
10	14.77
12	22.23
12	24.82
14	32.89
13	36.94
15	35.99
11	23.11
14	62.56
10	21.31

Based on data from Statistics Canada.

13. Refer to Data Set 16 in Appendix B.
   a. Use the paired data for durations and intervals after eruptions of the Old Faithful geyser. Is there a significant linear correlation, suggesting that the interval after an eruption is related to the duration of the eruption?
   b. Use the paired data for intervals after eruptions and heights of eruptions of the Old Faithful geyser. Is there a significant linear correlation, suggesting that the interval after an eruption is related to the height of the eruption?
   c. Assume you want to develop a method for predicting the time interval to the next eruption. Based on the results from parts (a) and (b), which factor would be more relevant: eruption duration or eruption height? Why?

14. Refer to Data Set 4 in Appendix B and use the paired columns for annual temperature and precipitation. Based on the result, does there appear to be a significant linear correlation between annual temperature and precipitation? If so, can researchers reduce their expenses by measuring only one of these two variables?

15. Refer to Data Set 21 in Appendix B.
   a. Use the paired data consisting of price and carat (weight). Is there a significant linear correlation between the price of a diamond and its weight in carats?
   b. Use the paired price/colour data. Assuming the colour data is recorded in an interval scale, is there a significant linear correlation between the price of a diamond and its colour?
   c. Assume that you are planning to buy a diamond engagement ring. In considering the value of a diamond, which characteristic should you consider to be more important: the carat weight or the colour? Why?

16. Refer to Date Set 4 in Appendix B and use the paired columns for annual temperature and snowfall. Based on the results, does there appear to be a significant correlation between annual temperature and snowfall? If so, can researchers reduce their expenses by measuring only one of these two variables?

17. Unlike Data Set 4, Data Set 7 in Appendix B records precipitation levels and temperatures in terms of *deviations from seasonal norms*, rather than in absolute terms. Use the columns in Data Set 7 in Appendix B for temperature departures and precipitation departures to test whether there appears to be a significant linear correlation between annual spring temperature

departures and precipitation departures from seasonal norms. Is there a contradiction between the results from this exercise and the results from Exercise 14?

18. The data below are extracted from the top ten entries in the *Financial Post* list of top 500 companies. The number of employees is given in thousands and the revenues for 1997 are given in billions of dollars. Is there a significant linear correlation between these companies' revenues and their numbers of employees? Would you necessarily expect that your results for these top companies would apply to all companies on the list, or to those that did not make the list?

Employees	29	122	24	30	16	3	83	50	43	33
Revenues	34.2	33.2	27.9	17.2	16.7	14.2	13.9	12.1	11.2	10.8

In Exercises 19–22, describe the error in the stated conclusion. (See the list of common errors included in this section.)

19. *Given:* The paired sample data of the ages of subjects and their scores on a test of reasoning result in a linear correlation coefficient very close to 0.
    Conclusion: Younger people tend to get higher scores.

20. *Given:* There is a significant linear correlation between personal income and years of education.
    Conclusion: More education causes a person's income to rise.

21. *Given:* Subjects take a test of verbal skills and a test of manual dexterity, and those pairs of scores result in a linear correlation coefficient very close to 0.
    Conclusion: Scores on the two tests are not related in any way.

22. *Given:* There is a significant linear correlation between provincial average tax burdens and provincial average incomes.
    Conclusion: There is a significant linear correlation between individual tax burdens and individual incomes.

9-2 Exercises B: Beyond the Basics

23. How is the value of the linear correlation coefficient r affected in each of the following cases?
    a. Each x value is switched with the corresponding y value.
    b. Each x value is multiplied by the same nonzero constant.
    c. The same constant is added to each x value.

24. In addition to testing for a linear correlation between x and y, we can often use *transformations* of data to explore for other relationships. For example, we might replace each x value by x^2 and use the methods of this section to determine whether there is a linear correlation between y and x^2. Given the paired data in the accompanying table, construct the scatter diagram and then test for a linear correlation between y and each of the following. Which case results in the largest value of r?

    a. x b. x^2 c. $\log x$ d. $\sqrt{x}$ e. $1/x$

x	1.3	2.4	2.6	2.8	2.4	3.0	4.1
y	0.11	0.38	0.41	0.45	0.39	0.48	0.61

25. The critical values of r in Table A-6 are found by solving

$$t = \frac{r}{\sqrt{\dfrac{1-r^2}{n-2}}}$$

for r to get

$$r = \frac{t}{\sqrt{t^2 + n - 2}}$$

where the t value is found from Table A-3 by assuming a two-tailed case with $n-2$ degrees of freedom. Table A-6 lists the results for selected values of n and α. Use the formula for r given here and Table A-3 (with $n-2$ degrees of freedom) to find the critical values of r for the given cases.
a. $H_0: \rho = 0$, $n = 50$, $\alpha = 0.05$
b. $H_1: \rho \neq 0$, $n = 75$, $\alpha = 0.10$
c. $H_0: \rho \geq 0$, $n = 20$, $\alpha = 0.05$
d. $H_0: \rho \leq 0$, $n = 10$, $\alpha = 0.05$
e. $H_1: \rho > 0$, $n = 12$, $\alpha = 0.01$

26. Given n pairs of data from which the linear correlation coefficient r can be found, use the following procedure to construct a confidence interval about the population parameter ρ.

Step a.   Use Table A-2 to find $z_{\alpha/2}$ that corresponds to the desired degree of confidence.

Step b.   Evaluate the interval limits w_L and w_R:

$$w_L = \frac{1}{2} \ln\left(\frac{1+r}{1-r}\right) - z_{\alpha/2} \cdot \frac{1}{\sqrt{n-3}}$$

$$w_R = \frac{1}{2} \ln\left(\frac{1+r}{1-r}\right) - z_{\alpha/2} \cdot \frac{1}{\sqrt{n-3}}$$

Step c.   Now evaluate the confidence interval limits in the expression below:

$$\frac{e^{2w_L} - 1}{e^{2w_L} + 1} < \rho < \frac{e^{2w_R} - 1}{e^{2w_R} + 1}$$

Use this procedure to construct a 95% confidence interval for ρ, given 50 pairs of data for which $r = 0.600$.

27. Refer to Table 9-1, used for the Chapter Problem. This table includes paired data representing the recorded latitudes and magnitudes of seismic activity (earthquakes). These data can only be recorded if an earthquake is picked up by monitors, and the great majority of these are located in Canada's lower latitudes. If it is possible that the widely spaced monitors in northern Canada are failing to detect lower-magnitude earthquakes in those latitudes, what effect could this have on our interpretation of this chapter's correlation results?

9-3 Regression

In Section 9-2 we analysed paired data with the goal of determining whether there is a significant linear correlation between two variables. We now want to describe the relationship by finding the graph and equation of the straight line that represents the relationship. This straight line is called the *regression line*, and its equation is called the *regression equation*. Sir Francis Galton (1822–1911) studied the phenomenon of heredity and showed that when tall or short couples have children, the heights of those children tend to *regress*, or revert to a more typical mean height. We continue to use his terminology.

DEFINITIONS

Given a collection of paired sample data, the **regression equation**

$$\hat{y} = b_0 + b_1 x$$

algebraically describes the relationship between the two variables. The graph of the regression equation is called the **regression line** (or *line of best fit*, or *least-squares line*).

This definition expresses a relationship between x (called the **independent variable** or **predictor variable**) and $\hat{y}$ (called the **dependent variable** or **response variable**). In the preceding definition, the typical equation of a straight line ($y = mx + b$) is expressed in the format of $\hat{y} = b_0 + b_1 x$, where b_0 is the y-intercept and b_1 is the slope. The following notation box shows that b_0 and b_1 are sample statistics used to estimate the population parameters β_0 and β_1.

Notation for Regression Equation		
	Population Parameter	Sample Statistic
y-intercept of regression equation	β_0	b_0
Slope of regression equation	β_1	b_1
Equation of the regression line	$y = \beta_0 + \beta_1 x$	$\hat{y} = b_0 + b_1 x$

For the regression methods given in this section, we make these assumptions:

Assumptions:

1. We are investigating only *linear* relationships.
2. For each x value, y is a random variable having a normal (bell-shaped) distribution. All of these y distributions have the same variance. Also, for a given value of x, the distribution of y values has a mean that lies on the regression line. (Results are not seriously affected if departures from normal distributions and equal variances are not too extreme.)

An important goal of this section is to use sample paired data to estimate the regression equation. Using only sample data, we can't find the exact values of the population parameters β_0 and β_1, but we can use the sample data to estimate them with b_0 and b_1, which are found by using Formulas 9-2 and 9-3:

Formula 9-2 $$b_0 = \frac{(\Sigma y)(\Sigma x^2) - (\Sigma x)(\Sigma xy)}{n(\Sigma x^2) - (\Sigma x)^2} \quad \text{(y-intercept)}$$

Formula 9-3 $$b_1 = \frac{n(\Sigma xy) - (\Sigma x)(\Sigma y)}{n(\Sigma x^2) - (\Sigma x)^2} \quad \text{(slope)}$$

These formulas might look intimidating, but they are programmed into many calculators and computer programs, so the values of b_0 and b_1 can be easily found (see Using Technology at the end of this section). In those cases when we must use formulas instead of a calculator or computer, the required computations will be much easier if we keep the following facts in mind:

1. If the linear correlation coefficient r has been computed using Formula 9-1, the values of Σx, Σy, Σx^2, and Σxy have already been found and they can be used again in Formula 9-3. (Also, the numerator for r in Formula 9-1 is the same numerator for b_1 in Formula 9-3; the denominator for r includes the denominator for b_1. If the calculation for r is set up carefully, the calculation for b_1 requires the simple division of one known number by another.)

2. If you find the slope b_1 first, you can use Formula 9-4 to find the y-intercept b_0. [The regression line always passes through the centroid $(\bar{x}, \bar{y})$ so that $\bar{y} = b_0 + b_1\bar{x}$ must be true, and this equation can be expressed as Formula 9-4. It is usually easier to find the y-intercept b_0 by using Formula 9-4 than by using Formula 9-2.]

Formula 9-4 $$b_0 = \bar{y} - b_1\bar{x}$$

Once we have evaluated b_0 and b_1, we can identify the estimated regression equation, which has the following special property: *The regression line fits the sample points best.* (The specific criterion used to determine which line fits "best" is the least-squares property, which will be described later.) We will now briefly discuss rounding and then illustrate the procedure for finding and applying the regression equation.

Rounding the y-Intercept b_0 and the Slope b_1

It's difficult to provide a simple universal rule for rounding values of b_0 and b_1, but we usually try to round each of these values to *three significant digits* or use the values provided by a statistical software package or calculator. Because these values are very sensitive to rounding at intermediate steps of calculations, you should try to carry at least six significant digits (or use exact values) in the intermediate steps. Depending on how you round, this book's answers to examples and exercises may be slightly different from your answers.

EXAMPLE   In Section 9-2 we used the Table 9-1 data (x = latitudes of seismic activity; y = magnitudes of seismic activity) to find that the linear correlation coefficient of $r = 0.623$ indicates that there is a significant linear correlation. Now find the regression equation of the straight line that relates x and y.

SOLUTION   We will find the regression equation by using Formulas 9-3 and 9-4 and these values already found in Table 9-2 from Section 9-2:

$$n = 13 \qquad\qquad \Sigma x = 742.3 \qquad\qquad \Sigma y = 35.1$$
$$\Sigma x^2 = 43344.79 \qquad\qquad \Sigma y^2 = 119.87 \qquad\qquad \Sigma xy = 2100.84$$

First find the slope b_1 by using Formula 9-3:

$$b_1 = \frac{n(\Sigma xy) - (\Sigma x)(\Sigma y)}{n(\Sigma x^2) - (\Sigma x)^2}$$

$$= \frac{13(2100.84) - (742.3)(35.1)}{13(43344.79) - (742.3)^2} = \frac{1256.19}{12472.98} = 0.100713$$

$$= 0.101 \quad \text{(rounded)}$$

Next, find the y-intercept b_0 by using Formula 9-4:

$$b_0 = \bar{y} - b_1\bar{x}$$

$$= \frac{35.1}{13} - (0.100713)\frac{742.3}{13} = -3.05 \quad \text{(rounded)}$$

Knowing the slope b_1 and y-intercept b_0, we can now express the estimated equation of the regression line as

$$\hat{y} = -3.05 + 0.101x$$

We should realize that this equation is an *estimate* of the true regression equation $y = \beta_0 + \beta_1 x$. This estimate is based on one particular set of sample data listed in Table 9-1, but another sample drawn from the same population would probably lead to a somewhat different equation.

The Excel display below shows the regression line plotted on the scatter diagram. We can see that this line fits the data reasonably well. (The data points tend to be distributed uniformly above and below the line.) Note that even though the regression line "fits the data," it does not actually pass through any of the original data points. This is common,

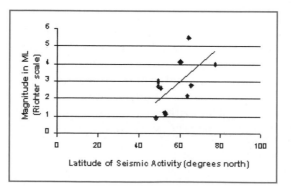

Excel Display   Scatter Diagram with Regression Line

although in a minority of cases, the regression line might pass through one or more of the sample data points.

Using the Regression Equation for Predictions

Regression equations can be helpful when used in *predicting* the value of one variable, given some particular value for the other variable. If the regression line fits the data quite well, then it makes sense to use its equation for predictions, provided that we don't go beyond the scope of the available scores. However, *we should use the equation of the regression line only if r indicates that there is a significant linear correlation. In the absence of a significant linear correlation, we should not use the regression equation for projecting or predicting; instead, our best estimate of the second variable is simply its sample mean.*

In predicting a value of y based on some given value of x . . .

1. If there is *not* a significant linear correlation, the best predicted y value is $\bar{y}$.
2. If there *is* a significant linear correlation, the best predicted y value is found by substituting the x value into the regression equation.

Figure 9-7 summarizes this process, which is easier to understand if we think of r as a measure of how well the regression line fits the sample data. If r is near -1 or $+1$, then the regression line fits the data well, but if r is near 0, then the regression line fits poorly (and should not be used for predictions).

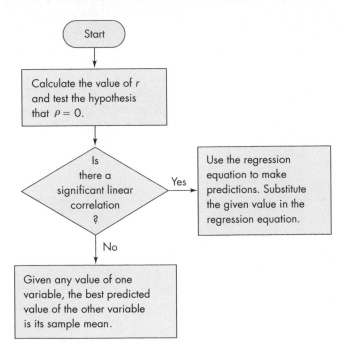

Figure 9-7 Predicting the Value of a Variable

● **EXAMPLE**   Using the sample data in Table 9-1, we found that there is a significant linear correlation between latitudes of earthquakes and their magnitudes, and we also found that the regression equation is $\hat{y} = -3.05 + 0.101x$. If an earthquake is recorded at latitude 64°N, predict its magnitude.

SOLUTION   There's a strong temptation to jump in and substitute 64.0 for x in the regression equation, but we should first consider whether there is a significant linear correlation that justifies the use of that equation. In this example, we do have a significant linear correlation (with $r = 0.623$), so our predicted value is found as follows:

$$\hat{y} = -3.05 + 0.101x$$
$$= -3.05 + 0.101(64.0) = 3.41$$

The predicted magnitude of an earthquake recorded at 64°N is 3.41 ML. (If there had not been a significant linear correlation, our best predicted weight would have been $\bar{y} = 2.7$ ML.)

● **EXAMPLE**   The Excel scatter diagram opposite compares, for each of the first 35 Parliaments, the number of days it was in session versus its approximate duration in years. Using Data Set 5 in Appendix B, find the best predicted number of days in session for a parliament that lasts 4.5 years.

SOLUTION   The diagram clearly shows that Assumption 2 for regressions (stated near the beginning of Section 9-3) does not apply to the relation between Parliament duration and number of days in session. There is *not* a consistent variance of y values around all parts of the trend line. For Parliaments lasting up to 3 years, it may be reasonable to find a regression equation, but the equation would not apply to Parliaments of at least 4 years' duration. Since there is no significant linear correlation between duration and days in session for Parliaments lasting 4 or more years, the mean number of days in session for these longer Parliaments would be a better predictor. The mean is $\Sigma(\text{days})/n = 21{,}619/25 = 864.8$.

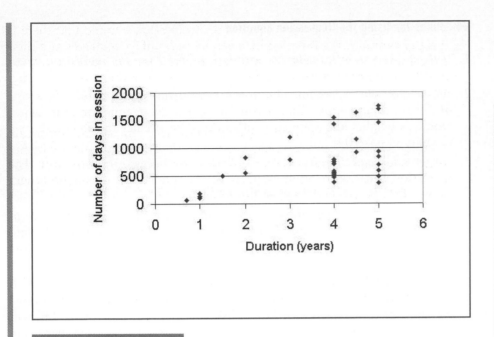

Excel Display Scatter Diagram
with No Linear Correlation

Carefully compare the solutions to the preceding two examples and note that we used the regression equation when there was a significant linear correlation, but in the absence of such a correlation, the best predicted value of *y* is simply the value of the sample mean $\bar{y}$.

Interpreting Predicted Values We should understand that when we determine a predicted value of *y* based on some given value of *x*, the predicted value will not necessarily be the exact result. There are other factors, such as random variation and characteristics not included in the study, that can also affect *y*. Based on the sample data in Table 9-1, we see that for an earthquake recorded at latitude 64°N, the best predicted magnitude (where the ML scale applies) is 3.41 ML. This does not mean that every recorded earthquake or other seismic activity at latitude 64°N will have a magnitude of exactly 3.41 ML; some will be less and some will be more. But the regression equation tells us that, on the whole, 3.41 ML is the single best estimate of magnitude whenever seismic activity is recorded at latitude 64°N. A common error is to use the regression equation when there is no significant linear correlation. That error violates the first of the following guidelines.

Identifying Risk Factors for Food Poisoning

In 1996, Canadians reported over 19,000 cases of food poisoning. No one knows how many other cases were simply dismissed as the flu or indigestion, and so went unreported. Health researchers and epidemiologists try to learn the factors that contribute to these outbreaks. A type of regression analysis confirmed that tainted strawberries and raspberries contributed to a significant outbreak of Cyclospora in May 1996, when 32 of 49 guests at a catered meal in North York, Ontario, became ill. Factors associated with increased food-poisoning risk include insufficient refrigeration of meat and dairy products, insufficient cooking of meat (especially poultry), and inadequate cleaning practices in food preparation. (See "Something You Ate?" *Chatelaine*, January 7, 1998, and Health Canada's Web pages.)

Guidelines for Using the Regression Equation

1. *If there is no significant linear correlation, don't use the regression equation to make predictions.*
2. *When using the regression equation for predictions, stay within the scope of the available sample data.* If you find a regression equation that relates women's heights and shoe sizes, it's absurd to predict the shoe size of a woman who is 10 ft tall.
3. *A regression equation based on old data is not necessarily valid now.* The regression equation relating used car prices and ages of cars is no longer usable if it's based on data from the 1970s.
4. *Don't make predictions about a population that is different from the population from which the sample data were drawn.* If we collect sample data from men and develop a regression equation relating age and TV remote control usage, the results don't necessarily apply to women.

Similarly, the regression for the chapter problem is based on data for which the Magnitude Local (ML) scale is appropriate. Magnitudes for events recorded by the Magnitude Nuttli (MN) scale (which involves different assumptions and calculations) cannot be predicted by the same regression equation.

Interpreting the Regression Equation: Marginal Change

We can use the regression equation to see the effect on one variable when the other variable changes by some specific amount.

DEFINITION

In working with two variables related by a regression equation, the **marginal change** in a variable is the amount that it changes when the other variable changes by exactly one unit.

The slope b_1 in the regression equation represents the marginal change resulting when x changes by one unit. For the earthquake data of Table 9-1, we can see that an increase in x of one unit will cause $\hat{y}$ to change by 0.101 units. That is, if an earthquake is recorded at 1° more north, its predicted magnitude increases by 0.101 ML.

Outliers and Influential Points

A correlation/regression analysis of bivariate data should include an investigation of *outliers* and *influential points,* defined as follows.

DEFINITIONS

In a scatterplot, an **outlier** is a point lying far away from the other data points. Paired sample data may include one or more **influential points,** which are points that strongly affect the graph of the regression line.

An outlier is easy to identify: Examine the scatterplot and identify a point that is far away from the others. To determine whether a point is an influential point, graph the regression line resulting from the data with the point included, then graph the regression line resulting from the data with the point excluded. If the graph changes by a considerable amount, the point is influential. Influential points are often found by identifying those outliers that are *horizontally* far away from the other points.

For example, refer to the preceding Excel display. If we include an additional earthquake at latitude 77°N that has a 9.0 ML magnitude, we have an outlier, because that point would fall in the upper-right corner of the graph and would be far away from the other points. This point would not be an influential point because the regression line would not change its position very much. If Canada annexed an island at 20°N, which then registered a 9.0ML earthquake, it would become an influential point because the graph of the regression line would change considerably, as shown by the following Excel display.

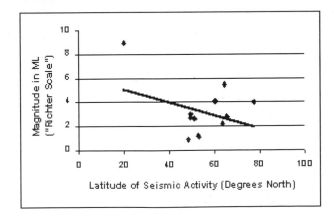

Excel Display   Scatter Diagram with Influential Point

Residuals and the Least-Squares Property

We have stated that the regression equation represents the straight line that fits the data "best," and we will now describe the criterion used in determining the line that is better than all others. This criterion is based on the vertical distances between the original data points and the regression line. Such distances are called *residuals*.

x	1	2	4	5
y	4	24	8	32

DEFINITION

For a sample of paired (x, y) data, a **residual** is the difference $(y - \hat{y})$ between an observed sample y value and the value of $\hat{y}$, which is the value of y that is predicted from the regression equation.

This definition might seem as clear as tax form instructions, but you can easily understand residuals by referring to Figure 9-8, which corresponds to the paired sample data in the margin. In Figure 9-8, the residuals are represented by the dashed lines. For a specific example, see the residual indicated as 7, which is directly above $x = 5$. If we substitute $x = 5$ into the regression equation $\hat{y} = 5 + 4x$, we get a predicted value of $\hat{y} = 25$. When $x = 5$, the *predicted* value of y is $\hat{y} = 25$, but the actual *observed* sample value is $y = 32$. The difference of $y - \hat{y} = 32 - 25 = 7$ is a residual.

The regression equation represents the line that fits the points "best" according to the *least-squares property*.

DEFINITION

A straight line satisfies the **least-squares property** if the sum of the squares of the residuals is the smallest sum possible.

 From Figure 9-8, we see that the residuals are -5, 11, -13, and 7, so the sum of their squares is

$$(-5)^2 + 11^2 + (-13)^2 + 7^2 = 364$$

Any straight line different from $\hat{y} = 5 + 4x$ will result in residuals with a sum of squares that is greater than 364.

Fortunately, we need not deal directly with the least-squares property when we want to find the equation of the regression line. Calculus has been used to

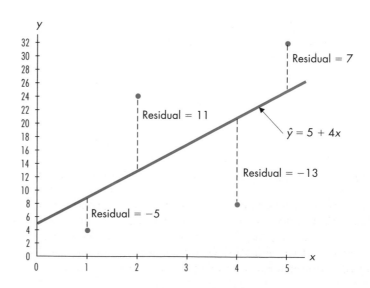

Figure 9-8   Scatter Diagram with Regression Line and Residuals

build the least-squares property into Formulas 9-2 and 9-3. Because the derivations of these formulas require calculus, we don't include them in this text.

Other Mathematical Models

In many cases, there is a relationship between two variables that is not linear. A **mathematical model** is similar to a regression, in that it is a mathematical function that "fits" or describes real-world data, and which can be used to predict the value of a dependent variable, given values of one or more independent variables.

For example, inspection of the table shown here shows that each y value is the square of the corresponding x value, so that the two variables are related by the equation $y = x^2$ instead of a linear equation, which has the form $y = b_0 + b_1 x$.

x	2	5	4	8	10
y	4	25	16	64	100

With specialized statistical software and calculators, it is possible to find directly the best curve-fitting equation for data, from a variety of complex options. Excel and STATDISK can be coaxed to assist in this process (see Using Technology), but the process is not so automatic.

The following are some common structures of equations which can be the basis of mathematical models:

Linear: $y = a + bx$
Quadratic: $y = ax^2 + bx + c$
Logarithmic: $y = a + b \ln x$
Exponential: $y = ab^x$
Power: $y = ax^b$
Logistic: $y = \dfrac{c}{1 + ae^{-bx}}$

These common models are illustrated on the following page. The particular model that you select depends on the nature of the sample data; a scatterplot can be very helpful in making that determination.

If you have the tools to assist you, there are three basic rules for developing a good mathematical model:

1. *Look for a pattern in the graph.* Examine the graph of the plotted points and compare the basic pattern to the known generic graphs illustrated on the next page. When trying to select a model, consider only those functions that visually appear to fit the observed points reasonably well.
2. *Find and compare values of R^2.* If your software can generate values of R^2, these can be interpreted as indicating degree of fit, similar to regression; select functions that result in larger values of R^2. However, don't place much importance on small differences, such as the difference between $R^2 = 0.984$ and $R^2 = 0.989$. (Another measurement used to assess the quality of a model is the sum of squares of the residuals.)

Excel Displays   Models

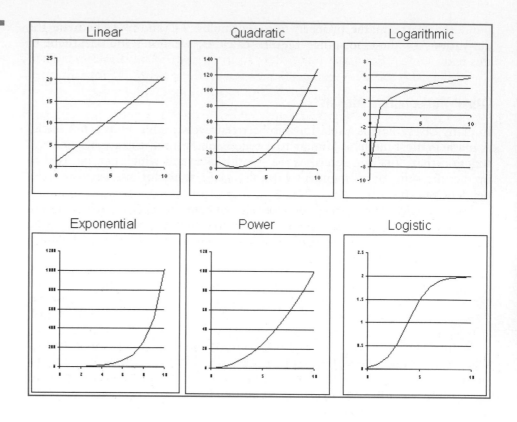

3. *Think.* Use common sense. Don't use a model that leads to predicted values known to be totally unrealistic. Use the model to calculate future values, past values, and values for missing years, then determine whether the results are realistic.

Using Technology

Because of the messy calculations involved, the linear correlation coefficient r and the slope and y-intercept of the regression line are usually found by using a calculator or computer software.

Excel: *Regression:* Use Excel's Data Analysis add-in by selecting **Tools** from the main menu, then selecting **Data Analysis** and **Regression**, then clicking **OK**. In the spaces provided, enter Excel ranges for the columns containing the y and x values, respectively. Specify an output location, then click **OK**. Among all the information provided by Excel, the slope and intercept of the regression equation can be found under the heading "Coefficient." The r value is found to the right of the heading "Multiple R."

Trend line: Once you have generated a scatter diagram for the x and y data (see Using Technology, Section 9-2), you can easily insert a trend line: Aim the mouse pointer at one of the plotted points, and left-click the mouse to highlight all the points. Then right-click the mouse without moving it. From the menu that appears, select **Add Trendline**. Then select the type **Linear**, and click on **OK**. (There are also some nonlinear options you can explore.)

Mathematical model: With patience, built-in Excel functions can be used to transform data, so the results can be analysed by the linear regression techniques of this chapter. For instance, if your model is that $y = x^2$, then the square root of each y should approximately equal its corresponding x value. Thus, use a conventional regression analysis to compare the transformed y values (that is, after taking the square root) with their corresponding x's. (See Exercise 25 in this section and Exercise 17 in Section 9-5 for more detailed examples.)

STATDISK: Select **Analysis** from the main menu bar, then use the option **Correlation and Regression**. Enter the paired data, or use Copy/Paste to copy in the data from, for example, Excel. Enter a value for the significance level. Click on the **Evaluate** button. The display will include the value of the linear correlation coefficient along with the critical value of r, the conclusion about correlation, and the intercept and slope of the regression equation, as well as some other results. Click on **Plot 1** to get a graph of the scatterplot with the regression line included.

STATDISK can also assist in testing mathematical models. Select **Data** from the main menu bar, then select the option of **Sample Transformations**, in order to transform columns of data mathematically. As described for Excel, transform the data in such a way that the results can be tested by regression.

9-3 Exercises A: Basic Skills and Concepts

In Exercises 1–4, use the given data to find the equation of the regression line.

1.
x	1	2	4	5
y	3	5	9	11

2.
x	5	3	2	1	0	2
y	-2	0	1	2	3	1

3.
x	2	3	5	5	10
y	6	9	14	16	30

4.
x	2	3	5	5	10
y	6	0	15	5	2

In Exercises 5–18, find the regression equation; unless the problem suggests otherwise, let the first variable be the independent (x) variable. Caution: When finding predicted values, be sure to follow the prediction procedure described in this section.

5.

x Chest (in.)	26	45	54	49	41	49	44	19
y Weight (lb)	90	344	416	348	262	360	332	34

Find the best predicted weight of a bear with a chest size of 52 in.

6.

Trees exported (1000s)	358	341	364	367
Export value ($1000s)	3978	3729	4073	4564

Find the best predicted export value when 362,000 Christmas trees are exported.

7.

Plastic (kg)	0.12	0.64	0.99	1.28	0.99	0.82	0.39	1.38
Household size	2	3	3	6	4	2	1	5

What is the best predicted size of a household that discards 0.25 kg of plastic?

8.

Paper (kg)	1.09	3.43	4.33	4.00	3.96	3.16	3.10	5.18
Household size	2	3	3	6	4	2	1	5

What is the best predicted size of a household that discards 5.00 kg of paper?

9.

Incubation period (days)	23	13	53	23	30	17	78	49	15	12	18
Fledgling period (days)	35	11	360	30	53	28	280	49	17	22	28

(Data from www.swishweb.com/Animal_Kingdom/Birds/animal03b.htm)

What is the best predicted fledgling period for a bird species whose incubation period is 36 days?

10.

TSE 300	9397.97	12061.95	13868.54	13648.84	17977.46	19309.36
Mining stock	0.450	0.600	0.210	0.160	0.335	0.400

(Data from *Management Information Circular*, January 26, 2001, TWIN Mining Corporation, Toronto)

What is the best predicted value for this mining stock, if the TSE 300 closes at 15445?

11. The salaries in the accompanying table are shown in thousands of dollars. What is the best predicted salary level for a person with 13 years of education? Does everyone with 13 years of education actually make that figure?

Years of education	Salary
16	61.10
10	26.53
11	29.57
11	28.38
13	37.62
13	27.22
12	36.70
10	14.77
12	22.23
12	24.82
14	32.89
13	36.94
15	35.99
11	23.11
14	62.56
10	21.31

Based on data from Statistics Canada.

12. What is the best predicted profit margin (as a percent) for a company whose ratio of current assets to current liabilities is 1.4?

Profit margin	3.9	2.9	9.4	6.1	–0.6	3.6	2.7	1.0	2.2	8.3	3.9
Assets/liabilities	1.3	1.3	1.1	1.5	1.7	1.5	1.6	1.5	1.0	1.1	0.9

13. Refer to Data Set 16 in Appendix B.
   a. Use the paired duration and interval data for eruptions of the Old Faithful geyser. What is the best predicted time before the next eruption if the previous eruption lasted for 210 seconds?
   b. Use the paired height and interval data for eruptions of the Old Faithful geyser. What is the best predicted time before the next eruption if the previous eruption had a height of 275 ft?
   c. Which predicted time is more reliable, the result from part (a) or the result from part (b)? Why?
14. Refer to Data Set 4 in Appendix B and use the paired columns for average annual temperature and precipitation. What is the best predicted amount of precipitation when the average annual temperature is 7.1°C?
15. Refer to Data Set 21 in Appendix B.
   a. Use the paired data consisting of price and carat (weight). What is the best predicted price of a diamond with a weight of 1.5 carats?
   b. Use the paired price/colour data. Assuming the colour data is recorded in an interval scale, what is the best predicted price of a diamond with a colour rating of 3?
   c. Which prediction is better, the result from part (a) or the result from part (b)? Why?
16. Refer to Data Set 4 in Appendix B and use the paired columns for average annual temperature and snowfall. What is the best predicted amount of snowfall when the average annual temperature is 7.1°C?
17. Refer to Data Set 7 of Appendix B and use the paired data consisting of temperature departures and precipitation departures from seasonal norms. What is the best predicted precipitation departure in a spring whose temperature was 0.9°C *below* the norm?

18.

Employees	29	122	24	30	16	3	83	50	43	33
Revenues	34.2	33.2	27.9	17.2	16.7	14.2	13.9	12.1	11.2	10.8

What is the best predicted revenue for a top company that employs 10,000 people? (Note that in the table the number of employees is given in thousands and revenues in billions of dollars.)

19. In each of the following cases, find the best predicted value of y given that $x = 3.00$. The given statistics are summarized from paired sample data.
   a. $r = 0.931$, $\bar{y} = 7.00$, $n = 10$, and the equation of the regression line is $\hat{y} = 4.00 + 2.00x$.
   b. $r = -0.033$, $\bar{y} = 2.50$, $n = 80$, and the equation of the regression line is $\hat{y} = 5.00 - 2.00x$.

20. In each of the following cases, find the best predicted value of y given that $x = 2.00$. The given statistics are summarized from paired sample data.

  a. $r = -0.882$, $\bar{y} = 3.57$, $n = 15$, and the equation of the regression line is $\hat{y} = 23.00 - 8.00x$.

  b. $r = 0.187$, $\bar{y} = 9.33$, $n = 60$, and the equation of the regression line is $\hat{y} = 4.00 + 8.00x$.

21. Refer to these data for Parliaments of up to 3 years' duration. If there were an additional Parliament to include, which lasted 1 year and was in session for 364 days, would the new point be an outlier? Would it be an influential point?

Duration (years)	0.7	1	1	1	1	1.5	2	2	3	3
Days in session	67	111	132	177	177	491	550	828	788	1189

22. Refer to the 13th pairs of data listed in Table 9-1. If we include a 14th data point, for an earthquake at 85°N latitude with magnitude 7.5ML, is the new point an outlier? Is it an influential point?

9-3 Exercises B: Beyond the Basics

23. Large numbers, such as those in the accompanying table, often cause computational problems. First use the given data to find the equation of the regression line, then find the equation of the regression line after each x value has been divided by 1000. How are the results affected by the change in x? How would the results be affected if each y entry were divided by 1000?

x	924,736	832,985	825,664	793,427	857,366
y	142	111	109	95	119

x	1	2	4	5
y	4	24	8	32

x	2.0	2.5	4.2	10.0
y	12.0	18.7	53.0	225.0

24. According to the least-squares property, the regression line minimizes the sum of the squares of the residuals. We noted that with the paired data in the margin, the regression equation is $\hat{y} = 5 + 4x$ and the sum of the squares of the residuals is 364. Show that the equation $\hat{y} = 8 + 3x$ results in a sum of squares of residuals that is greater than 364.

25. If the scatterplot reveals a nonlinear (not a straight line) pattern that you recognize as another type of curve, you may be able to apply the methods of this section. For the data given in the margin, find the linear equation ($y = b_0 + b_1 x$) that best fits the sample data, and find the logarithmic equation ($y = a + b \ln x$) that best fits the sample data. (*Hint:* Begin by replacing each x value with $\ln x$.) Which of these two equations fits the data better? Why?

26. Explain why a test of the null hypothesis H_0: $\rho = 0$ is equivalent to a test of the null hypothesis H_0: $\beta_1 = 0$, where ρ is the linear correlation coefficient for a population of paired data, and β_1 is the slope of the regression line for that same population.

27. See Data Set 19 in Appendix B. If you draw a scatter plot to compare (y) the maximum lifespans of the first six animals listed with (x) their metabolic rates, there appears to be a nonlinear relationship. For that data find the linear equation $(y = b_0 + b_1x)$ that best fits the sample data. Then find the exponential equation $(y = a \cdot e^{bx}$, where e represents the constant = 2.7182818) that best fits the sample data. (*Hint*: Begin by replacing each y (maxlife) value with ln y. Perform the linear regression versus x (metabolic rate). To transform the results of the regression: a for the exponential equation equals the constant e raised to the power b_0 (from the linear regression), and b for the exponential equation equals b_1.) Which of these two equations fits the data better? Explain.

9-4 Variation and Prediction Intervals

We have said that for paired variables, the actual y values rarely lie exactly on the regression line. There is usually variation between the actual and predicted values for y. We now examine this variation for these two major applications:

1. To determine the proportion of the variation in y that can be explained by the linear relationship between x and y.

2. To construct confidence interval estimates of predicted y-values. Such confidence intervals are called *prediction intervals*.

Explained and Unexplained Variation

In Section 9-2 we introduced the concept of correlation and used the linear correlation coefficient r in determining whether there is a significant linear correlation between two variables denoted by x and y. In addition to serving as a measure of the linear correlation between two variables, the value of r can also provide us with additional information about the variation of sample points about the regression line. We begin with a sample case, which leads to an important definition.

Suppose we have a large collection of paired data, which yields the following results:

- There is a significant linear correlation.
- The equation of the regression line is $\hat{y} = 3 + 2x$.
- The mean of the y values is given by $\bar{y} = 9$.
- One of the pairs of sample data is $x = 5$ and $y = 19$.
- *Figure 9-9* shows that the point $(5, 13)$ is one of the points on the regression line, because substitution of $x = 5$ into the regression equation yields the following:

$$\hat{y} = 3 + 2x = 3 + 2(5) = 13$$

Figure 9-9 shows that the point $(5, 13)$ lies on the regression line, but the point $(5, 19)$, which is from the original data set, does not lie on the regression line because it does not satisfy the regression equation. Take time to examine Figure 9-9 carefully and note the differences defined as follows.

Figure 9-9 Unexplained,
Explained, and Total
Deviation

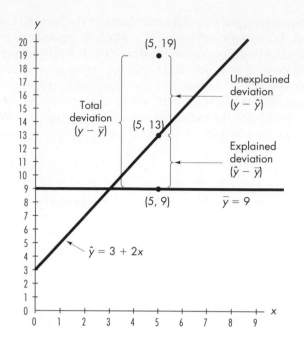

DEFINITION

Assume that we have a collection of paired data containing the particular point (x, y), that $\hat{y}$ is the predicted value of y (obtained by using the regression equation), and that the mean of the sample y values is $\bar{y}$.

The **total deviation** (from the mean) of the particular point (x, y) is the vertical distance $y - \bar{y}$, which is the distance between the point (x, y) and the horizontal line passing through the sample mean $\bar{y}$.

The **explained deviation** is the vertical distance $\hat{y} - \bar{y}$, which is the distance between the predicted y value and the horizontal line passing through the sample mean $\bar{y}$.

The **unexplained deviation** is the vertical distance $y - \hat{y}$, which is the vertical distance between the point (x, y) and the regression line. (The distance $y - \hat{y}$ is also called a *residual*, as defined in Section 9-3.)

For the specific data under consideration, we get these results:

total deviation of $(5, 19) = y - \bar{y} = 19 - 9 = 10$

explained deviation of $(5, 19) = \hat{y} - \bar{y} = 13 - 9 = 4$

unexplained deviation of $(5, 19) = y - \hat{y} = 19 - 13 = 6$

If we were totally ignorant of correlation and regression concepts and wanted to predict a value of y given a value of x and a collection of paired (x, y) data, our best guess would be $\bar{y}$. But we are not totally ignorant of correlation and regression concepts: We know that in this case (with a significant linear correlation) the way to predict the value of y when $x = 5$ is to use the regression equation, which yields $\hat{y} = 13$, as calculated before. We can explain the discrepancy between $\bar{y} = 9$ and $\hat{y} = 13$ by simply noting that there is a significant linear correlation best described by the regression line. Consequently, when $x = 5$, y should be 13 and not the mean y value of 9. But whereas y should be 13, it is 19. The discrepancy between 13 and 19 cannot be explained by the regression line and is called an *unexplained deviation* or a *residual*. The specific case illustrated in Figure 9-9 can be generalized as follows:

(total deviation) = (explained deviation) + (unexplained deviation)

or $(y - \bar{y})$ = $(\hat{y} - \bar{y})$ + $(y - \hat{y})$

This last expression applies to a particular point (x, y), but it can be further generalized and modified to include all of the pairs of sample data, as shown in Formula 9-5. In that formula, the **total variation** is expressed as the sum of the squares of the total deviation values, the **explained variation** is the sum of the squares of the explained deviation values, and the **unexplained variation** is the sum of the squares of the unexplained deviation values.

Formula 9-5

(total variation) = (explained variation) + (unexplained variation)

or $\Sigma(y - \bar{y})^2$ = $\Sigma(\hat{y} - \bar{y})^2$ + $\Sigma(y - \hat{y})^2$

Coefficient of Determination

The components of Formula 9-5 are used in the following important definition.

DEFINITION

The **coefficient of determination** is the amount of the variation in y that is explained by the regression line. It is computed as

$$r^2 = \frac{\text{explained variation}}{\text{total variation}}$$

We can compute r^2 by using the definition just given with Formula 9-5, or we can simply square the linear correlation coefficient r, which is found by using the methods described in Section 9-2. As an example, if $r = 0.8$, then the coefficient of determination is $r^2 = 0.64$, which means that *64% of the total variation in y can be explained by the regression line. It follows that 36% of the total variation in y remains unexplained.*

EXAMPLE   Referring to the earthquake data in Table 9-1, find the percentage of the variation in y (magnitude) that can be explained by the regression line.

SOLUTION   Recall that Table 9-1 contains 13 pairs of sample data, with each pair consisting of the recorded latitude and magnitude of seismic activity. In Section 9-2 we found that the linear correlation coefficient is $r = 0.623$. The coefficient of determination is $r^2 = 0.623^2 = 0.388$, indicating that the ratio of explained variation in y to total variation in y is 0.388.

Interpretation   38.8% of the total variation in y can be explained by the regression line. That is, 38.8% of the total variation in earthquake magnitudes can be explained by the variation in their recorded latitudes; most of the variation (61.2%) is attributable to other factors.

Prediction Intervals

In Section 9-3 we used the Table 9-1 sample data to find the regression equation $\hat{y} = -3.05 + 0.101x$, where $\hat{y}$ represents the predicted magnitude and x the recorded latitude of the seismic activity. We then used that equation to predict the y value, given that $x = 64°N$. We found that the best predicted magnitude of an earthquake recorded at 64°N is 3.41 ML. Because 3.41 is a single value, it is referred to as a *point estimate*. In Chapter 6 we saw that point estimates have the disadvantage of not conveying any sense of how accurate they might be. Here, we know that 3.41 is the best predicted value, but we don't know how accurate that value is. In Chapter 6 we developed confidence interval estimates to overcome that disadvantage, and in this section we follow that precedent. We will use a **prediction interval**, which is a confidence interval estimate of a **predicted value** of y.

The development of a prediction interval requires a measure of the spread of sample points about the regression line. Recall that the unexplained deviation (or residual) is the vertical distance between a sample point and the regression line, as illustrated in Figure 9-9. The *standard error of estimate* is a collective measure of the spread of the sample points about the regression line; it is formally defined as follows.

DEFINITION

The **standard error of estimate**, denoted by s_e, is a measure of the differences (or distances) between the observed sample y values and the predicted values $\hat{y}$ that are obtained using the regression equation. It is given as

$$s_e = \sqrt{\frac{\Sigma(y - \hat{y})^2}{n - 2}}$$

where $\hat{y}$ is the predicted y value.

Formula 9-6 can also be used to compute the standard error of estimate s_e. It is algebraically equivalent to the expression in the definition, but this form is generally easier to work with because it doesn't require that we compute each of the predicted values y by substitution in the regression equation. However, Formula 9-6 does require that we find the y-intercept b_0 and the slope b_1 of the estimated regression line.

Formula 9-6 $s_e = \sqrt{\dfrac{\Sigma y^2 - b_0 \Sigma y - b_1 \Sigma xy}{n - 2}}$ (standard error of estimate)

In both Excel and STATDISK, the value of the standard error of estimate is displayed as part of the output when their regression procedures are executed.

Rationale for the s_e definition

The development of the standard error of estimate s_e closely parallels that of the ordinary standard deviation introduced in Chapter 2. Just as the standard deviation is a measure of how scores deviate from their mean, the standard error of estimate s_e is a measure of how sample data points deviate from their regression line. The reasoning behind dividing by $n - 2$ is similar to the reasoning that led to division by $n - 1$ for the ordinary standard deviation, and we will not pursue the complex details. It is important to note that smaller values of s_e reflect points that stay close to the regression line, and larger values are from points farther away from the regression line.

EXAMPLE   Use Formula 9-6 to find the standard error of estimate s_e for the earthquake measurement data listed in Table 9-1.

SOLUTION   In Section 9-2 we used the Table 9-1 data to find that

$$n = 13 \qquad \Sigma y^2 = 119.87 \qquad \Sigma y = 35.1 \qquad \Sigma xy = 2100.84$$

In Section 9-3 we used the Table 9-1 data to find the y-intercept and slope of the regression line. Those values are given here with extra decimal places for greater precision:

$$b_0 = -3.05071 \qquad b_1 = 0.100713$$

We can now use these values to find the standard error of estimate s_e:

$$s_e = \sqrt{\frac{\Sigma y^2 - b_0 \Sigma y - b_1 \Sigma xy}{n - 2}}$$

$$= \sqrt{\frac{119.87 - (-3.05071)(35.1) - (0.100713)(2100.84)}{13 - 2}}$$

$$= 1.18199 = 1.18 \quad \text{(rounded)}$$

We can measure the spread of the sample points about the regression line with the standard error of estimate $s_e = 1.18$.

Wage Gender Gap

Data from Statistics Canada indicate that, on average, full-time female workers earn about 73¢ for each $1 earned by full-time male workers. Researchers have found that about one-third of the discrepancy can be explained by differences in education, seniority, work interruptions, and job choices. The other two-thirds remains unexplained by such labour factors.

We can use the standard error of estimate s_e to construct interval estimates that will help us see how dependable our point estimates of y really are. Assume that for each fixed value of x, the corresponding sample values of y are normally distributed about the regression line, and those normal distributions have the same variance. The following interval estimate applies to an *individual y*. (For a confidence interval used to predict the *mean* of all y values for some given x value, see Exercise 20.)

Prediction Interval for an Individual y

Given the fixed value x_0, the *prediction interval for an individual y* is
$$\hat{y} - E < y < \hat{y} + E$$
where the margin of error E is
$$E = t_{\alpha/2}s_e\sqrt{1 + \frac{1}{n} + \frac{n(x_0 - \bar{x})^2}{n(\Sigma x^2) - (\Sigma x)^2}}$$
and x_0 represents the given value of x, $t_{\alpha/2}$ has $n - 2$ degrees of freedom, and s_e is found from Formula 9-6.

● **EXAMPLE**   Refer to the Table 9-1 sample data listing earthquake latitudes (x) along with their magnitudes (y). In previous sections we have shown that

- There is a significant linear correlation (at the 0.05 significance level).
- The regression equation is $\hat{y} = -3.05 + 0.101x$.
- When $x = 64.0$, the predicted y value is 3.41ML, but a more accurate value of 3.39 ML is obtained if we calculate the predicted value using unrounded values of slope and intercept.

Construct a 95% prediction interval for the magnitude of an earthquake that is recorded at 64°N. This will provide a sense of how reliable the estimate of 3.39 ML really is.

SOLUTION   We have already used the Table 9-1 sample data to find the following values:

$$n = 13 \quad \bar{x} = 57.1 \quad \Sigma x = 742.3 \quad \Sigma x^2 = 43344.79$$
$$s_e = 1.18199$$

From Table A-3 we find $t_{\alpha/2} = 2.201$. (We used $13 - 2 = 11$ degrees of freedom with $\alpha = 0.05$ in two tails.) We can now calculate the margin of error E by letting $x_0 = 64.0$, because we want the prediction interval of y for $x = 64.0$.

$$E = t_{\alpha/2}s_e\sqrt{1 + \frac{1}{n} + \frac{n(x_0 - \bar{x})^2}{n(\Sigma x^2) - (\Sigma x)^2}}$$

$$= (2.201)(1.18199)\sqrt{1 + \frac{1}{13} + \frac{13(64.0 - 57.1)^2}{13(43344.79) - (742.3)^2}}$$

$$= (2.201)(1.18199)(1.06139) = 2.76$$

With $\hat{y} = 3.39$ and $E = 2.76$, we get the prediction interval as follows:

$$\hat{y} - E < y < \hat{y} + E$$
$$3.39 - 2.76 < y < 3.39 + 2.76$$
$$0.63 < y < 6.15$$

That is, for seismic activity recorded at latitude 64°N, we have 95% confidence that its true magnitude is between 0.63 ML and 6.15 ML (considering only events recorded in the ML scale). For earthquakes, that is a very large range. (One factor contributing to the large range is the small sample size of 13.)

Interpretation Although we have an equation to predict a magnitude (3.39 ML) for seismic activity at 64°N, we have discovered that the estimate is not very reliable. The 95% prediction interval shows that the magnitude estimate can vary considerably—from a very minor tremor up to a serious earthquake.

Using Technology

Excel: For procedures, see Using Technology in Section 9-3. Outputs include b_0 and b_1 (for the regression equation), the standard error estimate s_e, and the coefficient of determination (labelled as R square).

STATDISK: For procedures, see Using Technology in Section 9-3. Outputs include the linear correlation coefficient r, the equation of the regression line, the standard error estimate s_e, the total, explained, and unexplained variation, and the coefficient of determination.

9-4 Exercises A: Basic Skills and Concepts

In Exercises 1–4, use the value of the linear correlation coefficient r to find the coefficient of determination and the percentage of the total variation that can be explained by the regression line.

1. $r = 0.2$ 2. $r = -0.6$
3. $r = -0.225$ 4. $r = 0.837$

In Exercises 5–8, find the (a) explained variation, (b) unexplained variation, (c) total variation, (d) coefficient of determination, and (e) standard error of estimate s_e.

5. The accompanying table lists numbers x of patio tiles and costs y (in dollars) of having them manually cut to fit. (The equation of the regression line is $\hat{y} = 2 + 3x$.)

x	1	2	3	5	6
y	5	8	11	17	20

6. The paired data below consist of the chest sizes (in inches) and weights (in pounds) of a sample of male bears. (The equation of the regression line is $\hat{y} = -187.462 + 11.2713x$.)

x Chest (in.)	26	45	54	49	41	49	44	19
y Weight (lb)	90	344	416	348	262	360	332	34

7. The paired data below consist of the weights (in kilograms) of discarded plastic and sizes of households. (The equation of the regression line, for predicting household size from the weight of discarded plastic, is $\hat{y} = 0.5486 + 3.2694x$.)

Plastic (kg)	0.12	0.64	0.99	1.28	0.99	0.82	0.39	1.38
Household size	2	3	3	6	4	2	1	5

8. The paired data below consist of annual closing values of the TSE 300 stock index and of corresponding closing prices for a Canadian mining stock. (The equation of the regression line, for predicting the stock closing value from the TSE value, is $\hat{y} = 0.5013 - 0.000009886x$.)

TSE 300	9397.97	12061.95	13868.54	13648.84	17977.46	19309.36
Mining stock	0.450	0.600	0.210	0.160	0.335	0.400

9. Refer to the data given in Exercise 5 and assume that the necessary conditions of normality and variance are met.
   a. For $x = 4$, find $\hat{y}$, the predicted value of y.
   b. How does the value of s_e affect the construction of the 95% prediction interval of y for $x = 4$?

10. Refer to Exercise 6 and assume that the necessary conditions of normality and variance are met.
   a. For a bear with a chest size of 52 in., find $\hat{y}$, the predicted weight.
   b. Find the 99% prediction interval of y for $x = 52$.

11. Refer to the data given in Exercise 7 and assume that the necessary conditions of normality and variance are met.
   a. Find the predicted size of a household that discards 1.25 kg of plastic.
   b. Find the 95% prediction interval for the size of a household that discards 1.25 kg of plastic.

12. Refer to the data given in Exercise 8, and assume that the necessary conditions of normality and variance are met.
   a. For a year that the TSE 300 closes at 14447.99, find the predicted closing price for the mining stock.

b. Find the 99% prediction interval for the closing price of the mining stock, given that the TSE closed at 14447.99.

c. For this data set, does the answer from part (b) appear very useful? Why or why not?

In Exercises 13–16, refer to the data in Exercise 11 in Section 9-3. Let x represent the number of years of a person's education, and let y represent his or her salary (in thousands of dollars). Construct a prediction interval estimate of the salary of a person who has the given years of education. Use the given degree of confidence. (See the example in this section.)

13. 12 years; 95% confidence
14. 14 years; 90% confidence
15. 13.5 years; 90% confidence
16. 13 years; 99% confidence

9-4 Exercises B: Beyond the Basics

17. Confidence intervals for the y-intercept β_0 and slope β_1 for a regression line ($y = \beta_0 + \beta_1 x$) can be found by evaluating the limits in the intervals below:

$$b_0 - E < \beta_0 < b_0 + E$$

where

$$E = t_{\alpha/2} s_e \sqrt{\frac{1}{n} + \frac{\bar{x}^2}{\Sigma x^2 - \frac{(\Sigma x)^2}{n}}}$$

$$b_1 - E < \beta_1 < b_1 + E$$

where

$$E = t_{\alpha/2} \cdot \frac{s_e}{\sqrt{\Sigma x^2 - \frac{(\Sigma x)^2}{n}}}$$

In these expressions, the y-intercept b_0 and the slope b_1 are found from the sample data and $t_{\alpha/2}$ is found from Table A-3 by using $n - 2$ degrees of freedom. Using the earthquake data in Table 9-1, find the 95% confidence interval estimates of β_0 and β_1.

18. a. If a collection of paired data includes at least three pairs of values, what do you know about the linear correlation coefficient if $s_e = 0$?

b. If a collection of paired data is such that the total explained variation is 0, what do you know about the slope of the regression line?

19. a. Find an expression for the unexplained variation in terms of the sample size n and the standard error of estimate s_e.

b. Find an expression for the explained variation in terms of the coefficient of determination r^2 and the unexplained variation.

c. Suppose we have a collection of paired data for which $r^2 = 0.900$ and the regression equation is $\hat{y} = 3 - 2x$. Find the linear correlation coefficient.

20. From the expression given in this section for the margin of error corresponding to a prediction interval for y, we can get the expression

$$s_{\hat{y}} = s_e \sqrt{1 + \frac{1}{n} + \frac{n(x_0 - \bar{x})^2}{n(\Sigma x^2) - (\Sigma x)^2}}$$

Making Music with Multiple Regression

Sony manufactures millions of compact discs. At one step in the manufacturing process, a laser exposes a photographic plate so that a musical signal is transferred into a digital signal coded with 0s and 1s. This process was statistically analysed to identify the effects of different variables, such as the length of exposure and the thickness of the photographic emulsion. Methods of multiple regression showed that among all of the variables considered, four were most significant. The photographic process was adjusted for optimal results based on the four critical variables. As a result, the percentage of defective discs dropped and the tone quality was maintained. The use of multiple regression methods led to lower production costs and better control of the manufacturing process.

which is the *standard error of the prediction* when predicting for a *single* y, given that $x = x_0$. When predicting for the *mean* of all values of y for which $x = x_0$, the point estimate $\hat{y}$ is the same, but $s_{\hat{y}}$ is as follows:

$$s_{\hat{y}} = s_e \sqrt{\frac{1}{n} + \frac{n(x_0 - \bar{x})^2}{n(\Sigma x^2) - (\Sigma x)^2}}$$

Use the data from Table 9-1 and extend the last example of this section to find a point estimate and a 95% confidence interval estimate of the mean magnitude of all earthquakes which occur at latitude 64°N.

	A	B	C	D	E	F	G	H
34								
35		Coefficients	Standard Error	t Stat	P-value	Lower 95%	Upper 95%	
36	Intercept	-351.659891	127.4100874	-2.76006	0.032851	-663.42137	-39.89841	
37	Length of Bears	9.659785345	1.939444009	4.980698	0.0025	4.9141333	14.405437	

21. An alternate approach to calculating standard errors and confidence intervals for regression is to apply them to the calculated b_0 and x coefficient(s), instead of to the y estimate. For example, this is part of Excel's regression output for comparing the weights and lengths of bears.

   This shows that the b_0 term, which the regression formula would estimate as -352, could, in fact, range from -663 to -40 in the 95% confidence interval. Similarly, the x coefficient, which is estimated as 9.66, could range from 4.9 to 14.4.

   Refer to the data in Exercise 11 in Section 9-3. Let x represent the number of years of a person's education, and let y represent his or her salary (in thousands of dollars). Use Excel to find the confidence limits for the intercept and x coefficient for the regression between education and salary.

9-5 Multiple Regression

So far, we have examined relationships between exactly *two* variables. In this section we develop a method for analysing relationships involving *more than two* variables. For example, in addition to considering the relationship between the magnitude of an earthquake and its recorded latitude, we might also include variables such as the depth of focus (hypocentre) of the earthquake, or its recorded longitude. We will focus on three key elements: the multiple regression equation, the value of adjusted R^2, and the P-value. As in the preceding sections, we will work with linear relationships only.

Multiple Regression Equation

> **DEFINITION**
>
> A **multiple regression equation** expresses a linear relationship between a dependent variable y and two or more independent variables (x_1, x_2, . . . , x_k). The general form of a multiple regression equation is $\hat{y} = b_0 + b_1x_1 + b_2x_2 + \ldots + b_kx_k$.

We will use the following notation, which follows naturally from the notation used in Section 9-3.

Notation

$\hat{y} = b_0 + b_1x_1 + b_2x_2 + \cdots + b_kx_k$ (General form of the estimated multiple regression equation)

n = sample size

k = number of *independent* variables. (The independent variables are also called predictor variables or x variables.)

$\hat{y}$ = predicted value of the dependent variable y (computed by using the multiple regression equation)

$x_1, x_2, \ldots, x_k$ are the independent variables

β_0 = the y-intercept, or the value of y when all of the predictor variables are 0. (This value is a population parameter.)

b_0 = estimate of β_0 based on the sample data (b_o is a sample statistic)

$\beta_1, \beta_2, \ldots, \beta_k$ are the coefficients of the independent variables x_1, $x_2, \ldots, x_k$

$b_1, b_2, \ldots, b_k$ are the sample estimates of the coefficients $\beta_1, \beta_2, \ldots, \beta_k$

Although it is not easy, the calculations of the preceding sections of this chapter can all be done with any scientific calculator. The computations required for multiple regression are so complicated that a statistical software package must be used. We will focus here on *interpreting* the outputs of a statistical computer display. (See Using Technology in the section on how to generate such displays in Excel or STATDISK.)

EXAMPLE   Table 9-3 is drawn from data in Data Set 3 in Appendix B, which contains measurements from anesthetized bears. Based on Table 9-3, find the multiple regression equation in which the dependent (y) variable is weight and the independent variables are head length (HEADLEN) and total overall length (LENGTH).

SOLUTION   Based on the computer output illustrated below, we can formulate the multiple regression equation as

$$\text{WEIGHT} = -374 + 18.8\ \text{HEADLEN} + 5.87\ \text{LENGTH}$$

Using the notation presented earlier in this section, we could write this equation as

$$\hat{y} = -374 + 18.8x_3 + 5.87x_6$$

This equation best fits the given data (for weight, head length, and overall length) according to the same least-squares criterion described in Section 9-3. That is, when we use the Table 9-3 data for WEIGHT, HEADLEN, and LENGTH, this equation fits the data best, although if we used another sample, we might find a slightly different equation. If the equation fits the data well, it can be used for predictions. For example, if we determine that the equation is suitable for predictions, and if we have a bear with a 14.0 in. head length and a 71.0 in. overall length, we can predict its weight by substituting those values into the regression equation to get a predicted weight of 306 lb. Also, the coefficients of $b_3 = 18.8$ and $b_6 = 5.87$ can be used to determine *marginal change*, as described in Section 9-3. For example, the coefficient of $b_3 = 18.8$ shows that when the overall length of a bear remains constant, the predicted weight increases by 18.8 lb for each 1 in. increase in the length of the head.

TABLE 9-3	Data from Anesthetized Male Bears						
Sample Number	y WEIGHT	x_2 AGE	x_3 HEADLEN	x_4 HEADWTH	x_5 NECK	x_6 LENGTH	x_7 CHEST
1	80	19	11.0	5.5	16.0	53.0	26
2	344	55	16.5	9.0	28.0	67.5	45
3	416	81	15.5	8.0	31.0	72.0	54
4	348	115	17.0	10.0	31.5	72.0	49
5	262	56	15.0	7.5	26.5	73.5	41
6	360	51	13.5	8.0	27.0	68.5	49
7	332	68	16.0	9.0	29.0	73.0	44
8	34	8	9.0	4.5	13.0	37.0	19

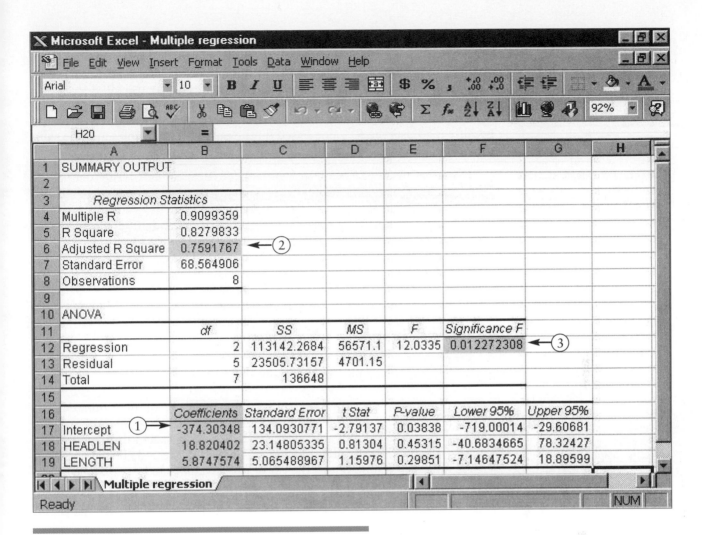

Excel Display   Multiple Regression.
The annotated Excel display has three key components, which are shaded here and identified with circled numbers:

1. Coefficients for the multiple regression equation
2. Adjusted R^2 = 0.759
3. Overall significance of multiple regression equation: ρ = 0.012

Adjusted R^2

R^2 denotes the **multiple coefficient of determination,** which is a measure of how well the multiple regression equation fits the sample data. A perfect fit would result in R^2 = 1. A very good fit results in a value near 1. A very poor fit results in a value of R^2 close to 0. The value of R^2 = 0.828 in the Excel display indicates that 82.8% of the variation in bear weight can be explained by the head length x_3 and overall length x_6. *The multiple coefficient of determination R^2 is a measure of how well the regression equation fits the sample*

Statistics in Court

Owners of a five-building apartment complex filed a lawsuit because of extensive damage to bricks. The damage occurred when water was absorbed by the brick face, followed by freezing and thawing cycles, causing part of the brick face to separate. With about 750,000 bricks, it was not practical to inspect each one, so methods of sampling were used instead. Statisticians used regression methods to predict the total number of damaged bricks. The independent variables included which of the five buildings was used, direction of wall exposure, height, and whether the wall faced an interior courtyard or was an exterior wall. The estimate of total damage appears to have strongly influenced the final settlements. (See "Bricks, Buildings, and the Bronx: Estimating Masonry Deterioration," by Fairley, Izenman, and Whitlock, *Chance*, Vol. 7, No. 3.)

data, but it has a serious flaw: As more variables are included, R^2 increases. (Actually, R^2 could remain the same, but it usually increases.) Although the largest R^2 is thus achieved by simply including all of the available variables, the best multiple regression equation does not necessarily use all of the available variables. Consequently, it is better to use the adjusted coefficient of determination when comparing different multiple regression equations, because it adjusts the R^2 value based on the number of variables and the sample size.

DEFINITION

The **adjusted coefficient of determination** is the multiple coefficient of determination R^2 modified to account for the number of variables and the sample size. It is calculated by using Formula 9-7.

Formula 9-7 $$\text{Adjusted } R^2 = 1 - \frac{(n-1)}{[n-(k+1)]}(1-R^2)$$ where

n = sample size
k = number of independent (x) variables

The Excel display shows the adjusted coefficient of determination as 0.759. If we use Formula 9-7 with the R^2 value of 0.828, $n = 8$, and $k = 2$, we find that the adjusted R^2 value is 0.759, confirming Excel's displayed value. For the weight, head length, and length data in Table 9-3, the R^2 value of 82.8% indicates that 82.8% of the variation in weight can be explained by the head length x_3 and overall length x_6, but when we compare this multiple regression equation to others, it is better to use the adjusted R^2 of 75.9% (or 0.759).

P-Value

The Excel display shows a P-value (labelled "Significance F") of 0.012. This value is a measure of the overall significance of the multiple regression equation. In this case, the small value of 0.012 suggests that the multiple regression equation has good overall significance and is usable for predictions. That is, it makes sense to predict weights of bears based on their head lengths and overall lengths. Like the adjusted R^2, this P-value is a good measure of how well the equation fits the sample data. The value of 0.012 results from a test of the null hypothesis that $\beta_3 = \beta_6 = 0$. Rejection of $\beta_3 = \beta_6 = 0$ implies that at least one of β_3 and β_6 is not 0, suggesting that this regression equation is effective in determining bear weights.

A complete analysis of the Excel results might include other important elements, such as the significance of the individual coefficients, but we will limit our discussion to the three key components—multiple regression equation, adjusted R^2 and P-value.

TABLE 9-4	Searching for the Best Multiple Regression Equation				
	LENGTH	CHEST	HEADLEN/ LENGTH	AGE/NECK/ LENGTH/CHEST	AGE/HEADLEN/HEADWTH/ NECK/LENGTH/CHEST
R^2	0.805	0.983	0.828	0.999	0.999
Adjusted R^2	0.773	0.980	0.759	0.997	0.996
Overall significance	0.002	0.000	0.012	0.000	0.046

Finding the Best Multiple Regression Equation

So far, we have considered only the multiple regression equation relating bear weights to the independent variables of head length and overall length, but there are several other variables that could be included. Perhaps some other combination of variables would result in an equation that fits the sample data better and is more likely to provide better predictions of bear weights. Table 9-4 lists a few of the combinations of variables.

Although *determination of the best multiple regression equation is often quite difficult and beyond the scope of this book*, we can provide some help with the following guidelines:

1. *Use common sense and practical considerations to include or exclude variables.* For example, we might exclude the variable of age because inexperienced researchers might not know how to determine the age of a bear and, when questioned, bears are reluctant to reveal their ages.

2. *Include relatively few independent (x) variables.* In weeding out independent variables that don't have an effect on the dependent variable, it might be helpful to find the linear correlation coefficient r for each pair of variables being considered. For example, using the data in Table 9-3, we will find that there is a 0.955 linear correlation for the paired NECK/ HEADLEN data. Because there is such a high correlation between neck size and head length, there is no need to include both of those variables. In choosing between NECK and HEADLEN, we should include NECK for this reason: NECK is a better predictor of WEIGHT because the NECK/ WEIGHT paired data have a linear correlation coefficient of $r = 0.971$, which is higher than $r = 0.884$ for the paired HEADLEN/WEIGHT data.

3. *Use adjusted R^2.* Select an equation having a value of adjusted R^2 with this property: If an additional independent variable is included, the value of adjusted R^2 does not increase by a substantial amount. For example, Table 9-4 shows that if we use only the independent variable of CHEST, the adjusted R^2 is 0.980, but when we include all six variables the adjusted R^2 increases to 0.996. Using six variables instead of only one is too high a price to pay for such a small increase in the adjusted R^2. We're better off with the single independent variable of CHEST than using all six independent variables.

Model for Alumni Contributions

Colleges and universities can improve their fundraising strategies by using multiple regression to predict alumni donations. The dependent variable would be the amount of money given by a donor in a year, while independent variables could include the donor's income, age, marital status, fraternity/sorority membership, major, distance from college, and level of participation in alumni events. External factors, such as a measure of the national economy, may also be deemed significant independent variables.

4. *For a given number of independent (x) variables, select the equation with the largest value of adjusted R^2.* That is, choose those variables with the property that no other combination of the same number of independent variables will yield a larger value of adjusted R^2. For example, if we decide to use a single independent variable, we should use CHEST, because its adjusted R^2 of 0.980 is larger than the adjusted R^2 for any other single variable. Consequently, CHEST is the best single predictor of WEIGHT.

5. *Consider the P-value.* Select an equation having overall significance, as determined by the *P*-value (Significance *F*) in the computer display. For example, see the values of overall significance in Table 9-4. The use of all six independent variables results in an overall significance of 0.046, which is just barely significant at the $\alpha = 0.05$ level; we're better off with the single variable of CHEST, which has overall significance of 0.000.

Using these guidelines in an attempt to find the best equation for predicting weights of bears, we find that for the data of Table 9-3, the best regression equation uses the single independent variable of CHEST. The best regression equation appears to be

$$\text{WEIGHT} = -195 + 11.4\,(\text{CHEST})$$

or
$$\hat{y} = -195 + 11.4x_7$$

For cases involving a large number of independent variables, many statistical software packages include a program for performing **stepwise regression,** whereby different combinations are tried until the best model is obtained. (However, in some cases, the validity of such solutions may be questionable.)

When we discussed regression in Section 9-3, we listed four common errors that should be avoided when using regression equations to make predictions. These same errors should be avoided when using multiple regression equations. Be especially careful about concluding that a cause–effect relationship exists.

Using Technology

Excel: First enter the sample data in columns. Select **Tools** from the main menu, then select **Data Analysis** and **Regression.** In the dialog box, enter the range of values for the dependent (*y*) variable, then enter the range of values for the independent (*x*) variables, which must be in adjacent columns. An example output is illustrated in this section.

STATDISK: Select **Analysis,** then **Multiple Regression.** Either enter the data in the different columns, or use Copy/Paste from another data source. Click on **Evaluate** and you will get a dialog box. Identify the columns that you want included, and identify the column representing the dependent (*y*) variable. Outputs include the multiple regression equation, the multiple coefficient of determination R^2 and the adjusted R^2.

9-5 Exercises A: Basic Skills and Concepts

In Exercises 1–4, refer to the Excel display below and answer the given questions.

1. Construct the multiple regression equation that expresses earthquake magnitude in terms of latitude, longitude, and depth.
2. Identify
   a. the *P*-value corresponding to the overall significance of the multiple regression equation
   b. the value of the multiple coefficient of determination R^2
   c. the adjusted value of R^2

	A	B	C	D	E	F	G
1	SUMMARY OUTPUT						
2							
3	*Regression Statistics*						
4	Multiple R	0.409795					
5	R Square	0.167932					
6	Adjusted R Square	0.145239					
7	Standard Error	1.067112					
8	Observations	114					
9							
10	ANOVA						
11		*df*	*SS*	*MS*	*F*	*Significance F*	
12	Regression	3	25.28057	8.426856	7.400232	0.000146209	
13	Residual	110	125.2601	1.138728			
14	Total	113	150.5407				
15							
16		*Coefficients*	*Standard Err*	*t Stat*	*P-value*	*Lower 95%*	*Upper 95%*
17	Intercept	-2.02693	1.26949	-1.59665	0.113212	-4.542766075	0.488899215
18	Lat	0.069004	0.017405	3.964659	0.000131	0.034511774	0.103496089
19	Long	0.008697	0.005985	1.453163	0.149025	-0.00316379	0.020558711
20	Depth	-0.02623	0.012521	-2.09508	0.038459	-0.051045566	-0.001418796

Excel Display

3. Is the multiple regression equation usable for predicting an earthquake's magnitude based on its recorded latitude, longitude, and depth? Why or why not?

4. Seismic activity has been detected as 48.2°N latitude and 124.99°W longitude, at a depth of 1 m.

   a. Find the predicted magnitude of the earthquake.

   b. The seismic activity in question actually had a magnitude of 0.9 ML. How accurate is the predicted weight from part (a)?

In Exercises 5–8, refer to the bear data in Data Set 3 of Appendix B. Let the dependent variable be WEIGHT, and let the independent variables be those given in the exercise. (The data sets are already stored on the data disk and STATDISK.) Use software such as Excel or STATDISK to answer these questions:

a. Find the multiple regression equation that expresses the dependent variable WEIGHT in terms of the given independent variables.

b. Identify the values of the multiple coefficient of determination R^2, the adjusted R^2, and (if Excel is used) the P-value corresponding to the overall significance.

> c. Does the multiple regression equation seem suitable for predicting the weight of a bear based on the given independent variables?

5. LENGTH and CHEST
6. NECK, LENGTH, and CHEST
7. BEARAGE, NECK, LENGTH, and CHEST
8. HEADLEN, LENGTH, and NECK

In Exercises 9–14, refer to the weights of garbage in Data Set 1 of Appendix B. Let the dependent variable be HHSIZE (household size), and let the independent variables be those given in the exercise. (The data sets are already stored on the data disk and STATDISK.) Use software such as Excel or STATDISK to answer these questions:

> a. Find the multiple regression equation that expresses the dependent variable HHSIZE in terms of the given independent variables.
> b. Identify the values of the multiple coefficient of determination R^2, the adjusted R^2, and (if Excel is used) the P-value corresponding to the overall significance.
> c. Does the multiple regression equation seem suitable for making predictions of household size based on the given independent variables?

9. YARD
10. PLASTIC
11. PLASTIC and PAPER
12. METAL, PLASTIC, and FOOD
13. METAL and PLASTIC
14. PAPER and GLASS
15. Refer to Data Set 4 in Appendix B and find the multiple regression equation with snowfall as the dependent variable. (Don't include CITY as an independent variable.) Is this equation suitable for predicting snowfall in Canadian locations? Why or why not?
16. Refer to Data Set 5 in Appendix B and find the best multiple regression equation with number of Senate sittings as the dependent variable. (Don't include the number of each Parliament as an independent variable.) Is this equation suitable for predicting the number of Senate sittings in a given Parliament? Why or why not? (*Hint:* To efficiently try out the regressions of the dependent variable with various combinations of independent variables, try sending each output to its own (suitably labelled) spreadsheet page. Where the differences between significance levels are very small, the real-world judgment of "best" regression may depend partly on non-mathematical factors, such as the ease of getting data for the different variables.)

9-5 Exercises B: Beyond the Basics

x	1	3	4	7	5
y	5	14	19	42	26

17. In some cases, the best-fitting multiple regression equation is of the form $\hat{y} = b_0 + b_1 x + b_2 x^2$. The graph of such an equation is a parabola. Using the data set listed in the margin, let $x_1 = x$, and, creating an x^2 row, let $x_2 = x^2$. Find the multiple regression equation for the parabola that best fits the given data. Based on the value of the multiple coefficient of determination, how well does this equation fit the data?

....

Vocabulary List

correlation
bivariate data
bivariate normal distribution
scatterplot
scatter diagram
linear correlation coefficient
cross product
Pearson product moment
  correlation coefficient
lurking variable
centroid
regression equation
regression line
independent variable
predictor variable
dependent variable
response variable
marginal change
outlier
influential point

predicted values
residual
least-squares property
mathematical model
total·deviation
explained deviation
unexplained deviation
total variation
explained variation
unexplained variation
coefficient of determination
prediction interval
standard error of estimate
multiple regression equation
multiple coefficient of
  determination
adjusted coefficient of
  determination
stepwise regression

....

Review

In this chapter we presented basic methods for using paired data to investigate the relationship between two or more variables. We generally limited our discussion to linear relationships because consideration of nonlinear relationships requires more advanced mathematics.

- Section 9-2 used scatter diagrams and the linear correlation coefficient to decide whether there is a linear correlation between two variables.

- Section 9-3 presented methods for finding the equation of the regression line, which (by the least-squares criterion) best fits the paired data. When there is a significant linear correlation, the regression line can be used to predict the value of a variable, given some value of the other variable. We saw that regression equations exemplify the more general concept of a mathematical model, which is a function that can be used to describe a relationship between variables. The possibility of *nonlinear* relationships was discussed.

- Section 9-4 introduced the concept of total variation, with components of explained and unexplained variation. We defined the coefficient of determination r^2 to be the quotient obtained by dividing explained variation by total variation. We also developed methods for constructing prediction intervals, which are helpful in judging the accuracy of predicted values.

- In Section 9-5 we considered multiple regression, which allows us to investigate relationships among several variables. We discussed procedures for obtaining a multiple regression equation, as well as the values of the multiple coefficient of determination R^2, the adjusted R^2, and a P-value for the overall significance of the equation.

• •

Review Exercises

In Exercises 1–4, use the data in the accompanying table. The data come from a study of ice cream consumption that spanned the springs and summers of three years. The ice cream consumption is in litres per capita per week, price of the ice cream is in dollars, family income of consumers is in dollars per week, and temperature is in degrees Celsius.

Consumption	0.219	0.212	0.223	0.241	0.231	0.195	0.186	0.164	0.153	0.145
Price	2.38	2.48	2.45	2.46	2.39	2.31	2.43	2.36	2.34	2.45
Income	540	548	562	554	527	540	568	548	527	548
Temperature	5	13	17	20	21	18	16	8	0	–4

Based on data from Kadiyala, *Econometrica*, Vol. 38.

1. **a.** Use a 0.05 significance level to test for a linear correlation between consumption and price.
   b. Find the equation of the regression line that expresses consumption (y) in terms of price (x).
   c. What is the best predicted consumption amount if the price is $2.43?
2. **a.** Use a 0.05 significance level to test for a linear correlation between consumption and income.
   b. Find the equation of the regression line that expresses consumption (y) in terms of income (x).
   c. What is the best predicted consumption amount if the income is $562?
3. **a.** Use a 0.05 significance level to test for a linear correlation between consumption and temperature.
   b. Find the equation of the regression line that expresses consumption (y) in terms of temperature (x).
   c. What is the best predicted consumption amount if the temperature is 0°C?
4. Use software such as Excel or STATDISK to find the multiple regression equation of the form $\hat{y} = b_0 + b_1 x_1 + b_2 x_2 + b_3 x_3$, where the dependent variable y represents consumption, x_1 represents price, x_2 represents income, and x_3 represents temperature. Also identify the value of the multiple coefficient of determination R^2, the adjusted R^2, and the P-value representing the overall significance of the multiple regression equation. Can the regression equation be used to predict ice cream consumption? Are any of the equations from Exercises 1–3 better?

In Exercises 5–8, use the sample data in the accompanying table. The table includes the results for the top performers in the 1996 Molson Indy Toronto. Note that the data in the Final Position column are ordinal and thus should not be used in the regressions. The distance between the first and second final positions, for example, may be quite different from the distance between the second and third final positions. Intervals between starting positions, however, are assumed to correspond to consistent track distances. Times are given in seconds and speeds in miles per hour.

Final Position	Starting Position	Qualifying Time	Qualifying Speed	Points
1	3	58.471	109.838	20
2	2	58.145	110.455	17
3	8	59.016	108.825	14
4	5	58.519	109.748	12
5	13	59.189	108.507	10
6	12	59.175	108.533	8
7	14	59.220	108.450	6
8	11	59.120	108.634	5
9	18	59.680	107.615	4
10	4	58.490	109.803	3

Based on data from the Molson Indy Toronto Web pages.

5. a. Use a 0.05 significance level to test for a linear correlation between qualifying speed and starting position.
   b. Find the equation of the regression line that expresses starting position (y) in terms of qualifying speed (x).
   c. What is the best predicted starting position (rounded to a whole number) for a driver whose qualifying speed is 109.066?

6. a. Use a 0.05 significance level to test for a linear correlation between qualifying speed and points.
   b. Find the equation of the regression line that expresses points (y) in terms of qualifying speed (x).
   c. What is the best predicted number of points (rounded to a whole number) for a driver whose qualifying speed is 109.066?

7. Use only the paired data for starting position and qualifying speed. For a driver whose qualifying speed is 109.066, find a 95% prediction interval estimate of the starting position.

8. Let y = points, x_1 = starting position, and x_2 = qualifying time. Use software such as Excel or STATDISK to find the multiple regression equation of the form $\hat{y} = b_0 + b_1 x_1 + b_2 x_2$. Also identify the value of the multiple coefficient of determination R^2, the adjusted R^2, and the P-value representing the overall significance of the multiple regression equation. Based on the results, should the multiple regression equation be used for making predictions? Why or why not?

· ·

Cumulative Review Exercises

1. In 1970, the mean time between eruptions of the Old Faithful geyser was 66 minutes. Refer to the intervals (in minutes) between eruptions for the more recent data listed in Data Set 16 of Appendix B.

a. Test the claim of Yellowstone National Park geologist Rick Hutchinson that eruptions now occur at intervals that are longer than in 1970.

b. Construct a 95% confidence interval for the mean time between eruptions.

2. The Marc Michael Advertising Company has prepared two different television commercials for Taylor's women's jeans. One commercial is humorous and the other is serious. A test screening involves a standard scale with higher scores indicating more favourable responses. The results are listed here. Based on the results, does one commercial seem to be better? Is the issue of correlation relevant to this situation?

Consumer	A	B	C	D	E	F	G	H
Humorous commercial	26	33	19	18	29	27	23	24
Serious commercial	21	30	14	14	24	22	21	19

3. In studying the effects of heredity and environment on intelligence, it has been helpful to analyse IQs of identical twins who were separated soon after birth. Identical twins share identical genes inherited from the same fertilized egg. By studying identical twins raised apart, we can eliminate the variable of heredity and better isolate the effects of environment. The accompanying table shows the IQs of identical twins (older twins are x) raised apart. Use the sample data to determine whether there is a relationship between IQs of the twins. Write a summary statement about the effect of heredity and environment on intelligence. Note that your conclusions will be based on this relatively small sample of 12 pairs of identical twins.

x	107	96	103	90	96	113	86	99	109	105	96	89
y	111	97	116	107	99	111	85	108	102	105	100	93

Based on data from "IQs of Identical Twins Reared Apart," by Arthur Jensen, *Behavioral Genetics*.

Technology Project

Use Excel or STATDISK to retrieve the bear data found in Data Set 3 of Appendix B. (Data Set 3 is stored on the data disk.) Using the complete data set, find the linear correlation coefficient and equation of the regression line when the dependent variable of weight is paired with (a) head length, (b) head width, (c) neck size, (d) length, and (e) chest size. Which of the preceding regression equations is best for predicting the weight of a bear given its head length, head width, neck size, length, and chest size? Also, find the multiple regression equation obtained when the dependent variable of weight is expressed in terms of the independent variables of head length, head width, neck size, and chest size. Interpret the computer results. Is the resulting multiple regression equation suitable for making predictions of a bear's weight based on its head length, head width, neck size, and chest size? Why or why not?

When hiking (with a tape measure but no scale) on the Grizzly Lake trail in Yellowstone National Park, one of the authors once encountered a bear, which he wrestled to the ground and rendered temporarily unconscious. (*Editor's note*: The truth is that he saw a bear 250 m away.) Given all of the preceding results, what is the best predicted weight of the bear that was measured and found to have a 12.3 in. head length, a 4.9 in. head width, a 19.0 in. neck size, a 55.3 in. length, and a 31.4 in. chest size?

•••••••• **FROM DATA TO DECISION** ••••••••

How Much Hockey "Star Power" Should You Buy?

Hockey-team executives must regularly assess the value of buying (or trading away) expensive star players for their team. Do the expensive new players deliver when it comes to team wins? The accompanying table lists NHL teams' payrolls (in millions of dollars, assessed after the trading deadline for the 1995–96 season) and points for that season (as of March 29, 1996). Use the methods of this chapter to analyse the data. Assuming the 1996 data are representative of future years, determine whether there is a correlation between payroll and points. How much should a team's payroll be if its season ended with 75 points? What is the highest point total you could expect if payroll was capped at $15 million? Which was the better deal in 1996: Montreal's payroll or Toronto's? Why?

Team	Payroll	Points
Edmonton	11.24	66
Ottawa	11.58	34
N.Y. Islanders	13.02	48
San Jose	14.14	43
Anaheim	14.14	65
Calgary	14.36	73
Tampa Bay	14.83	77
Buffalo	17.19	63
Montreal	17.25	84
Washington	17.40	82
Los Angeles	17.51	61
Florida	17.69	85
Boston	20.12	79
Hartford	20.47	69
Dallas	20.77	61
Chicago	21.07	86
Colorado	21.25	96
Philadelphia	21.91	91
Winnipeg	22.78	69
Pittsburgh	22.83	94
Toronto	22.93	72
New Jersey	24.47	80
Vancouver	25.33	75
Detroit	28.42	119
St. Louis	30.45	76
N.Y. Rangers	33.84	90

Based on data from "Making a Point Is Expensive" in the *Toronto Star*, March 31, 1996.

········ COOPERATIVE GROUP ACTIVITIES ········

1. *Out-of-class activity:* Divide into groups of 3 or 4 people. Investigate the relationship between two variables by collecting your own paired sample data and using the methods of this chapter to determine whether there is a significant linear correlation. Also identify the regression equation and describe a procedure for predicting values of one of the variables when given values of the other variable. Suggested topics:

   - Is there a relationship between taste and cost of different brands of chocolate chip cookies (or colas)? (Taste can be measured on some scale, such as 1 to 10.)

   - Is there a relationship between salaries of professional baseball (or basketball, or football) players and their season achievements?

   - Rates versus weights: Is there a relationship between car fuel consumption rates and car weights? If so, what is it?

   - Is there a relationship between the lengths of men's (or women's) feet and their heights?

   - Is there a relationship between student grade-point averages and the amount of television watched? If so, what is it?

   - Is there a relationship between heights of fathers (or mothers) and heights of their first sons (or daughters)?

2. *In-class activity:* Divide into groups of 8 to 12 people. For each group member, *measure* his or her height and *measure* his or her arm span. For the arm span, the subject should stand with arms extended, like the wings on an airplane. It's easy to mark the height and arm span on a chalkboard, then measure the distances there. Using the paired sample data, is there a correlation between height and arm span? If so, find the regression equation with height expressed in terms of arm span. Can arm span be used as a reasonably good predictor of height?

3. *In-class activity:* Divide into groups of 8 to 12 people. For each group member, record the pulse rate by counting the number of heart beats in one minute. Also record height. Is there a relationship between pulse rate and height? If so, what is it?

4. *In-class activity:* Divide into groups of 8 to 12 people. For each group member, use a string and ruler to measure head circumference and forearm length. Is there a relationship between these two variables? If so, what is it?

INTERNET PROJECT

Linear Regression

The linear correlation coefficient is a tool that can be used to measure the strength of the linear relationship between two variables. We can evaluate the linear correlation coefficient for any two sets of paired data, and then we can proceed to analyse the resulting values. Does it make sense for the two variables to be linearly correlated? Could a high correlation be caused by a third variable that is correlated with each of the two original variables? The Internet Project for this chapter can be found at this site:

http://www.pearson.ca/triola

Click on Internet Project, then on Chapter 9. There you will be told how to find several paired data sets in the fields of sports, medicine, and economics. You will then apply the correlation and regression methods of this chapter to answer some of the questions that arise in this type of analysis.

10

Multinomial Experiments and Contingency Tables

10-1 Overview

Chapter objectives are identified. This chapter deals with sample data consisting of frequency counts arranged in one row with at least three categories (one-way frequency table), or a table with at least two rows and at least two columns (two-way frequency table).

10-2 Multinomial Experiments: Goodness-of-Fit

The goodness-of-fit procedure of hypothesis testing is presented for sample data in a one-way frequency table. This procedure is used to test claims that observed sample frequencies fit, or conform to, a particular distribution.

10-3 Contingency Tables: Independence and Homogeneity

Contingency tables (or two-way frequency tables) are defined and described. A standard method is presented for testing claims that in a contingency table, the row variable and the column variable are independent. Also presented is a method for a test of homogeneity, in which we test a claim that different populations have the same proportions of some characteristics.

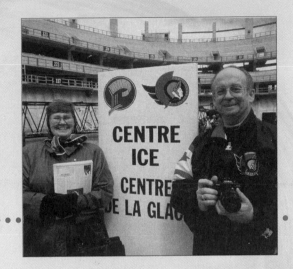

CHAPTER PROBLEM:

Are the same percentages of Quebeckers and Ontarians within different age brackets bilingual?

Although Canada is officially bilingual, this does not mean that all Canadian residents can speak both languages. Table 10-1 gives selected data from the 1996 Census, which provides statistics on French/English bilingualism. The table lists the numbers of bilingual residents in Quebec and Ontario, with reference to four different age groups. In these two provinces, 47% of bilingual youth who are less than 15 years old reside in Quebec. But 63% of bilingual residents between age 15 and 24 live in Quebec, and 73% of bilingual residents age 25 to 64 or 65 and over live in Quebec. Are these differences significant?

It is tempting for politicians or educators to make claims based on these apparent shifts in bilingualism rates. We can address the testing of such claims by analysing data of the type listed in Table 10-1. Section 10-3 will consider this particular set of data.

Table 10-1   Numbers of Bilingual Residents (in 10,000s) by Age in Quebec and Ontario

	Under 15	15–24	25–64	65 and Over
Quebec	19.25	44.77	176.87	25.17
Ontario	21.59	25.81	66.95	9.14

Based on data from Statistics Canada.

10-1 Overview

In this chapter we continue the pattern of applying inferential methods to different configurations of data. This chapter focuses on the analysis of categorical data (see Chapter 1) consisting of frequency counts for the different categories (or **cells**) into which the nonnumeric data can be separated. In Section 10-2 we will consider multinomial experiments, which consist of observed frequency counts arranged in a single row or column (called a one-way frequency table). In Section 10-3 we will consider contingency tables (or two-way frequency tables), which consist of frequency counts arranged in a table such as Table 10-1.

We will see that the two major topics of this chapter (multinomial experiments and contingency tables) use the same χ^2 (chi-square) test statistic that was introduced in Section 6-5. Recall the following important properties of the chi-square distribution:

1. Unlike the normal and Student t distributions, the chi-square distribution is not symmetric. (See Figure 10-1.)

2. The values of the chi-square distribution can be 0 or positive, but they cannot be negative. (See Figure 10-1.)

3. The chi-square distribution is different for each number of degrees of freedom. (See Figure 10-2.)

Critical values of the chi-square distribution are found in Table A-4.

10-2 Multinomial Experiments: Goodness-of-Fit

Each data set in this section consists of qualitative data that have been separated into different categories. We aim to determine whether the distribution agrees with or "fits" some claimed distribution.

The following assumptions apply when we test a hypothesis that the population proportion for each of the categories is as claimed.

Assumptions

1.   The data have been randomly selected.
2.   The sample data consist of frequency counts for each of the different categories.
3.   For each category, the *expected* frequency is at least 5. (The expected frequency for a category is the expected *mean* of the frequencies for that category that would occur if random samples of the same size were repeatedly selected from the same population. There is *no* minimum-size requirement for the *observed frequencies* in each category of the actual sample being analysed.)

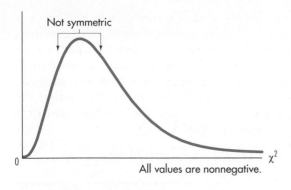

Figure 10-1 The Chi-Square Distribution

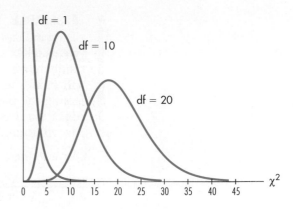

Figure 10-2 Chi-Square Distributions for 1, 10, and 20 Degrees of Freedom

We define a *multinomial experiment* the same way we defined a binomial experiment (Section 4-3), except that a multinomial experiment has more than two categories (unlike a binomial experiment, which has exactly two categories).

DEFINITION

A **multinomial experiment** is a procedure that meets the following conditions:

1. The number of trials is fixed.
2. The trials are independent.
3. All outcomes of each trial must be classified into exactly one of several different categories.
4. The probabilities for the different categories remain constant for each trial.

In this section we present a method for testing a claim that in a multinomial experiment, the frequencies observed in the different categories fit a particular distribution. Because we test for how well an observed frequency distribution conforms to some theoretical distribution, this method is often called a *goodness-of-fit test*.

DEFINITION

A **goodness-of-fit test** is used to test the hypothesis that an observed frequency distribution fits (or conforms to) some claimed distribution.

> **EXAMPLE**   Examine the *last digits* of each of the company Revenues listed in Data Set 6, in Appendix B. If dollar amounts are counted precisely, we usually expect that the last digits will occur with relative frequencies (or probabilities) that are roughly the same. In contrast, estimated or rounded-off values tend to have 0 or 5 occurring much more often as last digits. Using the methods of this section, we could test the hypothesis that the data (that is, the last digits of the company revenues) fit a uniform distribution, with all of the digits being equally likely.

Our goodness-of-fit tests will incorporate the following notation.

Notation
O represents the *observed frequency* of an outcome.
E represents the *expected frequency* of an outcome.
k represents the *number of different categories* or outcomes.
n represents the total *number of trials*.

Finding Expected Frequencies

In the typical situation requiring a goodness-of-fit test, we have *observed* frequencies (denoted by O) and must use the claimed distribution to determine the *expected* frequencies (denoted by E). In many cases, an expected frequency can be found by multiplying the probability p for a category by the number of different trials n, so

$$E = np$$

For example, if we test the claim that a die is fair by rolling it 60 times, we have $n = 60$ (because there are 60 trials) and $p = 1/6$ (because a die is fair if the six possible outcomes are equally likely with the same probability of 1/6). The expected frequency for each category or cell is therefore

$$E = np$$
$$= (60)(1/6) = 10$$

We know that sample frequencies typically deviate somewhat from the values we theoretically expect, so we now present the key question: Are the differences between the actual *observed* values O and the theoretically *expected* values E statistically significant? To answer this question we use the following test statistic, which measures the discrepancy between observed and expected frequencies.

Test Statistic for Goodness-of-Fit Tests in Multinomial Experiments
$$\chi^2 = \sum \frac{(O - E)^2}{E}$$

Critical Values

1. Critical values are found in Table A-4 by using $k - 1$ degrees of freedom, where k = number of categories.

2. Goodness-of-fit hypothesis tests are always right-tailed.

The form of the χ^2 test statistic is such that *close agreement* between observed and expected values will lead to a *small* value of χ^2. A large value of χ^2 will indicate strong disagreement between observed and expected values. A significantly large value of χ^2 will thus cause rejection of the null hypothesis of no difference between observed and expected frequencies. Our test is therefore always right-tailed because the critical value and critical region are located at the extreme right of the distribution.

Once we know how to find the values of the test statistic and critical value, we can test hypotheses by using the same procedure introduced in Chapter 7 and summarized in Figure 7-4.

EXAMPLE   Every year, the *Financial Post 500* ranks companies in a variety of categories, on a number of criteria. Two examples are the top 10 accounting firms as ranked by revenue and the top 500 companies ranked by assets. Table 10-2 shows successive years' rankings for a sample of companies that attained, in some category, a top-five ranking in 1997. Test the claim that regardless of companies' rankings in 1996, they all had the same probability of attaining a top-five ranking in 1997.

SOLUTION   Table 10-2 shows that 71 firms had top-five rankings for 1997. If the chance of a top-five rank in 1997 were the same regardless of the 1996 rank, then any 1996 rank (considering only ranks 1 to 7) would have equal probability ($p = 1/7$) of being the *previous* rank for a 1997 top-five company in a given category. The number of top-five companies expected to correspond to each of the 1996 rank numbers listed is as follows:

$$E = np = (71)(1/7) = 10.143$$

Safest Airplane Seats

Many of us believe that the rear seats are safest in an airplane crash. Safety experts do not agree that any particular part of an airplane is safer than others. Some planes crash nose first when they come down, but others crash tail first on takeoff. Goodness-of-fit tests can be used with a null hypothesis that all sections of an airplane are equally safe. Crashed airplanes could be divided into the front, middle, and rear sections. The observed frequencies of fatalities could then be compared to the frequencies that would be expected with a uniform distribution of fatalities. The χ^2 test statistic reflects the size of the discrepancies between observed and expected frequencies, and it would reveal whether some sections are safer than others.

TABLE 10-2	Successive Years' Rankings of "Top-Five" Companies						
	Ranking for 1996						
	1	2	3	4	5	6	7
Number with a top-five rank for 1997	14	15	14	14	9	5	0

Based on data in *The Financial Post 500*, 1998 edition.

The observed frequencies (denoted by O) are 14, 15, 14, . . . , 0, but the expected frequencies (denoted by E) are 10.143, 10.143, 10.143, . . . , 10.143. Having identified the observed and expected frequencies, we will now follow our standard procedure for testing hypotheses.

Step 1:   The original claim is that the probabilities of a top-five 1997 rank for the different 1996 ranks are not all the same. That is, at least one of the probabilities p_1, p_2, . . . , p_7 is different from the others.

Step 2:   If the original claim is false, then all of the probabilities are the same. That is, $p_1 = p_2 = \cdots = p_7$.

Step 3:   The null hypothesis must contain the condition of equality, so we have

$$H_0: p_1 = p_2 = p_3 = p_4 = p_5 = p_6 = p_7 \text{ (a uniform distribution)}$$

H_1: At least one of the probabilities is different from the others.

Step 4:   No significance level was specified, so we select $\alpha = 0.05$, a very common choice.

Step 5:   Because we are testing a claim about the distribution of the 1997 "top fives" being a uniform distribution, we use the goodness-of-fit test described in this section. The χ^2 distribution is used with the test statistic given earlier.

Step 6:   Using the observed frequencies O listed in Table 10-2 and the expected frequencies E (equal 10.143 for each rank in 1996), we compute the value of the χ^2 test statistic, as shown in Table 10-3. The test statistic is $\chi^2 = 19.607$. The critical value is $\chi^2 = 12.592$ (found in Table A-4 with $\alpha = 0.05$ in the right tail and degrees of freedom equal to $k - 1 = 6$). The test statistic and critical value are shown in Figure 10-3.

TABLE 10-3   Calculating the χ^2 Test Statistic for Top-Five Rankings for 1997

Rank in 1996	Observed Frequency O	Expected Frequency E	$O - E$	$(O - E)^2$	$\dfrac{(O - E)^2}{E}$
1	14	10.143	3.857	14.876	1.467
2	15	10.143	4.857	23.590	2.326
3	14	10.143	3.857	14.876	1.467
4	14	10.143	3.857	14.876	1.467
5	9	10.143	−1.143	1.306	0.129
6	5	10.143	−5.143	26.450	2.608
7	0	10.143	−10.143	102.880	10.143
	71	71.001			

$$\chi^2 = \sum \frac{(O - E)^2}{E} = 19.607$$

(Allowing for rounding, these two totals must closely agree.)

Step 7:   Because the test statistic falls within the critical region, there is sufficient evidence to reject the null hypothesis.

Interpretation There is sufficient evidence to support the claim that companies placing in different rankings of a category for 1996 had disproportionate probabilities of being placed in the top-five ranking of the same category for 1997. It appears that, if you to wish to forecast the top-five ranking companies for the next year, you should take the previous year's rankings into consideration.

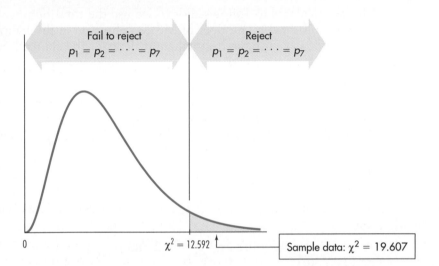

Figure 10-3   Goodness-of-Fit Test of $p_1 = p_2 = \cdots = p_7$

The techniques in this section can be used to test whether an observed frequency distribution conforms to some theoretical frequency distribution. The preceding example used a goodness-of-fit test to decide whether the observed frequencies conformed to a uniform distribution. Because many statistical analyses require a normally distributed population, we can use the chi-square test in this section to determine whether given samples are drawn from normally distributed populations (see Exercise 22).

The preceding example dealt with the null hypothesis that the probabilities for the different categories are all equal. The methods of this section can also be used when the hypothesized probabilities (or frequencies) are different, as in the next example.

EXAMPLE   Mars, Inc., claims that its M&M plain candies are distributed with the colour percentages of 30% brown, 20% yellow, 20% red, 10% orange, 10% green, and 10% blue. The colours of the M&Ms listed in Data Set 11 of Appendix B are summarized in Table 10-4. Using the sample data and a 0.05 significance level, test the claim that the colour distribution is as claimed by Mars, Inc.

Did Mendel Fudge His Data?

R.A. Fisher analysed the results of Mendel's famous work in hybridization, in which Mendel experimented with peas and other plants. Fisher noted that the data were unusually close to theoretically expected outcomes. He says, "The data have evidently been sophisticated systematically, and after examining various possibilities, I have no doubt that Mendel was deceived by a gardening assistant, who knew only too well what his principal expected from each trial made." Fisher used chi-square tests and concluded that only about a 0.00004 probability exists of such close agreement between expected and reported observations.

TABLE 10-4	Frequencies of M&M Plain Candies					
	Brown	Yellow	Red	Orange	Green	Blue
Observed frequency	33	26	21	8	7	5
Expected frequency	30	20	20	10	10	10

SOLUTION We extended Table 10-4 to include the expected frequencies, which are calculated as follows. For n, we use the total number of trials (100), which is the total number of M&Ms observed in the sample. For the probabilities, we use the decimal equivalents of the claimed percentages (30%, 20%, . . . , 10%).

Brown: $E = np = (100)(0.30) = 30$

Yellow: $E = np = (100)(0.20) = 20$

$\vdots$

Blue: $E = np = (100)(0.10) = 10$

In testing the given claim, Steps 1, 2, and 3 result in the following hypotheses:

H_0: $p_{br} = 0.3$ and $p_y = 0.2$ and $p_r = 0.2$ and $p_o = 0.1$ and $p_g = 0.1$ and $p_{bl} = 0.1$

H_1: At least one of the above proportions is different from the claimed value.

Steps 4, 5, and 6 lead us to use the goodness-of-fit test with a 0.05 significance level and a test statistic calculated from Table 10-5.

TABLE 10-5	Calculating the χ^2 Test Statistic for M&M Data				
Colour Category	Observed Frequency O	Expected Frequency $E = np$	$O - E$	$(O - E)^2$	$\dfrac{(O - E)^2}{E}$
Brown	33	30	3	9	0.3000
Yellow	26	20	6	36	1.8000
Red	21	20	1	1	0.0500
Orange	8	10	−2	4	0.4000
Green	7	10	−3	9	0.9000
Blue	5	10	−5	25	2.5000
	100	100		$\chi^2 = \sum \dfrac{(O - E)^2}{E} = 5.9500$	↑

The test statistic is $\chi^2 = 5.950$. The critical value of χ^2 is 11.071, and it is found in Table A-4 (using $\alpha = 0.05$ in the right tail with $k - 1 = 5$ degrees of freedom). The test statistic and critical value are shown in Figure 10-4. Because the test statistic does not fall within the critical region, there is not sufficient evidence to warrant rejection of the null hypothesis.

Interpretation There is not sufficient evidence to warrant rejection of the claim that the colours are distributed with the percentages given by Mars, Inc.

In Figure 10-5, we graph the claimed proportions of 0.30, 0.20, . . ., 0.10, along with the observed proportions of 33/100, 26/100, 21/100, 8/100, 7/100, 5/100, so that we can visualize the discrepancy between the distribution that was claimed and the frequencies that were observed. The

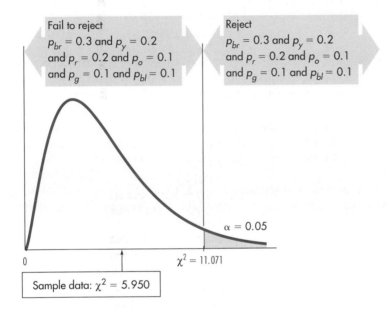

Figure 10-4 Goodness-of-Fit Test of $p_{br} = 0.3$ and $p_y = 0.2$ and $p_r = 0.2$ and $p_o = 0.1$ and $p_g = 0.1$ and $p_{bl} = 0.1$

Figure 10-5 Comparison of Claimed and Observed Proportions

Delaying Death

Sociologist David Phillips has studied the ability of people to postpone their death until after some important event. Analysing death rates of Jewish men who died near Passover, he found that the death rate dropped dramatically in the week before Passover, but rose the week after. He found a similar phenomenon occurring among Chinese-American women; their death rate dropped the week before their important Harvest Moon Festival, then rose the week after.

points along the solid line represent the claimed proportions, and the points along the broken line represent the observed proportions. The corresponding pairs of points are all fairly close, showing that all of the expected frequencies are reasonably close to the corresponding observed frequencies. In general, graphs such as Figure 10-5 are helpful in visually comparing expected frequencies and observed frequencies, as well as suggesting which categories result in the major discrepancies.

Rationale for the Test Statistic

The preceding examples should be helpful in developing a sense for the role of the χ^2 test statistic. It should be clear that we want to measure the amount of disagreement between observed and expected frequencies. Simply summing the differences between observed and expected values does not result in an effective measure because that sum is always 0, as shown below:

$$\Sigma(O - E) = \Sigma O - \Sigma E = n - n = 0$$

Squaring the $O - E$ values provides a more useful statistic, which reflects the differences between observed and expected frequencies. (The reasons for squaring the $O - E$ values are essentially the same reasons for squaring the $x - \bar{x}$ values in the formula for standard deviation.) The value of $\Sigma(O - E)^2$ measures only the magnitude of the differences, but we need to find the magnitude of the differences relative to what was expected. This relative magnitude is found through division by the expected frequencies, as in the test statistic.

The theoretical distribution of $\Sigma(O - E)^2/E$ is a discrete distribution because the number of possible values is limited. The distribution can be approximated by a chi-square distribution, which is continuous. This approximation is generally considered acceptable, provided that all values of E are at least 5. We included this requirement with the assumptions that apply to this section. In Section 5-6 we saw that the continuous normal probability distribution can reasonably approximate the discrete binomial probability distribution, provided that np and nq are both at least 5. We now see that the continuous chi-square distribution can reasonably approximate the discrete distribution of $\Sigma(O - E)^2/E$, provided that all values of E are at least 5. (There are ways of circumventing the problem of an expected frequency that is less than 5, such as combining categories so that all expected frequencies are at least 5.)

The number of degrees of freedom reflects the fact that we can freely assign frequencies to $k - 1$ categories before the frequency for every category is determined. Although we say that we can "freely" assign frequencies to $k - 1$ categories, we cannot have negative frequencies nor can we have frequencies so large that their sum exceeds the total of the observed frequencies for all categories combined.

P-Values

The examples in this section used the traditional approach to hypothesis testing, but the P-value approach can also be used. P-values can be obtained by using the same methods described in Sections 7-3 and 7-6. For instance, the preceding example resulted in a test statistic of $\chi^2 = 5.950$. That example had $k = 6$ categories, so there were $k - 1 = 5$ degrees of freedom. Referring to Table A-4, we see that for the row with 5 degrees of freedom, the test statistic of 5.95 is less than the lowest right-tailed critical value of 9.236, so the P-value is greater than 0.10. (If the preceding example is run on a computer, you can find a more precise P-value of 0.31111.) The high P-value suggests that the null hypothesis should not be rejected. Remember, we reject the null hypothesis only when the P-value is equal to or less than the significance level.

Using Technology

Excel: In Excel, you can analyse multinomial experiments using the template shown here. Type in the column and row headings shown in bold. Manually enter the data for the categories, observed frequencies, and expected frequencies. (If more rows are required, adjust the cell addresses in the formulas.) Enter the indicated formulas in Cells D4, E4, and F4. Select Cells D4:F4 then, under the **Edit** menu, select

	A	B	C	D	E	F	G	H
1		**Observed**	**Expected**					
2		**Frequency**	**Frequency**					
3	**Category**	**O**	**E**	**O-E**	**(O-E)^2**	**(O-E)^2/E**		
4	Brown	33	30	3	9	0.3		
5	Yellow	26	20	6	36	1.8		
6	Red	21	20	1	1	0.05		
7	Orange	8	10	-2	4	0.4		
8	Green	7	10	-3	9	0.9		
9	Blue	5	10	-5	25	2.5		
10								
11	**Alpha**	0.05						
12	**N**	6						
13	**Chi-Square**	5.95						
14	**Critical Chi-Sq.**	11.07048257						
15	**P value**	0.311114615						
16								
17								
18								

◄◄ ◄ ► ►◄ \ Multinomial experiments /

Ready

Excel Display Multinomial Experiments

Cell	Formula	Explanation
D4	=(B4-C4)	Table 10-5, fourth column
E4	=D4^2	Table 10-5, fifth column
F4	=E4/C4	Table 10-5, sixth column
B12	=COUNT(B4:B9)	n
B13	=SUM(F4:F9)	Table 10-5, chi-square calculation
B14	=CHIINV(B11,B12-1)	Critical value (always on right tail)
B15	=CHIDIST(B13,B12-1)	P-value

Use appropriate cell addresses for data.

Copy; select Cells D5:D9 then, under the **Edit** menu, select **Paste**. This completes the upper portion of the template. In the bottom portion of the template, enter the desired alpha. The n value can be input manually or else calculated by the **=COUNT** function. The formulas in Cells B13 to B15 complete the analysis.

STATDISK: Select **Analysis** from the main menu bar, then select the option **Multinomial Experiments**. Choose between "equal expected frequencies" and "unequal expected frequencies" and enter (or "paste" in) the data in the dialog box. If you choose "unequal expected frequencies," enter the expected values in the second column either as "counts" with the actual expected frequencies or as "proportions" (with the probabilities entered). Then click **Evaluate**.

10-2 Exercises A: Basic Skills and Concepts

1. One common way to test for authenticity of data is to analyse the frequencies of digits. When people are weighed and their weights are rounded to the nearest pound, we expect the last digits 0, 1, 2, . . . , 9 to occur with about the same frequency. In contrast, if people are asked how much they weigh, the digits 0 and 5 tend to occur at higher rates. The author randomly selected 80 students, obtained their weights, and recorded only the last digits, with the results shown in the following table. At the 0.01 significance level, test the claim that the last digits occur with the same frequency. Based on the results, does it appear that the students were actually weighed or were they asked to report their weights?

Last digit	0	1	2	3	4	5	6	7	8	9
Frequency	35	0	2	1	4	24	1	4	7	2

2. Excel can be used to generate random integers between 0 and 9 inclusive. Suppose the following results are obtained. Use a 0.05 significance level to test the claim that the computer generates digits that are uniformly distributed.

Digit	0	1	2	3	4	5	6	7	8	9
Frequency	32	29	37	21	41	24	33	32	25	26

3. One of the authors observed 500 spins of the roulette wheel at the Mirage Resort and Casino. For each spin, the ball can land in any one of the 38 different slots that are supposed to be equally likely. When computer software (STATDISK) was used to test the claim that the slots are in fact equally likely, the test statistic $\chi^2 = 38.232$ was obtained.
   a. Find the critical value, assuming that the significance level is 0.10.
   b. STATDISK displayed a P-value of 0.41331, but suppose you are working only with Table A-4. Given the known value for χ^2 and the number

of categories (38), what would be your estimate for the *P*-value, based on the table?

c. Write a conclusion about the claim that the 38 results are equally likely.

4. Such measures of inflation as the consumer price index can also be used to compare prices in different regions. A standardized "basket" of grocery or consumer items can be purchased in different cities and stores, and their prices compared. Suppose that 51 stores are randomly selected, from all grocery and convenience stores in the four cities shown that charged over $90 for a standard basket of consumer goods. At the 0.05 level of significance, test the claim that stores charging over $90 for the same grocery and convenience items are found in equal numbers in the four cities.

City	St. John's	Moncton	Regina	Victoria
Number	20	3	11	17

Based on data from Statistics Canada.

5. A labour specialist is analysing the numbers of work stoppages in the transportation industry. She claims that, in general, 10% of stoppages involve air transport, 10% involve rail transport, 20% water transport, and 60% road-based transport (including trucks, buses, and taxis). Based on the table below, drawn from a random selection of years from 1961 to 1999, test the specialist's claim. Use the 0.05 level of significance.

Mode of transport	Air	Rail	Water	Road
Number of stoppages	84	66	123	426

Based on data from Human Resources Canada.

6. A study was made of 147 industrial accidents that required medical attention. Among those accidents, 31 occurred on Monday, 42 on Tuesday, 18 on Wednesday, 25 on Thursday, and 31 on Friday (based on results from "Counted Data CUSUM's," by Lucas, *Technometrics*, Vol. 27, No. 2). Test the claim that accidents occur with equal proportions on the five workdays. If they are not the same, what factors might explain the differences?

7. Use a 0.05 significance level and the industrial accident data from Exercise 6 to test the claim of a safety expert that accidents are distributed on workdays as follows: 30% on Monday, 15% on Tuesday, 15% on Wednesday, 20% on Thursday, and 20% on Friday. Does rejection of that claim provide any help in correcting the industrial accident problem?

8. The Gleason Supermarket's manager must decide how much of each ice-cream flavour he should stock so that customer demands are satisfied but unwanted flavours don't result in waste. The ice-cream supplier claims that among the four most popular flavours, customers have these preference rates: 62% prefer vanilla, 18% prefer chocolate, 12% prefer neapolitan, and 8% prefer vanilla fudge. A random sample of 200 customers produces the results below. At the $\alpha = 0.05$ significance level, test the claim that the supplier has correctly identified customer preferences.

Flavour	Vanilla	Chocolate	Neapolitan	Vanilla Fudge
Customers	120	40	18	22

Data are based on results from the International Association of Ice Cream Manufacturers.

9. The number π is an irrational number with the property that when we try to express it in decimal form, it requires an infinite number of decimal places and there is no pattern of repetition. In the decimal representation of π, the first 100 digits occur with the frequencies described in the table below. At the 0.05 significance level, test the claim that the digits are uniformly distributed.

Digit	0	1	2	3	4	5	6	7	8	9
Frequency	8	8	12	11	10	8	9	8	12	14

10. The number 22/7 is similar to π in the sense that they both require an infinite number of decimal places. However, 22/7 is a rational number because it can be expressed as the ratio of two integers, whereas π cannot. When rational numbers such as 22/7 are expressed in decimal form, there is a pattern of repetition. In the decimal representation of 22/7, the first 100 digits occur with the frequencies described in the table below. At the 0.05 significance level, test the claim that the digits are uniformly distributed. How does the result differ from that found in Exercise 9?

Digit	0	1	2	3	4	5	6	7	8	9
Frequency	0	17	17	1	17	16	0	16	16	0

11. In a "Scratch & Save" promotion, Zellers promised all customers a discount ranging from 5% to 50%, depending on the value that appeared on their "Scratch & Save" card. In the accompanying table, the bottom row shows the expected distribution of discounts for every 1000 cards submitted. Suppose that the manager of one branch says the actual distribution of discounts for 1000 cards that were submitted in her store was as shown in the middle row. At the 0.05 level of significance, test the claim that this actual distribution of discounts is consistent with the distribution that Zellers promised.

Percent discount	5%	10%	15%	20%	25%	30%	50%
Actual quantity	203	715	35	22	8	14	3
Expected quantity	185	725	40	20	15	10	5

Based on promotional materials from Zellers.

12. In analysing hits by V-1 buzz bombs in World War II, South London was subdivided into regions, each with an area of 0.25 km^2. In Section 4-5 we presented an example and included a table of actual frequencies of hits and the frequencies expected with the Poisson distribution. Use the values listed here and test the claim that the actual frequencies fit a Poisson distribution. Use a 0.05 level of significance.

Number of bomb hits	0	1	2	3	4 or more
Actual number of regions	229	211	93	35	8
Expected number of regions (from Poisson distribution)	227.5	211.4	97.9	30.5	8.7

13. Refer to the Old Faithful geyser data in Data Set 16 of Appendix B. Test the claim that the time intervals are uniformly distributed among the five categories of 55–64, 65–74, 75–84, 85–94, 95–104.

14. Refer to Data Set 8 in Appendix B and record only the last digits of the pulse counts. Test for authenticity of the pulse counts by testing the claim that the last digits occur with equal frequency. Do the pulse counts appear to be authentic? (See Exercise 1.)

15. Refer to Data Set 10 in Appendix B and categorize the listed one-year returns for mutual funds as poor (up to 24%), fair (above 24% to 36%), good (above 36% to 48%), or excellent (above 48%). Test the claim that in the year sampled, the returns were evenly distributed among the four categories. Use the 0.05 level of significance.

16. Many lottery enthusiasts search for patterns that they hope will indicate winning combinations. Yuri thinks that sums of numbers in Lotto 6/49 draws are not evenly distributed. Refer to Data Set 12 in Appendix B and find the sum for each row of numbers (*not* including the bonus number). Place these numbers into categories by this procedure: Divide each sum by 20, then ignore the decimal portion of the result. (For example, the sum 57 would be placed in the category 2, since $57/20 = 2.85$, or 2 with the decimal portion dropped.) At the 0.05 level of significance, test the claim that the categories based on sums of the numbers occur with the same frequency. Do the results imply that the lottery is not fair?

10-2 Exercises B: Beyond the Basics

17. In doing a test for the goodness-of-fit as described in this section, does an outlier have much of an effect on the value of the χ^2 test statistic? Test for the effect of an outlier by repeating Exercise 4 after changing the frequency for Victoria from 17 to 170. Describe the general effect of an outlier.

18. In doing a test for goodness-of-fit as described in this section, suppose that we multiply each observed frequency by the same positive integer greater than 1. How is the critical value affected? How is the test statistic affected?

19. In this exercise we will show that a hypothesis test involving a multinomial experiment with only two categories is equivalent to a hypothesis test for a proportion (Section 7-5). Assume that a particular multinomial experiment has only two possible outcomes, A and B, with observed frequencies of f_1 and f_2, respectively.

   a. Find an expression for the χ^2 test statistic, and find the critical value for a 0.05 significance level. Assume that we are testing the claim that both categories have the same frequency, $(f_1 + f_2)/2$.

b. The test statistic

$$z = \frac{\hat{p} - p}{\sqrt{\dfrac{pq}{n}}}$$

is used to test the claim that a population proportion is equal to some value p. With the claim that $p = 0.5$, $\alpha = 0.05$, and

$$\hat{p} = \frac{f_1}{f_1 + f_2}$$

show that z^2 is equivalent to χ^2 [from part (a)]. Also show that the square of the critical z score is equal to the critical χ^2 value from part (a).

20. An observed frequency distribution is as follows:

Number of successes	0	1	2	3
Frequency	89	133	52	26

a. Assuming a binomial distribution with $n = 3$ and $p = 1/3$, use the binomial probability formula to find the probability corresponding to each category of the table.

b. Using the probabilities found in part (a), find the expected frequency for each category.

c. Use a 0.05 level of significance to test the claim that the observed frequencies fit a binomial distribution for which $n = 3$ and $p = 1/3$.

21. In a recent year, customers of Victoria Fridge and Stove (which is open 7 days a week) returned 146 appliances. If the frequencies of returns on different days conform to a Poisson distribution, they will be as shown on the bottom row of the following table. (For example, on about 245 days there will be no returns at all.) Use a 0.05 significance level to test the claim that the actual frequencies fit a Poisson distribution. (*Caution:* Not all of the expected frequencies are at least 5, as assumed by the hypothesis test.)

Number of returns on that day	0	1	2	3	4
Actual number of days	247	90	24	3	1
Expected number of days	244.7	97.9	19.6	2.6	0.2

22. An observed frequency distribution of sample IQ scores is as follows:

IQ score	Less than 80	80–95	96–110	111–120	More than 120
Frequency	20	20	80	40	40

a. Assuming a normal distribution with $\mu = 100$ and $\sigma = 15$, use the methods given in Chapter 5 to find the probability of a randomly selected subject belonging to each class. (Use class boundaries of 79.5, 95.5, 110.5, 120.5.)

b. Using the probabilities found in part (a), find the expected frequency for each category.

c. Use a 0.01 level of significance to test the claim that the IQ scores were randomly selected from a normally distributed population with $\mu = 100$ and $\sigma = 15$.

10-3 Contingency Tables: Independence and Homogeneity

The examples and exercises in Section 10-2 involved frequencies listed in a single row (or column) according to category. This section also involves frequencies listed according to category, but here we consider cases with at least two rows and at least two columns. For example, see Table 10-1, which has two rows (Quebec, Ontario) and four columns (the four categories for age groups). Tables similar to Table 10-1 are generally called *contingency tables*, or *two-way frequency tables*.

DEFINITIONS

A **contingency table** (or **two-way frequency table**) is a table in which frequencies correspond to two variables. (One variable is used to categorize rows, and a second variable is used to categorize columns.)

Contingency tables are especially important because they are frequently used to analyse survey results. Consequently, the methods presented in this section are among those used most often.

This section presents two types of hypothesis testing based on contingency tables. We first consider tests of independence, used to determine whether a contingency table's row variable is independent of its column variable. We then consider tests of homogeneity, used to determine whether different populations have the same proportions of some characteristic. Good news: Both types of hypothesis testing use the *same* basic methods. We begin with tests of independence.

Home Field Advantage

In the *Chance* magazine article "Predicting Professional Sports Game Outcomes from Intermediate Game Scores," authors Harris Cooper, Kristina DeNeve, and Frederick Mosteller used statistics to analyse two common beliefs: Teams have an advantage when they play at home, and only the last quarter of professional basketball games really counts. Using a random sample of hundreds of games, they found that for the four top sports, the home team wins about 58.6% of games. Also, basketball teams ahead after 3 quarters go on to win about 4 out of 5 times, but baseball teams ahead after 7 innings go on to win about 19 out of 20 times. The statistical methods of analysis included the chi-square distribution applied to a contingency table.

Test of Independence

> ### DEFINITION
>
> A **test of independence** tests the null hypothesis that the row variable and the column variable in a contingency table are not related. (The null hypothesis is the statement that the row and column variables are independent.)

It is very important to recognize that in this context, the word *contingency* refers to dependence, but this is only a statistical dependence and cannot be used to establish a direct cause-and-effect link between the two variables in question. For example, after analysing the data in Table 10-1, we might conclude that there is a relationship between age group and the likelihood of being a bilingual resident of a province, but that doesn't mean that age directly affects the causes for becoming bilingual.

When testing the null hypothesis of independence between the row and column variables in a contingency table, the following assumptions apply. (Note that these assumptions do not require that the parent population have a normal distribution or any other particular distribution.)

Assumptions

1. The sample data are randomly selected.
2. The null hypothesis H_0 is the statement that the row and column variables are *independent*; the alternative hypothesis H_1 is the statement that the row and column variables are dependent.
3. For every cell in the contingency table, the *expected* frequency E is at least 5. (There is no requirement that every *observed* frequency must be at least 5.)

Our test of independence between the row and column variables uses the following test statistic and critical values.

Test Statistic for a Test of Independence

$$\chi^2 = \sum \frac{(O - E)^2}{E}$$

Critical Values

1. The critical values are found in Table A-4 by using

$$\text{degrees of freedom} = (r - 1)(c - 1)$$

where r is the number of rows and c is the number of columns.

2. In a test of independence with a contingency table, the critical region is located in the *right tail only*.

The test statistic allows us to measure the degree of disagreement between the frequencies actually observed and those that we would theoretically expect when the two variables are independent. Small values of the χ^2 test statistic result from close agreement between observed frequencies and frequencies expected with independent row and column variables. Large values of the χ^2 test statistic are to the right of the chi-square distribution, and they reflect significant differences between observed and expected frequencies. In repeated large samplings, the distribution of the test statistic χ^2 can be approximated by the chi-square distribution, provided that all expected frequencies are at least 5.

The number of degrees of freedom $(r - 1)(c - 1)$ reflects the fact that because we know the total of all frequencies in a contingency table, we can freely assign frequencies to only $r - 1$ rows and $c - 1$ columns before the frequency for every cell is determined. [However, we cannot have negative frequencies or frequencies so large that any row (or column) sum exceeds the total of the observed frequencies for that row (or column).]

In the preceding section we knew the corresponding probabilities and could easily determine the expected values, but the typical contingency table does not come with the relevant probabilities. Consequently, we need to devise a method for obtaining the corresponding expected values. We will first describe the procedure for finding the values of the expected frequencies, and then we will justify that procedure. For each cell in the frequency table, the expected frequency E can be calculated by using the following equation.

Expected Frequency for a Contingency Table

$$\text{Expected frequency} = \frac{(\text{row total})(\text{column total})}{(\text{grand total})}$$

TABLE 10-6   Observed Frequencies (and Expected Frequencies) (in 10,000s)

	Age Group				Row totals
	Under 15	15-24	25-64	65 and Over	
Quebec	19.25	44.77	176.87	25.17	266.06
	(27.89)	(48.21)	(166.53)	(23.43)	
Ontario	21.59	25.81	66.95	9.14	123.49
	(12.95)	(22.37)	(77.29)	(10.88)	
Column totals:	40.84	70.58	243.82	34.31	Grand total: 389.55

Here *grand total* refers to the total of all observed frequencies in the table. For example, the expected frequency for the upper left cell of Table 10-6 (a duplicate of Table 10-1 with expected frequencies inserted in parentheses) is 27.89. It is found by noting that the total of all frequencies for that row is 266.06, the total of the column frequencies is 40.84, and the total of all frequencies in the table is 389.55, so we get an expected frequency of

$$E = \frac{(\text{row total})(\text{column total})}{(\text{grand total})} = \frac{(266.06)(40.84)}{389.55} = 27.89$$

EXAMPLE   The expected frequency for the upper left cell of Table 10-6 is 27.89. Find the expected frequency for the lower left cell, assuming independence between province of residence and the ages of bilingual people.

SOLUTION   The lower left cell lies in the second row (with total 123.49) and the first column (with total 40.84). The expected frequency is

$$E = \frac{(\text{row total})(\text{column total})}{(\text{grand total})} = \frac{(123.49)(40.84)}{389.55} = 12.95$$

Interpretation To interpret this result in the lower left cell, we can say that although (in 10,000s) 21.59 bilingual Ontarians were under 15, we would have expected 12.95 if the province of residence of a bilingual Canadian is independent of that person's age. There is a discrepancy between $O = 21.59$ and $E = 12.95$, and such discrepancies are key components of the test statistic.

It would be very helpful to stop here and verify that the other expected frequencies are 48.21, 166.53, 23.43, 22.37, 77.29, and 10.88.

Rationale for the procedure for finding expected frequencies:

Let us pretend that we know only the row and column totals and that we must fill in the cell expected frequencies by assuming independence (or no relationship) between the two variables involved—that is, pretend that we know only the row and column totals shown in Table 10-6. Let's begin with the cell in the upper left corner, and recall that all numbers represent tens of thousands of bilingual people. Because 266.06 of 389.55 bilingual persons were from Quebec, we have $P(\text{Quebec}) = 266.06/389.55$. Similarly, 40.84 of the bilingual individuals were under 15 years old, so $P(\text{under 15}) = 40.84/389.55$. Because we are assuming independence between the age and province of bilingual people, we can use the multiplication rule of probability to get

$$P(\text{Quebec and under 15}) = \frac{266.06}{389.55} \cdot \frac{40.84}{389.55}$$

This equation is an application of the multiplication rule for independent events, which is expressed in general as follows: $P(A \text{ and } B) = P(A) \cdot P(B)$.

Having found an expression for the probability of being in the upper left cell, we now proceed by finding the *expected value* for that cell, which we get by multiplying the probability for that cell by the total number of individuals, as shown in the following equation:

$$E = p \cdot n = \left[\frac{266.06}{389.55} \cdot \frac{40.84}{389.55} \right] \cdot 389.55 = 27.89$$

The form of this product suggests a general way to obtain the expected frequency of a cell:

$$\text{expected frequency } E = \frac{(\text{row total})}{(\text{grand total})} \cdot \frac{(\text{column total})}{(\text{grand total})} \cdot (\text{grand total})$$

This expression can be simplified to

$$E = \frac{(\text{row total}) \cdot (\text{column total})}{(\text{grand total})}$$

We can now proceed to use contingency table data for testing hypotheses, as in the following example, which uses the data given in the Chapter Problem.

EXAMPLE   At the 0.05 significance level, use the data in Table 10-1 to test the claim that the province of residence of a bilingual person is independent of the person's age.

SOLUTION   The null hypothesis and alternative hypothesis are as follows:

H_0: A bilingual person's province of residence is independent of his or her age bracket.

H_1: A bilingual person's province of residence and age bracket are dependent.

The significance level is $\alpha = 0.05$.

Because the data are in the form of a contingency table, we use the χ^2 distribution with this test statistic:

$$\chi^2 = \sum \frac{(O - E)^2}{E}$$

$$= \frac{(19.25 - 27.89)^2}{27.89} + \frac{(44.77 - 48.21)^2}{48.21} + \frac{(176.87 - 166.53)^2}{166.53}$$

$$+ \frac{(25.17 - 23.43)^2}{23.43} + \frac{(21.59 - 12.95)^2}{12.95} + \frac{(25.81 - 22.37)^2}{22.37}$$

$$+ \frac{(66.95 - 77.29)^2}{77.29} + \frac{(9.14 - 10.88)^2}{10.88}$$

$$= 2.6766 + 0.2455 + 0.6420 + 0.1292 + 5.7644 + 0.5290$$

$$+ 1.3833 + 0.2783$$

$$= 11.648$$

(The more accurate test statistic of 11.654 is obtained by carrying more decimal places in the intermediate calculations. Excel and STATDISK both agree that 11.654 is a better result.) The critical value is $\chi^2 = 7.815$, and it is found from Table A-4 by noting that $\alpha = 0.05$ in the right tail and the number of degrees of freedom is given by $(r - 1)(c - 1) = (2 - 1)(4 - 1) = 3$. The test statistic and critical value are shown in Figure 10-6. Because the test statistic falls within the critical region, we reject the null hypothesis that a bilingual person's province of residence is independent of his or her age bracket.

Interpretation At least with respect to Ontario and Quebec, there appears to be a connection between the province of residence of a bilingual person and his or her age bracket.

Figure 10-6 Test of Independence Between a Bilingual Person's Province of Residence and His or Her Age

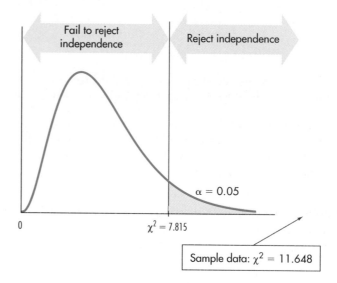

P-Values

The preceding example used the traditional approach to hypothesis testing, but we can easily use the *P*-value approach. Excel and STATDISK both provide the same *P*-value of 0.0087 (when rounded). Using the criterion given in Section 7-3, we reject the null hypothesis because the *P*-value is less than the significance level of $\alpha = 0.05$.

If we don't have a suitable calculator or statistical software package, we can estimate *P*-values by using the same methods introduced earlier. The preceding example resulted in a test statistic of $\chi^2 = 11.648$, and the critical value is based on 3 degrees of freedom. Refer to Table A-4 and note that for the row with 3 degrees of freedom, the test statistic of $\chi^2 = 11.648$ is between the displayed critical values of 11.345 and 12.838, so the *P*-value must be between the *P*-values (at the top of the table) of 0.01 and 0.005. This can be expressed as follows: $0.005 < P < 0.01$. On the basis of this relatively small *P*-value, we again reject the null hypothesis and conclude that there is sufficient sample evidence to warrant rejection of the claim that the province of residence of a bilingual person is independent of the person's age (for Ontario and Quebec).

If the *P*-value had been greater than the significance level of 0.05, we would have failed to reject the null hypothesis of independence.

Test of Homogeneity

In the preceding example, we illustrated a test of independence by using a sample of individuals drawn from a single population of bilingual Canadians. In some cases samples are drawn from different populations, and we want to determine whether those populations have the same proportions of the characteristics being considered.

DEFINITION

In a **test of homogeneity,** we test the claim that different populations have the same proportion of some characteristics.

Because a test of homogeneity uses data sampled from different populations, we have predetermined totals for either the rows or the columns in the contingency table. Consequently, a test of homogeneity involves random selections made in such a way that either the row totals are predetermined or the column totals are predetermined. In trying to distinguish between a test for homogeneity and a test for independence, we can therefore pose the following question:

> Were predetermined sample sizes used for different populations (test of homogeneity), or was one big sample drawn so both row and column totals were determined randomly (test of independence)?

As an example of a test of homogeneity, suppose we want to test the claim that the proportion of voters who are Canadian Alliance supporters is the same in British Columbia, Alberta, Saskatchewan, and Manitoba. If we choose to find the political party registrations for 250 British Columbians, 200 Albertans, 100 Saskatchewanians, and 80 Manitobans, then the contingency table summarizing the results will have either the row totals or the column totals (whichever represent the different provinces) predetermined as 250, 200, 100, 80.

In conducting a test of homogeneity, we can use the same procedures already presented in this section, as illustrated in the following example.

EXAMPLE   Does a pollster's gender have an effect on poll responses by men? In an article about polls, it was stated that people often give "acceptable" rather than honest responses on sensitive issues. The gender or race of the interviewer may influence the answers. To support that claim, data were provided for a poll in which surveyed men were asked if they agreed with this statement: "Abortion is a private matter that should be left to the woman to decide without government intervention." We will analyse the effect of gender on male survey subjects only. Table 10-7 shows the responses of surveyed men (based on data from *U.S. News and World Report*). Assume that the survey was designed so that male interviewers were instructed to obtain 800 responses from male subjects, and female interviewers were instructed to obtain 400 responses from male subjects. Using a 0.05 significance level, test the claim that the proportions of agree/disagree responses are the same for the subjects interviewed by men and the subjects interviewed by women.

TABLE 10-7	Gender and Survey Responses	
	Gender of Interviewer	
	Man	Woman
Men who agree	560	308
Men who disagree	240	92

SOLUTION   Because we have predetermined column totals of 800 subjects interviewed by men and 400 subjects interviewed by women, we test for homogeneity with these hypotheses:

H_0: The proportions of agree/disagree responses are the same for the subjects interviewed by men as the subjects interviewed by women.

H_1: The proportions are different.

Excel Display   Contingency Table for Test of Homogeneity

The significance level is $\alpha = 0.05$. We use the same χ^2 test statistic described earlier, and it is calculated by using the same procedure. Instead of listing the details of that calculation, we provide the accompanying Excel display that results from the data in Table 10-7.

The Excel display shows the expected frequencies of 578.67, 289.33, 221.33, and 110.67. The display also includes the test statistic of $\chi^2 = 6.529$ and the P-value of 0.011. Using the P-value approach to hypothesis testing, we reject the null hypothesis of equal (homogeneous) proportions. There is sufficient evidence to warrant rejection of the claim that the proportions are the same. It appears that response and the gender of the interviewer are dependent. It seems that men are influenced by the gender of the interviewer, although this conclusion is a statement of causality that is not justified by the statistical analysis.

Using Technology

Excel: In Excel, you can use the following template to find the test statistic, critical value, and P-value. Adjust the displayed formulas based on where you set up the template and whether you need to add extra rows or columns of data. First, set up an area for entering the row and column data. In Cell H2, input the formula shown to compute the row total; copy to Cell H3. In Cell D4, input the formula shown to compute the column total; copy to Cells E4:G4. In Cell H5, enter the formula for the grand total. Create a second area to find the expected frequencies for each cell. Input the formulas as shown in Cells D8 and D9, then copy to Cells E8:G8 and E9:G9, respectively. In the template area for subtotals, copy the formula shown for Cell D11 into the range D11:G12. In the bottom portion of the template, enter the desired alpha and the formulas for calculating the degrees of freedom, test statistic, critical value, and P-value.

STATDISK: The STATDISK display shows the results obtained for the data in Table 10-1. If you are using STATDISK, select **Analysis** from the main menu bar, then select **Contingency Tables** and proceed to enter the data as requested. The STATDISK results include the test statistic, critical value, P-value, and conclusion.

Excel Display Contingency Table for Test of Independence (or Test of Homogeneity)

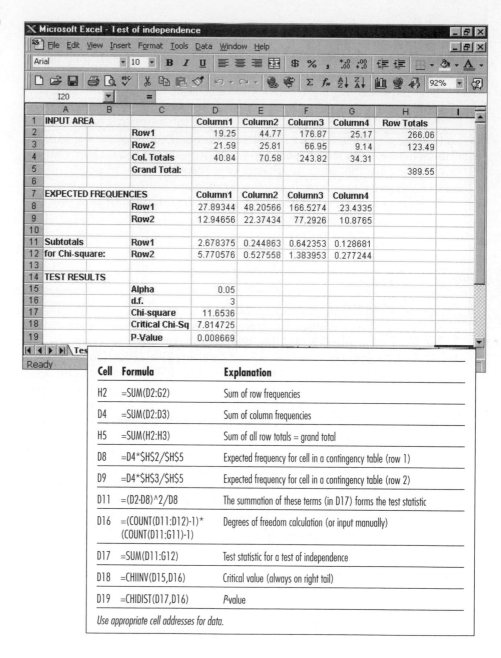

Cell	Formula	Explanation
H2	=SUM(D2:G2)	Sum of row frequencies
D4	=SUM(D2:D3)	Sum of column frequencies
H5	=SUM(H2:H3)	Sum of all row totals = grand total
D8	=D4*$H$2/$H$5	Expected frequency for cell in a contingency table (row 1)
D9	=D4*$H$3/$H$5	Expected frequency for cell in a contingency table (row 2)
D11	=(D2-D8)^2/D8	The summation of these terms (in D17) forms the test statistic
D16	=(COUNT(D11:D12)-1)*(COUNT(D11:G11)-1)	Degrees of freedom calculation (or input manually)
D17	=SUM(D11:G12)	Test statistic for a test of independence
D18	=CHIINV(D15,D16)	Critical value (always on right tail)
D19	=CHIDIST(D17,D16)	P-value

Use appropriate cell addresses for data.

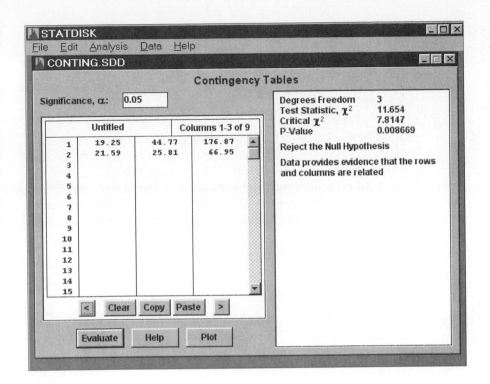

10-3 Exercises A: Basic Skills and Concepts

1. Table 10-7 summarizes data for male survey subjects, but the accompanying table summarizes data for a sample of women. Using a 0.01 significance level, and assuming that the sample sizes of 800 men and 400 women are predetermined, test the claim that the proportions of agree/disagree responses are the same for the subjects interviewed by men and the subjects interviewed by women.

	Gender of Interviewer	
	Man	Woman
Women who agree	512	336
Women who disagree	288	64

2. The number of overnight trips to Canada declined from 1996 to 1997, perhaps partly in response to the world financial conditions of 1997. Were these changes from year to year independent of the purposes of the trips made to Canada? Refer to the accompanying table showing the numbers of overnight trips (in thousands) for 1996 and 1997. At the 0.05 significance level, test the claim that the purposes of trips taken were independent of the year the trips were taken. Were some kinds of trips more affected than others?

	Business	Visit	Pleasure	Other
1996	671	1171	2360	174
1997	769	1204	2080	181

Based on data in *Industry Canada: Characteristics of International Travellers, 1997.*

3. Nicorette is a chewing gum designed to help people stop smoking cigarettes. Tests for adverse reactions yielded the results given in the accompanying table. At the 0.05 significance level, test the claim that the treatment (drug or placebo) is independent of the reaction (whether or not mouth or throat soreness was experienced). If you are thinking about using Nicorette as an aid to stop smoking, should you be concerned about mouth or throat soreness?

	Drug	Placebo
Mouth or throat soreness	43	35
No mouth or throat soreness	109	118

Based on data from Merrell Dow Pharmaceuticals, Inc.

4. Both proponents of and skeptics about health-store pills and nutritional supplements agree that to make valid claims about them, more clinical research on alternative medicines is necessary. One study has looked at a supplement for fighting the pain of arthritis. Based on the table below, test the claim that for those with arthritis, glucosamine hydrochloride has no effect on whether the subject feels improvement. Use the 0.05 level of significance. Does this study show that glucosamine hydrochloride is effective in reducing the pain of arthritis? If the study had a larger sample size and similar ratios were found within the contingency table, could this affect the outcome of the statistical test?

	Glucosamine Hydrochloride	Placebo
Felt improvement	22	24
Did not feel improvement	23	29

Based on data from the *Toronto Star*, September 19, 1998.

5. Firms that sponsor or participate in sporting events to gain marketing exposure like to represent winning teams. The accompanying table shows the numbers of cars of different makes in the top 14 and second 14 final positions in the 1996 Molson Indy Toronto. Does the evidence support a claim that the car model and the final position are independent? *Warning:* Not all expected frequencies are at least 5. If all the frequencies in the table had been five times greater than shown, the above warning would not be needed. In that scenario, would the *P*-value be greater than or less than the *P*-value that you get by using the original numbers in the table?

	Ford	Honda	Mercedes	Other
Top 14	5	3	6	0
Second 14	6	3	2	3

Based on data from the Molson Indy Toronto Web pages.

6. In a study of store checkout scanning systems, samples of purchases were used to compare the scanned prices to the posted prices. The accompanying table summarizes results for a sample of 819 items. When stores use scanners to check out items, are the error rates the same for regular-priced items as they are for advertised-special items? How might the behaviour of consumers change if they believe that disproportionately more overcharges occur with advertised-special items?

	Regular-Priced Items	Advertised-Special Items
Undercharge	20	7
Overcharge	15	29
Correct price	384	364

Based on data from "UPC Scanner Pricing Systems: Are They Accurate?" by Ronald Goodstein, *Journal of Marketing*, Vol. 58.

7. The Boeing Commercial Airplane Group conducted a survey of 133 planes being flown or on order from three airline companies based in different countries. The sample data are summarized in the accompanying table. Is there sufficient evidence to support the claim that the distribution of planes flying and planes ordered is independent of the airline company? Use a 0.01 significance level.

	United	British Air	Singapore
Boeing 777s flying	36	22	14
Boeing 777s ordered	16	23	22

8. A market researcher investigated cars and trucks sold in Canada to determine whether the proportions of sales for these two vehicle types were the same for all manufacturers. He examined randomly selected records for 50 sales of GM vehicles, 50 of Fords, 50 of Chryslers, 30 of Toyotas, and 20 of Volkswagens. (All sales were in December 1996.) The results are displayed below. At the 0.05 level of significance, test the claim that all these manufacturers sell cars and trucks in the same proportions.

	GM	Ford	Chrysler	Toyota	Volkswagen
Cars	24	14	16	24	19
Trucks	26	36	34	6	1

Based on data from *The Globe and Mail*, January 7, 1997.

9. A sports-medicine clinic is investigating the relation between types of sports injuries and the ages of patients involved. The accompanying table summarizes randomly selected sample data for patients with sports-based injuries. At the 0.05 significance level, test the claim that the sport where the accident occurred (basketball or other sport) is independent of the patient's age (under 10 or 10 and over). Does it follow from the results that playing basketball is safer at lower ages? Explain your answer.

	Sport Where Injury Occurred	
	Basketball	Other Sports
Under 10	23	124
10 and over	427	490

Based on data from *Chronic Diseases in Canada*, Vol. 16, No. 3.

10. A study of randomly selected car accidents and drivers who use cellular phones provided the following sample data. At the 0.05 level of significance, test the claim that the occurrence of accidents is independent of the use of cellular phones. Based on these results, does it appear that the use of cellular phones affects driving safety?

	Had Accident in Last Year	Had No Accident in Last Year
Cellular phone user	23	282
Not cellular phone user	46	407

Based on data from AT&T.

11. A provider of uniforms for CFL players is examining players' weights. The accompanying table compares the weights of 32 randomly selected offensive backs (including quarterbacks) in the league. At the 0.05 level of significance, do the data indicate that the weight distribution for offensive backs is independent of position played?

	Quarterback	Other Offensive Back
Less than 200 lb	7	9
At least 200 lb	3	13

Based on data from CFL Web site.

12. Winning team data were collected for teams in different sports, with the results given in the accompanying table. Use a 0.10 level of significance to test the claim that home/visitor wins are independent of the sport.

	Basketball	Baseball	Hockey	Football
Home team wins	127	53	50	57
Visiting team wins	71	47	43	42

Based on data from "Predicting Professional Sports Game Outcomes from Intermediate Game Scores," by Copper, DeNeve, and Mosteller, *Chance*, Vol. 5, No. 3–4.

13. The accompanying table lists sample data that statistician Karl Pearson used in 1909. Does the type of crime appear to be related to whether the criminal drinks or abstains? Are there any crimes that appear to be associated with drinking?

	Arson	Rape	Violence	Stealing	Coining	Fraud
Drinker	50	88	155	379	18	63
Abstainer	43	62	110	300	14	144

14. A study of people who refused to answer survey questions provided the randomly selected sample data in the accompanying table. At the 0.01 significance level, test the claim that the cooperation of the subject (response, refusal) is independent of the age category. Does any particular age group appear to be particularly uncooperative?

	Age					
	18–21	22–29	30–39	40–49	50–59	60 and over
Responded	73	255	245	136	138	202
Refused	11	20	33	16	27	49

Based on data from "I Hear You Knocking But You Can't Come In," by Fitzgerald and Fuller, *Sociological Methods and Research*, Vol. 11, No. 1.

15. Refer to Data Set 8 in Appendix B and test the claim that the gender of statistics students is independent of whether they smoke.

16. Refer to Data Set 8 in Appendix B and test the claim that whether statistics students exercise is independent of gender.

10–3 Exercises B: Beyond the Basics

17. The chi-square distribution is continuous, whereas the test statistic used in this section is discrete. Some statisticians use *Yates' correction for continuity* in cells with an expected frequency of less than 10 or in all cells of a contingency table with two rows and two columns. With Yates' correction, we replace

$$\sum \frac{(O - E)^2}{E} \quad \text{with} \quad \sum \frac{(|O - E| - 0.5)^2}{E}$$

Given the contingency table in Exercise 10, find the value of the χ^2 test statistic with and without Yates' correction. In general, what effect does Yates' correction have on the value of the test statistic?

18. **a.** For a contingency table with two rows and two columns and frequencies of a and b in the first row and frequencies of c and d in the second row, verify that the test statistic becomes

$$\chi^2 = \frac{(a + b + c + d)(ad - bc)^2}{(a + b)(c + d)(b + d)(a + c)}$$

b. Let $\hat{p}_1 = a/(a + c)$ and let $\hat{p}_2 = b/(b + d)$. Show that the test statistic

$$z = \frac{(\hat{p}_1 - \hat{p}_2) - 0}{\sqrt{\dfrac{\bar{p}\,\bar{q}}{n_1} + \dfrac{\bar{p}\,\bar{q}}{n_2}}}$$

where

$$\bar{p} = \frac{a + b}{a + b + c + d}$$

and

$$\bar{q} = 1 - \bar{p}$$

is such that $z^2 = \chi^2$ [the same result as in part (a)]. (This result shows that the chi-square test involving a 2×2 table is equivalent to the test for the difference between two proportions, as described in Section 8-6.)

• •

Vocabulary List

cells   two-way frequency table
multinomial experiment   test of independence
goodness-of-fit test   test of homogeneity
contingency table

• •

Review

Section 10-2 described the goodness-of-fit test for determining whether a single row (or column) of frequencies has some claimed distribution. Section 10-3 described contingency tables and the test of independence between the row and column variables, as well as the test of homogeneity, in which different populations have the same proportions of some characteristics. The following are some key elements of the methods discussed in this chapter.

• *Section 10-2 (Test for goodness-of-fit):*

Test statistic is $\chi^2 = \sum \dfrac{(O - E)^2}{E}$

Test is right-tailed with $k - 1$ degrees of freedom. All expected frequencies must be at least 5.

• *Section 10-3 (Contingency table test of independence or homogeneity):*

Test statistic is $\chi^2 = \sum \dfrac{(O - E)^2}{E}$

Test is right-tailed with $(r - 1)(c - 1)$ degrees of freedom. All expected frequencies must be at least 5.

Review Exercises

1. The latest product of a Dartmouth cat food manufacturer is apparently well liked and nutritious, but cans are reportedly going bad before the end of their stated shelf life. Tests are now being conducted with an improved product using a revised set of additives. Based on the accompanying results, and using a 0.05 level of significance, test the claim that the shelf life of their product is independent of the additives that are used.

	Below Standard	Acceptable	Above Standard
Current additives	34	25	5
Revised additives	7	44	10

2. In recent years, El Niño phenomena have been popularly blamed for a variety of weather effects. The accompanying table compares the number of springs with precipitation levels at least 2% above seasonal norms. Fourteen springs were sampled for each of three time periods related to El Niño cycles: (a) springs prior to a major El Niño cycle (either one or two years prior), (b) the springs within a major El Niño cycle (there are two springs per cycle), and (c) other springs, unrelated to an El Niño cycle. At the 0.05 level of significance, test the claim that the proportions of springs with above-normal precipitation are the same regardless of which part of the El Niño cycle is occurring.

	Prior Springs	El Niño Springs	Other Springs
Springs with above-normal precipitation	5	8	8
Springs without above-normal precipitation	9	6	6

Based on data from Environment Canada.

3. Based on seven years of data collected by Transport Canada, 72% of all bird strikes on moving aircraft involve gulls, sparrows, swallows, or snow buntings. The accompanying table is based on a random selection of bird strikes on planes, by other species than those just mentioned. Test the claim that the all the other bird species are involved in bird strikes with equal frequencies. Use the 0.05 level of significance. Would your results support a policy of focusing bird-strike prevention programs on particular species of birds? Why or why not?

Species	Hawks	Starlings	Ducks	Plovers	Owls	Sandpipers	Larks	Kestrels
Frequency	17	13	15	11	10	9	8	7

4. Refer to Data Set 18 in Appendix B, which shows the body temperatures for people who were sufficiently healthy to be accepted for voluntary surgery. Below, the temperature ranges of females and males in the sample are compared. Test the hypothesis that the patients' temperatures and genders are independent. Use the 0.05 level of significance.

	Female	Male
Below 37°C	43	51
At least 37°C	11	3

5. Clinical tests of the allergy drug Seldane yielded results summarized in the accompanying table. At the 0.05 significance level, test the claim that the occurrence of headaches is independent of the group (Seldane, placebo, control). Based on these results, should Seldane users be concerned about getting headaches?

	Seldane Users	Placebo Users	Control
Headache	49	49	24
No headache	732	616	602

Based on data from Merrell Dow Pharmaceuticals, Inc.

• •

Cumulative Review Exercises

TABLE 10-8

	A	B	C	D
x	66	80	82	75
y	77	89	94	84

1. Assume that Table 10-8 lists test scores for four people, where the x score is from a test of memory and the y score is from a test of reasoning. Test the claim that there is a relationship between the x and y scores.

2. Assume that Table 10-8 lists test scores for four people, where the x score is from a pretest taken before a training session on memory improvement and the y score is from a test taken after the training. Test the claim that the training session is effective in raising scores.

3. Assume that in Table 10-8, the letters A, B, C, D represent the choices on the first question of a multiple-choice quiz. Also assume that x represents men and y represents women, and the table entries are frequency counts, so that 66 men chose answer A, 77 women chose answer A, 80 men chose answer B, and so on. Test the claim that men and women choose the different answers in the same proportions.

4. Assume that in Table 10-8, the letters A, B, C, D represent different versions of the same test of reasoning. The x scores were obtained by four randomly selected men and the y scores were obtained by four randomly selected women. Test the claim that men and women have the same mean score.

Technology Project

Use Excel to randomly generate 100 digits between 0 and 9 inclusive, then use STATDISK to randomly generate another 100 digits between 0 and 9 inclusive. Record the results in the accompanying table, then test the claim that the digit selected is independent of whether you used Excel or STATDISK. Test the claim by using Excel or STATDISK, and obtain a printed copy of the display. Interpret the computer results and write your conclusions.

Digit	0	1	2	3	4	5	6	7	8	9
Frequency in Excel										
Frequency in STATDISK										

•••••••• FROM DATA TO DECISION ••••••••

In response to serious public allegations by a staff psychiatrist at a British Columbia hospital, British Columbia ordered an independent investigation ("B.C. Probes Big Increase in Shock Treatments," *The Globe and Mail*, Dec. 13, 2000). It was claimed that following a change in health policy, allowing doctors to be paid $62 for administering electroshock treatments to geriatric patients, the numbers of such treatments actually administered rose dramatically. The accompanying table shows the numbers of these treatments given during three consecutive time periods—one period *before* the policy of paying for treatments, and two subsequent periods.

Analyze the Results

Analyze the sample data and draw conclusions. Is there a significant difference in the numbers of

	Time Period		
	1996/1997	1997/1998	1998/1999
Number of electroshock treatments	689	1249	1533

electroshock treatments administered during the three time periods shown? If there does appear to be an upward change in the numbers of treatments, try to identify one factor *besides* the new payment policy that could be contributing to the higher numbers. Make a recommendation that might reduce any tendency for the payment system itself to be an incentive for ordering additional treatments.

⋯⋯⋯ COOPERATIVE GROUP ACTIVITIES ⋯⋯⋯

1. *Out-of-class activity:* Divide into groups of four or five students. Each group member should survey at least 15 male students and 15 female students at the same college by asking two questions: (1) Which political party does the subject favour most? (2) If the subject were to make up an absence excuse of a flat tire, which tire would he or she say went flat if the instructor asked? Ask the subject to write the two responses on an index card, and also record the gender of the subject and whether the subject wrote with the right or left hand. Use the methods of this chapter to analyse the data collected.

2. *Out-of-class activity:* In random sampling, each member of the population has the same chance of being selected. When the author asked 60 students to "randomly" select three digits each, the results listed below were obtained. Use this sample of 180 digits to test the claim that students select digits randomly.

Were the students successful in choosing their own random numbers? Select your own sample of students and ask each one to randomly select three digits. Test your results for randomness. Also test your results to determine whether they agree with those listed below. Write a report describing your experiment and clearly state your major conclusions.

3. *In-class activity:* Divide into groups of three or four students. Each group should be given a die along with the instruction that it should be tested for "fairness." Is the die fair or is it biased? Describe the analysis and results.

4. *In-class activity:* Divide into groups of six or more students. Each group member should provide the digits of his or her social insurance number. (The digits should be rearranged so that privacy is maintained.) Construct a combined list of those digits and test the claim that the digits 0, 1, 2, . . . , 9 occur with the same frequency.

213	169	812	125	749	137	202	344	496	348	714	765
831	491	169	312	263	192	584	968	377	403	372	123
493	894	016	682	390	123	325	734	316	357	945	208
115	776	143	628	479	316	229	781	628	356	195	199
223	114	264	308	105	357	333	421	107	311	458	007

INTERNET PROJECT

Contingency Tables

In all the examples in Section 10-3, data were sorted into categories formed by the rows and columns of a contingency table. We used contingency tables along with the associated chi-square test to form conclusions regarding qualitative population data. Characteristics such as gender, race, and geographic location become fair game for formal hypothesis testing procedures. Go to the Internet Project for this chapter, located at:

http://www.pearsoned.ca/triola

Click on Internet Project, then on Chapter 10. After collecting demographic data for a number of populations, you will apply the techniques of this chapter to form conclusions about the independence of interesting pairings of characteristics.

11

Analysis of Variance

11-1 Overview

Objectives are identified for this chapter, which introduces methods for testing the hypothesis that three or more populations have the same mean. In Chapter 8 we tested for equality between the means of two populations and used test statistics having normal or Student t distributions. The methods of this chapter, however, are very different. Because of the nature of the calculations required, this chapter will emphasize the use of computer software.

11-2 One-Way ANOVA

This section introduces the basic method of analysis of variance (ANOVA), which is used to test the claim that three or more populations have the same mean. One-way ANOVA involves different samples that are categorized according to a single characteristic.

11-3 Two-Way ANOVA

Section 11-2 deals with a single factor (or characteristic used to differentiate between populations), but this section considers two factors. Because the calculations are very difficult, the emphasis is on interpreting computer displays rather than performing manual calculations.

CHAPTER PROBLEM:

Are we spending more time on the Internet?

According to research published by the CBC, overall usage of the Internet has increased since 1997. The evidence that more people are using the "Net" than in the past, especially from home, is quite strong. But the evidence is less clear that, if a person has been using the Internet all along, they are now spending more time on it. Table 11-1 (which is based on summary distribution statistics in the CBC study) lists hours of Internet usage per week by samples of survey respondents in 1997, 1998, and 1999. The three samples have means of 4.56 hr., 5.56 hr., and 5.69 hr., respectively, so it appears that the mean time on the Internet per week is not the same for the three years. Figure 11-1 shows boxplots representing the three samples, and these also suggest that the samples come from populations with non-equal means. But, considering that each sample consists of only 19 values, are those differences statistically significant?

Chapter 8 included methods for testing equality between *two* population means. We now want to test for equality among *three* population means. Specifically, we want to test the claim that $\mu_{1997} = \mu_{1998} = \mu_{1999}$. This chapter introduces methods for testing such claims, and we will consider the data included in Table 11-1.

Table 11-1 Hours Per Week that Canadian Adults Spend on the Internet

Summer 1997	Summer 1998	Fall 1999
0	1.8	4.2
7.6	6.1	5.2
0.7	4.1	8.8
19.1	4.3	4.3
0.6	0.8	1.5
9.3	7.9	14.5
3.7	3.9	6.6
1.8	8.6	16.0
4.8	16.3	18.9
0	0	0
0.2	0.4	0.4
1.1	1.3	1.2
4.1	14.7	1.7
1.4	1.4	3.9
2.6	3.6	3.1
10.5	12.3	10.5
4.7	4.3	4.9
0	0	0.6
14.5	13.9	1.8
$n_1 = 19$	$n_2 = 19$	$n_3 = 19$
$\bar{x}_1 = 4.563$	$\bar{x}_2 = 5.563$	$\bar{x}_3 = 5.689$
$s_1 = 5.394$	$s_2 = 5.278$	$s_3 = 5.588$

Source: "Internet Users: Who Are They?" by B. Kiefl, presented at the Advertising Research Foundation, Oct. 17th, 2000, see www3.cbc.ca/research/Free/freet.html.

Figure 11-1 Comparison of Hours Spent on Internet per Week for Three Years

11-1 Overview

In Sections 8-2, 8-3, and 8-5 we developed procedures for testing the hypothesis that *two* population means are equal ($H_0: \mu_1 = \mu_2$). Section 11-2 introduces a procedure for testing the hypothesis that *three or more* population means are equal. (The methods used in this chapter can also be used to test for equality between two population means, but the methods used in Chapter 8 are more efficient.) A typical null hypothesis in Section 11-2 will be $H_0: \mu_1 = \mu_2 = \mu_3 = \mu_4$. The alternative hypothesis is H_1: At least one mean is different. The method we use is based on an analysis of sample variances.

DEFINITION

Analysis of variance (ANOVA) is a method of testing the equality of three or more population means by analysing sample variances.

ANOVA is used in applications such as the following:

- When three different groups of people (such as smokers, nonsmokers exposed to environmental tobacco smoke, and nonsmokers not so exposed) are measured for cotinine (a marker of nicotine), we can test to determine whether they have the same level.

- When the Canadian Nuclear Safety Commission is concerned with exposures of uranium miners to ionizing radiation, it can test to determine whether there are differences in mean annual exposures for various categories of mine workers.

Why bother with a new procedure when we can test for equality of two means by using the methods presented in Chapter 8, where we developed tests of $H_0: \mu_1 = \mu_2$? For example, if we want to use the sample data from Table 11-1 to test the claim (at the $\alpha = 0.05$ level) that the three populations have the same mean, why not simply pair them off and do two at a time by testing $H_0: \mu_1 = \mu_2$, then $H_0: \mu_2 = \mu_3$, and so on? This approach (doing two at a time) requires three different hypothesis tests, so the degree of confidence could be as low as 0.95^3 (or 0.857). In general, as we increase the number of individual tests of significance, we increase the likelihood of finding a difference by chance alone. The risk of a type I error—finding a difference when no such difference actually exists—is higher than is implied by the selected significance level for each test. The method of analysis of variance lets us avoid that particular pitfall (rejecting a true null hypothesis) by using one test for equality of several means.

F Distribution

The ANOVA methods use the F distribution, which was first introduced in Section 8-4. In Section 8-4 we noted that the F distribution has the following important properties (see Figure 11-2):

1. The *F* distribution is not symmetric; it is skewed to the right.

2. The values of *F* can be 0 or positive, but they cannot be negative.

3. There is a different *F* distribution for each pair of degrees of freedom for the numerator and denominator.

Critical values of *F* are given in Table A-5.

Analysis of variance (ANOVA) is based on a comparison of two different estimates of the variance common to the different populations. Those estimates (the *variance between samples* and the *variance within samples*) will be described in Section 11-2. The term *one-way* is used because the sample data are separated into groups according to one characteristic or factor. For example, the hours listed in Table 11-1 are separated into three different groups according to the one characteristic (or factor) of the year in which they were observed. Section 11-3 will introduce two-way analysis of variance, which allows us to compare populations separated into categories using two characteristics (or factors). For example, we might separate lengths of movies that are broadcast on television by using the following two criteria: (1) their star ratings (1 star, 2 stars, 3 stars, and 4 stars) and (2) the Canadian classification system for violence in programming (FAM, PA, 14+, and 18+).

Because the procedures used in this chapter require complicated calculations, we will emphasize the use of computer software, such as Excel and Statdisk.

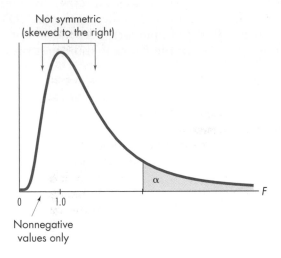

Figure 11-2   The *F* Distribution
There is a different *F* distribution for each different pair of degrees of freedom for numerator and denominator.

11-2 One-Way ANOVA

In this section we consider tests of hypotheses that three or more population means are all equal, for example, H_0: $\mu_1 = \mu_2 = \mu_3$. Because of the complexity of the calculations involved, we recommend the following approach to this section:

1. Develop a clear understanding of how to interpret a computer display that lists analysis of variance results.

2. Develop an understanding of the underlying rationale by studying the example in this section.
3. Become acquainted with the nature of the SS (sum of square) and MS (mean square) values and their role in determining the F test statistic, but depend on statistical software packages for finding those values.

The following assumptions apply when testing the hypothesis that three or more samples come from populations with the same mean.

Assumptions

1. The populations have distributions that are approximately normal.
2. The populations have the same variance σ^2 (or standard deviation σ).
3. The samples are random and independent of each other.
4. The different samples are from populations that are categorized in only one way.

The requirements of normality and equal variances are somewhat relaxed, as the methods in this section work reasonably well unless a population has a distribution that is very nonnormal or the population variances differ by large amounts. Statistician George E.P. Box showed that as long as the sample sizes are equal (or nearly equal), the variances can differ by amounts where the largest is up to nine times the smallest and the results of ANOVA will continue to be essentially reliable. (If the samples are independent but the distributions are very nonnormal, we can use the Kruskal-Wallis test presented in Section 13-5.)

The method we use is called **one-way analysis of variance** (or **single-factor analysis of variance**) because we use a single property, or characteristic, for categorizing the populations. This characteristic is sometimes referred to as a *treatment* or *factor*.

DEFINITION

A **treatment** (or **factor**) is a property, or characteristic, that allows us to distinguish the different populations from one another.

For example, the hours listed in Table 11-1 are sample data drawn from three different populations that are distinguished according to the treatment (or factor) of the year in which they were observed. The term *treatment* is used because early applications of analysis of variance involved agricultural experiments in which different plots of farmland were treated with different fertilizers, seed types, insecticides, and so on.

Interpreting Computer Results

Because the calculations required for analysis of variance are extremely involved, almost everyone uses computer software (except for one statistician living in a tent). We will first describe the interpretation of computer results, then we will consider the rationale underlying the method of analysis of variance.

Procedure for Testing H_0: $\mu_1 = \mu_2 = \mu_3 = \dots = \mu_k$

1. Use Excel, STATDISK, or other technology to obtain results.
2. Identify the P-value from the display.
3. Form a conclusion based on these criteria:
   - If P-value $\leq \alpha$, reject the null hypothesis of equal means.
   - If P-value $> \alpha$, fail to reject the null hypothesis of equal means.

EXAMPLE   Given the sample data in Table 11-1 and a significance level of $\alpha = 0.05$, use Excel or STATDISK to test the claim that the three samples come from populations with the same mean ($\mu_{1997} = \mu_{1998} = \mu_{1999}$).

SOLUTION   The Excel and STATDISK computer displays are shown on the next page. We will discuss specific computer procedures to generate these displays at the end of this section. A key element is the P-value, which is 0.78268. Because the P-value is not less than or equal to the significance level of $\alpha = 0.05$, we fail to reject the null hypothesis of equal means.

Interpretation   There is not sufficient evidence to warrant rejection of the claim that the three samples come from populations with the same mean. That is, the evidence in Table 11-1 is not sufficient to confirm that hours of Internet usage have been changing.

Rationale

The method of analysis of variance is based on this fundamental concept: With the assumption that the populations all have the same variance σ^2, we estimate the common value of σ^2 using two different approaches. The F test statistic is the ratio of those estimates, so that a significantly *large* F test statistic (located far to the right in the F distribution graph) is evidence against equal population means. The two approaches for estimating the common value of σ^2 are as follows:

1. The **variance between samples** (also called **variation due to treatment**) is an estimate of the common population variance σ^2 that is based on the variability among the sample *means*.
2. The **variance within samples** (also called **variation due to error**) is an estimate of the common population variance σ^2 based on the sample *variances*.

Excel Display   One-Way
ANOVA

STATDISK Display   One-Way
ANOVA

Test Statistic for One-Way ANOVA

$$F = \frac{\text{variance between samples}}{\text{variance within samples}}$$

The numerator of the test statistic measures variation between sample means. The estimate of variance in the denominator depends only on the sample variances and is not affected by differences among the sample means. Consequently, sample means that are close in value result in an F test statistic that is close to 1, and we conclude that there are no significant differences among the sample means. But if the value of F is excessively *large*, then we reject the claim of equal means. (The vague terms "close to 1" and "excessively large" are made objective by the use of a specific critical value, which clearly differentiates between an F test statistic that is in the critical region and one that is not.) Because excessively large values of F reflect unequal means, the test is right-tailed.

Calculations with Equal Sample Sizes

If the data sets all have the same sample size (as in Table 11-1), the required calculations aren't overwhelmingly difficult. First, find the variance between samples by evaluating $ns_{\bar{x}}^2$, where $s_{\bar{x}}^2$ is the variance of the sample means. That is, consider the sample means to be an ordinary set of values and calculate the variance. (From the central limit theorem, $\sigma_{\bar{x}} = \sigma/\sqrt{n}$ can be solved for σ to get $\sigma = \sqrt{n} \cdot \sigma_{\bar{x}}$, so that we can estimate σ^2 with $ns_{\bar{x}}^2$.) For example, the sample means in Table 11-1 are 4.563, 5.563, and 5.689. These three values have a standard deviation of $s_{\bar{x}} = 0.616948$, so that

$$\text{variance between samples} = ns_{\bar{x}}^2 = 19(0.616948)^2 = 7.2319$$

Compare the more precise value of 7.2344 in the Excel and STATDISK displays. Next, estimate the variance within samples by calculating s_{p}^2, which is the pooled variance obtained by finding the mean of the sample variances. The sample standard deviations in Table 11-1 are 5.394, 5.278, and 5.588, so that

$$\text{variance within samples} = s_{\text{p}}^2$$

$$= \frac{5.394^2 + 5.278^2 + 5.588^2}{3}$$

$$= 29.393 \text{ (or 29.391, using more precise values)}$$

Finally, evaluate the F test statistic as follows:

$$F = \frac{\text{variance between samples}}{\text{variance within samples}} = \frac{7.2319}{29.393} = 0.2460$$

Carrying more decimal places would result in the more accurate test statistic of $F = 0.2461$, as shown in the computer displays.

The critical value of F is found by assuming a right-tailed test, because large values of F correspond to significant differences among means. With k samples each having n scores, the numbers of degrees of freedom are computed as follows.

Poll Resistance

Surveys based on relatively small samples can be quite accurate, provided the sample is random or representative of the population. However, increasing survey refusal rates are now making it more difficult to obtain random samples. The head of one market research company said, "Everyone is fearful of self-selection and worried that generalizations you make are based on cooperators only." Results from the market research industry affect the products we buy, the television shows we watch, and many other facets of our lives.

Degrees of Freedom with k Samples of the Same Size n
numerator degrees of freedom $= k - 1$ denominator degrees of freedom $= k(n - 1)$

For the sample data in Table 11-1, $k = 3$ and $n = 19$, so the degrees of freedom are 2 for the numerator and $3(18) = 54$ for the denominator. With $\alpha = 0.05$, 2 degrees of freedom for the numerator, and 54 degrees of freedom for the denominator, the critical value is $F = 3.1504$. (Table A-5 does not include 54 degrees of freedom for the denominator, so we use the closest value, which corresponds to 60 degrees of freedom.) Note that statistical software packages such as Excel and STATDISK generally display the numbers of degrees of freedom along with the calculated F test statistic. Also, see Figure 11-3, which shows the test statistic and critical value. On the basis of these results, we fail to reject the null hypothesis of equal means. There is not sufficient evidence to warrant rejection of the claim that the three samples come from populations having the same mean.

Figure 11-3 *F* Distribution for Internet-Use Data

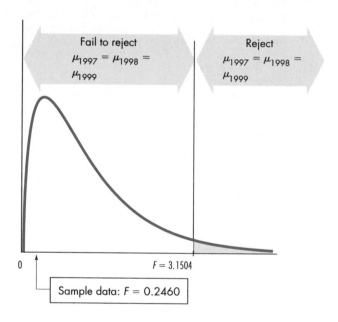

Calculations with Unequal Sample Sizes

While the calculations required for cases with equal sample sizes are reasonable, they become really complicated when the sample sizes are not all the same. The same basic reasoning applies because we calculate the F test statistic that is the ratio of two different estimates of the common population variance σ^2, but those estimates involve weighted measures that take the sample sizes into account, as shown below:

$$F = \frac{\text{variance between samples}}{\text{variance within samples}} = \frac{\left[\dfrac{\Sigma n_i(\overline{x}_i - \overline{\overline{x}})^2}{k - 1}\right]}{\left[\dfrac{\Sigma(n_i - 1)s_i^2}{\Sigma(n_i - 1)}\right]}$$

where $\overline{\overline{x}}$ = mean of all sample scores combined

k = number of population means being compared

n_i = number of values in the ith sample

N = total number of values in all samples combined

$\overline{x}_i$ = mean of values in the ith sample

s_i^2 = variance of values in the ith sample

Note that the numerator in this test statistic is really a form of the formula

$$s^2 = \frac{\Sigma(x - \overline{x})^2}{n - 1}$$

for variance that was given in Chapter 2. The factor of n_i is included so that larger samples carry more weight. The denominator of the test statistic is simply the mean of the sample variances, but it is a weighted mean with the weights based on the sample sizes.

Because calculating this test statistic can lead to large rounding errors, the various software packages typically use a different (but equivalent) expression that involves SS (for sum of squares) and MS (for mean square) notation. Although the following notation and components are complicated and involved, the basic idea is the same: The test statistic F is a ratio with a numerator reflecting variation *between* the means of the samples and a denominator reflecting variation *within* the samples. If the populations have equal means, the F ratio tends to be close to 1, but if the population means are not equal, the F ratio tends to be significantly larger than 1. Key components in our ANOVA method are identified in the following boxes.

SS(total), or total sum of squares, is a measure of the total variation (around $\overline{\overline{x}}$) in all of the sample data combined.

Formula 11-1 $SS(\text{total}) = \Sigma(x - \overline{\overline{x}})^2$

SS(total) can be broken down into the components of SS(treatment) and SS(error), described as follows.

SS(treatment) is a measure of the variation between the sample means. [In one-way ANOVA, SS(treatment) is sometimes referred to as SS(factor). Because it is a measure of variability *between* the sample means, it is also referred to as SS(between groups) or SS(between samples).]

Formula 11-2

$$SS(\text{treatment}) = n_1(\overline{x}_1 - \overline{\overline{x}})^2 + n_2(\overline{x}_2 - \overline{\overline{x}})^2 + \cdots + n_k(\overline{x}_k - \overline{\overline{x}})^2$$
$$= \Sigma n_i(\overline{x}_i - \overline{\overline{x}})^2$$

If the population means ($\mu_1, \mu_2, \ldots, \mu_k$) are equal, then the sample means $\bar{x}_1, \bar{x}_2, \ldots, \bar{x}_k$ will all tend to be close together and also close to $\bar{x}$. The result will be a relatively small value of SS(treatment). If the population means are not all equal, however, then at least one of $\bar{x}_1, \bar{x}_2, \ldots, \bar{x}_k$ will tend to be far apart from the others and also far apart from $\bar{\bar{x}}$. The result will be a relatively large value of SS(treatment).

SS(error) is a sum of squares representing the variability that is assumed to be common to all the populations being considered.

Formula 11-3

$$SS(error) = (n_1 - 1)s_1^2 + (n_2 - 1)s_2^2 + \cdots + (n_k - 1)s_k^2$$
$$= \Sigma(n_i - 1)s_i^2$$

Because SS(error) is a measure of the variance within groups, it is sometimes denoted as SS(within groups) or SS(within samples). Given the preceding expressions for SS(total), SS(treatment), and SS(error), the following relationship will always hold:

Formula 11-4   SS(total) = SS(treatment) + SS(error)

SS(treatment) and SS(error) are both sums of squares, and if we divide each by its corresponding number of degrees of freedom, we get *mean squares*, defined as follows (N = the total number of values in all samples combined).

MS(treatment) is a mean square for treatment.

Formula 11-5 $MS(treatment) = \dfrac{SS(treatment)}{k - 1}$

MS(error) is a mean square for error.

Formula 11-6 $MS(error) = \dfrac{SS(error)}{N - k}$

MS(total) is a mean square for the total variation.

Formula 11-7 $MS(total) = \dfrac{SS(total)}{N - 1}$

The SS and MS values are used for determining the F test statistic that applies when the samples do not all have the same size.

Test Statistic for ANOVA with Unequal Sample Sizes

In testing the null hypothesis H_0: $\mu_1 = \mu_2 = \cdots = \mu_k$ against the alternative hypothesis that these means are not all equal, the test statistic

Formula 11-8
$$F = \frac{MS(\text{treatment})}{MS(\text{error})}$$

has an F distribution (when the null hypothesis H_0 is true) with degrees of freedom given by

numerator degrees of freedom $= k - 1$
denominator degrees of freedom $= N - k$

This test statistic is essentially the same as the one given earlier, and its interpretation is also the same as described earlier. The denominator depends only on the sample variances that measure variation within the treatments and is not affected by the differences among the sample means. In contrast, the numerator does depend on differences among the sample means. If the differences among the sample means are extreme, they will cause the numerator to be excessively large, so F will also be excessively large. Consequently, very large values of F suggest unequal means, and the ANOVA test is therefore right-tailed.

Tables are a convenient format for summarizing key results in ANOVA calculations, and Table 11-2 has a format often used in computer displays. (See the preceding Excel display on page 566.) The entries in Table 11-2 result from the data in Table 11-1.

TABLE 11-2	ANOVA Table for Internet-Usage Data			
Source of Variation	Sum of Squares (SS)	Degrees of Freedom	Mean Square (MS)	F Test Statistic
Treatments	14.46877	2	7.234386	0.246141
Error	1587.126	54	29.39123	
Total	1601.595	56		

If we use ANOVA methods and conclude that there is sufficient evidence to reject (or fail to reject) the claim of equal population means, we cannot conclude that any particular mean is different from the others. There are several other tests that can be used to make such identifications, and those procedures are called **multiple comparison procedures.** Comparison of confidence intervals, the Scheffé test, the extended Tukey test, and the Bonferroni test are four common multiple comparison procedures that are usually included in more advanced texts.

As efficient and reliable as computer programs may be, they are worthless if you don't understand the relevant concepts. The methods in this section are used to test the claim that several samples come from populations with the same mean. These methods require normally distributed populations with the same variance, and the samples must be independent. We reject or fail to reject the null hypothesis of equal means by analysing these two estimates of variance: the variance between samples and the variance within samples. MS(treatment) is an estimate of the variation between samples, and MS(error) is an estimate of the variation within samples. If MS(treatment) is significantly greater than MS(error), we reject the claim of equal means; otherwise, we fail to reject that claim.

Even if we reject the hypothesis of equal means, we cannot be absolutely sure that the given factor is responsible for the differences. We must identify other relevant factors that could be causing the effect. In general, good results require that the experiments which generate the data be carefully designed and executed.

Using Technology

Earlier in this section we illustrated sample computer displays, and then discussed how to interpret them. Here we describe how to generate those displays.

Excel: Organize the raw data into an Excel range, with the data for each population in neighbouring columns (or rows). Select **Data Analysis** from the **Tools** menu. Choose **Anova: Single Factor**. Enter these details: For **Input Range**, specify the range that contains the data; input the desired **alpha**; and specify whether the input range is organized into columns or rows. Then select an **Output Option**, and click on **OK** to obtain the results.

STATDISK: Select **Analysis** from the main menu bar, then select **One-Way Analysis of Variance**, and proceed to enter (or "paste" in) the sample data. Click **Evaluate** when done.

11-2 Exercises A: Basic Skills and Concepts

1. Analysis of variance results generated by Excel are given below. The sample results are measured consumer reactions to television commercials for different products. Assume that we want to use a 0.05 significance level in testing the null hypothesis that the different products have commercials with the same mean reaction score.
   a. How many different samples are included in this study?
   b. Identify the value of the test statistic.
   c. Find the critical value from Table A-5.
   d. Identify the P-value.
   e. Based on the preceding results, what do you conclude about the equality of the population means?

Source of Variation	SS	df	MS	F	P-value
Between groups	50.00	5	10.00	3.33	0.032
Within groups	72.00	24	3.00		
Total	122.00	29			

2. Repeat Exercise 1 assuming that the Excel results are as shown below:

Source of Variation	SS	df	MS	F	P-value
Between groups	20.68	2	10.34	6.68	0.011
Within groups	18.59	12	1.55		
Total	39.27	14			

3. The following table is based on data in Data Sets 2 and 18 in Appendix B. Samples of human body temperatures in three contexts are compared. (Assume for this exercise that all three samples are independent.)
   a. Find the variance *between* samples by evaluating $ns_{\bar{x}}^2$. (Recall that $s_{\bar{x}}^2$ is the variance of the three sample means.)
   b. Find the variance *within* samples by evaluating the pooled variance s_p^2, which is the mean of the sample variances.
   c. Use the results from parts (a) and (b) to find the F test statistic.
   d. Find the F critical value. (Recall that with equal sample sizes, the degrees of freedom are $k - 1$ for the numerator and $k(n - 1)$ for the denominator.)
   e. Based on the preceding results, what do you conclude about the claim that the three populations have the same mean body temperature?

Three Samples of Body Temperatures (in degrees Celsius)

Awaiting Surgery	Sitting in Lab	Standing in Lab
36.0	37.61	37.63
35.0	37.07	37.17
36.0	37.20	36.93
36.0	37.23	37.35
36.7	37.38	37.73
36.5	37.28	37.39
36.3	37.12	37.57
35.5	37.55	37.89
36.1	37.04	37.50
36.7	37.78	37.98
37.1	37.59	37.36
$n_1 = 11$	$n_2 = 11$	$n_3 = 11$
$\bar{x}_1 = 36.17$	$\bar{x}_2 = 37.35$	$\bar{x}_3 = 37.50$
$s_1 = 0.588$	$s_2 = 0.249$	$s_3 = 0.307$

4. A large company is deciding between transportation methods for shipping its finished goods. Since the possibility of labour stoppages is a concern, a manager studied Data Set 20 in Appendix B, for annual person-days lost through work stoppages in different modes of transportation. For each of the transportation modes shown in the table below, she independently selected a random sample of 14 years' data. (The table shows annual person-days lost, in thousands.) At the 0.05 level of significance, test the claim that the four populations of annual person-days lost have the same mean. Based on the results, does it appear that the four modes are equally reliable, in terms of possible loss-of-service due to labour stoppage? Does any single category seem to be particularly reliable in this regard? Do we have enough information, from these results, to decide on the best mode of transportation to use? Explain.

Air	Rail	Water	Truck
$n_1 = 14$	$n_2 = 14$	$n_3 = 14$	$n_4 = 14$
$\bar{x}_1 = 60.805$	$\bar{x}_2 = 58.036$	$\bar{x}_3 = 12.631$	$\bar{x}_4 = 19.896$
$s_1 = 63.303$	$s_1 = 71.558$	$s_3 = 13.627$	$s_4 = 33.131$

For Exercises 5–7, use the data shown in the margin (based on the Financial Post *list of top 500 companies for 1998). Revenues, assets, and numbers of employees are compared for samples of companies from three industry groups: wholesale distributors (1), food production and sales industries (2), and conglomerates (3). Revenues and assets are in millions of dollars.*

5. At the 0.05 significance level, test the claim that the means of the revenues are the same in all three industry groups. Does any industry group seem to have higher revenues? If so, is this apparent difference significant?

6. At the 0.05 significance level, test the claim that the means of the assets are the same in all three industry groups. Does any industry group seem to have greater assets?

7. At the 0.05 significance level, test the claim that the means of the numbers of employees are the same in all three industry groups. Does any industry group seem to have greater numbers of employees?

8. A disgruntled University of Toronto employee reads the list (published in *The Globe and Mail*), of U of T staff who earn over $100,000 annually. The employee claims that for staff in this category, mean salaries are different based on the starting letters of their last names. A random sample from the full list follows. (Salaries are in thousands of dollars.) At the 0.05 level of significance, test the claim that the means are not equal for the three groups shown.

	Revenues	Assets	Employees
1	2,639	326	462
1	2,411	934	2,352
1	1,667	762	2,098
1	1,574	726	10,000
1	478	301	2,800
1	405	159	721
1	327	141	300
1	322	30	29
1	188	86	400
2	6,813	1,506	16,050
2	4,720	1,157	31,000
2	3,432	726	6,500
2	2,458	616	19,700
2	1,442	824	4,428
2	813	278	4,200
2	676	327	3,200
2	461	232	3,400
2	278	144	1,492
3	11,212	5,846	43,000
3	10,008	50,258	27,000
3	4,000	2,200	18,000
3	2,043	872	1,335
3	1,036	724	3,784
3	913	600	5,820
3	504	243	600
3	410	587	4,700
3	349	1,331	670

Names		
A to I	J to R	S to Z
113.7	108.0	114.7
106.4	109.2	111.0
120.3	100.9	121.5
104.7	105.4	156.1
143.8	103.0	107.7
118.3	102.5	112.1
166.7	102.7	108.1
116.7		102.0
		111.1
		158.1
		111.3

9. Flammability tests were conducted on children's sleepwear. The Vertical Semirestrained Test was used, in which pieces of fabric were burned under controlled conditions. After the burning stopped, the length of the charred portion was measured and recorded. Results are given in the margin for the same fabric tested at different laboratories. Because the same fabric was used, the different laboratories should have obtained the same results. Did they? Use a 0.05 significance level to test the claim that the different laboratories have the same population mean.

10. The values in the list below are measured maximum breadths of male Egyptian skulls from different epochs (in mm, based on data from *Ancient Races of the Thebaid,* by Thomson and Randall-Maciver). Changes in head shape over time suggest that interbreeding occurred with immigrant populations. Use a 0.05 significance level to test the claim that the mean is the same for the different epochs.

Laboratory				
1	2	3	4	5
2.9	2.7	3.3	3.3	4.1
3.1	3.4	3.3	3.2	4.1
3.1	3.6	3.5	3.4	3.7
3.7	3.2	3.5	2.7	4.2
3.1	4.0	2.8	2.7	3.1
4.2	4.1	2.8	3.3	3.5
3.7	3.8	3.2	2.9	2.8
3.9	3.8	2.8	3.2	
3.1	4.3	3.8	2.9	
3.0	3.4	3.5		
2.9	3.3			

4000 B.C.	1850 B.C.	150 A.D.
131	129	128
138	134	138
125	136	136
129	137	139
132	137	141
135	129	142
132	136	137
134	138	145
138	134	137

11. A political scientist claims that since Confederation, the number of times the House of Commons sits in each session of Parliament has been increasing. The table shows, in three samples grouped by Parliament number, how many times the House of Commons has sat in each Parliament. Parliaments lasting fewer than 1.5 years were not sampled. At the 0.05 level of significance, test the claim that all three groups have the same mean number of sittings.

Parliament		
1 to 12	13 to 24	25 to 35
460	507	447
283	355	418
568	605	687
303	292	405
254	366	707
262	565	767
458	390	590

Based on data from *Duration of Sessions of Parliament*, Library of Parliament.

12. The political scientist from Exercise 11 also claims that for Parliaments of 4, 4.5, and 5 years in length, the mean number of times the Senate has sat is equal. The table shows, in three samples grouped by length in years, the number of times that the Senate has sat in each Parliament. At the 0.05 level of significance, test the claim that all three groups have the same mean number of Senate sittings.

Length of Parliament in Years		
4	4.5	5
201	478	241
158	339	283
383	352	366
217		357
257		255
261		363

Based on data from *Duration of Sessions of Parliament*, Library of Parliament.

13. Refer to Data Set 21 in Appendix B. At the 0.05 significance level, test the claim that the mean weight (in carats) of diamonds is the same for each of the four clarity levels (2, 3, 4, or 5) shown. If you need to save money by compromising on clarity, does this necessarily limit the carat of the diamond that you choose?

14. Refer to Data Set 9 in Appendix B. Use a 0.01 significance level to test the claim that the mean cotinine level is different for these three groups: non-smokers not exposed to environmental tobacco smoke, nonsmokers who are exposed to tobacco smoke, and people who smoke. What do the results suggest about second-hand smoke?

11-2 Exercises B: Beyond the Basics

15. Repeat Exercise 3 after adding 1° to each temperature listed in the "Awaiting Surgery" group. Compare these results to those found in Exercise 3.

16. If Exercise 3 is repeated after changing the temperature readings from the Celsius scale to the Fahrenheit scale, are the results affected? In general, how is the analysis of variance F test statistic affected by the scale used?

17. How are analysis of variance results affected in each of the following cases?
    a. The same constant is added to every sample score.
    b. Every sample score is multiplied by the same constant.
    c. The order of the samples is changed.

18. Five independent samples of 50 scores each are randomly drawn from populations that are normally distributed with equal variances. We wish to test the claim that $\mu_1 = \mu_2 = \mu_3 = \mu_4 = \mu_5$.
    a. If we used only the methods given in Chapter 8, we would test the individual claims $\mu_1 = \mu_2, \mu_1 = \mu_3, \ldots, \mu_4 = \mu_5$. How many ways could we pair off 5 means?
    b. Assume that for each test of equality between two means, there is a 0.95 probability of not making a type I error. If all possible pairs of means are tested for equality, what is the probability of making no type I errors? (Although the tests are not actually independent, assume that they are.)
    c. If we use analysis of variance to test the claim that $\mu_1 = \mu_2 = \mu_3 = \mu_4 = \mu_5$ at the 0.05 level of significance, what is the probability of not making a type I error?
    d. Compare the results of parts (b) and (c). Which approach is better in the sense of giving us a greater chance of not making a type I error?

19. In this exercise you will verify that when you have two sets of sample data, the t test for independent samples (assuming equal variances) and the ANOVA method of this section are equivalent. Refer to the data used in Exercises 5–7, but exclude the data on conglomerates.
    a. Use a 0.05 level and the method of Section 8-5 to test the claim that wholesale distributors and companies in the food industry have the same revenues.

b. Use a 0.05 level and the ANOVA method of this section to test the claim made in part (a).

c. Verify that the squares of the t test statistic and critical value from part (a) are equal to the F test statistic and critical value from part (b).

20. Complete the following ANOVA table if it is known that there are three samples with sizes of 5, 7, and 7, respectively.

Source of Variation	Sum of Squares (SS)	Degrees of Freedom	Mean Square (MS)	Test Statistic
Treatments	?	?	?	
Error	100.00	?	?	$F = ?$
Total	123.45	?		

11-3 Two-Way ANOVA

Section 11-2 illustrated the use of analysis of variance to decide whether three or more populations have the same mean. We called those procedures *one-way* analysis of variance (or single-factor analysis of variance) because the data are categorized into groups according to a *single* factor (or treatment). A factor, or treatment, is a property used as the basis for categorizing the different groups of data. For example, in Table 11-3 the lengths of 30 movies are partitioned into three categories according to the single factor of star rating—a fair movie is rated with 2.0 or 2.5 stars, a good movie is rated with 3.0 or 3.5 stars, and an excellent movie is rated with 4.0 stars. Because the three samples in Table 11-3 are categorized according to a single factor (star rating), we can use the methods from Section 11-2 to test the claim that $\mu_1 = \mu_2 = \mu_3$. Following is the Excel display for the data in Table 11-3.

TABLE 11-3	Lengths (in min) of Movies Categorized by Star Ratings									
2.0–2.5 Stars (Fair)	98	100	123	92	99	110	114	96	101	155
3.0–3.5 Stars (Good)	93	94	94	105	111	115	133	106	93	129
4.0 Stars (Excellent)	103	193	168	88	121	72	120	106	104	159

From the Excel display on page 579 we can see that the test statistic is

$$F = \frac{MS(\text{treatment})}{MS(\text{error})} = \frac{791}{676} = 1.17$$

The P-value of 0.325 indicates that at the 0.05 significance level, we fail to reject the claim of equal means. Based on our sample data, it appears that the three categories of fair, good, and excellent movies have the same mean length.

	A	B	C	D	E	F	G	H
1	Anova: Single Factor							
2								
3	SUMMARY							
4	*Groups*	*Count*	*Sum*	*Average*	*Variance*			
5	2.0-2.5 Stars	10	1088	108.8	351.2889			
6	3.0-3.5 Stars	10	1073	107.3	219.3444			
7	4.0 Stars	10	1234	123.4	1456.489			
8								
9								
10	ANOVA							
11	*Source of Variation*	*SS*	*df*	*MS*	*F*	*P-value*	*F crit*	
12	Between Groups	1582.067	2	791.0333	1.170674	0.325409	3.354131	
13	Within Groups	18244.1	27	675.7074				
14								
15	Total	19826.17	29					

If we were investigating lengths of movies, a more complex analysis might include additional factors such as the budget for the movie, the actors and actresses who are featured, the director, and the musical score. **Two-way analysis of variance** involves two factors, such as the Table 11-4 factors of (1) the star rating, by which we categorize a movie as fair, good, or excellent, and (2) the CRTC-endorsed rating system for programs and films shown on TV, which includes the classifications FAM, PA, 14+, and 18+. Using the two factors of star rating and a grouping of CTR categories into "18+" versus "FAM/PA/14+," we partition the data into six categories, as shown in Table 11-4. Such subcategories are often called *cells,* so Table 11-4 consists of six cells containing five scores each. Tables 11-3 and 11-4 include the same numbers, but Table 11-3 classifies the data with the single factor of star rating, whereas Table 11-4 classifies the data with the two factors of star rating and CTR rating.

The following assumptions apply when testing with two-way analysis of variance.

Assumptions

1. For each cell, the sample values come from a population with a distribution that is approximately normal.
2. The populations have the same variance σ^2 (or standard deviation σ).
3. The samples are random and independent of each other.
4. The sample values are categorized in two ways.
5. All of the cells have the same number of sample values. (This is called a *balanced* design.)

In analyzing the sample data in Table 11-4, we have already discussed the one-way analysis of variance for the single factor of star rating, so it might seem reasonable to simply proceed with another one-way ANOVA for the factor of CTR rating. Unfortunately, that approach wastes information and totally ignores any effect from an interaction between the two factors.

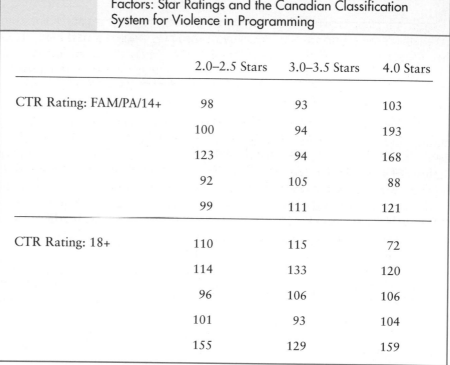

DEFINITION

There is an **interaction** between two factors if the effect of one of the factors changes for different categories of the other factor.

TABLE 11-4	Lengths (in min) of Movies on Television Categorized by Two Factors: Star Ratings and the Canadian Classification System for Violence in Programming

	2.0–2.5 Stars	3.0–3.5 Stars	4.0 Stars
CTR Rating: FAM/PA/14+	98	93	103
	100	94	193
	123	94	168
	92	105	88
	99	111	121
CTR Rating: 18+	110	115	72
	114	133	120
	96	106	106
	101	93	104
	155	129	159

Statistics and Baseball Strategy

Statisticians are using computers to develop very sophisticated measures of baseball performance and strategy. They have found, for example, that sacrifice bunts, sacrifice fly balls, and stolen bases rarely help win games and that it is seldom wise to have a pitcher intentionally walk the batter. They can identify the ballparks that favour pitchers and those that favour batters. Instead of simply comparing the batting averages of two different players, they can develop better measures of offensive strength by taking into account such factors as pitchers faced, position in the line-up, ballparks played, and weather conditions.

In using ANOVA for the data of Table 11-4, we will consider the effect of an *interaction* between star ratings and CTR ratings, as well as the effects of star ratings and the effects of CTR ratings on movie length. The calculations are quite involved, so *we will assume that a software package is being used.* The Excel display on page 581 shows results from the data in Table 11-4. (Excel can do two-way Anova, but STATDISK cannot. The Excel procedures are described at the end of this section.)

The Excel display includes SS (sum of square) components similar to those described in Section 11-2. Because the circumstances of Section 11-2 involved only a single factor, we used SS(treatment) as a measure of the variation due to the different treatment categories and we used SS(error) as a measure of the variation due to sampling error. We can now use SS(Stars) as a measure of variation among the star-rating means; this is SS for "Columns" in the Excel display. We use SS(CTR) as a measure of the variation among the CTR means; Excel labels this SS for the "Sample." Excel's SS for "Within" refers to variation within groups, and corresponds to what we call SS(error), a measure of variation due to sampling error. Similar to one-way ANOVA, the mean square values MS(Stars), MS(CTR), and MS(error) are obtained by dividing the corresponding SS values by their associated degrees of freedom (df).

	A	B	C	D	E	F	G	H
1	ANOVA							
2	*Source of Variation*	SS	df	MS	F	P-value	F crit	
3	Sample (*CTR*)	32.0333333	1	32.0333333	0.0481825	0.828113	4.259675	
4	Columns (*Stars*)	1582.06667	2	791.033333	1.18982201	0.321594	3.402832	
5	Interaction	2256.06667	2	1128.03333	1.69671597	0.20454	3.402832	
6	Within (*error*)	15956	24	664.833333				
7								
8	Total	19826.1667	29					

Excel Display Two-Way ANOVA (The labels in parentheses were added after Excel generated the table.)

Table 11-5 compares the analyses of the data in Tables 11-3 and 11-4. Some data appear the same in both cases. But note that as we go from the one-factor case (Table 11-3) to the two-factor case (Table 11-4), we partition the data according to the second factor of CTR rating, so that the value of SS(error) is partitioned into SS(CTR), SS(interaction), and SS(error). (You can see that $18,244 = 32 + 2256 + 15,956$.) Also, df(error) is partitioned into df(CTR), df(interaction), and df(error), which can be easily verified by noting that $27 = 1 + 2 + 24$. Similar partitioning does not apply to MS(error), where the value of MS(error) = 676 does not equal $32 + 1128 + 665$.

In executing a two-way analysis of variance, we consider three effects:

1. The effect due to the *interaction* between the two factors of star rating and CTR rating
2. The effect due to the *row* factor, which Excel calls the sample (CTR rating)
3. The effect due to the *column* factor (star rating)

TABLE 11-5 Comparison of Components Used in One-Way ANOVA and Two-Way ANOVA (rounded values)

One-Way ANOVA	Two-Way ANOVA
Sample data: Table 11-3	Sample data: Table 11-4
One factor: Star rating	Two factors: Star rating and CTR rating
SS(Stars) = 1582	Same
MS(Stars) = 791	Same
df(Stars) = 2	Same
SS(total) = 19,826	Same
df(total) = 29	Same
	SS(CTR) = 32
SS(error) = 18,244	SS(interaction) = 2256
	SS(error) = 15,956
	df(CTR) = 1
df(error) = 27	df(interaction) = 2
	df(error) = 24
	MS(CTR) = 32
MS(error) = 676	MS(interaction) = 1128
	MS(error) = 665

We now summarize the basic procedure for two-way analysis of variance. It is actually quite similar to the procedures presented in Section 11-2. We form conclusions about equal means by analysing two estimates of variance, and the test statistic F is the ratio of those two estimates. A significantly large value for F indicates that there is a statistically significant difference in means. The following procedure for two-way ANOVA is summarized in Figure 11-4. If you have generated an Excel output for this procedure, then the information you need is already on your screen.

Procedure for Two-Way ANOVA

Step 1:   *Interaction effect*
In two-way analysis of variance, begin by testing the null hypothesis that there is no interaction between the two factors. Using Excel for the data in Table 11-4, we get the following test statistic:

$$F = \frac{MS(\text{interaction})}{MS(\text{error})} = \frac{1128.0333}{664.8333} = 1.6967$$

Interpretation The displayed P-value for the interaction (0.2045) exceeds the desired alpha of 0.05. There is not sufficient evidence to conclude that movie length is affected by an interaction between star rating and CTR rating.

If we do reject the null hypothesis of no interaction between factors, then we should stop now; we should not proceed with the two additional tests. (If there is an interaction between factors, we shouldn't consider the effects of either factor without considering those of the other.)

Step 2:   *Row/column effects*
If we fail to reject the null hypothesis of no interaction between factors, then we should proceed to test the following two hypotheses:

H_0: There are no effects from the row factor (that is, the row means are equal).
H_0: There are no effects from the column factor (that is, the column means are equal).

In other words, if there is no apparent interaction between factors, there may still be an effect based on one or both of the factors, individually.

In Step 1, we did fail to reject the null hypothesis of no interaction between factors, so we proceed with the next two hypothesis tests.

For the row factor (CTR),

$$F = \frac{MS(\text{CTR})}{MS(\text{error})} = \frac{32.0333}{664.8333} = 0.0482$$

Figure 11-4 Procedure for Two-Way ANOVA

Interpretation Because the corresponding P-value for the CTR factor (0.8281) exceeds the significance level, we fail to reject the null hypothesis of no effects from CTR. The CTR rating does not appear to have an effect on movie length.

For the column factor (Stars),

$$F = \frac{\text{MS(Stars)}}{\text{MS(error)}} = \frac{791.0333}{664.8333} = 1.1898$$

Interpretation This value is not significant because the P-value for the stars factor (0.3216) exceeds the specified significance level. Thus, we fail to reject the null hypothesis of no effects from the star rating. The star rating of a movie does not appear to have an effect on the movie's length.

Special Case: One Observation per Cell and No Interaction

Table 11-4 contains five observations per cell. If our sample data consist of only one observation per cell, we lose MS(interaction), SS(interaction), and df(interaction) because those values are based on sample variances computed for each individual cell. If there is only one observation per cell, there is no variation within individual cells and those sample variances cannot be calculated. Here's how we proceed when there is one observation per cell: *If it seems reasonable to assume (based on knowledge about the circumstances) that there is no interaction between the two factors, make that assumption and then proceed as before to test the following two hypotheses separately:*

H_0: There are no effects from the row factor.

H_0: There are no effects from the column factor.

As an example, suppose that we have only the first score in each cell of Table 11-4. Note that the two row means are 98.0 and 99.0. Is that difference significant, suggesting that there is an effect due to CTR rating? The column means are 104.0, 104.0, and 87.5. Are those differences significant, suggesting that there is an effect due to star rating? If we believe the number of stars a movie receives seems to be totally unrelated to whether it is rated FAM, PA, 14+, or 18+, we can then assume that there is no interaction between star rating and CTR rating. (If we believe there is an interaction, the method described here does not apply.) To illustrate the method, we will make the assumption of no interaction. Following is the Excel display for the data in Table 11-4, with only the first score from each cell.

Excel Display Two-Way ANOVA Without Replication

Anova: Two-Factor Without Replication

SUMMARY	Count	Sum	Average	Variance
FAM/ PA/ 14+	3	294	98	25
18+	3	297	99	553
2.0-2.5 Stars	2	208	104	72
3.0-3.5 Stars	2	208	104	242
4.0 Stars	2	175	87.5	480.5

ANOVA

Source of Variation	SS	df	MS	F	P-value	F crit
Rows	1.5	1	1.5	0.003783	0.956549	18.51276
Columns	363	2	181.5	0.457755	0.685986	19.00003
Error	793	2	396.5			
Total	1157.5	5				

For testing the effect of the row factor (CTR), observe that Excel automatically displays the test statistic $F = 0.0038$, calculated as follows:

$$F = \frac{MS(CTR)}{MS(error)} = \frac{1.5}{396.5} = 0.0038$$

Because the displayed *P*-value for the CTR factor (0.9565) exceeds the significance level, we fail to reject the null hypothesis of no effect from the row factor (CTR rating). It seems that the CTR rating does not affect movie length.

For the column factors (Stars), the test statistic is

$$F = \frac{MS(Stars)}{MS(error)} = \frac{181.5}{396.5} = 0.4578$$

This value is not significant because the displayed *P*-value for the stars factor (0.6860) exceeds the significance level. We therefore fail to reject the null hypothesis of no effects from the star rating. The star rating of a movie does not appear to affect its length. Again, these conclusions are based on very limited data and might not be valid when more sample data are acquired.

Randomized Block Design

When we use the one-way (or single factor) analysis of variance technique and conclude that the differences among the means are significant, we cannot necessarily conclude that the given factor is responsible for the differences. It is possible that the variation of some other unknown factor is responsible for the differences. One way to reduce the effect of the extraneous factors is to design the experiment so that it has a **completely randomized design**, in which each element is given the same chance of belonging to the different categories or treatments. Another way to reduce the effect of extraneous factors is to use a **rigorously controlled design**, in which elements are carefully chosen so that all other factors have no variability. That is, select elements that are the same in every characteristic except for the single factor being considered.

Yet another way to control for extraneous variation is to use a **randomized block design**, in which a measurement is obtained for each treatment on each of several individuals that are matched according to similar characteristics. A **block** is a group of similar individuals. See the following example, where we use four different cars to test the mileage produced by three different grades (regular, extra, premium) of a gasoline. Using a randomized block design as a way to control differences among cars, we burn each grade of gas in each of the four cars, randomly selecting the order in which this is done. We have three treatments corresponding to the three grades of gas; we have four blocks corresponding to the four cars used.

EXAMPLE   When we burn each of three different grades of gas in each of four different cars, we obtain the results shown in Table 11-6. Use two-way analysis of variance to test the claim that the grade of gasoline does not affect mileage, and test the claim that the different cars do not affect mileage.

SOLUTION   The method we use is the same as the method used for the special case of one observation per cell, but we need not use special knowledge of the circumstances to assume that there is no interaction. We can assume that there is no interaction because of the way we designed the experiment. A portion of the Excel display for the data in Table 11-6 is shown below.

TABLE 11-6   Mileage (mi/gal) for Different Grades of Gasoline

		Block			
		Car 1	Car 2	Car 3	Car 4
Treatment	Regular gas	19	33	23	27
	Extra gas	19	34	26	29
	Premium gas	22	39	26	34

Excel Display   ANOVA for Randomized Block Design. (The labels in parentheses were added after Excel generated the table.)

	A	B	C	D	E	F	G	H
12	ANOVA							
13	Source of Variation	SS	df	MS	F	P-value	F crit	
14	Rows (Gas)	47.16667	2	23.58333	12.30435	0.007532	5.143249	
15	Columns (Cars)	390.25	3	130.0833	67.86957	5.08E-05	4.757055	
16	Error	11.5	6	1.916667				
17								
18	Total	448.9167	11					

Considering the treatment (row) effects, we calculate the test statistic

$$F = \frac{MS(Gas)}{MS(error)} = \frac{23.5833}{1.9167} = 12.3044$$

Because the displayed P-value for the gas factor is less than the significance level, we reject the null hypothesis. The grade of gas does seem to have an effect on the mileage.

For the block (column) effects

$$F = \frac{MS(Car)}{MS(error)} = \frac{130.0833}{1.9167} = 67.8696$$

This value is significant because the P-value for the cars factor (0.0000508, displayed by Excel in scientific notation) is much less than the specified alpha. We therefore reject the null hypothesis of equal block means, and conclude that the different cars have different mileage values. (If we interchange the roles played by the blocks and treatments by transposing Table 11-6, we obtain the same results.)

In this section we have briefly discussed an important branch of statistics, two-way analysis of variance. We have emphasized the interpretation of computer displays while omitting the manual calculations and formulas, which are quite formidable.

Using Technology

Excel: *For two-way tables with more than one entry per cell:* Entries from the same cell must be listed down a column, and not across a row. Enter the labels corresponding to the data set in column A and row 1, as in this example, which corresponds to Table 11-4.

A	B	C	D
	2.0–2.5 Stars	3.0–3.5 Stars	4.0–4.5 Stars
FAM/PA/14+	98	93	103
FAM/PA/14+	100	94	193
FAM/PA/14+	123	94	168
:	:	:	:
18+	101	93	104
18+	155	129	159

After entering the sample data and labels, select **Tools** from the main menu bar, then **Data Analysis**, then **Anova: Two-Factor With Replication**. In the dialog box, enter the input range (including row and column headings). For "rows per sample," enter the number of values in each cell (5, in the example shown in Table 11-4). Click **OK**.

For two-way tables with exactly one entry per cell: Enter the sample data as they appear in the table—but the labels are not required. Select **Tools** from the main menu bar, then **Data Analysis**, then **Anova: Two-Factor Without Replication**. In the dialog box, enter the input range (*excluding* headings). Click **OK**.

11-3 Exercises A: Basic Skills and Concepts

In Exercises 1–4, use the Excel display below, which corresponds to the data in the accompanying table.

	A	B	C	D	E	F	G	H
1	ANOVA							
2	Source of Variation	SS	df	MS	F	P-value	F crit	
3	Sample (CTR)	14.0625	1	14.0625	0.02023563	0.890398	5.317645	
4	Columns (Stars)	1049.1875	3	349.729167	0.50325269	0.690607	4.06618	
5	Interaction	3790.1875	3	1263.39583	1.81799922	0.221873	4.06618	
6	Within (error)	5559.5	8	694.9375				
7								
8	Total	10412.9375	15					

Lengths (in min) of Movies Categorized
by Star Ratings and the Canadian
Classification System for Violence in Programming

	Poor 0.0–1.5 Stars	Fair 2.0–2.5 Stars	Good 3.0–3.5 Stars	Excellent 4.0 Stars
CTR Rating: FAM/ PA/ 14+	108	98	93	103
	91	100	94	193
CTR Rating: 18+	105	110	115	72
	96	114	133	120

1. Identify the indicated values.
   a. MS(interaction)   b. MS(error)
   c. MS(Stars)   d. MS(CTR)
2. Find the test statistic and critical value for the null hypothesis of no interaction between star rating and CTR rating. What do you conclude?
3. Assume that the length of a movie is not affected by an interaction between its star rating and CTR rating. Find the test statistic and critical value for the null hypothesis that star rating has no effect on movie length. What do you conclude?
4. Assume that the length of a movie is not affected by an interaction between its star rating and CTR rating. Find the test statistic and critical value for the null hypothesis that CTR rating has no effect on movie length. What do you conclude?

In Exercises 5 and 6, use only the first value from each of the eight cells in the table used for Exercises 1–4. When we use only these first values, the Excel display includes the following.

	A	B	C	D	E	F	G	H
12	ANOVA							
13	Source of Variation	SS	df	MS	F	P-value	F crit	
14	Rows	0	1	0	0	1	10.12796	
15	Columns	459	3	153	0.574468	0.669941	9.276619	
16	Error	799	3	266.3333				
17								
18	Total	1258	7					

5. Assuming that there is no effect on movie length from the interaction between star rating and CTR rating, test the null hypothesis that CTR rating has no effect on movie length. Identify the test statistic and critical value, and state the conclusion. Use a 0.05 significance level.
6. Assuming that there is no effect on movie length from the interaction between star rating and CTR rating, test the null hypothesis that star rating has no effect on movie length. Identify the test statistic and critical value, and state the conclusion. Use a 0.05 significance level.

Exercises 7 and 8 refer to the sample data in the following table and the corresponding Excel display. The table entries are the numbers of support beams manufactured by four different operators using each of three different machines. In the Excel results, the operators are represented by rows and the machines are represented by columns.

		Machine		
		1	2	3
Operator	1	66	74	67
	2	58	67	68
	3	65	71	65
	4	60	64	66

	A	B	C	D	E	F	G	H
12	ANOVA							
13	Source of Variation	SS	df	MS	F	P-value	F crit	
14	Rows	59.58333	3	19.86111	2.474048	0.158993	4.757055	
15	Columns	93.16667	2	46.58333	5.802768	0.039583	5.143249	
16	Error	48.16667	6	8.027778				
17								
18	Total	200.9167	11					

7. Using a 0.05 significance level, test the claim of the hypothesis that the four operators have the same mean production output. Identify the test statistic and critical value, and state the conclusion.
8. Using a 0.05 significance level, test the claim that the choice of machine has no effect on the production output. Identify the test statistic and critical value, and state the conclusion.
9. Refer to Data Set 8 in Appendix B and construct a table with pulse rates categorized according to the two factors of gender and whether the individual smokes. Select 9 scores for each cell and test the null hypothesis of no interaction between gender and smoking.
10. Use the same data collected for Exercise 9, assume that pulse rates are not affected by an interaction between gender and smoking, and test the null hypothesis that gender has no effect on pulse rates.
11. Use the same data collected for Exercise 9, assume that pulse rates are not affected by an interaction between gender and smoking, and test the null hypothesis that smoking has no effect on pulse rates.

11-3 Exercises B: Beyond the Basics

12. Use a statistics software package, such as Excel or SPSS/PC, that can produce results for two-way analysis of variance. First enter the data in the table used for Exercises 1–4 and verify that the results are as given in this section. Then transpose the table by making the CTR rating the column factor and making the star rating the row factor. Obtain the computer

display for the transposed table, and compare the results to those previously given.

13. Refer to the data in the table used for Exercises 1–4 and subtract 10 from each table entry. Using a statistics software package with a two-way analysis of variance capability, determine the effects of subtracting 10 from each entry.

14. Refer to the data in the table used for Exercises 1–4 and multiply each table entry by 10. Using a statistics software package with a two-way analysis of variance capability, determine the effects of multiplying each entry by 10.

15. In analysing Table 11-4, we concluded that movie length is not affected by an interaction between star rating and CTR rating; it is not affected by star rating; and it is not affected by CTR rating.
    a. Change the table entries so that there is an effect from the interaction between star rating and CTR rating.
    b. Change the table entries so that there is no effect from the interaction between star rating and CTR rating, and there is no effect from star rating, but there is an effect from CTR rating.
    c. Change the table entries so that there is no effect from the interaction between star rating and CTR rating, and there is no effect from CTR rating, but there is an effect from star rating.

Vocabulary List

analysis of variance (ANOVA)	SS(error)
one-way analysis of variance	MS(treatment)
single-factor analysis of variance	MS(error)
treatment	MS(total)
factor	multiple comparison procedures
variance between samples	two-way analysis of variance
variation due to treatment	interaction
variance within samples	completely randomized design
variation due to error	rigorously controlled design
SS(total)	randomized block design
SS(treatment)	block

Review

In this chapter we used analysis of variance (or ANOVA) to test for equality of population means. This method requires (1) normally distributed populations, (2) populations with the same standard deviation (or variance), and (3) random samples that are independent of each other.

In Section 11-2 we considered one-way analysis of variance, characterized by sample data categorized according to a single factor. The following are key features of one-way analysis of variance:

- The F test statistic is based on the ratio of two different estimates of the common population variance σ^2, as shown below.

$$F = \frac{\text{variance between samples}}{\text{variance within samples}} = \frac{\text{MS(treatment)}}{\text{MS(error)}}$$

- Critical values of F are found in Table A-5, with the degrees of freedom (df) found as follows:

  df for numerator $= k - 1$ (where $k =$ number of samples)
  df for denominator $= N - k$ (where $N =$ the total number of values in all samples combined)

In Section 11-3 we considered two-way analysis of variance, characterized by data categorized according to two different factors. The method for two-way analysis of variance is summarized in Figure 11-4. We also considered two-way analysis of variance with one observation per cell and two-way analysis of variance with randomized block design.

Because of the nature of the calculations required throughout this chapter, we emphasized the interpretation of computer displays.

Review Exercises

1. In a study of the effects of drinking and driving, 3 groups of adult men were randomly selected for an experiment designed to measure their blood alcohol levels after consuming 5 drinks. Members of group A were tested after 1 hour, members of group B were tested after 2 hours, and members of group C were tested after 4 hours. The results are given in the accompanying table; the ANOVA table for these data is also shown. At the 0.05 level of significance, test the claim that the 3 groups have the same mean level.

A	B	C
0.11	0.08	0.04
0.10	0.09	0.04
0.09	0.07	0.05
0.09	0.07	0.05
0.10	0.06	0.06
		0.04
		0.05

ANOVA

Source of Variation	SS	df	MS	F
Between groups	0.007657143	2	0.003829	46.9
Within groups	0.001142857	14	8.16E-05	
Total	0.0088	16		

2. Is the mean cost of food items in a "typical" basket of products the same across Canada? The accompanying list shows the costs of the same items when purchased in four different cities. Do these sample data support the claim that the mean food costs are the same? Use a 0.05 significance level.

	St. John's	Moncton	Regina	Victoria
Food item 1	5.16	4.37	3.26	3.67
Food item 2	9.83	8.04	8.62	9.68
Food item 3	0.88	1.07	0.94	1.38
Food item 4	3.64	2.98	2.91	3.19
Food item 5	2.87	2.65	2.79	2.76
Food item 6	1.65	1.29	0.96	1.18
Food item 7	3.34	2.94	3.39	3.47
Food item 8	0.56	0.62	0.53	0.60

Based on data from Statistics Canada.

3. Twelve different 4-cylinder cars were tested for fuel consumption (in litres per 100 km) after being driven under identical highway conditions; the results are listed in the table and accompanying ANOVA table. At the 0.05 significance level, test the claim that fuel consumption is not affected by an *interaction* between engine size and transmission type.

Highway Fuel Consumption (L/100 km) of Different 4-Cylinder Compact Cars

	Engine Size (litres)		
	1.5	2.2	2.5
Automatic transmission	9.1, 8.8	10.1, 10.9	9.1, 12.3
Manual transmission	8.6, 7.8	8.6, 9.4	10.5, 8.1

ANOVA

Source of Variation	SS	df	MS	F	P-value	F crit
Sample	4.440833333	1	4.440833	2.958912	0.136196	5.987374
Columns	4.631666667	2	2.315833	1.543032	0.287956	5.143249
Interaction	0.331666667	2	0.165833	0.110494	0.897172	5.143249
Within	9.005	6	1.500833			
Total	18.40916667	11				

4. Refer to the same data used in Exercise 3 and assume that fuel consumption is not affected by an interaction between engine size and type of transmission. Use a 0.05 level of significance to test the claim that fuel consumption is not affected by engine size.

5. Refer to the same data used in Exercise 3 and assume that fuel consumption is not affected by an interaction between engine size and type of transmission. Use a 0.05 level of significance to test the claim that fuel consumption is not affected by type of transmission.

6. Transport Canada is concerned about the braking performance of snowmobiles. The following table shows the distances in metres that snowmobiles took to stop when the brakes were applied. The results are grouped by two factors: the speed of the snowmobile and the brand of the snowmobile. If you have access to a computer that can perform two-way analysis of variance, test the claim that the interaction of these two variables does affect mean brake performance, at the 0.01 significance level. What is the P-value for this test?

Snowmobile Braking Distances (in metres)
with Respect to Brand of Snowmobile and Speed

	Brand A	Brand B	Brand C	Brand D
10 km/h	3.0	4.4	9.5	1.1
	3.3	7.7	7.6	4.3
	4.8	7.0	6.8	3.5
20 km/h	15.8	24.7	18.0	13.7
	15.2	25.1	21.5	10.1
	19.5	35.7	20.3	12.6
30 km/h	37.9	66.4	48.9	32.2
	37.5	71.1	52.5	28.9
	31.6	66.4	55.5	28.7

● ●

Cumulative Review Exercises

1. The North of Superior Brewing Company plans to launch a major media campaign. Three advertising companies prepared trial commercials in an attempt to win a $2 million contract. The commercials were tested on randomly selected consumers, whose reactions were measured; the results are summarized in the accompanying table. (Higher scores indicate more positive reactions to the commercial.)

Aurora Advertising Co.	Solomon & Campbell Advertising	Gagné and Turner Advertising
52 68 75 40	69 73 82 59	42 73 69 53
77 63 55 72	66 84 75 70	57 61 73 74

a. Construct a boxplot for each of the three samples. Use the same scale so that the boxplots can be compared. Do the boxplots reveal any notable differences?

b. Find the mean and standard deviation for each of the three sets of sample data.

c. Use the methods of Section 8-5 to test the claim that the population of Aurora scores has a mean that is equal to the population mean for Solomon & Campbell scores. Use a 0.05 significance level.

d. For each of the three samples, construct a 95% confidence interval estimate of the population mean μ. Do the results suggest any notable differences?

e. At the 0.05 significance level, test the claim that the three populations have the same mean reaction score. If you were responsible for advertising at this brewery, which company would you select on the basis of these results? Why?

2. The tread life in kilometres of a certain model of radial tire is normally distributed, with a mean of 60,000 km and a standard deviation of 5000 km (based on data from Goodyear).

a. If one radial tire is randomly selected, what is the probability that it will have a tread life of more than 62,210 km?

b. If 16 radial tires are randomly selected, what is the probability that their mean tread life is more than 62,210 km?

c. What is the probability that each of the next 3 tires selected will have a tread life greater than 60,000 km?

3. Refer to the numbers of Newfoundland males in the labour force, in different SOC job categories, as listed in Data Set 14 in Appendix B.

a. Find the mean.

b. Find the standard deviation.

c. Construct a boxplot.

d. Identify any outliers.

e. Construct a histogram.

f. Assume that you want to test the null hypothesis that the mean number of workers per job category is the same for males in all provinces. Can you use one-way ANOVA? Why, or why not?

g. Based on the sample data, estimate the probability that a randomly selected male member of the labour force in Newfoundland works in the SOC job category "B5."

Technology Project

For prime ministers, popes, and British monarchs after 1690, the accompanying table lists the numbers of years that they lived after they first came to office or were crowned. Use boxplots and analysis of variance to determine whether the survival times for the different groups differ. Conduct the analysis of variance by running Excel or STATDISK or some other statistical software package. Obtain printed copies of the computer displays and write your observations and conclusions.

Prime Ministers		Popes		Kings and Queens	
Macdonald	24	Alexander VIII	2	James II	17
Mackenzie	19	Innocent XII	9	Mary II	6
Abbott	1	Clement XI	21	William III	13
Thompson	2	Innocent XIII	3	Anne	12
Bowell	23	Benedict XIII	6	George I	13
Tupper	19	Clement XII	10	George II	33
Laurier	23	Benedict XIV	18	George III	59
Borden	26	Clement XIII	11	George IV	10
Meighen	40	Clement XIV	6	William IV	7
Mackenzie King	29	Pius VI	25	Victoria	63
Bennett	17	Pius VII	23	Edward VII	9
St. Laurent	25	Leo XII	6	George V	25
Diefenbaker	22	Pius VIII	2	Edward VIII	36
Pearson	9	Gregory XVI	15	George VI	15
Trudeau	32	Pius IX	32		
		Leo XIII	25		
		Pius X	11		
		Benedict XV	8		
		Pius XII	17		
		Pius XIII	19		
		John XXIII	5		
		Paul VI	15		
		John Paul I	0		

Based on data from *Computer-Interactive Data Analysis*, by Lunn and McNeil, John Wiley & Sons.

•••••••• **FROM DATA TO DECISION** ••••••••

Was the Experiment Designed Correctly?

An experiment was designed to compare the effects of weight loss to the effects of aerobic exercise training on coronary artery disease risk factors in men who are healthy but sedentary, obese, and middle-aged or older. (See "Effects of Weight Loss vs. Aerobic Exercise Training on Risk Factors for Coronary Disease in Healthy, Obese, Middle-Aged and Older Men," by Katzel, Bleecker, et al., *Journal of the American Medical Association*, Vol. 274, No. 24.) The study involved 170 men divided into three groups: (1) 73 men were assigned to lose weight, (2) 71 men were assigned to aerobic exercise, and (3) 26 men were in a control group instructed not to lose weight or change the level of physical activity. In such a study, it is important to begin with groups that are similar in "baseline" characteristics of age, weight, body mass, body fat, and so on. In a report of the study, it was claimed that "there were no significant differences among the three groups in any of the baseline characteristics." The mean weights for the three sample groups are 94.3 kg, 93.9 kg, and 88.3 kg. Are these differences significant? Is there sufficient evidence to warrant rejection of the claim of no significant differences among the three groups? Analyse the data in the following list, form a conclusion, and write a report stating your results.

Weights (in kg) of men assigned to the weight loss group

95	82	94	87	84	111	98	101	85	117	111	86	114	85	98	102	97
92	76	95	88	107	89	81	93	77	91	106	97	107	78	101	88	92
101	110	96	83	92	106	107	106	110	102	105	84	93	69	96	70	80
108	87	86	93	78	98	86	93	101	94	85	107	74	101	105	93	89
90	103	103	80	116												

Weights (in kg) of men assigned to the aerobic exercise group

90	101	89	76	93	110	87	108	109	105	83	98	100	82	71	67	126
114	102	78	101	79	97	100	106	84	80	100	103	80	71	99	108	84
78	92	92	101	107	95	106	84	111	108	109	79	116	98	77	110	93
95	85	86	104	93	92	86	93	74	74	89	85	91	104	97	97	80
104	95	109														

Weights (in kg) of men assigned to the control group

91	71	74	86	97	78	81	82	78	106	79	110	91	93	87	72	95	
88	83	96	98	77	84	95	103	102									

········ COOPERATIVE GROUP ACTIVITIES ········

1. *In-class activity:* Divide into groups of five or six students. This activity is a contest of reaction times to determine which group is fastest, if there is a "fastest" group. Use the same reaction timer included with the Cooperative Group Activities in Chapter 5. Test and record the reaction time using the dominant hand of each group member. (Only one try per person.) Each group should calculate the values of n, $\bar{x}$, and s and record those summary statistics on the chalkboard along with the original list of reaction times. After all groups have reported their results, identify the group with the fastest mean reaction time. But is that group actually fastest? Use ANOVA to determine whether the means are significantly different. If they are not, there is no real "winner."

2. *Out–of–class activity:* The Web site **http://www.parl.gc.ca/information/about/people/house/mpsbo.asp** allows you to list, by country of origin, all the Members of the House of Commons who were born outside of Canada. In the **Search by Country** box, either type in a country, or click the arrow to choose a country from a list. Included in the list of past and present MPs from a given country are each member's date of birth, party affiliation, and year of election. Design and conduct an observational study that begins with the selection of samples from select groups, based on country of birth (such as England, the United States, the former Soviet Union, and so on). From these samples, compare the age when elected of members from the different groups. Do any particular groups appear to have a higher or lower mean age when elected than the other groups? Can you explain such differences?

INTERNET PROJECT   **Analysis of Variance**

Go to the Web site for this book, located at:

http://www.pearsoned.ca/triola

Click on Internet Project, then on Chapter 11. There you will find instructions for finding data sets. Each data set can be divided naturally into samples from different populations so that ANOVA methods may be applied. In applying ANOVA methods, you will be conducting analyses in areas as varied as the functioning of the human body, consumer product labelling, and performance in sports.

12

Statistical Process Control

12-1 Overview

The pattern of data over time is discussed as an important characteristic in a data set. The importance of quality control and monitoring processes is discussed.

12-2 Control Charts for Variation and Mean

A definition is presented for "process" data. Analysis of process data is described with run charts and control charts. Illustrations are provided of the construction and interpretation of (1) run charts (used to monitor the behaviour of individual process elements), (2) control charts for R (used to monitor process variation), and (3) control charts for $\bar{x}$ (used to monitor the process mean).

12-3 Control Charts for Attributes

This section describes the construction of p charts, which are used to monitor the proportion of items having some attribute, such as being defective.

CHAPTER PROBLEM:

Are production standards being maintained?

An axial load of an aluminum can is the maximum weight supported by its sides. It is important to have an axial load high enough so that the can isn't crushed when the top lid is pressed into place. The sample data in Table 12-1 came from a population of cans with a 0.0109 in. thickness. During each day of production, seven cans were randomly selected and tested. In this chapter we will analyse the manufacturing process by focusing on the pattern of axial loads over time.

Table 12-1 Axial Loads (in pounds) of Aluminum Cans

Day	Axial Load (pounds)							$\bar{x}$	Median	Range	s
1	270	273	258	204	254	228	282	252.7	258	78	27.6
2	278	201	264	265	223	274	230	247.9	264	77	29.7
3	250	275	281	271	263	277	275	270.3	275	31	10.6
4	278	260	262	273	274	286	236	267.0	273	50	16.3
5	290	286	278	283	262	277	295	281.6	283	33	10.7
6	274	272	265	275	263	251	289	269.9	272	38	11.8
7	242	284	241	276	200	278	283	257.7	276	84	31.4
8	269	282	267	282	272	277	261	272.9	272	21	7.9
9	257	278	295	270	268	286	262	273.7	270	38	13.5
10	272	268	283	256	206	277	252	259.1	268	77	25.9
11	265	263	281	268	280	289	283	275.6	280	26	10.1
12	263	273	209	259	287	269	277	262.4	269	78	25.3
13	234	282	276	272	257	267	204	256.0	267	78	27.8
14	270	285	273	269	284	276	286	277.6	276	17	7.3
15	273	289	263	270	279	206	270	264.3	270	83	27.0
16	270	268	218	251	252	284	278	260.1	268	66	22.3
17	277	208	271	208	280	269	270	254.7	270	72	32.2
18	294	292	289	290	215	284	283	278.1	289	79	28.1
19	279	275	223	220	281	268	272	259.7	272	61	26.5
20	268	279	217	259	291	291	281	269.4	279	74	25.9
21	230	276	225	282	276	289	288	266.6	276	64	27.2
22	268	242	283	277	285	293	248	270.9	277	51	19.3
23	278	285	292	282	287	277	266	281.0	282	26	8.4
24	268	273	270	256	297	280	256	271.4	270	41	14.3
25	262	268	262	293	290	274	292	277.3	274	31	14.1

(12-1) Overview

In Chapter 2 we noted that when describing, exploring, or comparing data sets, the following characteristics are usually very important: (1) a measure of *centre*, which is a representative or average value that gives us an indication of where the middle of the data set is located; (2) a measure of *variation*, which indicates the degree of scattering or spread among the data values; (3) the shape or nature of the data's *distribution*, such as bell-shaped, uniform, or skewed; (4) the presence of *outliers*, which lie very far away from the vast majority of the other sample values; and (5) the pattern of data over *time*. The main objective of this chapter is to address the fifth item: the changing characteristics of data over time. By monitoring this characteristic, we are better able to control the production of goods and services, thereby ensuring better quality.

There is currently a strong trend toward trying to improve the quality of manufactured goods and services, and the methods presented in this chapter are being used by growing numbers of businesses. Evidence of the increasing importance of quality is found in its greater role in advertising and the number of books and articles that focus on the issue of quality. Many job applicants have a distinct advantage when they can tell employers that they have studied statistics and methods of quality control. This chapter will present some of the basic tools commonly used to monitor quality.

(12-2) Control Charts for Variation and Mean

In this section we focus on the pattern of data over time. The data that we analyze are often referred to as *process data*.

DEFINITION

Process data are data arranged according to some time sequence. They are measurements of a characteristic of goods or services that results from some combination of equipment, people, materials, methods, and conditions.

For example, Table 12-1 includes process data consisting of the measured axial loads of aluminum cans over 25 consecutive days of production. Each day, 7 cans were randomly selected and tested. Because the data in Table 12-1 are arranged according to the time at which they were selected, they are process data. It is very important to recognize this point:

Important characteristics of process data can change over time.

In making aluminum cans, a manufacturer might use a good machine that is correctly calibrated, but if the machine wears with use, the cans may begin to become defective. Companies have gone bankrupt because they allowed manufacturing processes to continue without constant monitoring.

Run Charts

There are various methods that can be used to monitor a process to ensure that the important desired characteristics don't change—the *run chart* is one such method.

DEFINITION

A **run chart** is a sequential plot of *individual* data values over time. One axis (usually the vertical axis) is used for the data values, and the other axis (usually the horizontal axis) is used for the time sequence.

EXAMPLE   Treating the 175 axial loads in Table 12-1 as a string of consecutive measurements, construct a run chart by using a vertical axis for the axial loads and a horizontal axis to identify the order of the sample data.

SOLUTION   Figure 12-1 is an Excel-generated run chart for the data of Table 12-1. The vertical scale is designed to be suitable for axial loads ranging from 100 lb to 297 lb. The horizontal scale is designed to include the 175 values arranged in sequence. The first point represents the first value of 270 lb, the second point represents the second value of 273 lb, and so on.

Figure 12-1   Run Chart of Axial Loads in Table 12-1

In Figure 12-1, the horizontal scale identifies the sample number, so the number 20 indicates the 20th sample item. The vertical scale represents the measured axial load, so 250 indicates a load of 250 lb. Now examine Figure 12-1 and observe that there aren't any dramatic patterns that beg for attention. Figure 12-1 does not appear to reveal any problems that need correction.

The Flynn Effect: Upward Trend in IQ Scores

A run chart or control chart of IQ scores would reveal that they exhibit an upward trend, because IQ scores have been steadily increasing since they began to be used about 70 years ago. The trend is worldwide, and it is the same for different types of IQ tests, even those that rely heavily on abstract and nonverbal reasoning with minimal cultural influence. This upward trend has been named the *Flynn effect*, because political scientist James R. Flynn discovered the trend in his studies of military recruits. The amount of the increase is quite substantial: Based on a current mean IQ score of 100, it is estimated that the mean IQ in 1920 would have been about 77. The typical student of today is therefore brilliant when compared to his or her grandparents. So far, there is no generally accepted explanation for the Flynn effect.

Interpreting Run Charts

Only when a process is *statistically stable* can its data be treated as if they came from a population with a constant mean, standard deviation, distribution, and other characteristics.

DEFINITION

A process is **statistically stable** (or **within statistical control**) if it has only natural variation, with no patterns, cycles, or unusual points.

Figure 12-2 illustrates common patterns that may indicate that the process of filling 16-oz soup cans is not statistically stable:

- **Figure 12-2(a):** There is an obvious *upward trend* that corresponds to values that are increasing over time. If the filling process were to follow this type of pattern, the cans would be filled with more and more soup until they began to overflow, eventually leaving the employees swimming in soup.

- **Figure 12-2(b):** There is an obvious *downward trend* that corresponds to steadily decreasing values. The cans would be filled with less and less soup until they were extremely underfilled. Such a process would require a complete reworking of the cans in order to get them full enough for distribution to consumers.

- **Figure 12-2(c):** There is an *upward shift*. A run chart such as this one might result from an adjustment to the filling process, making all subsequent values higher.

- **Figure 12-2(d):** There is a *downward shift*—the first few values are relatively stable, and then something happened so that the last several values are relatively stable, but at a much lower level.

- **Figure 12-2(e):** The process is stable except for one *exceptionally high value*. The cause of that unusual value should be investigated. Perhaps the cans became temporarily stuck and one particular can was filled twice instead of once.

- **Figure 12-2(f):** There is an *exceptionally low value*.

- **Figure 12-2(g):** There is a *cyclical pattern* (or repeating cycle). This pattern is clearly nonrandom and therefore reveals a statistically unstable process. Perhaps periodic overadjustments are being made to the machinery, with the effect that some desired value is continually being chased but never quite captured.

- **Figure 12-2(h):** The *variation is increasing over time*. This is a common problem in quality control. The net effect is that products vary more and more until almost all of them are worthless. For example, some soup cans will be overflowing with wasted soup and some will be underfilled and unsuitable for distribution to consumers.

A common goal of many different methods of quality control is to *reduce variation* in a product or service. For example, Ford became concerned with

Figure 12-2 Processes with Patterns That Aren't Statistically Stable

variability when it found that its transmissions required significantly more warranty repairs than the same type of transmissions made by Mazda in Japan. A study showed that the Mazda transmissions had substantially less variation in the gearboxes; that is, crucial gearbox measurements varied much less in the Mazda transmissions. Although the Ford transmissions were built within the allowable limits, the Mazda transmissions were more reliable because of their lower variability. Variation in a process can be described in terms of two types of causes.

DEFINITIONS

Random variation is due to chance; it is the type of variation inherent in any process that is not capable of producing every good or service exactly the same way every time.

Assignable variation results from causes that can be identified (such as defective machinery, untrained employees, and so on).

Later in the chapter we will look at objective ways to distinguish between assignable variation and random variation.

The run chart is one tool for monitoring the stability of a process. We will now consider control charts, which are also extremely useful for that same purpose.

Control Chart for Monitoring Variation: The R Chart

DEFINITIONS

A **control chart** of a process characteristic (such as mean or variation) consists of values plotted sequentially over time, and it includes a **centre line** as well as a **lower control limit** (LCL) and an **upper control limit** (UCL). The centre line represents a central value of the characteristic measurements, whereas the control limits are boundaries used to separate and identify any points considered to be *unusual*.

We will assume that the population standard deviation σ is not known as we consider only two of several different types of *control charts:* **R charts** (or **range charts**) used to monitor variation and $\bar{x}$ **charts** used to monitor means. When using control charts to monitor a process, it is common to consider R charts and $\bar{x}$ charts together, because a statistically unstable process may be the result of increasing variation or changing means or both.

An **R chart** (or **range chart**) is a plot of the sample ranges instead of individual sample values, and it is used to monitor the *variation* in a process. (It might make more sense to use standard deviations, but range charts are used more often in practice. This is a carryover from times when calculators and computers were not readily available.) In addition to plotting the range values, we include a centre line located at $\overline{R}$, which denotes the mean of all sample ranges, as well as another line for the lower control limit and a third line for the upper control limit. The following is a summary of notation for the components of the R chart.

Notation

Given: Process data consist of a sequence of samples all of the same size, and the distribution of the process data is essentially normal.

n = size of each sample, or *subgroup*

$\overline{\overline{x}}$ = mean of the sample means (that is, the sum of the sample means, divided by the number of samples), which is equivalent to the mean of all sample scores combined

$\overline{R}$ = mean of the sample ranges (that is, the sum of the sample ranges, divided by the number of samples)

Monitoring Process Variation: Control Chart for *R*

Points plotted: Sample ranges

Centre line: $\overline{R}$

Upper control limit (UCL): $D_4\overline{R}$

Lower control limit (LCL): $D_3\overline{R}$

where the values of D_4 and D_3 are found in Table 12-2.

The values of D_4 and D_3 were computed by quality control experts, and they are intended to simplify calculations. The upper and lower control limits of $D_4\overline{R}$ and $D_3\overline{R}$ are values that are roughly equivalent to 99.7% confidence interval limits. It is therefore highly unlikely that values would fall beyond those limits. If a value does fall beyond the control limits, it's very likely that something is wrong with the process.

EXAMPLE   Refer to the axial loads in Table 12-1. Using samples of size $n = 7$ collected each working day, construct a control chart for R.

SOLUTION   We begin by finding the value of $\overline{R}$, the mean of the sample ranges:

$$\overline{R} = \frac{78 + 77 + \cdots + 31}{25} = 54.96$$

Don't Tamper!

Nashua Corp. had trouble with its paper-coating machine and considered spending a million dollars to replace it. The machine was working well with a stable process, but samples were taken every so often and, based on the results, adjustments were made. These overadjustments, called *tampering,* caused shifts away from the distribution that had been good. The effect was an increase in defects. When statistician and quality expert W. Edwards Deming studied the process, he recommended that no adjustments be made unless warranted by a signal that the process had shifted or had become unstable. The company was better off with no adjustments than with the tampering that took place.

TABLE 12-2	Control Chart Constants					
	$\bar{x}$		$\bar{s}$		$\bar{R}$	
Observations in Subgroup, n	A_2	A_3	B_3	B_4	D_3	D_4
2	1.880	2.659	0.000	3.267	0.000	3.267
3	1.023	1.954	0.000	2.568	0.000	2.574
4	0.729	1.628	0.000	2.266	0.000	2.282
5	0.577	1.427	0.000	2.089	0.000	2.114
6	0.483	1.287	0.030	1.970	0.000	2.004
7	0.419	1.182	0.118	1.882	0.076	1.924
8	0.373	1.099	0.185	1.815	0.136	1.864
9	0.337	1.032	0.239	1.761	0.184	1.816
10	0.308	0.975	0.284	1.716	0.223	1.777
11	0.285	0.927	0.321	1.679	0.256	1.744
12	0.266	0.886	0.354	1.646	0.283	1.717
13	0.249	0.850	0.382	1.618	0.307	1.693
14	0.235	0.817	0.406	1.594	0.328	1.672
15	0.223	0.789	0.428	1.572	0.347	1.653
16	0.212	0.763	0.448	1.552	0.363	1.637
17	0.203	0.739	0.466	1.534	0.378	1.622
18	0.194	0.718	0.482	1.518	0.391	1.608
19	0.187	0.698	0.497	1.503	0.403	1.597
20	0.180	0.680	0.510	1.490	0.415	1.585
21	0.173	0.663	0.523	1.477	0.425	1.575
22	0.167	0.647	0.534	1.466	0.434	1.566
23	0.162	0.633	0.545	1.455	0.443	1.557
24	0.157	0.619	0.555	1.445	0.451	1.548
25	0.153	0.606	0.565	1.435	0.459	1.541

Source: Adapted from *ASTM Manual on the Presentation of Data and Control Chart Analysis,* © 1976 ASTM, pp. 134–136. Reprinted with permission of American Society for Testing and Materials.

The centre line for our R chart is therefore located at $\bar{R} = 54.96$. To find the upper and lower control limits, we must first find the values of D_3 and D_4. Referring to Table 12-2 for $n = 7$, we get $D_3 = 0.076$ and $D_4 = 1.924$, so the control limits are as follows:

Upper control limit: $D_4\bar{R} = (1.924)(54.96) = 105.74$

Lower control limit: $D_3\bar{R} = (0.076)(54.96) = 4.18$

Using a centre line value of $\bar{R} = 54.96$ and control limits of 105.74 and 4.18, we now proceed to plot the sample ranges. The result is shown in the Excel display that follows.

Excel Display *R* Chart for Axial Load Samples

Quality Control at Perstorp

Perstorp Components, Inc., uses a computer that automatically generates control charts to monitor the thicknesses of the floor insulation the company makes for Ford Rangers and Jeep Grand Cherokees. The $20,000 cost of the computer was offset by a first-year savings of $40,000 in labour, which had been used to manually generate control charts to ensure that insulation thicknesses were between the specifications of 2.912 mm and 2.988 mm. Through the use of control charts and other quality-control methods, Perstorp reduced its waste by more than two-thirds.

Interpreting Control Charts

Here is an extremely important point:

> Upper and lower control limits of a control chart are based on the *actual* behaviour of the process, not the *desired* behaviour.

For example, control charts might suggest that 16-oz soup cans are being filled with a statistically stable process, but if they are being filled to a level of only 8 oz, then there is a major problem because the statistically stable actual behaviour is very different from the desired behaviour. Also, we should clearly understand the specific criteria for determining whether a process is in statistical control (that is, whether it is statistically stable). So far, we have noted that a process is not statistically stable if its pattern resembles any of those shown in Figure 12-2. This criterion is included with some others in the following list.

Criteria for Using Control Charts to Determine That a Process Is Not Statistically Stable (Out of Statistical Control)

1. There is a pattern, trend, or cycle that is obviously not random (such as those depicted in Figure 12-2).
2. There is a point lying beyond the upper or lower control limits.
3. **Run of 8 Rule:** There are 8 consecutive points all above or all below the centre line. (With a statistically stable process, there is a 0.5 probability that a point will be above or below the centre line, so it is very unlikely that eight consecutive points will all be above the centre line or all below it.)

We will use only the three out-of-control criteria listed, but some businesses use additional criteria such as these:

- There are 6 consecutive points all increasing or all decreasing.
- There are 14 consecutive points all alternating between up and down (such as up, down, up, down, and so on).
- Two out of three consecutive points are beyond control limits that are 1 standard deviation away from the centre line.
- Four out of five consecutive points are beyond control limits that are 2 standard deviations away from the centre line.

EXAMPLE   Examine the R chart shown in the Excel display in the previous example and determine whether the process variation is within statistical control.

SOLUTION   We can interpret control charts for R by applying the three out-of-control criteria just listed. Applying the three criteria to the Excel display of the R chart, we conclude that variation in this process is within statistical control because of the following:

1. There is no pattern, trend, or cycle that is obviously not random. (However, it would make sense to re-check soon with a new sample set. Although the last 8 samples do not exactly fit the above criteria, they *may* indicate a trend is emerging.)

2. No point lies beyond the upper or lower control limits.

3. There are not 8 consecutive points all above or all below the centre line.

We therefore conclude that the variation (not necessarily the mean) of the process is within statistical control. No action is required to correct the *variation* among the axial loads of the cans.

Control Chart for Monitoring Means: The $\bar{x}$ Chart

An $\bar{x}$ chart is a plot of the sample means, and it is used to monitor the *centre* in a process. In addition to plotting the sample means, we include a centre line located at $\bar{\bar{x}}$, which denotes the mean of all sample means (equal to the mean of all the sample values combined), as well as another line for the lower control limit and a third line for the upper control limit. Using the approach common in business and industry, the centre line and control limits are based on ranges (instead of standard deviations).

Monitoring Process Mean: Control Chart for $\bar{x}$

Points plotted: Sample means

Centre line: $\bar{\bar{x}}$

Upper control limit (UCL): $\bar{\bar{x}} + A_2\overline{R}$

Lower control limit (LCL): $\bar{\bar{x}} - A_2\overline{R}$

where the values of A_2 are found in Table 12-2.

EXAMPLE   Refer to the axial loads in Table 12-1. Using samples of size $n = 7$ collected each working day, construct a control chart for $\bar{x}$. Based on the control chart for $\bar{x}$ only, determine whether the process mean is within statistical control.

SOLUTION   Before plotting the 25 points corresponding to the 25 values of $\bar{x}$, we must first find the value for the centre line and the values for the control limits. We get

$$\bar{\bar{x}} = \frac{252.7 + 247.9 + \cdots + 277.3}{25} = 267.12$$

$$\bar{R} = \frac{78 + 77 + \cdots + 31}{25} = 54.96$$

Referring to Table 12-2, we find that for $n = 7$, $A_2 = 0.419$. Knowing the values of $\bar{\bar{x}}$, A_2, and $\bar{R}$, we are now able to find the control limits:

Upper control limit: $\bar{\bar{x}} + A_2\bar{R} = 267.12 + (0.419)(54.96) = 290.15$
Lower control limit: $\bar{\bar{x}} - A_2\bar{R} = 267.12 - (0.419)(54.96) = 244.09$

Interpretation   The resulting control chart for $\bar{x}$ will be as shown in the accompanying Excel display. Examination of the control chart shows that the process mean is within statistical control because none of the three out-of-control criteria is satisfied. Again, no corrective action is required.

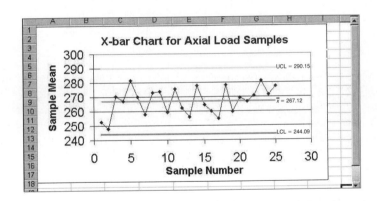

Excel Display $\bar{x}$ Chart for Axial Load Samples

Using Technology

Excel: To use the Data Desk XL add-in, click on **DDXL** and select **Process Control**. Proceed to select the type of chart that you want. (You must first enter the data in column A with sample identifying codes entered in column B. For the data of Table 12-1, for example, enter a 1 in column B adjacent to each value from day 1, enter a 2 for each value from day 2, and so on.)

To use Excel's built-in graphics features instead of Data Desk XL, see the following:

Run chart   Enter all of the sample data in a column (or row). To display a line for the sample mean, add a column to the right of (or a row below) the data consisting entirely of the sample mean, repeated. Click and drag the cell pointer to highlight the block of data you have input; then on the main menu bar, click on the **Chart Wizard** icon, which looks like a bar graph. For the chart type, select **Line**. For the chart subtype, select the first graph in the second row, then click **Next**. Continue to select **Next**, then **Finish**. The graph can be edited, as desired, to add a legend or labels, delete grid lines, and so on.

R chart The data need to be organized into a single data block, as shown below. The left column lists the sample numbers in sequence. The second column contains the range, R, of data for each sample. (Excel can calculate the range for any data block by using the formula = Max(data block) − Min(data block). The next three columns consist of the predetermined values for the lower control limit (LCL), mean of the sample ranges (R), and upper control limit (UCL), respectively—all of these repeated down the table.

Sample	Range	LCL	Mean R	UCL
1	78	4.18	54.96	105.74
2	77	4.18	54.96	105.74
3	31	4.18	54.96	105.74
4	50	4.18	54.96	105.74
5	33	4.18	54.96	105.74
6	38	4.18	54.96	105.74
.	.	.	.	.
.	.	.	.	.
.	.	.	.	.

To draw the chart, click on the **Chart Wizard** icon on the main toolbar. In Step 1, select **XY (Scatter)** and, for **Chart sub-type**, select the option illustrated by points connected with straight lines. In Step 2, enter the **Data Range** for the whole block of data, and indicate whether the data is in rows or columns. Continue to select **Next**, then **Finish**. The graph can be edited, as desired, to add a legend or labels, delete grid lines, change thickness for the control lines, and so on.

$\bar{x}$ chart The procedures for constructing an $\bar{x}$ chart in Excel are similar to those for constructing an R chart. First, organize the data into a single data block, as shown below. The left column lists the sample numbers in sequence. The second column contains the mean data $(\bar{x})$ for each sample. The next three columns consist of the predetermined values for the lower control limit (LCL), mean $\bar{x}$, and upper control limit (UCL), respectively—all of these repeated down the table.

To draw the chart, use Excel's Chart Wizard in exactly the same way as described above for constructing the R chart, adjusting the data range and using appropriate titles for the chart and the axes.

Sample	Means	LCL	Mean $\bar{x}$	UCL
1	252.7	244.09	267.12	290.15
2	247.9	244.09	267.12	290.15
3	270.3	244.09	267.12	290.15
4	267.0	244.09	267.12	290.15
5	281.6	244.09	267.12	290.15
6	269.9	244.09	267.12	290.15
.	.	.	.	.
.	.	.	.	.
.	.	.	.	.

12–2 Exercises A: Basic Skills and Concepts

In Exercises 1–3, use the following information:

The Old Faithful Geyser was monitored for 25 recent and consecutive years. In each year, six intervals (in minutes) between eruptions were recorded, with the results given in the accompanying table.

Intervals Between Eruptions

Year	Interval (min)						Mean	Range
1	65	72	60	69	65	67	66.3	12
2	74	65	60	69	68	59	65.8	15
3	68	66	69	64	70	73	68.3	9
4	73	65	71	77	63	77	71.0	14
5	79	67	64	61	81	77	71.5	20
6	74	76	65	69	76	64	70.7	12
7	70	73	74	77	65	73	72.0	12
8	71	68	70	79	75	82	74.2	14
9	62	63	61	48	59	77	61.7	29
10	60	74	77	57	52	78	66.3	26
11	67	73	47	81	92	57	69.5	45
12	79	84	79	72	61	80	75.8	23
13	83	78	83	74	61	68	74.5	22
14	57	68	72	75	56	79	67.8	23
15	59	76	78	86	64	72	72.5	27
16	63	63	71	77	81	65	70.0	18
17	67	84	72	75	70	70	73.0	17
18	93	83	85	79	90	74	84.0	19
19	81	74	80	65	70	84	75.7	19
20	83	67	71	67	97	88	78.8	30
21	62	61	57	86	70	77	68.8	29
22	67	75	67	89	93	81	78.7	26
23	86	65	70	74	83	74	75.3	21
24	74	67	99	75	41	83	73.2	58
25	97	93	73	81	85	90	86.5	24

Bribery Detected with Control Charts

Control charts were used to help convict a person who bribed jai alai players to lose. (See "Using Control Charts to Corroborate Bribery in Jai Alai," by Charnes and Gitlow, *The American Statistician*, Vol. 49, No. 4.) An auditor for one jai alai facility noticed that abnormally large sums of money were wagered for certain types of bets, and some contestants didn't win as much as expected when those bets were made. *R* charts and $\bar{x}$ charts were used in court as evidence of highly unusual patterns of betting. Examination of the control charts clearly shows points well beyond the upper control limit, indicating that the process of betting was out of statistical control. The statistician was able to identify a date at which assignable variation appeared to stop, and prosecutors knew that it was the date of the suspect's arrest.

1. Construct a run chart for the 150 values. Does there appear to be a pattern suggesting that the process is not within statistical control? What are the implications for tourists wishing to see Old Faithful erupt?
2. Construct an R chart and determine whether the process variation is within statistical control. If it is not, identify which of the three out-of-control criteria lead to rejection of statistically stable variation. How would tourists be affected by out-of-control variation?
3. Construct an $\bar{x}$ chart and determine whether the process mean is within statistical control. If it is not, identify which of the three out-of-control criteria lead to rejection of a statistically stable mean. How would tourists be affected by an out-of-control mean?

In Exercises 4–6, use the following information:

An aircraft plant fabricates trap panels for commercial jet airliners. Each day the final pocket thickness is measured on four randomly selected fabrications. The results for 16 days are listed in the accompanying table.

Pocket Thickness for Trap Panels

Sample	Thickness				Mean	Range
1	4	7	2	9	5.5	7
2	0	3	6	3	3.0	6
3	5	10	4	5	6.0	6
4	0	1	2	1	1.0	2
5	0	0	2	2	1.0	2
6	2	2	3	1	2.0	2
7	2	5	2	2	2.8	3
8	10	10	6	17	10.8	11
9	4	5	7	10	6.5	6
10	2	4	9	5	5.0	7
11	0	0	3	1	1.0	3
12	6	2	3	1	3.0	5
13	0	2	0	2	1.0	2
14	2	3	2	1	2.0	2
15	2	10	5	10	6.8	8
16	2	6	2	7	4.3	5

4. Construct a run chart for the 64 values. Does there appear to be a pattern suggesting that the process is not within statistical control? What are the practical implications of the run chart?
5. Construct an R chart and determine whether the process variation is within statistical control. If it is not, identify which of the three out-of-control criteria lead to rejection of statistically stable variation.
6. Construct an $\bar{x}$ chart and determine whether the process mean is within statistical control. If it is not, identify which of the three out-of-control criteria lead to rejection of a statistically stable mean. Does this process need corrective action?

In Exercises 7–9, use the following information:

The Monetary Conditions Index (MCI) is one of many financial indicators that the Bank of Canada compiles. The Bank states that the index "captures the effect monetary policy has on the economy both through interest rates and the exchange rate" (www.bankofcanada.ca/en/mci2.htm). Actual MCI data for 15 years are shown in the accompanying table. Each 6-value sequence of monthly observations is interpreted as a sample.

Monetary Conditions Index

Sample	Index Value					
1	9.70	9.68	8.19	7.70	7.90	7.72
2	7.98	8.37	8.31	8.93	8.35	7.99
3	7.34	7.96	8.77	9.36	9.78	9.77
4	8.91	9.08	9.14	9.13	9.00	8.63
5	8.66	8.37	8.14	8.21	8.92	9.49
6	9.75	10.49	10.94	11.34	12.44	13.13
7	13.37	13.06	13.19	14.91	16.01	15.69
8	15.84	15.91	15.45	14.92	13.95	14.11
9	11.51	9.98	9.74	9.72	9.70	9.57
10	9.81	10.54	11.68	11.67	12.34	12.78
11	12.73	12.96	14.12	14.22	14.00	14.24
12	14.16	13.90	14.17	13.99	13.29	11.66
13	11.40	10.47	9.60	9.56	9.36	8.75
14	8.54	8.46	8.38	7.47	7.14	7.21
15	6.88	6.54	6.44	6.59	7.18	7.13
16	6.93	6.73	6.27	6.17	7.46	7.27
17	7.32	7.24	8.00	9.02	8.87	8.24
18	8.44	8.81	9.15	10.42	11.21	11.16
19	11.14	11.52	12.10	13.16	10.19	9.04
20	8.35	7.78	7.84	8.59	9.65	13.07
21	13.51	13.77	13.63	14.15	15.67	16.17
22	16.54	18.64	17.61	15.89	13.75	13.35
23	12.32	12.11	12.51	12.50	11.88	12.46
24	12.02	11.28	10.43	9.13	8.29	7.10
25	6.62	6.57	6.35	6.18	6.13	6.28
26	6.34	6.53	6.41	6.27	6.34	6.58
27	6.62	6.52	6.26	6.46	6.95	7.1
28	7.99	7.93	7.65	7.39	6.46	5.85
29	5.2	5.56	5.54	4.45	3.83	3.75
30	3.57	3.19	2.86	2.17	1.86	1.78

Source: Economic Time Series Page, www.economagic.com.

7. Construct a run chart for the 180 values. Does there appear to be a pattern suggesting that the process is not within statistical control?
8. Complete the table as needed, then construct an R chart and determine whether the process variation is within statistical control. If it is not, identify which of the three out-of-control criteria lead to rejection of statistically stable variation.

9. Complete the table as needed, then construct an $\bar{x}$ chart and determine whether the process mean is within statistical control. If the process mean is unstable, this suggests that the results of monetary policy are not consistent. Based on your analysis, does the Bank of Canada have reason to be concerned?

In Exercises 10–12, use the following information:

The Medassist Pharmaceutical Supply Company provides drugstores with bulk packages of phenobarbital, all labelled as containing 2.2 kg. Each day, a sample of five packages is randomly selected and weighed. The results for 20 consecutive days are given in the table.

Weight (in kilograms) of Phenobarbital

Sample	Weight (kg)					Mean	Range
1	2.26	2.28	2.26	2.21	2.26	2.254	0.07
2	2.29	2.28	2.28	2.28	2.28	2.282	0.01
3	2.25	2.22	2.29	2.28	2.26	2.260	0.07
4	2.29	2.25	2.25	2.25	2.25	2.258	0.04
5	2.29	2.25	2.25	2.27	2.26	2.264	0.04
6	2.27	2.24	2.25	2.25	2.28	2.258	0.04
7	2.26	2.27	2.30	2.27	2.28	2.276	0.04
8	2.25	2.24	2.27	2.28	2.29	2.266	0.05
9	2.23	2.24	2.25	2.23	2.26	2.242	0.03
10	2.25	2.25	2.28	2.26	2.30	2.268	0.05
11	2.25	2.30	2.29	2.27	2.24	2.270	0.06
12	2.19	2.01	2.24	2.37	2.60	2.282	0.59
13	2.23	2.35	2.13	2.28	2.23	2.244	0.22
14	2.44	2.17	2.31	2.20	2.60	2.344	0.43
15	2.35	2.17	2.70	2.28	2.52	2.404	0.53
16	2.12	2.20	2.79	2.20	2.40	2.342	0.67
17	2.07	2.54	2.28	2.18	2.18	2.250	0.47
18	2.51	2.36	2.39	2.23	2.45	2.388	0.28
19	2.70	2.49	2.38	2.37	2.06	2.400	0.64
20	2.44	2.40	2.68	2.41	2.31	2.448	0.37

10. Construct a run chart for the 100 values. Is there a pattern indicating that the process is not statistically stable?

11. Construct an R chart and determine whether the process variation is within statistical control. If it is not, identify which of the three out-of-control criteria lead to rejection of statistically stable variation.

12. Construct an $\bar{x}$ chart and determine whether the process mean is within statistical control. If it is not, identify a consequence of not correcting the process to make it statistically stable.

12–2 Exercises B: Beyond the Basics

13. In this section we described control charts for R and $\bar{x}$ based on ranges. Control charts for monitoring variation and centre (mean) can also be based on standard deviations. An s *chart* for monitoring variation is made by plotting sample standard deviations with a centre line at $\bar{s}$ (the mean of the sample standard deviations) and control limits at $B_4\bar{s}$ and $B_3\bar{s}$, where B_4 and B_3 are found in Table 12-2. Construct an s chart for the data in Table 12-1. Compare the result to the R chart given in this section.

14. An $\bar{x}$ chart based on standard deviations (instead of ranges) is made by plotting sample means with a centre line at $\bar{\bar{x}}$ and control limits at $\bar{\bar{x}} + A_3\bar{s}$ and $\bar{\bar{x}} - A_3\bar{s}$, where A_3 is found in Table 12-2 and $\bar{s}$ is the mean of the sample standard deviations. Use the data in Table 12-1 to construct an $\bar{x}$ chart based on standard deviations. Compare the result to the $\bar{x}$ chart based on sample ranges (as shown in this section).

12–3 Control Charts for Attributes

In this section we construct a control chart for an attribute, such as the proportion p of defective items. Instead of monitoring *quantitative* data (as in Section 12-2), we now consider *qualitative* data, such as whether an item is defective, or weighs under 16 oz or is nonconforming. (A good or a service is nonconforming if it doesn't meet specifications or requirements. Nonconforming goods are sometimes discarded, repaired, or called "seconds" and sold at reduced prices.) As in Section 12-2, we select samples of size n at regular time intervals and plot points in a sequential graph with a centre line and control limits. (There are ways to deal with samples of different sizes, but we don't consider them here.) The **control chart for p** (or p **chart**) is a control chart used to monitor the proportion p; the relevant notation and control chart values are as shown below (where the attribute of "defective" can be replaced by any other relevant attribute).

We use $\bar{p}$ for the centre line because it is the best estimate of the proportion of defects from the process. The expressions for the control limits correspond to 3 standard deviations away from the centre line. (In Section 6-4 we noted that the standard deviation of sample proportions is $\sqrt{pq/n}$, and this is expressed in the control limits shown in the box.)

Notation
$\bar{p}$ = pooled estimate of the proportion of defective items in the process
$= \dfrac{\text{total number of defects found among all items sampled}}{\text{total number of items sampled}}$
$\bar{q}$ = pooled estimate of the proportion of process items that are *not* defective
$= 1 - \bar{p}$
n = size of each sample (not the number of samples)

AMP, Inc.

AMP, Inc., makes electrical connectors. In 1983 it instituted a quality improvement plan that so far has resulted in savings of about $75 million. While some companies continue to use a system of management decree by higher-level supervisors, AMP and many other successful companies are committed to the total involvement of employees. One aspect of this total involvement is that each of the more than 10,000 AMP employees receives training in statistical procedures related to control of processes.

Control Chart for p

Centre line: $\bar{p}$

Upper control limit: $\bar{p} + 3\sqrt{\dfrac{\bar{p}\,\bar{q}}{n}}$

Lower control limit: $\bar{p} - 3\sqrt{\dfrac{\bar{p}\,\bar{q}}{n}}$

(If the calculation for the lower control limit results in a negative value, use 0 instead. If the calculation for the upper control limit exceeds 1, use 1 instead.)

• **EXAMPLE**   An aircraft plant fabricates assemblies for commercial jet airliners. Each shipment is inspected for up to thirteen types of defect, such as rivets not seating properly, gaps between panels and supports, and uneven surfaces. Suppose that for each shipment, 200 rivets are inspected for proper seating. Construct a control chart for p given the following numbers of rivets that are not seated properly for 20 successive inspections. Determine whether the process of seating those rivets is within statistical control. If not, identify which of the three out-of-control criteria apply.

Improperly seated rivets:

5 3 3 4 3 3 2 0 0 0 0 2 0 0 2 1 2 2 2 1

SOLUTION   The centre line for our control chart is located by the value of $\bar{p}$:

$$\bar{p} = \frac{\text{total number of defectively seated rivets from all samples combined}}{\text{total number of rivets sampled}}$$

$$= \frac{5 + 3 + 3 + \cdots + 1}{20 \times 200} = \frac{35}{4000} = 0.00875$$

Because $\bar{p} = 0.00875$, it follows that $\bar{q} = 1 - \bar{p} = 0.99125$. Using $\bar{p} = 0.00875$, $\bar{q} = 0.99125$, and $n = 200$, we find the control limits as follows:

Upper control limit:

$$\bar{p} + 3\sqrt{\frac{\bar{p}\,\bar{q}}{n}} = 0.00875 + 3\sqrt{\frac{(0.00875)(0.99125)}{200}} = 0.02851$$

Lower control limit:

$$\bar{p} - 3 \sqrt{\frac{\bar{p}\,\bar{q}}{n}} = 0.00875 - 3 \sqrt{\frac{(0.00875)(0.99125)}{200}} = -0.01101$$
(Use 0.)

Having found the values for the centre line and control limits, we can proceed to plot the proportion of defectively seated rivets in each sample. The Excel control chart for p is shown in the accompanying display.

Interpretation   We can interpret the control chart for p by considering the same three out-of-control criteria listed in Section 12-2. Using those criteria, we conclude that this process is not out of statistical control. There is no clear trend or cyclical pattern, none of the points is beyond the control limits, and there are not eight consecutive points above or below the centre line (Run of 8 Rule). Based on these data, the fabrication process can continue without adjustments.

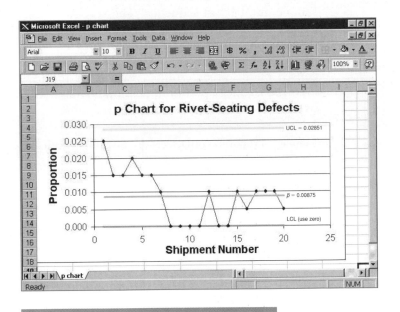

Excel Display p Chart for Rivet-Seating Defects

A variation of the control chart for p is the **np chart** in which the *actual numbers* of defects are plotted instead of the *proportions* of defects. The np chart will have a centre line value of $n\bar{p}$, and the control limits will have values of $n\bar{p} + 3\sqrt{n\bar{p}\,\bar{q}}$ and $n\bar{p} - 3\sqrt{n\bar{p}\,\bar{q}}$. The p chart and the np chart differ only in the scale of values used for the vertical axis.

Motorola and the Six-Sigma (σ) Quality Standard

From the 1950s to the 1970s, manufacturers sought to make 99.8% of their components good, with only 0.2% defective. This rate corresponds to a "three-sigma" level of tolerance. This would seem to be a high level of quality, but Motorola recognized that when many such components are *combined*, the chance of getting a defective product is quite high. The company sought to reduce the variation in all processes by one-half. This standard became known as the "six-sigma" program. A six-sigma level corresponds to about two defects per *billion* items. Motorola found that it could achieve this level with many components and processes. The extra cost was more than offset by reduced costs of repair, scrap, and warranty work.

Using Technology

Excel:

Using the **Data Desk XL** *add-in:* First enter the numbers of defects or successes in an Excel column, and the corresponding sample sizes in a neighbouring column. (For the example in this section, the first four items would be entered in a spreadsheet as shown in the margin.)

5	20
3	20
3	20
4	20

Click on **DDXL** and select **Process Control**, then select **Summ Prop Control Chart** (for summary proportions control chart). A dialog box should appear. Click on the pencil icon for "Success Variable" and enter the range of values containing numbers of successes. Then click on the pencil icon for "Totals Variable" and enter the range of values containing sample sizes. Click **OK**. Next, click on the **Open Control Chart** bar and the control chart will be displayed.

Using Excel's Chart Wizard: First, organize the data into a single data block, as shown below. The left column lists the sample numbers in sequence. The second column contains the proportion, p, of defects for each sample. (Depending on the form of your raw data, those p values may need to be calculated using an Excel formula.) The next three columns consist of the predetermined values for the lower control limit (LCL), mean p, and upper control limit (UCL), respectively—all of these repeated down the table.

Sample	Proportion of Defects	LCL	Mean p	UCL
1	0.025	0	0.00875	0.0285
2	0.015	0	0.00875	0.0285
3	0.015	0	0.00875	0.0285
4	0.020	0	0.00875	0.0285
5	0.015	0	0.00875	0.0285
6	0.015	0	0.00875	0.0285
.	.	.	.	.
.	.	.	.	.
.	.	.	.	.

To draw the chart, click on the **Chart Wizard** icon on the main toolbar. In Step 1, select **XY (Scatter)** and, for **Chart sub-type**, select the option illustrated by points connected with straight lines. In Step 2, enter the **Data Range** for the whole block of data, and indicate whether the data are in rows or columns. Continue to select **Next**, then **Finish**. The graph can be edited, as desired, to add a legend or labels, delete grid lines, change thickness for the control lines, and so on.

12–3 Exercises A: Basic Skills and Concepts

In Exercises 1–4, examine the given control chart for p and determine whether the process is within statistical control. If it is not, identify which of the three out-of-control criteria apply.

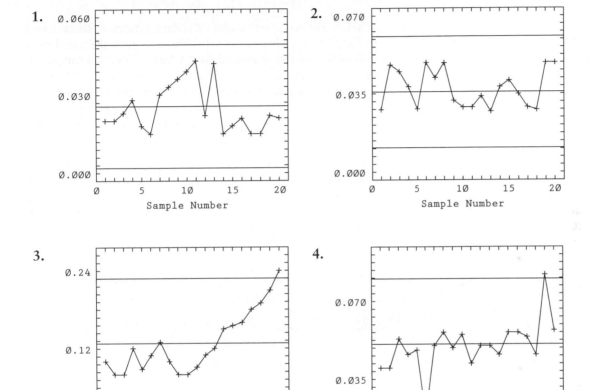

In Exercises 5–8, use the given process data to construct a control chart for p. In each case, use the three out-of-control criteria listed in Section 12-2 and determine whether the process is within statistical control. If it is not, identify which of the three out-of-control criteria apply.

5. An aircraft plant fabricates assemblies for commercial jet airliners. Each shipment is inspected for up to thirteen types of defect, including a "centre fall out" defect for a certain part. Suppose that for each shipment, 350 parts that can have that defect are inspected. Below are the numbers of this defect found in each of 26 inspections. Construct a control chart for *p* for the "centre fall out" defect. Do the results suggest a problem that should be corrected?

$$4\ 0\ 1\ 2\ 2\ 1\ 0\ 0\ 5\ 0\ 0\ 0\ 0$$
$$0\ 0\ 0\ 0\ 0\ 0\ 1\ 0\ 0\ 2\ 4\ 3\ 6$$

6. For each of five successive two-year periods, 3500 newborn babies are sampled. Shown below are the numbers of babies, in each of those samples, whose parents had never lived together before the birth (based on data from Statistics Canada). Do the data suggest that, relative to older norms, parenting patterns are out of statistical control (in other words, are social patterns changing)?

95   105   112   144   172

7. A labour researcher examines the raw data that are summarized in Data Set 20 in Appendix B. For each year from 1976 to 1999, she randomly selects records for 1000 of the person-days of labour lost due to work stoppages in transportation industries. The accompanying table shows how many of each year's sample of person-days lost were in the air transportation industry. Do the data represent a statistically stable process? What are the apparent implications for companies which rely on air transportation when shipping their finished products?

125   139   269   53   74   308   243   496   39   829   558   357
 46   4   11   110   827   252   38   14   12   731   384   146

8. Each year hundreds of thousands of hectares of Canadian forests are sprayed with insecticides. One such product is *Bacillus thuringiensis* (B.t.). An ecologist sampled 10000 hectares of Canadian forest in each of the years 1988 to 1998, inclusive. The accompanying table shows the number of hectares in each sample which were located in Newfoundland. Do the data represent a statistically stable process? Is there any factor which could drive this process out of control?

513   137   154   0   469   950   1123   1964   3203   589   361

12-3 Exercises B: Beyond the Basics

9. Construct the np chart for the example given in this section. Compare the result with the control chart for p given in this section.

10. a. Identify the locations of the centre line and control limits for a p chart representing a process that has been having a 5% rate of nonconforming items, based on samples of size 100.

b. Repeat part (a) after changing the sample size to 300.

c. Compare the two sets of results. What are an advantage and a disadvantage of using the larger sample size? Which chart would be better in detecting a shift from 5% to 10%?

Vocabulary List

process data	lower control limit
run chart	upper control limit
statistically stable	R chart
within statistical control	range chart
random variation	$\bar{x}$ chart
assignable variation	p chart
control chart	np chart
centre line	

Review

Whereas earlier chapters focused on the important data characteristics of centre, variation, distribution, and outliers, this chapter focused on pattern over time. Process data were defined to be data arranged according to some time sequence, and such data can be analysed with run charts and control charts. Control charts have a centre line, an upper control limit, and a lower control limit. A process is statistically stable (or within statistical control) if it has only natural variation with no patterns, cycles, or unusual points. Decisions about statistical stability are based on how a process is actually behaving, not how we might like it to behave because of such factors as manufacturer specifications. The following graphs were described:

- *Run chart*: a sequential plot of *individual* data values over time.

- *R chart*: a control chart that uses ranges in an attempt to monitor the *variation* in a process.

- *x̄ chart*: a control chart used to determine whether the process *mean* is within statistical control.

- *p chart*: a control chart used to monitor the proportion of some process *attribute*, such as whether items are defective.

Review Exercises

In Exercises 1–3, use the following information:

The Conestoga Chemical Company supplies epoxy cement hardener in containers that are designed to hold 142 mL of the liquid. Too much or too little of the hardener results in a mixture with little strength. Each hour, a sample of 5 containers of hardener is carefully measured; the table shows the results for 20 consecutive hours of operation.

Amounts of Epoxy Cement Hardener

Sample	Amount (mL)					Mean	Range
1	140.58	142.28	142.00	140.58	138.31	140.750	3.97
2	139.16	140.86	138.88	142.00	142.00	140.580	3.12
3	143.14	142.28	143.42	143.14	144.27	143.250	1.99
4	138.88	140.86	142.00	142.85	142.85	141.488	3.97
5	143.14	139.16	142.57	143.14	143.14	142.230	3.98
6	142.00	142.85	141.15	143.14	138.31	141.490	4.83
7	141.72	142.28	144.84	143.70	142.00	142.908	3.12
8	140.58	142.57	139.73	142.28	141.72	141.376	2.84
9	142.28	143.42	143.99	143.70	140.58	142.794	3.41
10	140.86	142.28	142.85	140.30	141.43	141.544	2.55
11	143.70	143.99	143.42	142.28	143.14	143.306	1.71
12	145.69	140.30	141.15	143.42	141.43	142.398	5.39
13	142.28	142.57	145.41	141.15	142.85	142.852	4.26
14	140.86	140.58	141.43	140.86	138.02	140.350	3.41
15	143.14	142.57	143.42	142.28	143.42	142.966	1.14
16	143.14	141.43	143.70	140.30	141.43	142.000	3.40
17	142.00	142.85	141.15	140.86	142.00	141.772	1.99
18	142.57	141.15	139.16	141.43	143.99	141.660	4.83
19	140.58	143.70	145.69	138.59	142.85	142.282	7.10
20	136.60	138.02	137.74	137.74	140.01	138.022	3.41

1. Construct a run chart for the 100 values. Does there appear to be a pattern suggesting that the process is not within statistical control?
2. Construct an R chart and determine whether the process variation is within statistical control. If it is not, identify which of the three out-of-control criteria lead to rejection of statistically stable variation.
3. Construct an $\bar{x}$ chart and determine whether the process mean is within statistical control. Does this process appear to be working well, or does it require correction?
4. The Joliette Cosmetics Company manufactures lipstick tubes that dispense (you guessed it) lipstick. Each day, 200 tubes are randomly selected and tested for defects. The results are given below for 20 consecutive days. Construct a control chart for p (proportion of defects), then determine whether the process is within statistical control. If not, identify which criteria lead to rejection of statistical stability.

4 2 3 6 1 4 3 0 5 5 2 1 9 3 4 1 0 2 6 3

• •

Cumulative Review Exercises

1. The Telektronic Company produces 20-amp fuses used to protect car radios from too much electrical power. Each day 400 fuses are randomly selected and tested; the results (numbers of defects per 400 fuses tested) for 20 consecutive days are as follows:

   10 8 7 6 6 9 12 5 4 7 9 6 11 4 6 5 10 5 9 11

   a. Use a control chart for p to verify that the process is within statistical control, so the data can be treated as coming from a population with fixed variation and mean.
   b. Using all of the data combined, construct a 95% confidence interval for the proportion of defects.
   c. Using a 0.05 significance level, test the claim that the rate of defects is 1% or less.

2. When interpreting control charts, one of the three out-of-control criteria is based on 8 consecutive points that are all above or all below the centre line. For a statistically stable process, there is a 0.5 probability that a point will be above the centre line and there is a 0.5 probability that a point will be below the centre line. In each of the following, assume that sample values are independent and the process is statistically stable.
   a. Find the probability that when 8 consecutive points are randomly selected, they are all above the centre line.
   b. Find the probability that when 8 consecutive points are randomly selected, they are all below the centre line.
   c. Find the probability that when 8 consecutive points are randomly selected, they are all above or all below the centre line.

3. The accompanying table is based on three-month (i.e., quarterly) increases in total consumer credit, over seven and half years (based on data from www.economagic.com). Sets of three successive data values are interpreted as samples. Use appropriate control or run charts to determine whether the data appear to be part of a statistically stable process.

Increases in Total Consumer Credit		
Sample	Quarterly Increase ($billion Canadian)	
1	1.2	1.7	2.3
2	1.9	1.1	1.6
3	1.1	1.9	2.8
4	2.1	2.2	2.1
5	3.1	2.8	2.5
6	2	2.3	2.9
7	2.7	3.2	1.3
8	0.6	1	0.4
9	0.9	0.3	-0.1
10	-0.4	0.4	0.3

4. Refer to the data below for quarterly increases in total consumer and business credit in Canada (based on data from www.economagic.com.

   a. Is there a significant linear correlation between the sizes of quarterly increases in total consumer and business credit? Explain.

   b. Identify the linear regression equation that relates increases in consumer credit (x) and business credit (y).

   c. What is the best predicted increase in business credit for a quarter when consumer credit has increased by $2.4 billion?

Quarter	Increase in Consumer Credit	Increase in Business Credit
1	1.2	5.0
2	1.7	7.8
3	2.3	6.0
4	1.9	6.3
5	1.1	8.0
6	1.6	5.2
7	1.1	7.3
8	1.9	5.5
9	2.8	7.4
10	2.1	11.2
11	2.2	9.6
12	2.1	7.3
13	3.1	8.1
14	2.8	9.7
15	2.5	11.5
16	2.0	9.1
17	2.3	11.2
18	2.9	12.4
19	2.7	13.2
20	3.2	10.2
21	1.3	9.9
22	0.6	7.9
23	1.0	1.9
24	0.4	3.7
25	0.9	2.0
26	0.3	4.9
27	-0.1	2.4
28	-0.4	2.8
29	0.4	1.1
30	0.3	1.3
31	0.0	2.2

Technology Project

a. Simulate 20 days of manufacturing heart pacemakers with a 1% rate of defective units, assuming that 200 pacemakers are sampled each day. If you are using Excel, select **Data Analysis** from the **Tools** menu, then select **Random Number Generation**. Enter 20 for the **Number of Variables** and 200 for the **Number of Random Numbers**. (Each column of output will represent the sample data for one day.) For **Distribution**, select **Bernoulli** from the pull-down list. For **p Value**, enter the simulated probability that any given unit is defective, which in this example is 0.01. It is usual to enter 0 for the **Random Seed**. (If you enter a different seed number, then you can reproduce the same simulated sample by choosing the same seed number later.) Now select an output option and click on **OK** to obtain the results. Consider a "1" in the output set to be the occurrence of a defective pacemaker, whereas a "0" represents an acceptable pacemaker.

If you are using STATDISK, select **Data** from the main menu bar, then select **Uniform Generator** and proceed to generate 200 scores with a minimum of 1 and a maximum of 100. Display the ranked data by using the **Format** menu in **Sample Editor**. Consider an outcome beginning with 1 to be defective and all other outcomes to be acceptable. Repeat this procedure until results for 20 days have been simulated.

b. Construct a p chart for the proportion of defective pacemakers, and determine whether the process is within statistical control. Since we know the process is actually stable with $p = 0.01$, the conclusion that it is not stable would be a type I error; that is, we would have a false positive signal, causing us to believe that the process needed to be adjusted when in fact it should be left alone.

c. The result from part (a) is a simulation of 20 days. Now simulate another 10 days of manufacturing pacemakers, but modify these last 10 days so that the nonconforming rate is 3% instead of 1%. (Modify the preceding Excel and STATDISK commands for the change from 1% to 3%.)

d. Combine the data generated from parts (a) and (c) to represent a total of 30 days of sample results. Construct a p chart for this combined data set. Is the process out of control? If we concluded that the process was not out of control, we would be making a type II error; that is, we would believe that the process was okay when in fact it should be repaired or adjusted to correct the shift to the 3% nonconforming rate.

•••••••• FROM DATA TO DECISION ••••••••

Is the Process of Manufacturing Cans Proceeding as It Should?

The Chapter Problem listed process data from a company that manufactures 0.0109-in. thick aluminum cans for a major beverage supplier, and those data were analysed in Section 12-2. Refer to Data Set 15 in Appendix B and conduct an analysis of the process data for the cans that are 0.0111 in. thick. The values in the data set are the measured axial loads of cans. The top lids are pressed into place with pressures that vary between 158 lb and 165 lb.

Should you take any corrective action? Write a report summarizing your conclusions.

Address not only the issue of statistical stability, but also the ability of the cans to withstand the pressures applied when the top lids are pressed into place. Also compare the behaviour of the 0.0111-in. cans to the behaviour of the 0.0109-in. cans and recommend which thickness should be used.

•••••••• COOPERATIVE GROUP ACTIVITIES ••••••••

1. *Out-of-class activity:* Collect your own set of process data and analyse them using the methods of this section. It would be ideal to collect data from a real manufacturing process, but that is usually difficult to implement. Instead, consider using a simulation or referring to published data, such as those found in an almanac. Here are some suggestions:

   • Shoot 5 crumpled sheets of paper into a wastebasket and record the number of shots made, then repeat this procedure 20 times and use a *p* chart to test for statistical stability in the proportion of shots made.

   • Select 5 candies from a bag of M&Ms and record the number that are brown. Repeat this procedure 20 times and pretend that the 20 samples were selected on 20 consecutive days of production. Use a *p* chart to test for statistical stability of the proportion of brown M&Ms.

   • Through the job-placement department at your college or university, you can find the annual placement rates for graduates with your major. If these are expressed in the form *rate*%, then assume that each year 100 students with your major are sampled, and that the *rate* represents the number of such students who were placed in a given year. Use a *p* chart to test the statistical stability of the placement rate over several years. (Other possible rates: placement rates within the area trained for; placement rates for graduates with different areas of specialization; rates of graduates going on to attain further education.)

   Obtain a printed copy of the computer results, and write a report summarizing your conclusions.

2. *In-class activity:* If the instructor can distribute the numbers of absences for each class meeting, groups of three or four students can analyse them and make recommendations based on the conclusions.

INTERNET PROJECT

Control Charts

This chapter introduced different charting techniques for summarizing and analyzing process data. The run chart is based on individual values, but the others are based on summary statistics. The R chart is constructed from sample ranges, the $\bar{x}$ chart is based on sample means, and the p chart is based on sample proportions. Except for the run chart, we do not need the original sample data; we need only the statistics that summarize each sample for determining whether the process is within statistical control.

Go to the Web site for this book, located at:

http://www.pearsoned.ca/triola

Click on Internet Project, then on Chapter 12. There you will be directed to several data sets to be used for constructing appropriate control charts. From your charts you will be asked to interpret and discuss trends in the underlying process.

13

Nonparametric Statistics

CHAPTER PROBLEM:

Do short and long Parliaments occur in a nonrandom pattern?

Of the first 35 Parliaments since Confederation, most lasted for more than three years (typically four to five years). Yet nearly a quarter of the Parliaments (8 of them) were relatively brief, lasting only one or two years. Is there any evidence that the short and long Parliaments occur in a nonrandom pattern? If there is, would you want to run for an election if you knew a brief session was coming up next? Or, in fact, does the alternation between Parliament lengths appear to be random?

The sequence of typical-length Parliaments (T) and brief Parliaments (B) is listed in Figure 13-1. (The sequence is read from left to right, continuing on the next row.) In Section 13-7 we will consider a test for determining whether such a sequence is random.

Figure 13-1 Length of Parliaments in Session

```
T B T T T T T T T B T T T B T T T
T T T B T B T B T B T B T T T T
```

(13-1) Overview

The methods of inferential statistics presented in Chapters 6, 7, 8, 9, and 11 are called *parametric methods* because they are based on sampling from a population with specific parameters, such as the mean μ, standard deviation σ, or proportion p. Those parametric methods usually must conform to some fairly strict conditions, such as a requirement that the sample data come from a normally distributed population. In this chapter we introduce nonparametric methods, which do not have such strict requirements.

DEFINITIONS

Parametric tests require assumptions about the nature or shape of the populations involved; **nonparametric tests** do not require such assumptions. Consequently, nonparametric tests of hypotheses are often called **distribution-free tests**.

Although the term *nonparametric* strongly suggests that the test is not based on a parameter, there are some nonparametric tests that do depend on a parameter such as the median, but they don't require a particular distribution. Although *distribution-free* is a more accurate description, the term *nonparametric* is more commonly used. The following are major advantages and disadvantages of nonparametric methods.

Advantages of Nonparametric Methods

1. Nonparametric methods can be applied to a wide variety of situations because they do not have the more rigid requirements associated with parametric methods. In particular, nonparametric methods do not require normally distributed populations.

2. Unlike parametric methods, nonparametric methods can often be applied to nonnumerical data, such as the genders of survey respondents.

3. Nonparametric methods usually involve simpler computations than the corresponding parametric methods and are therefore easier to understand and apply.

Disadvantages of Nonparametric Methods

1. Nonparametric methods may appear to waste information in cases where exact numerical data are converted to a qualitative form. For example, in the nonparametric sign test (described in Section 13-2), weight losses by dieters are recorded simply as negative signs; the actual magnitudes of the weight losses are ignored.

2. Nonparametric tests are not as efficient as parametric tests, so with a nonparametric test we generally need stronger evidence (such as a larger sample or greater differences) before we reject a null hypothesis.

			Efficiency of Nonparametric Test with Normal Population
Application	Parametric Test	Nonparametric Test	
Matched pairs of sample data	*t* test or *z* test	Sign test	0.63
		Wilcoxon signed-ranks test	0.95
Two independent samples	*t* test or *z* test	Wilcoxon rank-sum test	0.95
Several independent samples	Analysis of variance (*F* test)	Kruskal-Wallis test	0.95
Correlation	Linear correlation	Rank correlation test	0.91
Randomness	No parametric test	Runs test	No basis for comparison

TABLE 13-1   Comparison of Parametric and Nonparametric Tests

When the requirements of population distributions are satisfied, nonparametric tests are generally less efficient than their parametric counterparts, but the reduced efficiency can be compensated for by an increased sample size. For example, Section 13-6 will deal with a concept called *rank correlation,* which has an efficiency rating of 0.91 when compared to the linear correlation presented in Chapter 9. This means that all other things being equal, nonparametric rank correlation requires 100 sample observations to achieve the same results as 91 sample observations analysed through parametric linear correlation, assuming the stricter requirements for using the parametric method are met.

Table 13-1 lists the nonparametric methods covered in this chapter, along with the corresponding parametric approach and **efficiency** rating. Table 13-1 shows that several nonparametric tests have efficiency ratings above 0.90, so the lower efficiency might not be a critical factor in choosing between parametric or nonparametric methods. More important is that we avoid using the parametric tests when their required assumptions are not satisfied.

Ranks

Sections 13-3 through 13-6 use methods based on ranks. First, we look briefly at the nature of ranks.

DEFINITION

Data are *sorted* when they are arranged according to some criterion, such as smallest to largest or best to worst. A **rank** is a number assigned to an individual sample item according to its order in the sorted list. The first item is assigned a rank of 1, the second item is assigned a rank of 2, and so on.

EXAMPLE   The numbers 5, 3, 40, 10, and 12 can be arranged from lowest to highest as 3, 5, 10, 12, and 40, and these numbers have ranks of 1, 2, 3, 4, and 5, respectively:

| 5 | 3 | 40 | 10 | 12 | Original values |
| 3 | 5 | 10 | 12 | 40 | Values arranged in order |

↑   ↑   ↑   ↑   ↑

| 1 | 2 | 3 | 4 | 5 | Ranks |

Handling ties in ranks: If a tie in ranks occurs, the usual procedure is to find the mean of the ranks involved and then assign this mean rank to each of the tied items, as in the following example.

EXAMPLE   The numbers 3, 5, 5, 10, and 12 are given ranks of 1, 2.5, 2.5, 4, and 5, respectively. In this case, ranks 2 and 3 were tied, so we found the mean of 2 and 3 (which is 2.5) and assigned it to the values that created the tie:

| 3 | 5 | 5 | 10 | 12 | Original values |

↑   ↑   ↑   ↑   ↑

| 1 | 2.5 | 2.5 | 4 | 5 | Ranks |

↑_____↑

2 and 3 are tied

(13-2) Sign Test

In this section we introduce the *sign test* procedure, which is among the easiest for nonparametric tests.

> **DEFINITION**
>
> The **sign test** is a nonparametric (distribution-free) test that uses plus and minus signs to test different claims, including:
>
> 1. Claims involving matched pairs of sample data
> 2. Claims involving nominal data
> 3. Claims about the median of a single population

Assumptions

1. The sample data have been randomly selected.
2. There is no requirement that the sample data come from a population with a particular distribution, such as a normal distribution.

Basic Concept of the Sign Test: To prepare for the sign test, we convert the raw data into plus and minus signs. Then we test whether the frequencies of these plus and minus signs are significantly different. Figure 13-2 summarizes the sign test procedure, which will be illustrated with examples in this section.

For consistency and ease, we will stipulate the following notation.

Notation for the Sign Test

x = the test statistic representing the number of times the *less frequent* sign occurs

n = the total number of positive and negative signs combined

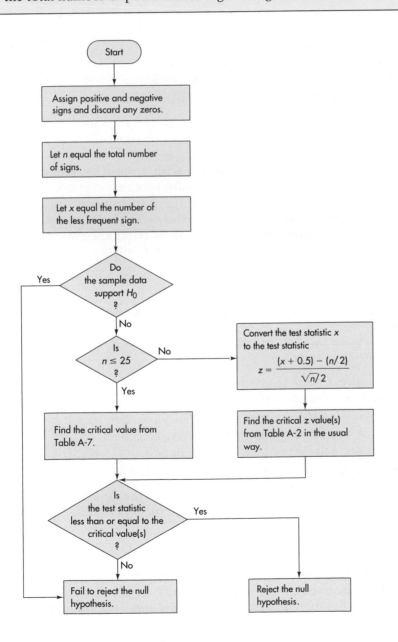

Figure 13-2   Sign Test Procedure

> **Test Statistic for the Sign Test**
>
> For $n \leq 25$: Use x (the number of times the less frequent sign occurs)
>
> For $n > 25$: Use $$z = \frac{(x + 0.5) - \left(\dfrac{n}{2}\right)}{\dfrac{\sqrt{n}}{2}}$$
>
> (based on a normal approximation)

Critical Values

1. For $n \leq 25$: Find critical x values in Table A-7.
2. For $n > 25$: Find the left critical z value in Table A-2.

Caution: When applying the sign test in a one-tailed test, be very careful to avoid making the wrong conclusion when one sign occurs significantly more often than the other, but the sample data are *consistent with* the null hypothesis. If the sense of the data is consistent with (instead of conflicting with) the null hypothesis, then fail to reject the null hypothesis and don't proceed with the sign test. Figure 13-2 summarizes the procedure for the sign test and includes this check: Do the sample data "support" (in the sense of being consistent with) H_0? If the answer is yes, fail to reject the null hypothesis. *It is always important to think about the data and to avoid relying on blind calculations or computer results.*

Claims Involving Matched Pairs of Sample Data

When using the sign test with data that are matched by pairs, we convert the raw data to plus and minus signs as follows:

1. We subtract each value of the second variable from the corresponding value of the first variable.
2. We record only the sign of the difference found in Step 1. We *exclude ties*: That is, we exclude from further analysis any matched pairs in which both values are equal. (For other ways to handle ties, see Exercise 14.)

   The key concept underlying the sign test is this:

   If the two sets of data have equal medians, the number of positive signs should be approximately equal to the number of negative signs.

EXAMPLE   Table 13-2 consists of sample data obtained when 14 subjects are tested for reaction times with their left and right hands. (Only right-handed subjects were used.) Use a 0.05 significance level to test the claim of no difference between the right- and left-hand reaction times.

TABLE 13-2	Reaction Times (in thousandths of a second) of 14 Subjects													
Right hand	191	97	116	165	116	129	171	155	112	102	188	158	121	133
Left hand	224	171	191	207	196	165	177	165	140	188	155	219	177	174
Sign of difference (right hand − left hand)	−	−	−	−	−	−	−	−	−	−	+	−	−	−

SOLUTION   Here's the basic idea: If people generally have the same reaction times with their right and left hands, the numbers of positive and negative signs should be approximately equal—but in Table 13-2 we have 13 negative signs and 1 positive sign. Are the numbers of positive and negative signs approximately equal, or are they significantly different? We follow the same basic steps for testing hypotheses as outlined in Figure 7-4.

Steps 1, 2, 3:   The null hypothesis is the claim of no difference between the right- and left-hand reaction times, and the alternative hypothesis is the claim that there is a difference.

H_0:   There is no difference.
    (The median of the differences is equal to 0.)
H_1:   There is a difference.
    (The median of the differences is not equal to 0.)

Step 4:   The significance level is $\alpha = 0.05$.
Step 5:   We are using the nonparametric sign test.
Step 6:   The test statistic x is the number of times the less frequent sign occurs. Table 13-2 includes differences with 13 negative signs and 1 positive sign. We let x equal the smaller of 13 and 1, so $x = 1$. Also, $n = 14$ (the total number of positive and negative signs combined). Our test is two-tailed with $\alpha = 0.05$, and reference to Table A-7 shows that the critical value is 2. (See Figure 13-2.)
Step 7:   With a test statistic of $x = 1$ and a critical value of 2, we reject the null hypothesis of no difference. (See Note 2 included with Table A-7: "Reject the null hypothesis if the number of the less frequent sign (x) is less than or equal to the value in the table." Because $x = 1$ is less than or equal to 2, we reject the null hypothesis.)

Interpretation   There is sufficient evidence to warrant rejection of the claim that the median of the differences is equal to 0; that is, there is sufficient evidence to warrant rejection of the claim that there is no difference between the right- and left-hand reaction times. This is the same conclusion reached in Section 8-2 where we used a parametric t test, but sign test results do not always agree with parametric test results.

Product Testing

The United States Testing Company in Hoboken, New Jersey, is the world's largest independent product-testing laboratory. It's often hired to verify advertising claims. A vice president has said that the most difficult part of his job is "telling a client when his product stinks. But if we didn't do that, we'd have no credibility." He says that there have been a few clients who wanted positive results fabricated, but most want honest results. The United States Testing Company evaluates laundry detergents, cosmetics, insulation materials, zippers, pantyhose, football helmets, toothpastes, fertilizers, and a wide variety of other products.

Claims Involving Nominal Data

Recall that nominal data consist of names, labels, or categories only. Although such a nominal data set limits the calculations that are possible, we can identify the *proportion* of the sample data that belong to a particular category, and we can test claims about the corresponding population proportion *p*. The following example uses nominal data consisting of genders (male/female). The sign test is used by representing women with + signs and men with − signs. (Those signs are chosen arbitrarily, honest.) Also note the procedure for handling cases in which $n > 25$.

EXAMPLE   The Gagné and Turner Advertising Company claims that its hiring practices are fair: "We do not discriminate on the basis of gender, and the fact that 40 of the last 50 new employees are men is just a fluke." The company acknowledges that applicants are about half men and half women, and all have met the basic job-qualification standards. Test the null hypothesis that men and women are hired equally by this company. Use a significance level of 0.05.

SOLUTION   Let *p* denote the population proportion of hired men. The claim of no discrimination implies that the proportions of hired men and women are both equal to 0.5, so that $p = 0.5$. The null and alternative hypotheses can therefore be stated as follows.

H_0: $p = 0.5$ (The proportion of hired men is equal to 0.5.)
H_1: $p \neq 0.5$

Denoting hired women by + and hired men by −, we have 10 positive signs and 40 negative signs. Refer now to the flowchart in Figure 13-2. The test statistic *x* is the smaller of 10 and 40, so $x = 10$. This test involves two tails because a disproportionately low number of either gender will cause us to reject the claim of equality. The sample data are not consistent with the null hypothesis because 10 and 40 are not precisely equal. Continuing with the procedure in Figure 13-2, we note that the value of $n = 50$ is above 25, so the test statistic *x* is converted (using a correction for continuity) to the test statistic *z* as follows:

$$z = \frac{(x + 0.5) - \left(\frac{n}{2}\right)}{\frac{\sqrt{n}}{2}}$$

$$= \frac{(10 + 0.5) - \left(\frac{50}{2}\right)}{\frac{\sqrt{50}}{2}} = -4.10$$

With $\alpha = 0.05$ in a two-tailed test, the critical values are $z = \pm 1.96$. The test statistic $z = -4.10$ is less than these critical values (see Figure 13-3), so we reject the null hypothesis of equality.

Interpretation There is sufficient sample evidence to warrant rejection of the claim that the hiring practices are fair. This company is in trouble.

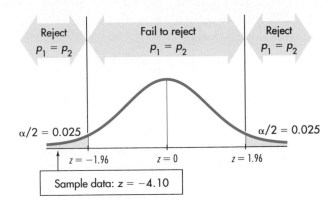

Figure 13-3   Testing the Claim That Hiring Practices Are Fair

Claims About the Median of a Single Population

In the next example, we illustrate how to use the sign test for testing a claim about the median of a single population. Observe that in such applications, the negative and positive signs are based on the claimed value of the median.

EXAMPLE   In Chapter 7 we used sample data to test the claim that the mean body temperature of adults accepted for voluntary surgery is not 37.0°C. With the same data, use the sign test to test the claim that the median is less than 37.0°C. The data set used in Chapter 7 has 108 subjects—94 subjects with temperatures below 37.0°C, 12 subjects with temperatures above 37.0°C, and 2 temperatures equal to 37.0°C.

SOLUTION   The claim that the median is less than 37.0° C is the alternative hypothesis, while the null hypothesis is the claim that the median is at least 37.0° C:

H_0:   Median is at least 37.0° C. (Median $\geq$ 37.0° C)
H_1:   Median is less than 37.0° C. (Median $<$ 37.0° C)

Following the procedure outlined in Figure 13-2, we discard the 2 zeros, we use the negative sign $(-)$ to denote each temperature that is below 37.0° C, and we use the positive sign $(+)$ to denote each temperature that is above 37.0° C. We therefore have 94 negative signs and 12 positive signs, so $n = 106$ and $x = 12$ (the number of the less frequent sign). The sample data thus conflict with the null hypothesis, because fewer than half of the 106 temperatures are at least 37.0° C. We must now proceed to determine whether this conflict is significant. (If the sample data did not conflict with the null hypothesis, we could immediately terminate the test by concluding that we fail to reject the null hypothesis.) The value of n exceeds 25, so we convert the test statistic x to the test statistic z:

$$z = \frac{(x + 0.5) - \left(\frac{n}{2}\right)}{\frac{\sqrt{n}}{2}}$$

$$= \frac{(12 + 0.5) - \left(\frac{106}{2}\right)}{\frac{\sqrt{106}}{2}} = -7.867$$

In this one-tailed test with $\alpha = 0.05$, we use Table A-2 to get the critical z value of -1.645. From Figure 13-4 we can see that the test statistic of $z = -7.867$ does fall within the critical region. We therefore reject the null hypothesis.

Interpretation On the basis of the available sample evidence, we support the claim that the median body temperature of adults accepted for voluntary surgery is less than $37.0°$ C.

Figure 13-4 Testing the Claim That the Median Is Less Than $37.0°$ C

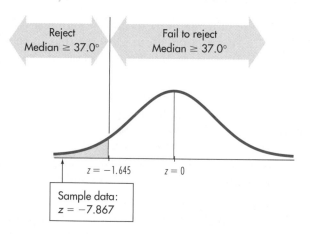

In this sign test of the claim that the median is below $37.0°$ C, we get a test statistic of $z = -7.867$, but a parametric test of the claim that $\mu < 37.0°$ C results in a test statistic of $z = -10.12$. Because -7.867 isn't as extreme as -10.12, we see that the sign test isn't as sensitive as the parametric test. Both tests lead to rejection of the null hypothesis, but the sign test doesn't consider the sample data to be as extreme, partly because the sign test uses only information about the direction of the differences between pairs of data, ignoring the magnitudes of those differences. The next section introduces the Wilcoxon signed-ranks test, which largely overcomes that disadvantage.

Rationale for the Test Statistics Used with the Sign Test

Rationale for the test statistic used when n ≤ 25: The critical values for the sign test, when n ≤ 25, are found in Table A-7 in Appendix A. The entries in Table A-7 were found by using the binomial probability distribution (Section 4-3). The binomial probability distribution applies because the results fall into two categories (positive sign, negative sign) and we have a fixed number of independent cases (or pairs of values).

Rationale for the test statistic used when $n > 25$: Table A-7 applies only for n up to 25, so we need another procedure for finding critical values when $n > 25$. When $n > 25$, the test statistic z is based on a normal approximation to the binomial probability distribution with $p = q = 1/2$. Recall that in Section 5-6 we saw that the normal approximation to the binomial distribution is acceptable when both $np \geq 5$ and $nq \geq 5$. Recall also that in Section 4-4 we saw that $\mu = np$ and $\sigma = \sqrt{npq}$ for binomial experiments. Because this sign test assumes that $p = q = 1/2$, we meet the $np \geq 5$ and $nq \geq 5$ prerequisites whenever $n \geq 10$. Also, with the assumption that $p = q = 1/2$, we get $\mu = np = n/2$ and $\sigma = \sqrt{npq} = \sqrt{n/4} = \sqrt{n}/2$, so

$$z = \frac{x - \mu}{\sigma} \quad \text{becomes} \quad z = \frac{x - \left(\frac{n}{2}\right)}{\frac{\sqrt{n}}{2}}$$

Finally, we replace x by $x + 0.5$ as a correction for continuity. That is, the values of x are discrete, but because we are using a continuous probability distribution, a discrete value such as 10 is actually represented by the interval from 9.5 to 10.5. Because x represents the less frequent sign, we act conservatively by concerning ourselves only with $x + 0.5$; we thus get the test statistic z, as given in the equation and in Figure 13-2.

Using Technology

Excel: You can perform the sign test using the following Excel template.

It relies on the fact that the sign test is really based on binomial probabilities: That is, what is the probability, given n positive or negative differences between paired samples and assuming the null hypothesis of no difference between the samples, of randomly getting x or fewer occurrences of the

	I19		=	
	A	B	C	
1	x	1		
2	n	14		
3	P (one tail)	0.0009155		
4	P (two tails)	0.0018311		
5				
6				

Cell	Formula	Explanation
B3	=BINOMDIST(B1,B2,0.5, TRUE)	Calculate as a binomial test, for specified x and n, and p = 0.5
B4	=2*B3	P-value doubles for a two-tailed test

Use appropriate cell addresses for data.

less frequent sign? For the one-tailed test, the *P*-value is taken directly from the binomial result; for a two-tailed test, it is the binomial result times 2. On your worksheet, type the indicated labels. Enter the values for *x* (the number of times the less frequent sign appears) and *n* (the number of positive and negative signs combined) and the given formulas for the *P*-values. If the displayed *P*-value is less than or equal to the significance level of α, we reject the null hypothesis; otherwise, we fail to reject the null hypothesis.

STATDISK: Select **Analysis** from the main menu bar, then select **Sign Test**. Select the option **Given Number of Signs** if you know the number of plus and minus signs, or select **Given Pairs of Values** if you prefer to enter matched pairs of data. After making the required entries in the dialog box, the displayed results will include the test statistic, critical value, and conclusion.

(13-2) Exercises A: Basic Skills and Concepts

In Exercises 1–12, use the sign test.

1. Do strong El Niño phenomena increase temperatures during springtime? Using the data in the following table, test the claim that the progression of a strong El Niño, from the spring of onset to the next spring, has no effect on Canadian temperature departures from seasonal norms. Use a 0.05 level of significance.

El Niño Cycle	A	B	C	D	E	F	G
Spring of El Niño onset	0.5	0.2	−1.2	−1	0.6	1.3	−0.4
Second spring of El Niño	1.5	0.0	0.9	−0.5	1.0	0.1	3.1

   Based on data from Environment Canada.

2. An environmental study compared the use of motorized vehicles in different countries over time. The accompanying table shows comparative data (in billions of vehicle-kilometers driven) for two countries in selected years. Use a 0.025 significance level to test the claim that there are more vehicle-kilometers driven annually in Japan than in France. What might explain this result?

	A	B	C	D	E	F
Japan	226.0	286.3	389.1	447.0	471.1	520.7
France	208.0	260.7	328.1	328.1	376.0	414.0

   Based on data from www.swishweb.com.

3. The Alumni Association of the University of British Columbia tries to track the whereabouts and careers of UBC graduates. In a sample of 88 graduates known to be living outside of Canada, 51 are living in the United States. At the 0.05 significance level, test the claim that most (more than half) of UBC graduates who live outside of Canada are living in the United States (based on data in *UBC Reports*, May 21, 1998.).

4. A college aptitude test was given to 100 randomly selected high school seniors. After a period of intensive training, a similar test was given to the same students: 59 students received higher grades, 36 received lower grades, and 5 received the same grades. At the 0.05 level of significance, test the claim that the training is effective.

5. The Joliette Manufacturing Company claims that hiring is done without any gender bias. If 18 of the last 25 new employees are women, and job applicants are about half men and half women who are all qualified, is there sufficient evidence to charge gender bias? Use a 0.01 level of significance, because we don't want to make such a serious charge unless there is very strong evidence.

6. Refer to Data Set 16 in Appendix B. Test the claim that the intervals between eruptions of the Old Faithful geyser have a median greater than 77 min, which was the median about 20 years ago.

7. Using the weights of only the *brown* M&Ms listed in Data Set 11 of Appendix B, test the claim that the median is greater than 0.9085 g. (For the 1498 M&Ms to produce a total package weight of 1361 g, the mean weight must be at least 0.9085 g.) Use a 0.05 significance level. Based on the result, does it appear that the package is labelled correctly?

8. Refer to Data Set 6 in Appendix B. Use the paired data consisting of the return on invested capital (%) and return on equity (%) for the top 50 companies. If either value is not available (n.a.) for a company, omit that company from the analysis. Using a 0.05 level of significance, test the claim that for top companies, the median difference in these two types of financial return is 0. Based on these results for top companies, do return on invested capital and return on equity appear to be about the same?

9. Refer to Data Set 20 in Appendix B. If annual person-days lost due to work stoppages from 1976 to 1999 are analysed, for six groups of transportation industries, the median annual number of person-days lost overall is 10,595. Find the median number of person-days lost due to work stoppages in just the truck-based transportation industry for 1976 to 1999. Test at the 0.05 level of significance, and assume that the data in Data Set 20 are representative of *all* years. Test the claim that the median number of person-days lost in the truck-based group is smaller than the median of 10,595 for all transportation groups combined.

10. The Life Trust Insurance Company funded a university study of drinking and driving. After 30 randomly selected drivers were tested for reaction times, they were given two drinks and tested again, with the result that 22 had slower reaction times, 6 had faster reaction times, and 2 received the same scores as before the drinks. At the 0.01 significance level, test the claim that the drinks had no effect on the reaction times. Based on these very limited results, does it appear that the insurance company is justified in charging higher rates for those who drink and drive?

11. Mental measurements of young children are often made by giving them blocks and telling them to build a tower as tall as possible. One experiment of block building was repeated a month later, with the times (in seconds) listed on page 646. Use a 0.01 level of significance to test the claim that there is no difference between the two times.

First trial	30	19	19	23	29	178	42	20	12	39	14	81	17	31	52
Second trial	30	6	14	8	14	52	14	22	17	8	11	30	14	17	15

Based on data from "Tower Building," by Johnson and Courtney, *Child Development,* Vol. 3.

12. Refer to the number of Senate sittings for Parliaments in Data Set 5 of Appendix B. Use the data for Parliaments of at least three years' duration. Assuming past Parliaments are representative of Parliaments in general, test the claim that the median number of Senate sittings for Parliaments of at least three years' duration is less than 300.

13-2 Exercises B: Beyond the Basics

13. A sample of 10 randomly selected IQ scores is obtained from the population of professional athletes. We want to test the claim that the population is centred at the IQ score of 100.

   a. Is it possible to have sample data such that the sign test leads to rejection of the null hypothesis that the median is equal to 100 while the t test conclusion (Chapter 4) is failure to reject the null hypothesis of $\mu = 100$? If so, construct such a data set.

   b. Is it possible to have sample data such that the sign test conclusion is failure to reject the null hypothesis that the median is equal to 100 while the t test conclusion (Chapter 4) is rejection of the null hypothesis of $\mu = 100$? If so, construct such a data set.

14. In the sign test procedure described in this section, we excluded ties (represented by 0 instead of a sign of $+$ or $-$). A second approach is to treat half of the 0s as positive signs and half as negative signs. (If the number of 0s is odd, exclude one so that they can be divided equally.) With a third approach, in two-tailed tests make half of the 0s positive and half negative; in one-tailed tests make all 0s either positive or negative, whichever supports the null hypothesis. Assume that in using the sign test on a claim that the median score is at least 100, we get 60 scores below 100, 40 scores above 100, and 21 scores equal to 100. Identify the test statistic and conclusion for the three different ways of handling differences of 0. Assume a 0.05 significance level in all three cases.

15. Table A-7 lists critical values for limited choices of α. Use Table A-1 to add a new column in Table A-7 (down to $n = 15$) that represents a significance level of 0.03 in one tail or 0.06 in two tails. For any particular n we use $p = 0.5$, as the sign test requires the assumption that

$$P(\text{positive sign}) = P(\text{negative sign}) = 0.5$$

The probability of x or fewer like signs is the sum of the probabilities for values up to and including x.

13-3 Wilcoxon Signed-Ranks Test for Two Dependent Samples

In Section 13-2 we used the sign test to analyse data, including sample data consisting of matched pairs. The sign test used only the signs of the differences and did not use their actual magnitudes (how large the numbers are). This section introduces the *Wilcoxon signed-ranks test*, which is also used with sample paired data. By using ranks (as defined in section 13-1), this test takes the magnitudes of the differences into account. Because the Wilcoxon signed-ranks test incorporates and uses more information than the sign test, it tends to yield conclusions that better reflect the true nature of the data.

DEFINITION

The **Wilcoxon signed-ranks test** is a nonparametric test that uses ranks of sample data consisting of matched pairs. It is used to test for differences in the population distributions, so the null and alternative hypotheses are as follows:

H_0: The two samples come from populations with the same distribution.
H_1: The two samples come from populations with different distributions.

(The Wilcoxon signed-ranks test can also be used to test the claim that a sample comes from a population of a specified median. See Exercise 10 for this application.)

Assumptions

1. The sample data have been randomly selected.
2. The population of differences (found from the pairs of data) has a distribution that is approximately *symmetric*, meaning that the left half of its histogram is roughly a mirror image of its right half. (There is no requirement that the data have a normal distribution.)

Procedure for Finding the Value of the Test Statistic

Step 1: For each pair of data, find the difference d by subtracting the second value from the first value. Keep the signs, but discard any pairs for which $d = 0$.

Step 2: *Ignore the signs of the differences*, then sort the differences from lowest to highest, and replace the differences by the corresponding rank value (as described in Section 13-1). When differences have the same numerical value, assign to them the mean of the ranks involved in the tie.

Step 3: Attach to each rank the sign of the difference from which it came. That is, insert those signs that were ignored in Step 2.

Step 4:   Find the sum of the absolute values of the negative ranks. Also find the sum of the positive ranks.

Step 5:   Let T be the *smaller* of the two sums found in Step 4. Either sum could be used, but for a simplified procedure we arbitrarily select the smaller of the two sums. (See the notation for T in the Notation box.)

Step 6:   Let n be the number of pairs of data for which the difference d is not 0.

Step 7:   Determine the test statistic and critical values based on the sample size, as shown in the Test Statistic box.

Step 8:   When forming the conclusion, reject the null hypothesis if the sample data lead to a test statistic that is in the critical region—that is, the test statistic is less than or equal to the critical value(s). Otherwise, fail to reject the null hypothesis.

Notation

$T =$ the smaller of the following two sums:

1. The sum of the absolute values of the negative ranks
2. The sum of the positive ranks

Test Statistic for the Wilcoxon Signed-Ranks Test for Two Dependent Samples

For $n \leq 30$: T

For $n > 30$: $z = \dfrac{T - \dfrac{n(n + 1)}{4}}{\sqrt{\dfrac{n(n + 1)(2n + 1)}{24}}}$

Critical values

If $n \leq 30$, the critical T value is found in Table A-8.
If $n > 30$, the critical z values are found in Table A-2.

TABLE 13-3	Reaction Times (in thousandths of a second) of 14 Subjects												
Right hand	191	97	116	165	116	129	171	155	112	102	188	158	121	133
Left hand	224	171	191	207	196	165	177	165	140	188	155	219	177	174
Differences d	−33	−74	−75	−42	−80	−36	−6	−10	−28	−86	+33	−61	−56	−41
Ranks of differences	4.5	11	12	8	13	6	1	2	3	14	4.5	10	9	7
Signed ranks	−4.5	−11	−12	−8	−13	−6	−1	−2	−3	−14	+4.5	−10	−9	−7

EXAMPLE   Table 13-3 consists of sample data obtained when 14 subjects are tested for reaction times with their left and right hands. (Only right-handed subjects were used.) Use the Wilcoxon signed-ranks test to test the claim of no difference between reaction times with right and left hands. Use a significance level of $\alpha = 0.05$.

SOLUTION   The null and alternative hypotheses are as follows:

H_0:   There is no difference between right- and left-hand reaction times.
H_1:   There is a difference between right- and left-hand reaction times.

The significance level is $\alpha = 0.05$. We are using the Wilcoxon signed-ranks test procedure, so the test statistic is calculated by using the eight-step procedure presented earlier in this section.

Step 1:   In Table 13-3, the row of differences is obtained by computing $d = $ right hand − left hand for each pair of data.

Step 2:   Ignoring their signs, we rank the absolute differences from lowest to highest. Note that the differences of −33 and +33 are tied for ranks of 4 and 5, so we assign a rank of 4.5 to each of them.

Step 3:   The bottom row of Table 13-3 is created by attaching to each rank the sign of the corresponding difference. If there is no difference between right- and left-hand reaction times, we expect the number of positive ranks to be approximately equal to the number of negative ranks.

Step 4:   We now find the sum of the absolute values of the negative ranks, and we also find the sum of the positive ranks.

Sum of absolute values of negative ranks: 100.5, which is

$$4.5 + 11 + 12 + 8 + 13 + 6 + 1 + 2 + 3 + 14 + 10 + 9 + 7$$

Sum of positive ranks: 4.5

Step 5:   Letting T be the smaller of the two sums found in Step 4, we find that $T = 4.5$.

Step 6:   Letting n be the number of pairs of data for which the difference d is not 0, we have $n = 14$.

Step 7:   Because $n = 14$, we have $n \leq 30$, so we use a test statistic of $T = 4.5$ (and we do not calculate a z test statistic). Also, because $n \leq 30$, we use Table A-8 to find the critical value of 21, given $\alpha = 0.05$ (two tails).

Step 8:   The test statistic $T = 4.5$ is less than or equal to the critical value of 21, so we reject the null hypothesis.

Interpretation It appears that there is a difference between right- and left-hand reaction times. Examining the sample data, we see that there are 13 negative signs and only 1 positive sign. Because negative signs result from lower values with the right hand, it appears that right-handed people have faster reaction times with their right hands.

If we use the sign test with the preceding example, we will arrive at the same conclusion. Although the sign test and the Wilcoxon signed-ranks test agree in this particular case, there are other cases in which not all tests agree.

Rationale: In this example the unsigned ranks of 1 through 14 have a total of 105, so if there are no significant differences, each of the two signed-rank totals should be around $105 \div 2$, or 52.5. The table of critical values shows that at the 0.05 level of significance with 14 pairs of data, a 21–84 split represents a significant departure from the null hypothesis, and any split that is farther apart (such as 20–85 or 19–86 or 4.5–100.5) will also represent a significant departure from the null hypothesis. Conversely, splits like 22–83 do not represent significant departures away from a 52.5–52.5 split, and they would not be a basis for rejecting the null hypothesis. The Wilcoxon signed-ranks test is based on the lower rank total, so instead of analysing both numbers constituting the split, we consider only the lower number.

The sum $1 + 2 + 3 + \cdots + n$ of all the ranks is equal to $n(n + 1)/2$; if this is a rank sum to be divided equally between two categories (positive and negative), each of the two totals should be near $n(n + 1)/4$, which is half of $n(n + 1)/2$. Recognition of this principle helps us understand the test statistic used when $n > 30$. The denominator in that expression represents a standard deviation of T and is based on the principle that

$$1^2 + 2^2 + 3^3 + \cdots + n^2 = \frac{n(n + 1)(2n + 1)}{6}$$

The Wilcoxon signed-ranks test can only be used for dependent (matched) data. The next section will describe a rank-sum test that can be applied to two sets of independent data that are not paired.

Using Technology

STATDISK: Select **Analysis** from the main menu bar, then select **Wilcoxon Tests** and proceed to use the Wilcoxon signed-ranks test for dependent samples. The STATDISK display will include the test statistic, critical value, and conclusion.

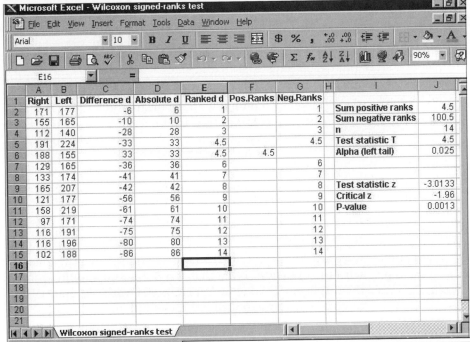

Excel Display Wilcoxon Signed-Ranks Test

	A	B	C	D	E	F	G	H	I	J
1	Right	Left	Difference d	Absolute d	Ranked d	Pos.Ranks	Neg.Ranks			
2	171	177	-6	6	1		1		Sum positive ranks	4.5
3	155	165	-10	10	2		2		Sum negative ranks	100.5
4	112	140	-28	28	3		3		n	14
5	191	224	-33	33	4.5		4.5		Test statistic T	4.5
6	188	155	33	33	4.5	4.5			Alpha (left tail)	0.025
7	129	165	-36	36	6		6			
8	133	174	-41	41	7		7			
9	165	207	-42	42	8		8		Test statistic z	-3.0133
10	121	177	-56	56	9		9		Critical z	-1.96
11	158	219	-61	61	10		10		P-value	0.0013
12	97	171	-74	74	11		11			
13	116	191	-75	75	12		12			
14	116	196	-80	80	13		13			
15	102	188	-86	86	14		14			

Cell	Formula	Explanation
C2	=A2-B2	The difference d between the paired scores
D2	=ABS(C2)	Ignores the signs of the differences
F2	=IF(C2>0,E2,"")	Records absolute ranks for the positive differences
G2	=IF(C2<0,E2,"")	Records absolute ranks for the negative differences
J2	=SUM(F2:F15)	Finds sum of recorded ranks for positive differences
J3	=SUM(G2:G15)	Finds sum of recorded ranks for negative differences
J4	=COUNT(F2:G15)	n (does not include cases of no difference)
J5	=MIN(J2:J3)	T (the smaller of the two sums for + and − ranks)
J9	=(J5-(J4*(J4+1)/4))/ SQRT(J4*(J4+1)*(2*J4+1)/24)	z (see boxed formula for test statistic, for $n > 30$)
J10	=NORMSINV(J6)	Lower critical value for z, for $n > 30$
J11	=NORMSDIST(J9)	P-value, for $n > 30$ (for two-tailed test, multiply by 2)

Use appropriate cell addresses for data.

Note: Ignore calculations for Cells J9:J11 if $n \le 30$.

Excel: In Excel, the Wilcoxon signed-ranks test can be partly auto-mated with the following templates. Set up the column headings as shown in the left part of the figure on the previous page, placing the headings and data for the two matched variables in the two left columns. Enter the given formulas for the first values of the difference and absolute difference; copy and paste them to fill the columns. Then sort the four left columns in order of the absolute differences. To do so, highlight those columns, including the headings. Select **Sort** from the **Data** menu and, in the dialog box that appears, select "Absolute d" for the **Sort by** option. Then specify **Ascending** and **Header** row, and click on OK. Fill the "Ranked d" column with the ordered numbers from 1 to the number of data pairs. Inspect the "Absolute d" column for tied values. If there are any, manually replace their ranks in the "Ranked d" column with the mean of the ranks that first appear in that column. (For example, in the sorted display shown, there are two 33s in the "Absolute d" column. Originally, the first 33 had a rank of 4 and the second 33 had a rank of 5. Both ranks were manually replaced with 4.5.) Next, complete Columns F and G by entering and copying the appropriate formulas, which are shown. These distinguish between the positive and negative ranks.

Input the indicated labels in Column I and formulas in Column J to complete the calculations. For alpha, enter only the left-tailed portion. Note that if n ≤ 30, you should look up the displayed T value in Appendix A-8 rather than use the z test statistic at the bottom of the template.

13-3 Exercises A: Basic Skills and Concepts

In Exercises 1–4, refer to the sample data for the given exercises in Section 13-2. Instead of the sign test, use the Wilcoxon signed-ranks test to test the claim that both samples come from populations having the same distribution. Use the significance level α that is given below.

1. Exercise 1; $\alpha = 0.05$
2. Exercise 2; $\alpha = 0.05$
3. Exercise 8; $\alpha = 0.01$
4. Exercise 11; $\alpha = 0.01$

In Exercises 5–8, use the Wilcoxon signed-ranks test.

5. A study was conducted to investigate the effectiveness of hypnotism in reducing pain. Results for randomly selected subjects are given below. The measurements are in centimetres on a pain scale. At the 0.01 significance level, test the claim that hypnotism has no effect.

Subject	A	B	C	D	E	F	G	H
Before hypnosis	6.6	6.5	9.0	10.3	11.3	8.1	6.3	11.6
After hypnosis	6.8	2.4	7.4	8.5	8.1	6.1	3.4	2.0

Based on "An Analysis of Factors That Contribute to the Efficacy of Hypnotic Analgesia," by Price and Barber, *Journal of Abnormal Psychology*, Vol. 96, No. 1.

6. In a study of the effect of posture on body temperature, data were collected for 11 subjects. The values given in the table are in degrees Celsius and represent the measured body temperatures of the 11 subjects first in a sitting position and then in a supine (lying face up) position. At the 0.01 level of significance, test the claim that there is no significant difference between the measurements taken in the two positions.

Sitting	37.61	37.07	37.2	37.23	37.38	37.28	37.12	37.55	37.04	37.78	37.59
Supine	37.19	36.91	36.7	36.80	36.96	37.11	36.82	37.36	36.92	37.22	37.25

Data courtesy of Michel B. Ducharme, Defence and Civil Institute of Environmental Medicine, Toronto.

7. According to a paid promotional article in *The Globe and Mail*, installation of an automotive accessory called the Platinum Vapor Injector (P.V.I.) can significantly increase a vehicle's gas mileage. Fifteen identical 5.0 litre vehicles were tested without, then with, this additive, and the results, in miles per gallon, are as shown.

Vehicle	A	B	C	D	E	F	G	H	I	J	K	L	M	N	O
Without P.V.I.	14.4	13.5	16.9	15.6	14.6	11.5	15.9	11.7	17.2	13.0	16.9	19.0	17.3	15.7	15.5
With P.V.I.	21.3	19.9	24.8	22.5	20.5	15.9	21.5	15.7	22.1	16.7	21.1	21.0	19.1	16.8	13.5

  a. Assume that the tested cars are representative of cars in general, and use the Wilcoxon signed-ranks test at the 0.05 level of significance. Test the claim that the P.V.I. additive does affect vehicles' gas mileage.

  b. Note that the vehicles tested in this example were not randomly selected, and in fact they all represent the same model of car under standardized conditions. Is the assumption made in Part (a), that the test results can be potentially applied to all cars, a reasonable one? Explain why or why not.

8. A company offers a daily list of stock picks to paid subscribers. Its web page called *Track Record for TSE* shows the prices of stocks it has recommended (1) on the day the "buy" recommendation was made, and (2) on a subsequent day within the next week or two. The accompanying table is a sample from this data, for November to December 2000. At the 0.05 significance level, do the data support the company's claim that, for stocks bought and sold at the prices cited, the buy and sell prices are different? If clients make their own decisions about when to sell a stock, is the displayed data sufficient to support a claim that the clients of this company made money? Explain.

Stock Pick Number	1	2	3	4	5	6	7	8	9	10	11	12
Entry price	4.87	22.85	14.05	13.80	22.70	10.00	25.45	18.90	20.90	4.50	31.30	14.00
Exit price	5.35	23.65	14.25	14.80	25.25	9.65	26.70	20.50	25.25	9.15	41.25	14.40

Based on data from www.activetrading.com.

13-3 Exercises B: Beyond the Basics

9. Assume that the Wilcoxon signed-ranks test is being used for a two-tailed hypothesis test with a significance level of 0.05.
   a. With $n = 10$ pairs of data, find the lowest and highest possible values of T.
   b. With $n = 50$ pairs of data, find the lowest and highest possible values of T.
   c. If there are $n = 100$ pairs of data with no differences of 0 and no tied ranks, find the critical value of T.
10. The Wilcoxon signed-ranks test can be used to test the claim that a sample comes from a population with a specified median. The procedure used is the same as the one described in this section, except that the differences (Step 1) are obtained by subtracting the value of the hypothesized median from each score. Use the sample data consisting of the 108 body temperatures listed in Data Set 18. At the 0.05 level of significance, test the claim that adults accepted for voluntary surgery have a median body temperature that is equal to 37.0° C.

13-4 Wilcoxon Rank-Sum Test for Two Independent Samples

In this section we introduce the *Wilcoxon rank-sum test*, which is a nonparametric test that can be applied to two independent sets of sample data. Recall that two samples are independent if the sample values selected from one population are not related or somehow matched or paired with the sample values from the other population.

DEFINITION

The **Wilcoxon rank-sum test** is a nonparametric test that uses ranks of sample data from two independent populations. It is used to test the null hypothesis that the two independent samples come from populations with the same distribution. (That is, the two populations are identical.) The alternative hypothesis is that the two population distributions are different in some way.

H_0: The two samples come from populations with the same distribution. (That is, the two populations are identical.)

H_1: The two samples come from populations with different distributions. (That is, the two distributions are different in some way.)

The Wilcoxon rank-sum test is equivalent to the **Mann-Whitney U test** (see Exercise 9), which is included in some other textbooks and software packages. The basis for the procedure used in the Wilcoxon rank-sum test is this principle: If two samples are drawn from identical populations and the individual values are all ranked as one combined collection of values, then the high and low ranks should fall evenly between the two samples. If the low ranks are found predominantly in one sample and the high ranks are found predominantly in the other sample, we suspect that the two populations are not identical.

Assumptions

1. There are two independent samples that were randomly selected.

2. Each of the two samples has more than 10 values. (For samples with 10 or fewer values, special tables are available in reference books, such as *CRC Standard Probability and Statistics Tables and Formulae,* published by CRC Press.)

3. There is no requirement that the two populations have a normal distribution or any other particular distribution.

Note that unlike the corresponding hypothesis tests in Sections 8-3 and 8-5, the Wilcoxon rank-sum test does *not* require normally distributed populations. Also, the Wilcoxon rank-sum test can be used with data at the ordinal level of measurement, such as data consisting of ranks. In contrast, the parametric methods of Sections 8-3 and 8-5 cannot be used with data at the ordinal level of measurement.

In Table 13-1 we noted that the Wilcoxon rank-sum test has a 0.95 efficiency rating when compared with the parametric t test or z test. Because this test has such a high efficiency rating and involves easier calculations, it is often preferred to the parametric tests presented in Sections 8-3 and 8-5, even when the requirement of normality is satisfied.

Gender Gap in Drug Testing

A study of the relationship between heart attacks and doses of aspirin involved 22,000 male physicians. This study, like many others, excluded women. However, results of medical tests on males do not necessarily apply to females. For example, women's hearts are different from men's in many important ways. When forming conclusions based on sample results, we should be wary of an inference that extends to a population larger than the one from which the sample was drawn.

Procedure for Finding the Value of the Test Statistic

1. Temporarily combine the two samples into one big sample, sort and then replace each sample value with its rank. (The lowest value gets a rank of 1, the next lowest value gets a rank of 2, and so on. For more details about ranks, see Section 13-1.)

2. Find the sum of the ranks for either one of the two samples.

3. Calculate the value of the z test statistic as shown in the Test Statistic box. Note that either sample can be used as sample 1.)

Notation for the Wilcoxon Rank-Sum Test

n_1 = size of sample 1

n_2 = size of sample 2

R_1 = sum of ranks for sample 1

R_2 = sum of ranks for sample 2

R = same as R_1 (sum of ranks for sample 1)

μ_R = mean of the sample R values that is expected when the two populations are identical

σ_R = standard deviation of the sample R values that is expected when the two populations are identical

---

If you are testing the null hypothesis of identical populations and both sample sizes are greater than 10, then the sampling distribution of R is approximately normal with mean μ_R and standard deviation σ_R, and the test statistic is as follows.

Test Statistic for the Wilcoxon Rank-Sum Test for Two Independent Samples

$$z = \frac{R - \mu_R}{\sigma_R}$$

where $\mu_R = \dfrac{n_1(n_1 + n_2 + 1)}{2}$

$\sigma_R = \sqrt{\dfrac{n_1 n_2 (n_1 + n_2 + 1)}{12}}$

n_1 = size of the sample from which the rank sum R is found

n_2 = size of the other sample

R = sum of ranks of the sample with size n_1

Critical values: Critical values can be found in Table A-2 (because the test statistic is based on the normal distribution). The expression for μ_R is a variation of the following result of mathematical induction: The sum of the first n positive integers is given by $1 + 2 + 3 + \cdots + n = n(n + 1)/2$. The expression for σ_R is a variation of a result that states that the integers $1, 2, 3, \ldots, n$ have standard deviation $\sqrt{(n^2 - 1)/12}$.

Weights (in grams) of M&Ms			
Red		Yellow	
0.870	(2)	0.906	(19)
0.933	(35)	0.978	(45)
0.952	(42)	0.926	(34)
0.908	(21)	0.868	(1)
0.911	(24.5)	0.876	(5)
0.908	(21)	0.968	(44)
0.913	(27)	0.921	(30)
0.983	(46)	0.893	(15)
0.920	(29)	0.939	(38)
0.936	(37)	0.886	(10.5)
0.891	(13)	0.924	(32)
0.924	(32)	0.910	(23)
0.874	(4)	0.877	(6)
0.908	(21)	0.879	(7.5)
0.924	(32)	0.941	(40)
0.897	(16)	0.879	(7.5)
0.912	(26)	0.940	(39)
0.888	(12)	0.960	(43)
0.872	(3)	0.989	(47)
0.898	(17)	0.900	(18)
0.882	(9)	0.917	(28)
		0.911	(24.5)
		0.892	(14)
		0.886	(10.5)
		0.949	(41)
		0.934	(36)
$n_1 = 21$		$n_2 = 26$	
$R_1 = 469.5$		$R_2 = 658.5$	

EXAMPLE   Samples of M&M plain candies are randomly selected, and the red and yellow M&Ms are weighed, with the results listed in the margin (from Data Set 11 in Appendix B). Use a 0.05 level of significance to test the claim that weights of red M&Ms and yellow M&Ms have the same distribution.

SOLUTION   The null and alternative hypotheses are as follows:

H_0:   Red and yellow M&M plain candies have weights with identical populations.

H_1:   The two populations are not identical.

Rank all 47 weights combined, beginning with a rank of 1 (assigned to the lowest weight of 0.868 g). Ties in ranks are handled as described in Section 13-1: Find the mean of the ranks involved and assign this mean rank to each of the tied values. The ranks corresponding to the individual sample values are shown in parentheses in the table. R denotes the sum of the ranks for the sample we choose as sample 1. If we choose the red M&Ms, we get

$$R = 2 + 35 + 42 + \cdots + 9 = 469.5$$

Because there are 21 red M&Ms, we have $n_1 = 21$. Also, $n_2 = 26$, because there are 26 yellow M&Ms. We can now determine the values of μ_R, σ_R, and the test statistic z:

$$\mu_R = \frac{n_1(n_1 + n_2 + 1)}{2} = \frac{21(21 + 26 + 1)}{2} = 504$$

$$\sigma_R = \sqrt{\frac{n_1 n_2(n_1 + n_2 + 1)}{12}} = \sqrt{\frac{(21)(26)(21 + 26 + 1)}{12}} = 46.73$$

$$z = \frac{R - \mu_R}{\sigma_R} = \frac{469.5 - 504}{46.73} = -0.74$$

The test is two-tailed because a large positive value of z would indicate that the higher ranks are found disproportionately in the first sample, and a large negative value of z would indicate that the first sample had a disproportionate share of lower ranks. In either case, we would have strong evidence against the claim that the two samples come from identical populations.

The significance of the test statistic z can be treated in the same manner as in previous chapters. We are now testing (with $\alpha = 0.05$) the hypothesis that the two populations are the same, so we have a two-tailed test with critical z values of 1.96 and -1.96. The test statistic of $z = -0.74$ does not fall within the critical region, so we fail to reject the null hypothesis that red and yellow M&Ms have the same weights.

We can verify that if we interchange the two sets of weights and consider the sample of yellow M&Ms to be first, $R = 658.5$, $\mu_R = 624$, $\sigma_R = 46.73$, and $z = 0.74$, so the conclusion is the same.

Figure 13-5   Stoppages

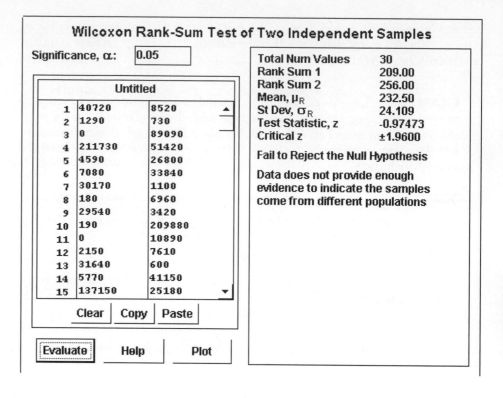

Wilcoxon Rank-Sum Test of Two Independent Samples

Significance, α: 0.05

Untitled		
1	40720	8520
2	1290	730
3	0	89090
4	211730	51420
5	4590	26800
6	7080	33840
7	30170	1100
8	180	6960
9	29540	3420
10	190	209880
11	0	10890
12	2150	7610
13	31640	600
14	5770	41150
15	137150	25180

Clear   Copy   Paste

Evaluate   Help   Plot

Total Num Values   30
Rank Sum 1   209.00
Rank Sum 2   256.00
Mean, μ_R 232.50
St Dev, σ_R 24.109
Test Statistic, z -0.97473
Critical z ±1.9600

Fail to Reject the Null Hypothesis

Data does not provide enough evidence to indicate the samples come from different populations

Rail	Air
40720	8520
1290	730
0	89090
211730	51420
4590	26800
7080	33840
30170	1100
180	6960
29540	3420
190	209880
0	10890
2150	7610
31640	600
5770	41150
137150	25180

EXAMPLE   A labour specialist has compiled Data Set 20 in Appendix B, in order to compare the annual amounts of work time lost (in person-days) in the rail and air transportation industries due to work stoppages. Because these data are not normally distributed, you suggest that she use the Wilcoxon rank-sum test. Based on annual totals for 15 different, randomly selected years for each transportation group (see margin), test the claim that the person-days lost per year both come from the same distribution.

SOLUTION   The null and alternative hypotheses are as follows:

H_0: Numbers of person-days lost per year due to work stoppages, in the rail and air transportation industries, come from populations with the same distribution.

H_1: The two distributions differ in some way.

Instead of manually calculating the rank sums, we refer to the STATDISK display shown in Figure 13-5. The display shows that the first rank sum (for rail transportation) is 209.0, which equals R. The test statistic z is −0.97473, and (assuming α = 0.05) the critical z values are ±1.9600. The conclusion is we fail to reject the null hypothesis that the distributions are the same.

Interpretation   The annual numbers of person-days lost due to work stoppages in the rail and air transportation industries show great variation, and have nonnormal distributions. That is why we avoided a parametric test. Based on the Wilcoxon rank-sum test, there is insufficient evidence to conclude that the data are distributed differently for these two groups.

Using Technology

STATDISK: Select **Analysis** from the main menu bar, then select **Wilcoxon Tests** and proceed to use the Wilcoxon rank-sum test for *independent* samples. The STATDISK display will include the rank sums, sample size, test statistic, critical value, and conclusion.

Excel: In Excel, the Wilcoxon ranked-sum test can be partly automated with the following template. Set up the column headings as

Excel Display   Wilcoxon Rank-Sum Test

Cell	Formula	Explanation
F5	=DCOUNT(A1:C48,1,E2:E3)	n for the first sample, whose ID is specified in E3
F6	=DCOUNT(A1:C48,1,F2:F3)	n for the second sample, whose ID is specified in F3
F7	=DSUM(A1:C48,3,E2:E3)	Sum of the ranks for the first sample
F8	=F5*(F5+F6+1)/2	μ_R (see the formula box for the test statistic)
F9	=SQRT(F5*F6*(F5+F6+1)/12)	σ_R (see the formula box for the test statistic)
F10	=(F7-F8)/F9	Test statistic z (see the formula box)
F11	=NORMSINV(1-F4)	Upper critical value
F12	=1-NORMSDIST(ABS(F10))	P-value (for two-tailed test, multiply by 2)

Use appropriate cell addresses for data.

Class Attendance *Does* Help

In a study of 424 undergraduates, it was found that students with the worst attendance records tended to get the lowest grades. (Is anybody surprised?) Those who were absent less than 10% of the time tended to receive grades of B or above. The study also showed that students who sit in the front of the class tend to get significantly better grades.

shown in the left part of the figure. Fill in the leftmost column with the data from *both* samples. Then, in the second column, identify the sample that each data value comes from. Once the data are entered, sort the two left columns in order of values. To do so, highlight those two columns, including the headings. Select **Sort** from the **Data** menu and, in the dialog box that appears, select "Values" for the **Sort** by option. Then specify **Ascending** and **Header** row, and click on **OK**. Now fill the "Ranks" column with the ordered numbers from 1 to the number of data values (in both samples combined). Inspect the "Values" column for tied values. If there are any, manually replace their ranks in the "Ranks" column with the mean of the ranks that first appear in that column. (For example, since 0.879 appears twice in the "Values" column, with the first 0.879 having a rank of 7 and the second having a rank of 8, both ranks have been manually replaced with 7.5.)

Also shown is the template for completing the calculations. For alpha, enter only the right-tailed portion. In Cells E2 and F2, enter the same heading that is in the middle column of your input block; use Cells E3 and F3 to enter the IDs you used, in the input block, for the first and second samples, respectively. All other values will be calculated, based on the indicated formulas.

(13–4) Exercises A: Basic Skills and Concepts

In Exercises 1–8, use the Wilcoxon rank-sum test.

1. The example in this section tested the null hypothesis that red and yellow M&M plain candies have weights with identical populations. Refer to Data Set 11 in Appendix B and test the claim that red and brown M&M plain candies have weights with identical populations. Use a 0.05 level of significance.

2. Listed below are time intervals (in minutes) between eruptions of the Old Faithful geyser in Yellowstone National Park. Using a 0.05 significance level, test the claim that the times are the same for both years.

1951	74	60	74	42	74	52	65	68	62	66	62	60
1996	88	86	85	89	83	85	91	68	91	56	89	94

Based on data from geologist Rick Hutchinson and the National Park Service.

3. Provincial governments have been re-examining their delivery of services, such as health care. The accompanying table is based on one random sample of hospitals in New Brunswick and another in Nova Scotia, and shows the total number of beds in each hospital. At the 0.05 significance level, test the claim that the two provinces have the same distribution of

hospital-bed numbers. If the distributions are different, do we have sufficient information to conclude that the numbers of hospital beds per person are different in the two provinces? Explain.

New Brunswick		Nova Scotia	
23	47	15	13
153	47	27	136
397	15	8	26
12	500	85	311
15	56	12	132
398		64	

Based on data from *Guide to Canadian Healthcare Facilities*, 1998-1999, vol. 6

4. An umbrella maker is deciding whether to concentrate on eastern or western Canada. To help decide, she randomly selects cities from both parts of the country, and obtains the corresponding annual precipitation data (in millimetres). At the 0.01 significance level, test the claim that, in general, eastern and western cities have the same amount of annual precipitation. Based on your result, can we conclude that one side of Canada would be a better market for umbrellas than the other?

Eastern Cities				Western Cities			
1169	1174	879	1097	398	647	402	266
1282	712	1109	1514	467	454	628	424
762	1444	769	908	526	2523	467	384
1491	909	946		1113			

5. The "bootstrap" (simulated) samples below are based on summary data for building statistics, in *The Durham Business News*, June 1998. They show the values of building permits, in thousand of dollars, in large and small communities in the region. At the 0.05 significance level, test the claim that both sizes of community are issuing the same dollar values of building permits. Is there evidence that one size of community is attracting larger-value projects than the other?

Large Communities				Small Communities			
118	118	118	57	29	203	29	203
111	118	123	123	203	29	52	77
57	111	118	118	203	203	203	29
111	111	111	111	203	203	77	77
57	57			203	52		

6. Sample data were collected in a study of calcium supplements and their effects on blood pressure. A placebo group and a calcium group began the study with measures of blood pressures. At the 0.05 significance level, test the claim that the two sample groups come from populations with the same blood pressure levels. (The data are based on "Blood Pressure and Metabolic Effects of Calcium Supplementation in Normotensive White

and Black Men," by Lyle et al., *Journal of the American Medical Association*, Vol. 257, No. 13.)

Placebo Group				Calcium Group			
124.6	104.8	96.5	116.3	129.1	123.4	102.7	118.1
106.1	128.8	107.2	123.1	114.7	120.9	104.4	116.3
118.1	108.5	120.4	122.5	109.6	127.7	108.0	124.3
113.6				106.6	121.4	113.2	

7. The arrangement of test items was studied for its effect on anxiety. Sample results are as follows:

Easy to Difficult				Difficult to Easy			
24.64	39.29	16.32	32.83	33.62	34.02	26.63	30.26
28.02	33.31	20.60	21.13	35.91	26.68	29.49	35.32
26.69	28.90	26.43	24.23	27.24	32.34	29.34	33.53
7.10	32.86	21.06	28.89	27.62	42.91	30.20	32.54
28.71	31.73	30.02	21.96				
25.49	38.81	27.85	30.29				
30.72							

At the 0.05 level of significance, test the claim that the two samples come from populations with the same scores. (The data are based on "Item Arrangement, Cognitive Entry Characteristics, Sex and Test Anxiety as Predictors of Achievement Examination Performance," by Klimko, *Journal of Experimental Education*, Vol. 52, No. 4.)

8. Refer to Data Set 9 in Appendix B. Use a 0.01 significance level to test the claim that the population of cotinine levels is the same for these two groups: Nonsmokers who are not exposed to environmental tobacco smoke (labelled as NOETS), and nonsmokers who are exposed to tobacco smoke (labelled as ETS). What do the results suggest about "second-hand" smoke?

13–4 Exercises B: Beyond the Basics

9. The Mann-Whitney U test is equivalent to the Wilcoxon rank-sum test for independent samples in the sense that it applies to the same situations and always leads to the same conclusions. In the Mann-Whitney U test we calculate

$$z = \frac{U - \frac{n_1 n_2}{2}}{\sqrt{\frac{n_1 n_2 (n_1 + n_2 + 1)}{12}}}$$

where

$$U = n_1 n_2 + \frac{n_1(n_1 + 1)}{2} - R$$

Show that if the expression for U is substituted into the preceding expression for z, we get the same test statistic (with opposite sign) used in the Wilcoxon rank-sum test for two independent samples.

10. Assume that we have two treatments (A and B) that produce measurable results, and we have only two observations for Treatment A and two observations for Treatment B. We cannot use the test statistic given in this section because both sample sizes do not exceed 10.

Rank				Rank sum for treatment A
1	2	3	4	
A	A	B	B	3

   a. Complete the accompanying table by listing the five rows corresponding to the other five cases, and enter the corresponding rank sums for treatment A.
   b. List the possible values of R, along with their corresponding probabilities. (Assume that the rows of the table from part (a) are equally likely.)
   c. Is it possible, at the 0.10 significance level, to reject the null hypothesis that there is no difference between treatments A and B? Explain.
11. When using the Wilcoxon rank-sum test, is the effect of an outlier large or small? Explain.

13-5 Kruskal-Wallis Test

In this section we introduce the *Kruskal-Wallis test*, which is used to test the claim that several different independent samples come from identical populations. In Section 11-2 we used one-way analysis of variance (ANOVA) to test hypotheses that differences in means among several samples are significant, but that method requires that all of the involved populations have normal distributions. The Kruskal-Wallis test does not require normal distributions.

DEFINITION

The **Kruskal-Wallis test** (also called the **H-test**) is a nonparametric test that uses ranks of sample data from three or more independent populations. It is used to test the null hypothesis that the independent samples come from populations with the same distribution. The alternative hypothesis is that the population distributions are different in some way.

H_0: The samples come from populations with the same distribution.

H_1: The samples come from populations with different distributions.

Drug Approval

According to the Pharmaceutical Manufacturers Association of Canada, the development and approval of a new drug can cost up to $500 million and take up to 15 years. Extensive laboratory testing precedes approval for human testing, which is granted by the Therapeutic Products Directorate of Health Canada. Phase One clinical trials involve a group of 20 to 100 healthy volunteers. In Phase Two, the drug is given to 100 to 300 people who suffer from the disease or condition for which it is intended. In Phase Three, 1000 to 3000 or more patients are treated, and the results are compared to those obtained with other available therapies for the disease or condition. Overseeing such a complex, extensive, and time-consuming process would be enough to give anyone a headache, but the process does protect us from dangerous or worthless drugs.

Assumptions

1. We have at least three samples, all of which are random.
2. Each sample has at least five observations. (If samples have fewer than five observations, refer to special tables of critical values, such as *CRC Standard Probability and Statistics Tables and Formulae,* published by CRC Press.)
3. There is no requirement that the populations have a normal distribution or any other particular distribution.

In applying the Kruskal-Wallis test, we compute the **test statistic H, which has a distribution that can be approximated by the chi-square distribution as long as each sample has at least five observations.** When we use the chi-square distribution in this context, the number of degrees of freedom is $k - 1$, where k is the number of samples. (For a quick review of the key features of the chi-square distribution, see Section 6-5.)

Procedure for Finding the Value of the Test Statistic

1. Temporarily combine all samples into one big sample and assign a rank to each sample value. (Sort the values from lowest to highest, and in cases of ties, assign to each observation the mean of the ranks involved.)
2. For each sample, find the sum of the ranks and find the sample size.
3. Using the results from Step 2, calculate the test statistic H. The relevant notation and test statistic are as follows.

Notation for the Kruskal-Wallis Test

N = total number of observations in all samples combined

k = number of samples

R_1 = sum of ranks for sample 1

n_1 = number of observations in sample 1

For sample 2, the sum of ranks is R_2 and the number of observations is n_2, and similar notation is used for the other samples.

Test Statistic for the Kruskal-Wallis Test

$$H = \frac{12}{N(N + 1)} \left(\frac{R_1^2}{n_1} + \frac{R_2^2}{n_2} + \cdots + \frac{R_k^2}{n_k} \right) - 3(N + 1)$$

where degrees of freedom = $k - 1$

Critical Values

1. The test is *right-tailed*.
2. Use Table A-4 (because the test statistic H can be approximated by a chi-square distribution).
3. Degrees of freedom = $k - 1$.

The test statistic H is basically a measure of the variance of the rank sums $R_1, R_2, \ldots, R_k$. If the ranks are distributed evenly among the sample groups, then H should be a relatively small number. If the samples are very different, then the ranks will be excessively low in some groups and high in others, with the net effect that H will be large. Consequently, only large values of H lead to rejection of the null hypothesis that the samples come from identical populations. **The Kruskal-Wallis test is therefore a right-tailed test.**

EXAMPLE   In an example for the previous section, we illustrated how Data Set 20 in Appendix B could be used to compare the annual amounts of work time lost (in person-days) due to work stoppages, in two related industries. The data are not normally distributed. Suppose you need data compared for three industries. Based on annual totals for 15 different, randomly selected years for each of three transportation groups—water-based, truck, and bus/urban transport—use the Kruskal-Wallis test for testing the claim that the annual person-days lost due to work stoppages in the three industries come from the same population.

TABLE 13-4	Annual Person-Days Lost in Three Transportation Industries Due to Work Stoppages	
Water	Truck	Bus & Urban
0 (1.5)	30850 (28)	71630 (38)
56830 (35)	10740 (15)	28150 (26)
20160 (22)	3680 (8)	84640 (40)
15010 (18)	15450 (19)	65430 (36)
32500 (30)	98740 (42)	37570 (31)
10360 (13)	820 (5)	25400 (25)
19620 (21)	19400 (20)	42460 (32)
0 (1.5)	100390 (43)	43050 (34)
9540 (12)	8860 (11)	31070 (29)
13450 (16)	129920 (44)	223720 (45)
8080 (10)	1700 (60)	6000 (9)
210 (3)	29600 (27)	83910 (39)
85550 (41)	550 (4)	42820 (33)
1850 (7)	21620 (24)	70990 (37)
10510 (14)	14100 (17)	21490 (23)
$n_1 = 15$ $R_1 = 245$	$n_2 = 15$ $R_2 = 313$	$n_3 = 15$ $R_3 = 477$

SOLUTION   We will follow the hypothesis testing procedure summarized in Figure 7-4.

Steps 1, 2, and 3:   The null and alternative hypotheses are:

H_0: The annual numbers of person-days lost per year due to work stoppages for the three industries come from the same population.
H_1: These numbers do not come from the same population.

Step 4:   No significance level was specified. In the absence of any overriding circumstances, we use $\alpha = 0.05$.

Step 5:   Because the three populations are not normally distributed, we use the Kruskal-Wallis test.

Step 6:   In determining the value of the test statistic H, we must first rank all of the data. We begin with the lowest value of 0; because there are two zeros, we follow the rule for ties, and assign both of the zeros the rank 1.5, which is the mean of ranks 1 and 2. Ranks are shown in parentheses with the original data in Table 13-4. Next we find the sample size, n, and sum of ranks, R, for each sample; these values are shown at the bottom of Table 13-4. Because the total number of observations is 45, we have $N = 45$. We can now evaluate the test statistic as follows:

$$H = \frac{12}{N(N+1)} \left(\frac{R_1^2}{n_1} + \frac{R_2^2}{n_2} + \cdots + \frac{R_k^2}{n_k} \right) - 3(N+1)$$

$$= \frac{12}{45(45+1)} \left(\frac{245^2}{15} + \frac{313^2}{15} + \frac{477^2}{15} \right) - 3(45+1)$$

$$= 10.994$$

Because each sample has at least five observations, the distribution of H is approximately a chi-square distribution with $k - 1$ degrees of freedom. The number of samples is $k = 3$, so we have $3 - 1 = 2$ degrees of freedom. Refer to Table A-4 to find the critical value of 5.991, which corresponds to 2 degrees of freedom and a 0.05 significance level.

Step 7:   The test statistic $H = 10.994$ is in the critical region bounded by 5.991, so we reject the null hypothesis that the populations are the same.

Interpretation The annual numbers of person-days lost due to work stoppages in these industry groups do not appear to come from the same population.

Rationale: The test statistic H, as presented earlier, is the rank version of the test statistic F used in the analysis of variance discussed in Chapter 11. When we deal with ranks R instead of raw scores x, many components are predetermined. For example, the sum of all ranks can be expressed as $N(N + 1)/2$, where N is the total number of scores in all samples combined. The expression

$$H = \frac{12}{N(N+1)}\Sigma n_i (\overline{R}_i - \overline{\overline{R}})^2$$

where
$$\overline{R}_i = \frac{R_i}{n_i} \qquad \overline{\overline{R}} = \frac{\Sigma R_i}{\Sigma n_i}$$

combines weighted variances of ranks to produce the test statistic H given here. This expression for H is algebraically equivalent to the expression for H given earlier as the test statistic. The earlier form of H (not the one given here) is easier to work with. In comparing the procedures of the parametric F test for analysis of variance and the nonparametric Kruskal-Wallis test, we see that in the absence of computer software, the Kruskal-Wallis test is much simpler to apply. We need not compute the sample variances and sample means. We do not require normal population distributions. Life becomes so much easier. However, the Kruskal-Wallis test is not as efficient as the F test, and it may require more dramatic differences for the null hypothesis to be rejected.

Using Technology

STATDISK: Select **Analysis** from the main menu bar, then select **Kruskal-Wallis Test**. STATDISK will display the sum of the ranks for each sample, the H test statistic, the critical value, and the conclusion.

Excel: In Excel, use the following template. Set up the column headings as shown in the left part of the figure. Fill in the leftmost column with the data from all of the samples. Then, in the second column, identify the sample that each data value comes from. Once the data are entered, sort the two left columns in order of values. To do so, highlight those two columns, including the headings. Select **Sort** from the **Data** menu and, in the dialog box that appears, select "Values" for the **Sort by** option. Then specify **Ascending** and **Header row**, and click on **OK**. Now fill the "Ranks" column with the ordered numbers from 1 to the number of data values (in all samples combined). Inspect the "Values" column for tied values. If there are any, manually replace their ranks in the "Ranks" column with the mean of the ranks that first appear in that column. (For example, since 65 appears twice in the "Values" column, with the first 65 having a rank of 15 and the second having a rank of 16, both ranks have been manually replaced with 15.5.)

We show the template for completing the calculations. Enter the full (right-tailed) alpha manually. In Cells E2, F2, E4, and F4, enter the same heading that is in the middle column of your input block. Use Cells E3, F3, E5, and F5 to enter the IDs you used, in the input block, for the samples (such as 1951 and 1985 in the example). In Cell F15, indicate whether three or four samples were used; the template does not handle more than four samples. All other values will be calculated, based on the indicated formulas.

Excel Display   Kruskal-Wallis
Test

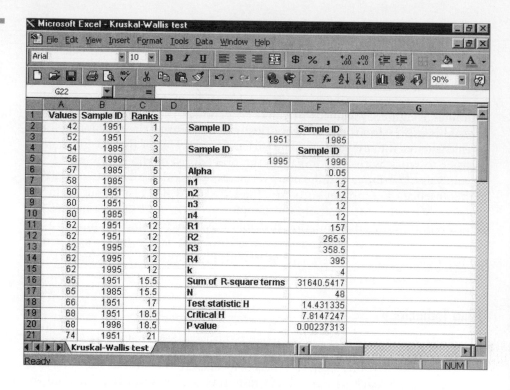

Cell	Formula	Explanation
F7	=DCOUNT(A1:C49,1,E2:E3)	n for the first sample, whose ID is specified in E3
F8	=DCOUNT(A1:C49,1,F2:F3)	n for the second sample, whose ID is specified in F3
F9	=DCOUNT(A1:C49,1,E4:E5)	n for the third sample, whose ID is specified in E5
F10	=DCOUNT(A1:C49,1,F4:F5)	n for the fourth sample, whose ID is specified in F5 (Leave F10 blank if there is no fourth sample.)
F11	=DSUM(A1:C49,3,E2:E3)	Sum of the ranks for the first sample
F12	=DSUM(A1:C49,3,F2:F3)	Sum of the ranks for the second sample
F13	=DSUM(A1:C49,3,E4:E5)	Sum of the ranks for the third sample
F14	=DSUM(A1:C49,3,F4:F5)	Sum of the ranks for the fourth sample (Leave F14 blank if there is no fourth sample.)
F16	=IF(F15=4,F11^2/F7+F12^2/F8+ F13^2/F9+F14^2/F10,F11^2/F7+ F12^2/F8+F13^2/F9)	Sum of each sample's R^2/n (an intermediate calculation within the boxed formula for the test statistic) (Based on 3 or 4 samples)
F17	=SUM(F7:F10)	Total number of observations in all samples combined
F18	=(12/(F17*(F17+1)))*F16- (3*(F17+1))	Test statistic H (see boxed formula for the test statistic)
F19	=CHIINV(F6,F15-1)	Critical value, based on the chi-square approximation
F20	=CHIDIST(F18,F15-1)	P-value, based on the chi-square approximation

Use appropriate cell addresses for data.
Note: The chi-square approximation assumes that each sample has at least 5 observations.

13–5 Exercises A: Basic Skills and Concepts

In Exercises 1–8, use the Kruskal-Wallis test.

1. The accompanying table lists the numbers of House sittings in each of 18 Parliaments, randomly selected from three different time periods. Parliaments lasting less than a year were not sampled. Using a significance level of $\alpha = 0.05$, test the claim that for the three periods sampled, the numbers of House sittings per Parliament are identical.

	Time Period	
1	2	3
283	355	447
568	605	687
303	292	405
254	366	707
262	565	767
458	390	590

Based on data from *Duration of Sessions of Parliament*, Library of Parliament.

2. Has usage of the Internet increased? Very likely, more people are using the Net than in the past, especially from home. But if a person has been using the Internet all along, are they are now spending more time on it? The table in the margin shows results from three independent surveys, conducted in 1997, 1998, and 1999; the specific values are the hours that respondents spend per week on the Internet. Use the 0.05 significance level to test the claim that the three samples come from identical populations.

3. Refer to Data Set 21 in Appendix B. A desirable trait for a top-rate diamond is to be flawless. Clarity is a measure of this characteristic—with 1 being the best. At the 0.05 level, test the claim that the prices of diamonds are not the same for each of the four clarity values listed (2, 3, 4, and 5). Would you conclude that clarity is a major determinant of price? If you need more information to answer the question, explain.

4. Flammability tests were conducted on children's sleepwear. The Vertical Semirestrained Test was used, in which pieces of fabric were burned under controlled conditions. After the burning stopped, the length of the charred portion was measured and recorded. Results are given on the following page for the same fabric tested at different laboratories (based on data from Minitab, Inc.). Because the same fabric was used, the different laboratories should have obtained the same results. Did they?

Hours per Week that Canadian Adults Spend on the Internet

Summer 1997	Summer 1998	Fall 1999
0.0	1.8	4.2
7.6	6.1	5.2
0.7	4.1	8.8
19.1	4.3	4.3
0.6	0.8	1.5
9.3	7.9	14.5
3.7	3.9	6.6
1.8	8.6	16.0
4.8	16.3	18.9
0.0	0.0	0.0
0.2	0.4	0.4
1.1	1.3	1.2
4.1	14.7	1.7
1.4	1.4	3.9
2.6	3.6	3.1
10.5	12.3	10.5
4.7	4.3	4.9
0.0	0.0	0.6
14.5	13.9	1.8

Laboratory

1	2	3	4	5
2.9	2.7	3.3	3.3	4.1
3.1	3.4	3.3	3.2	4.1
3.1	3.6	3.5	3.4	3.7
3.7	3.2	3.5	2.7	4.2
3.1	4.0	2.8	2.7	3.1
4.2	4.1	2.8	3.3	3.5
3.7	3.8	3.2	2.9	2.8
3.9	3.8	2.8	3.2	
3.1	4.3	3.8	2.9	
3.0	3.4	3.5		
2.9	3.3			

5. Refer to Data Set 11 in Appendix B. At the 0.05 significance level, test the claim that the weights of M&Ms are the same for each of the six different colour populations. If it is the intent of Mars, Inc., to make the candies so that the different colour populations are the same, do your results suggest that the company has a problem that requires corrective action?

6. Refer to Data Set 9 in Appendix B. Use a 0.01 significance level to test the claim that the populations of cotinine levels are identical for these three groups: nonsmokers who are not exposed to environmental tobacco smoke, nonsmokers who are exposed to tobacco smoke, and people who smoke. What do the results suggest about second-hand smoke?

7. The accompanying table lists the lengths, in minutes, and star ratings of televised movies rated 18+. Use a 0.05 significance level to test whether there is any difference in movie length based on star rating. Based on the results, does it appear that bad adult-rated movies are longer than good ones, or does it just seem that way?

(2.0–2.5 Stars) Fair	(3.0–3.5 Stars) Good	(4.0 Stars) Excellent
110	115	72
114	133	120
96	106	106
101	93	104
155	129	159

8. The City Resource Recovery Company (CRRC) collects the waste discarded by households in a region. Discarded waste must be separated into categories of metal, paper, plastic, and glass. In planning for the equipment needed to collect and process the garbage, CRRC refers to the data in Data Set 1 in Appendix B and uses Excel to obtain the results shown in the following display. At the 0.05 level of significance, test the claim that the four specific populations of garbage (metal, paper, plastic, glass) are the same. Based on the results, does it appear that these four categories require the same collection and processing resources? Does any single category seem to be a particularly large part of the waste management problem? (*Hint:* Look at the sums of the ranks. Also note that the P-value is in scientific notation.)

	E	F	G	H	I
2	Sample ID	**Sample ID**			
3	1	2			
4	Sample ID	**Sample ID**			
5	3	4			
6	Alpha	0.05			
7	n1	62			
8	n2	62			
9	n3	62			
10	n4	62			
11	R1	5604.8			
12	R2	12784.4			
13	R3	4730.6			
14	R4	7756.2			
15	k	4			
16	Sum of R-square terms	4474062.6			
17	N	248			
18	Test statistic H	122.4253012			
19	Critical H	7.814724703			
20	P value	2.31774E-26			
21					

Kruskal-Wallis test

Ready   NUM

13–5 Exercises B: Beyond the Basics

9. a. In general, how is the value of the test statistic H affected if a constant is added to (or subtracted from) each score?

   b. In general, how is the value of the test statistic H affected if each score is multiplied (or divided) by a positive constant?

   c. In general, how is the value of the test statistic H affected if a single sample value is changed to a value that causes it to become an outlier?

10. For three samples, each of size 5, what are the largest and smallest possible values of H?

11. In using the Kruskal-Wallis test, there is a correction factor that should be applied whenever there are many ties: Divide H by

$$1 - \frac{\Sigma T}{N^3 - N}$$

Here $T = t^3 - t$, where t is the number of observations that are tied for a group of tied scores. That is, find t for each group of tied scores, then compute the value of T, then add the T values to get ΣT. For the example presented in this section, use this procedure to find the corrected value of H. Does the corrected value of H differ substantially from the value of 14.431 that was found in this section?

12. Show that for the case of two samples, the Kruskal-Wallis test is equivalent to the Wilcoxon rank-sum test. This can be done by showing that for the case of two samples, the test statistic H equals the square of the test statistic z used in the Wilcoxon rank-sum test. Also note that with 1 degree of freedom, the critical values of χ^2 correspond to the square of the critical z score.

13-6 Rank Correlation

In this section we describe how the nonparametric method of rank correlation is used with paired data to test for an association between two variables. In Chapter 9 we used paired sample data to compute values for the linear correlation coefficient r, but in this section we use *ranks* as the basis for measuring the strength of the correlation between two variables.

DEFINITION

The **rank correlation test** (or **Spearman's rank correlation test**) is a nonparametric test that uses ranks of sample data consisting of matched pairs. It is used to test for an association between two variables, so the null and alternative hypotheses are as follows (where ρ_s denotes the rank correlation coefficient for the entire population.)

H_0: $\rho_s = 0$ (There is no correlation between the two variables.)

H_1: $\rho_s \neq 0$ (There is a correlation between the two variables.)

Assumptions

1. The sample data have been randomly selected.
2. Unlike the parametric methods of Section 9-2, there is no requirement that the sample pairs of data have a bivariate normal distribution. There is no requirement of a normal distribution for any population.

Advantages: Rank correlation has some distinct advantages over the parametric methods discussed in Chapter 9:

1. The nonparametric method of rank correlation can be used in a wider variety of circumstances than the parametric method of linear correlation. With rank correlation, we can analyse paired data that can be ranked but not measured. For example, if two judges rank 30 different gymnasts, we can use those ranks to test for a correlation between the two judges, but we cannot test for a correlation using linear correlation.

    Even when measured data are available, we can sometimes get a clearer result by converting the data into ranks. For example, the severity of industrial accidents is often reported in number of days of lost work time. But these exact numbers may cluster near arbitrary values, such as cutoffs for time-off support by Workers' Compensation. If you are comparing the magnitudes of energy sources and the severity of related accidents, converting the data to ranks may provide clearer results.

2. Rank correlation can be used to detect some (not all) relationships that are not linear. (An example will be given later in this section.)

3. The computations for rank correlation are much simpler than those for linear correlation, as can be readily seen by comparing the formulas used to compute these statistics. If calculators or computers are not available, the rank correlation coefficient is easier to compute.

Disadvantage: A disadvantage of rank correlation is its efficiency rating of 0.91, as described in Section 13-1. This efficiency rating indicates that with all other circumstances being equal, the nonparametric approach of rank correlation requires 100 pairs of sample data to achieve the same results as only 91 pairs of sample observations analysed through the parametric approach, assuming the stricter requirements of the parametric approach are met.

We will use the following notation, which closely parallels the notation used in Chapter 9 for linear correlation. (Recall from Chapter 9 that r denotes the linear correlation coefficient for sample paired data, ρ denotes the linear correlation coefficient for all paired data in a population, and n denotes the number of pairs of data.)

Notation

r_s = rank correlation coefficient for sample paired data (r_s is a sample statistic)

ρ_s = rank correlation coefficient for all the population data (ρ_s is a population parameter)

n = number of pairs of data

d = difference between ranks for the two observations within a pair

---

We use the notation r_s for the rank correlation coefficient so that we don't confuse it with the linear correlation coefficient r. The subscript s has nothing to do with standard deviation; it is used in honour of Charles Spearman (1863–1945), who originated the rank correlation approach. In fact, r_s is often called **Spearman's rank correlation coefficient**.

The procedure for using the rank correlation procedure is summarized in Figure 13-6. That figure includes the following test statistic.

Test Statistic for the Rank Correlation Coefficient

$$r_s = 1 - \frac{6\Sigma d^2}{n(n^2 - 1)}$$

where each value of d is a difference between the ranks for a pair of sample data

---

Critical values:

If $n \le 30$, critical values are found in Table A-9.
If $n > 30$, critical values are found by using Formula 13-1.

Formula 13-1 $r_s = \dfrac{\pm z}{\sqrt{n - 1}}$ (critical values when $n > 30$)

where the value of z corresponds to the significance level.

Direct Link Between Smoking and Cancer

When we find a statistical correlation between two variables, we must be extremely careful to avoid the mistake of concluding that there is a cause–effect link. The tobacco industry has consistently emphasized that correlation does not imply causality. However, Dr. David Sidransky of Johns Hopkins University now says that "we have such strong molecular proof that we can take an individual cancer and potentially, based on the patterns of genetic change, determine whether cigarette smoking was the cause of that cancer." Based on his findings, he also said that "the smoker had a much higher incidence of the mutation, but the second thing that nailed it was the very distinct pattern of mutations . . . so we had the smoking gun." Although statistical methods cannot prove that smoking *causes* cancer, they add to the weight of evidence that a causual relationship exists.

Handling Ties: We handle ties in ranks of the original sample values as in the preceding sections of this chapter: Find the mean of the ranks involved in the tie, and then assign the mean rank to each of the tied items. This test statistic yields the exact value of r_s only if there are no ties. With a relatively small number of ties, the test statistic is a good approximation of r_s. (When ties occur, we can get an exact value of r_s by ranking the data and using Formula 9-1 for the linear correlation coefficient; after finding the value of r_s, we can proceed with the methods of this section.)

● **EXAMPLE**   Every year, *Maclean's* magazine ranks Canadian universities by a number of criteria. The universities are grouped into categories such as primarily undergraduate, comprehensive, and so on, and ranked within these categories. Table 13-5 is based on one year's results for the 13 comprehensive universities. Is there a correlation between the universities' rankings for numbers of student awards and their rankings for number of faculty awards? The linear correlation coefficient r (Section 9-2) should not be used because it requires normal distributions, but the data consist of ranks that are not normally distributed. Instead, use the rank correlation coefficient to test the claim that there is a relationship between the rankings for student awards and faculty awards (that is, $\rho_s \neq 0$). Use a significance level of $\alpha = 0.05$.

TABLE 13-5	Rankings of Comprehensive Universities						
University	Simon Fraser	Guelph	Victoria	Waterloo	York	Memorial	Carleton
Student awards	3	2	4	1	11	12	6
Faculty awards	1	9	5	4	2	12	7
d	2	−7	−1	−3	9	0	−1
d^2	4	49	1	9	81	0	1
University	Windsor	New Brunswick	Regina	Concordia	UQAM	Trois-Rivières	
Student awards	13	5	10	7	8	9	
Faculty awards	6	13	11	8	3	10	
d	7	−8	−1	−1	5	−1	
d^2	49	64	1	1	25	1	→Total = 286

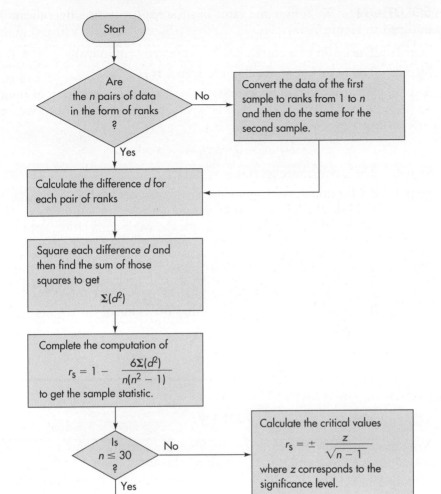

Figure 13-6   Rank Correlation
for Testing H_0: $\rho_s = 0$

Start

Are
the n pairs of data
in the form of ranks
?

No → Convert the data of the first
sample to ranks from 1 to n
and then do the same for the
second sample.

Yes

Calculate the difference d for
each pair of ranks

Square each difference d and
then find the sum of those
squares to get
$$\Sigma(d^2)$$

Complete the computation of
$$r_s = 1 - \frac{6\Sigma(d^2)}{n(n^2 - 1)}$$
to get the sample statistic.

Is
$n \leq 30$
?

No → Calculate the critical values
$$r_s = \pm \frac{z}{\sqrt{n - 1}}$$
where z corresponds to the
significance level.

Yes

Find the critical values of r_s in
Table A-9.

If the sample statistic r_s is positive and exceeds the positive critical value, there is a
correlation. If the sample statistic r_s is negative and is less than the negative critical
value, there is a correlation. If the sample statistic r_s is between the positive and negative
critical values, there is no correlation.

Manatees Saved

Manatees are large mammals that like to float just below the water's surface, where they are in danger from powerboat propellers. A Florida study of the number of powerboat registrations and the numbers of accidental manatee deaths confirmed that there was a significant positive correlation. As a result, Florida created coastal sanctuaries where powerboats are prohibited so that manatees could thrive. (See Program 1 from the series *Against All Odds: Inside Statistics* for a discussion of this case.) This is one of many examples of the beneficial use of statistics.

SOLUTION   We follow the same basic steps for testing hypotheses as outlined in Figure 7-4.

Step 1: The claim of a correlation is expressed symbolically as $\rho_s \neq 0$.

Step 2: The negation of the claim in Step 1 is $\rho_s = 0$.

Step 3: Because the null hypothesis must contain the condition of equality, we have

$$H_0: \rho_s = 0$$
$$H_1: \rho_s \neq 0 \quad \text{(original claim)}$$

Step 4: The significance level is $\alpha = 0.05$.

Step 5: As we noted, we cannot use the linear correlation approach of Section 9-2 because ranks do not satisfy the requirement of a normal distribution. We will use the rank correlation approach instead.

Step 6: We now find the value of the test statistic. Table 13-5 shows the calculation of the differences d and their squares d^2, which results in a value of $\Sigma d^2 = 286$. With $n = 13$ (for 13 pairs of data) and $\Sigma d^2 = 286$, we can find the value of the test statistic r_s as follows:

$$r_s = 1 - \frac{6\Sigma d^2}{n(n^2 - 1)} = 1 - \frac{6(286)}{13(13^2 - 1)}$$
$$= 1 - \frac{1716}{2184} = 0.214$$

Now refer to Table A-9 to determine that the critical values are ± 0.566 (based on $\alpha = 0.05$ and $n = 13$). Because the test statistic $r_s = 0.214$ does not exceed the critical value of 0.566, we fail to reject the null hypothesis.

Interpretation When the universities' rankings for numbers of student awards and faculty awards are compared, there is not sufficient evidence to support the claim of a correlation. It appears that different unrelated university features are associated with student and faculty awards.

EXAMPLE   Suppose that there were 40 comprehensive universities in Canada, and that *Maclean's* ranked them with respect to numbers of student awards and the numbers of faculty awards. If the test statistic r_s is found to be 0.291, and if the significance level is $\alpha = 0.05$, what do you conclude about the correlation between the two rankings?

SOLUTION   Because there are 40 pairs of data, we have $n = 40$. Because n exceeds 30, we find the critical values from Formula 13-1 instead of Table A-9. With $\alpha = 0.05$ in two tails, we let $z = 1.96$ to get

$$r_s = \frac{\pm 1.96}{\sqrt{40 - 1}} = \pm 0.314$$

The test statistic of $r_s = 0.291$ does not exceed the critical value of 0.314, so we fail to reject the null hypothesis. There is not sufficient evidence to support the claim of a correlation between the rankings for student and faculty awards.

The next example is intended to illustrate the principle that rank correlation can sometimes be used to detect relationships that are not linear.

EXAMPLE   Ten students study for a test; the following table lists the number of hours studied (x) and the corresponding number of correct answers (y).

Hours studied (x)	5	9	17	1	2	21	3	29	7	100
Correct answers (y)	6	16	18	1	3	21	7	20	15	22

At the 0.05 level of significance, test the claim that there is a relationship between hours studied and the number of correct answers.

SOLUTION   In part because of the x value of 100 hours (an outlier), the distribution requirements are not met for using the linear regression methods of Chapter 9. (Examine Figure 13-7.) We could choose to discard the outlier, but this wastes a potentially useful data pair. Instead we will use the Spearman's rank correlation approach. Testing the null hypothesis of null rank correlation, we have:

$$H_0: \rho_s = 0$$
$$H_1: \rho_s \neq 0$$

Refer to Figure 13-6, which we follow in this solution. Following the procedures of Section 13-1, we convert the original values into ranks as shown in the table.

Ranks for hours studied	4	6	7	1	2	8	3	9	5	10
Ranks for correct answers	3	6	7	1	2	9	4	8	5	10
d	1	0	0	0	0	−1	−1	1	0	0
d^2	1	0	0	0	0	1	1	1	0	0 → Total = 4

After expressing all data as ranks, we calculate the differences, d, and then square them. The sum of the d^2 values is 4. We now calculate

$$r_s = 1 - \frac{6\Sigma d^2}{n(n^2 - 1)} = 1 - \frac{6(4)}{10(10^2 - 1)}$$
$$= 1 - \frac{24}{990} = 0.976$$

Proceeding with Figure 13-6, we have $n = 10$, so we answer yes when asked if $n \leq 30$. We use Table A-9 to get the critical values of ± 0.648. Finally, the sample statistic of 0.976 exceeds 0.648, so we reject the null hypothesis of no significant correlation.

Interpretation   More hours of study appear to be associated with higher grades. (You didn't really think we would suggest otherwise, did you?)

In the preceding example, if we compute the linear correlation coefficient r (using Formula 9-1) for the original data, we get $r = 0.629$, which leads to the conclusion that there is not enough evidence to support the claim of a significant linear correlation at the 0.05 level of significance. If we examine the scatter diagram in Figure 13-7, we can see that there does seem to be a relationship, but it's not linear. This last example illustrates these two advantages of the nonparametric approach over the parametric approach: (1) With rank correlation, we can sometimes detect relationships that are not linear, and (2) Spearman's rank correlation coefficient r_s is less sensitive to an outlier, such as the 100 hours in the preceding data.

Figure 13-7   Scatter Diagram for Hours Studied and Correct Answers

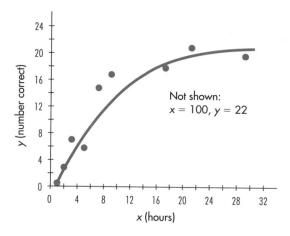

Not shown:
$x = 100, y = 22$

Using Technology

STATDISK: Select **Analysis** from the main menu bar, then select **Rank Correlation**. Next, click **Evaluate**.

Excel: Create a data range in which each sample value has been replaced by its corresponding rank, and these ranks are in neighbouring columns; then, using the data range as input, calculate the linear correlation coefficient with the same Excel procedures used in Section 9-2.

If the data are not already ranked, align the data in two neighbouring columns and add the headings as shown in the following figure. The original data are in the columns "Variable 1" and "Variable 2." Sort the table in order of the "Variable 1" column. Now fill the "Ranks 1" column with the ordered numbers from 1 to the number of data pairs. Inspect the "Variable 1" column for tied values. If there are any, then manually replace their ranks in the "Ranks 1" column with the mean of the ranks that first appear there. (If, for example, the two smallest values in the "Variable 1" column were both 1, then they would both be assigned the rank 1.5, which is the mean of the original ranks 1 and 2.) Now re-sort the full data range, including the "Ranks 1" column, based on the "Variable 2" column, and repeat the above procedures to fill in the "Ranks 2" column. When this is complete, the "Ranks 1" and "Ranks 2" columns can be the input range for the Excel procedures for calculating the linear correlation coefficient r.

	A	B	C	D	E	F	G	H	I
1	Variable 1	Variable 2	Ranks 1	Ranks 2					
2	1	1	1	1					
3	2	3	2	2					
4	5	6	4	3					
5	3	7	3	4					
6	7	15	5	5					
7	9	16	6	6					
8	17	18	7	7					
9	29	20	9	8					
10	21	21	8	9					
11	100	22	10	10					
12									

Excel Display   Rank
Correlation

13–6 Exercises A: Basic Skills and Concepts

1. For each of the following samples of paired ranks, sketch a scatter diagram, find the value of r_s, and state whether there appears to be a correlation between x and y.

   a. | x | 1 | 3 | 5 | 4 | 2 |
      |---|---|---|---|---|---|
      | y | 1 | 3 | 5 | 4 | 2 |

   b. | x | 1 | 2 | 3 | 4 | 5 |
      |---|---|---|---|---|---|
      | y | 5 | 4 | 3 | 2 | 1 |

   c. | x | 1 | 2 | 3 | 4 | 5 |
      |---|---|---|---|---|---|
      | y | 2 | 5 | 3 | 1 | 4 |

2. Find the critical value(s) for r_s by using either Table A-9 or Formula 13-1, as appropriate. Assume two-tailed cases, where α represents the level of significance and n represents the number of pairs of data.

   a. $n = 20, \alpha = 0.05$ b. $n = 50, \alpha = 0.05$
   c. $n = 40, \alpha = 0.02$ d. $n = 15, \alpha = 0.01$
   e. $n = 82, \alpha = 0.04$

In Exercises 3–18, use the rank correlation coefficient to test the claim of no correlation between the two variables. Use a significance level of $\alpha = 0.05$.

3. The accompanying table lists salary rankings and stress rankings for randomly selected jobs. Does it appear that salary increases as stress increases?

Job	Salary Rank	Stress Rank
Stockbroker	2	2
Zoologist	6	7
Electrical engineer	3	6
School principal	5	4
Hotel manager	7	5
Bank officer	10	8
Occ. safety inspector	9	9
Home economist	8	10
Psychologist	4	3
Airline pilot	1	1

Based on data from *The Jobs Rated Almanac.*

4. Exercise 3 includes paired salary and stress level ranks for 10 randomly selected jobs. The physical demands of the jobs were also ranked; the salary and physical demand ranks are given below. Does there appear to be a relationship between the salary of a job and its physical demands?

Salary	2	6	3	5	7	10	9	8	4	1
Physical demand	5	2	3	8	10	9	1	7	6	4

Based on data from *The Jobs Rated Almanac.*

5. Ten jobs were randomly selected and ranked according to stress level and physical demand, with the results given below. Does there appear to be a relationship between the stress levels of jobs and their physical demands?

Stress level	2	7	6	4	5	8	9	10	3	1
Physical demand	5	2	3	8	10	9	1	7	6	4

Based on data from *The Jobs Rated Almanac.*

6. Most truck industry carriers operate within a single province or region. About 1% operate across multiple jurisdictions, including nationally. Comparing ranked years (from the period 1984–94) and ranked numbers of multi-jurisdiction carriers per year, assess whether the number of these carriers and the year sequence are related.

Years	7	2	9	11	1	10	3	5	4	8	6
Numbers of carriers	7	2	9.5	11	1	8	3	9.5	5.5	4	5.5

Based on data from Transport Canada.

7. In studying the effects of heredity and environment on intelligence, scientists have learned much by analysing the IQ scores of identical twins who were separated soon after birth. Identical twins have identical genes, which they inherited from the same fertilized egg. By studying identical twins raised apart, we can eliminate the variable of heredity and better isolate the effects of environment. Following are the IQ scores of identical twins (first-born twins are x) raised apart.

x	107	96	103	90	96	113	86	99	109	105	96	89
y	111	97	116	107	99	111	85	108	102	105	100	93

Based on data from "IQ's of Identical Twins Reared Apart," by Arthur Jensen, *Behavioral Genetics.*

8. It's a baseball cliché that "pitching wins games." Test that claim based on the accompanying data. For eight randomly selected American League teams for the 2000 season, the following data compares the Earned Run Average (ERA) for the teams' pitchers (lower is considered better) and total team wins (based on data from the CNN/Sports Illustrated Web site).

Team ERA	4.53	4.58	4.84	5.02	5.16	5.17	5.48	5.52
Team wins	91	91	90	82	69	83	77	71

9. Researchers have studied bears by anesthetizing them in order to obtain vital measurements. The data in the table represent the first eight male bears in Data Set 3 from Appendix B.

x Length (in.)	53.0	67.5	72.0	72.0	73.5	68.5	73.0	37.0
y Weight (lb)	80	344	416	348	262	360	332	34

10. An amateur biologist has read that the life spans of mammals are related to their metabolic rates. The relation, if any, is not linear, so she will test the claim based on the rank correlation coefficient. She begins by randomly selecting six species, and then recording their maximum life spans and their typical metabolic rates (see Data Set 19 in Appendix B for more details). Is there a significant correlation between these variables?

Metabolic rate	0.6	0.9	1.3	1.4	11	36
Maximum life	70	45	115	20	3.5	0.3

11. The accompanying table lists educational requirements (in years) and typical salary (in thousands of dollars) for a sample of professions. Based on the result, can you expect to earn more if you choose a profession that requires more years of education? How do the results change if the salaries are entered as 61,100, 36,000, . . . , 14,800?

Years of education	16	15	14	14	13	13	12	11
Income	61.1	36.0	62.6	32.9	27.2	36.9	36.7	29.6

Years of education	13	11	10	12	11	12	10	10
Income	37.6	28.4	26.5	22.2	23.1	24.8	21.3	14.8

Based on data from Statistics Canada.

12. Refer to Data Set 21 in Appendix B and use the paired data for the price and weight (carats) of diamonds. Is there a correlation, suggesting that heavier diamonds are generally of greater value?

13. Refer to Data Set 16 in Appendix B and use the paired data for durations and intervals after eruptions of the Old Faithful geyser. Is there a correlation, suggesting that the interval after an eruption is related to the duration of the eruption?

14. Refer to Data Set 16 in Appendix B and use the paired data for intervals after eruptions and heights of eruptions of the Old Faithful geyser. Is there a correlation, suggesting that the interval after an eruption is related to the height of the eruption?

15. Refer to Data Set 2 in Appendix B and use the paired data consisting of the first and second columns of body temperatures for subjects who are initially sitting. Based on the result, does there appear to be a correlation between temperatures in the initially sitting postures and supine postures? If so, could researchers reduce their laboratory expenses by measuring only one of these two variables?

16. Refer to Data Set 2 in Appendix B and use the paired data consisting of the first and second columns of body temperatures for subjects who are initially standing. Based on the result, does there appear to be a correlation between temperatures in the initially standing postures and supine postures? If so, could researchers reduce their laboratory expenses by measuring only one of these two variables?

17. Refer to Data Set 7 in Appendix B, which looks at temperature and precipitation departures from seasonal norms. Pick out the data pairs corresponding to years of strong El Niños. Compare (a) the temperature departure for the first spring of El Niño and (b) the temperature departure for the second spring of El Niño. Based on the result, does there appear to be a correlation between temperatures in the first spring and those in the second spring of El Niño phenomena? If so, could researchers use this information to help predict the temperature departures for the second spring of El Niño?

18. Refer to Data Set 7 in Appendix B, which looks at temperature and precipitation departures from seasonal norms. Pick out the data pairs corresponding to years of strong El Niños. Compare (a) the precipitation departure for the first spring of El Niño and (b) the precipitation departure for the second spring of El Niño. Based on the result, does there appear to be a correlation between precipitation in the first spring and that in the second spring of El Niño phenomena? If so, could researchers use this information to help predict the precipitation departures for the second spring of El Niño?

13-6 Exercises B: Beyond the Basics

19. One alternative to using Table A-9 involves an approximation of critical values for r_s given as

$$r_s = \pm \sqrt{\frac{t^2}{t^2 + n - 2}}$$

Here t is the t score from Table A-3 corresponding to the significance level and $n - 2$ degrees of freedom. Apply this approximation to find critical values of r_s for the following cases.

a. $n = 8, \alpha = 0.05$ b. $n = 15, \alpha = 0.05$

c. $n = 30, \alpha = 0.05$ d. $n = 30, \alpha = 0.01$

e. $n = 8, \alpha = 0.01$

20. a. How is r_s affected if the scale for one of the variables is changed from feet to inches?
   b. How is r_s affected if one variable is ranked from low to high while the other variable is ranked from high to low?
   c. How is r_s affected if the two variables are interchanged?
   d. One researcher ranks both variables from low to high, while another researcher ranks both variables from high to low. How will their values of r_s compare?
   e. How is r_s affected if each value of x is replaced by $\log x$?

13-7 Runs Test for Randomness

We have seen many statistical procedures used in this book that require the random selection of data. In this section we describe the runs test, which is one method used to determine whether a sequence of sample data have the desired characteristic of randomness.

DEFINITIONS

A **run** is a sequence of data having the same characteristic; the sequence is preceded and followed by data with a different characteristic or by no data at all.

   The **runs test** uses the number of runs in a sequence of sample data to test for randomness in the order of the data.

Assumptions

1. The sample data are arranged according to some ordering scheme such as the order in which the samples were obtained.
2. Each data value can be categorized into one of two separate categories.
3. The runs test for randomness is based on the order in which the data occur; it is not based on the frequency of the data. (For example, a sequence of 3 men and 20 women might appear to be random by this test; whether 3 men and 20 women constitute a biased sample is not addressed by the runs test.)

Notation

n_1 = number of elements in the sequence that have one particular characteristic. (The characteristic chosen for n_1 is arbitrary.)

n_2 = number of elements in the sequence that have the other characteristic

G = number of runs

EXAMPLE   Manufacturers of cola conduct market research to determine consumer preferences. When 10 consumers are asked whether they prefer diet cola or regular cola, the responses of the first 10 subjects are listed in the order in which they were obtained. We use D to denote a consumer who prefers *diet* cola and R to denote a consumer who prefers *regular* cola. Find the number of runs G, and also identify the values of n_1 and n_2.

$$\underbrace{D\,D\,D\,D}_{\text{1st run}} \quad \underbrace{R\,R}_{\text{2nd run}} \quad \underbrace{D\,D\,D}_{\text{3rd run}} \quad \underbrace{R}_{\text{4th run}}$$

SOLUTION   There are exactly four runs, as shown, so $G = 4$. Letting n_1 represent the number of diet (D) colas, we have $n_1 = 7$ because there are seven diet colas present. It follows that the number of regular (R) colas is described by $n_2 = 3$.

Fundamental Principle of the Runs Test

The fundamental principle of the runs test can be briefly stated as follows: **Reject randomness if the number of runs is very low or very high**.

- Example: DDDDDRRRRR is not random because it has only 2 runs, so the number of runs is very low.

- Example: DRDRDRDRDR is not random because there are 10 runs, which is very high (relative to a 10-value data set).

We reject randomness if the number of runs G is too small or too large, but how do we determine exactly which values of G are too small or too large? We use the following criterion:

5% Cutoff Criterion
Reject randomness of the data if the number of runs G is so small or so large that in repeated samplings, a value at least as extreme as G will occur 5% of the time or less.

Although this criterion wins no prizes for simplicity, it's quite easy to apply if we use Table A-10. Table A-10 identifies those values of G that are so small or so large that they belong to the category of exceptional sequences that happen 5% of the time or less. Using Table A-10, the 5% criterion can be simply restated as follows:

Simplified 5% Cutoff Criterion

Reject randomness if the number of runs G is
- less than or equal to the smaller Table A-10 entry or
- greater than or equal to the larger entry in that table

Sports Hot Streaks

It is a common belief that athletes often have "hot streaks"—that is, brief periods of extraordinary success. Psychologist Amos Tversky and other researchers used statistics to analyse the thousands of shots taken by a professional basketball team for one full season and half of another. They found that the number of "hot streaks" was no different than you would expect from random trials with the outcome of each trial independent of any preceding results. That is, the probability of a hit doesn't depend on the preceding hit or miss.

For example, the sequence

$$D \quad D \quad D \quad D \quad R \quad R \quad R \quad R \quad R$$

results in these values: $n_1 = 4$, $n_2 = 5$, and $G = 2$ runs. With $n_1 = 4$ and $n_2 = 5$, Table A-10 indicates that we should reject randomness if the number of runs is 2 or less or 9 or greater. With $G = 2$ runs, we therefore reject randomness according to the simplified 5% cutoff criterion based on Table A-10.

Rationale: How do we find the cutoff values separating random sequences from those that are not? That is, how do we find the critical values displayed in Table A-10? Let's reconsider the sequence DDDDRRRRR (from the previous paragraph), for which $G = 2$, $n_1 = 4$ and $n_2 = 5$. If we refer to Table A-10, we find that for $n_1 = 4$ and $n_2 = 5$, the cutoff values are 2 and 9. If we had an abundance of time and patience, we could list all possible sequences of 4 diet colas and 5 regular colas. Examination of that list would reveal these facts:

- There are 126 different possible sequences of 4 diet and 5 regular colas.
- Among the 126 different possible cases, 2 cases have 2 runs, 7 cases have 3 runs, and so on, as summarized in Table 13-6.

Based on the 5% cutoff criterion, and based on the 126 cases summarized in Table 13-6, we should reject randomness if the number of runs G is 2 or 9 because, with randomly selected data, we will get 2 runs or 9 runs only 2.38% of the time. (With only 2 cases having 2 runs and with only 1 case having 9 runs, the number of runs G is excessively low or high in 3 cases, which is 3/126 or 2.38% of the total number of cases.) It is easy to get 3, 4, 5, 6, 7, or 8 runs, because these values occur more than 95% of the time; but it is unusual to get 2 or 9 runs because these values occur only 2.38% of the time. Table A-10 is constructed by this same principle: It displays the G values, for

TABLE 13-6	Frequency Table of the Number of Runs							
Number of runs	2	3	4	5	6	7	8	9
Frequency in 126 cases	2	7	24	30	36	18	8	1

Random Walk and Stocks

In the book *A Random Walk Down Wall Street*, Burton Malkiel states, "When the term (random walk) is applied to the stock market, it means that short-run changes in stock prices cannot be predicted. Investment advisory services, earnings predictions, and complicated chart patterns are useless." He also writes that "taken to its logical extreme, it means that a blindfolded monkey throwing darts at a newspaper's financial pages could select a portfolio that would do just as well as one carefully selected by the experts." This suggests that investors could save money by no longer securing the expensive advice of financial consultants. They can simply select stocks in a way that is random.

Country	Relative Currency Valuation
U.S.	H
Japan	L
U.K.	H
China	L
Germany	L
South Korea	L
Mexico	L
Belgium	L
France	L
Italy	L

each case, such that there is a 5% chance or less of such a G value occurring if the sequence of data is random.

EXAMPLE   Canada is a trading nation that depends on exports to other countries. A factor that influences trade is the foreign exchange value of the Canadian dollar in relation to the currencies of our trading partners. An ordered list of the top 10 countries for Canadian exports is given in the margin. Next to each country is indicated whether, in the international currency markets, its currency trades at a higher (H) or lower (L) value than the Canadian dollar. Use the (simplified) 5% cutoff criterion to test a claim that the sequence of higher and lower currency valuations is random. (Note that we are not testing for a *bias* in favour of one classification or the other. There are 2 H currencies and 8 L currencies; we are investigating only the randomness in the way they appear in the given sequence.)

SOLUTION   We must first find the values of n_1, n_2, and the number of runs G:

n_1 = number of currencies valued higher than the Canadian dollar = 2
n_2 = number of currencies valued less than the Canadian dollar = 8
G = number of runs = 4

We refer to Table A-10 to find the cutoff values of 1 and 6. Because $G = 4$ is not less than or equal to 1, nor is it greater than or equal to 6, we do not reject randomness.

Interpretation The sequence in which higher-valued and lower-valued currencies appear in the ordered list of Canada's export partners appears to be random.

Large Sample Cases

Table A-10 applies when the following three conditions are all met:

1. We are using 5% as the cutoff for sequences that have too few or too many runs.
2. $n_1 \leq 20$.
3. $n_2 \leq 20$.

If we wish to use the runs test for randomness but $n_1 > 20$ or $n_2 > 20$ or $\alpha \neq 0.05$, we use the property that the number of runs G has a distribution that is approximately normal with mean μ_G and standard deviation σ_G described as follows:

Formula 13-2
$$\mu_G = \frac{2n_1 n_2}{n_1 + n_2} + 1$$

Formula 13-3
$$\sigma_G = \sqrt{\frac{(2n_1 n_2)(2n_1 n_2 - n_1 - n_2)}{(n_1 + n_2)^2 (n_1 + n_2 - 1)}}$$

After finding the values of μ_G and σ_G, the test statistic can be computed as $z = (G - \mu_G)/\sigma_G$. The normal approximation (with test statistic z) is quite good. If the entire table of critical values (Table A-10) had been computed using this normal approximation, no critical value would be off by more than one unit.

Test Statistic for the Runs Test for Randomness

If $\alpha = 0.05$ and $n_1 \leq 20$ and $n_2 \leq 20$, the test statistic is G.
If $\alpha \neq 0.05$ or $n_1 > 20$ or $n_2 > 20$, the test statistic is

$$z = \frac{G - \mu_G}{\sigma_G} \quad \text{(where } \mu_G \text{ and } \sigma_G \text{ are from Formulas 13-2 and 13-3)}$$

Critical Values:

1. If the test statistic is G, critical values are found in Table A-10.
2. If the test statistic is z, critical values are found in Table A-2 by using the same procedures introduced in Chapter 6.

Figure 13-8 summarizes the procedures for the runs test for randomness and includes cases in which the test statistic is G as well as cases in which the test statistic is z.

EXAMPLE   Refer to the sequence of typical length (T) and brief (B) Parliaments in Figure 13-1. Is there any evidence that these T and B Parliaments occur in a nonrandom pattern? Use a 0.05 significance level in testing the sequence for randomness.

Figure 13-8 Runs Test for Randomness

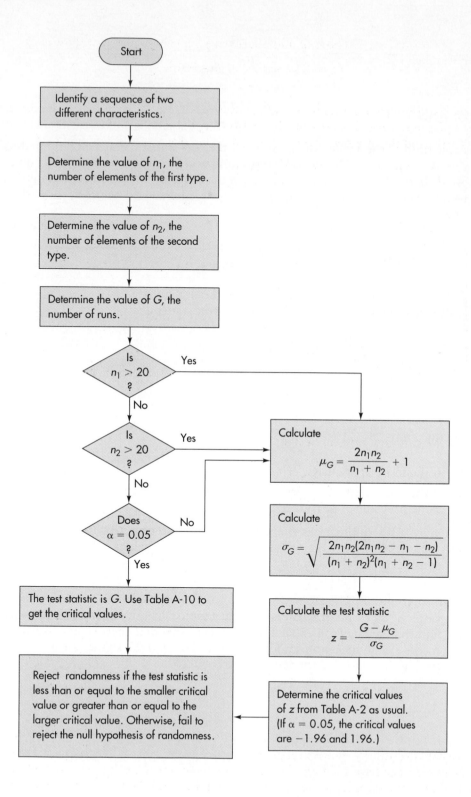

SOLUTION   The null and alternative hypotheses are as follows:

H_0:   The sequence is random.

H_1:   The sequence is not random.

The significance level is $\alpha = 0.05$; we are using the runs test for randomness. The test statistic is obtained by first finding the number of Ts, the number of Bs, and the number of runs. After analysing the sequence, we find that

$$n_1 = \text{number of Ts} = 27$$
$$n_2 = \text{number of Bs} = 8$$
$$G = \text{number of runs} = 17$$

As we follow Figure 13-8, we answer yes to "Is $n_1 > 20$?" We therefore need to evaluate μ_G and σ_G before we can determine the test statistic. Using Formulas 13-2 and 13-3 we get

$$\mu_G = \frac{2n_1 n_2}{n_1 + n_2} + 1 = \frac{2(27)(8)}{27 + 8} + 1 = 13.343$$

$$\sigma_G = \sqrt{\frac{(2n_1 n_2)(2n_1 n_2 - n_1 - n_2)}{(n_1 + n_2)^2(n_1 + n_2 - 1)}}$$

$$= \sqrt{\frac{[2(27)(8)]\,[2(27)(8) - 27 - 8]}{(27 + 8)^2(27 + 8 - 1)}} = 2.029$$

We can now find the test statistic:

$$z = \frac{G - \mu_G}{\sigma_G} = \frac{17 - 13.343}{2.029} = 1.802$$

Because the significance level is $\alpha = 0.05$ and we have a two-tailed test, the critical values are $z = -1.96$ and $z = 1.96$. The test statistic of $z = 1.802$ does not fall within the critical region, so we do not reject the null hypothesis of randomness.

Interpretation   The given sequence appears to be random. No matter what pattern has come before, the pattern provides no basis to guess whether the next Parliament is likely to be brief or long.

Alternative Application: Test for Randomness Above or Below the Mean or Median

In each of the preceding examples, the data clearly fit into two categories, but we can also test for randomness in the way numerical data fluctuate above or below a mean or median. To test for randomness above and below the median, for example, we use the sample data to find the value of the median, then replace each individual score with the letter A if it is *above* the median, and replace it with B if it is *below* the median. Delete any values that are equal to the median. It is helpful to write the As and Bs directly above the numbers they represent because this makes checking easier and also reduces the chance of having the wrong number of letters.

After finding the sequence of A and B letters, we can apply the runs test as described earlier. Economists use this test to help identify trends or cycles. An upward economic trend would contain a predominance of Bs at the beginning and As at the end, so the number of runs would be small. A downward trend would have As dominating at the beginning and Bs at the end, with a low number of runs. A cyclical pattern would yield a sequence that systematically changes, so the number of runs would tend to be large.

Using Technology

STATDISK: STATDISK will perform the runs test, but, because of the nature of the data, you must first determine the values of n_1, n_2, and the number of runs G. Select **Analysis** from the main menu bar, then select **Runs Test**. The STATDISK display will include the upper and lower critical values, the mean and standard deviation for the number of runs expected with a random sequence, and the conclusion.

Excel: To create a template in Excel, enter the right-tailed portion of alpha, n_1, n_2, and G. The formulas shown will calculate the other values. But for a two-tailed test, multiply the displayed *P*-value by 2. (Note that if n_1 and n_2 are both ≤ 20 and two-tailed $\alpha = 0.05$, the G cutoff returned by the template, which is based on a normal approximation, may differ slightly from the cutoff given in Table A-10.)

Excel Display   Runs Test for Randomness

	A	B
2	Alpha (right tail)	0.025
3	n1	27
4	n2	8
5	G	17
6	Mean G	13.342857
7	Std dev G	2.0292223
8	Test statistic z	1.8022387
9	Critical z	1.9599611
10	P value	0.0357539

Cell	Formula	Explanation
B6	=(2*B3*B4)/(B3+B4)+1	Formula 13-2
B7	=SQRT(((2*B3*B4)*(2*B3*B4-B3-B4)) /((B3+B4)^2*(B3+B4-1)))	Formula 13-3
B8	=(B5-B6)/B7	Test statistic *z* (see boxed formula)
B9	=NORMSINV(1-B2)	Upper critical value
B10	=1-NORMSDIST(ABS(B8))	*P*-value (for two-tailed test, multiply by 2)

Use appropriate cell addresses for data.

(13-7) Exercises A: Basic Skills and Concepts

In Exercises 1–4, use the given sequence to determine the values of n_1, n_2, the number of runs G, and the 5% cutoff values from Table A-10.

1. A A A B B B B B A A A A A A
2. T F T F T F T F T T T T T T T T T T
3. O O O O O O O O O O E E O O E E
4. M F F F F M F F M M M F F F F

In Exercises 5–12, use the runs test of this section to determine whether the given sequence is random. Use a significance level of $\alpha = 0.05$. (All data are listed in order by row.)

5. In conducting research for this book, one of the authors recorded the outcomes of a roulette wheel in the Stardust Casino. (Yes, it was hard work, but somebody had to do it.) Test for randomness of odd (O) and even (E) numbers for the results given in the following sequence. What would a lack of randomness mean to the author? To the casino?

   O O E E E E O O E O E O O O O O O E O E

6. The Niko Music Company uses a machine to produce compact discs that must meet certain specifications. When a sample of discs is selected in sequence from the assembly line, they are examined and judged to be defective (D) or acceptable (A), with the following results.

   A A A A A A A A A D D A A A A A A A A D D

7. Natural Resources Canada reports regularly on seismic events (earthquakes) in Canada. In just the three days—January 15 to 17, 2001—there were 24 such events. Earthquake magnitudes are recorded in a variety of scales, of which Canada primarily uses ML (Magnitude Local = Richter Scale) and MN (Magnitude Nuttli). For that January sequence of 24 seismic events, the sequence in which the two reporting scales (L for ML, N for MN) were used is shown below. Test the claim that the order in which the two scales appear is random.

   N N N N N N L N L L L N L N N L N L L N L L L L

8. Test the claim that the sequence of World Series wins by American League and National League teams is random. Given below are recent results with American and National league teams represented by A and N, respectively. What does the result suggest about the abilities of the two leagues?

   A N A A A N N A A N N N N A A A N A N A N A A A N A

9. Since 1935, there have been 11 changes of prime minister in Canada, including Pierre Trudeau's re-election in 1980 after a period in Opposition. The political party of each new prime minister is indicated by L for Liberal and P for Progressive Conservative. Does it appear that the Liberal and Progressive Conservative parties became the party of new prime ministers in a random sequence?

   L L P L L P L L P P L

10. As an aid to its farming industries, Alberta tracks the dates of last frost across the province. At some sites, the last frost occurs in mid-May, while others reach this event a month or more later. Tracking this information in five-day intervals, the accompanying list shows the sequence in which new sites are added to the last-frost list. (For example, two sites had their last frost within the first interval, 12 sites had their last frost in the next interval, and so on.) Find the median of the values, then replace each value by A if it is above the median and by B if it is below the median. Omit from the analysis any values that are exactly at the median. Then apply the runs test to the resulting sequence of As and Bs. What does the result suggest about the pattern in which sites across Alberta are added to the last-frost list? If you knew more about the latitude of each site in relation to its last frost date, might this cause you to reassess your conclusion from the runs test?

$$2 \quad 12 \quad 17 \quad 15 \quad 8 \quad 10 \quad 3 \quad 0 \quad 0 \quad 0 \quad 1$$

Based on "Freezing Dates for Alberta Locations," by Peter Dzikowski,
Conservation and Development Branch of Alberta Agriculture.

11. Business trends and economics applications are often analysed with the runs test. The accompanying list shows, in order by row, the net gain or loss in the TSE 300 Composite index over each month in a recent sequence of months. Replace each value by G if it is a gain (above zero) or L if it is a loss (below 0). Then apply the runs test to the resulting sequence of Gs and Ls. What does the result suggest about the pattern of net monthly gains and losses in the index? Given the pattern you have identified, is it possible to make money?

69.07	48.26	−307.62	135.75	405.69	136.26	181.24
−176.18	428.46	−209.30	−379.16	218.38	289.38	428.31
294.61	−151.52	−92.01	−322.26	−608.80		

12. Listed below are the bonus numbers selected in consecutive Lotto 6/49 drawings. Test for randomness of odd (0) and even (E) numbers. What would lack of randomness mean for those who play the lottery?

30 27 25   8 26 45 31 19 31 11 23   9 12 46   5 18
22 18 49 49 28 14 25 41 17   3 20 10 36 37 45 37

13. The Restaurant Market Research Company hires Diana Kriplani to survey adults about their dining habits. A check of her first 40 results shows that their genders are represented in the following sequence. Use the runs test to determine whether the subjects are randomly selected with respect to gender.

F F F   F F M M M M M F F F F M M M M F F
F F F M M M M M M M M M M M F F F F F F

14. Many mathematicians agree that the decimal digits of π cannot be distinguished from any random sequence. Given below are the first 100 decimal places of π. Test for randomness of odd (O) and even (E) digits.

```
1 4 1 5 9 2 6 5 3 5 8 9 7 9 3 2 3 8 4 6
2 6 4 3 3 8 3 2 7 9 5 0 2 8 8 4 1 9 7 1
6 9 3 9 9 3 7 5 1 0 5 8 2 0 9 7 4 9 4 4
5 9 2 3 0 7 8 1 6 4 0 6 2 8 6 2 0 8 9 9
8 6 2 8 0 3 4 8 2 5 3 4 2 1 1 7 0 6 7 9
```

15. Use the 100 decimal digits for π given in Exercise 14. Test for randomness above (A) and below (B) the value of 4.5.

16. Test the claim that the sequence of World Series wins by American League and National League teams is random. Given below are recent results, with American and National League teams represented by A and N, respectively.

```
A N A N N N A A A A N A A A N A N N A
A N N A A A A N A N N A A A A A N A N A
N A N A A A A A A A N N A N A N N A A N
N N A N A N A N A A A N N A A N N N N A
A A N A N A N A A A N A
```

13-7 Exercises B: Beyond the Basics

17. Using the elements A, A, B, B, what is the minimum number of possible runs that can be arranged? What is the maximum number of runs? Now refer to Table A-10 to find the 5% cutoff G values for $n_1 = n_2 = 2$. What do you conclude about this case?

18. a. Using all of the elements A, A, A, B, B, B, B, B, B, list the 84 different possible sequences.
    b. Find the number of runs for each of the 84 sequences.
    c. Use the results from parts (a) and (b) to find your own 5% cutoff values for G.
    d. Compare your results to those given in Table A-10.

● ●

Vocabulary List

parametric tests
nonparametric tests
distribution-free tests
efficiency
rank
sign test
Wilcoxon signed-ranks test
Wilcoxon rank-sum test

Mann-Whitney U test
Kruskal-Wallis test
H-test
rank correlation test
Spearman's rank correlation
    test
run
runs test

● ●

Review

In this chapter we examined six different nonparametric methods for analysing sample data. Nonparametric tests are also called distribution-free tests because they do not require that the populations have a particular distribution, such as a normal distribution. However, if the population distribution is normal, then nonparametric tests are not as efficient as parametric tests, so we would need stronger evidence before we reject a null hypothesis.

Table 13-7 lists the nonparametric tests presented in this chapter, along with their functions. The table also lists the corresponding parametric tests.

TABLE 13-7   Summary of Nonparametric Tests

Nonparametric Test	Function	Parametric Test
Sign test (Section 13-2)	Test for claimed value of average with one sample	t test or z test (Sections 7-2, 7-3, 7-4)
	Test for difference between two dependent samples	t test or z test (Section 8-2)
Wilcoxon signed-ranks test (Section 13-3)	Test for difference between two dependent samples	t test or z test (Section 8-2)
Wilcoxon rank-sum test (Section 13-4)	Test for difference between two independent samples	t test or z test (Sections 8-3, 8-5)
Kruskal-Wallis test (Section 13-5)	Test for more than two independent samples coming from identical populations	Analysis of variance (Section 11-2)
Rank correlation (Section 13-6)	Test for relationship between two variables	Linear correlation (Section 9-2)
Runs test (Section 13-7)	Test for randomness of sample data	(No parametric test)

• •

Review Exercises

In Exercises 1–12, use a 0.05 significance level with the indicated test. If no particular test is specified, use the appropriate nonparametric test from this chapter.

1. The accompanying table shows samples of data about prime ministers, popes, and British monarchs. The values are the numbers of years the subjects lived after they were first elected or were crowned. Test the claim that the three populations are not all the same.

Prime ministers	17	23	22	23	29	40	9	19	25
Popes	3	18	25	6	15	11	19		
Monarchs	17	13	12	33	10	7	25		

2. A number of companies sell both cars and trucks in Canada. Do a company's car sales go up (or down) in tandem with its truck sales? The accompanying table shows the annual percent changes in car and truck sales for a selection of companies that offer both. Use the Wilcoxon signed-ranks test to test the hypothesis that there is no difference in a company's percent change in sales for cars and trucks. By its use of ranks, the Wilcoxon test is not sensitive to the magnitude of differences where they occur. Inspecting these data, would you be inclined to predict changes in car sales based on changes in truck sales?

Car change	34.3	9	–3.7	–31.9	79.6	27.8	6.4	2.7	–20.8
Truck change	24.1	73	13.3	–8.6	–33.3	0	33.9	59.3	–19.4

Based on data in *The Globe and Mail.*

3. A Regina manufacturing company uses a machine to produce surgical knives that must meet certain specifications. A sample of knives is randomly selected and each knife is judged to be defective (D) or acceptable (A), with the results given below. Use the runs test for randomness to determine whether the sequence of defective and acceptable knives is random.

D A A A A D A A A A D A A A A
D A A A A D A A A A D A A A A

4. The accompanying table shows a sample from the poll results, by *The Globe and Mail Report on Business* and *Angus Reid*, which compare two years' evaluations, by CEOs, of the 25 top-performing firms. For the 2000 results, each company is given a score that reflects the respondents' choices. For 1999, the companies' scores have been converted to ranks (where 1 is best). Test the claim that there is a correlation between a company's scores in the two years.

2000 score	58	42	61	346	70	85	41	903	95
1999 rank	18	21	15	7	10	31	61	3	14

5. Internet search engines often return large lists of results for the search lists that are entered. Some guides suggest refining the search by adding more words to the search list. To test whether this suggestion is effective, the accompanying table shows the numbers of results returned by Yahoo Canada for each of eight randomly generated, two-word search lists. The bottom row

shows the numbers of results returned when each two-word search list is supplemented by a randomly generated third word. Use the sign test to test the claim that there is no difference in the numbers of results returned before and after adding the additional word to the search list. Is simply adding more words to a search list an effective strategy to reduce the numbers of results?

Trial	A	B	C	D	E	F	G	H
Two words	3,589	1,071,575	387,835	88,535	71,640	1,369	236,140	208,375
Three words	3,610	793,961	695,933	72,468	66,339	1,861	166,103	315,455

6. The Medassist Pharmaceutical Company conducted a study to determine whether a drug affects eye movements. A standardized scale was developed, and the drug was administered to one group, while a control group was given a placebo that produces no effects. The eye movement ratings of subjects are listed below. Test the claim that the drug has no effect on eye movements. Use the Wilcoxon rank-sum test.

Drugged group	Control group
652 512 711 621 508 603 787	674 676 821 830 565 821 837 652 549
747 516 624 627 777 729	668 772 563 703 789 800 711 598

7. To test the effectiveness of the use of technology in a statistics course, four different sections were taught with different combinations of calculators and computer software, with final course averages listed below for randomly selected students from each section. Test the claim that the samples come from populations that are not all the same.

Calculators Only	Computers Only	Calculators and Computers	No Calculators and No Computers
74 85 91 62	82 87 60 71	78 89 82 64	66 78 83 55
73 87 66 80	77 63 84 70	77 91 73 85	72 57 81 65

8. A statistics quiz consists of true-false questions with the answers listed as shown.
   a. Examine the sequence and try to identify a pattern showing that the answers are not random.
   b. What do you conclude from using the runs test for randomness?
   c. How do you explain the discrepancy between parts (a) and (b)?

   T F T T T T F T T T T F T T T T F T T T T F TT T

9. A consumer investigator obtained prices from mail-order companies and computer stores. The accompanying lists show the prices (in dollars) quoted for cartons of floppy disks from various manufacturers. Use the Wilcoxon rank-sum test to test the claim that there is no difference between mail order and store prices.

Mail Order				Computer Store			
23.00	26.00	27.99	31.50	30.99	33.98	37.75	38.99
32.75	27.00	27.98	24.50	35.79	33.99	34.79	32.99
24.75	28.15	29.99	29.99	29.99	33.00	32.00	

10. A study was conducted to investigate some effects of physical training. Sample data (weights in kilograms) are listed in the margin. (See "Effect of Endurance Training on Possible Determinants of VO_2 During Heavy Exercise," by Casaburi et al., *Journal of Applied Physiology*, Vol. 62, No. 1.) Use the sign test to test the claim that the training has no effect on weight.

11. Do Exercise 10 using the Wilcoxon signed-ranks test.

12. Two measures of health care are the mean number of people per physician, and the percentage of the population who reside fewer than 5 km from a physician. In the table below, the 10 provinces are ranked based on these measures. For "People/physician," a rank of 1 signifies the fewest people per physician; for "% < 5 km," a rank of 1 signifies the largest proportion of people who reside less than 5 km from a physician. Is there a correlation between these two measures of health care?

Pre-training	Post-training
99	94
57	57
62	62
69	69
74	66
77	76
59	58
92	88
70	70
85	84

Province	BC	AB	SK	MB	ON	PQ	NB	NS	PE	NF
People/physician	1	7	8	5	4	3	9	2	10	6
% < 5 km	1	4	8	5	3	2	10	7	9	6

Based on data from Statistics Canada.

• •

Cumulative Review Exercises

1. The Broadbent Opinion Research Organization assigned a pollster to collect data from 30 randomly selected adults. As the data were submitted to the company, the genders of the interviewed subjects were noted. The sequence obtained is shown in the accompanying list.
   a. At the 0.05 significance level, test the claim that the sequence is random.
   b. At the 0.05 significance level, test the claim that the proportion of women is different from 0.5.
   c. Use the sample data to construct a 95% confidence interval for the proportion of women.
   d. What do the preceding results suggest? Is the sample biased against either gender? Was the sample obtained in a random sequence? If you are the manager, do you have any problems with these results?

   M M F M M F M M F M F M M F M
   F M F M M F M M F M M F M M M

2. The Kamloops Weight Clinic claims that everyone can lose weight after two weeks in its program. The table at the top of the next page lists the weights, in kilograms, of randomly selected clients before and after the program. Use the indicated test with a 0.05 level of significance to test the hypothesis that the program has no effect on people's weight.
   a. Sign test
   b. Wilcoxon signed-ranks test
   c. *t* test for a claim about two dependent samples (Section 8-2)
   d. How do the preceding results support the statement that nonparametric tests lack the sensitivity of parametric tests (so stronger evidence is required before a null hypothesis is rejected)?

Client	A	B	C	D	E	F	G	H	I	J
Weight before entering program	75	81	77	87	85	74	77	104	95	100
Weight after entering program	70	82	77	85	80	75	79	100	84	93

3. Refer to the annual numbers of person-days lost in the water-based transportation industry due to work stoppages in Data Set 20 in Appendix B. Find the following:
   a. Mean
   b. Median
   c. Mode
   d. Range
   e. Standard Deviation
   f. Any outliers

Technology Project

In Section 13-4 we saw that the Wilcoxon rank-sum test can be used to test the null hypothesis that two independent samples come from the same distribution, and the alternative hypothesis is the claim that the two distributions differ in some way. Use Excel, STATDISK, or any other statistical software package to run the Wilcoxon rank-sum test and determine whether it detects the difference in the two distributions. The two samples are from populations with the same mean of 100 and the same standard deviation of 15, but the distributions are different (normal, uniform).

Sample randomly selected from a *normally* distributed population with mean 100 and standard deviation 15:

82	92	84	107	104	130	84	125	110	96
98	83	87	99	108	97	84	122	106	114
78	117	105	100	94	114	135	99	109	79
106	83	72	105	108	102	100	106	109	119
95	124	95	86	113	83	93	95	99	122
77	106	87	94	92	95	112	95	101	65
69	108	125	105	132	107	101	94	122	80
101	111	108	107	96	134	105	51	85	141
94	102	74	84	101	99	109	83	116	119
118	114	129	98	101	117	92	96	83	114

Sample randomly selected from a *uniformly* distributed population with a minimum of 74 and a maximum of 126 (such a population has a mean of 100 and a standard deviation of 15):

111	104	96	109	93	78	88	85	88	91
92	108	124	114	82	110	100	104	84	113
111	116	95	121	82	120	110	115	93	124
118	94	102	106	104	126	114	123	115	82
84	100	118	76	82	110	81	123	108	96
107	91	89	122	92	100	122	108	81	107
89	123	81	111	118	97	94	86	109	74
87	113	97	78	115	95	117	77	125	109
77	82	111	80	117	108	107	102	94	93
114	94	112	94	116	111	88	101	81	110

•••••••• **FROM DATA TO DECISION** ••••••••

Is Hockey Attendance Random?

Owners of hockey franchises, and many others, are vitally interested in the attendance patterns at hockey games. If there is evidence of nonrandom trends in attendance, then future marketing plans, budgets, and scheduling may all be affected. The accompanying list shows the attendance figures for the Vancouver Canucks' 41 home games during the 1996–97 and 1997–98 seasons.

a. Consider the sequence from the first game in the 1996–97 season to the last game of the 1997–98 season. Use the runs test to test the sequence for randomness above and below the median, which is 17,507.

b. Consider these four time segments within the data: (**1A**) games 1 to 20 of the 1996–97 season; (**1B**) games 21 to 41 of the 1996/97 season; (**2A**) games 1 to 20 of the 1997–98 season; and (**2B**) games 21 to 41 of the 1997–98 season. Use the Kruskal-Wallis test to test the claim that the four time segments all had attendance numbers drawn from the same population.

c. Draw a run chart based on the full sequence of 82 games, combining the two 41-game seasons in order, with the horizontal scale plotting the game numbers from 1 to 82 and the vertical scale plotting the attendance number corresponding to each game number. (See Section 12-2 for more details on run charts.) Note any pattern that may suggest the attendance numbers are not randomly sequenced.

d. In the data, there is one attendance number that appears much more frequently than the others. Identify that number and speculate as to why it appears so often. Does the recurrence of that number have an effect on the tests performed in parts (a), (b), and (c)? If it does, how? If not, do you think if there were *more* recurrences of that value, it could have an effect on the tests? Explain your answer.

Game	1996-97 Season Attendance	1997-98 Season Attendance
1	17,501	10,500
2	14,109	17,312
3	15,691	18,422
4	15,142	14,535
5	17,807	16,304
6	18,422	16,880
7	17,546	17,437
8	18,422	18,422
9	16,202	18,422
10	17,411	14,740
11	18,422	16,454
12	16,605	18,422
13	18,422	18,422
14	16,313	15,860
15	18,422	18,422
16	17,854	15,401
17	18,422	17,128
18	16,125	18,422
19	18,422	18,422
20	17,378	18,422
21	18,105	14,549
22	18,422	17,003
23	15,017	17,679
24	16,010	15,822
25	17,331	17,808
26	17,243	18,422
27	18,422	17,421
28	18,422	18,422
29	18,422	18,422
30	17,595	18,422
31	17,492	15,613
32	17,513	15,370
33	18,422	16,452
34	17,535	18,422
35	16,740	17,699
36	15,076	17,478
37	16,050	15,662
38	18,028	17,794
39	18,422	15,239
40	16,809	16,602
41	18,422	17,787

•••••••• COOPERATIVE GROUP ACTIVITIES ••••••••

1. *In-class activity:* Use the existing class seating arrangement and apply the runs test to determine whether the students are arranged randomly according to gender. After recording the seating arrangement, analysis can be done in subgroups of 3 or 4 students.

2. *In-class activity:* Divide into groups of 8 to 12 people. For each group member, *measure* his or her height and *measure* his or her arm span. For the arm span, the subject should stand with arms extended, like the wings on an airplane. It's easy to mark the height and arm span on a chalkboard, then measure the distances there. Divide the following tasks among subgroups of 3 or 4 people.

   a. Use rank correlation with the paired sample data to determine whether there is a correlation between height and arm span.
   b. Use the sign test to test for a difference between the two variables.
   c. Use the Wilcoxon signed-ranks test to test for a difference between the two variables.

3. *In-class activity:* Do Activity 2 using pulse rate instead of arm span. Measure pulse rates by counting the number of heartbeats in one minute.

4. *In-class activity:* Divide into groups of about 10 or 12 students and use the same reaction timer included with Chapter 5. Each group member should be tested for right-hand reaction time and left-hand reaction time. Analyse the results using methods from this chapter. State the methods used and the conclusions reached.

5. *Out-of-class activity:* See the preceding From Data to Decision project, which involves analysis of attendance data for all home games played by a hockey team over two seasons. Suppose you are helping to write a video game that incorporates simulated attendance data over two fictional seasons (to simulate crowd-noise effects and so on). Design a procedure that could produce 82 random numbers, such that the sequence will have the same minimum, maximum, and median values as the actual attendances in the preceding project. Once you have generated the 82 numbers, test your results by using the techniques suggested in parts (a), (b) and (c) of the From Data to Decision project. How do your results compare to those obtained in that project? Write a report that clearly describes the process you designed. Include your analyses and conclusions.

INTERNET PROJECT   Nonparametric Tests

This chapter introduced several different nonparametric or distribution-free tests. Such tests allow you to test hypotheses without making assumptions about the distributions underlying the associated data sets. The Internet Project for this chapter is found at:

   http://www.pearsoned.ca/triola

Click on Internet Project, then on Chapter 13. There you will be directed to revisit some of the hypotheses tested in earlier Internet Projects, but this time you will apply an appropriate nonparametric test. In the second part of the project, you will be asked to apply the runs test to determine randomness of a sequence.

14

Time Series

CHAPTER PROBLEM

What's the forecast for Canadian retail sales?

You work for a retail company, and your section has been asked to help in the planning process by forecasting Canadian retail sales for the next few quarters. The company's profit has always closely reflected the overall Canadian figures, so knowledge of what is likely to happen will be of considerable help in preparing budgets.

Table 14-1 lists Canadian retail sales from 1994 to 1997. Given these data, you would like to determine whether there is any long-term pattern of increasing or decreasing values. Identifying such a pattern is extremely helpful in forecasting future values. You would also like to know of any short-term patterns. For example, you know that retail sales peak in the fourth quarter of every year because of the demand for gifts, and drop off in the following first quarter, but you would like to have more specific knowledge of such seasonal changes. Just how much do the sales increase in the fourth quarter, and how much do they drop in the first quarter?

You want to forecast the total Canadian retail sales for the following year. Such a forecast, along with knowledge about long-term and short-term patterns, would be helpful to your company as it plans ahead.

What patterns are present, and how are they used to make a forecast for the following year? This chapter presents some answers to these questions.

Table 14-1 **Canadian Retail Sales (in billions of dollars)**

Year	Quarter	Canadian Retail Sales
1994	1	43.7
	2	53.6
	3	52.4
	4	57.2
1995	1	45.3
	2	55.2
	3	54.2
	4	56.9
1996	1	46.5
	2	56.0
	3	54.7
	4	59.7
1997	1	48.7
	2	60.7
	3	59.4
	4	64.1

Based on data from Statistics Canada.

14-1 Overview

In the early chapters of this book, we dealt mainly with collections of data consisting of single values. In more recent chapters we considered different configurations of data, such as the paired data of Chapter 9 and the contingency tables in Chapter 10. In this chapter we investigate sets of data called time series, which consist of values corresponding to different time intervals.

Such collections of data are extremely important in many applications, especially those involving business or economics. For example, investors and securities analysts work hard trying to predict stock and bond performances. Owners of a store attempt to predict sales activity with seasonal fluctuations and long-term trends taken into account. Prospective house builders set start-up dates based on business expectations. Time-series data are useful in all these applications.

A major objective of this chapter is to examine past time-series data and use the observations to *forecast*, or predict, future values. Although many different models can be used to represent a time series, this chapter only deals with the multiplicative model, which involves trend, cyclical, seasonal, and irregular components. Trend and seasonal components will be isolated, and *seasonally adjusted* values will be obtained. One of many different methods of forecasting will be shown.

Time-series data are often adjusted for inflation, using index numbers such as the consumer price index. The use of index numbers is discussed first.

14-2 Index Numbers

It is often helpful or necessary to compare scores to some appropriate basis or standard. In Chapter 2, we saw that z scores can be used to compare scores from populations with different means and standard deviations, and percentiles can be used to compare scores within the same set of data or between different sets of data. In this section we introduce *index numbers*, which allow us to measure and compare changes over time in prices, costs, inventory, production output, and other quantities used in business applications.

DEFINITION

An **index number** reflects changes in values for different time periods. A value for one particular time period is used as a basis for comparison, and the index number for another time period is obtained by forming a ratio that is usually multiplied by 100.

$$\text{index number for time period } t = \frac{\text{value for time period } t}{\text{value for base time period}} \times 100$$

Some common index numbers are price indexes, such as the Laspeyres price index, the Paasche price index, and Fisher's ideal price index.

Price Indexes

Price indexes are often employed as measures of price inflation or deflation.

> ### DEFINITION
>
> A **price index,** or **price relative,** is a value that represents changes in the price of some set of goods and/or services, as expressed below.
>
> $$\text{price index} = \frac{P_t}{P_0} \times 100$$
>
> where P_t = price in time period t
> P_0 = price in the base time period

EXAMPLE   Suppose we wish to compare over time the average prices of passenger cars made in North America. Table 14-2 lists prices for 1988 to 1997 (based on data from Statistics Canada). Using 1992 as the base time period, find the price index for 1997.

SOLUTION   Since 1992 is designated as the base year, P_0 = \$16,784. Because we want the price index for 1997, P_t = \$21,937. The price index is calculated as

$$\frac{P_t}{P_0} \times 100 = \frac{\$21,937}{\$16,784} \times 100 = 130.7$$

This result can be interpreted as follows: the price of a North American passenger car in 1997 was 130.7% of the price in 1992, giving an automobile-price inflation rate of 30.7% over the five-year period. As an exercise, verify that the North American passenger-car price index for 1988 is 91.1.

The preceding example uses 1992 as the base year. The selection of a base period is made carefully: It should be a time period of relative stability with no major disruptive influences such as wars or stock-market crashes. The base period should be changed when there is a dramatic change in consumer spending patterns. Both 1986 and 1992 have been used by Statistics Canada as base years.

The Consumer Price Index

The consumer price index (CPI) is a measure of the rate of price change for goods and services bought by Canadian consumers. It is the most widely used indicator of price changes in Canada.

The Canadian CPI began with a study conducted by the Department of Labour in the early 1900s. The study was based on a hypothetical family budget that represented weekly expenditures of an urban working class family of five. Retail prices of 29 food items and 5 fuel and lighting items were collected in approximately 60 cities. In addition, information was obtained on the rent for a representative worker's dwelling. Since then, the CPI has grown in comprehensiveness and detail to keep pace with increases in its use. (See Statistics Canada Catalogue No. 62-557-XPB.)

TABLE 14-2	Average Price of Passenger Cars Made in North America
Year	Average Price
1988	$15,290
1989	$16,339
1990	$16,858
1991	$15,766
1992	$16,784
1993	$17,459
1994	$18,478
1995	$20,009
1996	$21,066
1997	$21,937

The Laspeyres Price Index

The preceding example illustrates the construction of a simple price index for the average prices of just one type of item, passenger cars made in North America. With consumers buying hundreds of different items each year, it would be confusing to develop separate price indexes for each type of item. Instead, it is generally better to combine items. The **consumer price index (CPI)** is a well known and commonly used index designed to reveal changes in prices of a **fixed basket** of hundreds of goods and services, including such items as milk, lettuce, rent, cable-television rates, and babysitting costs. To illustrate the method used in calculating the consumer price index, we will use a more limited market basket containing only eggs, refined sugar, and chicken. The base year will be 1992. Consider the data in Table 14-3.

Any meaningful price index takes the consumption quantities into account. A **weighted aggregate index** combines the prices of several items, each multiplied (weighted) by a quantity. A common example is the Laspeyres price index, which is the method used for CPI calculations.

DEFINITION

The **Laspeyres price index**, based on a combination of several items, weights prices according to quantities consumed in the *base* year. It is calculated as follows:

$$\text{Laspeyres price index} = \frac{\sum P_t Q_0}{\sum P_0 Q_0} \times 100$$

where P_t = price of a good or service in year t
P_0 = price of a good or service in the base time period
Q_0 = quantity of a good or service consumed in the base time period

TABLE 14-3	Average October Retail Prices and Per Capita Consumption							
Year	1990	1991	1992	1993	1994	1995	1996	1997
Eggs								
Price (dollars/dozen)	1.56	1.50	1.52	1.44	1.50	1.63	1.76	1.75
Per capita consumption (dozens)	15.01	15.00	14.47	14.41	14.40	14.27	14.80	14.94
Refined sugar								
Price (dollars/kg)	1.03	0.81	0.76	0.83	0.88	0.98	1.05	1.17
Per capita consumption (kg)	37.25	37.14	40.42	41.19	42.25	38.51	39.04	39.37
Chicken								
Price (dollars/kg)	4.39	4.13	4.20	3.97	3.90	3.80	4.34	4.36
Per capita consumption (kg)	22.05	22.16	22.19	23.13	24.82	24.55	24.61	25.25

Based on data from Statistics Canada.

EXAMPLE   Using the data of Table 14-3 for eggs, refined sugar, and chicken, and using 1992 as the base year, find the Laspeyres price index for 1997.

SOLUTION   Using the prices for 1997 and the quantities for the base year 1992, $\sum P_t Q_0 = 169.3623$, as calculated below:

	$P_t(1997)$	$Q_0(1992)$	$P_t Q_0$
Eggs	1.75	14.47	25.3225
Refined sugar	1.17	40.42	47.2914
Chicken	4.36	22.19	96.7484
		$\sum P_t Q_0 =$	169.3623

Using the prices for the base year 1992 and the quantities for 1992, $\sum P_0 Q_0 = 145.9116$, as calculated below:

	$P_0(1992)$	$Q_0(1992)$	$P_0 Q_0$
Eggs	1.52	14.47	21.9944
Refined sugar	0.76	40.42	30.7192
Chicken	4.20	22.19	93.1980
		$\sum P_t Q_0 =$	145.9116

From the values of $\sum P_t Q_0$ and $\sum P_0 Q_0$, now compute the Laspeyres price index:

$$\frac{\sum P_t Q_0}{\sum P_0 Q_0} \times 100 = \frac{169.3623}{145.9116} \times 100 = 116.1$$

That is, if the same quantities of eggs, refined sugar, and chicken that were bought in 1992 were purchased in 1997, the cost would be 16.1% higher than in 1992.

The characteristic of the Laspeyres price index is that the *quantities* of goods are held constant at the base year level. Changing tastes, demands, and other factors can have dramatic effects on the quantities purchased. For example, as the price of an item goes up, consumers may buy less of it, so that per capita consumption decreases. The Laspeyres index, however, is based on the same quantity that was purchased in the base year, so it tends to exaggerate the effects of inflation on the consumer. On the other hand, there is the advantage that the same base quantities Q_0 are used year after year, so that there is no need to do an annual update of consumption quantities. The CPI (an example of a Laspeyres price index) is periodically adjusted with a new base time period so that the fixed initial quantities do not get too far out of line with current conditions. Before switching to 1992, Statistics Canada used 1986 as the base year.

The Paasche Price Index

The Laspeyres price index uses the quantities purchased in the base year to calculate expenditures in succeeding years. The Paasche price index uses *current* quantities for both the base time period and the current year.

DEFINITION

The **Paasche price index,** based on a combination of several items, weights prices according to quantities consumed in the *current* year. It is calculated as follows:

$$\text{Paasche price index} = \frac{\sum P_t Q_t}{\sum P_0 Q_t} \times 100$$

where P_t = price of a good or service in year t
P_0 = price of a good or service in the base time period
Q_t = quantity of a good or service consumed in year t

EXAMPLE   Using the data of Table 14-3 for eggs, refined sugar, and chicken, and using 1992 as the base year, find the Paasche price index for 1997.

SOLUTION   Using the prices for 1997 and the quantities for 1997, $\sum P_t Q_t = 182.2979$, which is calculated as shown:

	P_t(1997)	Q_t(1997)	$P_t Q_t$
Eggs	1.75	14.94	26.1450
Refined sugar	1.17	39.37	46.0629
Chicken	4.36	25.25	110.0900

$$\sum P_t Q_t = 182.2979$$

Using the prices for the base year 1992 and the quantities for 1997, $\sum P_0 Q_t = 158.6800$, which is calculated as shown:

	$P_0(1992)$	$Q_t(1997)$	$P_0 Q_t$
Eggs	1.52	14.94	22.7088
Refined sugar	0.76	39.37	29.9212
Chicken	4.20	25.25	106.0500
			$\sum P_0 Q_t = 158.6800$

From the values of $\sum P_t Q_t$ and $\sum P_0 Q_t$ now compute the Paasche price index:

$$\frac{\sum P_t Q_t}{\sum P_0 Q_t} \times 100 = \frac{182.2979}{158.6800} \times 100 = 114.9$$

That is, the 1997 expenditure is 14.9% higher than the 1997 quantities would have cost if they had been bought at the 1992 prices.

When the Paasche price index is calculated for each year, the prices are weighted by using the quantities for the current year, in contrast to the Laspeyres price index, where the prices are weighted by using the quantities for the base time period. The Paasche price index therefore has the advantage of reflecting the latest quantity levels used by consumers, but has the disadvantage of requiring the updating of the quantity values each year.

Fisher's Ideal Price Index

It is fairly common to have a period of several years during which prices rise and consumers decrease the quantities they use. For example, car prices have climbed dramatically in recent years, leading to the term "sticker shock" to describe the surprise of prospective car buyers when they learn how much costs have increased since their last purchase of a new car. Consequently, car sales have dropped, as drivers keep their old cars longer. The Laspeyres price index tends to overstate the problem of rising car prices, because it continues to use the same higher quantities of car purchases from the base time period, ignoring the fact that consumers soften the impact of higher prices by delaying purchases. The Paasche price index tends to understate the problem because the current lower purchase levels are used: The effect on consumers appears to be less than it really is. On the other hand, in a period of falling prices and rising quantities of consumption, the Laspeyres price index tends to understate the effect on consumers, and the Paasche price index tends to overstate it.

Because the Laspeyres price index and the Paasche price index are ratios, their opposing distortions of the effect of inflation can be balanced by finding their geometric mean. The **geometric mean** of two ratios is the square root of their product. This balance, known as Fisher's ideal price index, is expressed as follows.

The Standard of Living

Critics of the CPI note that it includes average costs, so some large expenses have a weight that substantially underemphasizes their impact on those who actually incur those costs. For example, the CPI currently assumes that the costs of alcoholic beverages and tobacco products account for 4.5% of the average consumer's budget (Statistics Canada Catalogue No. 62-557-XPB). For nondrinkers and nonsmokers, the figure is really 0%, and therefore those who actually consume alcohol and tobacco incur costs that are substantially larger than 4.5% of their total budgets.

The standard of living is affected by wages, not only prices. Wages and prices do not necessarily rise at the same rate: Sometimes the standard of living is only maintained through more household members working more hours. One way to gauge the standard of living is to compare costs of items in terms of time worked instead of dollars. For example, the average numbers of weeks that had to be worked to pay for a North American car in 1996 was 29.65, compared to 24.05 in 1986.

DEFINITION

Fisher's ideal price index $= \sqrt{(\text{Laspeyres price index})(\text{Paasche price index})}$

EXAMPLE   In the preceding examples, 1992 and 1997 prices and quantities of eggs, refined sugar, and chicken were used to find the Laspeyres price index of 116.1 and the Paasche price index of 114.9. Use these results to find Fisher's ideal price index for 1997, with a base year of 1992.

SOLUTION

Fisher's ideal price index

$$= \sqrt{(\text{Laspeyres price index})(\text{Paasche price index})}$$

$$= \sqrt{(116.1)(114.9)}$$

$$= 115.5$$

Although Fisher's ideal price index has much to recommend it in terms of reducing the distortion found in the Laspeyres and Paasche price indexes, it has the same disadvantage as the Paasche price index: new quantity weights must be determined every year. In practice the Laspeyres price index is used much more than either the Paasche price index or Fisher's ideal price index.

Interpreting Price Indexes

The preceding examples use 1992 and 1997 prices and quantities for eggs, refined sugar, and chicken. Based on those values, the Laspeyres price index was 116.1. If 1992 is the base year, and the entire collection of the more than 600 goods and services that make up the "market basket" used by Statistics Canada is taken into account, the Laspeyres price index (the consumer price index) for 1997 is 107.6, as shown in Table 14-4.

If all the items are included, in 1997 it would have cost 7.6% more to buy the market basket, and in 1990 it would have cost $100.0 - 93.3 = 6.7\%$ less than in 1992. Remember that the CPI values are ratios, so care must be taken when comparing years different from the base year. The increase from 1990 to 1997 in the CPI is $107.6 - 93.3 = 14.3$ *percentage points*, based on 1992, but it is wrong to say that there was a 14.3% increase from 1990 to 1997. The correct procedure is shown here:

$$\frac{1997 \text{ CPI}}{1990 \text{ CPI}} \times 100\% = \frac{107.6}{93.3} \times 100\% = 115.3\%$$

TABLE 14-4	All-Items Index for 1968–97, with 1992 as the Base Year

Year	All-Items Index	Year	All-Items Index	Year	All-Items Index
1968	22.4	1978	43.6	1988	84.8
1969	23.4	1979	47.6	1989	89.0
1970	24.2	1980	52.4	1990	93.3
1971	24.9	1981	58.9	1991	98.5
1972	26.1	1982	65.3	1992	100.0
1973	28.1	1983	69.1	1993	101.8
1974	31.1	1984	72.1	1994	102.0
1975	34.5	1985	75.0	1995	104.2
1976	37.1	1986	78.1	1996	105.9
1977	40.0	1987	81.5	1997	107.6

Based on data from Statistics Canada.

This result shows that there was a 15.3% increase from 1990 to 1997.

Another way to interpret the CPI is to determine the purchasing power of dollars in the current year, in terms of base-year dollars.

DEFINITION

The **purchasing power** of one dollar is computed as $\dfrac{100}{\text{CPI}}$.

● **EXAMPLE**   Use the data in Table 14-4 to find the purchasing power of the dollar in each of the years from 1989 to 1997 inclusive, in terms of 1992 dollars.

SOLUTION

Year	1989	1990	1991	1992	1993	1994	1995	1996	1997
Purchasing power of one dollar is 100/CPI	1.124	1.072	1.015	1.000	0.982	0.980	0.960	0.944	0.929

For example, a 1995 dollar had the same purchasing power that 100/104.2 = $0.96 had in 1992. In a context where all money amounts for different years have been adjusted in this way in order to be expressed in terms of base-year dollars, the amounts are said to be expressed in constant dollars.

When the base time period has to be changed, it is easy to get the new CPI figures. All the CPI values are divided by the CPI of the new base year, and multiplied by 100. Table 14-5 gives the CPI for Canada with 1986 as the base year. To get the figures for Table 14-4, with 1992 as the base year, simply

Other Canadian Indexes

The consumer price index is often perceived as the only measure of the rate of price change, but this is a misconception. Some of the many other price change measures are given below (from Statistics Canada Catalogue No. 62-557-XPB).

The **Industrial Product Price Indexes** measure the changes in prices received by Canadian manufacturers for goods as they leave the factory gate. Indirect taxes, transportation, and wholesale and retail costs are not included in the price. Almost 1300 basic indexes are available.

The **Raw Materials Price Indexes** measure price changes for the purchase of raw materials by Canadian industry. The term "raw material" refers either to a commodity that is sold for the first time after being extracted from nature, or a substitutable recycled product (for example, metal scrap).

The **New Housing Price Indexes** measure changes over time in the contractors' selling prices of new residential houses.

More Canadian Indexes

The **Machinery and Equipment Price Indexes** measure price changes for investment in machinery and equipment by industry of purchase. Price indexes are calculated for industries, major groups of industries, the total for all industries, as well as for commodities.

The **Nonresidential Building Construction Price Indexes** measure contractors' selling price changes of new nonresidential construction (that is, commercial, industrial, and institutional). The indexes relate to both general and trade contractors' work and exclude the cost of land, design, and real estate fees.

The **Farm Input Price Indexes** measure price changes of a basket of goods and services purchased by Canadian farmers for use in agricultural production.

The **Farm Product Price Indexes** measure the change through time in the prices received for agricultural commodities at the first transaction point.

The **Price Indexes of the National Accounts** measure the price change of broad categories of goods and services making up the gross domestic product (GDP).

TABLE 14-5   All-Items Index for 1974–97, with 1986 as the Base Year

Year	All-Items Index	Year	All-Items Index	Year	All-Items Index
1974	39.9	1982	83.7	1990	119.5
1975	44.2	1983	88.5	1991	126.2
1976	47.5	1984	92.4	1992	128.1
1977	51.3	1985	96.0	1993	130.4
1978	55.9	1986	100.0	1994	130.7
1979	61.0	1987	104.4	1995	133.5
1980	67.2	1988	108.6	1996	135.6
1981	75.5	1989	114.0	1997	137.8

Based on data from Statistics Canada.

divide the CPI values of Table 14-5 by 128.1, and multiply by 100. As an exercise, verify this last statement.

This section began with the concept of a general index number and proceeded to the definitions of different price indexes. A price index is a measure of price inflation or deflation. Since changes in buying patterns take place because of price increases, price indexes do not really give a true picture of *cost-of-living* increases. Nevertheless, the CPI is often used as the definition of the change in the cost of living. In labour contracts the CPI is used to calculate the cost-of-living adjustment (COLA), and Canada Pension Plan (CPP) payments are periodically adjusted taking into account changes in the CPI. Other indexes that can be used to measure the standard of living based on changes in the *quantities* of goods and services consumed are discussed in Exercise 20.

14-2 Exercises A: Basic Skills and Concepts

In Exercises 1–4, use the data in Table 14-2 to find the price relative for the average price of passenger cars made in North America for the given base year and reference year.

1. Base year = 1988; reference year = 1989
2. Base year = 1988; reference year = 1991
3. Base year = 1996; reference year = 1988
4. Base year = 1991; reference year = 1988

In Exercises 5–8, use the data in Table 14-3 for eggs, refined sugar, and chicken to find the Laspeyres price index for the given base year and reference year.

5. Base year = 1990; reference year = 1991
6. Base year = 1994; reference year = 1991
7. Base year = 1996; reference year = 1990
8. Base year = 1996; reference year = 1997

In Exercises 9–12, use the data in Table 14-3 for eggs, refined sugar, and chicken to find the Paasche price index for the given base year and reference year.

9. Base year = 1990; reference year = 1991
10. Base year = 1994; reference year = 1991
11. Base year = 1996; reference year = 1990
12. Base year = 1996; reference year = 1997

In Exercises 13–16, use the data in Table 14-3 for eggs, refined sugar, and chicken to find Fisher's ideal price index for the given base year and reference year.

13. Base year = 1990; reference year = 1991
14. Base year = 1994; reference year = 1991
15. Base year = 1996; reference year = 1990
16. Base year = 1996; reference year = 1997

14–2 Exercises B: Beyond the Basics

17. Table 14-6 extends Table 14-3 by giving prices and quantities for baked bean consumption in Canada. Use the data in Table 14-6 to calculate Laspeyres, Paasche, and Fisher's ideal price indexes for 1996, based on eggs, refined sugar, chicken, and baked beans. Take 1992 as the base time period.

TABLE 14-6   Average October Retail Prices and Per Capita Consumption

Year	1990	1991	1992	1993	1994	1995	1996	1997
Eggs								
Price (dollars/dozen)	1.56	1.50	1.52	1.44	1.50	1.63	1.76	1.75
Per capita consumption (dozens)	15.01	15.00	14.47	14.41	14.40	14.27	14.80	14.94
Refined sugar								
Price (dollars/kg)	1.03	0.81	0.76	0.83	0.88	0.98	1.05	1.17
Per capita consumption (kg)	37.25	37.14	40.42	41.19	42.25	38.51	39.04	39.37
Chicken								
Price (dollars/kg)	4.39	4.13	4.20	3.97	3.90	3.80	4.34	4.36
Per capita consumption (kg)	22.05	22.16	22.19	23.13	24.82	24.55	24.61	25.25
Baked and canned beans								
Price (dollars/kg)	3.14	2.81	2.66	2.31	n.a.	1.96	1.96	1.88
Per capita consumption (kg)	1.96	1.55	1.84	1.55	1.54	1.43	1.43	1.43

Based on data from Statistics Canada.

18. Use the data in Table 14-5 to find the purchasing power of dollars for the years 1990 to 1997 in terms of 1986 dollars.
19. Use the data in Table 14-5 to find the percentage increase in the CPI from 1984 to 1990.

20. A price index represents an attempt to measure price inflation or deflation. In contrast, a *quantity index* represents an attempt to measure the *standard of living*. The following are quantity indexes:

$$\text{Laspeyres quantity index} = \frac{\sum Q_t P_0}{\sum Q_0 P_0} \times 100$$

$$\text{Paasche quantity index} = \frac{\sum Q_t P_t}{\sum Q_0 P_t} \times 100$$

Fisher's ideal quantity index

$$= \sqrt{(\text{Laspeyres quantity index})(\text{Paasche quantity index})}$$

Refer to Table 14-6 for the egg, refined sugar, chicken, and baked bean data. Use 1992 as the base time period and find (a) the Laspeyres quantity index for 1997, (b) the Paasche quantity index for 1997, (c) Fisher's ideal quantity index for 1997, and (d) the total cost index for 1997, which is defined as follows:

$$\text{total cost index} = \frac{\sum P_t Q_t}{\sum P_0 Q_0} \times 100$$

14–3 Time-Series Components

The preceding section used index numbers to measure and compare *past* changes in such factors as prices or costs, but in many situations it is helpful, profitable, or necessary to predict some *future* activity. Textbook publishers must predict sales to print the appropriate number of copies. Financial advisors must predict a variety of economic factors so they can give investors better advice on stocks, bonds, and other investment opportunities. Municipal, provincial, and federal governments must predict future economic activity to make informed decisions concerning inflation, unemployment, recession, and other conditions. We *forecast* a future event when we attempt to predict its outcome. In this section we begin by examining the concept of a time series.

DEFINITION

A **time series** consists of a collection of observations of values that correspond to consecutive time intervals.

Table 14-7 reproduces the data on total Canadian retail sales, in billions of dollars, given in Table 14-1. Because observed values are listed with consecutive time intervals, this is an example of a time series.

In Figure 14-1, these data are depicted in a graph. From the graph we can easily see that farther to the right the points generally tend to be higher, forming a pattern of increasing values. There are, however, other patterns. Examine

TABLE 14-7	Canadian Retail Sales by Quarter, 1994–97 (in billions of dollars)

Year	Quarter	Canadian Retail Sales
1994	1	43.7
	2	53.6
	3	52.4
	4	57.2
1995	1	45.3
	2	55.2
	3	54.2
	4	56.9
1996	1	46.5
	2	56.0
	3	54.7
	4	59.7
1997	1	48.7
	2	60.7
	3	59.4
	4	64.1

Based on data from Statistics Canada.

Figure 14-1 for changes from the fourth quarters of 1994, 1995, and 1996 to the first quarters of their following years. In each case the first quarters have total retail sales that are less than the totals for the preceding quarters. Two patterns have become clear:

Figure 14-1   Canadian Retail Sales by Quarter, 1994–97 (in billions of dollars)

1. The general overall pattern of increasing values
2. The first-quarter drop in values

Once we recognize these two patterns, we may wonder whether there are other patterns as well. Instead of trying to identify all patterns through a subjective and intuitive examination of the graph, we will carry out a systematic procedure to describe patterns in terms of four distinct *types of variation* that occur in time series: trend, cyclical variation, seasonal variation, and irregular variation (random variation).

DEFINITIONS

The **trend** in a time series consists of a long-term increasing or decreasing pattern. See Figure 14-2(a).

The **cyclical variation** in a time series consists of patterns that *repeat* over time periods that exceed one year. See Figure 14-2(b).

The **seasonal variation** in a time series consists of patterns that *repeat* over time periods of one year or less. That is, the effects from seasonal influences are completed in a time period of one year, then they repeat on a yearly basis. See Figure 14-2(c).

The **irregular variation** in a time series consists of fluctuations that are not predictable, because they result from unusual events, such as El Niño, or from random fluctuation. See Figure 14-2(d).

Figure 14-2   Patterns in a Time Series for (a) Trend, (b) Cyclical Variation, (c) Seasonal Variation, and (d) Irregular Variation

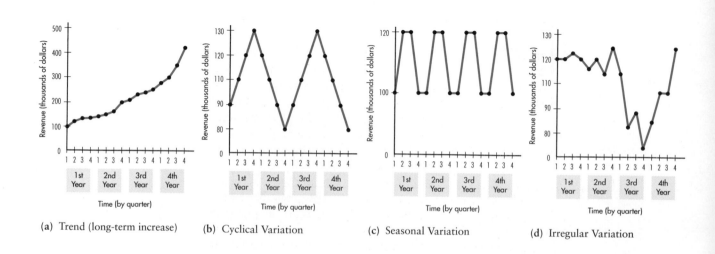

(a) Trend (long-term increase)   (b) Cyclical Variation   (c) Seasonal Variation   (d) Irregular Variation

> **Notation for Time Series**
>
> We denote the four components of a time series as follows:
>
> T denotes trend.
>
> C denotes the cyclical variation.
>
> S denotes the seasonal variation.
>
> I denotes the irregular (random) variation.

The trend T, cyclical C, seasonal S, and irregular I components are illustrated in Figure 14-2. Real-life patterns are usually not as perfect as those shown.

It is not difficult to think of real cases that illustrate the four different components of a time series. There is a *trend* in the number of television sets owned in Canada: that number has increased over the past several years. An Olympic fund-raising committee is likely to experience *cyclical variation* that corresponds to the Olympics occurring every two years. A manufacturer of women's perfume is likely to experience *seasonal variation* that includes increased sales around Christmas and Mother's Day. A business devastated by an ice storm experiences *irregular variation* that does not have a predictable pattern.

Figure 14-2 illustrates the four different components of time series, but actual time series typically consist of combinations of these components. Table 14-7 and Figure 14-1 correspond to a time series comprising a combination of components. The following sections show how these components can be identified. We will consider time series in which the Y values are expressed as a product of the trend T, cyclical C, seasonal S, and irregular I components. We will represent the time series as $Y = T \times C \times S \times I$, and decompose the product $T \times C \times S \times I$ by isolating individual factors.

Using Technology

Excel: Given a column of time-series data (such as the right column in Table 14-7), and a corresponding column of time-period identifiers (such as the middle (Quarter) column in Table 14-7), Excel can be used to easily generate a graph such as Figure 14-1. Highlight the spreadsheet column containing the data, then click the graph icon on the main Excel toolbar. For **Chart Type**, select **Line**, then click **Next**. Select the tab for **Series**, then in the box for **Category (X) Axis Labels** input the cell range containing the time-period identifiers; click on **Next**. When asked to input titles, type in the Y axis title, but type in the X axis title only if it requires just one line (compare Figure 14-1, which shows separate lines for the year numbers and the overall title). Click on **Finish**. If the X axis title was not completed, click on the Drawing icon on the main toolbar, and then on the Text Box icon.

Click and drag the mouse to create the text box below the time-period identifiers on the graph, and type in the desired lines of text.

(14-3) Exercises A: Basic Skills and Concepts

In Exercises 1–8, identify the time-series pattern as trend, cyclical variation, seasonal variation, or irregular variation.

1. A manufacturer of men's neckties experiences an increase in sales during December of each year.
2. A company that produces integrated circuits for computers finds that the number of units sold has grown steadily over the past decade.
3. When analysing the number of returned items, a retail store owner finds that the number fluctuates without any predictable pattern.
4. A supplier of campaign promotional products has a surge in revenue that corresponds to the month preceding each federal election.
5. A manager observes that over the past several years there has been a small but steady decrease in annual production.
6. For a certain bus route, the number of passengers rises and falls in a way that is unpredictable and without any pattern.
7. A pilot experiences increased expenses once every year as she prepares for the annual flight review required by Transport Canada.
8. A farmer has losses for most months of the year, but larger gains at the end of each growing season.

In Exercises 9–16, refer to the figure and identify the time series as trend, cyclical variation, seasonal variation, or irregular variation.

9.

10.

11.

12.

13.

14.

15.

16.

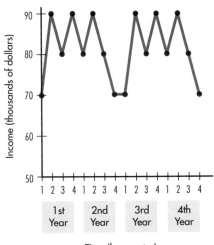

In Exercises 17–24, use the given time-series data to construct a graph and specify the time series as trend, cyclical variation, seasonal variation, or irregular variation. In each case, the data are listed in rows by consecutive quarters.

17.

600	570	542	514	489	464	441	419
398	378	359	341	324	308	293	278

18.

600	570	542	514	489	464	441	419
419	441	464	489	514	542	570	600

19.

600	620	625	610	650	560	570	540
615	605	630	570	580	585	575	615

20.

600	570	542	514	600	570	542	514
600	570	542	514	600	570	542	514

21.

367	386	350	405	367	386	350	405
367	386	350	405	367	386	350	405

22.

350	367	386	405	425	447	469	492
517	543	570	600	629	660	693	728

23.

492	469	447	425	405	386	367	350
350	367	386	405	425	447	469	492

24.

517	386	447	660	543	350	492	693
728	469	367	570	600	629	405	425

14-3 Exercises B: Beyond the Basics

In Exercises 25–28, use the given time series data to construct a graph and specify the time series as trend, cyclical variation, seasonal variation, or irregular variation. The 48 cost values correspond to 48 consecutive months (listed by rows), beginning with the first month of the first year.

25.

84	81	121	119	115	71	92	150	141	98	70	108
133	89	77	105	107	103	91	97	108	90	93	78
76	79	103	100	108	92	130	75	111	133	147	76
70	110	84	75	127	100	84	93	129	125	97	87

26.

27.6	27.3	27.1	27.0	26.8	26.6	26.5	26.2	25.9	25.6	25.2	24.9
24.6	24.4	24.2	24.0	23.8	23.5	23.2	22.9	22.6	22.3	22.0	21.8
21.8	22.0	22.3	22.6	22.9	23.2	23.5	23.8	24.0	24.2	24.4	24.6
24.9	25.2	25.6	25.9	26.2	26.5	26.6	26.8	27.0	27.1	27.3	27.6

27.

71	73	77	81	84	89	94	50	103	108	114	120
126	131	134	139	142	145	149	154	157	162	165	171
177	183	188	191	194	200	203	208	212	216	221	227
230	234	238	243	249	253	257	262	265	271	274	278

28.

5.8	5.6	5.9	6.2	6.6	5.9	5.9	6.4	6.6	6.0	5.8	5.7
5.8	5.6	5.9	6.2	6.6	5.9	5.9	6.4	6.6	6.0	5.8	5.7
5.8	5.6	5.9	6.2	6.6	5.9	5.9	6.4	6.6	6.0	5.8	5.7
5.8	5.6	5.9	6.2	6.6	5.9	5.9	6.4	6.6	6.0	5.8	5.7

Seasonal Components and Seasonal Adjustments

In Section 14-3 we identified and described the four basic patterns that occur in time series. Forecasting requires that the time series follow some pattern that can be identified and used. In each of the examples of Section 14-3, only one of the four basic patterns of variation was present. More typically time series involve combinations of the four patterns.

We assume that a time series comprises all four types of patterns. We further assume that Y represents the time-series values and the time-series model has the form

$$Y = T \times C \times S \times I$$

This model is called *multiplicative* because the components are multiplied. There are other models, such as the additive model $Y = T + C + S + I$ or mixed models (for example, $Y = T \times C \times S + I$). A major advantage of the multiplicative model is that it is easy to isolate the four different components. (This isolation of the four components assumes that they result from different causes.) The multiplicative model is the one most commonly used in business and economics applications.

In the multiplicative model, the values of T, C, S, and I are expressed as follows:

T is expressed in the same units as Y (such as dollars).
C is expressed as an index number, such as 1.05 or 0.90, that multiplies T.
S is expressed as an index number that multiplies T.
I is expressed as an index number that multiplies T.

Decomposition

We will develop a method for beginning with a known time series and *decomposing* it (breaking it down) into factors. For example, given a time series describing Canadian total retail sales for a few years, we can isolate the effect of seasonal variation, the trend effect, the effect of cyclical variation, and the effect of irregular variation.

In Table 14-8 and Figure 14-3 we present the same time series data given at the beginning of the chapter. The listed values of 43.7, 53.6, . . . , 64.1 can be considered values of Y, so that each is the product of the four time series components $T \times C \times S \times I$.

We begin the process by finding the effect of seasonal variation, denoted by S. There are several common ways of estimating the seasonal factors. The method used here has been chosen because it involves comparatively little computation. We separate the seasonal component S by finding a **seasonal index** for each quarter. We must assume that for each of the four quarters, the effect of S is the same every year. That is, the effect of S in the first quarter is the same every year, the effect of S in the second quarter is the same every year, and so on.

Figure 14-3   Canadian Retail Sales by Quarter, 1994–97 (in billions of dollars)

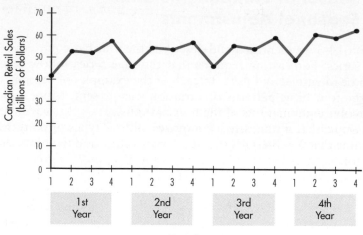

TABLE 14-8	Total Canadian Retail Sales by Quarter, 1994–97 (in billions of dollars)				
Quarter	1994	1995	1996	1997	Totals
1	43.7	45.3	46.5	48.7	184.2
2	53.6	55.2	56.0	60.7	225.5
3	52.4	54.2	54.7	59.4	220.7
4	57.2	56.9	59.7	64.1	237.9
					868.3

Based on data from Statistics Canada.

Over the four years, Quarter 1 accounts for 184.2/868.3 = 21.21% of total sales, Quarter 2 accounts for 225.5/868.3 = 25.97%, Quarter 3 accounts for 220.7/868.3 = 25.42%, and Quarter 4 accounts for 237.9/868.3 = 27.40%. If there were no seasonal effect, each quarter would, on the average, account for 25% of annual sales. The quarterly seasonal index numbers are therefore calculated as 21.21/25 = 0.8484 for Quarter 1, 25.97/25 = 1.0388 for Quarter 2, 25.42/25 = 1.0168 for Quarter 3, and 27.40/25 = 1.0960 for Quarter 4. If the annual total is available, it is reasonable to estimate the Quarter 1 contribution as 21.21% of it, or alternatively as 1/4 of the annual total multiplied by the seasonal index number 0.8484.

The use of data for several consecutive years reduces the chance that unusual values will distort the seasonal index values. The preceding example deals with quarters as the seasons, but analogous computations give monthly, weekly, and other seasonal index numbers. We now summarize the steps used in determining the values of the seasonal indexes:

1. Use a whole number of consecutive years, so that all n seasons ($n = 4$ for quarterly data, $n = 12$ for monthly data, and so on) occur the same number of times.

2. Calculate the Y totals for each of the n seasons, and the overall Y total.
3. The seasonal index for season i is calculated as $n \times (Y$ total for season $i)$ ÷ (overall Y total).

Seasonal Adjustments

When presenting time-series data, it is common practice to provide values that have been **seasonally adjusted** (or deseasonalized) by dividing the original time-series values by the seasonal indexes S. In the modified data the effect of seasonal variations is removed, thereby allowing more direct and equitable comparisons of results from different time periods. When analysing Canadian retail sales, for example, it wouldn't make sense to compare a first-quarter value to a fourth-quarter value for the same year, because sales have historically been higher in the fourth quarter than in any other quarter, mostly because of holiday shopping. The values can, however, be compared if the seasonal effect has been removed.

Table 14-9 lists the original, or *raw*, values of Canadian retail sales totals for the quarters, along with the seasonal index numbers calculated earlier. The column on the right consists of seasonally adjusted values:

$$\text{seasonally adjusted value} = \frac{\text{original value}}{\text{seasonal index}}$$

From the point of view of seasonally adjusted sales, Quarter 1 is the best quarter in 1996, but the worst quarter in 1997. The comparison is made according to the historical behaviour of sales in the four quarters.

TABLE 14-9		Seasonally Adjusted Values of Canadian Retail Sales by Quarter, 1994–97 (in billions of dollars)				
Year	Quarter	Retail Sales $(T \times C \times S \times I)$		S		Seasonally Adjusted Values
1994	1	43.7	÷	0.8484	=	51.5
	2	53.6		1.0388		51.6
	3	52.4		1.0168		51.5
	4	57.2		1.0960		52.2
1995	1	45.3		0.8484		53.4
	2	55.2		1.0388		53.1
	3	54.2		1.0168		53.3
	4	56.9		1.0960		51.9
1996	1	46.5		0.8484		54.8
	2	56.0		1.0388		53.9
	3	54.7		1.0168		53.8
	4	59.7		1.0960		54.5
1997	1	48.7		0.8484		57.4
	2	60.7		1.0388		58.4
	3	59.4		1.0168		58.4
	4	64.1		1.0960		58.5

Based on data from Statistics Canada.

Exercises A: Basic Skills and Concepts

Use the data in Table 14-10 to answer Exercises 1–3.

TABLE 14-10 Canadian Average Weekly Earnings, Industrial Aggregate, 1983–1997 (in dollars)

Year	Quarter	Average Weekly Earnings	Year	Quarter	Average Weekly Earnings	Year	Quarter	Average Weekly Earnings
1983	1	373.47	1988	1	453.99	1993	1	554.69
	2	381.37		2	459.14		2	556.91
	3	386.19		3	461.90		3	560.26
	4	389.67		4	467.34		4	559.80
1984	1	394.08	1989	1	473.62	1994	1	562.70
	2	397.36		2	481.64		2	568.03
	3	400.07		3	488.88		3	571.08
	4	402.80		4	492.26		4	570.94
1985	1	406.47	1990	1	495.79	1995	1	572.31
	2	411.19		2	502.81		2	570.98
	3	414.58		3	510.85		3	575.18
	4	418.49		4	515.26		4	576.39
1986	1	422.12	1991	1	520.90	1996	1	575.62
	2	422.35		2	528.47		2	584.07
	3	426.68		3	532.47		3	589.84
	4	429.34		4	536.14		4	594.36
1987	1	433.90	1992	1	539.71	1997	1	594.83
	2	438.01		2	546.07		2	599.65
	3	442.12		3	551.23		3	599.32
	4	450.48		4	554.72		4	599.63

Based on data from Statistics Canada.

1. Find the quarterly seasonal indexes for Canadian weekly earnings using the data from 1993 to 1997.
2. Find the quarterly seasonal indexes for Canadian weekly earnings using the data from 1983 to 1997, and compare them to your answers to Exercise 1. Have the indexes changed in the more recent years?
3. Deseasonalize the data for 1993 to 1997. Which quarter of 1997 had the highest seasonally adjusted average weekly earnings?

Use the data in Table 14-11 to answer Exercises 4–17.

4. Find the quarterly seasonal indexes for the numbers of building permits issued per quarter for single dwellings, using the data from 1989 to 1994.
5. Deseasonalize the single-dwelling data for 1989 to 1994. Which quarter of 1994 had the highest seasonally adjusted number of building permits for single dwellings?
6. Find the quarterly seasonal indexes for the numbers of building permits issued per quarter for cottages, using the data from 1989 to 1994.
7. Deseasonalize the cottage data for 1989 to 1994. Which quarter of 1994 had the highest seasonally adjusted number of building permits for cottages?
8. Find the quarterly seasonal indexes for the numbers of building permits issued per quarter for double dwellings, using the data from 1989 to 1994.

TABLE 14-11 Building Permits Issued in Canada for All Dwellings, 1989–94

Year	Quarter	Single Dwellings	Cottages	Double Dwellings	Row Housing	Apartments	Conversions	Total
1989	1	26,308	189	1,735	2,873	12,641	1,074	44,820
	2	42,647	912	2,425	4,369	17,572	1,086	69,011
	3	32,782	658	1,828	3,828	17,635	952	57,683
	4	25,093	334	1,671	3,921	17,792	712	49,523
1990	1	27,953	233	1,729	3,861	13,552	983	48,311
	2	34,269	870	2,315	4,681	14,784	939	57,858
	3	20,435	758	1,706	3,423	10,459	943	37,724
	4	13,305	258	1,188	2,825	12,360	1,108	31,044
1991	1	11,628	145	997	2,488	8,499	925	24,682
	2	32,560	734	2,451	4,008	12,769	1,186	53,708
	3	26,096	626	2,656	4,134	12,826	1,041	47,379
	4	18,050	276	2,474	5,470	13,506	989	40,765
1992	1	17,520	123	1,845	4,307	11,258	963	36,016
	2	31,835	587	2,727	4,410	12,903	1,073	53,535
	3	24,177	652	2,174	4,408	11,131	812	43,354
	4	18,872	267	2,624	4,015	9,567	797	36,142
1993	1	15,610	124	1,767	3,750	7,301	715	29,267
	2	29,304	574	2,769	5,480	11,021	989	50,137
	3	23,612	617	2,671	4,743	10,974	1,042	43,659
	4	17,118	229	2,365	4,461	10,121	1,119	35,413
1994	1	16,273	155	2,647	3,366	8,133	868	31,442
	2	33,950	548	4,135	5,727	10,779	1,070	56,209
	3	22,948	507	2,467	4,112	8,442	836	39,312
	4	15,639	229	1,873	3,547	7,948	826	30,062

Based on data from Statistics Canada.

9. Deseasonalize the double-dwelling data for 1989 to 1994. Which quarter of 1994 had the highest seasonally adjusted number of building permits for double dwellings?

10. Find the quarterly seasonal indexes for the numbers of building permits issued per quarter for row housing, using the data from 1989 to 1994.

11. Deseasonalize the row-housing data for 1989 to 1994. Which quarter of 1994 had the highest seasonally adjusted number of building permits for row housing?

12. Find the quarterly seasonal indexes for the numbers of building permits issued per quarter for apartments, using the data from 1989 to 1994.

13. Deseasonalize the apartment data for 1989 to 1994. Which quarter of 1994 had the highest seasonally adjusted number of building permits for apartments?

14. Find the quarterly seasonal indexes for the numbers of building permits issued per quarter for conversions, using the data from 1989 to 1994.

15. Deseasonalize the conversion data for 1989 to 1994. Which quarter of 1994 had the highest seasonally adjusted number of building permits for conversions?

16. Find the quarterly seasonal indexes for the total numbers of building permits issued per quarter, using the data from 1989 to 1994.

17. Deseasonalize the total building-permit data for 1989 to 1994. Which quarter of 1994 had the highest seasonally adjusted number of building permits?

14-4 Exercises B: Beyond the Basics

18. Modify the steps for quarterly indexes so that they can be used to get monthly seasonal indexes for monthly data.

Use the data in Table 14-12 to answer Exercises 19–22.

19. Find the seasonal indexes for the numbers of single-dwelling building permits issued per month, using the data from 1989 to 1994.

TABLE 14-12 Total and Single-Dwelling Building Permits Issued in Canada, 1989–94

Year	Month	Total	Single Dwellings	Year	Month	Total	Single Dwellings	Year	Month	Total	Single Dwellings
1989	Jan.	10,025	5,395	1991	Jan.	4,509	1,941	1993	Jan.	6,459	3,093
	Feb.	12,709	7,739		Feb.	8,072	3,372		Feb.	8,208	4,613
	Mar.	22,086	13,174		Mar.	12,101	6,315		Mar.	14,600	7,904
	Apr.	23,622	15,354		Apr.	19,336	11,261		Apr.	17,677	9,751
	May	24,038	14,696		May	18,044	11,538		May	16,071	9,786
	June	21,351	12,597		June	16,328	9,761		June	16,389	9,767
	July	18,671	11,127		July	16,382	9,249		July	14,482	7,798
	Aug.	20,223	11,363		Aug.	14,736	8,174		Aug.	14,458	7,735
	Sept.	18,789	10,292		Sept.	16,261	8,673		Sept.	14,719	8,079
	Oct.	19,461	10,117		Oct.	16,877	7,667		Oct.	12,978	6,855
	Nov.	17,608	8,991		Nov.	15,378	7,016		Nov.	13,088	6,154
	Dec.	12,454	5,985		Dec.	8,510	3,367		Dec.	9,347	4,109
1990	Jan.	12,235	6,648	1992	Jan.	7,806	3,280	1994	Jan.	6,661	2,939
	Feb.	14,379	8,116		Feb.	10,919	4,965		Feb.	8,879	4,126
	Mar.	21,697	13,189		Mar.	17,291	9,275		Mar.	15,902	9,208
	Apr.	21,903	13,222		Apr.	17,954	10,842		Apr.	18,737	11,493
	May	20,404	12,147		May	18,063	10,644		May	18,997	12,021
	June	15,551	8,900		June	17,518	10,349		June	18,475	10,436
	July	12,530	6,975		July	14,429	8,279		July	13,783	7,934
	Aug.	13,711	7,233		Aug.	13,675	7,625		Aug.	12,816	7,864
	Sept.	11,483	6,227		Sept.	15,250	8,273		Sept.	12,713	7,150
	Oct.	14,223	6,478		Oct.	15,195	8,380		Oct.	11,532	6,311
	Nov.	10,388	4,562		Nov.	11,906	6,310		Nov.	10,072	5,177
	Dec.	6,433	2,265		Dec.	9,041	4,182		Dec.	8,458	4,151

Based on data from Statistics Canada.

20. Deseasonalize the single-dwelling data for 1989 to 1994. Which month of 1994 had the highest seasonally adjusted number of building permits?

21. Find the seasonal indexes for the total numbers of building permits issued per month, using the data from 1989 to 1994.

22. Deseasonalize the total building-permit data for 1989 to 1994. Which month of 1994 had the highest seasonally adjusted number of building permits?

14–5 The Trend Component and Forecasting with Trend and Seasonal Factors

The Trend

The trend component is estimated using the linear regression methods of Chapter 9. While it is possible that the trend has a graph that is a curve (for example, exponential), this chapter will deal only with situations in which the graph of the trend is a straight line. The observed Y values of the time series are taken as the values of the variable to be predicted (sometimes called the *response* variable). The *predictor* (independent) variable is the time variable, which can be measured in years, months, weeks, or any other time unit. When a seasonal component is present, it is convenient to have the year as the unit; seasonal predictions are then made using seasonal index numbers.

Recall the formulas for regression, Formulas 9-3 and 9-4:

Formula 9-3
$$b_1 = \frac{n(\Sigma xy) - (\Sigma x)(\Sigma y)}{n(\Sigma x^2) - (\Sigma x)^2}$$

Formula 9-4
$$b_0 = \bar{y} - b_1\bar{x}$$

The Canadian total retail sales data will be used to show the methods for quarterly and annual trend equations.

The numbers in Table 14-13 enable the trend component to be calculated with a quarter year as the time unit. The 16 quarters for which the data are available are numbered consecutively from 1 to 16, and the following quarters have numbers consistent with this. For example, the first quarter of 1998 is considered to have $x = 17$. The regression calculations yield

$$b_1 = \frac{16(7625.3) - (136)(868.3)}{16(1496) - (136)^2} = \frac{3916}{5440} = 0.7199 \text{ (rounded)}$$

$$b_0 = \frac{868.3}{16} - (0.7199) \cdot \frac{136}{16} = 48.15 \text{ (rounded)}$$

From these equations, we obtain

$$\hat{y} = 48.15 + 0.7199x$$

Any calculator with two-variable statistics capability can be used for these calculations; computer statistics packages are even better for large data sets.

TABLE 14-13	Canadian Retail Sales by Quarter, 1994–97 (in billions of dollars)		
Year	Quarter	y = Sales	x = Time Period (quarters)
1994	1	43.7	1
	2	53.6	2
	3	52.4	3
	4	57.2	4
1995	1	45.3	5
	2	55.2	6
	3	54.2	7
	4	56.9	8
1996	1	46.5	9
	2	56.0	10
	3	54.7	11
	4	59.7	12
1997	1	48.7	13
	2	60.7	14
	3	59.4	15
	4	64.1	16

$n = 16, \Sigma x = 136, \Sigma x^2 = 1496, \Sigma y = 868.3, \Sigma y^2 = 47{,}622.41, \Sigma xy = 7625.3$

Based on data from Statistics Canada.

x	T
1	48.87
2	49.59
3	50.31
4	51.03
5	51.75
6	52.47
7	53.19
8	53.91
9	54.63
10	55.35
11	56.07
12	56.79
13	57.51
14	58.23
15	58.95
16	59.67

The trend equation can be used to find predicted values of y for each value of x from 1 to 16, which are approximations of the trend component at each of these times. The resulting estimated values of T are shown in the margin.

For each year, the sales total is found by summing the sales for the four quarters in the year (Table 14.14).

TABLE 14-14	Canadian Retail Sales by Year, 1994–97 (in billions of dollars)	
Year	y = Sales	x = Time Period (years)
1994	206.9	1
1995	211.6	2
1996	216.9	3
1997	232.9	4

Based on data from Statistics Canada.

The *annual* trend equation is $T = 196.25 + 8.33x$, and the estimated values of T are

x	1	2	3	4
T	204.58	212.91	221.24	229.57

It is interesting to note that if the *years* (1994, 1995, 1996, and 1997) had been used as the predictor variables instead of the x values 1, 2, 3, and 4, exactly the same estimated T values would have shown up:

Year	1994	1995	1996	1997
T	204.58	212.91	221.24	229.57

$$T = -16{,}405.44 + 8.33 \times \text{year}$$

Forecasting with Trend and Seasonal Factors

We can forecast values by assuming that past patterns and conditions will remain constant in the future. A **forecast** value in a time series is a predicted value for a time period beyond those for which values are known. Forecasting future values in a time series is a major reason for estimating the trend, seasonal, cyclical, and irregular components. In this section, however, not all of these components will be used to develop a forecast. The irregular component I is unpredictable, so it cannot be used, and inclusion of the cyclical component C is beyond the scope of this book. We therefore base forecasts on the trend and seasonal components. A forecast value Y is found for a particular time period by using

$$\hat{Y} = \left(\frac{T}{n}\right) \times S$$

where T is the value of the trend component for the year, n is the number of seasons in a year, and S is the corresponding seasonal index. Figure 14-4 describes a procedure in which the decomposition of a time series, as presented in Sections 14-4 and 14-5, can be used for forecasting.

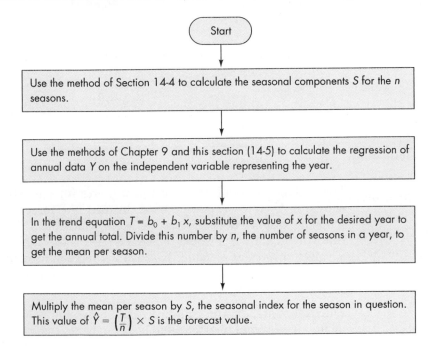

Figure 14-4 A Procedure for Using the Decomposition of a Time Series for Forecasting

This technique is applied to predict the total Canadian retail sales for the four quarters of 1998 (see Table 14-15). For the years from 1994 to 1997 the numbers in parentheses are the known Canadian retail sales totals, in billions of dollars, for the quarters.

The forecast Canadian retail sales for the four quarters of 1998 are $50.5 billion, $61.8 billion, $60.5 billion, and $65.2 billion.

TABLE 14-15	Forecasted Canadian Retail Sales by Quarter, 1994–98 (in billions of dollars)					
Year	Quarter	T	$\dfrac{T}{n} = \dfrac{T}{4}$	S	Forecast = $\left(\dfrac{T}{n}\right) \times S$	Actual Sales
1994	1	204.58	51.1450	0.8484	43.39	(43.7)
	2		51.1450	1.0388	53.13	(53.6)
	3		51.1450	1.0168	52.00	(52.4)
	4		51.1450	1.0960	56.05	(57.2)
1995	1	212.91	53.2275	0.8484	45.16	(45.3)
	2		53.2275	1.0388	55.29	(55.2)
	3		53.2275	1.0168	54.12	(54.2)
	4		53.2275	1.0960	58.34	(56.9)
1996	1	221.24	55.3100	0.8484	46.93	(46.5)
	2		55.3100	1.0388	57.46	(56.0)
	3		55.3100	1.0168	56.24	(54.7)
	4		55.3100	1.0960	60.62	(59.7)
1997	1	229.57	57.3925	0.8484	48.69	(48.7)
	2		57.3925	1.0388	59.62	(60.7)
	3		57.3925	1.0168	58.36	(59.4)
	4		57.3925	1.0960	62.90	(64.1)
1998	1	237.9	59.4750	0.8484	50.46	
	2		59.4750	1.0388	61.78	
	3		59.4750	1.0168	60.47	
	4		59.4750	1.0960	65.18	

Based on data from Statistics Canada.

Using Technology

Excel: For finding the trend, the Excel procedures for regression, shown in Chapter 9, can be used. Instead, the forecasting template displayed here uses the Excel function =**Trend** (**known_y's,known_x's,new_x**), which returns the predicted y value for a new_x value, based on a regression of two input data ranges (known_y's, using a range for annual totals, and known_x's, using a range for the years).

Enter the years, quarters, and raw data in Columns A to C, including year and quarter references for 1998, the forecast

Excel Display   Forecasting

Cell	Formula	Explanation
D2	=C2+C3+C4+C5	Annual total
C24	=TREND($A$24:$A$27,$B$24:$B$27,B24)	Trend total
E2:E5	=C24	Trend total for 1994
E6:E9	=C25	Trend total for 1995
E10:E13	=C26	Trend total for 1996
E14:E17	=C27	Trend total for 1997
E18:E21	=C28	Trend total for 1998
F2	=C2+C6+C10+C14	Quarter total
G2	=F2/($F$2+$F$3+$F$4+$F$5)	Quarter fractions calculated for one year
G6	=G2	Quarter fractions repeated for subsequent years
H2	=E2*G2	Forecast

Use appropriate cell addresses for data.

year. To calculate the annual totals in Column D, enter the formula shown in Cell D2 and copy to Cells D6, D10, and D14. In the section shown at the bottom of the display, use the annual totals as the dependent variable and the years as the independent variable to find the trend totals; copy the formula from Cell C24 to Cells C25:C28. Copy the trend totals to Column E, filling in the values for each quarter. In Column F, calculate the quarter totals by entering the given formula in Cell F2 and copying it to Cells F3:F5. In Column G, calculate quarter fractions for one year by entering the given formula in Cell G2 and copying it to Cells G3:G5; then fill in the column by entering =G2 in Cell G6 and copying to Cells G7:G21. Finally, calculate the seasonally adjusted forecasts by entering the given formula in Cell H2 and copying it to the rest of the column.

14-5 Exercises A: Basic Skills and Concepts

1. Refer to Table 14-10. Forecast the average weekly earnings for the four quarters of 1998 and of 1999, using the trend forecast and the seasonal index numbers that were calculated in Exercise 1 of Section 14-4.

Use the data in Table 14-11 to answer Exercises 2–8.

2. Forecast the number of single-dwelling building permits in Canada for the four quarters of 1995 and of 1999, using the trend forecast and the seasonal index numbers that were calculated in Exercise 4 of Section 14-4.
3. Forecast the number of cottage building permits in Canada for the four quarters of 1995 and of 1999, using the trend forecast and the seasonal index numbers that were calculated in Exercise 6 of Section 14-4.
4. Forecast the number of double-dwelling building permits in Canada for the four quarters of 1995 and of 1999, using the trend forecast and the seasonal index numbers that were calculated in Exercise 8 of Section 14-4.
5. Forecast the number of row-housing building permits in Canada for the four quarters of 1995 and of 1999, using the trend forecast and the seasonal index numbers that were calculated in Exercise 10 of Section 14-4.
6. Forecast the number of apartment building permits in Canada for the four quarters of 1995 and of 1999, using the trend forecast and the seasonal index numbers that were calculated in Exercise 12 of Section 14-4.
7. Forecast the number of conversion building permits in Canada for the four quarters of 1995 and of 1999, using the trend forecast and the seasonal index numbers that were calculated in Exercise 14 of Section 14-4.
8. Forecast the total number of building permits in Canada for the four quarters of 1995 and of 1999, using the trend forecast and the seasonal index numbers that were calculated in Exercise 16 of Section 14-4.
9. Using the annual data for Canadian exports to the Far East and Oceania in Data Set 22 in Appendix B, find the trend equation.

14-5 Exercises B: Beyond the Basics

Use the data in Table 14-12 to answer Exercises 11–13.

10. Using the annual data for person-days lost through work stoppages in the rail-based transportation industry, in Data Set 20 in Appendix B, find the trend equation. For the same data, use the methods from Chapter 9 to determine if the trend is *significant*. If you needed to predict the number of person-days that will be lost through work stoppages in the rail-based transportation industry next year, would you use the trend equation that you just calculated when formulating your prediction? Explain.

11. Forecast the number of single-dwelling building permits in Canada for the twelve months of 1995, using the trend forecast and the seasonal index numbers calculated in Exercise 19 of Section 14-4.

12. Forecast the total number of building permits in Canada for the twelve months of 1995, using the trend forecast and the seasonal index numbers calculated in Exercise 21 of Section 14-4.

13. Use the trend equation and the seasonal index numbers to estimate the number of single-dwelling building permits for the twelve months of 1994. These numbers will differ from the raw data in the table, but they should be close to the observed values. The *mean squared error* (MSE) is a measure of how well the time-series model fits the data, and is suitable for comparing different models. The MSE value is given by the formula

$$\text{MSE} = \frac{\Sigma(y - \hat{y})^2}{n}$$

where y is the actual value, $\hat{y}$ is the forecasted (predicted) value, and n is the number of periods in the forecast. Calculate MSE for the twelve months of 1994.

14. Use Excel to complete Exercises 1–13 of this section.

14–6 Smoothing Data with Moving Averages

There are various *smoothing* techniques that can be used with time-series data to minimize the effect of irregular variation. The easiest to apply is the method of **moving averages**. An n-point moving average is formed by summing n consecutive time-series values, and dividing this **moving total** by n. The term *moving* is used because after a set of n consecutive values is used, the next set of n consecutive values is chosen by deleting the initial value in the set and picking up the next number in the time series to form a new set that has a one-period *time lag*. The lag in time is thought of as motion along the time series.

The numbers computed in Table 14-16 show the smoothing effect. The four-point moving averages are clearly less variable than the three-point moving averages and the raw quarterly data. In fact, with only one exception, the four-point moving averages form an increasing sequence of numbers. Not only has irregular variation been smoothed out—seasonal variation has been obliterated as well! Seasonal variation is always eliminated when n equals the number of seasons in a year. If $n = 4$, quarterly variation disappears, and if $n = 12$, monthly variation disappears. When a time series has both the irregular and seasonal components smoothed out in this manner, the moving averages represent the $T \times C$ component of the time series.

With moving averages in time series, it is customary to associate the calculated value with the middle of the n time periods used. In Table 14-16, the three-point moving average 49.900 is associated with Quarter 2, and the four-point moving average 51.725 is associated with a point midway between Quarters 2 and 3. When n is even, for some applications it is desirable to *centre* the moving averages by taking the mean of each consecutive pair. Thus the centred moving average $(51.725 + 52.125)/2 = 51.925$ is associated with Quarter 3. Centring avoids the awkward situation of having calculated data not corresponding to the original time periods. The centred four-point moving

TABLE 14-16	Moving Totals and Averages of Canadian Retail Sales by Quarter, 1994–97 (in billions of dollars)					

Year	Quarter	Sales	3-Point Moving Total	3-Point Moving Average	4-Point Moving Total	4-Point Moving Average
1994	1	43.7	none	none		
	2	53.6	149.7	49.900	none	none
	3	52.4	163.2	54.400	206.9	51.725
	4	57.2	154.9	51.633	208.5	52.125
1995	5	45.3	157.7	52.567	210.1	52.525
	6	55.2	154.7	51.567	211.9	52.975
	7	54.2	166.3	55.433	211.6	52.900
	8	56.9	157.6	52.533	212.8	53.200
1996	9	46.5	159.4	53.133	213.6	53.400
	10	56.0	157.2	52.400	214.1	53.525
	11	54.7	170.4	56.800	216.9	54.225
	12	59.7	163.1	54.367	219.1	54.775
1997	13	48.7	169.1	56.367	223.8	55.950
	14	60.7	168.8	56.267	228.5	57.125
	15	59.4	184.2	61.400	232.9	58.225
	16	64.1	none	none	none	none

Based on data from Statistics Canada.

averages for the Canadian retail sales data are shown in Table 14-17, associated with their quarters. Quarter 3 is the first quarter for which there are enough data to calculate the four-point centred moving average, and Quarter 14 is the last.

TABLE 14-17	Centred Four-Point Moving Averages for Canadian Retail Sales							

Quarter	1	2	3	4	5	6	7	8
Centred 4-point moving average	none	none	51.925	52.325	52.750	52.938	53.050	53.300

Quarter	9	10	11	12	13	14	15	16
Centred 4-point moving average	53.463	53.875	54.500	55.363	56.538	57.675	none	none

With monthly data, the number of seasons is $n = 12$, and the effect of centring results in a lag of six months; the first month with an associated centred twelve-point moving average is the seventh month.

Using Technology

Excel: Excel can easily generate columns of moving averages, similar to those shown in Table 14-16. On Excel's main menu, select **Tools**, then **Data Analysis**, and select **Moving Average** from the list box that is presented. In the dialog box, indicate the spreadsheet range that contains the original data series, and specify an interval, that is, the value n that defines the n-point moving average. (Table 14-16 shows two intervals: 3 and 4.) Also input a cell address for the top of the output range, and then click **OK**.

14–6 Exercises A: Basic Skills and Concepts

Use the data in Table 14-11 to answer Exercises 1–3.

1. Find the centred four-point moving averages for the single-dwelling building permits.
2. Find the centred four-point moving averages for the double-dwelling building permits.
3. Find the centred four-point moving averages for the cottage building permits.

14–6 Exercises B: Beyond the Basics

4. Use the data in Table 14-12 to find, for the years 1989–91, the centred 12-point moving averages for the total monthly building permits.
5. What sort of moving average is used to smooth weekly data?
6. A frequently used different technique that reduces the short-term effects of seasonal and irregular variation is called *exponential smoothing*. The exponentially smoothed value for time period x is a weighted average of the current time series value and previous exponentially smoothed values. The exponentially smoothed value for time period x is denoted by E_x, and is found by using the formula

$$E_x = \alpha y_x + (1 - \alpha)E_{x-1}$$

where α is called a smoothing constant ($0 \le \alpha \le 1$), y_x is the time-series value for time period x, and E_{x-1} is the exponentially smoothed value for the time period preceding x. The choice of α depends on the amount of smoothing desired. Begin the process by letting E_1 be the first value in the time series. Let α be 0.04, and find the exponentially smoothed values for the first 16 values for total building permits in Table 14-12. Begin with $E_1 = 10{,}025$, and proceed to find $E_2, E_3, \ldots, E_{16}$. Plot the exponentially smoothed values on a graph.

7. Repeat Exercise 6 with a smoothing constant $\alpha = 0.9$. Compare the graphs to decide which α leads to more smoothing.

14-7 Other Forecasting Terms

The forecasts in Section 14-5 were based on a time-series model, but other models are available for different situations. A **causal model** has a variable that is dependent on (or caused by) other variables. For example, a dairy farmer may be able to forecast weekly milk production accurately simply by knowing the number of cows that are available. A **naïve model** is one that is extremely simple and does not require sophisticated statistical techniques. An example would be the organizing committee of a town fair always using the current year's attendance as a forecast of the following year's attendance.

Business indicators can be extremely helpful in forecasting. Such indicators allow the measurement and prediction of general business and economic conditions. **Leading indicators** tend to lead or precede a change in business conditions. For example, the values of new orders are considered to be leading indicators of business conditions. A drop in new orders tends to precede a drop in the level of business activity. **Coinciding indicators** tend, as might be expected, to coincide with changes in business conditions. The gross national product and the income earned by retail stores tend to reflect the current state of business activity. **Lagging indicators** tend to follow, or lag behind, changes in the state of the economy. A lowered level of business activity tends to be followed by lower expenditures on plant and capital equipment.

Forecasting is a tricky business. In this chapter the time-series examples have had relatively few observations. Time series covering longer spans of time with many more observations tend to produce much better results. Even so, forecasts are more unreliable the further into the future they predict. The reliability of the forecast is dependent on the patterns and conditions remaining constant in the future. Fires, earthquakes, wars, recessions, new technology, and pure chance are only a few of the factors that cause forecasts to be in error by embarrassing amounts.

. . . .

Vocabulary List

index number
price index
price relative
consumer price index (CPI)
fixed basket
weighted aggregate index
Laspeyres price index
Paasche price index
geometric mean
Fisher's ideal price index
purchasing power of the dollar
time series
trend
cyclical variation

seasonal variation
irregular variation
seasonal index
seasonally adjusted values
forecast
moving average
moving total
causal model
naïve model
business indicators
leading indicators
coinciding indicators
lagging indicators

. . . .

Review

In this chapter we began in Section 14-2 by considering index numbers. We described price indexes, including the Laspeyres price index, the Paasche price index, Fisher's ideal price index, and the purchasing power of the dollar. In Section 14-3, we studied methods for analysing a time series. We used the multiplicative model

$$Y = T \times C \times S \times I$$

where T is the trend component, C is the cyclical component, S is the seasonal component, and I is the irregular component. In Section 14-4 the isolation of S as a seasonal index was accomplished, and its use in seasonal adjustment was explained. The trend component T was calculated in Section 14-5, and the use of trend and seasonal factors in forecasting was then developed. Section 14-6 discussed smoothing with moving averages, and Section 14-7 briefly mentioned other terminology.

. . . .

Review Exercises

In Exercises 1–4, identify the time series pattern as trend, cyclical variation, seasonal variation, or irregular variation.

1. A manufacturer of golf equipment experiences a large increase in orders during the second quarter of each year.
2. A British Columbia ski resort has a surge of customers every four years during the Winter Olympics.

3. A Montreal restaurant finds that the number of cancelled reservations fluctuate without any pattern.

4. A supplier of laser disks finds that the number of units shipped has dropped steadily over the last several years.

In Exercises 5–8, refer to the figure and identify the time series pattern as trend, cyclical variation, seasonal variation, or irregular variation.

5.

6.

7.

8.

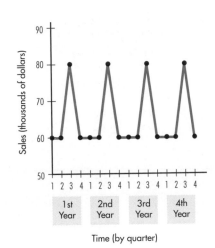

Use the data in Table 14-18 to answer Exercises 9–12.

TABLE 14-18	Representative Retail Prices of Regular Unleaded Gasoline (cents/litre)							
Year	1988	1989	1990	1991	1992	1993	1994	1995
Price	49.3	51.6	58.4	57.0	54.7	53.6	52.8	55.4

Based on data from Statistics Canada.

9. Use 1992 as the base year to find price relatives for regular unleaded gasoline in Canada for the years 1988 to 1995.

10. Use the data in Tables 14-4 and 14-18 to express the prices of a litre of gasoline from 1988 to 1995 in terms of constant (1992) dollars.

11. What was the percentage price increase from 1988 to 1995 if the prices are not adjusted for inflation?

12. What was the percentage price increase from 1988 to 1995 if all prices are expressed in terms of constant (1992) dollars?

13. Use the data in Table 14-19 to form a dairy-products price index by using the listed prices and quantities of milk, butter, and eggs. Take 1992 as the base year, and find the Laspeyres, Paasche, and Fisher's ideal price indexes for 1997. Do you think the general downward trend in consumption of these products is explained mostly by inflation?

TABLE 14-19   Average October Retail Prices and Per Capita Consumption

Year	1990	1991	1992	1993	1994	1995	1996	1997
Eggs								
Price (dollars/dozen)	1.56	1.50	1.52	1.44	1.50	1.63	1.76	1.75
Per capita consumption (dozens)	15.01	15.00	14.47	14.41	14.40	14.27	14.80	14.94
Milk—fresh, homogenized								
Price (dollars/L)	1.25	1.34	1.37	1.38	1.34	1.33	1.37	1.40
Per capita consumption (L)	21.86	19.89	18.31	17.04	16.66	15.77	15.22	14.79
Butter								
Price (dollars/kg)	6.28	6.19	6.21	6.15	6.08	6.28	6.37	6.50
Per capita consumption (kg)	3.27	2.98	2.79	2.93	2.86	2.75	2.69	2.53

Based on data from Statistics Canada.

Use the data in Table 14-20 to answer Exercises 14–18.

TABLE 14-20   Number of Canadians Not in the Labour Force, by Quarter, 1994–1997 (in thousands)

Year	Quarter	Not in Labour Force	Year	Quarter	Not in Labour Force
1994	1	8112	1996	1	8405
	2	7777		2	8127
	3	7576		3	7925
	4	8072		4	8369
1995	1	8264	1997	1	8603
	2	7999		2	8222
	3	7822		3	8017
	4	8313		4	8488

Based on data from Statistics Canada.

14. Estimate the quarterly seasonal indexes for Table 14-20.
15. Deseasonalize the quarterly data in Table 14-20.
16. Use the trend equation and the seasonal indexes to calculate seasonally adjusted estimates for the number of Canadians not in the labour force for the four quarters of 1997, and calculate MSE for these 1997 estimates.
17. Use the trend equation and the seasonal indexes obtained in Exercise 16 to give seasonally adjusted forecasts for the four quarters of 1998.
18. Smooth the quarterly data in Table 14-20 using a centred four-point moving average.

Use the data in Table 14-21 to answer Exercises 19–23.

TABLE 14-21	Number of Canadians Not in the Labour Force, by Month, 1994–1997 (in thousands)				
Year	Month	Not in Labour Force	Year	Month	Not in Labour Force
1994	Jan.	8163	1996	Jan.	8454
	Feb.	8107		Feb.	8389
	Mar.	8065		Mar.	8371
	Apr.	8046		Apr.	8391
	May	7717		May	8098
	June	7569		June	7892
	July	7384		July	7731
	Aug.	7452		Aug.	7796
	Sept.	7891		Sept.	8248
	Oct.	8015		Oct.	8266
	Nov.	8036		Nov.	8355
	Dec.	8166		Dec.	8486
1995	Jan.	8292	1997	Jan.	8618
	Feb.	8307		Feb.	8621
	Mar.	8193		Mar.	8569
	Apr.	8297		Apr.	8542
	May	7947		May	8174
	June	7753		June	7951
	July	7581		July	7853
	Aug.	7699		Aug.	7874
	Sept.	8187		Sept.	8325
	Oct.	8205		Oct.	8378
	Nov.	8349		Nov.	8475
	Dec.	8385		Dec.	8611

Based on data from Statistics Canada.

19. Estimate the monthly seasonal indexes for Table 14-21.
20. Deseasonalize the monthly data in Table 14-21.
21. Use the trend equation and the seasonal indexes obtained in Exercise 19 to give seasonally adjusted forecasts for the twelve months of 1998.
22. Use the trend equation and the seasonal indexes to calculate seasonally adjusted estimates for the number of Canadians not in the labour force for the twelve months of 1997, and calculate MSE for these 1997 estimates.
23. Smooth the monthly data of Table 14-21 using a centred twelve-point moving average.

Technology Project

Table 14-22 gives the average residential mortgage rates on five-year mortgages in Canada for every month from January 1978 to December 1997. Predicting mortgage rates is of interest to both potential home buyers and those who invest in mortgages. One group hopes they will decrease, and the other hopes they will increase.

Using computer software, obtain twelve-point centred moving averages for the time-series data, and plot both the raw time series and the smoothed series on a line graph. If you use Excel, this is easily done with the Chart Wizard. Both graphs show the same thing: There was an upward cycle for the first few years, and a downward cycle for the following years. Delete the upward-cycle data from an appropriate number of years at the beginning, and use the remaining data up to the end of 1996 to get a trend line.

Find monthly seasonal indexes by extending the computer method given in Section 14-6, or by some other suitable computer method. Do the seasonal factors appear to be significant? Would you expect mortgage rates to be seasonal?

Find the trend-line predictions for the twelve months of 1997, then adjust them with the seasonal indexes you have calculated. Calculate MSE for each of the sets of predictions on the computer. Does the seasonal adjustment give a better set of predictions?

Is it reasonable to extend this method of prediction into the future? What eventually happens?

TABLE 14-22	Average Residential Lending Rate on Five-Year Mortages										
Year	Jan.	Feb.	Mar.	Apr.	May	June	July	Aug.	Sept.	Oct.	Nov.	Dec.
1978	10.32	10.31	10.33	10.42	10.43	10.32	10.31	10.31	10.67	10.93	11.25	11.53
1979	11.28	11.25	11.11	11.05	11.06	11.16	11.20	11.80	12.25	13.50	14.46	13.58
1980	13.26	13.50	14.69	16.94	13.99	12.92	13.09	13.44	14.50	14.87	15.00	15.60
1981	15.17	15.27	15.75	16.45	17.82	18.55	18.90	21.30	21.46	20.54	18.80	17.79
1982	18.21	18.97	19.41	19.28	19.11	19.10	19.22	18.72	17.49	16.02	14.79	14.34
1983	14.05	13.60	13.45	13.26	13.16	12.98	13.08	13.57	13.88	13.10	12.84	12.55
1984	12.55	12.52	12.82	13.51	14.26	14.53	14.96	14.45	13.99	13.72	13.25	12.74
1985	12.44	12.57	13.43	12.77	12.38	11.89	11.75	11.77	11.85	11.96	11.75	11.61
1986	11.67	11.94	11.66	11.12	10.60	10.87	11.06	11.00	11.10	11.25	11.25	11.17
1987	10.85	10.46	10.20	10.39	11.04	11.26	11.26	11.49	11.72	11.97	11.49	11.56
1988	11.73	11.49	11.08	11.04	11.29	11.41	11.40	11.92	12.16	11.79	11.78	12.13
1989	12.24	12.23	12.41	12.72	12.29	11.93	11.85	11.76	11.75	11.75	11.75	11.95
1990	12.01	12.42	12.92	13.67	14.21	14.03	13.97	13.56	13.40	13.21	13.04	12.49
1991	12.13	11.58	11.45	11.27	11.23	11.24	11.31	11.47	11.38	10.84	10.14	9.84
1992	9.71	9.68	10.06	10.37	10.14	9.72	9.26	8.72	8.54	9.23	9.33	9.48
1993	9.47	9.44	8.97	8.89	8.88	8.86	8.68	8.58	8.57	8.55	7.84	7.71
1994	7.33	7.20	7.89	9.43	9.48	9.80	10.69	10.33	10.01	9.84	9.85	10.25
1995	10.60	10.48	9.93	9.66	8.98	8.67	8.54	8.94	8.95	8.75	8.66	8.46
1996	8.02	7.79	8.16	8.48	8.47	8.48	8.48	8.01	7.94	7.50	7.01	6.94
1997	7.14	7.12	7.06	7.56	7.46	7.22	6.98	7.00	6.96	6.73	6.69	6.90

Based on data from the Canada Mortgage and Housing Corporation.

Can a Cottage Industry Benefit from the Time-Series Approach?

A few years ago, a former employee of a financial house decided to go into business for himself. For three years he ran a firm constructing futon frames, hiring a small number of employees with the help of some government grants. He then switched to cottage industry, making bagpipe accessories in his home workshop, with the help of family members. He had kept his cash reserves in Treasury bills until the end of 1995, when the rate of return began to sink.

The return on Treasury bills appeared to be recovering by the end of 1997, and he had begun to wonder whether to invest in them again. Use the given data to establish a trend prediction for the first six months of 1998. Should all the data be used? If there appears to be a seasonal effect, use seasonal indexes to improve the forecasts. If it looks as if the rate of return will be greater than 5% for at least four of the first six months of 1998, advise investment in the Treasury bills.

Average Yields for Three-Month Treasury Bills

Month	1994	1995	1996	1997
Jan.	3.63	7.98	5.12	2.84
Feb.	3.85	7.77	5.18	2.86
Mar.	5.39	8.22	5.03	3.19
Apr.	5.82	7.92	4.73	3.14
May	6.34	7.39	4.65	3.01
June	6.67	6.72	4.70	2.86
July	5.79	6.62	4.43	3.32
Aug.	5.35	6.34	4.03	3.13
Sept.	5.29	6.46	3.96	3.10
Oct.	5.37	5.93	3.19	3.63
Nov.	5.79	5.82	2.69	3.57
Dec.	7.18	5.54	2.80	4.46

Based on data from Bank of Canada, Department of Monetary and Financial Analysis.

········ COOPERATIVE GROUP ACTIVITIES ········

1. *Out-of-class activity:* Each class member is assigned two or three months of the past five years for which she or he will get the daily maximum temperature. The information should be readily available from newspaper files or the Internet.

   Use the data to get the mean daily high temperature for each month. Use the monthly means to get monthly seasonal index numbers. From the annual trend equation and the monthly seasonal index number obtained, forecast the mean daily high temperature for the current month.

   For the current month, use the daily data to get *daily* seasonal index numbers. Devise a method for forecasting the daily high temperature for the remaining days in the current month. Calculate the MSE when the actual data become available.

2. *In-class activity:* Either go to a library or use the Internet to find the rates of return on Treasury bills for the first six months of 2001, in order to see how well the predictions made in the From Data to Decision section match the real-life performance. For the first six months of 2001, use the exponential smoothing technique to predict the rates, with $\alpha = 0.2$. Use the MSE to compare the two prediction methods.

3. *In-class activity:* In small groups, think of kinds of data that are readily available in a library or on the Internet, and that you think should exhibit seasonality. Collect as much time-series data of one kind as you can handle, and find the seasonal indexes and trend equation, preferably using Excel or some other computer package.

INTERNET PROJECT   Time Series Data on the Internet

The Internet is a host to a wealth of information that comes in the form of time-series data, which can be analysed using the techniques introduced in this chapter. As just one example, select the site

http://www.sunmedia.ca/BaseballMoneyMatters

Click on the menu item on the left for Payroll Comparisons, and on the resulting screen, find the payroll data for the Toronto Blue Jays. Use the historical data for all years except the most current (at the time of writing, the newest date displayed is 1999), and create a graph. Identify any trends and cycles. Try to predict the value for the most current year, based on the previous years' data. How accurate is your prediction? What factors might make accurate prediction difficult?

15

Project and Epilogue

15–1 A Statistics Group Project

A great way to conclude an introductory statistics course is to do a project in which methods of statistics are actually applied to real data collected by students. A list of suggested topics follows. Some of these topics can be addressed by actually conducting experiments, whereas others might require researching results already obtained. For example, testing the effectiveness of air bags by actually crashing cars is strongly discouraged, but destructive taste tests of chocolate chip cookies can be an easy and somewhat enjoyable experiment. In addition to a 5- to 10-minute-long oral report, students should submit a report that includes the following components:

1. List of data collected
2. Description of the method of analysis
3. Relevant graphs and/or statistics, including Excel or STATDISK displays
4. Statement of conclusions
5. Reasons why the results might not be correct, along with a description of ways in which the study could be improved, given more time and money

Suggested Topics

1. Are the ages of student cars different from those of faculty? If so, how?
2. Is the proportion of foreign cars the same for students and faculty?
3. Car ages in the parking lot of a discount store compared to car ages in the parking lot of an upscale shopping mall
4. Are husbands older than their wives?
5. Are husband/wife age differences the same for young married couples as for older married couples?

6. Analysis of the ages of books in the college library

7. How do the ages of books in the college library compare to those in the library of a nearby college?

8. Comparison of the ages of science books and English books in the college library

9. How many hours do students study each week?

10. Is there a relationship between hours studied and grades earned?

11. Is there a relationship between hours worked and grades earned?

12. A study of *reported* heights compared to *measured* heights

13. A study of the accuracy of wristwatches

14. Is there a relationship between taste and cost of different brands of chocolate chip cookies?

15. Is there a relationship between taste and cost of different brands of peanut butter?

16. Is there a relationship between taste and cost of different brands of cola?

17. Is there a relationship between salaries of professional baseball (or basketball, or football) players and their season achievements?

18. Rates versus weights: Is there a relationship between car fuel-consumption rates and car weights? If so, what is it?

19. Is there a relationship between the lengths of men's (or women's) feet and their heights?

20. Are there differences in taste between ordinary tap water and different brands of bottled water?

21. What is the probability that a dropped tack will land with the pointed end up?

22. Were auto fatality rates affected by laws requiring the use of seat belts?

23. Were auto fatality rates affected by the presence of air bags?

24. Is there a difference in taste between Coke and Pepsi?

25. Is there a relationship between student grades and the amount of television watched? If so, what is it?

26. Is there a relationship between the selling price of a home and its living area (in square feet), lot size (in acres), number of rooms, number of baths, and the annual tax bill?

27. A comparison of the numbers of keys carried by males and females

28. A comparison of the numbers of credit cards carried by males and females

29. Are murderers now younger than they were in the past?

30. Do people who exercise vigorously tend to have lower pulse rates than those who do not?

31. Do people who exercise vigorously tend to have reaction times that are different from those of people who do not?

32. Do people who smoke tend to have higher pulse rates than those who do not?

33. For people who don't exercise, how is pulse rate affected by climbing a flight of stairs?

34. Do statistics students tend to have pulse rates that are different from those of people not studying statistics?

35. A comparison of grades of statistics students versus students not taking statistics

36. Do left-handed people tend to be involved in more car crashes?

37. Do men have more car crashes than women?

38. Do young drivers have more car crashes than older drivers?

39. Are drivers who get tickets more likely to be involved in crashes?

40. Do smokers tend to be involved in more car crashes?

41. Do people with higher pulse rates tend to be involved in more/fewer car crashes?

42. A comparison of reaction times measured with right and left hands

43. Are the proportions of male and female smokers equal?

44. Do statistics students tend to smoke more (or less) than the general population?

45. Are people more likely to smoke if their parents smoked?

46. Evidence to support/refute the belief that smoking tends to stunt growth

47. Does a sports team have an advantage by playing at home instead of away?

48. Analysis of service times (in seconds) for a car drive-up window at a fast-food restaurant

49. A comparison of service times for car drive-up windows at two different fast-food restaurants

50. Analysis of times that Tim Horton's patrons are seated at a table

51. Analysis of times that Tim Horton's patrons wait in line

52. Analysis of times that cars require for refuelling

53. Is the provincial lottery a wise investment?

54. Comparison of casino games: craps versus roulette

55. Starting with $1, is it easier to win a million dollars by playing casino roulette or by playing a provincial lottery?

56. Bold versus cautious strategies of gambling: When gambling with $100, does it make any difference if you bet $1 at a time or if you bet the whole $100 at once?

57. Designing and analysing results from a test for extrasensory perception

58. Analysing paired data consisting of heights of fathers (or mothers) and heights of their first sons (or daughters)

15–2 Which Procedure Applies?

Data Collection and Exploration You can collect your own data through experiments or observational studies. For your conclusions to be valid, it is absolutely essential that the data be collected without bias—in either the selection of samples, or on the part of those who collect the data. Many of the procedures in this book are based on the assumption that we are working with a simple random sample, meaning that every possible sample of the same size has the same chance of being selected. But under appropriate conditions other randomized methods can be substituted (for example, if a large population can be listed in a randomly ordered list, then a systematic sample can be used.) After collecting the data, use the basic tools presented in Chapter 2 to find measures for *centre*, *variation*, and *distribution*, and also to examine the impact of *time* and possible *outliers*.

Inferences: Estimating Parameters and Hypothesis Testing When trying to use sample data for making inferences about a population, it is often difficult to choose the particular procedure that should be applied. This text includes a wide variety of procedures that apply to many different circumstances. Here are some key questions that should be addressed:

- What is the level of measurement (nominal, ordinal, interval, ratio) of the data?
- Does the study involve one, two, or more populations?
- Is there a claim to be tested or a parameter to be estimated?
- What is the relevant parameter (mean, standard deviation, proportion)?
- Is the sample large ($n > 30$) or small?
- Is there reason to believe that the population is normally distributed?
- What is the basic question or issue that you want to address?

In Figure 15-1 we list the major methods included in this book, along with a scheme for determining which of those methods should be used. To use Figure 15-1, start at the extreme left side of the figure and begin by identifying the level of measurement of the data. Proceed to follow the path suggested by the level of measurement, the number of populations, and the claim or parameter being considered.

  Note: The figure applies to a fixed population. If the data are from a process that may change over time, the figure applies to such process data only if the process is statistically stable. This condition can be tested by constructing a control chart (see Chapter 12). If the data represent a time series, then the methods of Chapter 14 may apply.

15–3 A Perspective

No one expects a single introductory statistics course to transform anyone into an expert statistician. After studying several of the chapters in this book, it is natural for students to feel that they have not yet mastered the material to the extent necessary for using statistics in real applications. Many important

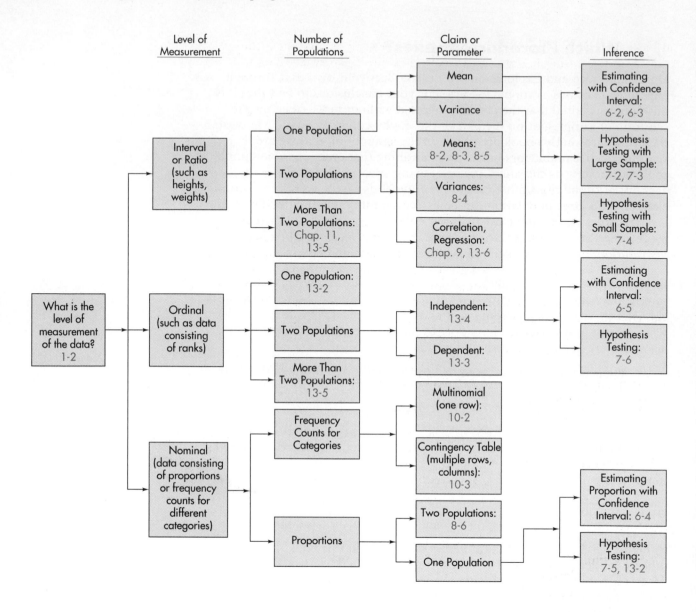

Figure 15-1   Inferential Statistics: Applicable Text Sections

topics (such as factor analysis and discriminate analysis) are not included in this text because they are too advanced for this introductory level. Some easier topics have been excluded for other reasons. It is important to know that professional help is available from expert statisticians, and this introductory statistics course will help you open a dialogue with one of these experts.

Although this course is not designed to make you an expert statistician, it is designed to make you a better educated person with improved job marketability. You should know and understand the basic concepts of probability and chance. You should know that in attempting to gain insight into a set of data, it is important to investigate measures of centre (such as mean and median), measures of dispersion (such as range and standard deviation), and the nature of the distribution (via a frequency table or graph), as well as whether the population is stable or changing over time, and whether outliers are present. You should know and understand the importance of estimating population parameters (such as a mean, standard deviation, and proportion), as well as testing claims made about population parameters. You should realize that the nature and configuration of the data can have a dramatic effect on the particular statistical procedures that are used.

Throughout this text we have emphasized the importance of good sampling. You should recognize that a bad sample may be beyond repair by even the most expert statisticians, using the most sophisticated techniques. There are many mail, magazine, and telephone call-in surveys that allow respondents to be self-selected. The results of such surveys are generally worthless when judged according to the criteria of sound statistical methodology. Keep this in mind when you are exposed to self-selected surveys, so that you don't let them affect your beliefs and decisions. You should also recognize, however, that many surveys and polls obtain very good results, even though the sample sizes might seem to be relatively small. Although many people refuse to believe it, a nationwide survey of only 1700 voters can provide good results if the sampling is carefully planned and executed.

At one time a person was considered educated if he or she could read, but in the new millennium society has become much more demanding. A modern education typically provides students with specific skills, such as the ability to read, write, understand the significance of the Renaissance, operate a computer, and do algebra. The larger picture involves several disciplines that use different approaches to a common goal—seeking the truth. The study of statistics helps us see the truth that is sometimes distorted by others or concealed by data that are disorganized or perhaps not yet collected. Understanding statistics is essential for a growing number of future employees, employers, and citizens.

Appendices

Appendix A: Tables

| TABLE A-1 | Binomial Probabilities |

n	x	.01	.05	.10	.20	.30	.40	.50	.60	.70	.80	.90	.95	.99	x
2	0	980	902	810	640	490	360	250	160	090	040	010	002	0+	0
	1	020	095	180	320	420	480	500	480	420	320	180	095	020	1
	2	0+	002	010	040	090	160	250	360	490	640	810	902	980	2
3	0	970	857	729	512	343	216	125	064	027	008	001	0+	0+	0
	1	029	135	243	384	441	432	375	288	189	096	027	007	0+	1
	2	0+	007	027	096	189	288	375	432	441	384	243	135	029	2
	3	0+	0+	001	008	027	064	125	216	343	512	729	857	970	3
4	0	961	815	656	410	240	130	062	026	008	002	0+	0+	0+	0
	1	039	171	292	410	412	346	250	154	076	026	004	0+	0+	1
	2	001	014	049	154	265	346	375	346	265	154	049	014	001	2
	3	0+	0+	004	026	076	154	250	346	412	410	292	171	039	3
	4	0+	0+	0+	002	008	026	062	130	240	410	656	815	961	4
5	0	951	774	590	328	168	078	031	010	002	0+	0+	0+	0+	0
	1	048	204	328	410	360	259	156	077	028	006	0+	0+	0+	1
	2	001	021	073	205	309	346	312	230	132	051	008	001	0+	2
	3	0+	001	008	051	132	230	312	346	309	205	073	021	001	3
	4	0+	0+	0+	006	028	077	156	259	360	410	328	204	048	4
	5	0+	0+	0+	0+	002	010	031	078	168	328	590	774	951	5
6	0	941	735	531	262	118	047	016	004	001	0+	0+	0+	0+	0
	1	057	232	354	393	303	187	094	037	010	002	0+	0+	0+	1
	2	001	031	098	246	324	311	234	138	060	015	001	0+	0+	2
	3	0+	002	015	082	185	276	312	276	185	082	015	002	0+	3
	4	0+	0+	001	015	060	138	234	311	324	246	098	031	001	4
	5	0+	0+	0+	002	010	037	094	187	303	393	354	232	057	5
	6	0+	0+	0+	0+	001	004	016	047	118	262	531	735	941	6
7	0	932	698	478	210	082	028	008	002	0+	0+	0+	0+	0+	0
	1	066	257	372	367	247	131	055	017	004	0+	0+	0+	0+	1
	2	002	041	124	275	318	261	164	077	025	004	0+	0+	0+	2
	3	0+	004	023	115	227	290	273	194	097	029	003	0+	0+	3
	4	0+	0+	003	029	097	194	273	290	227	115	023	004	0+	4
	5	0+	0+	0+	004	025	077	164	261	318	275	124	041	002	5
	6	0+	0+	0+	0+	004	017	055	131	247	367	372	257	066	6
	7	0+	0+	0+	0+	0+	002	008	028	082	210	478	698	932	7
8	0	923	663	430	168	058	017	004	001	0+	0+	0+	0+	0+	0
	1	075	279	383	336	198	090	031	008	001	0+	0+	0+	0+	1
	2	003	051	149	294	296	209	109	041	010	001	0+	0+	0+	2
	3	0+	005	033	147	254	279	219	124	047	009	0+	0+	0+	3
	4	0+	0+	005	046	136	232	273	232	136	046	005	0+	0+	4
	5	0+	0+	0+	009	047	124	219	279	254	147	033	005	0+	5
	6	0+	0+	0+	001	010	041	109	209	296	294	149	051	003	6
	7	0+	0+	0+	0+	001	008	031	090	198	336	383	279	075	7
	8	0+	0+	0+	0+	0+	001	004	017	058	168	430	663	923	8

(The column group header above the probability columns is labeled p.)

NOTE: 0+ represents a positive probability less than 0.0005.

(continued)

TABLE A-1   Binomial Probabilities (continued)

n	x	.01	.05	.10	.20	.30	.40	.50	.60	.70	.80	.90	.95	.99	x
9	0	914	630	387	134	040	010	002	0+	0+	0+	0+	0+	0+	0
	1	083	299	387	302	156	060	018	004	0+	0+	0+	0+	0+	1
	2	003	063	172	302	267	161	070	021	004	0+	0+	0+	0+	2
	3	0+	008	045	176	267	251	164	074	021	003	0+	0+	0+	3
	4	0+	001	007	066	172	251	246	167	074	017	001	0+	0+	4
	5	0+	0+	001	017	074	167	246	251	172	066	007	001	0+	5
	6	0+	0+	0+	003	021	074	164	251	267	176	045	008	0+	6
	7	0+	0+	0+	0+	004	021	070	161	267	302	172	063	003	7
	8	0+	0+	0+	0+	0+	004	018	060	156	302	387	299	083	8
	9	0+	0+	0+	0+	0+	0+	002	010	040	134	387	630	914	9
10	0	904	599	349	107	028	006	001	0+	0+	0+	0+	0+	0+	0
	1	091	315	387	268	121	040	010	002	0+	0+	0+	0+	0+	1
	2	004	075	194	302	233	121	044	011	001	0+	0+	0+	0+	2
	3	0+	010	057	201	267	215	117	042	009	001	0+	0+	0+	3
	4	0+	001	011	088	200	251	205	111	037	006	0+	0+	0+	4
	5	0+	0+	001	026	103	201	246	201	103	026	001	0+	0+	5
	6	0+	0+	0+	006	037	111	205	251	200	088	011	001	0+	6
	7	0+	0+	0+	001	009	042	117	215	267	201	057	010	0+	7
	8	0+	0+	0+	0+	001	011	044	121	233	302	194	075	004	8
	9	0+	0+	0+	0+	0+	002	010	040	121	268	387	315	091	9
	10	0+	0+	0+	0+	0+	0+	001	006	028	107	349	599	904	10
11	0	895	569	314	086	020	004	0+	0+	0+	0+	0+	0+	0+	0
	1	099	329	384	236	093	027	005	001	0+	0+	0+	0+	0+	1
	2	005	087	213	295	200	089	027	005	001	0+	0+	0+	0+	2
	3	0+	014	071	221	257	177	081	023	004	0+	0+	0+	0+	3
	4	0+	001	016	111	220	236	161	070	017	002	0+	0+	0+	4
	5	0+	0+	002	039	132	221	226	147	057	010	0+	0+	0+	5
	6	0+	0+	0+	010	057	147	226	221	132	039	002	0+	0+	6
	7	0+	0+	0+	002	017	070	161	236	220	111	016	001	0+	7
	8	0+	0+	0+	0+	004	023	081	177	257	221	071	014	0+	8
	9	0+	0+	0+	0+	001	005	027	089	200	295	213	087	005	9
	10	0+	0+	0+	0+	0+	001	005	027	093	236	384	329	099	10
	11	0+	0+	0+	0+	0+	0+	0+	004	020	086	314	569	895	11
12	0	886	540	282	069	014	002	0+	0+	0+	0+	0+	0+	0+	0
	1	107	341	377	206	071	017	003	0+	0+	0+	0+	0+	0+	1
	2	006	099	230	283	168	064	016	002	0+	0+	0+	0+	0+	2
	3	0+	017	085	236	240	142	054	012	001	0+	0+	0+	0+	3
	4	0+	002	021	133	231	213	121	042	008	001	0+	0+	0+	4
	5	0+	0+	004	053	158	227	193	101	029	003	0+	0+	0+	5
	6	0+	0+	0+	016	079	177	226	177	079	016	0+	0+	0+	6
	7	0+	0+	0+	003	029	101	193	227	158	053	004	0+	0+	7
	8	0+	0+	0+	001	008	042	121	213	231	133	021	002	0+	8
	9	0+	0+	0+	0+	001	012	054	142	240	236	085	017	0+	9
	10	0+	0+	0+	0+	0+	002	016	064	168	283	230	099	006	10
	11	0+	0+	0+	0+	0+	0+	003	017	071	206	377	341	107	11
	12	0+	0+	0+	0+	0+	0+	0+	002	014	069	282	540	886	12

NOTE: 0+ represents a positive probability less than 0.0005.

(continued)

TABLE A-1	Binomial Probabilities *(continued)*

n	x	.01	.05	.10	.20	.30	.40	p .50	.60	.70	.80	.90	.95	.99	x
13	0	878	513	254	055	010	001	0+	0+	0+	0+	0+	0+	0+	0
	1	115	351	367	179	054	011	002	0+	0+	0+	0+	0+	0+	1
	2	007	111	245	268	139	045	010	001	0+	0+	0+	0+	0+	2
	3	0+	021	100	246	218	111	035	006	001	0+	0+	0+	0+	3
	4	0+	003	028	154	234	184	087	024	003	0+	0+	0+	0+	4
	5	0+	0+	006	069	180	221	157	066	014	001	0+	0+	0+	5
	6	0+	0+	001	023	103	197	209	131	044	006	0+	0+	0+	6
	7	0+	0+	0+	006	044	131	209	197	103	023	001	0+	0+	7
	8	0+	0+	0+	001	014	066	157	221	180	069	006	0+	0+	8
	9	0+	0+	0+	0+	003	024	087	184	234	154	028	003	0+	9
	10	0+	0+	0+	0+	001	006	035	111	218	246	100	021	0+	10
	11	0+	0+	0+	0+	0+	001	010	045	139	268	245	111	007	11
	12	0+	0+	0+	0+	0+	0+	002	011	054	179	367	351	115	12
	13	0+	0+	0+	0+	0+	0+	0+	001	010	055	254	513	878	13
14	0	869	488	229	044	007	001	0+	0+	0+	0+	0+	0+	0+	0
	1	123	359	356	154	041	007	001	0+	0+	0+	0+	0+	0+	1
	2	008	123	257	250	113	032	006	001	0+	0+	0+	0+	0+	2
	3	0+	026	114	250	194	085	022	003	0+	0+	0+	0+	0+	3
	4	0+	004	035	172	229	155	061	014	001	0+	0+	0+	0+	4
	5	0+	0+	008	086	196	207	122	041	007	0+	0+	0+	0+	5
	6	0+	0+	001	032	126	207	183	092	023	002	0+	0+	0+	6
	7	0+	0+	0+	009	062	157	209	157	062	009	0+	0+	0+	7
	8	0+	0+	0+	002	023	092	183	207	126	032	001	0+	0+	8
	9	0+	0+	0+	0+	007	041	122	207	196	086	008	0+	0+	9
	10	0+	0+	0+	0+	001	014	061	155	229	172	035	004	0+	10
	11	0+	0+	0+	0+	0+	003	022	085	194	250	114	026	0+	11
	12	0+	0+	0+	0+	0+	001	006	032	113	250	257	123	008	12
	13	0+	0+	0+	0+	0+	0+	001	007	041	154	356	359	123	13
	14	0+	0+	0+	0+	0+	0+	0+	001	007	044	229	488	869	14
15	0	860	463	206	035	005	0+	0+	0+	0+	0+	0+	0+	0+	0
	1	130	366	343	132	031	005	0+	0+	0+	0+	0+	0+	0+	1
	2	009	135	267	231	092	022	003	0+	0+	0+	0+	0+	0+	2
	3	0+	031	129	250	170	063	014	002	0+	0+	0+	0+	0+	3
	4	0+	005	043	188	219	127	042	007	001	0+	0+	0+	0+	4
	5	0+	001	010	103	206	186	092	024	003	0+	0+	0+	0+	5
	6	0+	0+	002	043	147	207	153	061	012	001	0+	0+	0+	6
	7	0+	0+	0+	014	081	177	196	118	035	003	0+	0+	0+	7
	8	0+	0+	0+	003	035	118	196	177	081	014	0+	0+	0+	8
	9	0+	0+	0+	001	012	061	153	207	147	043	002	0+	0+	9
	10	0+	0+	0+	0+	003	024	092	186	206	103	010	001	0+	10
	11	0+	0+	0+	0+	001	007	042	127	219	188	043	005	0+	11
	12	0+	0+	0+	0+	0+	002	014	063	170	250	129	031	0+	12
	13	0+	0+	0+	0+	0+	0+	003	022	092	231	267	135	009	13
	14	0+	0+	0+	0+	0+	0+	0+	005	031	132	343	366	130	14
	15	0+	0+	0+	0+	0+	0+	0+	0+	005	035	206	463	860	15

NOTE: 0+ represents a positive probability less than 0.0005.

From Frederick C. Mosteller, Robert E. K. Rourke, and George B. Thomas, Jr., *Probability with Statistical Applications,* 2nd ed., © 1970 Addison-Wesley Publishing Co., Reading, MA. Reprinted with permission.

752

TABLE A-2	Standard Normal (z) Distribution									
z	.00	.01	.02	.03	.04	.05	.06	.07	.08	.09
0.0	.0000	.0040	.0080	.0120	.0160	.0199	.0239	.0279	.0319	.0359
0.1	.0398	.0438	.0478	.0517	.0557	.0596	.0636	.0675	.0714	.0753
0.2	.0793	.0832	.0871	.0910	.0948	.0987	.1026	.1064	.1103	.1141
0.3	.1179	.1217	.1255	.1293	.1331	.1368	.1406	.1443	.1480	.1517
0.4	.1554	.1591	.1628	.1664	.1700	.1736	.1772	.1808	.1844	.1879
0.5	.1915	.1950	.1985	.2019	.2054	.2088	.2123	.2157	.2190	.2224
0.6	.2257	.2291	.2324	.2357	.2389	.2422	.2454	.2486	.2517	.2549
0.7	.2580	.2611	.2642	.2673	.2704	.2734	.2764	.2794	.2823	.2852
0.8	.2881	.2910	.2939	.2967	.2995	.3023	.3051	.3078	.3106	.3133
0.9	.3159	.3186	.3212	.3238	.3264	.3289	.3315	.3340	.3365	.3389
1.0	.3413	.3438	.3461	.3485	.3508	.3531	.3554	.3577	.3599	.3621
1.1	.3643	.3665	.3686	.3708	.3729	.3749	.3770	.3790	.3810	.3830
1.2	.3849	.3869	.3888	.3907	.3925	.3944	.3962	.3980	.3997	.4015
1.3	.4032	.4049	.4066	.4082	.4099	.4115	.4131	.4147	.4162	.4177
1.4	.4192	.4207	.4222	.4236	.4251	.4265	.4279	.4292	.4306	.4319
1.5	.4332	.4345	.4357	.4370	.4382	.4394	.4406	.4418	.4429	.4441
1.6	.4452	.4463	.4474	.4484	.4495 *	.4505	.4515	.4525	.4535	.4545
1.7	.4554	.4564	.4573	.4582	.4591	.4599	.4608	.4616	.4625	.4633
1.8	.4641	.4649	.4656	.4664	.4671	.4678	.4686	.4693	.4699	.4706
1.9	.4713	.4719	.4726	.4732	.4738	.4744	.4750	.4756	.4761	.4767
2.0	.4772	.4778	.4783	.4788	.4793	.4798	.4803	.4808	.4812	.4817
2.1	.4821	.4826	.4830	.4834	.4838	.4842	.4846	.4850	.4854	.4857
2.2	.4861	.4864	.4868	.4871	.4875	.4878	.4881	.4884	.4887	.4890
2.3	.4893	.4896	.4898	.4901	.4904	.4906	.4909	.4911	.4913	.4916
2.4	.4918	.4920	.4922	.4925	.4927	.4929	.4931	.4932	.4934	.4936
2.5	.4938	.4940	.4941	.4943	.4945	.4946	.4948	.4949 *	.4951	.4952
2.6	.4953	.4955	.4956	.4957	.4959	.4960	.4961	.4962	.4963	.4964
2.7	.4965	.4966	.4967	.4968	.4969	.4970	.4971	.4972	.4973	.4974
2.8	.4974	.4975	.4976	.4977	.4977	.4978	.4979	.4979	.4980	.4981
2.9	.4981	.4982	.4982	.4983	.4984	.4984	.4985	.4985	.4986	.4986
3.0	.4987	.4987	.4987	.4988	.4988	.4989	.4989	.4989	.4990	.4990
3.10 and higher	.4999									

NOTE: For values of z above 3.09, use 0.4999 for the area.
*Use these common values that result from interpolation:

z score	Area
1.645	0.4500
2.575	0.4950

From Frederick C. Mosteller and Robert E. K. Rourke, *Sturdy Statistics*, 1973, Addison-Wesley Publishing Co., Reading, MA. Reprinted with permission of Frederick Mosteller.

Left tail

Student *t* distribution
Right tail

Two tails

α

Critical *t* score
(negative)

α

Critical *t* score
(positive)

$\alpha/2$ $\alpha/2$

Critical *t* score
(negative)

Critical *t* score
(positive)

TABLE A-3   *t* Distribution

			α			
Degrees of freedom	.005 (one tail) .01 (two tails)	.01 (one tail) .02 (two tails)	.025 (one tail) .05 (two tails)	.05 (one tail) .10 (two tails)	.10 (one tail) .20 (two tails)	.25 (one tail) .50 (two tails)
1	63.657	31.821	12.706	6.314	3.078	1.000
2	9.925	6.965	4.303	2.920	1.886	.816
3	5.841	4.541	3.182	2.353	1.638	.765
4	4.604	3.747	2.776	2.132	1.533	.741
5	4.032	3.365	2.571	2.015	1.476	.727
6	3.707	3.143	2.447	1.943	1.440	.718
7	3.500	2.998	2.365	1.895	1.415	.711
8	3.355	2.896	2.306	1.860	1.397	.706
9	3.250	2.821	2.262	1.833	1.383	.703
10	3.169	2.764	2.228	1.812	1.372	.700
11	3.106	2.718	2.201	1.796	1.363	.697
12	3.054	2.681	2.179	1.782	1.356	.696
13	3.012	2.650	2.160	1.771	1.350	.694
14	2.977	2.625	2.145	1.761	1.345	.692
15	2.947	2.602	2.132	1.753	1.341	.691
16	2.921	2.584	2.120	1.746	1.337	.690
17	2.898	2.567	2.110	1.740	1.333	.689
18	2.878	2.552	2.101	1.734	1.330	.688
19	2.861	2.540	2.093	1.729	1.328	.688
20	2.845	2.528	2.086	1.725	1.325	.687
21	2.831	2.518	2.080	1.721	1.323	.686
22	2.819	2.508	2.074	1.717	1.321	.686
23	2.807	2.500	2.069	1.714	1.320	.685
24	2.797	2.492	2.064	1.711	1.318	.685
25	2.787	2.485	2.060	1.708	1.316	.684
26	2.779	2.479	2.056	1.706	1.315	.684
27	2.771	2.473	2.052	1.703	1.314	.684
28	2.763	2.467	2.048	1.701	1.313	.683
29	2.756	2.462	2.045	1.699	1.311	.683
Large (z)	2.575	2.327	1.960	1.645	1.282	.675

TABLE A-4	Chi-Square (χ^2) Distribution

Area to the Right of the Critical Value

Degrees of freedom	0.995	0.99	0.975	0.95	0.90	0.10	0.05	0.025	0.01	0.005
1	—	—	0.001	0.004	0.016	2.706	3.841	5.024	6.635	7.879
2	0.010	0.020	0.051	0.103	0.211	4.605	5.991	7.378	9.210	10.597
3	0.072	0.115	0.216	0.352	0.584	6.251	7.815	9.348	11.345	12.838
4	0.207	0.297	0.484	0.711	1.064	7.779	9.488	11.143	13.277	14.860
5	0.412	0.554	0.831	1.145	1.610	9.236	11.071	12.833	15.086	16.750
6	0.676	0.872	1.237	1.635	2.204	10.645	12.592	14.449	16.812	18.548
7	0.989	1.239	1.690	2.167	2.833	12.017	14.067	16.013	18.475	20.278
8	1.344	1.646	2.180	2.733	3.490	13.362	15.507	17.535	20.090	21.955
9	1.735	2.088	2.700	3.325	4.168	14.684	16.919	19.023	21.666	23.589
10	2.156	2.558	3.247	3.940	4.865	15.987	18.307	20.483	23.209	25.188
11	2.603	3.053	3.816	4.575	5.578	17.275	19.675	21.920	24.725	26.757
12	3.074	3.571	4.404	5.226	6.304	18.549	21.026	23.337	26.217	28.299
13	3.565	4.107	5.009	5.892	7.042	19.812	22.362	24.736	27.688	29.819
14	4.075	4.660	5.629	6.571	7.790	21.064	23.685	26.119	29.141	31.319
15	4.601	5.229	6.262	7.261	8.547	22.307	24.996	27.488	30.578	32.801
16	5.142	5.812	6.908	7.962	9.312	23.542	26.296	28.845	32.000	34.267
17	5.697	6.408	7.564	8.672	10.085	24.769	27.587	30.191	33.409	35.718
18	6.265	7.015	8.231	9.390	10.865	25.989	28.869	31.526	34.805	37.156
19	6.844	7.633	8.907	10.117	11.651	27.204	30.144	32.852	36.191	38.582
20	7.434	8.260	9.591	10.851	12.443	28.412	31.410	34.170	37.566	39.997
21	8.034	8.897	10.283	11.591	13.240	29.615	32.671	35.479	38.932	41.401
22	8.643	9.542	10.982	12.338	14.042	30.813	33.924	36.781	40.289	42.796
23	9.260	10.196	11.689	13.091	14.848	32.007	35.172	38.076	41.638	44.181
24	9.886	10.856	12.401	13.848	15.659	33.196	36.415	39.364	42.980	45.559
25	10.520	11.524	13.120	14.611	16.473	34.382	37.652	40.646	44.314	46.928
26	11.160	12.198	13.844	15.379	17.292	35.563	38.885	41.923	45.642	48.290
27	11.808	12.879	14.573	16.151	18.114	36.741	40.113	43.194	46.963	49.645
28	12.461	13.565	15.308	16.928	18.939	37.916	41.337	44.461	48.278	50.993
29	13.121	14.257	16.047	17.708	19.768	39.087	42.557	45.722	49.588	52.336
30	13.787	14.954	16.791	18.493	20.599	40.256	43.773	46.979	50.892	53.672
40	20.707	22.164	24.433	26.509	29.051	51.805	55.758	59.342	63.691	66.766
50	27.991	29.707	32.357	34.764	37.689	63.167	67.505	71.420	76.154	79.490
60	35.534	37.485	40.482	43.188	46.459	74.397	79.082	83.298	88.379	91.952
70	43.275	45.442	48.758	51.739	55.329	85.527	90.531	95.023	100.425	104.215
80	51.172	53.540	57.153	60.391	64.278	96.578	101.879	106.629	112.329	116.321
90	59.196	61.754	65.647	69.126	73.291	107.565	113.145	118.136	124.116	128.299
100	67.328	70.065	74.222	77.929	82.358	118.498	124.342	129.561	135.807	140.169

From Donald B. Owen, *Handbook of Statistical Tables,* © 1962 Addison-Wesley Publishing Co., Reading, MA. Reprinted with permission of the publisher.

Right tail

α

χ^2

To find this value, use the column with the area α given at the top of the table.

Left tail

Area = $1 - \alpha$

α

χ^2

To find this value, determine the area of the region to the right of this boundary (the unshaded area) and use the column with this value at the top. If the left tail has area α, use the column with the value of $1 - \alpha$ at the top of the table.

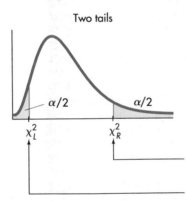

Two tails

$\alpha/2$ $\alpha/2$

χ_L^2 χ_R^2

To find this value, use the column with area $\alpha/2$ at the top of the table.

To find this value, use the column with area $1 - \alpha/2$ at the top of the table.

0.01

F

TABLE A-5   F Distribution ($\alpha = 0.01$ in the right tail)

Numerator degrees of freedom (df_1)

df_2	1	2	3	4	5	6	7	8	9
1	4052.2	4999.5	5403.4	5624.6	5763.6	5859.0	5928.4	5981.1	6022.5
2	98.503	99.000	99.166	99.249	99.299	99.333	99.356	99.374	99.388
3	34.116	30.817	29.457	28.710	28.237	27.911	27.672	27.489	27.345
4	21.198	18.000	16.694	15.977	15.522	15.207	14.976	14.799	14.659
5	16.258	13.274	12.060	11.392	10.967	10.672	10.456	10.289	10.158
6	13.745	10.925	9.7795	9.1483	8.7459	8.4661	8.2600	8.1017	7.9761
7	12.246	9.5466	8.4513	7.8466	7.4604	7.1914	6.9928	6.8400	6.7188
8	11.259	8.6491	7.5910	7.0061	6.6318	6.3707	6.1776	6.0289	5.9106
9	10.561	8.0215	6.9919	6.4221	6.0569	5.8018	5.6129	5.4671	5.3511
10	10.044	7.5594	6.5523	5.9943	5.6363	5.3858	5.2001	5.0567	4.9424
11	9.6460	7.2057	6.2167	5.6683	5.3160	5.0692	4.8861	4.7445	4.6315
12	9.3302	6.9266	5.9525	5.4120	5.0643	4.8206	4.6395	4.4994	4.3875
13	9.0738	6.7010	5.7394	5.2053	4.8616	4.6204	4.4410	4.3021	4.1911
14	8.8616	6.5149	5.5639	5.0354	4.6950	4.4558	4.2779	4.1399	4.0297
15	8.6831	6.3589	5.4170	4.8932	4.5556	4.3183	4.1415	4.0045	3.8948
16	8.5310	6.2262	5.2922	4.7726	4.4374	4.2016	4.0259	3.8896	3.7804
17	8.3997	6.1121	5.1850	4.6690	4.3359	4.1015	3.9267	3.7910	3.6822
18	8.2854	6.0129	5.0919	4.5790	4.2479	4.0146	3.8406	3.7054	3.5971
19	8.1849	5.9259	5.0103	4.5003	4.1708	3.9386	3.7653	3.6305	3.5225
20	8.0960	5.8489	4.9382	4.4307	4.1027	3.8714	3.6987	3.5644	3.4567
21	8.0166	5.7804	4.8740	4.3688	4.0421	3.8117	3.6396	3.5056	3.3981
22	7.9454	5.7190	4.8166	4.3134	3.9880	3.7583	3.5867	3.4530	3.3458
23	7.8811	5.6637	4.7649	4.2636	3.9392	3.7102	3.5390	3.4057	3.2986
24	7.8229	5.6136	4.7181	4.2184	3.8951	3.6667	3.4959	3.3629	3.2560
25	7.7698	5.5680	4.6755	4.1774	3.8550	3.6272	3.4568	3.3239	3.2172
26	7.7213	5.5263	4.6366	4.1400	3.8183	3.5911	3.4210	3.2884	3.1818
27	7.6767	5.4881	4.6009	4.1056	3.7848	3.5580	3.3882	3.2558	3.1494
28	7.6356	5.4529	4.5681	4.0740	3.7539	3.5276	3.3581	3.2259	3.1195
29	7.5977	5.4204	4.5378	4.0449	3.7254	3.4995	3.3303	3.1982	3.0920
30	7.5625	5.3903	4.5097	4.0179	3.6990	3.4735	3.3045	3.1726	3.0665
40	7.3141	5.1785	4.3126	3.8283	3.5138	3.2910	3.1238	2.9930	2.8876
60	7.0771	4.9774	4.1259	3.6490	3.3389	3.1187	2.9530	2.8233	2.7185
120	6.8509	4.7865	3.9491	3.4795	3.1735	2.9559	2.7918	2.6629	2.5586
∞	6.6349	4.6052	3.7816	3.3192	3.0173	2.8020	2.6393	2.5113	2.4073

Denominator degrees of freedom (df_2)

From Maxine Merrington and Catherine M. Thompson, "Tables of Percentage Points of the Inverted Beta (F) Distribution," *Biometrika 33* (1943): 80–84. Reproduced with permission of the Biometrika Trustees.

(continued)

TABLE A-5 F Distribution ($\alpha = 0.01$ in the right tail) (continued)

Numerator degrees of freedom (df_1)

df_2	10	12	15	20	24	30	40	60	120	∞
1	6055.8	6106.3	6157.3	6208.7	6234.6	6260.6	6286.8	6313.0	6339.4	6365.9
2	99.399	99.416	99.433	99.449	99.458	99.466	99.474	99.482	99.491	99.499
3	27.229	27.052	26.872	26.690	26.598	26.505	26.411	26.316	26.221	26.125
4	14.546	14.374	14.198	14.020	13.929	13.838	13.745	13.652	13.558	13.463
5	10.051	9.8883	9.7222	9.5526	9.4665	9.3793	9.2912	9.2020	9.1118	9.0204
6	7.8741	7.7183	7.5590	7.3958	7.3127	7.2285	7.1432	7.0567	6.9690	6.8800
7	6.6201	6.4691	6.3143	6.1554	6.0743	5.9920	5.9084	5.8236	5.7373	5.6495
8	5.8143	5.6667	5.5151	5.3591	5.2793	5.1981	5.1156	5.0316	4.9461	4.8588
9	5.2565	5.1114	4.9621	4.8080	4.7290	4.6486	4.5666	4.4831	4.3978	4.3105
10	4.8491	4.7059	4.5581	4.4054	4.3269	4.2469	4.1653	4.0819	3.9965	3.9090
11	4.5393	4.3974	4.2509	4.0990	4.0209	3.9411	3.8596	3.7761	3.6904	3.6024
12	4.2961	4.1553	4.0096	3.8584	3.7805	3.7008	3.6192	3.5355	3.4494	3.3608
13	4.1003	3.9603	3.8154	3.6646	3.5868	3.5070	3.4253	3.3413	3.2548	3.1654
14	3.9394	3.8001	3.6557	3.5052	3.4274	3.3476	3.2656	3.1813	3.0942	3.0040
15	3.8049	3.6662	3.5222	3.3719	3.2940	3.2141	3.1319	3.0471	2.9595	2.8684
16	3.6909	3.5527	3.4089	3.2587	3.1808	3.1007	3.0182	2.9330	2.8447	2.7528
17	3.5931	3.4552	3.3117	3.1615	3.0835	3.0032	2.9205	2.8348	2.7459	2.6530
18	3.5082	3.3706	3.2273	3.0771	2.9990	2.9185	2.8354	2.7493	2.6597	2.5660
19	3.4338	3.2965	3.1533	3.0031	2.9249	2.8442	2.7608	2.6742	2.5839	2.4893
20	3.3682	3.2311	3.0880	2.9377	2.8594	2.7785	2.6947	2.6077	2.5168	2.4212
21	3.3098	3.1730	3.0300	2.8796	2.8010	2.7200	2.6359	2.5484	2.4568	2.3603
22	3.2576	3.1209	2.9779	2.8274	2.7488	2.6675	2.5831	2.4951	2.4029	2.3055
23	3.2106	3.0740	2.9311	2.7805	2.7017	2.6202	2.5355	2.4471	2.3542	2.2558
24	3.1681	3.0316	2.8887	2.7380	2.6591	2.5773	2.4923	2.4035	2.3100	2.2107
25	3.1294	2.9931	2.8502	2.6993	2.6203	2.5383	2.4530	2.3637	2.2696	2.1694
26	3.0941	2.9578	2.8150	2.6640	2.5848	2.5026	2.4170	2.3273	2.2325	2.1315
27	3.0618	2.9256	2.7827	2.6316	2.5522	2.4699	2.3840	2.2938	2.1985	2.0965
28	3.0320	2.8959	2.7530	2.6017	2.5223	2.4397	2.3535	2.2629	2.1670	2.0642
29	3.0045	2.8685	2.7256	2.5742	2.4946	2.4118	2.3253	2.2344	2.1379	2.0342
30	2.9791	2.8431	2.7002	2.5487	2.4689	2.3860	2.2992	2.2079	2.1108	2.0062
40	2.8005	2.6648	2.5216	2.3689	2.2880	2.2034	2.1142	2.0194	1.9172	1.8047
60	2.6318	2.4961	2.3523	2.1978	2.1154	2.0285	1.9360	1.8363	1.7263	1.6006
120	2.4721	2.3363	2.1915	2.0346	1.9500	1.8600	1.7628	1.6557	1.5330	1.3805
∞	2.3209	2.1847	2.0385	1.8783	1.7908	1.6964	1.5923	1.4730	1.3246	1.0000

Denominator degrees of freedom (df_2)

From Maxine Merrington and Catherine M. Thompson, "Tables of Percentage Points of the Inverted Beta (F) Distribution," *Biometrika 33* (1943): 80–84. Reproduced with permission of the Biometrika Trustees.

(continued)

758

0.025

F

| TABLE A-5 | F Distribution ($\alpha = 0.025$ in the right tail) | | | | | | | | |

Numerator degrees of freedom (df_1)

df_2	1	2	3	4	5	6	7	8	9
1	647.79	799.50	864.16	899.58	921.85	937.11	948.22	956.66	963.28
2	38.506	39.000	39.165	39.248	39.298	39.331	39.335	39.373	39.387
3	17.443	16.044	15.439	15.101	14.885	14.735	14.624	14.540	14.473
4	12.218	10.649	9.9792	9.6045	9.3645	9.1973	9.0741	8.9796	8.9047
5	10.007	8.4336	7.7636	7.3879	7.1464	6.9777	6.8531	6.7572	6.6811
6	8.8131	7.2599	6.5988	6.2272	5.9876	5.8198	5.6955	5.5996	5.5234
7	8.0727	6.5415	5.8898	5.5226	5.2852	5.1186	4.9949	4.8993	4.8232
8	7.5709	6.0595	5.4160	5.0526	4.8173	4.6517	4.5286	4.4333	4.3572
9	7.2093	5.7147	5.0781	4.7181	4.4844	4.3197	4.1970	4.1020	4.0260
10	6.9367	5.4564	4.8256	4.4683	4.2361	4.0721	3.9498	3.8549	3.7790
11	6.7241	5.2559	4.6300	4.2751	4.0440	3.8807	3.7586	3.6638	3.5879
12	6.5538	5.0959	4.4742	4.1212	3.8911	3.7283	3.6065	3.5118	3.4358
13	6.4143	4.9653	4.3472	3.9959	3.7667	3.6043	3.4827	3.3880	3.3120
14	6.2979	4.8567	4.2417	3.8919	3.6634	3.5014	3.3799	3.2853	3.2093
15	6.1995	4.7650	4.1528	3.8043	3.5764	3.4147	3.2934	3.1987	3.1227
16	6.1151	4.6867	4.0768	3.7294	3.5021	3.3406	3.2194	3.1248	3.0488
17	6.0420	4.6189	4.0112	3.6648	3.4379	3.2767	3.1556	3.0610	2.9849
18	5.9781	4.5597	3.9539	3.6083	3.3820	3.2209	3.0999	3.0053	2.9291
19	5.9216	4.5075	3.9034	3.5587	3.3327	3.1718	3.0509	2.9563	2.8801
20	5.8715	4.4613	3.8587	3.5147	3.2891	3.1283	3.0074	2.9128	2.8365
21	5.8266	4.4199	3.8188	3.4754	3.2501	3.0895	2.9686	2.8740	2.7977
22	5.7863	4.3828	3.7829	3.4401	3.2151	3.0546	2.9338	2.8392	2.7628
23	5.7498	4.3492	3.7505	3.4083	3.1835	3.0232	2.9023	2.8077	2.7313
24	5.7166	4.3187	3.7211	3.3794	3.1548	2.9946	2.8738	2.7791	2.7027
25	5.6864	4.2909	3.6943	3.3530	3.1287	2.9685	2.8478	2.7531	2.6766
26	5.6586	4.2655	3.6697	3.3289	3.1048	2.9447	2.8240	2.7293	2.6528
27	5.6331	4.2421	3.6472	3.3067	3.0828	2.9228	2.8021	2.7074	2.6309
28	5.6096	4.2205	3.6264	3.2863	3.0626	2.9027	2.7820	2.6872	2.6106
29	5.5878	4.2006	3.6072	3.2674	3.0438	2.8840	2.7633	2.6686	2.5919
30	5.5675	4.1821	3.5894	3.2499	3.0265	2.8667	2.7460	2.6513	2.5746
40	5.4239	4.0510	3.4633	3.1261	2.9037	2.7444	2.6238	2.5289	2.4519
60	5.2856	3.9253	3.3425	3.0077	2.7863	2.6274	2.5068	2.4117	2.3344
120	5.1523	3.8046	3.2269	2.8943	2.6740	2.5154	2.3948	2.2994	2.2217
∞	5.0239	3.6889	3.1161	2.7858	2.5665	2.4082	2.2875	2.1918	2.1136

Denominator degrees of freedom (df_2)

(continued)

TABLE A-5   F Distribution (α = 0.025 in the right tail) (continued)

Numerator degrees of freedom (df_1)

df_2	10	12	15	20	24	30	40	60	120	∞
1	968.63	976.71	984.87	993.10	997.25	1001.4	1005.6	1009.8	1014.0	1018.3
2	39.398	39.415	39.431	39.448	39.456	39.465	39.473	39.481	39.490	39.498
3	14.419	14.337	14.253	14.167	14.124	14.081	14.037	13.992	13.947	13.902
4	8.8439	8.7512	8.6565	8.5599	8.5109	8.4613	8.4111	8.3604	8.3092	8.2573
5	6.6192	6.5245	6.4277	6.3286	6.2780	6.2269	6.1750	6.1225	6.0693	6.0153
6	5.4613	5.3662	5.2687	5.1684	5.1172	5.0652	5.0125	4.9589	4.9044	4.8491
7	4.7611	4.6658	4.5678	4.4667	4.4150	4.3624	4.3089	4.2544	4.1989	4.1423
8	4.2951	4.1997	4.1012	3.9995	3.9472	3.8940	3.8398	3.7844	3.7279	3.6702
9	3.9639	3.8682	3.7694	3.6669	3.6142	3.5604	3.5055	3.4493	3.3918	3.3329
10	3.7168	3.6209	3.5217	3.4185	3.3654	3.3110	3.2554	3.1984	3.1399	3.0798
11	3.5257	3.4296	3.3299	3.2261	3.1725	3.1176	3.0613	3.0035	2.9441	2.8828
12	3.3736	3.2773	3.1772	3.0728	3.0187	2.9633	2.9063	2.8478	2.7874	2.7249
13	3.2497	3.1532	3.0527	2.9477	2.8932	2.8372	2.7797	2.7204	2.6590	2.5955
14	3.1469	3.0502	2.9493	2.8437	2.7888	2.7324	2.6742	2.6142	2.5519	2.4872
15	3.0602	2.9633	2.8621	2.7559	2.7006	2.6437	2.5850	2.5242	2.4611	2.3953
16	2.9862	2.8890	2.7875	2.6808	2.6252	2.5678	2.5085	2.4471	2.3831	2.3163
17	2.9222	2.8249	2.7230	2.6158	2.5598	2.5020	2.4422	2.3801	2.3153	2.2474
18	2.8664	2.7689	2.6667	2.5590	2.5027	2.4445	2.3842	2.3214	2.2558	2.1869
19	2.8172	2.7196	2.6171	2.5089	2.4523	2.3937	2.3329	2.2696	2.2032	2.1333
20	2.7737	2.6758	2.5731	2.4645	2.4076	2.3486	2.2873	2.2234	2.1562	2.0853
21	2.7348	2.6368	2.5338	2.4247	2.3675	2.3082	2.2465	2.1819	2.1141	2.0422
22	2.6998	2.6017	2.4984	2.3890	2.3315	2.2718	2.2097	2.1446	2.0760	2.0032
23	2.6682	2.5699	2.4665	2.3567	2.2989	2.2389	2.1763	2.1107	2.0415	1.9677
24	2.6396	2.5411	2.4374	2.3273	2.2693	2.2090	2.1460	2.0799	2.0099	1.9353
25	2.6135	2.5149	2.4110	2.3005	2.2422	2.1816	2.1183	2.0516	1.9811	1.9055
26	2.5896	2.4908	2.3867	2.2759	2.2174	2.1565	2.0928	2.0257	1.9545	1.8781
27	2.5676	2.4688	2.3644	2.2533	2.1946	2.1334	2.0693	2.0018	1.9299	1.8527
28	2.5473	2.4484	2.3438	2.2324	2.1735	2.1121	2.0477	1.9797	1.9072	1.8291
29	2.5286	2.4295	2.3248	2.2131	2.1540	2.0923	2.0276	1.9591	1.8861	1.8072
30	2.5112	2.4120	2.3072	2.1952	2.1359	2.0739	2.0089	1.9400	1.8664	1.7867
40	2.3882	2.2882	2.1819	2.0677	2.0069	1.9429	1.8752	1.8028	1.7242	1.6371
60	2.2702	2.1692	2.0613	1.9445	1.8817	1.8152	1.7440	1.6668	1.5810	1.4821
120	2.1570	2.0548	1.9450	1.8249	1.7597	1.6899	1.6141	1.5299	1.4327	1.3104
∞	2.0483	1.9447	1.8326	1.7085	1.6402	1.5660	1.4835	1.3883	1.2684	1.0000

From Maxine Merrington and Catherine M. Thompson, "Tables of Percentage Points of the Inverted Beta (F) Distribution," *Biometrika 33* (1943): 80–84. Reproduced with permission of the Biometrika Trustees.

(continued)

0.05

F

TABLE A-5   F Distribution ($\alpha = 0.05$ in the right tail)

Numerator degrees of freedom (df_1)

Denominator degrees of freedom (df_2)	1	2	3	4	5	6	7	8	9
1	161.45	199.50	215.71	224.58	230.16	233.99	236.77	238.88	240.54
2	18.513	19.000	19.164	19.247	19.296	19.330	19.353	19.371	19.385
3	10.128	9.5521	9.2766	9.1172	9.0135	8.9406	8.8867	8.8452	8.8123
4	7.7086	6.9443	6.5914	6.3882	6.2561	6.1631	6.0942	6.0410	6.9988
5	6.6079	5.7861	5.4095	5.1922	5.0503	4.9503	4.8759	4.8183	4.7725
6	5.9874	5.1433	4.7571	4.5337	4.3874	4.2839	4.2067	4.1468	4.0990
7	5.5914	4.7374	4.3468	4.1203	3.9715	3.8660	3.7870	3.7257	3.6767
8	5.3177	4.4590	4.0662	3.8379	3.6875	3.5806	3.5005	3.4381	3.3881
9	5.1174	4.2565	3.8625	3.6331	3.4817	3.3738	3.2927	3.2296	3.1789
10	4.9646	4.1028	3.7083	3.4780	3.3258	3.2172	3.1355	3.0717	3.0204
11	4.8443	3.9823	3.5874	3.3567	3.2039	3.0946	3.0123	2.9480	2.8962
12	4.7472	3.8853	3.4903	3.2592	3.1059	2.9961	2.9134	2.8486	2.7964
13	4.6672	3.8056	3.4105	3.1791	3.0254	2.9153	2.8321	2.7669	2.7144
14	4.6001	3.7389	3.3439	3.1122	2.9582	2.8477	2.7642	2.6987	2.6458
15	4.5431	3.6823	3.2874	3.0556	2.9013	2.7905	2.7066	2.6408	2.5876
16	4.4940	3.6337	3.2389	3.0069	2.8524	2.7413	2.6572	2.5911	2.5377
17	4.4513	3.5915	3.1968	2.9647	2.8100	2.6987	2.6143	2.5480	2.4943
18	4.4139	3.5546	3.1599	2.9277	2.7729	2.6613	2.5767	2.5102	2.4563
19	4.3807	3.5219	3.1274	2.8951	2.7401	2.6283	2.5435	2.4768	2.4227
20	4.3512	3.4928	3.0984	2.8661	2.7109	2.5990	2.5140	2.4471	2.3928
21	4.3248	3.4668	3.0725	2.8401	2.6848	2.5727	2.4876	2.4205	2.3660
22	4.3009	3.4434	3.0491	2.8167	2.6613	2.5491	2.4638	2.3965	2.3419
23	4.2793	3.4221	3.0280	2.7955	2.6400	2.5277	2.4422	2.3748	2.3201
24	4.2597	3.4028	3.0088	2.7763	2.6207	2.5082	2.4226	2.3551	2.3002
25	4.2417	3.3852	2.9912	2.7587	2.6030	2.4904	2.4047	2.3371	2.2821
26	4.2252	3.3690	2.9752	2.7426	2.5868	2.4741	2.3883	2.3205	2.2655
27	4.2100	3.3541	2.9604	2.7278	2.5719	2.4591	2.3732	2.3053	2.2501
28	4.1960	3.3404	2.9467	2.7141	2.5581	2.4453	2.3593	2.2913	2.2360
29	4.1830	3.3277	2.9340	2.7014	2.5454	2.4324	2.3463	2.2783	2.2229
30	4.1709	3.3158	2.9223	2.6896	2.5336	2.4205	2.3343	2.2662	2.2107
40	4.0847	3.2317	2.8387	2.6060	2.4495	2.3359	2.2490	2.1802	2.1240
60	4.0012	3.1504	2.7581	2.5252	2.3683	2.2541	2.1665	2.0970	2.0401
120	3.9201	3.0718	2.6802	2.4472	2.2899	2.1750	2.0868	2.0164	1.9588
∞	3.8415	2.9957	2.6049	2.3719	2.2141	2.0986	2.0096	1.9384	1.8799

(continued)

TABLE A-5   F Distribution ($\alpha = 0.05$ in the right tail) (continued)

Numerator degrees of freedom (df_1)

df_2	10	12	15	20	24	30	40	60	120	∞
1	241.88	243.91	245.95	248.01	249.05	250.10	251.14	252.20	253.25	254.31
2	19.396	19.413	19.429	19.446	19.454	19.462	19.471	19.479	19.487	19.496
3	8.7855	8.7446	8.7029	8.6602	8.6385	8.6166	8.5944	8.5720	8.5494	8.5264
4	5.9644	5.9117	5.8578	5.8025	5.7744	5.7459	5.7170	5.6877	5.6581	5.6281
5	4.7351	4.6777	4.6188	4.5581	4.5272	4.4957	4.4638	4.4314	4.3985	4.3650
6	4.0600	3.9999	3.9381	3.8742	3.8415	3.8082	3.7743	3.7398	3.7047	3.6689
7	3.6365	3.5747	3.5107	3.4445	3.4105	3.3758	3.3404	3.3043	3.2674	3.2298
8	3.3472	3.2839	3.2184	3.1503	3.1152	3.0794	3.0428	3.0053	2.9669	2.9276
9	3.1373	3.0729	3.0061	2.9365	2.9005	2.8637	2.8259	2.7872	2.7475	2.7067
10	2.9782	2.9130	2.8450	2.7740	2.7372	2.6996	2.6609	2.6211	2.5801	2.5379
11	2.8536	2.7876	2.7186	2.6464	2.6090	2.5705	2.5309	2.4901	2.4480	2.4045
12	2.7534	2.6866	2.6169	2.5436	2.5055	2.4663	2.4259	2.3842	2.3410	2.2962
13	2.6710	2.6037	2.5331	2.4589	2.4202	2.3803	2.3392	2.2966	2.2524	2.2064
14	2.6022	2.5342	2.4630	2.3879	2.3487	2.3082	2.2664	2.2229	2.1778	2.1307
15	2.5437	2.4753	2.4034	2.3275	2.2878	2.2468	2.2043	2.1601	2.1141	2.0658
16	2.4935	2.4247	2.3522	2.2756	2.2354	2.1938	2.1507	2.1058	2.0589	2.0096
17	2.4499	2.3807	2.3077	2.2304	2.1898	2.1477	2.1040	2.0584	2.0107	1.9604
18	2.4117	2.3421	2.2686	2.1906	2.1497	2.1071	2.0629	2.0166	1.9681	1.9168
19	2.3779	2.3080	2.2341	2.1555	2.1141	2.0712	2.0264	1.9795	1.9302	1.8780
20	2.3479	2.2776	2.2033	2.1242	2.0825	2.0391	1.9938	1.9464	1.8963	1.8432
21	2.3210	2.2504	2.1757	2.0960	2.0540	2.0102	1.9645	1.9165	1.8657	1.8117
22	2.2967	2.2258	2.1508	2.0707	2.0283	1.9842	1.9380	1.8894	1.8380	1.7831
23	2.2747	2.2036	2.1282	2.0476	2.0050	1.9605	1.9139	1.8648	1.8128	1.7570
24	2.2547	2.1834	2.1077	2.0267	1.9838	1.9390	1.8920	1.8424	1.7896	1.7330
25	2.2365	2.1649	2.0889	2.0075	1.9643	1.9192	1.8718	1.8217	1.7684	1.7110
26	2.2197	2.1479	2.0716	1.9898	1.9464	1.9010	1.8533	1.8027	1.7488	1.6906
27	2.2043	2.1323	2.0558	1.9736	1.9299	1.8842	1.8361	1.7851	1.7306	1.6717
28	2.1900	2.1179	2.0411	1.9586	1.9147	1.8687	1.8203	1.7689	1.7138	1.6541
29	2.1768	2.1045	2.0275	1.9446	1.9005	1.8543	1.8055	1.7537	1.6981	1.6376
30	2.1646	2.0921	2.0148	1.9317	1.8874	1.8409	1.7918	1.7396	1.6835	1.6223
40	2.0772	2.0035	1.9245	1.8389	1.7929	1.7444	1.6928	1.6373	1.5766	1.5089
60	1.9926	1.9174	1.8364	1.7480	1.7001	1.6491	1.5943	1.5343	1.4673	1.3893
120	1.9105	1.8337	1.7505	1.6587	1.6084	1.5543	1.4952	1.4290	1.3519	1.2539
∞	1.8307	1.7522	1.6664	1.5705	1.5173	1.4591	1.3940	1.3180	1.2214	1.0000

Denominator degrees of freedom (df_2)

From Maxine Merrington and Catherine M. Thompson, "Tables of Percentage Points of the Inverted Beta (F) Distribution," *Biometrika 33* (1943): 80–84. Reproduced with permission of the Biometrika Trustees.

TABLE A-6	Critical Values of the Pearson Correlation Coefficient r	
n	$\alpha = .05$	$\alpha = .01$
4	.950	.999
5	.878	.959
6	.811	.917
7	.754	.875
8	.707	.834
9	.666	.798
10	.632	.765
11	.602	.735
12	.576	.708
13	.553	.684
14	.532	.661
15	.514	.641
16	.497	.623
17	.482	.606
18	.468	.590
19	.456	.575
20	.444	.561
25	.396	.505
30	.361	.463
35	.335	.430
40	.312	.402
45	.294	.378
50	.279	.361
60	.254	.330
70	.236	.305
80	.220	.286
90	.207	.269
100	.196	.256

NOTE: To test H_0: $\rho = 0$ against H_1: $\rho \neq 0$, reject H_0 if the absolute value of r is greater than the critical value in the table.

	.005 (one tail) .01 (two tails)	.01 (one tail) .02 (two tails)	.025 (one tail) .05 (two tails)	.05 (one tail) .10 (two tails)
TABLE A-7				

TABLE A-7 Critical Values for the Sign Test

			α		
n	.005 (one tail) .01 (two tails)	.01 (one tail) .02 (two tails)	.025 (one tail) .05 (two tails)	.05 (one tail) .10 (two tails)
1	*	*	*	*
2	*	*	*	*
3	*	*	*	*
4	*	*	*	*
5	*	*	*	0
6	*	*	0	0
7	*	0	0	0
8	0	0	0	1
9	0	0	1	1
10	0	0	1	1
11	0	1	1	2
12	1	1	2	2
13	1	1	2	3
14	1	2	2	3
15	2	2	3	3
16	2	2	3	4
17	2	3	4	4
18	3	3	4	5
19	3	4	4	5
20	3	4	5	5
21	4	4	5	6
22	4	5	5	6
23	4	5	6	7
24	5	5	6	7
25	5	6	7	7

NOTES:
1. * indicates that it is not possible to get a value in the critical region.
2. Reject the null hypothesis if the number of the less frequent sign (x) is less than or equal to the value in the table.
3. For values of n greater than 25, a normal approximation is used with

$$z = \frac{(x + 0.5) - \left(\frac{n}{2}\right)}{\frac{\sqrt{n}}{2}}$$

TABLE A-8	Critical Values of T for the Wilcoxon Signed-Ranks Test			

| | α | | | |
n	.005 (one tail) .01 (two tails)	.01 (one tail) .02 (two tails)	.025 (one tail) .05 (two tails)	.05 (one tail) .10 (two tails)
5	*	*	*	1
6	*	*	1	2
7	*	0	2	4
8	0	2	4	6
9	2	3	6	8
10	3	5	8	11
11	5	7	11	14
12	7	10	14	17
13	10	13	17	21
14	13	16	21	26
15	16	20	25	30
16	19	24	30	36
17	23	28	35	41
18	28	33	40	47
19	32	38	46	54
20	37	43	52	60
21	43	49	59	68
22	49	56	66	75
23	55	62	73	83
24	61	69	81	92
25	68	77	90	101
26	76	85	98	110
27	84	93	107	120
28	92	102	117	130
29	100	111	127	141
30	109	120	137	152

NOTES:

1. * indicates that it is not possible to get a value in the critical region.
2. Reject the null hypothesis if the test statistic T is less than or equal to the critical value found in this table. Fail to reject the null hypothesis if the test statistic T is greater than the critical value found in this table.

From *Some Rapid Approximate Statistical Procedures,* Copyright © 1949, 1964 Lederle Laboratories Division of American Cyanamid Company. Reprinted with the permission of the American Cyanamid Company.

TABLE A-9	Critical Values of Spearman's Rank Correlation Coefficient r_s			
n	$\alpha = 0.10$	$\alpha = 0.05$	$\alpha = 0.02$	$\alpha = 0.01$
5	.900	—	—	—
6	.829	.886	.943	—
7	.714	.786	.893	—
8	.643	.738	.833	.881
9	.600	.683	.783	.833
10	.564	.648	.745	.794
11	.523	.623	.736	.818
12	.497	.591	.703	.780
13	.475	.566	.673	.745
14	.457	.545	.646	.716
15	.441	.525	.623	.689
16	.425	.507	.601	.666
17	.412	.490	.582	.645
18	.399	.476	.564	.625
19	.388	.462	.549	.608
20	.377	.450	.534	.591
21	.368	.438	.521	.576
22	.359	.428	.508	.562
23	.351	.418	.496	.549
24	.343	.409	.485	.537
25	.336	.400	.475	.526
26	.329	.392	.465	.515
27	.323	.385	.456	.505
28	.317	.377	.448	.496
29	.311	.370	.440	.487
30	.305	.364	.432	.478

NOTE: For $n > 30$ use $r_s = \pm z/\sqrt{n-1}$, where z corresponds to the level of significance. For example, if $\alpha = 0.05$, then $z = 1.96$.

To test $H_0: \rho_s = 0$
against $H_1: \rho_s \neq 0$

From "Distribution of sums of squares of rank differences to small numbers of individuals," *The Annals of Mathematical Statistics*, Vol. 9, No. 2. Reprinted with permission of the Institute of Mathematical Statistics.

TABLE A-10 | Critical Values for Number of Runs G

		Value of n_2																		
Value of n_1		2	3	4	5	6	7	8	9	10	11	12	13	14	15	16	17	18	19	20
2		1	1	1	1	1	1	1	1	1	1	2	2	2	2	2	2	2	2	2
		6	6	6	6	6	6	6	6	6	6	6	6	6	6	6	6	6	6	6
3		1	1	1	1	2	2	2	2	2	2	2	2	3	3	3	3	3	3	3
		6	8	8	8	8	8	8	8	8	8	8	8	8	8	8	8	8	8	8
4		1	1	1	2	2	2	3	3	3	3	3	3	3	4	4	4	4	4	4
		6	8	9	9	9	10	10	10	10	10	10	10	10	10	10	10	10	10	10
5		1	1	2	2	3	3	3	3	3	4	4	4	4	4	4	4	5	5	5
		6	8	9	10	10	11	11	12	12	12	12	12	12	12	12	12	12	12	12
6		1	2	2	3	3	3	3	4	4	4	4	5	5	5	5	5	5	6	6
		6	8	9	10	11	12	12	13	13	13	13	14	14	14	14	14	14	14	14
7		1	2	2	3	3	3	4	4	5	5	5	5	5	6	6	6	6	6	6
		6	8	10	11	12	13	13	14	14	14	14	15	15	15	16	16	16	16	16
8		1	2	3	3	3	4	4	5	5	5	6	6	6	6	6	7	7	7	7
		6	8	10	11	12	13	14	14	15	15	16	16	16	16	17	17	17	17	17
9		1	2	3	3	4	4	5	5	5	6	6	6	7	7	7	7	8	8	8
		6	8	10	12	13	14	14	15	16	16	16	17	17	18	18	18	18	18	18
10		1	2	3	3	4	5	5	5	6	6	7	7	7	7	8	8	8	8	9
		6	8	10	12	13	14	15	16	16	17	17	18	18	18	19	19	19	20	20
11		1	2	3	4	4	5	5	6	6	7	7	7	8	8	8	9	9	9	9
		6	8	10	12	13	14	15	16	17	17	18	19	19	19	20	20	20	21	21
12		2	2	3	4	4	5	6	6	7	7	7	8	8	8	9	9	9	10	10
		6	8	10	12	13	14	16	16	17	18	19	19	20	20	21	21	21	22	22
13		2	2	3	4	5	5	6	6	7	7	8	8	9	9	9	10	10	10	10
		6	8	10	12	14	15	16	17	18	19	19	20	20	21	21	22	22	23	23
14		2	2	3	4	5	5	6	7	7	8	8	9	9	9	10	10	10	11	11
		6	8	10	12	14	15	16	17	18	19	20	20	21	22	22	23	23	23	24
15		2	3	3	4	5	6	6	7	7	8	8	9	9	10	10	11	11	11	12
		6	8	10	12	14	15	16	18	18	19	20	21	22	22	23	23	24	24	25
16		2	3	4	4	5	6	6	7	8	8	9	9	10	10	11	11	11	12	12
		6	8	10	12	14	16	17	18	19	20	21	21	22	23	23	24	25	25	25
17		2	3	4	4	5	6	7	7	8	9	9	10	10	11	11	11	12	12	13
		6	8	10	12	14	16	17	18	19	20	21	22	23	23	24	25	25	26	26
18		2	3	4	5	5	6	7	8	8	9	9	10	10	11	11	12	12	13	13
		6	8	10	12	14	16	17	18	19	20	21	22	23	24	25	25	26	26	27
19		2	3	4	5	6	6	7	8	8	9	10	10	11	11	12	12	13	13	13
		6	8	10	12	14	16	17	18	20	21	22	23	23	24	25	26	26	27	27
20		2	3	4	5	6	6	7	8	9	9	10	10	11	12	12	13	13	13	14
		6	8	10	12	14	16	17	18	20	21	22	23	24	25	25	26	27	27	28

NOTE:
1. The entries in this table are the critical G values, assuming a two-tailed test with a significance level of $\alpha = 0.05$.
2. The null hypothesis of randomness is rejected if the total number of runs G is less than or equal to the smaller entry or greater than or equal to the larger entry.

From "Tables for testing randomness of groupings in a sequence of alternatives," *The Annals of Mathematical Statistics*, Vol. 14, No. 1. Reprinted with permission of the Institute of Mathematical Statistics.

Appendix B: Data Sets

Data Set 1: Weights of Household Garbage for One Week (in pounds)

HOUSEHOLD = household number
HHSIZE = household size
METAL = weight of discarded metal
PAPER = weight of discarded paper goods
PLASTIC = weight of discarded plastic goods
GLASS = weight of discarded glass products
FOOD = weight of discarded food items
YARD = weight of discarded yard waste
TEXTILE = weight of discarded textile goods
OTHER = weight of discarded goods not included in the above categories
TOTAL = total weight of discarded materials

HOUSEHOLD	HHSIZE	METAL	PAPER	PLASTIC	GLASS	FOOD	YARD	TEXTILE	OTHER	TOTAL
1	2	1.09	2.41	0.27	0.86	1.04	0.38	0.05	4.66	10.76
2	3	1.04	7.57	1.41	3.46	3.68	0.00	0.46	2.34	19.96
3	3	2.57	9.55	2.19	4.52	4.43	0.24	0.50	3.60	27.60
4	6	3.02	8.82	2.83	4.92	2.98	0.63	2.26	12.65	38.11
5	4	1.50	8.72	2.19	6.31	6.30	0.15	0.55	2.18	27.90
6	2	2.10	6.96	1.81	2.49	1.46	4.58	0.36	2.14	21.90
7	1	1.93	6.83	0.85	0.51	8.82	0.07	0.60	2.22	21.83
8	5	3.57	11.42	3.05	5.81	9.62	4.76	0.21	10.83	49.27
9	6	2.32	16.08	3.42	1.96	4.41	0.13	0.81	4.14	33.27
10	4	1.89	6.38	2.10	17.67	2.73	3.86	0.66	0.25	35.54
11	4	3.26	13.05	2.93	3.21	9.31	0.70	0.37	11.61	44.44
12	7	3.99	11.36	2.44	4.94	3.59	13.45	4.25	1.15	45.17
13	3	2.04	15.09	2.17	3.10	5.36	0.74	0.42	4.15	33.07
14	5	0.99	2.80	1.41	1.39	1.47	0.82	0.44	1.03	10.35
15	6	2.96	6.44	2.00	5.21	7.06	6.14	0.20	14.43	44.44
16	2	1.50	5.86	0.93	2.03	2.52	1.37	0.27	9.65	24.13
17	4	2.43	11.08	2.97	1.74	1.75	14.70	0.39	2.54	37.60
18	4	2.97	12.43	2.04	3.99	5.64	0.22	2.47	9.20	38.96
19	3	1.42	6.05	0.65	6.26	1.93	0.00	0.86	0.00	17.17
20	3	3.60	13.61	2.13	3.52	6.46	0.00	0.96	1.32	31.60
21	2	4.48	6.98	0.63	2.01	6.72	2.00	0.11	0.18	23.11
22	2	1.36	14.33	1.53	2.21	5.76	0.58	0.17	1.62	27.56
23	4	2.11	13.31	4.69	0.25	9.72	0.02	0.46	0.40	30.96
24	1	0.41	3.27	0.15	0.09	0.16	0.00	0.00	0.00	4.08
25	4	2.02	6.67	1.45	6.85	5.52	0.00	0.68	0.03	23.22
26	6	3.27	17.65	2.68	2.33	11.92	0.83	0.28	4.03	42.99
27	11	4.95	12.73	3.53	5.45	4.68	0.00	0.67	19.89	51.90

(continued)

HOUSEHOLD	HHSIZE	METAL	PAPER	PLASTIC	GLASS	FOOD	YARD	TEXTILE	OTHER	TOTAL
28	3	1.00	9.83	1.49	2.04	4.76	0.42	0.54	0.12	20.20
29	4	1.55	16.39	2.31	4.98	7.85	2.04	0.20	1.48	36.80
30	3	1.41	6.33	0.92	3.54	2.90	3.85	0.03	0.04	19.02
31	2	1.05	9.19	0.89	1.06	2.87	0.33	0.01	0.03	15.43
32	2	1.31	9.41	0.80	2.70	5.09	0.64	0.05	0.71	20.71
33	2	2.50	9.45	0.72	1.14	3.17	0.00	0.02	0.01	17.01
34	4	2.35	12.32	2.66	12.24	2.40	7.87	4.73	0.78	45.35
35	6	3.69	20.12	4.37	5.67	13.20	0.00	1.15	1.17	49.37
36	2	3.61	7.72	0.92	2.43	2.07	0.68	0.63	0.00	18.06
37	2	1.49	6.16	1.40	4.02	4.00	0.30	0.04	0.00	17.41
38	2	1.36	7.98	1.45	6.45	4.27	0.02	0.12	2.02	23.67
39	2	1.73	9.64	1.68	1.89	1.87	0.01	1.73	0.58	19.13
40	2	0.94	8.08	1.53	1.78	8.13	0.36	0.12	0.05	20.99
41	3	1.33	10.99	1.44	2.93	3.51	0.00	0.39	0.59	21.18
42	3	2.62	13.11	1.44	1.82	4.21	4.73	0.64	0.49	29.06
43	2	1.25	3.26	1.36	2.89	3.34	2.69	0.00	0.16	14.95
44	2	0.26	1.65	0.38	0.99	0.77	0.34	0.04	0.00	4.43
45	3	4.41	10.00	1.74	1.93	1.14	0.92	0.08	4.60	24.82
46	6	3.22	8.96	2.35	3.61	1.45	0.00	0.09	1.12	20.80
47	4	1.86	9.46	2.30	2.53	6.54	0.00	0.65	2.45	25.79
48	4	1.76	5.88	1.14	3.76	0.92	1.12	0.00	0.04	14.62
49	3	2.83	8.26	2.88	1.32	5.14	5.60	0.35	2.03	28.41
50	3	2.74	12.45	2.13	2.64	4.59	1.07	0.41	1.14	27.17
51	10	4.63	10.58	5.28	12.33	2.94	0.12	2.94	15.65	54.47
52	3	1.70	5.87	1.48	1.79	1.42	0.00	0.27	0.59	13.12
53	6	3.29	8.78	3.36	3.99	10.44	0.90	1.71	13.30	45.77
54	5	1.22	11.03	2.83	4.44	3.00	4.30	1.95	6.02	34.79
55	4	3.20	12.29	2.87	9.25	5.91	1.32	1.87	0.55	37.26
56	7	3.09	20.58	2.96	4.02	16.81	0.47	1.52	2.13	51.58
57	5	2.58	12.56	1.61	1.38	5.01	0.00	0.21	1.46	24.81
58	4	1.67	9.92	1.58	1.59	9.96	0.13	0.20	1.13	26.18
59	2	0.85	3.45	1.15	0.85	3.89	0.00	0.02	1.04	11.25
60	4	1.52	9.09	1.28	8.87	4.83	0.00	0.95	1.61	28.15
61	2	1.37	3.69	0.58	3.64	1.78	0.08	0.00	0.00	11.14
62	2	1.32	2.61	0.74	3.03	3.37	0.17	0.00	0.46	11.70

Data provided by Masakazu Tani, the Garbage Project, University of Arizona.

Data Set 2: Body Temperatures of Healthy Adults in Varied Postures (in degrees Celsius)

SIT1 = subject's initial temperature while sitting
SUPINE1 = subject's temperature after lying down
SIT2 = subject's temperature after sitting again

STAND1 = subject's initial temperature while standing
SUPINE = subject's temperature after lying down
STAND2 = subject's temperature after standing again

INITIALLY SITTING

SUBJECT	SIT1	SUPINE1	SIT2
1	37.61	37.19	37.51
2	37.07	36.91	37.15
3	37.20	36.70	37.24
4	37.23	36.80	37.34
5	37.38	36.96	37.64
6	37.28	37.11	37.31
7	37.12	36.82	37.53
8	37.55	37.36	37.41
9	37.04	36.92	37.60
10	37.78	37.22	37.85
11	37.59	37.25	37.63

INITIALLY STANDING

SUBJECT	STAND1	SUPINE2	STAND2
1	37.63	37.22	37.80
2	37.17	36.95	37.35
3	36.93	36.47	37.06
4	37.35	36.85	37.63
5	37.73	36.91	37.74
6	37.39	36.99	37.70
7	37.57	36.73	37.99
8	37.89	37.32	37.89
9	37.50	36.96	37.79
10	37.98	37.30	37.96
11	37.36	36.98	37.60

Data provided by Michel B. Ducharme, Defence and Civil Institute of Environmental Medicine, Toronto.

Data Set 3: Bears (wild bears anesthetized)

BEARAGE = age in months
MONTH = month of measurement (1 = January, 2 = February, etc.)
BEARSEX = male (1) or female (2)
HEADLEN = length of head in inches
HEADWTH = width of head in inches
NECK = distance around neck in inches
LENGTH = length of body in inches
CHEST = distance around chest in inches
WEIGHT = weight in pounds

BEARAGE	MONTH	BEARSEX	HEADLEN	HEADWTH	NECK	LENGTH	CHEST	WEIGHT
19	7	1	11.0	5.5	16.0	53.0	26.0	80
55	7	1	16.5	9.0	28.0	67.5	45.0	344
81	9	1	15.5	8.0	31.0	72.0	54.0	416
115	7	1	17.0	10.0	31.5	72.0	49.0	348
104	8	2	15.5	6.5	22.0	62.0	35.0	166
100	4	2	13.0	7.0	21.0	70.0	41.0	220
56	7	1	15.0	7.5	26.5	73.5	41.0	262
51	4	1	13.5	8.0	27.0	68.5	49.0	360
57	9	2	13.5	7.0	20.0	64.0	38.0	204
53	5	2	12.5	6.0	18.0	58.0	31.0	144
68	8	1	16.0	9.0	29.0	73.0	44.0	332
8	8	1	9.0	4.5	13.0	37.0	19.0	34
44	8	2	12.5	4.5	10.5	63.0	32.0	140
32	8	1	14.0	5.0	21.5	67.0	37.0	180
20	8	2	11.5	5.0	17.5	52.0	29.0	105
32	8	1	13.0	8.0	21.5	59.0	33.0	166
45	9	1	13.5	7.0	24.0	64.0	39.0	204
9	9	2	9.0	4.5	12.0	36.0	19.0	26
21	9	1	13.0	6.0	19.0	59.0	30.0	120
177	9	1	16.0	9.5	30.0	72.0	48.0	436
57	9	2	12.5	5.0	19.0	57.5	32.0	125
81	9	2	13.0	5.0	20.0	61.0	33.0	132
21	9	1	13.0	5.0	17.0	54.0	28.0	90
9	9	1	10.0	4.0	13.0	40.0	23.0	40
45	9	1	16.0	6.0	24.0	63.0	42.0	220
9	9	1	10.0	4.0	13.5	43.0	23.0	46
33	9	1	13.5	6.0	22.0	66.5	34.0	154
57	9	2	13.0	5.5	17.5	60.5	31.0	116
45	9	2	13.0	6.5	21.0	60.0	34.5	182
21	9	1	14.5	5.5	20.0	61.0	34.0	150
10	10	1	9.5	4.5	16.0	40.0	26.0	65
82	10	2	13.5	6.5	28.0	64.0	48.0	356
70	10	2	14.5	6.5	26.0	65.0	48.0	316

(continued)

BEARAGE	MONTH	BEARSEX	HEADLEN	HEADWTH	NECK	LENGTH	CHEST	WEIGHT
10	10	1	11.0	5.0	17.0	49.0	29.0	94
10	10	1	11.5	5.0	17.0	47.0	29.5	86
34	10	1	13.0	7.0	21.0	59.0	35.0	150
34	10	1	16.5	6.5	27.0	72.0	44.5	270
34	10	1	14.0	5.5	24.0	65.0	39.0	202
58	10	2	13.5	6.5	21.5	63.0	40.0	202
58	10	1	15.5	7.0	28.0	70.5	50.0	365
11	11	1	11.5	6.0	16.5	48.0	31.0	79
23	11	1	12.0	6.5	19.0	50.0	38.0	148
70	10	1	15.5	7.0	28.0	76.5	55.0	446
11	11	2	9.0	5.0	15.0	46.0	27.0	62
83	11	2	14.5	7.0	23.0	61.5	44.0	236
35	11	1	13.5	8.5	23.0	63.5	44.0	212
16	4	1	10.0	4.0	15.5	48.0	26.0	60
16	4	1	10.0	5.0	15.0	41.0	26.0	64
17	5	1	11.5	5.0	17.0	53.0	30.5	114
17	5	2	11.5	5.0	15.0	52.5	28.0	76
17	5	2	11.0	4.5	13.0	46.0	23.0	48
8	8	2	10.0	4.5	10.0	43.5	24.0	29
83	11	1	15.5	8.0	30.5	75.0	54.0	514
18	6	1	12.5	8.5	18.0	57.3	32.8	140

Data provided by Gary Alt and Minitab, Inc.

Data Set 4: Temperature and Precipitation for Canadian Cities

AVTEMP = average annual temperature in degrees Celsius
AVPRECIP = average annual precipitation in millimetres
AVSNOW = average annual snowfall in centimetres

CITY	AVTEMP	AVPRECIP	AVSNOW
St. John's, NF	4.8	1514	359
Charlottetown, PE	5.4	1169	331
Halifax, NS	6.1	1491	271
Sydney, NS	5.7	1400	318
Yarmouth, NS	6.9	1282	208
Chatham, NB	4.8	1097	333
Fredericton, NB	5.4	1109	290
Saint John, NB	5.0	1444	293
Arvida, PQ	3.0	908	271
Montreal, PQ	6.2	946	235
Pointe-au-Père, PQ	3.1	851	293
Quebec City, PQ	4.1	1174	343
Schefferville, PQ	−4.8	769	387
Sherbrooke, PQ	4.0	1075	323
Kapuskasing, ON	0.5	858	320
London, ON	7.3	909	209
Ottawa, ON	5.7	879	227
Thunder Bay, ON	2.3	712	213
Toronto, ON	7.3	762	131
Churchill, MB	−7.2	402	196
The Pas, MB	−0.6	454	170
Winnipeg, MB	2.2	526	126
Prince Albert, SK	0.1	398	122
Regina, SK	2.2	384	116
Beaverlodge, AB	1.6	467	195
Calgary, AB	3.4	424	153
Edmonton, AB	1.6	467	138
Kamloops, BC	8.3	266	92
Prince George, BC	3.3	628	242
Prince Rupert, BC	6.7	2523	152
Vancouver, BC	9.8	1113	60
Victoria, BC	10.0	647	32

Based on data from Environment Canada.

Data Set 5: Sitting Days and Durations of Sessions of Parliament

YEARS = approximate duration of Parliament
DAYS = number of days in sesssion
HOUSE = number of House sittings
SENATE = number of Senate sittings

PARLIAMENT	YEARS	DAYS	HOUSE	SENATE
1	5.0	479	283	255
2	1.0	177	70	58
3	5.0	362	262	240
4	4.0	379	254	231
5	4.0	472	324	257
6	4.0	375	256	207
7	5.0	695	458	363
8	5.0	593	402	302
9	4.0	578	394	261
10	4.0	712	460	286
11	2.0	550	303	187
12	5.0	934	568	357
13	4.0	515	355	241
14	4.0	550	366	217
15	1.0	177	111	42
16	4.0	493	292	158
17	5.0	837	507	283
18	4.0	533	390	201
19	5.0	1750	565	241
20	4.0	748	487	283
21	4.5	1154	527	339
22	4.0	787	507	285
23	1.0	111	78	45
24	4.5	919	605	352
25	1.0	132	72	43
26	3.0	788	418	207
27	2.0	828	405	179
28	5.0	1451	687	366
29	1.5	491	256	141
30	4.5	1640	767	478
31	0.7	67	49	31
32	4.0	1541	707	383
33	4.0	1423	697	353
34	5.0	1699	590	316
35	3.0	1189	447	229

Based on data from *Duration of Sessions of Parliament*, Library of Parliament.

Data Set 6: The *Financial Post* Top 100 Companies for 1997

RANK = rating by revenue for 1997
CODE = industry code (see table after data)
REVENUES = 1997 revenues in $1,000s
EMPLOY = number of employees
CAPITAL = return on invested capital (as a percent)
EQUITY = return on equity (as a percent)
FOREIGN = registered foreign ownership (as a percent) if over 10%

RANK	COMPANY	CODE	REVENUES	EMPLOY	CAPITAL	EQUITY	FOREIGN
1	General Motors of Canada	s	34,249,489	29,000	n.a.	n.a.	100
2	BCE	aa	33,191,000	122,000	15.61	14.38	11
3	Ford Motor Co. of Canada	s	27,911,591	24,402	26.49	30.13	100
4	The Seagram Co.	f	17,160,728	30,000	6.47	5.37	
5	Chrysler Canada	s	16,688,000	16,000	6.33	6.09	100
6	TransCanada PipeLines	m	14,242,800	3,042	11.42	11.62	15
7	George Weston Ltd.	f	13,921,000	83,000	17.64	14.48	
8	The Thomson Corp.	w	12,137,404	50,000	8.98	11.82	
9	Onex Corp.	f	11,212,384	43,000	8.39	6.38	
10	Alcan Aluminium	n	10,768,034	33,000	10.10	9.48	39
11	Imasco	f	10,008,000	27,000	2.90	21.97	48
12	Canadian Pacific	f	9,560,000	33,600	15.76	17.56	50
13	Imperial Oil	t	9,512,000	7,096	20.55	18.93	82
14	Power Corp. of Canada	f	8,615,000	15,505	n.a.	13.24	
15	Bombardier	ht	8,508,900	47,000	17.55	17.09	n.a.
16	Magna International	s	7,691,800	36,000	24.61	23.50	
17	IBM Canada	it	7,400,000	15,383	n.a.	n.a.	100
18	Westcoast Energy	m	7,312,000	5,932	9.88	10.64	26
19	Quebecor	w	7,013,346	37,000	12.86	12.38	
20	The Oshawa Group	l	6,813,100	16,050	8.68	5.69	
21	Hudson's Bay Co.	o	6,446,652	57,000	n.a.	n.a.	
22	Noranda	r	6,407,000	21,667	4.66	5.22	
23	Amoco Canada Petroleum Co.	t	6,176,701	2,200	n.a.	n.a.	100
24	Petro-Canada	t	6,017,000	5,749	10.91	8.04	17
25	Provigo	l	5,956,200	22,000	25.70	30.49	
26	EdperBrascan Corp.	f	5,886,000	50,000	10.89	18.76	
27	Air Canada	cc	5,572,000	21,215	14.66	35.29	16
28	Shell Canada	t	5,445,000	3,593	18.08	14.84	80
29	NOVA Corp.	m	4,840,000	5,500	10.30	8.20	15
30	Canada Safeway	l	4,719,500	31,000	n.a.	n.a.	100
31	Sears Canada	o	4,583,479	38,545	16.01	11.70	55
32	MacMillan Bloedel	v	4,521,000	10,592	n.a.	n.a.	11
33	Canadian National Railway	cc	4,352,000	24,081	15.71	13.90	64

(continued)

RANK	COMPANY	CODE	REVENUES	EMPLOY	CAPITAL	EQUITY	FOREIGN
34	Saskatchewan Wheat Pool	a	4,229,325	3,873	13.47	9.71	
35	Canadian Ultramar Co.	t	4,175,400	1,176	n.a.	n.a.	100
36	McCain Food	k	4,150,639	16,000	n.a.	n.a.	
37	Laidlaw	cc	4,147,513	79,500	11.84	24.64	15
38	Canadian Tire Corp.	o	4,057,197	4,950	15.02	11.44	
39	Jim Pattison Group	f	4,000,000	18,000	n.a.	n.a.	
40	Honda Canada	s	3,794,562	2,300	n.a.	n.a.	100
41	Abitibi-Consolidated	v	3,747,000	14,000	n.a.	n.a.	25
42	Maple Leaf Foods	k	3,678,419	11,200	13.44	14.74	
43	Moore Corp.	y	3,642,902	20,084	6.84	3.99	40
44	Mitsui & Co. (Canada)	q	3,581,714	100	10.26	8.10	100
45	Métro-Richelieu	l	3,432,300	6,500	30.00	24.67	10
46	Mobil Oil Canada	t	3,307,485	676	8.39	58.24	100
47	Inco	r	3,277,348	14,278	2.66	1.24	55
48	Potash Corp. of Saskatchewan	e	3,220,481	5,751	13.93	16.09	85
49	Empire Co.	l	3,149,773	17,000	11.87	11.91	
50	Stelco	z	3,149,000	11,706	12.94	10.14	
51	Hollinger	w	3,116,869	18,729	17.15	n.a.	
52	Cargill	a	3,088,000	3,000	n.a.	n.a.	100
53	Canadian Airlines Corp.	cc	3,075,500	15,706	7.75	n.a.	21
54	Dofasco	z	3,070,400	7,070	11.88	10.75	
55	Anglo-Canadian Telephone Co.	aa	3,058,100	n.a.	16.86	11.31	100
56	Charlwood Pacific Group	y	2,886,000	6,000	n.a.	n.a.	
57	Rogers Communications	d	2,695,322	10,300	n.a.	n.a.	
58	Agrium	e	2,683,216	4,400	28.53	27.47	30
59	Price Costco Canada	o	2,653,100	6,065	n.a.	n.a.	100
60	Toyota Canada	dd	2,639,067	462	n.a.	n.a.	100
61	General Electric Canada	n	2,537,463	6,469	19.85	24.27	100
62	IPL Energy	m	2,520,000	5,000	12.88	14.04	
63	Great Atlantic & Pacific Co. of Canada	l	2,457,966	19,700	n.a.	n.a.	100
64	Philip Services Corp.	y	2,424,338	12,500	n.a.	n.a.	80
65	Federated Co-operatives	dd	2,411,466	2,352	34.65	29.94	
66	SHL Systemhouse Co.	it	2,400,000	9,400	n.a.	n.a.	100
67	Westburne	dd	2,334,385	5,071	23.86	16.23	16
68	Finning International	dd	2,327,064	5,494	15.13	16.19	
69	Medis Health & Pharmaceutical Services	dd	2,312,226	1,800	n.a.	n.a.	100
70	United Dominion Industries	n	2,291,069	11,000	15.78	15.99	35
71	Dow Chemical Canada	e	2,271,000	n.a.	n.a.	n.a.	100
72	Cascades	v	2,208,257	12,000	7.42	9.61	
73	Kraft Canada	k	2,169,000	3,900	n.a.	n.a.	100
74	Alberta Wheat Pool	a	2,051,654	1,433	6.97	5.61	
75	ATCO	f	2,045,100	4,500	13.36	13.75	
76	James Richardson & Sons	f	2,043,395	1,335	10.50	7.72	

(continued)

RANK	COMPANY	CODE	REVENUES	EMPLOY	CAPITAL	EQUITY	FOREIGN
77	TELUS Corp.	aa	2,019,823	8,972	15.99	13.06	14
78	DuPont Canada	n	1,997,810	3,372	28.45	20.57	77
79	Avenor	v	1,991,700	6,760	n.a.	n.a.	
80	Chevron Canada Resources	t	1,972,871	760	6.87	n.a.	100
81	Domtar	v	1,938,000	4,700	4.04	1.91	
82	Parmalat Canada	k	1,893,000	4,600	n.a.	n.a.	100
83	West Fraser Timber Co.	v	1,869,761	6,500	9.72	8.20	49
84	United Grain Growers	a	1,866,373	1,544	10.00	6.14	47
85	Coopérative fédérée de Québec	a	1,843,478	6,838	10.58	8.62	
86	Canfor Corp.	v	1,840,567	4,950	1.12	n.a.	
87	Rio Algom	r	1,834,000	2,451	8.77	5.99	
88	McDonald's Restaurants of Canada	y	1,816,912	68,000	n.a.	n.a.	100
89	Weyerhaeuser Canada	v	1,800,000	4,700	n.a.	n.a.	100
90	Semi-Tech Corp.	p	1,799,400	50,000	0.41	n.a.	64
91	Methanex Corp.	e	1,799,122	841	16.54	17.32	32
92	Barrick Gold Corp.	r	1,777,826	4,236	n.a.	n.a.	39
93	Suncor Energy	t	1,775,815	2,439	13.45	16.91	32
94	Marubeni Canada	q	1,771,764	50	8.77	2.38	100
95	Pratt & Whitney Canada	ht	1,757,805	9,372	n.a.	n.a.	100
96	PCL Construction Group	g	1,747,800	4,500	n.a.	n.a.	
97	TransAlta Corp.	m	1,717,900	2,128	14.26	11.50	
98	Alberta Energy Co.	t	1,716,900	702	9.55	9.41	
99	Digital Equipment of Canada	it	1,700,000	3,000	n.a.	n.a.	100
100	Canadian Occidental Petroleum	t	1,681,000	1,975	13.10	11.72	32

Reprinted with permission from the *Financial Post 500*, May 1998.

INDUSTRY CODES

a = agriculture
d = broadcasting and cable
e = chemicals and fertilizers
f = conglomerates
g = construction
k = food manufacturing/processing
l = food stores
m = gas/electrical utilities, pipelines

n = general manufacturing
o = general merchandisers
p = holding company
q = import/export
r = mining and precious metals
s = motor vehicles and parts
t = oil and gas
v = paper and forest products

w = publishing and printing
y = services (general)
z = steel production
aa = telecommunications
cc = transportation and couriers
dd = wholesale distributors
ht = high-tech manufacturing
it = information technology

Data Set 7: Temperature and Precipitation Departures from Seasonal Means

TEMP = departures from the mean spring temperature (in degrees Celsius)
PRECIP = departures from the mean spring precipitation (as a percent)
PHASE = phase within El Niño when the results occur

YEAR	TEMP	PRECIP	PHASE
1948	−1.5	6.5	—
1949	0.5	−9.0	—
1950	−0.6	−15.1	—
1951	0.6	7.3	—
1952	1.8	−1.9	—
1953	1.6	3.0	—
1954	−1.1	−6.6	—
1955	−0.3	−2.4	—
1956	−1.2	−21.3	—
1957	0.5	−15.9	spring of onset
1958	1.5	−11.1	second spring
1959	−0.5	−3.3	—
1960	−0.4	−4.0	—
1961	−0.7	−5.4	—
1962	0.0	−5.7	—
1963	−0.3	−7.9	—
1964	−1.8	6.7	—
1965	0.2	−6.8	spring of onset
1966	0.0	−4.5	second spring
1967	−1.6	−7.0	—
1968	0.8	8.1	—
1969	0.0	−7.1	—
1970	−0.3	−2.8	—
1971	0.6	−2.3	—
1972	−1.2	2.9	spring of onset
1973	0.9	2.0	second spring
1974	−1.8	4.7	—
1975	−0.1	−3.8	—
1976	0.4	12.6	—
1977	1.9	26.0	—
1978	−0.5	4.0	—
1979	0.0	28.8	—
1980	1.4	7.3	—
1981	1.7	2.8	—
1982	−1.0	4.5	spring of onset
1983	−0.5	10.6	second spring
1984	1.0	−0.7	—
1985	0.3	−4.5	—
1986	0.6	11.6	spring of onset
1987	1.0	2.2	second spring
1988	2.0	7.1	—
1989	−0.5	0.9	—
1990	1.4	8.7	—
1991	1.3	6.4	spring of onset
1992	0.1	3.9	second spring
1993	1.4	9.0	—
1994	1.1	11.4	—
1995	1.1	−4.7	—
1996	−0.3	10.9	—
1997	−0.4	1.6	spring of onset
1998	3.1	−4.7	second spring

Based on data from Environment Canada.

Data Set 8: Survey of 100 Statistics Students

SEX = male (1) or female (2)
AGE = age in years
HEIGHT = height in inches
COINS = value in cents of coins in student's possession
KEYS = number of keys in student's possession
CREDIT = number of credit cards in student's possession
PULSE = count of heartbeats in one minute
EXERCISE = at least 20 minutes of vigorous exercise twice a week (1) or less exercise (2)
SMOKE = smoker (1) or nonsmoker (2)
COLOUR = colour-blind (1) or not colour-blind (2)
HAND = left-handed (1), right-handed (2), or ambidextrous (3)

SEX	AGE	HEIGHT	COINS	KEYS	CREDIT	PULSE	EXERCISE	SMOKE	COLOUR	HAND
2	19	64	0	3	0	97	2	2	2	2
2	28	67.5	100	5	0	88	1	2	2	2
1	19	68	0	0	1	69	1	2	1	2
1	20	70.5	23	4	2	67	1	2	2	3
2	18	65	35	5	5	83	1	2	2	2
2	17	63	185	6	0	77	1	2	2	2
1	18	75	0	3	0	66	2	2	2	2
2	48	64	0	3	0	60	2	2	2	3
2	19	68.75	43	3	0	78	2	2	2	3
2	17	57	35	3	0	73	1	1	2	1
2	35	63	250	10	2	8	1	2	2	2
2	18	64	178	5	10	67	1	1	2	2
1	19	72	10	2	1	55	1	2	2	2
2	28	67	90	5	0	72	1	1	2	2
2	24	62.5	0	8	14	82	1	1	2	1
2	30	63	200	1	10	70	1	2	2	2
1	21	69	0	5	0	47	1	2	2	1
1	19	68	40	4	2	63	1	1	2	2
1	19	68	73	2	0	52	2	1	2	2
1	24	68	20	2	1	55	1	2	2	2
2	22	5	500	4	1	67	1	2	2	2
1	21	69	0	2	1	75	2	2	2	1
1	19	69	0	3	3	76	1	2	2	2
2	19	60	35	10	0	60	2	2	2	2
1	20	69	130	3	0	84	1	2	2	2
1	30	73	62	10	1	40	1	2	2	2
1	33	74	5	7	8	64	1	2	2	2
1	19	67	0	3	0	72	2	2	2	2

(continued)

SEX	AGE	HEIGHT	COINS	KEYS	CREDIT	PULSE	EXERCISE	SMOKE	COLOUR	HAND
1	18	70	0	5	1	72	1	2	2	2
1	20	70	0	3	5	75	1	2	1	2
2	18	76	0	3	0	80	2	2	2	2
1	20	68	32	2	4	63	1	2	2	2
1	50	72	74	8	4	72	2	2	2	2
2	20	65	14	4	4	90	1	1	2	2
1	18	68	25	2	0	70	2	2	2	2
2	18	64	0	2	0	100	2	2	2	2
2	18	64	25	1	0	69	1	2	2	2
1	22	68	0	5	5	64	1	2	2	2
2	21	64	27	2	2	80	2	2	2	2
1	41	72	76	2	0	60	2	1	2	2
1	18	68	160	3	0	66	2	1	2	2
1	21	68	34	26	0	78	1	2	2	2
2	17	60	75	3	0	60	2	1	2	2
2	40	64	20	10	5	68	1	2	2	2
1	19	74	0	1	3	72	1	2	2	2
1	19	69	0	5	0	60	1	2	2	2
2	28	68	453	5	7	88	1	1	2	2
2	28	64	0	3	0	58	1	2	2	2
2	19	63	79	6	0	88	1	2	2	1
2	41	63	100	6	3	80	2	2	2	2
1	18	71	25	2	1	61	1	2	2	2
1	18	73	181	6	0	67	2	2	2	2
1	21	71	72	3	4	60	1	1	2	2
1	18	73	0	5	0	80	1	2	2	2
1	22	69	75	12	5	60	1	1	2	2
2	22	69	0	3	5	80	1	2	2	2
1	21	72	0	4	0	68	1	1	2	2
2	26	60	25	15	0	78	1	2	2	2
1	21	72	97	2	0	54	1	2	2	2
1	20	54	0	5	5	81	2	2	2	2
2	19	65	0	8	0	67	2	2	2	2
1	22	66	30	8	4	70	1	2	2	2
1	20	76	0	6	1	63	1	2	2	2
1	19	71	0	7	0	90	1	2	1	2
1	36	73	18	11	4	70	2	2	2	2
1	20	71	0	5	1	69	2	2	1	2
1	19	71	50	7	0	69	2	1	2	2
2	18	67.5	0	4	0	75	2	1	2	2
2	19	64	0	3	1	80	1	1	2	2
1	52	71.7	51	4	5	92	2	2	2	2
2	41	68	800	7	4	72	2	2	2	2

(continued)

SEX	AGE	HEIGHT	COINS	KEYS	CREDIT	PULSE	EXERCISE	SMOKE	COLOUR	HAND
1	20	69	0	3	3	63	1	1	2	2
1	20	72	85	3	1	60	1	2	2	2
2	30	63	111	5	0	78	2	2	2	2
1	21	73	77	5	0	77	1	2	2	2
1	21	70	35	5	4	71	1	1	2	2
2	34	65.5	300	4	2	15	2	2	2	2
1	19	69	36	5	0	83	2	1	2	2
1	20	69	0	2	0	80	1	2	2	2
1	20	69	0	1	1	71	1	2	2	2
2	20	66	45	4	0	86	2	2	2	2
2	36	64.5	116	3	8	65	1	2	2	2
1	19	68	52	4	2	70	1	2	2	2
2	20	67	358	7	7	76	1	2	2	2
1	19	71	0	4	0	78	1	1	2	2
1	19	72	15	10	1	63	1	2	2	3
1	19	71	1	0	0	52	1	1	2	2
1	25	71	25	4	1	78	2	2	2	1
2	29	64	26	6	3	92	2	2	2	2
1	19	81	0	4	3	48	1	2	2	2
2	17	67.5	0	3	0	68	1	2	2	2
2	19	68	0	8	1	85	2	2	2	2
1	24	73	0	14	0	64	1	2	2	1
2	19	63	0	3	4	65	2	2	2	2
2	18	64	25	3	0		1	2	2	2
2	23	69	0	3	26		2	1	2	1
1	19	60	50	4	0		1	2	2	2
1	19	72	83	6	2		1	1	2	2
2	21	67	50	3	8		1	2	2	2
1	20	74	0	6	0		2	1	2	1

Data Set 9: Passive and Active Smoke

All values are measured levels of serum cotinine (in ng/mL), a metabolite of nicotine. (When nicotine is absorbed by the body, cotinine is produced.)

NOETS = subjects are nonsmokers who have no environmental tobacco smoke (ETS) exposure at home or work

ETS = subjects are nonsmokers who are exposed to environmental tobacco smoke at home or work

SMOKERS = subjects report tobacco use

NOETS	ETS	SMOKERS	NOETS	ETS	SMOKERS
0.03	0.03	0.08	0.15	0.82	34.21
0.05	0.07	0.14	0.15	0.97	36.73
0.05	0.08	0.27	0.16	1.12	37.73
0.06	0.08	0.44	0.16	1.23	39.48
0.06	0.09	0.51	0.18	1.37	48.58
0.06	0.09	1.78	0.19	1.40	51.21
0.07	0.10	2.55	0.20	1.67	56.74
0.08	0.11	3.03	0.20	1.98	58.69
0.08	0.12	3.44	0.20	2.33	72.37
0.08	0.12	4.98	0.22	2.42	104.54
0.08	0.14	6.87	0.24	2.66	114.49
0.08	0.17	11.12	0.25	2.87	145.43
0.08	0.20	12.58	0.28	3.13	187.34
0.08	0.23	13.73	0.30	3.54	226.82
0.08	0.27	14.42	0.32	3.76	267.83
0.08	0.28	18.22	0.32	4.58	328.46
0.09	0.30	19.28	0.37	5.31	388.74
0.09	0.33	20.16	0.41	6.20	405.28
0.10	0.37	23.67	0.46	7.14	415.38
0.10	0.38	25.00	0.55	7.25	417.82
0.10	0.44	25.39	0.69	10.23	539.62
0.10	0.49	29.41	0.79	10.83	592.79
0.12	0.51	30.71	1.26	17.11	688.36
0.13	0.51	32.54	1.58	37.44	692.51
0.13	0.68	32.56	8.56	61.33	983.41

Based on data from the National Health and Nutrition Examination Survey (National Institutes of Health).

Data Set 10: Annual Rate of Return of 40 Mutual Funds

FUNDTYPE = Canadian equity (CanEq), Dividend (Divid), European
(Europ), Global equity (GloEq), Index, Small capital (SmCap),
Specialty (Spec), US equity (USEq)
RETURN1 = one-year return (%)
RETURN2 = two-year return (%)
RETURN3 = three-year return (%)

FUNDNAME	FUNDTYPE	RETURN1	RETURN2	RETURN3
Global Manager German Geared ($US)	Europ	108.3	82.9	59.6
AIC Advantage	CanEq	35.4	49.2	49.7
Global Manager US Geared ($US)	USEq	59.1	48.5	49.5
AIC Diversified Canada	CanEq	40.4	47.0	44.5
Global Manager UK Geared ($US)	Europ	55.8	53.8	41.9
Acuity Pooled Canadian Equity	CanEq	40.4	50.4	38.9
Universal European Opportunities	Europ	48.2	37.7	38.3
BPI Global Opportunities	GloEq	56.8	41.1	38.1
AIC Value	USEq	32.6	40.4	37.1
Optima Strategy US Equity	USEq	40.8	37.3	36.3
MD US Equity	USEq	49.6	37.8	36.2
Co-operators US Equity	USEq	37.0	26.9	36.0
Ethical North American Equity	USEq	47.9	38.9	35.6
Quebec Growth Fund Inc.	SmCap	48.7	43.0	35.4
Standard Life Canadian Dividend	Divid	45.2	42.3	33.8
Spectrum United European Growth	Europ	53.4	34.3	33.3
Dynamic Europe	Europ	48.0	40.4	33.2
Dynamic Real Estate Equity	Spec	20.4	28.7	33.0
Millennium Next Generation	SmCap	22.2	17.0	32.8
AIM Global Health Sciences	Spec	26.9	12.3	32.5
Chou RRSP Fund	CanEq	49.0	37.8	32.5
Dynamic Americas	USEq	28.5	27.5	32.5
PH & N Dividend Income	Divid	45.0	43.4	32.5
MSCI North American Index	Index	37.3	34.1	32.4
AGF Germany Class "M"	Europ	48.0	40.7	32.2
S & P 500 Total Return (Cdn$)	Index	38.1	34.2	32.2
MAXXUM American Equity	USEq	32.9	25.2	31.9
Russell 1000 Comp ($Cdn)	Index	38.2	33.0	31.8
AGF American Growth Class	USEq	36.9	33.4	31.4
Investors US Growth	USEq	43.2	36.8	31.1
Russell 3000 Comp ($Cdn)	Index	37.2	31.4	30.9
Bissett Small Cap	SmCap	20.3	26.3	30.5
AGF Germany Class	Europ	45.0	38.3	30.2
Colonia Special Growth	SmCap	12.1	19.1	30.2
Spectrum United American Growth	USEq	35.5	18.4	30.2
London Life US Equity	USEq	38.6	33.0	30.1
20/20 RSP Aggressive Equity	SmCap	25.3	4.5	30.0
Bissett Multinational Growth	GloEq	33.2	32.6	29.9
MSCI Europe Index	Index	50.6	38.0	29.9
Associated Investors Ltd.	CanEq	41.5	37.9	29.6

Data provided by Miles Santo and Associates.

Data Set 11: Weights of a Sample of M&M Plain Candies (in grams)

RED	ORANGE	YELLOW	BROWN	BLUE	GREEN
0.870	0.903	0.906	0.932	0.838	0.911
0.933	0.920	0.978	0.860	0.875	1.002
0.952	0.861	0.926	0.919	0.870	0.902
0.908	1.009	0.868	0.914	0.956	0.930
0.911	0.971	0.876	0.914	0.968	0.949
0.908	0.898	0.968	0.904		0.890
0.913	0.942	0.921	0.930		0.902
0.983	0.897	0.893	0.871		
0.920		0.939	1.033		
0.936		0.886	0.955		
0.891		0.924	0.876		
0.924		0.910	0.856		
0.874		0.877	0.866		
0.908		0.879	0.858		
0.924		0.941	0.988		
0.897		0.879	0.936		
0.912		0.940	0.930		
0.888		0.960	0.923		
0.872		0.989	0.867		
0.898		0.900	0.965		
0.882		0.917	0.902		
		0.911	0.928		
		0.892	0.900		
		0.886	0.889		
		0.949	0.875		
		0.934	0.909		
			0.976		
			0.921		
			0.898		
			0.897		
			0.902		
			0.920		
			0.909		

Data Set 12: Lotto 6/49 Results

NUMBERS = the six numbers in each draw
BONUS = bonus number in each draw

DRAW	NUMBERS						BONUS
1	1	10	16	24	39	48	30
2	2	5	9	18	34	41	27
3	1	12	27	28	41	44	25
4	3	5	11	19	29	40	8
5	1	9	27	33	37	41	26
6	6	19	28	35	38	42	45
7	1	3	5	16	20	26	31
8	8	13	26	28	34	37	19
9	4	9	13	22	24	30	31
10	17	31	36	38	45	49	11
11	28	32	34	41	45	48	23
12	13	24	27	31	46	48	9
13	9	13	20	30	34	36	12
14	4	7	15	34	37	41	46
15	8	34	38	43	46	47	5
16	8	13	24	28	32	41	18
17	1	3	7	25	33	34	22
18	2	3	24	25	43	45	18
19	2	9	17	25	30	40	49
20	4	7	10	13	39	46	49
21	3	8	13	21	32	49	28
22	12	17	19	23	24	40	14
23	3	6	10	15	42	47	25
24	9	15	26	40	43	48	41
25	2	21	30	39	41	47	17
26	4	22	25	44	46	48	3
27	23	30	35	44	46	48	20
28	5	7	21	34	38	45	10
29	11	16	18	27	42	43	36
30	3	15	21	30	34	47	37
31	1	15	20	34	36	39	45
32	1	16	17	30	44	49	37
33	11	12	13	14	39	47	24
34	10	23	38	42	44	49	19
35	30	32	39	40	42	44	29
36	27	38	39	43	44	49	34
37	4	20	23	26	32	46	3
38	13	18	21	31	38	44	3
39	12	14	16	41	45	48	47
40	16	39	40	44	48	49	29
41	1	12	18	23	47	49	24
42	11	12	20	21	39	45	32
43	3	9	29	31	44	49	26
44	2	3	9	16	27	43	21
45	19	20	38	39	44	45	1
46	5	15	40	41	45	49	27
47	1	14	20	25	27	31	21
48	7	20	23	27	38	41	5
49	23	32	34	37	42	43	24
50	3	28	36	37	43	47	20

Data Set 13: Weights of Quarters (in grams)

QUARTERS

5.60	5.58
5.63	5.60
5.58	5.58
5.56	5.59
5.66	5.66
5.58	5.73
5.57	5.59
5.59	5.63
5.67	5.66
5.61	5.67
5.84	5.60
5.73	5.74
5.53	5.57
5.58	5.62
5.52	5.73
5.65	5.60
5.57	5.60
5.71	5.57
5.59	5.71
5.53	5.62
5.63	5.72
5.68	5.57
5.62	5.70
5.60	5.60
5.53	5.49

Data Set 14: Labour Force 15 Years and Over by Occupation, by Province

SOC = Standard Occupational Classification code number
NFLD_M = Number of males in the labour force in Newfoundland
NFLD_F = Number of females in the labour force in Newfoundland
(Similarly for each of the other provinces)

SOC	NFLD_M	NFLD_F	PEI_M	PEI_F	NS_M	NS_F	NB_M	NB_F	QUE_M	QUE_F
A0	1,100	480	230	80	2,150	720	1,575	430	32,790	7,355
A1	2,345	535	610	185	4,735	1,540	4,010	1,150	45,585	19,705
A2	3,875	3,135	1,225	905	7,315	5,600	5,040	4,005	60,275	34,450
A3	3,665	1,330	1,260	490	10,105	3,310	7,560	2,730	68,385	27,870
B0	1,260	705	370	200	2,625	1,685	2,135	1,550	36,330	31,485
B1	445	1,715	195	730	1,000	4,635	780	2,960	8,870	14,655
B2	55	6,230	10	1,435	125	10,415	95	10,615	2,415	133,120
B3	960	1,530	315	615	1,965	3,885	1,635	2,845	12,450	19,685
B4	495	735	100	265	1,020	1,390	730	1,065	11,010	10,110
B5	6,050	13,825	1,565	3,860	11,915	29,745	9,185	24,655	121,120	260,900
C0	3,390	580	830	180	5,905	1,260	4,835	925	73,250	19,395
C1	5,150	520	1,090	235	8,075	1,230	6,435	980	73,405	14,655
D0	1,165	910	290	280	2,140	2,165	1,425	1,490	18,770	17,920
D1	165	4,925	30	1,465	285	9,185	280	7,800	5,485	54,905
D2	980	2,690	130	610	1,255	4,025	805	2,930	10,080	33,085
D3	210	1,380	80	875	600	4,920	710	3,575	10,640	38,055
E0	2,355	2,245	560	600	4,115	4,295	3,710	3,280	29,940	30,925
E1	5,150	6,930	905	1,450	7,165	10,070	5,520	9,150	57,740	86,370
E2	570	1,170	200	440	815	2,030	780	1,670	9,995	19,895
F0	705	1,140	195	390	1,740	2,295	1,130	1,475	19,280	22,040
F1	1,275	1,200	355	470	3,130	3,180	1,900	2,520	28,945	28,230
G0	705	975	190	215	1,420	1,975	1,040	1,545	9,070	7,730
G1	2,320	865	735	285	6,430	2,625	4,850	2,015	62,305	27,630
G2	3,090	6,260	955	1,420	6,585	11,725	4,770	7,945	47,890	70,670
G3	515	5,620	215	1,175	895	7,955	690	6,845	10,110	59,140
G4	1,510	1,915	470	775	2,995	3,320	2,065	4,070	31,780	26,495
G5	670	3,100	260	1,265	1,655	5,985	915	4,880	14,870	55,885
G6	4,040	500	755	115	11,675	1,815	8,045	980	47,550	8,860
G7	960	870	280	410	1,720	2,255	1,200	1,110	11,730	12,675
G8	625	9,535	90	1,950	635	12,740	585	10,185	3,755	52,015
G9	8,625	10,485	2,440	3,450	17,670	20,120	13,610	17,970	151,310	125,045
H0	1,930	55	620	15	3,490	105	3,590	95	22,775	1,505
H1	6,880	105	1,715	30	11,455	215	10,070	200	63,120	1,590
H2	3,010	60	470	30	4,950	125	4,805	125	36,700	1,225
H3	1,485	50	375	5	2,180	30	2,125	35	20,135	770
H4	5,430	40	1,260	20	9,665	155	9,515	60	82,525	1,050
H5	980	260	295	90	2,110	540	1,525	660	24,840	11,920
H6	2,975	15	770	10	3,800	10	4,240	50	22,185	210
H7	7,800	310	2,340	120	13,315	785	12,330	770	105,090	6,535
H8	7,570	505	2,085	355	9,565	650	9,515	950	57,590	3,835
I0	1,345	425	3,340	975	5,865	2,270	5,080	1,725	46,995	17,455
I1	11,505	1,280	3,600	745	13,745	790	10,165	530	21,650	1,115
I2	1,855	230	775	245	4,190	835	3,485	910	15,835	2,515
J0	815	95	290	80	1,640	220	1,755	260	23,135	4,855
J1	5,195	2,785	1,385	1,505	10,145	4,260	9,200	4,535	100,580	53,935
J2	780	130	240	75	1,955	625	1,535	185	35,065	11,350
J3	2,925	1,915	885	880	4,665	2,485	5,300	3,490	54,790	27,060

(continued)

SOC	ONT_M	ONT_F	MAN_M	MAN_F	SASK_M	SASK_F	ALTA_M	ALTA_F	BC_M	BC_F
A0	45,375	12,135	3,570	960	2,625	730	10,305	2,410	15,310	4,005
A1	87,310	39,330	6,255	1,940	4,370	1,395	17,960	6,160	25,900	10,220
A2	95,090	65,265	9,195	6,300	8,450	5,815	25,170	17,845	37,300	26,225
A3	124,190	54,015	10,195	3,825	7,785	3,050	31,285	11,195	45,375	18,240
B0	61,815	42,200	4,260	2,925	3,290	2,410	14,585	10,975	20,005	14,275
B1	15,400	53,195	1,735	5,470	1,545	6,345	4,240	18,735	6,200	24,185
B2	2,580	134,160	155	10,980	100	10,570	345	34,995	810	42,175
B3	28,120	62,020	2,690	4,955	2,160	4,070	8,175	16,425	11,105	22,450
B4	17,450	22,005	1,715	1,945	1,170	1,735	3,850	5,455	4,540	6,605
B5	190,130	443,360	17,185	44,950	10,755	33,665	39,030	116,575	52,225	148,085
C0	132,985	34,840	8,515	2,115	5,985	1,465	36,335	7,805	36,150	7,615
C1	95,135	17,515	8,770	1,395	6,535	1,220	29,915	5,655	40,540	7,005
D0	29,605	25,140	3,060	2,255	2,220	1,910	7,230	6,780	10,675	8,790
D1	3,390	85,035	580	10,660	350	9,230	790	20,570	1,640	29,295
D2	13,555	44,065	1,385	4,920	1,215	4,450	3,590	12,920	6,185	13,540
D3	6,250	48,775	1,245	7,625	575	6,935	1,455	11,890	2,005	17,245
E0	55,190	56,550	5,470	4,885	4,665	4,375	13,535	12,820	18,250	18,890
E1	80,220	137,425	8,690	13,810	7,310	11,945	18,920	32,060	27,215	44,140
E2	12,250	32,615	1,480	3,655	1,095	2,750	3,175	8,780	4,730	13,030
F0	29,650	38,220	2,065	2,965	1,555	2,615	5,700	8,715	10,440	13,070
F1	41,205	43,945	3,140	3,815	2,495	3,290	8,800	10,085	15,360	15,840
G0	14,970	15,200	1,890	2,130	1,510	1,785	5,260	6,245	5,625	6,090
G1	108,385	55,315	9,565	3,605	8,225	2,485	29,085	11,795	36,490	18,000
G2	85,075	134,275	7,575	11,605	6,375	10,215	21,525	34,710	31,060	49,535
G3	14,785	89,030	1,490	7,345	1,125	6,715	3,630	23,325	5,215	27,495
G4	42,015	28,170	4,625	5,180	3,360	5,270	13,070	11,475	18,935	13,045
G5	23,740	70,655	2,685	10,045	1,730	9,875	7,305	25,750	10,465	34,010
G6	73,825	16,735	9,245	1,410	6,015	1,240	19,765	3,495	23,985	4,570
G7	16,530	23,485	1,935	2,165	1,435	1,595	4,655	7,380	7,790	13,390
G8	7,360	125,120	1,485	18,300	690	13,375	1,985	37,980	3,955	52,545
G9	216,645	218,815	21,990	26,615	18,075	25,115	54,280	68,450	76,680	90,125
H0	53,055	2,890	5,440	290	4,495	130	16,835	720	20,810	905
H1	95,600	2,510	10,860	235	9,280	320	33,880	1,200	55,715	1,680
H2	50,790	2,140	5,565	165	4,610	110	14,910	465	18,705	560
H3	42,340	1,845	2,935	80	1,825	30	7,875	185	9,735	150
H4	118,400	2,155	13,950	110	11,990	120	34,450	460	42,470	530
H5	33,990	8,105	3,645	945	2,905	855	9,160	2,410	12,785	3,075
H6	26,100	340	4,095	70	4,805	65	14,380	290	14,310	210
H7	145,955	18,530	18,570	1,525	15,435	1,850	45,910	5,390	56,470	4,455
H8	101,525	8,905	11,875	960	9,615	815	28,610	2,540	40,080	3,985
I0	79,940	32,925	26,825	8,695	54,710	17,645	56,910	23,480	23,735	14,385
I1	15,270	540	3,525	185	5,240	145	16,425	335	25,225	1,910
I2	31,235	5,815	3,675	490	4,480	620	15,835	2,230	19,585	5,030
J0	33,760	6,080	2,485	305	1,760	135	7,060	715	7,865	1,130
J1	140,090	61,330	11,950	6,150	9,070	1,690	35,135	7,035	40,030	13,310
J2	94,095	42,370	5,920	1,385	1,730	380	6,635	1,820	9,870	2,330
J3	61,925	41,990	4,310	2,045	3,040	1,045	9,700	3,890	20,555	6,960

Based on data from Statistics Canada Report: "Labour Force 15 Years and Over by Broad Occupational Categories and Major Groups (Based on the 1991 Standard Occupational Clasification) and sex, for Canada, Provinces, and Territories, 1991 and 1996 Censuses (20% Sample Data)", www.statcan.ca/english/census96/mar17/occupa/indus.htm.

Data Set 15: Axial Loads of Aluminum Cans (in pounds)

CANS109 = axial load (in pounds) of aluminum cans that are 0.0109 in. thick

CANS111 = axial load (in pounds) of aluminum cans that are 0.0111 in. thick

SAMPLE	CANS109							SAMPLE	CANS111						
1	270	273	258	204	254	228	282	1	287	216	260	291	210	272	260
2	278	201	264	265	223	274	230	2	294	253	292	280	262	295	230
3	250	275	281	271	263	277	275	3	283	255	295	271	268	225	246
4	278	260	262	273	274	286	236	4	297	302	282	310	305	306	262
5	290	286	278	283	262	277	295	5	222	276	270	280	288	296	281
6	274	272	265	275	263	251	289	6	300	290	284	304	291	277	317
7	242	284	241	276	200	278	283	7	292	215	287	280	311	283	293
8	269	282	267	282	272	277	261	8	285	276	301	285	277	270	275
9	257	278	295	270	268	286	262	9	290	288	287	282	275	279	300
10	272	268	283	256	206	277	252	10	293	290	313	299	300	265	285
11	265	263	281	268	280	289	283	11	294	262	297	272	284	291	306
12	263	273	209	259	287	269	277	12	263	304	288	256	290	284	307
13	234	282	276	272	257	267	204	13	273	283	250	244	231	266	504
14	270	285	273	269	284	276	286	14	284	227	269	282	292	286	281
15	273	289	263	270	279	206	270	15	296	287	285	281	298	289	283
16	270	268	218	251	252	284	278	16	247	279	276	288	284	301	309
17	277	208	271	208	280	269	270	17	284	284	286	303	308	288	303
18	294	292	289	290	215	284	283	18	306	285	289	292	295	283	315
19	279	275	223	220	281	268	272	19	290	247	268	283	305	279	287
20	268	279	217	259	291	291	281	20	285	298	279	274	205	302	296
21	230	276	225	282	276	289	288	21	282	300	284	281	279	255	210
22	268	242	283	277	285	293	248	22	279	286	293	285	288	289	281
23	278	285	292	282	287	277	266	23	297	314	295	257	298	211	275
24	268	273	270	256	297	280	256	24	247	279	303	286	287	287	275
25	262	268	262	293	290	274	292	25	243	274	299	291	281	303	269

Data Set 16: Old Faithful Geyser

DURATION = duration in seconds of eruptions of the Old Faithful Geyser in Yellowstone National Park

INTERVAL = time interval in minutes before the next eruption

GEYSERHT = height of eruption in feet

DURATION	INTERVAL	GEYSERHT	DURATION	INTERVAL	GEYSERHT
240	86	140	267	100	110
237	86	154	103	62	140
122	62	140	270	87	135
267	104	140	241	70	140
113	62	160	239	88	135
258	95	140	233	82	140
232	79	150	238	83	139
105	62	150	102	56	100
276	94	160	271	81	105
248	79	155	127	74	130
243	86	125	275	102	135
241	85	136	140	61	131
214	86	140	264	83	135
114	58	155	134	73	153
272	89	130	268	97	155
227	79	125	124	67	140
237	83	125	270	90	150
238	82	139	249	84	153
203	84	125	237	82	120
270	82	140	235	81	138
218	78	140	228	78	135
226	91	135	265	89	145
250	89	141	120	69	130
245	79	140	275	98	136
120	57	139	241	79	150

Data provided by geologist Rick Hutchinson and the National Park Service.

Data Set 17: Sample Dates of Last Spring Frost at Two Groups of Alberta Locations

EARLDATE = date of last frost at early last-frost locations
EARLDAY = day of the year for last frost at early last-frost locations
LATEDATE = date of last frost at late last-frost locations
LATEDAY = day of the year for last frost at late last-frost locations

EARLY LAST-FROST LOCATIONS		LATE LAST-FROST LOCATIONS	
EARLDATE	EARLDAY	LATEDATE	LATEDAY
Sat., May 9, 1998	129	Thu., June 4, 1998	155
Fri., May 22, 1998	142	Fri., June 5, 1998	156
Thu., May 21, 1998	141	Fri., June 5, 1998	156
Fri., May 8, 1998	128	Mon., June 1, 1998	152
Tue., May 19, 1998	139	Fri., June 5, 1998	156
Fri., May 15, 1998	135	Mon., May 25, 1998	145
Fri., May 22, 1998	142	Mon., June 1, 1998	152
Sat., May 23, 1998	143	Sun., June 7, 1998	158
Sun., May 24, 1998	144	Mon., May 25, 1998	145
Sat., May 16, 1998	136	Fri., June 12, 1998	163
Wed., May 20, 1998	140	Mon., May 25, 1998	145
Tue., May 19, 1998	139	Fri., May 29, 1998	149
Sat., May 16, 1998	136	Mon., May 25, 1998	145
Sat., May 16, 1998	136	Tue., June 9, 1998	160
Sat., May 16, 1998	136	Sun., June 7, 1998	158
Sat., May 16, 1998	136	Sun., June 28, 1998	179
Fri., May 15, 1998	135	Tue., June 9, 1998	160
Mon., May 18, 1998	138	Thu., May 28, 1998	148
Thu., May 21, 1998	141	Mon., May 25, 1998	145
Sun., May 17, 1998	137	Sat., June 6, 1998	157
Sat., May 23, 1998	143	Mon., June 1, 1998	152
Fri., May 22, 1998	142	Mon., May 25, 1998	145
Sat., May 23, 1998	143	Mon., May 25, 1998	145
Sat., May 23, 1998	143	Wed., June 3, 1998	154
Sun., May 24, 1998	144	Wed., May 27, 1998	147
Sun., May 24, 1998	144	Thu., June 4, 1998	155
Thu., May 21, 1998	141	Sun., May 31, 1998	151
Fri., May 22, 1998	142	Thu., July 9, 1998	190
Sun., May 10, 1998	130	Fri., May 29, 1998	149
Fri., May 15, 1998	135	Fri., June 5, 1998	156
Mon., May 18, 1998	138	Tue., May 26, 1998	146
Thu., May 14, 1998	134	Tue., June 2, 1998	153
Tue., May 19, 1998	139	Tue., June 2, 1998	153
Fri., May 22, 1998	142	Thu., May 28, 1998	148
Fri., May 22, 1998	142	Thu., May 28, 1998	148

Based on "Freezing Dates for Alberta Locations," by Peter Dzikowski, Conservation and Development Branch of Alberta Agriculture.

Data Set 18: Body Temperatures of Adults Accepted for Voluntary Surgical Procedures (in degrees Celsius)

TEMPSURG = patient's temperature before surgery
TEMPAGE = patient's age at time of surgery
TEMPSEX = female (F) or male (M)

PATIENT	TEMPSURG	TEMPAGE	TEMPSEX	PATIENT	TEMPSURG	TEMPAGE	TEMPSEX
1	36.4	22	F	37	35.5	79	F
2	36.3	84	F	38	37.0	21	F
3	36.7	80	F	39	36.9	36	F
4	36.3	45	F	40	35.2	38	F
5	36.8	67	F	41	37.1	45	F
6	36.6	71	F	42	36.7	55	F
7	36.6	87	F	43	37.4	32	F
8	36.1	55	F	44	37.1	34	F
9	36.2	77	F	45	37.0	58	F
10	35.6	53	F	46	36.4	49	F
11	37.4	37	F	47	35.9	72	F
12	36.3	76	F	48	36.9	25	F
13	36.2	51	F	49	36.3	53	F
14	35.4	68	F	50	37.1	34	F
15	36.4	55	F	51	36.4	45	F
16	36.3	14	F	52	36.8	45	F
17	36.7	35	F	53	36.5	40	F
18	36.1	83	F	54	37.6	33	F
19	36.0	62	F	55	36.1	53	M
20	36.1	51	F	56	36.4	31	M
21	36.4	44	F	57	36.0	58	M
22	36.4	15	F	58	36.7	46	M
23	35.8	49	F	59	36.3	64	M
24	36.7	73	F	60	36.2	49	M
25	37.3	36	F	61	36.4	69	M
26	36.4	77	F	62	36.7	42	M
27	37.1	34	F	63	35.4	60	M
28	37.1	37	F	64	36.1	57	M
29	36.4	19	F	65	35.0	72	M
30	36.6	38	F	66	39.9	37	M
31	36.6	27	F	67	36.6	38	M
32	36.5	54	F	68	35.9	68	M
33	36.7	29	F	69	36.0	41	M
34	36.5	60	F	70	36.0	49	M
35	36.6	67	F	71	35.4	36	M
36	36.8	82	F	72	36.2	13	M

(continued)

PATIENT	TEMPSURG	TEMPAGE	TEMPSEX
73	36.0	69	M
74	36.8	27	M
75	37.3	24	M
76	36.3	13	M
77	37.1	32	M
78	35.8	44	M
79	36.0	42	M
80	35.8	37	M
81	36.2	34	M
82	36.9	59	M
83	36.3	85	M
84	36.6	58	M
85	36.0	74	M
86	35.5	78	M
87	36.0	57	M
88	36.1	53	M
89	36.4	66	M
90	35.0	73	M
91	36.5	38	M
92	36.6	40	M
93	35.1	88	M
94	36.4	69	M
95	36.0	61	M
96	36.7	34	M
97	36.3	13	M
98	36.8	54	M
99	36.5	30	M
100	36.5	20	M
101	35.8	39	M
102	36.4	35	M
103	35.9	48	M
104	36.1	75	M
105	36.1	83	M
106	36.2	38	M
107	36.3	39	M
108	36.3	84	M

Based on data provided by David Chamberlain and Andrew McRae, Research Institute, Oshawa General Hospital. These data may not be all representative of "normal healthy" temperatures, but they are temperatures of people who are deemed sufficiently nonfevered to be accepted for voluntary scheduled surgical procedures. Cases are omitted where there is reason to suspect underlying fevers. Also, a randomization procedure has been used to reduce the list by about 40%.

Data Set 19: Lifespans of Animals

SPECIESNAME = Common name of species
MAXLIFE = Estimated maximum lifespan (yrs) for species
WEIGHTS = Approximate weight (in kg) of adult of species
METABOLIC_RATE = Approximate metabolic rate for selected species
(in calories/gram/hour)

SPECIESNAME	MAXLIFE	WEIGHTS	METABOLIC_RATE
Elephant	70	3780	0.6
Horse	45	850	0.9
Human	115	85	1.3
Dog	20	26	1.4
Mouse	3.5	0.025	11
European shrew	0.3	0.005	36
Sparrow	13	0.051	
Rat	3.9	0.29	
Fruit bat	30	0.32	
Opossum	8	4.8	
Baboon	36	42	
(Giant) tortoise	180	48	
Chimpanzee	55	59	
Gorilla	35	210	
Cow	30	700	

Based on graphical displays in the following sources: Clark, William R. *A Means to an End: The Biological Basis of Aging and Death* (Oxford: Oxford University Press, 1999), pp. 15, 17. Tobin, Allan J, and Dusheck, Jennie. *Asking About Life.* (Fort Worth, Toronto, et al: Saunders College Publishing, Harcourt Brace, 1998), p. 756.

Data Set 20: Person-Days Lost in Labour Stoppages in the Transportation Industry

YEAR = Year
AIR etc. = Person-days lost in the AIR-transportion industry
(etc. for the other modes of transportation)
CAN_UNEMPLT = The Canadian national unemployment rate for that year

YEAR	AIR	RAIL	WATER	TRUCK	BUS&URBAN	TAXI	CAN_UNEMPLT
1976	41150	61710	41810	98740	84640	0	7.0
1977	13860	5770	8080	19400	52760	30	8.0
1978	81040	115660	16860	21620	65430	290	8.3
1979	25180	20820	85550	100390	245340	30	7.5
1980	7610	31640	10360	10740	43050	0	7.5
1981	51720	0	2770	29600	83910	120	7.6
1982	107250	0	42190	129920	161720	90	11.0
1983	26800	4590	1850	5750	14160	880	11.9
1984	9240	0	0	3680	223720	0	11.3
1985	209880	0	230	550	42460	130	10.7
1986	107660	190	46740	820	37570	0	9.6
1987	153590	173790	14400	8860	80010	60	8.8
1988	10620	137150	9540	9910	61990	1080	7.8
1989	730	17440	56830	30850	71630	0	7.5
1990	1100	29540	20160	14100	31070	630	8.1
1991	10890	0	13450	1900	70990	1920	10.3
1992	89090	1290	10070	4200	1090	1950	11.2
1993	15460	40720	210	2970	1020	1030	11.4
1994	6960	30170	32500	1750	25400	86150	10.4
1995	3420	211730	15010	1000	6000	13260	9.4
1996	600	2150	0	850	42820	3440	9.6
1997	51420	0	1499	14220	2340	850	9.1
1998	33840	180	10510	15450	28150	0	8.3
1999	8520	7080	19620	1700	21490	110	7.6

Based on data from Human Resources Canada, Workplace Information Directorate and Labour Force Survey, Statistics Canada, "Historical Labour Force Statistics", #71–201

Data Set 21: Diamonds

CANPRICE = Price in Canadian dollars
CARAT = A unit of weight for diamonds
DEPTH = 100 times the ratio of height to diameter
TABLE = Size of the upper flat surface; Depth and table determine "cut"
COLOUR = From 1 representing colourless to increasingly more yellow
CLARITY = From 1 representing flawless up to 6 representing inclusions that can be seen by eye

CANPRICE	CARAT	DEPTH	TABLE	COLOUR	CLARITY
10367	1	60.5	65	3	4
8768	1	59.2	65	5	4
9436	1.01	62.3	55	4	4
6405	1.01	64.4	62	5	5
14287	1.02	63.9	58	2	3
10312	1.04	60	61	4	4
6594	1.04	62	62	5	5
10258	1.07	63.6	61	4	3
8680	1.07	61.6	62	5	5
5468	1.11	60.4	60	9	4
10692	1.12	60.2	65	2	3
11170	1.16	59.5	60	5	3
7703	1.2	62.6	61	6	4
8265	1.23	59.2	65	7	4
27708	1.25	61.2	61	1	2
11206	1.29	59.6	59	6	2
10817	1.5	61.1	65	6	4
12127	1.51	63	60	6	4
18172	1.67	58.7	64	3	5
22347	1.72	58.5	61	4	3
14506	1.76	57.9	62	8	2
14689	1.8	59.6	63	5	5
18473	1.88	62.9	62	6	2
37729	2.03	60.1	62	2	3
16401	2.03	62	63	8	3
57803	2.06	58.2	63	2	2
99502	3	63.3	62	1	3
69685	4.01	57.1	51	3	4
42912	4.01	63	63	6	5
43013	4.05	59.3	60	7	4

Data Set 22: Canadian Exports and Imports by World Area

$$
\begin{array}{rcl}
\text{YEAR} &=& \text{Year} \\
\text{X\_NORTHAM} &=& \text{Exports to North America} \\
\text{X\_FAR E/OCEANIA} &=& \text{Exports to the Far East and Oceana} \\
\text{X\_EUROPE} &=& \text{Exports to Europe} \\
\text{X\_CTL/S AMER} &=& \text{Exports to Central and South America, and Mexico} \\
\text{X\_MID E/AFRICA} &=& \text{Exports to the Middle East and Africa} \\
\text{I\_NORTHAM} &=& \text{Imports from North America} \\
\text{I\_FAR E/OCEANIA} &=& \text{Imports from the Far eEast and Oceana} \\
\text{I\_EUROPE} &=& \text{Imports from Europe} \\
\text{I\_CTI/S AMER} &=& \text{Imports from Central and South America, and Mexico} \\
\text{I\_MID E/AFRICA} &=& \text{Imports from the Middle East and Africa}
\end{array}
$$

Year	X_NorthAm	X_Far E/ Oceania	X_Europe	X_Ctl/ S Amer	X_Mid E/ Africa	I_NorthAm	I_Far E/ Oceania	I_Europe	I_Ctl/ S Amer	I_Mid E /Africa
1980	48205	8288	13440	4006	2220	47765	6023	7400	4029	4057
1981	55514	8521	12756	4201	2821	53973	7809	8491	5106	4103
1982	57722	9044	11360	3337	3067	47272	7070	7392	4307	1815
1983	66040	9306	9946	2927	2394	53233	8802	8008	3786	1691
1984	84960	10696	10755	3142	2831	66928	11574	10666	4693	1598
1985	93094	11024	10101	2917	2339	72682	12686	13077	4420	1490
1986	93237	11203	10866	3355	2007	75888	15504	15412	3932	1774
1987	94544	13262	11802	3352	2127	77412	16573	16553	4110	1590
1988	100887	17741	14490	3118	2262	87045	18701	19505	4534	1387
1989	101632	16889	14846	2787	2548	89810	19640	18569	5235	1937
1990	111600	16291	15794	2764	2530	89597	19535	20227	4582	2283
1991	109733	15887	15139	2800	2448	88759	20780	18722	5208	1992
1992	125712	16105	15485	3356	2171	99199	22902	18482	5395	2039
1993	150689	16688	13928	3696	2515	116965	25208	18747	6463	2571
1994	183337	20089	14686	4600	2966	140870	28322	22993	7998	2554
1995	207792	26596	18681	5554	3645	154559	31702	26994	9457	2840
1996	223217	24587	18509	5739	3767	161144	29820	27650	10497	3446
1997	245143	25129	17644	6848	4551	188848	35343	32629	12047	3989
1998	269961	19407	19001	6464	3689	208439	39937	33834	12963	3372
1999	308361	18983	17834	5589	3341	220662	43573	37326	14845	3503

Based on data from Statistics Canada, Catalogues 65–202, 65–001.

Appendix C: The Internet

The following Web sites are helpful sources of data sets and information about statistics. Be aware that information available on the Internet is constantly changing; some of these sites may be at new addresses or may no longer exist.

Elementary Statistics (Triola). **http://www.pearsoned.ca/triola**
Supplement to the latest American edition of *Elementary Statistics*. The site contains information about and data sets for STATDISK, articles and exercises related to the use of statistics in current events, and links to other statistics sites.

Statistics Canada. **http://www.statcan.ca**
Health Canada. **http://www.hc-sc.gc.ca**
Industry Canada. **http://strategis.ic.gc.ca**
Transportation Canada. **http://www.tc.gc.ca/pol/en/t-facts_e/T-FACTS_menu.htm**
Government of Canada. **http://canada.gc.ca**
These sites provide Canadian government statistics.

Statistics and Statistical Graphics Resources.
http://www.math.yorku.ca/SCS/StatResource.html
Offers links to data collections, statistical journals and associations, statistical software, statistical humour, and other related sites.

Chance Database. **http://www.dartmouth.edu/~chance**
Includes a collection of data sets, news about statistics, and a forum for discussion.

Department of Statistics, Carnegie Mellon University. **http://lib.stat.cmu.edu**
Includes the *Data and Story Library* (http://lib.stat.cmu.edu/DASL), the data archive for the *Journal of the American Statistical Association* (http://lib.stat.cmu.edu/jasadata), and links to other statistics sites.

Department of Statistics, University of Florida.
http://www.stat.ufl.edu/vlib/statistics.html
Provides links to data archives, information on statistical software, statistics departments at universities worldwide, and related sites.

Journal of Statistics Education. **http://www.amstat.org/publications/jse**
Includes a data archive as well as articles relevant to post-secondary statistics.

Dr. B's Wide World of Web Data.
http://seamonkey.ed.asu.edu/~behrens/siip/webdata/index.html
Provides links to statistical data on sites worldwide.

http://www.execpc.com/~helberg/statistics.html
http://www.2ndmoment.org
List statistics resources available on the Internet.

Minitab Home Page. **http://www.minitab.com**

http://www.stats.gla.ac.uk/steps/glossary/index.html
A statistics glossary.

Appendix D: Bibilography

*An asterisk denotes a book recommended for reading. Other books are recommended as reference texts.

Andrews D., and A. Herzberg. 1985. *Data: A Collection of Problems from Many Fields for the Student and Research Worker*. New York: Springer.

Bennett, D. 1998. *Randomness*. Cambridge, MS: Harvard University Press.

*Campbell, S. 1974. *Flaws and Fallacies in Statistical Thinking*. Englewood Cliffs, NJ: Prentice-Hall.

*Crossen, C. 1996. *Tainted Truth: The Manipulation of Fact in America*. New York: Simon & Schuster.

Devore, J., and R. Peck. 1997. *Statistics: The Exploration and Analysis of Data*. 3rd ed. St. Paul, MN: West Publishing.

*Fairley, W., and F. Mosteller. 1977. *Statistics and Public Policy*. Reading, MS: Addison-Wesley.

Fisher, R. 1966. *The Design of Experiments*. 8th ed. New York: Hafner.

*Freedman, D., R. Pisani, and R. Purves. 1998. *Statistics*. 3rd ed. New York: Norton.

*Gonick, L., and W. Smith. 1993. *The Cartoon Guide to Statistics*. New York: HarperCollins.

Good, P. 1999. *Resampling Methods: A Practical Guide to Data Analysis*. Boston: Birkhauser.

*Hacking, I. 1990. *The Taming of Chance*. Cambridge: Cambridge University Press.

Hoaglin, D., F. Mosteller, and J. Tukey, eds. 2000. *Understanding Robust and Exploratory Data Analysis*. New York: Wiley. (1st paperback edition)

*Hollander, M., and F. Proschan. 1984. *The Statistical Exorcist: Dispelling Statistics Anxiety*. New York: Marcel Dekker.

*Holmes, C. 1990. *The Honest Truth About Lying with Statistics*. Springfield, IL: Charles C. Thomas.

*Hooke, R., and J. Liles. 1983. *How to Tell the Liars from the Statisticians*. New York: Marcel Dekker.

*Huff, D., and I. Geis. 1993. *How to Lie with Statistics*. New York: Norton.

Kotz, S., and D. Stroup. 1983. *Educated Guessing— How to Cope in an Uncertain World*. New York: Marcel Dekker.

Lunnenborg, C. 2000. *Data Analysis by Resampling: Concepts and Applications*. Pacific Grove, CA: Duxbury Press.

*Moore, D. 2000. *Statistics: Concepts and Controversies*. 5th ed. San Francisco: Freeman.

Mosteller, F., R. Rourke, and G. Thomas, Jr. 1970. *Probability with Statistical Applications*. 2nd ed. Reading, MS: Addison-Wesley.

Ott, L., and W. Mendenhall. 1994. *Understanding Statistics*. 6th ed. Boston: Duxbury Press.

Owen, D. 1962. *Handbook of Statistical Tables*. Reading, MS: Addison-Wesley.

*Paulos, J. 1988. *Innumeracy: Mathematical Illiteracy and Its Consequences*. New York: Hill and Wang.

*Reichard, R. 1974. *The Figure Finaglers*. New York: McGraw-Hill.

*Reichmann, W. 1962. *Use and Abuse of Statistics*. New York: Oxford University Press.

*Rossman, A. 1996. *Workshop Statistics: Discovery with Data*. New York: Springer.

Scheaffer, R., M. Gnanadesikan, A. Watkins, and J. Witmer. 1996. *Activity-Based Statistics: Student Guide*. New York: Springer.

Schmid, C. 1983. *Statistical Graphics*. New York: Wiley.

Simon, J. 1992. *Resampling: The New Statistics*. Belmont, CA: Duxbury Press.

Smith, G. 1998. *Statistical Process Control and Quality Improvement*. 3rd ed. Upper Saddle River, NJ: Prentice Hall.

*Spirer, H., L. Spirer, and A. Jaffe. 1998. *Misused Statistics*. New York: Marcel Dekker.

*Stigler, S. 1999. *Statistics on the Table: The History of Statistical Concepts and Methods*. Cambridge, MS: Harvard University Press

*Tanur, J., ed. 1989. *Statistics: A Guide to the Unknown*. 3rd ed. Belmont, CA: Wadsworth.

Triola, M. 1998. STATDISK 7.0 *Student Laboratory Manual and Workbook*. 7th ed. Reading, MS: Addison-Wesley.

*Tufte, E. 2000 (2nd ed.). *The Visual Display of Quantitative Information*. Cheshire, CT: Graphics Press.

Tukey, J. 1977. *Exploratory Data Analysis*. Reading, MS: Addison-Wesley.

Utts, J. 1999. *Seeing Through Statistics*. 2nd ed. Pacific Grove, CA: Duxbury Press.

Zabowski, Glenn. 1999. *Using Excel for Statistics and Data Analysis*. Don Mills, ON: Addison-Wesley.

Zwillinger, D. and Kokoska, M.: 1999. *CRC Standard Probability and Statistics Tables and Formulae*. Boca Raton, FL: CRC Press.

Appendix E: Answers to Odd-Numbered Exercises (and ALL Review Exercises and Cumulative Review Exercises)

Section 1-2

1. Continuous   3. Discrete   5. Statistic   7. Parameter
9. Ordinal   11. Nominal   13. Interval   15. Nominal
17. Ordinal
19. The calculated result is meaningless. Although the different categories (political parties) have each been arbitrarily assigned a number, these numbers have no real computational significance.

Section 1-3

1. People with unlisted numbers and people without telephones are excluded.
3. A study sponsored by the fruit industry is much more likely to reach conclusions favourable to that industry.
5. Because the respondents are self-selected, the survey results are not likely to be valid at all.
7. 62% of 8% of 1875 is only 93.
9. Mothers who eat lobsters tend to be wealthier and therefore healthier.
11. A maker of shoe polish has an obvious interest in the importance of the product and there are many ways in which this could affect the survey results.
13. The mean of 69.5 for all males is measured from birth, whereas males don't become conductors until they have already survived for about 30 years. When this is taken into account, the mean of 73.4 years is not significant.
15. The wording of the question is biased and tends to encourage negative responses. The sample size of 20 is too small. Survey respondents are self-selected instead of being selected by the newspaper. If 20 readers respond, the percentages should be multiples of 5; 87% and 13% are not possible results.

Section 1-4

1. Observational study   3. Experiment   5. Convenience
7. Stratified   9. Random   11. Stratified   13. Cluster
15. Random
17. Answers can vary. For example, you may design a procedure based on randomly generating students' ID numbers.
19. a. An advantage of open questions is that they provide the subject and the interviewer with a much wider variety of responses; a disadvantage is that open questions can be very difficult to analyse.
   b. An advantage of closed questions is that they reduce the chance of misinterpreting the topic; a disadvantage is that

closed questions prevent the inclusion of valid responses the pollster might not have considered.
   c. Closed questions are easier to analyse with formal statistical procedures.
21. a. Not always. No.
   b. Not always. No.

Chapter 1 Review Exercises

1. a. Continuous   b. Ratio   c. Cluster
   d. Observational study
   e. The products that use the batteries may be damaged.
2. a. Ratio   b. Ordinal   c. Ordinal   d. Interval
   e. Nominal
3. Because it is a mail survey, the respondents are self-selected and will likely include those with strong opinions about the issue. Self-selected respondents do not necessarily represent the views of everyone who invests.
4. a. Design the experiment so that the subjects don't know whether they are using Statistiszene or a placebo, and design it so that those who observe and evaluate the subjects do not know which subjects are using Statistiszene and which are using a placebo.
   b. Blinding will help to distinguish between the effectiveness of Statistiszene and the placebo effect, whereby subjects and evaluators tend to believe that improvements are occurring just because some given treatment is given.
   c. Subjects are put into different groups through a process of *random selection*.
   d. Subjects are carefully chosen for the different groups so that those groups are made to be similar in ways that are important for the study.
   e. Replication is used when the experiment is repeated. The sample size should be large enough so that we can see the true nature of any effects. It is important so that we are not misled by erratic behaviour of samples that are too small.
5. a. Systematic   b. Random   c. Cluster   d. Stratified
   e. Convenience
6. Respondents often tend to round off to a nice even number like 50.
7. The sample could be biased by excluding those who work, those who don't eat at school, those who commute, and so on.
8. The figure is very precise, but it is probably not very accurate. The use of such a precise number may incorrectly suggest that it is also accurate.

Chapter 1 Cumulative Review Exercises

1. The second version of the question is substantially less confusing because it doesn't include a double negative. One possibility for a better question:
   "Which of the following two statements do you agree with more?
   - The Nazi extermination of Jews never happened.
   - The Nazi extermination of Jews definitely happened."
2. Answer varies

Section 2-2

1. Class width: 6. Class midpoints: 2.5, 8.5, 14.5, 20.5, 26.5. Class boundaries: -0.5, 5.5, 11.5, 17.5, 23.5, 29.5.
3. Class width: 2.0. Class midpoints: 0.995, 2.995, 4.995, 6.995, 8.995.
Class boundaries: -.005, 1.995, 3.995, 5.995, 7.995, 9.995

5.
Relative Absences	Frequency
0–5	0.195
6–11	0.205
12–17	0.190
18–23	0.200
24–29	0.210

7.
Weight (kg)	Relative Frequency
0.0–1.99	0.133
2.0–3.99	0.213
4.0–5.99	0.327
6.0–7.99	0.207
8.0–9.99	0.120

9.
Absences	Cumulative Frequency
Less than 6	39
Less than 12	80
Less than 18	118
Less than 24	158
Less than 30	200

11.
Weight (kg)	Cumulative Frequency
Less than 2.00	20
Less than 4.00	52
Less than 6.00	101
Less than 8.00	132
Less than 10.00	150

13. In Exercise 1, the numbers of absences are (approximately) evenly spread over the five classes, but the absences in Exercise 2 have frequencies that start relatively low, increase to a maximum in the middle class, then decrease to the last class.
15. Possible solutions include 0.25–0.74, or 0.26–0.75.

17.
Size of Group	Frequency
0 – 999	17
1000 – 1999	9
2000 – 2999	5
3000 – 3999	5
4000 – 4999	1
5000 – 5999	4
6000 – 6999	2
7000 – 7999	2
8000 – 8999	1
9000 – 9999	0
10000 –10999	0
11000 –11999	1

(1) The first two classes contain over half the total frequency. That is, most SOC occupational groups in Newfoundland contain fewer than 2000 males.
(2) Although the first two classes contain over half the total frequency, the remaining frequencies are stretched across eight additional classes. (*We say that such distributions are highly "skewed".*)

19.
Unemployment Rate	Frequency
7.0–7.49	1
7.5–7.99	6
8.0–8.49	4
8.5–8.99	1
9.0–9.49	2
9.5–9.99	2
10.0–10.49	2
10.5–10.99	1
11.0–11.49	4
11.5–11.99	1

These data do not appear random with respect to time. For example, the eight unemployment rates with values greater than 10% appear to occur in clusters—in sequences of several years in a row.

21. Relative frequencies for precipitation: 0.250, 0.125, 0.219, 0.188, 0.063, 0.125, 0.00, 0.00, 0.00, 0.031. Relative frequencies for snowfall: 0.063, 0.031, 0.156, 0.094, 0.125, 0.125, 0.063, 0.125, 0.156, 0.063. The distributions are quite dissimilar; the relative amounts of precipitation and snowfall do not seem to correspond.

23.

Axial Loads Without Outlier

Axial Load	Frequency
200-219	6
220-239	5
240-259	12
260-279	36
280-299	87
300-319	28

Axial Loads With Outlier

Axial Load	Frequency
200-219	6
220-239	5
240-259	12
260-279	36
280-299	87
300-319	28
320-339	0
340-359	0
360-379	0
380-399	0
400-419	0
420-439	0
440-459	0
460-479	0
480-499	0
500-519	1

Including the outlier dramatically changes the frequency table. Ten additional classes have to be added; yet all but one of the extra classes is empty.

25 Yes. Here is just one possible example of a dramatic change in apparent distribution due to changing the number of classes in a frequency table.

Illustrative Data Set

0	12	17
1	12	17
3	13	17
3	15	26
3	16	27
4	16	27
5	16	27
5	16	27
5	16	28
5	17	28
5	17	29

Distribution With Five Classes

Classes	Frequency
0-5	11
6-11	0
12-17	14
18-23	0
24-29	8

Distribution With Six Classes

Classes	Frequency
0-4	6
5-9	5
10-14	3
15-19	11
20-24	0
25-29	8

Section 2-3

1. Only one eruption out of 200 took as long as 109 min from the time of the preceding eruption, so allocating 100 min would please almost all bus trip participants.

3.

5. 570 571 577 581 583 583 584 589
   594 595 596 596 597 598 602 603

7. 3   67
   4   00133
   4   667889
   5   022334
   5   778999
   6   0011123333444
   6   556778
   7   00222233
   7   56

9. Networking appears to dominate as the most effective approach in getting a job.

11.

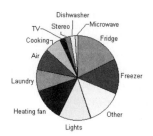

13. The distribution of job-group-sizes appears to be similar for male and female Newfoundlanders. However, the number of job groups with about 500 members appears to be greater for women. The graph does not tell us if the groups with the higher (or lower) frequencies for men and women are actually the same SOC job categories in both cases.

15.

17. Skewed

19. Bell-shaped

21. a. The two figures are given below. The histogram for π represents a more even distribution.

b. The number π is irrational (i.e., it cannot be represented as the quotient of two whole numbers). The decimal representation of the rational number 22/7 is obtained by dividing 7 into 22; because there are a maximum of 6 possible remainder digits at each step (1,2,3,4,5,6) that keep generating digits in the quotient, there are a maximum of six possible quotient digits that will repeat forever in a regular cycle.

23. The heights of the bars will be approximately halved. Also, depending on the nature of the data, the general shape may be changed.

Section 2-4

1. $\bar{x} = 16.2$; median = 16; mode = 16; midrange = 16
3. $\bar{x} = 6.14$; median = 5.62; mode: none; midrange = 6.63
5. Regular Coke: $\bar{x} = 0.37232$; median = 0.37215; (no mode); midrange = 0.37270.
   Diet Coke: $\bar{x} = 0.35603$; median = 0.35690; (no mode); midrange = 0.35575.
   Regular Coke does appear to weigh a small amount more than Diet Coke. Three measures of centre, the mean, median, and midrange, suggest the same result. It is possible that the sugar in Regular Coke weighs more than the artificial sweetener in Diet Coke.
7. 4000 B.C.: $\bar{x} = 128.7$; median = 128.5; mode = 131; midrange = 128.5
   150 A.D.: $\bar{x} = 133.3$; median = 133.5; mode = 126; midrange = 133.5
   Yes. Three measures of centre, the mean, median, and midrange, suggest that head sizes increased over time. The modes appear to contradict this finding, but they are based on just two data values for each time period—and could just be coincidences.
9. $\bar{x} = 37.00$; median = 36.96; mode = 36.91, 36.96, 37.22; midrange = 36.92
11. $\bar{x} = 182.9$; median = 150.0; mode = 140, 150, 166, 202, 204, 220; midrange = 270.0
13. 74.4 min 15. 380. This year's level of 492 Mt is much higher than the average. 17. 82.0

19. a. $\bar{x} = 226,500$; median = 175,600; mode: none; midrange = 251,450
    b. Each result is increased by k.
    c. Each result is multiplied by k.
    d. They're not equal.
21. 1.092
23. a. 58,701 b. 60,067 c. 61,433
    In this case, the open-ended class doesn't have too much effect on the mean. The mean is likely to be around 60,000, give or take about 1000.
25. a. 182.9 lb b. 171.0 lb c. 159.2 lb
    The results differ by substantial amounts, suggesting that the mean of the original set of weights is strongly affected by extreme scores.

Section 2-5

1. range = 4; $s^2 = 1.64$; $s = 1.28$
3. range = 3.33; $s^2 = 1.223$; $s = 1.106$
5. Regular Coke: Range = 0.0044; $s^2 = 0.0000025337$; $s = 0.0015917$.
   Diet Coke: Range = 0.0063; $s^2 = 0.0000063507$; $s = 0.0025201$.
   By all these measures, there seems to be slightly more variation in the weight of Diet Coke than in the weight of Regular Coke.
7. 4000 B.C.: range = 19.0; $s^2 = 21.5$; $s = 4.6$
   150 A.D.: range = 15.0; $s^2 = 25.2$; $s = 5.0$
9. 0.233 11. 121.8 13. 14.7 15. 53.09 Mt
17. The population of batteries with $\sigma = 1$ month are much more consistent, so they have a smaller chance of failing much earlier than expected.
19. Dollars. Dollars.^{2}
21. a. 68% b. 95% c. 50, 110
23. a. range = 259,700; $s = 112,707$
    b. The results will be the same.
    c. The range and standard deviation will be multiplied by k.
    d. No, they are not equal. The standard deviation of the log x values is 0.2062, but log $s = 5.0520$.
    e. $\bar{x} = 97.45$; $s = 0.63$
25. Section 1: range = 19.0; $s = 5.7$
    Section 2: range = 17.0; $s = 6.7$
    The ranges suggest that Section 2 has less variation, but the standard deviations suggest that Section 1 has less variation.
27. $I = -0.80$; there is not significant skewness.

Section 2-6

1. a. -1.8 b. 1.0 c. 0.2 3. 2.77 5. 2.56; unusual
7. -2.43; no 9. 2.00; 2.50; 250 is better
11. 1.50; 1.54; 1.47; 398 is highest
13. 17 15. 60 17. 279 19. 276.5 21. 282 23. 230
25. 13 27. 58 29. 30850 31. 1825 33. 98740 35. 9385

37. a. 20   b. 272   c. 59   d. Yes; yes   e. No
39. a. Uniform   b. Bell-shaped   c. The shape of the distribution remains the same.   d. There is no effect on the distribution of z scores.

Section 2-7

1.

3.

Actors:

Actresses:

Oscar-winning actresses tend to be younger than actors.

5.   Male:

Female:

The two groups do not appear to be different.

7.   Red:

Yellow:

Red and yellow M&Ms appear to have weights that are about the same.

9.

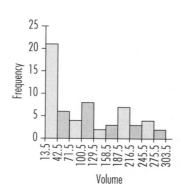

11. Both distributions are skewed.

Chapter 2 Review Exercises

1.
Volume	Frequency
14–42	21
43–71	6
72–100	4
101–129	8
130–158	2
159–187	3
188–216	7
217–245	3
246–274	4
275–303	2

2.
Volume	Relative Frequency
14–42	0.350
43–71	0.100
72–100	0.067
101–129	0.133
130–158	0.033
159–187	0.050
188–216	0.117
217–245	0.050
246–274	0.067
275–303	0.033

3.

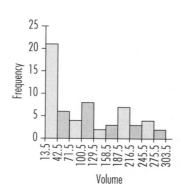

4. a. 25.5   b. 72.5   c. P_{62}
5. $s \approx 72.25$
6. $\bar{x} = 112.6$; $s = 85.5$

7.
0–4	*45788*4*4*2
5–9	78**5*3*
10–14	*68*56**
15–19	***1*2
20–24	3*2***
25–29	4*3***2
30–34	3****

8.

9. a. 124.4   b. 121.0   c. 135   d. 148.0   e. 158.0   f. 48.6
   g. 2364.5
10. a. 23.08   b. 23   c. 23   d. 30   e. 30   f. 5.77
    g. 33.28   h. 19   i. 19   j. 24
11. a. No, the z score is 1.5, so 260 is within 2 standard deviations
       of the mean.
    b. −0.38
    c. About 95% of the scores should fall between 120 and 280.
    d. 220   e. 40
12. 5.15; 1.67; 8 years is not unusual because it is within 2 standard
    deviations of the mean.

13.

14. The score of 450 is better because its z score of −0.63 is greater
    than the other z score of −0.75.
15. The mean appears to be greater in 150 A.D., so there does appear
    to be an upward shift in the maximum skull breadth.
16.

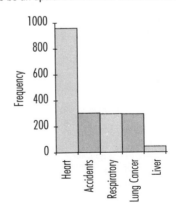

Chapter 2 Cumulative Review Exercises

1. a. $\bar{x}$ = 2.40; median = 2.20; mode: 0.0, 2.0, 2.1, 2.4, 4.4;
      midrange = 2.25
   b. s = 1.29; s^2 = 1.67; range = 4.50
   c. Continuous
   d. Ratio
2. a. Mode, because the other measures of central tendencies
      require calculations that cannot (or should not) be done with
      data at the nominal level of measurement.
   b. Convenience
   c. Cluster
3. No, the values should be weighted according to the corresponding number of cars sold. The weighted mean is $29,411.76.

Section 3-2

1. −0.2, 3/2, $\sqrt{2}$ 3. 1/2   5. 0.210   7. 0.25; no
9. 0.320   11. 0.450. Not unusual.
13. a. 1/365. Unusual.   b. 6/73 (reduced from 30/365). Not
    unusual.   15. 0.130. Not unusual!
17. 0.340; Not unusual; yes   19. 0.0896. Not unusual; yes.
    21. 0.200. Not unusual.
23. a. bb, bg, gb, gg   b. 1/4   c. 1/2
25. b. 1/8   c. 1/8   d. 1/2
27. 4:1
29. a. 37:1   b. 35:1   c. The casino pays off at 35:1 so that it will
    make a profit, instead of paying off at 37:1, which would not
    yield a profit.
31. 3/13   33. 0.600   35. a. 4/1461   b. 400/146,097

Section 3-3

1. a. No   b. No   c. Yes   3. a. 3/5   b. 0.72
5. a. 4/13 (reduced from 16/52)   b. 2/13 (reduced from 8/52)
7. 0.698   9. 0.290   11. 0.580   13. 0.62   15. 0.740
17. 0.54   19. 0.23   21. 0.15   23. 0.17
25. a. 17/60   b. $P(A \text{ or } B) = 0.9$ c. $P(A \text{ or } B) < 0.9$
27. $P(A \text{ or } B) = P(A) + P(B) - 2P(A \text{ and } B)$

Section 3-4

1. a. Dependent   b. Independent   c. Dependent
3. a. 0.17361 b. 0.15152 5. 0.00000369 7. 0.999992 9. 1/64
11. a. 0.0542   b. 0.799
13. 0.0643; not common.
15. 0.0000416   17. 0.787   19. 0.00000410; fraud
21. 0.0728
23. a. 0.210   b. 0.0530   c. 0.593   d. 0.0637 (not 0.0638)
25. 0.05   27. 0.95
29. 0.95
31. a. 0.431   b. 0.569   33. 0.0192

Section 3-5

1. 0.14; the simulated result is a bit higher. With n equal 50 in the simulated sample, the closest matches to the actual probability of 0.125 are 7/50 = 0.14 (a bit high), or 6/50 = 0.12 (a bit low). Neither result would be unusual.

     However, the simulation does have limitations: The gender-probabilities of each child in a family should be independent, but in Lotto 6/49, the numbers (representing genders) are drawn without replacement. Also, there are more odd numbers (representing girls) among the 49 balls than even numbers.

3. 0.58; the result is a little low. With n equal to 50 in the simulated sample, the closest match to the actual probability of 0.603 is 30/50 = 0.600. The simulation result of 29/50 = 0.58 would not be considered unusual. However, the simulation does have a limitation: The defect-probabilities of each phone in a sample should be independent, but in Lotto 6/49, the numbers (representing defect/no defect) are drawn without replacement. Instead, you could let each Bonus number represent one cell phone, and each sequence of six independently selected Bonus numbers represent one sample of six phones.

5. One possible method is to interpret every random digit in the range 1-6 as a throw of the die and ignore all digits that are outside the range. Interpret the digit 1 as a throw of 1 on the die. This technique leads to 8 ones out of 66 throws, for a probability = 8/66 = 0.121—which, for the sample size, would not be considered unusually far from 0.167 (the actual probability).

7. Begin by representing birthdays by integers from 1 through 365 as follows: 1 = January 1; 2 = January 2;.....; 365 = December 31. Using any source of equally likely integers (such as the uniform random generators in Excel or STATDISK), we can generate a list of 50 random integers between 1 and 365. That list can be ranked so that it becomes easy to determine whether there are any sequences of three or more identical "birthdays." If we repeat this process many times, we can simulate many different groups of 50 people, and we can then estimate the probability that among 50 randomly selected people, at least three of them have the same birthday. {Based on 8000 repetitions of this procedure, the author obtained 1037 instances where at least three of the 50 people shared the same simulated birthday—for a probability = 1037/8000 = 0.130.}

Section 3-6

1. 720   3. 970,200   5. 720   7. 15   9. 79,833,600
11. 3,838,380   13. 1   15. $n!$ 17. a. 10,000   b. 13.9 hours
19. 1/1,000,000,000   21. 43,758   23. 5040
25. a. 3,838,380   b. 1/3,838,380   c. 3,838,379:1
27. 14,348,907   29. a. 230,300   b. 1/230,300
31. 259,459,200   33. a. 17,576,000   b. 1/17,576,000
35. 1/76,904,685; yes, if all other factors are equal.
37. 1/479,001,600; yes   39. 1,000,000; 151,200; 786,240

41. 2,095,681,645,538 (about 2 trillion)
43. a. Calculator: 3.0414093×10^{64}; approximation: 3.0363452×10^{64}
    b. 615

Chapter 3 Review Exercises

1. 0.35   2. 0.57   3. 0.0896   4. 0.18   5. 0.6
6. 0.27   7. 0.55   8. 0.51
9. 0.877   10. 0.0483; should not speed.
11. a. 1/56   b. 336   12. 0.513   13. a. 9/19   b. 10:9   c. $5
14. 1/120   15. 0.000000531; no.   16. 1/12,870

Chapter 3 Cumulative Review Exercises

1. a. 67.5   b. 13.09   c. 0.683   d. 0.049   e. 0.0000011
2. a. 1/4   b. 3/4   c. 1/16
3. a. 151.3 b. 90.5   c. 130.0 d. 337 e. 0.667 f. 0.424

Section 4-2

1. Continuous   3. Discrete
5. Probability distribution with $\mu = 1.799$, $\sigma^2 = 0.613$, $\sigma = 0.782$
7. Not a probability distribution because $\Sigma P(x) \neq 1$.
9. Probability distribution with $\mu = 1.3$, $\sigma^2 = 0.71$, $\sigma = 0.84$
11. Probability distribution with $\mu = 0.5001$, $\sigma^2 = 0.4504$, $\sigma = 0.6711$
13. $-26¢$; 5.26¢   15. $2.00
17. $\mu = 1.5$, $\sigma^2 = 0.8$, $\sigma = 0.9$; minimum $= -0.3$ and maximum $= 3.3$, but reality dictates that the minimum and maximum are 0 and 3.
19. $\mu = 0.4$, $\sigma^2 = 0.3$, $\sigma = 0.5$
21. a. Yes   b. No, $\Sigma P(x) > 1$ c. Yes   d. Yes
23. a. $\mu = 4.5$, $\sigma = 2.9$ b. $\mu = 0$, $\sigma = 1$ c. Yes
25. Same as the table given in Exercise 6; $\mu = 2.0$, $\sigma = 1.0$

Section 4-3

1. Not binomial; more than two outcomes   3. Binomial
5. Not binomial; more than two outcomes
7. Not binomial; trials are not independent
9. 0.243   11. 0.075   13. 0.141   15. 0.238   17. 0.032816
19. 0.993785   21. a. 0.205   b. 0.828   c. 0.120   23. 0.250
25. 0.007; study
27. 0.0095
29. 0.392 suggests that the defect rate could easily be 10%; there isn't sufficient evidence to conclude that the newly instituted measures were effective in lowering the defect rate.
31. 0.297; the results could occur by chance.
33. 0.0524   35. 0.000535

Section 4-4

1. $\mu = 32.0$, $\sigma^2 = 16.0$, $\sigma = 4.0$
3. $\mu = 267.0$, $\sigma^2 = 200.3$, $\sigma = 14.2$
5. $\mu = 12.5$, $\sigma^2 = 6.3$, $\sigma = 2.5$ Yes, because 20 randomly guessed correct answers is more than two standard deviations above the mean. 7. $\mu = 13.2$, $\sigma = 3.6$ Yes, because zero sevens in 500 trials is more than two standard deviations below the mean.
9. a. $\mu = 1140.0$, $\sigma = 7.5$ b. Yes
11. a. $\mu = 153$, $\sigma = 11.27$ b. No; the result is within two standard deviations.
13. a. $\mu = 1160$, $\sigma = 28.7$
    b. Yes, the result is higher than usual (not within two standard deviations); perhaps it was an exciting game!
15. a. $\mu = 1365$, $\sigma = 31.5$ b. Yes, the result is unusual (not within two standard deviations).
17. a. $\mu = 44.6$, $\sigma = 6.1$ b. 32.4, 56.9

Section 4-5

1. 0.180   3. 0.153   5. a. 0.039   b. 0.127   c. 0.181
7. a. 0.819   b. 0.164   c. 0.0164   9. 0.594
11. a. 0.497   b. 0.348   c. 0.122   d. 0.0284   e. 0.00497
    The expected frequencies of 139, 97, 34, 8, and 1.4 compare reasonably well to the actual frequencies of 144, 91, 32, 11, and 2. The Poisson distribution does provide good results.
13. Table: 0.130; Poisson formula: 0.129

Chapter 4 Review Exercises

1. a. A random variable is a variable that has a single numerical value (determined by chance) for each outcome of an experiment.
   b. A probability distribution gives the probability for each value of the random variable.
   c. Yes, because each probability value is between 0 and 1 and the sum of the probabilities is 1.   d. $\mu = 3.4$ e. $\sigma = 0.7$
2. a. 7.5   b. 7.5   c. 2.5
   d. Yes, using the range rule of thumb, the number is usually between 2.5 and 12.5, so 15 is unusually high.   e. 0.123
3. a. 0.216   b. 0.798   c. $\mu = 5.8$, $\sigma = 1.56$
4. a. 0.394   b. 0.00347   c. 0.000142   d. 0.0375
5. a. 0.85   b. 0.84   c. Yes, because 4 is more than two standard deviations above the mean.
6. a. $\mu = 0.230$ b. 0.0210

Chapter 4 Cumulative Review Exercises

1. a.

x	r.f.
4	0.146
5	0.247
6	0.225
7	0.382

   b. Yes, each cumulative frequency is a value between 0 and 1, and the sum of the frequencies is 1.
   c. 0.854   d. 0.143   e. 5.8   f. 1.1
   g. 5.8 games; about 175,000 hot dogs

2. a. $\bar{x} = 9.7$, $s = 2.9$ b. 0.4 isn't close to 0.0278.   c. 0.431
   d. Claim that the sample of 20 results is too small to obtain meaningful results.

Section 5-2

1. 0.6   3. 0.4   5. 0.4987   7. 0.4901   9. 0.0049
11. 0.0183   13. 0.0863   15. 0.1203   17. 0.5319
19. 0.9890   21. 0.9545   23. 0.8412   25. 0.0099
27. 0.9759   29. 1.28°   31. −0.67°   33. 1.75°
35. −2.05°
37. a. 0.92   b. 0.41   c. 0.72   d. −0.68   e. −0.23
39. $\mu = 2.5$; $\sigma = 1.443$

Section 5-3

1. 0.1217   3. 0.9906   5. 0.2364   7. 0.1379   9. 0.0244
11. 0.0038; either a very rare event has occurred or the husband is not the father.
13. 0.9554   15. a. 0.0179   b. 1343
17. 0.1706 This answer assumes a normal distribution, but the expenditure distribution is more likely to be bimodal: Many households will spend nothing on postsecondary textbooks (because no one is attending postsecondary institutions); and the minority who are buying textbooks will spend a great deal.
19. 0.0013 No, it is rare for a person in this age group to have a seriously elevated serum cholesterol level.
21. a. Normal distribution   b. $\bar{x} = 0.9147$, $s = 0.0369$
    c. 0.0104
23. a. Normal distribution   b. $\bar{x} = 35.66$, $s = 9.35$
    c. 0.271

Section 5-4

1. 66.9 in.   3. 61.5 in.   5. a. 9.1 years   b. 0.0018   c. 5.6 years.
   7. 3.5 kg
9. 242 days   11. 135 Perhaps the employees of a "think tank" company could be held to this standard.   13. a. 0.9656   b. 658.9
15. 3497.4   17. 11.9   19. 131.6; 782

Section 5-5

1. a. 0.1480   b. 0.4896   3. a. 0.3783   b. 0.0146
5. 0.1251   7. a. 0.0274   b. 0.12%; level is acceptable   9. a. 0.3446   b. 0.0838
   c. Because the original population has a normal distribution, samples of *any* size will yield sample means that are normally distributed.
11. 0.0668   13. 0.9345   15. 0.0392
17. a. 0.2981   b. 0.0038
    c. Yes, because it is highly unlikely (with a probability of only 0.0038) that the mean will be that low because of chance.

19. a. 0.5675   b. 0.9999   c. Yes
21. a. 8; 5.385   b. 2,3; 2,6; 2,8; 2,11; 2,18; 3,6; 3,8; 3,11; 3,18; 6,8;
    6,11; 6,18; 8,11; 8,18; 11,18   c. 2.5; 4.0; 5.0; 6.5; 10.0; 4.5;
    5;5; 7.0; 10.5; 7.0; 8.5; 12.0; 9.5; 13.0; 14.5   d. 8; 3.406
    e. $\mu_{\bar{x}} = 8 = \mu$;
    $\sigma_{\bar{x}} = 3.406 = \sigma/\sqrt{n} \cdot \sqrt{[(N-n)/(N-1)]} = 3.80777 \cdot 0.894427$
23. They are all near 0.975.

Section 5-6

1. The area to the right of 35.5
3. The area to the left of 41.5
5. The area to the left of 72.5
7. The area between 124.5 and 150.5
9. a. 0.183   b. 0.1817
11. a. 0.996   b. Normal approximation is not suitable.
13. 0.1841   15. 0.1020   17. 0.1159
19. 0.0668; not *very* unusual   21. 0.4207
23. 0.9821; possibly yes—depending on desired significance level.
25. 0.1922; not unusual. The claim is accurate.
27. 0.7734   29. 0.2946
31. a. $0.4129 - 0.3264 = 0.0865$
    b. $0.3192 - 0.2643 = 0.0549$
    c. $0.0256 - 0.0228 = 0.0028$
    As n gets larger, the difference becomes smaller.

Chapter 5 Review Exercises

1. 60.83 in., 75.17 in.   2. 8.4%   3. 40.6%   4. 0.9381
5. 0.5198   6. a. 0.3944   b. 0.3085   c. 0.8599
    d. 0.6247   e. 0.2426   7. 79 (rounded)   8. 671
9. 0.4168
10. a. 0.9115   b. 0.8212   c. 44,375 km
11. The histogram suggests a normal distribution—except for one
    outlier (5). Removing the outlier, a normal probability plot is
    constructed, which also suggests that the distribution is approxi-
    mately normal.

Chapter 5 Cumulative Review Exercises

1. a. 0.0005   b. 0.243
    c. The requirement that $np \geq 5$ is not satisfied, indicating that the
       normal approximation would result in errors that are too large.
    d. 8.1   e. 2.73
    f. No, 10 is within two standard deviations of the mean and is
       within the range of values that could easily occur by chance.
2. a. 200.46 ms   b. 200.45 ms   c. 200.5 ms
    d. 0.29 ms   e. 0.14   f. 7.5%
    g. 3.14% (using $\bar{x} = 200.46$ and $s = 0.29$)   h. Yes

Section 6-2

1. 2.575   3. 2.33   5. a. 0.7 in.   b. 63.5 in. $< \mu <$ 64.9 in.
7. a. 1.9   b. 75.7 $< \mu <$ 79.5   9. 133.3 mm $< \mu <$ 135.7 mm;
    we are 95% confident that the interval from 133.3 mm to 135.7
    mm actually does contain the true population mean.
11. 0.9499 mm $< \mu <$ 0.9513 mm. We are 90% confident that the
    mean length is very close to the specification (0.950 mm). With
    regard to the range specification (0.945 to 0.955), some measure
    of variation for the sample would be needed.
13. 543
15. 5.600 g $< \mu <$ 5.644 g; no, the quarters become lighter as they
    wear down.
17. 432   19. 3453.98 $< \mu <$ 3476.94. No, the value claimed for the
    mean is outside the confidence interval.   21. 236   23.
    $\sigma = 3$, n = 782
25. $n = 62, \bar{x} = 9.428, s = 4.168$; 8.502 lb $< \mu <$ 10.354 lb
27. $n = 33, \bar{x} = 0.9128, s = 0.0395$; 0.8979 $< \mu <$ 0.9277; no, the
    sample is small.
29. a. 129.1 $< \mu <$ 134.9   b. 147
31. Given confidence level is 95%. Men: 1.7324 $< \mu <$ 1.7616
    Women: 1.5978 $< \mu <$ 1.6222. No. Because their respective confi-
    dence intervals do not overlap, it is unlikely that the populations
    of men's and women's heights have the same mean; so it is
    reasonable to conclude that the populations are different.

Section 6-3

1. 3.250   3. 2.528   5. a. 1.86 in.   b. 62.3 in. $< \mu <$ 66.1 in.
7. a. 6.2   b. 71.4 $< \mu <$ 83.8   9. $1066 $< \mu <$ $2506
11. 1.79 h $< \mu <$ 3.01 h. No, based on the sample, I am 47.5% confident that for the population, the mean hours required for paperwork is actually in the range from above 2.4h to 3.01h—which would leave less than 5.6 hours available for other work.
    13. 3.84 $< \mu <$ 4.04
15. 43.13 h $< \mu <$ 45.37 h
17. $\bar{x}$ = 7.96, s = 1.60; 7.11 $< \mu <$ 8.81
19. n = 100, $\bar{x}$ = 0.9147 g, s = 0.0369 g; 0.9075 g $< \mu <$ 0.9219 g; there is reasonable agreement with the result from Exercise 18.
21. The confidence interval limits are closer than they should be.
23. 90% (approx.)

Section 6-4

1. 0.0300   3. 0.0174   5. 0.720 $< p <$ 0.780
7. 0.385 $< p <$ 0.417   9. 2401   11. 664
13. a. 64.0%   b. 61.3% $< p <$ 66.7%   15. a. 0.134% $< p <$ 6.20% using x = 7, n = 221.   b. It has not been shown that Ziac is causing dizziness as an adverse reaction.
17. 72.8% $< p <$ 92.0%   19. 9.53% $< p <$ 18.5%; yes
21. 2944   23. 82.8% $< p <$ 85.2%; yes
25. a. 0.00916 $< p <$ 0.0233   b. 4229
27. 0.424 $< p <$ 0.764; yes, since 0.50 is within the interval
29. 1853   31. 89%
33. $p >$ 0.818; 81.8%

Section 6-5

1. 13.120, 40.646   3. 43.188, 79.082
5. 1.79 in. $< \sigma <$ 4.75 in.
7. 11.0 $< \sigma <$ 20.4   9. 767   11. 171
13. 38.2 mL $< \sigma <$ 95.7 mL; no, the fluctuation appears to be too high.
15. 3.0 mm $< \sigma <$ 5.0 mm
17. a. 0.33 min $< \sigma <$ 0.87 min   b. 1.25 min $< \sigma <$ 3.33 min
    c. The variation appears to be significantly lower with a single line. The single line appears to be better.
19. a. $s \approx$ 81.75
    b. 66.22 $< \sigma <$ 130.65   c. Yes (Exclude the data for Victoria)
21. a. 98%   b. 27.0

Chapter 6 Review Exercises

1. a. 22039.6 $< \mu <$ 53991.8   b. We can see (from the wide difference between mean and median) that the distribution is far from normal; but the methods in Section 6-5 have a strong requirement of normality.

2. 2944   3. 5.47 yr $< \mu <$ 8.55 yr   4. 2.92 yr $< \sigma <$ 5.20 yr
5. 0.509 $< p <$ 0.571; 3.1 percentage points   6. 221
7. n = 16, $\bar{x}$ = 72.6625, s = 2.5809236; 71.29 cm $< \mu <$ 74.04 cm
8. 36.5 $< \mu <$ 44.9   9. 110   10. 21.5% $< p <$ 26.5%

Chapter 6 Cumulative Review Exercises

1. a. 70.20 in.   b. 70.45 in.
   c. 70.4 in.   d. 69.65 in.
   e. 7.5 in.   f. 4.26 in.^{2} g. 2.07 in.   h. 68.95 in.
   i. 70.45 in.   j. 71.75 in.   k. ratio
   l.

   m. Answer varies, depending on the choices for the number of classes and the starting point. The histogram is approximately bell shaped.
   n. 69.02 in. $< \mu <$ 71.38 in.   o. 1.49 in. $< \sigma <$ 3.25 in.
   p. 707
   q. No, as neither the mean nor the variance are in the confidence intervals.
2. a. 0.0089   b. 0.260 $< p <$ 0.390
   c. Because the confidence interval limits do not contain 0.25, it is unlikely that the expert is correct.

Section 7-2

1. Reject the claim that the coin is fair.
3. Do not accept the claim that women who eat blue M&M candies have a better chance of having a boy.
5. a. $\mu \neq$ 650 mg   b. H_0: $\mu =$ 650 mg   c. H_1: $\mu \neq$ 650 mg
   d. Two-tailed
   e. The error of rejecting the claim that the mean equals 650 mg when it really does equal 650 mg.
   f. The error of failing to reject the claim that the mean is equal to 650 mg when it is really different from 650 mg.
   g. There is sufficient evidence to support the claim that the mean is different from 650 mg.
   h. There is not sufficient evidence to support the claim that the mean is different from 650 mg.
7. a. $p >$ 0.5   b. H_0: $p \leq$ 0.5   c. H_1: $p >$ 0.5   d. Right-tailed
   e. The error of rejecting the claim that she is favoured by at most 1/2 of the voters when she really is favoured by at most 1/2 of them.
   f. The error of failing to reject the claim that she is favoured by at most 1/2 of the voters when she is really favoured by more than 1/2 of them.
   g. There is sufficient evidence to support the claim that she is favoured by more than 1/2 of the voters.

h. There is not sufficient evidence to support the claim that she is favoured by more than 1/2 of the voters.

9. a. $p > 0.02$ b. $H_0: p \le 0.02$ c. $H_1: p > 0.02$ d. Right-tailed
   e. The error of rejecting the hypothesis that the proportion is at most 0.02 when it really is at most 0.02.
   f. The error of failing to reject the hypothesis that the proportion is at most 0.02 when it really is greater than 0.02.
   g. There is sufficient evidence to support the claim that the proportion is greater than 0.02.
   h. There is not sufficient evidence to support the claim that the proportion is more than 0.02.

11. a. $p < 0.1$ b. $H_0: p \ge 0.1$ c. $H_1: p < 0.1$ d. Left-tailed
    e. The error of rejecting the hypothesis that the proportion is at least 0.1 when it really is at least 0.1.
    f. The error of failing to reject the hypothesis that the proportion is at least 0.1 when it is really less than 0.1.
    g. There is sufficient evidence to support the claim that the proportion is less than 0.1.
    h. There is not sufficient evidence to support the claim that the proportion is less than 0.1.

13. 1.645   15. -2.33 17. ± 1.645 19. -1.96
21. 14.61   23. -38.82
25. There must be a fixed value of μ so that a specific normal distribution can be used for calculation of the test statistic.
27. a. 0.0294 b. 0.9706; the probability that the null hypothesis will correctly be rejected if the alternate hypothesis is true.

Section 7-3

1. Test statistic: $z = 2.00$. Critical values: $z = \pm 1.96$. Reject $H_0: \mu = 75$. There is sufficient evidence to warrant rejection of the claim that the mean equals 75. P-value: 0.0456.
3. Test statistic: $z = -0.50$. Critical value: $z = -2.05$. Fail to reject $H_0: \mu \ge 2.50$. There is not sufficient evidence to support the claim that the mean is less than 2.50. P-value: 0.3085.
5. Test statistic: $z = 1.87$. Critical values: $z = \pm 1.96$. Fail to reject $H_0: \mu = 92.14$ in. There is not sufficient evidence to support the claim that the mean is different from 92.14 in. These balls do not appear to be "juiced." P-value: 0.0614.
7. Test statistic: $z = 14.61$. Critical value: $z = 2.33$. Reject $H_0: \mu \le 0.21$. There is sufficient evidence to support the claim that the mean is greater than 0.21. Compulsive buyers do seem to get substantially higher scores than the general population. P-value: 0.0001.
9. Test statistic: $z = -1.30$. Critical value: $z = -1.645$ (assuming a significance level of 0.05). Fail to reject $H_0: \mu \ge 10\%$. There is not sufficient evidence to support the claim that Canadian equity funds fail to meet your investment criterion for foreign equity percentage. If the conclusion is a type II sampling error, it is possible that you would invest in a funds group that does not in fact meet your investment criterion. P-value: 0.0968

11. Test statistic: $z = 3.36$. Critical value: $z = \pm 2.575$. Reject $H_0: \mu = 0.075$. There is sufficient evidence to warrant rejection of the claim that the mean accident rate for young adult males undergoing voluntary treatment for substance abuse equals the general driving population's mean accident rate of 0.075. The Ministry of Transportation has grounds to encourage these at-risk drivers who are seeking help. P-value: 0.0002.
13. Test statistic: $z = -1.31$. Critical value: $z = -1.645$. Fail to reject $H_0: \mu \ge 7.5$ yr. There is not sufficient evidence to support the manager's claim that the mean is less than 7.5 yr. P-value: 0.0951.
15. Test statistic: $z = -4.22$. Critical values: $z = \pm 2.575$. There is sufficient evidence to warrant rejection of the claim that the mean is equal to 600 mg. Don't buy this cold medicine because it is not as described on the label. P-value: 0.0002.
17. Test statistic: $z = -4.16$. Critical value: $z = -2.575$. Reject $H_0: \mu \ge 12$ mo. The sample data support the claim that the mean shelf life is less than 12 months. P-value: 0.0001.
19. Test statistic: $z = -8.63$. Critical value: $z = 1.645$. Fail to reject $H_0: \mu \le 420$ hr. There is not sufficient evidence to support the claim of improved reliability. (In fact, it appears that quality has deteriorated by a significant amount.) P-value: 0.9999.
21. Test statistic: $z = -4.78$. Critical value: $z = -2.33$. Reject $H_0: \mu \ge 35$ lb. There is sufficient evidence to support the claim that the mean is less than 35 lb. P-value: 0.0001.
23. Test statistic: $z = 0.7135$. Critical value: $z = \pm 1.96$. Fail to reject $H_0: \mu = 4.5$. There is not sufficient evidence to warrant rejection of the claim that the mean of the last digits of the numbers of sitting days is 4.5. In this respect, the numbers give no evidence of inaccurate reporting. P-value: 0.4755.
25. 11.0   27. a. $\beta = 0.2176$ b. $\beta = 0.0000$

Section 7-4

1. a. ± 2.447 b. -1.796 c. 2.896
3. Test statistic: $t = -1.991$. Critical values: $t = \pm 2.201$. Fail to reject $H_0: \mu = 64.8$. There is not sufficient evidence to support the claim that the mean is not equal to 64.8. From Table A-3, we get 0.05 < P-value < 0.10; which leads to the same conclusion.
5. Test statistic: $t = 1.489$. Critical values: $t = \pm 3.250$. P-value: 0.171. Fail to reject $H_0: \mu = \$1750$ (based on either the test statistic or the P-value > 0.01). There is not sufficient evidence to warrant rejection of the claim that the prices quoted in the paper have the same mean as the industry average.
7. Test statistic: $t = 0.626$. Critical value: $t = 2.132$. Fail to reject $H_0: \mu \le 377$ yd. There is not sufficient evidence to support the scout's claim that the mean annual punt-return yardage for his recruits is greater than the mean for top-level punt returners.
9. Test statistic: $t = 4.662$. Critical values: $t = \pm 2.228$. Reject $H_0: \mu = 37.0°C$. There is sufficient evidence to warrant rejection of the claim that the mean is equal to 37.0°C.

11. Test statistic: $t = 3.344$. Critical value: $t = 2.718$. Reject H_0: $\mu \le$ $1800. There is sufficient evidence to support the claim that the mean exceeds $1800.

13. Test statistic: $z = 1.00$. Critical value: $z = 1.96$. Fail to reject H_0: $\mu \le$ $2000. There is not sufficient evidence to support the claim that the mean is greater than $2000. The new monitoring system will not be implemented.

15. Test statistic: $t = -3.408$. Critical value: $t = -2.602$. Reject H_0: $\mu \ge 10.00$. There is sufficient evidence to support the claim that the mean rating is less than 10.00.

17. Test statistic: $t = -6.158$. Critical value: $t = -2.764$. Reject H_0: $\mu \ge 2.4$ h. There is sufficient evidence to support the claim that the mean flight time is less than 2.4 h.

19. Test statistic: $t = -0.277$. Critical value: $t = -2.132$. Fail to reject H_0: $\mu \ge 0.9085$. There is not sufficient evidence to warrant rejection of the claim that the mean is at least 0.9085 g. We cannot conclude that the package contents disagree with the claimed weight printed on the label.

21. $n = 7$, $\bar{x} = 10601.2857$, $s = 1026.7175$. Test statistic: $t = -1.027$. Critical values: $t = \pm 2.447$. Fail to reject H_0: $\mu = 11,000$ kWh. There is not sufficient evidence to warrant rejection of the claim that the mean is equal to 11,000 kWh.

23. $n = 15$, $\bar{x} = 69.5$, $s = 19.3$. Test statistic: $t = 1.264$ (1.271 is more accurate). Critical value: $t = 1.761$ (assuming that $\alpha = 0.05$). Fail to reject H_0: $\mu \le 63.2$ s. There is not sufficient evidence to support the claim that the mean is greater than 63.2 s. Her new show does not appear to be significantly better.

25. Critical t changes to 2.821; P-value changes to 0.0855.

27. With $z = 1.645$, the table and the approximation both result in $t = 1.833$.

Section 7-5

1. Test statistic: $z = 2.19$. Critical values: $z = \pm 1.96$. Reject H_0: $p = 0.01$. There is sufficient evidence to warrant rejection of the claim that with scanners, 1% of sales are overcharges. Based on these results, scanners appear to increase overcharges instead of helping to avoid them. P-value: 0.0286.

3. Test statistic: $z = 1.25$. Critical value: $z = 1.645$. Fail to reject H_0: $p \le 0.04$. There is not sufficient evidence to warrant rejection of the claim that production is within control. No corrective actions appear to be necessary. P-value: 0.1056.

5. Test statistic: $z = 1.33$. Critical value: $z = 1.645$. Fail to reject H_0: $p \le 0.5$. There is not sufficient evidence to support the claim that most students don't know what the Holocaust is. P-value: 0.0918.

7. Test statistic: $z = 1.42$. Critical value: $z = 1.645$. Fail to reject H_0: $p \le 0.054$. There is not sufficient evidence to support the claim that the the proportion of civilian doctors leaving the country who are from Saskatchewan has increased from its previous rate of 5.4%. P-value: 0.0778.

9. Test statistic: $z = -1.758$. Critical value: $z = -1.645$. Reject H_0: $p \ge 0.458$. There is sufficient evidence to support the claim that the proportion of air-strike incidents involving gulls has decreased. P-value: 0.0394

11. Test statistic: $z = 5.96$. Critical values: $z = \pm 2.33$. Reject H_0: $p = 0.10$. There is sufficient evidence to warrant rejection of the claim that 10% of drivers use telephones. P-value: 0.0002.

13. Test statistic: $z = 0.99$. Critical values: $z = \pm 1.645$. Fail to reject H_0: $p = 0.08$. There is not sufficient evidence to warrant rejection of the claim that 8% of Seldane users experience drowsiness. P-value: 0.3222.

15. Test statistic: $z = -4.37$. Critical value: $z = -2.33$. Reject H_0: $p \ge 0.10$. There is sufficient evidence to support the claim that fewer than 10% of medical students prefer pediatrics. P-value: 0.0001.

17. Test statistic: $z = 0.83$. Critical value: $z = 1.28$. Fail to reject H_0: $p \le 0.5$. There is not sufficient evidence to support the claim that the majority are smoking a year after therapy. Although many of the smokers did not stop with the nicotine patch therapy, there are many who did stop smoking, so the therapy is effective for them. P-value: 0.2033.

19. Test statistic: $z = -14.00$. Critical values: $z = \pm 2.575$. Reject H_0: $p = 0.5$. There is sufficient evidence to reject the claim that half of all adults eat their fruitcakes. Fruitcake producers should consider changes. P-value: 0.0002.

21. a. $n \cdot p = 4.884$; so the condition of $np \ge 5$ and $nq \ge 5$ is not met.
    b. Using binomial probability calculations, given $n = 44$, and $p = 11.1\%$, $P(5) = 0.1860$.
    c. We do not reject the null hypothesis that the proportion of cold/flu sufferers in Ottawa is less than or equal to 11.1%, because, under that hypothesis it would not be at all unusual (probability = 0.1860) to find 5 cold/flu sufferers among 44 people tested.

23. 47% is not a possible result because, with 20 new businesses, the only possible success rates are 0%, 5%, 10%, ..., 100%.

Section 7-6

1. a. 1.735, 23.589   b. 45.642   c. 10.851

3. Test statistic: $\chi^2 = 114.586$. Critical values: $\chi^2 = 57.153$, 106.629. Reject H_0: $\sigma^2 = 43.7$ ft. There is sufficient evidence to support the claim that the standard deviation is different from 43.7 ft. Because the standard deviation seems to be larger than it was, the new production method results in less consistency and is therefore worse.

5. Test statistic: $\chi^2 = 9.016$. Critical value: $\chi^2 = 13.848$. Reject H_0: $\sigma \ge 6.2$ min. There is sufficient evidence to support the claim that there is lower variation with a single line. Although the waiting times are more consistent (so perceived by customers as fairer), the wait is not necessarily shorter.

7. Failing to meet the requirement means the standard deviation is greater than the allowed value. Test statistic: $\chi^2 = 22.036$. Critical value: $\chi^2 = 30.144$. Fail to reject H_0: $\sigma \leq 2.6$. There is not sufficient evidence to support the claim that the standard deviation for the X-ray tubes' peak-value voltages is greater than the permitted value of 2.6 kV.

9. Test statistic: $\chi^2 = 44.800$. Critical value: $\chi^2 = 51.739$. Reject H_0: $\sigma \geq 0.15$ oz. There is sufficient evidence to support the claim that the new machine fills bottles with lower variation. Based on the sample variation, the new machine should be purchased.

11. Test statistic: $\chi^2 = 69.135$. Critical value: $\chi^2 = 67.505$ (approximately). Reject H_0: $\sigma \leq 19.7$. There is sufficient evidence to support the claim that women have more variation.

13. $s = 2.340$. Test statistic: $\chi^2 = 15.628$. Critical values: $\chi^2 = 12.401, 39.364$ (assuming $\alpha = 0.05$). Fail to reject H_0: $\sigma = 2.9$ in. There is not sufficient evidence to support the claim that the standard deviation is different from 2.9 in.

15. a. $0.01 < P\text{-value} < 0.02$ b. $P\text{-value} < 0.005$
    c. $0.005 < P\text{-value} < 0.01$

17. a. Estimated values: 74.216, 129.565; Table A-4 values: 74.222, 129.561
    b. $\chi^2 = 117.093, 184.690$

19. Yes, this can happen. Try changing the first value in Example 13 to 48 (a rather moderate example of an outlier); χ^2 jumps almost fourfold in value, and this reverses the conclusion of the hypothesis test.

Chapter 7 Review Exercises

1. a. $t = -1.833$ b. $z = \pm2.575$ c. $\chi^2 = 8.907, 32.852$
2. a. $z = \pm1.645$ b. $\chi^2 = 19.023$ c. $z = -2.33$
3. a. $\mu = \$90,000$ b. Two-tailed
   c. Rejecting the claim that the mean equals $90,000 when it actually does equal that amount.
   d. Failing to reject the claim that the mean equals $90,000 when it is actually different from that amount.
   e. 0.05
4. a. $\sigma \geq 15$ s
   b. Left-tailed
   c. Rejecting the claim that the standard deviation is at least 15 s when it actually is at least 15 s.
   d. Failing to reject the claim that the standard deviation is at least 15 s when it is actually less than 15 s.
   e. 0.01
5. Not having one's teeth checked during the survey period means not having them checked annually. Test statistic: $z = 3.11$. Critical value: $z = 2.33$. Reject H_0: $p \leq 0.25$. There is sufficient evidence to support the claim that more than a quarter of people with dental insurance do not have their teeth checked annually.
6. Test statistic: $z = -2.73$. Critical value: $z = -2.33$. Reject

H_0: $\mu \geq 5.00$. There is sufficient evidence to support the claim that the mean radiation dosage is below 5.00 mR.

7. Test statistic: $\chi^2 = 20.429$. The critical value is between 14.954 and 22.164, but it should be close to 18.559. Fail to reject H_0: $\sigma \geq 2.50$ mR. There is not sufficient evidence to support the claim that the standard deviation is less than 2.50 mR. If the standard deviation is too high, there may be some machines that emit dangerously high levels of radiation.

8. Test statistic: $z = 0.78$. Critical value: $z = 2.33$. Fail to reject H_0: $p \leq 0.267$. There is not sufficient evidence to support the claim that the proportion of farms with gross receipts over $100,000 is greater than it was in the 1991 census.

9. Test statistic: $t = -2.758$. Critical value: $t = -2.500$. Reject H_0: $\mu \geq 355$ mL. There is sufficient evidence to support the claim that the mean contents of the company's cola cans is less than the amount printed on the cans. If this is intentional, it would be cheating customers.

10. $\bar{x} = 23.29$, $s = 4.53$. Test statistic: $t = 3.240$. Critical values: $t = \pm2.861$. Reject H_0: $\mu = 20$ mg. There is sufficient evidence to warrant rejection of the claim that the mean equals 20 mg. These pills are unacceptable because their contents do not correspond to the label.

11. Test statistic: $\chi^2 = 11.402$. Critical values: $\chi^2 = 2.180, 17.535$. Fail to reject H_0: $\sigma = 188.3$ days. There is not sufficient evidence to support the claim that the standard deviation is different from 188.3 days.

Chapter 7 Cumulative Review Exercises

1. a. 0.2358
   b. 0.0020
2. a. $\bar{x} = 124.23$, $s = 22.52$
   b. Test statistic: $t = 1.675$. Critical values: $t = \pm2.132$. Fail to reject H_0: $\mu = 114.8$. There is not sufficient evidence to warrant rejection of the claim that the mean is equal to 114.8.
   c. $112.23 < \mu < 136.23$; yes
   d. Test statistic: $\chi^2 = 44.339$. Critical values: $\chi^2 = 6.262$, 27.488. Reject H_0: $\sigma = 13.1$. There is sufficient evidence to warrant rejection of the claim that the standard deviation is equal to 13.1.
   e. Although the mean does not appear to change by a significant amount, the variation among the values appears to be significantly larger.
3. a. 6.3
   b. 2.2
   c. 0.0024 (or 0.0019 if unrounded statistics are used)
   d. Based on the low probability value in part (c), reject H_0: $p = 0.25$. There is sufficient evidence to reject the claim that the subject made random guesses.
   e. 423

4. a.

35.	24
35.	5689
36.	0111223333344444444
36.	555666667777788899
37.	0011111344
37.	6

   b. The distribution appears to be approximately normal.

   c. A histogram could also be used to test for a normal distribution.

Section 8-2

1. a. $\bar{d} = 2.8$

   b. $s_d = 3.6$

   c. $t = 1.757$

   d. $t = \pm 2.776$

3. $-1.6 < \mu_d < 7.2$

5. a. Test statistic: $t = -1.496$. Critical values: $t = \pm 2.447$. Fail to reject H_0: $\mu_d = 0$. There is not sufficient evidence to support the claim that the progression of an El Niño from the spring of onset to the next spring affects temperature departures from spring seasonal norms.

   b. $-2.30 < \mu_d < 0.55$. We have 95% confidence that the interval from -2.30 to 0.55 really does contain the true population mean difference.

7. a. If sales are growing, the mean difference (1987 minus 1997) will be negative. Test statistic: $t = -1.774$. Critical value: $t = -1.833$. Fail to reject H_0: $\mu_d < 0$. There is not sufficient evidence to support the claim that the fastest-growing companies do grow in sales after 10 years.

   b. $-22.18 < \mu_d < 2.68$

9. a. Test statistic: $t = 0.384$. Critical values: $t = \pm 2.306$. Fail to reject H_0: $\mu_d = 0$. There is not sufficient evidence to reject the claim that the starting salaries of university graduates in Ontario and Quebec are equal. In both provinces, graduates with comparable degrees appear to earn about the same starting income.

   b. $-1223.65 < \mu_d < 1712.53$

11. a. Test statistic: $t = -0.101$. Critical values: $t = \pm 2.365$. Fail to reject H_0: $\mu_d = 0$. There is not enough evidence to support the claim that simply adding a third word to the search strings makes any difference in the mean number of words returned by the browser.

   b. $0.711 < \mu_1 - \mu_2 < 6.674$

13. a. $0.402 < \mu_d < 0.657$

   b. Test statistic: $t = 9.247$. Critical values: $t = \pm 2.228$. Reject H_0: $\mu_d = 0$. There is sufficient evidence to reject the claim that temperatures are the same in the two postures. The differences in body temperatures for the two postures are not large, but they are significant.

15. Yes, the value of 64 ($64 million) for 1997 is far removed from all the other data. If the data pair that includes 64 is excluded from the analysis, the t test results are reversed: Test statistic t changes from -1.774 to -2.476; the critical value changes from -1.833 to -1.860. As a result, we now reject H_0: $\mu_d < 0$. The confidence interval changes dramatically, to $-8.692 < \mu_d < -0.308$. Yes, as shown here.

17. $\alpha = 0.025$

Section 8-3

1. Test statistic: $z = 0.79$. Critical values: $z = \pm 1.96$. Fail to reject H_0: $\mu_1 = \mu_2$. There is not sufficient evidence to warrant rejection of the claim that the two samples come from populations with the same mean.

3. $-3 < \mu_1 - \mu_2 < 7$; yes. The control group and experimental group do not appear to be significantly different.

5. a. Test statistic: $z = -0.47$. Critical values: $z = \pm 2.575$. Fail to reject H_0: $\mu_1 = \mu_2$. There is not enough evidence to reject the claim that there is no difference in foreign content between Canadian equity funds and Canadian balanced equity funds.

   b. $-5.74 < \mu_1 - \mu_2 < 3.78$

7. a. Test statistic: $z = 2.06$. Critical values: $z = \pm 2.575$. Fail to reject H_0: $\mu_1 = \mu_2$. There is not sufficient evidence to warrant rejection of the claim that the two populations have the same mean. Advertise, because there does not appear to be a difference.

   b. $-3.5 < \mu_1 - \mu_2 < 31.5$

9. a. H_0: $\mu_1 \leq \mu_2$ and H_1: $\mu_1 > \mu_2$. Test statistic: $z = 0.28$. Critical value: $z = 1.645$. Fail to reject H_0: $\mu_1 \leq \mu_2$. There is not sufficient evidence to support the claim that faculty whose last names begin with A to R earn more than faculty whose last names begin with S to Z.

   b. $-8.31 < \mu_1 - \mu_2 < 11.11$. Yes. This indicates that there is not a significant difference between the two means.

11. a. Test statistic: $z = -2.54$. Critical value: $z = -2.05$. Reject H_0: $\mu_1 \geq \mu_2$. There is sufficient evidence to support the claim that non-smokers with exposure to environmental tobacco smoke have higher levels of serum cotinine than nonsmokers without such exposure.

   b. $-6.674 < \mu_1 - \mu_2 < -0.711$. No. Yes, exposed nonsmokers appear to have significantly raised levels of serum cotinine.

13. Test statistic: $z = -0.954$. Critical value: $z = -1.645$. Fail to reject H_0: $\mu_1 \geq \mu_2$. There is not sufficient evidence to support the claim that the population of smaller communities has a higher mean value for building permits issued.

15. a. Test statistic: $z = -3.95$. Critical values: $z = \pm 1.96$. Reject H_0: $\mu_1 = \mu_2$. There is sufficient evidence to reject the claim that male and female statistics students have the same mean pulse rate.

b. P-value (based on tables) = 0.0002 < α = 0.05; reject H_0: $\mu_1 = \mu_2$.

c. $-13.2 < \mu_1 - \mu_2 < -4.4$; reject H_0: $\mu_1 = \mu_2$.

d. The results all agree.

17. P-value = 0.0278 > α = 0.02. Fail to reject H_0: $\mu_1 = \mu_2$. There is not sufficient evidence to support the claim that the treatment group comes from a population with a different mean from the mean for the placebo population. (Note: The critical values shown in the display do not apply, since they are based on α = 0.05.)

19. The boxplot for the 0.0111 in. cans uses a 5-number summary of 205, 275, 285, 294, 317. Before the deletion of the outlier, the 5-number summary was 205, 275, 285, 295, 504, so the only major change is shortening of the right whisker. In the hypothesis test, the test statistic changes from -5.48 to -5.66, so the conclusions will be the same. After deleting the outlier of 504, the confidence interval limits change from $(-21.6, -7.8)$ to $(-19.5, -7.3)$, so those changes are not substantial.

21. a. 50/3   b. 2/3   c. 52/3

e. The range of the x-y values equals the range of the x values plus the range of the y values.

Section 8-4

1. Test statistic: $F = 2.2222$. Critical value: $F = 2.2090$. Reject H_0: $\sigma_1^2 = \sigma_2^2$. There is sufficient evidence to support the claim that the two population variances are different.

3. Test statistic: $F = 1.2949$. Critical value: $F = 1.6928$ (approximately). Fail to reject H_0: $\sigma_1 = \sigma_2$. There is not sufficient evidence to support the claim that the samples come from populations with different standard deviations.

5. Although these samples are not truly independent—they involve the same individuals—we do not possess the "before" and "after" data pairs for each specific individual that methods based on *dependent* samples would require. Test statistic: $F = 1.7831$. Critical value: $F = 1.3272$. (If using table, can use df$_1$ = df$_2$ = 120. $F = 1.3519$.) Reject H_0: $\sigma_1 \leq \sigma_2$. There is evidence to support the claim that the individuals who have received treatment represent a population with a standard deviation for an accident rate which is greater than the standard deviation for the accident rate among those who have not yet received treatment. (Due to the dependency in that data, apply this conclusion only for individuals who do go on to get treatment at some point.)

7. Test statistic: $F = 1.1142$. Critical value: $F = 1.9508$. (If using table, can use df$_1$ = 40 and df$_2$ = 30, F = 2.0089) Fail to reject H_0: $\sigma_1 = \sigma_2$. There is not sufficient evidence to reject the claim that the standard deviation for shelf life is the same at both plants.

9. Test statistic: $F = 1.1707$. Critical value: $F = 5.4613$. Fail to reject H_0: $\sigma_1^2 = \sigma_2^2$. There is not sufficient evidence to warrant rejection of the claim that both groups of flight times come from populations with the same variance.

11. Test statistic: $F = 2.234$. Critical value: $F = 3.912$. (If using table, can use df$_1$ = 10; df$_2$ = 9. $F = 3.9639$.) Fail to reject H_0: $\sigma_1 = \sigma_2$. There is not sufficient evidence to reject the claim that both groups of ages come from populations with the same variance.

13. a. Reject H_0: $\sigma_1^2 = \sigma_2^2$.
    b. Fail to reject H_0: $\sigma_1^2 = \sigma_2^2$.
    c. Reject H_0: $\sigma_1^2 = \sigma_2^2$.

15. a. $F_L = 0.2484$, $F_R = 4.0260$
    b. $F_L = 0.2315$, $F_R = 5.5234$
    c. $F_L = 0.1810$, $F_R = 4.3197$
    d. $F_L = 0.3071$, $F_R = 4.7290$
    e. $F_L = 0.2115$, $F_R = 3.2560$

17. a. It doesn't change.
    b. It doesn't change.
    c. It doesn't change.

Section 8-5

1. F-test results: Test statistic is $F = 1.5625$. Critical value: $F = 2.8801$. Fail to reject $\sigma_1^2 = \sigma_2^2$. Test of means: Test statistic is $t = -0.990$. Critical values: $t = \pm 2.048$. Fail to reject H_0: $\mu_1 = \mu_2$. There is not sufficient evidence to warrant rejection of the claim that the two populations have equal means.

3. $-15 < \mu_1 - \mu_2 < 5$

5. a. $0.1748 < \mu_1 - \mu_2 < 0.4373$; no. There is sufficient evidence to reject the equality of mean flight times in both directions.
   b. Test statistic: $t = 4.945$. Critical values: $t = 1.746$. P-value = 0.00007338. Reject H_0: $\mu_1 \leq \mu_2$ There is sufficient evidence to support the claim that flights from Vancouver to San Francisco take longer.

7. a. F-test results: Test statistic: $F = 1.1276$. Using a Computer: Critical value: $F = 2.1952$. Fail to reject H_0: $\sigma_1^2 = \sigma_2^2$. Test of means: Test statistic: $t = 0.132$. Critical values: $t = \pm 1.975$. Fail to reject H_0: $\mu_1 = \mu_2$. There is not sufficient evidence to reject the claim that the past clients of both clinics have the same mean accident rate. The competing clinic is not justified in making its boast.
   b. $-0.097 < \mu_1 - \mu_2 < 0.111$

9. Test statistic: $t = 1.243$. Critical value: $t = 1.701$. Fail to reject H_0: $\mu_1 \leq \mu_2$. There is not sufficient evidence to support the claim that less flawed ("clearer") diamonds sell at a higher price than more flawed diamonds. Inspection of the raw data shows that, for the sampled high-quality diamonds, clarity never exceeds 5 (higher numbers indicate more visible flaws). To be sure that clarity is unrelated to price, we would need to also sample diamonds where clarity exceeds 5.

11. F-test results: Test statistic is $F = 2.9459$. Critical value: $F = 3.0074$. Fail to reject H_0: $\sigma_1^2 = \sigma_2^2$. Test of means: Test statistic is $t = -1.099$. Critical values: $t = \pm 2.052$. Fail to reject H_0: $\mu_1 = \mu_2$. There is not sufficient evidence to warrant rejection of the

claim that red and orange M&Ms have the same mean weight. No corrective action is necessary.

13. F-test results: Test statistic: $F = 5.2849$. Critical value: $F = 2.7689$. Reject H_0: $\sigma_1^2 = \sigma_2^2$. Test of means: Test statistic: $t = -2.295$. Critical values: $t = \pm 2.179$ (based on the approximate method for finding df). Reject H_0: $\mu_1 = \mu_2$. There is sufficient evidence to reject the claim that the East and West have the same mean annual precipitation.

15. Test statistic: $t = 1.301$. Critical values: $t = \pm 2.086$. Fail to reject H_0: $\mu_1 = \mu_2$. There is not sufficient evidence to reject the claim that the ages of CEOs from top growth companies in Western Canada and in Quebec are the same.

17. F-test results: The test statistic doesn't exist, because it would be calculated with division by 0. However, the standard deviations do not appear to be equal, so reject H_0: $\sigma_1^2 = \sigma_2^2$. Test of means: Test statistic is $t = 15.322$. Critical values: $t = \pm 2.080$. Reject H_0: $\mu_1 = \mu_2$. There is sufficient evidence to warrant rejection of the claim that the two groups come from populations with the same mean. (There is a serious question about the requirement that the samples come from normally distributed populations, because the 22 scores in the second sample appear to be the same.)

19. The number of degrees of freedom changes from 9 to 10. The test statistic doesn't change, the critical value changes from $t = 1.833$ to $t = 1.812$, but the conclusions remain the same. The confidence interval limits change from $(-16.6, 192.6)$ to $(-15.1, 191.1)$.

Section 8-6

1. a. 8/15
   b. -0.58
   c. ± 1.96
   d. 0.5620
3. 49
5. Test statistic: $z = 2.17$. Critical value: $z = 1.645$. Reject H_0: $p_1 \leq p_2$. There is sufficient evidence to support the claim that Facility A has the greater proportion of product that contains below half the allowable level of foreign matter. We cannot conclude from this that Facility A necessarily has a more consistent level of quality than Facility B. For example, of the 70% of Facility A's output which is not below half the allowable level of foreign matter, we have no indication of how much extra impurity these samples contain.
7. Test statistic: $z = -2.85$. Critical value: $z = -2.33$. Reject H_0: $p_1 \geq p_2$. There is sufficient evidence support the claim that fewer people, proportionally, support free trade in 2001 than in 1999. Yes. If, for example, n was 500 in 1999, the test statistic would change to $z = -2.31$, resulting in non-rejection of H_0: $p_1 \geq p_2$.
9. a. Test statistic: $z = -0.41$. Critical values: $z = \pm 2.575$. Fail to reject H_0: $p_1 = p_2$. There is not sufficient evidence to reject the claim that both industry groups have the same proportion of companies with a foreign ownership level of at least 10%.
   b. $-0.40 < p_1 - p_2 < 0.29$

11. Test statistic: $z = 3.86$. Critical value: $z = 2.33$. Reject H_0: $p_1 \leq p_2$. There is sufficient evidence to support the claim that arson is committed by a proportion of drinkers that is greater than the proportion of drinkers convicted of fraud. It does seem reasonable that drinking would have an effect on the type of crime.

13. Test statistic: $z = 4.47$. Critical value: $z = \pm 2.575$. Reject H_0: $p_1 = p_2$. There is sufficient evidence to reject the claim that the central-city refusal rate is the same as the refusal rate in other areas.

15. $-0.052 < p_1 - p_2 < 0.184$. Yes. There is no significant difference between the proportions of home wins for basketball and for football. To decide whether there is a home advantage at all, we would have to see whether each sport's individual confidence intervals for p at home include the value 0.50.

17. Test statistic: $z = 0.84$. Critical values: $z = \pm 1.96$. Fail to reject H_0: $p_1 - p_2 = 0.1$. There is not sufficient evidence to warrant rejection of the claim that when women are exposed to glycol ethers, their percentage of miscarriages is 10 percentage points more than the percentage for women not exposed to glycol ethers.

19. 2135

Chapter 8 Review Exercises

1. Test statistic: $z = 2.41$. Critical value: $z = 1.645$. Reject H_0: $p_1 \leq p_2$. There is sufficient evidence to support the claim that the percentage of people who stop after first seeing someone else being helped is greater than the percentage of people who stop without first seeing someone else being helped.

2. a. Test statistic: $t = -3.847$. Critical value: $t = -1.796$. Reject H_0: $\mu_d \geq 0$. There is sufficient evidence to support the claim that the Dozenol tablets are more soluble after the storage period.
   b. $12.4 < \mu_d < 45.6$

3. a. Test statistic: $z = 4.48$. Critical value: $z = 1.645$ (assuming a 0.05 significance level). Reject H_0: $p_1 \leq p_2$. There is sufficient evidence to support the claim that dyspepsia occurs at a higher rate among Viagra users.
   b. $0.0277 < p_1 - p_2 < 0.0699$; no; they are significantly different.

4. Test statistic: $t = -3.356$. Critical value: $t = \pm 3.106$ (based on the approximate method for finding df). Reject H_0: $\mu_1 = \mu_2$. There is sufficient evidence to reject the claim that the mean price for both types of flight is the same.

5. Test statistic: $F = 5.4505$. Critical values: $F = 4.2509$. Reject H_0: $\sigma_1^2 = \sigma_2^2$. The samples provide evidence to reject the claim of equal variances in the cost data for the two types of flights.

6. Test statistic: $z = 3.67$. Critical value: $z = 1.645$. Reject H_0: $p_1 \leq p_2$. There is sufficient evidence to support the claim that the

question was answered correctly by a greater proportion of pre-pared students.

7. Test statistic: $t = 1.185$. Critical values: $t = \pm 2.262$. Fail to reject H_0: $\mu_d = 0$. There is not sufficient evidence to warrant rejection of the claim that the position has no effect.

8. Test statistic: $z = 0.96$. Critical value: $z = 2.33$. Fail to reject H_0: $\mu_1 \leq \mu_2$. There is not sufficient evidence to support the claim that the 10-day program results in scores with a lower mean.

9. F-test results: Test statistic is $F = 12.0013$. Critical value: $F = 2.5598$. Reject H_0: $\sigma_1^2 = \sigma_2^2$. Test of means: Test statistic is $t = 2.444$. Critical values: $t = \pm 2.110$. Reject H_0: $\mu_1 = \mu_2$. There is sufficient evidence to warrant rejection of the claim that both systems have the same mean.

10. a. F-test results: Test statistic is $F = 2.3623$. Critical value: $F = 3.4737$. Fail to reject H_0: $\sigma_1^2 = \sigma_2^2$. Test of means: Test statis-tic: $t = -1.335$. Critical values: $t = \pm 2.074$. Fail to reject H_0: $\mu_1 = \mu_2$. There is not sufficient evidence to reject the claim that men and women in these circumstances have the same mean temperature.

   b. $-0.659 < \mu_1 - \mu_2 < 0.143$

Chapter 8 Cumulative Review Exercises

1. a. 0.0707
   b. 0.369
   c. 0.104
   d. 0.054
   e. Test statistic: $z = -2.52$. Critical value: $z = -1.645$. Reject H_0: $p_1 \geq p_2$. There is sufficient evidence to support the claim that women are ticketed at a lower rate. We cannot conclude that men generally speed more, only that they are ticketed more. Perhaps men drive more or perhaps they are more likely to get a ticket when speeding.

2. a. Test statistic: $z = 1.95$. Critical values: $z = \pm 1.96$. Fail to reject H_0: $\mu = 0$. There is not sufficient evidence to warrant rejection of the claim that the sample comes from a popula-tion with a mean equal to 0.

   b. Test statistic: $z = -1.87$. Critical values: $z = \pm 1.96$. Fail to reject H_0: $\mu = 0$. There is not sufficient evidence to warrant rejection of the claim that the sample comes from a popula-tion with a mean equal to 0.

   c. Test statistic is $z = 2.68$. Critical values: $z = \pm 1.96$. Reject H_0: $\mu_1 = \mu_2$. There is sufficient evidence to warrant rejection of the claim that both shifts manufacture scales with the same mean error.

   d. $0.0\,g < \mu < 2.4\,g$
   e. $-2.9\,g < \mu < 0.1\,g$
   f. $0.7\,g < \mu_1 - \mu_2 < 4.5\,g$
   g. 234

Section 9-2

1. a. Significant linear correlation; 98.4%
   b. Significant linear correlation; 11.1%
   c. No significant linear correlation; 20.8%

3. a. Significant linear correlation
   b. $n = 5$, $\Sigma x = 25$, $\Sigma x^2 = 163$, $(\Sigma x)^2 = 625$, $\Sigma xy = 489$, $r = 0.997$

5. Test statistic: $r = 0.993$. Critical values: $r = \pm 0.707$. Reject the claim of no significant linear correlation. There does appear to be a linear correlation between chest size and weight. The results do not change if the chest measurements are converted to feet.

7. Test statistic: $r = 0.841$. Critical values: $r = \pm 0.707$. Reject the claim of no significant linear correlation. There does appear to be a linear correlation between weight of discarded plastic and household size.

9. a. Test statistic: $r = 0.819$. Critical value: $r = \pm 0.602$. Reject the null hypothesis of no significant correlation. There does appear to be a significant correlation between species' incubation and fledgling periods.

   b. For samples created by randomly selecting one individual bird from each of the 11 species, the mean r approaches the r cal-culated in (a); since randomly selected higher or lower values for incubation or fledgling periods will tend to cancel out. For samples created by randomly selecting *any* 11 birds from among the 11 species (not necessarily one per species), the mean of the r's is greater than in (a); because the correlation is weak for a few of the species, and by chance, many samples will not include data from those species.

11. Test statistic: $r = +0.772$. Critical values: $r = \pm 0.497$. Reject the claim of no significant linear correlation. There does appear to be a linear correlation between salary and years of education.

13. a. Test statistic: $r = 0.870$. Critical values: $r = \pm 0.279$. Reject the claim of no significant linear correlation. There does appear to be a linear correlation between the interval after an eruption and the duration of the eruption.

   b. Test statistic: $r = -.00978$. Critical value: $r = \pm 0.279$. Do not reject the null hypothesis of no significant correlation. There does not appear to be a correlation between the interval after an eruption and the height of an eruption.

   c. For predicting the time interval after an eruption before the next eruption, eruption duration would be more relevant than height—because, of these two, only duration has a significant correlation to the time interval.

15. a. Test statistic: $r = 0.767$. Critical values: $r = \pm 0.361$. Significant linear correlation.

   b. Test statistic: $r = -0.441$. Critical values: $r = \pm 0.361$. Significant linear correlation.

   c. Part (a) because there is a higher correlation.

17. Test statistic: $r = 0.199$. Critical values: $r = \pm 0.279$ (approxi-mately). Fail to reject the claim of no significant linear correla-

tion. There does not appear to be a linear correlation between annual spring temperature departures and precipitation departures from seasonal norms. This does not directly contradict the results from Exercise 14. Exercise 14 compares temperature and precipitation data for individual cities; Exercise 17 aggregates (combines) data from all across Canada into single, annual values.

19. With a linear correlation coefficient very close to 0, there does not appear to be a correlation, but the conclusion suggests that there is a correlation.

21. Although there is no *linear* correlation, the variables may be related in some other *nonlinear* way.

23. In parts (a), (b), and (c), the value of r does not change.

25. a. ± 0.272
    b. ± 0.189
    c. -0.378
    d. 0.549
    e. 0.658

27. The apparent correlation between earthquake magnitude and latitude is conditional on an earthquake's being detected. Earthquakes *detected* at higher latitudes tend to have greater magnitude, but we do not know whether *all* earthquakes (even undetected ones) tend to have greater magnitudes in the North.

Section 9-3

1. $\hat{y} = 1 + 2x$ 3. $\hat{y} = 0 + 3x$ 5. $\hat{y} = -187 + 11.3x$; 399 lb

7. $\hat{y} = 0.549 + 3.27x$; 1.4 persons

9. $\hat{y} = -56.4 + 4.63x$; 110.3 days.

11. $\hat{y} = -36.1 + 5.58x$; $36,400 (36.4, in $1000s). No; for the three samples with $x = 13$, the actual incomes range from $27,220 to $37,620.

13. a. $\bar{y} = 41.9 + 0.179x$; 79 min
    b. Use $\bar{y} = 80.7$ min.
    c. Use part (a), since part (b) simply uses mean y for prediction, but the significant regression explains some of the variation of data from the mean.

15. a. $\bar{y} = -9175.3 + 18179x$; $18,093
    b. $\hat{y} = 42684 - 4535.9x$; $29,076
    c. Part (a) because the carat (weight) has a higher correlation with price.

17. $\hat{y} = 0.633 + 1.70x$; -0.90%

19. a. 10.00   b. 2.50

21. It is not an outlier because the point lies relatively close to the other data in the sample. It is not an influential point because it does not appreciably change the position or slope of the regression line.

23. $\hat{y} = -182 + 0.000351x$; $\hat{y} = -182 + 0.351x$. The slope is multiplied by 1000 and the y-intercept doesn't change. If each y entry is divided by 1000, the slope and y-intercept are both divided by 1000.

25. The linear equation $\hat{y} = -49.9 + 27.2x$ is better because it has $r = 0.997$, which is higher than $r = 0.963$ for $\hat{y} = -103.2 + 134.9 \ln x$.

27. Linear equation: $\hat{y} = 58.38 - 1.88x$
                            $r = 0.597$; not significant
    Exponential equation: $\hat{y} = 50.744e^{-0.1507x}$
                            $r = 0.942$; significant

    The exponential equation; because the correlation using the transformed data has the higher r value, and tests as significant.

Section 9-4

1. 0.04; 4%   3. 0.051; 5.1%

5. a. 154.8   b. 0   c. 154.8   d. 1   e. 0

7. a. 13.788646   b. 5.711257   c. 19.5   d. 0.70711
   e. 0.9756

9. a. 14
   b. Because $s_e = 0$, $E = 0$ and there is no "interval" estimate.

11. a. 4.64 persons   b. $1.95 < y < 7.32$

13. $11,800 < y < $49,900   15. $23,400 < y < $55,100

17. $-7.9004 < \beta_0 < 1.7990; 0.0167 < \beta_1 < 0.1847$

19. a. $(n-2)s_e^2$

    b. $\dfrac{r^2 \cdot \text{(unexplained variation)}}{1 - r^2}$ c. $r = -0.949$

21. $-68.77 < \text{intercept} < -3.35; 2.95 < x \text{ coefficient} < 8.21$

Section 9-5

1. $\hat{y} = -2.03 + 0.0690x_1 + 0.00870x_2 - 0.0262x_3$

3. Of limited usefulness. With a P-value of 0.00015, the equation has overall significance. However, the low r suggests that actual y values may vary considerably from predicted values.

5. a. $\hat{y} = -274 + 0.426x_1 + 12.1x_2$ b. 0.928; 0.925; 0.000 (Excel's P-value of 7.4×10^{-30} is a *very* small number.)
   c. Yes

7. a. $\hat{y} = -235 + 0.403x_1 + 5.11x_2 - 0.555x_3 + 9.19x_4$
   b. 0.942; 0.938; 0.000 (in Excel, 1.1×10^{-29})   c. Yes

9. a. $\hat{y} = 3.56 + 0.0980x_1$ b. 0.021; 0.005; 0.256   c. No

11. a. $\hat{y} = 1.15 + 1.41x_1 - 0.0144x_2$ b. 0.564; 0.549; 0.000 (Excel's P-value of 2.33×10^{-11} is a *very* small number.)
    c. Yes

13. a. $\hat{y} = 0.554 + 0.491x_1 + 1.08x_2$ b. 0.613; 0.600; 0.000 (in Excel, 7×10^{-13})   c. Yes

15. $\hat{y} = 163 - 12.5x_1 + 0.120x_2$ (where x_1 represents annual temperature). A qualified yes: The P-value = 0.0017, so the regression results are significant. Yet the R^2 value of only 0.356 indicates a great deal of unexplained variation in actual y values. (Also, note that the x_i's are averages, so the equation should be used advisedly for day-by-day predictions.)

17. $\hat{y} = 2.17 + 2.44x + 0.464x^2$. Because $R^2 = 1$, the parabola fits perfectly.

Chapter 9 Review Exercises

1. a. Test statistic: $r = 0.320$. Critical values: $r = \pm 0.632$. Fail to reject the claim of no significant correlation. There does not appear to be a linear correlation between consumption and price.
   b. $\hat{y} = -0.258 + 0.189x$ c. 0.202
2. a. Test statistic: $r = 0.112$. Critical values: $r = \pm 0.632$. Fail to reject the claim of no significant linear correlation. There does not appear to be a linear correlation between consumption and income.
   b. $\hat{y} = 0.0421 + 0.000283x$ c. 0.2011
3. a. Test statistic: $r = 0.784$. Critical values: $r = \pm 0.632$. Reject the claim of no significant correlation. There does appear to be a linear correlation between consumption and temperature.
   b. $\hat{y} = 0.162 + 0.00305x$ c. 0.162
4. $\hat{y} = 0.0301 + 0.250x_1 - 0.000862x_2 + 0.00317x_3$; $R^2 = 0.736$; adjusted $R^2 = 0.605$; P-value $= 0.0358$. This equation is a good predictor of ice cream consumption; but accounting for adjusted R^2, the equation from Exercise 3 is better.
5. a. Test statistic: $r = -0.976$. Critical values: $r = \pm 0.632$. Reject the claim of no significant correlation. There does appear to be a linear correlation between starting position and qualifying speed.
   b. $\hat{y} = 667.138 - 6.036x$ c. 9 (rounded from 8.8)
6. a. Test statistic: $r = 0.598$. Critical values: $r = \pm 0.632$. Fail to reject the claim of no significant linear correlation. There does not appear to be a linear correlation between qualifying speeds and points.
   b. $\hat{y} = -421 + 3.95x$ c. 10
7. $5.99 < y < 11.71$
8. $\hat{y} = -245 - 1.05x_1 + 4.48x_2$; $R^2 = 0.402$; adjusted $R^2 = 0.231$; P-value $= 0.166$. The multiple regression is not usable for predicting points, because the P-value is 0.166 and the adjusted R^2 is very small.

Chapter 9 Cumulative Review Exercises

1. $n = 50$, $\bar{x} = 80.7$, $s = 12.0$.
   a. Test statistic: $z = 8.66$. Critical value: $z = 1.645$ (assuming $\alpha = 0.05$). Reject H_0: $\mu \leq 66$. There is sufficient evidence to support the claim that the mean interval is now longer than 66 min.
   b. $77.3 < \mu < 84.0$
2. (Use the methods of Section 8-2 for two matched samples.) Test statistic: $t = 10.319$. Critical values: $t = \pm 2.365$ (assuming $\alpha = 0.05$). Reject H_0: $\mu_d = 0$. There does appear to be a significant difference between the scores on the humorous commercial and those on the serious commercial. The humorous commercial appears to have higher scores and is therefore better. The issue of correlation is not relevant here; the issue is whether either commercial gets significantly higher scores than the other, not whether the scores are related.
3. Test for a significant linear correlation between the two variables: Test statistic: $r = 0.702$. Critical values: $r = \pm 0.576$ (assuming $\alpha = 0.05$). Reject the claim of no significant linear correlation. There does appear to be a significant linear correlation between the IQs of identical twins who were raised apart. Because $r^2 = 0.493$, we can conclude that 49.3% of the total variation in the IQs of the younger twins can be explained by the variation in IQs of the older twins. This suggests that 49.3% of the variation in IQs can be explained by heredity, and the other 50.7% is attributable to other factors.

Section 10-2

1. Test statistic: $\chi^2 = 156.500$. Critical value: $\chi^2 = 21.666$. Reject H_0: The last digits occur with the same frequency. There is sufficient evidence to warrant rejection of the claim that the last digits occur with equal frequency. It appears that the students reported their weights.
3. a. df $= 37$, so $\chi^2 = 51.805$ (approximately)
   b. $0.10 < P\text{-value} < 0.90$
   c. There is not sufficient evidence to warrant rejection of the claim that the roulette slots are equally likely.
5. Test statistic: $\chi^2 = 5.185$. Critical value: $\chi^2 = 7.815$. There is not sufficient evidence to reject the claim that the work stoppages occur in the proportions indicated.
7. Test statistic: $\chi^2 = 23.431$. Critical value: $\chi^2 = 9.488$. Reject H_0: Accidents are distributed with the given percentages. There is sufficient evidence to warrant rejection of the claim that accidents are distributed with the given percentages. Rejection of the claim does not provide help in correcting the problem.
9. Test statistic: $\chi^2 = 4.200$. Critical value: $\chi^2 = 16.919$. Fail to reject H_0: The digits are uniformly distributed. There is not sufficient evidence to warrant rejection of the claim that the digits are uniformly distributed.
11. Test statistic: $\chi^2 = 8.381$. Critical value: $\chi^2 = 12.592$. Fail to reject H_0: The distribution of discounts is consistent with Zellers promotional claims. The data do not provide sufficient evidence to warrant rejection of the claim that discounts based on using Zellers' "Scratch and Save" cards are distributed in the proportions indicated.
13. Test statistic: $\chi^2 = 11.800$. Critical value: $\chi^2 = 9.488$ (assuming $\alpha = 0.05$). Reject H_0: The time intervals are uniformly distributed among the five categories. There is sufficient evidence to warrant rejection of the claim that the time intervals are uniformly distributed among the five categories.
15. Test statistic: $\chi^2 = 10.400$. Critical value: $\chi^2 = 7.815$. Reject H_0: The returns were evenly distributed among the four categories.

There is sufficient evidence to warrant rejection of the claim that the returns from one-year funds were evenly distributed among the four categories from poor to excellent. There seems to have been a disproportionate number of good returns for mutual funds that year.

17. The test statistic changes from 13.325 to 373.059, so the outlier can have a dramatic effect on the value of χ^2.

19. a.
$$\chi^2 = \frac{\left(f_1 - \frac{f_1 + f_2}{2}\right)^2}{\frac{f_1 + f_2}{2}} + \frac{\left(f_2 - \frac{f_1 + f_2}{2}\right)^2}{\frac{f_1 + f_2}{2}}$$

$$= \frac{(f_1 - f_2)^2}{f_1 + f_2}$$

b. $$z^2 = \frac{\left(\frac{f_1}{f_1 + f_2} - 0.5\right)^2}{\frac{1/4}{f_1 + f_2}} = \frac{(f_1 - f_2)^2}{f_1 + f_2}$$

Critical values: The χ^2 critical value is 3.841 and it is approximately equal to the square of $z = 1.96$.

21. Combine the last three cells. Test statistic: $\chi^2 = 2.059$. Critical value: $\chi^2 = 5.991$. Fail to reject H_0: The frequencies fit a Poisson distribution. There is not sufficient evidence to warrant rejection of the claim that the frequencies fit a Poisson distribution.

Section 10-3

1. Test statistic: $\chi^2 = 51.458$. Critical value: $\chi^2 = 6.635$. Reject the claim (H_0) that the proportions of agree/disagree responses are the same for the subjects interviewed by men and the subjects interviewed by women.

3. Test statistic: $\chi^2 = 1.174$. Critical value: $\chi^2 = 3.841$. Fail to reject the claim that the treatment is independent of the reaction. There is not enough evidence to be concerned.

5. Test statistic: $\chi^2 = 5.091$. Critical value: $\chi^2 = 7.815$ (assuming $\alpha = 0.05$). Fail to reject the claim that the car model and final position are independent. If all the same ratios held up in a sample five times larger, the test statistic χ^2 would equal 25.455, and the P-value would be much less than the P-value for the table in the original problem.

7. Test statistic: $\chi^2 = 8.642$. Critical value: $\chi^2 = 9.210$. There is not sufficient evidence to warrant rejection of the claim that the distribution of planes flying and planes ordered is independent of the airline company.

9. Test statistic: $\chi^2 = 49.624$. Critical value: $\chi^2 = 3.841$. Reject the claim (H_0) that the patient's age and the sport where the injury occurred are independent variables. The data suggest that these two variables are, in fact, related. This test result does not establish a *causal* relationship between age and risk of injury. It may

be that, proportionally, fewer children under 10 engage in basketball as their sport, compared with older people; perhaps that explains why fewer of the young people's sports injuries occur while playing basketball.

11. Test statistic: $\chi^2 = 2.327$. Critical value: $\chi^2 = 3.841$. There is not sufficient evidence to warrant rejection of the claim that the distribution of weights for offensive backs is independent of whether the player is a quarterback.

13. Test statistic: $\chi^2 = 49.731$. Critical value: $\chi^2 = 11.071$ (assuming $\alpha = 0.05$). Reject the claim that the type of crime is independent of whether the criminal drinks. Fraud appears to be unique in the sense that it is associated with drinkers at a much lower rate than the other crimes.

15. Test statistic: $\chi^2 = 0.122$. Critical value: $\chi^2 = 3.841$ (assuming $\alpha = 0.05$). Fail to reject the claim that gender of statistics students is independent of whether they smoke.

17. With Yates' correction: $\chi^2 = 1.205$. Without Yates' correction: $\chi^2 = 1.505$. In general, the test statistic decreases with Yates' correction.

Chapter 10 Review Exercises

1. Test statistic: $\chi^2 = 24.621$. Critical value: $\chi^2 = 5.991$. Reject the claim (H_0) that shelf life is independent of the additive formula that is used. The data suggest that the revised additives are associated with a changed distribution of product shelf life.

2. Test statistic: $\chi^2 = 1.714$. Critical value: $\chi^2 = 5.991$. Fail to reject the claim (H_0) that there is no difference in the proportion of springs with above-normal precipitation for the three categories of springs.

3. Test statistic: $\chi^2 = 7.600$. Critical value: $\chi^2 = 14.067$. There is not sufficient evidence to warrant rejection of the claim that all these species strike with equal frequencies. These data do not, of themselves, support a prevention policy that is focused on particular species.

4. Test statistic: $\chi^2 = 5.252$. Critical value: $\chi^2 = 3.841$. Reject the claim (H_0) that the patients' temperatures and genders are independent. The data provide evidence that patients' temperatures and genders are related.

5. Test statistic: $\chi^2 = 7.607$. Critical value: $\chi^2 = 5.991$. Reject the claim that the occurrence of headaches is independent of the group. The Seldane users had a lower headache rate than the placebo group, so headaches don't seem to be a problem.

Chapter 10 Cumulative Review Exercises

1. (Use the linear correlation coefficient, as in Section 9-2.) Test statistic: $r = 0.978$. Critical value: $r = 0.950$ (assuming $\alpha = 0.05$). Reject the claim of no significant linear correlation. There does appear to be a relationship between the memory test score and the reasoning test score.

2. (Use the test for two dependent means, as in Section 8-2.) With $\bar{d} = -10.25$ and $s_d = 1.5$, the test statistic is $t = -13.667$. The critical value is $t = -2.353$ (assuming $\alpha = 0.05$). Reject H_0: $\mu_d \geq 0$. There is sufficient evidence to support the claim that the scores are higher after the training session. It appears that the training session is effective in raising scores.

3. (Use a test of homogeneity in a contingency table, as in Section 10-3.) Test statistic: $\chi^2 = 0.055$. Critical value: $\chi^2 = 7.815$ (assuming $\alpha = 0.05$). Fail to reject the claim that men and women choose the different answers in the same proportions. The letter selections appear to be the same for men and women.

4. (Use a test for equality between two independent means, as in Section 8-5.) Preliminary F test: Test statistic is $F = 1.0344$. Critical value: $F = 15.439$ (assuming $\alpha = 0.05$). Fail to reject $\sigma_1^2 = \sigma_2^2$. Test of means: Test statistic is $t = -2.014$. Critical values: $t = \pm 2.447$ (assuming $\alpha = 0.05$). Fail to reject H_0: $\mu_1 = \mu_2$. There is not sufficient evidence to warrant rejection of the claim that men and women have the same mean score.

Section 11-2

1. a. 6   b. $F = 3.33$ c. $F_c = 2.6207$ d. 0.032
   e. There is sufficient evidence to reject the null hypothesis that the means are equal.

3. a. 5.836967   b. 0.167331   c. $F = 34.8828$
   d. 3.3158 (assuming $\alpha = 0.05$)
   e. There is sufficient evidence to warrant rejection of the claim that the three populations have the same mean body temperature.

5. Test statistic: $F = 1.4468$. Critical value: $F = 3.4028$. Fail to reject the null hypothesis of equal means. Although conglomerates appear to have a higher mean revenue, there is insufficient evidence to indicate that apparent differences in mean revenue are significant.

7. Test statistic: $F = 2.1188$. Critical value: $F = 3.4028$. Fail to reject the null hypothesis of equal means. Although conglomerates appear to have a greater mean number of employees, there is insufficient evidence to indicate that apparent differences in mean numbers of employees are significant.

9. Test statistic: $F = 2.9493$. Critical value: $F = 2.6060$. Reject the claim of equal means. The different laboratories do not appear to have the same mean.

11. Test statistic: $F = 4.3465$. Critical value: $F = 3.5546$. Reject the claim of equal means. The mean number of sittings appears to be different for different eras of Parliament.

13. Test statistic: $F = 0.0221$. Critical value: $F = 2.9752$. Fail to reject the claim that the mean weight (in carats) is the same for all four clarity levels. If you must compromise on clarity, it appears that your selection of carat levels is not affected.

15. a. 0.300300   b. 0.167331   c. $F = 1.794647$
    d. 3.3158 (assuming $\alpha = 0.05$)

e. Fail to reject the claim of equal means for the three groups. The three groups now appear to have the same mean body temperature. By adding 1° to each temperature for the first sample, the variance between the samples decreased. The variance within samples did not change. The F test statistic decreased to reflect the decreased disparity among the three samples.

17. In each case, the test statistic F is not affected.

19. a. Test statistic: $t = -1.506$. Critical values: $t = \pm 2.120$. Fail to reject the null hypothesis that the two industry groups have the same mean revenue.
    b. Test statistic: $F = 2.2693$. Critical value: $F = 4.4940$. Fail to reject the null hypothesis that the two industry groups have the same mean revenue.
    c. Test statistics: $t^2 = 2.2680 \approx F = -2.2693$. Critical values: $t^2 = 4.4944 \approx F = 4.4940$.

Section 11-3

1. a. 1263.396   b. 694.938   c. 349.729   d. 14.063

3. Test statistic: $F = 0.5033$. Critical value: $F = 4.0662$, assuming that the significance level is $\alpha = 0.05$. It appears that star rating does not have an effect on movie length.

5. Test statistic: $F = 0$. Critical value: $F = 10.1280$. It appears that CTR rating does not have an effect on movie length.

7. Test statistic: $F = 2.4740$. Critical value: $F = 4.7571$. Fail to reject the null hypothesis of no effects from the operators. It appears that the operators do not affect the numbers of support beams manufactured.

9. (The given results use the first nine values for each cell, but the pulse rate of 8 was excluded as being not feasible.) Test statistic: $F = 0.4200$. Critical value: $F = 4.1709$ (approximately). There does not appear to be an interaction between gender and smoking.

11. Test statistic: $F = 0.1814$. Critical value: $F = 4.1709$ (approximately, assuming $\alpha = 0.05$). Smoking does not appear to have an effect on pulse rates. (This is not surprising, because college students haven't been smoking very long.)

13. Nothing changes.

15. Answers vary.

Chapter 11 Review Exercises

1. Test statistic: $F = 46.90$. Critical value: $F = 3.7389$. Reject the null hypothesis of equal means.

2. Test statistic: $F = 3.0693$. Critical value: $F = 3.0725$. Fail to reject the claim (H_0) that the mean food costs are the same in the three cities.

3. Test statistic: $F = 0.1105$. Critical value: $F = 5.1432$. Fuel consumption does not appear to be affected by an interaction between transmission type and engine size.

4. Test statistic: $F = 1.5430$. Critical value: $F = 5.1432$. Fuel consumption does not appear to be affected by the engine size.
5. Test statistic: $F = 2.9589$. Critical value: $F = 5.9874$. The type of transmission does not appear to have an effect on fuel consumption.
6. Test statistic: $F = 24.2948$. Critical value: $F = 3.6667$. Reject the claim (H_0) that the interaction between the two variables does not affect brake performance. It appears that the interaction between snowmobile brand and speed does affect the mean brake performance of the vehicles. The P-value is 0.00000000438423.

Chapter 11 Cumulative Review Exercises

1. a.

Aurora Advertising and Gagné and Turner Advertising appear to be very similar, but Solomon & Campbell Advertising seems to be somewhat higher.

b. Aurora: $\bar{x} = 62.8$, $s = 12.9$; Solomon & Campbell: $\bar{x} = 72.3$, $s = 8.2$; Gagné and Turner: $\bar{x} = 62.8$, $s = 11.6$

c. F test results: Test statistic is $F = 2.4592$. Critical value: $F = 4.9949$. Fail to reject H_0: $\sigma_1^2 = \sigma_2^2$. Test of means: Test statistic is $t = -1.760$. Critical values: $t = \pm 2.145$. Fail to reject H_0: $\mu_1 = \mu_2$. There is not sufficient evidence to warrant rejection of the claim that the population of Aurora scores has a mean equal to the population mean for Solomon & Campbell scores.

d. Aurora: $52.0 < \mu < 73.5$; Solomon & Campbell: $65.4 < \mu < 79.1$; Gagné and Turner: $53.1 < \mu < 72.4$. Solomon & Campbell seems slightly higher.

e. Test statistic: $F = 1.9677$. Critical value: $F = 3.4668$. Fail to reject the null hypothesis of equal means. There is not sufficient evidence to warrant rejection of the claim that the three populations have the same mean reaction score. No single company stands out as being significantly better than the others.

2. a. 0.3300   b. 0.0384   c. 1/8
3. a. 2700.1   b. 2602.8

c.

d. 11505 is clearly an outlier ($z = 3.38$).
Although the boxplot also highlights the value 8625, because $z = 2.37$, the value appears consistent with the right-skewed data-distribution pattern (see the histogram for part (e)).

e.

f. No, the populations are not normally distributed.
g. $P(B5) = 0.0477$

Section 12-2

1.

There is an upward trend indicating that the intervals between eruptions are increasing, with the result that tourists must wait longer. There is increasing variation, with the result that predicted times of eruptions are becoming less reliable.

3.

There are points lying beyond the upper control limit and there is an upward trend, so the process mean is out of statistical control. An out-of-control process mean indicates that we cannot make accurate predictions.

5.

The process variation is out of statistical control because there is a point above the upper control limit.

7.

Yes, several patterns suggest that the process is not within statistical control. The last 39 observations are all below the mean, and apparently continue a downward trend that begins at about observation 130. There are also repeated sequences when 20 or more observations in a row are all one side or the other of the mean.

9.

The process mean is far from statistical control. If the Bank of Canada has intended to bring monetary conditions under statistical control, it has not been successful.

11.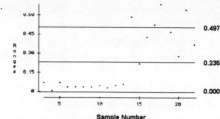

The process is out of control because there is a shift up, there are 8 consecutive points below the centre line, and there are points beyond the upper control limit.

13.

Using Table 12-1 values, $\bar{s} = 20.05$ and LCL $= 2.366$. The result and conclusions are very similar to those for the R chart.

Section 12-3

1. Process appears to be within statistical control.
3. Process appears to be out of statistical control because there is a pattern of an upward trend and there is a point that lies beyond the upper control limit.

5.

This process is out of statistical control because there are points above the upper control limit, and there are 10 consecutive points all lying below the centre line. Having samples with less than the mean proportion of defects is, in itself, a good result—but the chart shows that the situation is unstable. Causes for periods of instability should be identified.

7.

The process is out of statistical control because there are points beyond the upper control limit. Companies which rely on air transportation will be concerned about the apparent instability of that mode, with respect to the proportion of person-days lost due to work stoppages compared to alternative modes. This instability may result in air-based transportation service being unreliable.

9.

Except for the scale used, the charts are identical.

Review Exercises

1.

The process appears to be within statistical control.

2.

The process appears to be within statistical control.

3.

The process mean appears to be out of statistical control because there is a point lying beyond the lower control limit. The process should be corrected because too little epoxy cement hardener is being put into some containers.

4.

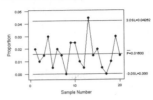

The process is out of statistical control because there is a point lying beyond the upper control limit.

Cumulative Review Exercises

1. a.

The process is in statistical control.

b. $0.0158 < p < 0.0217$

c. Test statistic: $z = 5.77$. Critical value: $z = 1.645$. Reject $H_0: p \leq 0.01$. There is sufficient evidence to warrant rejection of the claim that the rate of defects is 1% or less.

2. a. 1/256

b. 1/256

c. 1/128

3.

The process is out of statistical control because the run chart displays a shift up, followed by a shift down.

4. a. Yes. Test statistic: $r = 0.779$. Critical values: $r = \pm 0.361$ (approximate; assuming significance level $\alpha = 0.05$).

b. $\hat{y} = 2.72 + 2.65x$

c. \$9.08 billion.

Section 13-2

1. The test statistic $x = 2$ is not less than or equal to the critical value of 0. Fail to reject the claim that the temperature departures from seasonal norms do not differ between the first and second springs of an El Niño.

3. Because n > 25, use z test. (Instead of a right-tailed test to determine whether $x = 51$ is large enough to be significant, use a left-tailed test to determine whether $x = 88 - 51 = 37$ is small enough to be significant.) Test statistic: $z = -1.386$. Critical value: $z = -1.645$. Fail to reject the null hypothesis. There is not sufficient evidence to support the claim that more than half the UBC graduates living outside of Canada are living in the United States.

5. The test statistic $x = 7$ is not less than or equal to the critical value of 5. Fail to reject the null hypothesis that the proportions of men and women are equal. There is not sufficient evidence to charge gender bias.

7. (Instead of a right-tailed test to determine whether $x = 18$ is large enough to be significant, use a left-tailed test to determine whether $x = 15$ is small enough to be significant.) Convert $x = 15$ to the test statistic $z = -0.35$. Critical value: $z = -1.645$. Fail to reject H_0. There is not sufficient evidence to support the claim that the median is greater than 0.9085 g. We cannot conclude that the package is labelled incorrectly, because the median could be equal to 0.9085 g.

9. Person-days lost for the truck-based group were less than 10595 thirteen times and greater than 10595 eleven times, so use $x = 11$ and $n = 24$. The test statistic x is not less than or equal to the critical value of 7. Fail to reject the null hypothesis that person-days lost for the truck group were at least equal to 10595. There is not sufficient evidence to support the claim that truck-based transportation loses less time due to work stoppages than the median for all transportation groups combined.

11. The test statistic $x = 2$ is not less than or equal to the critical value of 1. Fail to reject the null hypothesis of no difference. There is not sufficient evidence to warrant rejection of the claim of no difference between the two times.

13. a. Yes. Example data set:

20   120   120   120   120   120   140   160   180   200

Sign test: Test statistic: $x = 1$. Critical values: $x = 1$ (assuming significance level $\alpha = 0.05$). Reject null hypothesis of median = 100.

t test: Test statistic: $t = 1.964$. Critical values: $t = \pm 2.262$ (assuming significance level $\alpha = 0.05$). Fail to reject null hypothesis of mean = 100.

b. Yes. Example data set:

80   90   160   160   160   160   160   160   180   200

Sign test: Test statistic: $x = 2$. Critical values: $x = 1$ (assuming significance level $\alpha = 0.05$). Fail to reject null hypothesis of median = 100.

t test: Test statistic: $t = 4.329$. Critical values: $t = \pm 2.262$ (assuming significance level $\alpha = 0.05$). Reject null hypothesis of mean = 100.

15. *, *, *, *, *, 0, 0, 0, 1, 1, 1, 2, 2, 3, 3

Section 13-3

1. Test statistic: $T = 6$. Critical value: $T = 2$. Fail to reject the null hypothesis that both samples come from the same population distribution.

3. For $n > 30$; $T = 326.5$. Test statistic: $z = -0.64$. Critical values: $z = \pm 2.575$. Fail to reject the null hypothesis that both samples come from the same population distribution.

5. Test statistic: $T = 1$. Critical value: $T = 0$. Fail to reject the null hypothesis that both samples come from the same population distribution. Based on the available results, hypnotism does not appear to be effective.

7. a. Test statistic: $T = 3.5$. Critical value: $T = 25$. Reject the null hypothesis of no difference. There is sufficient evidence to support the claim that the populations have different distributions.

b. No. The data provide no basis for assuming that gas mileage would improve for all cars which use P.V.I. Perhaps the experimental results are unique to 5.0 litre vehicles, or to the one model that was tested. Or perhaps the standardized test conditions are not representative of actual urban or rural driving conditions.

9. a. 0, 27.5

b. 0, 637.5

c. 1954

Section 13-4

1. $\mu_R = 577.5$, $\sigma_R = 56.358$, $R = 569$. Test statistic: $z = -0.15$. Critical values: $z = \pm 1.96$. Fail to reject the null hypothesis that red and brown M&Ms have weights with identical populations. They appear to be the same.

3. $\mu_R = 126.5$, $\sigma_R = 15.229$, $R = 139.5$, Test statistic: $z = 0.85$. Critical values: $z = \pm 1.96$. Fail to reject the null hypothesis that the two provinces have the same distribution of hospital bed numbers. (Regardless of these test results, we would need data about the two provinces' populations to determine whether the numbers of hospital beds per person differed between the provinces.)

5. $\mu_R = 333$, $\sigma_R = 31.607$, $R = 321$. Test statistic: $z = -0.38$. Critical values: $z = \pm 1.96$. Fail to reject the null hypothesis that both samples come from populations that have the same dollar values of building permits.

7. $\mu_R = 525$, $\sigma_R = 37.417$, $R = 437$, $z = -2.35$. Test statistic: $z = -2.35$. Critical values: $z = \pm1.96$. Reject the null hypothesis that the two samples come from populations with the same scores.

9. The denominators are the same, so you need to consider only the numerators. First set $R - \mu_R = -U + n_1 n_2/2$, and then replace U by $n_1 n_2 + n_1(n_1 + 1)/2 - R$ and replace μ_R by $n_1(n_1 + n_2 + 1)/2$. Remove parentheses and simplify to see that both sides are equal.

11. An outlier has no effect on the Wilcoxon rank-sum test, insofar as the ranks of the highest and lowest data values are the same, regardless of the exact magnitudes of those values. If a data value is mistakenly mis-copied, to become an outlier, the effect on the test is minimal, since at most the value will be assigned the highest (or lowest) of the ranks.

Section 13-5

1. Test statistic: $H = 7.240$. Critical value: $\chi^2 = 5.991$. Reject the null hypothesis that the three samples come from identical populations. There appears to be a difference in the number of House sittings per Parliament, for the three time periods.

3. Test statistic: $H = 5.717$. Critical value: $\chi^2 = 7.815$. Fail to reject the null hypothesis that the four samples come from identical populations. There is not sufficient evidence to support the claim that the prices of diamonds are different for different clarity levels. However, the data do not include diamonds of level 6 (the least clear). It may be useful to compare prices for diamonds of clarity 6 with the other diamonds.

5. Test statistic: $H = 2.075$. Critical value: $\chi^2 = 11.071$. Fail to reject the null hypothesis that the samples come from identical populations. No corrective action is necessary.

7. Test statistic: $H = 0.185$. Critical value: $\chi^2 = 5.991$. Fail to reject the null hypothesis that the three samples come from identical populations. There is not sufficient evidence to indicate that the samples of movie lengths come from different populations.

9. a. The test statistic H does not change.
   b. The test statistic H does not change.
   c. The value of the test statistic does not change much (because the rank is used instead of the magnitude of the outlier).

11. $\Sigma T = 366$. Dividing H by the correction factor results in $14.431335 \div 0.99668910$, which is rounded to 14.479. Even though 35 of the 48 scores are involved in ties, the correction factor does not change H by a substantial amount.

Section 13-6

1. a. $r_s = 1$ and there appears to be a correlation between x and y.
   b. $r_s = -1$ and there appears to be a correlation between x and y.

c. $r_s = 0$ and there does not appear to be a correlation between x and y.

3. $r_s = 0.855$. Critical values: $r_s = \pm0.648$. Significant correlation. There appears to be a correlation between salary and stress.

5. $r_s = -0.067$. Critical values: $r_s = \pm0.648$. No significant correlation. There does not appear to be a correlation between stress level and physical demand.

7. $r_s = 0.715$. Critical values: $r_s = \pm0.591$. Significant correlation. There appears to be a correlation between the IQ scores of identical twins separated at birth.

9. $r_s = 0.363$. Critical values: $r_s = \pm0.738$. No significant correlation. There does not appear to be a correlation between length and weight.

11. $r_s = 0.766$. Critical values: $r_s = \pm0.507$. Significant correlation. There appears to be a correlation between the income levels for professions and the number of years of education they require. The results do not change if each income is multiplied by 1000.

13. $r_s = 0.786$. Critical values: $r_s = \pm0.280$. Significant correlation. There appears to be a correlation between durations and intervals between eruptions.

15. $r_s = 0.736$. Critical values: $r_s = \pm0.623$. Significant correlation. For persons who move from an initially sitting position to a supine position, there appears to be a correlation between body temperatures in those two states. Yes, but not if the estimates need to be exact.

17. $r_s = 0.143$. Critical values: $r_s = \pm0.786$. No significant correlation. There does not appear to be a correlation between the temperature departures in the first and second springs of an El Niño. Neither of these variables can be used to predict the other.

19. a. ±0.707
    b. ±0.514
    c. ±0.361
    d. ±0.463
    e. ±0.834

Section 13-7

1. $n_1 = 10$, $n_2 = 5$, $G = 3$, 5% cutoff values: 3, 12

3. $n_1 = 12$, $n_2 = 4$, $G = 4$, 5% cutoff values: 3, 10

5. $n_1 = 12$, $n_2 = 8$, $G = 10$, 5% cutoff values: 6, 16. Fail to reject the null hypothesis of randomness. A lack of randomness could result in large gains for the author and large losses to the casino. Fat chance.

7. $n_1 = 12$, $n_2 = 12$, $G = 12$, cutoff values (for $\alpha = 0.05$): 7, 19. Fail to reject the null hypothesis of randomness. There is not sufficient evidence to warrant rejecting the claim that the order is random.

9. $n_1 = 7$, $n_2 = 4$, $G = 7$, 5% cutoff values: 2, 10. Fail to reject the null hypothesis of randomness. It appears that we elect Liberals and Conservatives to become the party of the new prime minister in a sequence that is random.

11. $n_1 = 11$, $n_2 = 8$, $G = 8$, 5% cutoff values: 5, 15. Fail to reject the null hypothesis of randomness. There is not sufficient evidence to suggest that the sequence of monthly gains and losses is not random. Someone investing in a TSE 300–based fund could still make money—if the *magnitudes* of monthly gains, when they occur, are greater than the magnitudes of the losses.

13. $n_1 = 21$, $n_2 = 19$, $G = 7$, $\mu_G = 20.95$, $\sigma_G = 3.11346$. Test statistic: $z = -4.48$. Critical values: $z = \pm 1.96$. Reject the null hypothesis of randomness.

15. $n_1 = 49$, $n_2 = 51$, $G = 54$, $\mu_G = 50.98$, $\sigma_G = 4.9727$. Test statistic: $z = 0.61$. Critical values: $z = \pm 1.96$. Fail to reject the null hypothesis of randomness.

17. Minimum is 2, maximum is 4. Critical values of 1 and 6 can never be realized so that the null hypothesis of randomness can never be rejected.

Chapter 13 Review Exercises

1. Test statistic: $H = 4.037$. Critical value: $\chi^2 = 5.991$. Fail to reject the null hypothesis that the three populations are the same. There is not sufficient evidence to support the claim that the three populations are not all the same.

2. Test statistic: $T = 17$. Critical value: $T = 6$. Fail to reject the null hypothesis that both samples come from the same population distribution. But because the data are so variable, it would be imprudent to predict changes in car sales based on changes in truck sales.

3. $n_1 = 6$, $n_2 = 24$, $G = 12$, $\mu_G = 10.6$, $\sigma_G = 1.6873$. Test statistic: $z = 0.83$. Critical values: $z = \pm 1.96$. Fail to reject randomness.

4. Convert 2000 scores to ranks, and re-number 1999 ranks into a sequence beginning at 1. $r_s = -.800$. Critical values: $r_s = \pm 0.683$. Significant correlation. There is sufficient evidence to support the claim that 1999 Ranks and 2000 Scores are rank correlated.

5. Test statistic: $x = 4$. Critical value: $x = 0$. Fail to reject the claim that there is no difference in the number of search results before and after adding a third word to the search list. Simply adding more words to the search list does not appear to be an effective strategy to reduce the number of results. (*Hint:* Try prefixing the most important words in your search list with +.)

6. $\mu_R = 201.5$, $\sigma_R = 23.894$, $R = 163$, $z = -1.61$. Test statistic: $z = -1.61$. Critical values: $z = \pm 1.96$. Fail to reject the null hypothesis that the drug has no effect on eye movements.

7. Test statistic: $H = 4.096$. Critical value: $\chi^2 = 7.815$. Fail to reject the null hypothesis that the four populations are identical. There is not sufficient evidence to support the claim that the samples come from populations that are not all the same.

8. a. Every answer "F" is followed by four answers of "T".
   b. $n_1 = 20$, $n_2 = 5$, $G = 11$, cutoff values (for $\alpha = 0.05$): 5, 12. Fail to reject the null hypothesis of randomness.
   c. The pattern shows evidence of a sequence that is not

random, but that evidence is not sufficient to warrant rejection of the null hypothesis of randomness.

9. $\mu_R = 144$, $\sigma_R = 16.25$, $R = 84$, $z = -3.69$. Test statistic: $z = -3.69$. Critical values: $z = \pm 1.96$. Reject the null hypothesis of no difference between mail order and store prices.

10. The test statistic $x = 0$ is less than or equal to the critical value of 0. Reject the claim that the training has no effect on weight. There does appear to be an effect.

11. Test statistic: $T = 0$. Critical value: $T = 1$. Reject the null hypothesis that training has no effect on weight. There does appear to be an effect.

12. $r_s = 0.770$. Critical values: $r_s = \pm 0.648$. There appears to be a significant correlation between the two measures of health care.

Cumulative Review Exercises

1. a. $G = 21$, $n_1 = 20$, $n_2 = 10$. Critical values: 9, 20. Reject randomness.
   b. Test statistic: $z = -1.83$. Critical values: $z = \pm 1.96$. Fail to reject null hypothesis that $p = 0.5$. There is not sufficient evidence to support the claim that the proportion of women is different from 0.5.
   c. $0.165 < p < 0.502$
   d. There isn't sufficient evidence to support a claim of bias against either gender, but the sequence does not appear to be random. It's possible that the pollster is using selection methods that are unacceptable.

2. a. Test statistic: $x = 3$. Critical value: $x = 1$. Because the test statistic is not less than or equal to the critical value, fail to reject the claim that there is no difference between the weights before and after the program.
   b. Test statistic: $T = 6.5$. Critical value: $T = 6$. Because the test statistic is not less than or equal to the critical value, fail to reject the claim that there is no difference between the weights before and after the program.
   c. Test statistic: $t = 2.279$. Critical values: $t = \pm 2.262$. Reject the null hypothesis that there is no difference between the weights before and after the program. The program does appear to have an effect.
   d. Both nonparametric tests (the sign test and the Wilcoxon signed-ranks test) failed to detect a difference, whereas the t test resulted in the conclusion of a significant difference. The t test fully utilizes the magnitudes of the differences, the sign test does not use the magnitudes at all, and the Wilcoxon signed-ranks test only uses the ordered rankings of the magnitudes. The two nonparametric tests will therefore be less sensitive in cases where the magnitudes have a potential impact on the test results.

3. a. 19176.6   b. 11980   c. 0   d. 85550
   e. 21538.3 {*Hint.* If your calculator cannot handle the large χ^2's,

you can make the numbers manageable by converting the original data into units of 1000 (for example, convert 41810 to 41.810); then multiply the final answer for *s* times 1000.

f. The largest value of 85550: Its corresponding *z* score is greater than 3, and it is quite far from the next highest value. However, the data set is highly skewed, so this single high value does not necessarily suggest an input or data-collection error.

Section 14-2

1. 106.9
3. 72.6
5. 90.6
7. 98.6
9. 90.7
11. 98.4
13. 90.6
15. 98.5
17. Laspeyres = 111.3; Paasche = 110.9; Fisher = 111.1
19. 29.3%

Section 14-3

1. Seasonal variation
3. Irregular variation
5. Trend
7. Seasonal variation
9. Seasonal variation
11. Trend
13. Cyclical variation
15. Irregular variation
17. Trend
19. Irregular variation
21. Seasonal variation
23. Cyclical variation
25. Irregular variation
27. Trend

Section 14-4

1.

Quarter	Quarterly Index
1	0.9917
2	0.9984
3	1.0040
4	1.0059

3.

Year	Quarter	Deseasonalized Earnings
1993	1	559.34
	2	557.78
	3	558.03
	4	556.52
1994	1	567.42
	2	568.92
	3	568.81
	4	567.60
1995	1	577.11
	2	571.87
	3	572.89
	4	573.02
1996	1	580.45
	2	584.98
	3	587.49
	4	590.88
1997	1	599.82
	2	600.59
	3	596.93
	4	596.12

Quarter 2 had the highest seasonally-adjusted average weekly earnings in 1997.

		5.	7.	9.	11.	13.	15.	17.
Year	Quarter	Single Dwellings	Cottages	Double Dwellings	Row Housing	Apartments	Conversions	Total
1989	1	32,972	517	2154	3417	14,620	1119	54,686
	2	30,124	572	1919	3741	15,627	987	53,060
	3	31,569	457	1802	3813	17,518	975	56,108
	4	33,549	556	1824	3972	17,717	739	58,145
1990	1	35,034	638	2147	4592	15,673	1025	58,946
	2	24,206	546	1832	4008	13,148	853	44,485
	3	19,679	526	1682	3410	10,390	966	36,694
	4	17,788	429	1297	2861	12,308	1150	36,449
1991	1	14,573	397	1238	2959	9,829	964	30,115
	2	22,999	461	1939	3432	11,356	1077	41,294

(continued)

(continued)

		5.	7.	9.	11.	13.	15.	17.
	3	25,130	435	2618	4118	12,741	1066	46,086
	4	24,132	459	2700	5541	13,449	1027	47,862
1992	1	21,958	337	2291	5122	13,020	1004	43,944
	2	22,487	368	2158	3776	11,475	975	41,161
	3	23,282	453	2143	4391	11,057	832	42,170
	4	25,231	444	2864	4067	9,527	827	42,434
1993	1	19,564	339	2194	4460	8,444	745	35,710
	2	20,699	360	2191	4692	9,801	898	38,548
	3	22,738	428	2633	4724	10,901	1067	42,467
	4	22,886	381	2581	4519	10,078	1162	41,578

Year	Quarter	Single Dwellings	Cottages	Double Dwellings	Row Housing	Apartments	Conversions	Total
1994	1	20,395	* 424	* 3286	4003	9,406	905	38,363
	2	* 23,981	344	3272	* 4904	* 9,586	* 972	* 43,217
	3	22,099	352	2432	4096	8,386	856	38,239
	4	20,909	381	2044	3593	7,914	857	35,296

* Quarter of 1994 with the highest seasonally adjusted number of building permits.

	19.	21.
Month	Index for Single Dwellings	Index for Total Permits
Jan.	.4836674	0.5466183
Feb.	.6837075	0.7239269
Mar.	1.2262969	1.1882115
Apr.	1.4932524	1.3664484
May	1.4706013	1.3250523
June	1.2832881	1.2103880
July	1.0663686	1.0346381
Aug.	1.0379664	1.0270969
Sept.	1.0109761	1.0224668
Oct.	.9510575	1.0345120
Nov.	.7933092	0.8989777
Dec.	.4995086	0.6216630

Section 14-5

1. Year	Quarter	Predicted Mean Weekly Earnings
1998	1	601.34
	2	605.46
	3	608.86
	4	610.07
1999	1	611.12
	2	615.31
	3	618.76
	4	620.00

		3.	5.	7.
		Seasonally Adjusted Predictions		
Year	Quarter	Cottages	Row Housing	Conversions
1995	1	114	3877	874
	2	499	5385	1003
	3	451	4629	890
	4	188	4552	878
1999	1	60	4376	821
	2	264	6079	942
	3	239	5225	836
	4	99	5138	825

9. $\hat{y} = 6856.8 + 850.5x$

11. Month	Monthly Adjusted Forecasts
Jan.	4745
Feb.	5792
Mar.	7769
Apr.	8762
May	8369
June	7352
July	6408
Aug.	5993
Sept.	5471
Oct.	5288
Nov.	4834
Dec.	3849

13.

Month	Monthly Adjusted Forecasts
Jan.	5140
Feb.	6273
Mar.	8414
Apr.	9489
May	9064
June	7963
July	6941
Aug.	6490
Sept.	5925
Oct.	5727
Nov.	5235
Dec.	4169

MSE = 2,805,957

Section 14-6

1.   3.

Centred 4-Point Moving Averages

Year	Quarter	Single Dwellings	Cottages
1989	1	none	none
	2	none	none
	3	31,913.125	528.750
	4	31,071.500	529.000
1990	1	28,480.875	536.250
	2	25,464.000	539.250
	3	21,949.875	518.750
	4	19,695.625	490.750
1991	1	20,189.625	457.250
	2	21,490.375	443.000
	3	22,820.000	442.500
	4	23,465.875	421.375
1992	1	23,135.375	406.250
	2	22,998.250	408.375
	3	22,862.250	407.375
	4	22,307.125	405.875
1993	1	21,920.125	399.875
	2	21,630.250	390.750
	3	21,493.875	389.875
	4	22,157.500	390.500
1994	1	22,655.250	373.500
	2	22,387.375	359.750
	3	none	none
	4	none	none

5. 52-point moving averages

7.

Total Permits	Alpha = 0.9
10,025	10,025
12,709	12,440.600
22,086	21,121.460
23,622	23,371.946
24,038	23,971.395
21,351	21,613.039
18,671	18,965.204
20,223	20,097.220
18,789	18,919.822
19,461	19,406.882
17,608	17,787.888
12,454	12,987.389
12,235	12,310.239
14,379	14,172.124
21,697	20,944.512
21,903	21,807.151

It is clear from the charts that $\alpha = 0.04$ leads to more smoothing.

Chapter 14 Review Exercises

1. Seasonal variation   2. Cyclical variation
3. Irregular variation   4. Trend
5. Cyclical variation   6. Trend
7. Irregular variation   8. Seasonal variation

9.

Year	1988	1989	1990	1991	1992	1993	1994	1995
Price relative	90.1	94.3	106.8	104.2	100	98.0	96.5	101.3

10.

Year	1988	1989	1990	1991	1992	1993	1994	1995
Price in 1992 $s	58.1	58.0	62.6	57.9	54.7	52.7	51.8	53.2

11. 12.4%   12. −8.5%

13. Laspeyres = 107.3; Paasche = 107.9; Fisher = 107.6. The general downward trend may be caused by other factors as well, such as health consciousness.

14. Quarterly indexes: 1.0265, 0.9878, 0.9636, 1.0221

Year	Quarter	Deseasonalized Data
1994	1	7903
	2	7873
	3	7862
	4	7897
1995	1	8051
	2	8098
	3	8117
	4	8133
1996	1	8188
	2	8228
	3	8224
	4	8188
1997	1	8381
	2	8324
	3	8320
	4	8304

Quarter	16. 1997 Adjusted Forecast	17. 1998 Adjusted Forecast
1	8569.7	8718.7
2	8246.6	8390.0
3	8044.6	8184.5
4	8533.0	8681.3

MSE = 1123.9

18.

Raw Data	Centred 4-Point Moving Average
8112	
7777	
7576	31,613.0
8072	31,800.0
8264	32,034.0
7999	32,277.5
7822	32,468.5
8313	32,603.0
8405	32,718.5
8127	32,798.0
7925	32,925.0
8369	33,071.5
8603	33,165.0
8222	33,270.5
8017	
8488	

19.

Month	Monthly Index
Jan.	1.03090
Feb.	1.02770
Mar.	1.02080
Apr.	1.02320
May	0.98200
June	0.95820
July	0.93930
Aug.	0.94770
Sept.	1.00390
Oct.	1.01050
Nov.	1.02130
Dec.	1.03460

20.	Year	Month	Deseasonalized Data
	1994	Jan.	7918
		Feb.	7888
		Mar.	7901
		Apr.	7864
		May	7858
		June	7899
		July	7861
		Aug.	7863
		Sept.	7860
		Oct.	7932
		Nov.	7868
		Dec.	7893
	1995	Jan.	8043
		Feb.	8083
		Mar.	8026
		Apr.	8109
		May	8093
		June	8091
		July	8071
		Aug.	8124
		Sept.	8155
		Oct.	8120
		Nov.	8175
		Dec.	8105
	1996	Jan.	8201
		Feb.	8163
		Mar.	8200
		Apr.	8201
		May	8246
		June	8236
		July	8231
		Aug.	8226
		Sept.	8216
		Oct.	8180
		Nov.	8181
		Dec.	8202
	1997	Jan.	8360
		Feb.	8389
		Mar.	8394
		Apr.	8348
		May	8324
		June	8298
		July	8360
		Aug.	8309
		Sept.	8293
		Oct.	8291
		Nov.	8298
		Dec.	8323

Month	21. 1998 Adjusted Forecast	22. 1997 Adjusted Estimate
Jan.	8756.1	8606.5
Feb.	8728.9	8579.7
Mar.	8670.3	8522.1
Apr.	8690.7	8542.2
May	8340.8	8198.2
June	8138.6	7999.5
July	7978.1	7841.7
Aug.	8049.4	7911.9
Sept.	8526.8	8381.0
Oct.	8582.9	8436.1
Nov.	8674.6	8526.3
Dec.	8787.5	8637.3

MSE = 1531.7

23.	Raw Data	Centred 12-Point Moving Average
	8163	
	8107	
	8065	
	8046	
	7717	
	7569	
	7384	7889.6250
	7452	7903.3333
	7891	7917.0000
	8015	7932.7917
	8036	7952.8333
	8166	7970.0833
	8292	7985.9583
	8307	8004.4583
	8193	8027.0833
	8297	8047.3333
	7947	8068.2917
	7753	8090.4583
	7581	8106.3333
	7699	8116.5000
	8187	8127.3333
	8205	8138.6667
	8349	8148.8750
	8385	8160.9583
	8454	8173.0000
	8389	8183.2917
	8371	8189.8750
	8391	8194.9583
	8098	8197.7500
	7892	8202.2083
	7731	8213.2500
	7796	8229.7500
	8248	8247.6667
	8266	8262.2083
	8355	8271.6667
	8486	8277.2917
	8618	8284.8333
	8621	8293.1667
	8569	8299.6250
	8542	8307.5000
	8174	8317.1667
	7951	8327.3750
	7853	
	7874	
	8325	
	8378	
	8475	
	8611	

Index